Stalinist Planning
for Economic Growth,
1933–1952

Stalinist Planning for Economic Growth, 1933–1952

by Eugène Zaleski

Translated from the French and edited by Marie-Christine MacAndrew and John H. Moore

The University of North Carolina Press
Chapel Hill

© 1980 The University of North Carolina Press
All rights reserved
Manufactured in the United States of America
ISBN 0-8078-1370-2
Library of Congress Catalog Card Number 78-31453

Library of Congress Cataloging in Publication Data

Zaleski, Eugène.
   Stalinist planning for economic growth, 1933–1952.
   Bibliography: p.
   Includes index.
   1. Russia—Economic policy—1917–
I. MacAndrew, Marie-Christine.   II. Moore, John
Hampton, 1935–   III. Title.
HC335.5.Z34   338.947   78-31453
ISBN 0-8078-1370-2

In memory of my mother

Contents

Tables

Charts

Acknowledgments

The French and American versions of this book were prepared almost simultaneously, which explains the time since the publication of *Planning for Economic Growth in the Soviet Union, 1918–1932*. It is difficult for me in these few words to acknowledge the debt I have incurred, in the course of long years, to many people or even to enumerate them all.

Today, as this book goes to press in the United States, my thoughts turn first of all to G. Warren Nutter, who played a major part in the publication of two earlier works on Soviet planning. Since then, he has never ceased encouraging my work, which was pursued in France, despite immense difficulties arising from the scope of the project. His constant advice, his friendly support, and his vital assistance enabled me to carry my studies as far as I have and to complete the present volume in particular.

The American edition is, above all, the work of Marie-Christine MacAndrew. She contributed to this task much more than her talents as translator and editor. Day in, day out, she struggled to improve the quality of the work, checking and rechecking all references and calculations. I shall never be able to express fully my warm feelings and my gratitude to her.

During long years, the preparation of this American edition was supervised by John H. Moore of the Law and Economics Center, University of Miami. I am very grateful to him for the useful advice that he so willingly gave me. I should also like to express my appreciation to the staff of the Thomas Jefferson Center Foundation, particularly to Becky Strode, Anne Hobbs, and Carolyn Southall.

The research for this book was done at the Centre National de la Recherche Scientifique in Paris (CNRS). It was initiated many years ago by Professor André Piatier, who has been kind enough to sponsor the publication of this book in French. It is with deep appreciation that I recall his constant support, his advice, and his unstinting assistance.

A work of this scope would certainly never have been possible without the advice and encouragement of many academics and researchers in France. It would be difficult to mention all of them, but it is impossible not to acknowledge the vital support provided by Maurice Allais, Pierre Bauchet, Henri Chambre, Henri Guitton, Basile Kerblay, Edmond Lisle, and Jean Marczewski, and I take this occasion to express my gratitude.

My appreciation also goes particularly to my colleagues and friends at the CNRS. I should like to thank on this occasion Henri Wronski, maître de recherche at the CNRS, and the members of the research group on the Economy and Planning Techniques of Eastern Countries: Madame Agota Dezsenyi-Gueullette, attaché de recherche at the CNRS, Madame Jeanne Delamotte, Wilhelm Jampel, Madame Michèle Legrand, Georges Mink, Madeleine Tchimichkian, and T. Wyrwa, chargé de recherche at the CNRS.

I also owe particular thanks to R. W. Davies of the Centre for Russian and East European Studies at the University of Birmingham for his help and useful advice and for the rare documents that he was kind enough to make available to me. My thanks also go to the skilled researchers at that Centre, Julian Cooper and Steve Wheatcroft, who are working with Davies on a study of Soviet economic history of the 1930's for which this documentation was obtained; the study is financed by the British Social Science Research Council.

This list of people who have been so generous with their assistance and advice is far from complete, but I cannot end it without thanking at least a few of the scholars whose support was particularly important to me: Renato Mieli of the Centro Studi e Ricerche su Problemi Economico-Sociali of Milan, Marie Lavigne of the University of Paris I, Henri Dunajewski of Aix-Marseille III, Gregory Grossman of the University of California at Berkeley, Andrzej Brzeski of the University of California at Davis, Holland Hunter of Haverford College, Murray Feshbach of the Department of Commerce, John Hardt of the Congressional Research Service, Zbigniew Fallenbuchl of the University of Windsor in Canada, Alec Nove and J. G. Zielinski of the University of Glasgow, and Peter Wiles of the University of London.

All the advice and criticism generously offered by these well-known specialists have been of inestimable help. Nevertheless, I alone remain responsible for the opinions expressed in this book.

Paris   Eugène Zaleski
April 1978

Preface

This is the third in a series of works on Soviet economic planning by Dr. Eugène Zaleski whose translation into English I have had the good fortune to be associated with. The first work, *Planning Reforms in the Soviet Union, 1962–1966*, appeared in 1967; the second, *Planning for Economic Growth in the Soviet Union, 1918–1932*, in 1971. Both were published by the University of North Carolina Press, publisher of the present volume as well. Taken together, the three volumes encompass most of the history of Soviet economic planning. The purpose of these translations has been to make the results of Zaleski's masterful and lifelong research available to as broad an audience as possible.

In the case of the present volume, the English version is the original one to be published. A French edition is planned by the author to follow at a later date.

No enterprise of the scope involved in preparing the present volume could have been undertaken without substantial financial assistance. A special debt of gratitude is owed to the Earhart Foundation, the Thomas Jefferson Center Foundation, the Olin Foundation, and the Scaife Foundation for the generous support that made this publication possible.

The Library of Congress system of transliterating the Russian alphabet has been used, except that diphthong marks and apostrophes for hard and soft signs have been eliminated.

Charlottesville, Virginia   G. Warren Nutter
April 1978

Foreword

During the Stalinist period, the Soviet economy underwent a vast transformation. The relative decentralization of the 1920's was replaced by a centralized, administrative system; agriculture was forcibly collectivized; investment consumed an unprecedented share of national product; and industry grew at a pace unequalled before or since. Along with these and other dramatic events, another development of lasting importance took place. The system of economic planning, begun in the 1920's, was elaborated, extended, and formed into much the same system as the one in existence today. In a previous volume (*Planning for Economic Growth in the Soviet Union, 1918–1932*), Eugène Zaleski described and analyzed the early development of the planning system. He now has extended his study of that system over the period of Stalin's personal dictatorship. In this monumental work, he has made a contribution of fundamental importance not only to knowledge of the operation of the system during that period but also to understanding of the nature of the system today. The political leaders of the 1970's are the economic heirs of the Stalinist period in more ways than one; in addition to the path of development fixed by decisions from the past, they have inherited a system of planning that was molded under the powerful dictator.

Zaleski's work is characterized by careful, patient, and detailed analysis of vast quantities of information. Even more than in the previous study, he here presents a wealth of data gathered from Soviet and Western sources, a collection of information that itself represents a lasting and important contribution to scholarship on the Soviet economy. In addition, his perceptive analysis of these data leads him to new insights about the operation of the Soviet planning system and, more broadly, the socialist system as a whole. Because his conclusions are so carefully and extensively documented, his insights into the system and his conclusions about its operation seem certain to require changes in the thinking of students of the Soviet Union. The full extent of these changes can only be seen by a reading of the book, but an example will serve to illustrate the point.

Zaleski concludes that the planning system is best seen as a mechanism for managing the economy. The system is less important as a means of planning for the future, in the sense of setting out alternative courses of action to be pursued under different contingencies, or even for projecting outcomes to be achieved, than it is as a tool for maintaining the grip of the leadership on the economy. This conclusion has many important implications. It results in a different interpretation of the importance and function of the long-range, medium-range, and even annual plans. It leads to re-evaluation of the prospects and motivations for reform. It revises one's view of the terms in which the performance of the planning system is evaluated.

The Nature of Stalinist Planning

Zaleski presents (p. 482) a compelling characterization of the main objective of the Stalinist planner: "The main job of the Stalinist planner is not the coordination of plans. He has a more ambitious goal—to impose his vision of the future on the country." In the Stalinist system, imposing a vision of the future is a task that requires planners to translate objectives articulated by the political leadership into specific orders to specific economic units and then to oversee the carrying out of those orders. It is an exercise in administration, the operation of a necessarily hierarchical order. The familiar process of plan formation—passing control figures down through the hierarchy, modifying them in the bargaining process between enterprise and ministry, and reaggregating them into a final plan—is more clearly understood in the light of Zaleski's interpretation of the nature of the process. As a means of formulating a consistent plan, a procedure of this sort has obvious and inevitable defects. But as a means of managing the system, it appears much more sensible. That is one reason why Zaleski is led to a new interpretation of Stalinist planning: instead of being a mechanism for formulating a set of foreseeably feasible and consistent planned objectives, it is primarily one for allocating specific tasks through the hierarchy to the basic economic units.

Allocation of tasks is, in a sense, a necessary function in any planned economy. To execute any plan, its constituent parts must be assigned, directly or indirectly, to individual economic units that will perform the indicated tasks. It is one thing to argue that the Stalinist hierarchical system of task allocation is less efficient than conceivable alternatives, but quite another to aver that task allocation takes precedence over planning per se in the planning system. Zaleski does not argue that the formal plans are unimportant in affecting economic policy; rather, he concludes that management is relatively more important. If planning took precedence, plans ought to remain relatively unchanged during the period to which they are supposed to apply, there should be a reasonable relation among plans meant to apply to the same period (annual plans as "slices" of longer-range plans, and so forth), and there should be a clear relation between the plan statements and the sets of orders used to implement them. Perhaps most important, the allocation of tasks should be based on the plans in force at the time. Zaleski finds that none of this was true of planning in the Stalinist period. The plans themselves were not the actual guides to the allocation of tasks; plans were continually adjusted and changed to conform to the outcome of the economic process as it unfolded under the management of the planning system. Plans followed performance, rather than the other way around.

Moreover, the plans had a heterogeneous nature. They were mixtures of direct and implied goals, projections of observed trends, and estimates of the impact of uncontrollable phenomena on the economy. They were not, in other words, intended to be operational. Instead, they were supposed to serve as documents to form the basis for making managerial decisions as the course of events developed. The plans did not—could not—specify what would actually be done in the face of alternative outcomes of uncertain events and therefore could not be considered contingency plans. Nor were they used in that way. Projections and estimates were included, but the decisions to be made were unspecified—that is, left to the discretion of the authorities. Not only were the organization and process of plan formation and execution primarily instruments for the management of the economic system, but also the plans themselves served as managerial tools.

The Significance of Five-Year Plans

The perception of the planning system as an instrument for managing the economy leads to deeper understanding of the role of the medium-term plans. Zaleski painstakingly demonstrates that, while the Stalinist five-year plans took the form of policy statements, the policies set out in them were not actually implemented. The five-year plans were not put into operation, and, in fact, were modified continually, often well into the periods they were supposed to deal with. Furthermore, the annual plans—which, Zaleski argues, were not really operational—and the quarterly plans (the shortest-term national plans that were operational) actually consisted of amalgams of a network of decisions continuously made by the government during the year. The results of managerial responses to the exigencies arising during the course of events, they could, in fact, hardly be expected to reflect the policies laid out in the five-year plan or even to be mutually consistent, since the decisions they embodied were taken at different times.

Consequently, the operation of the planning system in practice did not reflect the balanced growth strategy of the five-year plans, but rather revealed a different policy for economic growth, a Stalinist model of growth not stated in the five-year plans. This Stalinist model is the familiar one of unbalanced growth, with high priority given to producer goods, industries that contribute to military power, heavy industry, freight traffic, and the like. Consumer goods and agriculture brought up the rear, the residual claimants in the Soviet economy. Actions speak louder than words; if the function of the planning system is to allocate assignments in accord with the policies of the leaders, Zaleski argues, the real policy of the leaders is not that stated in the five-year plans but that reflected by the actual outcomes.

This leads to the conclusion that the Stalinist five-year plans have a function other than that of seriously stating economic policy. Zaleski sees that function as creating propaganda, intended not only to influence external opinion but also, and perhaps even more importantly, to obtain the cooperation and enthusiastic support of the population. By holding out the prospect of higher standards of living, by dramatizing the great leaps forward to be achieved by the economic policies of the plan, the leadership seeks to stimulate maximum effort. As Zaleski shows in detail, the hopes for a better life held out in the five-year plans were not met, and it is reasonable to wonder how long such a strategy could continue enjoying success. Perhaps that is one reason why the Bacchanalian planning of the 1930's was later abandoned. But consumer hopes raised by five-year plan statements continue to be dashed, as with the Ninth Plan, suggesting either that there have been genuine miscalculations or that the leadership continues to use the Stalinist strategy.

Evaluation of Plan Fulfillment

Summing up what has been noted so far, we may observe that, according to Zaleski's analysis, the purpose of the planning system was to manage the economy, to assign tasks that would implement the desire of the authorities (Stalin) to impose their will on the economy. The vision of the future that was to be imposed is revealed not by the five-year plans but by the actual outcome of the planning process. In addition, Zaleski argues that the authorities' main objectives were not fundamentally economic, but political and ideological. These observations have implications for the evaluation of plan fulfillment and for prospects for economic reform.

First, it is clear that fulfillment in the sense of meeting goals laid down in the plans is of little importance, at least insofar as the goals relate to the propaganda aspects of the plan. Success to the leaders will be measured in other ways. One of these is success in maintaining their control over the economic system; in view of the great importance of this function to the personal careers and ambitions of the leaders, performance of the system in this respect almost certainly takes precedence over all others. The other obvious dimension of success for the system is its effectiveness in imposing the will of the leaders. This is evidently not to be measured in terms of the five-year plan or even in primarily economic terms. Success in meeting basic political and ideological objectives might well not be reflected in the goals and objectives of the annual or quarterly plans or in measurable quantities at all. Satisfactory economic performance is important, especially insofar as it bears on the power of the nation and of its leaders, but it is not the essential factor. It is important only insofar as it contributes to the furtherance of the basic objectives.

In this light, thinking about the motivation and prospects for reform and change in the system must be revised. First, reforms based on criticism of the economic performance of the system are probably doomed if they adversely affect or do not improve the system's ability to manage the economy or if they fail to conform to the political and ideological objectives of the leaders. This may be one of the reasons for the failure of the Sovnarkhoz reforms, although there are many plausible ways to explain that particular episode. The objective of improving control may have been one of the motivating factors behind the formation of the associations, and disappointment in that regard one of the reasons for their limited success. Failure to improve managerial capabilities, not to mention incompatibility with ideology and political objectives, may have been partly to blame for the failure of the 1965 reforms. Substantive reform in a bureaucracy as immense as that of the Soviet economy is inevitably hindered by the vested interests of entrenched bureaucrats, but that often seems an inadequate explanation for the failure of reforms, especially where individual rights mean as little as they do in the Soviet Union. Zaleski's analysis provides a deeper and more satisfactory insight into the great conservatism exhibited by the Soviet system of economic planning and management.

This coin has another side. If, to be successful, reform must not only lead to better managerial control but also be consistent with the political and ideological objectives of the leaders, then there will be no major changes in the system until those objectives change. Until there is evidence of such changes, we can expect to see only continuation of the past tinkering with the details of the system and experimentation with minor modifications intended to improve its operation, where improvement is measured in the terms discussed here. Major reform will not occur until major changes in objectives do. To date, there is no such evidence and no reason to expect important change.

Inconsistencies in the Plans

If the purpose of the planning system is to manage, then inconsistencies and incoherences in the outcome are likely to emerge; outcomes are not tied to the plan statements, and therefore there is no reason to expect close correspondence between plans and outcomes. But Zaleski documents numerous inconsistencies within the plans themselves. Why should this be so? The answer provides further evidence to support the argument that the planning system was primarily a managerial instrument.

Inconsistencies in the plans could result from inconsistencies in the economic policy they allegedly embodied or simply from errors by the planners. But Zaleski argues that these are not necessarily the causes of the observed incoherence; instead, the inconsistencies are the result of the Stalinist planning process itself. He provides a number of reasons.

There is first the constant reorganization of the planning agencies and the reassignment of planning tasks among them, not to mention the purges. As Zaleski puts it, in Gosplan during this period, " . . . working conditions were not always very good." The purges, at least on the grand scale of Stalin, are a thing of the past, but reorganizations did not end with Stalin, as Zaleski has shown in his book *Planning Reforms in the Soviet Union, 1962–1966*. The reshuffling of personnel and functions necessarily had a deleterious effect on ability to develop coherent plans.

In addition, the federal structure of the Soviet Union caused difficulties in achieving coherence in the plans. The simultaneous preparation of plans by republic Gosplans for the areas of their competence and by USSR Gosplan for the country as a whole caused problems in overlapping jurisdictions that evidently could not be overcome during the Stalinist period. These problems were especially important in the case of the Russian Republic Gosplan, of course. The jurisdictional problem created difficulties for plan consistency for which there was no easy solution. To find one would have involved overcoming grave political and bureaucratic obstacles.

These causes of incoherence arise partly from the particular circumstances of the Soviet Union, although similar problems would almost certainly arise in any politicized, bureaucratic planning organization. Two other causes mentioned by Zaleski would be present in any hierarchical socialist planning system. One is the bargaining between enterprises and ministries during plan formation. In the absence of alternative methods of ascertaining enterprise capacities, the bargaining process is an essential element of plan formation and therefore a continuing source of plan incoherence. The second is the fact that, to achieve equilibrium in the plans, the Stalinist system aggregated physical quantities in value terms by applying centrally determined prices. The prices used were not scarcity prices. The resulting equilibrium was an artificial one; the monetary aggregates could not correspond to the underlying real magnitudes. For that reason, attaining consistency in the plans inevitably was destined to failure. The hoary problems of socialist calculations persist in the administered economy, here manifested in the incoherence of the central plans.

If the plans are necessarily inconsistent for the reasons just discussed, it is hopeless to expect that they will be implemented. This point cannot have been lost on the Soviet authorities; they must have known that inconsistent plans could not form the basis for consistent action. Consequently, they must have had different purposes in mind for the plans. The process of forming the plans can be seen as a means of gathering information about enterprise capabilities (although the information obtained is flawed by the bargaining process) and as a mechanism for monitoring enterprise performance and the behavior and abilities of enterprise directors. As already noted, the plans themselves played a propaganda role in securing the cooperation of the populace in meeting the real objectives of the planners. But the fact that the planners must have known that plan inconsistencies were inevitable and have realized that inconsistent plans could not be the basis for action lends weight to Zaleski's conclusion that priority in the planning system was given to management, not to planning.

Post-Stalinist Planning

Zaleski's study of the development of the Soviet planning system now extends to the end of the Stalinist period. In the quarter of a century that has elapsed since Stalin's death, many changes have taken place in the Soviet Union. And yet, the framework of the economic system remains essentially the same as that developed during Stalin's reign. Thus, besides providing an unexcelled scholarly analysis of a particular historical period, Zaleski's work contains insights and perceptions that are important in understanding the nature of Soviet planning today.

To be sure, some aspects of the Stalinist period were peculiar to the time. Purges on a grand scale seem to be a relic of the past. The wildly optimistic targets of the early five-year plans have been replaced by more modest and, so it is said, more realistic goals (although overoptimism still prevails on a lesser scale). There seems to be more stability in the organization of the system, although the Sovnarkhoz experiment and the reassignments of responsibilities that continued at least into the late 1960's show that instability has not been eliminated. The great, sweeping changes that resulted from Stalin's quest for power and the course of industrialization policy have not recurred. Adjustments and changes continue, but the cataclysmic transformations typified by collectivization seem to be a thing of the past. World war has been replaced by preparation for war. Instead of the battleground, virtual and real, of the twenty years of Stalin's personal supremacy, the Soviet Union has become a gray bureaucracy operated by an elite that answers to venerable ideological doctrine. Still revolutionary and still committed to that doctrine, the system is nevertheless more stable than during Stalin's time.

Nevertheless, much of what Zaleski describes is pertinent to the Soviet system of today. The pricing system remains fundamentally the same. The introduction of capital charges and rents and talk about profit as a motivating force are only tinkering with the system; in the absence of market relations which could create genuine scarcity prices, such economic signals are just as arbitrary as the artificial prices upon which they are based. The planning process remains basically unchanged, the widely publicized and theoretically interesting Soviet developments in mathematical economics notwithstanding. Such techniques as input-output analysis and improved forecasting methods have found their way into Gosplan's kit of tools, and their use along with appreciation of the implications of mathematical programming probably has had a favorable impact on planning practice. Soviet planners of 1975 surely were better at their craft than their counterparts of forty years earlier, and the quality of the forecasts and the consistency of the plans reflect this. But the basic procedures followed in plan formation remain largely the same; it is still a process of assembling, after the familiar process of bargaining, a huge dossier of orders to specific economic organizations. It is still, in short, a process of assignment of tasks through the planning hierarchy. Management seems still to take priority over planning, just as it did during the Stalinist period. This can be seen in the continued practice of goal modification, in the use of the consumer goods and agricultural sectors as buffers when things go wrong, in the reliance on foreign trade to open bottlenecks, and even in the resort to imported Western technology in an effort to resolve problems of economic growth.

Most fundamentally, there is still the same basic chain of authority, the same ostensible objectives, and—finally—the same underlying problem. The new constitution notwithstanding, there can be no doubt that the first consideration of the leadership is maintaining its control over society. They may aspire to continued control for personal motives or ideological commitment or both. But in any case, the ostensible objectives are political and ideological. The cynical leader has to clothe his ambitions in ideological trappings and so appears to have the same motivations as the true ideologue. Thus, the objectives to be pursued through the maintenance of control turn out to be the same in either case.

To operate an authoritarian society, control of the economy is essential, a *sine qua non* for maintaining power. In the authoritarian society of Stalinist Russia, as in the Soviet Union today, control was and is exercised through the hierarchy of the planning system. It is an organization, a bureaucracy, for performing what is, in its essential respects, a bureaucratic job. In Russia at least, with its centuries of authoritarian and bureaucratic tradition and with the ideological commitment of the Communist Party to authoritarian rule, not to mention its own hierarchical structure, it is hard to see any other form for an organization essential to the survival of the ruling group. Decentralization of the Soviet system is incompatible with historical tradition and ideology, and nearly inconceivable for that reason. There is no basis for expecting a change away from the hierarchical order.

The same elementary problem underlies the planners' efforts, as Zaleski notes. The planners must try to impose their will on men and women who remain individuals with their own wants and desires. The success of the planners is permanently limited by this inescapable fact. Even after 60 years, the new socialist man has not emerged, and individualism stubbornly refuses to die, even in the Soviet Union.

Conclusion

Thus, the same general objectives are pursued today in basically the same hierarchical system and with the same human material to work with as during Stalin's personal dictatorship. Zaleski's observations and conclusions based on that period retain their validity and importance for understanding the purposes, operation, and evaluation of the Soviet system of economic planning. In dealing with a closed society like that in the Soviet Union, it is always possible that new information will turn up that may modify understanding or fill gaps in our knowledge. But because of the broad range of sources and exhaustive investigation of available literature that Zaleski has presented, and because of his outstanding ability to analyze and interpret the information at hand, it seems unlikely that any important changes in our knowledge of the planning system will emerge in the future. His works seem certain to stand as landmarks in scholarship on the Soviet economy.

Miami, Florida   John H. Moore
April 1978

Stalinist Planning
for Economic Growth,
1933–1952

CHAPTER 1

Introduction

The first volume of this work[1] described the formation of the Stalinist system of planning in the Soviet Union and its effects on economic fluctuations and growth before World War II. The present volume attempts to explain the operation of this system, the methods used to draft plans and the effects these methods have on growth, and the resulting economic equilibrium. Taken together, the study of the First Five-Year Plan (1928–1932) in the first volume and the present work (extending from 1933 through 1952) cover the entire period of Stalinist planning.

It was impractical to hold completely to the chronological division of the subjects handled in these two volumes. The system of management and planning was studied only incidentally in the first volume and the powers of the enterprise discussed hardly at all. This gap has been filled in Part One (Chapters 2–5) of the present volume, which describes the whole Soviet system of management and planning from the beginning of the New Economic Policy in 1921 until the death of Stalin in 1953.

In the first volume the study of economic fluctuations and growth was extended to 1940 in order to bring out more clearly the observed trends. However, including the study of fluctuations for 1940–1952 in this volume would have been beyond the scope of the work, since that period was overly influenced by the war and reconstruction. On the other hand, economic growth is studied here when plans and results are analyzed and when economic policy intended to promote growth is discussed.

The study of the planning and management system has a definite goal—to show how and at what level decisions are made and to what extent the process of management and planning promotes the coherence of the plans. Four main authorities are involved here: the Communist Party, administrative agencies at different levels (people's commissariat or ministry, central administration or *Glavk*, trust, and enterprise), various planning agencies, and agencies control-

---

1. Eugène Zaleski, *Planning for Economic Growth in the Soviet Union, 1918–1932*, translated and edited by Marie-Christine MacAndrew and G. Warren Nutter, Chapel Hill, N.C., 1971.

ling material and equipment supply (rationing). Although the Stalinist system is a more or less homogeneous entity, the jurisdiction of these agencies changed continuously during the period under study. The stability of the system as a whole, along with constant shifting of the powers of the management and planning agencies, came to be a characteristic feature of the Soviet system. Therefore, it was necessary to study the powers of these agencies in a historical perspective, for the growth of the economic bureaucracy became a phenomenon inseparable from economic growth itself.

The study of management and planning agencies and of the decision-making process also is intended to make it possible to distinguish within the system various spheres for decision-making in the coordination of the plans of economic units. The most important sphere, the authoritarian allocation of goals and resources, is adjacent to the sphere of the organized market and the small sector of the free market. The historical survey is intended to bring out the shifts of these spheres. Particular attention is paid, in this connection, to wartime planning (1941–1945) in Part Four (Chapters 14 and 15).

Long-term (five-year and longer) and current (annual and quarterly) plans are studied separately because of the different problems raised by the launching of long-term plans and current operational plans. The object is to show how these plans actually influenced the decisions taken by the management agencies.

The study of long-term planning is broken down by five-year plans: the second (Chapters 6 and 7), the third (Chapters 8 and 9), and the fourth (Chapter 16). It is intended to show, first, the extent to which the different versions of the five-year plan led to an equilibrated growth, a problem studied from the available statistical data. Then a study is made of the extent to which the visions of growth represented in these plans, coherent or not, actually influenced the annual plans through which they were meant to be put into operation. The life of a five-year plan, then, is measured by the number of annual plans that it influenced during the five-year period. A comparison of the goals of the five-year plans and the actual economic results achieved makes it possible to see the difference between the vision of growth and economic efficiency envisaged in the plans, on the one hand, and the concrete results of the economic policy actually followed, on the other.

The prewar annual plans[2] are all treated together in Chapters 10 and 13. An attempt is made to show their coherence, their operational nature, and also the particular, peculiar manner in which their goals were drafted and fulfilled. Ordinarily, the launching of annual plans ought to be studied through the quarterly plans. This has been done here only for 1936 (Chapter 12). In order to confirm these results, this analysis could be extended to cover 1934, 1935, and 1937, for which statistical data, although brief, might be found.

Several chapters (10, 11, 17, and 18) are devoted to an analysis of economic equilibrium. On the one hand, this is an extension of the study of annual plans. It examines their operational nature and the many revisions made during the

2. Only one postwar annual plan—for 1947—is known, and it was studied along with the postwar five-year plans.

year, and it shows the concrete measures of economic policy that the government took during the year and the actual choices that it made. On the other hand, the study of economic equilibrium represents an analysis of the economic situation, made separately for the two sectors: the investment sector that determines equilibrium in the production sector and the planned market sector that controls consumption.

Chapters 11 and 17 deal with investment. Plans are compared with results, and the origins of disturbances are examined, along with their real causes and their effect on the investment sector, production, and consumption. In addition, an attempt is made to show to what extent disturbances are transmitted "spontaneously," through *ad hoc* government decisions or through the national plans.

The object of the study of market equilibrium is to show the limits of the equilibrium of the "organized," institutional market, its capacity to cushion shocks coming from the centralized sector, and the government's use of classical economic tools (prices, money, finance) to defend its equilibrium. In this connection, the role of the free (collective farm) market as a barometer of tensions and a cushion for shocks is analyzed.

The work as a whole seeks to clarify the role of authoritarian administrative plans, which have the power of law. Has the Soviet economy actually operated in accordance with these plans? If not, by what mechanism are the plans of economic units coordinated *ex post*? What role is played by centrally made plan revisions and by decisions made at lower levels of the management hierarchy and taken more or less independently by the enterprises? And, to the extent that the plans are not revised, what role is played by the institutional barriers of the management system, on the one hand, and by the market, on the other?

The relation between authoritarian plans and growth is also examined. If the authoritarian plans are not carried out, what happens to the economic policy that they embody? Are the multiple plan revisions and daily government decisions based on the same economic policy or on another, less popular policy? Are the authoritarian plans, then, only a tool in the strategy of growth of a centrally directed economy? Does the stability of this austere and unpopular policy, then, replace the instability and ephemeral nature of national plans that promise abundant growth?

PART ONE

The Stalinist System of Administrative Planning

CHAPTER 2

System of Management

Supreme Authority in Administration and Planning

The essential feature of Soviet planning is that plan goals are transmitted through administrative channels to the executors. In order to understand Soviet planning, therefore, it is necessary to describe the authorities that set the principal goals and give the orders, the agencies charged with carrying out these directives, and the actual executors.

The Communist Party

A study of economic power in the Soviet Union is made difficult by the subordination of all government institutions to the Communist Party, by the monolithic nature of the Party, and, for the period under consideration here, by the absolute personal power Stalin wielded within the Party. The subordination of the government to the Party dates from the time the Party seized power by a coup d'etat. According to Lenin, "No important political or organisational question is decided by any state institution in our republic without the guidance of the Party's Central Committee."[1]

The Party exercises its power and control on all levels of Soviet life concurrently with official government bodies and social organizations such as trade unions. The Soviet parliament (the Supreme Soviet), the Council of Ministers, ministries, institutions, administrations, and enterprises are all directly subordinated to the Party through the intermediary of the appropriate Party organizations. Thus a Soviet ministry is subordinated to the Party not only through the intermediary of the minister, who should be loyal to it, but also through all the agencies of the ministry and the enterprises under it, which are directly responsible to their own Party cells or committees.

This subordination to the Party is all the more oppressive because of the

1. V. I. Lenin, " 'Left-Wing' Communism—An Infantile Disorder," *Selected Works*, New York and Moscow, 1967, Vol. 3, p. 360.

monolithic nature of the Party. The concentration of power within the governing bodies of the Party—the secretariat, the Politburo, and the Central Committee—is reflected in the internal organization of the Central Committee, the subordination of local organizations to the Central Committee, and the regulation of freedom of discussion within the Party.[2] This subordination of local Party organizations to the Central Committee derives from the official doctrine of *democratic centralism*. According to Michel Lesage, this doctrine tries to show that it is possible to reconcile centralization and democracy, but it does not indicate the balance of power between central agencies and local organizations in formulating Party decisions and in controlling their execution.[3] In fact, the supremacy of the superior agencies was affirmed at the Eighth Party Conference in December 1919, which left to lower Party organizations control only over local matters. The principle of democratic centralism was promulgated at the Eighth Party Congress (March 18–23, 1919), which declared the necessity for a single centralized Communist Party with a single Central Committee and stressed the importance of centralism and discipline:

The Party is in a position where the strictest centralism and the most rigorous discipline are absolute necessities. All decisions made by the higher echelons are absolutely binding on the lower echelons. Every decision should be carried out first of all, and only then may it be appealed to the appropriate Party agency. In this sense, at the present time, real military discipline is indispensable in the Party. All Party activities requiring centralization (publishing, propaganda, etc.) should, in the interests of the cause, be centralized.
 All conflicts should be settled by the appropriate higher echelons of the Party.[4]

These principles of internal Party organization have remained practically unchanged until today, except that the powers of the highest echelons of the Party—the Central Committee, the Politburo, and the secretariat—have been questioned on a few occasions.

In the period under study here, which ends with his death in 1953, Stalin's personal and arbitrary power constantly increased at the expense of the Politburo's authority over the other Party and government agencies. What is important for this study is not as much the tragic history that led to Stalin's absolute tyranny as the principal stages of this rise to power and its effect on the nature of economic and planning authority.[5]

The first step was taken in November–December 1927, when L. D. Trotsky

2. Michel Lesage, *Les régimes politiques de l'U.R.S.S. et de l'Europe de l'Est*, Paris, 1971, p. 51.

3. *Ibid.*, pp. 52–53. See also Patrice Gelard, *Les systèmes politiques des états socialistes*, Vol. 1: *Le modèle soviétique*, Paris, 1975, pp. 155–58.

4. *KPSS v rezoliutsiiakh i resheniiakh sezdov, konferentsii i plenumov Ts.K.* [The Communist Party of the Soviet Union: Resolutions and Decisions at Congresses, Conferences, and Plenary Sessions of the Central Committee], Moscow, 1954, Part I, p. 444.

5. On the nature and history of Stalin's power, see Lev Trotskii, *Stalin: An Appraisal of the Man and His Influence* (translated from the Russian), New York, 1967; Boris Souvarine, *Stalin: A Critical Survey of Bolshevism* (translated from the French), New York, 1939; I. Deutscher, *Stalin: A Political Biography*, New York, 1949; Roy A. Medvedev, *Let History Judge: The Origins and Consequences of Stalinism* (translated from the Russian), New York, 1973; and Hélène Carrère d'Encausse, *L'Union Soviétique de Lénine à Staline, 1917–1953*, Paris, 1972. On the mechanism of Stalinist power, see also Zbigniew K. Brzezinski, *The Permanent Purge*, Cambridge, Mass., 1956, and Khrushchev's report to the Twentieth Party Congress in 1956.

and G. E. Zinoviev were expelled from the Party[6] and when the Fifteenth Party Congress (December 2–19, 1927) passed a resolution requiring, after a report by Stalin, severe self-criticism from the opposition within the Party. The exile of Trotsky and the recantations of L. B. Kamenev and Zinoviev, along with those of the 21 other members of the opposition, enabled Stalin to turn against "the right wing."[7]

Forced collectivization was preceded by an attack on N. I. Bukharin, who tried to restrain the looting of the peasantry. In a joint session with the Party Central Control Commission (April 16–23, 1929), the Central Committee condemned the views of Bukharin, A. I. Rykov, and M. P. Tomskii; Bukharin and Tomskii were dismissed from their posts on *Pravda*, the Comintern, and the trade unions,[8] and Rykov was replaced as chairman of the Council of People's Commissars by V. M. Molotov.[9]

Stalin further consolidated his personal power through the purges and the political trials held during collectivization until the "official end" of the purge campaign was decreed by the Central Committee on December 25, 1935.[10] The purges took different forms, affecting government administrative personnel[11] as well as Party members. The simplest form was checking Party cards or exchanging them for new ones. Between 1921 and 1928, 260,144 Party members were expelled, and between April 1929 and the Sixteenth Party Congress (held in July 1930) 130,500 more, 10 per cent of all Party members, were expelled. Stalin launched a new checking campaign in January 1933, which ended with 206,934 members being expelled by the end of 1934 and 64,371 members being demoted to candidates or "sympathizers." Adding to these figures the 47,000 members deprived of their Party cards, this purge covered about 12 per cent of all Party members.[12] After the official end of the purges, the exchange of old Party cards for new ones was retained as a convenient way to get rid of undesirable members. Thus the December 26, 1936, resolution of the Party Central Committee declared invalid, as of February 1, 1937, Party cards of the 1926 stage and the old type of candidate cards.[13] There was another exchange of Party cards after the war.

The political trials were another means for Stalin to consolidate his absolute power. The trials of 1928–1931 have already been mentioned in my earlier book.[14] After 1933, trials became much more widespread. Among many others

6. Trotsky was readmitted on December 18, 1927.
7. Lesage, *Régimes politiques*, pp. 78–79.
8. *KPSS v rezoliutsiiakh*, Part II, pp. 429–47.
9. *Key Officials of the Government of the USSR*, Part I: *The Soviet Union, 1917–1966*, Munich, 1966, p. 2.
10. "Results of Checking Party Documents" (*KPSS v rezoliutsiiakh*, Part II, p. 831). See also Carrère d'Encausse, *L'Union Soviétique*, pp. 251–76.
11. According to Brzezinski (*Permanent Purge*, p. 52), some 450,000 civil servants were screened for security, 30 per cent of whom were dismissed.
12. *Ibid.*, pp. 52 and 62.
13. *Ibid.*, p. 69.
14. See my *Planning for Economic Growth in the Soviet Union, 1918–1932*, translated and edited by Marie-Christine MacAndrew and G. Warren Nutter, Chapel Hill, N.C., 1971, pp. 106–9. Among the political trials of that period, mention should be made of the trial of the "Donbass engineers" (May

the sentencing of the "anti-Party" group of N. B. Eismont, V. N. Tolmachev, and A. P. Smirnov on January 12, 1933, the trial of the Metro-Vickers engineers in April 1933, and the great wave of arrests that followed Kirov's assassination in December 1934 are noteworthy. Stalin personally directed the repression through the intermediary of N. I. Yezhov, a member of the purge committee created in April 1933, who became deputy chairman of the Central Control Commission and joined the Orgbureau.[15] The November 5, 1934, decree of the Central Executive Committee and the Party Central Committee granted the People's Commissariat of Internal Affairs the right to order forced residence and internment of "persons recognized as a danger to society" and organized a "special conference" to impose these sanctions.[16] Yezhov replaced G. G. Yagoda as Commissar of Internal Affairs on September 26, 1936, a post he held during the period of great terror of 1936–1938. He was replaced by L. P. Beria on December 8, 1938, arrested at the beginning of 1939, and shot in the summer of 1940.[17]

The Stalinist terror was made official by the great public trials. The trial during August 19–24, 1936, of the "sixteen" (Zinoviev, Kamenev, G. E. Evdokimov, I. N. Smirnov, S. V. Mrachkovskii, and others) is one of the best known. They were accused of having organized a terrorist center on direct instructions from Trotsky. The January 23–30, 1937, trial of the "seventeen" (G. L. Piatakov, K. B. Radek, G. Ia. Sokolnikov, N. I. Muralov, L. P. Serebriakov, and others), accused, among other things, of trying to dismember the Soviet Union for the benefit of Japan and Germany, is also well known.[18] The March 2–13, 1938, trial of the "twenty-one" (Bukharin, Rykov, N. N. Krestinskii, K. G. Rakovskii, Yagoda, and others) should also be mentioned.[19] Another secret trial, in June 1937, of M. N. Tukhachevsky, I. E. Yakir, and Ia. B. Gamarnik, attacked the Red Army leadership.[20] The full extent of the purges of Party and government personnel during 1936–1938 came to be known only thirty years later. In his report to the Twentieth Party Congress, Nikita Khrushchev declared that, of the 139 members of the Central Committee who were elected at the Seventeenth Congress in 1934, 98 (70 per cent) were arrested and most of them shot during 1937–1938. Of the 1,966 delegates to that congress, 1,108 were arrested and charged with counterrevolutionary crimes.[21] On the whole, if government personnel are included, the Stalinist terror took on the proportions of a tragedy. According to Roy Medvedev, the most cautious estimate of the number of people subjected to repression for political reasons between 1936 and 1939 is four to five million; at least 400,000 to 500,000 of these, mostly high officials, were executed without

12–July 5, 1928), the trial of the "Moscow industrialists" (November 25–December 8, 1930), and the trial of the "Mensheviks" (March 1931).

15. Lesage, *Régimes politiques*, p. 89.

16. *Ibid.*, pp. 89–90.

17. Medvedev, *Let History Judge*, pp. 240–41.

18. For further detail, see *Report of Court Proceedings in the Case of the Anti-Soviet Trotskyist Center Heard before the Military Collegium of the Supreme Court of the USSR* (January 23–30, 1937), Moscow, 1937.

19. For further detail, see *Le procès du bloc des droitistes et des Trotskistes antisoviétiques* (March 2–13, 1938), Moscow, 1938.

20. See Deutscher, *Stalin*, pp. 379–80. For further detail, see the sources cited in footnote 5 above.

21. Lesage, *Régimes politiques*, p. 92.

trial.[22] The terror also decimated the staff of the economic administration and the State Planning Committee (Gosplan). All the directors of USSR Gosplan were replaced during that period.[23]

The internal struggle within the Party and the persecution did not stop before the war nor during 1941–1953. But after the Party had been completely subjected to Stalin's will, the repression consisted of disgrace (N. A. Voznesenskii in 1948), struggles for succession ("the doctors' plot" of 1952), or outright persecution of peoples annexed by the Soviet Union during 1939–1940 (Poles, Lithuanians, Estonians, Latvians) or suspected of lack of enthusiasm for the regime (Ukrainians, Crimean Tatars, Volga Germans, and others). But the apparatus for repression and the population of the concentration camps did not stop growing during the last years of Stalin's reign.[24]

This Stalinist persecution, which reached a peak during 1936–1939, does not officially show up in the texts of the long- and short-term plans drafted during 1933–1952. But it must not be forgotten when trying to explain the changes in the agencies of economic administration and planning and the changes in the plan goals. The threat of repression, as Michel Lesage points out, remained a basic element in the Stalinist system, which was the political regime in the Soviet Union until 1953.[25]

Legislative Power

The limited information given above on the role played by the Communist Party in general, and Stalin in particular, is sufficient to explain the lack of importance of the legislature in the Soviet Union during this period. It served largely as a "registry office," a role that it kept long after Stalin's death.

After the creation of the Union of Soviet Socialist Republics by the agreement of December 30, 1922, and in accordance with the Soviet Constitution, which went into effect in July 1924, the central legislative power in the USSR was invested in the Congress of Soviets. This body, elected by restricted, indirect, and public vote, was supposed to meet once a year. In actual fact, it met only

22. Medvedev, *Let History Judge*, p. 239.

23. On the purges in the economic administrative and planning agencies, see Chapter 8, section on purges.

24. To estimate the population of Soviet concentration camps would require a special study. Naum Jasny's estimate, derived from the 1941 annual plan, was 3.5 million in 1941 (see his "Labor and Output in Soviet Concentration Camps," *Journal of Political Economy*, October 1951, pp. 405–19). S. Swianiewicz (*Forced Labour and Economic Development*, London, New York, Toronto, 1965, p. 31) contests this figure, claiming that it does not include the cases handled by the Commissariat of Internal Affairs and the persons deported from the annexed territories. Swianiewicz suggests a figure of 6.9 million in 1941. During the war the population of Soviet concentration camps increased considerably because of the influx of German, Japanese, Hungarian, and Italian prisoners-of-war and because of the deportation of the Crimean Tatars, the Kalmyks, the Moslems from the Caucasus, and others. According to the estimates of the British government, cited during the August 1950 meeting of the Economic and Social Council of the United Nations by Corley Smith, there were more than 10 million people in Soviet concentration camps in 1948. Other sources estimate 15 million at the time of the amnesty after Stalin's death in 1953. See *ibid.*, pp. 44–45. See also David J. Dallin and Boris I. Nicolaevsky, *Forced Labor in Soviet Russia*, New Haven, 1947.

25. Lesage, *Régimes politiques*, p. 92.

eight times during 1922–1936.[26] In the intervals between sessions, the Central Executive Committee was the body with supreme authority; it was a bicameral body consisting of the Council of the Union and the Council of Nationalities. The Central Executive Committee was supposed to meet three times a year according to the constitution and had the same powers as the Congress (except in constitutional matters). It was, however, a large body, comprising 300 members. The members of the Council of the Union were elected by the Congress of Soviets from among the representatives of the federal republics in a number proportional to the population. The Council of Nationalities was made up of five representatives from each federal or autonomous republic and one from each autonomous province of the Russian Republic or the Transcaucasian Republic.[27]

A new constitution, adopted on December 5, 1936, by the Eighth Congress of Soviets, changed the structure of legislative power. The Congress of Soviets and its Central Executive Committee were replaced by the USSR Supreme Soviet, which is made up of the Council of the Union and the Council of Nationalities. The former is elected for four years in electoral districts with one deputy for each 300,000 voters. The latter is also elected by Soviet citizens in the federal and autonomous republics, autonomous provinces, and national districts at the rate of 25 deputies per federal republic, 11 per autonomous republic, 5 per autonomous province, and 1 per national district.[28]

The USSR Supreme Soviet is the only body that can pass laws, change the constitution, admit new republics, and change the frontiers of republics that are already part of the Union. It is responsible for settling the most important problems of foreign and domestic policy and voting on the USSR budget and plan. The Supreme Soviet elects its own presidium, which is supposed to convene it at least twice a year. It can also be convened at the request of the federal republics. It appoints the USSR Council of Ministers, the members of the USSR Supreme Court, and the Attorney General.[29] All these powers, however, are more formal than real. During the Stalinist period—and this is still true today—the Supreme Soviet passed all laws unanimously[30] and exercised very little supervision over subordinate bodies. It is intended above all to provide a sort of popular endorsement of decisions taken elsewhere.

Restricted Committee of Council of Ministers

Actual administrative power is concentrated in the Council of Ministers (Council of People's Commissars until 1946). Since this is too large a body to make decisions effectively, the real power—to the extent that the decisions have not

26. In 1922, 1924, 1925, 1927, 1929, 1931, 1935, and 1936 (*ibid.*, p. 71).
27. *Ibid.*, p. 72.
28. *Ibid.*, p. 93.
29. M. P. Kareva, *Konstitutsiia SSSR* [The USSR Constitution], Moscow, 1948, pp. 161–62.
30. In all the proceedings of the meetings of the Supreme Soviet that could be found for 1938–1941 and 1946–1953, every decision was unanimous. See *Zasedaniia Verkhovnogo Soveta SSSR* [Meetings of USSR Supreme Soviet] for various years.

already been made by the Party[31]—has always been exercised by the Restricted Committee of the Council of Ministers.

On November 30, 1918, during the Civil War, the All-Russia Central Executive Committee created the Council for Worker and Peasant Defense, the chairmanship of which was given to Lenin. Its objective was to coordinate the work of civilian and military organizations in order to mobilize resources. In April 1920, toward the end of the Civil War, this body was transformed into the Council for Labor and Defense (*Sovet Truda i Oborony*), still with Lenin as chairman. On December 29, 1920, the Eighth All-Russia Congress of Soviets granted it a statute, stressing its economic duties.[32] The Council for Labor and Defense became a commission of the Council of People's Commissars, with that Council's chairman its presiding officer. As a commission, it was composed of the People's Commissars of War, Labor, Transportation, Agriculture, and Food Supply; the chairmen of the Supreme Council of the National Economy (VSNKh) and of the Workers' and Peasants' Inspection Board; and a representative of the Central Union of Trade Unions. The director of the Central Statistical Administration had a consultative status. The duties of the Council for Labor and Defense were, as before, to coordinate the activities of government agencies handling military and civilian affairs, but its jurisdiction over economic matters became much broader. It issued decisions, decrees, and instructions and took all the necessary measures for their fulfillment. In particular, it drafted the single economic plan for the Russian Republic[33] and presented it for approval to the All-Russia Central Executive Committee, directed the work of the economic commissariats in accordance with this plan, supervised its fulfillment, and made the necessary revisions in the plan. All the decisions of the Council for Labor and Defense were binding on all the agencies of the Russian Republic, but they could be revised by the All-Russia Central Executive Committee and by the Council of People's Commissars.

The economic responsibilities of the Council for Labor and Defense were further increased after it was split up into the Defense Committee (*Komitet Oborony*) and Economic Council (*Ekonomicheskii Sovet*).[34] According to the November 28,

31. The members of the Restricted Committee of the Council of Ministers (or Council of People's Commissars) held the highest posts in the Party. Therefore it is difficult to distinguish between decisions taken by the Communist Party and those taken by the Soviet government. To do so, it would be necessary to know the relations between Stalin, his secretariat, and the Party Politburo.

32. December 29, 1920, decree of Eighth All-Russia Congress of Soviets, "On the Council for Labor and Defense" (*Upravlenie narodnym khoziaistvom SSSR, 1917–1940 gg.* [Management of USSR National Economy, 1917–1940], Moscow, 1968, pp. 44–45).

33. It should be noted that the Union of Soviet Socialist Republics had not yet come into existence. Jurisdiction over the entire USSR took effect on December 30, 1922.

34. The Economic Council was created by the November 28, 1937, decree of the Council of People's Commissars, "On the Creation of the Economic Council," *Sobranie zakonov i rasporiazhenii raboche-krestianskogo pravitelstva SSSR* [Collection of Laws and Decrees of the Workers' and Peasants' Government of the USSR], No. 75, December 15, 1937, Art. 365. The Defense Committee, attached to the Council of People's Commissars, was created in April 1937. In January 1938 it was endowed with a permanent Military and Industrial Commission, which was to mobilize and prepare the defense industry and industry in general and to guarantee the fulfillment of the plans and orders of the Defense Committee for the production and supply of armaments. ("On the Creation of the Military and

1937, decree, the Economic Council was composed of the chairman of the Council of People's Commissars (as before), the deputy chairmen of the Council (a sizable number[35]), and a representative of the Council of Trade Unions. It retained its status as a permanent commission of the Council of People's Commissars and its right to promulgate decrees that were binding on the people's commissariats, the republic councils of people's commissars, and all government agencies. Its economic powers, which were given in some detail, included examining annual and quarterly plans, presenting them to the Council of People's Commissars, and confirming plans for material and equipment supply, consumer goods supply, railroad and water transportation, agricultural work, and procurements. It was also to examine reports on plan fulfillment, government decisions, and the economic situation in various branches. It was responsible for reviewing problems of prices, employment, and wages; problems involved in creating and abolishing economic agencies and transferring state goods from one agency to another; and, in general, all current economic problems.[36] Moreover, it had its own staff.

In addition to decisions taken on its own initiative, the Economic Council coordinated the activities of the people's commissariats. For this purpose a special 15-member office of coordination was set up on November 4, 1939, with precise regulations on how it should function.[37] By 1940 the coordination duty had apparently become predominant, so the government issued a decree creating, under the Economic Council, six councils charged with coordinating and directing the work of the commissariats.[38] These councils were specialized by economic activity: metals and chemicals (presided over by N. A. Bulganin), machine-building (V. A. Malyshev), defense industry (Voznesenskii), fuel and electric power (M. G. Pervukhin), consumer goods (A. N. Kosygin), and agriculture and procurement (unknown). This same organization of the central authority in economic administration and planning on the national level was then

Industrial Commission under the Defense Committee," *KPSS o vooruzhennykh silakh Sovetskogo Soiuza* [The Communist Party of the Soviet Union on the Soviet Armed Forces], Moscow, 1969, p. 278, as cited by David Holloway, "Soviet Military R and D: Managing the 'Research-Production Cycle,'" *Soviet Science and Technology. Domestic and Foreign Perspectives*, edited by John R. Thomas and Ursula M. Kruse-Vaucienne, Washington, D.C., 1977, p. 194.)

35. From December 19, 1930, to May 6, 1941, V. M. Molotov was the head of the government of the USSR. The following persons were deputy chairmen of the Council at different periods (*Key Officials*, pp. 2–4): A. A. Andreev (1930–1931), L. P. Beria (March 1–May 6, 1941), N. A. Bulganin (May 1938–1941), N. A. Voznesenskii (May 1939–May 6, 1941), K. E. Voroshilov (May 1940–May 6, 1941), A. Ia. Vyshinskii (May 1939–May 6, 1941), R. S. Zemliachka (May 1939–?), L. M. Kaganovich (August 1938–May 6, 1941), S. V. Kosior (January 1938–February 1939), A. N. Kosygin (April 17, 1940–May 6, 1941), V. V. Kuibyshev (December 19, 1930–January 1935), V. A. Malyshev (April 17, 1940–May 6, 1941), V. I. Mezhlauk (1934–February 1937, October 1937–1938), L. Z. Mekhlis (March 1, 1941–May 6, 1941), A. I. Mikoyan (August 1937–May 6, 1941), M. G. Pervukhin (April 17, 1940–May 6, 1941), Ia. Z. Rudzutak (December 19, 1930–1937), V. Ia. Chubar (April 1934–?).

36. *Sobranie zakonov*, No. 75, December 15, 1937, Art. 365.

37. Decree of Economic Council, "On the Coordination of Problems Submitted by the People's Commissariats to the Economic Council under the USSR Council of People's Commissars" (*Sobranie postanovlenii i rasporiazhenii pravitelstva SSSR* [Collection of Resolutions and Decrees of the USSR Government], No. 57, December 16, 1939, Art. 610, signed by A. Mikoyan, chairman of the Economic Council).

38. *Izvestia*, April 18, 1940. On this occasion the government annulled the November 4, 1939, decree of the Economic Council (*Sobranie postanovlenii*, No. 12, May 31, 1940, Art. 291).

introduced into several federal republics, including the Ukraine, Uzbekistan, Turkmenistan, Belorussia, and Tadzhikistan.[39]

During the war the supreme decisions were made by the State Committee for Defense (*Gosudarstvennyi Komitet Oborony*), presided over by Stalin.[40] It is doubtful whether the Economic Council continued to operate during the war period. It no longer appears in official texts, but no mention of its abolition could be found in the sources consulted.

The State Committee for Defense was abolished on September 4, 1945.[41] Since that time the function of the restricted committee of the USSR Council of Ministers seems to have been exercised by its presidium, composed of the Council chairman, the deputy chairmen, and certain individuals appointed by the Council.[42] A very important body as it now operates, the presidium of the Council of Ministers was not provided for in the Soviet Constitution. On this point, a Soviet author said: "When the new constitution is drafted, it is essential that it specify the method of formation, the composition, and the extent of jurisdiction of this important government agency."[43] Indeed, the new constitution of 1977 (article 132) recognized the presidium as a permanent body of the Council of Ministers in charge of all government and economic matters.

The names and the positions of the presidium members other than the deputy chairmen are not known. There were a great many deputy chairmen of the Council during the period that Stalin was its chairman (from May 6, 1941, until March 5, 1953).[44] With twelve deputy chairmen in 1953 and the appointed members, the presidium of the Council of Ministers seems to have become quite an important agency, a real "Council of Ministers" within the legally existing Council. Therefore, it is not surprising that knowledge of which matters were to be settled in the plenary assembly of the Council of Ministers was of vital interest to Soviet economists; the presidium of the Council of Ministers played the same role as the presidium of the Supreme Soviet, with its decisions to be confirmed later by the whole assembly.[45] To judge from the evolution and composition of this body, this seems to have been the only way to handle the "inflation" of the staff of the Council of Ministers.

39. See *Sobranie postanovlenii*, No. 15, June 15, 1940, Art. 358; No. 21, August 30, 1940, Art. 511; No. 24, October 12, 1940, Art. 593; and No. 29, November 16, 1940, Art. 696 and 697.

40. On wartime administration (1941–1945), see beginning of Chapter 14.

41. *Ekonomicheskaia zhizn SSSR. Khronika sobytii i faktov, 1917–1965* [Economic Life of the USSR. Chronology of Events and Facts, 1917–1965], Moscow, 1967, Book I, p. 386.

42. N. A. Volkov, *Vysshie i tsentralnye organy gosudarstvennogo upravleniia SSSR i soiuznykh respublik v sovremennyi period* [Superior and Central Agencies of the State Administration of the USSR and the Union Republics in the Contemporary Period], Kazan, 1971, p. 26.

43. *Ibid.*

44. V. M. Molotov (May 6, 1941–March 5, 1953); L. P. Beria (May 6, 1941–March 5, 1953); A. A. Andreev (June 19, 1946–1953); A. I. Mikoyan (May 6, 1941–March 5, 1953); K. E. Voroshilov (May 6, 1941–March 5, 1953); N. A. Voznesenskii (May 6, 1941–March 14, 1949); L. M. Kaganovich (May 6, 1941–March 6, 1947); I. F. Tevosian (June 13, 1949–March 5, 1953); M. G. Pervukhin (May 6, 1941–1944; January 17, 1950–March 5, 1953); A. I. Efremov (March 18, 1949–?); V. A. Malyshev (May 6, 1941–March 5, 1953); G. M. Malenkov (October 18, 1946–March 5, 1953); M. Z. Saburov (May 6, 1941–1944; February 8, 1947–March 5, 1953); N. A. Bulganin (March 5, 1947–March 5, 1953); A. N. Kosygin (May 6, 1941–March 5, 1953): A. Ia. Vyshinskii (May 6, 1941–1944); and A. D. Krutikov (July 13, 1948–?) (*Key Officials*, pp. 3 and 5).

45. Volkov, *Vysshie organy*, pp. 26–27.

USSR Council of Ministers

The December 30, 1922, agreement establishing the Union of Soviet Socialist Republics gave the country a federal structure and provided for the distribution of authority between the Union and the federal republics.[46] Five Union (*obshchesoiuznye*) people's commissariats were to manage the affairs of the Union: foreign affairs, war and navy, foreign trade, transportation, and post and telegraph. Another group of people's commissariats, first called "unified" (*obedinennye*) and later Union-republic (*soiuzno-respublikanskie*), operated at both the Union and federal republic levels: Workers' and Peasants' Inspection Board, labor, food supply, finance, and VSNKh.

The 1924 Constitution maintained this distribution of authority. Until 1931 the Council of People's Commissars remained relatively restricted. Only one new Union commissariat (for water transport) was formed by splitting up the Commissariat of Transportation in 1931, and there were only six "unified" commissariats.[47] Meetings of the Council were attended by the people's commissars, by the chairmen of the various committees, offices, and administrations directly under the Council,[48] and, in certain cases, by the chairmen of the federal republic councils of people's commissars.

An "inflation" of the Council of People's Commissars began in 1932 and eventually made it so huge a body that it could no longer take decisions effectively. This "inflation" came about in several ways. People's commissariats (mainly industrial ones) were split up into commissariats of more limited jurisdiction; various state committees, commissions, or agencies operating under the Council were transformed into commissariats (or ministries); new state committees, commissions, or agencies were created; and the number of federal republics was increased.

The subdivision of commissariats into more specialized bodies began with the abolition of VSNKh on January 5, 1932, and its replacement by people's commissariats for heavy industry, light industry, and the timber industry.[49] The councils of the national economy (Sovnarkhozes) of the federal and autonomous republics were transformed into republic commissariats of light industry at the same time. The number of commissariats continued to increase during the prewar years (see Tables E-1 and E-2), more so in industry than elsewhere.[50] In 1934 the People's Commissariat of Food Supply was split into two—one for domestic trade and one for the food industry. The Commissariat of the Defense Industry was created in 1936 and the Commissariat of Machine-Building in 1937; both had

46. I. N. Ananov, *Ministerstva v SSSR* [Ministries in the USSR], Moscow, 1960, p. 68.

47. The 1924 Constitution provided for five "unified" people's commissariats (VSNKh, Labor, Finance, Workers' and Peasants' Inspection Board, and the Central Statistical Administration). The creation in 1929 of the Commissariat of Agriculture and in 1930 of the Commissariat of Food Supply and the subordination of the Central Statistical Administration to USSR Gosplan raised the number of "unified" commissariats to six.

48. An (incomplete) list of these agencies is given in Tables E-1 and E-2. On their jurisdiction, see below pp. 20–22.

49. On this subject, see my *Planning*, pp. 186–89.

50. *Sotsialisticheskoe narodnoe khoziaistvo SSSR v 1933–1940 gg.* [The USSR Socialist National Economy in 1933–1940], Moscow, 1963, p. 46.

previously been included in the Commissariat of Heavy Industry. During 1938–1939, there was further subdivision of commissariats: the food industry was split into three parts, machine-building into three, light industry into two, and heavy industry into six.[51] Separate commissariats were also created for construction, the rubber industry, and machine tools.

During the war, there was little variation in the number of people's commissariats. The government preferred to make use of the existing organizations, entrusting war goals to the existing commissariats and special tasks to *ad hoc* committees or commissions. There is mention of creating only two new industrial commissariats, for the tank industry and for mortars, and they were changed after the war.[52]

As can be seen from Table 1, the number of people's commissariats increased between 1936 and 1941, stabilized during the war,[53] and increased again later. It is hard to understand the purpose of the changes made during the Stalinist period. The people's commissars were given the title of minister (during the March 12–19, 1946, session of the Supreme Soviet) apparently for reasons of prestige.[54] The increase in the number of industrial ministries might be explained by the growth of industry, but the largest increase occurred between 1937 and 1941, a period of industrial stagnation. The changes made after the war are also difficult to explain by economic growth. Immediately after the war, the number of ministries increased to 59 (in July 1946) and even further, only to be reduced during the amalgamations of ministries carried out in 1948 and 1949. After Stalin's death, there was a sizable, but temporary, reduction; then the number of ministries increased to 46 in 1954 and 52 by January 20, 1957, only to drop to 16 by October 1, 1959, after the creation of the Sovnarkhozes.[55] The successive

51. The fuel industry, electric power stations and the electrical industry, the ferrous metal industry, the nonferrous metal industry, the chemical industry, and the construction materials industry (January 24, 1939, decree of Supreme Soviet presidium [*Upravlenie*, pp. 222–23]).

52. The Commissariat of the Tank Industry (created on September 11, 1941) became the Commissariat of Transport Machine-Building on October 14, 1945. The Commissariat of Mortars (created on November 26, 1941, to replace the Commissariat of General Machine-Building) became the Commissariat of Machine and Instrument Building on February 17, 1946. (*Ekonomicheskaia zhizn*, Book I, pp. 336, 338, 387, and 392.)

53. The Commissariats of Defense and of Foreign Affairs, nevertheless, became Union-republic commissariats on February 1, 1944. The creation of new industrial commissariats began, for the most part, after the end of the war. Thus, the People's Commissariat of Industrial Crops was created on November 11, 1945; the People's Commissariat of Agricultural Machine-Building on January 7, 1946 (see Table E–2, note i); and the People's Commissariats for the Construction of Heavy Industrial Enterprises and for the Construction of Military and Naval Enterprises on January 19, 1946. On this last date the People's Commissariat of the Coal Industry was split into separate commissariats for the western regions and the eastern regions. On March 4, 1946, the Commissariat of the Petroleum Industry was, in its turn, split into a commissariat for the southern and western regions, on the one hand, and one for the eastern regions, on the other. The People's Commissariat of Construction and Highway Machine-Building was created on February 17, 1946. See *ibid.*, Book I, pp. 388, 391, and 392.

54. *Ibid.*, Book I, p. 392. According to Ananov (*Ministerstva*, p. 27), the new title of "minister" given to the people's commissars of the USSR and the federal republics reflected the jurisdiction and responsibilities of central administration agencies and distinguished them from other administrative agencies. The term "commissar" or "commissariat" was used by not only central but also some local agencies (for instance, the district revision councils called themselves "military commissariats" and their chiefs "commissars").

55. *Ibid.*, pp. 71 and 74 and Table 3.

Table 1   Change in Number of People's Commissariats or Ministries,[a] 1922–1954

	Union People's Commissariats or Ministries[b]	"Unified" or Union-Republic People's Commissariats or Ministries[b]	Total
1922–1924	5	5	10
1931	6	6	12
1935	12	3	15
1936	8	10	18
1941	29	14	43
March 1946	30	19	49
July 1946	33[c]	22[c]	59
1949	28	20	48
February 1953	27[d]	20[d]	48
March 15, 1953	12	13	25
April 26, 1954	24	22	46

Source: Ananov, *Ministerstva*, pp. 71 and 74; Tables E-1 and E-2; and *Istoriia Sovetskoi Konstitutsii*, pp. 843–44.

a. People's commissariats became ministries in March 1946.

b. On the distinction between Union and "unified" or Union-republic commissariats or ministries, see Table E-1, note a, and pp. 22–23 below.

c. It was not possible to ascertain whether the following four ministries were Union or Union-republic: the Pharmaceutical Industry, Food Reserves, Material Reserves, Urban Construction.

d. It was not possible to ascertain whether the Ministry of Motor Transport was a Union or Union-republic ministry.

splits and amalgamations of ministries—such as that in the coal industry, the petroleum industry, the ferrous metal industry, electric power stations, the chemical industry, light industry, the fishing industry, the food industry, or agriculture (see Table E-2)—obviously had no direct connection with growth but simply reflected the proclivity, typical of the Stalinist period, for solving all problems by administrative order. That these solutions were not always good ones can be seen from the commentary in an official Soviet work describing these reorganizations: "As early as the Second, and particularly in the Third, Five-Year Plan, the harmful consequences of the cult of personality of Stalin began to be seen in management."[56]

The explanation of the revisions made in the number and function of the different committees, commissions, and working organizations under the USSR Council of Ministers is even more difficult. The organizations that can be identified are listed in Tables E-1 and E-2. These come under the Soviet definition of "specialized central agencies of state administration."[57] In 1959 the classification given in Table 2 was proposed. The formal distinction between the agencies listed in groups I and II, on the one hand, and those in group III, on the other, lies in the authority by which they are constituted. The former are created, reorganized, and abolished by the USSR Supreme Soviet, and the latter by the

56. *Sots. narodnoe khoziaistvo*, p. 50.
57. Ananov, *Ministerstva*, p. 30.

Table 2   Categories of Agencies Operating under USSR Council of Ministers, as of October 1, 1959[a]

I. Agencies assimilated to ministries
    Committee on State Security
    USSR Central Statistical Administration
    USSR State Bank (*Gosbank*)
II. State committees, councils, and commissions
    of USSR Council of Ministers
    A. State Committees for:
        Planning (Gosplan)
        Labor and Wages
        Aircraft Technology
        Defense Technology
        Radio Electronics
        Shipbuilding
        Chemistry
        Automation and Machine-Building
        Construction
        Foreign Economic Relations
        Grain Products
        Vocational-Technical Education
    B. State councils
        State Scientific Economic Council
    C. State commissions
        Soviet Control Commission

III. Special agencies
    A. State committees under USSR Council
        of Ministers for:
        Cultural Relations with Foreign Countries
        Radio Broadcasting and Television
    B. Central Administrations (*Glavki*) under
        USSR Council of Ministers for:
        Civil Air Fleet
        State Material Reserves
        Hydrometeorological Service
        Utilization of Atomic Energy
        Gas Industry
    C. Committees under USSR Council of
        Ministers for:
        Standards, Measures, and Measuring
            Instruments
        Inventions and Discoveries
    D. Councils under USSR Council of
        Ministers for:
        Russian Orthodox Church Affairs
        Religious Cults
    E. State Commission for Mining Resources
    F. Legal Commission
    G. USSR Telegraph Agency (TASS)
    H. State Board of Arbitration

Source: Ananov, *Ministerstva*, pp. 27–30.

a. Such a complete list is not available for the period under study here (1933–1953). Even this list could be much longer because of the creation of new state committees after the abolition of the industrial ministries in 1957 and 1958.

USSR Council of Ministers. Hence the agencies in groups I and II have the rank of ministry and their chairmen have full rights to participate in the work of the Council of Ministers. The agencies in group III (called special agencies, *spetsialnye vedomstva*) have a lower ranking. Their directors, who are appointed and dismissed by the Council of Ministers, have only a consultative status in that body.[58]

In Soviet practice, the state committees were often like "antechambers" of the ministries (or people's commissariats). Promotion (to ministry) theoretically was made according to the growth of the economic branch administered by the committee. Several such examples can be cited. The Committee for Domestic Trade became the People's Commissariat of Domestic Trade in 1924. The Committee for Agricultural Procurement under the Council of People's Commissars became the People's Commissariat of Agricultural Procurement in January 1938. The ministries of higher education (1946), the film industry (1946), geology (1946), forestry (1947), material reserves, and food reserves (1946) were created from existing state committees. But the reverse also happened, and several

58. *Ibid.*, pp. 28–31, and Volkov, *Vysshie organy*, pp. 16–19.

ministries became state committees (the Ministry of State Security in 1954, the Ministry of Urban Construction in 1950, the Central Administration for Construction of Motor Highways in 1956, and the Central Administration for Labor Reserves in 1958).[59]

In fact, the state committees and the various agencies operating under the USSR Council of Ministers were created and abolished according to the same principles as the ministries: the delegation (and revocation) of special powers to cope with immediate problems. It is pointless, therefore, to search for profound principles. But it is possible to observe the effects of this practice on the role of the Council of Ministers. The very composition of the Council became fluid, and the participation of assorted people with a "deliberative" voice (as if the others had a decisive voice) distorted the will of the majority and the process of the deliberations. The real weight of various agencies also became changeable. There was a clear tendency toward a "swelling" of the plenary assembly, which could only reduce its real role to the advantage of the presidium of the Council of Ministers.

Republic, Province, and Local Management Agencies

Officially, management powers are divided among Union agencies and bodies lower in the hierarchy according to the federal principle. Thus, at the Union level, part of the economy is under the direct administration of the Union people's commissariats and another part comes under the jurisdiction of the federal republics. The latter authority is exercised, on the one hand, through the intermediary of the Union-republic commissariats (or ministries), whose branches in the republics come under double jurisdiction, and, on the other, through direct management by the republic agencies.

The same federal type of jurisdictional setup is repeated at the level of federal republics, autonomous republics, and provinces, where, alongside enterprises directly under the republic (or province executive committee), are enterprises supervised indirectly through the intermediary of lower-ranking administrative agencies (autonomous republics, provinces, territories, districts, etc.). (See Chart 1.)

Before 1932 the federal republics managed the economy through the "unified" people's commissariats, as mentioned earlier, and the "nonunified" people's commissariats, which were under the sole jurisdiction of the republics. In 1924 there were six republic commissariats—for agriculture, internal affairs, justice, education, health, and social security. But the 1936 Constitution provided for only four—for education, local industry, communal economy, and social security.[60]

Among the "unified" people's commissariats, the most important before 1932 was VSNKh (Supreme Council of the National Economy). The federal republic VSNKh's operated at the federal level; the central Sovnarkhozes of autonomous

---

59. Created out of the former Ministry of Labor Reserves, which was integrated into the Ministry of Culture between 1953 and 1958 (see Table 2 and Ananov, *Ministerstva*, pp. 35–36).

60. *Ibid.*, p. 109.

republics and the province or territory Sovnarkhozes operated at the regional level. As mentioned earlier, after VSNKh was abolished in the beginning of 1932, three separate people's commissariats were created;[61] two of these (for heavy industry and the timber industry) were Union commissariats (*obshchesoiuznye*) and one (for light industry) a "unified" commissariat. The government decree issued on this matter on March 27, 1932, stipulated that this reorganization was not intended to result in the elimination of republic and local trusts and the automatic subordination of republic and local enterprises to Union agencies.[62]

Two organizational approaches were adopted at this time. For the Commissariat of Light Industry, the general rule of "unified" commissariats was applied: republic and local enterprises were subordinated to the republic commissariats of light industry and to the province departments of light industry. The republic and local enterprises under the Sovnarkhozes of the republics, provinces, or territories, which were not included under the Commissariat of Light Industry, came under a double jurisdiction—that of the Union Commissariats of Heavy Industry and of the Timber Industry and that of the councils of people's commissars of the republics in which they were located. The functions of the commissariats were to be limited to general planning of production and investment and exercised through the intermediary of delegates from the republic councils of people's commissars and the local executive committees. These delegates had their own staff and came under a double jurisdiction—that of their commissariat and that of the agencies to which they were attached. In actual fact, as pointed out by A. V. Venediktov, these delegates for the most part followed the instructions of their own commissars, especially in heavy industry. For the timber industry, the commissariat's right of management was formally recognized in the May 28, 1932, statute on the delegates of this commissariat, and, actually, the management of republic and local enterprises by that commissariat did not differ from that of the enterprises directly under Union jurisdiction.[63]

A general reform of the management of republic and local industry was introduced by the August 10, 1934, decree.[64] The enterprises of republic and local industry administered by the commissariats of heavy industry, light industry, and the timber industry were regrouped into commissariats of local industry created in the federal and autonomous republics and in the administrations of local industry operating under the territory and province executive committees. The new administrations were to manage, plan, and control directly the enterprises under their jurisdiction.

Enterprises were divided between the newly created people's commissariats of local industry, on the one hand, and the commissariats of heavy industry,

61. "On the Creation of the People's Commissariats of Heavy Industry, Light Industry, and the Timber Industry" (*Upravlenie*, pp. 189–90).

62. Decree of Central Executive Committee and USSR Council of People's Commissars, "On the Organization of the Management of Republic and Local Industry in Connection with the Reorganization of VSNKh" (*ibid.*, pp. 190–92).

63. A. V. Venediktov, *Organizatsiia gosudarstvennoi promyshlennosti v SSSR* [Organization of State Industry in the USSR], Leningrad, 1961, Vol. II, pp. 582–83.

64. Decree of USSR Central Executive Committee, "On the Creation of People's Commissariats of Local Industry in the Federal and Autonomous Republics" (*Upravlenie*, pp. 206–7).

Chart 1   Administration of the National Economy, 1933–1956

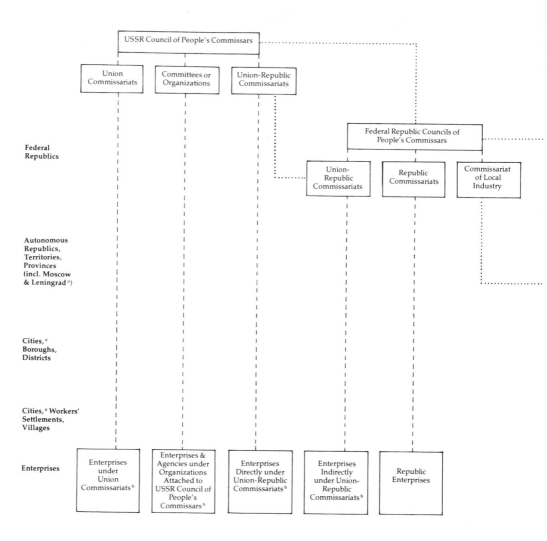

Note: After 1946, the Council of People's Commissars became the Council of Ministers and all commissariats became ministries.

a. The position of cities in the administrative hierarchy depends on their size. The largest cities (such as Moscow and Leningrad) come directly under the federal republic and are on the same level as provinces with their own districts. Other cities are assimilated to districts, and the smallest ones come under districts.

b. Between these enterprises and the people's commissariats, there are intermediaries (associations, combines, trusts, institutions, etc.) whose main activities are not subordinated to republic, province, or district agencies.

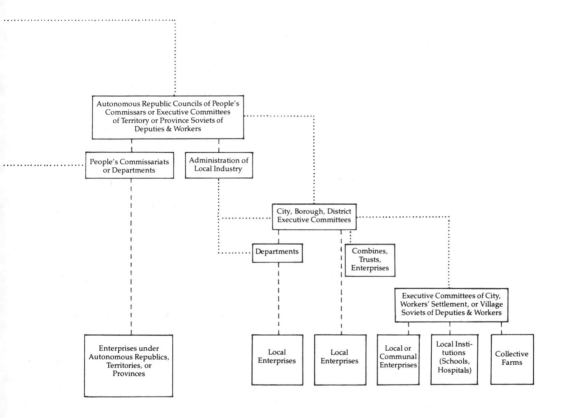

light industry, the timber industry, and the food industry, on the other, according to a decision of the Council of People's Commissars of September 29, 1934.[65] This decision approved eight lists of enterprises assigned to the commissariats of local industry and four lists of local industry and republic enterprises assigned to the commissariats of heavy industry, light industry, the timber industry, and the food industry. The enterprises previously under the jurisdiction of the republic or province agencies of these commissariats and not included on the above-mentioned lists or on other lists were henceforth to come under the jurisdiction of the commissariats of local industry.[66] This was the last general decision concerning republic and local industry. Thereafter management powers were divided between Union and republic or province agencies in two main ways: by classifying people's commissariats (or ministries) as Union, Union-republic, or republic commissariats and by the internal division of management powers within the Union-republic ("unified" before the 1936 Constitution) people's commissariats.

The division of people's commissariats into Union and Union-republic commissariats is given in Table 1 and Tables E-1 and E-2. The number of people's commissariats, which was six in 1931, was reduced to three in 1935 (agriculture, finance, domestic trade) after the abolition of VSNKh, the reorganization of the Commissariat of Food Supply, and the amalgamation of the Commissariat of Labor with the Central Union of Trade Unions.[67] The 1936 Constitution provided for ten Union-republic people's commissariats (agriculture, finance, domestic trade, food industry, light industry, timber industry, state farms, justice, health, and internal affairs). Since then the number of Union-republic commissariats has grown continuously (see Table 1).

According to Article 76 of the 1936 Constitution, the Union-republic commissariats manage the enterprises under their jurisdiction, as a rule, through the intermediary of the commissariats of the same name located in the federal republics and manage directly only a limited number of enterprises on a list approved by the USSR Supreme Soviet.[68] Hence there are two forms of management here: one jointly with the federal republics and the other directly by Union agencies. The trend toward centralization of management was very pronounced during the Stalinist period. It followed the reorganization of VSNKh and the creation of the Commissariat of the Food Industry in 1934. The number of enterprises under direct Union jurisdiction within the Union-republic commissariats was considerably increased and the drafters of the 1936 Constitution felt obliged to make direct mention of it. But the centralization of management was also manifested within the Union-republic commissariats in another form. The idea of joint management developed in the sense of an increase in the powers of the Union agencies. It was recognized that a Union ministry not only had the right to give orders but also had to organize and supervise directly by its orders and instructions the over-all work of the branch in question and that it

65. Venediktov, *Organizatsiia*, Vol. II, p. 589.
66. *Ibid.*
67. Ananov, *Ministerstva*, pp. 72–73 and 111. See also footnote 47 above.
68. *Ibid.*, p. 87.

held in its hands the principal tools for management, such as the appointment of personnel and checking on performance.[69]

Direct management by republic agencies was thus limited to that exercised by the people's commissariats under the sole jurisdiction of the councils of ministers of the federal republics. The number of these ministries increased from four in 1936 (see above) to seven in 1948 and nine on January 20, 1957.[70] Hence direct management of industry by the federal republics remained very limited, especially since in industry the new assignments of March 13, 1948, concerned only motor transportation and private housing construction.[71] In actual fact, most of heavy industry,[72] transportation, state farms, and Machine and Tractor Stations were under the direct jurisdiction of Union agencies.

As can be seen from Chart 1, the enterprises under the direct jurisdiction of local administrations (districts, cities, villages) were separated from the central power by a long chain of intermediary powers. Direct Union management was also carried out through a system of several stages, but according to an independent hierarchy outside the jurisdiction of the republic, province, and local powers.

The complexity of the system of management reappears at the regional level. As can be seen from Chart 1, enterprises under the jurisdiction of different administrations exist in the same area, which makes regional as well as branch planning particularly difficult.

Industrial Management Agencies at the Branch Level

Management by Trusts with Market Relations Predominating

The regrouping of industrial enterprises into trusts coincided with the introduction of the New Economic Policy (NEP), which was intended to re-establish the market.[73] Most of these trusts were created between December 1921 and September 1922. By October 1, 1922, there were 430 trusts containing 4,144 enterprises with 977,000 workers.[74] The number of trusts increased to 478 by the summer of 1923 and the number of workers was around one million, representing 75 per cent of the total number of workers in nationalized industry.[75]

---

69. *Ibid.*, p. 92. In light of these explanations, not much weight should be given to the centralization criterion of direct management by Union agencies. Direct management by Union agencies was extended even further during the last years of the Stalinist period; in industry it covered 67 per cent of the total value of production in 1950 and 70 per cent in 1952 (*Narodnoe khoziaistvo SSSR v 1956 godu* [The USSR National Economy in 1956], Moscow, 1957, p. 47).

70. The three new republic ministries formed between 1936 and 1948 were for the local fuel industry, motor transport, and civilian housing construction. Between 1948 and 1957 three new republic ministries were created (water management, inland waterway fleet, and justice) and the Ministry of Civilian Housing Construction was abolished. (Ananov, *Ministerstva*, p. 109.)

71. *Ibid.*

72. Except for small enterprises working with local resources.

73. See my *Planning*, pp. 22–23 and 29.

74. There were 172 trusts containing 2,281 enterprises with 816,000 workers under VSNKh and the *Promburo* and 258 trusts with 1,863 enterprises and 159,000 workers under the Sovnarkhozes (Venediktov, *Organizatsiia*, Vol. II, p. 55).

75. But the number of enterprises was only 3,561 (Maurice Dobb, *Soviet Economic Development since 1917*, London, 1951, p. 135).

The main provisions on trusts were set forth in the September 12, 1922, decree of VSNKh and in the April 10, 1923, decree of the Central Executive Committee and the Council of People's Commissars, which defined trusts as "state industrial enterprises granted autonomy of operation by the state in accordance with the statute approved for each of them and operating on a commercial basis with profit as an objective."[76] VSNKh put fixed and working capital at the disposal of the trust, but the material responsibility of the trust was limited by the volume of its capital. The government, although the owner of the trust, was not responsible for its debts. The April 10 decree provided three agencies to handle the trust: VSNKh, the board of management of the trust, and its control commission. The powers of VSNKh consisted mainly in appointing and dismissing the board of management, drafting instructions, and approving production estimates and plans, the balance sheet, and the distribution of profits. Changes in the volume of capital and reserve funds also required the approval of VSNKh.[77]

The provisions of 1922–1923 put most stress on the trust's autonomy in management and on the ban on interference in the trust's administration and operation by VSNKh or other government agencies or authorities. Management on an "autonomous commercial basis" (*kommercheskii raschet*) was understood in a broad sense,[78] and government provisions guaranteed the trust such rights as managing its own capital, acquiring its own materials, and selling its production where it wished (abroad or at home). In addition, the trust was entitled to transact all financial operations (participate in the capital of other enterprises or associations), set the number of jobs, and conclude collective contracts. Limitations on the trust's powers concerned only production reserved for the state by the Council for Labor and Defense decrees, the obligation to fulfill planned goals (according to the schedule and conditions specified in the contracts), and giving priority in producer goods and procurements to the state and cooperatives when conditions were otherwise equal. The VSNKh note accompanying the September 12 regulation stressed the market nature of the trust's operations and the fact that it was not to depend on state financing.

76. September 12, 1922, decree of VSNKh, "Model Statute on Associations (Trusts) and Explanatory Note" (*Upravlenie*, pp. 71–77); April 10, 1923, decree, "On State Industrial Enterprises Operating on a Commercial Basis (Trusts)" (excerpts published in *ibid.*, pp. 80–90). The first texts on the legal position of the trusts were published by the Council of People's Commissars on August 9, 1921, and then by the Council for Labor and Defense on August 12, 1921; these were followed by several texts on the trusts published by the Council for Labor and Defense, Gosplan, and VSNKh (Venediktov, *Organizatsiia*, Vol. II, pp. 56–57).

77. September 12 decree and April 10 decree (*Upravlenie*, pp. 71–77 and 80–90) and Venediktov, *Organizatsiia*, Vol. II, p. 58.

78. Venediktov (*ibid.*, Vol. II, pp. 25 and 58) considered that replacing the term *khoziaistvennyi raschet* or *khozraschet* (economic accounting in the literal translation, an inaccurate description after 1930) by the term *kommercheskii raschet* (commercial accounting) was not a real change since Lenin used both terms alternatively. This is no doubt true, but *khozraschet* should be used in the meaning that it had before 1930 when administrative planning was introduced. By insisting on the *khozraschet* of enterprises, administrative planning drained the term of the meaning given it, according to Venediktov, by Lenin as a symbol of commercial autonomy permitting the achievement of the enterprise's objective of profit.

The 1927 Reform of the Trust Statute

The reform of the trust statutes was widely discussed after the publication in early 1926 of the draft law on industrial trusts.[79] The very existence of trusts was questioned by the partisans of greater autonomy for the enterprise. The February 1927 plenary session of VSNKh recommended maintaining the existing structure of industry and emphasized the role of the trusts and the syndicates (*sindikaty*). The June 29, 1927, regulation on state industrial trusts, which applied to all trusts at the Union, republic, and local level (except for local trusts with a capital of less than 100,000 rubles), nevertheless tightened planned supervision of the trusts by higher echelons.[80] The definition of the trust no longer contained the statement that profit was its objective but declared that the trust operated on an "autonomous commercial basis" in conformity with planned goals. The use of profit as the trust's goal was not set aside; it was even mentioned in the text apropos of the deliveries the trust was to make on orders from the Council for Labor and Defense: the trust was given the right to include average profit in the prices fixed by contract. The stipulations of the April 10, 1923, decree on the three trust agencies (VSNKh, board of management, and control commission) were abolished. This last provision, which in conformity with Articles 349 and 353 of the Russian Republic civil code applied to joint-stock companies, was evidently out of date by 1927. Thus the trust became an economic agency of the state.[81]

The supervisory agency of which the trust was a part was granted jurisdiction over investments and capital repairs and the right to set the trust's selling prices. Considerable changes were made in the provisions for the distribution of trust profits. The profits that remained after deductions were appropriated by the budget.[82]

The June 29 decree did not change the relations between the trusts and the syndicates, which had been based in principle on voluntary associations for sales of production and supply.[83] But the emphasis on the subordination of management to planning, reaffirmed by the fourth plenary session of VSNKh in the fall of 1928, led to a sizable increase in the obligatory associations of trusts and syndicates for supply and sales. In the textile industry compulsory deliveries by the trusts to the Syndicate of the Textile Union were introduced on August 26, 1927, and the trusts of several branches were obliged to deliver all their production to the syndicate according to the Council for Labor and Defense regulation issued jointly with VSNKh and the People's Commissariat of Trade on February 29, 1928.[84] The role of the trust as an autonomous, market-oriented, and profit-operated economic agency became increasingly compromised.

79. *Ibid.*, Vol. II, pp. 261–63.
80. *Ibid.*, Vol. II, pp. 262–64.
81. *Ibid.*, Vol. II, p. 265.
82. Articles 15 and 38 of the June 29, 1927, "Statute on State Industrial Trusts Approved by the Central Executive Committee and the USSR Council of People's Commissars" (*Upravlenie*, pp. 133–51). See also Venediktov, *Organizatsiia*, Vol. II, pp. 265–66.
83. On the syndicates, see Chapter 5, section on supply management during NEP.
84. Venediktov, *Organizatsiia*, Vol. II, p. 297.

*Creation of Associations and Organization of Management
at the Branch Level, 1930–1934*

The powers of the syndicates were increased during 1928–1929 at the expense not only of the trusts but also of the central administrations (*Glavki*) of VSNKh and of the people's commissariats; this affected not only supply and sales but also financing the trusts and planning production and investment in enterprises.[85] The reorganization of industrial management put into effect on December 5, 1929, was the logical outcome of this development. The *Glavki* of VSNKh were abolished and, using the syndicates as a basis, a Central Committee decision set up "associations" in the various branches of industry.[86] Three types of associations were formed: federal, mixed (regrouping enterprises and trusts of federal, republic, and local industry), and republic and local. The powers of these associations were very broad. They made plans for production and investment and supervised investment, technical problems, and commercial and financial operations. They organized supply and sales and handled employment problems, personnel training, and the appointment and dismissal of managerial staff. Research institutes operating under a branch were directly subordinated to the associations. Trusts and enterprises were to be supplied either directly by the associations or through general contracts with the supply agencies.

The December 5 decree considerably reduced the powers of the trusts. The new powers granted to the enterprises under trusts in connection with the extension of accounting autonomy (*khozraschet*) are discussed at the end of this chapter. But, above all, the independence of trusts from higher echelons was reduced. The role of the trusts was limited to technical supervision of enterprises with the abolition of their jurisdiction over supply and sales. The creation of new trusts was no longer the duty of the Council for Labor and Defense; now VSNKh could create or abolish trusts on its own authority by using its own resources (decree of February 13, 1930). This action was followed by a regrouping of trusts and their enterprises, the creation of some new trusts, and the abolition of others.[87]

Following the December 5 decree, 26 associations in the principal branches of light and heavy industry were formed at the end of 1929 and the beginning of 1930. The size of these associations can be judged from the facts that the entire fuel industry was grouped into only three associations (*Soiuzugol* for coal, *Soiuztorf* for peat, and *Souizneft* for petroleum), that the entire timber and wood-processing industry was grouped into a single association (*Soiuzles*), and that the metallurgical industry was covered in only three associations (one each for ferrous metals, nonferrous metals, and the construction of new ferrous metal enterprises). One of the largest associations was for machine-building (*Mashinobedinenie*), which covered the entire machine-building industry along with

---

85. *Ibid.*, Vol. II, p. 545.

86. December 5, 1929, decree of Party Central Committee, "On the Reorganization of the Management of Industry" (*Upravlenie*, pp. 171–80).

87. Venediktov, *Organizatsiia*, Vol. II, pp. 555–56.

the associations for agricultural machinery, motor vehicles and tractors, ship-building, and the electrical industry.[88]

In order to carry out the immense tasks entrusted to them, the associations were authorized to organize separate sections (*chasti obedineniia*)—for sales, construction, etc.—and to grant them *khozraschet* with separate accounting and a certain independence of operation. Production planning and technical direction were entrusted to different administrations (*upravleniia*). The creation of administrations endowed with *khozraschet* within the associations was very important because of the January 30, 1930, credit reform. These administrations had separate accounts in the State Bank, which gave a certain independence to the supply and sales agencies.

The size of the associations made them cumbersome. They were not agencies capable of uniform management and adaptable to market conditions, but rather were huge economic administrations of enterprises located all over the country. This brought about a process of disintegration that started with the creation on March 26, 1930, of the association *Kotloturbina*, which had previously been part of *Mashinobedinenie*. After criticisms at the Sixteenth Party Congress (June 26–July 13, 1930) of mistakes in the reorganization of management, the process of splitting up the associations was accelerated.[89]

A little later, in the middle of 1931, the *Glavki* began to be re-established with the creation of *Glavlesprom* (Central Administration for the Timber Industry) within VSNKh. Associations specializing in sales were also formed in 1931, such as *Stalsbyt* (Steel Sales), *Soiuzkhimsbyt* (Sales of Chemical Products), and *Tsvetmetsbyt* (Nonferrous Metals Sales). As a result, the number of associations increased from 26 on January 31, 1930, to 82 (including 190 trusts) on September 8, 1931.[90]

Splitting up the associations was only one step toward their elimination, which occurred mainly during 1932–1933 and took different forms. In some cases the associations were replaced by trusts, which were subordinated to the *Glavki* of the commissariats; in other cases they were simply abolished and the trusts and enterprises that had been under their jurisdiction were subordinated to the *Glavki*; in still other cases they were reorganized into *Glavki*.[91] The November 8, 1932, decree of the Council of People's Commissars provided for the almost complete elimination of associations.[92]

Accordingly, during 1933 most associations were eliminated and the number of trusts was considerably reduced.[93] A resolution of the Seventeenth Party

88. *Ibid.*, Vol. II, pp. 552–53.
89. *Ibid.*, Vol. II, pp. 561–63.
90. *Ibid.*, Vol. II, pp. 566–67.
91. Thus the association *Vsekhimprom* was abolished May 11, 1932, and replaced by two new trusts directly under the jurisdiction of *Glavkhimprom* (the Central Administration for the Chemical Industry) of the People's Commissariat of Heavy Industry. And the July 23, 1932, decree created 16 branch *Glavki* while simultaneously abolishing the corresponding associations belonging to the People's Commissariat of Light Industry. (Venediktov, *Organizatsiia*, Vol. II, p. 568.)
92. *Ibid.*, Vol. II, p. 569.
93. Thus the August 31, 1933, decree of the Council of People's Commissars, "On the Specialization

Congress (held January 10–February 10, 1934) ordered that the number of intermediary management agencies (associations, trusts, etc.) be reduced and that the direct links between the people's commissariats and the large enterprises be strengthened.[94] The March 15, 1934, decision of the Central Executive Committee and the Council of People's Commissars, which followed this resolution, ordered that the associations be abolished and the number of trusts reduced.[95]

Consolidation of Glavki of Commissariats as Principal Management Agencies at the Branch Level

The elimination of associations and the subdivision of VSNKh was accompanied by an increase in the number and a consequent decrease in the size of the *Glavki*. This reorganization was carried out separately within the new industrial commissariats, the successors of VSNKh—the Commissariat of Heavy Industry, the Commissariat of Light Industry, and the Commissariat of the Timber Industry.

The Commissariat of Heavy Industry was reorganized by the August 31, 1933, decree of the Council of People's Commissars,[96] which split the machine-building *Glavk* (*Glavmashprom*) into four new *Glavki*, transformed several sections of existing *Glavki*[97] into separate *Glavki*, and created other new *Glavki*. Thus, after this reform, the Commissariat of Heavy Industry contained 25 *Glavki* instead of the previous 13.[98]

The Commissariat of Light Industry was reorganized on July 17, 1934, and the Commissariat of the Timber Industry on September 19, 1934. The new *Glavki* formed at this time administered entire branches or had territorial jurisdiction within a given branch.[99]

The resolution of the Seventeenth Party Congress and the March 15, 1934, decree also provided for the abolition of the so-called "functional" system of management. Under that system, management authority was scattered among departments of the commissariats, making it difficult to apply the principle of one-man management, dispersing responsibility, and giving rise to a plethora of administrative personnel.[100] This system was replaced by the regional produc-

---

and Reduction in Size of the *Glavki* of the People's Commissariat of Heavy Industry and on the Elimination of Several Associations and Trusts" (*Sobranie zakonov*, No. 58, 1933, Art. 346) abolished 15 associations of the People's Commissariat of Heavy Industry (Venediktov, *Organizatsiia*, Vol. II, p. 570).

94. *KPSS v rezoliutsiiakh*, Part II, p. 771.

95. The March 15 decree formulates this matter in terms very similar to those of the resolution of the Seventeenth Party Congress. See Venediktov, *Organizatsiia*, Vol. II, p. 571.

96. See footnote 93 above.

97. Those for the electrical industry, the nonferrous metal industry, and the chemical industry.

98. Venediktov, *Organizatsiia*, Vol. II, pp. 583–84.

99. *Ibid.*, Vol. II, pp. 586–88. Examples of regional production *Glavki* (*proizvodstvenno-territorialnye Glavki*) are the three *Glavki* of the cotton industry: one for the Moscow and Leningrad area, one for the Ivanovo area, and one for new construction and regions. In the timber industry four regional production *Glavki* were created for (1) the Urals, Siberia, and Gorkov Territory, (2) the northern regions, (3) the regions where heavy and valuable wood predominates, and (4) the timber industry of the far east. (See *ibid.*, Vol. II, pp. 587–88.)

100. A. M. Rubin, *Organizatsiia upravleniia promyshlennostiu v SSSR (1917–1967 gg.)* [Organization of Industrial Management in the USSR, 1917–1967], Moscow, 1969, pp. 123–24. The functional system was based on the predominance of "functional" departments. The structure of VSNKh, for

tion (*proizvodstvenno-territorialnyi*) system, a change that entailed an internal reorganization of the commissariats. The branch production (*proizvodstvenno-otraslevye*) *Glavki* and the regional production *Glavki* became the basic management agencies.[101] The commissariats were to manage only the enterprises of national interest and to do so through the intermediary of their *Glavki* set up in geographical areas. The existing collegia of the administrative and economic agencies were abolished in order to strengthen the system of one-man management; they were replaced by councils of people's commissariats with 40 to 70 members.[102]

The abolition of the "functional" system of management meant that responsibility at the *Glavk* level was strengthened and that the "functional" departments of the commissariats (for the plan, personnel, wages, finances, etc.) were not allowed to interfere in the work of the lower echelons. These departments were kept solely as auxiliary agencies to formulate certain specified problems and present conclusions to the commissariats.[103] Hence the question was one of redefining the powers of these departments. The number of "functional" departments maintained after the March 15 decree was to be specified in the new structure of each commissariat.[104] This internal structure seems to have varied considerably during the Stalinist era, and the principle of the noninterference of "functional" departments in management seems to have been violated occasionally.

The abolition of the associations and the reduction in the number of trusts created a new management structure in Soviet industry. In contrast with the former four-level system (commissariat, association, trust, enterprise), the new system consisted of either two levels (commissariat's *Glavk* and enterprise) or three levels (*Glavk*, trust, enterprise).[105] The three-level system gradually diminished in importance during the 1930's after the abolition of the numerous trusts. Thus, while on January 1, 1934, there were 182 enterprises of the Commissariat of Heavy Industry not under trusts or associations, by January 1, 1936, that number had increased to 355.[106] Although they represented only 13 per cent of

instance, which was decreed November 29, 1930, provided for 7 branch departments (machine-building, metals, chemicals, fuel and energy, wood construction, mining, and light industry) and 12 functional departments (planning, accounting, finance, supply and sales, personnel, labor, organization, rationalization and direction of production, scientific research, control over fulfillment, etc.). (Venediktov, *Organizatsiia*, Vol. II, p. 579.)

101. Rubin, *Organizatsiia*, p. 124. In the branch production *Glavki* the functions of management were exercised by operational (*proizvodstvenno-rasporiaditelnye*) sections.

102. Venediktov, *Organizatsiia*, Vol. II, pp. 585–86.

103. Rubin, *Organizatsiia*, p. 124.

104. Decree of March 15, 1934, "On Organizational Measures in Soviet Administrative Institutions and Economic Agencies" (*Sobranie zakonov*, March 23, 1934, Art. 103).

105. Venediktov, *Organizatsiia*, Vol. II, p. 580, and Rubin, *Organizatsiia*, p. 125. It is hard to say if the *Glavk* was replacing the association or the commissariat that represented it. Venediktov (*Organizatsiia*, Vol. II, p. 580) talks of the old system of four levels and includes the *Glavk* as a special agency of VSNKh alongside the association.

106. A. V. Venediktov, *Gosudarstvennaia sotsialisticheskaia sobstvennost* [State Socialist Property], Moscow-Leningrad, 1948, p. 725, as cited by David Granick, *Management of the Industrial Firm in the USSR*, New York, 1955, p. 18, note 24.

the number of enterprises under the Commissariat of Heavy Industry, these 355 enterprises accounted for 70 to 75 per cent of total production.[107]

There was also a one-level system of management in which certain large enterprises of national interest were subordinated directly to the commissariat without the intermediary of the *Glavk*.[108] The number of these enterprises increased during 1935–1940.[109]

As the sizes of the *Glavki* were reduced, their powers tended to increase considerably. This increase was effected mainly by the July 15, 1936, decree and by the July 21, 1938, order of the Commissar of Finance and the Chairman of the State Bank on the application of this decree.[110] The powers of the *Glavki* were extended in two basic areas—supply and sales, on the one hand, and finance, on the other. The supply and sales bases of the industrial commissariats became sections of the *Glavki*, which thereby acquired the right to draw up contracts and to have their own account for sales and purchasing.[111] Another account in the State Bank opened in the name of the *Glavki* was for the management of funds belonging to enterprises under the jurisdiction of the *Glavki*.[112]

Having concentrated in their hands the power to allocate physical resources and having, through the allocation of financial resources, a decisive say in the total volume of funds allotted to the enterprises, the *Glavki* became the most powerful management agencies. Their reorganization during and after the war affected only the definition of their jurisdiction over the production sectors that they controlled[113] or their regional jurisdiction but not the extent of their powers, which seem to have changed very little until the reforms of 1965.[114] Under these conditions, however, one might wonder what role the enterprises had in management.

107. *Trud v SSSR* [Labor in the USSR], Moscow, 1936, p. 71, and Venediktov, *Gosudarstvennaia*, p. 725, as cited by Granick, *Management*, p. 18, note 24.

108. Rubin, *Organizatsiia*, p. 125.

109. At the beginning of 1935 there were 9 enterprises in this category. In July 1940 another 42 enterprises were placed directly under the People's Commissariat of General Machine-Building and there were at least 8 other enterprises not under the *Glavki* in the two other heavy industry commissariats. (Granick, *Management*, pp. 18–19.)

110. July 15, 1936, decree, "On *Khozraschet* Rights for the *Glavki* of the Industrial People's Commissariats" (*Upravlenie*, pp. 211–12); and July 21, 1938, instructions (*ibid.*, pp. 218–22).

111. Separate accounts were introduced for supply and for sales.

112. This account was funded by profits from enterprises to be deposited in long-term investment banks and had several purposes: payments to the budget and to cover planned losses and working capital of other enterprises belonging to the same *Glavki*; deductions for amortization to be deposited in long-term investment banks; working capital appropriated from enterprises for distribution within the *Glavki*; payment by enterprises of turnover tax, current payments to research institutions for accounts with the security offices, etc.; and payments by enterprises of other *Glavki* in accordance with the regulation in effect ("Instructions on Putting into Effect the July 15, 1936, Decree of the Central Executive Committee and the People's Commissariats" [*ibid.*, pp. 218–22]).

113. The Commissariat of Heavy Industry regulation, for instance, which was issued November 10, 1937, provided for the operation of 30 *Glavki* under this commissariat (*Finansovoe i khoziaistvennoe zakonodatelstvo* [Financial and Economic Legislation], No. 1–2, January 1938, pp. 15–17). Several examples of such administrative reorganizations could be cited.

114. Except for the allocation of material and equipment supplies (see Chapter 5, section on supply management under Stalinist administrative planning). We are ignoring the 1957 reforms which, in creating the Sovnarkhozes, abolished (until 1965) the industrial ministries.

Management Powers at the Industrial Enterprise Level

Autonomous Enterprises during NEP

As mentioned in the section on trusts, when the New Economic Policy was introduced the trust became the basic unit in the administration of industry. Several government decrees, promulgated at that time, nevertheless mentioned the possibility of granting accounting autonomy (*khozraschet*) to certain industrial enterprises and of applying the provisions intended for the trusts to them.[115] These enterprises would be directly subordinated to VSNKh or to the government (later federal republic) councils of the national economy.

The autonomous status granted to state industrial enterprises was nevertheless an exception. At that time the Soviet government was engaged in a struggle against the private sector and did not want to support it by authorizing state enterprises to place their orders with the private sector. The trusts, on the other hand, directly controlled the material and equipment supply and sales of their enterprises. The syndicates, which were regrouping purchasing and sales of enterprises, were voluntary and therefore could not control the operations of autonomous enterprises, which had the right to deal freely on the market.[116]

In its struggle against private capital, the government went as far as forbidding state enterprises to have recourse to the private sector in placing their orders and forbidding state enterprise officials to receive commissions on contracts they concluded in the name of their enterprises.[117]

In granting autonomous enterprises the same legal status as trusts, the decrees cited above[118] defined their powers very clearly. They were constituted by the same procedure as the trusts, operating on the basis of the statutes governing them, and possessed a legal entity. The total volume of their capital was fixed by statute. VSNKh (or local councils) directed their work in the same way as that of the trusts: it appointed the director and deputy director, approved the accounts and balance of the enterprise, and had the same proprietary rights as for trusts. The autonomous enterprise took all legal actions itself, concluded contracts in its own name, and was responsible for its own obligations. The funds of autonomous enterprises were constituted by the same regulations as the funds and special capital of the trusts.[119]

Legal Status of Enterprises Subordinated to Trusts during NEP

The August 12, 1921, provisions of the Council for Labor and Defense were not concerned with the legal position of enterprises subordinated to trusts.[120] The first regulations on trusts issued in 1921–1922 were limited to specifying the

---

115. See the August 12, 1921, decree (Art. 1) of the Council for Labor and Defense on the restoration of large-scale industry and the April 10 and July 17, 1923, decrees on trusts (Venediktov, *Organizatsiia*, Vol. II, pp. 74–75).
116. *Ibid.*, Vol. II, p. 72.
117. *Ibid.*, Vol. II, p. 74.
118. See footnote 115 above.
119. Venediktov, *Organizatsiia*, Vol. II, p. 75.
120. *Ibid.*

procedure for appointing directors and staff and for fixing norms and wages in the enterprises under their jurisdiction.[121]

The necessity of extending the powers of enterprises was first mentioned by the Twelfth Party Congress (April 17–25, 1923). The Party stated that "the root of the success or failure of production lies in the *basic production unit* [italics added], that is, in the factory or the plant. The correct organization of work at every individual enterprise, not only from the standpoint of production technique but also from the commercial standpoint, is a problem of decisive importance."[122]

These ideas, however, were not fully implemented in the legislative and administrative provisions drawn up during NEP. The model statute for the trusts, approved by VSNKh on May 26, 1923, stipulated only that the relationship between the trust and the enterprise administration should be based on the mandate given to the director and on instructions "providing for its autonomy within the limits necessary for its economic activities."[123] The first model regulation on the management of enterprises under a trust, approved by the VSNKh presidium on July 9, 1923, proclaimed simultaneously the *unit of the trust* considered as a single enterprise and the *autonomy of industrial establishments* within the limits determined by the trust management.[124] The director of the establishment was to formulate a draft production program with cost estimates and to present it to the trust management, along with a request for materials, financial means, and manpower. After examining these requests jointly with the director of the establishment, the trust management was to provide raw materials, fuel, the principal materials, and financial means in accordance with the approved plans and estimate costs. Only minor orders could be placed directly by the director of the establishment. And even in this case the director placed the order in the name of the trust, and his obligations were legally those of the trust.[125]

The July 9 regulation did not lay down any general rule for the relations between the trust and its enterprises, but it recommended that relations be introduced between establishments and trusts concerning delivery of production on the basis of planned administrative orders, which would replace civil law relations. Such administrative relations were introduced by the second regulation (of May 14, 1924) on the management of establishments under trusts.[126] While still maintaining the mandate as the essential document determining the relationship of a trust to its enterprises, the regulation introduced the system of "order-goals" (*zakaz-zadanie*) addressed to enterprises, which specified the quantity and quality of a product, the delivery schedule, and the price. Raw materials, fuel, and materials were to be supplied to the enterprise by the trust at

121. For instance, the regulation on the administration of the flax industry, approved by the Council for Labor and Defense on August 8, 1921; see also other regulations of this type in *ibid.*, Vol. II, p. 76.

122. *KPSS v rezoliutsiiakh*, Part I, p. 697.

123. Venediktov, *Organizatsiia*, Vol. II, pp. 76–77.

124. *Ibid.*, Vol. II, p. 77.

125. *Ibid.*, Vol. II, pp. 77–78.

126. *Ibid.*, Vol. II, pp. 79–80.

prices calculated by the trust, and finished products were to be supplied by the enterprises at prices corresponding to cost.[127]

The idea of extending *khozraschet* to the enterprises under trusts was very slow to catch on. The introduction of commercial accounting in the 32 administrations of the *Donugol* mines by the September 4, 1923, regulation was short-lived, and the new regulation of November 6, 1924, transferred them to the "order-goal" system introduced on May 14.[128] Another attempt, a little more conclusive, was the transfer to commercial accounting of the enterprises of the Gomza Trust in 1924. These enterprises obtained an extension of their supply rights and a separate accounting within the Gomza Trust.[129]

In actual practice, the degree of managerial autonomy of the enterprises under trusts was small and there was a tendency to limit the powers of enterprise directors, mainly in supply and sales.[130] The notion of transferring enterprises to contractual bases was nevertheless gaining ground, and proposals were even made to transform the trusts into state joint-stock companies, in which the shareholders would be the enterprises under the trusts. But these ideas were rejected by VSNKh as conflicting with the principle of the economic and legal entity of the trust.[131]

In practice, Soviet management turned toward granting *khozraschet*. Following an appeal by VSNKh Chairman F. E. Derzhinskii on November 21, 1924, for greater enterprise independence within the trusts, attempts in this direction were expanded. As of October 1, 1926, all the enterprises of *Yugostal* were transferred to *khozraschet*. Since the results of this experiment were judged successful, *Glavmetal* of VSNKh recommended that all the trusts of the metallurgical industry should transfer their enterprises to *khozraschet*.[132] A little later, while still maintaining the legal entity of the trust, the February 1927 plenary session of VSNKh advocated an emphasis on the full responsibility of enterprise directors for production and financial operations.[133] On the basis of the resolution of this plenary session, the June 29, 1927, regulation on industrial trusts[134] contained a special section on production enterprises (*proizvodstvennye predpriiatiia*)[135] and advocated measures that amounted to transferring these enterprises to *khozraschet*.[136] Important among these measures were the definition of the powers of the enterprise director and the confirmation of the principle of one-man management, stipulations guaranteeing the director's right to dispose of savings realized by the enterprise, to open a bank account, to obtain credits, to conclude contracts, and to sell used equipment.[137]

127. *Ibid.*, Vol. II, p. 80.
128. *Ibid.*, Vol. II, p. 81.
129. *Ibid.*, Vol. II, p. 82.
130. *Ibid.*, Vol. II, pp. 79–80.
131. *Ibid.*, Vol. II, p. 80.
132. *Ibid.*, Vol. II, pp. 269–70.
133. *Ibid.*, Vol. II, p. 271.
134. On this regulation, see the section on the 1927 reform of the trust statute on p. 29 above.
135. The term "establishment" (*zavedenie*) was replaced at this time by "enterprise" (*predpriiatie*).
136. As Venediktov (*ibid.*, Vol. II, p. 271, note 48) points out, the June 29, 1927, regulation did not use the term *khozraschet*, but all the measures adopted amounted to the same thing.
137. *Ibid.*, Vol. II, pp. 271–72.

The trust was to approve for each enterprise a special statute based on the VSNKh model statute. Such a statute was issued on October 4, 1927, stating that at the beginning of the year the trust management had to specify the financial and material resources necessary to fulfill the enterprise's industrial and financial plan (*promfinplan*). Since the enterprise plan included inventory stocks, total credits and supplies provided to the enterprise by the trust (called the special list, *osoboe raspisanie*) were examined by the trust, together with the enterprise director, and then approved and made more concrete in quarterly orders (*nariady-zakazy*). All the losses suffered by the enterprises because of inadequate supplies were to be covered by the trust, and all the losses suffered by the trust because of late deliveries were to be covered by the enterprise.[138]

Nevertheless, the model statute of October 4 let stand several important limitations on the powers of the enterprise. The fact that only the trust was a legal entity meant that the enterprise's bank account and the contracts concluded by the enterprise director were in the name of the trust. The *khozraschet* status affected only the internal organization of the trust. The relationship between the enterprise and the trust did not become contractual but remained administrative. The trust's order (*nariad-zakaz*) became obligatory not because of a contract but because of a command issued by the trust management. If the enterprise director refused to accept the order, the trust could issue an administrative command, and the only recourse for the enterprise director was to lodge a complaint with VSNKh without the order being suspended.[139]

Putting into operation the provisions granting *khozraschet* to the enterprises under trusts was a very slow process. This was the case for the metallurgical industry, which was to be transferred to *khozraschet* as of September 1926,[140] as well as for all industry under VSNKh covered by the July 29, 1927, regulation. Even the April 11, 1928, Party plenary session was concerned with this problem and declared that the provisions of the July 29 decree "have, for all practical purposes, not been put into effect."[141] The Fourth Plenary Session of VSNKh in the fall of 1928 again took up this matter, but it was not settled until December 5, 1929, the date of the important reorganization in enterprise management.

138. *Ibid.*, Vol. II, pp. 272–73.
139. *Ibid.*, Vol. II, pp. 275–76.
140. The Leningrad Trust of Machine-Building transferred its enterprises to *khozraschet* as of October 19, 1928. It seems that at the beginning of 1928 only one trust in the Ukrainian Republic (the Machine-Building Trust of the South) had introduced *khozraschet* into its factories (*ibid.*, Vol. II, p. 270). Venediktov believes that the machine-building industry as a whole experienced delays.
141. In June 1928 the Collegium of the Workers' and Peasants' Inspection Board of the USSR established that, out of the 13 trusts surveyed, 9 had not yet started to put the new July 29 regulation into effect, 2 had just started the preparatory work, and only 2 had actually put it into operation. According to the Workers' and Peasants' Inspection Board of the Russian Republic, out of 36 Russian Republic trusts, not one had put the regulation fully into effect. VSNKh of the Ukraine declared in March 1928 that many trusts had not even bothered to inform themselves about the October 4, 1927, model regulation of the enterprise under trusts (*ibid.*, Vol. II, p. 278).

Powers of Industrial Enterprises in the Administrative Planning System

The main document defining the powers of the industrial enterprise under Stalinist planning was the December 5, 1929, decree of the Party Central Committee, "On the Reorganization of Industrial Management."[142] This decree defined the enterprise as the basic link in the administration of industry and specified the areas in which it could exercise its powers. The autonomy of the enterprise was loudly proclaimed, but "with the strictest respect for planned production and financial discipline within the framework of the fixed goals or 'limits' (*limity*)." The enterprise management bore the entire responsibility for the fulfillment of its program.[143] The decree declared the transfer of enterprises to *khozraschet* satisfactory, but stated that this measure had not yet been applied to all enterprises. The means at the disposal of the enterprise were to be determined every year by the financial-industrial plan, on the basis of which the production costs and the deductions for not respecting planned conditions were specified in the orders.[144]

The December 5 decree emphasized the enterprise's success criterion, the difference between planned and actual costs. Part of any cost saving was to remain at the enterprise's disposal. In order to permit an exact calculation of an enterprise's costs, the decree stipulated that the enterprise was to be granted *autonomous accounting* and to be guaranteed raw material and material supplies at prices fixed in advance.[145]

The new powers granted to the enterprises under trusts by this decree were preceded by another decree on one-man management.[146] This decree stressed the direct responsibility of the enterprise management (director) for the fulfillment of the industrial-financial plan and of all the production goals. All its economic and operational directives were to be unconditionally binding on the lower echelons and workers, regardless of their position in Party or syndicate organizations. The management was to appoint directly all enterprise staff.[147] The September 5 decree also stipulated that the syndicates were not to interfere directly in the management of the enterprise nor take the place of enterprise management. The same advice was given to the Party cells, especially with regard to operational management and the appointment of the management staff.[148]

While strengthening the powers of the enterprise and its management, the September 5 and December 5 decrees of the Party did not make the enterprise a legal entity. The trust under whose jurisdiction the enterprises fell was the legal entity, and the enterprise director could conclude contracts only in the name of the trust on the basis of the mandate and the orders. In practice, however, at

142. *Upravlenie*, pp. 171–80.
143. *Ibid.*, p. 172.
144. *Ibid.*
145. *Ibid.*, p. 173.
146. September 5, 1929, decree of the Party Central Committee, "On Measures to Introduce Order into the Management of Production and to Introduce One-Man Management" (*ibid.*, pp. 163–71).
147. *Ibid.*, p. 165.
148. *Ibid.*, p. 167.

least some enterprises became legal entities, although legislation in the matter lagged.

On April 1, 1930, enterprises under trusts acquired rights to receive credits directly from the State Bank and to open separate accounts in their names.[149] This provision was made to implement the January 30, 1930, decree on credit reform, which banned reciprocal credit between economic organizations and stipulated that the State Bank should grant credits directly (and automatically) to the enterprises belonging to associations and trusts on the basis of the credit plans drafted by the trusts.[150]

Another step toward making the enterprise a legal entity was the February 18, 1931, decree on the conclusion of contracts by the directors of enterprises under trusts.[151] Nevertheless, this provision did not change the legal status of the enterprise, which still had to make contracts under the trust's mandate, thus leading to such legal absurdities as making a contract concluded between two enterprises belonging to the same trust appear legally as a contract concluded by the trust with itself.[152]

The decisive step in making enterprises under a trust legal entities was the July 23, 1931, decree of the Council for Labor and Defense granting these enterprises, as of November 1, 1931, their own working capital.[153] This decree changed the nature of the internal relations within the trust, which had until then been based on a system of orders. The *khozraschet* provided by the July 29, 1927, decree was no longer only an internal matter but became, in the official terminology, "complete"; that is, it allowed the enterprises belonging to trusts to have their own working capital and to conclude civil law contracts autonomously.[154] Nevertheless, the trusts and the associations at first continued placing orders, but gradually these orders were replaced by quarterly planned goals with the trust no longer obliged to provide supplies nor the enterprise obliged to

149. Venediktov, *Organizatsiia*, Vol. II, pp. 616–17.

150. January 30, 1930, decree of Central Executive Committee and the USSR Council of People's Commissars, "On the Credit Reform" (*Upravlenie*, pp. 180–82).

Automatic distribution of credits based solely on the plan goals and applied generally was replaced in the January 14 and March 20, 1931, decrees of the Council of People's Commissars by the granting of credits for specific goals, in accordance with contracts concluded, and solely to the extent that they were put into actual use (Venediktov, *Organizatsiia*, Vol. II, p. 619). The original automatic process was replaced by what was called "ruble control," which consisted of a detailed checking of accounts by the State Bank, an administrative and bureaucratic procedure that often interfered with the autonomy of the enterprise because of the obligation to make arbitrarily decreed appropriations. The "ruble control" often gave rise to irregularities because of the inflexibility of the provisions and the incompatibility of these provisions with the production and investment goals set in other parts of the plan.

151. Decree of Central Executive Committee and Council of People's Commissars, "On Responsibility for Not Fulfilling Orders and Deliveries under Contract to the Socialist Sector of the National Economy" (*Sobranie zakonov*, No. 10, 1931, Art. 10, as cited by Venediktov, *Organizatsiia*, Vol. II, p. 620). This decree granted the right and the obligation to directors of enterprises under trusts to conclude contracts in their names and to be personally responsible for their fulfillment.

152. Venediktov, *Organizatsiia*, Vol. II, p. 620.

153. *Ibid.*, Vol. II, pp. 620–21.

154. The term *vnutrennyi khozraschet* (internal accounting autonomy) was applied to enterprises under trusts mainly in writings during 1927–1930. In official terminology, this term was used only after 1931, in distinction to *polnyi* or *zakonchennyi khozraschet* (complete accounting autonomy), which was tied to the existence of a separate bank account, the possession of the enterprise's own working

deliver its production solely to the trust.[155] In practice, however, the trust was still held responsible for the enterprise's obligations, but after August 3, 1932, this responsibility was not binding unless the trust or the association had agreed to guarantee payment when the contract was concluded.[156] The enterprises also remained liable for payment of taxes of the trust to which they belonged, but enterprises that belonged to the same trust were not mutually responsible for each other's debts.[157]

In actual fact, A. V. Venediktov points out, granting their own working capital to enterprises belonging to trusts gave them status as legal entities as defined by Articles 13 and 19 of the RSFSR Civil Code. This provision conflicted with Article 33 of the July 29, 1927, regulation on trusts that considered enterprises belonging to trusts as not having status as legal entities. According to Venediktov, however, it remained the only one in effect, since a later law in conflict with an earlier law renders the earlier law null and void.[158] In practice, legal entity was recognized only for those enterprises belonging to trusts that had their own working capital. The other enterprises (very few) continued to operate on the internal *khozraschet* system.[159]

The claim that the enterprise was "the basic link" in the administration of industry and its recognition as a legal entity mark the limit of the powers that the government decided to grant the enterprise. The legal autonomy of the enterprise was very limited in view of its administrative dependence on superior agencies, which kept for themselves complete authority in setting plan goals. The situation is described by a Western specialist in Soviet industrial management as follows:

If we ask what is more "basic" about it [the firm] than about units above or below, it is difficult to find a clear-cut theoretic answer. The best that can be said is that it possesses a different sort of financial independence and responsibility from that of any other unit, but even this distinction cannot be pushed too far. In practice, however, the answer is clear: Ordinarily and in essence, higher organs treat the firm as the lowest unit of industry to be dealt with in plans and in checks on the execution of these plans.[160]

This position of the enterprise was maintained throughout the whole period of Stalinist administrative planning; in fact, it survived that period and is still the same today. But in order to understand the real powers of the Soviet industrial enterprise, one must examine the structure of the planning agencies and the planning process.

---

capital (as of November 1, 1931), and the right to conclude contracts autonomously. Later the term *polnyi khozraschet* (or more rarely *zakonchennyi, razvernutyi,* or *samostoiatelnyi*—completed, extended, or independent) became a technical term to indicate the *khozraschet* granted to an economic agency with its own working capital, which was directly tied to the opening of a separate bank account and the right to conclude contracts in its own name. (*Ibid.,* Vol. II, p. 621, note 202.)

155. *Ibid.,* Vol. II, p. 622.
156. August 3, 1932, declaration of the presidium of the RSFSR Supreme Court (*ibid.,* Vol. II, p. 624).
157. *Ibid.,* Vol. II, pp. 628 and 630.
158. *Ibid.,* Vol. II, pp. 630–31.
159. *Ibid.,* Vol. II, p. 633.
160. Granick, *Management,* p. 21.

CHAPTER 3

Planning Agencies

General System of Planning Agencies

Since the Soviet plan was intended to encompass all the economic activities of the country, one should expect to find planning offices at all administrative levels. The Soviet literature usually distinguishes three groups of planning agencies:[1] (1) general planning agencies operating under executive bodies (councils of people's commissars or ministers of the Union, federal republics, or autonomous republics and executive committees of territories, provinces, districts, or cities); (2) branch planning agencies operating under people's commissariats (or ministries), central administrations (*Glavki*), and regional or local administration of industry, agriculture, etc.; and (3) planning agencies of enterprises, trusts, combines, and other direct management bodies. A general outline of the planning agencies is given in Chart 2.

The basic feature of this system is that there is no direct jurisdictional hierarchy among the various commissions or committees or among the planning bodies. They come directly under the agencies to which they are attached or integrated and have to make up their own economic staff.[2] Hence they cannot give or receive orders to or from other commissions or planning agencies except by following the normal administrative channels.

In order to cope with this split between USSR Gosplan and the republic and province management and planning agencies, the February 2, 1938, Gosplan statute provided for plenipotentiaries (*upolnomochennye*) of USSR Gosplan.[3] A corps of Gosplan plenipotentiaries actually worked between 1938 and 1949 in

1. N. R. Bychek, *Organizatsiia planirovaniia narodnogo khoziaistva SSSR* [Organization of Planning of the USSR National Economy], Moscow, 1956, pp. 15–17.

2. I. A. Evenko, *Voprosy planirovaniia v SSSR na sovremennom etape* [Problems of Planning in the USSR at the Present Stage], Moscow, 1959, p. 26.

3. "Statute on Gosplan under USSR Council of People's Commissars," decree of USSR Council of People's Commissars (*Sobranie postanovlenii i rasporiazhenii pravitelstva SSSR* [Collection of Resolutions and Decrees of the USSR Government], No. 7, March 28, 1938, Art. 41).

the republics and provinces checking on the fulfillment of the plan.[4] Thus, after 1938 there were two republic and province planning agencies—one under the jurisdiction of the local executive body entrusted with drafting (and no doubt also fulfilling) the plan and the other directly under the jurisdiction of USSR Gosplan entrusted solely with checking on the fulfillment of the plan. This solution does not appear to have been satisfactory, and the institution of Gosplan plenipotentiaries was abolished in 1949 "in order to strengthen the responsibility of local agencies for plan fulfillment."[5]

The status of the planning agencies also raised problems in the relationship between the general planning committees and the branch planning bodies. The former formulated the plan on the basis of directives from the councils of people's commissars or executive committees to which they were attached, whereas the latter and the enterprise planning agencies received orders from their *Glavki* (eventually from trusts) or people's commissariats. There was not necessarily any coordination among the directives, among the indexes for the planned goals, or among the delivery schedules. The general planning commissions could not give orders to the branch planning agencies and had to follow all the channels of the hierarchy in order to satisfy their needs.

Another problem was the relationship among the branch planning agencies. Since they were attached to the management agencies, they suffered from the effects of the complexity of that system, described in the preceding chapter. The further down the line toward local units a planning body was, the more likely it was to come under the jurisdiction of several agencies.

The complexity of this setup of planning agencies increased considerably during the years before the war because of the creation in 1931 of the district planning committees (*raiplany*),[6] which created a difficult problem since the work of these committees often had to be reorganized because of an increase in the number of districts, changes in administrative boundaries, and shortage of staff.[7]

USSR Gosplan

The principal role in formulating the final text of the national plan for the whole country has always fallen to the State Planning Commission (or Committee) under the USSR Council of People's Commissars— i.e., USSR Gosplan. The

4. A. Zelenovskii ("Dvadtsat piat let Gosplana" [Twenty-Five Years of Gosplan], *Planovoe khoziaistvo* [Planned Economy], No. 1, 1946, pp. 35–36) mentions a Gosplan statute "approved by the government" (no doubt in 1946) that provided for the institution of USSR Gosplan plenipotentiaries charged with checking on plan fulfillment in their republics, territories, or provinces.

5. *Po edinomu planu* [According to a Single Plan], Moscow, 1971, p. 115.

6. September 23, 1931, decree of Central Executive Committee and Council of People's Commissars (*Sobranie zakonov i rasporiazhenii raboche-krestianskogo pravitelstva SSSR* [Collection of Laws and Decrees of the Workers' and Peasants' Government of the USSR], 1931, as cited in *Plan*, No. 12, 1935, p. 4). This decree, which was put into effect quite slowly (see below), changed the departments of the plan and of statistics of the district central executive committees into district planning committees.

7. Around 1953–1954 there were more than 5,000 district and city planning committees (B. I. Braginskii and N. S. Koval, *Organizatsiia planirovaniia narodnogo khoziaistva SSSR* [Organization of

Chart 2 Planning Agencies of the National Economy, 1933–1956

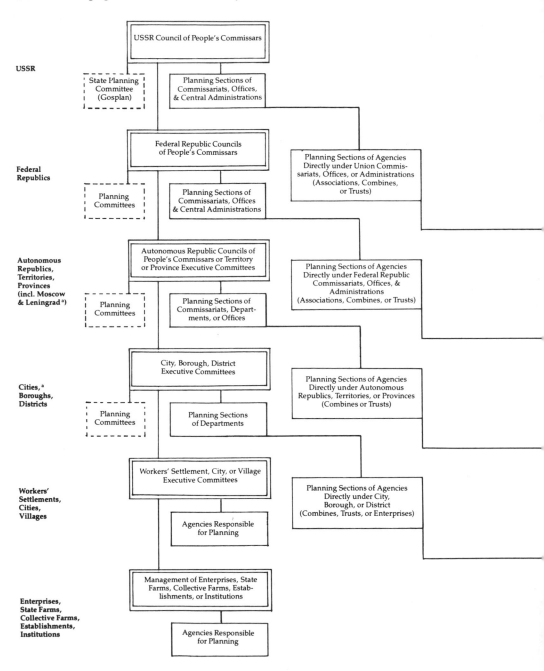

Note: After 1946, the Council of People's Commissars became the Council of Ministers and all commissariats became ministries.

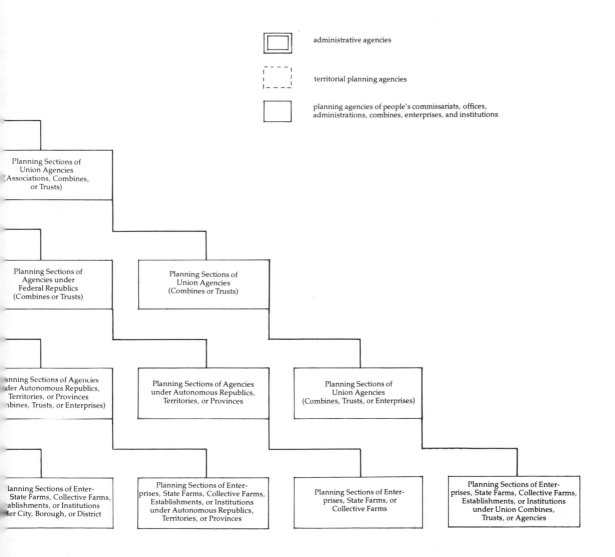

administrative agencies

territorial planning agencies

planning agencies of people's commissariats, offices, administrations, combines, enterprises, and institutions

Planning Sections of
Union Agencies
(Associations, Combines,
or Trusts)

Planning Sections of
Agencies under
Federal Republics
(Combines or Trusts)

Planning Sections of
Union Agencies
(Combines or Trusts)

Planning Sections of Agencies
under Autonomous Republics,
Territories, or Provinces
(Combines, Trusts, or Enterprises)

Planning Sections of Agencies
under Autonomous Republics,
Territories, or Provinces

Planning Sections of
Union Agencies
(Combines, Trusts, or Enterprises)

Planning Sections of Enterprises, State Farms, Collective Farms,
Establishments, or Institutions
under City, Borough, or District

Planning Sections of Enterprises, State Farms, Collective Farms,
Establishments, or Institutions
under Autonomous Republics,
Territories, or Provinces

Planning Sections of Enterprises, State Farms, or
Collective Farms

Planning Sections of Enterprises, State Farms, Collective Farms,
Establishments, or Institutions
under Union Combines,
Trusts, or Agencies

a. The position of cities in the administrative hierarchy depends on their size. The largest cities (such as Moscow and Leningrad) come directly under the federal republic and are on the same level as provinces with their own districts. Other cities are assimilated to districts, and the smallest ones come under districts.

functions of Gosplan were defined in the February 22, 1921, decree, signed by Lenin, and in the July 8, 1922, statute.[8] Gosplan was to draw up a single state plan, including means and procedures for its fulfillment, and to examine the production plans and projections of the different agencies and regional economic organizations in order to coordinate them with the general state plan and to draw up the work schedule. It was also to formulate general measures to promote the growth of knowledge and the organization of the necessary research to carry out the plan, as well as measures to train the labor force, and to draft measures to disseminate information on the plan, on ways of fulfilling it, and on methods of organizing planning work. Furthermore, it was to draw up the production plan of the state sector, as well as the plan to regulate the entire economy, and to draft long-range plans as well as current plans.

The revisions made in the Gosplan statutes during 1922–1941 did not change these provisions importantly.[9] However, the new Gosplan statute of February 2, 1938, specified Gosplan's complete responsibility for examining and drafting quarterly plans, for checking on plan fulfillment, and for supervising national accounts and statistics.[10] It also mentioned the responsibility for developing planning methods and forming *ad hoc* commissions of experts. The latter two provisions were not repeated in the new Gosplan statute of March 21, 1941, which did reiterate other provisions of the February 2 statute.[11]

If the functions of USSR Gosplan and of the Economic Council (*Ekonomicheskii Sovet*) are compared, it is apparent that the two bodies were concerned with basically the same problems. In the Economic Council, however, the stress was on examination of plans and only incidentally on confirmation. Gosplan, on the other hand, was concerned primarily with drafting plans and, on a lower level, with examining the plans of the commissariats, administrations, and federal republics. The advisory status of Gosplan is stressed by S. G. Strumilin, who, nevertheless, is aware of its actual authority as the "economic headquarters."[12] It is hard to agree with Strumilin on this matter, especially in view of Gosplan's responsibility for the allocation of resources. It is clear, however, that Gosplan could not be held responsible for the main decisions about the plan nor, for the most part, for its coherence.

The internal structure of USSR Gosplan and the functions of its departments and sections were revised several times between 1933 and 1941. Gosplan was a huge body divided into three categories of departments or sections (see Table E-3): a general production department responsible for making a synthesis of the

Planning of the USSR National Economy], Moscow, 1954, p. 114). See also last section of this chapter.

8. See Bychek, *Organizatsiia*, pp. 17–19, and G. M. Sorokin, *Planirovanie narodnogo khoziaistva SSSR* [Planning of the USSR National Economy], Moscow, 1961, pp. 257–58. See also my *Planning for Economic Growth in the Soviet Union, 1918–1932*, translated and edited by Marie-Christine MacAndrew and G. Warren Nutter, Chapel Hill, N.C., 1971, pp. 40–41.

9. Sorokin, *Planirovanie*, p. 262.

10. See footnote 3 above.

11. See S. G. Strumilin, *Planirovanie v SSSR* [Planning in the USSR], Moscow, 1957, pp. 32–33, and Sorokin, *Planirovanie*, p. 262.

12. Strumilin, *Planirovanie*, p. 32.

plan; aggregative departments responsible for examining the coherence of the plan in investment, finance, employment, material and equipment supply, and on a regional level; and branch departments. In addition, several agencies, the most important of which was for accounting and statistics, were attached to Gosplan.

The most frequent changes affected the general production department, which suffered the burden of arbitration within Gosplan and was often criticized for being "a Gosplan within Gosplan." Other important changes were made in the responsibilities for calculating materials and equipment balances, which were the basis for allocating resources. These functions belonged sometimes to the specialized departments and sometimes to the branch departments (see Table E-3, notes e and f); in general, it is hard to understand why, for example, the fuel and power balance was always made up in the branch departments, while other balances were calculated sometimes by the aggregative departments and sometimes by the branch departments.

Some of these changes no doubt reflected the new or enlarged functions of Gosplan. This was the case with the creation of several regional departments (see Table E-3, note c), the Office of Prices, the Office of Inventions, the Office of Economizing and Substitute Products, and the Corps of Gosplan Plenipotentiaries.[13]

Still other changes that can be seen in Table E-3 were purely formal and were basically adaptations of the Gosplan structure to changes made in the structure of the economic management apparatus. No information is available on the changes in the internal structure of Gosplan during the war years. The prominent role played by its chairman, N. A. Voznesenskii, its increased authority to draw up balances and allocation plans, and its functions as the principal agency entrusted with drafting the wartime economic plans all are signs of the increased importance of Gosplan.[14]

The internal structure of Gosplan was modified by a new regulation approved by the government in 1946.[15] In the place of a single general production department, two departments were created: the Department for Long-Range Plans and the Department for the National Economic Plan. Thus, the drafting of long-range plans was separated from the drafting of annual plans. But even this separation does not seem to have been sufficient, and the government felt obliged to split up Gosplan itself into two parts, in the June 4, 1955, decree, creating the USSR State Commission (USSR Gosplan) for long-range planning and the Economic Commission of the USSR Council of Ministers (*Gosekonomkomissiia*) for current planning.[16]

13. See first section of this chapter.

14. See beginning of this section.

15. "Planirovanie v poslevoennyi period i novaia struktura Gosplana" [Planning in the Postwar Period and the New Structure of Gosplan], *Planovoe khoziaistvo*, No. 5, 1946, pp. 19–20. G. A. Ivanov and A. S. Pribluda, *Planovye organy v SSSR* [Planning Agencies of the USSR], Moscow, 1967, p. 41.

16. June 4, 1955, decree of the Party Central Committee and the USSR Council of Ministers, "On the Reorganization of the Work of USSR Gosplan and on Measures to Improve State Planning" (*Direktivy KPSS i sovetskogo pravitelstva po khoziaistvennym voprosam* [Directives of the Communist Party of the Soviet Union and of the Soviet Government on Economic Matters], Moscow, 1958, Vol. 4, pp. 421–24).

The 1946 regulation also reorganized other departments and sections of Gosplan. A new department was set up to draft aggregate plans for industry and to ensure the coherence of the plans of different branches. It was made up of a sector for producer goods, a sector for consumer goods, and a sector for balancing production.[17] The 1946 regulation amalgamated and enlarged certain departments and formed special administrations (*upravleniia*) for planning the principal branches of the national economy: fuel, machine-building, transportation, construction, and agriculture. These administrations included aggregative sections that were to draft plans by branch. In the Finance Department a special section was created for balancing money income and expenditures of households, which was to ensure equilibrium between the growth of retail trade and services and household income. The Department for Regional Distribution (*Upravlenie territorialnogo razmeshcheniia*) was reorganized and sections for each federal republic were created within it.[18]

Another reorganization of Gosplan was made by the December 15, 1947, decree of the Party Central Committee.[19] The USSR State Planning Commission became the USSR State Planning Committee (the abbreviation Gosplan remaining unchanged), and its control over material and equipment supply[20] and over the introduction of new technology was removed. These Gosplan departments—the Administration of Inventories and Distribution of Material Stocks (*Upravlenie ucheta i raspredeleniia materialnykh fondov*) and the Department of Technology (*Otdel tekhniki*)—were transferred to newly created state committees: the State Committee for Material and Equipment Supply under the USSR Council of Ministers (*Gossnab*) and the State Committee for the Introduction of New Technology in the USSR National Economy (*Gostekhnika*).[21]

There is no indication of any change in the internal structure of Gosplan from 1948 until March 15, 1953, when, after Stalin's death, with power concentrated in the hands of the key ministers, Gosplan reintegrated *Gossnab* along with *Gosprodsnab*, which had been created on April 26, 1951 (see Table E-2).

Staff Problems of the Planning Apparatus

The worth of a plan depends directly on the quality of the men who draft it. Hence a study of planning agencies should ordinarily include a survey of planning personnel. The trouble with such a survey is that we are confronted

17. *Planovoe khoziaistvo*, No. 5, 1946, p. 20.

18. *Ibid.*, pp. 20–21. See also Ivanov and Pribluda, *Planovye organy*, pp. 41–42. It is hard to see to which Gosplan departments, according to the December 31, 1940, statute, this reform of the regional department was to apply. It is possible that this department was reorganized between December 31, 1940, and 1946.

19. "On the Reorganization of USSR Gosplan and on the Formation of the State Committee for Supply of the USSR National Economy and the State Committee for the Introduction of New Technology in the USSR National Economy" (*Direktivy*, Vol. 3, pp. 261–62).

20. See Table E-2 and p. 95 in Chapter 5.

21. The following *Glavki* under the USSR Council of Ministers were transferred to *Gossnab* at this time: *Glavmetallosnab* (for metal supply), *Glavsnabugol* (for coal supply), *Glavneftesnab* (for petroleum supply), and *Glavsnables* (for wood supply). And the following committees under the USSR Council of Ministers were transferred to *Gostekhnika*: the Committee for Inventions and Discoveries, the

with a veritable army of planners. Practically no information is available on most of these people, those who worked in the planning offices and the administrative apparatus (people's commissariats or ministries, *Glavki*, enterprises, etc.).[22] We can only study the staff of the regional planning agencies (see Chart 2), among which must be distinguished the staff of USSR Gosplan, the staff of federal republic and province planning committees, and the staff of the district planning committees.

Staff of USSR Gosplan

Estimates of the number of people employed in USSR Gosplan are very uncertain. The first Gosplan team consisted of 40 people. It was only in 1923 that this figure increased to 300.[23] Since that time there has been a continuous increase in the Gosplan staff. In 1934, 425 people were employed in this agency (not counting statisticians and instructors), of whom 150 were in management positions, 67 were engineers, 13 agronomists, and 142 economists.[24] The total number of employees, however, seems to have been much greater.[25] More recent data indicate that in 1962 the Moscow staff of USSR Gosplan numbered 2,700 people, 90 of whom were attached to the Office of Prices.[26] Around 1966 the staff of Gosplan, including office personnel, had increased to 3,000.

The increase in the size of the Gosplan staff was not matched by a corresponding improvement in quality. During 1922–1930, Gosplan seems to have been run by the most competent men in the field in the country at that time. Since planning was an art in its infancy, these men were pioneers. The most representative names of that period—V. G. Groman, S. G. Strumilin, G. M. Krzhizhanovskii, Ivan Kalinnikov, Viktor Larichev, E. I. Kviring, I. S. Ginzburg —certainly have their place in the history of planning.

This first management team of Gosplan was liquidated during the first wave of purges within that agency in 1929–1931.[27] The name of V. V. Kuibyshev, who replaced Krzhizhanovskii in November 1930 as head of Gosplan, is associated with these changes. From that time on, political criteria, and particularly Party membership, took precedence over all other qualifications. "Bourgeois" or Menshevik[28] elements were deliberately eliminated: "It was with difficulty, as Com-

---

Committee on Standards, and the Technical Council for the Mechanization of Labor-Intensive and Difficult Work. (*Ibid.*, p. 262.)

22. The hypertrophy of the planning and management apparatus was criticized during the discussions that preceded the 1965 reforms. According to academician N. P. Fedorenko, the number of persons engaged in the "sphere of administration" was about 12 million in 1961. According to academician V. M. Glushkov, planning work multiplied by the square of production and one would have to multiply by 36 the number of economists engaged in planning to attain a sixfold increase in production. See my *Planning Reforms in the Soviet Union, 1962–1966*, translated by Marie-Christine MacAndrew and G. Warren Nutter, Chapel Hill, N.C., 1967, pp. 54–55.

23. See my *Planning* (1971), p. 40, footnote 118.

24. L. Maizenberg, "Planovye kadry" [Planning Personnel], *Plan*, No. 11, 1934, p. 42.

25. In 1926 the staff of Russian Republic Gosplan was 900, but this figure might have included the staff of regional committees. See my *Planning* (1971), p. 40, footnote 118.

26. Mission to the USSR led by Louis Dufau-Peres (*Cahiers de l'I.S.E.A.*, No. G–18, 1963, p. 11).

27. See my *Planning* (1971), pp. 106–9.

28. Before the purges of 1930–1931, the USSR Gosplan staff included 20 former Mensheviks and 80

rade Kuibyshev observed, that position after position had to be filled and the bourgeois specialists, who were at that time our avowed enemies disguised as 'priests of pure science,' had to be evicted from the planning agencies and, to start with, from Gosplan."[29] The purge of the Gosplan staff continued during 1931; in the first half of the year alone, 237 employees were dismissed from Gosplan. Whereas in July 1930, Party and Young Communist League members accounted for only 24.2 per cent of Gosplan employees, at the beginning of 1932 they accounted for 68.4 per cent.[30]

At the same time, Party membership stopped providing immunity from being purged. Already in 1935 some Gosplan employees were accused of belonging to the Zinoviev group and, "in their struggle against the Party and the Soviet regime, of double-dealing, treason, and treachery."[31] Despite all these purges and the political nature of Gosplan, the team in power at the beginning of 1937 still included a large number of qualified specialists. Jack Miller points out that the heads of Gosplan departments were such people as Basiutin (regional planning), B. S. Borilin (general plan), Fishzhon (machine-building), and B. V. Troitskii (finances), who were specialists in their fields. He is much more skeptical about the head of the agriculture department, Krener. In general, however, Miller emphasizes, the departments did not have many employees (the regional planning department employed only 23 people) and hired specialized personnel.[32]

The most severe purges in Gosplan occurred in 1937 and 1938[33] and practically eliminated these specialists to replace them by former students, especially chosen from Party circles, of the planning institutes. Whatever the qualifications of these new people, it was obvious that the turnover of Gosplan personnel and the lack of experience of the new staff doomed the coherence of the plan that they were called upon to draft. Moreover, the government directives of that period did not allow coherence to be considered as a criterion of the success of the plan. Everything had to be considered in light of its usefulness to the Party:

The essential condition for the correct solution of economic planning problems lies in a political approach to any planning problem, to any figure, to every project. . . . These directives of Comrade Stalin's form the basis of Bolshevik management. In order to formulate an economic plan correctly and to direct the struggle for its realization, it is indispensable to keep firmly in mind the indissoluble link between politics and economics.

All the work of Gosplan and all the planning agencies should be permeated with the spirit of the Party and should ensure the Bolshevik implementation of Party and government directives.[34]

---

persons who had been members of the nobility, well-off citizens, or clergymen before the revolution (Maizenberg, *Plan*, No. 11, 1934, p. 42).

29. *Ibid.*, p. 41.

30. *Ibid.*, p. 42.

31. "Vyshe revoliutsionnuiu bditelnost!" [For Greater Revolutionary Vigilance], *Plan*, No. 2–3, 1935, p. 7. This article criticized Shvarts, Rozovskii, and B. Reznik of USSR Gosplan; Gorshenin of RSFSR Gosplan; Golendo of Belorussian Gosplan; and Radomyslskii and Liviant, professors at planning institutes.

32. Jack Miller, "Soviet Planners in 1936–37," *Soviet Planning: Essays in Honour of Naum Jasny*, Oxford, 1964, pp. 129–39.

33. See pp. 169–71 in Chapter 8 and pp. 11–13 in Chapter 2.

34. "Do kontsa likvidirovat posledstvii vreditelstva v planovykh organakh" [Eliminate Entirely the

The purge of Gosplan personnel during 1937–1938 did not spare its principal directors. V. I. Mezhlauk, Gosplan chairman from May 14, 1934,[35] was arrested in 1937. His successor, former deputy chairman of Gosplan, G. I. Smirnov, was arrested at the end of 1937 or the beginning of 1938 and in turn replaced on January 19, 1938, by N. A. Voznesenskii. The new list of deputy chairmen contained not one former director of Gosplan.[36] According to A. Zelenovskii, almost all the staff of Gosplan was replaced during 1938–1940.[37]

The new staff that was installed during 1938–1940 seems to have stayed on during and immediately after the war. It is impossible to know, for lack of information, to what extent Voznesenskii's disgrace in 1948 (he remained officially chairman of USSR Gosplan until March 14, 1949) affected the staff of this agency. His successor, M. Z. Saburov, stayed in his job until Stalin's death and then, after a short interval from March 6 to August 8, 1953, when Gosplan was run by G. P. Kosiachenko, returned to the job until May 25, 1955.[38]

Staff of Republic and Province Planning Committees

The information that could be assembled on the staff of the planning committees of the Russian Republic is presented in Table 3. A slow but sure increase in this apparatus occurred mainly because of the increase in the staff of the lower-echelon (district) bodies. Soviet authors commented on the shortage of personnel and on how the needs were greater than the number of positions available. Despite the lack of data, it can be assumed that the problem of personnel for republic and province planning agencies was not resolved during the Stalinist period.

The data are equally inadequate on personal qualifications, although some information is available on the agencies of the largest republic—the RSFSR. As of January 1, 1937, 28.2 per cent of the employees of autonomous republic and province planning committees in the Russian Republic (not counting technical and subordinate personnel) had a higher education. For 20.3 per cent of the total staff, this higher education was obtained at the Higher Institutes of Planning. These specialists were scattered among different areas; the larger cities attracted the best of them. Thus, out of 68 section heads, their assistants, economists, agronomists, and engineers of the Leningrad Province Planning Committee, 62 had completed their higher education.[39]

The turnover of employees in regional planning committees was, nevertheless, very high. In 1936, a year when political purges played a minor role, 644 new employees were hired in these agencies and 632 were dismissed. On January 1, 1937, these agencies had only 1,924 employees altogether. And 1936

Consequences of Sabotage in Planning Agencies], *Planovoe khoziaistvo*, No. 5–6, 1937, pp. 8–9.

35. On this date Mezhlauk replaced V. V. Kuibyshev as chairman (*Key Officials of the Government of the USSR*, Part I: *The Soviet Union, 1917–1966*, Munich, 1966, p. 62).

36. See p. 170 in Chapter 8.

37. A. Zelenovskii, "Ocherednye zadachi Gosplana" [The Immediate Tasks of Gosplan], *Planovoe khoziaistvo*, No. 2, 1941, p. 17. Following the official explanations, Zelenovskii attributed these changes to sabotage on the part of the former Gosplan staff.

38. *Key Officials*, p. 63.

39. Tonkov, *Plan*, No. 10, 1937, p. 48.

Table 3   Staff[a] of Planning Committees in Russian Republic, 1934–1937

	Actual Number in 1934 (1)	Actual Number in 1935 (2)	Number Requested by Committees for 1936 (3)	Actual Number on Jan. 1, 1937 (4)
Planning committees for:				
Russian Republic	171	173		
Territories, provinces, and autonomous republics	1,235	1,340	1,520	1,973
Provinces of far east and Kazakhstan	114	129		
Districts	2,064	2,374	3,365	2,903
Cities	614	624	737	} 786
Boroughs	41	62		
Total	4,239	4,702		

Source: N. Bogrov, "Planovye kadry RSFSR v 1936 g." [Personnel in Planning Agencies in the Russian Republic in 1936], *Plan*, No. 24, 1935, p. 40; S. Tonkov, "Kadry mestnykh planovykh organov RSFSR" [Personnel in Local Planning Agencies in the Russian Republic], *Plan*, No. 10, 1937, p. 47.

a. Excluding statisticians and office personnel.

was not an exceptional year. On January 1, 1937, 20.2 per cent of these province planning committee employees in the Russian Republic had worked for more than three years and only 8 per cent had worked for more than five years.[40] All these data are for the period before the large-scale purges of 1937–1938. Since the purges were general throughout the administrative and economic apparatus, it can be assumed that the regional planning committees were severely affected by them and that it was rarely the same people who drafted plans from one year to the next.

Political pressure seems to have been less strong at the regional level. On January 1, 1937, 18.2 per cent of the province and territory planning committee employees were Party members and 9.1 per cent were members of the Young Communist League.[41]

Staff of District Planning Committees

The shortcomings of the staff of the district planning committees were not due solely to their poor qualifications; a more general problem was posed by the government's attitude toward the committees themselves. The advisability of creating these district planning committees, which was decided upon by the government in 1931,[42] was discussed in the following years. These agencies were subordinated to the local executive committees, which did not control the major part of the industry or transportation in the districts.[43] For this reason,

40. *Ibid.*
41. *Ibid.*
42. See p. 43 above.
43. On October 1, 1936, 3,316 districts each controlled an average of 19 village committees, 70–80 collective farms, 2–3 Machine and Tractor Stations (MTS), a few state farms, 20–30 industrial enter-

their plans were mainly for the local economy, and the over-all characteristics of the district economy could only be estimated from information that the enterprises under the jurisdiction of higher authorities were obliged to transmit to them.

The position of the district planning committees was strengthened a little after the statutes of August 10, 1935, and November 10, 1937, which stressed their operational subordination to the province planning committees and insisted on their authority to draft the plan for the whole economy of the district.[44] Nevertheless, the organizational setup left much to be desired.

Even the creation of the district planning committees experienced considerable delays. On February 1, 1935, only 11 of 52 districts in Orenburg Province had planning committees.[45] In the Stalingrad Territory in September 1935 planning committees were not organized in 21 districts, and in October 1935 only 22 districts out of 52 in Krasnoiarsk Territory had planning committees.[46] Very often, moreover, the creation of district planning committees was purely formal. These agencies usually consisted of only two positions (chairman and economist), and even these posts were not always filled.

On July 1, 1933, out of 1,451 planning committees in 38 provinces or territories where a survey was made, only 1,034 had their position of chairman officially filled.[47] On February 1, 1935, out of 1,746 district planning committees in the Russian Republic, only 683 had chairmen. For these same agencies, 1,820 positions were provided for economists, but only 1,271 of them were actually filled.[48] On September 1, 1937, in the Russian Republic 33 per cent of the posts of chairmen and 22.2 per cent of the posts of economists were vacant. While at this period there was an average of 1.9 posts provided for each district planning committee in the Russian Republic, these posts were distributed unequally among the districts (3.6 in Gorky Province, for instance, but 1.2 in Sverdlovsk District and 1.1 in the Azov-Black Sea Territory).[49] The situation was hardly better in the Ukraine, where in 1937 the posts provided for chairmen and statisticians in the district planning committees were replaced by posts simply for clerical employees.[50]

Moreover, the number of positions provided for the district planning commit-

prises, industrial cooperatives, or commercial enterprises, schools, hospitals, libraries, etc. (*Planovoe khoziaistvo*, No. 11–12, 1937, p. 128).

44. "On Confirmation of the Statute on District Planning Committees," November 10, 1937, decree of Party Central Committee and RSFSR Council of People's Commissars (*Planovoe khoziaistvo*, No. 11–12, 1937, pp. 126–27).

45. "O strukture Respublikanskikh, kraevykh i oblastnykh Planovykh Komissii i Raiplanakh" [On the Structure of Republic, Territory, Province, and District Planning Committees], *Plan*, No. 4, 1935, p. 28.

46. A. Pimenov, "Stalingradskii krai" [Stalingrad Territory], *Plan*, No. 17, 1935, p. 57; G. Magoril, "Povysit kachestvo raboty Krasnoiarskogo Kraiplana" [Improve the Quality of the Work in the Krasnoiarsk Territory Planning Committee], *Plan*, No. 20, 1935, p. 72. It should be pointed out that the Krasnoiarsk Territory was established only in the first half of 1934.

47. Maizenberg, *Plan*, No. 11, 1934, p. 44.

48. *Plan*, No. 4, 1935, p. 30.

49. Tonkov, *Plan*, No. 10, 1937, p. 47.

50. A. Kagan, "V Kievskom oblplane" [In the Kiev Province Planning Committee], *Plan*, No. 15, 1937, p. 51.

tees did not correspond to the number of people actually employed. The chairmen of these agencies were usually deputy chairmen of the district executive committees at the same time, the latter job having priority on their time. The entire apparatus of the district planning committees was often occupied by current administrative work that had nothing to do with planning: "The apparatus of the district planning committees is generally used for carrying out various orders of the District Executive Committee that often have absolutely nothing to do with planning work, and the chairmen of district planning committees spend most of their time on missions in the district performing various jobs in political and economic campaigns as 'titular plenipotentiaries' of the District Executive Committee or the District Party Committee."[51]

Various complaints were heard from 1934 to 1938 protesting against the use of district planning committee staff for the numerous campaigns (for spring sowing, harvests, etc.) and, in general, for work that had no connection with district planning and against part-time work.[52] All this resulted from the attitude of the district executive committees which considered the work of their planning committees as not very important. This attitude is well illustrated by the following description of the situation in the Ukraine in 1937:

Not a single district has a real planning committee. Their staff is subordinated to the chairmen of the district executive committees or (in most cases) to the deputy chairmen. They are flooded by an infinite number of small operational jobs that have no connection with planning; they write out permissions and organize the recruiting of workers; they carry out orders for construction, prepare materials for meetings of the presidiums of the district executive committees, etc. Since their qualifications are poor and in view of the absence of a statute on district planning committees, they have very little power in the district. The district planning committees usually do not have their own quarters and have to share space with two or three other sections of the District Executive Committee and in some cases even occupy the waiting room of the chairman of the Executive Committee.[53]

The lack of respect accorded to employees of the district planning committees is reflected in their salaries. In 1934, for example, the salaries of planning committee economists ranged from 150 to 180 rubles a month. In other district organizations, the same qualifications commanded much higher salaries: 180 to 225 rubles in the Central Statistical Administration, 275 to 350 rubles in the

51. V. Cherepanov and P. Kuzmin, "Kuibyshevskii kraiplan ne rukovodit rabotoi raiplanov" [The Kuibyshev Territory Planning Committee Is Not Directing the Work of the District Planning Committees], *Plan*, No. 2–3, 1935, p. 82.

52. In 1934 in the Russian Republic, 46 per cent of the district planning committees had chairmen who worked full time. See "Zadachi raionnykh planovykh komissi" [Tasks of District Planning Committees], *Planovoe khoziaistvo*, No. 8–9, 1934, pp. 3–12. On the same subject, see also: S. Tonkov, "O sostoianii planovoi raboty v Kurskoi Oblasti" [On the Planning Work in Kursk Province], *Plan*, No. 14, 1936, p. 56; S. Shiriaev, "Predvaritelnye itogi konkursa raiplanov po Moskovskoi Oblasti" [Preliminary Results of the Competition of the District Planning Committees of Moscow Province], *Plan*, No. 17, 1935, p. 43; S. Shiriaev, "Kraevaia konferentsiia rabotnikov Oblraigorplanov Severokavkazskogo kraia" [Territory Conference of Employees of Province, District, and City Planning Committees of the Northern Caucasus Territory], *Plan*, No. 16, 1936, p. 53; and E. Ginzburg, "Soveshchanie raigorplanov Dnepropetrovskoi oblasti" [Conference of District and City Planning Committees of Dnepropetrovsk Province], *Plan*, No. 9, 1937, p. 48.

53. Kagan, *Plan*, No. 15, 1937, p. 51.

District Trade Center, and 300 to 400 rubles on state farms and Machine and Tractor Stations.[54] The average monthly salary for all employees in the state administration (economic or not) was 224.50 rubles in 1934.[55] The salaries of district planning committee employees were raised several times between 1934 and 1941, following the general rise in money wages and in retail prices.[56] Sometimes these raises were limited to certain regions (such as to western Siberia in 1935 or to Bashkiria in 1936) and sometimes they were general (such as the one on January 1, 1938).[57] The relatively lower standing of employees of the district planning committees was, nevertheless, not eliminated.

This discriminatory treatment evidently resulted in considerable switching to other employment. Out of 1,500 graduates from the Higher Institutes of Planning sent to work in the local planning committees of the Russian Republic during 1930–1937, less than half were still in their jobs at the beginning of 1937.[58] During 1936, of a total of 1,017 employees of RSFSR district planning committees, 443 chairmen were hired and 361 dismissed. A similar turnover rate existed for economists, of whom 728 were hired and 598 dismissed in 1936 out of a total of 1,598 in all Russian Republic districts.[59] In some areas of the Russian Republic, turnover was even greater. In Kursk Province, of 176 employees in district planning committees on January 1, 1937, 114 were hired and 116 dismissed during 1936. In the Mordovian Autonomous Republic, the number of employees in district planning committees hired or dismissed in 1936 was almost double the total number employed on January 1, 1937. The situation was little better in the provinces of Voronezh, Saratov, and Iaroslav, and even in Leningrad Province the turnover rate was 30 per cent in 1936.[60]

The result of this high turnover rate was a lack of experienced personnel. At the beginning of 1937, 46.6 per cent of district planning committee chairmen had been in their jobs for less than a year and only 10 per cent had been working for more than three years. For the economists, of whom 40.3 per cent had been in their jobs for less than one year and only 20.7 per cent for more than three years,

54. Maizenberg, *Plan*, No. 11, 1934, p. 44.

55. *Sotsialisticheskoe stroitelstvo SSSR* [Socialist Construction in the USSR], Moscow, 1936, pp. 512–13.

56. For changes in retail prices and money wages, see my *Planning* (1971), Table A-17, pp. 391–92.

57. In western Siberia the raise was from 170–180 rubles to 300–310 rubles per month for employees in the 37 largest districts. See S. Tonkov, "K itogam vserossiiskogo konkursa raiplanov" [On the Results of the Competition of District Planning Committees for All Russia], *Plan*, No. 19, 1935, p. 53. Another raise in the salaries of chairmen and economists of the district planning committees was noted in 1936. See Sh. Zigangirov, "Soveshchanie Predsedatelei Raigorplanov Bashkirskoi ASSR" [Conference of the Chairmen of the District and City Planning Committees of the Bashkir Autonomous Republic], *Plan*, No. 5, 1937, p. 57. On the general rise in wages of employees of the district planning committees on January 1, 1938, see the December 11, 1937, decree of the USSR Council of People's Commissars mentioned in *Planovoe khoziaistvo*, No. 11–12, 1937, p. 129.

58. "Sobranie aktiva Gosplana RSFSR" [Meeting of the Staff of RSFSR Gosplan], *Plan*, No. 8, 1937, p. 32.

59. Tonkov, *Plan*, No. 10, 1937, pp. 47–48. The same situation existed in the city and borough planning committees in the Russian Republic: out of 786 employees on January 1, 1937, 245 were hired and 186 dismissed in 1936.

60. *Ibid.*, and T. Sergeev, "Leningradskii Oblplan plokho zabotitsia o kadrakh raiplanov" [The Leningrad Province Planning Committee Is Not Concerned about the Staff of the District Planning Committees], *Plan*, No. 23, 1936, p. 53.

the situation was not much better.[61] To this lack of experience should be added the mediocre professional skills of these employees, which deteriorated even further in 1937 because of the high turnover rate. Whereas in 1936, 24.1 per cent of the chairmen and 20.6 per cent of the economists of the district planning committees in the Russian Republic had a college education, these percentages dropped to 14.6 and 11.0, respectively, in 1937. The number of chairmen with only elementary school education or no schooling at all (listed in the statistics as "educated at home") reached 43.5 per cent in 1937 for the Russian Republic.[62] In some provinces, such as Smolensk, this percentage exceeded 90.[63] Only 22 per cent of the district planning committee chairmen had finished secondary school, 3 per cent had finished secondary planning schools, and 13 per cent had taken planning courses.[64] Although the educational level of these chairmen may have dropped considerably in 1937, their political loyalty was strengthened: 69.3 per cent of them were members of the Party and 7.5 per cent were members of the Young Communist League.[65]

The situation was a little different for economists in the district planning committees. Only 18.5 per cent of them had elementary school education or were educated "at home," 40 per cent had finished secondary school, 13.9 per cent had gone through planning schools, and 24 per cent had taken planning courses. Although the economists had a higher level of education than their immediate superiors, their political credentials were inferior in the eyes of the government: only 5.2 per cent were Party members and 19.2 per cent were members of the Young Communist League.[66]

All these figures apply to the period before the large-scale purges of 1937–1938. After that time the inadequacy of the district planning committee personnel increased: the number of unfilled jobs and the turnover of staff increased, while professional qualifications dropped, all of which was supposedly compensated by increased Party membership among the staff. But the drafting of coherent plans was rendered even more difficult.

A detailed survey of the situation in the district planning committees during and after the war is not possible. The total number of employees in these agencies, which was from 5,000 to 6,000 around 1938,[67] certainly increased since the number of district and city planning committees exceeded 5,000 in 1953–1954.[68]

61. Tonkov, *Plan*, No. 10, 1937, p. 47.
62. *Ibid.*
63. I. Gaisimovich, "Bolshe vnimaniia raiplanam" [More Attention to District Planning Committees], *Planovoe khoziaistvo*, No. 7, 1938, p. 90.
64. Tonkov, *Plan*, No. 10, 1937, p. 47.
65. *Ibid.*
66. *Ibid.*
67. Gaisimovich, *Planovoe khoziaistvo*, No. 7, 1938, p. 95.
68. See footnote 7 above.

CHAPTER 4

The Planning Process

Development of Planning System

Uniform Plan Indicators

A system of uniform indicators is particularly important in administrative and authoritarian planning of the Stalinist type. Since every plan indicator is in principle an order, it should follow the proper channels of the hierarchy to the basic units. For any order to be transmitted effectively, the economic units must use the same "language" for both definitions and recorded activities.

The first Soviet annual plans did not fulfill this requirement. They were amalgams of operational documents transmitted by people's commissariats and federal republics and of various estimates made by planning agencies. The estimates covered mainly small-scale industry, noncollectivized agricultural production, wages, employment, and social services. The data transmitted through administrative channels did not lend themselves readily to aggregation at the national level. Each commissariat and agency drafted its own forms and used the indicators and definitions that seemed most suitable.

The first system of uniform indicators was formulated by USSR Gosplan in 1930. According to official commentaries, this system was too extensive and too complicated and therefore did not obtain official approval,[1] but this explanation seems unlikely in view of the future trend toward an increasingly detailed system. It seems more plausible that when V. V. Kuibyshev became head of Gosplan in November 1930 and political control of Gosplan's work was strengthened,[2] the plan forms drawn up by the old staff could no longer satisfy the government.

---

1. "K itogam raboty Komissi po razrabotke metodologii sostavleniia plana na 1935 god" [On the Results of the Work of the Commission on the Methodology of Drafting the 1935 Plan], *Plan*, No. 8, 1934, p. 66.
2. On his point, see my *Planning for Economic Growth in the Soviet Union, 1918–1932*, translated and edited by Marie-Christine MacAndrew and G. Warren Nutter, Chapel Hill, N.C., 1971, pp. 106–9, and discussion later in this chapter.

Another system of uniform planning indicators was formulated in 1932 for the preparation of the annual plan for 1933. It was published in six parts,[3] but was not binding; neither the economic organizations nor the statistical agencies were obliged to follow it. The result was a considerable discrepancy between this system of indicators and the plans presented to Gosplan, to say nothing of the overlap between them.

A new effort—this time successful—to create uniform planning indicators was made by the government in 1934. The April 16, 1934, decree created a special commission comprised mainly of Gosplan members,[4] who were to draw up forms and methodological instructions for the plan by July 1, 1934. These forms and instructions were actually published in 1934.[5] The August 4, 1934, decree made them mandatory for all organizations presenting plans to Gosplan.[6]

Annual Drafting of Forms and Instructions

After 1934 the preparation of instructions and forms became an integral part of drafting annual plans. As early as February 22, 1935, the chairman of Gosplan set up a commission consisting of the most important members of that agency.[7] Then the forms and instructions for the 1936 plan were published in large numbers.[8] In 1936 the same procedure was used to draft the methodological instructions for the 1937 plan, and the Gosplan chairman called on almost the same people to make up the drafting commission.[9] The government directives were revised in July 1936, and the instructions and forms for the 1937 plan did not appear until September 1936.[10]

3. See *Plan*, No. 8, 1934, p. 66. These parts could not be found in the libraries consulted.

4. This commission was composed of: B. S. Borilin, Kats, B. Reznik, R. Riz, Sh. Turetskii, S. Aizenson (USSR Gosplan), I. A. Kraval, M. G. Pervukhin, K. Kristin (Central Statistical Administration), Kruglikov (People's Commissariat of Heavy Industry), N. Voznesenskii (Commission of State Control), Klevtsov (Gosplan Institute of Economic Research), and A. M. Anikst (RSFSR Gosplan). See "Za razrabotku edinoi metodologii v planirovanii i uchete" [For Working out a Uniform Methodology in Planning and Accounting], *Plan*, No. 4, 1934, p. 65.

5. *Ukazaniia i formy k sostavleniiu narodno-khoziaistvennogo plana na 1935 god* [Instructions and Forms for Drafting the National Economic Plan for 1935], Moscow, 1934. This document could not be found in the libraries consulted. It is cited by G. M. Sorokin, *Planirovanie narodnogo khoziaistva SSSR* [Planning of the USSR National Economy], Moscow, 1961, p. 426. A summary of it was published in *Plan*, No. 8, 1934, pp. 25–49 ("Metodicheskie ukazaniia Gosplana SSSR k sostavleniiu plana na 1935" [USSR Gosplan Instructions on Methods of Drafting the 1935 Plan]).

6. *Plan*, No. 8, 1934, p. 25.

7. This commission was made up of G. I. Smirnov (deputy chairman of USSR Gosplan), I. A. Kraval, B. V. Troitskii, B. S. Borilin, and I. D. Vermenichev. In addition, representatives of USSR Gosplan departments, the people's commissariats, and the Central Statistical Administration were to participate. See "Nachata rabota po sostavleniiu metodologicheskikh ukazanii k narodno-khoziaistvennomu planu na 1936 god" [Work on Drafting the Methodological Instructions for the 1936 National Economic Plan Has Begun], *Plan*, No. 4, 1935, p. 58.

8. *Ukazaniia i formy k sostavleniiu narodno-khoziaistvennogo plana na 1936 god* [Instructions and Forms for Drafting the National Economic Plan for 1936], Moscow, 1935.

9. The commission was composed of G. I. Smirnov, Kraval, Borilin, Troitskii, V. V. Belenko, and Vermenichev. In addition, representatives from the people's commissariats, the Central Statistical Administration, and USSR Gosplan were to participate. See Ia. Chadaev, "Razrabotka metodologicheskikh ukazanii k narodno-khoziaistvennomu planu na 1937 g." [Drafting the Methodological Instructions for the 1937 National Economic Plan], *Plan*, No. 9, 1936, p. 50.

10. V. Mezhlauk, "Prikaz tov. V. Mezhlauka v sviazi s materialami 'Pravdy' o zanizhennykh

The instructions and forms for the 1938 annual plan were also drawn up by Gosplan, but the work was impaired by the purges within Gosplan, and it is probable that the document was not completed.[11] After Gosplan was reorganized in 1938, annual drafting of instructions and forms was resumed, and the specialized journals mentioned them for the 1939 and 1940 plans (see Table E-4). However, no such publications were found in the sources consulted.

The need continually to draw up new instructions for the annual plans arose from the planners' desire to correct their mistakes and their obligation to take account of government directives. For instance, the instructions for 1935 were criticized on numerous grounds: lack of precision in the plans for districts and for local industry, lack of data on net investment (which made it impossible to draw up a balance of construction materials), lack of coordination between plan and budget (for public health), and inadequate agricultural indicators,[12] as well as lack of data on the production of industrial cooperatives and incomplete financial data. Lack of data on planned profits made it impossible to link financial plans to production plans, and incomplete data on planned costs made it impossible to show the sources of financing investment. Other gaps were found in planning national income and money income of households.[13] Finally, the 1935 instructions were criticized for lack of data on material and equipment supply and lack of coordination between future and past statistical data.[14]

The instructions and forms for 1936 were criticized mainly for maintaining what was called the "functional" approach, which simply meant the transposition of the administrative nature of the plan. The basic data (on production, investment, fixed capital, etc.) appeared in the plan only insofar as they were included in the plans of the people's commissariats or of the republics or provinces, and their aggregate presentation was incomplete.[15] The 1935 plan was also considered too imprecise with respect to product assortment, statistics on capacity, and technical and economic indicators.[16]

The criticisms of the instructions for 1937 were rather vague, concentrating mainly on accusing the authors of the instructions of sabotage.[17] In general,

planakh" [Order of Comrade V. Mezhlauk on Materials in *Pravda* on Underestimated Plans], *Plan*, No. 14, 1936, p. 1; and D. Ivenskii, "K perestroike planovoi raboty v mestnoi promyshlennosti" [On Reorganization of Planning Work in Local Industry], *Plan*, No. 19, 1936, p. 10. On the revision of the government directives, see p. 60 below.

11. See Table E-4 and "Do kontsa likvidirovat posledstviia vreditelstva v planovykh organakh" [Eliminate Entirely the Consequences of Sabotage in Planning Agencies], *Planovoe khoziaistvo* [Planned Economy], No. 5–6, 1937, p. 8.

12. F. Shikhinov, "Neskolko zamechanii po povodu 'Metodologicheskikh ukazanii Gosplana SSSR'" [A Few Remarks on the "Methodological Instructions of USSR Gosplan"], *Plan*, No. 6, 1935, p. 38.

13. A. Pimenov, "K sostavleniiu metodologicheskikh ukazanii k planu 1936 g." [On the Drafting of the Methodological Instructions for the 1936 Plan], *Plan*, No. 10, 1935, p. 35.

14. "Soveshchanie po razrabotke metodologicheskikh ukazanii k planu 1936 goda" [Conference on Drafting Methodological Instructions for the 1936 Plan], *Plan*, No. 8, 1935, pp. 55–56.

15. Ia. Chadaev, "Razrabotka metodologicheskikh ukazanii i form k planu na 1937 g." [Drafting the Methodological Instructions and Forms for the 1937 Plan], *Plan*, No. 10, 1936, pp. 53–54.

16. *Ibid.*, p. 54; and G. Tsybulskii, "O metodologicheskikh ukazaniiakh k planu promyshlennogo proizvodstva na 1937 g." [On the Methodological Instructions for the 1937 Industrial Production Plan], *Plan*, No. 16, 1936, p. 47.

17. "However, 'the instructions and forms' for 1937 contain a number of false and harmful solu-

since the complete texts of the instructions and forms for all the plans from 1935 to 1941 are not available, it is impossible to know precisely the contents of the annual plans drafted during that period. Nevertheless, the general trend was certainly toward extending the scope of centralized planning and continually adding new details to plans that were approved at the highest level.[18]

Each new drafting of instructions for annual plans was preceded by government directives. The texts of these directives are not known, but the most important points can be gathered from the official commentaries. Thus, the instructions for the 1936 plan stressed eliminating the defects mentioned above for the 1935 instructions and emphasized the plan for local industry, distribution by districts, and the plan for retail trade.[19] The preparation of the 1937 plan was marked by directives on the use of the index of marketed production (as an essential index of performance), on a better definition of losses, and on greater detail on product assortment.[20] The preparation of the instructions for the 1937 plan was, moreover, affected by new government instructions, which stipulated that the plans for the gross value of production should be replaced (as a criterion of success) by production plans with a detailed assortment and that consumer goods should be treated as by-products of heavy industry.[21] These last instructions seem not to have been maintained for long. Until the 1939 plan, gross value of production in 1926/27 prices was the main goal and criterion of success; marketed production was used to calculate the turnover of retail trade and to draw up the plan for costs and finances. Only in 1940 was marketed production approved in the annual and quarterly plans in current wholesale prices. The same system was used in the 1941 plan,[22] but the calculation of gross production in 1926/27 prices was not abandoned altogether and continued to be considered, despite all the reforms, as the criterion of plan fulfillment.

Drafting instructions and forms for the general economic plan was accompanied by similar work for the financial plans and the material and equipment supply plans. These instructions, however, are available only for the 1936 and 1937 plans,[23] and it is not even certain that such documents were ever drafted for the other years. Nevertheless, mention was made of Gosplan's sending instructions and forms for drawing up balances for manpower resources for 1939

---

tions which resulted in most cases from the fact that Trotskyite-Bukharinite saboteurs, with their dirty hands, contributed to this work" (M. Kozin, "Ob ukazaniiakh i formakh k sostavleniiu narodno-khoziaistvennykh planov" [On the Instructions and Forms for Drafting the National Economic Plans], *Planovoe khoziaistvo*, No. 7, 1938, p. 79).

18. See the next subsection below.

19. *Plan*, No. 8., 1935, pp. 55–56.

20. Tsybulskii, *Plan*, No. 16, 1936, p. 47.

21. Mezhlauk, *Plan*, No. 14, 1936, p. 1.

22. M. Kozin, "O planirovanii i uchete tovarnoi produktsii" [On Planning and Accounting of Marketed Production], *Planovoe khoziaistvo*, No. 4, 1941, p. 92.

23. *Ukazaniia i formy k sostavleniiu balansov i planov materialno-tekhnicheskogo snabzheniia na 1936 god* [Instructions and Forms for Drafting Balances and Plans for Material and Equipment Supply in 1936], Moscow, 1935. *Ukazaniia i formy k sostavleniiu finansovykh planov na 1936 god* [Instructions and Forms for Drafting Financial Plans for 1936], Moscow-Leningrad, 1935. *Ukazaniia i formy k sostavleniiu materialnykh balansov i planov snabzheniia oborudovaniem, materialami i syriem na 1937 god* [Instructions and Forms for Drafting Material Balances and Plans for Equipment, Material, and Raw Material Supply in 1937], Moscow, 1936.

and 1940 to republic, province, and local agencies in August 1939.[24] This might have been an exceptional case in accordance with the decisions of the Council of People's Commissars which promulgated several decrees on manpower during 1939 and 1940.

A more general practice was drafting instructions and forms at the republic and province level. Table E-4 shows some of this work, but it clearly was much more general. There were also some "avant-garde" areas, such as Leningrad Province, whose instructions and forms for the 1934 plan were taken as models for other province planning committees.[25] After 1938, information on this subject is almost nonexistent and, in view of the troubles involved in drafting instructions on the national level, it may be that province instructions were rare or not very original.

Unfortunately, the planning methods used during the war years are not known, nor is it certain that instructions and forms were drafted at this time for the national economic plan. Soviet sources mention only the instructions and new forms for annual plans, prepared by Gosplan and approved by the government on February 14, 1947; these forms remained in effect until the end of the five-year period (1950), but the methodological instructions accompanying them were very brief, their main defect, according to Soviet sources.[26]

These 1947 forms show that a very high degree of centralization was planned for agriculture, with detailed plans to be made at the center and almost all quantitative and qualitative indexes to be sent to the collective and state farms.[27] Only the goals for farm income, distribution and use of this income in farming (except for payments to the budget), and use of manpower were not sent to the collective farms. In the eyes of the Soviet planners, such a centralization of planning would promote the restoration of agricultural production and the supply of food products to the population.[28]

In 1950, Gosplan did considerable work to make the forms and indicators reflect the greater complexity of the economy, the more advanced technological level, and the changed structure of production. New methodological instructions were also prepared. In drafting new forms, indicators, and methodological instructions, Gosplan sought to introduce technical and economic calculations and norms for the utilization of resources that would make the principal goals realistic, to specify production in physical terms by quarter, and to include the calculation of balances that would allow the coordination of the goals of different branches and eliminate bottlenecks. Estimated (raschetnye) indicators were also introduced for ministry plans that were not submitted for official approval.[29]

24. B. Babynin, M. Sonin, and S. Trubnikov, "Protiv mestnicheskikh tendentsii planirovanii rabochei sily" [Against Local Tendencies in Manpower Planning], Planovoe khoziaistvo, No. 4, 1940, p. 58.

25. V. Smirnov, "Rabota Leningradskogo oblplana s raiplanami" [Work of Leningrad Province Planning Committee with District Planning Committees], Plan, No. 9, 1934, p. 36.

26. Po edinomu planu [According to a Single Plan], Moscow, 1971, pp. 112–13.

27. For sown area and yield by crop, head of livestock and productivity of livestock, tractor work to be done by Machine and Tractor Stations, procurements of various agricultural products, etc. (ibid., p. 113).

28. Ibid., pp. 113–14.

29. Ibid., p. 113.

Unfortunately, the instructions, forms, and indicators for 1947 and 1950 were never published, so they cannot be compared directly with those in effect before the war.

Trend to Extend Scope of Central Planning

The only way to estimate the degree of centralization of planning is to make a detailed comparison of plan indicators approved at different levels of the economic administration. Such a study has never been published by the Soviet planning agencies. Some data are available on the ever-growing number of indicators contained in the central plan approved by the Council of People's Commissars, but very little is known about the indicators approved at lower levels. In view of the long chain of intermediary links that separate the enterprise from the central authority, measures of "centralization" or "decentralization" based on the number of indicators in the central plan must be taken with a grain of salt.

Despite all these reservations, it is evident that the general trend during 1933–1941 was toward an extension of the scope of the central plan. That this was a conscious effort can be seen from a statement by Gosplan Chairman V. Mezhlauk in answer to a question about what constituted the great success of Soviet planning at that stage: "The socialist plan permeates all economic activity in our country; in fact, it shows in practice 'the transformation of every state economic mechanism into a single huge machine, or economic organism, working in such a way that hundreds of millions of people are directed by one single plan.' "[30]

A major step in this direction was taken with the publication of the instructions and forms for the 1935 annual plan. The first requirement of these instructions was a uniform classification of branches of industry. All the commissariats and economic organizations were obliged to list in the plan the entire production of principal and auxiliary enterprises according to the single system of classification established by Gosplan. The statistical and national accounting agencies had to make use of the same system of classification.

Until that time, considerable production was omitted from the plan because planning was limited to the principal activities of the various commissariats. The People's Commissariat of Transportation, for example, included only freight traffic in the plan that it submitted to the central authorities and itself managed the heavy industry production of its auxiliary enterprises, which amounted to about 1 billion rubles in 1934.[31] Other commissariats, such as Communications, Water Transport, Food Supply, and Light Industry, also manufactured heavy industrial products in their auxiliary enterprises, and these products were omitted from the central plan. Even within heavy industry, 1.5 billion rubles of

30. Quotation from V. I. Lenin, *Sochineniia*, Vol. XXV, p. 316, as cited by V. Mezhlauk, "K perestroike raboty planovykh organov" [On the Reorganization of the Work of Planning Agencies], *Planovoe khoziaistvo*, No. 3, 1934, p. 4.

31. B. Reznik, "Metodologicheskie voprosy planirovaniia promyshlennosti" [Methodological Problems in Industrial Planning], *Plan*, No. 8, 1934, p. 8. Gross industrial production in the USSR in 1934, in 1926/27 prices, amounted to 54.6 billion rubles (*Narodno-khoziaistvennyi plan na 1936 god* [The National Economic Plan for 1936], Moscow, 1936, 2nd ed., Vol. I, p. 392).

production from auxiliary enterprises was omitted from the central plan; this came mostly from machine-building workshops belonging to *Glavki* (central administrations) that specialized in other kinds of production, from timber enterprises, and from machine-building enterprises of the ferrous metal industry or electric power stations of factories that were not part of the *Glavenergo* system (Central Administration for Electric Power).[32]

The main argument advanced in favor of including this production in the central plan was that the lack of direct planned orders to the commissariats for their auxiliary enterprises weakened control over their operation and made it difficult to draft the aggregate parts of the central plan, such as employment, costs, finances, transportation, and material balances.[33] It is hard to understand why even more orders from above were issued on the basis of this argument. The transmission of decisions to lower echelons would no doubt have sufficed to make the plan more complete. Moreover, this practice was introduced in 1935 in the plans of the district planning committees. These plans were made up of two parts: one covered the economic activities under the jurisdiction of the district executive committee for which index-orders were transmitted in collaboration with the district planning committees, and the other covered the economic activities under the jurisdiction of higher echelons in the district for which the enterprises transmitted only their goals to the local planning committees.[34]

The trend toward increasing the number of indicators in the central plan can also be seen in the instructions and forms for the 1936 annual plan.[35] The list of industrial products given in physical terms was extended and differentiated in order to take more account of product assortment. And, on the other hand, the integration of the output of auxiliary enterprises became more complete. For agriculture, the 1936 plan proposed including the total production of the country by category of farms and by commissariats. A breakdown of the plan by districts was introduced, and in livestock breeding account was taken, for the first time, of the experiment of the special livestock plan drawn up in 1935. For transportation, an effort was made to include in the plan all categories of freight transportation. A few forms for railroad transportation were, nevertheless, abolished, and the plan for motor transportation was made obligatory only for enterprises with 1,000 trucks instead of 500, as established in the 1935 forms. For employment, the instructions for the 1936 plan for the first time made the distinction between the *estimated* wage fund and the *planned* wage fund. The plan forms for social and cultural construction, public health, and science were equally detailed. The distribution of the plan by districts was extended to all sections and

32. Reznik, *Plan*, No. 8, 1934, p. 8. The output of machines in the petroleum industry, for instance, was larger than that of oil equipment produced in the machine-building industry. The output of the ferrous metal machine-building industry exceeded 200 million rubles in 1934. The output of machine-building enterprises of the Commissariat of Food Supply was also greater than that of the industrial association specialized in this production. (*Ibid.*)

33. *Ibid.*

34. Shikhinov, *Plan*, No. 6, 1935, p. 38.

35. S. Aizenson, "Novoe v metodologicheskikh ukazaniiakh k planu 1936 g." [New Elements in the Methodological Instructions for the 1936 Plan], *Plan*, No. 18, 1935, p. 27.

to the principal indexes of the central plan. For the other sections of the plan, particularly for investments and costs, the plan forms were changed very little from 1935,[36] although an effort was made to establish a more direct link between the production plan and the distribution plan by including an appendix on the procedures for presenting requests for equipment, raw materials, and centrally allocated (*fondiruemye*) materials.[37]

Several new indexes were also introduced in the instructions for the 1937 annual plan. The plan for the assortment of industrial production became even more detailed (see Table 4), and both the make and the technical properties of the output of the principal and auxiliary enterprises were specified.[38] Several details were also introduced to stress the results of the Stakhanovite movement lauded by the December 1935 directives of the Party and the government.[39] Distribution by district became even more detailed, and more detail was given on the printing and publishing industry. A special section was devoted to the construction industry and a section was included on railroad freight transportation; the plan for livestock breeding was supplemented by data on the breed of animals, the mechanization of breeding, and new methods of feeding.[40] Four new forms were added to the agricultural part of the central plan.[41]

No information is available about the instructions for the annual plans for 1938–1941. Nevertheless, the text of the 1941 annual plan, which was found during the war and reproduced in the United States in 1952,[42] is voluminous, and it is not likely that the number of indexes it contains was reduced from 1937.

Still, Soviet authors seem to have been aware of a certain hypertrophy of the central plan. In 1934, G. Laptev wrote: "First of all, supervision of the enterprise must be eliminated. For that purpose, the number of indexes planned by superior organizations for factories as well as for the superior organizations themselves (trust, administration of the Commissariat of Light Industry) must be considerably reduced so that the factories can have the maximum opportunity to show their own initiative."[43] In 1935 this problem again was raised by Goldman during a discussion of the structure of the planning committees in which he criticized the "exaggerated centralization in adopting the most de-

36. For investment, the instructions and forms for 1936 specified that the plan should use estimated 1935 prices or prices taking into account the 8 per cent reduction in prices planned for 1935. See *ibid.*, p. 29.

37. On the planning of distribution, see pp. 96–101 in Chapter 5.

38. Chadaev, *Plan*, No. 10, 1936, p. 53, and Tsybulskii, *Plan*, No. 16, 1936, p. 47.

39. Chadaev, *Plan*, No. 9, 1936, p. 50.

40. *Ibid.*, p. 51.

41. These forms applied to the plan to supply Machine and Tractor Stations and state farms with petroleum products, the technical and repair centers for the MTS, the plan to lower costs in tractor work, and income in kind for the MTS. See G. Tsybulskii, "Novoe v ukazaniiakh i formakh k sostavleniiu plana po selskomu khoziaistvu na 1936 g." [New Elements in Instructions and Forms for Drafting the Agricultural Plan for 1937], *Plan*, No. 13, 1936, p. 53.

42. *Gosudarstvennyi plan razvitiia narodnogo khoziaistva SSSR na 1941 god* [State Plan for the Development of the USSR National Economy for 1941], Moscow, 1941 (reprinted by the American Council of Learned Societies, 1948).

43. G. Laptev, "Nuzhno uprostit planirovanie legkoi promyshlennosti" [Planning of Light Industry Must Be Simplified], *Plan*, No. 9, 1934, p. 10.

Table 4 Number of Indicators for Industrial Products in Annual Plans for 1936 and 1937

	1936 Plan (1)	1937 Plan (2)
1. Machine-building, total:	330	550
2. Machine tools	32	60
3. Metal consumer goods	20	130[a]
4. People's Commissariat of Food Industry (21 *Glavki*):	1,086[b]	1,358
5. *Glavryba* (Central Administration for Fishing Industry):[c]	130	186
6. Fish catch	22	32
7. Industrial processing of fish	36	61
8. *Glavkhleb* (Central Administration for Baking Industry)	18	42
9. *Glavkonserv* (Central Administration for Canned Food Industry):	68	169
10. Canned food:	52	90
11. Canned meat	11	35
12. Canned fish	18	25
13. *Glavchai* (Central Administration for Tea Industry)	8	36

Source: Lines 1–3: R. Dorogov, "Rabota nad planom 1937 g. v otdelakh i sektorakh Gosplana SSSR. V otdele mashinostroeniia" [Work on the 1937 Plan in Sectors and Departments of the USSR State Planning Committee. In the Machine-Building Sector], *Plan*, No. 18, 1936, p. 49; lines 4–13: P. Priputen, "Nomenklatura izdelii v plane NKPP SSSR na 1937 g." [List of Products in the Plan of the USSR People's Commissariat of the Food Industry for 1937], *Plan*, No. 23, 1936, p. 54. The changes for *Glavsakhar* (Central Administration for Sugar Industry) were largely in the accounting of different categories of refinement.

a. Covers 80–85 per cent of total production.

b. Based on number in 1937 (col. 2) and increase between 1936 and 1937 (given as 25 per cent in Priputen, *Plan*, No. 23, 1936, p. 54).

c. Includes auxiliary production.

tailed indexes."[44] The trend, even if hardly "spontaneous," toward the continuous adding of new indexes in the central plan was perhaps best defined by V. Troitskii: "Very often, in the people's commissariats as well as in USSR Gosplan, the revision of the forms consists of adding new indexes and new forms, thus further complicating all the work of drafting control figures."[45]

On the same occasion Troitskii advocated the maximum possible reduction in the forms and instructions for drafting plans. His advice does not seem to have been heeded, and both the 1937 plan and the postwar plans were much more detailed than their predecessors. Other proposals to simplify and reduce the indexes in the central plans that can be found in the Soviet literature met the same fate.[46]

44. "O strukture Respublikanskikh, kraevykh i oblastnykh Planovykh Komissii i Raiplanakh" [On the Structure of Republic, Territory, Province, and District Planning Committees], *Plan*, No. 4, 1935, p. 28.

45. V. Troitskii, "Nashi predlozheniia k metodologicheskim ukazaniiam Gosplana SSSR k planu 1937 g." [Our Proposals on the Methodological Instructions of USSR Gosplan for the 1937 Plan], *Plan*, No. 13, 1936, p. 37.

46. See, for example, G. Vizhnitser, "K itogam aktiva Mosoblplana" [On the Results of the Meeting of the Leaders of the Moscow Province Planning Committee], *Plan*, No. 8, 1937, p. 56. Another

In actual fact, far from being simplified, the list of products in the annual plans increased considerably during the postwar years. The list of industrial products, which in the 1946 plan contained 1,637 entries (about double the number included in the Third Five-Year Plan), increased to 3,390 in the annual plan for 1950.[47] The total number of indexes in the national economic plan increased in approximately the same proportions: from 4,744 in 1940 to 9,490 in 1953, and down to 6,308 in 1954 after Stalin's death.[48]

Rather than being a question of good or bad will on the part of the planners, this development seems to have been due to a certain inner logic of administrative and authoritarian planning. The process of plan approval reflected a particular division of power among the various administrative levels. Since the central authority was by definition infallible, logically it should have borne the responsibility for all the decisions which, for any reason, may have attracted its attention. The reduction in the number of centrally planned indexes after Stalin's death reflected the changes in the central authority in the Soviet Union. It was the nature of the new powers to impose limits both on decentralization and on the number of indexes planned centrally.[49]

Drafting of Annual Plans

Problems Peculiar to the Soviet System

A Western reader looking for a coherent system and a well-defined procedure for drafting Soviet plans risks being disappointed. A Western researcher who worked for a year from 1936 to 1937 at the Gosplan Institute of Economic Research described the system as follows:

> The reason why I did not get any coherent picture of the Soviet planning system— apart from lack of ability and the increasing secrecy during the period—was that a coherent planning system did not exist. What existed was a priorities system of a fairly simple kind. The effective priorities were limited to products and services important enough to merit decisions by the Politburo and its permanent staff (the relevant Departments of the Central Committee and Stalin's personal secretariat). Gosplan USSR was, in effect, the specialist economic agency of these bodies. The elaborate governmental procedure for drawing up the plans was, in principle, the means of handling the Politburo's economic decisions while preventing the economy from breaking up.[50]

---

proposal made just before the instructions and forms for the 1939 plan were drafted is typical: " 'The instructions and forms for drafting annual plans for the national economy' should be reviewed, particularly with the aim of shortening and simplifying them" ("V Gosplane SSSR—V otdele svodnogo narodno-khoziaistvennogo plana" [In USSR Gosplan—In the Department of the General Economic Plan], *Planovoe khoziaistvo*, No. 3, 1938, p. 165).

47. *Po edinomu planu*, p. 112.

48. Sorokin, *Planirovanie*, p. 234.

49. The number of indexes was reduced from 6,308 in 1954 to 3,081 in 1955, 3,390 in 1957, and 1,780 in 1958 (*ibid.*). In 1968, besides the 1,965 indexes approved by Gosplan, there were 12,000 approved by *Gossnab* and 25,000 by the ministries and the republic councils of ministers (P. Krylov and M. Chistiakov, "Voprosy sovershenstvovaniia metodiki planirovaniia promyshlennosti" [Questions of Improving Methods of Industrial Planning], *Planovoe khoziaistvo*, No. 3, 1968, pp. 11–12).

50. Jack Miller, "Soviet Planners in 1936–37," *Soviet Planning: Essays in Honour of Naum Jasny*, Oxford, 1964, p. 120.

In the economic literature, the procedure for drafting the annual plan was usually presented chronologically. The preliminary work and four stages of actual drafting were distinguished. The first stage consisted of drafting control figures with a limited number of indexes (around June or July). In the second stage, the complete draft of the annual plan was drawn up in Gosplan, the people's commissariats, and the republics (around August, September, or October). The third stage comprised arbitration and coordination of the different parts of the plan before approval of the Council of People's Commissars (around October, November, or December). Finally, the fourth stage consisted of the approval of the plan and its transmittal through the administrative units to the executors (January–April and later).[51]

This ideal scheme, however, is not completely corroborated by the information that could be obtained on the practice of drafting plans. First, drafting was done simultaneously at different levels of the economic administration.[52] This can be seen clearly in Table E-4. In other words, several planning bodies belonging to different agencies worked at the same time and often their work was coordinated only later. In view of the number of administrative levels that the draft plan had to go through, it was inevitable that the drafting procedure be carried on simultaneously:

In the present system, the plan passes through four to six levels of government agencies before reaching the enterprise (People's Commissariat of Light Industry, *Glavk*, republic people's commissariat, province administration, trust, enterprise). Each of these organizations considers it its duty to make additions, to check, to judge, and only then to send the plan (sometimes with its corrections) on to the lower body. Each of these organizations considers it essential to include in the plan (for greater safety) the largest possible number of indexes, often completely useless.

If the chronological order of plan drafting were to be maintained, the time available for drawing up the plan would be insufficient. For this reason, the plan is usually drafted simultaneously (in a parallel and overlapping fashion) by different organizations.[53]

The distinction between plan drafting by different bodies was often artificial. The superior agencies did not transmit their directives once and for all but often did so gradually as they received directives themselves. The lower agencies did not limit their estimates of resources to the directives given them but often drew up their own requests for investment credits, wage funds, etc., by soliciting certain directives and avoiding others. Thus, permanent relations were established among the different planning agencies, which often gave rise to bargaining.[54]

51. Some authors accept these stages. See, for instance, B. I. Braginskii and N. S. Koval, *Organizatsiia planirovaniia narodnogo khoziaistva SSSR* [Organization of Planning of the USSR National Economy], Moscow, 1954, pp. 331–43; Sorokin, *Planirovanie*, p. 274 (Sorokin makes no distinction between the third and fourth stages); Miller in *Soviet Planning*, pp. 126–27 (Miller does not mention the transmittal of the plan to the executors); N. R. Bychek, *Organizatsiia planirovaniia narodnogo khoziaistva SSSR* [Organization of Planning of the USSR National Economy], Moscow, 1956, p. 33 (Bychek adds another stage, that of analyzing the results of the preceding year, and fails to mention arbitration before approval).

52. This feature is emphasized by Braginskii and Koval (*Organizatsiia*, p. 337), Bychek (*Organizatsiia*, p. 32), and many others.

53. Laptev, *Plan*, No. 9, 1934, p. 9.

54. On this subject, see pp. 79–80 below.

The different phases of drawing up the plan were not the same for all levels of planning. At the higher level—Party, government, USSR Gosplan—the process began earlier but ended with plan approval in December or January. For the lower bodies, the first task was to draw up provisional drafts based on very brief directives (or sometimes on no directives at all) and the last one was to draft documents justifying requests for investments. For the basic units, the final plans transmitted after official approval of the general plan were so different from the control figures that they required complete revision of the plan.

In order to understand the complexity of the procedure for drafting the annual plan, it may be useful briefly to survey the work actually done during the different periods of the year. This survey is based largely on the information given in Table E-4.

Preliminary Work

This is the period on which information is the least adequate. The preliminary work consisted of drafting both instructions and forms for the plans, as described above, and basic directives. Very little is known about the roles of the Party, the government, and Gosplan at this stage. Another point that is not clear is the destination of these directives. Were they to stay in Gosplan to serve as a basis for drafting the control figures in the first stage of the work or were they also transmitted to the republic and regional agencies and to the people's commissariats? The fact that some republic and regional agencies began their work in April or May makes the second hypothesis the more likely. The districts, on the other hand, do not seem to have participated in this stage of the work.

First Stage: Drafting Control Figures

The first stage consisted mainly of Gosplan's drafting control figures on the basis of government directives. This work was done around June or July, with government approval toward the beginning of August. An abbreviated version of the plan was drafted covering the principal goals for production, investment, etc. These goals, which were both authorizations and directives at the same time, were called "limits." The content of these "limits" was defined every year by the chairman of Gosplan.[55]

Once approved by the government, these "limits" were sent to the Union commissariats and to the republics. At this stage the "limits" were aggregated and included only over-all figures by commissariats or federal republic.[56] The commissariats and the republics distributed these "limits" among the agencies that they controlled: associations or *Glavki* and territories or provinces. Before

55. On the contents of these "limits" for 1936 and 1937, see Ia. Chadaev, "O podgotovke k razrabotke plana na 1936 g." [On Preparations for Drafting the 1936 Plan], *Plan*, No. 11, 1935, p. 56, and Ia. Chadaev, "Razrabotka limitov k narodno-khoziaistvennomu planu 1937 g." [Drafting "Limits" for the 1937 National Economic Plan], *Plan*, No. 12, 1936, p. 52.

56. S. Slavin, "K sostavleniiu raionnogo razreza narodnokhoziaistvennogo plana 1937 g." [On the Breakdown by Districts of the 1937 National Economic Plan], *Plan*, No. 17, 1936, p. 39.

this distribution, the commissariats and the federal republic councils of people's commissars made up their own definition of the contents of these "limits" as they affected their own sphere.[57]

At this stage, the "limits" did not go down beyond provinces, although districts were sometimes called upon to present their requests or development projects. It is clear that the "limits" approved by the government and distributed by the republic councils of people's commissars could not arrive at the province planning committees before the middle of August and perhaps even later. It appears, nevertheless, that the province planning committees usually began their work at the beginning of July and sometimes even earlier. Was this preparatory work done on their own initiative or was it based on preliminary orders transmitted by Gosplan around May or June and distributed in a provisional manner among republics and provinces? It also might have been based on orders given by Gosplan at the preliminary stage of its work in June before Gosplan's work was sent in for government approval. This last hypothesis seems the most likely, but it is also possible that different approaches were adopted each year. All that is certain is that work on drafting the plan was done simultaneously in different agencies. The lower echelons could, in that case, only have been working on old hypotheses that were being corrected at the center at the same time.

Second Stage: Drafting the Annual Plan

The second stage consisted of drawing up a complete draft of the annual plan and transmitting it to the government for approval. Here, too, work was done simultaneously at different levels. USSR Gosplan may have continued to work on the plan in preparation for distributing it among districts, but it did not submit a new variant for approval at this stage. The province planning committees submitted their plans for approval to the province executive committees and then through the republic agencies to Gosplan and the government.

Until 1936, all these draft plans were transmitted to USSR Gosplan, which was then to prepare an integrated text and submit it to the government. An October 1936 decree stipulated that the commissariats and the republics were to send their draft plans directly to the Council of People's Commissars, with only a copy going to USSR Gosplan.[58] The point of this operation seems to have been to give more freedom to Gosplan in drawing up its own variant. In actual fact, according to Jack Miller, after 1935, Gosplan prepared a version that was not a simple integration of the draft plans of the commissariats or the republics.[59]

At this stage, the district planning committees received instructions, forms, and "limits" approved by higher authorities and had to start drafting their own control figures. It is not certain when the "limits" were approved for the districts. Gosplan had to prepare the distribution of the plan by districts around

57. V. L., "Razrabotka proekta osnovnykh direktiv plana 1937 g. v Gosplane RSFSR" [Drawing up a Draft of the Basic Directives of the 1937 Plan in RSFSR Gosplan], *Plan*, No. 13, 1936, pp. 56–57.
58. Slavin, *Plan*, No. 17, 1936, p. 40.
59. Miller in *Soviet Planning*, p. 133.

August or September, but it does not always seem to have succeeded in doing so. In general, the level of economic administration at which the "limits" for the districts were approved is not known.

Third Stage: Arbitration and Coordination

The third stage covered the period between the time the draft plans were deposited with the Council of People's Commissars and Gosplan and the time they were approved at the highest level. Here four categories of work can be distinguished: that done by Gosplan, arbitration within the Council of People's Commissars (and, no doubt, also its restricted committee—the Council for Labor and Defense until 1937 and the Economic Council thereafter), revisions in the draft plans by the commissariats, the republics, and the provinces, and drafting the first (incomplete) variant of district plans.

The most important work at this stage was done by Gosplan. The draft plans of the commissariats were sent first to its branch department and the republic and province plans to its regional departments to be transmitted, after checking and revising, to the functional departments.[60] In its revisions, Gosplan also took into account the most recent information it had received (for instance, on harvests) and the latest government directives.[61] In November or the beginning of December, Gosplan sent its findings on the plans of the commissariats,[62] material balances, and the draft of the general plan for the whole country to the Council of People's Commissars.[63]

Very little is known on arbitration within the USSR Council of People's Commissars during this period. It can be assumed that substantial revisions were made before the complete version of the plan was drafted since often more than two months elapsed.

During 1934 and 1935 the government tried to force the commissariats to present a draft plan that included a breakdown by districts. These directives were seldom implemented because the economic organizations had little concern for plan equilibrium at the district level.[64] The role of districts in drafting the plan became more important at this stage. The district planning committees were to examine the draft plans of organizations in their districts, especially the parts on investments, and to give their recommendations to the province planning committee.[65] After receiving instructions and "limits," they were also to draw up

60. S. G. Strumilin, *Planirovanie v SSSR* [Planning in the USSR], Moscow, 1957, p. 38. On the internal organization of USSR Gosplan, see second section of Chapter 3.

61. Thus, after the plan for procurement of agricultural materials (mainly raw cotton) was overfulfilled, USSR Gosplan increased the 1937 production plan for several light industry and food products. See G. Ivanov, "Analiz syrevykh balansov legkoi i pishchevoi promyshlennosti" [Analysis of Raw Material Balances of the Light and Food Industries], *Plan*, No. 24, 1936, p. 45. See also Table E-4.

62. USSR Gosplan no doubt also sent in its findings on the draft plans of the republics and provinces.

63. Miller in *Soviet Planning*, p. 134.

64. A. Kurskii and S. Slavin, "Raionnyi razrez narodno-khoziaistvennogo plana" [Breakdown by Districts of National Economic Plan], *Planovoe khoziaistvo*, No. 3, 1936, p. 153.

65. E. Novskaia, "Rabota nad planom 1936 g. na mestakh: Leningradskaia oblast" [On-the-Spot Work on 1936 Plan: Leningrad Province], *Plan*, No. 17, 1935, pp. 56–57.

their own draft plan. There seems to have been some indecision here. Drafting complete district plans proved to be premature (for example, for Moscow and Leningrad Provinces), and the work could not be used.[66] Therefore, the instructions for drawing up the 1936 annual plan in Moscow Province provided at this stage for drafting investment plans for enterprises under the district executive committees and drafting complete control figures for agriculture. When the requests for investments were drawn up, the main production goals were to be specified clearly but the districts were not to draft a general plan, even for the part of the economy under district control. (This was not true for the agricultural part of the plan, which was extended relative to other years.[67])

Not only was the third stage of work carried out simultaneously at all levels, but it also involved personal contacts that required arbitration and coordination. Several republic representatives traveled to Moscow,[68] and conferences or individual meetings of those in charge of the district planning committees were organized at the province level.

Fourth Stage: Approving the Plan and Transmitting It to Executors

The Council of People's Commissars and the Central Executive Committee (which became the Supreme Soviet in 1938) usually approved the plan in the middle of January. The plan and the budget were approved separately. Once approved, the plan was transmitted to the executors through the regular channels —the commissariats and economic organizations for the bodies that came under their jurisdiction, and the federal republics for the republic, province, and local organizations.

Theoretically, transmitting the plan should have been a mere formality since all the goals were coordinated after consultation with the agencies concerned during the third stage, but this was not the case. During 1933–1935 the final plan was supposed to be presented around April for the districts. In actual fact, these plans were usually presented in May or June and some districts were incapable of drafting a final plan. It is impossible to have an over-all view of the industry under the jurisdiction of the commissariats, but some examples cited for 1933 and 1934 mentioned receipt of government approval in April or May. There were also extreme cases of enterprises working the whole of 1933 without a finally approved plan.[69] The lack of a final plan generally entailed a multitude of provisional plans:

66. S. Shiriaev, ''Raiplany Moskovskoi Oblasti rabotaiut nad planom 1936 g.'' [The District Planning Committees of Moscow Province Are Working on the 1936 Plan], *Plan*, No. 20, 1935, p. 70.

Other Soviet authors mention the drafting of a more complete district plan at this stage. For example, see V. Lavrov, ''K sostavleniiu planov na 1937 g. v raionakh Moskovskoi Oblasti'' [On Drafting Plans for 1937 in the Districts of Moscow Province], *Plan*, No. 22, 1936, p. 69.

67. Data on agrotechnical measures, yields, livestock breeding, and the fodder balance were included. See Shiriaev, *Plan*, No. 20, 1935, p. 70.

68. The trips of representatives of the Uzbek Republic are mentioned by Jack Miller (*Soviet Planning*, p. 128). Other instances of such trips could easily be found. Closer contacts seem to have been formed among the province staff. See Table E–4.

69. The plan for the Moscow knitwear factory *Krasnaia Zvezda* was examined by five agencies (the Commissariat of Light Industry of the USSR and that of the RSFSR, *Glavtrikotazh*—the Central Ad-

In the middle of February there was still no annual or quarterly plan for all the indexes. The Rostov Agricultural Machine-Building Plant (*Rostselmash*) did not even have an approved annual production program; the plant workers, on the other hand, knew of seven variants of the plan, which barely resembled each other; we shall mention only three of them:

Tractor-drawn plows	50,000	40,000	35,000
Harrows	7,400	4,000	3,300
Combines	1,500	5,000	3,500
Mowers	3,000	6,000	2,000[70]

Thus, it happened that, even in priority sectors, the actual results for the first months of the year came in before the plans: "For the electrical industry, for example, the final annual goals are given in January or February, which means that the plan is drawn up after the year has started and often the actual data for January arrive before the plan."[71]

The situation improved a little in 1935 and 1936 but, particularly at the district level, the presentation of the final formulation of the plan became less prompt. Moreover, in 1937 the annual plan was not approved by the Council of People's Commissars until March 29, 1937, and some commentators, such as Jack Miller, attribute this delay to revisions made in the plan after sabotage.[72] In any case, after 1937 official publication of the texts of annual plans was suspended. For 1938, only partial government decrees are available, scattered between November 29, 1937, and August 14, 1938, and concerning different parts of the plan and the budget. It is even doubtful whether the complete final text of the 1938 annual plan was ever published.[73]

The plans for 1939 and 1940 were approved by the Council of People's Commissars earlier than usual (in November and December), but the belated adoption of the budget (May 31, 1939, and April 3, 1940) make unlikely any real progress in the final publication of the annual plan at the executant level. The

---

ministration for the Knitted Goods Industry, the Moscow Province Administration of Light Industry, and the Moscow Knitted Goods Trust) and in 46 departments of these agencies. The factory received 19 directives, each invalidating the previous one. The plans for 1933 were revised seven times for production, four times for employment, and eight times for costs. In conclusion, the factory worked the whole year without a plan. The plan for 1933 was approved definitively on January 4, 1934. See R. Riz, "O poriadke i srokakh prokhozhdeniia narodno-khoziaistvennykh planov" [On the Procedure and Schedule for Transmitting National Economic Plans], *Plan*, No. 2, 1934, p. 38.

70. N. Koltunov, "Svoevremenno dovodit plan do predpriiatiia" [Transmit the Plan to the Enterprise on Schedule], *Plan*, No. 6, 1935, p. 42.

71. N. Ksenofontov, "Bolshe chetkosti i operativnosti v planirovanii i uchete na predpriiatii" [More Accuracy and Operational Work in Planning and Accounting of Enterprises], *Plan*, No. 7, 1934, p. 16.

72. Miller in *Soviet Planning*, p. 134. Some of the basic goals of the 1937 plan were published in December 1936 or January 1937, that is, before the revisions mentioned by Miller. There was no difference between these goals and those approved March 29, 1937. The drafting of the 1937 plan, on the other hand, followed its normal course and the final text was to be ready at the beginning of January 1937. A special study remained to be made to deal with the revisions made between January and the end of March 1937.

73. P. M. Alampev (*Ekonomicheskoe raionirovanie SSSR* [Economic Regionalization of the USSR], Moscow, 1959, p. 176) mentions the 1938 plan: *Gosudarstvennyi plan razvitiia narodnogo khoziaistva Soiuza SSR v 1938 g.* [State Plan for the Development of the National Economy of the USSR in 1938], Moscow, 1938. This may have been a preliminary text, like the ones published in 1935, 1936, and probably 1937. In this case, the final text is missing, as was probably the case in 1937.

few examples of plan approval known for that period strengthen this impression.

As for the war and postwar years, information on procedures for drafting annual plans is very limited. Nevertheless, it appears that delays in sending the final plans to the production units were quite considerable. The only annual plan published during this period, one for 1947 in a very brief version, was published only on March 1, 1947.[74] To judge by the dates of the sessions of the Supreme Soviet examining the state budget, during the period of reconstruction there continued to be considerable delays in transmitting the final text of the annual plan.[75]

Requirements for Coherence

The preceding chapters listed a few of the conditions necessary for coherence—the existence of a plan covering the basic economic activities of the country[76] and the existence of agencies and staff capable of drafting the plan. It is clear that these conditions were far from being met in the Soviet Union.

Further obstacles to coherence arose directly from the administrative nature of plan preparation, from the fact that in the Soviet Union the plan was not a study but a dossier or, rather, a huge collection of hundreds of thousands of dossiers at different stages of the administrative process—directives, projects, requests, authorizations, decrees, or laws. The method of drafting the plan, hence, was not independent of its content. The method directly affected the solutions adopted and the physical goals made mandatory for the executors. Therefore, it is of interest to see how certain aspects of the administrative procedure, the division of power among various agencies, the nature of decisions, and the method of transmitting the directives affected the coherence of the plan.

Division of Power among Various Planning Agencies

The powers of the regional planning committees attached to the different administrative agencies are not easy to identify. Their plans were made up of two distinct parts—one covering the economic activities under the jurisdiction of the agency to which they were attached and the other covering the economic activities under the jurisdiction of superior authorities (see Chart 2 in Chapter 3). In other words, their plans were made up of heterogeneous elements—compulsory directives that they helped transmit to the local level and estimates based on the figures transmitted by the planning bodies of agencies under the jurisdiction of higher authorities. Hence in every case there were elements of administrative

74. *Komsomolskaia pravda* [Truth of the Young Communist League], March 1, 1947, pp. 1–2.

75. The sessions of the USSR Supreme Soviet devoted to examining the state budget during the postwar years were held on the following dates: October 15–18, 1946; February 20–25, 1947; January 30–February 4, 1948; March 10–14, 1949; June 12–19, 1950; March 6–12, 1951; March 5–8, 1952; and August 5–8, 1953 (*Ekonomicheskaia zhizn SSSR* [Economic Life of the USSR], Moscow, 1967, Book I, pp. 397, 402, 413, 423, 433; and Book II, pp. 444, 451, and 461).

76. It is obviously not necessary for all the goals to be distributed in an automatic and authoritarian fashion among economic units.

dossiers and statistical data that made it possible to draft long-range economic plans and tentative monograph-like plans.

Regional planning committees did not have the same significance at all administrative levels. At the level of a very large republic like the RSFSR and at the district level, the disadvantages often predominated. The Russian Republic (RSFSR) alone contained 68.6 per cent of the population living on 92.8 per cent of the territory of the Soviet Union.[77] To draft a regional plan for this republic was almost as much of a job as to prepare a general plan for the whole country. Until 1933, RSFSR Gosplan attempted to plan all the economic activities on its territory, but it became apparent that this work was duplicating the work of USSR Gosplan. It was all the more useless since USSR Gosplan did not take into account the results of RSFSR Gosplan's work and, as Soviet authors commented, the latter "was working in a vacuum." Furthermore, while doing parallel work on some points, the two Gosplans ignored several important problems, such as ship repairs and urban renewal.[78]

The solution adopted from 1934 on was to limit the work of RSFSR Gosplan to economic activities under republic jurisdiction. This solution was a hybrid one, since a distinction was made between the republic economy, which was *handled* by RSFSR Gosplan, and the rest of the economy, which was *taken into account* by RSFSR Gosplan on the basis of local materials and documents transmitted by USSR Gosplan and the agencies directly under the USSR Council of People's Commissars.[79]

Jurisdiction was also poorly defined in the district planning committees. Directly responsible for those parts of the economy under the district executive committees, these planning committees were also supposed to test the coherence of the national plan in the district's territory. With the help of material and financial balances, these committees were to see if the goals of the branches under the jurisdiction of higher authorities were in accord with those of local enterprises, to find bottlenecks in the plan, and to discover means of eliminating them by reducing to the minimum the requests of local enterprises addressed to enterprises under Union jurisdiction. But because they did not have government directives on long-range plans for the branches under Union jurisdiction, the district planning committees could perform only purely formal and mechanical work that did not stand much chance of being retained at higher echelons. In general, USSR Gosplan tended to examine mostly the materials of the commissariats and to neglect those of the local administration.[80]

Because of the lack of precise definition of the responsibilities of the regional planning committees, the powers of superior authorities and especially of USSR Gosplan tended to be interpreted broadly. In 1933 and 1934 the "limits" for

77. Population as of January 1, 1933, and territory as of May 1, 1936 (the territory of the USSR did not change between 1933 and 1938). *Sotsialisticheskoe stroitelstvo SSSR* [Socialist Construction in the USSR], Moscow, 1936, pp. xvi–xvii.

78. A. Samsonov, "Uporiadochit sistemu prokhozhdeniia respublikanskikh i oblastnykh (kraevykh) planov" [Regulate the System of Transmitting Republic and Province (Territory) Plans], *Plan*, No. 12, 1934, pp. 34–35.

79. *Plan*, No. 4, 1935, pp. 29–30.

80. Slavin, *Plan*, No. 17, 1936, pp. 39–40.

lower agencies were drafted in USSR Gosplan without consultation with the parties concerned.[81] The 1935 plan for local industry was drafted by USSR Gosplan without taking into account drafts made by local agencies. This was true for both the allocation of raw materials, which was entrusted to the *Glavki*, and the total volume of decentralized investments. This plan remained thus "suspended in mid-air" since the local planning committees had no means of integrating it into their regional plan.[82] The imposition of unrealistic and incompletely considered tasks on the district planning committees was criticized in 1937, as was the reluctance of Gosplan to cooperate with lower agencies.[83] Current practice was to invite the district planning committees to cooperate in drawing up the plan once the targets had been fixed by USSR Gosplan and the commissariats, a procedure that often meant fixing goals and leaving the executors to find the means to carry them out.[84]

The regular administrative procedure was not always followed. The district planning committees requested that directives be sent to them quickly, even a few of them, in order to be able to draft their plans. When they received no official answer, they had to ask the advice of the regional planning department of RSFSR Gosplan or of the USSR Gosplan department for the regional distribution of production. Very little came of this procedure; the consultations produced no concrete results, and it was "not very useful to take their advice into account."[85] Other planning agencies were similarly and frequently short-circuited during the process of drafting the plan. Sometimes the enterprises in a district went directly to the executive committee, going over the head of the planning committee, and sometimes the commissariats gave directives directly to trusts, ignoring the regional administrations.[86] This procedure disorganized the work of the planning agencies and cast doubt on the very usefulness of their work.

The Nature of Decision-Making

In a market economy the decision to produce follows an agreement or expectation of one. The entrepreneur agrees to produce in exchange for a promise or a hope of receiving a given price, a price that will cover the costs of production. In administrative planning, an order from the central authority replaces the agreement and everything in it; that is, it simultaneously determines the quantity and

81. Riz, *Plan*, No. 2, 1934, p. 37.
82. A. Volin, "O rassmotrenii Gosplanom Soiuza Raionnykh Planov" [On the Examination of District Plans by USSR Gosplan], *Plan*, No. 12, 1934, pp. 36–37.
83. "Usilit vnimanie k rabote raiplanov" [Pay More Attention to the Work of District Planning Committees], *Plan*, No. 5, 1937, p. 5. *Planovoe khoziaistvo*, No. 5–6, 1937, p. 12.
84. "Shire privlekat raiplany k sostavleniiu plana na 1936 god" [Involve the District Planning Committees More Closely in the Drafting of the 1936 Plan], *Plan*, No. 15, 1936, p. 63.
85. V. Lukianov, "Ustranit nedostatki v organizatsii rabot nad godovym planom" [Eliminate Shortcomings in the Organization of Work on the Annual Plan], *Plan*, No. 14, 1935, pp. 35–36.
86. V. Cherepanov and P. Kuzmin, "Kuibyshevskii kraiplan ne rukovodit rabotoi raiplanov" [The Kuibyshev Territory Planning Committee Is Not Directing the Work of the District Planning Committees], *Plan*, No. 2–3, 1935, p. 82. An example of the latter practice was cited about the RSFSR People's Commissariat of Light Industry (see Vizhnitser, *Plan*, No. 8, 1937, p. 56).

the quality of the good to be produced and the means to carry it out. Once this principle has been laid down, planning becomes the art of giving economic orders. The procedure for drafting Soviet-type plans, with successive orders (called "limits") becoming more and more detailed at every phase, makes it possible to implement this concept. The essence of this system, then, lies in the fact that at every stage[87] the government determines both *what must be produced or consumed* and the *means* at the disposal of the economic units. The only difference between the preliminary and the final directives lies in the degree of precision, but the decision to produce and the means to do so are determined at every stage of the procedure of plan drafting.[88]

If the planners were omniscient and the executors machines, the only problem would be to find the optimal solution. But the level of knowledge of the top Party leadership is probably inversely proportional to its political power. Therefore it cannot help but call on the huge planning and management apparatus to specify what should be produced and the resources needed for that purpose. And it is at this moment that the discussion occurs which, in an administrative planned economy, replaces negotiation in a market economy. The margin of freedom of the executors is narrow since they cannot dispute the order to produce, the quantity, or the prices. However, while avoiding any questioning of the order given, they can conceal their real resources or try to show that they deserve a larger share of the available means, fixed globally by the planners for the republics, provinces, districts, or commissariats.

In general, the means requested are of three types: total investments, raw materials and equipment, and manpower resources. The Soviet literature of 1933–1934 abounds in examples of excessive investment requests. In this connection, a distinction must be made between requests for production capital and requests for social and cultural investments. In the first case, the Soviet state, in exchange for its production order, furnishes capital free to enterprises, the only charge made—for amortization—being clearly underestimated throughout this period. Nevertheless, requests for capital are examined and cut at every stage of the process of plan preparation. Since there is no way to protect against reductions in credits, the only tactic is to request more than needed. Conversely, since there is neither the time nor the means to check on these requests, the authorities can do only one thing—reduce them automatically. Some results of this procedure of evaluating investment needs are given in Table 5. It appears that the requests of the federal republic and province planning committees generally were cut by half or two-thirds. Other large reductions were also mentioned in

---

87. Whether at the moment the preliminary instructions are drawn up in April or May, when the control figures are approved in the end of July or in August, or when the final text of the plan is drafted in November.

88. Information on the preliminary orders of April or May is quite rare, but already at this stage the principal goals are set for production and investment. More is known about the "limits" drawn up in July by Gosplan. They cover not only goals for industrial and agricultural production and retail trade but also the means to carry them out—employment and productivity, wages, costs, budgetary credits, and even the main technical-economic indexes. The first attempts at coherence between these goals and means are made at this stage through the calculation of quite brief balances of raw materials, fuel, electric power, materials, and equipment. See Chadaev, *Plan*, No. 12, 1936, p. 52.

Table 5   Reduction of Requests for Investment Made during Drafting the 1936 Plan (million rubles)

Planning Committees	Requests Made by Planning Committees	Amounts Approved in Plan
Autonomous Republic of Karelia	529.9	182.4
Leningrad Province	2,287.5	1,386.5
Kalinin Province	515.5	224.8
Kirov Territory	666.3	167.9
Stalingrad Territory	831.0	319.1
Azov-Black Sea Territory	1,444.4	524.6
Northern Caucasus Territory	515.2	219.3
Autonomous Republic of Bashkiria	515.2	219.3
Sverdlovsk Province	2,200.00	1,084.8
Cheliabinsk Province	1,584.5	550.7
Omsk Province	524.1	151.4
Western Siberia Territory	1,401.7	617.8
Federal Republic of Transcaucasia	2,552.0	1,379.0
Republic of Uzbekistan	994.5	483.5
Republic of Turkmenia	351.1	152.4
Republic of Tadzhikistan	345.2	167.3

Source: Slavin, *Plan*, No. 17, 1936, p. 39.

the 1935 plan for the Russian Republic and in the 1936 plan for other parts of the RSFSR, such as Moscow Province and the Kara-Kalpak Autonomous Republic.[89] The requests of the industrial commissariats seem to have been handled in the same way. Those of the People's Commissariat of Light Industry, for example, were cut from 65 to 35 million rubles for investments in the 1936 annual plan.[90]

In making their requests for investments for social and cultural purposes, the local agencies could not take advantage of the priorities imposed from above. Nevertheless, they usually presented considerably overestimated requests.[91] For the draft plans for housing construction in 1935, these requests were double or triple the "limits" set and were not taken into consideration even at the preliminary stage of plan work.[92]

In their directives on the volume of production, the central authorities also implicitly (and explicitly at the later stages) fixed norms for consumption of materials and purchases of equipment. Every year these norms provided for an over-all reduction below the results of the previous year, these goals then being allocated through administrative channels among executors. It was on the basis of these norms, often very vague, that enterprises had to draft their requests for

89. "Rabota nad planom 1935 goda v Gosplane RSFSR" [Work on the 1935 Plan in RSFSR Gosplan], *Plan*, No. 9, 1934, p. 65. "V Moskovskom Oblplane" [In the Moscow Province Planning Committee], *Plan*, No. 18, 1935, p. 60. K. Kristin, "V Gosplane Kara-Kalpakskoi ASSR" [In the Kara-Kalpak Autonomous Republic], *Plan*, No. 18, 1935, p. 59.

90. V. S., "Finplan legkoi promyshlennosti v 1936 g." [The Financial Plan for Light Industry in 1936], *Plan*, No. 23, 1935, p. 53.

91. "Sostavlenie plana na 1935 god v Gosplane RSFSR" [Drafting the Plan for 1935 in RSFSR Gosplan], *Plan*, No. 8, 1934, p. 67.

92. G. Shcherbakov, "Sostavlenie plana po zhilishchno-kommunalnomu stroitelstvu" [Drafting the Plan for Communal Housing Construction], *Plan*, No. 12, 1934, p. 52.

materials. Because they often considered these norms unrealistic and also because of existing shortages,[93] enterprises tended to make their requests as high
as possible. The authorities, on the other hand, often automatically considered
the requests overestimated and reduced them arbitrarily.

In 1936, for instance, on the basis of regulation norms, the requests of the
People's Commissariat for Communications were cut by half, those of the
Commissariat of Light Industry by almost 30 per cent, and those of the Commissariat of Heavy Industry (for machine tools) by 35 or 40 per cent.[94] In the 1937
plan, the plans for material and equipment supply drawn up by the commissariats consisted, according to official statements, simply of the sum of the
requests of the *Glavki*. The commissariats were unable to present the justifica-
tions required by Gosplan, especially since the requests often were above the
limits for investments set by the government.[95] While the 1938 plan was being
drafted, it was pointed out that the requests for materials from the People's
Commissariat of Transportation were artificially inflated and that, after checking
them over in April or May of 1938, the commissariat itself had reduced them
substantially.[96]

The same problems arose with the requests for manpower. Exaggerated requests appeared mainly in 1939 and 1940 when the shortage of manpower was
especially acute because of food shortages and the stress on war production. The
authorities accused the commissariats of trying to recruit the largest possible
number of workers and of increasing their requests by 50 to 100 per cent above
"actual needs." Table 6 shows that these requests were considerably reduced in
the 1940 plan.

"Overestimated" requests and "arbitrary" reductions seem to be an inherent
feature of the administrative system of planning. Personal interests, excluded
from the setting of goals and means, take refuge in the underbrush of technical
discussions, a realm in which the authorities have to take account of the advice
of the executors. The negotiation of a market economy is replaced by a discussion full of distrust, based largely on the power of the participants. There is no
reason at all why the estimation of needs made in this manner should produce a
coherent solution. One could even say that the more arbitrary the administrative
system of planning becomes at the top, the less likely it is to produce coherence,
which was the case with the Stalinist system during most of the prewar years.

The arbitrary nature of decision-making was not denied in the prewar Soviet
literature. The bureaucratic approach, the lack of analysis, and the avoidance of
responsibility were often emphasized.[97] The planning committees were also

93. On this subject, see Chapter 5.

94. A. Shmaev, "K razrabotke balansa oborudovaniia na 1937 god" [On Drawing up a Balance
of Equipment for the Year 1937], *Plan*, No. 19, 1936, p. 6.

95. P. Tsarkov, "Pervye itogi razrabotki planov materialnogo snabzheniia na 1937 g." [Preliminary
Results of Drafting Material Supply Plans for 1937], *Plan*, No. 1, 1937, p. 45.

96. For example, profile iron was reduced by 206,000 metric tons and cement by 180,000 metric tons.
F. Gaposhkin and A. Ambartsumov, "O materialno-tekhnicheskom snabzhenii" [On Material and
Equipment Supply], *Planovoe khoziaistvo*, No. 11, 1938, p. 105.

97. Mezhlauk, *Planovoe khoziaistvo*, No. 3, 1934, pp. 15–16. "V Gosplane pri SNK SSSR" [In
Gosplan under USSR Council of People's Commissars], *Planovoe khoziaistvo*, No. 2, 1940, p. 120. L.
Maizenberg, "O khoziaistvennom plane" [On the Economic Plan], *Planovoe khoziaistvo*, No. 10, 1940,
p. 12.

reproached for contenting themselves with simply summing up the requests presented to them or distributing the "limits" mechanically.[98] Even ordinary mistakes in arithmetic can be found in plan calculations.[99]

Before the war the idea became accepted that the essential consideration was not an optimal calculation of resources but drafting a "good" plan. From this theory arose the practice of bargaining, centered mostly on the investment limits, bargaining which, because of changes in the limits, compromised "the fragile structure of the plan."[100] This plan bargaining had its own rules of the game.[101] Planning officials listened attentively to their visitors from the provinces but often disregarded their suggestions after their departure.[102] It was mainly in the final stage of plan preparation in October or November that the

Table 6 Plan for Recruitment[a] of Outside Manpower in 1940 (thousand persons)

People's Commissariats	Requests Made by People's Commissariats	"Actual" Needs
Ferrous Metal Industry	46.0	29.0
Electrical Industry	36.4	10.4
Construction Materials Industry	15.5	5.0
Fishing Industry	47.0	45.0
Food Industry	16.5	13.5
Maritime Fleet	11.5	7.0

Source: Babynin, Sonin, and Trubnikov, *Planovoe khoziaistvo*, No. 4, 1940, p. 63.

a. Organized outside the provinces in which enterprises were located.

pressures from below became the strongest. The leaders from the provinces, territories, and republics came personally to Moscow to complain of the inadequacy of investments. Turned down, they not only complained to the management of USSR Gosplan but also wrote letters to Party and government leaders, enclosing documents to support their contentions.[103] This "bargaining outside

98. This applied mainly to the "limits" (authorizations for utilization of funds) allocated for investments. See A. Pimenov, "Stalingradskii krai" [Stalingrad Territory], *Plan*, No. 17, 1935, p. 57; and Slavin, *Plan*, No. 17, 1936, p. 39.

99. "It should also be noted that it is difficult to make use of the control figures presented by regions, in particular by the planning committees of the Northern Caucasus and Gorky Territories, Transcaucasia, the Crimea, and others, because of the large number of mistakes in calculation and in the computation of percentages, etc., in other words, because of sloppy arithmetic. Moreover, data in different units are often reproduced and added together in the tables: tons are added to centners, etc." (M. Urev, "Rabota nad planom zhivotnovodstva na 1935 god" [Work on the Plan for Livestock Breeding for 1935], *Plan*, No. 12, 1934, p. 51).

100. E. Novskaia, "Organizovanno provesti podgotovku k sostavleniiu plana na 1936 g." [Preparation for Drafting the 1936 Plan Must Be Conducted in an Organized Fashion], *Plan*, No. 11, 1935, p. 39.

101. On this subject, see Joseph S. Berliner, *Factory and Manager in the USSR*, Cambridge, Mass., 1957, Chapter XII, "The Tolkach and Uses of Influence."

102. "Sobranie aktiva Gosplana RSFSR" [Meeting of the Staff of RSFSR Gosplan], *Plan*, No. 8, 1937, p. 35.

103. K. Kostiushin, "Kak 'planiruetsia' dorozhnoe khoziaistvo" [How the Road System Is "Planned"], *Plan*, No. 18, 1935, p. 25.

the market" was much more inclusive than that in liberal economies. It took into account human elements, group interests, and privileges, which did not necessarily lead to a solution that balanced goals and the means provided to realize them.

Transmittal of Directives

It has been mentioned above (in the section on drafting annual plans earlier in this chapter) that the directives were transmitted in the aggregate at each stage of plan preparation. Changes in the directives, made outside the "official" periods, even within a stage, were considered completely normal. The simultaneous work of different agencies, changes in the economic situation, and changes in government policy certainly justified such decisions. The advantages of such a procedure, however, risked being outweighed by the disadvantages. The new directives forced the planning agencies to redo the major part of their work and caused delays that had repercussions on other echelons in the system. But the most serious changes were those made after the approval of the national plan, that is, after December. The new directives prevented the enterprises from receiving the final annual plan on schedule and forced them to produce on the basis of old directives, outdated by definition; in other words, inconsistencies in the plan were transformed into actual disproportions in the economy.

A few examples of such late and multiple changes in directives have been cited in the Soviet press. Between November 25, 1933, and April 9, 1934, the directives of the *Glavk* for the Cotton Industry to the Moscow Cotton Trust changed six times; the trust's 1934 plan was approved in the middle of May 1934 instead of on April 15.[104] The example of the Rostov Agricultural Machine-Building Plant, which had seven variants of its annual plan for 1935 without having a final plan approved in February 1935, was cited earlier.[105] A factory that produced movable parts for tractors had its production plan revised three times by the People's Commissariat of Machine-Building during the first quarter of 1938. The directives of January 26, 1938, aimed at a production of 4.3 million rubles; those of February 2, 1938, at 3.0 million rubles; and the plan approved on April 11, 1938, provided only for 2.6 million rubles.[106] The Soviet press is reluctant to mention such examples and usually cites changes in directives without giving any details.[107] But the delays in obtaining final approval of the plans for basic units (see Table E-4) show that this was current practice. Only changes in directives can explain the general delays of several months in the final variants of the plans.

Aside from changes in directives by central agencies, there were also changes in directives made by intermediate echelons. Regional agencies had the right to add to the assortment of centrally determined goals, particularly in local industry, but this practice jeopardized the coherence of the central plan at the branch

104. Laptev, *Plan*, No. 9, 1934, p. 9.
105. See text around footnote 70 above.
106. E. Gaposhkin, "Kapitalnyi remont v 1938 godu" [Capital Repairs in 1938], *Planovoe khoziaistvo*, No. 9, 1938, p. 59.
107. See, for instance, Novskaia, *Plan*, No. 11, 1935, p. 39.

level. If the product assortment was too aggregated, the coherence of the plan would be fragile. If an attempt were made to test the coherence in current selling prices, the provisions that had been valid for the total aggregate value would be considerably out of line for different provinces or districts[108] and discrepancies would appear during the execution of the plan.

On the other hand, some illegal practices were introduced in the transmittal of the plans. They consisted sometimes of understating and sometimes (more often) of overstating goals which the commissariats or *Glavki* distributed among the enterprises. Overstating the aggregate production goals was a kind of insurance against the risk of failing to fulfill the plan by making it possible to hide the nonfulfillment of the plan for the first quarter by including the "debt" in the program for the second quarter. Sometimes, simultaneously with overstating production goals, in order to create "reserves," goals were reduced for investments, wage funds, and purchase of raw materials, fuel, or construction materials. This practice was opposed by the government, which deplored such violations of plan discipline. Alongside the official plan appeared a parallel plan, with uncertain resources, which risked not only failing to be fulfilled but also compromising the fulfillment of the centrally fixed plan. The November 29, 1937, decree of the Council of People's Commissars condemned and forbade these deviations from government goals that made up the so-called "operational" plans.[109]

It was not always easy to transmit government directives to the enterprises, especially since they often consisted of demands for additional economizing or supplementary production. The *Glavki* then slowed down the transmittal of these directives. An example was cited about the reduction of the norms for the consumption of metal ordered by the government in the March 4, 1938, decree.[110] The new norms and the saving in metal to be thus obtained were to be presented on September 1, 1938. In actual fact, by the fourth quarter of 1939, only the People's Commissariats of the Ferrous Metal Industry and of Defense had presented their draft plans. But even the former commissariat, which drafted norms for economizing metal, only passed a decree distributing the tasks of the *Glavki* in this field without supervising the transmittal of these goals to the enterprises. Thus, the *Glavk* for the Metal Industry, which was to ensure a saving of 865,000 metric tons in the production of metal and of 5,000 metric tons in equipment repairs in 1939, transmitted these directives to the enterprises only partially (for 226,600 metric tons in production), leaving the other goals "without addressee."[111] Also in 1939 the People's Commissariat of Heavy Machine-Building did not transmit to the factories the directive on expanding the production of machine tools decreed by the USSR Council of People's Commissars.[112]

The lack of precise definition of the responsibilities of planning agencies also raised problems in transmitting directives, as occurred during 1933–1934 with

108. Ivenskii, *Plan*, No. 19, 1936, p. 10.
109. Maizenberg, *Planovoe khoziaistvo*, No. 10, 1940, pp. 22–23.
110. A. Zosimov and I. Sirovskii, "Puti ekonomii metalla" [Ways of Economizing Metal], *Planovoe khoziaistvo*, No. 12, 1939, pp. 112–13.
111. *Ibid.*, p. 113.
112. September 4, 1939, decree, "On the Development of the USSR Machine Tool Industry" ("V

the plans of some enterprises for which goals were set both by their *Glavki* and by the district planning committees.[113] The same was true for some goals, such as costs, for local industry. The aggregate goals were transmitted by the Commissariat of Local Industry in the 1935 plan to both the branch administrations and the regional agencies. Each of these intermediary bodies allotted the goals to the enterprises in its own fashion. Thus, different goals were sent to the same enterprises, creating considerable confusion.[114] Local enterprises were confused by this procedure and did not know which plan to carry out—the one drawn up by USSR Gosplan and transmitted through the people's commissariats and institutions or the one approved by the local agencies.[115]

This procedure, called "duplicate planning," was also observed in the plans for retail trade. In Moscow Province, *Tsentrosoiuz* set the 1936 plan at a turnover of 1,200 million rubles for the Moscow Union of Cooperatives, the province agencies approved a plan of 1,350 million for the same body, and the Moscow Union of Cooperatives itself allotted these goals among the district or regional organizations for a total of 1,469 million rubles.[116] Such "duplicate planning" was in principle forbidden by the People's Commissariat of Domestic Trade, and its regional agencies should have refused to accept different plans adopted by the province or district executive committees. The distribution of responsibilities was not clear, however, and during all of 1936 the fight continued about who was to draft the plans for the local trade agencies—the regional domestic trade agencies or *Glavtorg* (Central Administration for Trade). Since each agency considered its plan as "final" and binding, the local retail trade agencies were completely confused.[117]

It is difficult to judge to what extent all these changes and the lack of clearly defined channels for transmitting directives actually jeopardized the coherence of the central plan. It is clear, however, that the administrative and formal unity of the plan, such as it existed under the law on annual planning, was much more apparent than real. Another question also arises: even if it were real, would this administrative and formal unity have been sufficient to ensure the coherence of the plan? Did the search for administrative unity and legal authority not arise from the absence of consistency between the goals and the means of implementing them, a consistency that the calculation of material, financial, and manpower balances was meant to ensure?

Gosplane pri SNK SSSR" [In Gosplan under USSR Council of People's Commissars], *Planovoe khoziaistvo*, No. 1, 1940, p. 123).

113. Riz, *Plan*, No. 2, 1934, p. 37.

114. I. Ivenskii, "Voprosy planirovaniia mestnoi promyshlennosti" [Questions of Planning Local Industry], *Plan*, No. 1, 1935, p. 24.

115. Kurskii and Slavin, *Planovoe khoziaistvo*, No. 3, 1936, p. 153.

116. T. Biazrov, "Uporiadochit planirovanie tovarooborota" [Bring Order to the Planning of Trade Turnover], *Plan*, No. 2, 1937, p. 20.

117. The conflict of jurisdiction was settled during the first quarter of 1937. *Glavtorg* was to limit itself to setting general goals for regional trade agencies, which were to allocate these amounts among the local trade agencies (see *ibid.*, p. 21). Although actual examples of "duplicate planning" were rare, complaints on the subject were frequent (see, for instance, Mezhlauk, *Planovoe khoziaistvo*, No. 3, 1934, p. 6, and "Za bolshevistskuiu proverku vypolneniia narodnokhoziaistvennogo plana" [For a Bolshevist Checking on the Fulfillment of the National Economic Plan], *Planovoe khoziaistvo*, No. 7, 1938, p. 7).

CHAPTER 5

Centralized Allocation of Resources and Planning of Priorities

The Plan, Rationing, and Priorities

In a centralized planning system that eliminated the market completely, there would be no need to draft separate plans for the allocation of material and human resources and to introduce a system of priorities for fulfilling the plan. Setting production and consumption goals would automatically be accompanied by the allocation of the means to fulfill them.

In the Stalinist centralized planning system, market forces were not completely eliminated. As a result, the central plan was made up of two different plans—that for the centralized sector, with centralized allocation of material and human resources, and that for the market sector, however imperfect the market. The dividing line between these two sectors, moreover, was not fixed; often it ran through a state enterprise that might sometimes have its resources allocated centrally and sometimes be authorized (in fact, obliged) to find its own resources, relying on its planned goals and the financial means at its disposal. Under Stalinist planning, the centralized sector automatically had priority, and extensive measures were taken to insulate it from the effects of disturbances in the "market" sector. The centralized sector was protected by three forms of rationing. First, raw materials, materials, and equipment for certain production and certain construction projects were centrally allocated. Second, labor was controlled by allocating specialized manpower to certain sectors. Finally, funds in wholesale and retail trade were centrally allocated, and direct rationing of consumer goods was introduced at certain times.

This chapter will deal only with the first form of rationing—that of raw materials, materials, and equipment. The other two forms will be discussed later, along with the government's economic policy and its relation to the plans.

[83]

Supply Management after the Communist Party Take-Over

After the October 1917 coup d'etat, supply of materials and equipment to enterprises, like all the production activities of enterprises, was submitted to worker control.[1] This control was exercised by factory committees, within which were created commissions for controlling production, supply, sales, etc. Worker control over supply and sales was carried out through control of accounting, deliveries and use of materials, and sales of products.

After the creation on December 2, 1917, of the Supreme Council of the National Economy (VSNKh),[2] which was to control all the economic activities of the country, its offices began to handle both supply and sales.[3] At the beginning of 1918, 13 production departments (metals, mining, fuel, etc.) covering the sectors of supply and sales were set up under VSNKh. These sectors handled the allocation of production (sales) by issuing authorization permits for acquiring materials and supplying enterprises in their branches. At the same time a specialized department for "supply and norms" was created, whose principal function was to evaluate and distribute abandoned equipment among interested agencies.[4]

After the outbreak of the Civil War and the June 28, 1918, decree on nationalization of industry,[5] severe shortages led to strict centralization of the allocation of material resources. Within the VSNKh central administrations (*Glavki*), sectors for supply and distribution were created, and this allocation was carried out through the *Glavki*. The powers of the *Glavki* were extensive: they controlled, either directly or through their agencies, all raw material and equipment supply in their branch and distributed the final production. Enterprises were deprived of all power: they received money according to estimates (*smeta*), food products according to lists (*spiski*), and material and equipment supplies according to warrants (*nariady*).[6]

Besides the branch supply agencies under the *Glavki*, VSNKh also set up specialized agencies to handle the allocation of products according to plan: *Prodrasmet* for supplies of metals and metal products; *Glavtop* for allocation of fuel; *Khimsnabzhenie* for supplies of chemical products; *Tramot* for transportation and materials, handling depots and the distribution of unallocated (*beskhoziaistvennye*) goods; and *Komissiia ispolzovaniia* (literally Utilization Commission), which drew up plans for the allocation of industrial products, mainly consumer goods. These agencies had no direct connection with each other, which contri-

---

1. *Ekonomika materialno-tekhnicheskogo snabzheniia* [The System of Material and Equipment Supply], edited by E. Iu. Lokshin, Moscow, 1960, p. 78.
2. See my *Planning for Economic Growth in the Soviet Union, 1918–1932*, translated and edited by Marie-Christine MacAndrew and G. Warren Nutter, Chapel Hill, N.C., 1971, p. 24.
3. *Ekonomika*, p. 79.
4. *Ibid.*
5. See my *Planning*, p. 17.
6. *Ekonomika*, p. 80. This same source mentions that at the end of December 1918 the Second Congress of Soviets adopted a resolution whereby nationalized and state enterprises were to be supplied with raw materials and fuel and railroad transportation of freight delivered to state agencies without payment in money (*ibid.*).

buted to the poor supply situation at the time.[7] Although under the institutional jurisdiction of VSNKh, these agencies worked according to directives from the Council for Worker and Peasant Defense.

In September 1920, in order to coordinate all this work, VSNKh formed the Council for Supply and Allocation, to which the specialized agencies were subordinated. A certain degree of decentralization of allocation was introduced at the end of 1920 with the reorganization of the VSNKh *Glavki* into agencies that could only issue directives and control the work of the regional Sovnarkhozes according to the state plan and with the transfer of the direct management of enterprises (except the largest ones) to the Sovnarkhozes.[8]

Supply Management during the New Economic Policy

When market relations were introduced during the New Economic Policy (NEP), centralized resource allocation was replaced by direct commercial relations between suppliers and clients.[9] Reorganization of the administrative apparatus became indispensable. One of the first measures taken was the extension of the functions of the Utilization Commission, which was entrusted with drafting the plans for allocating the total resources of the country except for fuel. At the same time the Commission was subordinated directly to the Council for Labor and Defense. In March 1921 the VSNKh Council for Supply and Allocation became the VSNKh Supply Section, then the VSNKh Central Administration for Supply (*Tsentrosnab*), and thereafter its activities came under the allocation plans drawn up by the Utilization Commission. Local supply agencies (*Gubsnaby*) controlled local supply in the provinces (*guberniia*) and carried out the orders of *Tsentrosnab*.[10]

Once NEP was in effect, the state stopped supplying some enterprises, leaving them to purchase their own materials on the market. At the same time the number of products centrally allocated was reduced. Material and equipment supply was reorganized again at the beginning of 1922. VSNKh *Tsentrosnab* and the Utilization Commission were abolished and replaced by the VSNKh Industrial Planning Commission (*Promplan*), empowered to allocate state industrial production (which remained centralized) and to coordinate production and the needs of the most important enterprises and agencies.[11] This reorganization was accompanied by changes in administration at intermediary and local levels. The direct management of enterprises was transferred from the VSNKh *Glavki* to the trusts,[12] whose functions included organizing supply and sales for the enterprises under their jurisdiction. At the local level, organization of commercial

---

7. *Ibid.*, p. 81.
8. *Ibid.*, p. 82.
9. See my *Planning*, pp. 20–34.
10. *Ekonomika*, p. 83.
11. *Ibid.*, p. 84.
12. See Chapter 2, section on industrial management agencies at the branch level.

agencies began for local industry (*Gubtorg*) under the local Sovnarkhozes, with much the same function.

Although the trusts were free to organize supply and sales for their enterprises, after 1922 VSNKh encouraged them to form syndicates (*sindikaty*) to fulfill the goals for trade and money circulation. The syndicates were state commercial organizations voluntarily formed by the trusts. Their main objective was selling the production entrusted to them by the trusts. Some trusts also supplied their members with raw materials, materials, and equipment and lent them financial assistance. The syndicate statutes adopted by the members were approved by the VSNKh presidium. The statutes granted the syndicates the same power in administration and planning as the trusts.[13] The first syndicates —for textiles, matches, salt, leather—were created at the beginning of 1922.[14] Between February 1922 and 1923, 15 syndicates were formed in different branches of industry.[15] Despite their supposedly voluntary character, some of these syndicates were mandatory associations, controlling sales of the entire production of all the trusts in a branch. This was the case with the syndicates for salt, petroleum, coal, and Urals metals.[16] In 1926 the coordination of all the syndicates was entrusted to the USSR Council of Syndicates.[17]

A model statute for the syndicates was adopted on March 26, 1925, but a regulation was not approved by the Central Executive Committee and the USSR Council of People's Commissars until February 29, 1928. This regulation defined the syndicate as a commercial joint-stock company (*torgovoe paevo*) joining together state trusts with the aim of selling the members' production and supplying them with the main materials so as to replace their independent commercial activity. The syndicate was made a legal entity and had operating and commercial autonomy (*kommercheskii raschet*). It was to work on the basis of goals planned by USSR or federal republic VSNKh's. Trusts were not subordinated to the syndicates but were members of them, owning part of their capital. The syndicate was run by an assembly of representatives of the trusts and by its own administration. Trusts had the right to leave the syndicate and to appeal its decisions to VSNKh or their commissariat.[18]

The voluntary nature of the trusts' membership in the syndicates, much discussed during 1922–1923, was confirmed again by the February 29, 1928, regulation. The output to be delivered by the trusts to the syndicate was to be

13. A. V. Venediktov, *Organizatsiia gosudarstvennoi promyshlennosti v SSSR* [Organization of State Industry in the USSR], Leningrad, 1961, Vol. II, p. 38. Venediktov also mentions the creation of syndicates called "offices" (Office of Starch and Syrup) or "council of the congress of representatives" (of the basic chemical industry, for instance), which had no operating functions and were to coordinate the sales and supply of the trusts (*ibid.*, Vol. II, p. 84).

14. In July 1922 a syndicate was organized for the coal industry, then one for petroleum, one for the Urals metal industry, one for the construction of agricultural machinery, and others.

15. *Materialnye balansy v narodnokhoziaistvennom plane* [Material Balances in the National Economic Plan], edited by G. I. Grebtsov and P. P. Karpov, Moscow, 1960, p. 7.

16. Venediktov, *Organizatsiia*, Vol. II, pp. 280–83.

17. *Materialnye balansy*, p. 8.

18. VSNKh approved the annual plan of the syndicate, the decisions of the assembly of representatives of the trusts on the appointment of the administrative staff, as well as the accounts, balance sheets, and the distribution of profits, or covering of losses (Venediktov, *Organizatsiia*, Vol. II, pp. 280–83).

decided by the trusts. But even after the February 29 regulation, the Council for Labor and Defense, VSNKh, and the People's Commissariat of Trade required the trusts of some industrial branches to deliver all their production to the syndicates.[19] The powers of the syndicates continued to grow during NEP. Contractual links between trusts and syndicates for sales were extended. General contracts between syndicates and cooperatives developed, which gave a monopoly to the syndicates as an intermediary between the trusts and the cooperatives. The syndicates' powers were extended in delegation of the authority of the Council for Labor and Defense, VSNKh, and the Commissariat of Trade. Thus the syndicates became powerful administrative agencies and the basic planning instrument in state industry.[20]

Along with the organization of syndicates for Union, republic, and regional industry, commercial trading agencies for local industry were organized under the jurisdiction of the local Sovnarkhozes. Called *Gubtorgi*, these state organizations were to serve local industry by selling its production and supplying it with raw materials, fuel, and materials. They also sold the production of the associations and the trusts, supplied them on a contractual basis, and carried out various orders of the local Sovnarkhozes. In fact, they played the part of "syndicates" for local industry.[21] The functions of these trading agencies were defined in a legislative act, after a certain delay, by the April 27, 1928, decree of the Council for Labor and Defense. These functions were later extended by the August 29, 1929, decree of the Council for Labor and Defense,[22] which empowered the trading agencies to supply Union and republic industry with materials from supply depots and to sell the production of nonunionized industry on the market. In 1927/28 the producer goods going through this network represented 26.2 per cent of the turnover; in 1930/31 the figure was 73.7 per cent.[23]

These figures summarize the main trends in the development of the trading organizations during 1927–1930. From general supply agencies specializing in consumer goods, they became a supply network with depots for producer goods for state industry. For this reason, they were reorganized at the beginning of 1931 into regional supply and sales organizations (*Raisnabsbyty*) of VSNKh, and other trading agencies handling mainly consumer goods were subordinated to the People's Commissariat of Trade. Along with the republic, territory, and province supply agencies, the *Raisnabsbyty* were regrouped in 1931 into an

---

19. It should be noted that around 1926/27 trusts and syndicates supplied more than half of their production to state and communal enterprises as material and equipment supply (*Ekonomika*, p. 85). The best-known example of compulsory deliveries of the trusts' production to the syndicates is the August 26, 1927, decree of the Council for Labor and Defense requiring the trusts of the cotton industry and all the syndicate trusts of the linen fabrics industry to deliver 100 per cent of their production to the USSR Textile Syndicate. Immediately thereafter, in 1928, this syndicate was amalgamated with *Glavtekstil* (Central Administration for the Textile Industry) of VSNKh. (Venediktov, *Organizatsiia*, Vol. II, p. 297.)

20. *Ibid.*, Vol. II, pp. 296–97.

21. *Ekonomika*, p. 85.

22. "On the Work of the Trading Agencies" (*ibid.*, p. 87).

23. *Ibid.*, pp. 87–88.

association (*Soiuzsnabsbyt*), which included 32 *Snabsbyty* with 564 supply depots located in 240 spots across the country.[24]

Supply Management under Stalinist Administrative Planning

After the December 5, 1929, reorganization of industrial management,[25] associations were formed regrouping the syndicates and the *Glavki*, and at that time the administration of supply and sales under the syndicates was transferred to their control. They were authorized to organize "autonomous departments" endowed with *khozraschet* and operating autonomy, which were administrations (*upravleniia*) for supply (*snaby*) and sales (*sbyty*).[26] With the decentralization of the associations' powers, these administrations often became "associations" themselves, joining together the management of supply and sales or running them separately. The most important association was *Stalsbyt* for selling steel, which was organized after the association *Stal* was split up into *Stal* and *Vostokostal* (Eastern Steel) in 1930. Other such associations were organized during 1930 and 1931: *Soiuzkhimsbyt* for selling chemical products, *Tsvetmetsbyt* for selling nonferrous metals, *Lessnabsbyt* for selling timber products. After VSNKh was split up into three commissariats in January 1932, the number of autonomous supply and sales organizations tended to grow.[27]

.The supply associations in light industry were formed on the same legal bases as the trusts. They were autonomous units enjoying legal entity and were registered in the agencies of the Commissariat of Finance. They had their own branches and offices located in different parts of the country which exercised the functions of planning and management of the commercial bases under these associations. The commercial bases were organized after the March 23 and August 19, 1932, decrees of the Council of People's Commissars; they operated on the same principles as the enterprises under trusts and had their own working capital.[28] In light industry, for example, *Soiuzkhlopkosbyt* (with a network of 115 wholesale units) was organized for selling cotton products, *Soiuzshelkosbyt* (with 18 units) was created for silk products, and *Soiuztrikotazhsbyt* (with 27 units) was set up for knitted goods. The sales associations could assign the commercial bases only those functions specified in the government directives.[29]

The sales and supply associations (*Snabsbyty*) operated simultaneously with the specialized associations of the People's Commissariat of Heavy Industry,[30] which caused a jurisdictional problem. The Commissariat of Heavy Industry tried to resolve this problem by a regulation promulgated on November 10, 1932. This regulation established a list of enterprises serviced by the *Snabsbyty*, reserved raw material and fuel supplies for the specialized associations, and

24. *Ibid.*, p. 88.
25. See p. 30 ff. in Chapter 2.
26. Venediktov, *Organizatsiia*, Vol. II, pp. 558–60.
27. *Ibid.*, Vol. II, pp. 560 and 597.
28. *Ibid.*, Vol. II., p. 599.
29. *Ibid.*, Vol. II, p. 598.
30. *Ibid.*, Vol. II, pp. 599–601. On *Snabsbyty*, see end of previous section.

forbade the *Snabsbyty* to conclude contracts monopolizing the supply of enterprises. Most of the trusts were removed from the supply and sales operations of their enterprises and were limited to giving them directives based on the plans for the allocation of their production belonging to the trust, the conclusion of general contracts, etc. Direct supply and sales by the trusts were exceptions.[31]

The organization of material and equipment supply was revised when the powers of the *Glavki* were consolidated on July 15, 1936. As mentioned earlier,[32] branch sales and supply agencies of the commissariats were transformed into sections of the *Glavki*. But the autonomous departments for sales and supply (*Glavsbyty* and *Glavsnaby*) continued to be organized under the commissariats after 1936. Thus, a *Glavk* for supply was organized under the Commissariat of Heavy Industry in 1937, and its job was to organize and manage the supply of the enterprises of that commissariat.[33]

Until 1938 industrial production was sold through the numerous sales departments of the *Glavki*. In order to obtain ferrous metals, consumers had to present requests to seven sales agencies, each of which delivered supplies independently from the others. This forced the government to organize *Glavki* for sales in the main branches of industry: *Glavmetallosbyt* for metals, *Glavneftesbyt* for petroleum, *Glavuglesbyt* for coal, *Glavkhimsbyt* for chemicals, *Glavelektrosbyt* for electric power, etc. These *Glavki* planned and organized the sales of their own commissariat and also the production of enterprises of other commissariats that were included in their prescribed list of products.[34]

Splitting up the commissariats during the 1930's resulted in the organization of many new supply and sales agencies.[35] Each commissariat had *Glavsnaby* and supply and sales sections of the *Glavki*. When new commissariats were created, the local offices of these agencies were also automatically split up. Moreover, several *Glavsnaby* created their own trusts with jurisdiction over the entire branch to run the operations and carry out the supply plans of both the offices and local bases. Thus several agencies were doing the same work. For instance, the following agencies operated simultaneously for supply:[36] the *Glavki* for supplies (*Glavsnaby*); branch trusts with local networks of offices, bases, and supply depots; and supply sections of the *Glavki* (with their own local network). All this slowed down the supply mechanism and caused an accumulation of stocks. For some commissariats, more than 70 per cent of the operations required storage in supply depots.[37]

The organization of supply and sales thus became cumbersome and inefficient. In 1939, 36 Union commissariats had a turnover of supply and sales agencies of

31. Such as by *Leningradodezhda* (Leningrad Clothing Trust) or timber trusts other than those of Moscow, Leningrad, or Belorussia (*ibid.*, Vol. II, pp. 602–3).

32. See p. 34 in Chapter 2.

33. At the same time the *Soiuzsnabsbyt* of the Commissariat of Heavy Industry was abolished. See end of previous section and *Ekonomika*, pp. 88 and 91.

34. *Ibid.*, p. 91.

35. See Table E–1.

36. *Ekonomika*, p. 92.

37. *Ibid.* This seems to refer to the share of supply depots in the total value of the commissariat's material and equipment supply.

20.2 billion rubles, 75 per cent of which fell on the supply *Glavki*. There were around 5,000 supply and sales agencies with a staff of over 126,000, to whom wages of 518 million rubles had to be paid. If we add to this figure the supply offices of production trusts, enterprises, construction sites, province and territory administrations, and republic commissariats, the total number of workers in supply agencies for industry and construction was on the order of 400,000 with a wage fund of more than 1.5 billion rubles in 1939.[38] This represented some 4 per cent of total industrial employment and 3.5 per cent of the total wage fund in industry.[39]

An attempt to eliminate the defects of the supply system was made by a decree of the Council of People's Commissars issued on April 5, 1940.[40] This decree abolished the branch trusts in industry, transferring their functions to the supply *Glavki*, abolished the local agencies (offices, bases, supply depots) under the branch supply sections of the *Glavki*, established a ceiling for storage operations (which was not to exceed 25 to 30 per cent of total turnover), and reduced taxes paid for supply depots. After this reorganization, the general organization of material and equipment supply followed the diagram presented in Chart 3.

Very few changes were made in this setup during the war and postwar years (until 1957). During the war, material and equipment supply was supervised directly by the State Committee for Defense, headed by Stalin.[41] The allocation of materials was highly centralized, and control over expenditures was tightened. Some sales *Glavki*—*Glavneftesbyt* for petroleum, *Glavlesosbyt* for timber, and *Glavuglesbyt* for coal—were subordinated directly to the USSR Council of People's Commissars and called supply *Glavki*—*Glavneftesnab*, *Glavsnables*, and *Glavuglesnab*. During the war the practice of special supply was extended through direct government decisions. The greatest difficulty lay in obtaining deliveries from producer factories, which was solved by creating the plenipotentiaries of supply agencies at producer factories, whose job was to supervise product shipment and supply to the main industrial enterprises.[42]

The supply *Glavki* directly under the USSR Council of Ministers were subordinated in January 1948 to the recently created State Committee for Material and Equipment Supply (*Gossnab SSSR*). They were soon removed from this agency, called sales *Glavki*, and attached to the corresponding ministries—*Glavmetallosbyt* for metals, *Glavlesosbyt* for timber, *Glavavtotraktorosbyt* for motor vehicles and tractors, etc.[43] *Gossnab* kept only its planning functions.[44]

The sales *Glavki* operated mainly in heavy industry. Aside from the *Glavki* cited above, those specializing in coal (*Glavuglesbyt*), petroleum (*Glavneftesbyt*),

38. A. Nesterovskii and R. Tsetlin, "Uporiadochit materialno-tekhnicheskoe snabzhenie promyshlennosti" [Put Order in Industrial Material and Equipment Supply], *Planovoe khoziaistvo* [Planned Economy], No. 3, 1940, p. 51.

39. See Table A-3. The cost of the offices of the supply agencies amounted to about 10 to 11 per cent of their turnover (*ibid.*, p. 55).

40. "On the Organizational Structure of the Supply Agencies of the Economic Commissariats" (*Ekonomika*, p. 92).

41. See pp. 286–87 in Chapter 14.

42. *Ekonomika*, pp. 93–94.

43. *Ibid.*, p. 94.

44. See p. 95 below.

and chemicals and rubber (*Glavkhimsbyt*) should be mentioned. In the food industry, products were sold through production *Glavki*—*Glavkonditer* for confectionery, *Glavsakhar* for sugar, and *Glavchai* for tea.[45] The sales *Glavki* were to study needs, coordinate the assortment and quantities produced in enterprises, supervise deliveries of production to consumers, control the fulfillment of the delivery plans, draft plans for "planned" production,[46] and set up accounts with suppliers and buyers. They also handled transportation plans and presented requests to the appropriate agencies. The sales *Glavki* were divided into operational administrations and had the offices, bases, and supply depots under their jurisdiction. Their local agencies operated under *khozraschet*.[47]

The supply *Glavki* were to check on enterprise needs for raw materials, materials, fuel, and equipment; draft demands for material funds; prepare for the ministry the plan for the allocation of funds among enterprises; draw up specifications; organize decentralized procurement; and mobilize internal resources. They also ran supply depots and organized the accounts of the bases and depots. They were divided into sections by products (metals, fuel, etc.) and into aggregate sections (plan, finances, etc.).

The lowest level in the system of material and equipment supply was made up of the enterprise supply sections. These sections were to run the enterprise supply depots and study the needs and draft requests for materials and funds for the enterprises. They also organized workshop and section supply by providing them with monthly "limits" according to the norms authorized for the expenditure of materials.[48]

Jurisdiction over Supply Planning

During the first months after the take-over by the Communist Party and during the Civil War, there was no clear distinction between managing and planning material and equipment supply. Enterprise requests for materials, raw materials, and fuel were presented to VSNKh production and planning agencies, which determined the over-all needs of each branch.[49] With its creation under VSNKh in September 1920, the Council for Supply and Allocation had the task, among others, of drafting general plans for allocation. At the beginning of NEP, the jurisdiction of the Utilization Commission was extended.[50] When it was transferred from VSNKh to the Council for Labor and Defense, it was given the new function of drawing up plans for allocating among the commissariats all material resources of the country, except for fuel allocated by the Central Commission for Planning Fuel under the *Glavk* for fuel (*Glavtop*).[51]

---

45. E. Iu. Lokshin, *Planirovanie materialno-tekhnicheskogo snabzheniia narodnogo khoziaistva SSSR* [Planning of Material and Equipment Supply in the USSR National Economy], Moscow, 1952, pp. 33–34.
46. On the distinction between "funded" and "planned" products, see p. 96 below.
47. Lokshin, *Planirovanie*, p. 34.
48. *Ibid.*, pp. 34–36.
49. *Ekonomika*, pp. 80–81.
50. See p. 85 above.
51. *Ekonomika*, p. 83.

Chart 3   Diagram of Organization of Material and Equipment Supply, May 1940[a]

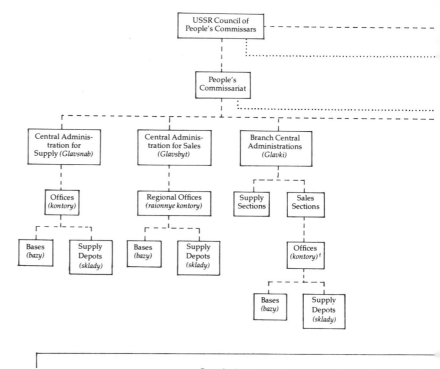

Supply Sections of Enterprises, Construction Projects,

Source: B. Sukharevskii, "Materialnye balansy promsyshlennoi produktsii v narodnokhoziaistvennom plane" [Material Balances for Industrial Production in the National Economic Plan], *Planovoe khoziaistvo*, No. 11–12, 1937, pp. 27–39; Nesterovskii and Tsetlin, *Planovoe khoziaistvo*, No. 3, 1940, p. 49; A. Shmaev, "K razrabotke balansa oborudovaniia na 1937 god" [On Drawing up a Balance of Equipment for the Year 1937], *Plan*, No. 19, 1936, pp. 5–8; B. I. Braginskii and N. S. Koval, *Organizatsiia planirovaniia narodnogo khoziaistva SSSR* [Organization of Planning of the USSR National Economy], Moscow, 1954, pp. 92–106; *Ekonomika*, pp. 86–100; *Materialnye balansy*, pp. 7–8; G. L. Dubinskii, *Organizatsiia snabzheniia narodnogo khoziaistva v Respublike i ekonomicheskom raione* [Organization of Supplies to the National Economy in the Republic and in the Economic Region], Moscow, 1964, pp. 22–23.

a. This simplified diagram does not show all the people's commissariats, republic Gosplans, *Glavki*, trusts, enterprises, etc.

b. For more details, see Table E-3, notes e and f.

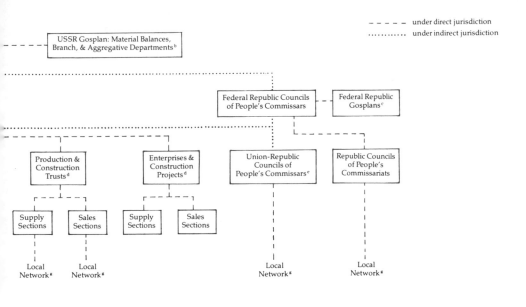

- - - - - under direct jurisdiction
.... under indirect jurisdiction

USSR Gosplan: Material Balances, Branch, & Aggregative Departments[b]

Federal Republic Councils of People's Commissars

Federal Republic Gosplans[c]

Production & Construction Trusts[d]

Enterprises & Construction Projects[d]

Union-Republic Councils of People's Commissars[e]

Republic Councils of People's Commissariats

Supply Sections

Sales Sections

Supply Sections

Sales Sections

Local Network[g]

Local Network[g]

Local Network[g]

Local Network[g]

Various Organizations

c. The federal republic Gosplans exercise control only indirectly over the material and equipment supply of the people's commissariats (ministries after 1946) and organizations on their territory. They are under the administrative jurisdiction of the republic councils of people's commissars and also receive directives from USSR Gosplan.

d. These (few) trusts and enterprises are under the direct jurisdiction of the people's commissariat without the intermediary of the *Glavki*.

e. The Union-republic people's commissariats (ministries after 1946) come under both the corresponding Union commissariat and the federal republic councils of people's commissars.

f. The sales sections (*otdely sbyta*) of the *Glavki* have a regular network of offices, bases, and supply depots only when a given branch does not have a Central Administration for Sales (*Glavsbyt*).

g. The local network usually includes offices under which are bases and supply depots. The organization of this local network for trusts and for republic industry is not known in any detail for 1940. Therefore, its existence is only indicated here.

The Utilization Commission was abolished at the beginning of 1922 when *Promplan* was created under VSNKh.[52] This agency seems to have handled allocation plans at the same time as USSR Gosplan. But drawing up balances of metals and basic industrial products systematically was not begun until 1926. VSNKh drew up a list of materials that would be supplied on demand, drafted forms, and set schedules. At the end of NEP, USSR Gosplan was given the basic responsibility for drawing up the balances on which the allocation of resources was based.

The distribution of power between USSR Gosplan and the commissariats varied considerably during 1931–1941. Until 1933, Gosplan drew up both the annual balances and the quarterly balances. After 1933, drafting quarterly balances was entrusted to the commissariats, with Gosplan retaining control over this work only insofar as it was affected by general economic policy.[53] This work, as well as the actual administration of funds, was entrusted to the supply and sales agencies of the commissariats.[54]

The decree of June 10, 1934, handed the task of drawing up material balances and plans for the allocation of materials and equipment back to Gosplan; the commissariats had only to supply Gosplan with the necessary information and requests 40 days before the beginning of the quarter or the year. At this time a special Section of Material Balances was created under Gosplan.[55]

Gosplan's jurisdiction over material and equipment supply was again narrowed by the December 2, 1937, decree of the Economic Council.[56] The Department of Material Balances was abolished, and the calculation of balances and the coordination of all problems concerning any particular product were transferred to the sector agencies of Gosplan. The Gosplan regulation of February 2, 1938, confirmed this decree.[57] Thenceforward the commissariats that produced the goods for which the balances were calculated were to present annual and quarterly draft plans for supplies to the Economic Council. When several different commissariats handled the same product, the principal producer was to draw up the supply plan. Gosplan's functions were limited to giving advice on plans for material and equipment supply.[58]

52. *Ibid.*, p. 84.

53. V. I. Mezhlauk, "Boevye zadachi organov planirovaniia" [The Fighting Tasks of Planning Agencies], *Plan*, No. 1, 1937, p. 2.

54. B. Sukharevskii, "Materialnye balansy promyshlennoi produktsii v narodnokhoziaistvennom plane" [Material Balances for Industrial Production in the National Economic Plan], *Planovoe khoziaistvo*, No. 11–12, 1937, p. 28.

55. Decree of the Council of People's Commissars, "On Procedure for Drafting and Approving Material Balances for the Allocation of Materials and Equipment" (*Sobranie zakonov i rasporiazhenii raboche-krestianskogo pravitelstva SSSR* [Collection of Laws and Decrees of the Workers' and Peasants' Government of the USSR], No. 33, 1934, Art. 259).

56. "Novoe v organizatsii materialno-tekhnicheskogo snabzheniia" [Something New in the Organization of Material and Equipment Supply], *Planovoe khoziaistvo*, No. 5, 1938, pp. 167–68.

57. See Table E–3, note e.

58. *Planovoe khoziaistvo*, No. 5, 1938, p. 168. At this time USSR Gosplan drafted a regulation, approved by the USSR Economic Council, on "the procedure and schedule for the establishment by the people's commissariats of plans for material and equipment supply." This regulation listed the "funded" (centrally allocated) products; the number of nondeficit products may have been reduced.

In 1939 Gosplan's powers to plan supplies were again broadened. The Section of Material Balances was re-established on April 13, 1939, and after that date Gosplan had to present plans for the distribution of the principal industrial and agricultural products to the government for its approval.

During the war years USSR Gosplan remained the principal agency in charge of planning material and equipment supply and establishing the balances of centrally allocated products, the number of which increased considerably.[59]

Planning material and equipment supply and drafting the corresponding balances seem to have occupied an increasingly important place in Gosplan's work. As the volume of production increased during the postwar years, it appeared necessary to set up a special agency for this work. This was done when USSR Gosplan was reorganized on December 15, 1947.[60] A new agency was created called the State Committee for Material and Equipment Supply under the USSR Council of Ministers (*Gossnab SSSR*). The function of this agency included planning the allocation of material resources, drafting annual and long-term material balances and norms for the expenditure of materials, and preparing suggestions for eliminating "bottlenecks."[61] At the same time the sections for calculating and allocating material funds, which had been under USSR Gosplan, were transferred to *Gossnab*. Also, some supply *Glavki* that had been attached directly to the USSR Council of Commissars during the war were transferred to *Gossnab*.[62] On April 26, 1951, the Ministry of Food and Material Reserves became the State Committee for Supply of Food and Industrial Goods (*Gosprodsnab*), which had to plan and allocate food products, manufactured industrial products, and agricultural raw materials.[63]

According to O. I. Andreev, one of the co-authors of the basic work on material and equipment supply, this organization was considered too cumbersome and too centralized.[64] The separation of material and equipment supply from Gosplan had its disadvantages, since different agencies handled production and construction planning (USSR Gosplan) and material and equipment supply planning (*Gossnab* and *Gosprodsnab*). When the ministries were reorganized on March 15, 1953, *Gossnab* and *Gosprodsnab* were absorbed into USSR Gosplan.[65] *Gossnab* was reorganized as an independent state committee only after the economic reforms of 1965.

---

59. See pp. 99–100 below.

60. Decree of Party Central Committee, "On the Reorganization of USSR Gosplan and the Formation of the State Committee for Supply of the USSR National Economy and the State Committee for the Introduction of New Technology in the USSR National Economy" (*Direktivy KPSS i sovetskogo pravitelstva po khoziaistvennym voprosam* [Directives of the Communist Party of the Soviet Union and of the Soviet Government on Economic Matters], Moscow, 1957, Vol. 3, pp. 261–62).

61. *Ekonomika*, p. 94.

62. See p. 90 above.

63. See Table E–2. It is not known whether the Ministry of Food and Material Reserves allocated only reserves that Gosplan planned or also drew up balances and allocation plans.

64. *Ekonomika*, p. 94.

65. See Table E–2.

Drafting Supply Plans

The official Soviet term for material and equipment supply (*materialno-tekhniche-skoe snabzhenie*) very inadequately conveys the nature and forms of this supply. In reality, it amounted to a rationing system, like those in operation in Western Europe during the world wars. In the Soviet Union rationing was carried out on different levels. First, the so-called "funded" (*fondiruemye*) products were allocated according to plans established by USSR Gosplan (or *Gossnab* or other agencies in different periods) and approved by the USSR Council of People's Commissars.[66] Second, "centrally planned" products[67] were allocated according to plans drawn up by the commissariats with the approval of Gosplan or *Gossnab*. Third, products "planned in a decentralized way" were allocated directly by local agencies and by local organizations of the commissariats or by the enterprises through direct economic links between producers and consumers.

Drawing up balances and plans for material and equipment supply was divided into two stages. Material balances and balances for production, allocation, and consumption were drawn up first, and then supply plans, indicating allocation of raw materials, semimanufactured products, and manufactured products among different users, were drafted.[68] The first stage was intended to provide a general idea of needs and available resources and the second was to ensure supply for priority sectors. In actual fact, according to Soviet economists, the distinction between the two stages became illusory since the planned balances became the direct tools of the supply plans instead of the means of guaranteeing a balance between needs and resources.[69]

The general outline of a material balance usually included two aspects. On the one hand were resources, including production (broken down by producers), imports, other sources, and surplus stocks of suppliers at the beginning of the year. On the other hand was distribution, showing needs of production, capital construction, trade funds, exports, payment to state reserves, reserves of USSR Council of Ministers, and surplus stocks of suppliers at the end of the year.[70] The balances and distribution plans were drawn up for the whole year and often also for quarters.

66. A. Kurskii and B. Sukharevskii, "Burmistrov N. S. 'Ocherki tekhniko-ekonomicheskogo planirovaniia promyshlennosti' ONTI 1936" [N. S. Burmistrov's "Outline of Technical Economic Planning of Industry," 1936], *Planovoe khoziaistvo*, No. 9–10, 1936, p. 21; *Materialnye balansy*, p. 8; Lokshin, *Planirovanie*, pp. 27–29.

67. As Lokshin (*Planirovanie*, p. 29, note 1) points out, the term "planned production" is a conventional one since "funded" (*fondiruemaia*) production is also planned.

68. Discussed by Kurskii and Sukharevskii in *Planovoe khoziaistvo*, No. 9–10, 1936, p. 210.

69. "Do kontsa likvidirovat posledstvii vreditelstva v planovykh organakh" [Eliminate Entirely the Consequences of Sabotage in Planning Agencies], *Planovoe khoziaistvo*, No. 5–6, 1937, p. 11; Sukharevskii, *Planovoe khoziaistvo*, No. 11–12, 1937, p. 28. According to F. Gaposhkin and A. Ambartsumov ("O materialno-tekhnicheskom snabzhenii" [On Material and Equipment Supply], *Planovoe khoziaistvo*, No. 11, 1938, p. 102), "one of the most serious defects in the material balances is that they do not include all sources of supply. . . . Until now the balances have not reflected the specific needs of the national economy for material and equipment supply for each period (month, quarter, season, etc.)."

70. B. I. Braginskii and N. S. Koval, *Organizatsiia planirovaniia narodnogo khoziaistva SSSR* [Organization of Planning of the USSR National Economy], Moscow, 1954, pp. 282–83. On the role of balances in the planning process, see Marie Lavigne, *Les économies socialistes soviétiques et européenes*, Paris, 1970, pp. 258–75.

Material balances have been calculated since the beginning of the Soviet period. When the first production plans were drawn up for the *Glavki* under VSNKh in 1919, brief balances were calculated. The VSNKh Utilization Commission made considerable use of this method during the Civil War in order to guarantee priority to the needs of the army and the armament industry. Balances were also used in drawing up the first electrification plan (Goelro).[71]

All these balances were used simply in the calculations made by different agencies; they did not require government approval. The first balance approved by the government was that drawn up in 1926 for rolled steel. During the First Five-Year Plan a few balances were drawn up for machinery (locomotives, railroad cars, tractors) and the most important products. Not until 1928/29 were the first balances made for bricks, cement, and timber products. After the Second Five-Year Plan, the number of balances calculated and officially approved increased considerably.[72]

Table 7 gives some details on the balances calculated during 1934–1938 and presented for government approval. As can be seen, the total number of these balances nearly doubled between 1934 and 1938; the increase was much greater for materials than for equipment.[73] It is interesting to note that the quarterly balances submitted for government approval were calculated much less frequently, especially for equipment. The increase in the number of balances reflects increased centralization in supply planning, apparently particularly marked in 1938. In 1937, mention was made of only "more than 250 balances."[74] This increase in the number of centrally approved balances was not considered useful for planning needs; Soviet economists themselves admit that it was only a special measure taken in cases of deficits. Such was the case, for example, with the balances for bathtubs and radiators. Some progress was also made during this period in drawing up balances for the principal products along with their territorial distribution.[75]

The essential task in drafting balances and plans for the distribution of resources lay in drawing up utilization norms and technical coefficients. In the first balances and during the First Five-Year Plan, "average statistical data" for the preceding years for products in a very aggregated form were used as the basis for calculating expenditures of raw materials, fuel, and power.[76] Reductions in the consumption of raw materials were applied in a very general way.

Several government decrees and regulations were issued during 1933–1941 to improve setting norms. Among the most important were the October 13, 1936, decree of the USSR Council of People's Commissars and Ordzhonikidze's order

71. Braginskii and Koval, *Organizatsiia*, pp. 280–81.

72. *Ibid.*, p. 281, and Sukharevskii, *Planovoe khoziaistvo*, No. 11–12, 1937, pp. 37–38.

73. The statistics on the number of balances must be examined with some caution since they are sometimes given for broad categories (such as pipes) and sometimes in considerable detail. See Iu. I. Koldomasov, *Planirovanie materialno-tekhnicheskogo snabzheniia narodnogo khoziaistva v SSSR* [Planning of Material and Equipment Supply in the USSR National Economy], Moscow, 1961, p. 23.

74. Of these, 90 balances were for machinery and equipment, 45 for ferrous metals and metal products, and 16 for construction materials (*Planovoe khoziaistvo*, No. 5–6, 1937, p. 11).

75. Sukharevskii, *Planovoe khoziaistvo*, No. 11–12, 1937, pp. 38–39.

76. *Ibid.*, p. 33.

Table 7 Number of Materials and Equipment Balances Calculated by USSR Gosplan and Presented to USSR Council of People's Commissars, 1934 and 1938

	Decree of 9/8/34		Decree of 12/2/38	
	Annual Plans (1)	Quarterly Plans (2)	Annual Plans (3)	Quarterly Plans (4)
Materials				
Ferrous metals	21	17	56	21
Metal objects	4	2	15	6
Pipes	4	2	13	13
Pig iron			3	3
Ferroalloys			9	0
Nonferrous metals	12	12	18	18
Cables	3	3	15	7
Wood and timber products	10	5	23	18
Construction materials	7	2	13	13
Vegetable oil for production use	2	2	3	3
Alcohol	1	1	1	1
Raw materials and agricultural raw materials				
for the textile and leather industries	6	5	13	13
Paper, paperboard, and pulp	1	1	11	10
Chemical products	17	5	15	2
Rubber	1	0		
Tires	1	1	1	1
Fuel	15	0	14	10
Total materials	105	58	223	139
Equipment[a]				
Thermal power equipment (incl. cranes				
and accumulators)	12[b]	0	17	4
Electrical equipment	24	0	30	0
Machine tools	7	0	40	40
Forges and presses (incl. *liteinoe*)	5	0	10	0
Woodprocessing equipment	2	0	10	0
Tools and armatures	6	0	3	0
Equipment for conditioning gas and liquids	5	0	11	0
Transportation equipment and excavators	7	0	3	0
Railroad and urban transportation equipment	8	0	4	0
Ships	6	0	5	0
Motor vehicles and tractors[c]	2	2	3	0
Agricultural machinery[c]	1	0	4	3
Communal equipment	7	7	2	0
Highway machinery	2	0	2	0
Other equipment	17	0	12	2
Total equipment	111	9	156	51
Grand total	216	67	379	190

Source: Cols. 1–2: September 8, 1934, decree of USSR Council of People's Commissars, "On Procedure for Drafting and Approving Annual and Quarterly Balances and Plans for Material and Equipment Supply," *Sobranie zakonov*, No. 47, September 25, 1934, Art. 369; cols. 3–4: December 2, 1938, decree of the Economic Council under the USSR Council of People's Commissars, "On Procedure for Drafting and Approving Annual and Quarterly Balances and Plans for Material, Equipment, and Fuel Supply," *Sobranie postanovlenii i rasporiazhenii pravitelstva SSSR* [Collection of Resolutions and Decrees of the USSR Government], No. 56, December 30, 1938, Art. 316.

a. The September 8, 1934, decree lists types of equipment and gives specifications for different categories. In the cases where the specification is detailed, it was assumed that separate balances were given. For instance, it was assumed that, for railroad equipment, separate balances were drawn up for locomotives, railroad cars, electric locomotives, etc.

b. The September 8, 1934, decree states that in the balances specification is made "according to power." Therefore the specification by power used in the December 2, 1938, decree was accepted to make the methods in 1934 and 1938 comparable.

c. Specification by category of motor vehicle and tractor is mentioned in 1934 and in 1938 although the decrees give no details. Therefore it was impossible to take these specifications into account.

of August 29, 1936.[77] These new regulations included a number of provisions. There were to be periodic re-examinations and setting of norms for expenditure of materials (which norms were to be an integral part of the production plans of the *Glavki*). Measures were to be applied to rationalize the production apparatus in order to guarantee the supply of materials to the economy, to make use of substitutes and waste products, and to mobilize the internal resources of enterprises. Lists were established of so-called "prohibitions" (such lists were already in use for nonferrous metals at the end of the First Five-Year Plan), forbidding the allocation of certain materials—for instance, nonferrous metals, metals, petroleum, etc.—for certain production. Finally, disciplinary sanctions for exceeding norms for the utilization of materials were laid down.

Instructions to reduce norms for the utilization of materials were frequent and repeated in all the annual plans.[78] In 1938, Gosplan also organized committees of experts to examine the new norms for the principal products.[79] The government often requested the commissariats to submit for approval new norms that showed considerable saving.[80] These efforts apparently did not have the desired effect. Toward the end of 1938, Soviet economists summarized the situation in setting norms as follows: "Despite the many orders from the government, the people's commissariats have not drawn up technical norms for the expenditure of materials per unit of production. The situation is no better for norms for expenditure of materials in construction. Here norms . . . are practically nonexistent."[81]

Soviet economists also pointed out that the commissariats did not carry out the government's decrees on reducing norms for consumption of materials.[82]

It is impossible to judge the quality of the balances and allocation plans established during the war years of 1941–1945. The number of centrally allocated products more than doubled at the beginning of the war and the number of indexes in the supply plans exceeded 30,000.[83] But the number of balances drawn up during this period is not known.

77. Decree, "On Economizing Electric Power" and Ordzhonikidze's order, "On Economizing Metals," both cited in *ibid*.

78. See, for instance, the instructions of Gosplan Deputy Chairman Smirnov on drafting the 1938 plan (G. Aleshkovskii, "Sernokislotnaia promyshlennost v tretem piatiletii" [The Sulfuric Acid Industry in the Third Five-Year Period], *Plan*, No. 12, 1937, p. 38). Such examples could be cited for all the annual and quarterly plans published.

79. "V Gosplane pri SNK SSSR" [In Gosplan under the USSR Council of People's Commissars], *Planovoe khoziaistvo*, No. 4, 1939, p. 189.

80. See, for instance, the February 8, 1936, decree of the Council for Labor and Defense and the January 25, 1937, decree of the USSR Council of People's Commissars (Gaposhkin and Ambartsumov, *Planovoe khoziaistvo*, No. 11, 1938, p. 102). See also the March 4, 1938, decree of the Council of People's Commissars (A. Zosimov and I. Sirovskii, "Puti ekonomii metalla" [Ways of Economizing Metal], *Planovoe khoziaistvo*, No. 12, 1939, p. 112).

81. Gaposhkin and Ambartsumov, *Planovoe khoziaistvo*, No. 11, 1938, p. 101.

82. Gaposhkin and Ambartsumov (*ibid.*, pp. 102–3) cite several decrees on this matter that were not carried out: the February 8, 1936, decree of the Council for Labor and Defense and the January 25, 1937, decree of the Council of People's Commissars on reducing the norms for utilization of metals; the June 3, 1938, decree of the Council of People's Commissars on ferrous metals; the November 17, 1937, and the April 11, 1937, decrees of the Council of People's Commissars on economizing cement and wood in construction.

83. G. M. Sorokin, *Planirovanie narodnogo khoziaistva SSSR* [Planning of the USSR National Economy], Moscow, 1961, pp. 213–14. See also pp. 287–88 in Chapter 14.

After the war, with the organization of *Gossnab* at the beginning of 1948, the number of balances approved by the government increased considerably. In 1951 the list of these balances contained 1,600 items, covering 14 groups.[84] Of these, 11 groups were planned by *Gossnab* and 3 by *Gosprodsnab*.[85]

It is not known how many products and balances were "centrally planned" and how many were planned in a decentralized fashion in that period. Around 1956 there were 1,050 balances on the list of "funded" products set up by USSR Gosplan, that is, fewer than in 1951. During the same period there were about 5,000 "centrally planned" (industrial and agricultural) products allocated by the ministry *Glavsbyty*.[86]

Since it is not known how many products were planned in a decentralized way during the postwar years, it is impossible to estimate with any precision the total number of products that were "funded," "centrally planned," and "planned in a decentralized way." In 1960, after the distinction between "funded" and "planned" (whether centrally or not) products had been abolished (in 1959), the list of raw materials, fuels, materials, and equipment in the material and equipment supply plan drafted and approved by USSR Gosplan contained 12,750 items.[87]

In fact, it is difficult to judge the extent of centralization of Soviet rationing just from the number of items in the plan for material and equipment supply. The material and equipment supply plan had only two items for steel-rolling equipment until 1965, whereas in actual fact dozens of items were planned. Similarly, the centrally planned production of electric machinery appears as one single item, whereas it actually included 1,150 items.[88] Moreover, as A. Ia. Emdin notes, the list of centrally planned products was not comparable for each branch of industry, and the number of planned items did not give a precise idea of the extent of the work. For instance, drawing up the balance and plan for the allocation of rolled steel required as much work as drawing up balances and plans for hundreds of other less widely used materials.[89]

It is hard to specify an accurate measure of the extent of rationing in the Soviet Union. Rationing primarily affected deficit products, but it also affected new products needed for machine-building. Actually the trend was to include a

84. (1) Ferrous metals, (2) nonferrous metals, (3) solid fuels, (4) petroleum products, (5) electric power, (6) chemicals, (7) rubber products, (8) machinery and equipment, (9) construction materials, (10) timber products, (11) paper, (12) food products, (13) manufactured products, and (14) agricultural raw materials (Lokshin, *Planirovanie*, pp. 27–28 and 76).

85. *Ibid.*, p. 28.

86. *Materialnye balansy*, p. 13.

87. *Ibid.*, p. 21. It should be noted that in 1963 the list of centrally planned products included 24,790 items. USSR Gosplan prepared directly 3,308 balances and allocation plans; ministries and offices prepared 1,331; federal republics prepared 704; and *Glavki* for republic deliveries prepared 19,447. As Emdin pointed out, this list is heterogeneous; for some branches it covers groups of products and for others a detailed specification (A. Ia. Emdin, *Metodologiia planirovaniia i organizatsiia materialno-tekhnicheskogo snabzheniia* [Methods of Planning and Organizing Material and Equipment Supply], Moscow, 1966, pp. 17–18). Dubinskii (*Organizatsiia*, p. 15) gave the number as 14,000 in 1961.

88. Emdin, *Metodologiia*, p. 18. Emdin noted that during the same period amplifying receivers (*priemno-usilitelnye*) were specified in detail and appeared in the list of centrally planned products with 392 items.

89. *Ibid.*

larger and larger share of total production in rationing. In 1959 and 1960, years for which data exist, the material and equipment supply plan drawn up by Gosplan using technical and economic norms covered from 90 to 95 per cent of the total planned production of the principal raw materials.[90] Moreover, allocation was done according to a system of priority allocation for the productions considered the most important.

Allocation of funds was done on the basis of so-called progressive norms for the expenditure of materials, raw materials, and fuel per unit of production or per unit of labor (for instance, per hour of work of machine tools) as well as norms for stocks. The requests (zaiavki) of enterprises were presented through the appropriate channels to the supply sections of the Glavki or to the ministry Glavsnaby which established the aggregate requests for their branch. In 1951 these requests were presented for the first 11 groups of "funded" production to Gossnab and for the 3 other groups to Gosprodsnab.[91] For planned production, they were presented to the production ministries. The state plan for material and equipment supply included a list of agencies receiving funds approved by the USSR Council of Ministers. This list, revised after the splitting up, amalgamation, and creation of new ministries and offices, covered all the Union ministries and Union-republic ministries, the Glavki under the USSR Council of Ministers, the 16 federal republic councils of ministers, a few large economic organizations (for the large-scale construction projects of communism),[92] and the central offices on a special list. All other organizations and enterprises were supplied through supervisory channels.[93]

The material and equipment supply plan approved by the USSR Council of Ministers specified the ministry or organization to which the funds were allocated, the quantity, and the assortment. The consuming ministries allocated these funds among their enterprises according to the production plan. At this stage the enterprises specified the exact nature of the necessary materials, kinds, and dimensions. These specifications were sent through the supply sections of the Glavki to the Glavsnab of the ministry and were used as the basis for allocating vouchers (raznariady) and for drafting aggregate specifications. These were transmitted to the Glavsbyty of the production ministries, which then gave orders to the production enterprises for the corresponding production and assortment.[94]

It is clear that parallel planning occurred here and was even more cumbersome than in production planning, which involved a huge administrative and bureaucratic apparatus. The system of protecting government priorities required constant adjustments in the plans. It represented the basic element for protecting the plan from economic disturbances, which will be discussed in the following chapters.

90. *Materialnye balansy*, p. 24.
91. See list in footnote 84 above.
92. Lokshin, *Planirovanie*, pp. 30–31. See also pp. 386–95 in Chapter 16.
93. *Ibid.*, p. 31.
94. *Ibid.*, p. 32.

PART TWO

Long-Term Planning, 1931–1941

CHAPTER 6

Variants of Second Five-Year Plan

Principal Goals of the Plan

The principal goals and the different stages involved in drawing up the Second Five-Year Plan were described by the chairman of the State Planning Commission (Gosplan), V. V. Kuibyshev, in his speech at the plenary session of the commission on May 11, 1931.[1] While the goals of the First Five-Year Plan had been to lay the foundations for a socialist economy, the goals of the second plan were much more ambitious—to build a socialist economic system. The main feature of the second plan was the elimination of the differences between the countryside and the city, on the one hand, and between physical and intellectual work, on the other. The first objective was to be achieved through a considerable improvement in living conditions (the doubling of the urban and rural housing fund was to help eliminate the "stupidity" of rural life) and through the complete industrialization of agriculture. The second was to be accomplished through a plan for general technical education.

The predominance of social objectives in the plan was very clear. It was emphasized by V. Molotov and repeated by Kuibyshev during the Seventeenth Party Conference in February 1932: "Comrade Molotov has already mentioned the main point of the theses setting out the essential social and political objective of the Second Five-Year Plan: the complete elimination of capitalist elements, of classes in general, and of the factors causing the appearance of classes and exploitation; victory over relics of capitalism in the economy and in the make-up of men; and the transformation of all the working people into conscious and active builders of a classless socialist society."[2]

Although the authors of the plan stressed this predominance of social and political aims, they were not very precise about the connection between the aims

1. V. V. Kuibyshev, *Izbrannye proizvedeniia* [Selected Works], Moscow, 1958, pp. 269–86. Speech entitled "Ob organizatsii planirovaniia" [On the Organization of Planning], first published in *Planovoe khoziaistvo* [Planned Economy], No. 4, 1931.
2. Kuibyshev, *Izbrannye proizvedeniia*, p. 328.

and economic growth. Kuibyshev mentioned only that the transformation of society would be made through the most advanced technological means and would necessitate a considerable increase in the production of metals, electric power, and means of transportation in 1937. And, indeed, it is not to the political and social objectives that we must turn to find the origins of the quantitative targets of economic development. These targets were inspired, above all, by the example of "the most advanced" capitalist countries, which the Soviet Union had to catch up with and overtake. This idea was very clearly expressed by G. I. Lomov in a speech at the Conference on Drafting a General Electrification Plan for the USSR (May 5–10, 1931):

Right now we have to start putting into effect the slogan of "catching up with and overtaking" the [capitalist] economies. The Congress of Soviets has set this task and has given us about ten years to fulfill it. Comrades, in order to draft a long-range electrification plan, we have to start with some final goals for the increase in our production during the next few years. These goals should be determined first of all by the slogan "catch up with and overtake." To catch up with the [capitalist] production of the principal products means overtaking them in such areas as machine-building. In order to catch up with their production of pig iron, coal, and petroleum, we must overtake them tremendously in machine-building because there we have to cover in a few years what was originally to be covered in about fifty years.[3]

The communist leaders saw no contradiction in trying to achieve independent social and political objectives by copying the structure of economic development of the opposing system. This question did not even come up since it had been settled once and for all by Lenin in a pamphlet he had written before the revolution, where he declared that Russia had already overtaken the most advanced countries politically but, in order to survive, she had to overtake them economically as well.[4]

Work Program

The main stages in drafting the plan for 1933–1937 were outlined by Kuibyshev in his May 11 speech. In the initial directives, a few of the principal goals were to be given in physical units; but the main purpose was to describe the general aims of the plan. All levels of planning agencies were to collaborate in this work, which Gosplan had to submit to the government in the fall of 1931. After consultation with the government, in the spring of 1932 Gosplan was to draft the over-all figures or ranges. These were then to be submitted for additional checking to all the social organizations, all the planning agencies, and all the scientific research institutes. In the fall of 1932 the Second Five-Year Plan was to

3. G. I. Lomov, "Problema novogo plana elektrifikatsii SSSR" [Problem of New Electrification Plan for the USSR], *Problemy genplana elektrifikatsii SSSR* [Problems of the General Electrification Plan for the USSR], 2nd ed., Moscow, 1932, p. 17.

4. V. I. Lenin, *Groziashchaia katastrofa i kak s nei borotsia* [The Impending Catastrophe and How to Combat It], Moscow, 1917 (translated in V. I. Lenin, *Selected Works*, New York and Moscow, 1967, Vol. 2, pp. 213–54). Soviet writers always refer to this speech of Lenin's whenever they advocate overtaking capitalist countries economically. See also Stalin's speech cited in my *Planning for Economic Growth in the Soviet Union, 1918–1932*, translated and edited by Marie-Christine MacAndrew and G. Warren Nutter, Chapel Hill, N.C., 1971, p. 116, and Lomov, *Problemy genplana*, p. 17.

be definitively confirmed by the government; the goals for the first year (1933) would then be extracted and made into the current operational plan.

This procedure seemed reasonable, with the general directives going back and forth to the main agencies and the text of the plan becoming more complete and more precise each time. All this work was to be done in a year and a half and completed about three months before the beginning of the five-year period. Even assuming that the work could be accomplished according to this schedule, the procedure entailed first drawing up a plan for seven years (including annual plans for 1931 and 1932) and then a plan for six years (including an annual plan for 1932). The result was, indeed, a five-year plan for 1933–1937 but built on the very uncertain base of 1931 and 1932. In other words, the planners had no say about the immediate goals being implemented by the economic administrative agencies. They had to accept these goals as they were, without being able, for obvious political reasons, to submit them to analysis and criticism. But this tenuous point of departure made the goals for 1933–1937 hypothetical and necessitated constant revisions.[5] That is why drafting the final text of the plan dragged out over three and a half years and the plan was officially confirmed only in November 1934.

The exact number of variants drafted during the preparatory stages is not known. Nevertheless, the gradual transformation of the plan can be observed by analyzing, one by one, the variants that are known for each year from 1931 to 1934.

First Outline of Five-Year Plan in May 1931

In May 1931 no five-year plan for 1933–1937 existed, but the economists charged with drafting the plan had as reference points the few physical goals mentioned by Kuibyshev in his May speech. There is only scant knowledge of these goals, which are shown in Table 8. In retrospect and compared with the final goals, they seem absurd, but for two reasons they did not seem so absurd to the Soviet planners at that time. First, comparison with the capitalist countries made these goals seem feasible. The 50–60 million metric tons of pig iron planned was close to the American production of 40 million, and the 40–50 million kilowatts of planned capacity of electric power stations close to the 42 million kilowatts of installed power in the United States in 1930.[6] The beef cattle herd was to surpass that in the U.S. by 50 per cent and the number of cows by 100 per cent. The amount of ginned cotton to be produced in 1937, however, was less than that in the United States (1,670–2,100 thousand metric tons in the USSR in 1937 compared with 3,000–3,170 thousand metric tons in the U.S. around 1930).[7] Nearly all the physical goals given at that time were set according to levels already

5. In his article "K metodologii sostavleniia plana vtoroi piatiletki" [On the Methods of Drafting the Second Five-Year Plan] in *Planovoe khoziaistvo*, No. 3, 1932, pp. 17–26, I. Smilga stated that one of the main difficulties in drafting the five-year plan lay in knowing the point of departure, the results of the First Five-Year Plan in 1932.

6. Lomov, *Problemy genplana*, pp. 5 and 17.

7. Shigalovich, *ibid.*, p. 238.

Table 8   Evolution of 1937 Goals in Second Five-Year Plan

	Units	Directives of May 1931 (1)	Variant of Feb.–May 1932 (2)	Draft Plan of 1933 (3)	Final Plan of Jan.–Feb. 1934 (4)	Actual Results in 1937 (5)
1. Electric power (capacity)	mill. kw	40–50	24–25	10.7	10.9	8.2
2. Electric power	bill. kwh	150	100–110	38.0	38.0	36.2
3. Coal	mill. m. tons	390–500	250–275	152.5	152.5	128.0
4. Crude oil and gas	mill. m. tons	130–150	80–90	47.5	46.8	30.5
5. Pig iron	mill. m. tons	50–60	22–23	18.0	16.0	14.5
6. Aluminum	thous. m. tons	386–480	200–250		80.0	37.7
7. Refined copper	thous. m. tons	847	515–580		135.0	97.5
8. Total sown area	mill. hectares	200–210	160–170	140	139.7	135.3
9. Ginned cotton	thous. m. tons	1,670–2,100	1,100	722	700	716.7
Livestock (in spring)						
10. Cattle:	mill. head	70–90	70		65.5	57.0
11. Cows	mill. head	45	32		26.9	22.7
12. Railroad freight traffic	mill. m. tons	800–900	750–780	480	475	517.3

Source

COLUMN 1–Line 1: G. Sorokin, "Pervyi generalnyi plan razvitiia narodnogo khoziaistva" [First General Plan for the Development of the National Economy], *Planovoe khoziaistvo*, No. 2, 1961, p. 46. Given for oil only. B. Z. Esin (*Problemy genplana*, p. 233) gives a counterplan of 25–50 mill. kw, which was dropped from the second edition as a typographical error. However, it appears rather to have been a revision made between 1931 and 1932. Comparison of these original figures with those from other sources, as well as the fact that these "typographical errors" apply only to goals that are too high, leads one to conclude that these were the original 1931 goals, not errors. Line 2: Poplujko, "La faillite du sixième plan quinquennal," *Problèmes Soviétiques*, No. 1, 1958, p. 110. Esin (*Problemy genplana*, p. 233) gives a counterplan of 200–250 bill. kwh. Line 3: Kuibyshev (*Planovoe khoziaistvo*, No. 4, 1931, p. 70) gives 390 mill. m. tons; Sorokin (*Planovoe khoziaistvo*, No. 2, 1961, p. 46) gives 450–500; and Poplujko (*Problèmes Soviétiques*, No. 1, 1958, p. 110) gives 420–500. Line 4: Sorokin, *Planovoe khoziaistvo*, No. 2, 1961, p. 46. Line 5: Poplujko, *Problèmes Soviétiques*, No. 1, 1958, p. 110. Sorokin (*Planovoe khoziaistvo*, No. 2, 1961, p. 46) gives 60 mill. m. tons. Line 6: Golinskii (*Problemy genplana*, p. 169) gives 386 thous. m. tons; Gardin (*ibid.*, p. 162) gives 450–480. Line 7: Poplujko, *Problèmes Soviétiques*, No. 1, 1958, p. 110. Lines 8 and 9: Shigalovich, *Problemy genplana*, p. 238. Line 10: Gaister, *ibid.*, p. 225; Shigalovich, *ibid.*, p. 238. Line 11: Shigalovich, *ibid.* Line 12: Sokolovskii, *ibid.*, p. 196; Belousov, *ibid.*, p. 188. The latter also gives 1,500–1,700 mill. m. tons, but this figure is said to be an error in the addendum (see note to line 1 above).

COLUMN 2–Line 1: Lomov, *Planovoe khoziaistvo*, No. 1, 1932, pp. 60 and 64. Kuibyshev (*Izbrannye proizvedeniia*, pp. 330–32) gives 20 mill. kw, and Lomov gives 22 excluding reserves. Line 2: Kuibyshev (*Izbrannye proizvedeniia*, p. 332) gives 100 bill. kwh, and Lomov (*Problemy genplana*, p. 7) gives "more than" 100. Esin (*ibid.*, p. 233) gives 110 bill. kwh. Line 3: Kuibyshev, *Izbrannye proizvedeniia*, p. 330; Libin, *Generalnyi plan elektrifikatsii SSSR. Materialy k Vsesoiuznoi Konferentsi* [General Plan for the Electrification of the USSR. Materials for the All-Union Conference], edited by G. I. Lomov, Moscow-Leningrad, 1932, Vol. III, p. 44; and Zenkis, *ibid.*, Vol. I, p. 125. Line 4: Kuibyshev, *Izbrannye proizvedeniia*, p. 331. Zenkis (*Generalnyi plan*, Vol. I, p. 125) gives 73 mill. m. tons; Smirnov (*ibid.*, Vol. II, pp. 11–14) gives 80.0; F. Syromolotov ("Fond poleznykh iskopaemykh i ikh potrebnosti vo vtoroi piatiletke" [Mineral Resources and Needs in Second Five-Year Plan], *Planovoe khoziaistvo*, No. 1, 1932, p. 38) gives 80.5; and Libin (*Generalnyi plan*, Vol. III, p. 44) gives 82. Line 5: G. Lauer ("Osnovnye linii razvitiia chernoi metallurgii vo vtoroi piatiletke" [The Main Lines of Development of the Ferrous Metal Industry in the Second Five-Year Plan], *Planovoe khoziaistvo*, No. 1, 1932, p. 86) gives 22 mill. m. tons; Syromolotov (*Planovoe khoziaistvo*, No. 1, 1932, p. 49) gives 22.6; and Zenkis (*Generalnyi plan*, Vol. I, p. 125) gives 23. Line 6: Smirnov, *ibid.*, Vol. II, p. 15; and F. Gavrilov, G. Golubev, and S. Shneider, "Razvertyvanie tsvetnoi metallurgii" [Development of the Ferrous Metal Industry], *Planovoe khoziaistvo*, No. 2, 1932, p. 51. The latter source also gives 230 thous. m. tons (*ibid.*, p. 52). Line 7: Syromolotov (*Planovoe khoziaistvo*, No. 1, 1932, p. 43) gives 515 thous. m. tons; Poplujko (*Problèmes Soviétiques*, No. 1, 1958, p. 110) gives 540; Smirnov (*Generalnyi plan*, Vol. II, p. 15) gives 556; and Gavrilov *et al.* (*Planovoe khoziaistvo*, No. 2, 1932, p. 43) gives 580. Line 8: Kuibyshev, *Izbrannye proizvedeniia*, p. 346; P. Mesiatsev, "Sotsialisticheskaia rekonstruktsiia i razmeshchenie selskokhoziaistvennogo proizvodstva vo vtoroi piatiletke" [Socialist Reconstruc-

Table 8   *continued*

tion and Geographical Distribution of Agricultural Production in the Second Five-Year Plan], *Planovoe khoziaistvo*, No. 1, 1932, p. 102. **Lines 9-11:** Mesiatsev, *Planovoe khoziaistvo*, No. 1, 1932, pp. 100–101. **Line 12:** V. D. Kolyshev, *Generalnyi plan*, Vol. III, p. 188 (and p. v); Zenkis, *ibid.*, Vol. I, p. 121.

   COLUMN 3–All lines: *Proekt vtorogo piatiletnego plana razvitiia narodnogo khoziaistva SSSR (1933–1937 gg.)* [Draft of Second Five-Year Plan for the Development of the USSR National Economy, 1933–1937], Moscow, 1934, Vol. I, pp. 440, 446–47, 464, 528, and 473.

   COLUMN 4–Lines 1, 4, 8, and 10-11: *Vtoroi piatiletnii plan razvitiia narodnogo khoziaistva SSSR (1933–1937)* [Second Five-Year Plan for the Development of the USSR National Economy, 1933–1937], Moscow, 1934, pp. 430–33, 440, and 528. **Lines 2-3, 5-7, 9, and 12:** Table A-1, col. 1.

   COLUMN 5–Line 1: *Promyshlennost SSSR* [Industry of the USSR], Moscow, 1957, p. 171. **Lines 2-3, 5-7, 9, and 12:** Table A-1, col. 2. **Line 4:** *Tretii piatiletnii plan razvitiia narodnogo khoziaistva SSSR (1938–1942)* [Third Five-Year Plan for the Development of the USSR National Economy, 1938–1942], Moscow, 1939, p. 202. **Lines 8 and 11:** *Narodnoe khoziaistvo SSSR v 1958 godu* [The USSR National Economy in 1958], Moscow, 1959, pp. 387 and 445. For line 11, January 1, 1938. **Line 10:** Naum Jasny, *The Socialized Agriculture of the USSR*, Stanford, 1949, p. 797.

reached in the West (the United States), which had to be surpassed as rapidly as possible. The second reason that the Soviet goals seemed not only justified but also perfectly attainable was the rather naive interpretation by Soviet planners of the economic results achieved during the previous years. Since the great "leap forward" in 1929 had made high rates of growth possible in 1930 for certain basic industrial products and since the 1931 plan had to be considered sacrosanct and perfectly attainable, there was no reason to doubt that this growth could be continued in future years. Hence the 1937 goals were extrapolations of the rates of growth achieved in 1928–1930 and planned for 1931.

   In order to understand the origin of the 1937 goals, therefore, the actual rates of growth for the principal products should be compared with the planned ones, which has been done for electric power, pig iron, and coal in Charts 4, 5, and 6. The extrapolation of the past rates of growth is not very precise and, for some products like coal or pig iron, the growth planned for 1932–1937 is a bit slower than that envisaged in the 1931 annual plan.

   The physical goals given in Table 8 were used, mostly by economists and technicians, as orders of magnitude. They were not intended, however, to constitute a five-year plan. Like the long-range plan for the following 10 or 15 years, the plan for 1933–1937 was intended to be only a working paper. The preliminary stage was to consist of drafting a second "Goelro" plan, that is, the second General Electrification Plan for the USSR, to start in 1932 or 1933 and end in 1942 or even 1945. The Second Five-Year Plan was to become the first segment of this plan. Work on this new electrification plan was begun on February 25, 1931, by the Gosplan presidium, which issued a decree setting up an organizational committee under Lomov. This committee was divided into nine sections.[8] A meeting of specialists was planned for April 1931 and a general conference for the whole country for November 1931. The amount of work involved can be

---

   8. (1) Power resources, (2) electric power stations and networks, (3) electrification of industry, (4) electrification of transportation, (5) electrification of housing and towns, (6) electrification of agricultural production, (7) power equipment, (8) regional electrification, and (9) summary plan. (See *Generalnyi plan*, Vol. VIII, p. 3. See also *Pravda*, March 5, 1931, and Sorokin, *Planovoe khoziaistvo*, No. 2, 1961, pp. 44–46.)

Chart 4   Goals for Electric Power Production in Second and Third Five-Year Plan Variants, 1928–1942

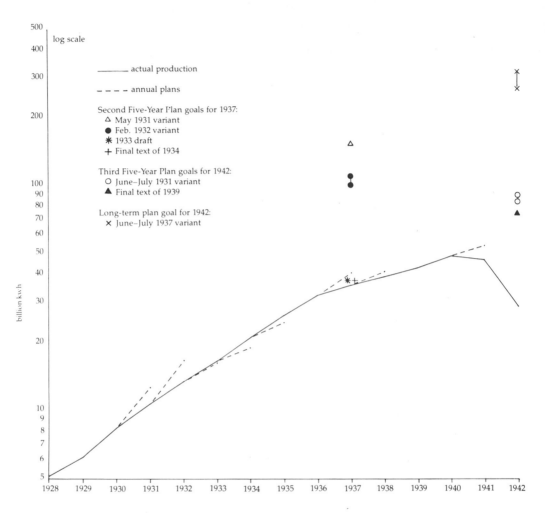

Source: Tables 8, 33, A-1, A-2, A-3, my *Planning* (Tables A-1 and A-2), and *Generalnyi plan*.

Chart 5 Goals for Pig Iron Production in Second and Third Five-Year Plan Variants, 1928–1942

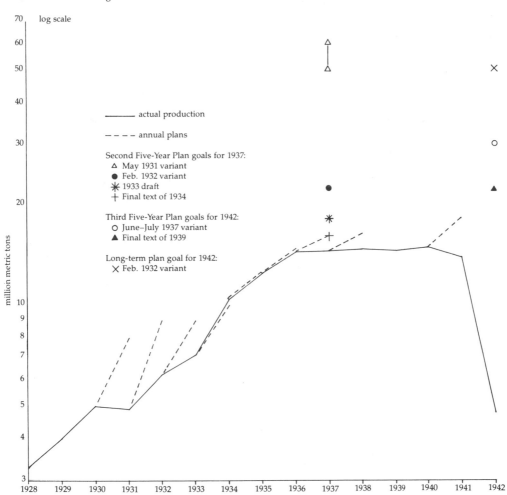

Source: Tables 8, 33, A-1, A-2, A-3, my *Planning* (Tables A-1 and A-2), and *Generalnyi plan*.

Chart 6   Goals for Coal Production in Second and Third Five-Year Plan Variants, 1928–1942

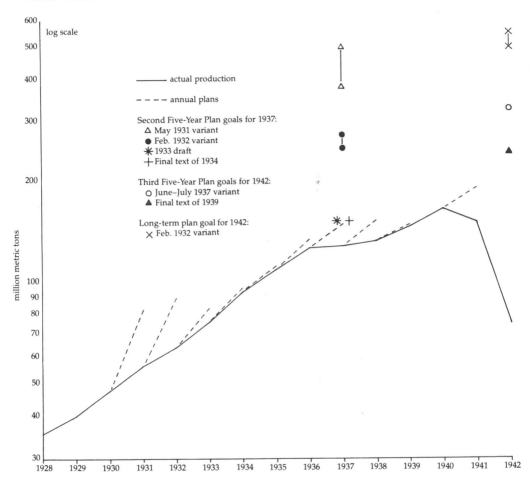

Source: Tables 8, 33, A-1, A-2, A-3, my *Planning* (Tables A-1 and A-2), and *Generalnyi plan*.

judged from the fact that by the end of 1931 more than a thousand researchers were taking part in it. The conference of May 5–10, 1931, was attended by 700 people and that of May 7–14, 1932, by 2,500 people.[9] The authors of the materials collected by this Gosplan organizational committee included more than a hundred specialists who worked with several research institutes and economic administrations.[10]

The first outline of the General Electrification Plan included an early variant of the Second Five-Year Plan since it covered all economic growth. This work reached only a preliminary stage and is known solely through the report on the May 1931 conference in Moscow.[11] Without more detail, it is difficult to assess the plan. The published reports were often technical; they envisaged development in very general terms and emphasized the possibilities of using electric power in the various sectors of the economy.[12] In the second edition of the report on the conference proceedings, which appeared in January, physical goals were rare but sufficient to place them in the unrealistic framework of the over-all directives announced by the government and the Party. B. Z. Esin proposed a "counterplan" with a production of 200–250 billion kilowatt-hours of electric power in 1937 (see Chart 4 to judge how realistic this was) and the installation of power stations with a total capacity of 25–50 million kilowatts.[13] Sokolovskii proposed for 1937 the electrification of 30 per cent of the railroad network carrying 50 per cent of the freight traffic, and Belousov thought that the railroad network could be doubled between 1931 and 1937.[14] The Party directives also had a direct effect on the agricultural section of the plan. Taner-Tanerbaum believed that, by the end of the Second Five-Year Plan, Soviet agriculture would be made up of 7,000 to 10,000 large state farming centers and large tractor centers, which would be agricultural towns with an average population of 15,000 to 20,000, and that this would change the structure of fuel consumption.[15] Agriculture would be entirely socialized, and the 45 million cows planned for 1937 were to belong solely to state and collective farms.[16]

Many more examples could be cited of the unrealistic directives that perme-

9. See editor's note to second edition of *Problemy genplana* and *Ekonomicheskaia zhizn SSSR* [Economic Life of the USSR], 2nd ed., edited by S. G. Strumilin, Moscow, 1967, Book I, p. 228.

10. *Generalnyi plan*, Vol. VIII, p. 9. Among the institutes were the Technical and Technological Policy Institute of the Communist Academy, the Leningrad Electrophysical Institute, the USSR Electrical Institute, the Thermal Power Institute, and Russian Republic Gosplan.

11. *Problemy genplana*. Some of the reports (those of G. I. Lomov, Iu. N. Flakserman, A. I. Ioffe, M. Ia. Lapirov-Skoblo) were published in *Planovoe khoziaistvo*, No. 6, 1931, but the book contains summaries of 49 reports.

12. Such as the one by Sazonov on power resources or the one by Simonov on the potential power capacity of rivers.

13. *Problemy genplana*, p. 233.

14. *Ibid.*, pp. 200 and 194.

15. *Ibid.*, pp. 52–53. According to him, agriculture would no longer be able to use fuels obtained in a decentralized way such as firewood, dried dung, or faggots. The thermal resources of agriculture would have to be used in thermal power stations for the agricultural production process. According to Gaister also (*ibid.*, p. 224), the predominant type of agricultural farm would be a large socialist enterprise using advanced technology and well adapted to electrification and mechanization of production. He believed there would be 4,000 to 4,500 Machine and Tractor Stations and 1,500 to 2,000 state farms.

16. Shigalovich, *ibid.*, p. 236.

ated all the work of these specialists. From the published texts, three approaches emerge. The first was limited to taking into account existing resources and did not set goals, except incidentally. A second consisted of discussing technical or technological problems without raising the question of means, and a third tried to create a link between the production goals of the sector under study and the means necessary to implement them. None of the specialists, however, analyzed the goals and the available resources as a whole.

Nevertheless, the technical discussion is still of interest to economists. Academician A. I. Ioffe emphasized that, in order to overtake the United States, technology had to be considered not statically, as it existed in May 1931, but dynamically, as it might develop during the next ten years.[17] According to him, it was necessary not only to foresee future technology but also to create it. The biggest difficulty was not calculating goals but evaluating possibilities realistically and organizing the necessary stages to implement them. Unfortunately, in concrete cases, Ioffe tended to exaggerate the possibilities open. For example, in the creation of a single interconnecting electrical network, he believed it would be possible to install in 1940 a network with line capacities of 400,000 volts. At the same time, he was more realistic than some others; he doubted the possibility of installing lines capable of transmitting one million volts, as proposed by another speaker at the same conference, Iu. N. Flakserman, or of making widespread use of direct current.[18]

B. B. Gartenshtein took a different approach. Although he began by expressing his confidence in precise calculations, he preferred the lessons of experience and cited the concrete experience of Western countries, particularly the electrification of railroads in Italy.[19] He felt that the implementation of any program depended on three factors: technical know-how, investment, and time. For the first factor, the contracts drawn up with foreign companies (mainly General Electric, but also Westinghouse, Metro-Vickers, Brown-Boveri, A.E.G., and Siemens) basically met Soviet needs. This was not the case for investment. The plan for the construction of electric locomotives in 1932–1934 depended heavily on credits being granted, and the lack of credits had already set it back several times, as can be seen from the various draft plans in Table 9. Thus the original plan for 830 electric locomotives was cut back to 590 at the beginning of 1931 and was further reduced in May. It is interesting to note that the 1934 goal gradually became imprecise because the question of building a new factory was still not settled. Obviously, under these conditions the long-term plans for 1937 or for 1942–1945 could not be taken very seriously. According to the architects of the plan, everything depended on the means the government would command. Hence they could only approach the matter like artisans working on order for a client. And it was up to the client—on this occasion, the government—to give a definite order by granting the necessary credits.

17. A. I. Ioffe, "Energeticheskie problemy vydvigaemye sovremennoi tekhnikoi" [Electric Power Problems Raised by Modern Technology], *Problemy genplana*, pp. 38–50.

18. *Ibid.*, p. 39. Iu. N. Flakserman, "Edinaia sotsialisticheskaia sistema energeticheskogo khoziaistva" [A Single Socialist Electric Power System], *ibid.*, p. 35.

19. B. B. Gartenshtein, "O proizvodstve elektrooborudovaniia dlia transporta" [On the Production of Electric Equipment for Transportation], *ibid.*, pp. 201–6.

Table 9   Changes in Construction Plan for Electric Locomotives, 1930–1931 (number of locomotives)

| | Potential Increase without Additional Investment | Draft Plan for Fall of 1930 (incl. additional investment)[a] | Draft Plan for Beginning of 1931: Electric Equipment[a] | May 1931 Plan | | Actual Production |
				Electric Equipment[a]	Mechanical Equipment	
1932	10	36	80	24	24	3
1933	22	214	110	80	[b]	17
1934	15	600	400			19
Total for 1932–1934	37	830	590			39

Source: B. B. Gartenshtein, *Problemy genplana*, pp. 203–6.

a. Subject to the allocation of the necessary credits, which consisted of 5.7 million rubles to enlarge the factory *Dynamo* and 38.5 million rubles to build a new factory.

b. *Parvagdiz*, which was supposed to produce the mechanical parts of the equipment for electric locomotives, did not confirm in May 1931 any commitment to produce the equipment for the 80 locomotives for which the electric equipment could have been produced if the necessary credits were supplied.

Five-Year Plan Variant of Early 1932

The first outline of the five-year plan, the one that served as the basis for discussion at the May 1931 conference, was to be submitted to the government in the fall of 1931. Unfortunately, neither the content of the discussion held in the Gosplan presidium on this subject nor the direct reactions of members of the government are known. Nevertheless, it is of interest to note that after October 1931 all discussion of the Second Five-Year Plan ceased in the Soviet press and Gosplan's specialized journal *Planovoe khoziaistvo* temporarily suspended publication.[20]

The silence was short-lived, and after four or five months a new draft of the five-year plan was presented by two eminent members of the government, Molotov and Kuibyshev, at the Seventeenth Party Conference (January 30–February 4, 1932). No mention was made on this occasion of the earlier work and the original goals. The two speakers stressed that this draft was not a real plan but rather directives, sometimes approximate, for drafting a plan. For this reason, the February 1932 draft only gave goals for the final year of the plan and a regional breakdown for "purposes of orientation."[21] The 1932 annual plan was put aside because, in the eyes of the planners, it was a final operational plan quite distinct from the five-year plan and had to be presented separately by a different speaker (G. K. Ordzhonikidze).

The figures that were made public in February are presented in Table 10. In addition to these data, the speeches of Molotov and Kuibyshev contained much precise information on the factories to be built in 1933–1937, on the railroad lines

20. The last issue of *Planovoe khoziaistvo* in 1931 (No. 5–6) went to press on October 3, 1931, and the first issue of 1932 (No. 1) on May 26, 1932.

21. Kuibyshev, *Izbrannye proizvedeniia*, pp. 334 and 350.

to be laid, and on such political measures as complete socialist ownership. So the original text must have been quite important and must have given details on regional breakdowns, at least for the principal products. The method of balances in physical and value terms for such important products as fuel, electric power, and pig iron must have been used at this stage of the work. Some kind of over-all balance must have been drawn up since there were figures on national income, consumption, and investment.

There is no need to stress the considerable discrepancies between this plan and the preliminary directives of 1931 (Table 8). The poor fulfillment of the 1931 annual plan and the abandonment of the three-year plan for 1931–1933 are sufficient explanation.[22] It is interesting to note that these goals were not abandoned but were simply postponed to a future date—1942–1945, the end of the general plan.

Table 11 shows a certain stability in the principal goals, the only real increase being in the production of electric power. This means that the fluctuation in the goals was more apparent than real, the factor of time being simply an element of cost that had to be increased.

Detailed Drafting of the Plan

The directives of the Seventeenth Party Conference made possible a new start in drafting the Second Five-Year Plan. The March 25, 1932, decree of the Council of People's Commissars recommended that workers and collective farmers join technicians and research organizations in this work.[23] At the same time Gosplan authorized the organization of 24 general conferences for the whole country to study the main problems: geographical distribution of production, electrification, development of the chemical industry, specialization and coordination of machine-building, and development of transportation, agriculture, trade, and culture.[24] Directives on methods to be used in drafting the plan were also published at this time.[25] Gosplan itself drew up detailed directives based on the

22. See my *Planning*, pp. 189–204, and also Charts 4–6 above.

23. "On the Organization of Work to Draft the Second Five-Year Plan (*Ekonomicheskaia zhizn*, Book I, p. 242). *Silami millionov razrabotat plan postroeniia sotsializma. Direktivnye ukazaniia VTsSPS i Gosplana SSSR ob uchasti rabochikh i ITR v razrabotke plana vtoroi piatiletki* [The Efforts of Millions Are Drafting the Plan to Build Socialism. Directives of the Union of Trade Unions and of USSR Gosplan on the Participation of Workers, Engineers, and Technicians in Drafting the Second Five-Year Plan], Moscow, 1932.

24. Kuibyshev, *Izbrannye proizvedeniia*, pp. 401–8, and *Ekonomicheskaia zhizn*, Book I, p. 242. According to G. M. Sorokin (*Planirovanie narodnogo khoziaistva SSSR* [Planning of the USSR National Economy], Moscow, 1961, p. 193), the USSR Academy of Sciences, 200 research institutes, and more than 300 eminent specialists participated in drafting the Second Five-Year Plan.

25. *Osnovnye ukazaniia k sostavleniiu vtorogo piatiletnego plana narodnogo khoziaistva SSSR (1933–1937)* [Basic Instructions for Drafting the Second Five-Year Plan for the USSR National Economy, 1933–1937], Moscow, 1932. *Sistema pokazatelei i formy tablits k sostavleniiu vtorogo piatiletnego plana narodnogo khoziaistva SSSR* [The System of Indexes and Forms to Draft the Second Five-Year Plan for the USSR National Economy], Moscow-Leningrad, 1932. S. M. Sarov, "O poriadke raboty obshchikh planovykh organov nad vtorym piatiletnim planom" [On Procedure for Work of General Planning Agencies on Second Five-Year Plan], *Organizatsiia upravleniia* [Organization of Management], No. 4, 1932, pp. 45–55. I. Ia. Tseitlin, E. P. Sokolova, and M. V. Kurman, *K metodologii planirovaniia naseleniia na vtoruiu piatiletku* [On Methods of Planning Population for the Second Five-Year Plan], Leningrad, 1932.

Table 10 Seventeenth Party Conference Directives on Second Five-Year Plan

	Units	Total Planned for 1933–1937	Goals for 1937 Physical Units	Goals for 1937 Index (1932 = 100)
National income	bill. rubles			200[a]
Industrial production	bill. rubles			250[a]
Coal:	mill. m. tons		250	
Donbass and northern Caucasus	mill. m. tons		110–120	
Kuzbass	mill. m. tons		50	
Moscow Basin	mill. m. tons		20–22	
Urals	mill. m. tons		25	
Kazakhstan (Karaganda)	mill. m. tons		15	
Central Asia	mill. m. tons		10	
Eastern Siberia	mill. m. tons		12	
Far east	mill. m. tons		10–12	
Transcaucasia	mill. m. tons		3	
Crude oil:				
Northern Caucasus (Grozneft and Maikopneft)	mill. m. tons		28–30	
Transcaucasia (new regions excl. Baku)	mill. m. tons		10	
Central Asia	mill. m. tons		3	
Coke:				
Urals	mill. m. tons		8	
Eastern Siberia	mill. m. tons		4	
Electric power (capacity)	mill. kw		20	
Electric power	bill. kwh		100	
Pig iron:	mill. m. tons		22	
Ukraine	mill. m. tons		11	
Urals	mill. m. tons		6	
Eastern Siberia	mill. m. tons		2	
Mineral fertilizer, total:	mill. m. tons		7,000[b]	
Phosphoric fertilizer	mill. m. tons		[b]	
Ammonium sulfate	mill. m. tons		[b]	
Machine-building:	bill. rubles			300–350
Tractors	thousands		170	
Sown area, total	mill. hectares		160–170	
Grain harvest, total	mill. m. tons		130[c]	
Average yield of grain	quintals per hectare		140	
Construction of new railroad track	thous. km	25–30		
Industrial population[d]	millions	over 15	50	
National income	bill. rubles	500[e]		200
Per capita consumption of industrial and food products				200–300
Total investment in national economy	bill. rubles	140–150[f]		

Source: Speeches of V. Molotov and V. V. Kuibyshev at the Seventeenth Party Conference (*Pravda*, February 4 and 8, 1932, and Kuibyshev, *Izbrannye proizvedeniia*, pp. 321–79).

a. The prices used to calculate these are not known. They may be 1926/27 prices. See also note e.

b. U.S. production in 1931; in 1929, it was 9,320 (*Biennial Census of Manufactures: 1933*, Washington, 1936, p. 342). "In the production of fertilizers we should not only be the first in Europe but also catch up with the United States." "In phosphoric fertilizer and ammonium sulfate, we should catch up with and overtake even America" (Kuibyshev, *Izbrannye proizvedeniia*, pp. 331 and 342).

c. Resolutions of the Seventeenth Party Conference (*KPSS v rezoliutsiiakh i resheniiakh sezdov, konferentsii i plenumov Ts. K.* [The Communist Party of the Soviet Union: Resolutions and Decisions at Congresses, Conferences, and Plenary Sessions of the Central Committee], Moscow, 1953, Part II, p. 696).

d. The coverage of this term (*industrialnoe naselenie*) is not clear. It seems to refer to urban population with a few adjustments.

e. G. F. Grinko, *Pravda*, March 6, 1932. It is not clear whether this figure is expressed in the same prices as the index for 1937 based on 1932.

Table 10   *continued*

f. Kuibyshev does not specify the prices in which investment was expressed. Earlier investments (e.g., for the electrification of agricultural production, see S. V. Shchurov, *Generalnyi plan*, Vol. IV) were expressed in 1931 prices either with or without allowance for the reduction in construction costs. (On the cost of new urban housing, see Smirnov, *ibid.*, Vol. V, p. 32.)

Table 11   Comparison of Goals in First Variant of Second Five-Year Plan and in General Plan for 1942–1945

	Units	Feb.–May 1931 Goals for 1937 (1)	Feb.–May 1931 Goals for 1942–1945 (2)
1. Electric power (capacity)	mill. kw.	40–50	50–65
2. Electric power	bill. kwh	150–250	320–350
3. Coal	mill. m. tons	390–500	500–550
4. Crude oil and gas	mill. m. tons	130–150	
5. Pig iron	mill. m. tons	50–60	50
6. Steel	mill. m. tons		57
7. Rolled steel	mill. m. tons		44

Source

COLUMN 1: Table 8, col. 1.

COLUMN 2–Line 1: G. I. Lomov, *Generalnyi plan*, Vol. VIII, p. 33. **Lines 2 and 5–7:** Kaplan *et al.*, *ibid.*, Vol. I, pp. 16, 17, and 29. **Line 3:** Prigorovskii, *ibid.*, Vol. I, p. 149, and Kaplan *et al.*, *ibid.*, Vol. I, p. 17.

recommendations of the Seventeenth Party Conference. Goals were set for each year of the plan and the most important indexes were specified for the main regions.[26]

On the whole, these directives and recommendations were followed, and several important projects were carried out during the first three quarters of 1932. Several of the conferences organized should be mentioned. The conference on the geographical distribution of production was held in Moscow, April 15–26, 1932, with nearly 1,000 delegates, and the conference on the General Electrification Plan was held in Moscow on May 7–14 with nearly 2,500 delegates. The conference on the development of mining resources should be noted also.[27] Detailed work was done on planning the development of the ferrous metal industry, the timber industry, the food industry, agriculture, and transportation during the five-year plan.[28] Draft plans were made by different insti-

26. These directives were not published, but they were mentioned by some writers. On this subject, see A. K. Shmidt, "Energeticheskie resursy ot obogashcheniia sibirskikh i uralskikh uglei" [Power Resources Obtained from the Enrichment of Siberian and Urals Coal], *Generalnyi plan*, Vol. I, p. 231. Shmidt cited the Gosplan data based on the decisions of the Seventeenth Party Conference and reproduced the goals for the production of pig iron for the factories of the Urals and western Siberia for each year from 1932 to 1937. It should be recalled that the February 1932 directives were given only for the last year of the plan (see previous section of text and footnote 76 in this chapter).

27. *Trudy Pervoi Vsesoiuznoi Konferentsii po razmeshcheniiu proizvoditelnykh sil SSSR* [Papers of the First All-Union Conference on the Geographical Distribution of the Production of the USSR], Moscow, 1932. (See also *Ekonomicheskaia zhizn*, Book I, p. 243.) *Generalnyi plan* (11 volumes). *Rezoliutsiia Vsesoiuznoi Konferentsii po sostavleniiu generalnogo plana elektrifikatsii SSSR 7–14 maia 1932 g.* [Resolution of the All-Union Conference on Drafting a General Electrification Plan for the USSR, May 7–14, 1932], Moscow-Leningrad, 1932. Syromolotov, *Planovoe khoziaistvo*, No. 1, 1932, pp. 36–59.

28. See the articles by G. Lauer, G. I. Lomov, I. N. Dolinskii, A. Braude, P. Mesiatsev, and I. Unshlikht in *Planovoe khoziaistvo*, Nos. 1, 2, and 3, 1932.

tutions, such as those for the development of communications, for geological prospecting, for the timber and woodprocessing industry, for the petroleum industry, and for the cultivation of forests.[29] Also published at this time were studies of particular aspects of the five-year plan, such as technical progress, organization and rationalization of production, geographical distribution, and the development of certain regions and of certain cities.[30]

Since this detailed work on drafting a final text of the plan is only partially available, it cannot be evaluated as a whole. Nevertheless, the tenor of it can be understood by examining in greater detail the most important part—the General Electrification Plan. Since all the drafts of the Second Five-Year Plan were made according to the same principles and methods, the same problems come up here as in the plans for other sectors.

Draft of Second General Electrification Plan

The final text of this plan was never published, but work on it had progressed sufficiently in May 1932, at the time of the Moscow conference, to warrant a

29. The main data in physical terms from the (preliminary) draft plan for communications were cited by I. N. Anisin, Ia. I. Rosolovskii, and V. P. Khoven, "Voprosy tekhnicheskoi rekonstruktsii narodnoi sviazi vo vtoroi piatiletke" [Problems of the Technical Reconstruction of Communications in the Second Five-Year Plan], *Generalnyi plan*, Vol. III, pp. 270–304.

Information on geological prospecting comes from V. P. Novikov, "O perspektivnom plane geologo-razvedochnykh rabot na 1933–1937" [On the Long-Range Plan for Geological Prospecting in 1933–1937], *Generalnyi plan*, Vol. I, pp. 464–80. Although presented at the conference on electrification, this plan was separate and specified the prospecting work to be done, along with its cost (by years in some cases), and must have been drawn up by an official agency. Novikov was a member of the Power Resources Section of the Gosplan Organizational Committee for Drafting the General Electrification Plan.

A detailed project of the Commissariat of the Timber Industry is partially reproduced by A. A. Boronets in *Voprosy organizatsii i ratsionalizatsii proizvodstva vo vtoroi piatiletke* [Problems of Organization and Rationalization of Production in the Second Five-Year Plan], edited by I. Burdianskii, Moscow-Leningrad, 1933, pp. 269 ff.

The figures from the draft plan of the Petroleum Section of the Supreme Council of the National Economy are partially reproduced by L. I. Loginovich, "Perspektivy khoziaistvennogo ispolzovaniia prirodnykh gazov v SSSR" [Prospects for the Use of Natural Gas in the USSR Economy], *Generalnyi plan*, Vol. I, pp. 393, 406, and 410.

On forest cultivation, see Malkov, Sazin, Turitsyn, "Lesnye resursy SSSR. Materialy k postroeniiu perspektivnogo plana lesnoi promyshlennosti i lesnogo khoziaistva" [Forestry Resources of the USSR. Materials for Drafting a Long-Range Plan for the Timber Industry and for Forestry], *Generalnyi plan*, Vol. I, pp. 417–39.

30. Of the abundant literature on this subject, the following may be mentioned: *K voprosu o tekhnicheskikh sdvigakh vo vtoroi piatiletke. Materialy* [On the Problem of Technological Progress in the Second Five-Year Plan. Materials], edited by I. M. Burdianskii, V. I. Veits, G. M. Krzhizhanovskii, F. V. Lengnik, and M. I. Rubinshtein, Moscow, 1932; *Voprosy organizatsii*, edited by the Technological Policy Section of Gosplan with the collaboration of the Committee on Rationalization under the Society for the Propagation of Technical Progress; *Geograficheskoe razmeshchenie pishchevoi promyshlennosti vo vtorom piatiletii* [The Geographical Distribution of the Food Industry in the Second Five-Year Plan], edited by I. N. Dolinskii and M. F. Sass, Moscow-Leningrad, 1932; *Severnyi Krai vo vtoroi piatiletke. Vtoroi piatiletnii plan Severnogo Kraia na 1933–1937 gg. Pervyi variant* [The Northern Territory in the Second Five-Year Plan. The Second Five-Year Plan of the Northern Territory for 1933–1937. First Variant], edited by M. Ia. Rozner, Arkhangelsk, 1932; *Elektrifikatsiia i toplivo respublik Srednei Azii vo vtoroi piatiletke* [Electrification and Fuel in the Republics of Central Asia in the Second Five-Year Plan], Tashkent, 1932; *Perspektivy Donbassa vo vtoroi piatiletke* [Prospects for the Donbass in the Second Five-Year Plan], edited by N. S. Popov, Kharkov, 1931–1932 (2 volumes); *Rekonstruktsiia gorodov SSSR, 1933–1937* [Reconstruction of the Cities of the USSR, 1933–1937], edited by N. Ushakov, Moscow, 1933 (2 volumes).

huge publication of 11 volumes and 4,000 pages.[31] Although this text represented the work of more than 100 researchers attached to different specialized institutes and was more precise and better documented than its predecessor (the Goelro plan), it is hardly ever mentioned in the contemporary Soviet literature. A brief summary of its contents and methods will make the reasons for this reticence clear.

The failure of this plan can certainly not be attributed to the lack of conscientiousness or the unrealistic approach of its authors. In the introduction to Volume I, the organizational committee stressed the provisional nature of all the projections and the lack of coordination among different projects published at that stage. This does not mean, however, that the plan was the work of utopians or dreamers; rather it was the work of engineers, among the best in each field, who accompanied every projection with reservations about its conditional and tentative nature.[32] Only a more detailed examination of the methods used will make it possible to understand the apparent contradiction between the cautious approach of the authors and the fantastic prospects for development that were very soon refuted by the facts.

The second General Electrification Plan was a document made up of several heterogeneous parts. For our purposes we can distinguish the retrospective technical monograph, the projections for the future made for the electrification plan, and the projections for the future made by other organizations and picked up by the authors of this work. The technical monograph is no doubt the most important part. It constituted half of the total plan and was composed of a number of reports, including international comparisons of power resources and power equipment production, a study of electric railroads in Italy, and a detailed evaluation of the resources of the USSR in coal, oil shale, peat, subterranean water, natural gas, and even wind power. It contained technical studies of different aspects of the electrification of railroads, agricultural work, communications, and the production of power equipment. The line between purely technical studies and projections for the future was not always clear, and some authors, such as M. Ia. Lapirov-Skoblo, studied how to direct research so as to introduce advanced techniques into the electrical industry in the future.[33] Another author, M. G. Evreimov, in a research piece on the introduction of electric power in agricultural production, raised questions about such major technical discoveries of worldwide interest as the transportation of power over a distance without a conductor and the use of atomic energy.[34] He made a

31. *Generalnyi plan*.

32. *Ibid.*, Vol. I, pp. vi–ix. On the authors' reservations, see, for instance, the introduction to *ibid.*, Vol. III, pp. viii and ix. Libin (*ibid.*, Vol. III, p. 89) pointed out that the chronological data on the development of railroads contained nothing new. Reservations were also made by Kolychev (*ibid.*, Vol. III, p. 189), Eremin (*ibid.*, Vol. IV, p. 84), in the introduction to Volume IV on agriculture and in the introduction to Volume VI on power equipment, and Lomov in his introductory article to Volume VIII on the summary plan for electrification (*ibid.*, Vol. VIII, pp. 32–33).

33. M. Ia. Lapirov-Skoblo, "Tekhnicheskie sdvigi elektropromyshlennosti i problemy nauchno-issledovatelnoi raboty" [Technical Progress in the Electrical Industry and Problems of Scientific Research], *ibid.*, Vol. VI, pp. 61–131.

34. M. G. Evreimov, "Nauchno-issledovatelskie problemy v oblasti elektrifikatsii selskogo khoziaistva" [Problems of Scientific Research in Electrification of Agriculture], *ibid.*, Vol. IV, pp. 158–59.

number of proposals for agriculture, including the application of discoveries already in use in other branches of the economy (particularly the electric motor industry), the introduction of methods used abroad, the use of local sources of power, the study of new sources of power (wind, sun, tides, etc.), the effect of electromagnetic fields on cattle and plants, and ways of controlling climatic conditions (artificial rain, etc.). Evreimov did not set any schedule for carrying out these research projects but indicated only that they should be examined to see whether they were feasible and to what extent they met the needs of agriculture that would arise at given stages of development.

It should be noted that none of the monograph and technical section of this plan was absurd. On the contrary, the ideas it contained and the documentation it provided made a valuable contribution, and the authors hardly even mentioned the long-term goals imposed by the party at the Seventeenth Conference in February 1932. These studies were certainly not outdated after the general plan was abandoned and could have been integrated in various later versions of long-range plans.[35]

Excluding the monograph and technical part, the General Electrification Plan was much less important; it covered barely 2,000 pages, of which 600 pages were subsidiary projections. These included projections for the expansion of industry to enable calculating electric power use in industry, long-range prospects for housing and the communal economy, a plan for geological prospecting, a plan for forest cultivation, and long-range prospects for the development of communications. Excluding these, only 1,400 pages remained for the electrification plan as such. Moreover, even this remaining part was not one single plan but a collection of plans of varying importance.

The major part was taken up by a project for building electric power stations. Precise goals for these stations (total capacity of 22.7 million kilowatts in 1937 and 60 million kilowatts by the end of the general plan) were given in the resolutions of the May 1932 conference, which listed all the power stations to be built and specified their type and the kind of fuel to be used. The regional detail was so abundant that this section occupied all of Volume VIII of the general plan (856 pages).

Another plan worked out in great detail was for the electrification of railroads. Precise goals were set for lines to be electrified for each year from 1933 to 1937 (21,000 kilometers altogether for 1933–1937) and for the whole plan period (50,000 kilometers). These were followed by studies by different authors of railroad needs for electric power, equipment, investment, and manpower; one study was devoted to showing the savings in operating costs compared with the required investments.[36] This plan covered about 180 pages of Volume III.

35. Sorokin (*Planovoe khoziaistvo*, No. 2, 1961) was thinking of this part of the plan when he said that everything that was still valid in this work was integrated into the Second Five-Year Plan. Sorokin, whose main criticism was directed against the authors of the plan, did not mention that a large part of this work was also included in other long-range plans drawn up in 1941 and 1946. His criticism of the planners seems unjust. This matter will be discussed in more detail later.

36. V. D. Kolyshev, "Effektivnost elektrifikatsii zheleznykh dorog" [Efficiency of Electrification of Railroads], *Generalnyi plan*, Vol. III, pp. 186–220.

Another important part of the plan concerned the electrical industry, which was studied from the standpoint of the needs of other sectors of the economy: electric power stations, transportation by electric railroad, the ferrous metal industry, the motor vehicle and tractor industry, production of motors, and the cable and electric bulb industry. The total value of production was estimated at 1.0 billion rubles for the 1932 plan, 7.5 billion for the 1937 plan, and 11.5 billion for the 1942–1945 plan (all in 1926/27 prices).[37] The plan covered production by old and new factories, provided a regional breakdown, and evaluated raw material needs of the industry and investment in new factories (from 2 to 2.5 billion rubles for the whole plan period).[38] This plan was quite short, covering only some 80 pages.[39]

The last plan of any importance in the General Electrification Plan was for the electrification of agricultural production.[40] Electric power was to be introduced only in certain agricultural processes: livestock breeding, raising industrial crops (cotton, flax), fruit and vegetable growing in urban areas, dairy production, and certain soil and crop improvements. By 1937 all of this work was to be done with electric power on state farms and 10 to 50 per cent on collective farms.[41] The plan also contained estimates of the required power-station capacity for each category of agricultural work and separately for state and collective farms, as well as the corresponding electric power needs. Having established the number and capacity of electric power stations, the plan estimated required gross and net investment (in value terms), the required quantity of equipment and materials (in physical terms), and manpower needs.

Besides these detailed plans, the General Electrification Plan also included outlines of other plans that formed an integral part of it. First was a plan to build a single interconnecting network. According to A. I. Kolpakova, by the end of the Second Five-Year Plan, the single interconnecting network was to have a capacity on the order of 17 million kilowatts and, by the end of the general plan, of 50 million kilowatts, that is, 70 and 80 per cent, respectively, of the total electric power capacity of the USSR.[42] Then came a plan to use wind power, drawn up by the engineer N. V. Krasovskii, who estimated that Soviet resources in wind power were 16.7 times as great as the total of all other sources of power

37. I. Iu. Kaplan, A. M. Nikolaev, P. P. Ovsiannikov, D. M. Bernshtein, and I. E. Nelidov, "Gipoteza razvitiia elektrotekhnicheskoi promyshlennosti v razreze Generalnogo Plana" [Model of Development of the Electrical Industry in the General Plan], *ibid.*, Vol. VI, pp. 15–60.

38. *Ibid.*, Vol. VI, p. 52.

39. In addition to the article by Kaplan *et al.* cited above, there is an article by A. E. Maleev, "Perspektivy razvitiia kotloturbinnoi promyshlennosti vo vtorom piatiletii" [Prospects for the Development of the Boiler and Turbine Industry in the Second Five-Year Plan], *ibid.*, Vol. VI, pp. 343–64.

40. *Ibid.*, Vol. IV, pp. 1–157 and 170–238. Articles by I. B. Geronimus, S. V. Shchurov, A. S. Eremin, B. N. Rastov, A. A. Krasnov, and V. S. Krasnov.

41. Except for soil improvement and electrification of harvesting, for which the percentage of electrification was to be only 3.2 for state farms and 0.1 for collective farms (*ibid.*, Vol. IV, pp. 50–51).

42. Engineer A. I. Kolpakova, "Edinaia vysokovoltnaia set Soiuza" [A Single Interconnecting Network in the USSR], *ibid.*, Vol. IX, p. 85. See also engineer E. A. Palitsyn, "Nauchno-issledovatelskie raboty v oblasti edinoi vysokovoltnoi seti" [Scientific Research Work on the Single Interconnecting Network], *ibid.*, Vol. IX, pp. 267–79.

in the country.[43] He studied the technical problems involved in installing wind-mills, as well as the cost of investment and operation, and concluded that, in some cases, wind power was cheaper than other sources of power. Krasovskii also mentioned projects of the Commissariat of Agriculture that envisaged an installed windmill capacity of 1.5 million kilowatts in 1937 for water supply, irrigation, and electrification of agricultural processes. The Power Administration (*Energotsentr*) envisaged a capacity of 0.5 million kilowatts for the electrification of industrial production. Thus the total installed capacity of windmills was to reach 2 million kilowatts in 1937 (9 per cent of total Soviet power) and the share of wind in total power sources used in the USSR was to reach 34 per cent by the end of the general plan.[44]

Since the major part of the plan was devoted to the construction of electric power stations, the methods used there are the most interesting. First, the planners had to work under certain constraints. They were not free to establish the total capacity of the power stations to be built, that is, the principal goal of the plan. The directives of the Party conference of February 1932 stipulated in no uncertain terms that the production of 100 billion kilowatt-hours of electric power was indispensable in 1937.[45] These directives were repeated several times by the authors of the general plan and in the resolutions of the May 1932 conference.[46] The only discussion centered around how this order was to be carried out. If power stations operated an average of 5,000 hours in 1937 (compared with 3,500 in 1928 and 4,000 planned for 1932),[47] total capacity would have to be around 23 to 24 million kilowatts, taking account of reserves and the stations' own needs. As a precautionary measure, Lomov proposed two variants: one of 22 million kilowatts and the other of 24 million.[48]

In fact, the principal task facing the authors of the General Electrification Plan was to determine the geographical distribution of the power stations.[49] They were to be guided by the principles of a balanced distribution of production, maximum industrialization, increased defense strength, and consolidation of economic independence. Their work was to be based on a detailed study of power sources and power consumption of different branches of the national economy (mainly industry). They were also to lay the groundwork for rural electrification by preparing for the establishment of a single interconnecting network and for the electrification of transportation and agricultural production. The emphasis placed on the geographical distribution of power stations explains

43. N. V. Krasovskii, "Vetrovye energoresursy SSSR i perspektivy ikh ispolzovaniia" [Wind Power Resources of the USSR and Prospects for Their Use], *ibid.*, Vol. I, pp. 440–63.

44. *Ibid.*, Vol. I, p. 462. These figures might not have been approved by the conference. Lomov, the president of the Organizational Committee, talked in the summary section of 100,000 to 300,000 kilowatts of installed capacity using wind power for 1937 (*ibid.*, Vol. VIII, p. 33).

45. *KPSS v rezoliutsiiakh*, Part II, p. 694.

46. See, for instance, *Generalnyi plan*, Vol. VIII, pp. 19, 32–33, and 57–58, and Vol. I, pp. vii and 120–21.

47. Lomov, *ibid.*, Vol. VIII, p. 19.

48. Lomov, *ibid.*, Vol. VIII, p. 32.

49. "The main goal of the electrification plan is the geographical distribution of the industrial power stations" (Lomov, *ibid.*, Vol. VIII, p. 21).

the predominance given to regional planning. The May conference resolutions on building electric power stations went over only the work done by the regional planning committees.[50] It is this work, therefore, that should be studied in order to understand the methods used to draw up the general plan.

The methods used to draft the regional electrification plans were quite uniform. First, the power and mining (or timber) resources of the region were listed; then there was a brief summary of the earlier economic development of industry, agriculture, transportation, etc.; and, finally, projections were made for 1937 (often for all the years from 1933 to 1937 and for the end of the general plan). In most cases long-range forecasts of population and employment were also given. The projections for the future, based largely on the directives of superior agencies (of USSR Gosplan) and on the resolutions of specialized conferences, were compared with the capacity of the electric power stations specified by the higher authorities for the region.[51] The work of the regional planning committee then consisted of coordinating the electric power needs of different branches of the economy and distributing within a given region the power stations that region would have in 1937 and 1942–1945. The relation between needs and available resources was determined by norms for electric power consumption established for each major production process. In setting these norms, the regional planning committee had considerable authority. The principle was that, as industrialization progressed, norms would increase; that is, production processes would require more electric power. Data for earlier years (in kilowatt-hours per ruble of production) were the basis for this rule.[52] Generally the norms gave the amount of power consumed in each production process in physical terms. In practice, since these norms varied considerably, the choice of the "average" norm was a delicate matter.[53] The number of hours of operation of the power stations also had to be determined in order to compute the required capacity.[54]

50. Volume VIII of *Generalnyi plan* reproduces the electrification plans for the provinces of Leningrad and Karelia, the Northern Territory, Urals, western Siberia, Bashkiria, Kazakhstan, Nizhnyi Novgorod Territory, the Central Black Earth Province, the Western Province, and the Belorussian Republic.

51. "We can assume that the point of departure in planning the construction of electric power stations was the total capacity specified for the province which was calculated from the total for the whole country. After this total had been established at 22 million kilowatts, the increase in capacity of the province (Leningrad) was set at 1.6 million kilowatts. Not very different from this figure is the province Gosplan draft, according to which the capacity of the electric power stations in Leningrad Province is set at 1,697 megawatts for 1937 and 4,230 for the general plan" (M. S. Shatelen and N. V. Den, *ibid*, Vol. VIII, pp. 205–6).

According to the Organizational Committee (*ibid.*, Vol. VIII, p. 4), the regions asked for a total capacity of 36 million kilowatts for 1937, of which only 22.7 million were approved.

52. See the figures for the Urals (*ibid.*, Vol. VIII, p. 342).

53. From 8 to 12 kilowatt-hours per ton of Martin steel, from 75 to 300 kwh per metric ton of rolled steel, from 40 to 80 kwh for pig iron from foundries, from 450 to 1,000 kwh for copper working, from 40 to 120 kwh for the production of salt, from 75 to 120 kwh for cement, etc. (given for the Urals in *ibid.*, Vol. VIII, pp. 337–40).

54. The plans always envisaged a fuller utilization of capacity than the existing one. In the Urals, for example, the number of hours of operation was to increase from 5,000 in 1932 to 7,500 in 1937 for ferrous metals, from 3,000 to 5,000 for ores, from 3,000 to 5,500 for coal, from 4,000 to 7,000 for nonferrous metals, from 3,000 to 5,500 for machine-building, etc. (*ibid.*, Vol. VIII, pp. 343–47). Similar increases can be found in nearly all the regional electrification plans.

The next stage was to estimate the investment required for the construction of new power stations. In most cases, this was done by regional planning agencies which presented investment figures in constant (usually 1931) prices for all years from 1933 to 1937 and for the whole plan period. This work was apparently unsatisfactory to the participants in the May 1932 conference, since they recommended further studies on the subject.[55]

Plans for the construction of electric power stations basically were drawn up at the regional level, while the other two plans (for the electrification of railroads and for the electrical industry) were drafted by the central authorities. But the central planners' freedom of decision-making was no greater. For the electrification of railroads, the main part of the plan—the length of railroad line to be electrified—was decided by superior agencies.[56] The planners simply had to demonstrate needs or, in other words, the additional requests implied by the implementation of the government's wishes. For the electrical industry, production was also determined from the outside. The production of hydroelectric generators and turbogenerators, transformers, turbines, and boilers was determined by the total new capacity to be installed. The production of electric locomotives (3,540 in the five years 1933–1937) had been calculated by the Commissariat of Transportation when the plan for the electrification of railroads was drawn up.[57] The needs of the metal industry for motors were fixed by the projects to build new factories, which set plans according to production of various products.[58] The needs of the motor vehicle and tractor industry were also determined by the industry's production plans.[59] The plan for the electrical industry could only try to coordinate these disparate elements, determine the raw material and investment needs,[60] study the regional distribution of production, and evaluate the over-all production of that industry.

55. "The lack of preparation on the part of our planning agencies, combined with a considerable increase in the work required to build electric power stations (compared with the estimates), resulted in the conference being unable to set and to project the exact total cost of one kilowatt of capacity and the cost of producing one kilowatt-hour of power, since amortization is one of the basic elements of cost. It is essential that all the organizations in charge of building power stations, and above all the Electric Power Stations Section of the Organizational Committee and the Central Power Administration (*Glavenergo*), rectify this situation" (*ibid.*, Vol. VIII, p. 6).

56. The electrification of railroads was decided by the June 15, 1931, resolution of the plenary session of the Central Committee, which proposed the electrification of 3,690 kilometers of line (3,215 for freight transportation) in 1932 and 1933. The July 28, 1931, decree of the Council of People's Commissars reduced these goals to 3,540 kilometers for the three years 1932–1934, with 3,065 for freight transportation. (*Zheleznodorozhnyi transport SSSR v dokumentakh kommunisticheskoi partii i sovetskogo pravitelstva, 1917–1957* [Railroad Transportation in the USSR in Documents of the Communist Party and Soviet Government, 1917–1957], Moscow, 1957, pp. 244–55.)

The plan for the electrification of railroads presented in May 1932 repeated the same length of line to be electrified in 1932–1934 (3,043 kilometers for freight transportation) with a few minor modifications. For 1935–1937 and for the end of the general plan, it simply continued the same trend, and there is no doubt that the directives on the length of network to be electrified came from above.

57. *Generalnyi plan*, Vol. VI, p. 28.

58. For example, the plans set the capacity of motors at 10 kilowatts per 1,000 metric tons of pig iron, 6.7 kilowatts per 1,000 metric tons of steel, and 125 kilowatts per 1,000 metric tons of rolled steel (*ibid.*, Vol. VI, p. 30).

59. *Ibid.*, Vol. VI, p. 31.

60. Only the total volume of investment for new construction is given: 400 million rubles for 1928/29–1932, 1.5 billion rubles for 1933–1937, and 2–2.5 billion rubles for the whole period of the general plan (Kaplan *et al.*, *ibid.*, Vol. VI, p. 52).

Different methods were used to draft the plan for the electrification of agricultural production. The main work was done by the Union for Rural Electrification (*Soiuzselelektro*), the All-Union Electrotechnical Association (*Vsesoiuznoe Elektrotekhnicheskoe Obedinenie*), and the scientific research institutes of the state and collective farms, based on proposed models of certain state farms and certain Machine and Tractor Stations.[61] At the time the plan was undertaken, government policy favored the creation of very large farms, so the planners used as the basic unit a state farm with a herd of 40,000 cattle and 500,000 poultry.[62] But while the planners were working on their model, the government changed its policy and decided to have separate state farms specializing in livestock breeding.[63] The norms based on large farms became obsolete and new ones had to be drawn up. The task could not be finished by May 1932, so the planners published only part of their work, excluding the most important part on introducing electric power in livestock breeding (cattle, pigs, and poultry) and citing outdated norms for very large farms.[64] The discussion about farm size was really ideological, not economic. The first projects for the electrification of agricultural processes were condemned because they dared to suggest providing individual farmers (even kulaks) with electric plows and proposed producing small electric plows of 10 to 15 horsepower.[65]

Like the authors of the other parts of the General Electrification Plan, these authors had to observe not only the limitations on farm size but also several underlying compulsory assumptions. Electrification was basically reserved for industry and transportation, and agriculture was to be mechanized primarily through the use of tractors. The agricultural planners were to count on only 7 to 10 billion kilowatt-hours of electric power.[66] The share of various processes to be electrified on state and collective farms was also determined in advance. The same was true of the goals for agricultural production for 1933–1937, which were transmitted to the planners by the Office of the Five-Year Plan of the Commissariat of Agriculture.[67]

In view of these restrictions, the main task of the authors of the plan was to

61. These proposed models included prospects for changing the type and structure of production of farms with electric power, lists of processes to be electrified, methods of introducing electric power in each category of work, estimation of costs of electrification and of operation, specification of equipment required and method of electric power supply (*ibid.*, Vol. IV, p. 4).

62. *Ibid.*, Vol. IV, p. 11, and Vol. VIII, p. 51.

63. *Ibid.*, Vol. IV, pp. 4 and 105. See also the March 31, 1932, decree of the Council of People's Commissars, the Party Central Committee, and the USSR Commissariat of Agriculture, "On the Work of State Farms Specialized in Livestock Breeding" (*Ekonomicheskaia zhizn*, Book I, p. 242). The average size of state farms during the Second Five-Year Plan was to be 1,000 milk cows, 3,000 beef cattle, and 400 to 1,000 sows (*Generalnyi plan*, Vol. IV, p. 70).

64. Once the idea of large farms had been abandoned, the authors of the General Electrification Plan put forward the argument that in the United States the largest livestock farms had only 4,200 head of beef cattle. But opposition to the structure of American agricultural production had long been a favorite topic of Communist ideologists. (See Lomov, *ibid.*, Vol. III, p. 51. See also the attack on the Kondratiev-Oganovskii Plan in my *Planning*, pp. 45–47.)

65. I. B. Geronimus, *Generalnyi plan*, Vol. IV, pp. 9–10, and Lomov, *ibid.*, Vol. VIII, p. 51.

66. Geronimus (*ibid.*, Vol. IV, p. 14) put agricultural electric power consumption at 10 billion kilowatt-hours, whereas the resolutions of the May 1932 conference put it at only 7 billion (*ibid.*, Vol. VIII, p. 84).

67. A. S. Eremin, *ibid.*, Vol. IV, p. 105.

draw up norms for power needs and norms for the capacity of power stations necessary for various agricultural work. On the basis of these norms, they had to estimate equipment and investment needs.[68] All this work was reproduced in great detail, but the authors specified that they had in mind large-scale farms. Estimates of manpower and electric equipment needs for agriculture, by region, were also included.[69]

Later Variants of Second Five-Year Plan

There is a very definite gap in our knowledge of the drafting of the Second Five-Year Plan between the summer of 1932 and the beginning of 1934. We know only that Gosplan was to present a preliminary version of the plan by November 15, 1932, at the latest and a final version by January 15, 1933.[70]

Despite the covertness of the Soviet authorities, it is possible to get an idea of what happened to the vast amount of data amassed in the beginning of 1932. If the needs listed by the authors of the partial plans as necessary to implement the mandatory Party directives are aggregated, it is clear that the resulting totals are impossible to achieve. Thus, the work of the lower-echelon agencies was not useless because it showed the absurdity of the Party directives, an absurdity that no one could have pointed out directly. Was this lack of coordination in the Party directives demonstrated in physical terms or in the excessive requests for investment funds?

An examination of several partial plans shows that the investments requested were not far from half the total volume of investments envisaged in February for the second plan (140 to 150 billion rubles).[71] Just how inadequate that total was is made obvious by comparing the investments requested in May 1932 and those allocated in February 1934 (see Table 12). In the February 1934 variant the measures for which investments are specified (and thus can be compared) represent less than a quarter of total investments, while in the May 1932 variant they represent nearly half the total. Hence, if the May 1932 goals had been maintained, the investments required should have been more than doubled, amounting to 300 to 400 billion rubles. Just how tenuous the original plan was can be judged by remembering that total national income, according to the

68. Average norms were calculated for 1,000 milk cows, 1,000 head of beef cattle, 100,000 sheep, 1,000 hectares of cotton, etc., and applied to the projected production proportionately to the percentage of electrification of the various activities of state and collective farms (S. V. Shchurov, *ibid.*, Vol. IV, pp. 50–52 and 74–75).

The norms for equipment were drawn up by the Office of the Five-Year Plan of *Soiuzselelektro* according to models of electrification of types of state and collective farms. The norms were calculated per 1,000 kilowatts of installed capacity (large and small power stations) and separately for the various sectors: livestock breeding, milk, poultry, etc. This part of the plan was very detailed. (*Ibid.*, Vol. IV, pp. 73–79 and 104–57.)

69. According to Shchurov (*ibid.*, Vol IV, p. 80), electrification would necessitate the employment of 147,097 specialists in 1937. To understand why this figure is so large, we note that from 6,000 to 7,000 electrical engineers alone were needed and from 15,000 to 20,000 technicians, compared with the 200 engineers and 200 electrical technicians employed in *Soiuzselelektro* in 1932 (see Geronimus, *ibid.*, Vol. IV, p. 16).

70. Smilga, *Planovoe khoziaistvo*, No. 3, 1932, p. 17, note.

71. Kuibyshev, *Izbrannye proizvedeniia*, p. 351.

Table 12   Comparison of Investments Requested in May 1932 and Investments in Final Draft of Second Five-Year Plan (billion rubles)

	Total Investments for 1933–1937	
	Feb.–May 1932 Variant (1)	Feb. 1934 Final Draft (2)
1. Total investments:	140–150	133.4
2. Construction of electric power stations and network	15–20	5.4
3. Food industry (People's Commissariat of Food Supply)	10	5.3
4. Electrification of railroads	3.6	0.6
5. Housing construction, urban	25.0	13.4
6. Water and cleaning of cities	4.0	1.7
7. Urban transportation	3.5	1.1
8. Public baths and laundries	1.0	0.4
9. Urban electrification	1.5	0.6
10. Total of specified items	63.6–68.6	28.5
11. Electrification of agriculture	4.3	
12. Electrical industry, new plants	1.5	
13. Prospecting work	3.0	
14. Total of items specified in Feb.–May 1932 variant only	72.4–77.4	

Source
COLUMN 1–Line 1: Kuibyshev, *Izbrannye proizvedeniia*, p. 351. Kuibyshev does not specify the prices in which investment was expressed, but, to judge from the computations in *Generalnyi plan*, 1931 prices were probably used. **Line 2:** According to E. G. Nedler, "Elektrifikatsiia Kazakhstana" [The Electrification of Kazakhstan] in *Generalnyi plan*, Vol. VIII, p. 559, Kazakhstan Gosplan assumed a cost of 400 rubles for power stations (*kondensatsionnye aggregaty*) of up to 50,000 kw, 365 rubles for those of 50,000 to 100,000 kw (15 per cent more for heating plants, *teplofikatsionnye aggregaty*), and 1,000 rubles for hydraulic power stations. To this should be added the cost of building the interconnecting network, which was to amount to 1 billion rubles in 1931 prices. See A. I. Kolpakova, *Generalnyi plan*, Vol. IX, p. 99, and Vol. VIII for regional data (Vol. VIII, p. 559, for Kazakhstan). **Line 3:** I. Dolinskii, "O tempakh razvitiia pishchevoi promyshlennosti vo vtoroi piatiletke" [On Rates of Growth in the Food Industry in the Second Five-Year Plan], *Planovoe khoziaistvo*, No. 3, 1932, p. 63. **Line 4:** *Generalnyi plan*, Vol. III, p. viii. Excluding the cost of rolling stock. **Lines 5–9:** *Ibid.*, Vol. V, p. 32, and Vol. VIII, pp. 103–4. For housing construction, the figures take into account the following reduction in construction cost per square meter of floorspace: 80 rubles in 1933, 75 in 1934, 70 in 1935, 65 in 1936, and 60 in 1937. **Line 10:** Sum of lines 2–9. **Line 11:** Shchurov, *ibid.*, Vol. IV, p. 71. In 1931 prices without taking into account the reduction in costs. **Line 12:** Kaplan *et al.*, *ibid.*, Vol. VI, p. 52. No specification of prices. **Line 13:** V. P. Novikov, *ibid.*, Vol. I., p. 479. No specification of prices. **Line 14:** Sum of lines 2–9 and 11–13.
     COLUMN 2–Lines 1-9: *Vtoroi plan*, pp. 442, 444, 557, 646, 677, and 719. In 1933 plan prices. **Line 10:** Sum of lines 2–9.

February 1932 estimates, was to have been 500 billion rubles for the whole period 1933–1937.[72]

The lack of coherence of the draft plan of February 1932 is so obvious that it is pointless to inquire whether it was drawn up from balances in physical terms or in value terms. The needs listed by the authors of the sector plans could not help but snowball once they went to USSR Gosplan. To satisfy them, it would have been necessary to increase production goals, hence investment goals, etc., and reduce consumption goals.

The reaction of the central planning agencies was not long in coming. Already Smilga's article, published during the third quarter of 1932 and obviously in-

72. Grinko, *Pravda*, February 6, 1932.

spired by Gosplan, had criticized the arbitrary calculation of "needs" (in quotation marks in the text) and several precise goals, such as for the electrification of 18,000 to 20,000 kilometers of railroad line during 1933–1937; it also emphasized the importance of the figures in the annual plan for 1932, which were taken as a solid fixed base.[73] The poor fulfillment of the 1932 annual plan must have further diminished the coherence of the original plan draft (February–May 1932).[74] As already mentioned, Gosplan was to present a preliminary version of the five-year plan on November 15, 1932, and a final version on January 15, 1933, but no trace of one has been found in any of the sources consulted. Only the abridged text of the annual plan for 1933 was adopted at a plenary session of the Party Central Committee on January 7–12, 1933.[75]

Despite the silence of the Soviet authorities on the subject of the five-year plan, there is no doubt that it was revised at the end of 1932 and the beginning of 1933. That can be seen in Table 13, which compares the annual plan for 1933 with the earlier five-year plan goals drafted for 1933 in February–May 1932.[76] The reduction of the earlier 1933 goals by 30 to 50 per cent proves that the goals for 1937 must also have been reduced at that time. However, an examination of the projections in Charts 4–6, which, for the five-year plans, generally extrapolate the results of the preceding years and the annual plan forecasts, shows that the new variant of the five-year plan (of November 1932–January 1933) still contained some rates of growth higher than those adopted definitively a year later. The poor fulfillment of the 1933 plan and the (very slight) reduction of the growth rates made during the Seventeenth Party Congress (January 26–February 10, 1934) again entailed considerable changes in the plan.[77]

What matters in the final text of the plan is not the slower rates of growth as much as its coherence. In other words, the question to be examined is the viability of the plan.

Final Text of Second Five-Year Plan

The revisions made in the draft of the Second Five-Year Plan at the Seventeenth Party Congress seem minor. Ordzhonikidze, People's Commissar of Heavy Industry, proposed the reduction of the average rate of growth of industrial production from 18.9 to 16.5 per cent and small reductions in the 1937 goals for

73. Smilga, *Planovoe khoziaistvo*, No. 3, 1932 (this issue went to press on September 15, 1932), pp. 25 and 18.

74. On this subject, see my *Planning*, pp. 228–35.

75. In the decree, "Results of the First Five-Year Plan and the National Economic Plan for 1933, the First Year of the Second Five-Year Plan," *KPSS v rezoliutsiiakh*, Part II, pp. 717–42. See also *O narodnokhoziaistvennom plane i finansovoi programme pervogo goda vtoroi piatiletki. Doklady i Rezoliutsii, III Sezd TsIK SSSR, Ianvar 1933* [On the National Economic Plan and Financial Program of the First Year of the Second Five-Year Plan. Reports and Resolutions, Third Congress of USSR Central Executive Committee, January 1933], Leningrad, 1933, reports of Molotov and Kuibyshev.

76. The annual goals of the February–May 1932 variant are only partly known from the reports of the participants in the May 1932 Conference on the General Electrification Plan, but the information is sufficient to show the fundamental difference between the earlier drafts and the 1933 plan.

77. *KPSS v rezoliutsiiakh*, Part II, pp. 743–97. The reductions made at the Seventeenth Party Congress were proposed by Ordzhonikidze, Commissar of Heavy Industry, on February 4, 1934. When he declared that the new rates of growth were still very high, all the delegates applauded him (G. K. Ordzhonikidze, *Statii i rechi* [Articles and Speeches], Moscow, 1957, pp. 556–58.)

Table 13   Revisions of Original Goals of Second Five-Year Plan Made in Annual Plan for 1933

	Units	Goals for 1933 in Feb.–May 1932 Variant of Five-Year Plan (1)	Annual Plan for 1933 (2)	Actual Results in 1933 (3)
1. Electric power (capacity)	mill. kw	7.5	5.7	5.6
2. Coal, Kuzbass	thous. m. tons	21,000	10,700	9,160
3. Pig iron	thous. m. tons	13,000	9,000	7,110
4. Steel	thous. m. tons	14,500	8,950	6,889
5. Rolled steel	thous. m. tons	10,000	6,255	5,065
6. Rails, deliveries to RR	thous. m. tons	700		517
7. Steam turbines	thous. kw	1,900	608	635
8. Steam boilers	thous. m²	465	158	154
9. Electric locomotives	units	107		17

Source
COLUMN 1–Lines 1 and 7-8: A. E. Maleev, *Generalnyi plan*, Vol. VI, pp. 347, 349, and 360. **Line 2:** A. K. Shmidt, *ibid.*, Vol. I, p. 229. **Lines 3-5:** Kaplan *et al.*, *ibid.*, Vol. VI, p. 31. **Line 6:** Libin, *ibid.*, Vol. III, p. 56. **Line 9:** *Ibid.*, Vol. III, p. ix.
   COLUMN 2–Line 1: *Pravda*, January 31, 1933, p. 1. **Line 2:** *Vtoraia ugolnaia baza SSSR—Kuzbass* [Second Coal Basin of the USSR—Kuzbass], Moscow, 1935–1936, Vol. I, p. 29. **Lines 3-5 and 7-8:** Table A-2, col. 1.
   COLUMN 3–Line 1: *Promyshlennost*, p. 171. **Lines 2 and 6:** *Sotsialisticheskoe stroitelstvo SSSR* [Socialist Construction in the USSR], Moscow, 1936, pp. 100–101. **Lines 3-5 and 7-9:** Table A-2, col. 2.

machine-building and the principal metallurgical products (see Table 15). The revisions proposed by A. I. Mikoyan for the food industry and by I. E. Liubimov for light industry were hardly more substantial. Nor were these reductions spontaneous; Molotov announced to the Congress that they had been approved by the Party Politburo.[78]

In theory, the revisions merely entailed reducing the growth rates of industrial production, for both producer and consumer goods; but only the share of industry in the growth of national income was reduced; for the other sectors, the same goals were maintained (see Table 14). In actual fact, the purpose of the revisions was to make the plan less taut by introducing greater austerity. The investment goals (133.4 billion rubles in 1933 plan prices) were maintained untouched. The resulting reduction in national income (7.9 billion rubles in 1926/27 prices in 1937 alone) came entirely from consumption, for which the index relative to 1932 was reduced from 257.6 to 242.1 (see Table 14). This had a direct effect on the volume of state and cooperative retail trade, reducing it from 94.6 billion rubles to 80.0 billion (in 1932 prices).[79] That this policy was carried out at the expense of the Soviet consumer can also be seen from the reduction of the goals for gross industrial production in 1937 (see Table 14). For heavy industry the reduction

78. *XVII Sezd Vsesoiuznoi Kommunisticheskoi Partii, 26 ianvaria–10 fevralia 1934 g.* [Seventeenth Congress of the USSR Communist Party, January 26–February 10, 1934], Moscow, 1934, p. 522. This explains why the official summary quotes the approving remarks of Voroshilov, Vareikis, and Kirov (*ibid.*, p. 436).
79. Excluding tobacco and alcohol. See *Proekt vtorogo plana*, p. 522, and *Vtoroi plan*, p. 521.

Table 14 Comparison of 1937 Goals for Principal Indexes in Last Two Variants of Second Five-Year Plan

	Draft Plan (end of 1933)		Final Plan (Feb. 1934)	
	Billion Rubles (1)	Index (1932 = 100) (2)	Billion Rubles (3)	Index (1932 = 100) (4)
National income (1926/27 prices):	108.1	237.6	100.2	220.2
Industry	51.5	250.0	46.4	225.2
Agriculture	17.6	210.0	17.6	210.0
Construction	14.3	230.0	14.3	230.0
Transportation (rail, water, and motor)	4.8	190.0	4.8	190.0
National income (1932 prices):				
Accumulation		180.1		180.3
Consumption		257.6		242.1
Reserves		160.9		160.9
Accumulation (per cent of total)	18.7		19.4	
Consumption (per cent of total)	79.5		78.7	
Gross industrial production (1926/27 prices):	102.7	237.2	92.7	214.1
Commissariat of Heavy Industry	35.7	250.1	33.5	234.6
Commissariat of Timber Industry	3.6	202.4	3.6	200.0
Commissariat of Light Industry	23.5	300.0	19.5	249.0
Commissariat of Food Supply	13.1	282.7	11.9	256.1
Producer goods (group A)	48.4[a]	209.4[a]	45.5	197.2
Consumer goods (group B)	54.3[a]	268.8[a]	47.2	233.6

Source: Unless otherwise indicated, cols. 1–2: *Proekt vtorogo plana*, pp. 411 and 422–45; cols. 3–4: *Vtoroi plan*, pp. 427, 429, and 686–87.

a. V. M. Molotov, *XVII Sezd*, pp. 356 and 358.

was only 2.2 billion rubles, whereas for light industry and the food industry it was 5.2 billion rubles and for local industry 0.4 billion.

The importance of these figures is purely relative. The chances for complete fulfillment of the plan were minimal at best, and Soviet planners no doubt remembered the fate of other long-range plans drawn up since 1925. Much more important was the immediate effect of the decision to revise the annual goals of the Second Five-Year Plan, whose results are presented in Table 15. Unfortunately, the only information available is for industry.[80] In any case, the revisions do not appear to have been easily made. Although the Seventeenth Party Congress finished its work on February 10, 1934, the final text of the Second Five-Year Plan appeared only on November 17, 1934. No doubt the revision of the goals and the balances for the next few years gave rise to discussions and bargaining, but absolutely no mention of this could be found in the sources consulted.

80. Several other goals for each of the plan years are also given for investment, transportation, and percentages of the reduction in cost of production. But since this part of the plan was not substantially revised, these figures were not included in Table 15. More important revisions were made in employment, wages, gross agricultural production, and especially in retail trade. But the annual goals of the five-year plan for these sectors are not available.

Table 15 Effect of Revisions of 1937 Goals on Annual Goals of Second Five-Year Plan

	Second Five-Year Plan Goals for			
	1934	1935	1936	1937
Gross industrial production (1926/27 prices)				
Draft plan (billion rubles)	55.8	67.8	82.5	102.7
Final plan (billion rubles)	55.8	64.8	76.9	92.7
Draft plan (per cent of preceding year)	119.0	121.5	121.7	124.5
Final plan (per cent of preceding year)	119.0	116.1	118.7	120.5
Commissariat of Heavy Industry (1926/27 prices)				
Draft plan (billion rubles)	19.6	23.6	29.0	35.7
Final plan (billion rubles)	19.3	22.8	27.6	33.5
Draft plan (per cent of preceding year)	123.2	120.6	122.7	123.4
Final plan (per cent of preceding year)	124.3	117.8	121.0	121.5
Commissariat of Timber Industry (1926/27 prices)				
Draft plan (billion rubles)	2.1	2.5	2.9	3.6
Final plan (billion rubles)	2.1	2.5	2.9	3.6
Draft plan (per cent of preceding year)	115.5	119.0	119.9	123.7
Final plan (per cent of preceding year)	114.7	118.0	118.7	123.3
Commissariat of Light Industry (1926/27 prices)				
Draft plan (billion rubles)	8.9	12.1	16.4	23.5
Final plan (billion rubles)	8.9	10.8	14.2	19.5
Draft plan (per cent of preceding year)	110.2	135.4	136.1	143.3
Final plan (per cent of preceding year)	110.7	120.2	132.3	137.0
Commissariat of Food Supply (1926/27 prices)				
Draft plan (billion rubles)	5.9	7.6	9.8	13.1
Final plan (billion rubles)	6.0	7.2	9.1	11.9
Draft plan (per cent of preceding year)	122.1	128.1	130.1	133.0
Final plan (per cent of preceding year)	123.9	119.6	126.7	130.7
Machine-building and metalworking [a] (1926/27 prices)				
Draft plan (billion rubles)	9.7	11.7	14.1	17.1
Final plan (billion rubles)	9.6	11.2	13.3	15.8
Pig iron				
Draft plan (million metric tons)	10.0	12.7	15.1	18.0
Final plan (million metric tons)	10.0	12.2	14.0	16.0
Steel ingots and castings				
Draft plan (million metric tons)	9.8	12.0	15.5	19.0
Final plan (million metric tons)	9.8	12.1	14.8	17.0
Rolled steel				
Draft plan (million metric tons)	6.6	8.3	11.0	14.0
Final plan (million metric tons)	6.6	8.0	10.5	13.0
Cotton fabrics (incl. unfinished)				
Draft plan (million meters)	3,059.2	3,650	4,800	6,250
Final plan (million meters)	3,059.2	3,475	4,215	5,100
Raw sugar				
Draft plan (thousand metric tons)	1,400	1,700	2,100	2,800
Final plan (thousand metric tons)	1,400	1,650	2,000	2,500
Fish catch				
Draft plan (thousand metric tons)	1,500	1,600	1,750	1,900
Final plan (thousand metric tons)	1,500	1,550	1,660	1,800

Source: Draft plan from *Proekt vtorogo plana*, pp. 442–47 and 454–57; final plan from *Vtoroi plan*, pp. 686–87, 690–91, and 704–5.

a. In the Commissariat of Heavy Industry.

The first conclusion that can be drawn from Table 15 is that the revision had no effect on the goals for 1934. The few minor changes that appear resulted from changes in methods of calculation, a fact noted in the official text. Apparently the agencies in charge of revising the five-year plan had no authority to touch the figures in the 1934 annual plan. If they had had such authority, they would certainly have revised the volume of investments planned for 1934 and changed by the government during the year.[81] Actually, it was a three-year plan (1935–1937) that the authors of the final text of the five-year plan were instructed to draft. This new text was simply to be stuck onto the 1934 annual plan without any critical evaluation of its chances of fulfillment.

The real concern of the authors of this new three-year plan seems, moreover, not to make the plan as a whole more coherent but to make it more feasible in the immediate future, that is, in 1935. The indexes of annual growth are actually lower for 1935 than for 1936 and 1937. This increase in the growth indexes for the later years of the long-range plan is theoretically justified by the return expected on investments. In fact, the authors of the new plan knew very well that it was impossible to plan the exact date when new factories would be opened and start operating efficiently (which depended largely on the workers mastering the new technology). Pushing the high growth rates forward to the later years of the plan simply meant relaxing the tautness of the plan in the expectation that it would be modified eventually or put in a state of abeyance. These methods are probably largely responsible for the silence of Soviet authorities about the annual sections of the five-year plans published after 1934. We can still find traces of these practices in the seven-year plan for 1959–1965, in which lower growth rates were planned for industrial production in the first years and much higher ones for the later years of the plan. But the planners were reluctant to publish these data and did so only when the plan was revised.[82]

It is impossible to judge from the published figures how successful the planners were in making the first year (1935) of the three-year plan (1935–1937) coherent. The success of their work depended on the results of the 1934 annual plan, and the extent to which it was possible to "launch" the five-year (three-year) plan in 1935 will become clear later. Meanwhile, the coherence of the final text of the plan should be examined briefly.

81. The volume of investment planned for 1934 (25.11 billion rubles in current prices) was reduced during the year to 23.52 billion, and the corresponding changes were undoubtedly known in November 1934. See *Narodno-khoziaistvennyi plan na 1935 god* [The National Economic Plan for 1935], 1st ed., Moscow, 1935, p. 93n.

82. The main difficulty is that the growth rates for industrial production and starting up new productive capacities were set at much higher levels for the last years of the Seven-Year Plan than for the first years. To achieve an average annual rate of growth of gross industrial production of 8.8 per cent, the average annual rate set for the first three years was 8.3 per cent and for the last three years 9.5 per cent (with 9.8 per cent for 1965). See "Rezervy semiletki—v deistvie" [Reserves of the Seven-Year Plan in Operation], *Planovoe khoziaistvo*, No. 7, 1962, p. 5.

CHAPTER 7

Internal Coherence of Second Five-Year Plan

Principal Goals and Success Criteria of the Plan

The final text of the Second Five-Year Plan fully incorporated the basic political and social goals presented at the Seventeenth Party Conference in February 1932.[1] Molotov gave details on progress in planned collectivization in his speech on February 3, 1934, at the Seventeenth Party Congress. The priority given in the plan to social goals, especially to collectivization, can be seen in Table 16. But, while there is no doubt about their intentions regarding collectivization, the Soviet planners seemed to be trying to prove too much in setting the 1937 share of the socialist sector at 100 per cent in all branches of the economy. In discussing industry, Molotov made no mention of small-scale or artisan industry, and, in discussing agriculture, he passed off the private plots of collective and state farmers as socialist forms of agriculture. In discussing retail trade, he ignored the collective farm market and the "bazaar" (a sort of free market for consumer goods), and he said nothing about construction of private houses. One therefore wonders just how the 100 per cent of national income to be obtained from socialist forms of production was calculated. But it is obvious that the other goals were secondary, to be achieved only if convenient; the same is true of the two-and-a-half to threefold increase[2] in the standard of living of the workers and collective farmers and the technical reconstruction of the economy. Therefore, it was possible for Molotov to declare that, despite the changes made in the text of the plan after the Seventeenth Party Conference, particularly in industry, "the

1. V. M. Molotov's statement at that conference is given *in toto* in his speech at the Seventeenth Party Congress. See *XVII Sezd Vsesoiuznoi Kommunisticheskoi Partii, 26 ianvaria–10 fevralia 1934 g.* [Seventeenth Congress of the USSR Communist Party, January 26–February 10, 1934], Moscow, 1934, pp. 351 ff.
2. Here Molotov is referring to the draft of the plan and not to the final text, which provided for an increase of 142.1 per cent in consumption between 1932 and 1937 (see Table 14 in Chapter 6).

Table 16 Share of Socialist Sector in Various Branches of the Economy, 1928, 1932, and 1937 (per cent of total)

	1928	1932	Planned for 1937
Share in:			
Gross industrial production	99.0	99.93	100.0
Gross agricultural production [a]	3.0	74.7	100.0
Total sown area [a]	2.8	79.7	100.0
National income	44.0	93.0	100.0
Retail trade	75.2	99.0	100.0
Percentage of peasant farms collectivized	1.7	61.5	100.0

Source: Molotov, *XVII Sezd*, p. 352.

a. Including private plots of collective farmers.

principal goals of the Second Five-Year Plan are expressed in the proposals presented to the congress in complete accord with the decisions of the Seventeenth Party Conference."[3]

The main economic goals of the Second Five-Year Plan are presented in Table 17. On the average, the principal indexes were to double in four years, starting from the preliminary results for 1933. This was true of national income as well as industrial and agricultural production and real wages. The outstanding features of the plan were the more rapid growth of consumption than of accumulation and the greater increase planned for consumer goods (Group B) than for producer goods (Group A) in gross industrial production. This relative favoring of Group B, unusual in Soviet planning, reflects the very low level of consumption in 1932 and the crisis experienced that year, rather than any change in policy. High planned rates of growth do not necessarily imply a high priority. Such an implication would be justified only in an entirely coherent plan that had a chance of being wholly fulfilled. What must be examined, then, is the extent to which the final text of the plan reflected these requirements and the realism of the premises on which the plan's chances for success rested.

It must be emphasized that the statistical data published on the Second Five-Year Plan do not facilitate studying its coherence. Contrary to their practice in the First Five-Year Plan, the Soviet authorities kept secret all the physical balances, and only in the course of discussion did it become clear how precarious these balances were. Thus, Iu. L. Piatakov pointed out the fragile balance for petroleum and the deficit balance for rolled steel, which was to be alleviated after 1935; he also stressed that the solution to the problem of nickel was one of the most difficult in the five-year plan.[4]

The value balances were also kept secret. Only the financial plan was published (and in only an aggregated version), and the main data given in value terms were very incomplete, usually for the last year of the plan, and often in different prices, making their integration into value balances particularly diffi-

3. *XVII Sezd*, p. 353.
4. *Ibid.*, pp. 460 and 462.

cult. The prices used were sometimes 1926/27 prices, sometimes 1932, 1933 plan, 1933, and even current prices adjusted to take into account planned price reductions. Nevertheless, examination of the one balance that was published— the financial plan (see Table 18)—roughly shows the bases of the planned equilibrium. This equilibrium rests mainly on a planned reduction in prices, which was to reduce the total income of the socialist sector for 1933–1937 by 13 per cent. This reduction would allow expenditures for the national economy to increase only by 55 per cent in five years (while national income was to increase by 120 per cent) and expenditures for administration and defense to increase by 72 per cent. The doubling in five years of social expenditures is also particularly important in view of the planned reduction of prices.

Table 17 Principal Goals of Second Five-Year Plan (billion rubles, unless otherwise indicated)

	Final Results in 1932 (1)	Preliminary Results in 1933 (2)	Goals for 1937	
			Billion Rubles (3)	Index (1932 = 100) (4)
National income (1926/27 prices):	45.5	48.5[a]	100.2	220.2
Industry	20.6	23.0	46.4	225.2
Agriculture	8.4	9.2	17.6	210.0
Construction	6.2	5.6	14.3	230.0
Transportation (rail, water, and motor)	2.5	2.6	4.8	190.0
Trade	6.0[a]	6.0[a]		
Accumulation				180.3
Consumption				242.1
Reserves				160.9
Gross industrial production (1926/27 prices):	43.3	46.9	92.7	214.1
Producer goods (group A)	23.1		45.5	197.2
Consumer goods (group B)	20.2		47.2	233.6
Gross agricultural production (1926/27 prices):	13.1	14.0[a]	26.2	200.1
Investment:[b]				
Total in 1933 plan prices		18.0	32.0	133.4[c]
Total in current prices	20.1[d]	18.0	25.6	120.1[c]
Employment, workers and employees (millions):				
National economy	22.9	22.3[a]	28.9	126.0
Industry	8.0	7.9[e]	10.2	128.0
Wage fund, workers and employees, national economy	32.7	35.0[a]	50.7	155.0
Fund for services and housing for nonagricul. workers	4.3		9.3	215.5
Average money wage, workers and employees, nat. econ. (rubles per yr.)	1,427	1,566[a]	1,755	123.0
Average real wage				196.0
State and cooperative retail trade (excl. tobacco and alcohol):[f]				
In 1932 prices	27.1		67.3	248.2
In 1933 prices			81.6	
In current prices	27.1		53.0	195.6
Public eating places[g]	4.9	6.4	12.7	264.6

Table 17 *continued*

	Final Results in 1932 (1)	Preliminary Results in 1933 (2)	Goals for 1937 Billion Rubles (3)	Goals for 1937 Index (1932 = 100) (4)
State and cooperative retail trade (incl. tobacco and alcohol):				
In 1932 prices	40.4[a]			
In current prices	40.4[a]	49.8[a]		
Labor productivity (per worker):				
Large-scale industry				163.0
Construction (net)				175.0
Railroad transportation (ton-kilometers)				143.0
Reduction in cost of production (per cent):				
Industry		1.5[h]	8.5[h]	26.0[i]
Agriculture (state farms)				63.3[i]
Construction (net)		0[h]	11.5[h]	40.0[i]
Railroad transportation				10.5[i]
Trade (socialist sector)				26.0[i]
Saving effected by reduction in production costs, 1933–1937:				
Industry			13.0	
Construction (net)			8.8	
Price index in state and cooperative retail trade				65[j]

Source: Unless otherwise indicated, *Vtoroi piatiletnii plan razvitiia narodnogo khoziaistva SSSR (1933–1937)* [Second Five-Year Plan for the Development of the USSR National Economy, 1933–1937], Moscow, 1934, pp. 427–29, 435, 521, 530–31, 716–17, and 728. This final text of the plan was approved in February 1934 but published only on November 17, 1934.

a. Final results (*Sotsialisticheskoe stroitelstvo SSSR* [Socialist Construction in the USSR], Moscow, 1936, pp. xxxii, 4, 6, 8, 30, and 407).

b. Excluding investments made from collective farms' and farmers' own resources (5.0 billion rubles for 1933–1937 in 1933 plan prices, 0.5 billion in 1933, and 1.6 billion in 1937) and excluding public participation in road construction (1.7 billion rubles for 1933–1937 in 1933 plan prices, 285 million in 1933, and 405 million in 1937). See *Vtoroi plan*, p. 716.

c. Total for 1933–1937 in billion rubles.

d. *Sotsialisticheskoe stroitelstvo*, 1936, p. 394.

e. *Narodno-khoziaistvennyi plan na 1935 god* [The National Economic Plan for 1935], 2nd ed., Moscow, 1935, p. 640.

f. Excluding public eating places.

g. *Sotsialisticheskoe stroitelstvo*, 1936, p. 606. According to *Proekt vtorogo piatiletnego plana razvitiia narodnogo khoziaistva SSSR (1933–1937 gg.)* [Draft of Second Five-Year Plan for the Development of the USSR National Economy, 1933–1937], Moscow, 1934, Vol. I, pp. 522 and 530, prices in public eating places did not change between 1932 and 1933. The original 1937 goal for public eating places was 13,920 million rubles in both 1932 and 1933 prices.

h. Relative to preceding year.

i. Relative to 1932.

j. 1933 plan prices = 100.

The size of the planned price decrease is not completely known. For state and cooperative retail trade (excluding tobacco and alcohol), prices in 1935 were to be 35 per cent lower than in 1933. But it is likely that the prices of tobacco and alcohol were to go up. The price of bread was doubled on August 20, 1933, and

Table 18   Financial Resources in Second Five-Year Plan (billion rubles)

	1932	Planned for 1937	Total for 1933–1937
Income			
1. Accumulation of socialist sector without allowance			
for price reduction:	33.8	93.7	328.0
Profits	6.6	24.7	72.9
Turnover tax	19.6	59.4	216.1
2. Accumulation of socialist sector with allowance for			
price reduction:	33.8	65.1	273.0
Depreciation of fixed capital	2.0	5.9	20.2
Mobilized resources of the population	8.2	9.0	44.6
Other income	0.6	4.1	17.7
Total with allowance for price reduction	44.6	84.1	355.5
Total without allowance for price reduction	44.6	112.7	410.5
Expenditures			
1. Financing of national economy:	30.2	46.8	221.4
Investments	19.2	24.0	113.9
Increase in working capital	4.1	5.5	28.2
2. Financing of social and cultural measures (excl.			
resources of economic organizations):	9.5	20.2	75.4
Investments	0.4	1.7	5.5
3. Expenditures for administration and defense	2.5	4.3	19.0
4. Expenditures for state loans	1.0	2.8	10.0
5. Other expenditures	1.4	3.5	15.7
Total expenditures	44.6	77.6	341.5
State reserve		6.5	14.0
Grand total	44.6	84.1	355.5

Source: *Vtoroi plan*, pp. 540–41.

the retail price index was certainly higher in 1933 than in 1932. It can, therefore, be assumed that the reduction in prices planned for 1937 was much less than the 35 per cent cited.[5] Less can be said about wholesale prices because it was impossible to find any direct information. Reductions in the cost of production planned for 1934–1937 were sizable (see Table 17) and in 1937 alone represented a saving of 34.5 billion rubles over 1932.[6]

Planned price decreases made it possible to include several otherwise impossible goals in the five-year plan and still keep the plan officially balanced. Gross industrial production was to increase by 114 per cent but employment in industry by only 28 per cent. Real wages were to increase by 96 per cent, while average money wages were to go up by only 23 per cent. The cost of investment was also smaller in current prices. The source of all these anticipated achievements was the planned increase in productivity (see Table 17). In his

5. Naum Jasny (*Soviet Industrialization, 1928–1952*, Chicago, 1961, p. 156) estimates that the level of retail prices planned in the Second Five-Year Plan for 1937 would have been 2.7 times that in 1928. In my *Planning for Economic Growth in the Soviet Union, 1918–1932* (translated and edited by Marie-Christine MacAndrew and G. Warren Nutter, Chapel Hill, N.C., 1971, p. 395), the level of prices in state and cooperative retail trade in 1932 is estimated at 310 (1928 = 100). Thus the planned reduction would be only 13 per cent, but this figure is given with reservations.

6. *Vtoroi plan*, p. 518.

speech on the plan, Molotov explained the grounds for these expectations.[7]

The main source of the planned increase in productivity lay in technological progress. Thanks to a greater mastery of new technology, to the greater experience acquired by managerial personnel, to the utilization of reserves of unemployed labor,[8] and to socialist competition, production was to increase more than would arise merely from the new capacities put into operation (see Chapter 11). Planned increases in capacity and production, according to Piatakov's draft and shown in Table 19, imply substantial productivity increases.

Table 19   Increase in Capacity and Production Envisaged during Second Five-Year Plan (per cent)

	Capacity	Production
Tractor building	48	99
Steel ingots and castings	135	223
Zinc	445	585
Cement	64	105
Coal	104	136

Source: Iu. L. Piatakov, XVII Sezd, p. 463.

The statement of the sources of the planned increase in productivity shows regression from precise calculations into the vague realm of wish. How was measurement to be made of the experience acquired by peasants whom collectivization had chased from their villages? The premises of the plan were so vague that the real problem was not to fulfill the plan in 1937 but just to put it into operation in 1935.

1934 Annual Plan Fulfillment and Launching Five-Year Plan in 1935

Fulfillment of the annual plan for 1934 is important in studying the Second Five-Year Plan because it affected adoption of the final text of the plan. The principal data are summarized in Table 20. To a considerable extent, the plan was not fulfilled for individual series, especially in construction materials, machine-building, and transportation. There was also unwanted overfulfillment, mostly in employment and money wages. However, the aggregate indexes computed from official Soviet estimates give a significantly different picture of achievements in 1934. The plan for industrial and agricultural production was just about fulfilled, and the plan for retail trade, in current prices, was overfulfilled;[9]

7. *XVII Sezd*, pp. 364–65.

8. According to Molotov, in many enterprises the number of working hours was only five to five and a half a day (compared with the seven planned). See *ibid.*, p. 364. Labor turnover must also be taken into account. In 1934, for instance, the number of workers newly hired was about the same as the average number of workers on the payroll (accession rate of 100.5 per cent) and the number of workers quitting was also nearly the same (separation rate of 96.7 per cent). See *Socialist Construction in the U.S.S.R.*, Moscow, 1936, p. 388.

9. *Narodno-khoziaistvennyi plan na 1935 god* [The National Economic Plan for 1935], 1st ed., Moscow, 1935, pp. 79, 83, and 90.

Table 20   Fulfillment of 1934 Annual Plan (per cent)

National income (1926/27 prices)	92.7	Steam boilers	70.0
		Railroad freight cars (2-axle units)	68.9
Industry		Grain combines	68.7
Official Soviet Estimates		Hydraulic turbines	67.4[e]
Producer goods (1926/27 prices)	98.1	Spinning machines	65.5
Total value of production (1926/27 prices)	97.8	Looms	61.3
Consumer goods (1926/27 prices)	97.6	Turbogenerators	60.8
		Roofing tiles	58.8
Producer Goods		Ground natural phosphate	53.1
Synthetic dyes	114.1	Steam and gas turbines	52.0
Machine tools	111.2	Electric locomotives	47.5
Aluminum	110.7	Oil shale	45.9
Electric power	110.5	Diesel locomotives	40.0
Manganese ore	107.1	Metallurgical equipment	39.4
Rolled steel	106.6		
Nickel	106.6	*Consumer Goods*	
Soda ash	106.1	Knitted outer garments	248.9
Hydroelectric power	104.8	Refined sugar	121.8[f]
Coke	104.6	Cameras	120.4
Pig iron	104.3	Enameled kitchenware	114.3
Tires	103.1	Cheese	111.3
Phosphoric fertilizer (18.7% P_2O_5)	102.7	Butter	110.1
Tractors (15 hp)	102.4	Cotton yarn	109.9
Peat	101.4	Woolen fabrics	108.3
Trucks and buses	100.7	Fish catch (including whales and shellfish)	103.1
Motor vehicles, total	100.6	Leather shoes	102.5
Automobiles	100.6	Silk and rayon fabrics	101.9
Plywood	100.6	Fish catch	101.8[g]
Natural gas	99.6	Raw sugar	100.3
Steel ingots and castings	98.9	Starch and syrup	100.3
Phosphoric fertilizer (14% P_2O_5)	98.9	Rubber footwear	100.0
Tractors	98.9	Salt	98.5
Iron ore	98.7	Beer	98.3
Coal	97.3	Vegetable oil	97.9
Sulfuric acid	97.1	Rubber galoshes	97.9
Lumber	96.9	Watches	96.0[h]
Steam locomotives	96.6	Furniture	94.6[h]
Window glass (m²)	96.5	Cigarettes	92.9
Paper	94.3	Soap (40% fatty acid)	92.7
Lime	94.1	Low-grade tobacco (*makhorka*)	92.7
Synthetic rubber	92.5	Margarine	92.3
Zinc	90.5	Matches	91.1
Steel pipes	89.4	Hosiery	90.8
Turbogenerators (hydraulic)	89.1[a]	Meat	89.4
Paperboard	87.2	Cotton fabrics	89.4
Copper ore	86.8[b]	Yeast	89.3[h]
Industrial timber hauled	84.1	Felt footwear	89.3
Asbestos shingles	83.5	Metal beds	89.2
Refined copper	83.3	Flour (procurements)	88.1
Bricks	82.9	Canned food	86.9
Crude petroleum	82.8	Bicycles	85.8
Lead	82.4	Crude alcohol	85.8
Lead and zinc ore	82.4[c]	Confectionery	84.9
Cement	81.3	Linen fabrics (m²)	79.5
Excavators	81.0	Sewing machines, household	65.2
Railroad freight cars	78.2	Macaroni	64.7
Ammonium sulfate	75.3	Phonographs	45.5
Railroad passenger cars	74.7	Radios	32.0
Electrolytic copper	74.4[d]		

Table 20 *continued*

Agriculture

Official Soviet Estimates

Animal production (1926/27 prices)	105.9
Total agricultural production (1926/27 prices)	93.5
Vegetable production (1926/27 prices)	90.5

Harvest and Animal Production

Millet	133.1[i]
Oats	117.2
Meat and fat	108.6
Wheat	100.2
Wool	99.8
Milk	98.6
Grain (biological yield)	98.0
Pigs	96.4[j]
Beef cattle	95.8[j]
Sunflowers	95.7
Sheep and goats	94.8[j]
Cows	93.1[j]
Flax fiber	92.7
Horses	92.1[j]
Buckwheat groats	92.1[k]
Barley	89.2
Potatoes	89.0
Rye	84.5
Corn	84.2
Raw cotton	83.1
Sugar beets	80.3

Market Production

Milk and dairy products	106.3
Meat and fat	103.8
Grain, total	101.4
Raw cotton	82.9
Potatoes	81.2

Procurements

Grain, total	104.5
Meat and fat (dead weight)	93.3
Milk and dairy products	93.0

Transportation

Railroad

Average length of haul, total	106.2
Coal and coke (tons)	102.4
Ore (tons)	100.0
Length of network	99.9
Firewood (tons)	96.3
Freight traffic (ton-km)	95.7
Freight traffic (tons)	90.1
Timber (tons)	90.0
Ferrous metals (tons)	87.5
Passenger traffic (pass.-km)	87.1
Grain and flour (tons)	85.7
Average daily carloadings	81.9
Oil and oil products (tons)	81.2
Principal construction materials	71.4
Cement (tons)	50.1[l]

Inland Waterway

Timber transported in ships	102.9[h]
Length of network	98.7

Timber rafted	95.2[h]
Average length of haul	91.5
Freight traffic (tons)	89.3
Oil and oil products (tons)	87.8
Salt (tons)	83.3
Grain and flour (tons)	82.9
Freight traffic (ton-km)	81.7
Mineral construction materials (tons)	81.1
Coal and coke (tons)	75.4
Passenger traffic (pass.-km)	63.8

Maritime (Soviet ships)

Passenger traffic (pass.-km)	100.3
Average length of haul	98.2
Freight traffic (tons)	91.9
Freight traffic (ton-km)	90.2

Air

Freight traffic, incl. mail (tons)	157.5[m]
Passenger traffic (passengers)	137.0
Freight traffic, incl. mail (ton-km)	85.7
Average length of haul	55.8[n]

Employment

Credit institutions	116.5
Other transport (motor, etc.)	110.1
Maritime and inland waterway transport	109.4
Industry	107.7
Administration	106.7
Communications	105.7
Logging	104.9[o]
Railroad transport	102.9
Education	101.2
Workers and employees, national economy	100.9
State-owned agriculture and logging	98.6
Public health	98.1
State-owned agriculture	96.3
Public eating places	92.5
Trade, procurements, and supply	91.0
Construction	88.9

Wages

Wage Fund

Industry	117.9
National economy	115.4

Money Wage, Average

Construction	125.7
Administration	119.3
Logging	116.5
National economy	114.3
Public eating places	112.7
State-owned agiculture	109.9
Education	109.5
Industry	109.3
Maritime and inland waterway transport	108.9
Railroad transport	107.6
Public health	107.2
Trade	106.8
Communications	105.5
Credit institutions	103.9

Table 20 *continued*

Housing	
Housing fund, urban, total	97.2
Retail Trade	
State and cooperative, current prices	103.0

Source: Unless otherwise indicated, Table A-2, col. 6.

a. Calculated from annual plan goal (given in *Plan 1935*, 2nd ed., pp. 514–15) and 1934 results (given in *Narodno-khoziaistevennyi plan na 1936 god* [The National Economic Plan for 1936], Vol. I, 2nd ed., Moscow, 1936, p. 418).

b. Calculated from annual plan goal (estimated at 2,400 thous. m. tons from G. Lauer, "Metallurgicheskaia baza narodnogo khoziaistva v 1934 g." [Metallurgical Base of the National Economy in 1934], *Planovoe khoziaistvo*, No. 5–6, 1934, p. 80) and 1934 results (given in *Tsvetnye metally* [Nonferrous Metals], No. 11, 1937, p. 41, as cited in *Statistical Abstract of Industrial Output in the Soviet Union, 1913–1955*, National Bureau of Economic Research, New York, 1956, series 207.3).

c. Calculated from annual plan goal (given in Lauer, *Planovoe khoziaistvo*, No. 5–6, 1934, p. 82) and 1934 results (given in *Tsvetnye metally*, No. 11, 1937, p. 41, as cited in *Statistical Abstract*, series 211.6).

d. Calculated from annual plan goal and 1934 results (given in *Plan 1935*, 1st ed., p. 128).

e. Calculated from annual plan goal (given in *Plan 1935*, 2nd ed., pp. 514–15) and 1934 results (given in *Promyshlennost SSSR* [Industry of the USSR], Moscow, 1957, p. 217).

f. Calculated from annual plan goal (given in "Osnovnye pokazateli narodnokhoziaistvennogo plana 1934 g." [Main Indicators of National Economic Plan for 1934], *Planovoe khoziaistvo*, No. 5–6, 1934, p. 210) and 1934 results (given in *Plan 1936*, p. 430).

g. Calculated from annual plan goal (given in *Planovoe khoziaistvo*, No. 5–6, 1934, p. 210) and 1934 results (given in *Narodnoe khoziaistvo SSSR* [The USSR National Economy], Moscow, 1956, p. 89).

h. Calculated from annual plan goals and 1934 results (given in *Plan 1935*, 2nd ed., pp. 547, 629, and 668–70). For yeast, 1934 result from *Plan 1936*, p. 432.

i. Calculated from annual plan goal (given in *Plan 1935*, 2nd ed., p. 586) and 1934 results (given in Nancy Nimitz, "Statistics of Soviet Agriculture," RAND Research Memorandum 1250, Santa Monica, 1954, p. 5).

j. Calculated from annual plan goals (given for "spring of 1934 plan" in P. Mesiatsev and A. Kogan, "Selskoe khoziaistvo v 1934 g." [Agriculture in 1934], *Planovoe khoziaistvo*, No. 5–6, 1934, p. 131) and 1934 results as of July 1 (given for tax data in *Plan 1935*, 2nd ed., pp. 601–2).

k. Calculated from annual plan goal (estimated as 1,203 thous. m. tons from *Plan 1935*, 2nd ed., p. 588) and 1934 results (given in *Sotsialisticheskoe stroitelstvo*, 1936, p. 342).

l. Calculated from annual plan goal (given in B. Reznik, "Proizvodstvo stroitelnykh materialov v 1934 g." [Production of Construction Materials in 1934], *Planovoe khoziaistvo*, No. 5–6, 1934, p. 91) and 1934 results (given in *Sotsialisticheskoe stroitelstvo*, 1936, p. 421).

m. Calculated from annual plan goal (given in *Planovoe khoziaistvo*, No. 5–6, 1934, p. 216) and 1934 results (given in *Sotsialisticheskoe stroitelstvo*, 1936, p. 501).

n. Calculated from annual plan goal (derived as 734.4 km from planned air freight traffic in ton-kilometers given in Table A-2, col. 4, and in tons estimated from *Sotsialisticheskoe stroitelstvo*, 1936, p. 501) and 1934 results (derived as 410.0 km from actual air freight traffic in ton-kilometers and in tons given in *ibid.*).

o. Calculated from annual plan goal (given in *Planovoe khoziaistvo*, No. 5–6, 1934, p. 222) and 1934 results (given in *Trud v SSSR* [Labor in the USSR], Moscow, 1936, pp. 10–12).

nevertheless, only 92.7 per cent of the plan for national income, in 1926/27 prices, was fulfilled according to official Soviet calculations.

The over-all conclusion might be that cases of plan underfulfillment were minor. Achieved rates of growth were impressive: 14.5 per cent for national income, 17.4 per cent for gross industrial production, and 6.2 per cent for agricultural production.[10] Western estimates of the growth rates for this year are not very different, the Soviet Union having entered a period of expansion in

10. *Ibid.*, pp. 78, 79, and 83.

1934 after a slowdown in 1931–1933.[11] But putting a concrete plan into operation is not simply a question of growth rates. To make it work properly requires that the resources planned for accumulation and consumption actually exist, that the structure of prices and costs used in the calculations not be modified too much, and that the structure of production in the base year not be too different from that envisaged when the plan was made.

If fulfillment of the 1934 plan is examined from this angle, it is clear that none of these requirements was met. Underfulfillment of the plan for national income amounted to only 4.6 billion rubles in 1926/27 prices, but it was undoubtedly much higher in current prices. Underfulfillment of the investment plan alone, in current prices, amounted to 2 billion rubles.[12] But these prices were meant to go down in 1934 and they did not. Information on this subject is incomplete, but it is known from official sources that, instead of the planned 15 per cent decrease in costs in 1934, there was no reduction.[13] Part of these supplementary costs must have been borne by the population. Money wages increased by 18.6 per cent on the average, as opposed to the 3.7 per cent planned, but the increase in retail prices, as will be seen later, was considerable. The goal of a 96 per cent increase in real wages in five years was further away than ever.

Soviet planners could have tried to make up in the 1935 plan the loss incurred in 1934, but they do not seem to have seriously considered the idea, and perhaps it would not have been feasible. The increase in national income planned for 1935 (in 1926/27 prices) was 16.1 per cent, a little lower than the average rate in the five-year plan.[14] The discrepancy was greater for aggregate investment, totaling 21.2 billion rubles in current prices. The five-year plan set total investments for 1935 at 25.7 billion rubles,[15] but in lower prices including, among other things, the 15 per cent reduction in the cost of construction in 1934 which had not been realized.[16] No doubt the consumption plan also differed from the goals for 1935 in the five-year plan, but since these annual goals were not published it is impossible to measure the discrepancy.

The annual plan for 1935 differed most from the five-year plan in prices and costs. As mentioned earlier, the five-year plan provided for a reduction in retail prices. In actual fact, the government doubled the price of rye bread on June 20, 1934, raising it from 25 to 50 kopeks per kilogram.[17] There was another 100 per cent increase at the time rationing was abolished, which went into effect January 1, 1935.[18] During this same period prices of nonrationed goods in state trade were reduced in so-called "commercial" stores, so it is difficult to make an over-

11. See my *Planning*, pp. 255–61.

12. *Plan 1935*, 1st ed., p. 78.

13. A distinction must be made between the index of the cost of investment (for which the goals for the 1934 plan are not given) and the index of the cost of construction. *Plan 1935* (1st ed., p. 197) gives the planned reduction in 1934 as 15 per cent and the actual reduction as zero.

14. Which was 17.1 per cent. The five-year plan goal for 1935 is not known.

15. *Vtoroi plan*, pp. 716–17.

16. See footnote 13 above.

17. Jasny, *Soviet Industrialization*, p. 155.

18. December 7, 1934, decree (*Sobranie zakonov i rasporiazhenii raboche-krestianskogo pravitelstva SSSR* [Collection of Laws and Decrees of the Workers' and Peasants' Government of the USSR], No. 61, Art. 445, p. 860).

all evaluation. But the parts of the five-year plan pertaining to retail trade and real wages could no longer be maintained.

The policy of keeping the wholesale prices of producer goods stable, which the five-year plan implied, seems to have been maintained until 1936. But the structure of costs seems to have been strongly affected by overrunning the plan for wages and employment in 1934. As can be seen in Table 21, revisions in the 1935 annual plan goals for costs relative to the five-year plan for the same year were so large that they made the five-year plan estimates in value terms practically meaningless. And, in fact, not only were the 1934 annual plan goals for

Table 21   Changes in Cost of Production Envisaged in Second Five-Year Plan and Annual Plan Goals for 1934 and 1935 (per cent of change relative to preceding year)

	Annual Plan Goal for 1934 [a] (1)	Results in 1934 with or without Allowance for Increase in Prices and Salaries		Second Five-Year Plan Goal for 1935 (4)	Annual Plan Goal for 1935 with or without Allowance for Increase in Prices and Salaries	
		Without (2)	With (3)		Without (5)	With (6)
1. Industry:	−4.6	−3.9	0	−6.7[b]	−3.8	+21.2
Commissariat of Heavy Industry	−7.0	−8.0	−4.5	−8.0	−6.0	+3.0
Commissariat of Light Industry	−1.8	+1.0	+8.5	−5.0	+1.2	+51.6
Commissariat of Food Industry	−4.0	0	+4.5	−6.9	−3.1	+53.1
Commissariat of Timber Industry	−4.0	−1.2	+1.3	−6.0	−2.7	+13.0
2. Construction (net)	−15.0		0	−10.0	−15.0	−12.0
3. Committee for Agricultural Procurement under Council of People's Commissars	−4.8				−2.1	+11.0
4. Railroad transportation	−4.0				+5.8	+11.0
5. Water transportation	−15.8				−5.5	−1.9

Source: Cols. 1–3 and 5–6: *Plan 1935*, 1st ed., p. 197; col. 4: *Vtoroi plan*, p. 728.

a. The Second Five-Year Plan goals for 1934 are almost the same as the 1934 annual plan goals (cf. *Vtoroi plan*, p. 728).

b. Includes the four people's commissariats listed and the Committee for Agricultural Procurement under the Council of People's Commissars.

costs not fulfilled, but the 1935 annual plan targets bear no relation to the corresponding slice of the five-year plan. The revisions were made not only because of the increase in prices and wages in December 1934 but also quite independently of that increase. Furthermore, the plans for reducing production costs applied only to "comparable" production. New products were not included, which makes plans even less realistic.

In addition to the changes in the amount of resources available and in the structure of prices and costs, there were changes in the structure of production, which can be seen in Table 22 for the goals that are known.[19] There are two possible explanations of how these new goals for 1935 came to be set only a few weeks after the publication of the final text of the five-year plan. First, these changes could have been the result of a change in policy made after the publication of the five-year plan. In view of the small interval of time between the two documents, this would seem to apply only to exceptional cases. Second, the changes could reflect the extent of fulfillment of the 1934 annual plan. According to this hypothesis, only the rates of growth of the five-year plan would be maintained, while the absolute volume of production and input-output relations would be based mainly on the actual results in 1934 and not on the five-year plan goals for 1935.

Examination of Table 23 shows that the second hypothesis is the correct one. Of the 71 series for which the 1934 results can be compared with the five-year and annual plan goals for 1935, there is close correspondence in 42 cases. It is very close for gross industrial production, ferrous metals, construction materials, and the food industry, and quite close for light industry and transportation. The most substantial differences appear in machine-building, which is the most sensitive to disturbances experienced during the year. These differences arose because some products were replaced by others, and not because policy was changed. Thus, the reduction in motor vehicle output (relative to the five-year plan goal) basically reflected the need for increased production of grain combines. The increase in the production of railroad freight cars was compensated by decreased production of passenger cars. Similar substitutions seem to have been made in the fuel industry (coal was stressed to make up for the lack of petroleum and the low peat production) and in maritime transportation (where freight traffic was increased at the expense of passenger traffic). It seems quite clear that the authors of the 1935 annual plan based their calculations not on the five-year plan goals for that year but on the results achieved in 1934. But even if the actual goals of the five-year plan were not implemented, the pressure they exercised on the economy was maintained, and this pressure can be measured by the planned rates of growth that were maintained.

One might, then, ask which provisions of the five-year plan actually were put into effect in 1935. The most illuminating information on this subject can be obtained from the list of factories scheduled to be built during the five-year plan and actually transferred to the annual plan. It is clear from a study that I made of investment in the Kuznetsk Basin[20] that most of the construction projects in heavy industry listed in the Second Five-Year Plan actually were undertaken. But neither the estimates, nor the production capacity, nor the construction schedules were respected. The investment in light industry was planned primarily for the last years of the five-year plan and was to be put into operation in 1936 or 1937. All of this part of the five-year plan was transcribed with a few

19. In agriculture, the goals were calculated assuming equal production in all years. Lower rates may have been planned for the first years.

20. E. Zaleski, "Investissements en Sibérie occidentale et croissance du Kuzbass," *Cahiers de l'I.S.E.A.*, No. G–8, 1960, pp. 99–163.

Table 22   Goals for 1935: Annual Plan as Percentage of Five-Year Plan

Heavy Industry		Margarine	93.3
Railroad freight cars (2-axle units)	166.0	Beer	92.3
Grain combines	125.0	Soap (40% fatty acid)	90.1
Manganese ore	120.0	Bicycles	89.7
Tractors (units)	116.9	Leather shoes	89.5
Tractors (15 hp)	111.8	Linen fabrics	88.5
Machine tools	108.3	Cigarettes	88.2
Rolled steel	108.1[a]	Raw sugar	87.9
Electric power	103.7	Cheese	87.8
Pig iron	102.5	Confectionery	81.4
Coal	102.0	Hosiery	80.7
Steam locomotives	100.0	Cotton fabrics	80.6
Tires	100.0	Low-grade tobacco (*makhorka*)	80.0
Iron ore	98.7	Meat	78.5
Coke	98.5	Woolen fabrics	72.8
Steel ingots and castings	97.5	Radios	68.8
Lumber	96.0	Phonographs	63.9
Paper	94.7		
Window glass	93.8	*Agriculture*[b]	
Peat	93.0	Barley, harvest	117.5
Bricks	90.9	Oats, harvest	117.4
Electric locomotives	90.9	Potatoes, harvest	114.9
Industrial timber hauled	88.4	Grain, market production	111.1
Cement	88.0	Wheat, harvest	110.3
Steam boilers	87.5	Grain, harvest, total (biological yield)	106.5
Petroleum and gas	86.7	Potatoes, market production	101.6
Trucks and buses	85.2	Milk and dairy products, market	
Steel pipes	84.7	production	100.2
Motor vehicles, total	83.6	Rye, harvest	99.1
Phosphoric fertilizer (14% P_2O_5)	81.9	Sugar beets, harvest	98.4
Lime	80.0	Flax fiber, harvest	93.2
Automobiles	77.3	Raw cotton, harvest	91.9
Steam and gas turbines	75.9	Corn, harvest	87.0
Diesel locomotives	75.0	Milk, production	79.7
Ground natural phosphate	58.2	Sunflowers, harvest	74.5
Turbogenerators	58.1	Meat and fat, market production	71.6
Oil shale	53.6	Wool, production	63.7
Railroad passenger cars	26.3	Meat and fat, production	41.9
Light and Food Industries		*Transportation*	
Bread and breadstuffs (large-scale industry)	146.3[a]	Maritime freight traffic (ton-km)	108.8
Knitted underwear	111.0[a]	Railroad freight traffic, average length of	
Butter	106.3	haul	103.2
Sewing machines	102.0	Railroad freight traffic (ton-km)	102.6
Rubber footwear	100.0	Railroad freight traffic (tons)	99.4
Fish catch	100.0	Inland waterway freight traffic (tons)	95.2
Matches	97.1	Inland waterway freight traffic (ton-km)	89.7
Canned food	96.8	Railroad passenger traffic (pass.-km)	82.5
Hosiery	95.9	Maritime passenger traffic (pass.-km)	80.4
Crude alcohol	95.1	Inland waterway passenger traffic (pass.-km)	72.5

Source: Unless otherwise indicated, Table 23, col. 2.

a. Calculated from 1935 annual plan goals (Table A-2, col. 7) and Second Five-Year Plan goals for 1935 (given in *Vtoroi plan*, pp. 680–704).

b. Calculated from 1935 annual plan goals (Table A-2, col. 7) and Second Five-Year Plan interpolated goals for 1935 (estimated from actual results in 1932 in my *Planning*, Table A-1, col. 6, and five-year plan goals for 1937 in Table A-1, col. 1, by assuming an equal average annual planned rate of growth during 1933–1937).

Table 23   Effect of Fulfillment of 1934 Annual Plan on Five-Year Plan Goals for 1935

	Per Cent of Fulfillment of Annual Plan Goals for 1934 (1)	1935 Annual Plan Goals as Per Cent of Five-Year Plan Goals for 1935 (2)
National income	92.7	
Gross industrial production	97.8	96.5
Fuel and Energy		
Coal	97.3	102.0
Peat	101.4	93.0
Coke	104.6	98.5
Oil shale	45.9	53.6
Petroleum and gas	83.3[a]	86.7[b]
Electric power	110.6	103.7
Ferrous Metals		
Iron ore	98.7	98.7
Pig iron	104.3	102.5
Steel ingots and castings	98.9	97.5
Steel pipes	89.4	84.7
Manganese ore	107.1	120.0
Chemicals		
Phosphoric fertilizer (14% P_2O_5)	98.9	81.9
Phosphoric fertilizer (18.7% P_2O_5)	102.7	73.9
Ground natural phosphate	53.1	58.2
Tires	103.1	100.0
Construction Materials		
Cement	81.3	88.0
Lime	94.1	80.0
Window glass	96.5	93.8
Bricks	82.9	90.9
Industrial timber hauled	84.1	88.4
Lumber	96.9	96.0
Paper	94.3	94.7
Machine-Building		
Machine tools	111.2	108.3
Steam and gas turbines	52.0	75.9
Steam boilers	70.0	87.5
Turbogenerators	60.8	58.1[c]
Tractors (units)	98.9	116.9
Tractors (15 hp)	102.4	111.8
Motor vehicles:	100.6	83.6[d]
Trucks and buses	100.7	85.2[d]
Automobiles	100.6	77.3[d]
Grain combines	68.7	125.0[d]
Steam locomotives	96.6	100.0
Diesel locomotives	40.0	75.0
Electric locomotives	47.5	90.9
Railroad freight cars (2-axle units)	68.9	166.0
Railroad passenger cars	74.7	26.3
Light Industry		
Cotton fabrics	89.3	80.6
Woolen fabrics	108.3	72.8
Linen fabrics	79.5	88.5
Hosiery	90.8	80.7[e]
Leather shoes	102.5	89.5

Table 23 *continued*

	Per Cent of Fulfillment of Annual Plan Goals for 1934 (1)	1935 Annual Plan Goals as Per Cent of Five-Year Plan Goals for 1935 (2)
Rubber footwear	100.0	100.0
Bicycles	85.8	89.7
Radios	32.0	68.8
Sewing machines, household	65.2	102.0f
Phonographs	45.5	63.9
Soap (40% fatty acid)	92.7	90.1
Food Industry		
Raw sugar	100.3	87.9
Fish catch	103.1	100.0
Crude alcohol	85.8	95.1
Butter	110.1	106.3
Cheese	111.3	87.8
Meat	89.4	78.5
Canned food	86.9	96.8
Confectionery	84.9	81.4
Margarine	92.3	93.3
Beer	98.3	92.3
Cigarettes	92.9	88.2
Matches	91.1	97.1
Low-grade tobacco (*makhorka*)	92.7	80.0
Transportation		
Railroad freight traffic (ton-km)	95.7	102.6
Railroad freight traffic (tons)	90.1	99.4
RR freight traffic, average length of haul	106.2	103.2g
RR passenger traffic (pass.-km)	87.1	82.5
Inland waterway freight traffic (ton-km)	81.7	89.7
Inland waterway freight traffic (tons)	89.3	95.2
Inland waterway passenger traffic (pass.-km)	63.8	72.5
Maritime freight traffic (ton-km)	90.2	108.8
Maritime passenger traffic (pass.-km)	100.3	80.4

Source: Unless otherwise indicated, col. 1: Table A-2, col. 6; col. 2: calculated from 1935 annual plan goals (Table A-2, col. 7) and Second Five-Year Plan goals for 1935 (given in *Vtoroi plan*, pp. 680–704 and 712).

a. Calculated from the 1934 annual plan goal (given as 30,660 thous. metric tons in *Planovoe khoziaistvo*, No. 3, 1934, p. 69) and 1934 results (given as 25,532 thous. metric tons in *Plan 1935*, 2nd ed., p. 507).

b. The 1935 annual plan goal was taken from *Plan 1935*, 2nd ed., p. 507.

c. The five-year plan goal for 1935 was derived by reducing the goal for generators (given as 1,250 thous. kw in *Proekt vtorogo plana*, p. 448) in order to eliminate hydraulic generators.

d. The lowering of goals for motor vehicles in the 1935 annual plan is worded as follows: "The plan for the production of motor vehicles for 1935 was set at 92,000, which is less than envisaged in the five-year plan goals largely because of the necessity to allocate part of the GAZ motors to the production of combines" (*Plan 1935*, 1st ed., p. 11).

e. The five-year plan goal for 1935 was estimated by adding 150 million to the goal given for the People's Commissariat of Light Industry as 325 million (*Vtoroi plan*, p. 702).

f. The five-year plan goal for 1935 was calculated from actual results in 1932 (Zaleski, *Planning*, Table A-1, p. 310) and the Second Five-Year Plan goal for 1937 (Table A-1, col. 1) by assuming an equal average annual planned rate of growth during 1932–1937.

g. The five-year plan goal for 1935 was calculated from goals for railroad freight traffic in ton-kilometers and in tons in *Vtoroi plan*, p. 712.

changes into the future long-range plans, but some of the factories envisaged were still not built in 1960.

Second Five-Year Plan and Annual Plans for 1936 and 1937

Nothing seems to be gained from dwelling on the differences between the 1936 and 1937 annual plans and the five-year plan targets for those years. We are faced with an economy of very different dimensions from that originally envisaged, with a structure of prices and costs that in no way resembles the planned one, and with a different structure of production, employment, and population in general.

The information that could be collected to compare the five-year plan goals with the annual plan goals for 1936 and 1937 is given in Tables 24 and 25. The 1937 annual plan goals are based on a much larger quantity of data about actual production than the five-year plan goals for that year. The overrun of the money wage plan reflects mainly the difference in the price structure. For the other sectors, no general conclusion can be drawn other than that we are faced with quite different plans; in other words, the production structures bear no resemblance to each other.

Of most interest is the attitude of the Soviet authorities to this situation. On the one hand, despite the inflated aggregate indexes of national income, industrial production, and agricultural production, the deviation from the five-year plan goals is impossible to conceal.[21] The share of consumer goods in industrial production, which was to reach 50.9 per cent in 1937, was set at only 43.8 per cent in the 1936 plan.[22] According to the five-year plan, total investments in current prices were to reach 25.6 billion rubles in 1936. The annual plan for 1936 was 32.4 billion rubles in current prices, which were considerably higher than 1933 plan prices originally planned for 1936.[23] Therefore, it is hardly surprising that total budgetary financing of the national economy (in the financial plan), planned to be 46.8 billion rubles in 1937, reached 57.8 billion in the 1936 annual plan and that expenditures for administration and defense reached 20.2 billion in 1936, as opposed to the 4.3 billion envisaged by the five-year plan for 1937.[24] Statistics on the decrease in production costs are given without including changes in prices and wages. In other words, they do not reflect development of costs. The changes made in the five-year plan thus appear quite clearly in official texts. But the Soviet authorities refused to admit that the five-year plan was no longer in effect and passed off the changes as indexes of performance, citing only the cases when the goals were exceeded.

An example of this attitude can be seen in an official table comparing the 1936

---

21. The lack of annual data in the five-year plan makes impossible valid comparisons for national income and agricultural production. An over-all evaluation is attempted later (see Table 28) and estimates in the inflated 1926/27 prices are compared with Western estimates.

22. *Narodno-khoziaistvennyi plan na 1936 god* [The National Economic Plan for 1936], Vol. I, 2nd ed., Moscow, 1936, pp. 390–92.

23. *Ibid.*, p. 391, and *Vtoroi plan*, pp. 716–17.

24. *Plan 1936*, p. 381. See also Table 18 above.

Table 24   Goals for 1936: Annual Plan as Percentage of Five-Year Plan

Heavy Industry		Sewing machines, household	107.1 [e]
Grain combines	305.0	Crude alcohol	103.7
Trucks	140.3	Fish catch	103.3
Railroad freight cars (2-axle units)	133.5	Rubber footwear	100.0
Window glass	122.1	Low-grade tobacco	100.0
Manganese ore	121.7	Matches	96.4
Bricks	117.3	Phonographs	95.5
Rolled steel	116.2	Cheese	90.7
Motor vehicles, total	115.4	Cigarettes	88.6
Tractors (units)	114.5	Canned food	84.9
Steam and gas turbines	110.1 [a]	Confectionery	84.0
Cement	108.3	Leather shoes	78.6 [f]
Steel ingots and castings	108.1	Soap (40% fatty acid)	77.5
Steel pipes	107.5	Meat	76.5
Lumber	107.0 [b]	Cotton fabrics	76.3
Electric power	106.7	Margarine	76.2
Coal	106.6	Hosiery	70.1 [g]
Paper	106.4	Woolen fabrics	62.4
Tractors (15 hp units)	105.8		
Coke	104.4	*Agriculture* [h]	
Pig iron	103.6	Potatoes, harvest	130.0
Machine tools	103.2	Sugar beets, harvest	122.8
Plywood	101.3	Oats, harvest	120.5
Tires	100.0	Barley, harvest	118.1
Peat	95.7	Grain, market production	117.1
Iron ore	94.0	Wheat, harvest	113.7
Industrial timber hauled	93.0	Potatoes, market production	113.6
Lime	86.4	Milk and dairy products, market	
Steam boilers	86.0	production	112.6
Electric locomotives	76.5	Grain harvest, total (biological yield)	108.4
Petroleum and gas	74.1 [c]	Flax fiber, harvest	106.4
Phosphoric fertilizer (14% P_2O_5)	73.1	Rye, harvest	97.9
Turbogenerators	57.5 [d]	Milk, production	88.3
Oil shale	53.1	Sunflowers, harvest	87.1
Ground natural phosphate	52.6	Corn, harvest	81.5
Diesel locomotives	50.0	Meat and fat, market production	71.5
Automobiles	45.9	Wool, production	67.6
Railroad passenger cars	30.2	Meat and fat, production	52.1
Looms	25.6		
Spinning machines	20.8	*Tranportation*	
		Railroad freight traffic (ton-km)	116.1
Light and Food Industries		Railroad freight traffic (tons)	110.4
Bicycles	170.2	Maritime freight traffic (ton-km)	110.2
Radios	147.9	Railroad freight traffic, average length	
Bread and breadstuffs (large-scale		of haul	105.1 [i]
industry)	147.6	Inland waterway freight traffic (tons)	101.5
Knitted underwear	137.4	Maritime freight traffic (tons)	97.2
Butter	132.2	Inland waterway freight traffic	
Raw sugar	125.0	(ton-km)	87.6
Beer	116.1	Maritime passenger traffic (pass.-km)	71.4
		Inland waterway passenger traffic	
		(pass.-km)	56.2

Source: Unless otherwise indicated, calculated from 1936 annual plan goals (Table A-2, col. 10) and Second Five-Year Plan goals for 1936 (given in *Vtoroi plan*, pp. 680–704 and 712).

a. Five-year plan goal derived from planned output of steam and hydraulic turbines (given in *Vtoroi plan*, p. 695) by subtracting estimated planned output of hydraulic turbines, as in Table A-1, col. 1, series 47.

Table 24 *continued*

b. Five-year plan goal (given in *Vtoroi plan*, p. 701) increased to make coverage comparable with later sources, as in Table A-1, col. 1, series 42.

c. Annual plan goal given in *Plan 1936*, p. 411.

d. Five-year plan goal derived from planned output of all generators (given in *Proekt vtorogo plana*, pp. 448–49) by subtracting estimated planned output of hydraulic generators, as in Table A-1, col. 1, series 49.

e. Five-year plan goal estimated from actual output in 1932 (in my *Planning*, Table A-1, col. 1) and five-year plan goal for 1937 (in Table A-1, col. 1) by assuming an equal average annual planned rate of growth during 1933–1937.

f. Five-year plan goal derived from total output in 1932 (given in *ibid.*) and planned increase for 1936 (calculated from 1932 output and 1936 planned output of state and cooperative industry in *Vtoroi plan*, p. 703).

g. Five-year plan goal given in *Proekt vtorogo plana*, pp. 456–57.

h. Five-year plan goals for all agricultural series were estimated from actual output in 1932 (in my *Planning*, Table A-1, col. 6) and five-year plan goals for 1937 (in Table A-1, col. 1) by assuming an equal average annual planned rate of growth during 1933–1937.

i. Five-year plan goal was derived from railroad freight traffic series in tons and in ton-kilometers (given in *Vtoroi plan*, p. 704).

Table 25 Goals for 1937: Annual Plan as Percentage of Five-Year Plan

Heavy Industry		
Grain combines	275.0	
Steam and gas turbines	166.8	
Trucks	139.3	
Bricks	137.1	
Rolled steel	120.2	
Window glass	120.1	
Roofing tiles	120.0	
Steel ingots and castings	118.5	
Manganese ore	118.5	
Asbestos shingles	114.5	
Motor vehicles, total	110.0	
Refined copper	107.4	
Steel pipes	106.8	
Tires	106.7	
Electric power	106.6	
Plywood	106.6	
Tractors (15 hp)	103.6	
Coke	103.3	
Machine tools	102.5	
Zinc	101.1	
Lumber	100.5	
Pig iron	100.1	
Peat	100.0	
Cement	99.2	
Industrial timber hauled	98.8	
Coal	98.5	
Paper	95.5	
Natural gas	93.6	
Lime	93.0	
Iron ore	91.2	
Tractors	89.3	
Turbogenerators	83.5	
Phosphoric fertilizer (14% P_2O_5)	83.3	
Sulfuric acid	80.1	
Railroad freight cars (2-axle units)	79.9	
Soda ash	79.0	
Hydroelectric power	77.7	
Paperboard	77.1	
Steam boilers	75.1	

Crude petroleum	72.6
Railroad freight cars	72.5
Lead	69.6
Steam locomotives	62.8
Aluminum	62.5
Railroad passenger cars	42.9
Automobiles	41.7
Ground natural phosphate	40.2
Caustic soda	35.6
Electric locomotives	33.3
Oil shale	30.8
Spinning machines	30.0
Looms	13.1

Light and Food Industries	
Bread and breadstuffs (large-scale industry)	161.9
Bicycles	156.5
Radios	130.5
Knitted underwear	128.6
Butter	123.3
Beer	114.7
Sewing machines, household	113.3
Crude alcohol	106.9
Ginned cotton	104.3
Raw sugar	104.0
Felt footwear	103.1
Rubber footwear	100.0
Fish catch	100.0
Leather shoes	99.5
Cotton yarn	95.6
Cheese	91.9
Low-grade tobacco (*makhorka*)	91.7
Silk and rayon fabrics	91.1
Flour (procurements)	90.0
Cameras	85.3
Cigarettes	81.6
Cotton fabrics	80.1
Confectionery	79.5
Canned food	71.3
Meat	67.7

Table 25   *continued*

Phonographs	66.7		Maritime freight traffic (tons)	88.7
Matches	66.7		Railroad passenger traffic (pass.-km)	79.1
Vegetable oil	65.1		Inland waterway, coal and coke (tons)	78.5
Macaroni	64.2		Inland waterway, grain and flour (tons)	76.1
Salt	55.7		Inland waterway, average length of	
Margarine	54.2		haul	73.4
Woolen fabrics	49.1		Inland waterway freight traffic	
Hosiery	48.7		(ton-km)	71.1
Soap (40% fatty acid)	48.5		Maritime passenger traffic (pass.-km)	62.1
			Inland waterway, oil and oil products	
Agriculture			(tons)	48.9
Potatoes, harvest	121.8		Inland waterway passenger traffic	
Barley, harvest	109.3		(pass.-km)	44.6
Raw cotton, harvest	109.2		Air passenger traffic (pass.)	27.1
Wheat, harvest	108.1		Air freight traffic (ton-km)	20.8
Oats, harvest	107.5			
Grain, harvest, total (biological yield)	103.4		*Employment*	
Flax fiber, harvest	102.9		Credit institutions	134.1
Milk, production	90.8		Other transport (motor, etc.)	127.3
Sugar beets, harvest	88.8		Administration	116.3
Wool, procurements	83.3		Public health	113.3
Sunflowers, harvest	79.7		Communications	111.6
Corn, harvest	78.8		Education	106.1
Wool production	75.0		Industry	97.1
Meat and fat, production	69.6		Railroad transport	93.0
			Workers and employees	91.0
Transportation			Maritime and inland waterway	
Railroad, timber (tons)	140.0		transport	85.7
Inland waterway, mineral construction			Trade, procurements, and supply	85.2
materials (tons)	132.4		State-owned agriculture	72.4
Railroad freight traffic (ton-km)	129.3		Construction	51.1
Railroad, ferrous metals (tons)	126.1		Public eating places	48.0
Railroad, ore (tons)	124.1			
Railroad, average daily carloadings	120.3		*Wages*	
Railroad freight traffic (tons)	118.9		Money wage, education	205.2
Inland waterway, salt (tons)	118.5		Money wage, workers and employees	169.6
Railroad, firewood (tons)	113.2		Money wage, maritime and inland	
Railroad, coal and coke (tons)	112.8		waterway transport	168.7
Railroad freight traffic, average length			Money wage, railroad transport	165.7
of haul	108.4		Money wage, construction	165.1
Railroad, grain and flour (tons)	106.3		Money wage, industry	163.5
Maritime freight traffic, average length			Money wage, administration	163.4
of haul	103.1		Money wage, public eating places	161.1
Inland waterway, length of network	100.5		Wage fund, industry	158.7
Inland waterway freight traffic (tons)	96.8		Wage fund, national economy	154.4
Railroad, length of network	92.0		Money wage, trade	152.2
Maritime freight traffic (ton-km)	91.6		Money wage, state-owned agriculture	151.4
Railroad, oil and oil products (tons)	89.1		Money wage, public health	151.0
			Money wage, credit institutions	143.7
			Money wage, communications	128.8

Source: Calculated from 1937 annual plan goals (Table A-2, col. 13) and Second Five-Year Plan goals for 1937 (Table A-1, col. 1).

annual plan and the 1936 five-year plan goals.[25] By limiting coverage to industrial products, by citing only cases of plan overfulfillment, and by adding a few products of secondary interest, an impression is created of massive overfulfillment of the five-year plan goals. A comparison of this table with Table 24, which is much more comprehensive, very clearly shows the intentions of the Soviet authorities. The desire to present the 1936 annual plan as an integral part of the five-year plan theoretically in progress can be seen in the very title of the 1936 annual plan—"fourth year of the five-year plan."[26]

In fact, the Soviet authorities wanted to hide the absence of any serious attempt to revise the five-year plan, which became necessary as soon as the 1935 annual plan was published. Nevertheless, no trace of such a revision could be found. It is possible that partial revisions were made but certainly there was no general revision integrating these changes into a unified draft.

Fulfillment of Second Five-Year Plan Goals in 1937

Since the five-year plan for 1933–1937 was never, for practical purposes, operational, it seems useless to discuss the extent of its fulfillment. However, it is interesting to compare the goals and the results obtained in 1937 to see if the plan was of any interest as a forecast.

Table 26 presents the available data on the fulfillment of the plan.[27] If the value series, which are discussed later, are ignored, the "classic" picture of five-year plan fulfillment emerges clearly. Series representing the results of economic activity show the largest underfulfillment; series representing costs, such as transportation or wages, exceed planned targets. There are, however, a few exceptions due to the particular conditions of 1937. The good harvest (exaggerated because of its measurement by biological yield) made overfulfillment of the plan for grain possible in 1937, and difficulties in investment and the purges resulted in underfulfilling the employment plan (mainly in construction), although the urban population increased more than planned.

In industrial production there was considerable variation in plan fulfillment from one product to the next. The most sensitive seems to have been machine-building, a young industry in the Soviet Union in the 1930's, where relatively small changes in production and investment programs caused great differences in the percentage of plan fulfillment. In general, Table 26 should be viewed more as an illustration of the discrepancy between plan and results and less as an index of performance since the series cited are not of equal importance.

Another method is used in Table 27 to show discrepancies between the five-year plan and the results. The largest deviations are in the plans for wages, both money and real wages, and for housing and retail trade—areas directly affecting the standard of living. In industry, the largest deviations show up in machine-building, chemicals, and the food industry.

25. *Ibid.*, p. 15.
26. See footnote 22 above.
27. Table 26 covers the 229 series for which data could be found; 218 of these are included in Table A–1.

Table 26 Fulfillment of Second Five-Year Plan[a] Goals in 1937 (per cent)

National income (1926/27 prices)	96.1	Oil shale	19.8
Industry		Spinning machines	13.6
Producer goods (1926/27 prices)	121.3	Looms	12.8
Total value of production (1926/27 prices)	103.0	Diesel locomotives	3.6
Consumer goods (1926/27 prices)	85.4	*Consumer Goods*	
		Bread and breadstuffs	182.2
Producer Goods		Beer	119.5
Grain combines	219.5	Sewing machines, household	113.4
Trucks	128.8	Knitted underwear	111.5
Bricks	108.3	Butter	102.8
Steel ingots and castings	104.3	Ginned cotton	102.4
Manganese ore	101.9	Crude alcohol	102.3
Motor vehicles, total	99.9	Cameras	100.9
Rolled steel	99.7	Flour (procurements)	99.4
Lime	99.4	Raw sugar	96.4
Window glass	97.4	Leather shoes	95.8
Peat	96.2	Bicycles	94.0
Electric power	95.2	Silk and rayon fabrics	92.0
Coke	94.0	Fish catch	89.4
Plywood	92.4	Low-grade tobacco (*makhorka*)	89.1
Pig iron	90.5	Cotton yarn	87.2
Machine tools	90.3	Rubber footwear	84.6
Tires	89.9	Cheese	83.8
Zinc	85.0	Felt footwear	83.7
Asbestos shingles	85.0	Cigarettes	71.4
Coal	83.9	Confectionery	68.2
Steel pipes	83.9	Meat	67.7
Paper	83.2	Cotton fabrics	67.6
Steam and gas turbines	82.2	Vegetable oil	66.0
Iron ore	81.7	Margarine	61.7
Natural gas	79.2	Meat and subproducts of first category	60.9
Soda ash	75.5	Matches	59.7
Cement	72.7	Salt	53.3
Refined copper	72.2	Macaroni	51.7
Hydroelectric power	72.1	Soap (40% fatty acid)	49.5
Lumber	70.4	Woolen fabrics	49.2
Industrial timber hauled	67.2	Canned food	49.1
Paperboard	66.2	Phonographs	45.1
Sulfuric acid	65.8	Linen fabrics (m²)	42.3
Phosphoric fertilizer (18.7% P_2O_5)	65.6	Hosiery	40.9
Phosphoric fertilizer (14% P_2O_5)	65.4	Radios	40.0
Crude petroleum	64.3	Clocks and watches	23.5
Tractors (units)	57.6		
Lead	54.2	**Agriculture**	
Roofing tiles	54.0	Vegetable production (1926/27 prices)	83.1
Steam locomotives	51.6	Total value of production (1926/27 prices)	76.9
Mineral fertilizer	50.5	Animal production (1926/27 prices)	63.0
Railroad freight cars (2-axle units)	49.8		
Railroad freight cars	49.7	*Harvests and Animal Production*	
Aluminum	47.1	Barley[b]	126.3
Caustic soda	46.2	Wheat[b]	123.7
Turbogenerators	44.7	Raw cotton[b]	121.5
Steam boilers	44.3	Oats[b]	121.1
Tractors (15 hp)	39.9	Rye[b]	115.9
Automobiles	30.3	Grain, total (biological yield)	114.8
Ground natural phosphate	29.5	Grain, total (barn yield)	92.9
Railroad passenger cars	26.1	Potatoes[b]	89.9
Electric locomotives	21.3	Cows	88.1[c]
		Beef cattle	87.0[d]

Table 26 *continued*

Sheep and goats	84.7[d]
Milk	80.4
Sugar beets[b]	79.2
Horses	76.6[d]
Flax fiber[b]	70.6
Wool	66.4
Corn[b]	64.8
Sunflowers[b]	61.2
Eggs	61.2
Pigs	52.5[d]
Meat and fat (excl. rabbits and poultry)	46.6
Mineral fertilizer deliveries	41.7[e]
Market Production	
Raw cotton	120.7
Grain	110.1
Milk and dairy products	83.2
Sugar beets	77.7
Potatoes	71.2
Meat and fat (dead weight)	58.9
Procurements	
Raw cotton	120.8
Grain	106.2
Vegetables	98.5
Potatoes	92.1
Milk and dairy products	85.4
Sugar beets	77.6
Wool	69.2
Meat and fat (dead weight)	59.6
Flax fiber	42.6
Hemp	24.5
Transportation	
Railroad	
Oil and oil products, average length of haul	156.4
Ore, average length of haul	149.8
Timber, average length of haul	129.4
Ferrous metals, average length of haul	128.7
Grain and flour (tons)	121.6
Total freight traffic (ton-km)	118.3
Ferrous metals (tons)	113.9
Average daily carloadings	113.7
Ore (tons)	113.0
Total freight traffic (tons)	108.9
Total freight traffic, average length of haul	108.5
Grain and flour, average length of haul	106.0
Timber (tons)	104.2
Principal construction materials (tons)	103.8
Firewood (tons)	101.6
Firewood, average length of haul	100.4
Coal and coke, average length of haul	97.1
Coal and coke (tons)	93.3
Length of network	90.3
Total passenger traffic (pass.-km)	82.6
Oil and oil products (tons)	77.2

Inland Waterway	
Mineral construction materials (tons)	104.0
Length of network	100.1
Salt (tons)	100.0
Passenger traffic (passengers)	88.1
Freight traffic under ministries and economic organizations (tons)	74.3
Average length of haul under ministries and economic organizations	71.4
Grain and flour (tons)	67.4
Coal and coke (tons)	59.9
Freight traffic under ministries and economic organizations (ton-km)	52.5
Oil and oil products (tons)	44.9
Passenger traffic (pass.-km)	43.2
Maritime	
Average length of haul	98.6
Freight traffic (tons)	73.5
Freight traffic (ton-km)	72.2
Passenger traffic (pass.-km)	60.7
Passenger traffic (passengers)	53.6
Motor	
Freight traffic (ton-km)	54.4
Freight traffic (tons)	49.5[f]
Air	
Passenger traffic (passengers)	35.3
Freight traffic, incl. mail (ton-km)	20.7
Employment	
Credit institutions	143.0
Other transport (motor, etc.)	124.1
Administration	118.6
Communications	111.6
Education	111.5
Public health	109.6
Industry	99.1
National economy, total	93.4
Railroad transport	90.8
Trade, procurements, and supply	87.3
Maritime and inland waterway transport	78.3
State-owned agriculture	69.5
Construction	59.1
Public eating places	46.0
Wages	
Wage Fund	
Industry	167.4
National economy	162.1
Money Wage	
Coal industry	193.4
Railroad transport	176.0
Education	175.6
National economy (excl. collective farms)	173.6
Construction	172.1
Maritime and inland waterway transport	171.8

Table 26   *continued*

Cotton industry	171.1	**Housing**	
Public eating places	170.4	Housing fund, urban, total	84.1
Industry	168.9	Floorspace per inhabitant, urban	71.8
Textile industry	168.2	Housing construction, urban, total	19.8
Machine-building	167.5		
Administration	166.3	**Population**	
Trade	164.9	Urban	112.0
Ferrous metals	164.6	Total	92.5
Wool industry	164.6	Rural	85.3
State-owned agriculture	163.3		
Public health	157.4	**State and Cooperative Retail Trade**	
Credit institutions	149.4	*Constant Prices*	
Logging	148.7	Sugar	107.1[g]
Communications	142.4	Fish	73.1[g]
		Meat and meat products	63.5[g]
Real Wage		Food products	55.9[g]
National economy (calculated from		Total (calculated from Zaleski index)	54.9
Zaleski index)	68.1	Total (calculated from official Soviet	
National economy (calculated from		price index)	43.4
official Soviet index)	53.7	*Current Prices*	
		Total	139.9

Source: Table A-1, col. 3, unless otherwise indicated.

a. Final version published in November 1934.

b. Biological Yield. The barn yields for these crops are not known, but a general idea of the plan fulfillment for the two yields can be obtained from the percentages for both for total grain crops.

c. Derived from the plan for spring 1937 (given in *Vtoroi plan*, p. 432) and actual results in June 1937 (estimated at one million more than in December 1937, which was given in *Chislennost skota v SSSR* [Head of Livestock in the USSR], Moscow, 1957, p. 6, since that was the approximate difference in 1935).

d. Derived from the plan for spring 1937 (given in *Vtoroi plan*, p. 432) and actual results in June 1937 (given in Naum Jasny, *The Socialized Agriculture of the USSR*, Stanford, 1949, p. 797).

e. Derived from the plan for 1937 (sum of ammonium sulfate, phosphoric fertilizer converted to 18% P_2O_5, sylvanite, and ground natural phosphate given in *Vtoroi plan*, p. 472) and actual total deliveries in 1937 (given in Nancy Nimitz, "Statistics of Soviet Agriculture," RAND Research Memorandum 1250, Santa Monica, 1954, p. 55).

f. Derived from the plan for 1937 (given in *Vtoroi plan*, p. 713) and actual results in 1937 (given in *Transport i sviaz SSSR* [Transport and Communications in the USSR], Moscow, 1957, p. 155).

g. Derived from the plan for 1937 for foodstuffs intended for consumption by agricultural and nonagricultural population, excluding requirements for export, livestock breeding, and other nonconsumption purposes (given in *Vtoroi plan*, p. 390) and actual results in 1937 (estimated from 1932 results in *ibid.* and increase in 1937 over 1932 given in I. Merenkov, "Torgovlia v period sotsializma" [Trade in the Socialist Period], *Planovoe khoziaistvo*, No. 3, 1939, p. 142).

It is of interest to compare the forecasting performances of the First and the Second Five-Year Plans. On the whole, the planners' "ability to forecast" improved slightly, but it is difficult to draw definite conclusions in view of the lack of detail available; however, the data by industry groups and by individual sectors are a little more precise. The growth in machinery production and diversification seems to have made forecast of the future structure of production much more difficult. There was a definite improvement, on the other hand, in ferrous metals and construction materials, which might indicate that the crisis of 1937 was less severe than that of 1932.

As for agricultural production, the fact that 1937 was an exceptionally good

Table 27   Mean Absolute Deviation from 100 Per Cent Fulfillment of First and Second Five-Year Plans (percentage points)

	Absolute Deviation Based on 1932 Results Compared with First Five-Year Plan Maximum Goals for 1932/33 (1)	Absolute Deviation Based on 1937 Results Compared with Second Five-Year Plan Goals for 1937 (2)
1. Industry	43.8	31.1
2. Fuel and power	17.4	24.4
3. Ferrous and nonferrous metals	51.1	19.2
4. Machine-building	31.0	57.3
5. Chemicals	78.4	39.0
6. Construction materials	46.4	20.0
7. Light industry	47.3	28.4
8. Food industry	34.8	29.5
9. Agriculture	53.9	27.7
10. Animal production	66.5	36.3
11. Market production	54.1	23.3
12. Procurements		27.7
13. Harvests (biological yield)	41.2	23.4
14. Transportation	24.5	24.3
15. Employment	50.6	21.1
16. Average money wage	30.8	66.5
17. Average real wage	60.0	39.1
18. Housing	36.7	41.4
19. Population	11.7	11.4
20. Retail trade (in constant prices)	35.5	50.9
21. Foreign trade (in constant prices)	40.2	
22. All groups	38.8	34.8

Source: Col. 1: Zaleski, *Planning*, Table 44, col. 2, pp. 242–43; col. 2; the unweighted arithmetic mean of absolute deviations of the percentage fulfillments in Table A-1, col. 3, from 100 covers the series indicated below:

Line 1: unweighted arithmetic mean of lines 2–8. **Line 2:** series 5–12. **Line 3:** series 13–19 and 21–23. **Line 4:** series 46–56 and 58–64. **Line 5:** series 24–27 and 30–33. **Line 6:** series 35–45. **Line 7:** series 66–70, 72–73, 75–78, and 82–87. **Line 8:** series 88–89, 90b–92, 94–100, and 102–9. **Line 9:** unweighted arithmetic mean of lines 10–13. **Line 10:** series 125–28. **Line 11:** series 129–31 and 133–35. **Line 12:** series 137–39, 141–43a, 145–46, and 148. **Line 13:** series 113, 114–22, and 124. **Line 14:** series 149–58, 159a–60, 162–72, and 174–85. **Line 15:** series 186–88 and 190–200. **Line 16:** series 203, 205, 208–9a, 212–12b, and 215–26. **Line 17:** series 204 and 204a. **Line 18:** series 227–29. **Line 19:** series 230–32. **Line 20:** series 234a and 234b. **Line 22:** unweighted arithmetic mean of lines 1, 9, and 14–20.

Note: Some groups include aggregate series and their components. The comparison of the deviations in the two plans is made with reservations since the same series are not included in the two calculations.

year tends to make comparisons misleading. More significant are the comparisons of goals for money wages, which reflect greater disturbances in the structure of prices and wages in the Second than the First Five-Year Plan.

Nevertheless, all these statistics do not provide a clear judgment of the efficiency of Soviet planners. Only data comparing over-all costs and the results obtained can be significant here. Unfortunately, to collect adequate statistics on costs is almost impossible. It is extremely difficult to estimate the real cost of investment and to compare that estimate with the five-year plan goals. (For a more detailed discussion, see Chapter 11.) Statistics on investments, even those officially given in constant prices, are actually calculated in current prices (or in prices very close to current ones), and the result gives a false picture of the volume of investment. Thus, an attempt to recalculate in 1933 plan prices the figures recently published "in comparable prices" shows investment goals exceeded for 1933–1937, whereas all other indications imply the contrary.[28]

The difficulty involved in evaluating the results for 1933–1937 stems from two factors: the overevaluation of the official statistics using the notorious 1926/27 prices and the absence of a cost-of-living index for 1932–1937. To cope with these difficulties, use of independent Western calculations is indispensable. The results of these calculations, as well as the official Soviet ones, are reproduced in Table 28.

The main discrepancy concerns the growth of national income. The five-year plan in this sector was almost entirely fulfilled according to official Soviet estimates, but only two-thirds fulfilled according to Western estimates. The discrepancy for this period between Soviet and Western estimates is much less for industrial production and agricultural production. The argument may be summarized as follows. If the official Soviet figure for national income is accepted, then the official figure for growth of real wages (and consumption, see Table 28) must also be accepted, and the result is only a slight underfulfillment of the investment plan. If, on the other hand, the Soviet figure for national income is not accepted—and all Western studies agree that it should not be[29]—the necessary result is nonfulfillment of the investment and consumption plans.

For real wages, calculations that Naum Jasny and I made independently show a 62 or 66 per cent fulfillment of the five-year plan, that is, an increase in real wages of only 22 or 29 per cent during the five years. According to Jasny, total personal income increased 62.8 per cent during this period, which brings the fulfillment of the consumption plan to 67.2 per cent (see Table 28). The extent of the consumption plan underfulfillment is very close to that of the national income plan according to Jasny's calculations. A similar percentage of fulfillment for the investment plan for 1933–1937, therefore, seems likely. Unfortunately, there are no detailed Western studies on this subject, except for Jasny's rough calculations. On the basis of his data, fulfillment of the five-year investment plan can be estimated at about 75 to 80 per cent.[30]

28. According to *Narodnoe khoziaistvo SSSR v 1961 godu* [The National Economy of the USSR in 1961], Moscow, 1962, p. 537, total investment in 1933 in "constant" prices (July 1, 1955, estimate prices, taking later changes into account) was 20.62 billion old rubles. In 1933 plan prices, this same total was 18.8 billion rubles (see *Vtoroi plan*, p. 716). Hence the new prices were 9.7 per cent higher than the 1933 plan prices.

Total investment "in comparable prices" during 1933–1937 was 161.63 billion old rubles. In 1933 plan prices, then, it would be 147.3 billion rubles, whereas the five-year plan provided 139.1 billion rubles for investment in that period (including the work of collective farmers and the contribution of the population to road construction). See *ibid.*, p. 716.

29. Abram Bergson's study, *The Real National Income of Soviet Russia since 1928* (Cambridge, Mass., 1961, p. 177), shows an increase in national income (1937 ruble factor cost) of 67.6 per cent between 1928 and 1937, whereas Soviet sources give an increase of 282 per cent. A study by G. Warren Nutter ("The Effects of Economic Growth on Sino-Soviet Strategy" in *National Security: Political, Military, and Economic Strategies in the Decade Ahead*, edited by D. M. Abshire and R. V. Allen, New York, 1963, p. 166) shows an increase of 85 per cent in national income (composite national product) between 1928 and 1937. All these calculations are made with income originating weights.

30. According to Jasny (*Essays*, p. 239), planned investments in 1932 prices (which were very close

Table 28   Fulfillment of Principal Economic Indexes for Second Five-Year Plan: Comparison of Official Soviet and Western Estimates

	Level in 1937 (1932 = 100) (1)	Per Cent of Fulfillment of Five-Year Plan Goals for 1937 (2)
National Income		
1. Official Soviet estimate in 1926/27 prices	211.6	96.1
2. Jasny estimate	146.4	66.5
3. Moorsteen and Powell estimate	156.4	71.0
Industrial Production		
4. Official Soviet estimate in 1926/27 prices	219.5	103.0
5. Jasny estimate	173.9	81.2
6. Kaplan and Moorsteen estimate	162.0	75.7
7. Nutter estimate	199.3	93.1
Agricultural Production		
Official Soviet estimates:		
8. In 1926/27 prices	153.9	76.9
9. In "constant" prices (revised)	125.3	62.6
10. Jasny estimate	153.4	76.7
Johnson and Kahan estimates:		
11. In 1926/27 prices	138.1	69.0
12. In average 1925–1929 prices	137.6	68.8
13. In 1958 prices	132.2	66.1
Employment		
14. Workers and employees, national economy, official Soviet estimate	117.9	93.4
Wages		
15. Average money wage, workers and employees, national economy, official Soviet estimate	213.5	173.6
16. Real wage, official Soviet estimate	201	102.6
17. Real wage, Jasny estimate	122.4	62.4
18. Real wage, Zaleski estimate	129	65.8
19. Real income of peasants, Jasny estimate	152.8	
Total Personal Income		
20. Jasny estimate	162.8	67.2

Source

COLUMN 1–Lines 1, 4, and 14-15: Derived from Table A-1, col. 2, and my *Planning*, Table A-1, col. 6. **Line 2:** Derived from Jasny total national income less duplication for 1928 and 1937 (29.8 and 51.1 bill. rubles in Naum Jasny, *Soviet Industrialization, 1928–1952*, Chicago, 1961, p. 444) and 1932 figure derived by same method (34.9 in my *Planning*, Table 46, p. 248). **Line 3:** Derived from Richard Moorsteen and Raymond Powell, *The Soviet Capital Stock, 1928–1962*, Homewood, Ill., 1966, p. 361. **Line 5:** Derived from Naum Jasny, *The Soviet Price System*, Stanford, 1951, p. 173. In real 1926/27 prices. **Line 6:** Derived from Norman Kaplan and Richard Moorsteen, "Indexes of Soviet Industrial Output," RAND Research Memorandum 2495, Santa Monica, 1960, Vol. II, p. 235. In Soviet 1950 wholesale prices. Civilian production only. **Line 7:** Derived from G. Warren Nutter, *Growth of Industrial Production in the Soviet Union*, Princeton, 1962, p. 158. Total industrial production. **Lines 8–13:** Derived from my *Planning*, Table A-14, p. 387. **Line 16:** In a speech to the Eighteenth Party Congress, Molotov stated that real wages had increased by 101 per cent between 1932 and 1937 (Naum Jasny, *Essays on the Soviet Economy*, New York, 1962, p. 241). **Lines 17 and 19-20:** Derived from Jasny, *Soviet Industrialization*, pp. 446–47. **Line 18:** Derived from average money wage (line 15) and increase in price index between 1932 and 1937 (derived as 166 from my *Planning*, Table A-17, col. 3, p. 391).

COLUMN 2–Lines 1, 4, 8-9, and 14-15: Table A-1, col. 3. **Lines 2-3, 5-7, 10-13, 16-18, and 20:** Derived from col. 1 and planned increases given in Table 21, col. 4. For line 20, consumption goal under national income in Table 21, col. 4, was used.

On the whole, it appears that not only was the Second Five-Year Plan rejected by the Soviet authorities as a base for their operational plans, annual and quarterly, but it also did not forecast correctly the broad lines of economic development. Implementation of the plan was much more modest than anticipated, a result even more significant in view of the fact that the period 1933–1937 included the three best prewar years (1934–1936) and that the base from which the plan was calculated was particularly low. Still, the Soviet authorities could justly boast of the abolition of rationing and an increase in peasant income, which were much more important in the eyes of the people than index calculations.

---

to 1933 plan prices) were set at 73.9 billion rubles in the annual plans for 1935, 1936, and 1937. For lack of any more precise information, it has to be assumed that these plans were fulfilled. To this amount must be added investment in 1933 (18.8 billion rubles) and investment in 1934 (21.5 billion rubles in 1933 prices), which makes a total of 114.2 billion in 1932–1933 prices, compared with the 139.1 billion given in the plan in 1933 plan prices. Supposedly, 83 per cent of the investment plan was fulfilled, but since the investment plan was probably not fulfilled in 1937 (a depression year), a 75 to 80 per cent fulfillment seems more likely. Of course, this percentage covers only real expenditures for investment and does not reflect the cost increase that usually occurs relative to the original estimates.

CHAPTER 8

Drafting the Third Five-Year Plan

Campaign to Draw Up Third Five-Year Plan

Beginning in 1936

The initial stages of drafting the Third Five-Year Plan (1938–1942) seem to have coincided with celebrations commemorating the fifteenth anniversary of Gosplan (February 22, 1936). In a speech made on that occasion, Molotov launched a vast campaign, declaring that "this third five-year plan should prove to ourselves and to the whole world what we are worth."[1] Government directives were accompanied by a flood of medals for the Order of Lenin, the Red Star, and the Order of Merit awarded to former and present Gosplan directors by a decree issued February 21, 1936.[2] The actual content of the directives remains unknown. Gosplan Deputy Chairman E. I. Kviring mentioned only that this plan would "gradually strengthen the elements of communism and the victorious movement toward communism."[3] An agreement between Gosplan and the USSR Academy of Sciences listed eight areas for priority research.[4]

1. Quoted in G. Krzhizhanovskii, "Akademiia nauk i podgotovka tretego piatiletnego plana" [The Academy of Sciences and Preparation of the Third Five-Year Plan], *Planovoe khoziaistvo* [Planned Economy], No. 4, 1936, p. 10.

2. "O nagrazhdenii ordenami SSSR rabotnikov po planirovaniiu narodnogo khoziaistva" [On Awarding USSR Orders to Workers in National Economic Planning], *Plan*, No. 4, 1936, pp. 3–4. Among those decorated were such former Gosplan directors as G. M. Krzhizhanovskii, S. G. Strumilin, A. N. Dolgov, V. R. Viliams, E. Ia. Shulgin, Gosplan Chairman V. I. Mezhlauk, Gosplan Deputy Chairmen G. I. Smirnov and E. I. Kviring, Director of the Gosplan Institute of Economic Research and head of the Financial Section B. V. Troitskii, most of the heads of Gosplan departments (B. S. Borilin, G. B. Lauer, I. S. Ginzburg, etc.), and I. A. Kraval, head of the Central Administration of Statistics and National Accounting under Gosplan (*TsUNKhU*).

3. E. Kviring, "Ocherednye zadachi planirovaniia" [Immediate Tasks of Planning], *Planovoe khoziaistvo*, No. 3, 1936, p. 57.

4. Prospecting, searching for a new petroleum base, establishing a single interconnecting electric power network, supplying fuel to motor vehicles and tractors, developing the ferrous and nonferrous metal industry and the chemical industry, mechanization and automation, developing grain crops, and drawing up a balance of the national economy (Krzhizhanovskii, *Planovoe khoziaistvo*, No. 4, 1936, pp. 22–27).

It is probable that the government directives were more precise and that some actual goals for 1942 were given to the planning agencies. The government's experience of having to revise its directives when preparing the Second Five-Year Plan no doubt gave rise to some caution. In any case, only a few actual goals are known and these have no direct connection with the preparation of the Third Five-Year Plan. Examples are the goal given by Stalin "to increase during the next three or four years the grain harvest to 7 or 8 billion poods"[5] and the goals for the production of electric power (145 to 230 billion kilowatt-hours in 10 or 15 years, i.e., in 1945 or 1950) adopted as a base by specialists.[6]

The third plan was to be drafted in "one year or less"; that is, the plan was to be ready around the middle of 1937 and put into operation at the beginning of 1938. As with the previous five-year plans, all the people's commissariats and all the scientific institutes, led by the USSR Academy of Sciences, were to join in the work, and a large number of sectoral and regional conferences was planned.[7] The basic work was to be done under USSR Gosplan, which was charged with drawing up "methodological instructions, tables, and indicators" for drafting the plan, the main balances, and the outline of the geographical location of productive forces, as well as with deciding which problems were important enough to warrant study. In fact, these methodological instructions, tables, and indicators were to lay out the work to be done in the whole country. A special commission, headed by Gosplan Deputy Chairman G. I. Smirnov, was set up for that purpose within Gosplan and charged with preparing these instructions with a deadline of June 1, 1936.[8] Similar instructions for drafting the 1937 annual plan were to be prepared even earlier, by May 10, 1936. Thus, the two plans (the annual plan for 1937 and the five-year plan for 1938–1942) were directly linked, with the 1937 plan figures serving as the base for the five-year projections.[9]

Smirnov's commission was to calculate a number of preliminary balances, was to make long-range calculations of national income and the financial plan, and was to estimate projections for the increase in labor productivity and the reduction of wholesale and retail prices.[10] A list of projects to be undertaken under the

5. *Ibid.*, p. 26.

6. S. Kukel-Kraevskii, "O putiakh razvitiia edinogo energokhoziaistva SSSR" [On Means of Developing a Single Electric Power System in the USSR], *Planovoe khoziaistvo*, No. 1, 1936, p. 38.

7. Kviring, *Planovoe khoziaistvo*, No. 3, 1936, pp. 56–57.

8. The most important Gosplan directors were members of this commission: Kraval, head of *TsUNKhU*; Borilin, head of the General Department of Production of Gosplan; Troitskii, director of the Gosplan Institute of Economic Research and head of the Financial Section; V. V. Belenko, head of the Gosplan Department of Trade; and I. D. Vermenichev, head of the Gosplan Department of Agriculture. See Ia. Chadaev, "Razrabotka metodologicheskikh ukazanii k narodno-khoziaistvennomu planu na 1937 g." [Drafting the Methodological Instructions for the 1937 National Economic Plan], *Plan*, No. 9, 1936, p. 50.

9. *Ibid.*

10. The preliminary balances were fuel, electric power, the principal types of equipment, cement, wood, cotton, wool, linen, grain, trade and personal consumption, freight transportation, investment, and labor (Ia. Chadaev, "Razrabotka metodologicheskikh ukazanii i form k planu na 1937 g." [Drafting the Methodological Instructions and Forms for the 1937 Plan], *Plan*, No. 10, 1936, p. 53). According to Ts. Galperin ("Iz opyta sostavleniia vtorogo piatiletnego plana" [From the Experience of Drafting the Second Five-Year Plan], *Planovoe khoziaistvo*, No. 3, 1936, p. 93), the Third Five-Year Plan was to be divided into four sections: branches, institutions, regions, and an aggregative section.

auspices of Gosplan's Institute of Economic Research was to be presented as soon as possible with specification of who was to direct the projects and the schedules for carrying them out.

The same principles were to guide republic Gosplans and province planning committees in drawing up their plans. In the spring of 1936 the Russian Republic Council of People's Commissars named a special commission to direct the work on the third plan. Headed by D. E. Sulimov, this commission included the men responsible for the republic economy, including Russian Republic Gosplan Chairman S. B. Karp. Another office created under that Gosplan and headed by Karp was to direct the planning work within Gosplan and to publish a special bulletin, the first issue of which was to appear in May 1936.[11] In the middle of May, RSFSR Gosplan sent all the province and local planning committees instructions for drawing up the plan and starting projects to be undertaken on the spot. The departments of Gosplan were to draft a first version of the Third Five-Year Plan, which was to be discussed at a Gosplan meeting in June.[12]

During the first half of 1936, considerable work on the third plan seems to have been accomplished by province and regional planning committees. Several conferences were held to study the development of the Northern Province in February[13] and the development of the Northern Caucasus in March; reports published in the specialized press stressed the progress made in several other areas.[14] We should also point out that work seems to have been quite far advanced during the first half of 1936 in various branches of industry, agriculture, and social and cultural welfare.[15]

The impetus with which the planning work started contrasts sharply with the relative silence of the specialized press on the subject from September 1936 until the beginning of 1937. The commentaries that accompanied the resumption of planning work in April and May of 1937 may explain in part the reasons for the temporary lull that followed.

Restarting in Spring 1937

Work on the third plan was officially resumed in response to the April 28, 1937, decree of the Council of People's Commissars. That decree requested USSR Gosplan, the people's commissariats, and the federal republic councils of people's commissariats to present a complete draft of the third plan for approval by

11. "V respublikanskikh, oblastnykh i kraevykh komissiakh i UNKhU" [In Republic, Province, and Territory Planning Committees and the National Economic Statistical Administration], *Plan*, No. 11, 1936, pp. 54 and 57.

12. *Ibid.*, p. 57.

13. *Plan*, No. 5, 1936; No. 8, 1936; and No. 11, 1936, pp. 57 and 31.

14. Kalinin, Leningrad, Eastern Siberia, Kirov, the Crimea, Gorky, the Western Province, Volga, Belorussia, and Azov-Black Sea (*Plan*, No. 7–No. 14, 1936). To learn the details of work done on the third plan, it would be necessary to go through the local specialized press, access to which is difficult. A special investigation on this subject would have to be made, which could produce interesting results by showing the repercussions of government directives on the work done on the spot.

15. In chemicals, machine-building, peat extraction, electric power stations, and motor fuels; irrigation of the Volga area; and public health (*Plan*, Nos. 7, 10, 11, and 13, 1936).

July 1, 1937, at the latest, and recommended a vast press campaign on the subject.[16]

A change in government policy is certainly one of the main reasons for both slowing down and resuming the work on the third plan. This change lay mainly in the stress put on strengthening military power in the USSR: "Capitalist encirclement and the preparations of the fascist states for a war against the USSR oblige the planning agencies to guarantee by the plan a general strengthening of the defense capacities of the country. All the plans for the development of different sectors and the geographical distribution of new construction projects should be re-examined with a view to strengthening the military and defensive capacities of the USSR. Special impetus must be given to the development of the defense industry."[17] This reason alone is sufficient to explain the complete revision of the first variants of the Third Five-Year Plan. Nevertheless, it is logical to assume that other reasons, economic ones, also forced the government to modify its original goals. These goals were actually based not only on the preliminary directives of the 1937 plan but also on the forecasts of the 1936 annual plan. Although satisfactory in value terms, the fulfillment of this plan was very poor in some branches of industry (mainly machine-building, but also nonferrous metals, chemicals, and the food and light industries), in agriculture, and in investment.[18] The sizable increases in wholesale prices of April 1, 1936,[19] the abolition of rationing, and several changes in retail prices completely changed the structure of costs and prices of investment, which, according to the new instructions, were to be estimated in prices of December 1, 1936.[20] Unfortunately, it is difficult to judge the importance of the changes that necessitated revising the 1936 annual plan goals and the price reforms, since neither the original directives nor the progress made in 1936 is known in sufficient detail.

Changes in the personnel of the economic administration, the factories, and the planning and statistical agencies also forced revision of the original work. The effects of this purge are very clear-cut, and a special section will be devoted to this matter later.[21]

Technical difficulties may have been another reason that planning work was slowed and later restarted. When the work was resumed, a completely new set of methodological and technical instructions was drawn up for the local planning agencies. The April 28 decree on resumption of work on the plan stipulated that USSR Gosplan immediately had to begin drafting methodological instructions and a system of indicators for the people's commissariats and the republics. Immediately thereafter, on May 4, 1937, Gosplan Deputy Chairman Kviring set

16. *Direktivy KPSS i sovetskogo pravitelstva po khoziaistvennym voprosam* [Directives of the Communist Party of the Soviet Union and of the Soviet Government on Economic Matters], Moscow, 1957, Vol. 2, p. 514.

17. "Za razrabotku bolshevistskogo plana tretei piatiletki" [For Drafting a Bolshevik Third Five-Year Plan], *Plan*, No. 9, 1937, p. 2.

18. For more details on the fulfillment of the 1936 annual plan, see Table A–2.

19. Naum Jasny, *Soviet Prices of Producers' Goods*, Stanford, 1952, pp. 151–57 and 160.

20. V. Nikiforova, "V Gosplane RSFSR" [In RSFSR Gosplan], *Plan*, No. 9, 1937, p. 46. The new variant of the plan also made it necessary to revise the goals for retail trade; the figures on gross production were in constant "1926/27" prices, except for the cooperative industry, which was estimated in 1932 prices (*ibid*.).

21. See section below on purges of personnel in planning agencies.

up a special commission in Gosplan to draft these instructions and indicators and ordered the heads of Gosplan departments and sections to present their proposals as soon as possible.[22] At the same time, the RSFSR Gosplan Chairman Karp issued instructions on drawing up the third plan to province and local planning committees.[23]

This drafting of completely new instructions and indicators is all the more surprising since those drawn up in 1936 seemed ready. An article in the Gosplan journal *Plan* (on June 12, 1936) even gave some details, stating that the Third Five-Year Plan would cover all sectors of the economy more completely than the Second Five-Year Plan by estimating investment, fixed capital, employment, wages, etc., for each sector and giving a breakdown of production by commissariats and by industries. The provisions of the plan for electric power and petroleum were cited at that time.[24] No trace of the publication of these instructions could be found in the sources consulted, although the instructions for drafting the 1937 annual plan, which must have been prepared at the same time, were published.[25] The only possible explanation for reformulating all these instructions and indicators is that important changes in government policy necessitated a completely different conception of the entire work.

After the work on the third plan was restarted, it received considerable publicity in the press. The work was evidently done both at the Gosplan level and at the level of the local and province planning agencies. Many articles appeared on this subject during 1937, several of which gave detailed figures on the plan goals for 1942 both for different industries and for different regions. Nevertheless, the official press was very discreet about the fate of the draft plan that was to be presented by USSR Gosplan for the approval of the Council of People's Commissars on July 1, 1937. The closing down, probably in August or September of 1937, of the semimonthly Gosplan journal *Plan*, the best source of information on the practical problems of planning, made it impossible to continue following the work of Gosplan very closely.[26] The silence observed on this subject, the administrative reforms, and changes in planning agency personnel were sufficient indication even then that the draft plan, approved or not, could not be put into operation. New work on the Third Five-Year Plan hence became indispensable in 1938.

Drawing up a Draft in 1938

Very little is known of the history of work on the Third Five-Year Plan during 1938. It is possible only to reconstruct the broad outlines. There appear to have been two phases, one coinciding with the preparation of the 1938 annual plan

---

22. "V Gosplane i TsUNKhU SSSR" [In USSR Gosplan and *TsUNKhU*], *Plan*, No. 9, 1937, p. 42.

23. Nikiforova, *Plan*, No. 9, 1937, p. 46.

24. Ia. Chadaev, "O khode razrabotki metodologicheskikh ukazanii k sostavleniiu plana tretei piatiletki" [On Progress in Drafting Methodological Instructions for the Third Five-Year Plan], *Plan*, No. 11, 1936, p. 50.

25. *Ukazaniia i formy k sostavleniiu narodnokhoziaistvennogo plana na 1937 god* [Instructions and Forms for Drafting the National Economic Plan for 1937], Moscow, 1936.

26. The last issue of this journal (No. 16) appeared on August 25, 1937. It proved impossible to find Nos. 13, 14, and 16 of 1937.

toward the end of 1937 and the beginning of 1938, and a second coinciding with the inauguration of a new management team in Gosplan headed by N. A. Voznesenskii[27] just before the drafting of the 1939 annual plan.

Attempts to revise the third plan made at the end of 1937 or the beginning of 1938 can be perceived in an article on prospects for the development of retail trade during the third plan.[28] The figures published in this article clearly show that the draft in question came *after* the one to be presented to the government on July 1, 1937, and *before* the final text of the plan presented by Molotov to the Eighteenth Party Congress on March 14–17, 1939. The links between this text and the 1938 annual plan are mentioned directly by one of the commentators on the plan, B. Timofeev: "From the goals for 1938 the shape of the Third Five-Year Plan can be seen clearly. In this five-year plan retail trade is to increase two to two and a half times and to reach the immense volume of 250 to 300 billion rubles."[29]

From elsewhere it is known that the drafting of the 1939 annual plan was delayed, officially because instructions and forms were not received in time.[30] The economic difficulties of 1937 and the purges were no doubt the real reasons. In any case, the trade figures published, which take into account the 1937 results as well as the links with the 1938 annual plan, show that attempts were made to revise the projections of May–June 1937 in the light of the 1937 results and the 1938 plan.[31]

The failure of these attempts can be seen in the continuation of the work in 1938. A new Gosplan statute issued on February 2, 1938,[32] and the administrative reorganization of Gosplan that accompanied the inauguration of the new management team[33] were followed by a new surge of work on drafting the third plan. Most surprisingly, Gosplan seems to have started its preparatory work all over again. It was pointed out that, during the June 25, 1938, meeting, "Gosplan also examined the problem of drafting the Third Five-Year Plan and adopted a certain number of decisions. In particular, Gosplan decided to draw up methodological instructions and forms for drafting the third five-year plan and to organize some special conferences on technical and scientific problems raised by the third plan."[34]

27. Decree of April 21, 1938 (*Sobranie postanovlenii i rasporiazhenii pravitelstva SSSR* [Collection of Resolutions and Decrees of USSR Government], No. 19, May 7, 1938, Art. 118).

28. Iu. Shnirlin, "Zadachi sovetskoi torgovli v tretei piatiletke" [Tasks of Soviet Trade in Third Five-Year Plan], *Planovoe khoziaistvo*, No. 2, 1938, pp. 98–112.

29. B. Timofeev, "Sovetskaia torgovlia vo vtoroi piatiletke" [Soviet Trade in the Second Five-Year Plan], *Problemy ekonomiki* [Problems of Economics], No. 2, 1938, p. 162.

30. "Raboty Gosplana na uroven novykh zadach" [Work of Gosplan on Level of New Tasks], *Planovoe khoziaistvo*, No. 2, 1938, p. 25.

31. For a comparison of the different variants of the Third Five-Year Plan, see Table 31 below.

32. *Sobranie postanovlenii*, No. 7, March 28, 1938, Art. 41. An annex to this decree, published at the same time, gives the breakdown of Gosplan into departments, sections, and groups, which was confirmed by the Council of People's Commissars on February 28, 1938.

33. This is discussed in detail in the last part of the section on the purges in the planning agencies below.

34. "V Gosudarstvennoi Planovoi Komissii pri SNK SSSR" [In Gosplan under USSR Council of People's Commissars], *Planovoe khoziaistvo*, No. 7, 1938, p. 148.

Another decision taken on this occasion, probably not put into effect, was to publish a monthly Gosplan bulletin with M. A. Lagutin as editor-in-chief.[35]

Not a single figure from this new variant of the third plan was published, and it is impossible to know the extent to which the work in progress was affected by the economic difficulties of 1938. In any case, the final draft, approved by the Eighteenth Party Congress on March 14–17, 1939, was published for the first time only at the beginning of 1939 in the form of a report by Molotov.[36] Hence it was to include the preliminary results for 1938 and the figures of the 1939 annual plan.[37] From a five-year plan for 1938–1942, the final text thus became a three-year plan for 1940–1942 based on the actual results of 1938 and on the goals of the 1939 annual plan. Thus it bears considerable resemblance to the Second Five-Year Plan for 1933–1937, the final text of which included long-range goals for 1935–1937, the actual results of 1933, and the 1934 annual plan.[38]

Purges of Planning Agency Personnel

Extent of Purges

The purges within the planning agencies constituted only a fragment of the huge wave of purges orchestrated by Stalin during 1936–1938. From the second half of 1936 on, the atmosphere of political terror was carefully cultivated. The big show trials of the "Trotskyite" group of August and their reverberations served as a warning to all administrative and Party personnel.[39] The groundwork for installing an apparatus of repression was laid in September 1936, when the head of the Commissariat of Internal Affairs (NKVD) G. G. Yagoda was

---

35. *Ibid*.

36. "Tretii piatiletnii plan razvitiia narodnogo khoziaistva SSSR (1938–1942 gg). Tezisy doklada tov. V. Molotova" [Third Five-Year Plan for the Development of the USSR National Economy, 1938–1942. Theses of Comrade V. Molotov's Report], *Planovoe khoziaistvo*, No. 1, 1939, pp. 4–26. This issue was set in type on December 29, 1938; "permission to print" was received on February 20, 1939. *Tretii piatiletnii plan razvitiia narodnogo khoziaistva SSSR (1938–1942)* [Third Five-Year Plan for the Development of the USSR National Economy, 1938–1942], presented by N. A. Voznesenskii for government confirmation, was set in type on March 7, 1939, and "permission to print" was received on March 14, 1939. This plan was adopted by the Eighteenth Party Congress on March 14–17, 1939.

37. Gosplan ordered the drafting of the 1939 annual plan on September 20, 1938, after a report by Voznesenskii. The heads of the Gosplan departments and sections were to draw up their projects by October 15, 1938, at the latest. The resumption of work on the Third Five-Year Plan was announced June 25, 1938 (see above). Actually, Gosplan worked on the five-year plan and the 1939 annual plan simultaneously: "At this time Gosplan has taken up the preparation of the Third Five-Year Plan and the 1939 annual plan. The main objective of this work is the revision of the 'instructions and forms,' which should guarantee a unified system of comparable indicators and a single method of drafting the national economic plan." (M. Kozin, "Ob ukazaniiakh i formakh k sostavleniiu narodno-khoziaistvennykh planov" [On the Instructions and Forms for Drafting the National Economic Plans], *Planovoe khoziaistvo*, No. 7, 1938, p. 88.) See also "V Gosplane SSSR" [In USSR Gosplan], *Planovoe khoziaistvo*, No. 10, 1938, p. 159.

38. See the end of Chapter 6.

39. The main defendants in August were Kamenev, Zinoviev, Smirnov, and Mrachkovskii and in December Radek, Piatakov, Sokolnikov, and Serebriakov. See *Sudebnyi otchet po delu Trotskistskogo-Zinovevskogo Tsentra* [Court Proceedings of the Trial of the Trotskyite-Zinoviev Center], Moscow, 1936; and *Sudebnyi otchet po delu antisovetskogo Trotskistskogo Tsentra* [Court Proceedings of the Trial of the Anti-Soviet Trotskyite Center], Moscow, 1937.

replaced by N. I. Yezhov, since 1933 a specialist in organizing purges within the Party.[40]

The issuance of new Party cards (in exchange for the old ones) decreed by the Central Committee on December 26, 1936, was a good excuse to re-examine the loyalty of every Party member. In a speech to the plenary session of the Central Committee on February 28, 1937, Molotov denounced alleged acts of sabotage, cited several of those guilty, and incited the audience to self-criticism and denunciation.[41] Another violent speech, this time by Stalin on March 3, 1937, lent more weight to the campaign.[42]

The repression was general and covered the entire Party and government apparatus. Many of the victims were liquidated physically, with or without trial, and others went to swell the population of the concentration camps or to supply cheap labor for the regime's large-scale construction projects.[43] Economic sabotage (*vreditelstvo*) was the most common charge, but the system of arresting a certain number of people according to quotas imposed on the local NKVD authorities[44] led to repression, pure and simple, that was intended to eliminate elements judged to be politically unreliable. The wave of terror reached the high-water mark with the trial of "the twenty-one" of the "bloc of rightist Trotskyites" held in March 1938, with Bukharin, Rykov, Rakovskii, Krestinskii, G. F. Grinko, and former NKVD chief Yagoda as the main defendants.[45] A special study would be needed to present an accounting of the ravages that these purges caused in the economic administration. Practically all factory offices and personnel were affected. Several holders of ministerial posts (people's commissars), their deputies, and the heads of central administrations (*Glavki*) were arrested and most of them shot.[46]

---

40. Zbigniew K. Brzezinski, *The Permanent Purge*, Cambridge, Mass., 1956, p. 70. Yagoda was arrested in April 1937, tried at the trial of the "twenty-one" in March 1938, and shot. See *ibid.*, pp. 70–73; *Pravda*, April 4, 1937, p. 1. See also Roy A. Medvedev, *Let History Judge: The Origins and Consequences of Stalinism*, New York, 1973, pp. 175–78.

41. V. M. Molotov, "Nashi zadachi v borbe s trotskistskimi i inymi vrediteliami, diversantami i shpionami" [Our Tasks in the Struggle against Trotskyite and Other Saboteurs, Diversionists, and Spies], *Plan*, No. 8, 1937, pp. 4–21; and V. M. Molotov, "Uroki vreditelstva, diversii i shpionazha iapono-nemetsko-trotskistskikh agentov" [Lessons of Sabotage, Diversion, and Espionage by Japanese and German Trotskyite Agents], *Planovoe khoziaistvo*, No. 4, 1937, pp. 3–42.

42. I. V. Stalin, "O nedostatkakh partiinoi raboty i merakh likvidatsii trotskistskikh i inykh dvurushnikov" [On Shortcomings in Party Work and Measures to Liquidate Trotskyites and Other Double-Dealers], *Plan*, No. 7, 1937, pp. 1–15.

43. David J. Dallin and Boris I. Nicolaevsky, *Forced Labor in Soviet Russia*, New Haven, Conn., 1947, pp. 259–61; and S. Swianiewicz, *Forced Labour and Economic Development*, London, New York, Toronto, 1965, pp. 133–235.

44. Dallin and Nicolaevsky, *Forced Labor*, p. 259.

45. *Sudebnyi otchet po delu anti-sovetskogo i pravo-Trotskistskogo Bloka* [Court Proceedings of the Trial of the Anti-Soviet and Rightist Trotskyite Bloc], Moscow, 1938.

46. The following list is only a partial one: Ia. Livshits, Deputy Commissar of Transportation; G. Ia. Sokolnikov, Deputy Commissar of the Timber Industry; V. I. Zof, Deputy Commissar of Water Management; Markevich, Konar, Volf, and Isak Reingold, former Deputy Commissars of Agriculture; L. P. Serebriakov, former head of the Office of Transportation; N. G. Tumanov, chairman of the Industrial bank (*Prombank*); Arkus, deputy chairman of the State Bank (*Gosbank*); S. A. Rataichak, director of the Chemical Industry *Glavk*; G. F. Grinko, People's Commissar of Finance; A. I. Rykov, former chairman of the Council of People's Commissars; M. P. Tomskii, former chairman of the Trade Union Council; K. G. Rakovskii, former ambassador to London and Paris; and G. L. Piatakov, former de-

All these people were directly responsible not only for economic administration but also for drafting plans. The central and local planning agencies therefore must have found it impossible to work, even if their particular agency was not purged.

Purges within the Planning Agencies

Conferring high distinctions on and awarding medals to the Gosplan directors at the time work was begun on the Third Five-Year Plan[47] may have given the impression that they enjoyed the complete confidence of the government and the Party. Nevertheless they were put to a severe test from the very first manifestations of the wave of repression and particularly after the speeches of Molotov and Stalin in February and March of 1937.

A conference of Gosplan "activists," with 200 communists participating, was organized on March 13–15, 1937, to discuss the results of the February 23–March 5 plenary session of the Party Central Committee (at which Stalin and Molotov had made their speeches) as reported by Gosplan Deputy Chairman G. I. Smirnov. The real task of this meeting was to start a movement of self-criticism and denunciation for sabotage within Gosplan. To judge from an editorial in the journal *Plan*, the conference performed its task very poorly.[48] Smirnov did denounce a few "enemies of the people" who had infiltrated the Gosplan apparatus and who were arrested by the NKVD (Soldatov, Bronshtein) and others who were dismissed (Smirnov, Iakhontov), but the 31 participants in the discussion were very reticent in denouncing people for sabotage. The editorial criticized the contributions of such people as Belova, Kazarin, and Tokarev, and in particular that of the head of Gosplan's Mining and Metal Department, G. B. Lauer, who declared that "there is no sabotage in the ferrous metal industry."[49]

Similar conferences were also organized on the republic level. The one held by Russian Republic Gosplan was severely criticized in *Plan*, which reported that the participants talked a great deal about sabotage in general but very little about sabotage within Russian Republic Gosplan itself, even though enemies of the people had become entrenched in that organization. The *Plan* statement also denounced the insufficient self-criticism of the reporter, RSFSR Gosplan Chairman Karp, and of Deputy Chairman Anikst.[50]

These conferences were followed, during April and June of 1937, by a purge, the details of which are not fully known. An editorial in *Plan* (June 12, 1937) mentions several Gosplan directors as "enemies of the people," letting it be

puty chairman of the Supreme Council of the National Economy (VSNKh), arrested earlier (Molotov, *Planovoe khoziaistvo*, No. 4, 1937, pp. 3–42; and "Pravo-trotskistskaia banda shpionov i ubiits" [Rightist Trokskyite Band of Spies and Murderers], *Planovoe khoziaistvo*, No. 2, 1938, pp. i–vi).

47. See the beginning of this chapter.

48. "Sobranie aktiva Gosplana SSSR" [Meeting of the Staff of USSR Gosplan], *Plan*, No. 7, 1937, pp. 44–45.

49. *Ibid.*, p. 40.

50. "Sobranie aktiva Gosplana RSFSR" [Meeting of the Staff of RSFSR Gosplan], *Plan*, No. 8, 1937, p. 27.

understood that they were arrested.[51] They included the head of the Central Administration of Statistics and National Accounting (*TsUNKhU*), I. A. Kraval,[52] the head of Gosplan's Mining and Metal Department, Lauer, and Mrs. Muklevich, of Gosplan's Department of Material Balances. B. V. Troitskii, head of Gosplan's Finance Department and director of the Institute of Economic Research, also was violently attacked. He had been in charge of the journal *Plan* until the previous issue (No. 10 of May 25, 1937). He was denounced as an enemy of the people and a long-standing friend of the saboteurs from the State Bank, Mariasinym and Abezgauzov. Another USSR Gosplan director, Minaev, was denounced on the same occasion as a saboteur and a coward.[53]

The purge within USSR Gosplan continued during the second half of 1937 until the entire organization had been reorganized and its new statute published on February 2, 1938.[54] Gosplan Chairman V. I. Mezhlauk was arrested in the middle of 1937 and replaced temporarily by his deputy chairman G. I. Smirnov,[55] who in turn was arrested toward the end of 1937 or the beginning of 1938. Another important Gosplan director, E. I. Kviring, was also arrested, and the same fate was meted out to most of the heads of Gosplan departments and sections. The new Gosplan setup under the February 2 statute did not contain a single one of the former Gosplan directors.[56]

The accusations against the old management team were specified in the beginning of 1938:

Gaister, Kraval, Smirnov, and the other Trotskyite bandits of the right who installed themselves in Gosplan made use of their stay in the state planning headquarters to employ all their efforts to disorganize socialist planning and national accounting, to disrupt the national economy, and to undermine the defense strength of our country. The saboteurs and murderers in Gosplan and *TsUNKhU* acted in concert with the saboteurs and murderers who infiltrated the people's commissariats, organizations, and enterprises to prepare the downfall of the Soviet Union and the re-establishment of capitalism in our country.[57]

51. "Vykorchevat korni vreditelstva v planovoi rabote" [Extirpate the Roots of Sabotage in Planning Work], *Plan*, No. 11, 1937, pp. 1–3.

52. Kraval's arrest was linked to the purge within *TsUNKhU* that followed the census of 1937. The results of this census displeased Stalin and were never published.

53. *Plan*, No. 11, 1937, pp. 1–3. After the appearance of this issue, one single editor-in-chief, V. F. Vasutin, replaced the collegium of six who had been editing the journal until then.

54. *Sobranie postanovlenii*, No. 7, March 28, 1938, Art. 41. The connection between the new statute and the purge within Gosplan is stressed in "Raboty Gosplana na uroven novykh zadach" [Work of Gosplan on Level of New Tasks], *Planovoe khoziaistvo*, No. 2, 1938, p. 19.

55. Smirnov is mentioned as the chairman of USSR Gosplan in "O rabote nad limitami plana 1938 g." [On Work on the "Limits" of the 1938 Plan], *Plan*, No. 12, 1937 ("permission to print" this issue was received on August 11, 1937).

56. The new members of USSR Gosplan were: Chairman N. A. Voznesenskii, M. Z. Saburov, V. N. Emchenko, I. V. Sautin, M. I. Rubinshtein, V. P. Businskii, K. P. Kasatkin, and S. P. Demidov (*Sobranie postanovlenii*, No. 19, May 7, 1938, Art. 118). Two first deputy chairmen were appointed later: M. Z. Saburov and G. P. Kosiachenko (*ibid.*, No. 31, December 19, 1940, Art. 800, and No. 14, May 17, 1941, Art. 260); then five deputy chairmen were appointed: N. A. Borisov, A. N. Lavrishchev, M. V. Degtiar, V. N. Starovskii, V. P. Nikitin, who were also to become members of Gosplan at the same time (*ibid.*, No. 10, April 2, 1941, Art. 167).

57. *Planovoe khoziaistvo*, No. 2, 1938, p. vi.

These were followed by the particular accusations against the staff of *TsUNKhU*: "Thanks to the heroic work of the NKVD it was possible to destroy mercilessly the principal nests of the enemies of the people who had infiltrated the national accounting agencies. The apparatus of the *TsUNKhU* was thoroughly cleaned out and new fresh forces of young economists and statisticians were brought in. The Party sent in several hundred communists and Bolsheviks who, although not communists, were loyal to the Party."[58]

The immediate consequence of this purge, which took place in the first half of 1938, was a shortage of personnel and a lack of experience among the newly hired Gosplan personnel:

Gosplan announced that in 1938, with the help of the Party Central Committee and the government, considerable work was accomplished in purging Gosplan of hostile elements and strengthening the Gosplan apparatus by promoting to responsible positions new personnel, who were politically reliable and capable of eliminating altogether the consequences of sabotage in national economic planning and guaranteeing that the level of planning be raised in accordance with the goals of the Third Five-Year Plan.

At the same time, Gosplan recognized that in recruiting personnel there were several important problems still be resolved, for which purpose the Personnel Section had to take strong measures.

Gosplan paid special attention to speeding up the recruitment of responsible Gosplan personnel, department heads, and group directors.[59]

The inexperience of the new personnel was considered particularly alarming in the area of balances. The personnel section was given the job of raising the qualifications of the heads of Gosplan groups, sections, and departments, all of whom were encouraged to expose technical and economic problems within their jurisdiction at Gosplan plenary meetings.[60]

Another consequence of the purge was discrediting the work of the former Gosplan team. The instructions and forms for drafting the national economic plan for 1937 were judged "erroneous and harmful" and the "work of Trotskyite and Bukharinite saboteurs."[61] Thus, it is easy to understand why preparatory work had to be begun all over again in 1938. Also discredited was the work done by Gosplan's Institute of Economic Research and the tables on the balance of the national economy made up by academician Strumilin.[62]

Discrediting the personnel and work of Gosplan would have been sufficient to account for the redrafting of the plan and for the many successive variants. However, the fact that the work was dragged out for three years (1936–1938) would have made it necessary to revise the original variants.

58. "Za bolshevistskuiu perestroiku raboty TsUNKhU" [For the Bolshevist Reorganization of the Work of *TsUNKhU*], *Planovoe khoziaistvo*, No. 3, 1938, pp. 16–17.

59. Summary of proceedings of USSR Gosplan meeting of September 16, 1938 (*Planovoe khoziaistvo*, No. 10, 1938, p. 159).

60. *Ibid*.

61. Kozin, *Planovoe khoziaistvo*, No. 7, 1938, p. 79.

62. *Planovoe khoziaistvo*, No. 2, 1938, p. 24.

Successive Variants of Third Five-Year Plan

It would seem natural to assume that the goals of the Third Five-Year Plan had to be revised every year in light of the results of the annual plans. Nevertheless, it is impossible to compare the original directives of February–March 1936 with fulfillment of the 1936 annual plan because none of the actual goals in these directives are known. Hence the comparison can be started only with the June–July 1937 variant and an attempt made to interpret the changes in goals as having been due to the results of the fulfillment of the annual plans for 1937 and 1938.

June–July 1937 Variant of Third Five-Year Plan

At the time this variant was drafted, the Soviet planners had at their disposal only the results for 1936. Hence the 1937 annual plan served as the base for the projections for 1942.[63] Projections were made for every year from 1937 to 1942, but we know only the few scattered figures that were published in specialized journals and that were given only for 1942 compared with the 1937 annual plan.[64] The data that could be found are given in Table 29. Even though the amount of concrete information on this variant of the plan is very limited, it is possible to make out its main features.

In the first place, these figures and those derived from them in Table 30 reveal the continuation of the expansion realized in 1934–1936.[65] The average annual rates of growth planned for 1937–1942 are very high. For this entire period (the 1937 annual plan and the five-year plan), they reach 16.1 per cent for gross industrial production, 13.0 per cent for pig iron, and as high as 64.8 per cent for oil shale. For the same industrial products, the growth rates in the three best prewar years ranged from 8.5 per cent for crude petroleum to 47.5 per cent for hydroelectric power. Comparison of the average annual growth rates achieved for 1934–1936 with those planned for 1937–1942, made in Table 30, shows that, of the 22 series studied, the planned growth rates are higher than the actual rates for 1934–1936 in nine cases and slightly lower (1.7 to 13.7 per cent) in three cases. There are reductions from 30 to 55 per cent in ten cases, two of which are series in value terms (which are less precise) and two for railroad freight traffic. Even the reduced growth rates are still quite high.

In general, it is clear that the Soviet authorities thought they could continue the expansion of 1934–1936 without difficulties, while making certain important changes in the structure of production. In heavy industry, stress was put on increasing extraction of oil, natural gas, and oil shale and on building electric

---

63. See the beginning of this chapter.

64. The drafting of plans for every year of the five-year plan from 1937 to 1942 was ordered by the Russian Republic Gosplan chairman, and it can be safely assumed that this was general practice (Nikiforova, *Plan*, No. 9, 1937, p. 46).

65. On the alternating periods of expansion and contraction of Soviet industrial production, see my *Planning for Economic Growth in the Soviet Union, 1918–1932*, translated and edited by Marie-Christine MacAndrew and G. Warren Nutter, Chapel Hill, N.C., 1971, pp. 255–88.

Table 29   June–July 1937 Variant of Third Five-Year Plan

		Actual Results in 1936 (1)	Plan for 1937		Plan for 1942	
	Units		Physical Units (2)	Index (1936 = 100) (3)	Physical Units (4)	Index (1937 Plan = 100) (5)
1. Gross industrial production (1926/27 prices):	bill. rubles	85.8	103.0	120.0	205–215	200
2. Producer goods (1926/27 prices)	bill. rubles	50.2	60.0	119.5	111.0	185
3. Consumer goods (1926/27 prices)	bill. rubles	35.6	43.0	120.8	107.5	250
4. Coal	mill. m. tons	126.8	150.2	119	327	218
5. Peat	mill. m. tons	22.4	25.0	112	52	208
6. Oil shale	mill. m. tons	.48	.8	167	9.6	1,200
7. Crude petroleum	mill. m. tons	27.3	32.2	118	64	200
8. Natural gas	mill. m. tons	1.9	2.3	121	8–9	350–390
9. Electric power (capacity)	mill. kw	7.5	9	120	18	200
10. Electric power:	bill. kwh	32.8	40.5	123	85–90	210–220
11. Hydroelectric power	bill. kwh	4.0			15	
12. Pig iron	mill. m. tons	14.4	16.0	111	30	185–190
13. Steel ingots and castings	mill. m. tons	16.4	20.2	123	37–38	185–190
14. Industrial timber hauled	mill. m³	120.0	167.9	140	269–285	160–170
15. Plywood	thous. m³	674	770	114	1,232	160
16. Soda ash	thous. m. tons	503.4	553.3	110	1,450–1,500	262–271
17. Sulfuric acid	thous. m. tons	1,197	1,666	139	4,300	258
18. Cement	mill. m. tons	5.9	7.4	125	16.0	216
19. Synthetic fiber	thous. m. tons		8.6			1,000
20. Length of railroad network	thous. km	85.4	86.5	101	117	135
21. Railroad freight traffic	bill. m. ton-km	323.5	387.0	120	700	181
22. Railroad freight traffic	mill. m. tons	483.2	565.0	117	1,000	177
23. Inland waterway and maritime freight traffic	bill. m. ton-km	72.3	91.5	127	183	200

Source

COLUMN 1–Lines 1-3, 5-8, 14, and 20-21: *Narodno-khoziaistvennyi plan Souiza SSR na 1937 god* [The USSR National Economic Plan for 1937], Moscow, 1937, pp. 42, 64–66, 94–95, and 120–23. Natural gas is derived as the difference between crude petroleum including gas and crude petroleum excluding gas. **Lines 4, 9-13, and 15-18:** *Promyshlennost SSSR* [Industry of the USSR], Moscow, 1957, pp. 140, 171, 106, 261, 194, 196, and 277. **Line 22:** *Transport i sviaz SSSR* [Transport and Communications in the USSR], Moscow, 1957, p. 32. **Line 23:** Sum of inland waterway traffic (given as 31.2 billion m. ton-km in *ibid.*, p. 116) and maritime traffic (given as 41.1 billion m. ton-km in Ernest W. Williams, Jr., *Freight Transportation in the Soviet Union*, Princeton, 1962, p. 182).

COLUMN 2–Lines 1-8, 12-14, and 20-23: *Plan 1937*, pp. 42, 64–66, 68, 94–95, 120–23, and 130–32. Natural gas is derived as the difference between crude petroleum including gas and crude petroleum excluding gas. Line 23 is sum of inland waterway and maritime traffic. **Line 9:** Based on cols. 4 and 5. **Lines 10 and 16-17:** "Osnovnye pokazateli narodnokhoziaistvennogo plana na 1937 g." [Main Indicators of the National Economic Plan in 1937], *Planovoe khoziaistvo*, No. 3, 1937, pp. 228 and 233. **Line 15:** V. Vozdvizhenskii, "Razvitie lesnoi promyshlennosti i razmeshchenie ee v treti piatiletke" [Development of the Timber Industry and Its Geographical Distribution in the Third Five-Year Plan], *Planovoe khoziaistvo*, No. 9–10, 1937, p. 85. **Line 18:** *Planovoe khoziaistvo*, No. 3, 1937, p. 205; and A. Kazanskii, "Razmeshchenie tsementnoi promyshlennosti" [Distribution of the Cement Industry], *Planovoe khoziaistvo*, No. 7, 1937, p. 50. **Line 19:** *Promyshlennost*, p. 323.

COLUMN 3–Lines 1-7, 14, and 20-22: *Plan 1937*, pp. 42, 64–66, 94–95, and 120–23. **Lines 8-10, 12-13, 15-18, and 23:** Col. 2 as per cent of col. 1.

COLUMN 4–Line 1: Approximate range based on cols. 2 and 5 and on sum of lines 2 and 3 (taking into account that the figure for consumer goods is probably too high). **Lines 2-3, 7, 12-15, and 23:** Based on cols. 2 and 5. **Lines 4-5:** Derived from percentage breakdown of fuel in conventional units, given as 55.9 for coal, 18.5 for crude petroleum, and 4.3 for peat by V. I. Veits, A. E. Probst, and E. A. Rusakovskii ("Edinyi energeticheskii balans v

Table 29 *continued*

tretem piatiletii" [A Single Power Balance in the Third Five-Year Period], *Planovoe khoziaistvo*, No. 9–10, 1937, p. 37). Figure for crude petroleum (64 mill. m. tons in line 7) was converted into conventional units by 1940 conversion factor of 1.43 (derived from *Promyshlennost*, pp. 133 and 153), thus making it possible to derive total fuel in conventional units. From that total, coal and peat in conventional units were derived and then converted into tons by the respective 1940 conversion factors of .847 and .41 (derived from *Promyshlennost*, pp. 133, 144, and 165). **Line 6:** M. Sonin, "O razvitii slantsevoi promyshlennosti v tretem piatiletii" [On the Development of the Oil Shale Industry in the Third Five-Year Period], *Plan*, No. 12, 1937, p. 40. **Line 8:** According to Veits, Probst, and Rusakovskii (*Planovoe khoziaistvo*, No. 9–10, 1937, p. 63), production of natural gas was to reach 8–10 billion m³ by 1942. According to N. Sazonov ("Ob energosnabzhenii v tretei piatiletke" [On Electric Power Supply in the Third Five-Year Plan], *Planovoe khoziaistvo*, No. 5–6, 1937, p. 24), this 8–10 bill. m³ would make it possible to economize 8–9 million metric tons of oil and oil products. **Lines 9-11:** Veits, Probst, and Rusakovskii, *Planovoe khoziaistvo*, No. 9–10, 1937, pp. 42 and 64. **Line 16:** G. Aleshkovskii, "V otdele khimii" [In the Chemical Sector], *Plan*, No. 9, 1937, p. 44. Given as approximations. **Line 17:** Minimum requirements given by Kalmykov, president of *Glavkhimprom* of the People's Commissariat of Heavy Industry, according to G. Aleshkovskii, "Sernokislotnaia promyshlennost v tretem piatiletii" [The Sulfuric Acid Industry in the Third Five-Year Period], *Plan*, No. 12, 1937, p. 39. **Line 18:** Kazanskii, *Planovoe khoziaistvo*, No. 7, 1937, p. 50. **Line 20:** Based on freight traffic (700 billion m. ton-kilometers in line 21) and average density of traffic (given as 5.5 to 6.0 million m. tons by I. Libin, "Voprosy razmeshcheniia zheleznodorozhnoi seti v tretei piatiletke" [Problems of the Distribution of the Railroad Network in the Third Five-Year Plan], *Plan*, No. 9, 1936, p. 28). **Lines 21-22:** V. Obraztsov and S. Zemblinov, "Voprosy zheleznodorozhnogo transporta v tretei piatiletke" [Problems of Railroad Transportation in the Third Five-Year Plan], *Planovoe khoziaistvo*, No. 5–6, 1937, p. 61.

COLUMN 5—**Lines 1-3, 7, 12-13, and 23:** *Ibid.*, pp. 58–59. Approximations. For consumer goods, increase may be slightly high. **Lines 4-6, 8, 10, 16-18, and 20-22:** Col. 4 as per cent of col. 2. **Line 9:** G. Laptev, "K razrabotke plana tretei piatiletki BSSR" [On Drafting the Third Five-Year Plan for the Belorussian Republic], *Plan*, No. 14, 1936, p. 36. **Line 14:** Obraztsov and Zemblinov, *Planovoe khoziaistvo*, No. 5–6, 1937, p. 59. Given for procurements, which is very nearly the same as timber hauled. In the 1937 plan, industrial timber hauled was 167.9 mill. m³ and timber procurements was 168.9 (*Plan 1937*, p. 94). **Line 15:** Planned increase in 1942 of not less than 60 per cent over 1937 given by Veits, Probst, and Rusakovskii, *Planovoe khoziaistvo*, No. 9–10, 1937, p. 35. **Line 19:** S. Ginzburg, "O promyshlennosti iskusstvennogo volokna" [On the Synthetic Fiber Industry], *Planovoe khoziaistvo*, No. 7, 1937, p. 65.

power stations, especially hydroelectric plants.[66] The chemical industry was also to be considerably expanded. The growth of the ferrous metal industry and machine-building seems to have been slowed down, which is hard to explain in view of the increased emphasis on armaments.[67] The high rates of growth for consumer goods could reflect the high goals in agricultural production set by Stalin[68] and the desire to continue raising the standard of living observed in 1935 and 1936. There was also to be considerable investment in building railroads, electric power stations, and chemical plants, but the commentators stressed the need to utilize existing capacities.

The information available does not enable us to judge how the Soviet planners expected to reconcile these ambitious goals, including as they did an increase in the production of armaments, large-scale construction projects, and a considerable increase in consumption. One of the prerequisites for carrying out this program was an increase in labor productivity "sufficient to reach the level of advanced capitalist countries."[69] In the ferrous metal industry, for example, the

66. One should not be misled by the reduction of the growth rate in the production of hydroelectric power. The high rates in 1934–1936 were the result of an exceptionally large increase (90 per cent) in 1934, a sizable increase (54.7 per cent) in 1935, and only a small increase (9.2 per cent) in 1936 (see Table A-2).

67. See p. 164 above.

68. See p. 162 above.

69. "Za razrabotku bolshevistskogo plana tretei piatiletki" [For Drafting a Bolshevik Third Five-

Table 30   Comparison of Rates of Growth Planned for 1937–1942 with Actual Rates of Growth for 1934–1936 (per cent)

	Average Annual Rate of Growth		Col. 1 as Per Cent of Col. 2 (3)
	Planned for 6 Years (1937–1942) (1)	Achieved in 3 Years (1934–1936) (2)	
Oil shale	64.8	39.0	166.2
Natural gas	28.4	24.4	116.4
Hydroelectric power	24.6	47.5	51.8
Sulfuric acid	23.7	24.1	98.3
Consumer goods	20.2	19.8	102.0
Soda ash	19.6	15.1	129.8
Plywood	10.6	16.6	63.9
Cement	18.1	29.4	61.6
Electric power	17.8	26.1	68.2
Coal	17.1	18.4	92.9
Inland waterway and maritime freight traffic (ton-km)	16.7	12.8	130.5
Electric power (capacity)	15.7	10.5[a]	149.5
Gross industrial production	16.1	23.1	69.7
Crude petroleum	15.3	8.5	180.0
Peat	15.1	17.5	86.3
Steel ingots and castings	15.0	33.5	44.8
Industrial timber hauled	15.0	9.3	161.3
Producer goods	14.1	25.7	54.9
Railroad freight traffic (ton-km)	13.7	24.0	57.1
Pig iron	13.0	26.5	49.1
Railroad freight traffic (tons)	12.9	21.7	59.4
Length of railroad network	5.4	1.0	540.0

Source: Col. 1: Calculated from Table 29, cols. 1 and 4; col. 2: calculated from Table A-2, cols. 2 and 11.

a. Calculated from capacity for 1933–1936 (given in *Promyshlennost*, p. 171).

output of pig iron per worker, which was 675 metric tons in 1936, was to reach 1,720 metric tons in 1942.[70] In actual fact, this goal was not reached until 1952, when 1,741 metric tons were produced per worker.[71] Another source of growth was to be a reduction in costs, above all in construction, thanks to a reduction in the norms for expenditure of raw materials, materials, and fuel.[72]

All this brings to mind the balances of the First and Second Five-Year Plans. The increase in productivity and the reduction of costs were to make possible a reduction in prices and, as a result, create sources of accumulation. Everything depended, then, on achieving real reductions in costs and use of materials and fuel and on estimating resources correctly, especially agricultural resources. There was also another essential condition—the realism of the basic hypotheses used as a point of departure, that is, the provisions of the 1937 annual plan.

Year Plan], *Plan*, No. 9, 1937, p. 2. "The economic competition between the two systems will be crowned with success thanks to the efforts of the Soviet Union to catch up with and surpass the United States in level of labor productivity and in volume of industrial production" (*ibid.*, p. 4).

70. G. Paushkina, "Proizvoditelnost truda v chernoi metallurgii" [Productivity of Labor in the Ferrous Metal Industry], *Plan*, No. 10, 1937, p. 13.

71. *Promyshlennost*, p. 105.

72. *Plan*, No. 9, 1937, p. 3.

Therefore, the results of the 1937 annual plan must be examined in order to understand the revisions that had to be made in the draft of the third plan as soon as it was put into operation in 1938.

Revision of Third Plan at Beginning of 1938

The prerequisite for putting the five-year plan into operation—fulfilling the 1937 annual plan—was not met. The worst failures in fulfilling the plan were in industry, animal production in agriculture, and transportation.[73] The percentages of plan fulfillment varied from 64.4 to 96.2 for fuel and electric power, from 78.6 to 90.5 for ferrous metals, from 67.2 to 84.1 for nonferrous metals, from 45.0 to 86.6 for construction materials and wood (except for lime, where it was 106.9 per cent), and from 38.5 to 97.5 for machine-building.

It is not known whether a complete revised text of the five-year plan was drafted in 1938. Table 31 shows one fragment of that plan for retail trade. It is clear, however, that this fragment is different from the plan drafted in June–July 1937 and from the one presented for confirmation at the Eighteenth Party Congress in March 1939. This plan uses 1937 prices and actual results in 1937 as a base, which could not have been done in June–July 1937. It also differs considerably from the final text of the plan of March 1939, where the goals for total state and cooperative retail trade are from 73.6 to 76.3 per cent of the goals set in the beginning of 1938.

Since no other such fragments of the plan revised in the beginning of 1938 could be found, it seems reasonable to assume that they were drafted without being incorporated into a final text of the plan covering the whole economy. In any case, when the plan for 1938 was drawn up, the planners had to decide what to do about the June–July 1937 draft of the five-year plan. In view of the failure of the 1937 annual plan, they had two alternatives: to accomplish what was not done in 1937 or to renounce the June–July 1937 goals altogether, which in itself would imply a revision of the five-year plan.

To show which alternative was chosen, Table 32 compares rates of growth in the 1938 annual plan with rates necessary to achieve the June–July 1937 goals based on the actual results of 1937. For value of gross industrial production (in 1926/27 prices), the rate of growth of the 1938 annual plan was sufficient to achieve the earlier goals. But the 1926/27 prices that the Soviet authorities used to measure production in 1937 were no longer valid after the introduction of new products; they represent a very debatable unit of measurement.[74] For the other series (except cement)[75] for which the comparison was made, the rates of growth adopted in the 1938 annual plan range from 57.1 to 98.5 per cent of the rates

73. See Table A–2.
74. On this subject, see my *Planning*, pp. 256–60.
75. For cement, the rate of growth in the 1938 annual plan is 22.1 per cent higher than the rate needed to reach the old goals of the five-year plan set in 1937. But the high growth rate in the 1938 plan results largely from the failure to fulfill the 1937 plan (73.3 per cent only). The goal of the 1938 plan (7.05 million metric tons) is, in fact, lower than the 1937 annual plan goal, which was 7.44 million metric tons. Hence it was a question not of catching up with the goals for 1942 but, more modestly, of producing in 1938, 94.8 per cent of the amount planned for 1937.

Table 31   Variants of Third Five-Year Plan for State and Cooperative Retail Trade

	Actual Results in 1937 (billion rubles[a]) (1)	Plan for 1938		Preliminary Variant (beginning of 1938)		Final Plan March (1939)		Col. 6 as Per Cent of Col. 4 (8)
		Billion Rubles[a] (2)	Index (1937 = 100) (3)	Billion Rubles[a] (4)	Index (1937 = 100) (5)	Billion Rubles[a] (6)	Index (1937 = 100) (7)	
1. Total state and cooperative retail trade	126.3	140.5	111.2	270–280.0	over 200	206	163	73.6–76.3
2. Total state and cooperative retail trade (alternative)				250–300.0	200–250	206	163	68.7–82.4
3. Food products	69.3			127	183	106	153	83.5
4. Consumer durables	46.8			117	250	80	171	68.4
5. Public eating places	10.2	11.1	108.8			20	197	

Source

COLUMNS 1, 6, and 7–All lines: *Tretii plan*, p. 199.

COLUMN 2–All lines: B. Timofeev, "Sovetskaia torgovlia vo vtoroi piatiletke" [Soviet Trade in the Second Five-Year Plan], *Problemy ekonomiki*, No. 2, 1938, p. 161.

COLUMN 3–All lines: Based on cols. 1 and 2.

COLUMN 4–Line 1: Iu. Shnirlin, "Zadachi sovetskoi torgovli v tretei piatiletke" [Tasks of Soviet Trade in Third Five-Year Plan], *Planovoe khoziaistvo*, No. 2, 1938, p. 101. Line 2: Timofeev, *Problemy ekonomiki*, No. 2, 1938, p. 162. Line 3: Derived from consumer durables (line 4) and percentage shares of food products and consumer durables in total trade excluding public eating places (given as 52 and 48, respectively, in Shnirlin, *Planovoe khoziaistvo*, No. 2, 1938, p. 102). Line 4: Based on cols. 1 and 5. Line 5: Lines 1 or 2 minus the sum of lines 3 and 4 would yield a range of from 6 to 56 billion rubles depending on which total in lines 1 or 2 was used.

COLUMN 5–Lines 1 and 4: Shnirlin, *Planovoe khoziaistvo*, No. 2, 1938, pp. 101 and 103. Line 2: Timofeev, *Problemy ekonomiki*, No. 2, 1938, pp. 161–62. Line 3: Based on cols. 1 and 4.

a. In 1937 prices.

necessary to reach the earlier goals set for 1942. Hence the 1938 annual plan effectively sanctions the revision of the five-year plan goals set in June–July 1937, and the only question is whether this revision took the form of a new, coherent plan or whether it was done by sectors with little connection among the different goals. With existing documentation, this question cannot be answered.

Revision of Third Plan in Early 1939

As mentioned earlier, a new management team was inaugurated in Gosplan in the spring and summer of 1938 and ordered to draw up an entirely new draft of the Third Five-Year Plan. It is impossible to know how much of the work of its predecessors the new team could use. But it is nevertheless certain that the drafts of June–July 1937 and the beginning of 1938 had to be considerably revised. The revisions were required by the increased defense effort resulting from the international situation and the poor fulfillment of the annual plan for 1938, which was integrated as the first year in the variants drafted at the beginning of 1938 (which existed perhaps only by sectors).

Appendix Table A-3 gives an over-all view of the extent of fulfillment of the

Table 32   1938 Annual Plan Compared with June–July 1937 Variant of Third Five-Year Plan

	Per Cent of Fulfillment of 1937 Annual Plan (1)	Average Annual Rate of Growth in Five-Year Plan for 1937–1942 (June–July 1937 variant)		Rate of Growth in 1938 Plan (4)	Col. 4 as Per Cent of Col. 3 (5)
		Based on 1937 Annual Plan (2)	Based on Actual Results in 1937 (3)		
Gross industrial production (1926/27 prices)	92.7	15.3	17.1	16.2	94.7
Coal	85.2	16.8	20.6	20.3	98.5
Crude petroleum	88.6	14.7	17.5	10.5	60.0
Electric power (capacity)	91.5[a]	15.0	17.0[b]	9.7[c]	57.1
Electric power	89.3	16.7	19.3	13.9	72.0
Pig iron	90.5	13.4	15.7	12.5	79.6
Steel ingots and castings	88.0	13.4	16.5	14.5	87.9
Soda ash	95.5	21.7	22.8	16.1	70.6
Sulfuric acid	82.2	20.9	25.7	16.0	62.3
Cement	73.3	16.7	24.0	29.3	122.1
Railroad freight traffic (ton-km)	91.5	12.6	14.6	11.3	77.4
Railroad freight traffic (tons)	91.6	12.1	14.1	9.8	69.5

Source: Col. 1: Table A-2, col. 15; col. 2: calculated from Table 29, cols. 2 and 4; col. 3: calculated from Table A-1, col. 2, and Table 29, col. 4; col. 4: calculated from Table A-1, col. 2, and Table A-3, col. 1.

a. Calculated from 1937 annual plan goal (derived by adding the increase in capacity planned for the Commissariat of Heavy Industry for 1937 given in *Plan 1937*, p. 17, to the capacity at the end of 1936 given in *Promyshlennost*, p. 171) and actual capacity in 1937 (given in *ibid.*).

b. Actual capacity in 1937 given in *Promyshlennost*, p. 171.

c. Calculated from actual capacity in 1937 (given in *ibid.*) and increase planned for 1938 (given in A. Zelenovskii, "Promyshlennost v pervom godu tretei piatiletki" [Industry in the First Year of the Third Five-Year Plan], *Planovoe khoziaistvo*, No. 5, 1938, p. 18).

1938 annual plan. For the principal products of heavy industry, the percentages of plan fulfillment varied from 71 to 97; the plan was not fulfilled for a single one of the series known. The plan for light industry and the food industry came slightly closer to fulfillment, with some products like knitted outer garments, macaroni, vegetable oil, and butter overfulfilled by 5 to 19 per cent. But there were failures to fulfill the plan for such products as cotton fabrics, sugar, and fish catch. Only 90.9 per cent of the plan for railroad freight traffic in tons was fulfilled and 93.8 per cent in ton-kilometers.

Comparisons of the goals of the March 1939 final text of the five-year plan and those of earlier variants are presented in Table 31 for retail trade and in Table 33 for other plan indexes. It is clear at once that the new goals are considerably lower, even lower than would have been required by the poor fulfillment of the 1937 annual plan. In fact, the final plan indexes (see Table 33, data with 1937 = 100) are—with the three exceptions of producer goods, electric power capacity, and industrial timber hauled—lower than the rates of growth based on the 1937 annual plan and drafted in June–July 1937. Hence the planners must have taken into account not only the results of 1937 but also those of 1938.[76]

76. If the planners had wanted to revise the goals in the light of the degree of fulfillment of the

Table 33 Comparison of Final Goals (March 1939) of Third Five-Year Plan for 1942 and Goals in June–July 1937 Variant for 1942

	Units	Goals for 1942 in June–July 1937 Variant		Goals for 1942 in Final Text of March 1939		Col. 3 as Per cent of Col. 1
		Physical Units (1)	Index (1937 Plan = 100) (2)	Physical Units (3)	Index (1937 = 100) (4)	(5)
1. Gross industrial production (1926/27 prices)	bill. rubles	205–215	200	184	192[a]	86–90
2. Producer goods (1926/27 prices)	bill. rubles	111.0	185	114.5	207[a]	103.2
3. Consumer goods (1926/27 prices)	bill. rubles	107.5	250	69.5	172[a]	64.7
4. Coal	mill. m. tons	327	218	243.0	190[a]	74.3
5. Peat	mill. m. tons	52	208	49.0	206[b]	94
6. Oil shale	mill. m. tons	9.6	1,200	4.0	777[b]	41.7
7. Crude petroleum	mill. m. tons	64	200	49.5	174[b]	77
8. Natural gas	mill. m. tons	8–9	350–390	4.5[c]	227[d]	50–56
9. Electric power (capacity)	mill. kw	18	200	17.2[e]	212[f]	95.6
10. Electric power:	bill. kwh	85–90	210–220	75.0	206[b]	83–88
11. Hydroelectric power	bill. kwh	15		8.8	210	58.7
12. Pig iron	mill. m. tons	30	185–190	22.0	152[b]	73
13. Steel ingots and castings	mill. m. tons	37–38	185–190	28.0	156[b]	74–76
14. Industrial timber hauled	mill. m³	269–285	160–170	200	180[a]	70–74
15. Plywood	thous. m³	1,232	160	1,000	151[b]	81.2
16. Soda ash	thous. m. tons	1,450–1,500	262–271	1,125	218[b]	75–78
17. Sulfuric acid	thous. m. tons	4,300	258			
18. Cement	mill. m. tons	16.0	216	11.0	202[a]	68.7
19. Length of railroad network	thous. km	117	135	96	113	82.1
20. Railroad freight traffic	bill. m. ton-km	700	181	510	144[b]	72.9
21. Railroad freight traffic	mill. m. tons	1,000	177	745	144	74.5
22. Inland waterway and maritime freight traffic	bill. m. ton-km	183	200	109	156	59.6

Source: Unless otherwise indicated, cols. 1 and 2: Table 29, cols. 4 and 5; col. 3: Table A-1, col. 7; col. 4: col. 3 divided by Table A-1, col. 2.

a. "Tretii piatiletnii plan razvitiia narodnogo khoziaistva SSSR. Rezoliutsiia XVIII Sezda VKPb po dokladu tov. V. Molotova" [Third Five-Year Plan for the Development of the USSR National Economy. Resolution of the Eighteenth Party Congress on the Report of Comrade V. Molotov], *Planovoe khoziaistvo*, No. 4, 1939, p. 91.

b. *Tretii plan*, pp. 202, 203, 208, 204, 198.

c. *Ibid.*, p. 202. Crude petroleum and gas minus crude petroleum.

d. Derived from col. 3 and 1937 output (Table A-2, col. 14).

e. *Tretii plan*, p. 213.

f. Derived from col. 3 and 1937 capacity (given as 8,116.5 thous. kw in *ibid.*).

1937 annual plan, the indexes of growth for 1942 in the two variants of the plan would have remained unchanged.

Important changes were also made in the structure of production. In the June–July 1937 variant growth rates for consumer goods were considerably higher than for producer goods, but the opposite was true in the final variant. This change, moreover, was not the result of adapting the new text to revisions of the 1937 and 1938 annual plans. Significant changes were introduced in state and cooperative retail trade after the variant of early 1938 was drafted (see Table 31). The figure for retail trade in the final text is about 25 per cent lower than the one in the earlier variants (16.5 per cent lower for food products and 31.6 per cent lower for consumer durables). But the annual plan came very close to being fulfilled in this area (99.6 per cent in current prices)[77] and such a large reduction in goals was not required. Only plans for increased armaments production can explain this change in policy.

The efforts to change the structure of the balance of fuel envisaged in 1937 also seem to have been compromised. The production of peat, a low-quality fuel, was maintained at more or less the same level, whereas the production of natural gas was considerably reduced (almost by half). The production of hydro-electric power was reduced by half, which meant abandoning temporarily the construction of some hydroelectric power stations. The considerable cutting back of construction work compared with the earlier plans can be seen most clearly in the reduction by nearly 40 per cent of the goals for cement production. A reduction of the same order in inland waterway and maritime freight traffic goals reflected the same trend since increase in this traffic would require considerable investment.

To give an idea of the changes made in the long-range plans during 1936–1939, all the information on plans for the production of electric power has been gathered in Chart 7. The tendency to extrapolate rates of growth from previous years appears very clearly.

The connection between the annual and long-range plans also emerges clearly. The failure of the annual plan usually brings about a revision of the long-range plan. This seems to be true not only for five-year plans but also for longer-term plans for 10 or 15 years. In view of the actual evolution of production, the long-term plans seem to have been unrealistic. Nevertheless, these were the plans that inspired the investment plans, especially those for electric power stations. Hence the long-term fluctuations in goals seem to reflect rescheduling investment projects as much as lack of precision in planning construction projects and putting them into operation.

77. See Table A–3. Retail prices remained quite stable during 1938. Hence the percentage of plan fulfillment in current prices approximately reflects the fulfillment in constant prices. Still, account must be taken of the evolution of the collective farm market, where certain increases of moderate importance took place in 1938.

Chart 7   Goals for Electric Power Production in Long-Term Plans, 1936–1950

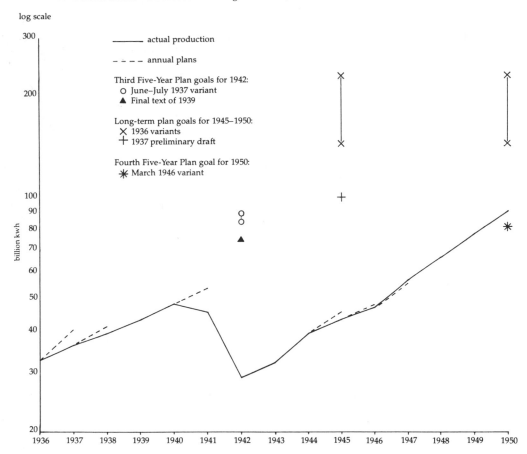

log scale

Legend:
——— actual production
– – – – annual plans
Third Five-Year Plan goals for 1942:
  O June–July 1937 variant
  ▲ Final text of 1939
Long-term plan goals for 1945–1950:
  X 1936 variants
  + 1937 preliminary draft
Fourth Five-Year Plan goal for 1950:
  ✳ March 1946 variant

billion kwh

Source: Tables 33, A-1, A-2, A-3, A-4, and A-5, and Kukel-Kraevskii, *Planovoe khoziaistvo*, No. 1, 1936, p. 38.

CHAPTER 9

Internal Coherence
of Third Five-Year Plan
and New Long-Term Prospects

Principal Goals

The goals in the final text of the Third Five-Year Plan were very ambitious. Although production capacities in the economy were considerably greater in 1937 than in 1932, the principal indexes of growth (gathered in Table 34) were much the same as those of the Second Five-Year Plan.[1] In some cases, such as agricultural production or retail trade, the lower indexes are obviously the result of a much higher base in 1937 than in 1932.

Austerity is another prominent feature of the third plan. Despite an 80 per cent increase planned for national income, personal consumption was to rise very little. The share of consumption in national income in 1942 was to be lower than in 1937, and perhaps even lower than indicated by the official percentages (see Table 34, source to cols. 1–3, lines 2–4). In industrial production, consumer goods were to increase much more slowly than producer goods, whereas just the opposite had been true in the second plan. The most striking feature is the movement of real wages. In the second plan they were to have increased 96 per cent, mostly thanks to reductions planned for retail prices (35 per cent below 1933); none of the variants of the third plan makes mention of any such de-

---

1. It should be noted that, according to official Soviet estimates in 1926/27 prices, national income increased 112 per cent between 1932 and 1937 (see Tables 17 and 34) and agricultural production only 25.2 per cent (official revised index cited in *Narodnoe khoziaistvo SSSR v 1958 godu* [The USSR National Economy in 1958], Moscow, 1959, p. 350). Industrial production in official 1926/27 prices increased 121 per cent (see Tables 17 and 34). Industrial production increased 99.3 per cent between 1932 and 1937 according to G. Warren Nutter (*Growth of Industrial Production in the Soviet Union*, Princeton, 1962, p. 158) and 62 per cent according to Norman Kaplan and Richard Moorsteen ("Indexes of Soviet Industrial Output," RAND Research Memorandum 2495, Santa Monica, 1960, Vol. II, p. 235).

Table 34   Principal Goals of Third Five-Year Plan[a]

	Units	Actual Results in 1937 (1)	Actual Results in 1938 (2)	Third Five-Year Plan Goals for 1942		Second Five-Year Plan Goals for 1937 (1932 = 100) (5)
				Physical Units (3)	Index (1937 = 100) (4)	
1. National income (1926/27 prices):	bill. rubles	96.3	105.0	173.6	180	220.2
2. Consumption	per cent	73.6		71.2		78.7
3. Accumulation:	per cent	26.4		28.8		21.3
4. Reserves	per cent	2.9		6.3		1.9
5. Gross industrial production (1926/27 prices):	bill. rubles	95.5	106.1	184.0	192	214.1
6. Producer goods (group A)	bill. rubles	55.2		114.5	207	197.2
7. Consumer goods (group B)	bill. rubles	40.3		69.5	172	233.6
8. Gross agricultural production (1926/27 prices)	bill. rubles	20.1	18.0	30.5	152	200.1
Investment						
9. Total including repairs[b]	bill. rubles	30.2		50.0	213.8	133.4
10. Total excluding repairs	bill. rubles	26.5	29.4	41.5	192.0	
Employment, workers and employees						
11. National economy	millions	27.0	27.8	32.7	121	126.0
12. Industry	millions	10.1	10.2	11.9	118	128.0
Wages						
13. Wage fund, workers and employees, national economy	bill. rubles	82.2	96.4	137.3	167	155.0
14. Average money wage, workers and employees, national economy	rubles per yr.	3,038	3,468	4,162	137	123.0
15. Average real wage					137	196.0
Trade						
16. State and cooperative retail trade (1937 prices)	bill. rubles	126.3	138.6	206.0	163	248.2
Labor productivity (per worker)						
17. Industry	1937 = 100	100.0	113.0		165	163.0
18. Construction	1937 = 100	100.0	117.0		175	175.0
19. Railroad transportation (ton-km)	1937 = 100	100.0	107.0		132	143.0
Reduction in cost of production						
20. Industry	per cent below 1937		2.8		11.0	26.0
21. Agriculture (state farms)	per cent below 1937		5.6		26.5	63.3
22. Construction (net)	per cent below 1937					40.0
23. Railroad transportation	per cent below 1937		2.3		3.0	10.5
24. Inland waterway and maritime transport	per cent below 1937		11.0		14.0	
25. Trade (Commissariat of Trade)	per cent below 1937		5.0		13.0	26.0

Table 34   *continued*

			Third Five-Year Plan Goals for 1942		
	Units	Actual Results in 1937 (1)	Actual Results in 1938 (2)	Physical Units (3)	Index (1937 = 100) (4)	Second Five-Year Plan Goals for 1937 (1932 = 100) (5)

Saving effected by reduction in production costs

26. Industry	bill. rubles			49–50		13
27. Construction	bill. rubles					8.8

Source

COLUMN 1–Lines 1, 6–7, 9–14, and 16: *Tretii piatiletnii plan razvitiia narodnogo khoziaistva SSSR (1938–1942)* [Third Five-Year Plan for the Development of the USSR National Economy, 1938–1942], Moscow, 1939, pp. 197–228. **Lines 2–4:** A. D. Kurskii, *Tretia stalinskaia piatiletka* [Third Stalinist Five-Year Plan], Moscow, 1940, p. 21. In 1937 prices. Voznesenskii (*Tretii plan*, p. 197) gives the following percentage breakdown: consumption, 75.5; accumulation, 21.6; and reserves, 2.9. **Lines 5 and 8:** "Tretii piatiletnii plan razvitiia narodnogo khoziaistva SSSR. Rezoliutsiia XVIII Sezda VKPb po dokladu tov. V. Molotova" [Third Five-Year Plan for the Development of the USSR National Economy. Resolution of the Eighteenth Party Congress on the Report of Comrade V. Molotov], *Planovoe khoziaistvo*, No. 4, 1939, pp. 91–109.

COLUMN 2–**Line 1:** D. Allakhverdian, *Natsionalnyi dokhod SSSR* [National Income of the USSR], Moscow, 1952, p. 56. **Line 5:** *Sotsialisticheskoe stroitelstvo Soiuza SSR, 1933–1938* [Socialist Construction in the USSR for 1933–1938], Moscow-Leningrad, 1939, p. 34, as cited by Naum Jasny, *The Soviet Price System*, Stanford, 1951, pp. 172–73. **Line 8:** Estimated from col. 1 and reduction of 10.4 per cent (derived from *Narodnoe khoziaistvo, 1958*, p. 350). **Line 10:** Kurskii, *Tretia*, p. 95. **Line 11:** A. I. Notkin, *Ocherki teorii sotsialisticheskogo proizvodstva* [Essays on the Theory of Socialist Reproduction], Moscow, 1948. **Line 12:** Estimated from increases in industrial production (derived as 11.1 per cent from line 2, cols. 1 and 2) and in labor productivity (given as 11.0 per cent in Walter Galenson, *Labor Productivity in Soviet and American Industry*, New York, 1955, p. 15). **Lines 13 and 16:** I. V. Stalin, *Voprosy Leninizma* [Problems of Leninism], 11th ed., Moscow, 1947, pp. 586 and 584. **Line 14:** Based on wage fund (line 13) and employment in national economy (line 11). The same figure is given by Jasny in *Soviet Price System*, p. 23. **Lines 17–21 and 23–25:** 1938 plan. A. D. Kurskii, *Narodno-khoziaistvennyi plan na 1938 god i ego vypolnenie* [The National Economic Plan for 1938 and Its Fulfillment], Moscow, 1938, p. 39. For line 18, net construction. For line 24, inland waterway transportation only.

COLUMN 3–**Lines 1, 9–10, 12, 16, and 26:** *Tretii plan*, pp. 197–228. Line 12 should probably be increased slightly since the final goals for employment in the whole national economy and wages were raised slightly by the Eighteenth Party Congress above those given in *Tretii plan*. Line 26 is total for five-year plan in billion rubles; since industrial production was estimated in 1926/27 prices in both plans, saving was probably also estimated in 1926/27 prices. **Lines 2–4:** Kurskii, *Tretia*, p. 21. In 1937 prices. Voznesenskii (*Tretii plan*, p. 197) gives the following percentage breakdown: consumption, 72.3; accumulation, 21.4; and reserves, 6.3. The revision of the percentage breakdown in the final text may have been made in order to reduce the importance of the relative decrease in consumption in the plan for 1942. **Lines 11 and 13–14:** Based on cols. 1 and 4.

COLUMN 4–**Lines 1, 5–8, 10–11, 13–14, and 17:** *Planovoe khoziaistvo*, No. 4, 1939, pp. 91–109. Line 10 is total for 1938–1942 in billion rubles (*Tretii plan*, pp. 197 and 26, gives 181.0 billion rubles). **Lines 9, 12, 16, 18–21, and 23–25:** *Tretii plan*, pp. 197–231. Line 9 is total for 1938–1942 in billion rubles.

COLUMN 5–**Lines 1, 5–8, 11–15, and 19:** Table 17, col. 4. **Lines 2–4:** *Vtoroi piatiletnii plan razvitiia narodnogo khoziaistva SSSR (1933–1937)* [Second Five-Year Plan for the Development of the USSR National Economy, 1933–1937], Moscow, 1934, p. 427. In 1932 prices. Reserves have been included in accumulation as in the Third Five-Year Plan. **Line 9:** Table 7, col. 4. Total for 1933–1937 in billion rubles in 1933 plan prices. In current prices, taking into account the reduction in cost of construction and machinery, it would be 120.1 billion rubles for 1933–1937. **Line 16:** Table 17, col. 4. In 1932 prices excluding tobacco and alcohol (13.3 billion rubles in 1932 out of a total of 40.4 billion rubles). If tobacco and alcohol were included, the index would probably be lower. **Line 17:** Table 17, col. 4. Large-scale industry. **Line 18:** Table 17, col. 4. Net construction. **Lines 20–23 and 25:** Table 17, col. 4. Per cent below 1932. **Lines 26–27:** Table 17, col. 3. Total for 1933–1937 in billion rubles, probably in 1926/27 prices for industry (line 26) and in 1933 prices for construction (line 27).

a. Final text approved by Eighteenth Party Congress on March 14–17, 1939.

b. In prices of December 1, 1936. Excluding autonomous (*vnelimitnye*) investments.

creases. This lack of any (significant) drop in retail prices can be seen by comparing the reductions in the cost of production provided in the two plans. This reduction was between two and three times as large in the second plan as in the third one for industry, agriculture (state farms), and trade. The reduction in the cost of construction was not given in the third plan but it can be assumed to be much less than the 40 per cent given in the second plan. The relatively small reduction in the cost of production in the third plan left very little margin for a decrease in prices. The index for the increase in money wages thus came very close, in the third plan, to that for the increase in real wages and remained extremely low.

The greater austerity of the third plan could have been offset by improved internal coherence but, to judge from Table 34, this does not seem to have been the case.

The 52 per cent increase planned for agricultural production was not an unrealistic goal since, despite the excellent harvest of 1937, production in 1937 was only 25.2 per cent higher than in 1932.[2] Actually, the planned increase should have been considered as 69.4 per cent higher than in 1938, a more normal year, but no practical measures were taken to facilitate such a performance. The fragility of the agricultural plan made it difficult to fulfill the plans for foreign trade and consumer goods. The 72 per cent increase planned for Group B goods was just as improbable as the 134 per cent increase in the second plan.

Another condition necessary to achieve equilibrium is the limitation of the increase in money wages. At the beginning of 1939, the planners' margin of safety was very small. By 1938 average money wages had increased 14.1 per cent, which left only 20 per cent for them to increase and stay within the goals planned for 1942. Was it possible to limit the increase in wages so strictly? The outcome of this policy depended mainly on fulfilling the goals for labor productivity. These goals are the only ones in the third plan that are as high (in index form) as those in the second plan. Since production was to increase less, these goals could be realized only by limiting the increase in employment.

The authors of the third plan stressed the importance of the labor productivity goals. The goal for industry (an average increase of 65 per cent between 1937 and 1942) was the result of relatively small increases planned for light industry (35 per cent), for local industry (50 per cent), and for the food and timber industries (53 per cent), and a large increase for heavy industry (95.7 per cent).[3] To obtain such results, the planners were relying on better production organization expected to result from abandoning the grandiose construction projects,[4] the return to a two-shift production schedule, the mechanization of industrial construction, and the tightening of labor discipline, all recently decreed by the government.[5] This part of the plan proved to be particularly fragile in 1939–1940

2. See footnote 1 above.
3. *Tretii plan*, pp. 103–4.
4. It was Molotov who criticized what he called "gigantomania" in his speech to the Eighteenth Party Congress in March 1939.
5. On this subject, see the December 20, 1938, decree proposing the introduction of work books and the December 28, 1938, joint decree of the Party Central Committee and the Council of People's Commissars on "measures to consolidate work discipline, improve the operation of social insurances, and combat abuses in this field" (Solomon Schwarz, *Labor in the Soviet Union*, New York, 1951,

when the stress was on armaments. In fact, when there were deficits in priority production or construction, it was simpler to have recourse to supplementary manpower than to wait for the effects of government measures, as was shown by the authors of the third plan when they presented a balance of manpower resources for collective farms which showed that the average annual number of unemployed persons on the collective farms was 5,350,000 in 1937 and would reach 5,953,000 in 1942.[6]

Difficulties in 1939 and Delays in Carrying Out Plan Goals

As mentioned earlier, the Third Five-Year Plan presented in March 1939 actually gave three-year goals for 1940–1942, the annual plan for 1939, and the actual results for 1938. Its "launching" in 1940, therefore, depended directly on fulfilling the 1939 annual plan. Unfortunately, this plan was not published and very few of its goals are known. Only plans for agricultural work and livestock breeding were published, and even these were largely for collective farms.[7] The other goals that could be found in different sources are very limited. The fulfillment of these goals is given in Table 35.

These figures on the 1939 annual plan fulfillment might give the impression that the plan was quite successful, at least for livestock breeding and light industry. Actually this table should be examined together with Table 36, which shows the progress made in the five-year plan by the end of 1939. It is surprising to see that by that time the five-year plan was already jeopardized. The median percentage of fulfillment of the five-year plan goals interpolated for 1939 was 85.1 for producer goods, 92.9 for consumer goods, and 87.6 for agricultural production and livestock breeding.[8] Transportation goals were just as poorly fulfilled, with notable failures in motor and maritime transportation. Those indexes which the planners tried to keep down because of their effect on costs— that is, total employment and money wages—exceeded five-year plan goals interpolated for 1939. In state and cooperative retail trade, goals were exceeded because of price increases in 1939. Between July 1, 1938, and July 1, 1939, this

---

p. 101). The authors of the third plan anticipated that these measures would increase the number of days actually worked per worker from 260 in 1937 to 268 or 270 (see *Tretii plan*, p. 104).

6. *Tretii plan*, p. 109.

7. February 8, 1939, decree of Council of People's Commissars, "On the State Plan for Agricultural Work in 1939" (*Sobranie postanovlenii i rasporiazhenii pravitelstva SSSR* [Collection of Resolutions and Decrees of the USSR Government], No. 14, March 1939, Art. 88, pp. 157–228). March 25, 1939, decree of Council of People's Commissars, "On the State Plan for the Development of Livestock Breeding for 1939" (*ibid.*, No. 22, April 16, 1939, Art. 137, pp. 329–59). The first of these decrees gives goals for sown areas for all farms and yields for collective farms only. The methods used to calculate these yields is not given, and it is difficult to make any estimates of planned production.

8. The method of calculation is explained in the notes to Table 36. In the case of the series for which the plan was poorly executed, this method of estimation tends to exaggerate slightly the five-year plan goals where the planners already knew the 1938 results. In general, the figures in Table 36 are only approximations. The fact that the overfulfillment of the 1939 annual plan for cotton fabrics, woolen fabrics, and hosiery still did not make it possible to fulfill the interpolated five-year plan goals for 1939 means that in light industry the greatest expansion was to be in the last years of the plan.

Table 35   Fulfillment of Known 1939 Annual Plan Goals (per cent)

Industrial production	
1. Equipment for forges and presses	67.9
2. Paper	90.4
3. Cotton fabric	102.8
4. Woolen fabrics	110.9
5. Linen fabrics	88.8
6. Hosiery	107.6
Mineral fertilizer (deliveries to agriculture):	
7. Plan for 1939 (thous. m. tons)	3,652.0
8. Actual results in 1940 (thous. m. tons)	3,159
State and cooperative retail trade	
9. Total in current prices	89.9
Collective farm livestock	
10. Horses	98.5
11. Cattle:	103.2
12. Cows	99.4
13. Pigs	86.6
14. Sheep and goats	102.5

Source: Line 1: December 29, 1940, decree of USSR Council of People's Commissars and of Party Central Committee, "On Developing the Construction of Forges and Presses in the USSR" (*Direktivy KPSS i sovetskogo pravitelstva po khoziaistvennym voprosam* [Directives of the Communist Party of the Soviet Union and of the Soviet Government on Economic Matters], Moscow, 1957, Vol. 2, p. 658); lines 2–6 and 9: Table A-3, col. 6; line 7: sum of phosphoric fertilizer (18.5% P_2O_5), ammonium sulfate, potash fertilizer, ground natural phosphate, and Thomas slag (February 8, 1939, decree of Council of People's Commissars, "On the State Plan for Agricultural Work in 1939," *Sobranie postanovlenii*, No. 14, March 1939, Art. 88, p. 216); see also footnote 7 in this chapter; line 8: *Dostizheniia sovetskoi vlasti za 40 let v tsifrakh* [Achievements of the Soviet Regime during 40 Years in Figures], Moscow, 1957, p. 153; lines 10–14: calculated from 1939 plan (given in *Sobranie postanovlenii*, No. 22, April 21, 1939, Art. 137, p. 329) and 1939 actual results (given in *Chislennost skota v SSSR* [Head of Livestock in the USSR], Moscow, 1957, p. 7).

increase was 9.6 per cent,[9] which means that the 1939 annual plan goal was not fulfilled, nor was the interpolated five-year plan goal for that year.[10]

The most striking feature of Table 36 is the great variation in the fulfillment of different goals for producer goods. Whereas 100.6 per cent of the interpolated five-year plan goal for lead was fulfilled, the percentage was only 45.6 for excavators and 54.4 for automobiles.

There seem to be three main reasons for this early failure of the five-year plan: revisions in the annual (and five-year) plan during the year, difficulties in certain branches of heavy industry, and imbalance between supply and demand of consumer goods. No direct information could be found on any important revision made in the 1939 annual plan. Nevertheless, this plan could not possibly have predicted the absolute drop in output of products for which high rates of growth

9. See my "Les fluctuations des prix de détail en Union Soviétique," *Etudes et Conjoncture*, April 1955, p. 326.

10. The price increase on the collective farm market must also be taken into account, for this was certainly not anticipated by the third plan, as it foresaw a sizable increase in agricultural production. Collective farm market prices, which did not differ much from state prices in 1937 and 1938, increased considerably on January 1, 1940. See *ibid.*, p. 381.

Table 36   Fulfillment of Third Five-Year Plan Goals Interpolated for 1939 (per cent)

National income	94.3	Cotton yarn	97.1
Industry		Cigarettes	96.6
Consumer goods (1926/27 prices)	100.0	Cotton fabrics	94.8
Total value of production (1926/27 prices)	99.9	Woolen fabrics	92.9
Producer goods (1926/27 prices)	99.7	Crude alcohol	92.6
		Canned food	91.8
Producer Goods		Hosiery	89.4
Lead	100.6	Confectionery	89.2
Roofing tiles	100.1	Knitted underwear	89.0
Tractors (15 hp)	99.1	Leather shoes	88.0
Tires	96.6	Butter	85.7
Refined copper	96.6	Fish catch	85.1
Peat	93.4	Linen fabrics	80.1
Ammonium sulfate	92.2	Rubber footwear	75.8
Iron ore	90.0	Raw sugar	65.0
Electric power (capacity)	89.5[a]		
Electric power	89.3	**Agriculture**	
Asbestos shingles	88.9	Animal production (1926/27 prices)	83.5[d]
Coal	88.6	Total value of production (1926/27	
Industrial timber hauled	88.2	prices)	76.3[d]
Coke	87.6	Vegetable production (1926/27 prices)	73.4[d]
Tractors (units)	86.7		
Paperboard	86.4[b]	*Harvests and Animal Production*	
Machine tools	85.9	Sunflowers	124.3
Zinc	85.8	Raw cotton	98.2
Lumber	85.6	Horses	96.6[e]
Crude petroleum	85.2	Flax fiber	94.6
Phosphoric fertilizer (14% P_2O_5)	85.0	Wool	94.5
Pig iron	84.9	Sheep	91.9[e]
Plywood	84.8	Cows	87.6[e]
Hydroelectric power	83.6	Sugar beets	86.8
Hydraulic turbines	82.6[c]	Grain, total	85.9
Steel ingots and castings	82.5	Milk	84.0
Trucks	82.4	Beef cattle	81.9[e]
Rolled steel	81.1	Potatoes	80.0
Lime	79.4	Pigs	67.1[e]
Soda ash	79.0		
Phosphoric fertilizer (18.7% P_2O_5)	78.0	*Procurements*	
Steam locomotives	77.0	Grain, total	99.4
Potash fertilzer	76.7	Sunflowers	97.4
Motor vehicles, total	76.5	Vegetables	93.4
Aluminum	75.6	Potatoes	52.3
Bricks	74.5		
Cement	72.0	**Transportation**	
Paper	69.5	*Railroad*	
Manganese ore	67.2	Average length of haul	103.2
Nickel	58.0	Mineral construction materials	98.9
Automobiles	54.4	Length of network	96.9
Excavators	45.6	Average daily carloadings	95.9
		Freight traffic (ton-km)	95.5
Consumer Goods		Freight traffic (tons)	92.5
Meat and subproducts of first category	123.7	Passenger traffic (pass.-km)	91.9
Vegetable oil	112.7		
Ginned cotton	109.5	*Inland Waterway*	
Matches	109.4	Passenger traffic (passengers)	96.5
Silk and rayon fabrics	108.0	Average length of haul under ministries	
Soap (40% fatty acid)	106.3	and economic organizations	94.2
Beer	100.4	Passenger traffic (pass.-km)	91.7
Knitted outer garments	99.8	Freight traffic (tons)	88.0
		Freight traffic (ton-km)	83.3

Table 36 *continued*

Maritime		**Wages**	
Freight traffic (tons)	87.0	Wage fund, national economy	115.3
Average length of haul	81.7	Wage fund, industry	114.4
Freight traffic (ton-km)	71.1	Money wage, railroad transport	114.0
Motor		Money wage, national economy	112.0
Freight traffic (ton-km)	49.4	**Trade**	
Employment		State and cooperative retail trade[f]	
National economy	103.4	(current prices)	108.2
Industry	93.6		

Source: Unless otherwise indicated, calculated from actual results in 1939 (Table A-3, col. 5) and Third Five-Year Plan goals interpolated for 1939 (estimated from actual results in 1937 in Table A-1, col. 2, and goals for 1942 in Table A-1, col. 7, by assuming an equal average annual planned rate of growth during 1938–1942).

a. Actual results in 1937 and in 1939 taken from *Promyshlennost SSSR* [Industry of the USSR], Moscow, 1957, p. 171; 1942 plan from *Tretii plan*, p. 213.

b. Actual results in 1939 taken from *Bumazhnaia promyshlennost* [The Paper Industry], No. 10, 1940, p. 62, as cited in *Statistical Abstract of Industrial Output in the Soviet Union, 1913–1955*, National Bureau of Economic Research, New York, 1956, series 450.3.

c. Actual results in 1939 taken from *Promyshlennost*, p. 217; actual results in 1937 from *Narodnoe khoziaistvo SSSR* [The USSR National Economy], Moscow, 1956, p. 56; and 1942 plan from *Tretii plan*, p. 35.

d. Actual results in 1939 derived from indexes for 1937 and 1939 (given as 109 and 119 for animal production, 134 and 121 for total value of production, and 150 and 125 for vegetable production, with 1913 = 100, in *Narodnoe khoziaistvo, 1958*, p. 350) and actual results in 1937 (Table A-1, col. 2).

e. Actual results in 1939 taken from *Chislennost*, p. 6; actual results in 1937 and 1942 from *Tretii plan*, pp. 219 and 221.

f. Includes public eating places.

had been envisaged in the five-year plan adopted in March 1939. For instance, it would have been impossible to plan a decrease in automobile production for 1939, since an increase of 100 per cent had been planned for 1942 (over 1937) in March 1939. Nevertheless, there was a drop in 1939.[11] The same was true of tractors, grain combines, steam and electric locomotives, and excavators.[12] It is hard to attribute these failures solely to economic difficulties. According to G. M. Sorokin, the rapid increase in the production of the armament industry (an average of 39 per cent for 1938–1940 as opposed to an average of 13 per cent for all industry) was the cause of the drop in the output of machines that required large quantities of metal—motor vehicles, tractors, and certain other machines.[13] The fact that absolute decreases appeared already in 1939 shows that the annual plan must have been revised during the second half of 1939.

11. This drop amounted to 4.5 per cent for all motor vehicles, 1.1 per cent for trucks, and 27.4 per cent for automobiles (see Table A–3). The 100 per cent increase over 1937 planned in March 1939 for motor vehicles in 1942 was comprised of a 66 per cent increase for trucks and buses and a 449 per cent increase for automobiles.

12. The decreases between 1938 and 1939 were as follows: 2.2 per cent for tractors (24 per cent increase in five-year plan); 35.4 per cent for grain combines; 16.9 per cent for steam locomotives (33 per cent increase in five-year plan); 46.9 per cent for electric locomotives; and 37.0 per cent of excavators (92 per cent increase in five-year plan). See Tables A-3 and A-1.

13. G. M. Sorokin, *Planirovanie narodnogo khoziaistva SSSR* [Planning of the USSR National Economy], Moscow, 1961, p. 201.

Certain difficulties arose in 1939 quite independently of the government's will. They seem to have resulted mainly from an incorrect estimation of inputs of raw materials, fuel, and manpower and from a general unplanned increase in costs. The failure to fulfill the plan for reducing industrial production costs in 1939 appears to have been quite important. The March 1939 variant of the five-year plan provided for a reduction in the cost of production of 11 per cent in industry and the 1938 annual plan for a reduction of 2.8 per cent in state-owned industry and in local industry.[14] In actual fact, instead of a decrease, there was an increase of 2.1 per cent in the cost of industrial production.[15] This rise was due to increases in both wholesale prices and wages.[16] The price of coal went up on February 1, 1939, that of petroleum on March 17, 1937, and those of steel and construction materials (cement, bricks, window glass) on January 1, 1940.[17] Railroad freight rates were increased on March 5, 1939.[18] According to Western calculations, the index of wholesale prices of producer goods rose 6.1 percent between 1938 and 1939.[19] In view of the goals for costs in the March 1939 variant of the five-year plan, the annual plan must certainly have envisaged a sizable drop in the cost of industrial production. In reality there was a further increase of 5.1 per cent in 1939.[20]

Another trouble spot was the investment plan; the causes were the redistribution of investment to favor the armament industries and the increase in costs.[21] Comparisons of plans and actual results for investment in 1939 are extremely

14. Kurskii, *Plan 1938*, p. 39.

15. In current prices, taking into account the price increases. Not taking the price increases into account, the rise in the cost of industrial production was only 0.9 per cent (A. N. Malafeev, *Istoriia tsenoobrazovaniia v SSSR, 1917–1963 gg.* [History of Pricing in the USSR, 1917–1963], Moscow, 1964, p. 406). It should be noted that the data on the development of production costs do not reflect the movement of costs accurately since they cover "comparable" production and exclude new products.

16. Wholesale prices increased 2.7 per cent in 1938 according to Western estimates (Abram Bergson, Roman Bernaut, and Lynn Turgeon, "Prices of Basic Industrial Products in the U.S.S.R., 1928–50," *Journal of Political Economy*, August 1956, p. 322). Average wages in industry were to increase 10.4 per cent in 1938 (A. Zelenovskii, "Promyshlennost v pervom godu tretei piatiletki" [Industry in the First Year of the Third Five-Year Plan], *Planovoe khoziaistvo*, No. 5, 1938, p. 21). This goal was exceeded by 3.9 per cent (see Table A–3).

17. Naum Jasny, *Soviet Prices of Producers' Goods*, Stanford, 1952, pp. 151–61.

18. The basic rates (for 50 kilometers) were increased 14 per cent by the March 5, 1939, decree of Council of People's Commissars, "On the Introduction of New Rates for Railroad Freight Transportation" (*Sobranie postanovlenii*, No. 25, April 25, 1939, Art. 159, pp. 381–404).

19. Bergson, Bernaut, and Turgeon, *Journal of Political Economy*, August 1956, p. 322.

20. Taking into account price increases. If price increases are not taken into account, the rise is only 0.1 per cent (Malafeev, *Istoriia*, p. 406).

21. In 1938, investments in armament industries were increased 70 per cent over 1937 (K. N. Plotnikov, *Biudzhet sotsialisticheskogo gosudarstva* [Budget of the Socialist State], Moscow, 1948, p. 217). A redistribution of investment funds to favor armament industries during 1938–1939 was pointed out by official sources (see *Sotsialisticheskoe narodnoe khoziaistvo SSSR v 1933–1940 gg.* [The USSR Socialist National Economy in 1933–1940], Moscow, 1963, p. 206). The budget of the armed forces (Commissariats of Defense and of the Navy) was increased from 23.2 billion rubles in 1938 to 39.2 billion in 1939, to which should be added expenditures for the armament industries (aircraft industry, shipbuilding, munitions, and armaments) that amounted to 8.5 billion rubles in the 1939 budget compared with 7.4 billion in the 1938 budget. Military expenditures were also included in the budget for special construction projects of the Commissariat of Internal Affairs, which increased from 1,882 million rubles in the 1938 budget to 2,884 million in the 1939 budget (*Zasedaniia Verkhovnogo Soveta SSSR*

difficult because of differences in statistical definitions.[22] In any case, out of 9.6 billion rubles of investment (excluding working capital) to have been financed by enterprises in 1939, only 6.2 billion rubles in current prices were spent that year (64.6 per cent);[23] the percentage was still lower in constant prices. The volume of unfinished construction rose from 25.2 billion rubles on December 31, 1937, to 29.1 billion at the end of 1938, to 31.5 billion by the end of 1939.[24] The failure to fulfill the investment plan in 1939 was serious in the ferrous metal industry. Investment in 1936 was 35 per cent lower than in 1935, and in 1938–1939 it reached only the 1936 level.[25] The Third Five-Year Plan stipulated that 23 blast furnaces, 56 open-hearth furnaces, and 34 rolling mills were to be put into operation during the five years; in fact, only 2 blast furnaces, 2 open-hearth furnaces, and 3 rolling mills were actually put into operation.[26]

All these data explain the difficulties experienced in heavy industry during 1939. The absolute drops in production were certainly not foreseen in the plan;

(*vtoraia sessiia*). *10–21 avg. 1938 g*. [Meetings of the USSR Supreme Soviet. Second Session, Aug. 10–21, 1938], Moscow, 1938; *Zasedaniia Verkhovnogo Soveta SSSR (tretia sessiia). 25–31 maia 1939 goda* [Meetings of USSR Supreme Soviet. Third Session, May 25–31, 1939], Moscow, 1939; *Zasedaniia Verkhovnogo Soveta SSSR (shestaia sessiia). 29 marta–4 aprelia 1940 g*. [Meetings of USSR Supreme Soviet. Sixth Session, March 29–April 4, 1940], Moscow, 1940).

According to Jasny (*Soviet Prices*, p. 165), construction costs increased as follows (with 1926/27 = 100):

	1937	1940
Industrial construction	170	208
New housing	300	350–400
New railroads	300	400
Total, state construction	180	225

The increase in costs was largely responsible for the overrun of the 1939 budget for expenditures in industry. Planned expenditures were 27.5 billion rubles, whereas actual expenditures were 31.1 billion (*Zasedaniia*, 1939, and *Zasedaniia*, 1940).

22. Total investments (centralized and noncentralized) were 39,660 million rubles in the 1938 plan, 39,430 million in the 1939 plan, and 41,630 million in the 1940 plan (Norman Kaplan, "Capital Investments in the Soviet Union, 1924–1951," RAND Research Memorandum 735, Santa Monica, 1951, p. 58).

According to Plotnikov (*Biudzhet*, p. 240), actual expenditures for investment were 95 billion rubles for the three years 1938–1940. Unfortunately, it is not known to which investments Plotnikov was referring, total or only centralized, or what prices he used for his estimates. They would seem to be total investments in current prices. The percentage of fulfillment of the three plans (1938, 1939, and 1940) would then be 78.7 (since the planned total was 120.72 billion rubles), but the effect of the increase in prices should be taken into account.

23. A. G. Zverev, *Gosudarstvennye biudzhety Soiuza SSR, 1938–1945 gg*. [State Budgets of the USSR for 1938–1945], Moscow, 1946, p. 105.

24. *Sots. narodnoe khoziaistvo*, p. 188.

25. *Ibid.*, p. 206.

26. The total number of blast furnaces, open-hearth furnaces, and rolling mills in operation during 1937–1940 was as follows (on December 31 of each year):

	1937	1938	1939	1940
Blast furnaces	112	113	112	99
Open-hearth furnaces	372	373	381	391
Rolling mills	332	340	343	346

(*Ibid.*, p. 261.)

they affected mainly construction materials, ferrous metals, and hydroelectric power.[27] There were also troubles in the coal industry.[28]

The imbalance between supply and demand of consumer goods got worse again in 1939 after a brief improvement in supply in 1936–1938. The statistics on production of consumer goods and trade were more favorable than those for heavy industry,[29] but these were goods for which demand was inelastic. The wage fund rose 21 per cent in 1939,[30] a little more than state and cooperative retail trade, which rose 18.4 per cent in current prices. However, supply became very irregular during the second half of 1939. Queues appeared in front of shops, and prices on the collective farm market rose.[31] According to Western calculations, prices in collective farm trade rose 78 per cent between 1937 and January 1940.[32]

1940 Annual Plan and Third Five-Year Plan Fulfillment

It is hard to study the "launching" of the five-year plan in 1940 because of the paucity of data on the 1940 annual plan goals. Only a few of these goals could be found; they are presented in Table 37. Although very incomplete, Table 37 nevertheless gives a few clues on the relation between the 1940 annual plan and the five-year plan goals interpolated for 1940. For industrial production, the annual plan goals were clearly lower than the five-year plan goals. In view of the evolution of industrial production between 1937 and 1940, the same was proba-

27. The drop in production in 1939 can be compared with the increase planned for 1942 in March 1939 for the following products:

	Actual Decrease, 1938–1939 (per cent)	Planned Increase, 1937–1942 (per cent)
Hydroelectric power	7.5	110
Pig iron	0.9	52
Steel	2.7	58
Rolled steel	4.0	62
Manganese ore	0.9	64
Cement	8.6	102
Window glass	13.9	
Paper	4.0	80

Calculated from Tables A–1 and A–3.

28. *Sots. narodnoe khoziaistvo*, p. 220. The delays in carrying out the plan for coal mining continued in 1938–1939 because of the incomplete utilization of the capacities of the mines, which, at the beginning of 1940, were operating at 75 per cent of capacity in the Kuzbass, 78 per cent in the Urals, and 67 per cent in Karaganda. See also Sorokin, *Planirovanie*, p. 201.

29. See Tables 35 and 36 above and Table A–3.

30. Franklyn D. Holzman, *Soviet Taxation: The Fiscal and Monetary Problems of a Planned Economy*, Cambridge, Mass., 1962, p. 40.

31. See footnote 10 above.

32. Franklyn D. Holzman, "Soviet Inflationary Pressures, 1928–1957: Causes and Cures," *Quarterly Journal of Economics*, May 1960, p. 168. Holzman estimates that collective farm market prices increased 283 per cent between the annual average for 1937 and the level in December 1940.

Janet Chapman (*Real Wages in Soviet Russia since 1928*, Cambridge, Mass., 1963, p. 97) estimates that collective farm market prices increased 100 per cent between 1937 and 1940 (annual averages).

Table 37   Selected Indexes from Annual Plan for 1940

	Annual Plan for 1940			Fulfillment of Annual Plan for 1940	
	Physical Units (1)	Index (1939 = 100) (2)	As Per Cent of Five-Year Plan Goals Interpolated for 1940 (3)	Physical Units (4)	Per Cent (5)
Industrial Production					
Oil industry					a
Forging and pressing equipment					57.2[b]
Automatic cold upsetters					47[b]
Pneumatic drills					52.7[b]
Steam and pneumatic hammers					25[b]
Friction presses					65.9[b]
Soda ash (thous. m. tons)	649	114.9	78.1	536.1	82.6
Paperboard (thous. m. tons)	115.8	118.6	87.7	120.0	103.6
Wage Fund					
Workers and employees, national economy (billion rubles)	129.3	111.0	115.5	123.7	95.7
State and Cooperative Retail Trade					
In current prices (billion rubles)	189.0	114.0	111.7	175.1	92.6
In constant prices (billion rubles):					
Based on official Soviet index				147.1	87.0[c]
Based on Zaleski index				110.9	65.6[c]

Source: Unless otherwise indicated, col. 1: Table A-3, col. 7; col. 2: col. 1 as percentage of Table A-3, col. 5; col. 3: col. 1 as percentage of Table A-1, col. 4; col. 4: Table A-1, col. 5; col. 5: Table A-3, col. 9.

a. Plan not fulfilled (*Kommunisticheskaia partiia v borbe za uprochenie i razvitie sotsialisticheskogo obshchestva, 1937 god–iiun 1941 goda* [The Communist Party in the Struggle to Strengthen and Develop the Socialist Society, 1937–June 1941], Moscow, 1962, p. 88).

b. December 29, 1940, decree of USSR Council of People's Commissars and of Party Central Committee (*Direktivy*, Vol. 2, p. 658). Covers eleven months of 1940 and output of People's Commissariat of Heavy Machine-Building.

c. Fulfillment of five-year plan goals interpolated for 1940. Calculated from 1940 results (col. 4) and five-year plan goal interpolated for 1940 (Table A-1, col. 4).

bly true of other branches of industry that were not directly connected with armament production.[33]

For wages, the five-year plan goals for 1940 were exceeded despite a very definite policy to limit monetary expenditures. This was due to the evolution of prices and wages during 1938 and 1939; the planners could not go backward in order to carry out the provisions of the Third Five-Year Plan.

Although they exceeded the five-year plan goals for 1940, the annual plan goals for wages and retail trade were clearly lower than the five-year plan goals, if changes in retail prices are taken into account. According to Holzman's estimates, retail prices in state and cooperative trade increased 42.9 per cent between 1937 and January 1940. Between July 1939 and January 1940 this

33. On the evolution of production in other branches of industry, see pp. 194–95 below and Table 39.

increase was 19 per cent,[34] and the projections for 1940 were supposed to be based on the level at the end of 1939, not the annual average for 1939. But a change in general policy would have been required to reorient the economy toward the five-year plan goals set in March 1939.

The policy of promoting massive production of armaments, established during the second half of 1939, can be seen clearly in the 1940 budget. Expenditures for the Commissariats of Defense and of the Navy increased from 39.2 billion rubles actually spent in 1939 to 57.1 billion rubles in the 1940 budget. Expenditures for the Commissariat of Internal Affairs (NKVD), which had its own army, increased from 5,455 million rubles in the 1939 budget to 7,045 million rubles in the 1940 budget. Expenditures for special construction projects for the NKVD increased from 2,884 million rubles in 1939 to 3,440 million rubles in the 1940 budget. Only expenditures for the four commissariats directly concerned with armaments (Aircraft Industry, Shipbuilding, Munitions, and Armaments) were slightly cut back in 1940 (8.0 billion rubles as opposed to 8.5 billion in 1939), but their absolute level remained very high.[35]

The effects of this policy can also be seen in machine-building, where the cutting back of certain products, begun in 1938, continued during 1940 (see Table 38). The cuts spread to other branches of machine-building and construction materials and reached the chemical industry. The ferrous metal industry barely started to recover, and the production of rolled steel remained 1.1 per cent lower in 1940 than in 1938.

Under these conditions, one might wonder what could have been retained of the five-year plan provisions in the 1940 annual plan. The structure of industrial production was changed, primarily in heavy industry; the light and food industry was falling behind schedule, and agriculture could not even pretend to catch up the 20 per cent (on the average) that it had fallen behind the five-year plan schedule by the end of 1939. The structure of prices and the provisions for consumption were incompatible, which made it impossible to maintain the sections of the plan for wages and retail trade. Thus the Third Five-Year Plan suffered the same fate as the other long-range plans. The plan guaranteed to put into operation many construction projects. Once in progress, these construction projects limited the planners' freedom to maneuver. In case of difficulties, the usual reaction of the planners was to try to extend the construction cycle and to do what they could to save the project, since abandoning it would entail sizable accounting losses. Hence it is the investments in the five-year plan taken separately, factory by factory, and the accompanying technical and economic studies that should be taken as the base of the annual plan for 1940.[36] Nevertheless, the planners did not feel tied by the construction schedules, nor by the capacities

34. Holzman, *Quarterly Journal of Economics*, May 1960, p. 168.

35. *Zasedaniia*, 1939; *Zasedaniia*, 1940; and Plotnikov, *Biudzhet*, p. 216.

36. A special study of investment projects would be necessary to understand the real significance of the Third Five-Year Plan in this respect and could be based on a list of construction projects that was published at the time the Commissariat of Construction was set up (*Sobranie postanovlenii*, No. 46, August 17, 1939, Art. 359).

Table 38   Decline in Output of Selected Industrial Products between 1939 and 1940 (per cent)

Automobiles	71.9[a]	Grain combines	13.8[a]
Looms	55.5[b]	Rubber footwear	13.2[a]
Electric locomotives	47.1[a]	Window glass	12.9
Tractors (units)	34.2[a]	Excavators	11.6[a]
Steam and gas turbines	29.4	Railroad passenger cars	9.9[c]
Tires	28.8	Steam locomotives	9.6[a]
Motor vehicles, total	27.9[a]	Mineral fertilizer	9.1
Trucks and buses	23.2[a]	Industrial timber hauled	6.5
Diesel locomotives	16.7[a]	Soda ash	5.1
Turbogenerators	16.2[c]	Sulfuric acid	2.3
		Bricks	1.8

Source: Derived from Table A-3, cols. 8 and 5.

a. Output in 1939 was lower than in 1938 also (see footnotes 11, 12, and 27 in this chapter).
b. Per cent below 1937 (Table A-2, col. 14) because data are missing for 1938 and 1939.
c. Per cent below 1938 (Table A-3, col. 2) because data are missing for 1939.

envisaged in the five-year plan, nor, in general, by the goals for production or the material and financial balances in the third plan.

This attitude on the part of the planners explains to a certain extent the state of fulfillment of the third plan at the end of 1940 (see Table 39). A comparison of the 1940 results with those achieved at the end of 1939 (see Table 36 above) clearly shows the disintegration of the third plan that took place during the year. In industry, to start with, the general level of plan fulfillment was lower. For producer goods, the median percentage of plan fulfillment was 85.1 in 1939 and 76.0 in 1940. For consumer goods, it was 92.9 in 1939 and 84.5 in 1940. The deviation from the median is equally large in 1940. Several goals in machine-building simply seem to have been abandoned altogether, such as those for motor vehicles, tractors, railroad passenger cars, spinning machines, and looms, among producer goods, and bicycles, motorcycles, sewing machines, and radios, among consumer goods.

The figures on agriculture are a bit distorted because of the territorial annexations that took place during 1939 and 1940. It is even more difficult to eliminate overreporting from use of biological yield estimates (such overreporting varied from year to year). It is interesting to note that value figures computed on the basis of recent Soviet estimates (recalculating previous estimates in terms of barn yield) show a very poor degree of fulfilling the agricultural plan for 1940: 80.3 per cent for the total, 84.9 per cent for vegetable production, and only 66.4 per cent for animal production.

The figures on employment and wages, which represent costs, exceed the planned figures—an almost permanent feature of Soviet plans, which minimize costs at the outset at the risk of having to authorize exceptions later on. Since the plan represents an authorization, planned costs set too high risk being automatically fulfilled! Since wage rates and employment are important parts of costs, the planners feel obliged to minimize them, thus creating disturbances due to a

Table 39 Fulfillment of Third Five-Year Plan Goals Interpolated for 1940 (per cent)

National income	93.6	Silk and rayon fabrics	111.7
Industry		Beer	103.7
Producer goods (1926/27 prices)	99.2	Knitted outer garments	99.8
Total value of production (1926/27		Meat and subproducts of first category	98.5
prices)	98.2	Meat	97.6
Consumer goods (1926/27 prices)	96.1	Soap (40% fatty acid)	97.1
		Metal beds	96.4
Producer Goods		Cotton yarn	96.3
Natural gas	94.7	Flour (centralized resources)	96.1
Oil shale	93.5	Ginned cotton	94.9
Paperboard	90.9	Matches	93.4
Lead	90.7	Cigarettes	93.0
Peat	90.2	Cotton fabrics	92.8
Potash fertilizer	90.0	Butter	92.2
Refined copper	88.9	Knitted underwear	87.2
Nickel	88.5	Hosiery	84.8
Coal	88.3	Leather shoes	84.3
Electric power (capacity)	87.4[a]	Linen fabrics	83.6
Electric power	86.2	Woolen fabrics	82.3
Plywood	85.5	Crude alcohol	76.8
Coke	84.4	Raw sugar	71.7
Hydraulic turbines	84.1[b]	Fish catch	71.3
Asbestos shingles	82.8	Sausages	70.2
Iron ore	82.2	Canned food	69.6
Machine tools	81.5	Confectionery	64.0
Railroad freight cars	81.0	Rubber footwear	58.6
Pig iron	80.1	Rubber galoshes	53.8
Ammonium sulfate	80.0	Enameled kitchenware	35.3
Lumber	79.1	Motorcycles	34.0
Steel ingots and castings	78.6	Phonographs	33.6
Crude petroleum	78.4	Sewing machines, household	31.2
Hydroelectric power	78.2	Bicycles	29.9
Zinc	76.0	Radios	27.8
Rolled steel	75.7		
Aluminum	74.9	**Agriculture**	
Industrial timber hauled	73.8	Animal production (1926/27 prices)	92.5
Lime	71.1	Total value of production (1926/27	
Manganese ore	69.2	prices)	90.2
Paper	68.6	Vegetable production (1926/27 prices)	89.7
Cement	68.3		
Bricks	67.5	*Harvests and Animal Production*	
Roofing tiles	66.0	Sunflowers	132.0
Steam locomotives	65.7	Meat and fat	102.3
Soda ash	64.5	Potatoes	99.7
Tractors (15 hp)	63.7	Cows	96.2[c]
Trucks	55.5	Grain, total (biological yield)	94.3
Phosphoric fertilizer (14% P_2O_5)	54.8	Milk	92.9
Tractors (units)	54.7	Sheep	92.7[c]
Phosphoric fertilizer (18.7% P_2O_5)	54.1	Grain, total (barn yield)	91.8
Tires	54.1	Raw cotton	90.3
Railroad passenger cars	52.3	Beef cattle	87.3[c]
Spinning machines	50.6	Wheat	82.9
Motor vehicles, total	48.0	Wool	82.9
Steam boilers	41.4	Sugar beets	82.3
Excavators	35.5	Flax fiber	78.0
Looms	18.3	Horses	74.5[c]
Automobiles	10.9	Pigs	68.4[c]
		Mineral fertilizer, deliveries	
Consumer Goods		to agriculture	57.4[d]
Vegetable oil	116.5		

Table 39 *continued*

Procurements			**Employment**	
Vegetables	146.7		Public eating places	135.1
Eggs	121.8		Credit institutions	121.9
Sunflowers	107.9		Construction	113.7
Meat and fat	100.3		Administration	113.2
Grain, total	98.2		Education	110.8
Milk and dairy products	90.8		Other transportation (motor, etc.)	109.8
Potatoes	83.2		Public health	108.7
Wool	82.2		Railroad transportation	108.1
Raw cotton	75.4		Trade, procurements, and supply	108.1
Sugar beets	66.2		Communications	107.4
Flax fiber	62.2		National economy	103.0
Hemp	52.4		State agriculture	99.7
			State agriculture and logging	99.2
Transportation			Industry	98.4
Railroad			Maritime and inland waterway	
Length of network	116.1		transport	96.7
Grain and flour	103.7			
Total freight traffic, average length			**Wages**	
of haul	102.2		*Wage Fund*	
Mineral construction materials	101.7		National economy	110.5
Average daily carloadings	96.9		Industry	109.8
Firewood	95.9			
Ore	95.4		*Real Wage* (national economy)	
Coal and coke	94.7		Calculated from official Soviet index	90.7
Freight traffic (ton-km)	94.1		Calculated from Zaleski index	68.4
Freight traffic (tons)	92.0			
Passenger traffic (pass.-km)	91.6		*Money Wage*	
Oil and oil products	89.4		Maritime and inland waterway	
Ferrous metals	80.2		transport	129.6
Timber	70.5		Communications	114.0
			Industry, workers and employees	111.6
Inland Waterway			Industry, workers	110.6
Passenger traffic (pass.-km)	100.0		Construction	108.2
Passenger traffic (passengers)	96.2		National economy	108.1
Average length of haul	94.4		Railroad transport	107.9
Oil and oil products	88.2		Administration	107.7
Freight traffic (tons)	81.9		Credit institutions	106.3
Freight traffic (ton-km)	77.5		State-owned agriculture	103.5
			Public health	101.9
Maritime			Education	89.6
Passenger traffic (pass.-km)	89.6			
Freight traffic (tons)	82.8		**Housing**	
Passenger traffic (passengers)	81.6		Housing construction, urban	84.9
Average length of haul	62.7			
Freight traffic (ton-km)	53.1		**State and Cooperative Retail Trade**	
			Total in current prices	103.5
Motor			Total in constant prices:	
Freight traffic (ton-km)	40.4		Calculated from official Soviet index	87.0
			Calculated from Zaleski index	65.6

Source: Table A-1, col. 6, unless otherwise indicated.

a. Actual results in 1937 and in 1940 taken from *Promyshlennost*, p. 171; 1942 plan from *Tretii plan*, p. 213.

b. Actual results in 1937 taken from *Narodnoe khoziaistvo*, 1956, p. 56; actual results in 1940 from *Promyshlennost*, p. 217; and 1942 plan from *Tretii plan*, p. 35.

c. Actual results in 1937 and 1942 plan taken from *Tretii plan*, pp. 219 and 221; actual results in 1940 from *Chislennost*, pp. 6–7.

d. Actual results in 1937 and 1942 plan taken from Nancy Nimitz, "Statistics of Soviet Agriculture," RAND Research Memorandum 1250, Santa Monica, 1954; actual results in 1940 from *Dostizheniia*, p. 153.

relative overestimation of planned benefits and available resources. (Overfulfillment of the planned wage fund represents underfulfillment of planned benefits.)

As for transportation, the poor fulfillment of the goals for maritime, inland waterway, and motor transportation reappeared, slightly worsened, in 1940. Actually, transportation is also an element of costs, especially in industry. Compared with a median plan fulfillment in industry on the order of 78 per cent, the plan fulfillment for railroad freight transportation (by far the most important) was 92.0 per cent in tons and 94.1 per cent in ton-kilometers, implying that more transportation services per unit of production were used.

On the whole, it is evident that the revisions made in the five-year plan provisions were definite because of changes in economic policy as much as in the economic situation and that it was useless to try to "revive" the third plan in 1941. The text of the 1941 annual plan, which is known in considerable detail, enables us to find out what the planners thought about this matter.

Abandonment of Third Five-Year Plan in 1941

The preservation of the Third Five-Year Plan was officially proclaimed by Gosplan Chairman N. A. Voznesenskii when the 1941 annual plan was presented to the Eighteenth Party Conference on February 18, 1941.[37] The Soviet government claimed to be pursuing the two primary objectives of the third plan: strengthening political and economic independence in the face of capitalist encirclement and strengthening socialist forms of production. Maintaining the principal goals of the third plan should, according to Voznesenskii, lead to higher rates of growth in the ferrous metal industry and machine-building than in the other producer goods, increased production of special machines and rare metals, and the construction of new enterprises in the metallurgical and machine-building industries. Socialist forms of production in industry, transportation, and agriculture were also to receive preferred treatment. In general, according to the February 18 resolution of the Eighteenth Party Conference, Party organizations were to turn their attention to industry and transportation, since "the grain problem in the USSR had already been largely solved thanks to the abundant harvests (7 to 8 billion poods)."[38]

The general aggregate goals of the 1941 annual plan did not appear to be in contradiction with those of the Third Five-Year Plan. The revisions were made to seem relatively unimportant. But a glance at the budget for 1941 shows that the 1941 annual plan stressed armaments, which in 1940 had already caused sizable deviations from the five-year plan provisions. Expenditures for the Commissariats of Defense and of the Navy increased from 56.7 billion rubles actually

37. "The tasks of the national economic plan for 1941 follow from the decisions of the Eighteenth Congress of the C.P.S.U. (B) on the Third Five-Year Plan of National Economic Development" (N. A. Voznesenskii, *Economic Results of the U.S.S.R. in 1940 and the Plan of National Economic Development for 1941* [translated from the Russian], Moscow, 1941, p. 12).

38. "On the Tasks of Party Organizations in Industry and Transportation," *Kommunisticheskaia partiia*, p. 91. The editors of this collection of documents declare that the harvest reports were exaggerated because they represented biological yield (*ibid.*, pp. 12 and 378). The barn yield averaged 4,756 million poods in 1938–1940.

spent in 1940 to 70.9 billion in the 1941 budget. Expenditures for the four commissariats directly concerned with armaments (Aircraft Industry, Shipbuilding, Munitions, and Armaments) increased from 8.0 billion rubles in the 1940 budget to 9.8 billion in the 1941 budget, and expenditures for special construction projects for the NKVD increased from 3.4 billion rubles in the 1940 budget to 7.0 billion in the 1941 budget. Expenditures for the Commissariats of Internal Affairs and of State Security (which, as mentioned earlier, maintained separate armed forces) remained at the high level of 7.3 billion rubles in the 1941 budget (compared with 7.0 billion in the 1940 budget).[39]

The continuation and the intensification of the policy adopted in the 1940 annual plan can be seen in Table 40, which expresses the goals of the 1941 annual plan as percentages of the five-year plan goals interpolated for the same year. For producer goods, the median is 79.3 per cent, compared with a median fulfillment of 76 per cent of the five-year plan goals for 1940 (see Table 39); the difference is the result of the recovery in the ferrous metal industry during the second half of 1940 and the increased production of armaments. Most of the products that received preferred treatment in 1940 continued to receive it in 1941, with special emphasis on the production of freight cars, oil shale, and ferrous metal products. This was done at the expense of the same products as before in machine-building (motor vehicles, textile machinery, railroad passenger cars), the chemical industry (fertilizer, soda ash), and the construction materials industry (bricks, lime). The level and structure of production in 1941 did not have much in common with those of the Third Five-Year Plan.

The same observations can be made about consumer goods and agriculture. The medians (81.5 per cent for consumer goods and 95.3 per cent for agriculture) are very close to those for 1940 (see Table 39). Consumer durables were the worst hit, as in 1940, and animal production seems to have suffered at the expense of vegetable production. For transportation, the level of fulfillment of the five-year plan in 1941 was the same as in 1940, with railroad transportation favored relative to the other forms. For maritime and motor transportation, as in 1940, the five-year plan can be considered as abandoned. The five-year plan goals for wages continued to be exceeded in 1941, but some attempt was made to limit the expansion of employment. Nevertheless, the distribution of employment by branches of the national economy did not in the least correspond to the five-year plan goals.

Table 40 shows figures for the whole country that conceal changes made in the five-year plan on the regional level. For coal, for instance, where the five-year plan goals for 1941 seem to have been more or less respected in the annual plan, the variation by region was much greater—from 74.3 per cent for central Asia to 108.7 per cent for Karaganda (see Table 41). It can be assumed that these regional variations were greater for products of lower priority than coal.

A keystone in the Third Five-Year Plan was its provision for a reduction in production cost, made possible by productivity increases, a reduction that was

39. *Zasedaniia*, 1940, and *Zasedaniia Verkhovnogo Soveta SSSR (vosmaia sessiia). 25 fevralia–1 marta 1941 g.* [Meetings of USSR Supreme Soviet. Eighth Session, February 25–March 1, 1941], Moscow, 1941. Plotnikov, *Biudzhet*, p. 216.

Table 40   Goals for 1941: Annual Plan as Percentage of Interpolated Third Five-Year Plan

Industry

Producer goods (1926/27 prices)	104.6
Total value of production (1926/27 prices)	100.6
Consumer goods (1926/27 prices)	93.7

Producer Goods

Railroad freight cars	149.5
Oil shale	144.4
Paperboard	127.9
Nickel	108.2
Roofing tiles	98.5
Refined copper	95.0
Machine tools	94.6
Peat	93.2
Coal	89.2
Pig iron	89.1
Potash fertilizer	88.9
Steam locomotives	88.3
Coke	88.1
Asbestos shingles	87.9
Steel ingots and castings	87.7
Iron ore	85.6
Industrial timber hauled	84.8
Cement	83.7
Electric power	83.3
Rolled steel	82.7
Hydraulic turbines	80.6[a]
Crude petroleum	78.1
Bricks	76.2
Manganese ore	76.0
Paper	72.9
Soda ash	69.6
Spinning machines	67.6
Lime	65.5
Phosphoric fertilizer (18.7% P_2O_5)	64.5
Phosphoric fertilizer (14% P_2O_5)	64.1
Ammonium sulfate	61.3
Lumber	60.2
Plywood	59.7
Tires	56.6
Excavators	55.7
Trucks	48.3
Steam boilers	47.1
Tractors (units)	46.4
Motor vehicles, total	40.2
Railroad passenger cars	34.5
Looms	23.5
Automobiles	12.7

Consumer Goods

Bread and breadstuffs (large-scale industry)	106.3
Flour (centralized resources)	105.6
Flour (procurements)	105.4
Silk and rayon fabrics	101.1
Beer	100.5
Vegetable oil	96.6
Matches	96.3
Cigarettes	95.7

Cotton yarn	95.7
Cotton fabrics	94.9
Leather shoes	92.0
Ginned cotton	89.4
Soap (40% fatty acid)	88.8
Meat	88.6
Knitted outer garments	86.0
Knitted underwear	85.5
Hosiery	84.1
Raw sugar	81.5
Confectionery	80.3
Canned food	79.4
Fish catch	78.9
Linen fabrics	78.3
Metal beds	77.7
Woolen fabrics	75.9
Butter	75.5
Crude alcohol	73.2
Sewing machines, household	70.2
Sausages	67.5
Rubber footwear	61.2
Rubber galoshes	57.1
Bicycles	37.7
Enameled kitchenware	33.0
Radios	32.2
Phonographs	25.9
Watches, pocket and wrist	19.6[b]

Agriculture

Sunflowers	110.5
Potatoes	106.0
Sheep and goats	105.8[c]
Horses	103.9[c]
Grain harvest, total	96.7
Raw cotton, biological yield	96.2
Flax fiber	95.5
Cows	95.1[c]
Sugar beets	90.2
Milk	89.1
Beef cattle	87.5[c]
Wool	79.8
Pigs	78.0[c]
Meat and fat	64.5

Transportation
Railroad

Grain and flour	102.2
Freight traffic, average length of haul	100.7
Average daily carloadings	97.2
Coal and coke	94.7
Ore	91.4
Freight traffic (ton-km)	90.8
Freight traffic (tons)	90.1
Oil and oil products	89.5
Mineral construction materials	89.0
Ferrous metals	82.9
Timber	81.7
Passenger traffic (pass.-km)	79.8
Firewood	77.3

Table 40   *continued*

Inland Waterway		Industry	96.3
Average length of haul	100.8	Maritime and inland waterway	
Passenger traffic (passengers)	92.7	transport	94.1
Passenger traffic (pass.-km)	91.7	State-owned agriculture	79.2
Oil and oil products	91.2	**Wages**	
Freight traffic (ton-km)	89.4	*Wage Fund*	
Freight traffic (tons)	88.7	Industry	116.2
Maritime		National economy	107.8
Freight traffic (tons)	84.4	*Money Wages*	
Passenger traffic (passengers)	79.5	Maritime and inland waterway	
Passenger traffic (pass.-km)	75.7	transport	127.7
Average length of haul	62.4	State-owned agriculture	127.6
Freight traffic (ton-km)	52.7	Industry, workers and employees	111.4
Motor		Public eating places	110.6
Freight traffic (ton-km)	32.3	Industry, workers	109.6
Employment		Communications	109.5
Construction	165.3	Trade	108.9
Public eating places	128.8	National economy	108.2
Credit institutions	125.0	Construction	107.5
Public health	110.5	Railroad transport	106.2
Education	103.8	Public health	97.2
Railroad transport	103.3	Credit institutions	96.0
Workers and employees, national		Education	92.8
economy	100.3	**Retail Trade**	
Trade, procurements, and supply	98.5	State and cooperative, total, current	
Communications	98.5	prices	105.5

Source: Unless otherwise indicated, calculated from 1941 annual plan goals (Table A-3, col. 10) and Third Five-Year Plan goals interpolated for 1941, estimated from actual results in 1937 (Table A-1, col. 2) and goals for 1942 (Table A-1, col. 7) by assuming an equal average annual planned rate of growth during 1938–42.

a. Actual results in 1937 taken from *Narodnoe khoziaistvo, 1956*, p. 56; 1941 plan from *Gosudarstvennyi plan razvitiia narodnogo khoziaistva SSSR na 1941 god* [State Plan for the Development of the USSR National Economy for 1941], Moscow, 1941, p. 28; and 1942 plan from *Tretii plan*, p. 35.

b. Actual results in 1937 and 1942 plan taken from *Tretii plan*, p. 208; 1941 plan from *Gosudarstvennyi plan, 1941*, pp. 169 and 171.

c. Actual results in 1937 and 1942 plan taken from *Tretii plan*, pp. 219 and 221; 1941 plan from *Gosudarstvennyi plan, 1941*, pp. 4 and 5.

to promote accumulation. A direct comparison of cost reductions in the third plan and in the 1941 plan is not sufficient to draw any conclusions (see Table 42). All that can be established is that the cost decreases planned for 1941 were generally more than one-fifth of the total reduction planned for 1938–1942.

The official figures show a decrease in the cost of industrial production of 0.5 per cent between 1937 and 1940.[40] These figures are hard to accept in view of the 21 per cent increase in prices of basic industrial products, the 6 per cent increase in prices of machinery, and the 35.8 per cent increase in money wages during

40. Not taking into account price changes. The cost of industrial production rose 0.9 per cent between 1938 and 1937, 0.1 per cent between 1939 and 1938, and decreased 1.5 per cent between 1940 and 1939 (Malafeev, *Istoriia*, p. 406).

Table 41   Comparison of 1941 Goals for Coal in Third Five-Year Plan and in Annual Plan, by Region (million metric tons)

	Actual Results in 1937 (1)	Third Five-Year Plan Goals Interpolated for 1941 (2)	Annual Plan Goals for 1941 (3)	Third Five-Year Plan Goals for 1942 (4)	Annual Plan Goals as Per Cent of Five-Year Plan Goals (5)
Coal, total:	127.26	204.3	190.8	230.0[a]	93.4
Donetsk Basin	75.04	104.3	95.0	113.3	91.1
Moscow Basin	7.51	15.1	12.3	18.0	81.5
Urals	8.1	18.0	15.0	22.0	83.3
Karaganda	3.94	6.9	7.5	8.0	108.7
Kuznetsk Basin	17.34	23.7	23.4	25.5	98.7
Central Asia	1.04	3.5	2.6	4.7	74.3
Far east	3.26	6.3	4.8	7.5	76.2

Source: Cols. 1 and 4: *Tretii plan*, p. 202; col. 2: estimated from actual results in 1937 (col. 1) and goals for 1942 (col. 4) by assuming an equal average annual planned rate of growth during 1938–1942; col. 3: *Gosudarstvennyi plan, 1941*, p. 13; col. 5: col. 3 as per cent of col. 2.

a. Preliminary goal. The final goal adopted by the Eighteenth Party Congress was 243 million metric tons (*Planovoe khoziaistvo*, No. 4, 1939, p. 91), but since the final goals by region are not known, it seemed preferable to use the preliminary goal for the total here.

that period (see Table 42). Increases in prices and wages were widespread during 1938–1940, and the structure of industrial costs bore no resemblance to the five-year plan provisions. Hence the reductions in the 1941 annual plan were based on a much higher level of costs and on a very different internal structure.

Official Soviet sources give absolute figures on costs for freight transportation. Table 43 shows that not only were changes in transportation costs very different from the five-year plan provisions, but there were also considerable variations in the different forms of transportation. The 1941 plan envisaged a rate increase over 1937 of only 5.2 per cent for inland waterway transportation but of 213.9 per cent for maritime transportation. The reductions in costs provided in the five-year plan (Table 43, col. 5) were thus completely forgotten.

It is in the light of these data on changes in costs and prices that the state of fulfillment of the five-year plan for investment should be examined. For centralized investment for which data are available, the five-year plan provided for expenditures of 192 billion rubles in December 1, 1936, prices.[41] The expenditures for four years (1938–1940 and the 1941 plan) were to reach 138.5 billion rubles, i.e., 72.1 per cent of the total.[42] It is not known what prices were used to estimate these figures but, in light of the changes in costs, it is doubtful that they are December 1, 1936, prices. In any case, whenever physical data are available for the planned and actual installation of new capacities, the percentage of

41. *Direktivy*, Vol. 2, p. 574.
42. In actual estimate prices, the total for 1938–1940 was given as 108 billion rubles, 17.5 billion of which was for decentralized investment; the total for the 1941 plan was 57 billion rubles, 9 billion of which was for decentralized investment (Voznesenskii, *Economic Results*, pp. 9 and 13).

Table 42   Changes in Costs, Prices, and Wages in Industry during Third Five-Year Plan

	Planned Increase or Decrease in Cost of Production		Wholesale Prices in 1940 (1937 = 100, 1937 weights) (3)	Money Wage of Workers in 1940 (1937 = 100) (4)
	Third Five-Year Plan for 1942 Compared with 1937 (per cent) (1)	1941 Annual Plan Compared with 1940 (per cent) (2)		
Industry, Total	−11.0	−3.7	121	135.8
Fuel industry:	−4.0			
Coal industry		−6.3	166	144.2
Petroleum industry		−1.0	97 [a]	126.3 [b]
Electric power stations	−13.0	−2.8	114	122.6 [c]
Ferrous metal industry	−13.5	−3.5	128	144.5
Nonferrous metal industry	−8.0	−2.0	224	
Chemical industry	−13.0	−4.0	111	142.5
Machine-building:			106 [d]	141.5
Heavy	−27.0	−6.0		
Medium	−36.0	−8.0		
General	−26.0	−7.0		
Construction materials industry	−10.0	−5.3	138	
Woodprocessing and timber industry	−4.5	−2.6	100	
Defense industry		−11.1		
Paper industry		+0.5		
Light industry	−6.0	−1.7		
Textile industry	−3.5	−1.1		146.9
Food industry	−6.0	−1.2		150.3
Meat and dairy industry	−9.5	−1.4		
Fishing industry	−11.0	−3.1		
Local industry (of republics)	−12.0	−2.6		

Source: Unless otherwise indicated, col. 1: *Tretii plan*, p. 230 (for industrial commissariats); col. 2: *Gosudarstvennyi plan, 1941*, pp. 566–67 (for industrial commissariats); col. 3: Bergson, Bernaut, and Turgeon, *Journal of Political Economy*, August 1956, p. 323; col. 4: derived from Table A-1, cols. 5 and 2.

a. Refined petroleum products.

b. Derived from 1937 wage (given as 3,688.6 in E. Vasilev and Kh. Kovalzon, "Za dostoinuiu sotsialisticheskogo obshchestva proizvoditelnost truda" [For a Labor Productivity Worthy of a Socialist Society], *Planovoe khoziaistvo*, No. 3, 1939, p. 163) and 1940 wage (estimated as 4,657 from 1941 planned wage for workers in People's Commissariat of Oil Industry and increase between 1940 and 1941 plan, both given in *Gosudarstvennyi plan, 1941*, pp. 513–14).

c. Derived from 1937 wage (given as 3,507.0 in Vasilev and Kovalzon, *Planovoe khoziaistvo*, No. 3, 1939, p. 163) and 1940 wage (estimated as 4,299 from 1941 planned wage for workers in People's Commissariat of Electric Power Stations and increase between 1940 and 1941 plan, both given in *Gosudarstvennyi plan, 1941*, pp. 513 and 515).

d. Richard Moorsteen, *Prices and Production of Machinery in the Soviet Union, 1928–1958*, Cambridge, Mass., 1962, p. 72.

fulfillment of the five-year plan is much lower than for production (see Table 44).

There is no point in emphasizing the abandonment of the five-year plan goals for personal consumption in the 1941 annual plan. The effort made in armament production and the stagnation of several sectors of the economy during 1938–1940 made it impossible for the planners to pursue their old objectives in 1941.

In retail trade, comparisons with the five-year plan goals are difficult because

Table 43   Changes in Freight Transportation Costs during Third Five-Year Plan

	Actual Costs in 1937	Actual Costs in 1940	Costs in 1941 Plan	Planned Increase or Decrease	
				1941 Annual Plan Compared with 1937 (per cent)	Third Five-Year Plan for 1942 Compared with 1937 (per cent)
	(kopeks per ton-kilometer)				
	(1)	(2)	(3)	(4)	(5)
Railroad freight transportation, Commissariat of Transportation	2.091	2.566	2.625	+25.5	−3.0
Inland waterway fleet	2.138		2.250	+5.2	−16.5
Maritime fleet	0.994		3.12	+213.9	−7.0

Source: Col. 1: Sh. Turetskii, "Sotsialisticheskoe nakoplenie v tretei piatiletke" [Socialist Accumulation in the Third Five-Year Plan], *Planovoe khoziaistvo*, No. 3, 1939, p. 172; col. 2: A. Arkhangelskii and A. Kreinin, "Voprosy tsenoobrazovaniia i sistema zheleznodorozhnykh gruzovykh tarifov" [Problems of Price Formation and the System of Railroad Freight Rates], *Voprosy ekonomiki* [Problems of Economics], No. 11, 1957, p. 113; col. 3: *Gosudarstvennyi plan, 1941*, p. 585; col. 4: derived from cols. 1 and 3; col. 5: *Tretii plan*, p. 231.

the 1941 goals are in current prices, which are definitely lower than 1937 prices (see Table 45 and source to col. 3). Using the official price estimates with 1940 weights, the 1941 annual plan goals would be only 13 per cent lower than the five-year plan goals interpolated for the same year (see Table 45). Western estimates indicate a much greater discrepancy between the annual plan goals and the five-year plan goals (from 18 to 22 per cent according to Mrs. Chapman and from 28 to 34 per cent according to my calculations shown in Table 45). If the changes in turnover and prices of the collective farm market[43] were included in these figures, the development of retail trade would be even less favorable. But the five-year plan provisions for collective farm trade are not known.

For wages, only the five-year plan goals in current prices were exceeded. Average real wages remained unchanged between 1937 and 1940 according to Mrs. Chapman and were 10 per cent lower in 1940 according to my calculations of the cost-of-living index. There is no question of fulfilling in 1941 a plan that provided for an increase in wages of 37 per cent in five years, when, during the fourth year of the plan period, the goal was to reach the 1937 level (according to Mrs. Chapman) or a level even 10 per cent lower than that (according to my index).

Preparation of Fourth Five-Year Plan (1943–1947) and New Long-Term Prospects

Whether the Soviet authorities themselves were aware of the abandonment of the five-year plan in 1941 is a matter of conjecture. In any event, they probably did not try to integrate the various partial plans for individual sectors into a new, over-all, coherent plan for 1942. These partial plans, which extended beyond

43. See footnotes 9 and 32 in this chapter.

Table 44   Installation of New Productive Capacity during Third Five-Year Plan

| | Units | Third Five-Year Plan (1938–1942) | | Installation of New Capacity between 1938 and 1940 (3) | Fulfillment of Third Five-Year Plan in 1940 (per cent) (4) |
		Installation of New Capacity (1)	Increase in Capacity (2)		
Coal industry	mill. m. tons	160[a]	120	51[b]	32
Electric power stations	mill. kw	9[a]	8.1	2.4[b]	27
Ferrous metals:					
Pig iron	mill. m. tons		8.7	2.9[b]	
Blast furnaces	units	23[c]		7[c]	30
Open-hearth furnaces	units	56[c]		14[c]	25
Rolling mills (hot)	units	34[c]		11[c]	32
Textile industry:					
Cotton spinning machines	thousands		3,606	1,000[b]	

Source: Col. 2: *Tretii plan*, pp. 226–27 (capacity planned for January 1, 1943, minus capacity on January 1, 1938); col. 4: col. 3 as per cent of col. 1.

a. "Tretii piatiletnii plan razvitiia narodnogo khoziaistva SSSR. Rezoliutsiia XVIII Sezda VKPb po dokladu tov. V. Molotova" [Third Five-Year Plan for the Development of the USSR National Economy. Resolution of the Eighteenth Party Congress on the Report of Comrade V. Molotov], *Planovoe khoziaistvo*, No. 4, 1939, p. 102.

b. Voznesenskii, *Economic Results*, pp. 9–10. For electric power stations, Voznesenskii states that 1,750,000 kw of new capacity was to be added at the end of 1940. He also states (*ibid.*, p. 13) that 850,000 spinning machines were to increase the capacity of the cotton industry in 1941.

c. *Sots. narodnoe khoziaistvo*, pp. 205–6. Between January 1, 1938, and January 1, 1941, the number of blast furnaces in operation decreased by 13 (but their capacity increased by 5,267 m³), the number of open-hearth furnaces increased by 19, and the number of rolling mills increased by 14.

1942 and paved the way for drawing up the Fourth Five-Year Plan (1943–1947), took no account of the goals of the 1938–1942 five-year plan.

New goals for sown areas in the Ukraine for 1942 appeared as early as a decree of March 5, 1940.[44] These goals seemed to constitute a three-year plan with no apparent connection to the five-year plan in progress. A four-year plan for the production of forges and presses, quite complete and including goals for all the years from 1941 to 1944, was included in the December 29, 1940, decree of the Council of People's Commissars.[45] This was a four-year projection quite obviously outside the five-year planning system.

During the first half of 1941, the government published three decrees. The last two of these were directly concerned with preparations for a new five-year plan (the fourth) for 1943–1947. The first of these decrees (February 3, 1941) was on "the development of fruit and vegetable production in the area of the Stalin Canal at Samur-Divinsk and in the Apsheronsk peninsula (near Baku) as well as the cultivation of tea and citrus fruit in the subtropical regions of the Azerbai-

44. Decree of Council of People's Commissars, "On the Introduction of Correct Crop Rotation on the Collective and State Farms of the Ukrainian Republic" (*Sobranie postanovlenii*, No. 5, March 1, 1940, Art. 149).

45. "On the Development of the Production of Forges and Presses in the USSR" (*Direktivy*, Vol. 2, pp. 657–64).

Table 45   Changes in Retail Trade and Real Wages during Third Five-Year Plan

	Units	Actual Results in 1937 (1)	Third Five-Year Plan Goals Interpolated for 1941 (2)	Annual Plan for 1941 — Physical Units (3)	Annual Plan for 1941 — Index (1937 = 100) (4)	1941 Annual Plan as Per Cent of Five-Year Plan Goals Interpolated for 1941 (5)
State and Cooperative Retail Trade						
1. Total in current prices	bill. rubles	125.9	190	197	156	104
Total in 1937 prices:						
2. Official Soviet	bill. rubles	125.9	190	165	131	87
3. Chapman (1940 weights)	bill. rubles	125.9	190	156	124	82
4. Chapman (1937 weights)	bill. rubles	125.9	190	149	118	78
5. Zaleski (1925/26 weights)	bill. rubles	125.9	190	137	109	72
6. Zaleski (1951 weights)	bill. rubles	125.9	190	126	100	66
Average Annual Money Wage						
7. National economy [a]	rubles	3,047	3,910	4,230	139	108
Average Annual Real Wage (national economy [a])						
8. Calculated from Chapman index (1940 weights)	rubles	3,047	3,910	3,110	102	80
9. Calculated from Chapman index (1937 weights)	rubles	3,047	3,910	2,979	98	76
10. Calculated from Zaleski index (1951 weights)	rubles	3,047	3,910	2,677	88	68

Source

COLUMN 1–Lines 1 and 7: Table A-1, col. 2. **Lines 2-6:** Assumed to be same as line 1. **Lines 8–10:** Assumed to be same as line 7.

COLUMN 2–Lines 1 and 7: Estimated from actual results in 1937 (col. 1) and goals for 1942 (Table A-1, col. 7) by assuming an equal annual planned increment in physical growth during 1938–1942. It was also assumed that no change was planned in the cost of living over this period. **Lines 2-6:** Assumed to be same as line 1. **Lines 8–10:** Assumed to be same as line 7.

COLUMN 3–Line 1: Table A-3, col. 10. **Line 2:** Total in current prices (line 1) deflated by official retail price index (derived as 119.2 for 1940, with 1937 = 100, from G. Dikhtiar, "Sovetskaia torgovlia i rost narodnogo potrebleniia" [Soviet Trade and Growth of Consumption], *Voprosy ekonomiki*, No. 10, 1957, p. 131). **Lines 3-4:** Total in current prices (line 1) deflated by Chapman retail price index (derived as 126 for 1940 with 1940 weights and 132 for 1940 with 1937 weights, both with 1937 = 100, in Chapman, *Real Wages*, p. 87). **Lines 5-6:** Total in current prices (line 1) deflated by my retail price index (derived as 143.3 for 1940 with 1925/26 weights and 156.8 for 1940 with 1951 weights, both with 1937 = 100, in Zaleski, *Etudes et Conjoncture*, April 1955, pp. 336–37). **Line 7:** Based on money wage in 1940 (Table A-1, col. 5) and increase planned for 1941 (given as 6.5 per cent in Voznesenskii, *Economic Results*, p. 33). **Lines 8-9:** Official Soviet wage (line 7) deflated by Chapman cost-of-living index (derived as 136 for 1940 with 1940 weights and 142 for 1940 with 1937 weights, both with 1937 = 100, in Chapman, *Real Wages*, p. 87). **Line 10:** Official Soviet wage (line 7) deflated by my cost-of-living index (derived as 158 for 1940 with 1951 weights and with 1937 = 100 in Zaleski, *Etudes et Conjoncture*, April 1955, pp. 336–37).

COLUMN 4–All lines: Col. 3 as per cent of col. 1.

COLUMN 5–All lines: Col. 3 as per cent of col. 2.

a. Workers and employees, excluding collective farms and cooperatives.

dzhan Republic."[46] This plan set goals for production, sowing, financing, and deliveries of wood, cement, and iron for each year from 1941 to 1945. Some goals were for 1946 (fruit and vegetables) and 1947 (vine planting); others did not go beyond 1942, 1943, or 1944. This was still a far cry from the five-year planning theoretically in effect for 1938–1942.

Another decree on drainage work in the Belorussian Republic[47] contained a detailed plan specifying, for each year from 1941 to 1947, the areas to be drained, the funds to be allocated, and the materials, equipment, and fertilizer to be delivered. The goals were given sometimes for 1941–1947, sometimes for 1942–1947 or 1943–1947, and sometimes for 1942–1945. An obvious effort was made to place this plan within the time span of the new five-year plan in preparation.

The last decree was on developing silk production[48] and was a plan covering a whole branch of agriculture for the entire country. The goals for planting, however, were given only for 1941 and the last year of the plan—1947—and occasionally for 1942 also. The plan specified the prices to be paid to collective and state farms and certain means of financing.

It is likely that these partial plans by branch or by region published in government decrees represented only a small proportion of the projects drafted by various offices of Gosplan and the commissariats. Hence the problem of integrating this work into the draft of a new five-year plan for 1943–1947 arose before the war with Germany started on June 22, 1941. But no trace of the instructions for the preparation of the Fourth Five-Year Plan has been found in the sources consulted. Nevertheless, the government was certainly less concerned with revising the Third Five-Year Plan goals for 1942 than with looking toward longer-range prospects, and the drafting of a new general plan for fifteen years was officially undertaken.

The decision was made at the Eighteenth Party Congress in March 1939 that such a plan should be drafted, and the task was entrusted to USSR Gosplan by the February 22, 1941, decree of the Party Central Committee and the USSR Council of People's Commissars.[49] The principal objective of this plan was to overtake the main capitalist countries in per capita production. Thus, by 1957 the Soviet per capita production of pig iron was to exceed that of Germany and Great Britain and was to reach the 1937 U.S. level. Soviet rolled steel production was to overtake that of Germany and Great Britain and almost to equal that of the United States.[50] The Russians were also to overtake the capitalist countries

46. *Sobranie postanovlenii*, No. 5, February 20, 1941, Art. 93.

47. March 6, 1941, decree of Party Central Committee and Council of People's Commissars, "On Draining Marshes in Belorussian Republic and Using the Drained Land for Collective Farms to Enlarge Their Sown Area and Pasture Land" (*ibid.*, No. 8, March 20, 1941, Art. 130).

48. March 13, 1941, decree of Party Central Committee and Council of People's Commissars, "On Measures for the Further Development of Silkworm Breeding" (*ibid.*, No. 9, March 25, 1941, Art. 149).

49. *Pravda*, February 22, 1941, as cited in *Ekonomicheskaia zhizn SSSR: Khronika sobytii i faktov, 1917–1965* [Economic Life of the USSR. Chronology of Events and Facts, 1917–1965], 2nd ed., edited by S. G. Strumilin, Moscow, 1967, Book I, p. 329.

50. A. Zalkind and B. Miroshnichenko, "Iz opyta Gosplana SSSR po podgotovke dolgosrochnykh planov" [From USSR Gosplan's Experience in Drafting Long-Term Plans], *Planovoe khoziaistvo*, No. 4, 1973, p. 47.

in the production of steel, fuel, electric power, machinery, and certain other producer and consumer goods. The list of objectives also included providing the whole country with electric power and eliminating rural and urban differences and differences between intellectual and manual work. The goals of the Second Five-Year Plan and of the second general electrification plan are quite recognizable.[51] The date for their scheduled fulfillment was simply pushed forward first from 1937 and then from 1942–1947 to 1957.

The scope of the preparation of the plan for 1943–1957 was broad. USSR Gosplan enlisted the Central Statistical Administration (TsUNKhU), the people's commissariats, the USSR Academy of Science, and other organizations in the work and formed several study groups. Materials were to be prepared by various sections of Gosplan according to directives approved by Gosplan Chairman N. A. Voznesenskii and later to be combined into a single two-volume document. The first volume was to give the results of growth for twenty-five years and the over-all long-range economic outlook. The second volume was to be devoted to provinces and republics. During the first stage, only hypotheses of development were drafted; during the second stage, a draft of a general plan was drawn up including growth rates by branch and presenting balances that tied the plans together by sectors. Computations were made for 1942, 1947, 1952, and 1957.[52]

This draft enabled Gosplan to present a report to the Party Central Committee and the USSR Council of People's Commissars on the 15-year plan, announcing the country's transition to a new stage of development—the gradual transition from socialism to communism. It was stressed that this transition would require a long period of time.[53]

The principal known goals of the 15-year (1943–1957) plan have been collected in Table 46. They seem to present the classical picture of Soviet plans: a higher rate of growth for producer goods than for consumer goods, ambitious goals for agriculture, more modest growth for freight transportation,[54] and a considerable increase in machine-building, mainly for new techniques. Growth of consumption is not forgotten (as in some other Stalinist plans), and a number of increases in per capita consumption (for 1957 relative to 1942) were planned.[55] The over-all consumption fund was to increase 2.7 times, and the share of fabrics, shoes, and other manufactured products in this fund was to increase at the expense of food products.[56]

51. See Chapter 6.
52. Zalkind and Miroshnichenko, *Planovoe khoziaistvo*, No. 4, 1973, p. 47.
53. *Ibid*.
54. The growth planned for fifteen years amounted to less than three times the total freight traffic planned for 1942 (659 billion ton-kilometers, derived as sum of different transportation series in Table A–1). A reduction in the average length of haul was hoped for but never achieved.
55. These planned increases in consumption between 1942 and 1957 were: meat, 2.8-fold; milk and dairy products, twofold; fish, 2.3–fold; sugar, 2.3–fold; vegetables, 2.3–fold; eggs, fourfold; cotton fabrics, 2.4–fold; woolen fabrics, 5.7–fold; and leather shoes, 2.3–fold (Zalkind and Miroshnichenko, *Planovoe khoziaistvo*, No. 4. 1973, p. 49).
56. The share of food products in the consumption fund was to decline from 67 to 61 per cent (*ibid*.). Such a change in the structure of consumption would have implied an increase in the standard of living.

The means of attaining this growth were classical: a threefold increase in total investment and a considerable increase in labor productivity, to be achieved through technical progress, tightening labor discipline, improving the organization of production, reducing the working day, etc.[57] The share of the eastern provinces in gross industrial production was to increase from 14.8 per cent in 1939 to 29–30 per cent in 1957. The number of specialists was to increase from 2.7 to 8 million, with highly skilled specialists in this total increasing from 1 to 6 million.[58]

The published data do not permit an examination of the internal coherence of the plan. Like the other Stalinist plans, this one seems to have stressed inflationary investment financing, making it possible to emphasize heavy industry goals at the expense of consumption. The overoptimistic agricultural production plan and the very high labor productivity goals were also weak points.

Comparison of these plan goals with the actual outcome presented in Table 46 seems to confirm this evaluation. Some value figures exceed the goals, but not too much importance should be attributed to this in view of the inflation of the Soviet index in constant 1926/27 prices.[59] With a few exceptions, percentage fulfillment of the 1957 plan runs from 56 to 71 for producer goods and from 40 to 60 for consumer goods. The shortfalls in agricultural production and the grain harvest are, as expected, large. It is also of interest to see when the various goals of the 1943–1957 plan were actually met. For producer goods (except for machine-building, which is expressed in value terms),[60] the 1957 goals were reached between 1960 and 1965. But the goal for coal production was not reached in 1975 and will still not be reached by the end of the Tenth Five-Year Plan,[61] as a result of a change in coal policy. The goal for motor vehicle production was reached only at the end of the ninth plan in 1975, thanks to a change in policy concerning private transportation.

For consumer goods, the earliest date by which a 1957 goal was reached was 1961, when the sugar production goal was reached. The goal for shoes was reached only in 1970, and the goal for fabrics will not be reached in the foreseeable future. For agriculture, the goals were fulfilled around 1970–1971, that is, around 14 years later than scheduled.

Thus, the fulfillment of the 15-year plan goals resembles that of the earlier long-range plan goals: growth was slower and more costly (cost indexes were exceeded) and the consumption goals fell by the wayside (they were never taken very seriously in drafting the long-range plans). Nevertheless, the 1943–1957

57. The increase in investment was made up of a 3.6–fold increase for industry, a 2.5–fold increase for agriculture, and a fourfold increase for transportation; the increase in labor productivity was to average 6.3 per cent per year (*ibid.*, pp. 49–50).

58. *Ibid.*

59. See my *Planning*, p. 256.

60. *Ibid.*

61. Output in 1975 was 701 million metric tons (*USSR in Figures, 1975*, p. 87) and planned output for 1980 was 805 million metric tons (*Ekonomicheskaia gazeta* [Economic Gazette], No. 45, 1976, p. 7).

According to G. Sorokin ("Pervyi generalnyi plan razvitiia narodnogo khoziaistva" [First General Plan for the Development of the National Economy], *Planovoe khoziaistvo*, No. 2, 1961, pp. 47–48), the 1943–1957 plan erred in underestimating the development of sources of power, in overemphasizing coal production, and in studying insufficiently the prospects for technical progress.

Table 46   Principal Goals of Fifteen-Year Plan for 1943–1957 and Their Fulfillment

	Units	Five-Year Plan Goals for 1942 (1)	Goals Revised for 1942 (2)	Goals for 1957 Index (1942 Goals = 100) (3)	Physical Units (4)
1. Gross industrial production (1926/27 prices)	1937 = 100	193		324	625
2. Producer goods (group A)	1937 = 100	207		350	725
3. Consumer goods (group B)	1937 = 100	172		280	482
4. Pig iron	mill. m. t.	22.0	21.0	310	65.0
5. Steel ingots	mill. m. t.	28.0	26.6	320	85.0
6. Rolled steel	mill. m. t.	21.0	18.7	332	62.0
7. Fuel, total	convent. units			344	
8. Coal	mill. m. t.	243.0		340	826.2
9. Petroleum	mill. m. t.	49.5		438	216.8
10. Electric power	bill. kwh	75.0		395	296.3
11. Machine-building	1937 = 100	229		354	810.7
12. Machine tools	thousands	70.0		278	195
13. Motor vehicles	thousands	400		475	1,900.0
14. Chemical industry	1937 = 100	237		375	888.8
15. Cement	mill. m. t.	11.0		400	44.0
16. Cotton fabrics	mill. m	4,900		270	13,230
17. Woolen fabrics	mill. m	177		385	681.5
18. Leather shoes	mill. pairs	258.0		250	645
19. Raw sugar	thous. m. t.	3,500		220	7,700
20. Gross agricultural production	1937 = 100	151.6	131.5	250	329
21. Grain harvest (barn yield)	mill. m. t.	108.1		162	175.1
22. Cotton harvest	thous. m. t.	3,290		218	7,172
23. Sugar beet harvest	thous. m. t.	28,200		192	54,144
24. Total freight traffic (excl. pipeline)	bill. ton-km			261	1,723
25. Average length of haul, railroad freight traffic	km	685			600

Source
COLUMN 1–Lines 1-3 and 20: Calculated from Table A-1, cols. 2 and 7. **Lines 4-10, 12-13, 15-19, 21-23, and 25:** Table A-1, col. 7. **Line 11:** *Direktivy*, Vol. 2, p. 564. **Line 14:** *Tretii piatiletnii plan razvitiia narodnogo khoziaistva SSSR. Rezoliutsiia XVIII Sezda VKPb po dokladu tov. V. Molotova* [Third Five-Year Plan for the Development of the USSR National Economy. Resolution of the Eighteenth Party Congress on the Report of Comrade V. Molotov], Moscow, 1939, p. 9.

COLUMN 2–Lines 4-6: Calculated from cols. 3 and 4. **Line 20:** Calculated from increase between 1937 and 1940 (5.2 per cent from *Narodnoe khoziaistvo SSSR v 1959 godu* [The USSR National Economy in 1959], Moscow, 1960, p. 308) and increase planned for 1941 and 1942 (arbitrarily estimated at 25 per cent).

COLUMN 3–Lines 1-23: Zalkind and Miroshnichenko, *Planovoe khoziaistvo*, No. 4, 1973, p. 48. **Line 24:** Calculated from col. 4 and 1942 goal for total transportation (derived by summing individual series in Table A-1).

COLUMN 4–Lines 1-3, 8-19, and 21-23: Calculated from cols. 1 and 3. These figures are probably too high since the five-year plan goals for 1942 were undoubtedly revised downward. **Lines 4-6:** Zalkind and Miroshnichenko, *Planovoe khoziaistvo*, No. 4, 1973, p. 47. **Line 20:** Calculated from cols. 2 and 3. **Line 24:** Calculated from 1937 traffic

| Actual Results in 1957 | | Fulfillment of 1957 Goals | | |
Physical Units (5)	As Per Cent of Planned Goals (6)	Year (7)	Physical Units (8)	Line No.
565	90.4	1958	623	1
738	101.8	1957	738	2
342	71.0	1962	498	3
37.0	56.9	1965	66.2	4
51.2	60.2	1964	85.0	5
40.2	64.8	1965	61.7	6
574.6				7
463.5	56.1			8
98.3	45.3	1964	223.6	9
209.7	70.8	1960	292.3	10
1,040	128.3	1955	810	11
131.0	67.2	1967	197.0	12
495.4	26.1	1975	1,964	13
				14
28.9	65.7	1960	45.5	15
5,588	42.2			16
283.6	41.6			17
317.3	49.2	1970	675.7	18
4,491	58.3	1961	8,376	19
148.3	45.1	1971	235.6	20
102.6	58.6	1970	186.8	21
4,210	58.7	1971	7,100	22
39,700	73.3	1958	54,400	23
1,443.9	83.8	1959	1,726.4	24
815	135.8			25

(given in *Transport i sviaz SSSR* [Transport and Communications in the USSR], Moscow, 1957, p. 7) and increase planned for 1957 (given as fourfold in Zalkind and Miroshnichenko, *Planovoe khoziaistvo*. No. 4, 1973, p. 49). **Line 25:** Zalkind and Miroshnichenko, *Planovoe khoziaistvo*, No. 4, 1973, p. 49.

COLUMN 5–Lines 1-3: Calculated from indexes for 1957 and 1937 with 1913 = 100 (given in *Narodnoe khoziaistvo v 1960 godu* [The USSR National Economy in 1960], Moscow, 1961, p. 219). **Lines 4-6:** *Ibid.*, p. 241. **Line 7:** *Ibid*, p. 253. **Line 8:** *Ibid.*, p. 255. **Line 9:** *Ibid.*, p. 262. **Line 10:** *Ibid.*, p. 269. **Line 11:** Calculated from indexes for 1937 and 1957 with 1913 = 1 (given in *ibid.*, p. 283). **Line 12:** *Ibid.* p. 285. **Line 13:** *Ibid.*, p. 291. **Line 15:** *Ibid.*, p. 307. **Lines 16-17:** *Ibid.*, p. 321. **Line 18:** *Ibid.*, p. 337. **Line 19:** *Ibid.*, p. 344. **Line 20:** Calculated from index for 1940 with 1937 = 100 (derived as 105.2 from *ibid.*, p. 362) and index for 1957 with 1940 = 100 (given as 141 in *ibid.*, p. 363). **Lines 21-23:** *Narodnoe khoziaistvo SSSR, 1922–1972* [The USSR National Economy, 1922–1972], Moscow, 1972, p. 217. **Line 24:** *Narodnoe khoziaistvo, 1958*, p. 539. Total minus pipelines. **Line 25:** *Ibid.*, p. 545.

COLUMN 6–All lines: Calculated from cols. 4 and 5. **Line 25:** Since a decrease was planned in the average length of haul, this "overfulfillment" represents a failure to carry out the plan.

COLUMNS 7-8–Line 1: Calculated from indexes for 1958 and 1937 with 1913 = 100 (given in *Narodnoe khoziaistvo*

Table 46   *continued*

SSSR v 1960 godu [The USSR National Economy in 1960], Moscow, 1961, p. 219). **Line 2:** Calculated from indexes for 1957 and 1937 with 1913 = 100 (given in *ibid.*, p. 219). **Line 3:** Calculated from index for 1940 with 1937 = 100 (derived as 133.2 from *ibid.*, p. 219) and index for 1962 with 1940 = 100 (given as 374 in *Narodnoe khoziaistvo SSSR v 1965 godu* [The USSR National Economy in 1965], Moscow, 1966, p. 122). **Lines 4-6:** *Narodnoe khoziaistvo, 1922–1972*, p. 165. **Line 8:** 1957 goal had not yet been attained in 1975 (output given as 701 mill. m. tons in *The USSR in Figures for 1975* (translated from the Russian), Moscow, 1976, pp. 86–87). **Line 9:** *Narodnoe khoziaistvo, 1922–1972*, p. 163. **Line 10:** *Ibid.*, p. 158. **Line 11:** Calculated from indexes for 1937 and 1955 with 1913 = 1 (given in *Narodnoe khoziaistvo, 1960*, p. 283). **Line 12:** *Narodnoe khoziaistvo, 1922–1972*, p. 179. **Line 13:** *USSR in Figures, 1975*, pp. 92–93. **Line 15:** *Narodnoe khoziaistvo, 1960*, p. 193. **Lines 16-17:** 1957 goals had not been reached in 1975 (output given as 7,856 and 541 mill. m in *Narodnoe khoziaistvo SSSR v 1974 godu* [The USSR National Economy in 1974], Moscow, 1975, p. 270). **Line 18:** *Narodnoe khoziaistvo, 1922–1972*, p. 202. **Line 19:** *Ibid.*, p. 209. Output declined to 7,800 thous. m. tons in 1962 and 6,219 in 1963 before increasing to 8,208 in 1964 (*ibid.*). **Line 20:** Calculated from index for 1940 with 1937 = 100 (derived as 105.2 from *Narodnoe khoziaistvo, 1960*, p. 362) and index for 1971 with 1940 = 100 (given as 224 in *Narodnoe khoziaistvo, 1922–1972*, p. 220). **Lines 21-23:** *Ibid.*, p. 217. **Line 24:** *Narodnoe khoziaistvo, 1960*, p. 531. Total minus pipelines. **Line 25:** The average length of haul continued to increase after 1957, rising to 894 in 1975 (derived from *USSR in Figures, 1975*, pp. 144–47).

plan does differ from other long-term plans in that it seems to have been better prepared than the two Goelro plans, the planners having profited from past experience. Moreover, the preliminary work was presented to a Gosplan meeting in April 1941.[62] Also a major event occurred in the meantime—the war against Germany. It is interesting to note that, despite the war, the style of carrying out a long-range Stalinist plan did not change.

62. *Ibid.*, p. 48.

PART THREE

Current Planning, 1933–1941

CHAPTER 10

Statistical Coherence
of Annual Plans, 1933–1941

The use of physical and value balances provides Soviet planners with an excellent tool for checking the coherence of planned goals and required resources. Unfortunately for this study, only some of these planned balances are available —those published for the First Five-Year Plan (1927/28–1932/33) and the first annual plans (until 1929/30). After that time, publication of these balances ceased, and data that would make it possible to calculate these balances indirectly also became very rare. Because a detailed examination of plan coherence is not possible, only a more aggregative approach to analyzing the assumptions on which the planned goals are based is attempted here. The analysis makes possible an appraisal of the real nature of the sources of the planned expansion and the planned balance of the money income and expenditures of households.

Over-All Equilibrium between Goals and Resources in Annual Plans

The basic feature of the prewar annual plans was that they attempted to transpose microeconomic rationality to a national scale. This approach can be partly explained by the tendency on the part of Soviet officials to consider the Soviet state as a single enterprise. The quest for such a transposition encouraged Soviet planners to adopt an approach in their annual plans that sought simultaneously to maximize results and minimize costs.

This approach can be seen clearly in Table 47. The aggregate goals are particularly high. The annual rates of growth vary from 13 to 26 per cent for national income, from 16 to 23 per cent for industrial production, and from 8 to 24 per cent for agricultural production. These results were to be attained through very large investments and a sizable increase in labor productivity. All this depended on realizing very ambitious goals to reduce costs (in construction, the

Table 47   Principal Goals of Annual Plans for 1933–1941 (per cent of increase or decrease relative to preceding year)

	1933	1934	1935	1936	1937	1938	1939	1940	1941
1. National income (1926/27 prices)	13.3	24.1	16.1	26.5	24.3				
2. Gross industrial production (1926/27 prices)	16.5	21.3	16.0	23.0	20.0	17.2			17–18
3. Gross agricultural production (1926/27 prices)		8.2	16.3	24.2					
4. Grain harvest	12.9	1.6	6.2	13.9	30.9		10.1		4.2
Labor Productivity									
5. Industry	14.0	13.5	11.0	20.0	19.5				12.0
6. Construction	25.0	17.5	20.0	30.0	22.4				12.0
7. Railroad transportation		10.0	−0.8	8.4	16.0				
Employment									
8. Workers and employees, total:	−6.6	5.1	4.8	4.0	2.1				1.3
9. Industry	2.0	4.2	6.1	4.3	2.3				1.8
Transportation									
10. Total freight traffic[a] (tons)		32.4	13.8	17.5	17.2				5.9
11. Railroad freight traffic (tons)	12.4	31.3	13.3	17.2	16.7	9.8			5.3
Investment									
12. Socialist sector	5.4	39.6	−1.4	34.8	3.0	22.9[b]	17.9[b]	18.4[b]	41.7[b]
Costs									
13. Industry	−3.9	−4.7	−3.7	−6.2	−3.1	−2.8			−3.7
14. Investment:[c]				−8.0	−10.5				
15. Construction[d]	−15.0	−15.0	−15.0	−14.5	−13.5				
16. Equipment					−5.0				

Source
1933–Lines 1, 9, and 11: V. Mezhlauk, "Za bolshevistskoe vypolnenie plana pervogo goda vtoroi piatiletki" [For a Bolshevik Fulfillment of the Plan for the First Year of the Second Five-Year Plan], *Planovoe khoziaistvo*, No. 1–2, 1933, pp. 47, 46, and 44. **Line 2:** *Pravda*, January 31, 1933, p. 1. **Lines 4 and 6:** *Pravda*, January 28, 1933, p. 2. **Lines 5, 13, and 15:** *KPSS v rezoliutsiiakh i resheniiakh sezdov, konferentsii i plenumov Ts. K.* [The Communist Party of the Soviet Union: Resolutions and Decisions at Congresses, Conferences, and Plenary Sessions of the Central Committee], Moscow, 1953, Part II, p. 728. **Line 8:** Based on 1933 plan (given as 21,310 thous. by Mezhlauk in *Planovoe khoziaistvo*, No. 1–2, 1933, p. 46) and 1932 employment (given as 22,804.3 thous. in *Itogi vypolneniia pervogo piatiletnego plana razvitiia narodnogo khoziaistva Soiuza SSR* [Fulfillment of the First Five-Year Plan for the Development of the USSR National Economy], Moscow-Leningrad, 1933, p. 229). **Line 12:** Based on 1933 plan (given as 18,000 mill. rubles in *KPSS v rezoliutsiiakh*, Part II, p. 728, in 1932 prices deflated by official reduction in construction costs in line 15) and 1932 investments (given as 20,086 mill. rubles in current prices in *Sotsialisticheskoe stroitelstvo SSSR* [Socialist Construction in the USSR], Moscow, 1936, p. 386).
1934–Lines 1, 2, 5, 7-11, and 15: *Narodno-khoziaistvennyi plan na 1935 god* [The National Economic Plan for 1935], 1st ed., Moscow, 1935, pp. 78–79, 88, 85, and 89. For line 9, large-scale industry. **Line 3:** P. Mesiatsev and A. Kogan, "Selskoe khoziaistvo v 1934 g." [Agriculture in 1934], *Planovoe khoziaistvo*, No. 5–6, 1934, p. 121. *Plan 1935*, 1st ed., p. 83, gives 11.7 per cent. **Lines 4, 6, and 13:** "Osnovnye pokazateli narodnokhoziaistvennogo plana 1934 g." [Main Indicators of the National Economic Plan for 1934], *Planovoe khoziaistvo*, No. 5-6, 1934, pp. 213, 220, and 224. **Line 12:** Based on 1934 plan and 1933 investments (given as 25,111 and 17,989 mill. rubles, respectively, in *Vtoroi piatiletnii plan razvitiia narodnogo khoziaistva SSSR, 1933–1937* [Second Five-Year Plan for the Development of the USSR National Economy, 1933–1937], Moscow, 1934, p. 717), both apparently in 1933 plan prices.
1935–Lines 1-3, 5-11, 13, and 15: *Plan 1935*, 1st ed., pp. 78–79, 83, 88, 85, and 89. For line 9, large-scale industry. **Line 4:** *Narodno-khoziaistvennyi plan na 1935 god* [The National Economic Plan for 1935], 2nd ed., Moscow, 1935, p. 586. **Line 12:** Based on 1935 plan and 1934 investments (given as 21,190 and 21,500 mill. rubles, respectively, in *Plan 1935*, 1st ed., p. 78). According to "Metodicheskie ukazaniia Gosplana SSSR k sostavleniiu plana na 1935 g." [USSR Gosplan Instructions on Methods to Draft the 1935 Plan], *Plan*, No. 8, 1934, p. 29, average annual prices in effect at the moment the plan was drafted were used for the 1934 plan, and current 1934 prices deflated by the planned reduction in construction and equipment costs were used for the 1935 plan.

Table 47   *continued*

1936—Lines 1-11, 13, and 15: *Narodno-khoziaistvennyi plan na 1936 god* [The National Economic Plan for 1936], Vol. 1, 2nd ed., Moscow, 1936, pp. 390–92, 433, 435, 285, 457, 449, 452, 453, 455, and 313. For line 10, sum of railroad, inland waterway, maritime, and air freight traffic. **Line 12:** Based on 1936 plan and 1935 investments (given as 32,365 and 24,015 mill. rubles in *ibid.*, p. 391). It is not clear whether the 1936 plan took into account the planned reduction in investment costs (line 14). **Line 14:** Decrease relative to 1935 price estimates for cost of investment (*kapitalnye raboty*). See *Ukazaniia i formy k sostavleniiu narodno-khoziaistvennogo plana na 1936 god* [Instructions and Forms for Drafting the National Economic Plan for 1936], Moscow, 1935, pp. 4 and 191–93.

1937—Lines 1-2, 5-11, 13, and 16: *Narodno-khoziaistvennyi plan Soiuza SSR na 1937 god* [The USSR National Economic Plan for 1937], Moscow, 1937, pp. 42, 224, 142–45, 27, 121–23, 128–31, 134–35, 241, and 16. For line 10, sum of railroad, inland waterway, maritime, and air freight traffic. For line 5, large-scale industry. **Line 4:** Based on 1937 plan and 1936 harvest (given as 108.32 and 82.73 mill. m. tons in Table A-2, cols. 13 and 11). **Line 12:** Based on 1937 plan and 1936 investments (given as 32,593 and 31,750 mill. rubles, respectively, in *Plan 1937*, pp. 142–43). Result rounded since the 1936 results are in current prices anticipated in 1936 and the 1937 plan is in 1935 prices deflated by planned reduction in investment costs (see *Ukazaniia i formy k sostavleniiu narodnokhoziaistvennogo plana na 1937 god* [Instructions and Forms for Drafting the National Economic Plan for 1937], Moscow, 1936, pp. 216–17).

1938—Line 2: A. Zelenovskii, "Promyshlennost v pervom godu tretei piatiletki" [Industry in the First Year of the Third Five-Year Plan], *Planovoe khoziaistvo*, No. 5, 1938, p. 20. Probably in 1926/27 prices. **Line 11:** Based on 1938 plan (given as 568 mill. m. tons in "K novomu podemu promyshlennosti i transporta" [Toward a New Advance in Industry and Transportation], *Planovoe khoziaistvo*, No. 11–12, 1937, p. 18) and 1937 traffic (given as 517.3 mill. m. tons in *Transport i sviaz SSSR* [Transport and Communications in the USSR], Moscow, 1957, p. 32). **Line 12:** Based on 1938 plan and 1937 investments (given as 40.8 and 33.2 mill. rubles, respectively, in Norman Kaplan, "Capital Investments in the Soviet Union, 1924–1951," RAND Research Memorandum 735, Santa Monica, 1951, p. 37). **Line 13:** A. D. Kurskii, *Narodno-khoziaistvennyi plan na 1938 god i ego vypolnenie* [The National Economic Plan in 1938 and Its Fulfillment], Moscow, 1938, p. 39.

1939—Line 4: Based on 1939 plan (estimated as 104.6 mill. m. tons from grain yield on collective farms and total area sown to grain according to 1939 plan, as given in *Sobranie postanovlenii i rasporiazhenii pravitelstva SSSR* [Collection of Resolutions and Decrees of the USSR Government], No. 14, 1939, Art. 88) and 1938 harvest (given as 94.99 mill. m. tons in Nancy Nimitz, "Statistics of Soviet Agriculture," RAND Research Memorandum 1250, Santa Monica, 1954, p. 4). See also I. V. Stalin, *Voprosy Leninizma* [Problems of Leninism], 11th ed., Moscow, 1947, p. 582. **Line 12:** Based on 1939 plan and 1938 investments (given as 48.0 and 40.7 mill. rubles, respectively, in Kaplan, "Capital Investments," p. 37).

1940—Line 12: Based on 1940 plan and 1939 investments (given as 47.5 and 40.1 mill. rubles, respectively, in *ibid.*, p. 37).

1941—Line 2: N. A. Voznesenskii, *Economic Results of the U.S.S.R. in 1940 and the Plan of National Economic Development for 1941* (translated from the Russian), Moscow, 1941, p. 13. **Line 4:** Based on 1941 plan and 1940 harvest (given as 123.76 and 118.8 mill. m. tons in Nimitz, "Statistics," p. 4). **Lines 5-6:** *Gosudarstvennyi plan razvitiia narodnogo khoziaistva SSSR na 1941 god* [State Plan for the Development of the USSR National Economy for 1941], Moscow, 1941, p. 5. **Line 8:** Based on 1941 plan (given as 31.6 mill. in *ibid.*, p. 512) and 1940 employment (given as 31.2 mill. in Nikolai A. Voznesensky, *The Economy of the USSR during World War II* [translated from the Russian], Washington, 1948, p. 7). **Line 9:** Based on 1941 plan (given as 11.092 mill. in *Plan 1941*, p. 512) and 1940 employment (calculated as 10.9 mill. from statement that industrial workers were 35 per cent of total in Voznesensky, *Economy*, p. 64). **Line 10:** Sum of railroad, inland waterway, and maritime (petty cabotage only) freight traffic. Based on 1941 plan (summed from *Plan 1941*, pp. 450, 454, 462–65) and 1940 traffic (summed from *Transport*, p. 17). **Line 11:** Based on 1941 plan (given as 624.0 mill. m. tons in *Plan 1941*, p. 450) and 1940 traffic (given as 592.6 mill. m. tons in *Transport*, p. 32). **Line 12:** Based on 1941 plan and 1940 investments (given as 63.2 and 44.6 mill. rubles, respectively, in Kaplan, "Capital Investments," p. 37). **Line 13:** *Plan 1941*, p. 5.

a. Railroad, inland waterway, maritime, and air traffic. Motor traffic is not included since it is measured in tons without distance transported, a meaningless quantity.

b. Total investments excluding collective farm investments made from their own resources. In 1936/37 prices.

c. The concept of investment (*kapitalnye raboty*) covers: (1) net construction (*chistoe stroitelstvo*); (2) equipment (*oborudovanie*); (3) equipment assembly; and (4) other work relating to construction (projects, geological prospecting, scientific research, acquiring tools, inventory, livestock purchases, planting). See *Plan*, No. 8, 1934, p. 29. The same definition is used in the instructions for the 1936 and 1937 plans.

d. For 1933, construction (*stroitelstvo*); for 1934–1936, net construction (*chistoe stroitelstvo*). The latter concept covers: (1) construction of all sorts of buildings, such as industrial, residential (*zdaniia*); (2) construction of all kinds of installations (*sooruzheniia*); and (3) capital repairs of buildings and installations. For 1937, construction work (*stroitelnaia rabota*).

planned annual reductions were on the order of 15 per cent) and to increase employment and wages as little as possible.

The plan objectives permitted very few exceptions due to special circumstances. Rates of growth of agricultural production were strongly influenced by the harvests of the preceding year, and decreases or a considerable slowing down of the growth rates for employment were anticipated at the time of a slowdown in growth in 1933 and 1937 (and no doubt in 1938 and 1939 also). The high rates of growth for freight traffic do not appear to be typical of this policy, but result from putting into operation transportation investment projects that had been delayed until 1933. For investment, the very low rates of 1935 and 1937 result from the accumulation of projects in progress (in 1935) and from the stagnation that developed in 1937.

Sources of Planned Expansion

Production increases depended on two factors: increased nonagricultural employment and increased labor productivity. Table 47 shows that increasing labor productivity was the preference of the planners. The low rates of growth for nonagricultural employment may seem surprising during the 1930's in a country with the Soviet Union's sizable surplus rural population, a surplus that would be further increased by the results anticipated for rural collectivization. Furthermore, this policy was in contradiction with trends evidenced during the First Five-Year Plan (1928–1932).[1] However, it can be easily explained. The huge influx of peasants into the towns during 1929–1932 considerably reduced the living space per inhabitant and raised serious infrastructure problems. To bring vast numbers of new workers into the towns would have been very costly, as would have been the assimilation and training of the newly arrived workers.

Was it realistic to depend so heavily on improved labor productivity? That dependence assumed a considerable upgrading of labor qualifications and made the expansion depend largely on the investment program. (For more details, see Chapter 11.) In fact, the rates of growth planned for investment were so high that, even without an increase in employment, the planned expansion should have been possible. Since it is not very likely that the Soviet planners anticipated a decrease in the return on capital, it must be assumed that they wanted to protect themselves against not fulfilling their investment program or failing to put new production capacities into operation. The problem, then, is to know whether it was possible to guarantee that and whether assurance of fulfillment could be translated into figures, in view of how investment plans were drafted.

All projects for the expansion of production showed the share to come from reconstruction and modernization and improvement of technology, on the one hand, and that to come from the introduction of new production capacities, on the other. The former was based largely on the results of advanced factories and on the effects of political and social actions (the Stakhanovite movement, actions

1. See my *Planning for Economic Growth in the Soviet Union, 1918–1932*, translated and edited by Marie-Christine MacAndrew and G. Warren Nutter, Chapel Hill, N.C., 1971, pp. 247–48.

of the Party and the Young Communist League, administrative reorganization, and improvement of labor qualifications); that is, it lent itself poorly to precise evaluation. The latter share was based largely on construction projects in progress or to be put into operation. For this purpose each annual plan contained a long list of the principal construction projects, which took up an important part of the total volume of the plan and, in fact, made up a collection of accepted estimates. The list specified the construction schedules and dates for putting construction projects into operation, the productive capacities, the total costs, and the values of work already done and that anticipated during the plan year. The prices used were sometimes those of the year preceding the plan (for the 1933 and 1935 plans), sometimes the estimate prices of the year preceding the plan (for the 1934 and 1936 plans), sometimes the estimate prices of two years before (for the 1937 plan), or sometimes constant prices (for the plans for 1938–1941).[2] In all cases, estimate prices were reduced by a fixed percentage, calculated separately for construction work and for equipment.[3] The plans for putting new capacities into operation linked the investment plans to the production plans.

Coordination of these investment projects with the available resources could be done only with the value estimates. In other words, investments were to be integrated into the financial plan not according to the real costs of the past but according to the costs desired by the central planner. The experience of 1930–1940 showed that these forecasts were too optimistic. The problem is knowing whether the real increase in costs could be predicted. There is no doubt that the planners thought it could. Investment planning did not differ much from that of 1931,[4] and the costs of industrial production, construction, and wages continued to increase steadily after 1931. But the increases mentioned in the official statistics were only for "comparable" production and did not cover new products, whose real weight must have been very great in an economy undergoing such extensive transformation.

In order to evaluate the coherence of Soviet plans, it would be necessary to distinguish between what was incomplete, calculated in summary fashion, and knowingly underestimated in the investment estimates, on the one hand, and the increases in investment costs due to poor forecasting of the movement of prices during the planned year, on the other. The present state of documentation does not allow such an evaluation. The impression is of a cumulative movement: underestimation of real investment costs encouraged starting many construction projects that wasted resources, compromised production plans, and increased the discrepancy between planned goals and available resources. The distribution of national income between accumulation and consumption, then, had to be changed from that provided in the plan, and the equilibrium of the Soviet market in that sense became one of the main preoccupations of the government.

2. See Table 47, sources to line 12.

3. The percentage of the reduction planned for total investment costs was rarely given. From the figures in the 1936 and 1937 plans, much more economizing seems to have been anticipated in reducing construction and assembly work than in reducing the cost of machinery (see Table 47).

4. See my *Planning*, pp. 163–64.

Planned Balance between Money Incomes and Expenditures of Households

The balance of money incomes and expenditures of households is the most important tool in the study of the equilibrium of the Soviet market. Yet it must not be forgotten that this market was influenced equally by the money stock and by operations that do not enter into the calculation of this balance. These operations are the purchases of organizations and institutions made directly in state stores and on the collective farm market and the in-kind distribution for *trudodni* (hypothetical working days) made to collective farmers, which had a direct effect on supply and demand of the food products of peasants and on the amount of cash they had.

Tables 48 and 49 present an attempt to calculate a balance of the money incomes and expenditures of Soviet households during 1932–1941. Although this calculation makes no claims to precision, it does enable discussion of a few questions on the coherence of annual plans in relation to the equilibrium of the consumer goods market.

The first question is whether there was an over-all balance between money incomes and expenditures of households in the annual plans. Although the planned balance could be estimated only for one year—1936—the answer is certainly positive. Table 48 shows that the most important item in money income —wages and salaries—was planned considerably below the actual results in all years (except 1940). Since the annual plan for state and cooperative retail trade— the most important item in expenditures—was well fulfilled in current prices, the implication is that a certain excess of money expenditures was generally planned.[5] In other words, the over-all balance of the market in the annual plans was based on a certain excess of money expenditures of households. Hence the government was trying to withdraw some of the money from circulation.

Even Soviet authors thought that this over-all balance could not be realized in the regional and local plans.[6] In seasonal activities and in construction, there were temporary workers who came from other areas and who took the money they earned away with them. Agricultural areas received money earned outside the area. Some cash was sent away by money orders. Some wages were paid in cities to workers who lived in the suburbs and spent their money there. It is not easy to estimate the money spent on business trips, holidays, health cures, and vacations in country houses. The same is true of the money received by collective farmers selling their products in large cities (for example, fruits and vegetables from the Caucasus sold in Moscow) and of the expenditures of the floating population in the big cities.[7] The corrections made in the estimates on these grounds before the war were very small.

To the problem of regional balances must be added that of the elasticity of supply and demand. Although studies of family budgets were made at that

5. The situation was a little different in 1939 and 1940, when there was a considerable rise in retail prices. It is not certain that the 1939 plan was deflationary. This effect, however, seems to have been sought in 1940 with a sizable increase (not realized) in the planned turnover of state and cooperative retail trade in increased current prices. See Table 53.

6. Margolin, *Balans*.

7. *Ibid.*, p. 39.

time, the production of consumer goods does not seem to have been taken into account in the structure of supply. In this connection, three periods should be distinguished during which supply and demand were balanced in different fashions: rationing in 1929–1935, relative abundance in 1936–1938, and scarcity in 1939–1941.[8]

The estimates made by Soviet authorities of the money incomes of households (see Table 48) do not seem to have been sufficiently precise to permit evaluation of the equilibrium. A distinction should be made here among income planned centrally, income planned in a decentralized way, and simple estimates. Among the centrally planned items were mainly pensions and allowances, stipends and scholarships, and interest receipts by households. Their over-all importance was slight, but they depended on the state budget and could be planned with precision. Among items planned in a decentralized way, the most important were wages and salaries.[9] Their volume depended in large part on the fulfillment of norms and production plans. Table 48 shows that plans in these areas were not very precise. All the other items of income were simple estimates based on economic legislation (other regular money income),[10] on the evaluation of the economic situation, and on the effect of planned orders on different sectors of the economy.

The most doubtful estimates seem to have been those based on goals for agricultural production. Income from procurements was based on the plan for sowing and delivery norms. Money payments for *trudodni* made up the residual part of the income of collective farmers, a flexible part, compared with the other fixed obligations of the collective farms to the state or to the Machine and Tractor Stations or compared with investment obligations.[11] Thus, the money payments depended not only on the harvest but also on the general economic situation. As for the sales of farm products on the collective farm market, neither their prices nor their quantities could be predicted with any precision.

On the whole, in view of the optimism of the annual plans in overestimating the expansion of agricultural production,[12] it is likely that all the items of the money incomes of households that depended on agriculture were overestimated. The overestimation of money income from agricultural sources compensated in part for the underestimation of income from salaries and wages.

In the money expenditures of households, the share of trade was both pre-

8. Over-all balancing was obtained during the rationing period (1929–1935) by increasing prices on the collective farm market (private trade in 1929–1931) and by organizing sales at higher prices in so-called "commercial" trade in state and cooperative stores. In 1936–1938, the balance was obtained by increasing retail prices for basic products and reducing collective farm market prices ("commercial" trade having been abolished). At the same time the supply of goods increased considerably. In 1939–1941, in the face of a sizable reduction in supply, market equilibrium was obtained by increasing considerably prices in state and cooperative trade and on the collective farm market.

9. Part of this item (wages in administration and education, and military pay) was planned centrally, but it was a small part of the total.

10. Income of independent artisans, payments to household help, hunters, gold miners, etc. See Bergson, *Soviet National Income, 1937*, p. 108.

11. On this subject, see Henri Wronski, *Rémunération et niveau de vie dans les kolkhoz: Le troudoden*, Paris, 1957.

12. Tables A–2 and A–3.

Table 48   Money Incomes of Households, 1932–1941 (billion rubles)

	1932 Actual (1)	1933 Planned (2)	1933 Actual (3)	1934 Planned (4)	1934 Actual (5)	1935 Planned (6)	1935 Actual (7)	1936 Planned (8)	1936 Actual (9)
1. Wages and salaries	32.7	30.8	35.0	38.1	44.0	49.8	56.2	63.4	71.4
2. Other payments	9.7	9.1	10.3	11.2	13.0	14.7	16.6	17.9	20.1
3. Money payments to collective farmers for *trudodni*, bonuses, and salaries of collective farm executives and administrative personnel	1.8		1.6		1.7		4.6	7.7	5.9
4. Income from sale of farm products on collective farm market	4.1		6.2		7.5		7.8	8.8	8.4
5. Income from sale of farm products to state procurement agencies	1.7		2.1	2.3	2.4		2.6		2.3
6. Pensions and allowances	2.3	(2.5)	2.5		2.7		2.9	(4.0)	4.0
7. Stipends and scholarships	0.6		0.8		1.2		1.4	(1.8)	1.8
8. Interest on loans and savings	1.0	1.3	1.3	1.7	1.9	1.8	1.8	2.7	2.2
9. Income of cooperative artisans and other regular money income	5.2		5.6		7.0		9.0	10.0	11.3
10. Total income	59.1		65.4		81.4		102.9	116.3	127.4
11. Surplus of income over expenditures	+5.4		−3.5		−2.5		−2.2	−9.2	−4.2
12. Net total	53.7		68.9		83.9		105.1	125.5	131.6

dominant and difficult to forecast. Aside from the uncertainty of planned agricultural production, the planning of retail trade prices could not be precise. The figures in the 1933 plan were given in 1932 prices (for state and cooperative trade). But the share of so-called "commercial" sales at higher prices was not specified, and no effort was made to evaluate the sales in the probable prices of 1933, which could only increase. The prices of the 1934 and 1935 plans were "constant" prices, and it is likely that they were in effect at the time the plan was drafted. The 1935 plan reflected in any case the increases in the prices of certain rationed products that took place on December 7 and 16, 1934.[13]

During 1933–1941, the Soviet government had a choice of two general approaches—that adopted in the 1936 plan and that adopted in the 1937 plan. The plan for the turnover of state and cooperative retail trade in 1936 was set in two categories of prices:[14] prices in effect at the time the plan was drafted; and prices planned for 1936, taking into account the reductions planned for each product separately (these being "current" prices). In the 1937 plan, the planned prices were those in effect at the time the plan was drafted—in fact, those of August 15, 1936.[15] The second approach—that of the 1937 plan—seems to have been most frequently used. Thus, the government was betting on a certain stability of

13. *Plan 1935*, 1st ed., p. 197.
14. *Ukazaniia, 1936*, p. 326.
15. *Ukazaniia, 1937*, pp. 343–44.

1937		1938		1939		1940		1941		
Planned (10)	Actual (11)	Planned (12)	Actual (13)	Planned (14)	Actual (15)	Planned (16)	Actual (17)	Planned (18)	Actual (19)	Line No.
78.3	82.2	94.0	96.4	140.6	116.5	129.3	123.7	136.4		1
22.1	23.2	25.7	26.4		31.9	39.9	38.3	38.9		2
	7.5		9.6		9.8		11.3			3
	9.6		15.5		18.9		25.6			4
	2.9		2.9		3.2		5.0		2.2	5
	6.1		6.5		7.0	7.6	7.3	8.1	7.7	6
	2.2		2.3		2.4		2.4	2.7		7
2.6	3.5	2.1	2.0	1.9	2.1	2.5	2.8	3.3		8
	13.7		16.0		19.3		20.6			9
	150.9		177.6		211.1		237.0			10
	−3.2		−0.6		−2.1		0			11
	154.1		178.2		213.2		237.0	281.9		12

Note: Figures in parentheses are estimates based on assumption, for lack of any other data, that planned income was the same as actual income in a given year.

Source

LINE 1: This item covers wages and salaries of workers and employees excluding collective farmers and workers in cooperatives but including state farmers. Data were collected by the Central Administration of National Economic Accounting (*Tsentralnoe Upravlenie narodnokhoziaistvennogo ucheta SSSR* or *TsUNKhU*) under USSR Gosplan and published directly as wage funds or calculated from published figures on average annual wages and average annual number of workers and employees in the following sources: **Cols. 1, 3, 5, and 7:** *Sotsialisticheskoe stroitelstvo*, 1936, p. 510. **Col. 2:** Mezhlauk, *Planovoe khoziaistvo*, No. 1–2, 1933, p. 46. **Col. 4:** *Planovoe khoziaistvo*, No. 5–6, 1934, p. 223. **Col. 6:** *Plan 1935*, 2nd ed., p. 642. **Col. 8:** *Plan 1936*, p. 458. **Cols. 9–10:** *Plan 1937*, pp. 146–47. **Col. 11:** *Tretii piatiletnii plan razvitiia narodnogo khoziaistva SSSR (1938–1942)* [Third Five-Year Plan for the Development of the USSR National Economy, 1938–1942], Moscow, 1939, p. 228. **Col. 12:** A. G. Zverev, *Gosudarstvennye biudzhety Soiuza SSR 1938–1945 gg.* [State Budgets of the USSR for 1938–1945], Moscow, 1946, p. 9. **Col. 13:** Stalin, *Voprosy Leninizma*, p. 586. **Col. 14:** See line 2, col. 14. **Col. 15:** Franklyn D. Holzman, *Soviet Taxation: The Fiscal and Monetary Problems of a Planned Economy*, Cambridge, Mass., 1955, p. 40. **Col. 16:** N. Sokolov, ''Kontrol gosbanka nad fondami zarabotnoi platy'' [The State Bank's Control over Wage Funds], *Dengi i kredit* [Money and Credit], No. 1, 1940, p. 8 (1940 plan given as 11 per cent increase over 1939). **Col. 17:** Voznesenskii, *Economic Results*, p. 10. **Col. 18:** Based on number of workers and employees (given as 31.6 mill. in *Plan 1941*, p. 512) and average annual wage, which was derived as 4,318 rubles from average annual wage in 1940 (given as 4,054 in M. Lifits, *Sovetskaia torgovlia* [Soviet Trade], Moscow, 1948, p. 2) and increase in average annual wage planned for 1941 (given as 6.5 per cent over 1940 in Voznesenskii, *Economic Results*, p. 33).

LINE 2: This item covers payments to workers and employees not included in the wage fund figures published by *TsUNKhU* (line 1 above). According to Abram Bergson (''A Problem in Soviet Statistics,'' *Review of Economics and Statistics*, November 1947, pp. 247 ff.), this item includes: (1) wages paid to workers in certain local industries and wages paid for work not included in the annual economic plan; (2) wages paid to hired workers by collective farms; (3) earnings of artisans belonging to cooperatives; (4) military pay; and probably (5) earnings of forced laborers. **Cols. 1–4, 6–12, and 15–16:** Estimated from wages and salaries in line 1 and their shares in total wages and salaries. These shares were extrapolated (from those given in cols. 5, 13, and 17) as 77.2 per cent for cols. 1–4 and 6–7, 78.0 per cent for cols. 8–11, 78.5 per cent for cols. 12 and 15, and 76.4 per cent for col. 16. **Cols. 5 and 13:** Based on wages

Table 48   *continued*

and salaries in line 1 and their share in total wages and salaries (given as 77.2 per cent for 1934 and 78.5 per cent for 1938 by Abram Bergson, *Soviet National Income and Product in 1937*, New York, 1953, p. 107, based on data from N. S. Margolin, *Voprosy balansa denezhnykh dokhodov i raskhodov naseleniia* [Questions of the Balance of Money Income and Expenditure of the Population], Moscow, 1939). **Col. 14:** Based on budget for state social insurance (given as 7.2 billion rubles in Zverev's annual speech in *Gosudarstvennye biudzhety, 1938–1945*) and its share in total wages and salaries (given as 5.12 per cent in *ibid.*). **Col. 17:** Total wages and salaries (given as 162.0 bill. rubles by N. A. Voznesensky in *Five-Year Plan for the Rehabilitation and Development of the National Economy of the USSR, 1946–50* [translated from the Russian], London, 1946, p. 24) minus wages and salaries in line 1. **Col. 18:** Total wages and salaries (given as 175.3 billion rubles in *Plan 1941*, p. 5) minus wages and salaries in line 1.

LINE 3: This item is the sum of three separate sources of income: money payments for *trudodni*, bonuses paid to collective farmers, and salaries of collective farm executives and administrative personnel. Sources for the first components were the following. **Cols. 1, 3, 5, 7, 11 and 13:** Serge N. Prokopovicz, *Histoire économique de l'U.R.S.S.*, Paris, 1952, p. 220. **Col. 8:** Estimated from assumption that 75 per cent of the plan was fulfilled (as for agricultural production in 1936 in Table A-2). **Col. 9:** Based on money payments for *trudodni* in 1935 (col. 7 above) and increase in 1936 (estimated at 26.4 per cent, increase in collective farm income between 1935 and 1936 for 13 provinces given by M. Nesmii, "Dokhody kolkhozov i kolkhoznikov" [Income of Collective Farms and Collective Farmers], *Planovoe khoziaistvo*, No. 9, 1938, p. 100). **Cols. 15 and 17:** Based on total money income of collective farmers (given as 18.3 bill. rubles in 1939 in Voznesenskii, *Economic Results*, p. 10, and 21.0 bill. rubles in 1940 in N. I. Anisimov, *Selskoe khoziaistvo SSSR za 30 let* [Agriculture in the USSR during 30 Years], Moscow, 1947, p. 14, as cited by Abram Bergson and Hans Heymann, Jr., *Soviet National Income and Product, 1940–48*, New York, 1954, pp. 112–13) and share of *trudoden* payments in that total (estimated at 50.35 per cent for 1940 in *ibid.*, p. 113). The 1940 share was used for 1939 also.

The second and third components were derived from total collective farm money income (given above for 1939 and 1940) and share of bonuses and executives' salaries in that total (estimated together at 3.5 per cent in 1932–1936 and 3.4 per cent in 1939 and 1940 on basis of data for 1937 and 1938 in M. Nesmii, "Finansovoe khoziaistvo kolkhozov" [Finances of Collective Farms], *Planovoe khoziaistvo*, No. 8, 1939, p. 92, and Bergson and Heymann, *Soviet National Income, 1940–48*, p. 115).

LINE 4: Table C-2, line 7.

LINE 5: Table C-2, line 9.

LINE 6: This item covers part of expenditures for state social insurance and all budget expenditures for social security and family allowances.

LINE 7–Cols. 1, 3, 5, 7, 9, 11, 13, 15, and 17: Holzman, *Soviet Taxation*, p. 330. **Col. 18:** Based on stipends and scholarships in 1940 (col. 17) and increase planned for 1941 (assumed to be same as increase planned for number of students in higher educational institutions, given as 13 per cent in Zverev, *Gosudarstvennye biudzhety, 1938–1945*, p. 111).

LINE 8–Col. 1: Holzman, *Taxation*, p. 330. Debt service. **Cols. 2-3:** *Industrializatsiia SSSR, 1933–1937* [Industrialization of the USSR, 1933–1937], Moscow, 1971, p. 31. **Cols. 4-5:** *Ibid.*, p. 62. **Cols. 6-7:** *Ibid.*, p. 92. **Cols. 8-9:** *Ibid.*, p. 123. **Cols. 10-11:** *Ibid.*, p. 124. **Col. 12:** *Zasedaniia Verkhovnogo Soveta SSSR (vtoraia sessiia). 10-21 avg. 1938 g.* [Meetings of USSR Supreme Soviet. Second Session, August 10–21, 1938], Moscow, 1938. **Col. 13:** *Industrializatsiia SSSR, 1938–1941* [Industrialization of the USSR, 1938–1941], Moscow, 1973, p.25. **Cols. 14-15:** *Ibid.*, p. 31. **Cols. 16-17:** *Ibid.*, p. 41. **Col. 18:** *Zasedaniia Verkhovnogo Soveta SSSR (vosmaia sessiia). 25 fevralia–1 marta 1941 g.* [Meetings of the USSR Supreme Soviet. Eighth Session, February 25–March 1, 1941], Moscow, 1941, p. 277.

LINE 9–Cols. 1, 3, and 7-9: Based on total wages and salaries (sum of lines 1 and 2) and the share that the income of cooperative artisans and other income was of that total in 1934 (derived as 12.3 per cent from col. 5). **Cols. 5 and 13:** Sum of income of cooperative artisans (derived as 2.05 and 5.45 billion rubles, respectively, by Bergson and Heymann, *Soviet National Income, 1940–48*, p. 130, from data in N. S. Margolin, *Balans denezhnykh dokhodov i raskhodov naseleniia* [Balance of Money Income and Expenditures of Households], Moscow, 1940, p. 8) and other regular money income (derived as 4.90 and 10.56 billion rubles, respectively, from Bergson's calculation that this item was 8.6 per cent of total wages and salaries in *Soviet National Income, 1937*, pp. 107–8). **Cols. 11 and 17:** Bergson and Heymann, *Soviet National Income, 1940–48*, p. 131. **Col. 15:** Based on total wages and salaries (sum of lines 1 and 2) and the share that the income of cooperative artisans and other income was of that total in 1938 (derived as 13.0 per cent from col. 13).

LINE 10: Sum of lines 1–9.

LINE 11: Line 10 minus line 12.

LINE 12: Table 49, line 7.

prices, which, in the light of the results of 1932–1941, could not be maintained.

The precariousness of the plans was even greater in collective farm trade. Unfortunately, no information is available on the prices planned for the collective farm market. Such information would have provided a basis for analysis of the government's agricultural and price policies.

It should be noted that the lack of coherence in the official estimates of supply and demand on the consumer goods market did not have the same importance that it would have had in a market economy. In the very frequent cases when the demand of consumers exceeded the supply, state management of retail trade made it possible to introduce hidden rationing at the wholesale trade level, and queues in front of stores took the place of price rises. But this "barrier" had limits that the government could not exceed; hence the periodic cascades of price rises, such as those in 1939–1941. In other words, while a relatively minor disequilibrium of the balance of incomes and expenditures of households could be supported, the government had to make an effort to avoid a major disequilibrium that would provoke a cumulative movement of wages and prices.

Table 49   Money Expenditures of Households, 1932–1941 (billion rubles)

	1932 Actual (1)	1933 Planned (2)	1933 Actual (3)	1934 Planned (4)	1934 Actual (5)	1935 Planned (6)	1935 Actual (7)
1. State and cooperative retail trade sales to households	35.7	43.4	44.1	53.1	54.7	70.8	72.3
2. Collective farm market sales to households	6.8		10.4		12.6		13.1
3. Housing and other services	5.8	6.9	7.0	8.2	8.4	10.6	10.9
4. Trade union, Party, and other dues	0.4	0.4	0.5	0.5	0.6	0.6	0.7
5. Direct taxes	2.4	3.0	3.5	3.2	3.8	2.8	3.2
6. Net increase in savings and loans	2.6	3.2	3.4	3.9	3.8	4.4	4.9
7. Total	53.7		68.9		83.9		105.1

Source

LINE 1: Total state and cooperative retail trade sales (taken from my *Planning*, Table A-2, for col. 1, and from Tables A-2 and A-3 in this volume for cols. 2–19) minus share of those sales that went to enterprises and institutions. On the basis of data for 1937 and 1938 (in Margolin, *Balans*, p. 89), that share was estimated at 11.5 per cent for 1932–1938 (cols. 1–13). On the basis of data for 1940 (in Bergson and Heymann, *Soviet National Income, 1940–48*, p. 144), that share was estimated at 7.5 per cent for 1939, 1940, and 1941 (cols. 14–17 and 19). For the 1941 plan (col. 18), the amount of that share was given as 6.5 billion rubles or 3.4 per cent (in *Plan 1941*, p. 590).

LINE 2: Total turnover on the collective farm market (see sources below) minus that which was sold to enterprises and institutions. On the basis of data for 1937 and 1938 (in Margolin, *Voprosy balansa*, p. 63), that share was estimated at 10 per cent for 1932–1938 (cols. 1–13). On the basis of data for 1940 (in Bergson and Heymann, *Soviet National Income, 1940–48*, p. 148), that share was estimated at 15 per cent for 1940 and 1941 (cols. 17–18). For 1939 (col. 15), that share was interpolated as 13 per cent. Total turnover on the collective farm market was taken from the following sources: **Col. 1:** *Sotsialisticheskoe stroitelstvo*, 1936, p. 606. **Cols. 3, 5, 7, 9, and 13:** Stalin, *Voprosy Leninizma*, p. 584. **Col. 8:** V. Voronov, "K voprosu ob ucheta roznichnogo tovarooborota" [On the Question of Retail Trade Turnover Accounting], *Plan*, No. 12, 1936, p. 27. **Cols. 15 and 17:** Based on total turnover of retail trade (see source to line 1) and share of collective farm market trade in total (given as 15.3 per cent in 1939 and 19.0 per cent in 1940 in B. I. Gogol et al., *Ekonomika sovetskoi torgovli* [Economics of Soviet Trade], Moscow, 1955, p. 236). **Col. 18:** Assumed as 43.6 bill. rubles on the basis of movement in previous years.

LINE 3: Based on total state and cooperative retail trade (see source to line 1) and share of housing and other services in total trade. On the basis of data for 1937 and 1938 (in Margolin, *Balans*, p. 9), Bergson (in *Soviet National Income, 1937*, p. 110) estimated that share at 13.6 per cent for 1934 (cols. 4 and 5), 12.5 per cent for 1937 (cols. 10 and 11), and 12.1 per cent for 1938 (cols. 12 and 13). By the same method, that share was estimated at 14.4 per cent for 1932 (col. 1), 14.0 per cent for 1933 (cols. 2 and 3), 13.3 per cent for 1935 (cols. 6 and 7), and 12.9 per cent for 1936 (cols. 8 and 9). On the basis of the trends in retail prices and prices of services (see my article "Les fluctuations des prix de détail en Union Soviétique," *Etudes et Conjoncture*, April 1955, pp. 345 and annex pp. 16–18), that share was estimated at 11.0 per cent for 1939 (cols. 14 and 15), 12.0 per cent for 1940 (cols. 16 and 17), and 11.9 per cent for 1941 (cols. 18 and 19).

LINE 4: Based on total wages and salaries (Table 48, lines 1 plus 2) and share of trade union, Party, and other dues in that total. On the basis of data for 1935 (V. Cherniavskii and S. Krivetskii, "Pokupatelnye fondy naseleniia i roznichnyi tovarooborot" [Disposable Income of the Population and Retail Trade Turnover], *Planovoe khoziaistvo*, No. 6, 1936) and for 1940 (in *Izvestiá*, February 27, 1941, p. 3), Bergson (in *Soviet National Income, 1937*, p. 110, and Bergson and Heymann, *Soviet National Income, 1940–48*, p. 158) estimated that share at 1 per cent in 1935, 1937, and 1940. This share has been applied to all years here.

LINE 5–Col. 1: Holzman, *Soviet Taxation*, p. 219. **Cols. 3, 5, 7, 9, and 11:** Plotnikov, *Biudzhet*, pp. 44, 102, and 112. Given for Union, republics, and local Soviets. **Cols. 2, 4, 6, 8, and 10:** Based on actual taxes (cols. 3, 5, 7, 9, and 11) and fulfillment of plan for wage fund increased slightly to take account of progressivity of income tax (derived as 115 per cent for 1933, 118 per cent in 1934, 115 per cent in 1935 and 1936, and 108 per cent in 1937 by increasing figures for fulfillment of wage fund plan in Table A-2). **Cols. 12–19:** Sum of (a) personal taxes, (b) local taxes and revenues, and (c) various other taxes. For cols. 12, 14, and 18, item (a) is taken from *Zasedaniia Verkhovnogo Soveta SSSR* [Meetings of USSR Supreme Soviet] for 1938, 1939, and 1941. For col. 16, item (a) is sum of planned taxes ex-

1936		1937		1938		1939		1940		1941		
Planned (8)	*Actual* (9)	*Planned* (10)	*Actual* (11)	*Planned* (12)	*Actual* (13)	*Planned* (14)	*Actual* (15)	*Planned* (16)	*Actual* (17)	*Planned* (18)	*Actual* (19)	*Line No.*
88.5	94.5	115.9	111.4	124.3	123.9	170.6	153.4	174.8	162.0	190.5	141.3	1
14.9	14.0		16.0		22.0		22.1		28.3	37.1		2
12.9	13.8	16.4	15.7	17.0	16.9	16.8	18.2	22.7	21.0	23.4	18.2	3
0.8	0.9	1.0	1.1	1.2	1.2	1.4	1.5	1.7	1.6	1.8		4
3.3	3.8	3.7	4.0	6.5	6.6	9.1	9.6	12.9	12.6	16.3		5
5.1	4.9	6.0	5.9	8.1	7.6	10.0	8.4	12.0	11.5	12.8	11.0	6
125.5	131.6		154.1		178.2		213.2		237.0	281.9		7

cluding those paid into local budget (given as 5.99 million rubles in *ibid.*) and taxes paid into local budget (assumed to be same as actual such taxes in 1940, given as 3.68 million rubles in Plotnikov, *Biudzhet*, p. 196). For cols. 13, 15, and 17, item (a) is taken from *ibid.*, p. 181. For col. 19, item (a) is taken from K. N. Plotnikov, *Ocherki istorii biudzheta sovetskogo gosudarstva* [Essays on the History of the Soviet State Budget], Moscow, 1954, p. 293. For cols. 12–17, item (b) is taken as three-quarters of figures given for local taxes and revenues and state taxes by A. Suchkov (*Dokhody gosudarstvennogo biudzheta SSSR* [Revenue from USSR State Budget], Moscow, 1955, p. 135). For lack of information, planned figures were assumed to be the same as actual figures. For col. 18, item (b) is taken as three-quarters of a similar figure given by N. N. Rovinskii, (*Gosudarstvennyi biudzhet SSSR* [State Budget of the USSR], Moscow, 1944, p. 48, as cited by Harry Schwartz, *Russia's Soviet Economy*, London, 1951, p. 425). For cols. 12–18, item (c) is taken as three-quarters of figures given for revenues other than taxes and miscellaneous taxes in *Zasedaniia* for 1938–1941.

LINE 6–Col. 1: Holzman, *Soviet Taxation*, pp. 251 and 325. Sum of purchases of government bonds (80 per cent of total purchases assumed to be by households) and increment in savings. **Cols. 2 and 3:** *Industrializatsiia SSSR, 1933–1937* [Industrialization of the USSR, 1933–1937], Moscow, 1971, p. 29. **Cols. 4 and 5:** *Ibid.*, p. 59. **Cols. 6 and 7:** *Ibid.*, p. 88. **Cols. 8 and 9:** *Ibid.*, p. 120. **Cols. 10 and 11:** *Ibid.*, p. 134. **Cols. 11 and 13:** *Industrializatsiia SSSR, 1938–1941* [Industrialization of the USSR, 1938–1941], Moscow, 1973, p. 22. **Cols. 14 and 15:** *Ibid.*, p. 29. **Cols. 16 and 17:** *Ibid.*, p. 36. **Col. 18:** Total state loans in budget minus loans to cooperatives, collective farms, and communal banks (both taken from *Zasedaniia*). **Col. 19:** Total state loans in budget (taken from Plotnikov, *Biudzhet*, p. 181, and Plotnikov, *Ocherki*, p. 293) minus loans to cooperatives, collective farms, and communal banks (estimated from plan fulfillment of total loans).

LINE 7: Sum of lines 1–6.

CHAPTER 11

Investment Planning and Economic Equilibrium, 1933–1941

Launching the Second Five-Year Plan for Investment

During the First Five-Year Plan investment grew extremely rapidly. In 1927/28 prices, including the private sector, it increased by 28.7 per cent in 1930 and 28.1 per cent in 1931. These precipitous increases were followed by a drop to 3.9 per cent in 1932, the result of an enormous increase (21.5 per cent) in construction costs and a continued steep rise in money credits allocated for investment.[1] The headlong pace of industrial growth, reflected in the decrease in its rate,[2] was also seen in a perceptible drop in real wages.[3] Nevertheless, at the time the Second Five-Year Plan (for 1933–1937) was drafted and presented to the Seventeenth Party Conference (January 30–February 4, 1932[4]), the Soviet leaders were still under the spell of the great leap forward of 1930–1931 and were convinced that the power to continue it lay in their hands.

Information on the original variant of the Second Five-Year Plan for investment drafted in 1931–1932 is very scarce (see Table 12 in Chapter 6). Total investments for 1933–1937 of 140–150 billion rubles, probably in 1931 prices (some 30 per cent of the total national income planned for the five years), seemed too high, even though sizable cuts had already been made in the requests of the various republic commissariats and councils. In any case, the variant of the second plan presented by V. Molotov and V. Kuibyshev in February 1932 was approved but not taken into account in subsequent work on drafting the plan.

The 1933 annual plan, therefore, had to be put into operation before the final

1. See my *Planning for Economic Growth in the Soviet Union, 1918–1932*, translated and edited by Marie-Christine MacAndrew and G. Warren Nutter, Chapel Hill, N.C., 1971, p. 246.
2. *Ibid.*, pp. 258–59.
3. The index of real wages was 65.4 in 1932 (with 1927/28 = 100), according to official Soviet calculations and 43.6 according to my calculations (*ibid.*, p. 392).
4. See Chapter 6.

version of the Second Five-Year Plan was approved by the Seventeenth Party Congress (January 26–February 10, 1934),[5] and it was probably part of a little-known version of the second plan drafted at the end of 1932 or the beginning of 1933. But fulfillment of the 1933 annual plan was a necessary condition for fulfilling the five-year plan in progress. Total investment in the socialist sector for the 1933 annual plan was set at 18 billion rubles (see Tables B–5 and B–6, line 1, col. 1). This sum can be assumed to be in 1933 plan prices, which were later used to calculate investment as a whole for the Second Five-Year Plan. In the annual plan this sum is compared with the 17,900 million rubles of actual investment in 1932.[6] Construction costs were to decrease by 15 per cent in 1933 (see Table B–15, line 1, col. 1). This was the first time that the plan did not envisage an increase in the real level of investment.

Even this goal, however, proved to be too ambitious. Actual expenditures on investment amounted in money terms to exactly the planned figure (17,989 million rubles), but complete silence was maintained about fulfillment in volume. The official commentator, G. Smirnov, emphasized only that the plan "was completely fulfilled in money terms."[7] In reality, to the extent that construction costs did not fall as planned, the investment plan was not fulfilled (see Table B–15, line 2, col. 1). In fact, actual costs exceeded planned costs by 16.2 per cent (see Table B–16, line 3, col. 12); this figure was used to deflate actual investments in 1933 in order to compare them with the goals in Table B–5 and B–6. The corresponding underfulfillment of the 1933 plan (around 14 per cent) was unevenly distributed among various sectors. But data on value of investment in current prices and on investment costs of individual sectors are fragmentary or nonexistent. Some rough calculations show the poorest plan fulfillments for light industry (where 44.1 per cent of the plan was fulfilled), for railroad transportation (60.4 per cent), and for housing, education, and other public facilities (78.5 per cent; see Tables B–5 and B–6).

It is difficult to establish a link between these investment plan failures and their repercussions on production. Investment expenditures, even expressed in constant prices, give only total resources allocated, not actually put into use, and total allocated resources could even be larger than anticipated. It is, therefore, necessary to compare planned productive capacities with capacities actually put into operation. But data for this purpose are fragmentary at best and exist only for a few years (not for 1933). Finally, installation of new capacities must be followed by a process of assimilation (whose duration depends on technical know-how and the effectiveness of installation) and, in the beginning, only a small part of the new capacities can be utilized efficiently.[8]

It should be noted that during 1932 and 1933 the Soviet authorities put con-

5. See Chapter 6, section on later variants of the plan.

6. *O narodnokhoziaistvennom plane i finansovoi programme pervogo goda vtoroi piatiletki. Doklady i rezoliutsii, III Sezd TsIk SSSR, Ianvar 1933* [On the National Economic Plan and Financial Program of the First Year of the Second Five-Year Plan. Reports and Resolutions, Third Congress of USSR Central Executive Committee, January 1933], Leningrad, 1933, p. 123.

7. G. Smirnov, "Kapitalnoe stroitelstvo 1934 g." [Capital Construction in 1934], *Planovoe khoziaistvo* [Planned Economy], No. 5–6, 1934, p. 24.

8. Concrete data on the degree of assimilation, for certain basic production processes, can be found for years after the Second Five-Year Plan. See Tables 52, 53, and 55 and pp. 239–41 below.

siderable stress on assimilation of new techniques (*osvoenie*). As early as January 7, 1933, in his speech on the results of the First Five-Year Plan, Stalin declared that enthusiasm for new construction must now be supplemented with enthusiasm for opening up new factories and mastering new techniques.[9] G. K. Ordzhonikidze, Minister of Heavy Industry, became a passionate advocate of this assimilation.[10]

The results of this campaign were, nevertheless, limited. For the first time in many years, in 1933 the volume of investment decreased—about 14 per cent below the preceding year (this decrease can be estimated at the same rate as that mentioned above for the increase in investment prices, 16.2 per cent over 1933 plan prices, see Table B–16, line 3, col. 12). The failure of the production plan, in which current investment difficulties played only a minor role, was particularly noticeable. The percentages of fulfillment of the 1933 annual production plan were: 90.7 for coal, 78.2 for peat, 88.1 for crude petroleum, 79.0 for pig iron, 77.0 for steel ingots and castings, and 81.0 for rolled steel (see Table A–2, col. 3). Moreover, they varied considerably from one sector to another and were relatively high (from 90.8 to 99.3 per cent) for the products of light industry, for which the 1933 investment plan was particularly poorly fulfilled (44.1 per cent). On the other hand, the percentages of fulfillment of the production plan were lower (from 73 to 100.9 per cent) for food products, for which 88.6 per cent of the investment plan was fulfilled. Only 60 per cent of the plan for urban housing construction in square meters of floorspace was fulfilled, whereas 78.5 per cent of the investment plan for housing, education, and other public facilities in value terms in constant prices was fulfilled.

Even though these are approximate estimates, they do seem to show the lack of any real links between the 1933 annual plan and the known variants of the Second Five-Year Plan. Clearly, the Soviet planners could not take account of the 1933 annual plan in drafting the five-year plan presented in January–February 1934, and they must have included in this plan not the 1933 annual plan figures but the actual results in 1933.[11] But the uncertain situation of the Soviet economy in 1933 certainly did not facilitate drafting the final variant of the Second Five-Year Plan, which, particularly in investment, seems to have contained several serious gaps.

The Burden of Investment

Of all the Soviet five-year plans, the second is the most precise on the subject of investment. It contains not only a breakdown by sector and commissariat for each year of the plan but also plans by sector and commissariat with itemized

9. I. V. Stalin, "Itogi pervoi piatiletki" [Results of the First Five-Year Plan], *Sochineniia* [Works], Moscow, 1952, Vol. 13, p. 186.

10. See, for example, G. K. Ordzhonikidze, "Pafos stroitelstva dopolnit pafosom osvoeniia" [Supplement Enthusiasm for Construction with Enthusiasm for Assimilation of Technology], speech of August 2, 1933, in *Statii i rechi* [Articles and Speeches], Moscow, 1957, pp. 491–504.

11. On this subject, see Smirnov (*Planovoe khoziaistvo*, No. 5–6, 1934, p. 25), who, in giving the same volume of investment for 1933 as for the first year of the five-year plan, stated that it represented actual investment in 1933.

lists of the principal construction projects, their capacity, their value, and the years in which construction was to begin and to be completed.[12] Despite this detail, the data on investment seem to contain certain serious errors and to lack precision. The errors and imprecision are so extensive that much of their value must have been lost. For this reason, the American economist Naum Jasny was led to make severe criticisms of the second plan.[13]

The main data on the investment plan for 1933–1937, in current prices and in 1933 plan prices, are summarized in Tables 50 and 51. More detailed figures are given in Appendix B. In order to evaluate the burden of investment, its volume should be compared with that of the First Five-Year Plan. Such a comparison is made in the second plan, for which investment is said to be 264.1 per cent of that in the first plan.[14] But the comparison is between total investment planned for 1933–1937 in 1933 prices and the total for the base period (50,502 million rubles) in prices that are not specified but are very close to current prices,[15] so it is difficult to draw any conclusions.

There is considerable confusion about the prices used to calculate the value of investments in constant (1933 plan) prices and in current prices. The second plan gives figures in current and constant prices for all the years of the plan (see Tables B-1 and B-2),[16] and it is possible to calculate an index of planned prices (Table B-3). The figures in current prices appear to be the same as those in constant prices for 1933 and 1934, which must mean that 1933 plan prices were the same as 1933 actual prices and that no reduction in prices was planned for 1934. This raises several serious inconsistencies.

It was mentioned above that the final text of the Second Five-Year Plan included the results achieved in 1933. To state that 1933 plan prices and 1933 actual prices were the same does not stand up to scrutiny. It appears from Table B-15 that a reduction in construction costs of 15 per cent was planned for 1933, and we have cautiously estimated the total planned reduction at 10 per cent in view of the possibly smaller reduction in cost of assembly work and equipment. But this was not the actual outcome. The most reliable official sources show not a reduction but an increase in construction costs of 4.6 per cent; other official sources give an increase of 1.1 per cent for a restricted sample (see Table B-15, line 2, col. 5). Therefore, the representation of the results for 1933 by the same figure—17,989 million rubles—in both current prices and 1933 plan prices (see Tables B-1, B-2, and B-3) does not make sense. Obviously, these are results

12. See *Vtoroi piatiletnii plan razvitiia narodnogo khoziaistva SSSR (1933–1937)* [Second Five-Year Plan for the Development of the USSR National Economy, 1933–1937], Moscow, 1934, pp. 553–683.

13. "The two-volume publication on the second FYP is impressive only if one does not look into it too carefully" (Naum Jasny, *Soviet Industrialization, 1928–1952*, Chicago, 1961, p. 126).

14. *Vtoroi plan*, pp. 442–43.

15. In current prices, the report on the fulfillment of the First Five-Year Plan gives the figure of 52.5 billion rubles for the socialist sector (*Itogi vypoleniia pervogo piatiletnego plana razvitiia narodnogo khoziaistva Soiuza SSR* [Fulfillment of the First Five-Year Plan for the Development of the USSR National Economy], Moscow-Leningrad, 1933, p. 285). In view of the evolution of prices during the First Five-Year Plan (see my *Planning*, p. 246), it is unlikely that the figures in 1933 plan prices would be lower. On the evolution of prices during the Second Five-Year Plan, see Tables B–3 and B–16.

16. Data by year in current prices have not been reproduced in Appendix B but were used to calculate the indexes in Table B-3.

Table 50   Fulfillment of Investment Goals of Second Five-Year Plan (1933–1937) in Current Prices (million rubles)

	Total Investment Planned for 1933–1937		Actual Investment for 1933–1937 with Capital Repairs and Extra-Limit Investments		
	Draft Second Five-Year Plan (1)	Final Second Five-Year Plan (2)	Included (3)	Excluded (4)	Per Cent of Plan Fulfilled (5)
1. National economy, total socialist sector	120,083	120,083	137,491[a]	114,675	114.5
2. Industry, total	62,437	62,497	65,763	58,613	105.2
3. Producer goods (Group A)	48,183	48,223	54,565	49,802	113.2
4. Consumer goods (Group B)	14,274	14,274	11,198	8,811	78.5
5. Agriculture, total	14,061	14,061	16,760	11,334[b]	119.2
6. State farms	5,093	5,093			
7. Machine and Tractor Stations	5,788	5,788			
8. Transportation, total	23,998	23,845	25,411	20,699	106.6
9. Railroad	15,850	15,765	17,077	13,292	108.3
10. Inland waterway and maritime	4,002	3,934	4,950	4,493	125.8
11. Motor	3,069	3,069	2,593	2,198	84.5
12. Civil aviation	1,077	1,077	791	716	73.4
13. Communications	1,566	1,566	1,336	1,162	85.3
14. Trade[c]	1,503	1,556	3,245	2,062	208.5
15. Housing, education, and other public facilities	16,518	16,558	24,976	20,805	150.8
16. Housing, education, and other public facilities, total[d]		28,033			
17. Housing construction		11,480			
18. Urban and industrial	10,902	10,723			
19. Communal construction	6,192	6,295			
20. Urban		5,459			
21. Education	3,396	3,378			
22. Vocational training		1,854			
23. Public health	2,939	2,931			
24. Supply		2,095			
Not included in national economy					
25. Public participation in road building			4,206		

Source

COLUMN 1: *Proekt vtorogo piatiletnego plana razvitiia narodnogo khoziaistva SSSR (1933–1937 gg)* [Draft of Second Five-Year Plan for the Development of the USSR National Economy, 1933–1937], Moscow, 1934, Vol. I, p. 427.

COLUMN 2: *Vtoroi plan*, pp. 442 and 444.

COLUMN 3–4: *Itogi vypolneniia vtorogo piatiletnego plana razvitiia narodnogo khoziaistva SSSR* [Results of Fulfillment of the Second Five-Year Plan for the Development of the USSR National Economy], Moscow, 1939, p. 71.

COLUMN 5: Col. 3 as a percentage of col. 2. It has been assumed here that the plan figures in col. 2 are comparable with the actual ones in col. 3 rather than with those in col. 4 since the source (*ibid.*) specifically compares the actual figures *including* capital repairs and extra-limit investment with the same First Five-Year Plan figure that the second plan uses for comparison. Also, it was common practice at this time to include capital repairs and extra-limit investments in total investment. However, doubts are raised about this assumption from reading an article by E. Lokshin ("Problemy kapitalnogo stroitelstva v tiazheloi promyshlennosti" [Problems of Capital Formation in Heavy Industry], *Problemy ekonomiki* [Problems of Economics], No. 2, 1938, p. 38), for he compares preliminary results of the Second Five-Year Plan with results of the first plan that seem to include collective farm investment from their own resources and public participation in road building. If it is assumed that the second plan figures in col. 2 include capital repairs but exclude extra-limit investment and if these are compared with the total figure of this coverage from *Tretii piatiletnii plan razvitiia narodnogo khoziaistva SSSR (1938–1942)* [Third Five-Year

Table 50   *continued*

Plan for the Development of the USSR National Economy, 1938–1942], Moscow, 1939, p. 26 (128,100 mill. rubles), and Lokshin's preliminary figures for industry and its breakdown (62,703 mill. rubles for industry, 51,969 mill. rubles for Group A, and 10,734 mill. rubles for Group B), then the percentages of plan fulfillment would be 106.7 for the total national economy, 100.3 for industry, 107.8 for Group A, and 72.9 for Group B.

a. Another source (A. Sarin, "Za bolshevistskii poriadok v uchete kapitalnogo stroitelstva" [For Bolshevist Order in Capital Construction Accounts], *Planovoe khoziaistvo*, No. 1, 1938, p. 88) gives more than 130 billion rubles. A third figure (130.25 billion rubles) can be derived from the statement (in "Uporiadochit stroitelnoe delo" [Put Order into Construction], *Planovoe khoziaistvo*, No. 3, 1938, p. 20) that total investment in 1933–1937 was two and a half times total investment in 1928–1932 (given as 52.1 bill. rubles).

b. 14,619 million rubles according to *Tretii plan*, p. 225. According to Norman Kaplan ("Capital Investments in the Soviet Union, 1924–1951," RAND Research Memorandum 735, Santa Monica, 1951, p. 85, note 3), the difference between this figure and the one given in the table here is that the former includes and the latter excludes Agricultural Bank loans to collective farmers.

c. Given as circulation and distribution in some sources (*Vtoroi plan*, p. 447, and *Plan*, No. 4, 1935, p. 11) and as trade turnover in others (*Narodno-khoziaistvennyi plan na 1936 god* [The National Economic Plan for 1936], Vol. I, 2nd ed., Moscow, 1936, p. 278), but figures for same years from different sources show that the category is the same.

d. This section includes investments for housing and education facilities that are normally included in the plans of various commissariats and other institutions and hence are included in different sectors above (such as industry or agriculture), not just in line 15.

expressed in *current* prices in both cases, which is what has been assumed in Tables B-5 and B-6.

The figures for 1934 in the Second Five-Year Plan are even less consistent. The same figure—25,111 million rubles—is given for 1934 in both 1933 plan prices and current prices and for the 1934 annual plan, which was incorporated into the final text of the five-year plan. This is quite impossible. The 1934 plan figures in 1933 plan prices cannot be the same as those in current prices since a reduction of 15 per cent in construction costs was planned for 1934 (see Table B-15, line 3, col. 1). Of course, it could be that the 1933 figure (17,989 million rubles) in current prices is higher than that in 1933 plan prices by the same proportion as the reduction planned in 1934. For example, if 1933 plan prices were 90 per cent of 1932 prices, then actual 1933 prices would be the same as 1932 prices, and 1934 plan prices would be 90 per cent of actual 1933 prices. Such an identity, which appears in Table B-3, would then be possible. But in that case a lower figure should be accepted for 1933 results in 1933 plan prices (which has been done in Table B-5).

Another inconsistency emerges from a comparison of the price indexes in Table B-3 and the reduction in construction costs planned for 1937 in comparison with 1932 (see Table B-3, note a). If the price index for investment is 60 in 1937 (with 1932 = 100), it would be 75 in the 1933 plan. This figure conflicts with the reductions in construction costs given in Table B-15 and is improbable in any event.

It is difficult to compare the burden of investment with the national income planned for the Second Five-Year Plan period. It is possible only to compare the rates of growth in 1937 relative to 1932 in constant prices. National income was to increase by 120 per cent (see Table 17 in Chapter 7) and investment in 1933 plan prices by 79 per cent.[17] Thus, some reduction in the burden of investment

17. For 1932, see p. 229 above, and for 1937, see Table B-1.

Table 51 Fulfillment of Investment Goals of Second Five-Year Plan (1933–1937) in 1933 Plan Prices (million rubles)

	Total Investment Planned for 1933–1937		Actual Investment for 1933–1937 (3)	Per Cent of Plan Fulfilled (4)
	Draft 2nd FYP (1)	Final 2nd FYP (2)		
1. National economy, total socialist sector	133,400	133,400	120,809[a]	90.6[a]
2. Industry	69,475	69,545	56,500	81.2
3. Producer goods (Group A)	53,402	53,442	46,900	87.8
4. Consumer goods (Group B)	16,073	16,103	9,600	59.6
5. Agriculture	15,239	15,239		
6. State farms	5,475	5,475		
7. Machine and Tractor Stations	6,360	6,360		
8. Transportation, total	26,522	26,342		
9. Railroad	17,464	17,364		
10. Inland waterway and maritime	4,396	4,316		
11. Motor	3,455	3,455		
12. Civil aviation	1,207	1,207		
13. Communications	1,679	1,679		
14. Trade[b]	1,679	1,740		
15. Housing, education, and other public facilities	18,806	18,855		
16. Housing, education, and other public facilities, total[c]		32,499		
17. Housing construction		13,412		
18. Urban and industrial	12,725	12,502		
19. Communal construction	7,052	7,145		
20. Urban		6,195		
21. Education, total	4,002	3,979		
22. Excluding institutions		3,167		
23. Vocational training		2,134		
24. Public health, total	3,515	3,498		
25. Excluding institutions		2,875		
26. Supply		2,331		
Not included in national economy				
27. Collective farm investment from own resources	5,000	5,000		
28. Public participation in road building	1,700	1,700		

Source: Col. 1: *Proekt vtorgo plana*, pp. 422–23; col. 2: *Vtoroi plan*, pp. 422 and 444; col. 3: *Industrializatsiia SSSR, 1933–1937* [Industrialization of the USSR, 1933–1937], Moscow, 1971, pp. 233–34; and col. 4: col. 3 as a percentage of col. 2.

a. The total obtained by summing the figures in Tables B-5 through B-14 is 105,862 mill. rubles, which would yield a fulfillment percentage of 79.4.

b. See Table 50, note c.

c. Included in various sectors above (see Table 50, note d).

seems to have been planned, a reduction that would correspond to higher rates planned for consumption (142 per cent) than accumulation (80 per cent, see Table 17).

The burden of investment, moreover, seems to have been distributed very unevenly over the five years; the increase was to have been 39.6 per cent for 1934, 11.5 per cent for 1935, 8.3 per cent for 1936, and only 5.6 per cent for 1937, in 1933 plan prices (see Table B-1). As Jasny emphasizes, this planning does not make much sense, with the heaviest burden being in the first actual year of the plan (1934), when total national income was relatively low, and the lightest in the last year of the plan, when national income was relatively higher.[18]

In fact, the planners do not seem to have had any precise idea of the burden of investment. The 1933 plan included 724 construction projects with a total value of 3,961 million rubles that did not have any estimate costs at the beginning of the construction season. In the 1934 plan, this number was reduced to 334, with a value of 2,547 million rubles.[19] But on December 10, 1935, 891 construction projects totaling 4,456 million rubles still did not have the necessary specifications or approved estimate costs.[20]

In looking at the investment plan, it can be seen that the share of investment under way, that is, simply being continued during the Second Five-Year Plan, was very high. In industry, the share of new construction was 58.9 per cent, but more than 40 per cent of this amount represented construction work carried over from the First Five-Year Plan.[21] These figures still do not reflect the true situation in 1933 and 1934. In industry the share of new investment carried over from the first plan was 88.5 per cent in 1933 and 81.2 per cent in 1934. The aggregate value of construction under way, moreover, increased rapidly, rising from 11.6 billion rubles in 1930 to 29.9 billion in 1932 and 34.2 billion in 1933.[22] The orientation toward construction in progress was imposed by circumstances, and the Second Five-Year Plan for investments looks like an attempt to estimate the needs of these construction projects. The Soviet central planners were trying to coordinate, adjust, or help along the movement that they had started without really being able to influence its direction. In fact, all investment in construction in progress is frozen investment and dictates the actions of the authorities, who risk loss of already committed funds. A consequence of this situation was that the value of construction in progress at the end of 1934 was planned to increase only marginally (by 1.6 billion rubles, or 4.7 per cent).[23]

An attempt to make the Second Five-Year Plan coherent is made in the table presenting the financial plan.[24] This plan is presented both in current and constant prices; the saving anticipated from the price reduction amounts to 55

18. Jasny, *Soviet Industrialization*, p. 126.

19. B. Reznik, "Podgotovitsia k razvertyvaniiu stroitelstva v 1934 g." [We Must Prepare for the Development of Construction in 1934], *Plan*, No. 3, 1934, p. 4.

20. S. Smirnov, "Planirovanie izyskatelskikh i proektirovochnykh rabot" [Planning Exploratory and Projection Work], *Plan*, No. 6, 1936, pp. 15 ff.

21. *Vtoroi plan*, p. 288.

22. Smirnov, *Planovoe khoziaistvo*, No. 5–6, 1934, p. 28.

23. *Ibid*.

24. *Vtoroi plan*, pp. 540–41.

billion rubles, or 41 per cent of the five-year plan investments in 1933 plan prices. Sizable cost reductions (see Table B-3, note a) and increases in labor productivity (63 per cent in industry, 75 per cent in construction, and 146 per cent on state farms[25]) were to make this goal achievable. An increase of 13.8 per cent in investment prices was observed between 1932 and 1937 (see Table B-16), an increase which seems normal since plans for money wages and employment had been exceeded during the First Five-Year Plan.[26] As we have noted, instead of a reduction in investment prices of around 10 per cent in 1933, there was an increase of 4.6 per cent, and there was nothing in the Soviet economy during 1930–1933 likely to bring about a rapid reversal of this trend. Hence the 55 billion rubles of saving planned from the price reductions represented inflationary financing.

Difficulties in 1933 and 1934 and Revision of Five-Year Plan for Investment

The 1934 annual plan, integrated into the Second Five-Year Plan, provided for an increase of 39.6 per cent in investment over 1933. But, as explained earlier, the five-year plan figures for 1933 were probably in current prices. In 1933 plan prices, which were used for the 1934 annual plan, 1933 actual investments were only 15,480 million rubles (see Table B-5), which would imply an increase in 1934 over 1933 of 62.2 per cent in constant prices.

It is difficult to accept this figure. But it can be assumed that a very sizable increase in investment was planned for 1934, probably more than 40 per cent. Was such an investment burden supportable? Jasny emphasizes that this increase was hardly compatible with a planned increase of 24.1 per cent in national income.[27] A sizable increase in the production of construction materials (55.6 per cent for cement, 64.4 per cent for bricks, 126.2 per cent for roofing tiles, and 35.9 per cent for lime, among others[28]) seemed to make such an effort possible. Actually the government was obliged to revise this plan during the year. The revision does not seem to have applied to the plan as a whole, and it may have consisted only of *ad hoc* decisions.[29]

The total reduction of planned investments for 1934 was 1.6 billion rubles (see Tables B-7 and B-8), or 6.3 per cent. The sector most affected was heavy industry (which was reduced by 1.1 billion rubles, 0.5 billion of which was in the ferrous metal industry) and then agriculture (0.3 billion). Moreover, neither the original plan nor the revised one was fulfilled (see Tables B-7 and B-8). For the whole national economy, 77.8 per cent of the original plan was fulfilled, with lower percentages for agriculture and transportation. The underfulfillment of the 1934

25. *Ibid.*, p. 509.

26. See my *Planning*, pp. 342–47.

27. Jasny, *Soviet Industrialization*, p. 126.

28. "Osnovnye pokazateli narodnokhoziaistvennogo plana 1934 g." [Main Indicators of the 1934 Plan], *Planovoe khoziaistvo*, No. 5–6, 1934, p. 207.

29. The 1935 annual plan (*Narodno-khoziaistvennyi plan na 1935 god* [The National Economic Plan for 1935], 2nd ed., Moscow, 1935, p. 461, note 1) specifies that the plan that was finally approved, taking into account the corrections made during the year, amounted to 23,525 million rubles.

plan for construction materials confirms this poor performance (see Table 20 in Chapter 7).

The over-all fulfillment of the investment plan, even if expressed in constant prices, is not the sole indicator of the success of the plan. In 1934, the value of construction under way was to increase by only 4.7 per cent. In fact, it reached the sum of 47.6 billion rubles, an increase of 39.2 per cent over 1933.[30] As a result, the value of the funds put into operation increased by only 25.7 per cent, which reduced their share in total investment from 74.0 per cent in 1932 and 92.0 per cent in 1933 to 83.2 per cent in 1934.[31] During the two first years of the Second Five-Year Plan, total investment tied up in unfinished construction increased by 5.6 billion rubles.[32]

To obtain a slightly more accurate picture of the fulfillment of the investment plan, the plans and the achievements in installation of new productive capacity should be compared. Unfortunately, data for this purpose are very fragmentary, but those available are gathered in Table 52. This table shows, by branch, planned and actual total productive capacity and planned and actual increase in capacity. The very poor implementation of the plan for increase in capacity had only a small effect on the fulfillment of the plan for total capacity. In fact, it is interesting to compare the fulfillment of the plan for increase in capacity with that for planned investment for the same year and the fulfillment of the plan for total capacity with that for production.

The first of these two comparisons reflects more than the extent of the real increase in expenditures (that is, expenditures in constant prices, increasing because of incomplete or inadequate estimate costs). Investment expenditures have a bearing on the construction projects to be put into operation during the year in question as well as those planned for other years. Furthermore, they show up the discrepancy between the planners' idea of investment costs and the costs that result in the end. The fulfillment of the plan for increases in productive capacity is also a more reliable indicator than the fulfillment of the investment plan (even in constant prices) of the contribution of investment to the expansion of production.

The fulfillment of investment plans for producer goods (the only ones shown in Table 52) was 84.8 per cent in 1933 and 78.6 per cent in 1934 (see Tables B-5 and B-7). Data on fulfillment of the plan for increases in productive capacity are much more fragmentary, but the unweighted average of these percentages is 62.3 per cent in 1933 and 50.1 per cent in 1934. But these percentages understate the degree of underfulfillment because the increase in investment costs (see Table B-16) does not enter into this comparison, which is made in physical quantities or in constant prices. The main cause for the poor fulfillment is increase in real costs (the necessity to use more materials or equipment). This

30. *Ibid.*, p. 309, and Smirnov, *Planovoe khoziaistvo*, No. 5–6, 1934, p. 28.
31. The corresponding percentages for industry were 65.0, 90.4, and 82.5 per cent (*Plan 1935*, 2nd ed., p. 305).
32. *Ibid.*

Table 52   Installation of New Productive Capacity, 1933 and 1934

	Units	1932 1/1/33 Actual (1)	1933 Plan (2)	1933 1/1/34 Actual (3)	1933 Per Cent of Plan Fulfilled (4)	1934 Plan (5)	1934 1/1/35 Actual (6)	1934 Per Cent of Plan Fulfilled (7)
Productive Capacity								
Electric power								
1. Total power stations	th. kw	4,696	5,700	5,426	95.2	6,624	6,212	93.8
Coal								
2. Mines	units	437	507	489	96.4	528		
3. Capacity	mill. m. t.	110.7	149.5	138.0	92.3	158.0	147.9	93.6
Pig iron								
4. Blast furnaces	units	103	118	110	93.2	122	117	95.9
5. Capacity	th. m³	36.9	50.8	41.7	82.1	53.5		
Steel								
6. Open-hearth furnaces	units	294	339	320	94.4	360	338	93.9
7. Capacity	th. m³	6.7		8.0		9.7		
Rolled steel								
8. Rolling mills	units	262	277	274	98.9	302	283	93.7
Increase in Productive Capacity								
Electric power								
9. Total power stations	th. kw		1,004	730	72.7	1,198	786	65.6
Coal								
10. Mines	units		70	52	74.3	39		
11. Capacity	mill. m. t.		38.8	27.3	70.4	20.0	9.9	49.5
Pig iron								
12. Blast furnaces	units		15	7	46.7	12	7	58.3
13. Capacity	th. m³		13.9	4.8	34.5	11.8		
Steel								
14. Open-hearth furnaces	units		45	26	57.8	40	18	45.0
15. Capacity	th. m²			1.3		1.7		
Rolled steel								
16. Rolling mills	units		15	12	80.0	28	9	32.1

Source

COLUMN 1–Lines 1-8: *Vtoroi plan*, p. 448.

COLUMN 2–Lines 1 and 8: *Plan 1933*, p. 46. **Lines 2-6:** Sum of actual capacity on January 1, 1933 (col. 1, lines 2–6) and increase in capacity planned for 1933 (col. 2, lines 10–14). **Lines 9 and 16:** Capacity planned for 1933 (col. 2, lines 1 and 8) minus actual capacity on January 1, 1933 (col. 1, lines 1 and 8). **Lines 10-14:** *Plan 1933*, p. 120.

COLUMN 3–Lines 1-8: Smirnov, *Planovoe khoziaistvo*, No. 5–6, 1934, p. 30. **Lines 9-16:** Actual capacity on January 1, 1934 (col. 3, lines 1–8) minus actual capacity on January 1, 1933 (col. 1, lines 1–8).

COLUMN 4–All lines: Col. 3 as a percentage of col. 2.

COLUMN 5–Lines 1-8: Smirnov, *Planovoe khoziaistvo*, No. 5–6, 1934, p. 30. **Lines 9-16:** Capacity planned for 1934 (col. 5, lines 1–8) minus actual capacity on January 1, 1934 (col. 3, lines 1–8).

COLUMN 6–Line 1: Ordzhonikidze, *Statii*, Vol. 2, p. 609. **Lines 3-4, 6, and 8:** Sum of actual capacity on January 1, 1934 (col. 3, lines 3–4, 6, and 8) and increase in capacity on January 1, 1935 (col. 6, lines 11–12, 14, and 16). **Line 9:** Actual capacity on January 1, 1935 (col. 6, line 1) minus actual capacity on January 1, 1934 (col. 3, line 1). **Line 11:** E. Kviring, "Problemy osvoeniia" [Problems of Assimilation], *Problemy ekonomiki*, No. 2, 1935, p. 37. **Line 12:** A. Tochinskii and V. Rikman, "Protsessy osvoeniia v chernoi metallurgii v 1934 g." [Processes of Assimilation in the Ferrous Metal Industry in 1934], *Planovoe khoziaistvo*, No. 1, 1935, p. 61. Including small-scale metal industry. **Line 14:** A. Margolin, "Perspektivy snabzheniia prokatom v 1935 g." [Prospects for Rolled Steel Supply in 1935], *Plan*, No. 2–3, 1935, p. 33. **Line 16:** *Ibid*. Also Tochinskii and Rikmann, *Planovoe khoziaistvo*, No. 1, 1935, p. 61.

rise seems to have been largely responsible for the increases in estimate costs experienced during 1934.[33]

The contrast between the plan for total capacity and for production is still more striking (see Table 53 below and Table 19 in Chapter 7). The extent to which plans for total capacity were fulfilled does not seem to have had a direct effect on production plans. In 1933, production plans (except for electric power) were less well fulfilled than capacity plans, but the discrepancy is not great. In 1934, the reverse is true, and the discrepancy is much greater. The economy was expanding in both years, so it was the degree of assimilation of new capacity that played the determining role.

Table 53   Fulfillment of Plans for Capacity and Production, 1933 and 1934

	1933			1934		
	Productive Capacity,	Production		Productive Capacity,	Production	
	Per Cent of Plan Fulfilled (1)	Per Cent of Plan Fulfilled (2)	Index of Increase (1932 = 100) (3)	Per Cent of Plan Fulfilled (4)	Per Cent of Plan Fulfilled (5)	Index of Increase (1933 = 100) (6)
Electric power stations [a]	95.2	100.3	120.8	93.8	110.6	128.5
Coal	92.3	90.7	118.6	93.6	97.3	123.4
Pig iron	82.1	79.0	115.4	95.9[b]	104.3	146.7
Steel ingots and castings [c]	94.4	77.0	116.2	93.9	98.9	140.7
Rolled steel [d]	98.9	81.0	114.4	93.7	106.6	138.9

Source: Cols. 1 and 4: Table 52, cols. 4 and 7; cols. 2 and 5: Table A-2, cols. 3 and 6; col. 3: calculated from my *Planning*, Table A-2, col. 14, pp. 330–31, and Table A-2, col. 2; col. 6: calculated from Table A-2, cols. 2 and 5.

a. Electric power capacity for cols. 1 and 4; electric power production for cols. 2, 3, 5, and 6.
b. Number of blast furnaces.
c. Number of open-hearth furnaces for cols. 1 and 4.
d. Number of rolling mills for cols. 1 and 4.

The definition of the term "assimilation" (*osvoenie*) is, in principle, very simple: it means the complete utilization of existing equipment.[34] Hence this capacity must be measured correctly, which was not easy to do, particularly for imported equipment for which special corrections were made to take account of the lack of training of technicians and workers. This practice was condemned by Ordzhonikidze.

At the same time an effort was made to extend the notion of assimilation. Mastery of the production process and obtaining production equal to the capacity planned in the specifications were no longer sufficient. A comparative

33. A check of estimate costs in effect for 401 construction projects in 1934 already in operation before that year showed that the costs, which amounted to 13 billion rubles in the 1934 plan, were planned by the commissariats to be 18.7 billion rubles in the 1935 plan (*ibid.*, p. 310). This increase was apparently not due to increases in investment costs, which were to be reduced by 6.6 per cent in the 1935 plan (see Table B–15).
34. Kviring, *Problemy ekonomiki*, No. 2, 1935, p. 23.

analysis was required of the indicators and coefficients obtained and those obtained in the best capitalist enterprises, as well as an examination of the saving in labor, costs, and labor productivity.[35] In a broader sense, assimilation also meant the elimination of seasonal fluctuations (especially in the production of agricultural machinery), the reduction of production losses, the production of various spare parts, and the appropriate supply of producer goods.[36]

This broader definition of assimilation confuses causes and effects, and there was certainly at that time a rather confused idea of what "complete utilization of equipment" meant. An example is provided in the September 20, 1934, speech of Ordzhonikidze.[37] First, Ordzhonikidze asserted that the machine-building industry was working at only 80 per cent of its maximum capacity and often even less than that. Defense industries worked at a considerably lower percentage. In citing the example of the Urals heavy machine-building factory, Ordzhonikidze states:

Last year when I visited this factory, it resembled a museum of beautiful machines. No production was to be seen. This year it is already a factory in operation. But can it be said that it is working at full capacity? Every time this factory is requested to produce something more, they answer: "It's difficult; we're not ready." And on how many shifts does this factory work? Only one. The machinery works seven hours and rests the rest of the time. Rest is a fine thing, but it makes no sense to have so much rest. This factory is not an exception.

The utilization of capacity according to "machine time" recommended by Ordzhonikidze[38] and the revising (upward[39]) of capacities in construction plans introduced a large element of uncertainty into what should have been ordinarily expected of new capacities. One might wonder if the technological problems of the complete utilization of equipment were not being swamped in the economic problems (material and equipment supply, seasonal fluctuations, productivity, shifts, etc.). One thing is sure: there were no clear and solid criteria to evaluate the repercussions of investment on production. The authoritarian nature of the production and investment plans was in complete contradiction with the rough estimates, which were, moreover, a compromise between the engineering experts and bureaucrats from the commissariats and Gosplan (themselves serving ideologues or prophets of growth). "Assimilation" became a real myth,[40] a master key, that could be blamed for all the defects of the system and made it possible to change at will authoritarian plans. The Soviet authorities were well aware of the spontaneous activity that such a situation encouraged, but their only course of action lay in strengthening controls over investment.[41]

35. *Ibid.*, p. 25.

36. *Ibid.*, p. 27.

37. Ordzhonikidze, *Statii*, Vol. 2, p. 584.

38. Cited by Kviring, *Problemy ekonomiki*, No. 2, 1935, p. 24.

39. As an example, Kviring (*ibid.*, p. 26) cites the Stalingrad and Kharkov tractor plants with a planned capacity (which was underestimated) of 40,000 tractors and a real capacity of 50,000–52,000 tractors, which number was to be produced in 1936.

40. The Second Five-Year Plan was even called "the five-year plan of the assimilation of new techniques." See V. V. Kuibyshev, *Izbrannye proizvedeniia* [Selected Works], Moscow, 1958, p. 422. This article also appeared in *Tekhnika molodezhi* [Technology for Youth], No. 1, 1934.

41. See the September 3, 1934, decree of the Council of People's Commissars, "On the Elimination

The delays in starting up new capacities and the accumulation of unfinished construction inevitably affected the 1935 annual plan. Particular stress was put on installing fixed capital, the value of which was to increase from 17.9 billion rubles in 1934 to 22.6 billion in the 1935 plan, or 26 per cent. Also, 1,220 large-scale construction projects were to be put into operation with a value of 8.6 billion rubles, of which 347 were in heavy industry but only 29 in light industry and 85 in the food industry.[42] The prices in which these estimates were made were not specified but they might well be 1935 plan prices. In these prices, total investments in the national economy in 1935 were to increase by only 8 per cent over 1934;[43] to reach the level envisaged by the five-year plan (taking account of the difficulties in 1934), investment would have had to increase by 49.6 per cent (see Tables B-1 and B-7, col. 6).

A marked increase in the installation of new capacities and a relative slow-down in the increase in investment was to permit a reduction in the value of construction in progress in 1935. The number of construction projects was to drop from 1,850 with a value of 47.6 billion rubles at the end of 1934 to 1,450 with a value of 44.56 billion at the end of 1935.[44]

Under these conditions, substantial revisions had to be made in the five-year plan goals for 1935. The main revisions of the five-year plan for production were examined earlier (see Table 23 and surrounding text, Chapter 7). These changes seemed to reflect largely fulfillment of the 1934 annual plan while the government maintained pressure on the economy (through high growth rates) and stuck to the general policy foreseen in the five-year plan without maintaining the planned goals for 1935. Did the same policy apply to investment?

A partial attempt is made to answer this question in Table 54. Not only did the government give up the investment goals in the five-year plan (at least for volume of investment), as it had the production goals, but it also considerably revised priorities and substantially reduced the volume of investment envisaged in the five-year plan for 1935. The 1935 annual plan for total investment amounted to two-thirds of the five-year plan for that year, and the share for agriculture and consumer goods was even lower. For agriculture, this drop can be explained by the government's desire not to develop any more state farms.[45] For consumer goods, it seems to result from poor preparation for starting up factories.[46] For railroad transportation, the explanation seems to lie in the necessity to make up for previous delays, the rate of increase of investment over 1934 being very high. Among the other investments that were higher than the average relative to

---

of Construction Projects without Specifications or Estimate Costs" (*Direktivy KPSS i sovetskogo pravitelstva po khoziaistvennym voprosam* [Directives of the Communist Party of the Soviet Union and of the Soviet Government on Economic Matters], Moscow, 1957–1958, Vol. 2, pp. 426–28). This decree forbade, as of October 1, 1934, the financing of construction projects not approved according to established procedures and defined the authority of various agencies according to the importance of the projects.

42. With a value of 327 million rubles in light industry and 389 million in the food industry (*Plan 1935*, 2nd ed., pp. 305–6).

43. *Ibid.*, p. 302.

44. *Ibid.*, p. 309.

45. *Ibid.*, p. 303.

46. See above and footnote 42.

Table 54   Five-Year and Annual Plan Investment Goals, 1934 and 1935 (1933 plan prices)

	1934 Actual Investment [a]		1935 Plan		
	As Per Cent of Annual Plan Goals for 1934	As Per Cent of FYP Goals for 1934	As Per Cent of FYP Goals for 1935	As Per Cent of 1934 Actual Investment [b]	
				Calculated	Official Soviet
	(1)	(2)	(3)	(4)	(5)
National economy, total	77.8	74.4	67.0	100.3	98.5
Industry, total	78.1	74.4	60.7	96.5	96.2
Producer goods	78.6	74.8	66.4	94.3	93.7
Consumer goods	76.0	72.7	44.9	107.0	107.9
Agriculture, state-owned	77.0	75.0	54.1	82.1	77.2
Transportation, total	73.9	70.6	83.5	126.7	121.6
Railroad	70.8	67.7	86.6	138.1	131.7
Inland waterway and maritime	69.9	66.8	87.1	122.4	
Motor	99.4	95.1	65.8	84.2	86.8
Communications	70.3	67.3	73.1	110.0	127.7
Trade [c]	102.3	97.8	116.8	100.5	123.9
Housing, education, and other public facilities	80.6	77.1	74.9	92.6	88.8
Housing, education, and other public facilities [d]	71.1	68.0 [e]		113.7	106.2
Communal economy	73.1	69.9 [e]		95.5	89.1
Education	80.0	76.5 [e]		108.7	101.6
Public health	73.7	70.4 [e]		132.0	123.0

Source: Unless otherwise indicated, col. 1: Table B-7, col. 7; col. 2: calculated from Table B-7, col. 6, and Table B-1, col. 2; col. 3: Table B-9, col. 3; col. 4: calculated from Table B-9, col. 2, and Table B-7, col. 6; and col. 5: *Plan 1935*, 2nd ed., pp. 302 and 460.

a. The difference between cols. 1 and 2 is simply a question of prices, the figures in col. 1 being based on 1934 goals deflated by price index of 1.046 (see Table B-16).

b. The figures in cols. 4 and 5 may differ not only because of the different prices used but also because the official Soviet sources use preliminary figures for actual investments in 1934.

c. See Table 50, note b.

d. See Table 50, note c.

e. Col. 1 deflated by price index of 1.046 (see Table B-16).

the five-year plan, the most noticeable are trade (no doubt the result of the planned abolition of rationing), inland waterway and maritime transportation, and housing, education, and other public facilities.

What is striking in this revision of the five-year plan in 1935 is the difference between the revisions made in the five-year plan for investment and the results expected in production (see Tables 22 and 54). For producer goods, the volume of investment in the 1935 plan came to 66.4 per cent of the volume in the five-year plan for that year. But the median of the individual products is 93.0 per cent (see Table 22). For consumer goods, the corresponding figures are 44.9 and 89.7 per cent; for agriculture, 54.1 and 98.7 per cent; and for transportation, 83.5 and 95.2 per cent. Even bearing in mind that these calculations are approximations, it still emerges very clearly that the government was counting on a better organization of production, higher employment (the lack of annual goals in the five-year plan on this subject makes it impossible to give precise figures), and above all a better "assimilation" of new productive capacities. But it is precisely in this area that the calculations of administrative plans are the most precarious.

Investment Planning and the Economic Situation in 1935–1937

The discrepancies between the relatively austere planning for investment and the rather optimistic planning for production in 1935 obliged the government to make adjustments in the investment plan. During 1935 this plan was increased by 3.65 billion rubles, or 17.2 per cent, over the original provisions (see Table B-9). The largest increases were in producer goods (1.5 billion), agriculture (0.4 billion), and housing, education, and public facilities (1.06 billion).

The original investment plan for 1935 was exceeded in most sectors of the national economy, except for consumer goods and public health (see Table B-9). But the revised plan was not fulfilled for the most part (even in current prices), except for heavy industry. If it is taken into account that the planned reduction in construction costs was not fulfilled (3 per cent realized instead of the 12 per cent planned, see Table B-15), the underfulfillment is even worse. The overfulfillment of the original plans and the relatively satisfactory implementation of the revised plan (to be seen in Table B-9) are not confirmed by the official Soviet calculations that could be found or by official commentaries.

According to N. Tumanov, who gives the fulfillment of the 1935 annual plan for 11 months in plan prices (see Table B-10, col. 8), 81 per cent of the capital construction plan for heavy industry was fulfilled and 73.3 per cent for the Commissariat of Light Industry, the percentages ranging from 72 to 86 for the main commissariats. Tumanov stresses that the plan to reduce the value of construction in progress was not carried out[47] and cites many examples of unfulfilled plans for installation of new productive capacity.[48] The 1936 annual plan also emphasizes that the main plan for putting new capacities into service was not executed in 1935, particularly in light industry and the lumber industry.[49]

Nevertheless, the failure of the plan for installing new productive capacity did

47. See p. 241 above.

48. "The underfulfillment of the investment plan very clearly had repercussions on the fulfillment of the plan for installation, approved by the Party Central Committee and the government. In the ferrous metal industry, a number of aggregates provided in the plan were not put into operation. The plans for installation were also not fulfilled in the coal industry, machine-building, and the electric power industry. In the food industry, planned schedules were not met for putting very important plants into operation. . . . Light industry also lagged in opening a number of important enterprises planned to be put into operation in 1936: the Barnaul Textile Combine, the Zvorinsk Linen Combine, etc. Construction works planned to be put into operation in the lumber industry and in water transportation were also behind schedule" (N. Tumanov, "Problemy udeshevleniia stroitelstva" [Problems in Reducing Construction Costs], *Planovoe khoziaistvo*, No. 4, 1936, p. 43).

49. According to *Plan 1936* (pp. 268–69), the original installation plan was 22,375 million rubles and actual installation was 23,124 million. But this does not take into account the increase in the original plan for capital investment from 21,190 to 24,800 million rubles; the value of the installation covers a large number of supplementary projects that were not included in the basic installation plan and this plan was not fulfilled. In the Commissariat of Light Industry, investment with a total value of 664 million rubles, including supplementary projects, was put into service, compared with the original plan of 732 million. In the lumber industry, investment with a value of 430 million rubles was put into service compared with a plan of 503 million.

not prevent the production plan from being fulfilled. Table 63 in Chapter 13 and Table A-2 show that the 1935 annual plan was the best fulfilled of all prewar annual plans, and the country experienced a considerable expansion, benefiting from the installation and assimilation (in the broader sense) of new productive capacity started largely during the First Five-Year Plan.

For 1935, the contrast between the failure to fulfill the plan for capacity and the overfulfillment of the production plan also had another aspect. The over-fulfillment of the original investment plan was due largely to additional investments, often unplanned, made to meet needs that arose during the year. Revisions were made in plans that had been established bureaucratically and mechanically, and these revisions certainly had a beneficial effect on production. But the conflict between the centralized investment plans and the requests made by people's commissariats, construction projects, and enterprises resulted in a multiplication of investment decisions in situations where the central plan could only register the requests, and in an unplanned rise in costs. This is why the government felt obliged to put order into investment planning by the February 11, 1936, decree, "On the Improvement of Construction and Reduction of Construction Costs."[50]

This decree was aimed mainly at promoting a large-scale building industry to replace small-scale, artisan-type construction work done by ministries and enterprises. It was also aimed at introducing into building the Stakhanovite movement, increasing labor productivity, and establishing obligatory rules for submitting specifications and estimate costs.

It is of interest to examine the government's attitude in face of the failure of the 1935 investment plan and the successful expansion of production. The policy adopted in the 1936 investment plan seems to reflect a certain euphoria on the part of the central planners. They thought they could conduct the fight on several fronts; they simultaneously attacked unfinished construction, particularly in the producer goods sector, and they substantially increased investment in the consumer goods sector. This latter approach seems to have been dictated by social policy, the elimination of rationing and the increase in the supply of consumer goods being consolidated by new investment.

The first consequence of this policy was a very sizable increase planned for total investment in 1936 (34.8 per cent), higher than that planned for national income for the same year (24.2 per cent in Table A-2). This increase was distributed unevenly among the various sectors. Investment in producer goods was to increase by 9.5 per cent, while investment in consumer goods was to rise by 55 per cent. Investment in transportation was to increase by 35.2 per cent and in housing by 58.8 per cent, while investment in education was to rise by 132.0 per cent. Investment in state-owned agriculture was to increase by only 20.7 per cent and its share in the total was to drop (from 9.1 to 8.1 per cent).[51]

Special emphasis was put on guaranteeing the installation of fixed capital. It was to increase from 23,124 million rubles in 1935 to 31,372 million in the 1936

50. Decree of the USSR Council of Ministers and the Party Central Committee (*Direktivy*, Vol. 2, pp. 495–510).
51. *Plan 1936*, p. 505.

plan,[52] or 8.2 billion rubles (compared with 4.7 billion in the 1935 plan[53]), of which 2.9 billion was in industry, 1.7 billion in transportation, and 3.0 billion in housing and communal construction.[54] The share of newly started construction in 1936 was to increase from 3.6 per cent in 1935 to 5.9 per cent in 1936,[55] and, in order to obtain the most effect, the central planners concentrated their efforts on very large factories or combines. In the construction of electric power stations, 50 per cent of investment was concentrated on 18 stations; in the ferrous metal industry, 8 construction sites received 53 per cent of total investment; in the nonferrous metal industry, 10 construction sites received 50 per cent of the total; and in machine-building, 4 construction projects received more than 50 per cent of the investment.[56] This attitude, dictated as much by reasons of prestige as by the planners' idea of efficiency, was to be condemned three years later as "gigantomania."

This concentration on the most important construction projects that could be put into operation the most rapidly should ordinarily have favored drafting of estimate costs and specifications approved by the government and higher agencies because of the priority these construction projects enjoyed. In actual fact,the 1936 annual plan shows that, of 2,683 large-scale construction projects with a value of 9.6 billion rubles, only 1,266 with a value of 4,233 million rubles had approved estimate costs and specifications.[57] This was very serious because the success of construction was controlled to a large extent by planning a reduction in investment costs of 11 per cent, which was meant to result in a saving of 3,568 million rubles; it provided for financing 28,797 million rubles to obtain a value of 32,365 million rubles in 1935 prices.[58]

The precariousness of the premises on which the investment plan for 1936 was based became apparent in the very first months of the year. Only 13.6 per cent of the annual plan was fulfilled in the first quarter and 19.3 per cent in the second quarter, a total of 32.9 per cent for the first half year.[59] This share was lower than in 1935 and unevenly distributed among sectors; 37.0 per cent of the annual plan for the Commissariat of Heavy Industry was fulfilled and only 26.7 per cent of the plan for the Commissariat of Transportation. Only 20.5 to 32.7 per cent of the annual goals were fulfilled for housing construction in the first half year by the principal commissariats.[60]

52. I. Morozov, "Osnovyne kontury stroitelnoi programmy" [The Main Features of the Construction Program], *Plan*, No. 2, 1936, p. 18.

53. *Plan 1935*, 2nd ed., p. 306.

54. Excluding construction in industry and other sectors of the economy (Morozov, *Plan*, No. 2, 1936, p. 18).

55. *Plan 1936*, p. 275.

56. *Ibid.*, p. 276. In the paper industry, seven construction projects received 70 per cent of the investments; in new railroad construction, five railroad lines received 58 per cent of the credits; and for secondary railroad lines, three construction projects received 92 per cent of the credits.

57. *Ibid.*, p. 280.

58. *Ibid.*, pp. 270 and 279.

59. E. Orlikova, "Kapitalnoe stroitelstvo v pervom polugodii 1936 g." [Capital Construction in the First Half of 1936], *Plan*, No. 17, 1936, p. 9.

60. *Ibid.*, p. 10. It should be noted that, according to the half-year plan (practically speaking, the sum of quarterly plans), 49 per cent of the total investment for the year was to be fulfilled by July 1,

The difficulties encountered in carrying out the investment plan were recognized by Soviet commentators of that period. An editorial in the journal *Plan*, commenting on the economic situation in the first half of 1936, indicates that construction continued to be one of the most lagging sectors because of unsatisfactory drafting of specifications and estimate costs and delays in drawing up contracts and approving construction plans. An additional major cause was delays in the transfer to contract work by new construction trusts.[61]

An additional cause of disruption was the disequilibrium imposed at the highest level by additional investment orders and by the redirection of credits to certain construction projects, with new ones added before the funds invested in the old ones had been put into service and assimilated according to plan. Revisions had to be made in the plans during the year, which resulted in adding some 4 billion rubles of new credits (see Table B-11). These revisions seem to have been made, as in previous years, *ad hoc*, and they must have filled gaps in the plan as well as compensating, at least in part, for the damage caused by the failure to fulfill the plan for reduction in investment costs (see Tables B-15 and B-16).[62]

All of these difficulties caused poor fulfillment of the 1936 investment plan

---

1936. See "Narodnoe khoziaistvo za ianvar-iiul 1936 g." [The National Economy for January–July 1936], *Plan*, No. 17, 1936. p. 4.

61. *Ibid.*

62. Investment in the 1937 plan, from which the figures on the fulfillment of the 1936 plan were taken (*Narodno-khoziaistvennyi plan Soiuza SSR na 1937 god* [The USSR National Economic Plan for 1937], Moscow, 1937, p. 143), was evaluated in 1935 estimate prices, as was actual 1937 investment, with allowance for planned cost reductions (*Ukazaniia i formy k sostavleniiu narodnokhoziaistvennogo plana na 1937 god* [Instructions and Forms for Drafting the National Economic Plan for 1937], Moscow, 1936, p. 216). If we assume that the revised plan was evaluated in the prices of the original plan, then only 77 per cent of the revised plan was fulfilled; if it was evaluated in actual 1936 prices, which were higher, then 87.4 per cent was fulfilled (calculated from Tables B-11 and B-16). In this latter case, the revisions would have just compensated for losses due to costs that were generally too high. This calculation can be only an approximation because of the ambiguity about the prices used in the 1937 annual plan (and the figures for 1936 cited there). After the 1937 plan was drafted in 1935 estimate prices, there were increases in prices for equipment, "funded" construction materials (on the meaning of this term, see last section of Chapter 5), and railroad rates during 1936. At the same time there were a few price reductions for construction materials produced locally (5 per cent for bricks, 10 per cent for nonmetallic materials) and an increase in output norms for construction and assembly work (averaging 25 per cent), while norms for administrative expenditures were reduced. According to I. Pokrovskii ("Osnovnye elementy snizheniia stoimosti stroitelstva" [Basic Elements in the Reduction of Construction Costs], *Plan*, No. 5, 1937, p. 8), the increases and decreases balanced out on a national level; for different construction projects the estimate costs, evaluated in 1935 estimate prices and in December 1, 1936, prices, varied largely according to the share of "funded" equipment and materials used.

The recalculation into December 1, 1936, prices was to be done by April 1, 1937, for construction projects that were to be finished during 1937 and by July 1, 1937, for construction projects that were to be carried over to 1938 (*ibid.*). This work was not done during 1937. Therefore, when the fulfillment of the 1937 plan had to be calculated, some of the construction organizations that were making the calculations presented the results in 1936 prices and others in 1935 estimate prices. Hence the over-all fulfillment of the 1937 investment plan was heterogeneous: for some projects, plan fulfillment was calculated in 1936 prices and for others in 1935 prices, but the share of each group was not given. The Central Statistical Administration did not even include in its forms and instructions a question on what prices were used to calculate the plan fulfillment (Sarin, *Planovoe khoziaistvo*, No. 1, 1938, p. 95). Contrary to what Pokrovskii stated at the beginning of 1937, Sarin indicated that 1936 estimate prices were higher than 1935 estimate prices (*ibid.*). On the discrepancy between planned and actual prices in 1936, see Table B-15.

(see Table B-11). The poor performance in 1936 is especially striking when it is compared with that in 1935; in that year, the original plan was exceeded by 12.4 per cent in constant prices (see Table B-9), even though official commentators considered it a failure. The shortfalls in the 1936 investment plan were distributed unevenly. The over-all percentage of fulfillment was 86.5 per cent; producer goods and trade were above average (95.3 per cent and 116.7 per cent, respectively), but consumer goods and housing, education, and other public facilities were below average (73.2 and 78.9 per cent). The latter two sectors were precisely those in which the 1936 investment plan provided for a particular advance.

The ambitious plan for the installation of fixed capital was not fulfilled in 1936; instead of the 31.4 billion rubles planned, about 25 billion[63] was put into service, an increase of only 2.0 billion over 1935. An increase of 8.2 billion had been planned. As for the installation of new capacity in physical terms, commentators on the 1936 annual plan fulfillment provide very little information. It is known that of 18 new coal mines planned, only 11 were actually put into operation in 1936; of 14 open-hearth furnaces planned, only 7 were put into operation; and 3 blast furnaces planned were actually put into operation.[64]

In contrast with the experience of 1935, the failure to fulfill the plan for investment and for installation of new productive capacity did have repercus-

63. This was estimated from the change in fixed capital, for which the 1936 plan was underfulfilled by 6.3 billion rubles (in 1933 plan prices). *Plan 1937*, p. 143, gives the total fixed capital put into service in 1936 as 30,500 million rubles. Since the 1936 plan provided for 31.4 billion rubles to be put into service (Morozov, *Plan*, No. 2, 1936, p. 18), the underfulfillment would be 0.9 billion rubles. There are several reasons not to accept such a small discrepancy between plan and fulfillment here. First, it is probable that, just as in 1935 (see footnote 49 above), the large volume of fixed capital put into service in 1936 was the result of additions and corrections to the original plan (see Table B-11) of around 4 billion rubles. The original plan for installation of fixed capital must also have been revised. Second, there was considerable ambiguity in 1936 about the prices used in calculating investment (see footnote 60 above). Third, the official commentary on the fulfillment of the 1936 annual investment plan states: "The 1936 investment plan was not completely fulfilled. As a result, many large-scale construction projects which were meant to be finished in 1936 were carried over unfinished into 1937. The huge reserves contained in the Stakhanovite movement were not altogether utilized. The goal for the reduction of construction costs was not completely fulfilled" ("Stroitelnaia programma zavershaiushchego goda vtoroi piatiletki" [The Construction Program of the Final Year of the Second Five-Year Plan], *Plan*, No. 4, 1937, p. 9). Fourth, if the plan for installation of fixed capital had been underfulfilled by only 0.9 billion rubles, nothing would have justified the underfulfillment of the plan for total value of fixed capital by 6.3 billion rubles, even if the figure is in 1933 plan prices. It should be noted that, according to Table B-16 which was based on official Soviet data of that time, actual 1936 investment prices were only 18.7 per cent higher than 1933 plan prices.

64. Planned capacities were given in *Plan 1936*, p. 276. Increase in new capacities put into service in 1936 was derived by subtracting the total for 1933–1935 (given in *ibid.*, p. 267) from the total for 1933–1936 (given by E. Lokshin, "Osvoenie proizvodstvennykh moshchnostei v tiazheloi industrii" [Assimilation of Productive Capacities in Heavy Industry], *Planovoe khoziaistvo*, No. 2, 1937, p. 42). These totals are 100 and 111 coal mines and 75 and 82 open-hearth furnaces. The opening of three blast furnaces in 1936 was estimated from the total number put into operation during 1933–1935 (17), the total number put into operation between January 1, 1933, and January 1, 1938 (see Table 55), and the statement by Lokshin (*Problemy ekonomiki*, No. 2, 1938, p. 40) that no blast furnaces were put into operation in 1937. Nevertheless, there is a certain inconsistency in the data on this subject, since the same author, Lokshin, states in his *Planovoe khoziaistvo* (No. 2, 1937, p. 41) article that 19 blast furnaces were put into operation during the four years 1933–1936. Thus there must have been only two furnaces in operation in 1936, and since there were 20 in service at the end of 1937 and none was started up in 1937, the date when the 20 were put into operation is unclear.

sions on the fulfillment of the production plan (see Tables 63 and A-2). Official overestimation of the output indexes (based on the notorious 1926/27 prices) made it possible for the official Soviet figures to show an overfulfillment of 3.5 per cent for national income and of 5.8 per cent for industrial production. Western estimates, however, show underfulfillments of 8.5 and 5.0 per cent, respectively. Official Soviet and Western calculations of agricultural production agree, showing an underfulfillment of around 25 per cent.

The failure of the 1936 plan should not obscure the fact that 1936 was still a year of expansion, at least for national income, industrial production, and transportation. According to official Soviet estimates (see Table A-2), national income increased by 28.6 per cent, gross industrial production by 28.4 per cent, and railroad freight transportation by 25.3 per cent. Western estimates give more modest growth rates for national income and industrial production—8.0 and 16.9 per cent.[65] For agricultural production, recent official Soviet calculations (see Table A-2) give a drop of 8.4 per cent, which is larger than that (6.0 per cent) estimated by D. Gale Johnson and A. Kahan in the West.[66]

The increase in industrial production and national income must have encouraged the Soviet planners to increase total investment in 1937 still further, even if to a more modest degree. But already sabotage was being blamed for failures in the investment plan by making the executant level responsible for serious policy errors of the highest level.[67] The disproportions that appeared during 1936 became the most common accusation in the trials of people that Stalin wanted liquidated (for example, former Deputy Commissar of Heavy Industry Piatakov[68]). A few examples of such accusations, cited by Lokshin in 1937, show that the chronic defects of the Stalinist planning system were simply presented as sabotage: incorrect use of equipment, failure to carry out capital repairs, reluctance to introduce new techniques, delays in installation of imported equipment, ordering equipment not corresponding to needs, failure to declare real productive capacities, frequent changing and poor drafting of specifications, dispersion of resources on multiple construction projects, extension of construction schedules, reduction of investment efficiency, disproportions among various

65. Gross national products calculated by Richard Moorsteen and Raymond Powell (*The Soviet Capital Stock, 1928–1962*, Homewood, Ill., 1966, p. 622); all industrial products, excluding miscellaneous machinery, calculated by G. Warren Nutter (*Growth of Industrial Production in the Soviet Union*, Princeton, 1962, p. 525).

66. D. Gale Johnson and Arcadius Kahan, "Soviet Agriculture: Structure and Growth" in *Comparisons of the United States and Soviet Economies*, Joint Economic Committee, U.S. Congress, Washington, 1959, Part I, p. 204. Recalculated from index based on 1928.

67. The text of the 1937 annual plan, sent to press April 8, 1937, states: "In order to eliminate as rapidly as possible the *consequences of sabotage*, the People's Commissariat of Heavy Industry must immediately draft and implement measures to eliminate the artificial disruptions and disproportions created by saboteurs among various workshops, factories, and branches of industry, to reduce delays in building vital plants and mines, to establish strict work rules for enterprises and regulations for technical security, and to supervise their implementation, particularly in the chemical and coal industries. It must also guarantee rapid investigation into all accidents by trained personnel and by special commissions appointed by the commissar to find those responsible and to eliminate the cause of accidents" (*Plan 1937*, p. 21).

68. See p. 12 in Chapter 2.

workshops, and putting into operation blast furnaces not completely finished.[69] These facts appear to be confirmed and indisputable. The accusations of sabotage and the language of repression, however, make it impossible to discuss true responsibility.[70]

The 1937 annual plan reflected only to a moderate extent the consequences of the serious 1936 crisis in construction.[71] Total investment in 1937 was to increase by 3 per cent, but a reduction of 2 per cent was planned for producer goods. The largest increases were for transportation (20 per cent) and public health (28 per cent); even state-owned agriculture was to increase more than the average.

Once again the chances for fulfilling the 1937 investment plan depended on the planned reduction in investment costs. This reduction, which averaged 10.5 per cent, varied by sector: 10.9 per cent in industry, 5.4 per cent in state-owned agriculture, 4.9 per cent for the Commissariat of Agriculture, and 9.0 per cent for state farms, among others.[72] It was to yield a saving of 3.4 billion rubles by paying out only 29,165 rubles to obtain investments valued at 32,593 million rubles (see Table B-13) in December 1, 1936, estimate prices.[73]

As might be expected after the failure of the annual investment plan in 1936, the official keynote was to concentrate effort on the installation of fixed capital,[74] which amounted to 34,861 million rubles in the plan,[75] or 3.3 billion rubles more than the investment planned for that year. The increase in installation over 1936 was 4.4 billion rubles. (This figure in fully comparable prices could be smaller since a large part of the 1936 results seems to have been evaluated in 1935 prices, which were lower than December 1, 1936, prices.[76])

Unfortunately, in contrast with practice in previous years, nothing was published on the share of new construction to be started in 1937. A Soviet commentator indicates only that the 1937 investment plan was distinguished by a high concentration of resources on large-scale projects (evidently the continuation of the 1936 policy) and that the completion of construction projects under way for several years was to be accompanied by setting up enterprises to guarantee a new increase in production during the Third Five-Year Plan.[77]

69. E. Lokshin, "Tiazhelaia industriia i tekhnicheskaia rekonstruktsiia narodnogo khoziaistva" [Heavy Industry and Technical Reconstruction of the National Economy], *Problemy ekonomiki*, No. 5–6, 1937, pp. 51–52.

70. These criticisms can be compared with the regular criticisms of construction at that time. For example, A. Pokrovskii ("Na puti k krupnoi stroitelnoi industrii" [On the Way to a Large-Scale Construction Industry], *Nashe stroitelstvo* [Our Construction], No. 3, 1937, p. 2) writes: "The utilization of machines and construction equipment was not organized and many important projects in this area were not started until toward the end of 1936. The Stakhanovite movement on construction projects developed spontaneously in many cases. A fixed technical plan was rare. Work on specifications and estimate costs was delayed; discipline was not always observed."

71. See *Plan 1937*, p. 143.

72. Antonina Smilga, "Finansy sotsialisticheskogo gosudarstva" [Finances of the Socialist State], *Problemy ekonomiki*, No. 2, 1937, pp. 116–17.

73. See footnote 62 above.

74. See *Plan*, No. 4, 1937, p. 9.

75. *Plan 1937*, p. 143.

76. See footnote 62 above.

77. B. Sukharevskii, "Tiazhelaia promyshlennost v 1937 g." [Heavy Industry in 1937], *Plan*, No. 3, 1937, p. 16.

The priority granted simultaneously to the construction projects to be put into operation, to large-scale construction projects, to starting construction for the Third Five-Year Plan, and to consumption, even if timidly, made the 1937 annual plan extremely taut. The chances of fulfilling it were very slender, resting as they did on a sizable reduction in costs, on an increase of 22.4 per cent in labor productivity in construction,[78] and on a considerable increase in the production of construction materials.[79] The precariousness was pointed out for the food industry plan for the second half of 1937.[80]

As soon as the 1937 annual plan had gotten under way, in the first quarter, special stress was put on better labor organization and the elimination of construction projects that lacked specifications or estimate costs.[81] The results of the quarterly plans (see Table 58) do not seem to show any improvement at the beginning of the year: only 16.6 per cent of the total for the year was fulfilled during the first quarter, whereas the plan specified 19.0 per cent. During the second quarter fulfillment was 26.3 per cent instead of the 28.8 per cent planned.[82]

Special difficulties appeared in the production of construction materials, particularly for local industry for which price reductions had been planned in the new rates of December 1, 1936. An increase in production by cooperatives and the additional installation of new capacities for the production of bricks, roofing tiles, and other locally produced materials had also been planned.[83] The lack of construction materials was the most noticeable in local industry because of the discrepancies between the planning of production and of supplies.[84] An article on the Ordzhonikidze territory plan indicates that the principal construction materials (bricks, lime, alabaster, roofing tiles) were in very short supply and that the main construction projects could not work even though they had speci-

78. *Plan 1937*, p. 143.

79. Increases of 27 per cent for cement, 17 per cent for lime, 21 per cent for asbestos shingles, 107 per cent for roofing tiles, 32 per cent for bricks, etc. (*Plan 1937*, pp. 93–94). The importance of construction materials was stressed in the March 29, 1937, decree of the Party Central Committee and the Council of People's Commissars on the 1937 annual plan (*ibid.*, p. 37).

80. A. Sakhtan, "Dve piatiletki pishchevoi promyshlennosti" [Two Five-Year Plans of the Food Industry], *Problemy ekonomiki*, No. 2, 1937, p. 91. The author insists that "the implementation of the current tasks of the food industry in 1937 necessitates an unflagging effort in all sectors of the plan, a struggle to overcome bottlenecks and eliminate all production disorders."

81. "Pervyi kvartal vtorogo stakhanovskogo goda" [The First Quarter of the Second Year of the Stakhanovite Movement], *Plan*, No. 1, 1937, p. 9.

82. It is not very clear how these percentages were calculated. The investment plan for the first quarter of 1937 was 6,686.9 million rubles and it represented 19.03 per cent of the annual investment plan, which was 35,139 million rubles and not 32,593. The sum of the percentages of the quarterly plans and of their fulfillments comes to 100.0 per cent. What represents the discrepancy between the plan and the fulfillment when the plan, even in current prices, was underfulfilled by about 2.4 billion rubles?

83. The 1937 plan provided for a production by industrial cooperatives of more than 1.2 billion bricks (compared with a total output of 11.0 billion) and a production of 27.5 per cent of the total output of tiles (excluding collective farms), and 22 per cent of lime. See S-ov, "Rasshirenie proizvodstva stroimaterialov po promkooperatsii" [Expansion of Production of Construction Materials by Industrial Cooperatives], *Plan*, No. 7, 1937, p. 62.

84. Several specific figures for sheet iron, among other products, were cited in support of the argument that disparities between the plan and supply affected mainly republic local industry (N. Gavrilov, "O nesoglasovannosti v planakh proizvodstva i snabzheniia" [On Lack of Coordination in Production and Supply Plans], *Plan*, No. 9, 1937, pp. 18–19).

fications, estimate costs, and credits. Nevertheless, the work of the construction projects depended on these factories.[85]

To what extent were the difficulties in carrying out the investment plan amplified by the campaign of purges and repression? Obviously, this campaign did not encourage enterprise managers to make a long-term effort; they had to ward off the immediate dangers. In any case, it is of interest to reproduce several accusations made about "sabotage" in construction that show, on the one hand, the crisis situation of the Soviet economy in 1937 and, on the other, several permanent defects of Stalinist planning, magnified by a brutal and very inexperienced industrialization policy. Enterprise managers and staff had to play the part of scapegoats, and criticisms of enterprise or technical management were meant to divert attention from the serious responsibilities of Stalin and his henchmen.

Among the accusations about investment planning, several taken from a 1937 article may be cited:[86] (1) dispersion of investments among too large a number of objectives; (2) intentionally undervalued estimate costs in order to obtain their necessary revision; (3) unfinished construction, giving rise to delays in operation; (4) grandiose plans in general, concealing disparities among certain sectors; (5) low efficiency of investment; and (6) use of phraseology concealing the true state of affairs.

These charges were accompanied by more general accusations of the political passivity of the staff, their defective theoretical and ideological perceptions, and their lack of desire to perform economic work. Accusations went as far as declaring that "a pernicious 'little theory' was being widely spread among planning workers claiming that the regular fulfillment of plans proved the absence of sabotage. The people blinded by this enemy idea no longer saw that the regular fulfillment of plans concealed their underestimation and the lack of a comprehensive evaluation of the colossal possibilities of the socialist economy."[87]

One might, then, wonder why the Soviet authorities wasted, and still waste, so much time proving that they fulfill the plans and that the plans are perfect. The charges were even more unfair because the personnel accused of fulfilling the plans correctly had had relatively little to do with drafting them and had been forced to do so under threat of reprisal. The same could not be said for the central authorities and for Stalin himself, who expressed his economic policy through the plans and imposed an inefficient system. By making reliable statistics for the whole country scarce and by multiplying individual pieces of information on microeconomic difficulties, the party leaders prevented any serious

85. "The tempo and schedule of the work on construction sites very often depends on the supply of local construction materials; unplanned stoppages result; bricklayers have to be transferred to other work; and the development of the Stakhanovite movement is slowed down. . . . Primitive artisan methods of work, lack of culture, and conservatism reign in the enterprises. They work by approximation, in the old-fashioned way, and the floors of the factories are littered with obstructions and dirt. The low quality of the materials and their high cost hold up construction just as much as shortages" (P. Pavlov, "Stroitelstvu—deshevye i vysokie po kachestvu stroimaterialy" [Cheaper and Higher-Quality Construction Materials for Construction], *Plan*, No. 11, 1937, pp. 24–25).

86. "Vykorchevat korni vreditelstva v planovoi rabote" [Extirpate the Roots of Sabotage in Planning Work], *Plan*, No. 11, 1937, p. 3.

87. *Ibid.*, p. 4.

study of the links between government investment policy and its inevitable repercussions. Even had strict censorship not made thorough study of this problem impossible in the Soviet Union, the maze of disconnected statistics on investment, costs, and prices, as well as the innumerable plans at different levels, discouraged any real research on this subject in the West.[88]

In view of the quality of the 1937 investment plan and the economic and social situation in the country at the time, considerable underfulfillment of the 1937 investment plan should have been expected. The official commentators summarized the situation as follows: "In 1937, as is known, the investment plan was not satisfactorily fulfilled either for volume or for value. Even less satisfactory was the fulfillment of the plan for putting into service."[89]

The data on the 1937 annual plan for investment are summarized in Tables B-13 and B-14. Only the fulfillment of the plan as a whole could be calculated (77.8 per cent), since the data by sectors were not available. But, because of the prices in which the plan and its fulfillment were evaluated, these results can only be considered approximations.[90]

The immediate cause for the failure of the 1937 plan was the failure to fulfill the plan for costs (see Table B-15). Instead of the planned cost reduction of 10.5 per cent, a reduction of 0.5 per cent was announced, a figure that did not include allowance for price changes. If such allowance is made, the increase in costs was more than 6 per cent.

The main reason that the cost plan was not fulfilled was the failure of the plan to increase productivity in construction (it was to reach 22.4 per cent). Productivity per worker in construction actually dropped by 2.1 per cent between 1936 and 1937,[91] only 80 per cent of the annual plan being fulfilled. More than 300,000 additional workers had to be employed for the same volume of work, and the wage fund was exceeded. Poor utilization of equipment in construction, high labor turnover, and an overly narrow range of workers' wages were mainly responsible for this result. The revision of norms (considerably exceeded in 1936) in 1937, increasing them by 8 per cent,[92] made the situation even more difficult, and these norms were not followed by 15 to 20 per cent of the workers. Losses of working time in construction are not fully known, but information for construction sites and brigades makes it possible to estimate work stoppages and losses

88. Among the best Western work giving evaluations of Soviet investment can be cited Kaplan, "Capital Investments"; Jasny, *Soviet Industrialization*; and Moorsteen and Powell, *Soviet Capital Stock*.

89. *Planovoe khoziaistvo*, No. 3, 1938, p. 27.

90. See footnote 62 above. Jasny (*Soviet Industrialization*, pp. 187–88) points out that the "difficulty with using the data at the prices and norms of 1936/37 is that various compensations and additions to those prices and norms were permitted from time to time and that nobody took the trouble to incorporate the compensations and additions into the basic prices and norms. There is also a suspicion that the purges brought into existence some inflationary factors, which affected the value in these prices and costs and were not taken care of by the compensations and additions."

91. E. Vasilev, "Proizvoditelnost truda v stroitelstve" [Labor Productivity in Construction], *Planovoe khoziaistvo*, No. 8, 1938, pp. 35–36 (data covering net construction of large-scale construction projects). Vasilev cited data by commissariat relative to 1936 (reductions of from 9.8 to 3.1 per cent, except for light industry which had an increase of 3.3 per cent) and relative to the 1937 plan (77.3 to 86.8 per cent fulfilled).

92. *Ibid.*, p. 36.

of working time at 20 to 35 per cent. Work stoppages of one day or more averaged 1.73 man-days per worker.[93] Work stoppages were particularly serious in the ferrous metal industry.[94] Commissar of Heavy Industry Kaganovich issued a special order on November 20, 1937, blaming the failure to fulfill the plan on negligence in work, the large number of accidents, and a lack of respect for production.[95]

The poor state of equipment in the construction agencies, caused largely by the low priority accorded capital repairs during the previous years, was responsible for many of the work stoppages. On the average, as a percentage of the value of fixed productive capital, expenditures on capital repairs were reduced from 2.1 per cent in 1934 to 1.7 per cent in 1935 and 1.5 per cent in 1936.[96]

Other reasons for the failure of the 1937 investment plan put forward at the time were more or less connected with the accusations of "sabotage." Many of these accusations are the same as the charges mentioned earlier. They seem perfectly valid as explanations of the failures of 1937, but here, too, the commentators accuse the wrong people, those to blame being Stalin's entourage and the system that he created. Among the accusations are the following: there was too much concentration on new construction without a simultaneous study of the possibilities of expanding production in existing enterprises, and the possibilities of increasing production without new investment were neglected.[97] There was a mania for the gigantic, a trend that was certainly apparent in the 1936 annual plan (discussed above) and was encouraged by the central authorities. The introduction of industrial methods in construction was too slow, and the old-fashioned artisan methods in use were incapable of coping with technical and economic problems.[98] The financial system made it difficult to obtain funds.[99] The norms used in construction were a hindrance.[100] There were disparities between construction intended for production and housing construction.

---

93. *Ibid.*

94. For open-hearth furnaces, they increased from 21.8 per cent of working time in 1936 to 22.4 per cent in 1937 (nine months); for rolling mills, they increased from 15.6 to 22.4 per cent. In some factories, like the Lysensk one, the open-hearth furnaces were not in operation 35 per cent of working time in 1937; in the Frunze plant, downtime was 31.4 per cent. The rolling mills of the Voikov factory were not in operation 39 per cent of the time, and those in the Kuznetsk plant, 35.3 per cent. (G. Kharatian, "Proizvodstvennye moshchnosti chernoi metallurgii SSSR i ikh osvoenie" [Productive Capacities of the USSR Ferrous Metal Industry and Their Assimilation], *Problemy ekonomiki*, No. 4, 1938, p. 38.)

95. *Ibid.*

96. P. Khromov, "Amortizatsiia i remont osnovnykh fondov promyshlennosti" [Amortization and Repairs of Fixed Capital in Industry], *Planovoe khoziaistvo*, No. 5, 1938, p. 52.

97. O. Osipov-Shmidt, "Likvidiruem posledstviia vreditelstva v khimicheskoi promyshlennosti" [Liquidate the Remnants of Sabotage in the Chemical Industry], *Planovoe khoziaistvo*, No. 4, 1937, pp. 43–44.

98. *Planovoe khoziaistvo*, No. 3, 1938, pp. 20–28.

99. *Ibid.*, pp. 21–22. A Council of People's Commissars decree was issued on this subject on February 2, 1938 ("On Improving the Drafting of Specifications and Estimate Costs and on Bringing Order to the Financing of Construction," cited in *ibid.*, p. 22), and a Construction Committee was created under the Council of People's Commissars.

100. The list of norms for estimate costs for construction projects that was approved November 29, 1937, replaced the 10,000 norms that were in effect by 900 aggregated norms (*ibid.*, p. 24).

The direct consequence of the failure of the 1937 annual investment plan was that the plan for installation of new productive capacity was not fulfilled (see above). But this time there is not the slightest doubt about the extent of this failure. Instead of the 34.9 billion rubles of fixed capital that were planned to be put into service, only some 27 billion rubles materialized, or nearly 8 billion less than planned.[101] For the People's Commissariat of Machine-Building, for which data exist, the 1937 plan provided for an increase in unfinished construction of from 1,710 million rubles in 1936 to 1,810 million. In actual fact, the total value of unfinished construction reached 2,300 million rubles at the beginning of 1938.[102]

The direct consequence of the difficulties encountered in carrying out the plan for investment and for installing fixed capital was the failure of the production plan, even more serious than in 1936 (see Table 63 in Chapter 13). This time the plan was poorly fulfilled according to official Soviet as well as Western calculations. Only agriculture fared better, thanks to an exceptionally good harvest. The growth rates of national income remained high, thanks to this harvest (8.0 per cent in 1936 and 10.1 per cent in 1937), even according to Western calculations (see Table 56 below); but the growth rate for industry dropped considerably (from 16.9 per cent in 1936 to 6.1 per cent in 1937).[103] In 1938 the trend toward a reduction in growth rates became general; national income grew at 1.8 per cent (see Table 56) and industrial production at 4.6 per cent.[104] Although it was not the sole cause, investment played an important part in the fluctuation of production.

Over-All View of the Fulfillment of the Second Five-Year Plan

The official Soviet results of the Second Five-Year Plan for investment were presented in Tables 50 and 51 above. The difficulties involved in comparing the plan and results in current prices were pointed out in Table 50 (notes to column 5). They arise from changes in statistical definitions. The total in current prices commonly accepted at the time was 130 billion rubles (see Table 50, note a), which would yield an overfulfillment of 8.3 per cent in current prices.

The figures in constant prices (1933 plan prices) should, in principle, be more reliable since they are given directly by USSR Gosplan (see Table 51). In fact, they, too, do not agree with the calculations made in this book, according to the movement of prices from 1932 to 1941 indicated by official Soviet authors (see Table B-16). The figure for total investment in 1933 plan prices that results from these calculations, presented in Tables B-5 through B-14, is 105,862 million rubles. According to that calculation, only 79.4 per cent of the five-year plan for investment would have been fulfilled for the national economy as a whole

101. The 1938 plan for fixed capital installation was "almost one and a half times that of the preceding year" (I. Bolshakov, "Stroitelnaia programma 1938 goda" [Construction Program for 1938], *Planovoe khoziaistvo*, No. 6, 1938, p. 32).

102. A. Zelenovskii, "Promyshlennost v pervom godu tretei piatiletki" [Industry in the First Year of the Third Five-Year Plan], *Planovoe khoziaistvo*, No. 5, 1938, p. 25.

103. Calculated from Nutter, *Growth*, p. 525 (industrial products excluding miscellaneous machinery).

104. *Ibid*.

(excluding the collective farm sector). In the light of what is known about prices and cost estimates at this time, this discrepancy is hardly surprising.[105] Moreover, Soviet authors pointed out this problem in 1937.[106]

In order to better understand the success or failure of the investment plan, it should be noted that its apparent overfulfillment, even in constant prices, is not meaningful. Real costs were often higher than estimate costs. For that reason, the meaningful comparison is between fulfillment of the investment plan in constant prices and that of the plan for installation of new productive capacity. An attempt at such a comparison has been made in Table 55. The data on fulfillment of the plans for installation of new productive capacity are very incomplete, but the results are striking. In heavy industry, the percentages of plan fulfillment for putting new capacity into service vary around 50 per cent, which means that the plan fulfillment percentages in constant prices of 80 to 90 per cent are considerably overestimated. The real effort that was required was much greater than planned. It should be remembered, moreover, that fulfillment of the plan for installation of new capacity does not automatically guarantee the production planned for that construction project. The problem of assimilation was one of the most serious during the 1930's.[107]

Another question that arises is the effect of the investment policy on the development of production. Did the acceleration or deceleration of investment have an effect on production? If so, with how much lag? An attempt has been made in Table 56 to gather the elements needed to answer this question. A certain correlation appears clearly between variations in the rate of growth (or decline) of investment in constant prices and variations in the Western calculations of national income,[108] with a lag of one year, but only after 1934. Thus, the increase in the growth rate of investment in 1934 is followed by an increase in the growth rate of national income in 1935, and so forth.

This correlation does not exist for the years of the First Five-Year Plan. Sizable migration of workers to the towns made possible the substitution of labor for capital. Disinvestment resulting from the slaughter of cattle and reduction of stocks made possible a temporary increase in national income.[109] The share of agriculture (excluding collective farm investment after 1933) was relatively much larger. Nevertheless, a regular fluctuation, based on the investment cycle, is clearly visible after a certain level of industrialization is reached.[110]

Moreover, it should not be forgotten that the success of the investment plan cannot be measured solely by plan fulfillment. The time element, vital in the

105. See footnote 62 above.
106. "A precise comparison of investments with five-year plan goals is particularly difficult at present, since it would entail making complicated calculations of the actual cost of construction. The five-year plan provided for a sizable reduction in construction costs which was not carried out, and, in fact, real costs did not decrease much in relation to 1933 prices" (E. Kviring, "Poslednii god vtoroi piatiletki" [The Last Year of the Second Five-Year Plan], *Problemy ekonomiki*, No. 2, 1937, pp. 37–38).
107. See pp. 239 ff. above.
108. On the defects of official Soviet calculations in 1926/27 prices, see my *Planning*, pp. 256 ff.
109. *Ibid.*, p. 247.
110. It is interesting to note that Gérard Duchene (*Essai sur la logique de l'économie planifiée soviétique, 1965–1975*, Paris, 1976, pp. 455 ff) uncovers investment cycles in the USSR during 1958–1970. I hope to return to this question in future work.

Table 55   Growth of Production Capacities during the Second Five-Year Plan, 1933–1937

	Units	Productive Capacity				Increase in Productive Capacity during Second Five-Year Plan		
		Actual, Jan. 1, 1933 (1)	Planned, Jan. 1, 1938 (2)	Actual, Jan. 1, 1938 (3)	Per Cent of Plan Fulfilled (4)	Planned, Jan. 1, 1938 (5)	Actual, Jan. 1, 1938 (6)	Per Cent of Plan Fulfilled (7)
Commissariat of Heavy Industry								
Electric Power Stations								
Total capacity:	th. kw	4,696	10,900	8,116.5	74.5	6,204	3,420.5[a]	55.1
Regional stations (*Glavenergo*)	th. kw	2,653	6,646	4,712.9	70.9	3,993	2,059.9	51.6
Industrial stations	th. kw	1,674	3,234			1,560		
Coal Industry								
Output	mill. m. t.	110.7	238.8	186.3[b]	78.0	128.1	75.6[b]	59.0
Number of mines	units	437	524	582[c]	111.1	87	145[d]	166.7
Petroleum Industry								
Crude petroleum	mill. m. t.	23.4	40.9	30.6	74.8	17.5	7.2	41.1
Refined petroleum products	mill. m. t.	3.0	15.8	9.3	58.9	12.8	6.3	49.2
Ferrous Metal Industry								
Pig iron:								
Number of blast furnaces	units	103	139	123[c]	88.5	36	20[d]	55.6
Capacity of blast furnaces	m³	36,911	78,429	55,715[c]	71.0	41,518	18,804[e]	45.3
Steel:								
Number of open-hearth furnaces	units	296[f]	437	372[f]	85.1	141	76[g]	53.9
Capacity of open-hearth furnaces	m²	6,688	13,093	10,266[c]	78.4	6,405	3,578[e]	55.9
Bessemer furnaces	th. m. t.	1,250	3,309			2,059		
Rolled steel:								
Number of rolling mills	units	262	362	311[c]	85.9	100	49[h]	49.0
Capacity of rolling mills	mill. m. t.	7.0	19.0	16.0	84.2	12.0	9.0	75.0
Nonferrous Metal Industry								
Copper	th. m. t.	94	207			113		
Machine-Building								
Tractors (15 hp), excl. tractor cultivators	th.	80	276.7	[i]		196.7		
Motor vehicles	th.	92	360	[j]		268		
Freight cars[k]	th. 2-axle units	40	155	77.8	50.2	115	37.8	32.9
Transformers	th. kw	3,500	7,000	4,400	62.9	3,500	900	25.7
Steam boilers	th. m²	250	625	[l]		375		
Commissariat of Light Industry								
Cotton fabrics	mill. m	3,600	5,300	[m]		1,700		
Shoes	mill. prs	100	200	154[n]	77.0	100	54[o]	54.0
Commissariat of Timber Industry								
Lumber	mill. m³	22.0	31.2	33	105.8	9.2	11.0	119.6
Paper	th. m. t.	625	1,120	830	74.1	495	205	41.4

Table 55 *continued*

	Units	Productive Capacity				Increase in Productive Capacity during Second Five-Year Plan		
		Actual, Jan. 1, 1933 (1)	Planned, Jan. 1, 1938 (2)	Actual, Jan. 1, 1938 (3)	Per Cent of Plan Fulfilled (4)	Planned, Jan. 1, 1938 (5)	Actual, Jan. 1, 1938 (6)	Per Cent of Plan Fulfilled (7)
Commissariat of Food Industry [p]								
Sugar, daily sugar processing capacity	th. m. t.	108.6	153.7	165.4 [q]	107.6	45.1	56.8 [r]	125.9
Flour (Commissariat of Agricultural Procurement)	mill. m. t.	18.0	28.8	[s]		10.8		

Source: Unless otherwise indicated, cols. 1–2: *Vtoroi plan*, pp. 448–49; col. 3: *Tretii plan*, pp. 226–27; col. 4: col. 3 as a percentage of col. 2; col. 5: col. 2 minus col. 1; col. 6: col. 3 minus col. 1; and col. 7: col. 6 as a percentage of col. 5.

a. *Dostizheniia sovetskoi vlasti za 40 let v tsifrakh* [Achievements of the Soviet Regime during 40 Years in Figures], Moscow, 1957, p. 212.

b. Another source (*Itogi vtorogo plana*, p. 41) gives 74.6 mill. m. t. for installation of new capacity during the Second Five-Year Plan, which, it states, is a 1.5–fold increase in productive capacity over the First Five-Year Plan. This would yield a figure of 166.05 mill. m. t. for January 1, 1938, in col. 3. Still another source (*Dostizheniia*, p. 212) gives 78.4 mill. m. t.

c. Col. 1 plus col. 6.

d. *Itogi vtorogo plana*, p. 41.

e. *Industrializatsiia, 1933–1937*, p. 236.

f. *Promyshlennost SSSR* [Industry in the USSR], Moscow, 1957, p. 124.

g. *Industrializatsiia, 1933–1937*, p. 236, gives 86, and *Itogi vtorogo plana*, p. 41, gives 88.

h. I. Bolshakov, "Stroitelnaia programma 1938 goda" [Construction Program for 1938], *Planovoe khoziaistvo*, No. 6, 1938, p. 33.

i. Production, which was 50.8 thous. in 1932, rose to 173.2 thous. in 1936, only to drop to 66.5 thous. in 1937 (*Promyshlennost*, p. 226).

j. Production, which was 23,879 in 1932, rose to 199,857 in 1937 (*Narodnoe khoziaistvo SSSR v 1959 godu* [The USSR National Economy in 1959], Moscow, 1960, p. 216).

k. Of the type used by the People's Commissariat of Transportation.

l. Production, which was 163.3 thous. m² in 1932, rose to 268.2 thous. m² in 1937 (*Promyshlennost*, p. 214).

m. Production, which was 2,694 mill. m in 1932, rose to 3,448 mill. m in 1937 (*ibid.*, p. 328).

n. Covers the main industrial commissariats. Between 1937 and 1941 several industrial commissariats were split into smaller units (see Table E-1).

o. Another source (*Dostizheniia*, p. 212) gives 44 mill. prs.

p. Commissariat of Food Supply in 1933 and Commissariat of Food Industry in 1937.

q. Given for capacity of sugar production. Assumed to be daily processing as in cols. 1 and 2.

r. Another source (*Dostizheniia*, p. 212) gives 11.77 th. m. t.

s. Production of Commissariat of Agriculture Procurement was 8.165 mill. m. t. in 1932 (*Vtoroi plan*, p. 462) and 13.918 mill. m. t. in 1937 (*Tretii plan*, p. 210).

Table 56   Growth of National Income and Investment, 1928–1940

	National Income					Investment		
	Official Soviet Estimates			Moorsteen and Powell				
	In 1926/27 Prices (bill. rubles)	Index (1928 = 100)	Change from Pre-ceding Year (per cent)	Index (1928 = 100)	Change from Pre-ceding Year (per cent)	In 1933 Plan Prices (bill. rubles)	Index (1928 = 100)	Change from Preceding Year (per cent)
	(1)	(2)	(3)	(4)	(5)	(6)	(7)	(8)
1928	24.4	100.0		100.0		4.9	100.0	
1929	27.5	112.7	12.7	102.7	2.7	11.2	228.6	128.6
1930	35.0	143.4	27.3	108.7	5.8	14.4	293.9	28.6
1931	40.9	167.6	16.9	110.9	2.0	18.5	377.6	28.5
1932	45.5	186.5	11.2	109.7	−1.1	19.2	391.8	3.8
1933	48.5	198.8	6.6	114.2	4.1	15.5	316.3	−19.3
1934	55.8	228.7	15.1	125.5	9.9	18.7	381.6	20.6
1935	66.9	274.2	19.9	144.4	15.1	21.1	430.6	12.8
1936	86.0	352.5	28.6	155.9	8.0	26.7	544.9	26.5
1937	96.3	394.7	12.0	171.6	10.1	23.9	487.8	−10.5
1938	105.0	430.3	9.0	174.7	1.8	26.0	530.6	8.8
1939	115.0	471.3	9.5	185.5	6.2			
1940	128.3	525.8	11.6	202.5	9.2			

Source
   COLUMN 1–1928–1929: Zaleski, *Planning*, pp. 306 and 330. 1930–1934: *Socialist Construction in the U.S.S.R.* (translated from the Russian), Moscow, 1936, p. 30. For 1930–1932, see also my *Planning*, pp. 330–31. For 1933–1934, see also Table A-2. 1935–1937: Table A-2. 1938–1940: Table A-3.
   COLUMN 2–1928–1940: Calculated from col. 1.
   COLUMN 3–1929–1940: Calculated from col. 1.
   COLUMN 4–1928–1940: Calculated from gross national product in rubles in 1937 prices in Moorsteen and Powell, *Soviet Capital Stock*, pp. 622–23.
   COLUMN 5–1929–1940: Calculated from col. 4.
   COLUMN 6–1928–1931: Investment in 1927/28 prices (Zaleski, *Planning*, p. 246, Table 47, col. 5, and source to col. 1) recalculated into 1933 plan prices by ratio of 1927/28 to 1933 plan prices for 1932 (derived as 1.192 from *ibid.* and 1932 figure below). 1932: Investment in current prices (*ibid.*, col. 3) deflated by price index (given as 1.111 in Table B-16, col. 12, line 1). 1933–1937: Tables B-5, B-7, B-9, B-11, and B-13. 1938: Investment in December 1, 1936, prices (given as 30.9 bill. rubles in *Industrializatsiia SSSR, 1938–1941* [Industrialization of the USSR, 1938–1941], Moscow, 1973, p. 45) deflated by price index for 1936 (given as 1.187 in Table B-16, col. 12, line 9).
   COLUMN 7–1928–1938: Calculated from col. 6.
   COLUMN 8–1929–1938: Calculated from col. 6.

fulfillment percentages, is no doubt less important than the fact that the movement of industrialization made an irreversible start. Success should also be measured in terms of new factories built and new capacities put into service, regardless of plan goals. From this viewpoint, the increase in productive capacity during the Second Five-Year Plan (see Table 55) represented a certain success. The Soviet authorities, moreover, did not fail to make capital of this increase by arguing that the Second Five-Year Plan goal to produce, in 1937, 80 per cent of industrial output in new or entirely rebuilt enterprises was completely fulfilled.[111] On January 1, 1938, more than 50 per cent of the existing stock of machine tools came from production obtained during the Second Five-

111. *Itogi vtorogo plana*, p. 20.

Year Plan. In agriculture, almost all the tractors and combines in 1938 came from production during the second plan.[112]

Thus the accomplishments are indisputable, and the increase of 56.4 per cent in national income between 1932 and 1937, obtained by independent calculations (see Table 56), confirms them fully. Nevertheless, the price paid for this increase in national income was exhorbitant and should be measured by the results of the first two five-year plans.

The first point that emerges from Table 56 is that the investment effort was extremely inefficient from the economic standpoint. From 1928 to 1937 national income increased only 71.6 per cent, while investment increased nearly fivefold. This ratio was even less favorable in 1938. Moreover, the cost of investment is easy to measure in terms of increase in material well-being. Between 1928 and 1937 real wages in industry decreased by 33.6 per cent according to official Soviet price indexes and by 43.9 per cent according to my calculations.[113] According to official Soviet calculations, the very low real wages of 1932 had hardly changed by 1937; according to my calculations, they increased by 28.7 per cent, still far from the very low level of 1928. Were the sacrifices imposed on the population necessary? Judgment of the very nature of the Stalinist industrialization policy rests on the answer.

The fulfillment of the Second Five-Year Plan for large-scale investment projects had a by-product in the consolidation of the Stalinist administrative and authoritarian system of planning, with interference from the government and the Party in the smallest details of economic activity and daily life. This was, as the eminent Polish economist Edward Lipinski pointed out in a more general way, one of the unforeseen (or unadmitted) consequences of intentional or conscious centralized planning.[114] This by-product of voluntaristic planning of the 1930's was made into dogma and represented a constraint which the Soviet leaders after Stalin did not want, or did not find it useful, to get rid of. Nevertheless, the defects of the system, particularly in its motive force, investment planning, remained intact. The "crimes" of which the "saboteurs" of 1936–1938 were accused[115] became ordinary practice, a method of giving a bit of flexibility to the system, while their "inventors" were liquidated or severely punished. But, despite these more or less tolerated means of adjustment, the problem of the rigidity and efficiency of the system remained intact.[116]

112. *Ibid.*
113. See my *Planning*, p. 392.
114. At a conference organized by Renato Mieli for Centro Studi e Ricerche su Problemi Economico-Sociali. See Edward Lipinski, *Karol Marks i zagadnienia wspolczesnosci* [Karl Marx and Contemporary Problems], Warsaw, 1969.
 It is of interest to note that similar ideas are expressed by Henri Guitton (*Maîtriser l'économie*, Paris, 1967, p. 10), who writes: "In the face of this astonishing growth, which has not stopped growing or astonishing, man, who is nevertheless an artisan, is uneasy and bewildered. He wonders what will become of him amidst these forces which he has loosed. He is afraid of no longer being their master." Perhaps the desire of the central planner to control everything is also an expression of the same fear.
115. See pp. 251 and 253 above.
116. The continuation of these practices in the postwar period is documented in Chapter 17.

CHAPTER 12

Quarterly Planning

Drafting Quarterly Plans

The quarterly plans during 1933–1941 are especially important because they were operational in two senses. They led to final intervention by the central authorities in drafting the national economic plan and they were used as a base for the balances and plans for centralized allocation of essential products.[1] The extent to which the quarterly plans were operational will be shown later. For now it should simply be noted that these plans consisted of only the "definitive" orders given by the central planners to their immediate subordinates, ministries (people's commissariats), institutions, and republic councils of ministers. Industrial enterprises and railroads had monthly plans as definitive orders, drawn up by the same commissariats and republic agencies on the basis of the quarterly plans.

Before the war and until 1946, quarterly plans were drafted separately from the annual plans and approved by the government.[2] In the beginning of 1947, this procedure was abolished and quarterly plans were replaced by appropriate slices of the annual plans.[3] Actually such quarterly slices of the annual plans existed before 1947, but they were part of the plans drawn up by the commissariats and transmitted to lower agencies such as the central administrations (*Glavki*) and enterprises. In the annual plan approved by the government, the quarterly slices were missing.[4]

1. A. Margolin, "K voprosu o srokakh sostavleniia balansov prokata" [On the Problem of the Schedules for Drawing up Balances of Rolled Steel], *Plan*, No. 5, 1934, p. 13.

2. August 29, 1946, decree of USSR Council of Ministers, "On Annual and Quarterly Economic Plans" (*Direktivy KPSS i sovetskogo pravitelstva po khoziaistvennym voprosam* [Directives of the Communist Party of the Soviet Union and of the Soviet Government on Economic Matters], Moscow, 1957, Vol. 3, pp. 89–91).

3. Except for the food product distribution plan, the State Bank credit plan, the State Bank cash plan, and the transportation plan (broken down by months), which still had to be drafted and approved separately by the government for each quarter.

4. On this subject, see *Ukazaniia i formy k sostavleniiu narodno-khoziaistvennogo plana na 1936 god* [Instructions and Forms for Drafting the National Economic Plan for 1936], Moscow, 1935, and *Ukazaniia i formy k sostavleniiu narodnokhoziaistvennogo plana na 1937 god* [Instructions and Forms for

Although during 1933–1941 all quarterly plans were approved separately by the government, the process of drafting and approving these plans was much less complicated than for the annual plans. The plans do not seem to have gone back and forth between the government and the enterprises. It was impossible to find in the sources consulted any trace of general government directives on the content of the quarterly plans. Only appeals were found, such as the one from USSR Gosplan Chairman Mezhlauk inveighing against the practice of underestimating plans (apropos of the plan for the fourth quarter of 1936).[5] Hence it seems that the draft quarterly plans presented to the government were based mainly on the annual plans in operation.

The quarterly plans were to be presented to the government for approval by the people's commissariats and USSR Gosplan no later than one month before the beginning of the quarter. The drafts were to be accompanied by brief notes giving the extent of plan fulfillment and justification of the principal measures and goals for the various branches of the economy.[6] Based on these draft quarterly plans, the commissariats, USSR Gosplan, and republic Gosplans made their own recommendations to the *Glavki* and planning committees at lower levels. For example, on February 10, 1933, the People's Commissariat of Heavy Industry transmitted to the lower-level agencies its instructions for drafting the plan for the second quarter of 1933,[7] and in the middle of May, USSR Gosplan requested the Kirov Territory Planning Committee to submit its draft of the plan for the third quarter of 1934.[8] Generally, draft quarterly plans were to be presented to the republic Gosplan no later than 35 days before the beginning of the quarter.[9] These deadlines seem to have aroused some objections from enterprises and local planning committees, which insisted that a month and a half before the beginning of the quarter they did not have the necessary data to estimate the results of the current quarter and the plan for the next quarter.[10]

Drafting the National Economic Plan for 1937], Moscow, 1936. In these publications the formulas submitted for government approval do not contain a breakdown of the annual goals into quarters. The quarterly slices of the annual plan drawn up by the People's Commissariat of Food Supply (which was subdivided into the People's Commissariat of the Food Industry and the People's Commissariat of Domestic Trade in 1934—see Table 1 in Chapter 2) can be found in *Plan promyshlennosti Narkomsnaba na 1933 god* [Plan for Industry of People's Commissariat of Food Supply for 1933], Moscow-Leningrad, 1933, pp. 20–26, 29, and 68–69.

5. Ia. Chadaev, "Novoe v sostavlenii plana IV kvartala 1936 g." [New Elements in Drafting Plan for Fourth Quarter of 1936], *Plan*, No. 18, 1936, p. 51.

6. July 4, 1937, decree of Council of People's Commissars, "On the Order of Presenting Quarterly Plans to the USSR Council of People's Commissars" (*Sobranie zakonov i rasporiazhenii raboche-krestianskogo pravitelstva SSSR* [Collection of Laws and Decrees of the Workers' and Peasants' Government of the USSR], No. 41, 1937, Art. 176).

7. February 10, 1933, edict of USSR People's Commissariat of Heavy Industry, "On the Control Figures for the Second Quarter of 1933" (*Bibliograficheskie materialy po vtoromu 5-letnemu planu tiazheloi promyshlennosti* [Bibliographical Material on the Second Five-Year Plan for Heavy Industry], Moscow-Leningrad, 1934, Issue II, No. 1105).

8. "O strukture Respublikanskikh, kraevykh i oblastnykh Planovykh Komissii i Raiplanakh" [On the Structure of Republic, Territory, Province, and District Planning Committees], *Plan*, No. 4, 1935, p. 28.

9. E. Ioffe, "V Gosplane USSR" [In the Ukrainian Gosplan], *Plan*, No. 8, 1935, p. 62. Ioffe is discussing the practice in the Ukrainian Gosplan, but the schedules seem to have been more general.

10. On this point, see Goldman of the Kirov Territory Planning Committee in *Plan*, No. 4, 1935, p. 28.

Although the deadlines for presenting the draft plans were moved back, the plans were still transmitted late to enterprises,[11] changes were still made in the directives while the plan was being drawn up,[12] and the plan was still transmitted in "little bundles."[13] There was a conflict between the deadlines that were indispensable for central planning and the need to take immediate decisions at the enterprise level. This conflict can be seen in enterprise complaints pointed out by a Soviet author in 1934:

[The problem of delays] . . . is even worse for operational quarterly plans [than for annual plans]. Ordinarily, a factory receives directives toward the end of the preceding month, around the 25th, that is, at the time when the goals have been allocated by shops and when the quotas have already been distributed for all the main indexes and for manpower (notifications should be distributed on the 15th of the preceding month). Any goal that is late endangers the accuracy and coherence of the plan and is reflected in the progress of the production process. . . .

The shop management should distribute the monthly plan to the brigades on the 25th of the preceding month at the latest. The planning section of the factory should draw up the plan by the 15th of the preceding month at the latest, but to do that it must have a definite program for the month following the planned month; otherwise it cannot include the production of semifabricated products (to say nothing of tools) in the program for the current month.

For the program, drawn up in the framework of the quarterly plan a month and a half in advance, is usually frozen in the trust until the last days before the planned quarter. As a result, the spurt in production and the ability to maneuver combine to "finish up" the plan but lead to irregular work [sturmovshchina] in the shops and agitation in the planning agencies.[14]

Clearly, if the government received the draft quarterly plan only 30 days before it had to be put into operation, it is obvious that the goals could not be transmitted all the way down to the enterprise level in two weeks, unless control were purely formal.

The plan for the first quarter was usually drafted at the same time as the annual plan but approved separately. When drafting of the annual plan was

11. Complaints against the late transmittal of quarterly plans to enterprises are very frequent. See R. Riz, "O poriadke i srokakh prokhozhdeniia narodno-khoziaistvennykh planov" [On the Procedure and Schedule for Transmitting National Economic Plans], *Plan*, No. 2, 1934, p. 37; I. Ivenskii, "Voprosy planirovaniia mestnoi promyshlennosti" [Problems of Planning Local Industry], *Plan*, No. 1, 1935, p. 23; and N. Koltunov, "Svoevremenno dovodit plan do predpriiatiia" [Transmit the Plan to the Enterprise on Schedule], *Plan*, No. 6, 1935, p. 42. These writers point out that toward the middle of the quarter the quarterly plan had not yet been transmitted to enterprises. In Leningrad Province the investment plan for the third quarter of 1936 was approved only on August 19, 1936 (Moroshkin, "Leningradskii oblpotrebsoiuz ne organizuet planovoi raboty" [The Leningrad Province Consumers' Union Is Not Organizing Planning Work], *Plan*, No. 1, 1937, p. 55). In Moscow the qualitative indexes of the plan for the first quarter of 1937 were transmitted to the enterprises in the last days of the quarter and sometimes even at the beginning of the second quarter (G. Vizhnitser, "K itogam aktiva Mosoblplana" [On the Results of the Meeting of the Leaders of the Moscow Province Planning Committee], *Plan*, No. 8, 1937, p. 56).

12. Riz, *Plan*, No. 2, 1934, p. 37. Many examples of such changes in the plan during drafting could be cited.

13. Moroshkin (*Plan*, No. 1, 1937, p. 55) points out that not one of the regional cooperatives received the plan in the form of a single document. Separate transmittal of the various plan indexes was current practice. See also footnote 11 above.

14. N. Ksenofontov, "Bolshe chetkosti i operativnosti v planirovanii i uchete na predpriiatii" [More Accuracy and Operational Work in Planning and Accounting of Enterprises], *Plan*, No. 7, 1934, p. 16. Ksenofontov gives examples of how the plan functions in machine-building industries.

delayed, the quarterly plan was approved earlier. Changes made in the annual plan after that required revisions in the quarterly plan, but it was not always possible to make them.[15]

In order to reduce the delays, the government tried to limit the number of indexes in the quarterly plans. Several proposals of this sort were made as early as 1934. For example, one suggested that republic and province planning committees be relieved of the obligation of including in their quarterly plans indexes for the production of commissariats under Union jurisdiction.[16] It was also suggested that province planning committees be given more power in the quarterly planning of local industry.[17] In practice, the texts of the quarterly plans published until 1936 were concerned mostly with industry under Union jurisdiction, local industry being included only in aggregate value form and cooperative industry usually absent altogether. But in 1936 there appeared a trend to extend the sphere of quarterly planning. Beginning with the fourth quarter of 1936, cooperative industry was also covered and information on assortment was included in accordance with the instructions and forms for the 1937 annual plan, which had just been drafted.[18] The plan for the fourth quarter of 1936 also included goals for market production. Following an unexplained reduction in the number of indexes in the plan for the first quarter of 1937, the increase of planned indexes continued after the second quarter of 1937, particularly in production quality, auxiliary production, and consumer goods.[19]

Even with these increases, the quarterly plans contained fewer indexes than the annual plans. Along with the short time periods available to the planners, this had an adverse effect on the coherence of the quarterly plans. There is no dearth of criticism on this subject in the specialized press. Various authors complained that these quarterly plans were unrealistic, of little practical interest, and drawn up mechanically (24 to 26 per cent of the annual plan goals)[20] without any attempt to coordinate the different figures: "How was the work done in drafting the plan for the third quarter [of 1937]? Just as during the previous quarters, a more or less comprehensible plan was drafted, which, with the exception of minor errors, amounted to a compilation of the indexes for the production plan, the construction plan, the material and equipment supply plan, goals for employment, costs, etc. In setting the actual goals, the essential criterion was the slice of the annual plan that corresponded to the third quarter. All this is obviously important and indispensable but far from sufficient."[21] This author also stresses the limited horizons of the compilers of the plan for the third quarter of 1937 and insists that they did not take sufficient account of the development of

15. This example from Leningrad Province was cited by E. Novskaia ("Organizovanno provesti podgotovku k sostavleniiu plana na 1936 g." [Preparation for Drafting the 1936 Plan Must Be Conducted in an Organized Fashion], *Plan*, No. 11, 1935, p. 39).

16. Riz, *Plan*, No. 2, 1934, p. 38.

17. Ivenskii, *Plan*, No. 1, 1935, p. 23.

18. Chadaev, *Plan*, No. 18, 1936, p. 51.

19. M. Kozin, "O rabote nad planom II kvartala 1937 g." [On Work on Plan for Second Quarter of 1937], *Plan*, No. 6, 1937, p. 48.

20. Ivenskii, *Plan*, No. 1, 1935, p. 23. Ivenskii is concerned mainly with local industry.

21. G. Smirnov, "Kontrol za vypolnenem plana—vazhneishaia zadacha planovykh organov" [Control over Fulfillment of Plan—the Most Important Task of the Planning Agencies], *Plan*, No. 12, 1937, p. 2.

the economy during the first half of 1937.[22] In other words, he reproaches the planners for having made no effort to coordinate the quarterly plan goals.

Quarterly Planning and Annual Plans

Seasonal Fluctuations

The government's over-all approval of the annual plan freed it, in a way, from any obligation to estimate seasonal fluctuations at the beginning of the year. But such estimates were made by the commissariats and republics, and they had direct effects on quarterly plan goals. Any interpretation of the quarterly plan goals thus had to take these estimates of the commissariats and republics into account. Unfortunately, the estimates of seasonal fluctuations made by these agencies are practically unknown. Therefore, it is necessary to resort to general data on seasonal fluctuations.[23] An over-all study of this problem was made by B. Sukharevskii, whose results are reproduced in Table 57. Seasonal fluctuations seem to have had considerable effect on the meat, butter and cheese, fishing, logging, lumber, sugar, and brick industries. On the other hand, production was less disrupted in coal, cotton textiles, and agricultural machine-building. Seasonal fluctuations also seem small in electric power production, ferrous metals, chemicals, and machine-building.

Distribution of Planned Goals within the Year

Although seasonal fluctuations were of considerable importance in planning goals during the year, another element—"the struggle to overfulfill the plan"— seems to have been of paramount importance. In fact, comparing distribution of the principal indexes of economic activity during the year, the fourth quarter considerably exceeds the other quarters (see Table 58). This cannot be explained by seasonal fluctuations. The authorities tried to discourage feverish fourth-quarter activity in the course of which much output was produced solely to exceed the plan rather than to satisfy needs. During this time enterprises concentrated their efforts on "easy" output. But the authorities appear to have had little success in their endeavor. The planned targets for the first quarter of the year remained relatively less important, and they were not always fulfilled, particularly in construction.

Problems for Planners in Disturbances in the Plan

Lack of material prevents a systematic study of this problem. Still it was possible to collect data for one prewar year—1936—for which the quarterly plans and their relation to the annual plan could be presented for industrial branches and for a large number of industrial products. It should be noted that 1936 was one

---

22. *Ibid*.

23. On seasonal fluctuations, see my *Planning for Economic Growth in the Soviet Union, 1918–1932*, translated and edited by Marie-Christine MacAndrew and G. Warren Nutter, Chapel Hill, N.C., 1971, pp. 283–88.

Table 57 Seasonal Fluctuations in Soviet Industry, 1937

	Length of Production Cycle	Ratio of Minimum to Maximum Volume of Production (per cent)	Ratio of Minimum to Maximum Number of Workers Employed (per cent)
Agricultural machine-building	year-round	77.4[a]	95.0
Cement industry	year-round	65.5	95.7
Brick industry	40% of factories operating year-round	29.5	37.8
Meat industry	year-round	31.3	65.5
Slaughtering of beef cattle	year-round	12.3	
Slaughtering of pigs	year-round	36.1	
Butter and cheese industry	part of indus. year-round	13.7	64.3
Sugar industry:			
Granulated sugar	129.8 days		48.0[b]
Lump sugar	262.5 days		29.2[b]
Canned fruit and vegetables industry	68–126.7 days		68.5
Flour industry		63.4	88.9
Groats industry		39.1	47.3
Butter industry (*masloboinaia*)		34.8	67.1
Crude alcohol industry	242.6 days		
Fish catch	225.6 days	36.5	
Peat industry	about 120 days		
Logging		23.3	36.9
Lumber industry	year-round	41.6	84.7
Coal industry	year-round	87.2	88.5
Cotton industry	year-round	83.2	95.0

Source: B. Sukharevskii, "Ispolzovanie oborudovaniia v promyshlennosti SSSR i kapitalisticheskikh stran" [Utilization of Equipment in Industry in the USSR and Capitalist Countries], *Planovoe khoziaistvo*, No. 5, 1939, p. 64.

a. In 1938.
b. In 1936.

of the best prewar years, the one when rationing of consumer goods was almost entirely abolished and when industrial production continued its forward surge, despite a few difficulties in the fourth quarter.

The data collected are presented in Appendix F. Those in value terms in 1926/27 prices complement those in physical units but are often less detailed. It can be assumed that the defects of calculations in 1926/27 prices were less important within a single year.

The plan for the first quarter was certainly better fulfilled, although still far from satisfactorily, than the plans for the other quarters of 1936. Of the 82 series in physical units in Tables F-2 and F-4, plans for only 35 were fulfilled or over-fulfilled, plans for 34 were not fulfilled (10 of which had a fulfillment percentage lower than 90), and the results for the remaining 13 were not known. Among those that were not fulfilled were the plans for petroleum, oil shale, construction materials (cement, timber, window glass), some machinery (machine tools, blast furnace equipment, steam turbines, steam boilers, tractors, and grain combines), and several food products (flour, raw sugar, fish, meat).[24]

24. There was also a sizable failure in the nonferrous metal industry, estimated in value terms (see Tables F-1 and F-3).

Table 58   Quarterly Distribution of Industrial Production, Retail Trade, and Construction, 1932–1938 (per cent)

	First Quarter		Second Quarter		Third Quarter		Fourth Quarter	
	Planned	Actual	Planned	Actual	Planned	Actual	Planned	Actual
Industrial production								
(1926/27 prices)[a]								
1934		23.8						
1935		23.3						
1936	24.0	24.5	24.8	24.7	27.2	25.2	31.9	30.6
1937	23.7							
Machine-building								
1934		23.4		25.2		25.7		28.4
1935		24.1		25.9		27.1		32.7
1936	23.0	23.6	26.8	25.4	29.0	25.2	31.9	29.8
State and cooperative retail trade								
1932		23.2		23.9		24.2		28.7
1933		23.9		24.2		23.5		28.4
1934		22.8		24.4		25.1		27.7
1935		22.6		24.6		24.9		27.9
1936		23.8		25.0	25.5			
Investment								
1935[b]		16.6		21.8		25.0		36.6
1936	20.6	15.8	27.1	22.5	31.2	27.5	21.2	34.2
1937	19.0	16.6	28.8	26.3	29.5	26.4	22.8	30.7
1938	19.0	12.1	28.7		32.8			

Source

Industrial production: for 1934–1935, "Narodnoe khoziaistvo v I kvartale 1936" [The National Economy in the First Quarter of 1936], *Plan*, No. 9, 1936, p. 3; for 1936, Table F-1; for 1937, *Plan*, No. 1, 1937, p. 4.

Machine-building: for 1934–1935, *Narodno-khoziaistvennyi plan na 1936 god* [The National Economic Plan for 1936], Vol. I, 2nd ed., Moscow, 1936, p. 63; for 1936, Table F-1.

Retail trade: "Kritika i bibliografii" [Criticism and Bibliography], *Planovoe khoziaistvo*, No. 7, 1936, p. 225.

Construction: For 1935, E. Tulchinskii, "O planirovanii i vypolnenii finansovykh planov kapitalnogo stroitelstva" [On Drafting and Fulfilling the Financial Plans for Capital Construction], *Plan*, No. 8, 1936, p. 30; for 1936–1938, E. Vasilev, "Proizvoditelnost truda v stroitelstve" [Labor Productivity in Construction], *Planovoe khoziaistvo*, No. 8, 1938, p. 39.

a. USSR and local industry.
b. Construction under the jurisdiction of USSR agencies.

The plan for the second quarter of 1936 shows the reactions of the planners to these results. In some cases, such as in seasonal industries, it is impossible to evaluate this reaction without eliminating seasonal movements. In other cases, three distinct approaches on the part of the planners can be seen. First, in several cases, the planners tried to make up the losses sustained during the first quarter. The goals for the second quarter, then, were set at more than one-quarter of the annual plan goals (assuming that originally the annual plan goals were evenly distributed among quarters). This approach can be seen in the plans for railroad freight cars (28 and 29.6 per cent of the annual plan), equipment for presses and forges (27.4 per cent), steam boilers (26.9 per cent), tractors (26.7 and 27.2 per cent), petroleum, refined copper, cement, and railroad passenger cars.

Second, in certain cases, the government made no attempt to make up losses suffered in the first quarter but continued planning the amounts originally scheduled, or at least so it seems (grain combines, 25.2 per cent of the annual plan; steam locomotives, 25.3 per cent; and paper, 24.7 per cent).

Third, in still other cases, the planned goals for the second quarter show a reduction in the annual plan goals. This was the case for blast furnace equipment (15.6 per cent of the annual plan), generators for steam turbines (19.7 per cent), lumber (20.9 per cent), oil shale (21.4 per cent), and steam turbines (24.3 per cent). For this last product, only 42.3 per cent of the first-quarter plan was fulfilled (see Table F-4).

During the second quarter, the failures of the plan in industry were more numerous, with the plans for 39 series of the 82 not being fulfilled, for 25 series being fulfilled or overfulfilled, and for the remaining 18 not known. The planners then took a stronger stand. If seasonal products such as timber, alcohol, sugar, and meat are excluded, most of the goals for the third-quarter plan were set at between 24.7 and 34.8 per cent of the annual plan, this percentage being clearly higher than that for the second-quarter plan. In these cases, it is clear that the planners wanted to make up for the losses sustained during the first two quarters. But in other cases, such as machine-building, the annual plan goals were evidently abandoned. Thus, the shares of the third-quarter plans in the annual plan were only 17.7, 7.95, and 19.4 per cent for blast furnace equipment, open-hearth furnace equipment, and equipment for presses and forges, respectively, whereas only 86.5, 71.5, and 61.0 per cent of their respective plans for the second quarters were fulfilled (see Table F-4).

The results of the third quarter were even worse than those of the second quarter. Of the 68 series for which data could be found (see Tables F-2 and F-4), the plan was not fulfilled for 65 (for 10 of which fulfillment was less than 60 per cent) and was fulfilled or overfulfilled for only 3. Again the approach of the government was very firm, and the goals set for the fourth quarter were even more ambitious than those for the previous quarters, exceeding 30 per cent of the annual plan goals in 35 cases (including seasonal products such as sugar or meat). But to the list of cases where the annual plan goals were abandoned during the second and third quarters must be added rolling mill equipment and matches.

It seems, therefore, that in most cases in 1936 the government set very high goals without taking actual possibilities into account. There followed a very poor fulfillment of the quarterly plans, which got worse with every quarter, the last one being the very worst. The ties between the quarterly plans and the annual plan became weaker and weaker, and the "defense" of the annual plan goals was gradually tranformed into pressure on the economic agents reacting to the needs of the moment.

Fulfillment of Quarterly Plans

Lack of adequate data forces us to concentrate again on the quarterly plans for 1936. It should be noted, first, that fulfillment of the production plan for a particular product does not imply an absence of disturbances. Very often the statistics cover a group of products for which average plan fulfillment is given. Moreover, even when the plan is overfulfilled, certain consumers are more favored than others. Thus, in 1936, the 2 per cent overfulfillment of the plan for rolled steel production made it possible to deliver from 101.5 to 106.2 per cent of the planned stocks of iron of different categories to the Commissariat of Heavy Industry enterprises. But at the same time republic industries received only from 30 to 90 per cent of the planned amount of structural steel.[25]

It might be expected that a plan for the relatively short period of three months would be fulfilled better than an annual plan. But it is clear from Table F-4 that this was not the case in 1936. The government intended to defend the annual plan goals as much as possible in industry, and it did so at the expense of the precision of the quarterly plans. Thus, in most cases, the annual plan is better fulfilled than the quarterly plans. Nevertheless, this is not true for series where the annual plan goal was abandoned during the year. As the quarterly plans became more realistic, they could be fulfilled better. For certain seasonal products, the average fulfillment of the quarterly plans was higher than that of the annual plan (see Table F-4). But the unequal distribution of the annual production goals over the year makes it impossible to draw any firm conclusions. For meat, for example, the overfulfillment by 40.3 per cent of the second-quarter plan raises the average fulfillment of the quarterly plans. But the plan for the second quarter amounted only to some 9 per cent of the production planned for the whole year (see Table F-4).

Three conclusions can be drawn from these observations. First, the defense of the annual plan was not very effective. The plan was not fulfilled for several basic products, such as coal, petroleum, and industrial timber hauled, and was very poorly fulfilled for such consumer durables as bicycles, motorcycles, and radios. Some successes in the food industry were largely the result of production in the fourth quarter and were quite independent of the policy on quarterly plans. Second, government interference no doubt succeeded in protecting certain priority sectors, such as ferrous metals or machine-building, but it proved incapable of continuing the expansion of Soviet industry beyond 1936. The retardation in growth and the decline of certain key sectors, which had been protected in 1936, could not be stopped in 1937.

The quarterly plans became, during the course of the year, more and more "independent" of the annual plan. As the quarterly plan goals were set in reaction to economic circumstances and to the desire for an immediate equilibrium, they gradually lost the proportions laid out by the annual plan. The economy regulated *ad hoc* and centralized management thus took precedence over the central plan.

25. N. Gavrilov, "O nesoglasovannosti v planakh proizvodstva i snabzheniia" [On Lack of Coordination in Production and Supply Plans], *Plan*, No. 9, 1937, p. 19.

CHAPTER 13

Analysis of Fulfillment of Prewar Annual Plans

Problems in Analyzing Fulfillment of Annual Plans

In my earlier book the fulfillment of each annual plan was analyzed individually.[1] This procedure allows comparison of the economic situation for every year but leads to repetition. In this book the analysis of the annual plan as an element in economic development is presented in Part Two on long-term planning. In the comments that follow, therefore, I shall try to give only a synthesis of the results of the annual plans.

It must not be forgotten that there is a basic difference between five-year plans and annual plans in the prewar period (1933–1941). Since the long-term plans were never operational, a study of their "fulfillment" should be restricted to studying the quality of the forecasts.[2] The annual plans were, in principle, considered capable of being implemented. Their successive variants were transmitted all the way down to the enterprises, so it is possible to study in them the fulfillment of *decisions* rather than of *forecasts*.

The fact that annual plans actually represent empirical decisions makes it difficult to consider them as indexes of *performance*. In Soviet planning during this period, the circumstances in which the goals were set were often more important than the competence of the executors. In fact, the quality of the goals depended to a great extent on the atmosphere that surrounded their drafting. Pressure from managers was felt at all administrative levels; it impaired the accuracy of the basic data and favored the fulfillment of certain goals at the expense of others.

During the discussion of the five-year plans, it was found to be unwise to use aggregate indexes (such as value of gross industrial or agricultural production, total investment, or investment by branch) for analysis of plan fulfillment. It

1. See my *Planning for Economic Growth in the Soviet Union, 1918–1932*, translated and edited by Marie-Christine MacAndrew and G. Warren Nutter, Chapel Hill, N.C., 1971.

2. See Chapter 7, last section, and Chapter 9, section on 1940 annual plan and Third Five-Year Plan fulfillment.

now appears to be just as unwise to study the planned figures for an individual product in isolation. These figures fit into a context of longer-range goals (for three, five, or more years), which are very sensitive to changes in the economic situation, just as much as into a set of economic relations which it is artificial to try to separate.

Analysis of annual plan fulfillment raises several technical questions. The amount of data available is not the same for all the prewar annual plans. There are plans about which much is known (those for 1934–1937 and 1941), plans about which little is known (those for 1933 and 1938), and plans about which almost nothing is known (those for 1939 and 1940). This diversity makes it more difficult to draw conclusions, for, as the number of series studied increases, it becomes possible to enter areas less controlled or less controllable by the planners, where deviations from the plan may be more important.

A synthetic analysis of annual plans also has another drawback. Overfulfillments of plans tend to be compensated by underfulfillments. The average statistical results thus come close to the plan, whereas in fact the imbalances which these deviations have created are not necessarily eliminated.

Deviations from Goals in Annual Plans for 1933–1938[3]

An attempt to summarize the fulfillment of the annual plans for 1933–1938 is presented in Tables 59 and 60.[4] It is apparent at once that the degree of plan fulfillment cannot be conveyed by one single figure (for instance, the median fulfillment or the mean absolute deviation from 100 per cent fulfillment). A few comments on these tables may clarify the problem.

The range of average fulfillment of the annual plans for 1933–1937 for producer goods is between 130 and 30 per cent. The median is 92.2 per cent for the 53 series covered. The significance of the degree of plan fulfillment, however, varies importantly according to the nature of the product. For steel, pig iron, or electric power, even a slight deviation from the plan represents a considerable change. For machinery, locomotives, railroad cars, and generators, sizable deviations simply entail a delay in putting investments or a new plant into operation. In certain cases, fulfillment of an index (total motor vehicles) may result from the unequal development of its component parts (the production of trucks was favored and the production of automobiles was restrained).

For consumer goods, the range in the average fulfillment of the annual plans is just as great (between 50 and 164 per cent), but on the whole these plans seem to have been carried out a little better. This "better" fulfillment, however, is largely a question of the kind of product. While it may not be harmful to fulfill only 50 to 77 per cent of the plans for bicycles, phonographs, or radios, the same does not hold for such products as sugar, shoes, bread, soap, or butter. The

3. Of the three other prewar plans, the 1941 plan is known in detail, but the results reflected the exigencies of the war. Only fragments of the plans for 1939 and 1940 are known.

4. Few data are available on the 1938 plan (only 44 series out of those studied here), so it seemed preferable to present those results separately. Moreover, the average of the annual plans for 1933–1937 could be compared with the five-year plan for the same years.

Table 59   Fulfillment of Annual Plans for 1933–1937[a] (per cent)

	Average Fulfillment of Annual Plans		Per Cent of Fulfillment of Second Five-Year Plan, 1933–1937
	Years Covered (1)	Per Cent (2)	(3)
Industry			
Producer Goods			
Caustic soda	1933, 1936–1937	104.5	46.2
Trucks	1933–1937	104.3	128.8
Tractors (units)	1933–1937	103.7	57.6
Synthetic dyes	1933–1937	103.4	
Lime	1934–1937	103.1	99.4
Electric power, total	1933–1937	101.7	95.2
Motor vehicles, total	1933–1937	101.1	99.9
Soda ash	1933–1937	100.9	75.5
Phosphoric fertilizer (18.7% P_2O_5)	1933–1937	100.8	65.6
Tractors (15 hp)	1933–1937	99.1	39.9
Phosphoric fertilizer (14% P_2O_5)	1933–1937	98.1	65.4
Machine tools	1934–1937	97.7	90.3
Hydroelectric power	1934–1937	97.0	72.1
Rolled steel	1933–1937	96.4	99.7
Coke	1933–1937	95.6	94.0
Tires	1934–1937	95.0	89.9
Paper	1933–1937	94.7	83.2
Pig iron	1933–1937	94.6	90.5
Steel ingots and castings	1933–1937	94.6	104.3
Manganese ore	1933–1937	94.5	101.9
Peat	1933–1937	94.5	96.2
Aluminum	1934–1937	93.5	47.1
Coal	1933–1937	93.0	83.9
Sulfuric acid	1933–1937	92.8	65.8
Iron ore	1933–1937	92.0	81.7
Lumber	1933–1937	90.9	70.4
Crude petroleum	1933–1937	90.9	64.3
Natural gas	1934–1937	90.7	79.2
Bricks	1934–1937	89.7	108.3
Zinc	1933–1937	88.9	85.0
Steam locomotives	1933–1937	88.5	51.6
Window glass (m²)	1933–1937	88.5	97.4
Asbestos shingles	1934–1937	87.3	85.0
Industrial timber hauled	1933–1937	85.4	67.2
Steel pipes	1933–1937	85.2	83.9
Railroad passenger cars	1933–1937	84.6	26.1
Refined copper	1933–1937	83.3	72.2
Automobiles	1933–1937	82.0	30.3
Cement	1933–1937	81.4	72.7
Ground natural phosphate	1934–1937	80.1	29.5
Railroad freight cars	1934–1937	79.0	49.7
Excavators	1934–1937	78.6	
Grain combines	1933–1937	78.1	219.5
Railroad freight cars (2-axle units)	1933–1937	74.0	49.8
Lead	1933–1937	71.0	54.2
Turbogenerators	1933–1937	70.3	44.7
Steam boilers	1933–1937	69.5	44.3
Roofing tiles	1934–1937	66.6	54.0
Spinning machines	1934–1937	65.5	13.6
Electric locomotives	1934–1937	63.4	21.3

Table 59   *continued*

	Average Fulfillment of Annual Plans		Per Cent of Fulfillment of Second Five-Year Plan, 1933–1937
	Years Covered (1)	*Per Cent* (2)	(3)
Steam and gas turbines	1933–1937	63.3	82.2
Oil shale	1933–1937	54.9	19.8
Diesel locomotives	1934–1937	30.1	3.6
Consumer Goods			
Knitted outer garments	1934–1937	144.6	
Sausages	1933, 1935–1937	135.9	
Beer	1934–1937	109.0	119.5
Bread and breadstuffs	1935–1937	108.4	182.2
Cameras	1934–1937	106.3	100.9
Woolen fabrics	1933–1937	105.7	49.2
Cotton yarn	1934–1937	104.0	87.2
Leather shoes	1933–1937	103.4	95.8
Enameled kitchenware	1934–1937	102.1	
Silk and rayon fabrics	1933–1937	102.0	92.0
Butter	1934–1937	101.5	102.8
Starch and syrup	1933–1937	101.0	
Flour (procurements)	1933–1937	99.9	99.4
Cheese	1933–1937	99.4	83.8
Metal beds	1934–1937	99.2	
Low-grade tobacco (*makhorka*)	1933–1937	98.1	89.1
Meat	1933–1937	97.9	67.7
Raw sugar	1933–1937	97.4	96.8
Rubber footwear	1933–1937	97.3	84.6
Knitted underwear	1935–1937	96.7	111.5
Margarine	1933–1937	96.7	61.7
Soap (40% fatty acid)	1934–1937	96.6	49.5
Fish catch	1934–1937	96.5	89.4
Salt	1933–1937	94.8	53.3
Crude alcohol	1933–1937	94.5	102.3
Vegetable oil	1933–1937	94.3	66.0
Cigarettes	1933–1937	93.9	71.4
Cotton fabrics	1933–1937	93.8	67.6
Sewing machines	1934–1937	93.7	113.4
Rubber galoshes	1934–1937	93.3	
Felt footwear	1934–1937	93.0	83.7
Confectionery	1933–1937	90.8	68.2
Hosiery	1933–1937	88.2	40.9
Canned food	1933–1937	87.8	49.1
Matches	1933–1937	87.1	59.7
Linen fabrics (m²)	1933–1936	86.0	42.3
Macaroni	1933–1937	78.0	51.7
Bicycles	1934–1937	77.1	94.0
Phonographs	1934–1937	59.3	45.1
Radios	1934–1937	50.4	40.0
Agriculture			
Harvests[b] *and Animal Production*			
Wheat	1934, 1935, 1937	103.7	123.7
Raw cotton	1933–1937	103.5	121.5
Barley	1934, 1935, 1937	103.3	126.3
Oats	1934–1937	100.5	121.1
Wool	1934–1937	100.5	66.4
Meat and fat	1934–1937	100.0	46.6

Table 59   *continued*

	Average Fulfillment of Annual Plans		Per Cent of Fulfillment of Second Five-Year Plan, 1933–1937
	Years Covered (1)	Per Cent (2)	(3)
Grain, total	1933–1937	99.0	114.8
Milk	1934–1937	94.1	80.4
Sunflowers	1933–1937	84.1	61.2
Flax fiber	1933–1937	83.6	70.6
Sugar beets	1933–1937	83.4	79.2
Corn	1934–1937	81.5	64.8
Potatoes	1934–1937	81.5	89.9
Transportation			
Railroad			
Average length of haul, total traffic	1933–1937	103.1	108.5
Grain and flour	1933–1937	102.6	121.6
Ore (tons)	1933–1937	100.8	113.0
Total freight traffic (ton-km)	1933–1937	100.1	118.3
Ferrous metals (tons)	1933–1937	97.5	113.9
Total freight traffic (tons)	1933–1937	97.1	108.9
Firewood (tons)	1933–1937	96.7	101.6
Average daily carloadings	1933–1937	96.5	113.7
Coal and coke (tons)	1933–1937	95.7	93.3
Timber (tons)	1933–1937	93.8	104.2
Passenger traffic (pass.-km)	1933–1935, 1937	92.3	82.6
Oil and oil products (tons)	1933–1937	90.9	77.2
Principal construction materials (tons)	1933–1936	90.8	103.8
Inland Waterway			
Mineral construction materials (tons)	1934–1937	98.6	104.0
Length of network	1934–1937	94.3	100.1
Salt (tons)	1934–1937	91.9	100.0
Total freight traffic (tons)	1933–1937	90.5	74.3
Grain and flour (tons)	1934–1937	90.1	67.4
Average length of haul, total traffic	1934–1937	89.0	71.4
Oil and oil products (tons)	1934–1937	88.2	44.9
Coal and coke (tons)	1934–1937	83.5	59.9
Total freight traffic (ton-km)	1933–1937	81.5	52.5
Passenger traffic (pass.-km)	1934–1937	79.5	43.2
Maritime [c]			
Passenger traffic (pass.-km)	1934–1937	100.0	60.7
Average length of haul	1933–1937	94.7	98.6
Total freight traffic (tons)	1933, 1934, 1936, 1937	90.2	73.5
Total freight traffic (ton-km)	1933–1937	87.0	72.2
Air			
Passenger traffic (pass.)	1934–1937	112.3	35.3
Total freight traffic (ton-km)	1933–1937	94.4	20.7
Employment			
Public health	1934–1937	105.7	109.6
Education	1934–1937	105.0	111.5
Administration	1934–1937	104.3	118.6
Other transport (motor, etc.)	1934–1937	103.2	124.1
Trade, procurements, and supply	1933–1937	103.0	87.3
Industry	1933–1937	102.4	99.1
National economy, excl. collective farms	1933–1937	102.0	93.4

Table 59   *continued*

	Average Fulfillment of Annual Plans		Per Cent of Fulfillment of Second Five-Year Plan, 1933–1937
	Years Covered (1)	Per Cent (2)	(3)
Construction	1933–1937	101.0	59.1
Communications	1933–1937	99.1	111.6
Railroad transport	1933–1937	99.0	90.8
Maritime and inland waterway transport	1933–1937	96.7	78.3
State-owned agriculture	1934–1937	95.8	69.5
Public eating places	1933–1937	91.9	46.0
Wages			
Wage Fund			
National economy, excl. collective farms	1933–1937	111.8	162.1
Industry	1933–1937	109.2	167.4
Average Annual Money Wage			
Construction	1934–1937	116.6	172.1
Administration	1934–1937	111.8	166.3
Education	1934–1937	111.4	175.6
Public eating places	1934–1937	110.6	170.4
Trade	1934–1937	110.4	164.9
State-owned agriculture	1934–1937	109.7	163.3
National economy, excl. collective farms	1933–1937	108.6	173.6
Railroad transport	1933–1937	107.5	176.0
Industry, workers and employees	1933–1937	106.3	168.9
Maritime and inland waterway transport	1933–1937	105.5	171.8
Public health	1934–1937	102.8	157.4
Housing			
Housing fund, urban, total	1934–1937	98.1	84.1
Retail Trade			
State and cooperative, total, current prices	1933–1937	101.9	139.9

Source: Unless otherwise indicated, col. 2: arithmetic average of fulfillment percentages in Table A-2, cols. 3, 6, 9, 12, and 15; col. 3: Table A-1, col. 3.

a. Only series for which data were available for at least three years were included.

b. The actual harvest figures are for biological yields, which are considerably overestimated, but the plans were similarly overestimated. For details, see Tables A-1 and A-2.

c. In Soviet ships only.

failure represented by the 90.5 per cent fulfillment of the annual plans for meat (excluding subproducts, which raise the percentage tremendously and artificially) is much more serious than that corresponding to the 50.5 per cent fulfillment of the plans for radios.

In railroad transportation, too, relatively slight deviations from the plan have a considerable effect. Only 96.5 per cent of the plan for average daily carloadings (perhaps the most representative index) was fulfilled, a sizable underfulfillment. In railroad transportation, the objective was to increase hauled tonnage to the maximum and to reduce the length of haul by means of a better regional distribution of freight traffic. The results were just the reverse. The plan for average length of haul was exceeded, while the plan for total traffic in tons was not realized. In inland waterway, maritime, and air transportation, on the other hand, an increase in length of haul was desired. Here, too, the results were the opposite of the goals: the length of haul was less than planned.

The "fulfillment" of the plans for employment and money wages does not have the same significance as for production. Employment is a cost that the planners try to minimize. Hence "overfulfilling" the plan is a counterperformance, especially in the annual plans where the current economic situation is already taken into account. And this is the meaning of the "overfulfillment" of the annual plans for employment in 1933–1937. The planners tried to restrain inflation by minimizing money wage increases. Table 59 shows that they did not succeed; the 8.5 per cent average overfulfillment of the plan for money wages during 1933–1937 was responsible for a large part of the prewar inflation.

The average percentages of fulfillment of the plans for housing and for state and cooperative retail trade given in Table 59 show the inadequacy of presenting overaggregated statistics. In housing, annual construction obviously represented a small share in the total housing stock, so construction failures could not have a large effect on the stock. In 1929/30, for instance, 100.5 per cent of the annual plan for the housing stock was fulfilled, and only 66.7 per cent of the plan for housing construction was fulfilled. In 1933, only 60 per cent of the housing construction plan was fulfilled, but no data on the housing stock are available for that year. Hence it can be assumed that the 98.1 per cent average fulfillment of the housing stock plans for 1934–1937 was accompanied by a considerable underfulfillment of the housing construction plans.

For state and cooperative retail trade, the 101.9 per cent average fulfillment of the annual plans for 1933–1937 is very low in view of the facts that the official retail price index (1940 weights) increased by 110 per cent between 1932 and 1937[5] and that the largest part of this increase was not included in the annual plans.

Table 59 also makes it possible to compare the fulfillment of the annual plans for 1933–1937 with the fulfillment of the five-year plan for the same period. The first conclusion is the same as the one already made in Part Two in studying five-year plans. The distribution of the percentages of fulfillment of the five-year

5. A. N. Malafeev, *Istoriia tsenoobrazovaniia v SSSR, 1917–1963 gg.* [History of Pricing in the USSR, 1917–1963], Moscow, 1964, p. 407.

plan for 1933–1937 does not correspond at all to that of the fulfillment of the annual plans, and the coefficient of correlation is weak. Some particularly sizable differences show that substantial changes took place in certain five-year plan goals. Moreover, a high correlation between the average fulfillment of the annual plans and of the five-year plan in 1937 in no way implies that the latter was actually followed.

For manganese ore, for instance, average fulfillment of the annual plans for 1933–1937 was 99.9 per cent and fulfillment of the five-year plan in 1937 was 101.9 per cent. But only the 1934 plan followed the goals of the five-year plan.[6] The other annual plans exceeded these goals: by 20 per cent in 1935, 21.7 per cent in 1936, and 18.5 per cent in 1937. Annual plan fulfillments were 107.1 per cent in 1934, 99.4 per cent in 1935, 107.1 per cent in 1936, and 86.0 per cent in 1937.[7] Fulfillment of the annual plans thus in no way resembled the fulfillment of the five-year plan. Many more examples of such a lack of correspondence could be cited.

The fulfillment of the 1938 annual plan is presented separately in Table 60. It is interesting to note that the percentages of plan fulfillment were low for producer goods (from 71.0 to 97.2 per cent), which reflects the deceleration of industrial growth rates that started that year. The percentages of plan fulfillment for consumer goods were very close to those for 1933–1937. It is also interesting to observe that inflationary pressure was weaker—the wage fund plan was exceeded by only 2.6 per cent. Only 99.6 per cent of the plan for state and cooperative retail trade in current prices was fulfilled because of the almost complete stabilization of consumer goods prices in 1938. Hence there is no doubt that the plan for retail trade was actually fulfilled much better in 1938 than in 1933–1937 when the plans were overfulfilled (by 1.9 per cent for the annual plans and 39.9 per cent for the five-year plan) in an inflationary period.

Despite the fact that no more than a relative significance should be attached to the statistics on the average fulfillment of annual plans, the results of such a calculation are presented in Table 61. The median fulfillment of the annual plans for 1933–1937 seems to be much better than that of the Second Five-Year Plan, with the largest differences between the two in heavy industry (90.4 for the average for the 1933–1937 annual plans and 72.1 per cent for the Second Five-Year Plan), food and light industry (95.1 and 83.7 per cent), and money wage (105.4 and 167.5 per cent). The same holds for agricultural production and employment. On the other hand, fulfillment of the five-year plan was better for transportation.

These data are supplemented by the mean absolute deviation from 100 per cent fulfillment of the goals set (see Table 62). Although suffering from the same drawbacks as the percentages of plan fulfillment, the data on mean deviation nevertheless bring out the extent to which the general structure of the economy differed from the planners' vision of future development.

The deviation for the Second Five-Year Plan is particularly striking. For the 12

6. The 1934 annual plan was actually an annual slice of the final variant of the five-year plan for 1933–1937, published in November 1934. On this point, see end of Chapter 6.
7. Table A-2.

Table 60   Fulfillment of 1938 Annual Plan (per cent)

Industry			
Total value of production (1926/27 prices)	95.6	Starch and syrup	110.5
		Margarine	109.4
Producer Goods		Soap (40% fatty acid)	108.2
Sulfuric acid	97.2	Knitted outer garments	105.5
Crude petroleum	95.8	Macaroni	105.5
Machine tools	95.7	Beer	105.2
Electric power	95.5	Bread and breadstuffs (ministries and	
Paper	90.5	local Soviets)	104.2
Phosphoric fertilizer (18.7% P_2O_5)	90.3	Low-grade tobacco (*makhorka*)	100.0
Pig iron	89.9	Sugar, lump	98.9[b]
Lead	89.4	Leather shoes	96.2
Steel ingots and castings	89.0	Fish catch	94.6
Plywood	88.8	Raw sugar	93.3
Soda ash	88.5	Cheese	92.4
Ammonium sulfate	88.4	Hosiery	87.6
Rolled steel	87.8	Cotton fabrics	85.7
Coal	86.6	Canned food	73.6
Iron ore	83.1		
Cement	80.7	**Railroad Transportation**	
Industrial timber hauled	75.0	Average length of haul, total freight	
Refined copper	74.0	traffic	103.3
Electrolytic copper	73.3[a]	Total freight traffic (ton-km)	93.8
Manganese ore	71.0	Average daily carloadings	92.6
		Total freight traffic (tons)	90.9
Consumer Goods			
Meat	126.7	**Wages**	
Sausages	119.7	Average money wage, industry	103.9
Vegetable oil	119.1	Wage fund, national economy, excl.	
Confectionery	111.6	collective farms	102.6
Butter	110.6	Wage fund, industry	99.0
		Retail Trade	
		State and cooperative in current prices	99.6

Source: Table A-3, col. 3, unless otherwise indicated.

a. Calculated from annual plan goal (derived as 133.5 th. m. tons from 1937 output in *Statistical Abstract of Industrial Output in the Soviet Union, 1913–1955*, New York, 1956, series 206.6, and increase planned for 1938 given in A. Zelenovskii, ''Promyshlennost v pervom godu tretei piatiletki'' [Industry in the First Year of the Third Five-Year Plan], *Planovoe khoziaistvo*, No. 5, 1938, p. 21) and 1938 results (given in *Sotsialisticheskoe stroitelstvo Soiuza SSR, 1933–1938* [Socialist Construction in the USSR for 1933–1938], Moscow-Leningrad, 1939).

b. Calculated from annual plan goal (given in *Statistical Abstract*, series 1117.3) and 1938 results (given in *Promyshlennost SSSR* [Industry of the USSR], Moscow, 1957, p. 373).

basic groups given in the table,[8] the average deviation for the annual plans for 1933–1937 is 10.8 percentage points, whereas it is 34.5 for the five-year plan for the same years. A similar deviation exists for all the groups except money wage; in that case, the average deviation for the annual plans is only 7.9 percentage points, but 66.5 points for the five-year plan.

For the five separate annual plans, the average deviation is similar for most groups, ranging from 6.9 to 16.4 percentage points. The exception is machine-building, where the deviation averaged 25.3 varying between 20.5 and 31.2

8. Excluding the total and subtotals. The data on housing and retail trade were not included in Table 62 because they were too aggregated.

Table 61 Median Fulfillment of Annual Plans for 1933–1938 (per cent)

	Annual Plans					Average for Annual Plans, 1933–1937	Second Five-Year Plan, 1933–1937	Annual Plan 1938
	1933 (1)	1934 (2)	1935 (3)	1936 (4)	1937 (5)	(6)	(7)	(8)
1. Heavy industry (producer goods)	81.4	95.4	100.8	92.1	82.2	90.4	72.1	88.8
2. Food and light industry (consumer goods)	88.9	92.7	103.3	99.1	91.3	95.1	83.7	105.3
3. Transportation	89.4	89.7	101.7	96.9	91.5	93.8	97.9	92.6
4. Agriculture	90.3	93.3	101.2	87.0	88.6	92.1	81.8	
5. Employment	98.7	101.2	104.5	98.9	100.9	100.8	96.3	95.3
6. Money wage	102.3	109.4	104.9	109.3	100.9	105.4	167.5	105.9
Number of series included	112	179	185	185	173		197	47

Source: Cols. 1–5: median of percentage fulfillments in Table A-2, cols. 3, 6, 9, 12, and 15; col. 6: arithmetic average of cols. 1–5; col. 7: median of percentage fulfillments in Table A-1, col. 3; col. 8: median of percentage fulfillments in Table A-3, col. 3. Cols. 1–5 and 7–8 cover the series listed below when available.

Line 1: series 5–65. Line 2: series 66–109. Line 3: series 149–85. Line 4: series 113–48. Line 5: series 186–200. Line 6: series 203 and 205–26.

percentage points. This is consistent with the view that machine-building, with a multitude of new factories under construction and with a large number of new products, did not lend itself to precise planning during the prewar years.

A comparison of the deviations from 100 per cent fulfillment of the annual plans for the different years brings out a great stability on the whole—from 9.2 to 12.3 percentage points. As could be expected, 1935, the year with the greatest expansion, had the smallest deviation and 1936 had the largest.[9] But, in all cases, it would be difficult to impute the difference in deviations solely to successes and failures in planning; many economic factors, as well as the peculiarities of individual sectors, must be taken into account.

Goals and Results of Prewar Annual Plans

In this work and particularly in the study of five-year plans, it seemed useful to compare the fulfillment of the goals representing results for outputs (consumer goods, real wages, investment) with the fulfillment of the goals representing costs (raw materials and electric power, transportation, employment, money wages). Such a comparison is not possible for the prewar plans, mainly because several price series are lacking. For this reason, only a rough and ready analysis could be made, based on comparison of plans and results for the principal economic goals (Table 63).

In the analysis of the results of the five-year plans, the aggregate series on

9. Had the number of series studied been the same, the deviation between goals and fulfillment would most likely have been the greatest in 1938.

national income, industrial production, etc., did not yield a true picture because of price distortions. However, the results of the annual plans were not so seriously affected by price distortions. Excesses of actual over planned costs can be seen in the series shown in Table 63. The actual cost of industrial production (which includes unplanned price increases) was higher than planned cost in every year. This result is not unexpected in view of the constant exceeding of employment and wage plans. The official Soviet statistics also show that in most cases the plan for industrial labor productivity was not fulfilled.

Poor results—actually even poorer than they at first appear, since they were obtained with higher costs—are evident for national income as well as for industrial and agricultural production. It is interesting to note, in this connection, that, except for 1936, Western estimates correspond quite well with the official Soviet estimates. Since there was a sizable increase in industrial prices and a very bad harvest in 1936, the lower estimates made in the West seem more probable. In any case, except for the very good year of 1935, national income was from 3 to 9 per cent lower than planned in the annual goals, which is an enormous discrepancy for an aggregate index.

The lack of data on the annual plans for 1939 and 1940 and the interruption of the 1941 annual plan make it impossible to find out whether the quality of annual plans improved after 1938. With the war (1941–1945) and the period of reconstruction (1946–1952), the Soviet Union entered a new phase of its economic history, during which it turned toward a new kind of planning.

Table 62   Mean Absolute Deviation from 100 Per Cent Fulfillment of Annual Plans for 1933–1938
(percentage points)

	Annual Plans					Average for Annual Plans, 1933–1937	Second Five-Year Plan, 1933–1937	Annual Plan 1938
	1933 (1)	1934 (2)	1935 (3)	1936 (4)	1937 (5)	(6)	(7)	(8)
1. Industry, total	16.1	15.5	11.7	11.9	16.9	14.4	30.5	10.4
2. Heavy industry	20.7	14.2	11.3	12.4	20.8	15.9	32.0	10.7
3. Fuel and power	21.9	12.0	7.2	10.7	13.5	13.1	24.4	7.4
4. Ferrous and nonferrous metals	27.9	8.4	8.1	9.0	18.0	14.3	19.2	16.5
5. Machine-building	20.5	25.6	22.9	26.4	31.2	25.3	57.3	4.3[a]
6. Chemicals	8.9	12.1	12.8	8.5	18.0	12.1	39.0	8.9
7. Construction materials	24.2	12.8	5.5	7.6	23.3	14.7	20.0	16.3
8. Light and food industry	11.4	16.7	12.0	11.5	13.1	12.9	28.9	10.1
9. Light industry	5.7	24.5	14.1	12.9	16.3	14.7	28.4	9.0
10. Food industry	17.1	8.9	14.6	10.1	10.0	12.1	29.5	11.1
11. Agricultural production	11.3	7.8	9.3	19.6	17.7	13.1	29.9	
12. Harvests	11.3	12.2	10.1	31.5	16.8	16.4	23.4	
13. Animal production		3.4	8.6	7.7	18.7	9.6	36.3	
14. Transportation	11.3	12.6	10.5	11.4	11.7	11.5	24.3	7.3
15. Employment	10.4	6.4	6.9	6.6	4.4	6.9	21.1	4.7[a]
16. Money wage	2.8	11.2	7.6	12.0	5.7	7.9	66.5	5.9
17. All groups	10.4	10.7	9.2	12.3	11.3	10.8	34.5	7.1
Number of series included	101	170	172	174	171		180	46

Table 62   *continued*

Source: Lines 3–7, 9–10, 12–13, and 14–16, cols. 1–5: unweighted arithmetic mean of absolute deviations from 100 of the percentage fulfillments in Table A-2, cols. 3, 6, 9, 12, and 15; col. 6: arithmetic mean of cols. 1–5; col. 7: Table 27, col. 2; and col. 8: unweighted arithmetic mean of absolute deviations from 100 of the percentage fulfillments in Table A-3, col. 3. Lines 1, 2, 8, 11, and 17: derived as explained below. Covers series indicated below when available.

Line 1: unweighted arithmetic mean of lines 2 and 8. **Line 2:** unweighted arithmetic mean of lines 3–7. **Line 3:** series 5–12. **Line 4:** series 13–23. **Line 5:** series 46–65. **Line 6:** series 24–34a. **Line 7:** series 35–45. **Line 8:** unweighted arithmetic mean of lines 9 and 10. **Line 9:** series 66–87. **Line 10:** series 88–109. **Line 11:** unweighted arithmetic mean of lines 12 and 13. **Line 12:** series 113–24. **Line 13:** series 125–28. **Line 14:** series 149–85. **Line 15:** series 186–200. **Line 16:** series 203 and 205–26. **Line 17:** unweighted arithmetic mean of lines 1, 11, and 14–16.

a. Rough estimate.

Table 63   Fulfillment of Principal Goals of Annual Plans for 1933–1938 (per cent)

	1933	1934	1935	1936	1937	1938
National Income						
1. Official Soviet estimate (1926/27 prices)	95.1	92.7	103.7	103.5	91.3	
2. Based on Moorsteen and Powell estimates	92.9	88.5	99.6	87.0	89.7	
Industrial Production						
3. Official Soviet estimate (1926/27 prices)	91.3	97.8	106.9	105.8	92.7	95.6
4. Based on Nutter index	91.5	98.7	103.3	96.3	88.4	90.0
Agricultural Production						
5. Official Soviet estimate (1926/27 prices)		93.5	93.8			
6. Official Soviet estimate ("comparable" prices)		94.3	95.0	75.3		
7. Based on Johnson and Kahan index		90.3	95.0	77.3	96.5	
Industrial Labor Productivity						
8. Official Soviet estimate	95.4	97.5	101.8	101.2	91.1	98.7
9. Based on Galenson index	96.0	98.2	97.6–100.4			
Cost of Industrial Production						
Official Soviet estimates ("comparable" prices):						
10. Without allowance for price changes	104.8	101.2	99.8	102.7	103.5	103.8
11. With allowance for price changes		104.9		113.4	105.2	105.0
Employment (official Soviet estimates)						
12. Workers and employees, national economy	104.7	100.9	101.2	100.4	102.7	
13. Workers and employees, industry	95.9	107.7	103.3	102.8	102.1	95.3
Wages (official Soviet estimates)						
14. Wage fund, national economy, excl. collective farms	113.4	115.4	112.8	112.6	105.0	102.6
15. Wage fund, industry	98.9	117.9	110.9	112.7	105.5	99.0
16. Average money wage, national economy, excl. collective farms	102.8	114.3	111.1	112.4	102.4	
17. Average money wage, industry	102.0	109.3	107.3	109.7	103.3	103.9

Source: Lines 1, 3, 5, 12-17: Table A-2, cols. 3, 6, 9, 12, and 15, and Table A-3, col. 3; line 2: derived from Moorsteen and Powell annual indexes of gross national product (calculated from ruble figures in their *The Soviet Capital Stock, 1928–1962*, Homewood, Ill., 1966, pp. 622–23) and official Soviet planned annual indexes (calculated from Tables A-2 and A-3); line 4: derived from Nutter's annual indexes of all civilian products excluding miscellaneous machinery (calculated from ruble figures in his *Growth of Industrial Production in the Soviet Union*, Princeton, 1962, p. 525) and official Soviet planned annual indexes (calculated from Tables A-2 and A-3); line 6: derived from revised official Soviet annual indexes for gross agricultural production (given in *Narodnoe khoziaistvo SSSR v 1958 godu* [The USSR National Economy in 1958], Moscow, 1959, p. 350) and official Soviet planned annual indexes

Table 63 *continued*

(calculated from Table A-2); line 7: derived from Johnson and Kahan annual indexes of gross agricultural output in 1926/27 prices (calculated from D. Gale Johnson and Arcadius Kahan, "Soviet Agriculture: Structure and Growth," *Comparisons of the United States and Soviet Economies*, Joint Economic Committee, U.S. Congress, Washington, 1959, Part I, p. 204) and official Soviet planned annual indexes (calculated from Table A-2, except for 1937, where plan was assumed to be 130 per cent of 1936, as was the grain harvest total); line 8: derived from official Soviet annual indexes for labor productivity in large-scale industry (given in *Socialist Construction in the U.S.S.R.* [translated from the Russian], Moscow, 1936, p. 25, for 1933–1934 and in Walter Galenson, *Labor Productivity in Soviet and American Industry*, New York, 1955, p. 15, for 1935–1938) and official Soviet planned annual indexes (given in Table 47, line 5, for 1933–1937 and in Zelenovskii, *Planovoe khoziaistvo*, No. 5, 1938, p. 21, for 1938); line 9: derived from Galenson's index of labor productivity (*ibid.* p. 17) and official Soviet planned annual indexes (given in Table 47, line 5); lines 10-11: derived from actual changes in costs with and without allowance for price changes (given in Malafeev, *Istoriia*, p. 406, except for 1934 which was taken from *Narodno-khoziaistvennyi plan na 1935 god* [The National Economic Plan for 1935], 2nd ed., Moscow, 1935, p. 352) and planned reduction in costs (Table 47, line 13); for 1935, there was a planned increase in costs of 21.2 per cent, taking into account the price increases of December 7 and 16, 1934 (*Plan 1935*, 2nd ed., p. 658); since these official estimates are in "comparable" prices and hence cover only "comparable" production and exclude new products (which accounted for an increasingly large share in total costs), they do not reflect the actual changes in costs; also, whenever the plan for a reduction in costs was *not* fulfilled, it shows up in the table as an "overfulfillment" of the plan since it means that the costs were higher than planned.

PART FOUR

Wartime Planning, 1941–1945

CHAPTER 14

Economic Plans during the War

Introduction of a War Economy

War Economy

The introduction of a war economy that followed the outbreak of hostilities with Germany on June 22, 1941, entailed a number of changes. Extraordinary legislation was adopted for wartime and for training new administrative personnel. Specific plans were introduced to meet the needs of the armed forces, and the nature and scope of traditional plans were modified. Human and material resources were mobilized to stimulate the war effort. Finally, more frequent recourse was had to the practices of a regulated market economy (*économie dirigée*) in order to supplement the system of economic plans and attempt to balance supply and demand.

This new system was not decreed in one stroke but was introduced by several government decisions, often taken on pragmatic grounds. The first of these was the June 22, 1941, decree of the presidium of the Supreme Soviet, "On the State of War,"[1] which established principles for mobilizing human and material resources and means of transportation to serve the armed forces, authorized local government agencies to introduce rationing, required them to give assistance to the armed forces, and prescribed necessary sanctions. Another special decree of the Supreme Soviet presidium, issued on June 26,[2] authorized enterprise managers to lengthen the working day by one to three hours and suspended all annual leave. Still other principles of a war economy were set forth in June 22 and 29 declarations of the government and the Party and in a July 3 radio speech made by Stalin as chairman of the Council of People's Commissars.[3]

1. *Direktivy KPSS i sovetskogo pravitelstva po khoziaistvennym voprosam* [Directives of the Communist Party of the Soviet Union and of the Soviet Government on Economic Matters], Moscow, 1957, Vol. 2, pp. 700–702.
2. "On the Working Time of Workers and Employees during Wartime," *ibid.*, Vol. 2, pp. 702–3.
3. G. S. Kravchenko, *Voennaia ekonomika SSSR, 1941–1945* [The Wartime Economy of the USSR, 1941–1945], Moscow, 1963, pp. 86–87.

Wartime Administration

Strictly speaking, there was no administrative reorganization after the introduction of the war economy. New agencies were usually superimposed on existing ones, and in a few cases new people's commissariats were created.

The most important agency created immediately after the beginning of the war was the State Committee for Defense (*Gosudarstvennyi Komitet Oborony*),[4] which was headed by Stalin. The full powers of the Party, the government, and the armed forces were drawn together in this committee. Some influential *ad hoc* committees were also created, the most important being the Evacuation Committee, set up on June 24, 1941, and headed by N. V. Shvernik, with A. N. Kosygin and M. G. Pervukhin as deputy chairmen.[5] This committee was replaced on December 25, 1941, by a committee chaired by A. I. Mikoyan, which was to handle freight remaining on the railroads.[6] Later, on June 22, 1942, after new advances by the German armies, an Evacuation Commission was set up, with Shvernik as chairman and Mikoyan and Kosygin as deputy chairmen.[7] Still another committee, headed by Mikoyan, was organized on October 25, 1941, for the purpose of evacuating food supplies, industrial products, and light industry equipment from the areas close to the front.[8] This committee was probably dissolved at the same time as the first Evacuation Committee, on December 25, 1941, to be replaced by the new committee headed by Mikoyan.

It should be noted that at the beginning of the war the Council of People's Commissars itself was split up, and a decree of October 25, 1941, authorized Council Deputy Chairman N. A. Voznesenskii to represent the Council in Kuibyshev and to direct the production of industries evacuated to the east, especially the production of planes, tanks, armaments, munitions, and ferrous metal enterprises.[9]

Other special committees or commissions with extraordinary powers, superimposed in some way on existing agencies, were also organized. These included the special commission, under USSR Gosplan Chairman Voznesenskii, that was entrusted on July 9, 1941, with drafting the wartime economic plan (a task that ordinarily fell to Gosplan);[10] the Transportation Committee under the State Commmittee for Defense, headed by Stalin, with A. A. Andreev as deputy chairman;[11] the Committee for the Registration and Allocation of Manpower;[12] and the USSR Academy of Sciences commission for mobilizing the resources of the Urals for defense needs, which was created in Sverdlovsk in August 1941.[13]

4. *Direktivy*, Vol. 2, p. 703.

5. *Istoriia Velikoi Otechestvennoi Voiny* [History of the Great Patriotic War], Moscow, 1960–1963, Vol. 2, pp. 143 and 148. G. I. Shigalin, *Narodnoe khoziaistvo SSSR v period velikoi otechestvennoi voiny* [The USSR National Economy during the Great Patriotic War], Moscow, 1960, pp. 48–49.

6. *Istoriia*, Vol. 2, p. 148.

7. *Ibid.*, Vol. 2, p. 501.

8. *Ibid.*, Vol. 2, p. 148.

9. *Ibid.*

10. Decree of State Committee for Defense (*Direktivy*, Vol. 2, p. 705).

11. Created on February 14, 1942 (*Istoriia*, Vol. 2, p. 526).

12. Shigalin, *Narodnoe khoziaistvo*, p. 242.

13. V. L. Komarov, chairman of the USSR Academy of Sciences, presided over this commission

The function of these bodies was to assure the execution of certain tasks of the highest priority above and beyond the existing institutional framework through the authority and high rank of their directors.

Very few new people's commissariats were created during the war, but their number, particularly in industry, was already very large in 1941 (see Table E-1). At the beginning of the war, to the four commissariats directly concerned with armaments (Aircraft Industry, Armaments, Munitions, and Shipbuilding) were added two more, Tank Industry (September 11, 1941) and Mortars (November 26, 1941), the latter replacing the Commissariat of General Machine-Building.[14] Later the reconstruction of destroyed cities required creating People's Commissariats for the Construction of Civilian Housing under the Russian Republic (February 9, 1944) and under the Belorussian Republic (September 11, 1944).[15] Both new commissariats seem to have enjoyed a certain autonomy from the People's Commissariat of Construction created before the war (see Table E-1).

Reorganization of Central Planning and Administrative Agencies

The centralization of planning and management and the mobilization of resources for the war economy required changes in the operations of the principal government agencies in charge of planning and management.

Soviet writers insist that the Soviet economy was centralized to a much greater degree than those of Western countries during the war.[16] This centralization consisted largely of increasing the number of products allocated centrally (i.e., the so-called "funded" products, allocated by USSR Gosplan).[17] Their number doubled at the beginning of the war, despite the fact that in 1940 and the first half of 1941 measures taken in preparation for war had already increased centralization.[18] The total number of indicators in the central plans for material and equipment supply exceeded 30,000, the materials and equipment being allocated among 120 large users.[19] Thus the balances and allocation plans drawn up by Gosplan covered all the basic factors of production (manpower, equipment, metals, fuel, raw materials) as well as military supplies. Food supplies and consumer goods for the urban population were also rationed according to centralized plans.[20]

The increased centralization of material and equipment supply considerably heightened the importance of Gosplan, the main body executing this policy, and Soviet writers did not hesitate to refer to Gosplan as "the indispensable partner

(B. V. Levshin, *Akademiia Nauk SSSR v gody Velikoi Otechestvennoi Voiny, 1941–1945* [The USSR Academy of Sciences during the Great Patriotic War, 1941–1945], Moscow, 1966, pp. 24–25.

14. *Ekonomicheskaia zhizn SSSR* [Economic Life of the USSR], edited by S. G. Strumilin, 2nd ed., Moscow, 1967, Book I, pp. 336 and 338; Kravchenko, *Voennaia ekonomika*, pp. 88–89.

15. *Ekonomicheskaia zhizn*, Book I, pp. 370 and 375.

16. *Shagi piatiletok: Razvitie ekonomiki SSSR* [Steps of the Five-Year Plans: Development of the USSR Economy], Moscow, 1968, p. 165.

17. On material and equipment supply in the USSR before 1941, see Chapter 5.

18. *Shagi*, p. 165.

19. G. M. Sorokin, *Planirovanie narodnogo khoziaistva SSSR* [Planning of the USSR National Economy], Moscow, 1961, pp. 213–14.

20. *Ibid.*, p. 214.

of the government and of the State Committee for Defense in organizing the war economy."[21] This increase in Gosplan's importance seems to have coincided with new functions entrusted to its chairman, Voznesenskii. He was appointed a member of the State Committee for Defense, headed the Council of People's Commissars (transferred to Kuibyshev at the beginning of the war), and was charged with drafting the first plan for the war economy.[22] But nevertheless this did not mean that the role of the annual or quarterly economic plans drafted by Gosplan was augmented or that their fulfillment was improved (see Table E-5).

While the administrative powers of Gosplan were being strengthened at the beginning of the war, so were those of the commissariats. The July 1, 1941, decree broadened their powers in managing material resources. Henceforward they could allocate these resources among their enterprises and construction agencies, authorize enterprise directors to relinquish resources, allocate investment funds, and authorize expenditures for the reconstruction of damaged enterprises.[23] All this was made possible only by weakening the role of the general central plan for the whole economy. Before the war, this plan had theoretically been unchangeable and binding on all executors, ministers, central administrations (*Glavki*), and enterprises.

Other reorganizations of economic administrative agencies during the war were relatively less important. To facilitate the construction and equipping of armament enterprises and of military plants, the State Committee for Defense, by a decree of July 8, 1941, created special sections for construction and assembly work under the People's Commissariat of Construction. Seventy-six such sections were set up; the Commissariat of Construction was empowered to use them as intervention teams, send them from one construction site to another, and provide for their staff.[24] The internal reorganization of the Commissariat of Transportation was decreed by the State Committee for Defense on March 22, 1942. The regional administrations of railroads were abolished and replaced by a Central Administration for Traffic.[25] Similarly, on August 28, 1942, the State Committee for Defense created the Central Administration for War Reconstruction, under the People's Commissariat of the Navy, whose job was to repair war damages and organize inland waterway traffic in areas liberated from enemy occupation.[26]

---

21. *Shagi*, p. 165.
22. See earlier in this chapter.
23. "On the Extension of the Rights of USSR People's Commissars under Wartime Conditions," July 1, 1941, decree of the Council of People's Commissars (*Direktivy*, Vol. 2, pp. 704–5). This decree was extended to apply to the people's commissars of the Russian Republic and the Ukraine on July 18, 1941 (*ibid.*, Vol. 2, p. 707).
24. *Istoriia*, Vol. 6, p. 110.
25. Commissar of Transportation L. M. Kaganovich was held responsible on this occasion and replaced by A. V. Khrulev (*ibid.*, Vol. 2, pp. 528–29).
26. *Ekonomicheskaia zhizn*, Book I, p. 349.

Wartime Economic Plans

Introduction of Wartime Economic Plans

There seems to have been no general plan for conversion to a wartime economy drawn up and approved before the beginning of the war. The only plans that existed at that time were partial plans "for the mobilization of production" in certain branches of industry. Thus, the plan for mobilizing munitions production, approved by the government on June 6, 1941, was put into effect the day after hostilities broke out.[27] But for the USSR Academy of Sciences, for instance, there was no plan for reorganizing research work in case of war.[28]

The conditions in which the "plan for the mobilization of the economy for the third quarter of 1941" was drafted show clearly how hurriedly the preparatory work had been done and how much the government had been taken by surprise. Although it approved the plan for the third quarter of 1941 on June 14, the day after the war started the government asked Gosplan to draft a plan for economic mobilization for the same period, which plan it approved on June 30 (see Table E-5). Drawn up in a few days, this plan could only partially modify the original quarterly plan. The production of armaments was increased by 26 per cent; investment was reduced, but concentrated in the armament factories far from the front (the Volga region, the Urals, western Siberia); and a list of superpriority construction projects was drawn up. Out of 22,000 machine tools produced, 14,000 were to be allocated to armament factories that evidently benefited from priorities in material and equipment supply. It is rather surprising to find that the plan for retail trade was reduced by only 12 per cent and that several plans for railroad traffic (coal, petroleum, metals, and grain) were maintained at their previous level.[29]

Because of its hasty drafting and also because of the rapid occupation of much Soviet territory, the first economic plan for mobilization in time of war was soon outdated. Its inadequacy, moreover, has been emphasized both by Voznesenskii, Gosplan chairman, and by more recent writers.[30] The government itself was aware of the preliminary nature of this first war plan and, immediately after its approval on July 4, named a special commission headed by Voznesenskii[31] to draw up a real wartime economic plan (*voenno-khoziaistvennyi plan*). This plan covered the fourth quarter of 1941 and all of 1942 but was limited to the Volga region, western Siberia, Kazakhstan, and central Asia. It was actually drafted

27. On June 23, 1941. See Kravchenko, *Voennaia ekonomika*, p. 87. The author also mentions the introduction of other plans for the mobilization of production but does not give any details.

28. Levshin, *Akademiia Nauk*, p. 11. It was only at the extraordinary meeting of the presidium of the USSR Academy of Sciences on June 23, 1941 (to which other scholars were also invited, a total of 60), that directives were issued to convert research to defense needs.

29. See sources to entry for 7/30/41 in Table E-5.

30. Nikolai A. Voznesensky, *The Economy of the USSR during World War II* (translated from the Russian), Washington, 1948, pp. 21–22; Kravchenko, *Voennaia ekonomika*, p. 90.

31. See the beginning of this chapter.

and approved by the Council of People's Commissars and the Party Central Committee on August 16, 1941.[32]

Place of Wartime Economic Plans in Economic Plans Drafted during 1941–1945

The wartime economic plans did not replace traditional planning, but were simply superimposed on it. Traditional planning was limited to partial plans that covered certain economic activities less essential to the war effort, that were not coordinated into an over-all plan (except for 1945), and that were frequently revised.

In general, the wartime economic plans were drawn up under the close supervision of the State Committee for Defense and promulgated under its authority. The traditional plans were drawn up by the appropriate agencies (ministries, republics, Gosplan), and the most important of them were published by the Council of People's Commissars, often together with the Party Central Committee (see Table E-5).

The system of plans in effect during the war can be summarized briefly by the following outline.

A. Wartime economic plans:
   General, annual, quarterly, and monthly plans
   Plans for certain priority sectors
   Revision of plans and strengthening of priorities
B. Specific economic plans or decisions necessitated by the war:
   Plans for evacuation and putting evacuated factories into operation
   Reconstruction plans
   Reconversion plans
C. Traditional economic plans:
   General, long-range, annual, and quarterly plans
   Plans for certain branches, regions, or activities
   Revised plans and strengthening of priorities

The available documentation does not make it possible to show the exact significance of all these plans nor their interrelations, but the specific features of Soviet planning during the war can be seen.

General Wartime Economic Plans

According to Soviet writers, annual, quarterly, and monthly wartime economic plans were drawn up for 1942, 1943, and 1944.[33] Unfortunately, only the decree on the plan for the fourth quarter of 1941 and the year 1942 was published;[34] the available sources do no more than mention the existence of plans for 1943 and 1944. However, many partial wartime economic plans, which cover certain sectors and revise earlier plans, have been published, at least partly. The main

32. *Direktivy*, Vol. 2, pp. 707–12. See also Table E-5.
33. Sorokin, *Planirovanie*, p. 208; *Shagi*, p. 120.
34. *Direktivy*, Vol. 2, pp. 707–12.

facts known on this subject are summarized in Table E-5. Information on the actual content of the general wartime economic plans can be gleaned only through the decree on the plan for the fourth quarter of 1941 and 1942, which set exceptionally high targets.

The German advance during the second half of 1941 was very rapid. According to Voznesenskii, the Soviet territory occupied by November 1941 accounted before the war for about 40 per cent of the total population and large proportions of the output of important industries.[35] Hence it is natural that the first general wartime plan should have covered only the eastern regions of the country, that is, the Volga, the Urals, western Siberia, Kazakhstan, and central Asia.

The main objectives of this plan were to convert industry to wartime needs and to put the full potential of the economy at the service of the army. For this reason, the plan covered only certain essential economic activities, particularly the production of armaments, heavy industry, railroad transportation, and "shock" (udarnyi) work. Other activities, such as the production of the textile, light, and food industries and agricultural production, were mentioned only briefly in the plan. The same was true of the problems connected with the front-line regions, for which the plan mentioned only maintaining the earlier goals for military production in the same factories installed in the east.

The main difference between this first wartime plan and the later plans for 1943 and 1944 lies in the fact that, after 1943, war production could not be increased through the redistribution of material and human resources. Output could be increased only by improving production technology and organization.[36] With successes occurring on the front line, these plans set goals for the reconstruction of liberated areas, set up schedules and priorities for this work, and allocated financial and material resources to the rebuilt enterprises, especially in war industries and heavy industry.[37]

A study of the wartime economic plans would be incomplete if it were limited solely to the general (or largely general) plans promulgated at regular intervals of a year, a quarter, or a month. It can be seen from Table E-5 that many additional plans were adopted during the war years, sometimes by the State Committee for Defense and sometimes by the USSR Council of People's Commissars, in order to direct, promote, and control the production of defense-related sectors. These plans applied mainly to the coal industry (more than 15 texts were mentioned), the ferrous metal industry (9 texts mentioned), electric power stations, the petroleum industry, and railroad transportation.

It is impossible to compare these texts since some of them were published in great detail, while others were merely mentioned. It is possible to gain some

35. 63 per cent of coal, 68 per cent of pig iron, 58 per cent of steel, 60 per cent of aluminum, 38 per cent of grain harvest, 84 per cent of sugar, 38 per cent of beef cattle, 60 per cent of pigs, and 41 per cent of the railroad network (Voznesensky, *Economy*, p. 24). It should be noted that, for Soviet writers, the term "Soviet territory" also includes Polish, Rumanian, Lithuanian, Latvian, Estonian, and Finnish territory annexed in 1939–1940.

36. *Shagi*, p. 123.

37. Ia. E. Chadaev, *Ekonomika SSSR v period Velikoi Otechestvennoi Voiny, 1941–1945* [The Economy of the USSR during the Great Patriotic War, 1941–1945], Moscow, 1965, pp. 88–89.

insight into the relation between these partial plans and the annual, quarterly, or monthly wartime economic plans by examining the case of the coal industry. Table E-5 contains information on 17 partial plans for the coal industry and 1 quarterly plan for the whole country (for the first quarter of 1945). Three of these plans covered the whole country but only for certain aspects of the industry: production of mining machinery (April 2, 1945), construction of factories under the jurisdiction of the People's Commissariat of the Coal Industry (July 18, 1945), and assignment to the mines of engineers and skilled workers who would not ordinarily have benefited from demobilization measures (June 20, 1945). Another plan covering the whole country (April 19, 1943) for opening coal mines was more general, but no details are known. The 13 other partial plans covered various coal basins—the Moscow Basin, the Pechora Basin, the Kuzbass, and, most important, the Donbass. In those cases when the information is sufficiently detailed to form conclusions,[38] it can be seen that these are genuine autonomous plans whose many provisions were intended to increase production. First, there were investment goals. These goals often included detailed allocations to open, equip, and operate individual mines, all of these activities being assigned to various trusts. Then there were precise production goals, often monthly. Then came measures to facilitate the allocation of manpower (most often by exemption from military service) and of materials and equipment. In some cases the decrees concerned the organization of production in factories that were intended to supply construction materials and mining equipment to mines. In other cases investments were facilitated by exemption from presentation of a draft project and an estimate to be approved before the reconstruction of mines. The ease of obtaining material and equipment supplies for production was accompanied by provisions favoring housing and supply of miners and making concessions on their wages. In some cases these measures were supplemented by financial estimates of their costs and by the administrative reorganization of management.

The decrees cited above certainly brought about revisions in the production plans set in the annual, quarterly, or monthly wartime economic plans. But the effects of these partial plans clearly went further. The plans for the allocation of raw materials, equipment, and fuel were the most affected. During the war these plans were highly centralized,[39] so clearly this centralization was accompanied by a considerable increase in revisions along the way. Hence the somewhat paradoxical conclusion is reached that the excessive centralization of material and equipment supply during the war served mainly to facilitate the very frequent revisions that were made during the year.

It is not difficult to guess the effects of these revisions of the plans for material and equipment supply on the general wartime economic plans. What was given to the coal industry or to the ferrous metal industry had to be taken away from some other industry, thus compromising that plan, and the mobilization of resources for military purposes made it impossible to draw much from civilian

38. The best known are the decrees of December 29, 1941, on the Moscow Basin and of October 26, 1943, and July 18, 1944, on the reconstruction of the Donetsk Basin.
39. See pp. 287–88 above.

consumption. Hence the annual, quarterly, and monthly wartime economic plans could not help but be divided into plans that someone wanted and was able to defend and other plans that suffered from the aftereffects. With, in addition, the general uncertainty resulting from the progress of the war, destruction, and reconstruction, it seems probable that the wartime economic plans were general, annual, quarterly, or monthly only in name. In actual fact, there were a multitude of quasi-autonomous plans of the industrial and transportation commissariats concerned with the war effort, whose executives competed in putting pressure on Gosplan and the State Committee for Defense for the allocation of human and material resources.

Plans for Evacuation, Reconstruction, and Reconversion

In principle, the plans for evacuation, reconstruction, and reconversion should have been integrated into the wartime economic plans. In actual fact, this integration, practically impossible at the beginning of the war, seems to have presented continuing serious difficulties.

The evacuation was directed by the Council for Evacuation. It was not conducted according to a general over-all plan. Certain regulations were laid down. Finished production was to be evacuated first, then unassembled equipment, and then basic equipment and raw materials. Next in line were power equipment and machine tools. Third, subsidiary materials, means of transportation, and other enterprise commodities were to be removed. The Council for Evacuation also drew up regulations to control the evacuation of workers, employees, and their families.[40] In fact, the plans for evacuation were drawn up at the level of factories or institutions and were only confirmed by the Council for Evacuation under the USSR Council of People's Commissars.[41] In view of the extent of the evacuation and the haste with which it was carried out, it is obvious that any plan made in advance was bound to fail. The evacuation took place on a huge scale; for example, during July–November 1941, 1,523 industrial enterprises, 1,360 of which were large, were evacuated to the east. The People's Commissariat for the Aircraft Industry was able to evacuate 85 per cent of its factories. The transportation required for evacuation during the second half of 1941 used about 1.5 million railroad cars.[42] Workers evacuated in January 1942 accounted for 30 to 40 per cent of the total number of workers originally employed in the enterprises that were removed to the east.[43]

In fact, the only plans actually executed concerned putting evacuated factories into operation and organizing their production after their transfer to the east.

40. Workers continued to receive their wages (average of the three preceding months) during the evacuation and a supplement in addition (Kravchenko, *Voennaia ekonomika*, pp. 99–100).

41. The evacuation plans drawn up by the Zaporozhstal and Azovstal plants were confirmed in this way (Shigalin, *Narodnoe khoziaistvo*, pp. 50–51). The plan for the evacuation of the USSR Academy of Sciences was confirmed on July 16, 1941 (Levshin, *Akademiia Nauk*, p. 15).

42. 667 industrial enterprises were evacuated to the Urals, 226 to the Volga region, 244 to western Siberia, 78 to eastern Siberia, and 308 to Kazakhstan and central Asia (Kravchenko, *Voennaia ekonomika*, p. 100).

43. Shigalin, *Narodnoe khoziaistvo*, p. 49.

Such plans were mentioned in the fall of 1941 for the metallurgical plants of the Volga, the Urals, central Asia, and Kazakhstan (see Table E-5). In this connection, a few production goals are cited for the end of 1941 and the beginning of 1942, but these do not represent real partial autonomous plans as much as a schedule for restarting production capacities that had been evacuated to the east.

It was mentioned above that the wartime economic plans for 1943 and 1944 included goals for reconstructing liberated and devastated areas. Nevertheless, the conclusion should not be drawn that reconstruction could really be integrated into the general annual, quarterly, or monthly planning. Table E-5 and the sources consulted indicate that most of the measures on reconstruction were taken separately and quite independently from the annual or quarterly plans. Three kinds of reconstruction decisions can be distinguished: (1) those representing real autonomous plans limited to a town, an area, or an industry; (2) those taken to prepare for reconstruction work, often including an obligation to draw up a concrete plan on the subject; and (3) those announcing a certain number of measures to help branches, sectors, or areas in trouble. Only the first of these types represented real revisions of plans or implied such short-term revisions. These decisions are listed in Table E-5. Particular note should be taken of the decrees of October 26, 1943, and July 18, 1944, on the reconstruction of the Donbass and the decrees of March 29 and May 27, 1944, on the reconstruction of the city of Leningrad. A decree of May 23, 1944, setting up a large-scale housing construction industry can also be included in this category (see Table E-5). Other decisions that could be classified in this group were undoubtedly made, but information about them was not sufficiently detailed to enable judgment of the effects they might have had on the economic plans in progress.

Other decrees on reconstruction were urgent but did not claim to be plans, only announcing the future drafting of plans. An example was a decree of February 22, 1943, of the State Committee for Defense on the "Reconstruction of Mines in the Donbass."[44] The measures taken were simply organizational, intended to obtain skilled labor and equipment and to give a certain number of orders to Party and industrial administration agencies to facilitate supply. The drafting of a reconstruction plan was formally requested. Another decree in this category, a little more precise, was issued on November 16, 1945, by the Council of People's Commissars on the reconstruction of 15 large cities (Smolensk, Kursk, Orel, Rostov-on-the-Don, and others).[45] This decree provided 764 million rubles for investment in 1946, material supplies, and recruiting "tens of thousands" of workers for the construction agencies involved.

The State Committee for Defense decree of October 1, 1944, on the reconstruction and development of the coal, petroleum, ferrous and nonferrous metal industries, and electric power stations fell into an intermediary position.[46] It specified directly the revision of plans for supplying materials and equipment to

44. *Direktivy*, Vol. 2, pp. 751–52.
45. *Ekonomicheskaia zhizn*, Book I, p. 388. See also Table E-5.
46. *Direktivy*, Vol. 2, pp. 854–55.

these industries for the fourth quarter of 1944 and ordered the drafting of plans for development and reconstruction in 1945 and 1946.

The largest number of government decisions taken on reconstruction belong in the third category: measures to help areas, sectors, or cities in trouble. Most of the published measures were for aid to agriculture and the reconstruction of cities and private housing. Among the former, the most important were the decrees of January 23 and August 21, 1943.[47] The first concerned rebuilding Machine and Tractor Stations in liberated areas that were to be guaranteed delivery of tractors, agricultural machinery, and spare parts that had been evacuated or were in the hands of various commissariats, including the People's Commissariat of Defense. It also provided for the "mobilization," to this end, of tractor drivers and for financial compensation. The second decree contained the most detailed agricultural measures. It provided for the restoration of the livestock evacuated from the collective farms (by granting authorizations for purchases), reduction of procurement quotas for 1943, help with seeds for winter sowing, assistance for each area in reorganizing the Machine and Tractor Stations, rebuilding the railroads, measures on housing and individual plots, organization of professional schools, etc. Although in less detail, similar measures for agriculture were published in 1944–1945 for Belorussia (decrees of February 3 and October 3, 1944, and June 13, 1945), Moldavia (June 24, 1944), Estonia (September 10, 1944), and sub-Carpathian Russia (March 16, 1945).[48]

Among the measures on the reconstruction of cities should be mentioned those for Stalingrad (decrees of April 4, 1943) and Sevastopol (decree of November 19, 1944), which were added to the other measures passed for devastated cities.[49] The measures to promote private housing construction in the cities in liberated areas (decree of May 29, 1944) provided mainly for financial credit (up to 10,000 rubles) and facilitated material supply.[50] Others, on the construction of the private houses of collective farmers in occupied areas of the Russian Republic (decree of July 8, 1945) and the construction of farm and recreational buildings on collective farms, also included financial assistance and material supplies.[51]

All these measures for assistance to devastated areas seem to have been more a matter of action than of planning. Their results and effects on production could not be evaluated with any precision. They influenced plans in operation largely through directives given to the agencies in charge of allocation of material resources and brought pressure to bear, which had an unavoidable effect on the

47. "On Measures to Rebuild the MTS and Collective Farms in Areas Liberated from the German Fascist Invaders" (January 23, 1943) and "On Essential Measures for the Reconstruction of the Economy in Areas Liberated from the German Occupation" (August 21, 1943), *ibid.*, Vol. 2, pp. 746–50 and 765–802.

48. *Istoriia*, Vol. 4, pp. 674 and 680; Vol. 5, p. 612; Vol. 4, p. 676; Vol. 4, p. 680; and Vol. 5, p. 609.

49. *Ibid.*, Vol. 3, p. 610 (*Pravda*, April 9, 1943, February 2 and 8, 1945, published the results of assistance given in the reconstruction of Stalingrad but did not mention any concrete plan on this subject); *Istoriia*, Vol. 4, p. 682.

50. *Sobranie postanovlenii i rasporiazhenii pravitelstva SSSR* [Collection of Resolutions and Decrees of the USSR Government], No. 7, 1944, Art. 109.

51. *SSSR v Velikoi Otechestvennoi Voine, 1941–1945* [The USSR during the Great Patriotic War, 1941–1945], Moscow, 1964, p. 762.

production plans of low-priority sectors. But they affected the sector of traditional planning much more than that of the wartime economic plans.

Operation of Traditional Planning in Wartime

Long-Range Planning

In the last section of Chapter 9 it was emphasized that the preparation of the Fourth Five-Year Plan for 1943–1947 was quite well along before the beginning of the war in June 1941. The outbreak of hostilities, the German invasion, and the conversion of the economy to military needs obviously interrupted this work. Nevertheless, it is interesting to note that the interruption did not last long. As early as 1943, Gosplan had drawn up a development plan for industry and transportation in the Urals; the plan was adopted in August 1943. This plan paid special attention to the ferrous metal industry, the fuel industry, and electric power stations.[52] Gosplan also studied the problems involved in developing the production of boilers, turbines, and generators for three or four years. Long-range plans were made for the liberated areas just as much as for the areas that had not been occupied by the enemy.[53]

The methods used in drawing up these plans, and the extent to which the various commissariats and regional planning committees were involved, are not known. Some work seems to have exceeded the five-year period and to have covered a longer term (10 years). This was the case for the "General Prospects for Soviet Science" drafted by the USSR Academy of Sciences. A program for the Academy was adopted at its September 1943 session. After a year of work, recommendations (called "notes") were drawn up on basic problems in physics and mathematics, technical sciences, chemistry, biology, geology, geography, and the social sciences. Problems concerning atomic reactors, semiconductors, computer electronics, and other advanced technology were studied in detail. This large-scale program of scientific work was summarized in more than 40 scientific reports.[54]

USSR Gosplan's use of this work in drafting the "long-range plan for the reconstruction and development of the USSR national economy for 1943–1947" is not known. According to this plan, national income was to rise above the 1940 level by 32 per cent, industrial production by 28 per cent, and railroad freight traffic by 8 per cent. Agricultural production was to have fallen by 7 per cent.[55] These few known goals of the Fourth Five-Year Plan are of particular interest because they give an idea of the leadership's perceptions of the development of the Soviet economy during the war.

First of all, these goals should be compared with those of the preceding five-year plan (for 1938–1942) and with those of the final version of the Fourth Five-Year Plan for 1946–1950 (see Table 64). The goals for 1947 seem to be very close to

52. Sorokin, *Planirovanie*, p. 210.
53. *Shagi*, p. 123.
54. After its examination in the scientific division of the Academy, the program was assessed by its General Assembly in October 1944 (Levshin, *Akademiia Nauk*, pp. 148–50).
55. *Shagi*, p. 124.

those for 1942 for national income and industrial production, but they are more than 10 per cent lower for railroad freight traffic and almost 30 per cent lower for agricultural production. The similarity of goals (apart from agriculture) shows that a very rapid recovery was expected. In fact, as can be seen in Chart 8, the point of departure for the 1938–1942 plan was much higher than that for the 1943–1947 plan. Actually the point of departure for the 1943–1947 plan was 1943, and the plan was adopted by Gosplan in August 1944. Hence it was a four-year plan, with the 1944 annual plan for the first year.[56] It can also be seen from Chart 8 that the planners' estimates of the speed of the economy's recovery

Table 64   Comparison of Goals for Original Fourth Five-Year Plan (1943–1947) and Goals for 1942 and 1950

	Units	Results in 1940 (1)	3rd Five-Year Plan (1938–1942) Goals for 1942 (2)	Original 4th Five-Year Plan (1943–1947) Goals for 1947 (3)	Final 4th Five-Year Plan (1946–1950) Goals for 1950 (4)
National income (1926/27 prices)	bill. rubles	128.3	173.6	169.4	177
Industrial production (1926/27 prices)	bill. rubles	138.5	184	177.3	205.0
Agricultural production (1926/27 prices)	bill. rubles	23.3	30.5	21.7	29.6
Railroad freight traffic	bill. m. ton-km	415.0	510.0	448.2	532

Source: Cols. 1, 2, and 4: Table A-1, cols. 5, 7, and 10; col. 3: calculated from col. 1 and planned percentage increases in *Shagi*, p. 124.

turned out to be wrong. Production in 1945 showed a substantial discrepancy from the goals of the 1943–1947 plan, and later on this discrepancy grew larger.

One may wonder at the reasons for the exaggerated optimism on the part of the Gosplan planners. After the Russian army had reached the middle of Poland and after the German front in France had been broken in the middle of 1944, did they expect a quick end to the war? Did they underestimate the difficulties of reconstruction? Was the statistical information at the disposal of Gosplan insufficient in 1944? There is no answer to all these questions at present. We can only assume that the Fourth Five-Year Plan for 1943–1947 was short-lived. Soviet writers do not mention its confirmation by the government.[57] On the contrary, a decree was issued by the State Committee for Defense on October 1, 1944 (see Table E-5), ordering USSR Gosplan to present within 20 days basic data on reconstruction and development of the coal industry, the petroleum industry, the ferrous and nonferrous metal industry, and electric power stations for 1945–1946 (with a breakdown by half years).[58] These plans were to be drafted in

56. The final version of the Third Five-Year Plan adopted in March 1939 was also a four-year plan (1939–1942). On this point, see Chapter 8.

57. *Shagi*, p. 124. This source mentions only the draft of the five-year plan for 1943–1947 drawn up by USSR Gosplan.

58. *Direktivy*, Vol. 2, pp. 854–55.

Chart 8 Principal Five-Year Plan Goals for 1942, 1947, and 1950

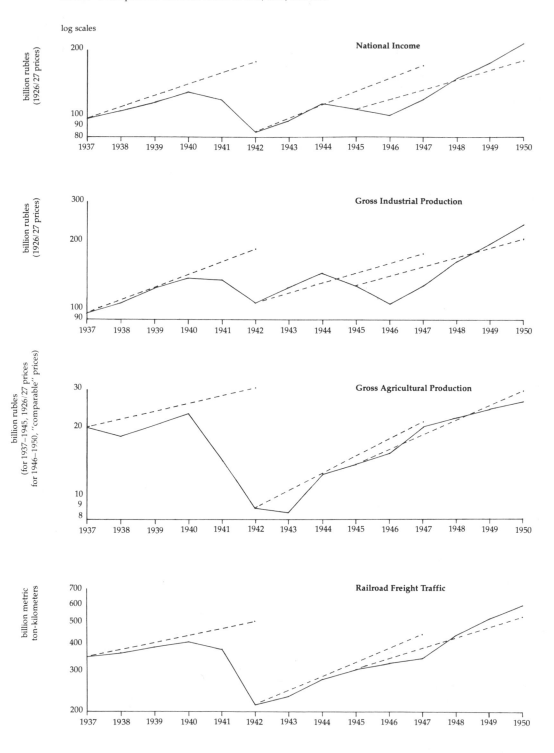

log scales

National Income

billion rubles
(1926/27 prices)

Gross Industrial Production

billion rubles
(1926/27 prices)

Gross Agricultural Production

billion rubles
(for 1937–1945, 1926/27 prices
for 1946–1950, "comparable" prices)

Railroad Freight Traffic

billion metric
ton-kilometers

———— actual production
‑ ‑ ‑ ‑ ‑ ‑ five-year plans

Source: For five-year plans, Table 64; for actual production, Tables A-2, A-3, A-4, and A-5.

collaboration with the appropriate commissariats. Soviet writers emphasized that these plans were drafted and that they served as the basis for the drafting of future annual plans.[59]

USSR Gosplan's August 1944 draft of the 1943–1947 plan must have been rejected. Otherwise there would have been no need to draw up other separate plans and this plan would have been used with the necessary revisions. In fact, the Soviet government seems to have soon abandoned the assumption of such a rapid reconstruction as provided for in the 1943–1947 plan. The new five-year plan, which was ordered to be drafted on August 19, 1945 (see Table E-5),[60] was to cover 1946–1950. The principal goals of this plan, as can be seen in Table 64 and Chart 8, were only slightly higher than the old goals for 1947, but they were to be attained three years later.

Traditional Annual Planning

The introduction of wartime economic plans in the second half of 1941 interrupted the drafting of the general annual and quarterly plans as it had been done before the war. Nevertheless, drafting was resumed before the end of the war, and as early as 1945 there can be found a traditional "plan for the reconstruction and development of the national economy" and quarterly plans in their usual form.[61] It is possible that such a plan was also drafted for 1944, but information on this point is unclear (see Table E-5, note to 1944a). In any case, it is certain that the reintroduction of traditional annual planning preceded the dissolution of the State Committee for Defense, the agency entrusted with executing wartime economic plans, which occurred on September 4, 1945.[62]

The interruption of traditional annual and quarterly planning did not, however, prevent the drafting of annual plans in certain branches. Because of their special nature and drafting schedule, the goals of these plans obviously could not have been integrated entirely into the wartime economic plans. Prominent among these were the plans for agriculture. Four categories of agricultural plans were drafted regularly during the war (see Table E-5): first, the state plan for the development of agriculture drafted in the spring; second, the plan for animal husbandry on collective and state farms; third, the plan for harvests and procurement of agricultural products; and fourth, the plan for the production and repair of tractors and agricultural machinery.[63]

---

59. Sorokin, *Planirovanie*, pp. 210–11; Chadaev, *Ekonomika*, p. 92.

60. It is surprising that the government ordered the separate drafting of a general plan and a plan for the reconstruction of railroad transportation, which ordinarily would have been part of the general plan.

61. See Table E-5. Only the plans for the first, third, and fourth quarters of 1945 are listed in Table E-5, but it seems likely that a plan for the second quarter of 1945 was also drafted.

62. *Ekonomicheskaia zhizn*, Book I, p. 386.

63. Plans in the first category were drafted on March 3, 1942; March 19, 1943; March 15, 1944; and February 24, 1945. Plans in the second category were drafted on March 13, 1942; April 13 and May 13, 1943; and April 6, 1945. Plans in the third category were drafted on July 11, 1942; July 18, 1943; July 20, 1944; and July 13, 1945. And plans in the fourth category were drawn up on November 17, 1941, and February 3, 1943. The March 13, 1945, plan for improving the work of the Machine and Tractor Stations could be included in this last category.

All of these agricultural plans had been drafted before the war as well, but then they constituted a kind of decree putting the general annual plans into operation (which they revised, however, to a greater or lesser extent). During the war, these plans seem to have been more or less autonomous.

In other sectors, the special annual plans belonging to this category are much less well known. Examples include the plan for training skilled workers for the first quarter of 1942 (December 1941), the plan for developing the fishing industry in the rivers of Siberia and the far east (January 6, 1942), the plan of work for the Academy of Sciences for 1942 and 1944 (May 8, 1942, and September 1944), and plans for railroad transportation in the first and second quarters of 1944 (see Table E-5). Whatever the extent to which they were integrated in the wartime economic plans, all these plans for branches or sectors seem to have been revised frequently. These revisions resulted largely from changes made in the wartime economic plans and from the priorities in allocation of resources (planned or not) given to industries working for defense. The plans for the reconstruction of agriculture in liberated areas or cities, which were made during the year and were influenced mainly by developments at the front, could not help but modify considerably the data on which were based the calculations of the traditional plans for branches and sectors of the economy.

Direct measures constituting revisions in the traditional plans in progress were noted mainly in agriculture. For example, there were decisions on changes to be made in sown areas (increase in technical crops in the republics producing cotton, September 3 and 22, 1942), restoration of areas sown to cotton in Uzbekistan (July 14, 1945), and increases in plans for meat procurement (February 15, 1942) and grain procurement (November 1943). (See Table E-5.)

New Forms of Annual and Quarterly Planning

The introduction of wartime economic plans and the corresponding reduction in importance of traditional annual plans deprived Soviet planners of a tool that provided an over-all view of the entire economy. To compensate for this lack, the planners supplemented the authoritarian planning of the wartime economic plans and what remained of the traditional annual and quarterly plans with calculations of financial balances for the whole country. The innovation lay not so much in the actual calculation of these balances (although changes were made in their form) as in their scope. They were used thenceforward to tie together the disparate elements of planning contained in the system of plans drawn up during the war and the sizable sector of the economy, mainly private consumption, that came under the command economy.

The most general balance was for the national economy. This balance contained estimates of gross national product and set the shares of producer and consumer goods, of industry and agriculture, and household incomes. It specified increases in the supply of consumer goods and services and changes in consumption and accumulation. It also integrated the data of the state budget, the allocation of national income for the mobilization of the necessary resources for military expenditures, and the balance of the money incomes and expenditures of households.[64] In calculating the balance of the national economy, use was also made of the balance of fixed capital, which controlled the volume of unfinished construction and the effect of investment on production, and of the balance of manpower, making possible the allocation of workers to priority branches.[65]

Obviously, all of these estimates could not be mandatory in the way the material balances or allocation plans were. They were largely economic calculations making use of data in aggregated value terms that did not lend themselves to a redistributon of tasks by direct administrative channels, as was the case in the annual and quarterly plans before the war. Hence it was impossible to seek the fulfillment of goals in the calculation of these balances or to hold economic agents responsible for the fulfillment or nonfulfillment of these plans. For that reason, there were no reports from USSR Gosplan during the war on the implementation of these over-all goals. The Gosplan reports covering the whole economy, then, took the form of reports on the economic situation. Such reports are mentioned for July 1941–December 1943, for 1942, and for 1943,[66] but apparently they were actually made more frequently and regularly.

Fulfillment of Wartime Economic Plans

In view of the nature of wartime planning, the exceptional measures taken, and the frequent revision of directives, it is understandable that the very idea of "plan fulfillment" became secondary. In order to analyze fulfillment, one would have had to engage in learned exercises on the variant of the plan used as a reference point (the original plan or its numerous revisions), its duration (short-term plans of one month or one quarter were often the most common), its coverage (wartime plans often covered a part of industrial or agricultural production or transportation), and the part of Soviet territory to which it applied. It is impossible to know the extent to which these calculations of wartime plan fulfillment were actually made by Gosplan offices or other agencies, but very few of them were made public.

Table 65 contains all the information that could be found on the fulfillment of economic plans during the war (1941–1945). Most of this information was taken from recent Soviet publications, whose authors had access to archives. The fragmentary nature of these data make general observations impossible. First, a distinction should be made between the annual plans for 1941–1944, on which information is very scanty, and the plan for 1945, for which several aggregate figures showing over-all development are available.

For 1941–1944, what is most striking is the paucity of information on the fulfillment of armament plans, whereas in other places statistics on armament production are given in a detail quite unexpected in Soviet practice in this area.[67]

64. Chadaev, *Ekonomika*, p. 91–92. Voznesensky (*Economy*, p. 44) also mentions the planning of the balance of the national economy during the war.

65. Chadaev, *Ekonomika*, p. 92.

66. *Shagi*, pp. 112, 123, and 133.

67. On this point, see Kravchenko, *Voennaia ekonomika*, pp. 163–207 and 291–374.

Table 65   Fulfillment of Selected Goals in Economic Plans, 1941–1945

	Units	Period of Plan	Original Plan (1)	Revised Plan (2)	Results (3)	Per Cent of Plan Fulfilled (4)
1941 (second half)						
1. Production of tanks		July–Dec.				61.7
2. Production of armaments		July–Dec.				not fulfilled
3. Production of planes		December				38.8
4. Repair of MTS tractors	no.	fall–winter			248,783	97
5. Repair of MTS combines	no.	summer			109,357	102
1942						
Wartime Economic Plan						
6. Gross (industrial) production		year				92
7. Coal mines put into operation, Urals, west Siberia, Kazakstan, and central Asia	no.	year	41	131		
8. Capacity	th. m. t.	year	12,170	19,000		
9. Daily mining of coal, Moscow Basin	m. t.	March	10,000	14,000		
10. Mining of coal, Kuznetsk Basin	mill. m. t.	Jan.–Aug.	17.8		12.6	70.8
11. Mining of coal, Kuznetsk Basin	mill. m. t.	Oct.–Dec.	7.9		7.2	91.1
12. Mining of coal, Karaganda Basin:	mill. m. t.	Jan.–Aug.	5.5		4.2	76.3
13. Coking coal		Jan.–Aug.				65.7
Ferrous Metal Industry						
14. Blast furnaces installed	no.	year	11		4	
15. Capacity	th. m. t.	year	1,815		730	
16. Open-hearth furnaces installed	no.	year	51		12	
17. Capacity	th. m. t.	year			820	
18. Rolling mills installed	no.	year	22		9	
19. Capacity	th. m. t.	year	3,239		841	
20. Coking furnaces installed	no.	year	22		4	
21. Capacity	th. m. t.	year	3,930		1,656	
Agriculture						
Total sown area:						
22. Spring sowing	mill. ha	March–June		60.6	58.1	96
23. Fall–winter sowing	mill. ha	Aug.–Dec.		21.8	21.8	99
24. Cotton crops	th. ha	year	1,494		1,449	97.0
Collective farm sown area:						
25. Spring sowing		spring				74
26. Fall–winter sowing		fall–winter				90
Livestock breeding, collective farms:						
27. Beef cattle	thous.	year	16,935		13,500	79.7
28. Pigs	thous.	year	5,800		3,300	56.9
29. Sheep and goats	thous.	year	50,260		35,500	70.6
30. Repair of MTS tractors	no.	fall–winter			202,798	92
31. Repair of MTS combines	no.	summer			89,659	92
1943						
32. Coal mining, daily average, Donbass	tons	December	40,000		35,000	87.5
Agriculture						
Total sown area:						
33. Spring sowing	mill. ha	March–June		51.3	44.8	87

Table 65 *continued*

	Units	Period of Plan	Original Plan (1)	Revised Plan (2)	Results (3)	Per Cent of Plan Fulfilled (4)
34. Fall–winter sowing	mill. ha	Aug.–Dec.		26.7	24.0	90
35. Cotton crops	mill. ha	year	1,100		1,099.6	100
Collective farm sown area:						
36. Spring sowing		spring				73
37. Fall–winter sowing		fall–winter				79
Livestock breeding:						
Collective farm:						
38. Beef cattle:	thous.	year	15,526		14,100	90.8
39. Cows	thous.	year	4,279		3,500	81.8
40. Pigs	thous.	year	3,972		2,200	55.4
41. Sheep and goats	thous.	year	41,785		35,900	85.9
42. Horses	thous.	year	6,900		6,200	89.9
State farms:						
43. Beef cattle:	thous.	year	1,393		1,100	79.0
44. Cows	thous.	year	505		400	79.2
45. Pigs	thous.	year	285		100	35.1
46. Sheep and goats	thous.	year	3,129		2,100	67.1
47. Horses	thous.	year	300		300	
48. Compulsory deliveries of pigs to state by collective farms	thous.	year	1,120		1,113	99.4
49. Repairs of MTS combines	no.	summer			75,951	79
1944						
Industry						
50. Coal mining, Kuzbass	mill. m. t.	year	28.0		28.1	100.4
Machine-building:						
51. Machine tools	units	year	21,000		34,049	
52. Tractors	units	year	5,500	7,000	3,154	57.3 or 45.1
Agricultural machinery:						
53. Tractor-drawn plows	units	year	25,000	8,000		
54. Horse-drawn plows	units	year	50,000	70,000		
55. Tractor-drawn drills	units	year	30,000	2,600		
56. Horse-drawn drills	units	year	35,000	7,500		
57. Combines	units	year	10,000	1,500		
58. Reapers	units	year	30,000	10,000		
59. Horse-drawn rakers	units	year	30,000	6,000		
60. Separators	units	year	30,000	14,200		
Deliveries of Mineral Fertilizer to Agriculture						
61. Ammonium sulfate	th. m. t.	year	69			
62. Phosphoric fertilizer (18.7%)	th. m. t.	year	296			
63. Potash fertilizer	th. m. t.	year	125			
64. Ground natural phosphate	th. m. t.	year	102			
Railroad Transportation						
65. Average daily carloadings		1st quart.				102.6
66. Average daily carloadings		2nd quart.				100.5
Agriculture						
Total sown area:						
67. Spring sowing	mill. ha	March–June		54.3	50.8	93
68. Fall–winter sowing	mill. ha	Aug.–Dec.		30.9	27.0	87
Collective farm sown area:						
69. Spring sowing		spring				79

Table 65   *continued*

	Units	*Period of Plan*	*Original Plan* (1)	*Revised Plan* (2)	*Results* (3)	*Per Cent of Plan Fulfilled* (4)
70. Fall–winter sowing		fall–winter				82
71. Repair of MTS tractors	no.	fall–winter			276,843	97
72. Repair of MTS combines	no.	summer			80,776	71

73. Investment, total excl.
     collective farms
     (current prices)
	bill. rubles	year	31.2		34.0	109

1945						
Gross Industrial Production *(1926/27 prices)*						
74. Total:	bill. rubles	year	152		127.4	83.8
75. Heavy industry	bill. rubles	year	122.2		95.0	77.7
76. Light and food industry	bill. rubles	year	29.8		31.7	106.4
77. Total:	bill. rubles	3rd quart.	28.6			
78. Military production	bill. rubles	3rd quart.	11.5			
79. Civilian production	bill. rubles	3rd quart.	17.1			
80. Coal	mill. m. t.	year	153		149.3	97.6
81. Steel ingots and castings	mill. m. t.	year	13		12.3	94.6
82. Electric power	mill. kwh	year	45,880		43,257	94.3
83. Tractors	units	year	27,000		7,728	28.6
84. Machine tools	units	year	35,000		38,419	
Railroad Transportation						
85. Average daily carloadings	units	year	63,000		62,200	98.7
Agriculture Total sown area:						
86. Spring sowing	mill. ha	March–June		55.7	54.6	98
87. Fall–winter sowing	mill. ha	Aug.–Dec.		30.9	27.7	90
Collective farm sown area:						
88. Spring sowing		spring				85
89. Fall–winter sowing		fall–winter				85
Livestock breeding:						
90. Beef cattle, total	mill.	year	45.2		47.6	105.3
91. Beef cattle, collective farms	mill.	year	17.1		15.9	93.0
92. Pigs, collective farms	mill.	year	3.3		2.7	81.8
93. Sheep and goats, total	mill.	year	88.9		70.0	78.7
94. Horses, collective farms	mill.	year	6.5		6.5	100

95. Investment, total excl.
     collective farms
     (current prices)
	bill. rubles	year	40		43.3	108.3

Source

LINES 1-2–Col. 4: *Ekonomicheskaia zhizn*, Book I, p. 340.

LINE 3–Col. 4: Kravchenko, *Voennaia ekonomika*, p. 172. Only 23. 6 per cent of the plan for the production of plane motors in December 1941 was fulfilled (*ibid*.).

LINES 4-5–Cols. 3-4: Iu. V. Arutiunian, *Sovetskoe krestianstvo v gody velikoi otechestvennoi voiny* [The Soviet Peasantry during the Great Patriotic War], Moscow, 1963, p. 138.

LINE 6–Col. 4: *Ekonomicheskaia zhizn*, Book I, p. 353. The 1942 plan for the assimilation and production of armaments and military equipment (*voennaia tekhnika*) was fulfilled and, in certain cases, overfulfilled in the eastern regions (Sorokin, *Planirovanie*, p. 208).

LINES 7-8–Col. 1: Goals of wartime economic plan in decree of August 16, 1941 (*Direktivy*, Vol. 2, p. 709). Col. 2: Goals of December 8, 1941, decree, "On Development of Coal Mining in Eastern Regions of USSR" (Kravchenko, *Voennaia ekonomika*, pp. 123–24). Even though the revised plan might have covered a larger territory, the original goals were certainly increased.

Table 65   *continued*

LINE 9–Col. 1: Decree of December 29, 1941 (*Direktivy*, Vol. 2, p. 713). **Col. 2:** Decree of February 5, 1942 (Kravchenko, *Voennaia ekonomika*, p. 123).

LINE 10–Cols. 1, 3–4: Derived from statement (*ibid.*, p. 124) that 70.8 per cent of the plan for coal mining in the Kuznetsk Basin for the first eight months of 1942 was fulfilled and that output was 5.2 mill. m. tons short of the planned output.

LINE 11–Col. 1: Derived from daily planned output of coal, given as 88,000 m. tons in August 24, 1942, decree of State Committee for Defense (*SSSR*, p. 245) and assumption that this goal applied to fourth quarter of 1942. **Col. 3:** Total output of coal in Kuzbass for 1942 (derived as 21.5 mill. m. tons from 1943 output for whole country and share of Kuzbass output in total and increase of 20 per cent in 1943, all given in Kravchenko, *Voennaia ekonomika*, pp. 247–48) minus output during first eight months of year (given as 12.6 mill. m. tons in line 10, col. 3) and minus output in September (estimated as 1.7 mill. m. tons from daily output of 57,000 m. tons given in *SSSR*, p. 245). **Col. 4:** Based on cols. 1 and 3.

LINE 12–Cols. 1 and 3: Based on col. 4 and amount of shortfall of plan (given as 1,300 thous. m. tons in Kravchenko, *Voennaia ekonomika*, p. 124).

LINES 12-13–Col. 4: *Ibid.*

LINES 14-21–Col. 1: April 13, 1942, decree of State Committee for Defense (*Direktivy*, Vol. 2, p. 724). For lines 16–17, col. 1, in addition to the 51 open-hearth furnaces installed, 22 electric furnaces and one Bessemer furnace were installed in 1942 with a total annual capacity for all three types of 3,550,000 m. tons of steel (*ibid.*). **Col. 3:** Kravchenko, *Voennaia ekonomika*, p. 234. Given for eastern regions and liberated areas, which were considered representative of the whole country. These areas do not include the northwest, the center, and the Volga region, whose total share in production of steel amounted to 16.1 per cent in 1942 (*ibid.*, p. 237). **Col. 4:** Not calculated since figures in cols. 1 and 3 do not have the same coverage, but it is obvious that plan fulfillment was very poor.

LINE 22–Col. 1: The wartime economic plan (*Direktivy*, Vol. 2, p. 711) gave total sown area for 1942 harvest as 62.7 mill. hectares for the regions of the Volga, the Urals, western Siberia, Kazakhstan, and central Asia. Arutiunian's data (col. 3), on the other hand, cover the area actually sown in 1942, i.e., partly for the 1943 harvest, and all the territory under Soviet control.

LINES 22-23–Cols. 2-4: Arutiunian, *Sovetskoe krestianstvo*, p. 406.

LINE 24–Cols. 1 and 3: *Ibid.*, p. 175. **Col. 4:** Based on cols. 1 and 3.

LINES 25-26–Col. 4: Arutiunian, *Sovetskoe krestianstvo*, p. 293.

LINES 27-29–Col. 1: Decree of March 13, 1942 (*Ekonomicheskaia zhizn*, Book I, p. 344). **Col. 3:** *Chislennost skota v SSSR* [Head of Livestock in the USSR], Moscow, 1957, p. 7. **Col. 4:** Based on cols. 1 and 3.

LINES 30-31–Cols. 3-4: Arutiunian, *Sovetskoe krestianstvo*, p. 138.

LINE 32–Col. 1: October 26, 1943, decree of State Committee for Defense (*Direktivy*, Vol. 2, p. 804). **Col. 3:** *Ekonomicheskaia zhizn*, Book I, p. 367. For end of 1943. **Col. 4:** Based on cols. 1 and 3.

LINE 33–Col. 1: The March 19, 1943, plan for the development of agriculture in 1943 (*Ekonomicheskaia zhizn*, Book I, p. 358) gave the plan for area sown for the 1943 harvest as 6.4 mill. hectares more than in 1942. This figure is not comparable with those given by Arutiunian (see line 22, col. 1), and it can be gathered from Arutiunian that Soviet statisticians did not know the area sown for the 1942 harvest.

LINES 33-34–Cols. 2-4: Arutiunian, *Sovetskoe krestianstvo*, p. 406.

LINE 35–Cols. 1 and 3: *Ibid.*, p. 175. **Col. 4:** Based on cols. 1 and 3.

LINES 36-37: Arutiunian, *Sovetskoe krestianstvo*, p. 293.

LINES 38-41, 43-46–Col. 1: Decree of April 13, 1943 (*Direktivy*, Vol. 2, p. 757).

LINES 38-42–Col. 3: *Chislennost*, p. 7.

LINES 38-46–Col. 4: Based on cols. 1 and 3.

LINE 42–Col. 1: Based on number of horses in 1942 (given as 6.6 mill. on January 1, 1943, in *Chislennost*, p. 7) and increase planned for 1943 (given as 5.3 per cent in May 13, 1943, decree in *Ekonomicheskaia zhizn*, Book I, p. 360).

LINES 43-46–Col. 3: Arutiunian, *Sovetskoe krestianstvo*, p. 309.

LINE 47–Cols. 1 and 3-4: The 1943 plan (*Ekonomicheskaia zhizn*, Book I, p. 360) gave an increase of 6.6 per cent over 1942, but the available figures for 1942 and 1943 are so rounded (0.3 mill. in Arutiunian, *Sovetskoe krestianstvo*, p. 309) that it is impossible to tell if the plan was fulfilled.

LINE 48–Col. 1: Decree of April 13, 1943 (*Direktivy*, Vol. 2, p. 759). **Col. 3:** Arutiunian, *Sovetskoe krestianstvo*, p. 438.

LINE 48–Col. 4: Based on cols. 1 and 3.

LINE 49–Cols. 3-4: Arutiunian, *Sovetskoe krestianstvo*, p. 138.

LINE 50–Col. 1: Based on workers' obligations (rather than actual plan), which planned to increase coal output by at least 2.2 mill. m. tons in 1944 over 1943 (*Ekonomicheskaia zhizn*, Book I, p. 369), and 1943 coal output in Kuzbass (derived as 25.8 mill. m. tons from total of 93,141,000 m. tons and Kuzbass share of 27.7 per cent, both given in Kravchenko, *Voennaia ekonomika*, p. 248). **Col. 3:** Based on total coal output for whole country and share of Kuzbass in total (given as 121,470,000 m. tons and 23.1 per cent, respectively, in Kravchenko, *Voennaia ekonomika*, p. 248). **Col. 4:** Based on cols. 1 and 3.

Table 65   *continued*

LINE 51–Col. 1: February 28, 1944, resolution of State Committee for Defense (*Direktivy*, Vol. 2, p. 823). Output of enterprises belonging to People's Commissariat of the Machine Tool Industry (*stankostroeniia*). **Col. 3:** Kravchenko, *Voennaia ekonomika*, p. 255. **Col. 4:** Not calculated since the coverage of cols. 1 and 3 is not comparable.

LINE 52–Col. 1: Decree of February 18, 1944 (*Direktivy*, Vol. 2, p. 818). Output of enterprises belonging to People's Commissariat of Medium Machine-Building. **Col. 2:** Decree of March 14, 1944 (*ibid.*, p. 827). **Col. 3:** Kravchenko, *Voennaia ekonomika*, p. 257. **Col. 4:** Based on cols. 1 and 3 and on cols. 2 and 3.

LINES 53–60–Col. 1: Decree of March 18, 1943, which gave goals for both 1943 and 1944 (*Direktivy*, Vol. 2, p. 755). **Col. 2:** Decree of March 14, 1944 (*ibid.*, Vol. 2, pp. 827–28). Output of People's Commissariat of Armaments (*Narkominvooruzheniia*). For line 60, includes output of NKVD and *Narkomlespron* RSFSR.

LINES 53–57–Col. 3: Deliveries to the Commissariat of Agriculture, the main client for agricultural machinery, were as follows: tractor-drawn plows—2,435; horse-drawn plows—22,700; tractor-drawn drills—0; horse-drawn drills—1,037; and combines—127 (Arutiunian, *Sovetskoe krestianstvo*, p. 273).

LINES 61–64–Col. 1: Decree of March 14, 1944 (*Direktivy*, Vol. 2, p. 828). **Col. 4:** Fulfillment of these goals appears unlikely. Kravchenko (*Voennaia ekonomika*, p. 264) emphasizes the poor development of the chemical industry for civil production during the war. Arutiunian (*Sovetskoe krestianstvo*) gives no information on the subject. See Table A-3.

LINE 65–66–Col. 4: *Pravda*, July 30, 1944, as cited in *Ekonomicheskaia zhizn*, Book I, p. 375.

LINES 67–68–Cols. 2–4: Arutiunian, *Sovetskoe krestianstvo*, p. 406.

LINE 69–Col. 1: The state plan for the development of agriculture in 1944 contained an increase of 7.55 mill. hectares of sown area on the collective farms, excluding areas liberated by the Red Army during the winter of 1943/44 (*Ekonomicheskaia zhizn*, Book I, p. 372). This figure may not be comparable to Arutiunian's figure in col. 4 and hence has not been entered.

LINES 69-70–Col. 4: Arutiunian, *Sovetskoe krestianstvo*, p. 293.

LINES 71-72–Cols. 3-4: *Ibid.*, p. 138.

LINE 73–Cols. 1 and 3: Norman Kaplan, "Capital Investments in the Soviet Union, 1924–1951," RAND Research Memorandum 735, Santa Monica, 1951, p. 37.

LINE 73–Col. 4: Based on cols. 1 and 3.

LINES 74-76–Cols. 1 and 3-4: Table A-4, series 2, 3, and 4, cols. 4-6.

LINES 77-79–Col. 1: *Istoriia*, Vol. 5, pp. 418–19. The same source also gives figures for the second quarter: 25.9 bill. rubles for total production, 18 bill. for military production, and 7.9 bill. for civilian production. This means a reduction of 6.5 bill. rubles in military production between the second and third quarters of 1945, which implies a revision of the annual plan.

LINES 80-82–Cols. 1 and 4: Table A-4, cols. 4 and 6.

LINES 80-85–Col. 3: Table A-4, col. 5.

LINE 83–Col. 1: Decree of February 18, 1944 (*Direktivy*, Vol. 2, p. 818).

LINES 83 and 85–Col. 4: Based on cols. 1 and 3.

LINE 84–Col. 1: February 28, 1944, resolution of State Committee for Defense (*Direktivy*, Vol. 2, p. 823). Only production of People's Commissariat of the Machine Tool Industry (*stankostroeniia*). **Col. 4:** Not calculated since the coverage of cols. 1 and 3 is not comparable.

LINE 85–Col. 1: *Istoriia*, Vol. 5, p. 368.

LINES 86-87–Cols. 2-4: Arutiunian, *Sovetskoe krestianstvo*, p. 406.

LINES 88-89–Col. 4: *Ibid.*, p. 293.

LINE 90–Col. 1: Based on 1940 head of cattle (given as 54.5 mill. on January 1, 1945, in *Chislennost*, p. 6) and percentage that 1945 plan was of 1940 (given as 83 in *Istoriia*, Vol. 5, p. 367).

LINES 90-94–Col. 3: *Chislennost*, pp. 6–7. **Col. 4:** Based on cols. 1 and 3.

LINE 91–Col. 1: Based on 1944 head of cattle on collective farms (given as 15.4 mill. on January 1, 1945, in *Chislennost*, p. 7) and increase planned for 1945 (given as 11 per cent in *Ekonomicheskaia zhizn*, Book I, p. 383).

LINE 92–Col. 1: Based on 1944 number of pigs on collective farms (given as 2.4 mill. on January 1, 1945, in *Chislennost*, p. 7) and increase planned for 1945 (given as 37 per cent in *Ekonomicheskaia zhizn*, Book I, p. 383).

LINE 93–Col. 1: Based on prewar (1940) number of sheep and goats (given as 91.6 mill. on January 1, 1941, in *Chislennost*, p. 6) and percentage that 1945 plan was of 1940 (given as 97 in *Istoriia*, Vol. 5, p. 367).

LINE 94–Col. 1: Based on 1944 number of horses on collective farms (given as 6.2 mill. on January 1, 1945, in *Chislennost*, p. 7) and increase planned for 1945 (given as 5 per cent in *Ekonomicheskaia zhizn*, Book I, p. 383).

LINE 95–Col. 1: *Istoriia*, Vol. 5, pp. 365–69. **Col. 3:** Kaplan, "Capital Investments," p. 37.

It appears from Table 65 that the production plan for armaments was very poorly carried out during the second half of 1941. The failure to fulfill the wartime economic plan for 1942, along with the simultaneous fulfillment of the plans for armament production in the eastern regions, also suggests shortcomings in this area in 1942. For 1943 and 1944, no information is available on the fulfillment of the armament plans; these results can only be inferred from the plan fulfillment of industries directly serving armaments, such as ferrous metals, fuel, and machine-building. In machine-building, the results were not good in 1942, but the silence is nearly as complete for 1943 and 1944, except for the machine-building and chemical industries supplying agriculture (tractors, agricultural machinery, fertilizer), whose plans were very poorly fulfilled. It can only be assumed that the failure of the plans for deliveries of tractors, agricultural machinery, and fertilizers to agriculture was largely due to failures in the armament industries that forced the government to change its original plans.

The agricultural plans mention the very poor fulfillment of plans for livestock breeding and sown areas on collective farms for almost all the years from 1941 to 1944, which leads one to assume failures in production plan fulfillment.

For 1945, the considerable underfulfillment of the production plan for heavy industry (77.7 per cent, see Table 65) resulted mainly from the reorientation of the economy to civilian needs, which was decided in the plan for the third quarter of 1945 and which, in all probability, was not foreseen in the annual plan. In fact, military production, which amounted to 18 billion rubles in the second quarter of 1945, was planned to drop by 6.5 billion rubles in the third quarter. Civilian production, on the other hand, was to increase from only 7.9 billion rubles in the course of the second quarter of 1945 to 17.1 billion rubles during the third quarter of 1945.[68]

In the 1945 plan, the production plan for heavy industry (except for tractors) was relatively well fulfilled for electric power, the ferrous metal industry, and railroad transportation. For agriculture, the sowing plans were better fulfilled than during the war years, but certain shortcomings appeared in the plans for the restoration of collective farm livestock, particularly pigs, sheep, and goats.

Soviet writers, moreover, make no mystery of the poor fulfillment of economic plans during the war. But the reasons given differ. G. I. Shigalin believes that military activities often required important changes in the material supply plans for the army, which were possible only because of greater flexibility and maneuverability in the production and distribution of industrial production. Hence, according to Shigalin, the quarterly and monthly plans for the principal industrial products and the monthly plans for railroad transportation took on greater importance during the war. The partial disproportions that occurred were due, according to Shigalin, to mistakes in prewar planning calculations and to temporary losses of territory during the first months of the war.[69]

But other authors, such as Ia. E. Chadaev, stress the major errors that were made in planning the wartime economy "due largely to the cult of the personality

68. See Table 65 and source note to lines 77–79, col. 1.
69. Shigalin, *Narodnoe khoziaistvo*, pp. 69–70.

of Stalin."[70] Chadaev emphasizes the unauthorized assimilation of objective economic laws to government laws on economic plans, the scorn for technical and economic calculations, and the "voluntarism" and "subjectivism" of the administrative agencies which impaired the scientific examination of the plan goals. He criticizes most strongly planning on the basis of results attained during the current year, which encourages enterprises to minimize their production capacities and in a way "legalizes" the errors and shortcomings of the reference period.[71]

These two explanations, however, do not seem to be incompatible, and they could both be accepted simultaneously. An additional explanation could be given, which would lay the failures of the wartime plans to the hybrid nature of planning during this period. Since wartime planning was ranked the highest in a sense, it disturbed lower-level plans (the remnants of the traditional plans), and particularly the whole area abandoned to the command economy covering private consumption, which, because of its low priority, tended to jeopardize the fulfillment of the plans in progress.

70. Chadaev, *Ekonomika*, p. 93.
71. *Ibid.*, pp. 93–94.

CHAPTER 15

Mobilization of Resources in the Wartime Economy

Mobilization of Human and Material Resources

Mobilization of Human Resources

The introduction of a wartime economy soon led to a tightening of labor discipline and the imposition of restrictions on free choice of employment and mobility of the labor force. Even before the war, on October 19, 1940, a decree of the Supreme Soviet presidium had authorized the compulsory transfer of engineers, technicians, and skilled workers from one enterprise to another.[1] Immediately after the war started, on July 23, 1941, this right was granted to the republic councils of people's commissars and to territory and province executive committees.[2] These decrees were followed by several measures that mobilized people at their places of work and provided for the forced assignment of certain military personnel and workers to jobs in agriculture, industry, and construction.

Direct mobilization of people at their places of work was introduced originally for war industries by a decree of December 26, 1941.[3] This decree forbade workers to leave their jobs for the duration of the war. It was soon extended to workers in areas near the front (decree of September 29, 1942)[4] and then to transportation personnel.[5] In addition, special decrees on labor discipline in the

1. G. I. Shigalin, *Narodnoe khoziaistvo SSSR v period velikoi otechestvennoi voiny* [USSR National Economy during the Great Patriotic War], Moscow, 1960, pp. 240–41.

2. *Ibid.*, p. 241; G. S. Kravchenko, *Voennaia ekonomika SSSR, 1941–1945* [The Wartime Economy of the USSR, 1941–1945], Moscow, 1963, p. 95.

3. *Ekonomicheskaia zhizn SSSR* [Economic Life of the USSR], edited by S. G. Strumilin, 2nd ed., Moscow, 1967, Book I, p. 339; Kravchenko, *Voennaia ekonomika*, p. 96.

4. *Ekonomicheskaia zhizn*, Book I, p. 350.

5. It was extended to inland waterway transport in October 1942, by a decree of the Supreme Soviet presidium; to railroad transport on April 15, 1943, by a decree of the Supreme Soviet, "On the Introduction of a State of Wartime Emergency on All Railroads"; and to the People's Commissariats

railroads and in inland waterway transport were issued in April and May of 1943.[6] These strict provisions, however, seem not always to have been followed to the letter. In fact, a Party Central Committee decree of July 3, 1944, condemned excessive mobility in the labor force and unauthorized job quits and ordered local Party agencies to deal with these infractions.[7]

Another series of regulations dealt with mobilizing workers. A decree of February 13, 1942, declared that all men from 16 to 55 and women from 16 to 45 could be mobilized for work in the cities where they were domiciled, with industries for war, metals, chemicals, and fuel having priority. Exemptions were made for women feeding babies, women alone with children under eight, and students.[8] This decree made possible the mobilization, by the end of 1942, of 565,900 able-bodied people in cities and 168,000 people in villages, or a total of 733,900 people, 191,300 of whom were sent directly to work in war industries.[9]

Requisitions were also made to assign people to jobs serving production directly and to send city workers temporarily to work in the fields.[10] M. I. Kalinin likened the importance of agricultural work to producing munitions.[11] Later, in 1944, the Commandant of the Army ordered some detachments to do certain agricultural work and to repair tractors and agricultural machinery. It should be noted that 1,395,600 people were mobilized in 1942 for temporary and seasonal work in industry, transportation, and construction alone (that is, excluding agricultural work) and 826,000 young people were sent for training in factory schools.[12]

Besides mobilizing civilian workers and occasionally making use of military personnel, the Soviet authorities tried to use military personnel incapable of regular service in a regiment for work in industry, transportation, and construc-

---

of the Inland Waterway Fleet and of the Navy and to the Central Administration for the Northern Sea Route on May 9, 1943 (*ibid.*, Book I, pp. 359–60).

6. On April 25 and May 19, respectively (*ibid.*, Book I, pp. 359–60).

7. *SSSR v Velikoi Otechestvennoi Voine, 1941–1945* [The USSR during the Great Patriotic War, 1941–1945], Moscow, 1964, p. 580.

8. February 13, 1942, decree of the presidium of the Supreme Soviet, "On the Wartime Mobilization of the Able-Bodied Urban Population for Work in Production and Construction" (*Direktivy KPSS i sovetskogo pravitelstva po khoziaistvennym voprosam* [Directives of the Communist Party of the Soviet Union and of the Soviet Government on Economic Matters], Moscow, 1957–1958, Vol. 2, p. 722). The age of women liable for mobilization was raised to 50 by the September 19, 1942, decree (Shigalin, *Narodnoe khoziaistvo*, pp. 341–42), and the age of children justifying exemption was lowered to 4 (when space was available in child-care centers) on August 7, 1943. Specific provisions on the work to be done, the duration of the work, quotas, remuneration, etc., were given in the August 10, 1942, decree (*Ekonomicheskaia zhizn*, Book I, pp. 344, 349, and 362).

9. Shigalin, *Narodnoe khoziaistvo*, p. 242.

10. November 4, 1942, decree (*Ekonomicheskaia zhizn*, Book I, p. 351); and April 13, 1942, decree, "On the Mobilization of the Able-Bodied Urban and Rural Population for Agricultural Work on Collective and State Farms and in the Machine and Tractor Stations" (*Sobranie postanovlenii i rasporiazhenii pravitelstva SSSR* [Collection of Resolutions and Decrees of the USSR Government], No. 4, 1942, Art. 60). The latter decree authorized the temporary mobilization for this work of the population not employed in industry or transportation, schoolboys in grades 6 to 10, and students, except those in the last year of their studies.

11. On March 5, 1942 (*Ekonomicheskaia zhizn*, Book I, p. 344).

12. Kravchenko, *Voennaia ekonomika*, p. 96. The factory schools were the FZO (*Fabrichno-Zavodskoe Obuchenie*, schools for factory and plant training) and the state labor reserve schools (*Uchilishcha gosudarstvennykh trudovykh rezervov*).

tion. "Construction battalions" and "labor columns" were formed. During the second half of 1941 alone, these organizations mobilized 700,000 men, 251,000 of whom were sent directly to work in war industries.[13]

Combating Manpower Shortages

Mobilization for military service and the occupation of a considerable part of Soviet territory during the first months of the war resulted in a severe manpower shortage.[14] The total number of workers and employees in the national economy fell from 31.2 million in 1940 to 18.4 million in 1942, the drop in industry going from 11.0 to 7.2 million in that period.[15] The labor shortage was worst during the first months of 1942. The People's Commissariat of Munitions was short 35,000 workers, the Commissariat of the Tank Industry 45,000 workers, the Commissariat of Armaments 64,000, the Commissariat of the Aircraft Industry 215,000, and the Commissariat of Heavy Machine-Building 50,000. Half of these requirements were for skilled workers.[16]

One of the first measures taken to meet the growing manpower needs lengthened the working day. A decree of June 26, 1941, authorized enterprise directors, with the approval of the USSR Council of People's Commissars, to increase the working day by one to three hours; vacations were suspended and replaced by financial compensation.[17] The number of mandatory hypothetical working days (*trudodni*) for collective farmers was increased, as of April 13, 1942.[18]

Special stress was put on replacing men with women.[19] Starting in the second half of 1941, 500,000 housewives and about 500,000 schoolgirls in grades 8 to 10 were put to work in the production process. The share of women in the total number of employees and workers in the national economy (excluding collective farms) rose from 38 per cent in 1940 to 53 per cent in 1942 (from 41 to 52 per cent in industry, from 21 to 40 per cent in railroad transportation) and reached 55 per cent in 1945.[20] In some military-related industries this share reached very high levels.[21]

An estimate of the active population was important for meeting manpower

13. *Ibid.*, pp. 96–97.

14. The territory occupied during the first months of the war contained 88 million inhabitants, 45 per cent of the total population (Shigalin, *Narodnoe khoziaistvo*, p. 231).

15. *Ibid.* See also Tables A–3 and A–4.

16. Kravchenko, *Voennaia ekonomika*, p. 95.

17. *Ekonomicheskaia zhizn*, Book I, p. 331. These compensation payments were frozen in savings banks. After vacations were restored on July 1, 1945 (*ibid.*, Book I, p. 385), the frozen sums were paid up to the amount of 100 rubles and above that in equal parts during four years (*Sobranie postanovlenii*, No. 10, 1945, Art. 120).

18. The increases varied: on cotton collective farms, the mandatory number was raised to 150 days per year; in some provinces (Moscow, Leningrad, Ivanovo, Yaroslav, Gorky, Kalinin, and others), it was 100; in still others, 120 (*Sobranie postanovlenii*, No. 4, 1942, Art. 61).

19. On the railroads, for instance, the Young Communist League organized training for 50,000 young girls (December 16, 1941, decree of the Komsomol in *Ekonomicheskaia zhizn*, Book I, pp. 338–39).

20. *Zhenshchina v SSSR* [Women in the USSR], Moscow, 1960, p. 35; Kravchenko, *Voennaia ekonomika*, p. 99.

21. It was 59 per cent in the electrical industry, but only 40.5 per cent in the aircraft industry at the end of 1942 (Shigalin, *Narodnoe khoziaistvo*, p. 233).

needs, but making this estimate was not easy under the tumultuous wartime conditions. On November 20, 1942, the government introduced monthly telegraph reports on manpower for a limited number of indicators and ordered that a census be taken of workers and employees in industrial enterprises on December 15, 1942.[22] On February 5, 1943, a census of the urban population was taken, and the government ordered the offices of the Central Statistical Administration to make an estimate of the rural population from data available in the village Soviets on January 1, 1944.[23]

Action was also taken to train skilled workers. A detailed plan on this subject was drafted in December 1941 for the first quarter of 1942, providing for training 365,400 people by 31 economic organizations.[24] It is likely that similar plans were also drafted for the other war years. In any case, training and improving worker skills were undertaken on a large scale. The official reports declare that in 1942, for example, 80 per cent of all industrial workers took courses and that this number increased to 131 per cent in 1945 (see Table 66).[25] However, it is difficult to estimate the actual improvement in skills. A considerable effort was also made at this time to make schools more accessible to adolescents working in enterprises and to re-educate invalids.[26]

A parallel effort was made to train tractor drivers and agricultural mechanics. A decree of August 18, 1942, organized individual instruction for tractor drivers in the Machine and Tractor Stations (MTS).[27] Another decree issued on January 9, 1943, mobilized collective farmers and the male rural population not working in industry or transportation for instruction in operating and maintaining agricultural machinery. A plan to train these people for MTS and for state farms was adopted in 1943. It provided, among other things, for training 250,000 tractor drivers, 46,410 combine operators, 42,110 combine-operator helpers, and 12,770 drivers for MTS, as well as 40,812 tractor drivers, 10,542 combine operators, 13,259 combine-operator helpers, and 8,197 drivers for state farms.[28] A comparison of these figures with those in Table 66 shows that this plan was not fulfilled in terms of sheer numbers. But the real criterion of fulfillment lay in the quality of the training rather than in the total number of machine operators trained, and it is difficult to judge this element.

22. *Ekonomicheskaia zhizn*, Book I, p. 351.

23. *Ibid.*, pp. 355 and 363.

24. Kravchenko, *Voennaia ekonomika*, p. 97.

25. The fact that the total number of workers who received this kind of training was higher than the total number of workers in industry shows that some workers must have been counted more than once, possibly having taken different courses or short courses.

26. See the decrees of July 15, 1943, March 5, 1944, and April 30, 1944 (*Ekonomicheskaia zhizn*, Book I, pp. 361, 371, and 373; and *Sobranie postanovlenii*, No. 8, 1944, Art. 130) and the decrees of May 6, 1942, and August 28, 1942 (*ibid.*, No. 5, 1942, Art. 76; and *Ekonomicheskaia zhizn*, Book I, pp. 346 and 349).

27. *SSSR*, p. 241.

28. January 9, 1943, decree, "On Training Tractor Drivers, Combine Operators, Mechanics, and Leaders of Tractor Brigades for MTS and State Farms" (*Direktivy*, Vol. 2, pp. 744–46).

Table 66 Training of Skilled Workers in Industry and Tractor Drivers and Combine Operators in Agriculture, 1940–1945 (thousands)

	1940	1941	1942	1943	1944	1945
Industry						
1. Average annual number of workers, total	8,290	7,827	5,491			7,189[a]
2. Number of new or newly trained workers	3,665.8	3,250.3	4,388.8	5,787	7,893	9,444
3. Line 2 as per cent of line 1	44.2	41.5	79.9			131
4. New workers	1,654.5	1,244.3	1,259.9	3,417	3,936	4,360
5. Workers with skills increased on the job	1,950.0	1,520.8	2,512.3	1,717	3,433	4,561
6. Workers trained in FZO and state labor reserve schools[b]		439.5	569.0	598	416	453
7. Workers trained in schools belonging to institutions	61.3	45.7	47.5	55	78	70
Agriculture						
8. Total number of tractor drivers trained	285.0	438.0[c]	354.2	276.6	233.0	230.2
9. Total number of combine operators trained	41.6	75.6[d]	54.2	42.0	33.0	26.0

Source: Lines 1–2 and 4–7: Kravchenko, *Voennaia ekonomika*, pp. 98 and 218; lines 8–9: Shigalin, *Narodnoe khoziaistvo*, p. 250.

a. *Promyshlennost SSSR* [Industry of the USSR], Moscow, 1964, p. 84.
b. See footnote 12 in this chapter.
c. Of these, 207,700 were trained in short courses.
d. Of these, 48,803 were trained in short courses.

Alleviating Transportation Shortages

From the very first days of the war the means of transportation were put at the service of the armed forces and the war effort. A new traffic schedule was put into effect, giving priority and assuring maximum speed to military transports and restricting civilian passenger transportation.[29] The number of carloadings shipped according to centralized plans was increased. Traffic capacity was increased on the Urals railroads and the main railroad networks (Cheliabinsk, Sverdlovsk, Tagil, Novosibirsk, Kirov). Several new railroad lines were built along the Volga, in the east, and in the north, such as the Vorkuta railroad and the new railroad line from Transcaucasia to Astrakhan.[30]

At the very beginning of the war, the priority given to military-related transports led to the introduction of special fast trains to transport raw materials or fuels that were particularly important to the Commissariat of Armaments. These special trains were treated like military transports.[31] Furthermore, there were

29. A. E. Gibshman *et al.*, *Ekonomika transporta* [The Economics of Transportation], Moscow, 1957, pp. 109–10.
30. Nikolai A. Voznesensky, *The Economy of the USSR during World War II* (translated from the Russian), Washington, 1948, p. 20.
31. See the December 26, 1941, decree of the State Committee for Defense (*Istoriia Velikoi*

measures mobilizing transportation workers (mentioned earlier) and the introduction of a state of wartime emergency on the railroads (by a decree of April 15,
1943).[32]

Nevertheless, wartime difficulties in Soviet transportation remained severe.
At the beginning of the war, the evacuation, the German invasion, and the ensuing destruction thoroughly disorganized traffic. Commissar of Transportation
Kaganovich was held responsible for the disorganization and was replaced.[33]
After 1943, when the Soviet army went over to the offensive, the extension of
lines considerably increased the average distance covered by freight cars and
their turnaround time. There was an imbalance in the direction of traffic, with
westbound traffic going toward the front predominating. On some railroad lines
traffic was largely in one direction, which considerably increased the proportion
of trips by empty cars. During this stage of the war, the shortage of freight cars
was felt acutely, particularly since no locomotive or railroad cars were replaced
during the war. Major repairs were cut down and wear and tear increased.
Enemy bombing also caused considerable damage.[34]

All this caused severe difficulties, especially during the winter when freight
piled up at the stations; particular difficulties were mentioned in February and
March of 1943.[35] The authorities tried several solutions. As well as the special
trains mentioned above, they authorized sending some of the mobilized machine operators and other specialists to work on the railroads. They eliminated
certain freight that was not used, had no accompanying documents, and stayed
in the stations; and they provided for an increase in the deliveries of material
and equipment to the railroads.[36]

The reconstruction of the railroads undertaken after 1943 in the liberated areas
played an important part in alleviating transportation shortages. It should be
emphasized that the total length of the railroad network in operation declined
by 40 per cent between 1941 and 1943, the stock of locomotives declined by 15
per cent, and the stock of freight cars by 20 per cent.[37] When the Soviet armies
recaptured territory, a large part of the railroads was destroyed. As Voznesenskii
points out, reconstruction of the railroads was often done under enemy fire.
During only the first two or three months of 1943, 6,600 kilometers of railroad
line were reopened; the figure was 19,000 kilometers for the whole of 1943 and

Otechestvennoi Voiny [History of the Great Patriotic War], Moscow, 1960–1963, Vol. 2, p. 526). The
March 1943 decree of the State Committee for Defense (ibid., Vol. 3, p. 192) set up special itineraries
and special defense trains, whereas the March 4, 1944, decree (ibid., Vol. 4, p. 604) organized transports exclusively for military or similar material on certain railroads.

32. Decree of the presidium of the Supreme Soviet, "On the Introduction of a State of Wartime
Emergency on All Railroads" (Zheleznodorozhnyi transport SSSR v dokumentakh kommunisticheskoi partii
i sovetskogo pravitelstva, 1917–1957 [Railroad Transportation in the USSR in Documents of the Communist Party and Soviet Government, 1917–1957], Moscow, 1957, pp. 339–40).

33. Istoriia, Vol. 2, pp. 528–29.

34. Gibshman et al., Ekonomika, p. 112.

35. The accumulation of supplies to be transported was considerable in February 1943 in the combines of Kuznetsk, Magnitogorsk, and Nizhnyi Tagil (Istoriia, Vol. 3, pp. 191–92). Many carloads that
had not reached their destination were also sitting in stations in August 1944 (ibid., Vol. 5, pp. 393–
94). Gibshman et al. (Ekonomika, p. 112) claim that these difficulties existed throughout the war.

36. Istoriia, Vol. 3, pp. 191–92; Sobranie postanovlenii, No. 1, 1944, Art. 23; and Istoriia, Vol. 4, p. 604.

37. Voznesensky, Economy, p. 59.

43,000 kilometers for 1944.[38] During 1943–1944 several decrees were issued in an attempt to organize this reconstruction, the most important of which seems to have been that of August 21, 1943.[39] This decree gave the People's Commissariat of Transportation the task (to be accomplished by January 1, 1944) of rebuilding 122 railroad stations and 520,000 square meters of housing in the liberated areas, and assigned to this project 15 battalions of militarized detachments of railroad workers, 3 reserve regiments of railroad workers, and other supporting resources. USSR Gosplan was to provide the timber, oil shale, lumber, and other materials.

Financing the War Effort

Burden of Military Expenditures

The exact volume of resources devoted to the war is difficult to estimate, but several indexes of national income, gross industrial and agricultural production, production of the armament industries, and over-all investment provide an idea of the extent of the changes that took place (see Table 67). In 1942, for example, national income was two-thirds and industrial production three-quarters of that of 1940. At the same time, the output of armament industries was almost double the 1940 level. In fact, the output of defense industries was far from representing the total industrial effort devoted to satisfying war needs. In July 1942, for instance, of a total value of production under Union and Union-republic industry of 8,018 million rubles (in 1926/27 prices), only 3,782 million rubles (that is, 47.2 per cent) was accounted for by the output of the four commissariats directly involved in war work (see Table 67, note a).[40] If the military orders filled by the other commissariats are taken into account, 70 to 80 per cent of total industrial production went to satisfy war needs.[41] For the whole of 1942, the share of industrial production devoted to war needs reached 68 per cent (compared with 26 per cent in 1940), the share of agricultural production was 24 per cent (compared with 9 per cent in 1940), and the share of transportation was 61 per cent (compared with 16 per cent in 1940).[42]

The redirection of production to satisfy war needs also considerably changed the distribution of gross national product and national income. The data in Table 68 suggest that the share of military expenditures (excluding consumption of military personnel) increased largely at the expense of accumulation. However, if the consumption of military personnel is excluded, the share of civilian

38. *Ibid.*, p. 60; Shigalin, *Narodnoe khoziaistvo*, p. 217. Kravchenko (*Voennaia ekonomika*, p. 281) gives the figure of 47,000 kilometers of railroad line rebuilt in 1944 and 1,214 large and medium bridges rebuilt. He includes in his figures railroad line within stations.

39. May 26, 1943, and April 27, 1944, decrees of the State Committee for Defense; November 1943 decree of the Party Central Committee and of the Ukrainian Council of People's Commissars (*Istoriia*, Vol. 3, pp. 190 and 611). August 21, 1943, decree of Council of People's Commissars and Central Committee (*Direktivy*, Vol. 2, pp. 791–94); cited in Chapter 14, footnote 49.

40. Kravchenko, *Voennaia ekonomika*, p. 199. On the organization of industrial management, see Chapter 2 above.

41. *Istoriia*, Vol. 2, p. 500.

42. *Shagi*, p. 121.

Table 67   Principal Economic Indexes, 1940–1945 (1940 = 100)

	1941	1942	1943	1944	1945
1. National income	92	66	74	88	83
2. Industrial production:	98	77	90	104	92
3. Armament industries[a]	140	186	224	251	[b]
4. Agricultural production	62	38	37	54	60
5. Investment, excl. collective farms (comparable prices)	86	53	53	72	89

Source: Lines 1–4: *Shagi piatiletok: Razvitie ekonomiki SSSR* [Steps of the Five-Year Plans: Development of the USSR Economy], Moscow, 1968, p. 121; line 5: *Narodnoe khoziaistvo SSSR v 1958 godu* [The USSR National Economy in 1958], Moscow, 1959, p. 618.

a. People's Commissariats of the Aircraft Industry, of the Tank Industry, of Armaments, and of Munitions.

b. There was a reduction in the output of the four commissariats handling armaments. The indexes for 1944 and 1945 (1940 = 100) were as follows: aircraft industry—239 and 177; tank industry—296 and 276; armaments—206 and 156; and munitions—310 and 171 (*Shagi*, p. 132).

consumption in national income dropped from 66 per cent in 1940 to 38–39 per cent in 1942–1943, a decrease made more serious by a sizable drop in aggregate national income (see Tables 67 and 68). It is tempting to measure the burden of military and war expenditures by the share of expenditures on the armed forces in the total expenditures of the state budget. As can be seen from Table 68, during 1942–1944 this share was more or less equal to that of total military expenditures (including the consumption of military personnel) in national income. It was just under 60 per cent in 1942 and 1943 and 52 per cent in 1944.

In reality, the expenditures on the armed forces that appear in the budget are noticeably lower than total military expenditures and probably do not include the cost of armaments and many expenditures for the conduct of the war. No official Soviet estimates of national income in current prices are available for the war years, but Abram Bergson and Hans Heymann estimate it at 458.0 billion rubles in 1940 and 487.4 billion in 1944.[43] Total budget expenditures, then, would represent about 38 per cent of national income (in current prices) in 1940 and 54 per cent in 1944. Total military expenditures in 1940, then, were about 21 per cent higher than the expenditures of the People's Commissariats of Defense and of the Navy in 1940 (that is, a total of about 69 billion rubles) and, in 1944, almost double the expenditures of those commissariats (that is, around 253 billion rubles).[44] It is likely that only part of these additional expenditures was included in the state budget, but it is certain that several expenditure items other than those of the Commissariats of Defense and of the Navy went to finance the war effort. This applies to the expenditures of the People's Commissariat of

43. Abram Bergson and Hans Heymann, Jr., *Soviet National Income and Product, 1940–48*, New York, 1954, p. 24.

44. That is, about 15 per cent of the national income estimated by Bergson and Heymann for 1940 and 52 per cent of that estimated for 1944. In view of the different methods of computation, these figures should be taken only as an order of magnitude.

Table 68   Changes in Composition of Gross National Product and National Income during World War II (per cent)

	1940 (1)	1941 (2)	1942 (3)	1943 (4)	1944 (5)	1945 (6)
Gross National Product (current prices)	100		100	100	100	
1. Consumption in production	43		43	43	43	
Personal consumption:						
2. Including consumption of military personnel	42		38	34.2	34.8	
3. Civilian consumption only	37		22			
4. Accumulation	11		2	4.0	8.5	
Military expenditures:						
5. Excluding consumption of military personnel	4		17	18.8	13.7	
6. Including consumption of military personnel	9		33			
National Income (1926/27 prices)	100	100	100	100	100	100
Personal consumption:						
7. Including consumption of military personnel	74		67	60	61	
8. Civilian consumption only	66		39	35	33	
9. Accumulation	19		4	7	15	
Military expenditures:						
10. Excluding consumption of military personnel	7		29	33	24	
11. Including consumption of military personnel	15	29	57	58	52	
12. Share of expenditures on armed forces in total budgetary expenditures	32.5	43.4	59.3	59.5	52.2	42.9

Source

LINES 1-2, 4-5, 7, and 9-10–Cols. 1 and 3: Voznesensky, *Economy*, pp. 38–39. Voznesenskii does not specify what prices were used in the estimates of national income and gross national product that he cites. According to information kindly provided by Vladimir Treml, GNP was estimated in current prices and national income in 1926/27 prices. For line 10, cols. 1 and 3, also *Voenno-ekonomicheskie voprosy v kurse politekonomii* [Military and Economic Problems in the Political Economy Course], edited by P. V. Sokolov, Moscow, 1968, p. 249. **Cols. 4-5:** M. L. Tamarchenko, *Sovetskie finansy v period Velikoi Otechestvennoi Voiny* [Soviet Finances during the Great Patriotic War], Moscow, 1967, pp. 50–51. For line 10, col. 4, also Kravchenko, *Voennaia ekonomika*, p. 221. For line 10, cols. 4–5, also *Voenno*, p. 249.

LINE 3: Line 2 minus consumption of military personnel, which is derived by taking 57 per cent (the share of national income in GNP in 1940 and 1942, since consumption in production in line 1 was 43 per cent) of the difference between military expenditures including and those excluding consumption of military personnel (line 11 minus 10).

LINE 6: Line 5 plus consumption of military personnel (derived as in line 3 above).

LINE 8: Line 7 minus consumption of military personnel (line 11 minus line 10).

LINE 11–Col. 1: *Shagi*, p. 121. Also *Voenno*, p. 250. **Cols. 2-5:** Kravchenko, *Voennaia ekonomika*, p. 221. In 1940 prices. For col. 3, *Shagi*, p. 121, and *Voenno*, p. 250, give 55 per cent.

LINE 12: Calculated from Table 69 (line 21 as a percentage of line 24).

Internal Affairs and State Security (see Table 69, note d) and to most of the expenditures for industry and transportation.

The war also had a direct effect on expenditures for education, which were considerably reduced in 1942 and 1943. But general education was replaced largely by the formation of State Labor Reserves, which from October 1940 to October 1945 trained 2,250,000 young people at a cost of 11 billion rubles.[45]

War mobilization also created problems with pensions.[46] A decree of June 26, 1941, granted the families of military personnel monthly pensions, the amount of which depended on the number of able-bodied persons in the home and the number of persons unable to work who were being supported by the mobilized person.[47] Various provisions in military pensions were extended to cover workers for the army and the navy.[48] All this increased considerably the social security pensions paid from the state budget; pension payments rose from 3.2 billion rubles in 1940 to 17.8 billion in 1945 (see Table 69). On several occasions the government also provided assistance in housing and food supplies to the families of mobilized persons.[49]

Increased Financial Pressure and Indirect Taxes

During the first days of the war, the Soviet government made some basic changes in the budget provisions for the second half of 1941. Military expenditures were increased by 20.6 billion rubles (an increase that could not be fully achieved), and expenditures for the national economy and for social and cultural measures were reduced by 21.6 and 16.5 billion rubles, respectively.[50] Extraordinary measures were taken at the same time to increase income and reduce expenditures. Thus, as of July 1, 1941, the sums remaining in enterprise directors' funds were appropriated, as were the liquid assets remaining in the industrial and invalids' cooperatives. Some expenditures of the state social insurance, enterprise administrative agencies, and republic budgets were thus reduced.

The main government effort, however, was to increase taxes paid by the population, to increase loans and semicompulsory gifts, and later to increase indirect taxes by the introduction of a double sector in state and cooperative retail trade (see pp. 321–22 and 334 below). Soon after the war started, on July

45. K. N. Plotnikov, *Biudzhet sotsialisticheskogo gosudarstva* [Budget of the Socialist State], Moscow, 1948, p. 264.

46. According to Plotnikov (*ibid.*), 110 million people were mobilized during the war.

47. *Ibid.*, p. 339.

48. The pensions granted in the case of the death of a person with a family to support, provided for military personnel by the July 16, 1940, and June 5, 1941, decrees, were extended to cover sailors operating near enemy action (by the September 12, 1942, decree in *Sobranie postanovlenii*, No. 8, 1942, Art. 131), to sailors of the inland waterway fleet operating in the same conditions (by the October 22, 1942, decree in *ibid.*, No. 9, 1942, Art. 152), and to medical workers of the maritime and inland waterway fleets operating in the same conditions (by the January 7, 1943, decree in *ibid.*, No. 1, 1943, Art. 20).

49. See decrees of January 22 and 27, 1943 (*Ekonomicheskaia zhizn*, Book I, pp. 356–57). The June 4, 1943, decree extended the benefits of the June 26, 1941, legislation for families of military personnel to the families of military personnel who were killed or missing in action (*Sobranie postanovlenii*, No. 8, 1943, Art. 140).

50. Plotnikov, *Biudzhet*, p. 254.

Table 69   Budget of Soviet Government, 1940–1945 (billion rubles)

	1940		1941		1942[a]	1943[a]	1944		1945	
	Planned (1)	Actual (2)	Planned (3)	Actual (4)	Actual (5)	Actual (6)	Planned (7)	Actual (8)	Planned (9)	Actual (10)
Income										
1. Turnover tax	108.3	105.9	124.5	93.2	66.4	71.0	80.2	94.9	118.1	123.1
2. Tax on profits of state-owned enterprises	22.4	21.7	31.3	23.5	15.3	20.1	23.0	21.4	17.3	16.9
3. Personal taxes	9.7	9.4	12.5	10.8	21.6	28.6	34.3	37.0	45.3	39.8
4. State loans	11.2	11.4	13.2	11.5	15.3	25.5	30.3	32.6	25.0	29.0
5. Defense Fund and Red Army Fund				1.8	5.3	5.3	5.0	5.0	0.5	0.5
6. Miscellaneous and unspecified income[b]	32.4	31.8	35.3	36.2	41.1	53.9	72.8	77.8	101.5	92.7
7. Total income	184.0	180.2	216.8	177.0	165.0	204.4	245.6	268.7	307.7	302.0
Expenditures										
8. National economy	57.1	57.1	73.2	51.7	31.6	33.1	44.7	53.7	64.7	74.4
9. Industry		27.8	39.2	30	18.0	18.0	24.7	27.3	35.9	43.9
10. Agriculture		12.6	13.5	9.4	5.1	5.1	7.2	7.0	9.2	9.1
11. Transportation		4.6	6.6			4.8	6.3	7.7	9.8	9.9
12. Trade and procurements						0.8	1.2	1.2	1.7	2.2
13. Communal economy and housing		2.5			1.1	1.7	1.8	2.9	2.4
14. Unspecified						3.3	3.6	8.7	5.2	6.9
15. Social and cultural expenditures[c]	42.9	40.9	47.8	31.4	30.3	37.7	51.4	51.3	66.1	62.7
16. Education	23.2	22.5	26.6	15.5	10.4	13.2	21.1	20.7	28.6	26.4
17. Public health and physical culture	9.8	9.0	10.9	6.8	6.8	8.5	10.4	10.2	13.2	11.5
18. Family allowances	1.2	1.2	1.2	1.2	0.8	0.7	0.8	0.9	1.4	2.1
19. Social insurance	5.8	5.0	5.6	3.4	2.5	2.8	3.7	3.7	5.2	5.0
20. Social security	2.9	3.2	3.5	4.5	9.8	12.4	15.4	15.7	17.7	17.8
21. People's Commissariats of Defense and of the Navy	57.1	56.7	70.9	83.0	108.4	125.0	128.4	137.8	137.9	128.2
22. Administration and justice	7.2	6.8	7.1	5.1	4.3	5.2	6.7	7.4	9.5	9.2
23. Miscellaneous and unspecified expenditures[d]	15.6	11.9	17.1	20.2	8.2	9.0	14.4	13.8	29.5	24.1
24. Total expenditures	179.9	174.3	216.1	191.4	182.8	210.0	245.6	264.0	307.7	298.6
25. Surplus of income over expenditures	+4.1	+5.9	+0.7	−14.4	−17.8	−5.6		+4.7		+3.4

Source

COLUMN 1–Lines 1–4, 7-8, 15-19, 21-22, and 24: A. G. Zverev, *Gosudarstvennye biudzhety Soiuza SSR 1938–1945 gg*. [State Budgets of the USSR for 1938–1945], Moscow, 1946, pp. 67–84 and 128. **Line 6:** Line 7 minus sum of lines 1-4. **Line 20:** Table C-5, col. 4. **Line 23:** Line 24 minus sum of lines 8, 15, 21, and 22. **Line 25:** Line 7 minus line 24.

COLUMN 2–Lines 1-4, 8-9, 11, 13, and 24: Zverev, *Gosudarstvennye biudzhety, 1938–1945*, pp. 95–96, 104, and 128–29. **Line 6:** Line 7 minus sum of lines 1–4. **Lines 7, 10, 15-19, and 21-22:** K. N. Plotnikov, *Ocherki istorii biudzheta sovetskogo gosudarstva* [Essays on the History of the Soviet State Budget], Moscow, 1954, pp. 293, 324, 335, and 340. **Line 20:** Line 15 minus sum of lines 16–19. **Line 23:** Line 24 minus sum of lines 8, 15, 21, and 22. **Line 25:** Line 7 minus line 24.

COLUMN 3–Lines 1-4, 7-8, 15, 21, and 24: Zverev, *Gosudarstvennye biudzhety, 1938–1945*, pp. 95–96, 104, and 128–30. **Line 6:** Line 7 minus sum of lines 1–4. **Lines 9-11, 16-20, and 22:** *Zasedaniia Verkhovnogo Soveta SSSR (vosmaia sessiia). 25 fevralia–1 marta 1941 g*. [Meetings of USSR Supreme Soviet. Eighth Session, February 25–March 1, 1941], Moscow, 1941, p. 275. **Line 23:** Line 24 minus sum of lines 8, 15, 21, and 22. **Line 25:** Line 7 minus line 24.

COLUMN 4–Lines 1-5, 7-8, 10, 15-19, 21-22, and 24: Plotnikov, *Ocherki*, pp. 293, 324, and 340. **Line 6:** Line 7 minus sum of lines 1–5. **Line 9:** Tamarchenko, *Sovetskie finansy*, p. 106. **Line 20:** Line 15 minus sum of lines 16–19. **Line 23:** Line 24 minus sum of lines 8, 15, 21, and 22. **Line 25:** Line 7 minus line 24.

Table 69 *continued*

COLUMN 5–Lines 1-5, 7-8, 10, 15-19, 21-22, and 24: Plotnikov, *Ocherki*, pp. 293, 314, 324, 335, and 340. **Line 6:** Line 7 minus sum of lines 1–5. **Line 9:** Tamarchenko, *Sovetskie finansy*, p. 106. **Line 20:** Line 15 minus sum of lines 16–19. **Line 23:** Line 24 minus sum of lines 8, 15, 21, and 22. **Line 25:** Line 7 minus line 24.

COLUMN 6–Lines 1-5, 7-8, 10-13, 15-19, 21-22, and 24: Plotnikov, *Ocherki*, pp. 293, 314, 324, 335, and 340. **Line 6:** Line 7 minus sum of lines 1-5. **Line 9:** Tamarchenko, *Sovetskie finansy*, p. 106. **Line 14:** Line 8 minus sum of lines 9–13. **Line 20:** Zverev, *Gosudarstvennye biudzhety, 1938–1945*, p. 124. **Line 23:** Line 24 minus sum of lines 8, 15, 21, and 22. **Line 25:** Line 7 minus line 24.

COLUMN 7–Lines 1-4, 7-13, 15-22, and 24: Zverev, *Gosudarstvennye biudzhety, 1938–1945*, pp. 131–32, 134, 136, and 146–48. **Line 5:** Assumed to be same as actual. **Line 6:** Line 7 minus sum of lines 1–5. **Line 14:** Line 8 minus sum of lines 9–13. **Line 23:** Line 24 minus sum of lines 8, 15, 21, and 22. **Line 25:** Line 7 minus line 24.

COLUMN 8–Lines 1-5, 7-8, 10-13, 15-17, 19, 21-22, and 24: Plotnikov, *Ocherki*, pp. 293, 314, 324, 335, and 340. **Line 6:** Line 7 minus sum of lines 1–5. **Line 9:** Tamarchenko, *Sovetskie finansy*, p. 106. **Line 14:** Line 8 minus sum of lines 9–13. **Lines 18 and 20:** Zverev, *Gosudarstvennye biudzhety, 1938–1945*, pp. 146–48. **Line 23:** Line 24 minus sum of lines 8, 15, 21, and 22. **Line 25:** Line 7 minus line 24.

COLUMN 9–Lines 1-2: *Zasedaniia Verkhovnogo Soveta SSSR (odinadtsataia sessiia). 24–27 aprelia 1945 g.* [Meetings of USSR Supreme Soviet. Eleventh Session, April 24–27, 1945], Moscow, 1945, p. 252. **Lines 3-4, 8-13, and 15-22:** Zverev, *Gosudarstvennye biudzhety, 1938–1945*, pp. 149, 152–53, 155, and 157. **Line 5:** Assumed to be same as actual. **Line 6:** Line 7 minus sum of lines 1–5. **Line 7 and 24:** *Zasedaniia Verkhovnogo Soveta SSSR (pervaia sessiia). 12–19 marta 1946 g.* [Meetings of USSR Supreme Soviet. First Session, March 12–19, 1946], Moscow, 1946, p. 7. **Line 14:** Line 8 minus sum of lines 9–13. **Line 23:** Line 24 minus sum of lines 8, 15, 21, and 22. **Line 25:** Line 7 minus line 24.

COLUMN 10–Lines 1-5, 7, and 22: Plotnikov, *Ocherki*, pp. 293, 314, and 324. **Line 6:** Line 7 minus sum of lines 1–5. **Lines 8-13, 15-21, and 24:** *Zasedaniia Verkhovnogo Soveta SSSR (vtoraia sessiia). 15–18 oktiabria 1946 g.* [Meetings of USSR Supreme Soviet. Second Session, October 15–18, 1946], Moscow, 1946, pp. 15–16 and 20. **Line 14:** Line 8 minus sum of lines 9–13. **Line 23:** Line 24 minus sum of lines 8, 15, 21, and 22. **Line 25:** Line 7 minus line 24.

a. Planned figures omitted because none are available for these years.

b. Miscellaneous income includes, among other items, income from the social insurance budget (9.1 billion planned and 8.1 billion actual in 1940 and 10.0 billion planned for 1941), income from Machine and Tractor Stations (2.6 billion planned and 2.0 billion actual in 1940 and 2.6 billion planned for 1941), local taxes, and the logging tax. Of unspecified income, the most important during the war was custom duties, for which the planned figures were 2.5 billion for 1940, 3.0 billion for 1941, 24.0 billion for 1944, and 27.0 billion for 1945. Also included are the funds not utilized during the preceding year (1.6 billion planned for 1940, 1.5 billion for 1940, and 5.5 billion planned for 1941), the carry-over of funds earmarked for investment (1 billion planned for 1941), and savings realized in the administrative apparatus (2.0 billion planned for 1941). (*Zasedaniia Verkhovnogo Soveta SSSR [shestaia sessiia]. 29 marta–4 aprelia 1940 g.* [Meetings of USSR Supreme Soviet. Sixth Session, March 29–April 4, 1940], Moscow, 1940, pp. 239, 429 and 431–32. *Zasedaniia*, 1941, pp. 29, 264, 267, 269, 282, 504, and 507. *Zasedaniia*, 1945, p. 253.)

c. Component parts in lines 16-20 may not sum to total in line 15 because of rounding.

d. This item includes mainly the expenditures of the Commissariat of Internal Affairs and State Security (and of the army under the jurisdiction of this commissariat) and reserve funds (for planned expenditures only, since the actual expenditures appear in the budgetary items for which they have been earmarked). These planned expenditures were as follows (in billion rubles):

	1940	1941	1944	1945
People's Commissariat of Internal Affairs and State Security	7.0	7.3	10.7	15.7
Reserve funds	5.0	5.2	7.0	11.1

(*Zasedaniia*, 1940, p. 248. *Zasedaniia*, 1941, p. 277. *Zasedaniia*, 1945, p. 256.)

3, 1941, the government increased the agricultural tax and the income tax. For the former, the increase was a uniform 100 per cent. For the latter, the increase was 50 per cent for workers and employees with a monthly income of 300–500 rubles and 100 per cent for workers and employees with a monthly income of 600 rubles or more and for all other categories of the population. Special terms and exemptions were provided for military personnel and their families.[51]

A new tax, the war tax, was introduced on January 1, 1942. This tax was levied on individuals, and all the able-bodied population, except for military personnel and their families, was subject to it.[52] Rates were progressive, rising from 10 rubles per month for incomes under 150 rubles a month to 225 rubles per month for incomes above 2,000 rubles a month. This tax accounted for more than half of total taxes on personal income: 14.0 billion rubles in 1942, 17.1 billion in 1943, 20.7 billion in 1944, and 20.3 billion in 1945.[53] Another, less important, tax introduced during the war was on single people and families with no children (a decree of the Supreme Soviet of November 21, 1941). Men aged 20 to 50 and women aged 20 to 45 were subject to this tax, which amounted to 5 rubles per month on incomes under 150 rubles a month and 5 per cent of all incomes over 150 rubles a month. This tax raised 123 million rubles in 1941, 1,092 million in 1942, 1,266 million in 1943, 2,231 million in 1944, and 3,373 million in 1945. Military personnel and their families, students and pensioners, as well as persons whose health did not allow them to have children, were exempt from this tax.[54]

During the war the government also revised existing taxes. The base for the agricultural tax was almost quadrupled on July 3, 1943, compared to its prewar level (which was still in effect in 1942), and a decree of June 3, 1941, made the agricultural tax more progressive, with the maximum subject to progression increasing from 4,000 to 10,000 rubles.[55] A decree of April 30, 1943, combined the personal income tax with taxes for cultural and housing needs. The rates of the tax varied with the amount of income and with the social category of the person taxed. The progression was from 3.6 per cent for an income of 3,600 rubles a year to 11.8 per cent for an income of 50,000 rubles a year for workers and employees, but from 6.8 to 39.1 per cent for the same income for artisans and people other than artists, doctors, lawyers, etc. After these reforms, the agricultural tax increased from 2,204 million rubles in 1942 to 5,571 million in 1945, and the income tax from 3.7 billion rubles in 1940 to 10.6 billion in 1954.[56]

Sizable sums were also raised for the state budget through war loans, which were compulsory for workers and collective farmers. The four war loans, issued successively for 10 billion rubles in 1942, 12 billion in 1943, and 25 billion in 1944 and 1945, raised 13.2 billion rubles in 1942, 20.8 billion in 1943, 29.0 billion in 1944, and 26.7 billion in 1945. The peasants' share in these loans increased

51. *Ibid.*, pp. 271–72.
52. The amount of the agricultural tax was based on the amount of income received from farming.
53. *Ibid.*, p. 277. To compare the income from this tax with total personal income taxes, see Table 69.
54. *Ibid.*, pp. 277–78.
55. *Ibid.*, p. 279.
56. *Ibid.*, pp. 253 and 278–81.

considerably, from 17.0 per cent in 1940 and 22.7 per cent in 1942 to 35.1 per cent in 1944, which made it possible to absorb the liquid assets held by the rural population.[57]

Another means of appropriating the available funds of the population during the war was the formation of a Fund for the Defense of the USSR and a Fund for the Red Army. These funds were set up during the first months of the war with the object of inspiring a spirit of sacrifice and support among the population. Payments in money, valuables, currency, bonds, etc., were accepted. The Fund for the Defense of the USSR managed to collect 6,011 million rubles and the Fund for the Red Army 10,114 million. (For the distribution of these funds by year, see Table 69.) In addition, the Fund for the Defense of the USSR collected 13 kilograms of platinum, 130.7 kilograms of gold, 9.5 tons of silver, 15.8 million rubles in currency, and 522 million rubles in savings bank deposits.[58]

Indirect taxation through the turnover tax, mainly on consumer goods,[59] was considerably reduced during the first years of the war because of the stability of prices in rationed retailed trade. The introduction of state trade at prices close to those of the collective farm market but not rationed brought a total of 15.7 billion rubles into the budget in 1944 and 1945,[60] which, together with the increase in the turnover of retail trade (see below), increased considerably the income from the turnover tax (see Table 69).

The Problem of Budgetary and Financial Equilibrium

The sizable increase in military expenses in the second half of 1941 was a heavy burden on the state budget. The burden was even heavier than the increased expenditures alone would suggest, since regular budgetary income was considerably reduced. This resulted as much from the disorganization of industrial production as from the reduction in retail trade, which, along with light industry, the food industry, and procurements, furnished most of the turnover tax.

The budgetary disequilibrium that appeared in 1941 can be seen by comparing the planned and actual state budgets for 1941 (see Table 69). Income from the turnover tax was 31.3 billion rubles less than planned and from the tax on profits of state-owned enterprises 7.8 billion rubles less. On the outlay side, expenditures for the national economy and for social and cultural measures were reduced considerably below the plan. The expenditures of the People's Commissariats of Defense and of the Navy exceeded the original provisions of the 1941 plan by 12.1 billion rubles (an increase actually lower than called for by the plan for the second half of 1941, which had anticipated additional expenditures of 20.6 billion rubles).

57. *Ibid.*, pp. 289–91.
58. *Ibid.*, pp. 284–88.
59. In 1941, out of the 124.5 billion rubles of income expected from the turnover tax (with only around 11 billion rubles from heavy industry, 8.3 billion of which were from the petroleum industry), 39 billion were paid by agencies for the procurement of agricultural products and for retail trade, with the rest coming from the light and food industries (*Zasedaniia*, 1941).
60. A. N. Malafeev, *Istoriia tsenoobrazovaniia v SSSR, 1917–1963 gg.* [History of Pricing in the USSR, 1917–1963], Moscow, 1964, p. 234.

These developments created a sizable budget deficit (14.4 billion rubles), quite exceptional in Soviet budgetary practice.[61] Budget deficits continued in 1942 and 1943, and it was only in 1944 and 1945 that balanced budgets or surpluses were possible (see Table 69).

Soviet writers indicate that the budget deficits were covered by issuing currency, increasing the public debt, and utilizing material stocks and reserves belonging to the state.[62] According to Voznesenskii, currency in circulation increased 2.4-fold during the three war years.[63] If Raymond P. Powell's estimate is accepted, total currency in circulation was 22 billion rubles on January 1, 1941.[64] Thus, three years later (that is, in 1944), currency in circulation would have been 52.8 billion rubles—an increase of 30.8 billion compared with a budgetary deficit of 39.5 billion rubles in three years.

Nevertheless, during the last year of the war, currency in circulation seems to have increased despite the improvement made in balancing the state budget. According to official Soviet sources, currency in circulation multiplied 3.8 times during the war years.[65] Again using Powell's January 1, 1941, estimate, this would imply 83.6 billion rubles for currency in circulation at "the end of the war" and an increase in currency in circulation of 30.8 billion rubles during the two last years of the war.[66] If so, the budget surpluses of 1944 and 1945 notwithstanding (see Table 69), currency in circulation increased at an even faster rate in this last period than during the first three war years with their sizable budget deficits.[67] The source of this increase is not clear. It might be looked for in the expansion of credit, but according to Voznesenskii there was a decline in the granting of short-term credits in 1941 and 1942 and an increase of only 6 billion rubles in 1943,[68] whereas during these years the total budget deficit amounted to 39.5 billion rubles. During the other war years, the expansion of credit was probably very small also, since total short-term bank loans to enterprises increased by only 4.5 billion rubles between 1941 and 1946.[69]

The increase in currency in circulation could have resulted, at least in part,

61. The budgets had shown no deficits for a long time and had even realized sizable surpluses in 1936–1940 (R. W. Davies, *The Development of the Soviet Budgetary System*, Cambridge, Mass., 1958, pp. 294–95).

62. See, for example, *Shagi*, p. 158, and Kravchenko, *Voennaia ekonomika*, p. 225. It is surprising to find the explanation that the budget deficit was covered by increasing the public debt, since in the Soviet Union the sums received from loans are part of budget income and the sums paid out for loans are part of the expenditures of the state budget. Other Treasury debts to the banks seem to have been incurred during the war, if this information is correct.

63. Voznesensky, *Economy*, p. 82.

64. See Table 111 in Chapter 18.

65. *Shagi*, p. 159. See also Table 111 in Chapter 18.

66. Or perhaps only from July 1, 1944, to July 1, 1945, since Voznesenskii's statement is not very precise about the time period.

67. Hence the situation was similar to the one before 1940 when between 1929 and 1937 the money in circulation increased from 2.1 to 11.3 billion rubles, despite a budget surplus of 15.1 billion rubles during the same period (Franklyn D. Holzman, *Soviet Taxation: The Fiscal and Monetary Problems of a Planned Economy*, Cambridge, Mass., 1955, pp. 53 and 57).

68. Voznesensky, *Economy*, pp. 80–81; and Holzman, *Soviet Taxation*, p. 230.

69. *Gosudarstvennyi bank SSSR* [The USSR State Bank], edited by V. F. Popov, Moscow, 1957, p. 243, as cited by Franklyn D. Holzman, "Soviet Inflationary Pressures, 1928–1957: Causes and Cures," *Quarterly Journal of Economics*, May 1960, p. 182.

from the government's increasing notes in circulation to offset a drain of currency to cash balances held by the rural population. According to Voznesenskii, although the cash holdings of the urban population were reduced in 1942 below 1940 levels, the decrease in the supply of goods in the state and cooperative stores caused money to flow from the cities to rural areas. After the increase in retail prices on the collective farm markets, the money income of the rural population increased faster than its expenditures, which immobilized some currency in peasants' savings.[70]

In any case, the government was very careful during the war not to compromise the budgetary and financial equilibrium by increasing wholesale prices of industrial products. According to Voznesenskii, these prices were at the following levels in 1942 (with 1940 = 100):[71]

General index of industrial wholesale prices	98
War industry	72
Machine-building industry	87
Heavy industry other than war and machine-building industries	98
Light and food industry	120

The index of industrial wholesale prices is not known for all the war years, but Soviet writers claim that it was more or less stable during the ten years preceding the 1949 reform.[72] These claims are consistent with detailed computations made in the West by Bergson, Bernaut, and Turgeon, showing that the index of wholesale prices of basic industrial products (with 1937 weights) increased only 6.0 per cent between 1940 and 1945 and only 2.9 per cent between 1941 and 1945.[73] Jasny, however, pointed out increases in various individual industrial products.[74]

To maintain industrial wholesale price stability while raising industrial wages required recourse to subsidies, which was the only way of controlling pecuniary costs.[75] In fact, several industries began to suffer from planned deficits that could not be covered by budget subsidies. These subsidies, which amounted to 5.1 billion rubles in 1940, came to 4.6 billion in 1943 and increased to 8.1 billion in

70. Voznesensky, *Economy*, p. 81.

71. *Ibid.*, p. 75.

72. D. D. Kondrashev, *Tsenoobrazovanie v promyshlennosti SSSR* [Price Formation in USSR Industry], Moscow, 1956, p. 131.

73. Abram Bergson, Roman Bernaut, and Lynn Turgeon, "Prices of Basic Industrial Products in the U.S.S.R., 1928–50," *Journal of Political Economy*, August 1956, p. 322.

74. Naum Jasny, *Soviet Prices of Producers' Goods*, Stanford, 1952, pp. 153, 157, 160, and 168. They were certain chemical products (hydrochloric acid, ammonium chloride, potassium hydroxide, caustic soda, soda ash), construction materials (window glass, bricks, cement), and certain categories of steel, tractors, and motors.

75. Official Soviet sources (*Shagi*, p. 158) lay claim to a reduction in costs of industrial production in constant prices: −6.9 per cent in 1941, −5.9 per cent in 1942, −2.5 per cent in 1943 and 1944; but there was an increase of 0.9 per cent in 1945 (Malafeev, *Istoriia*, p. 406). In fact, several industries showed a deficit. Kondrashev (*Tsenoobrazovanie*, p. 131) cites the example of the textile industry, whose profits dropped from 6.8 per cent in 1940 to 2.6 per cent in 1942 to 0.02 per cent in 1943, until the industry was working at a loss (of 2.3 per cent in 1944 and 5.3 per cent in 1945).

1944 and 13.9 billion in 1945.[76] Their allocation gave rise to complicated calculations and discussions with the financial administration, since over-all subsidies were fixed at the center and then distributed among enterprises according to the kind of production.[77]

Measures to Ensure Equilibrium between Supply and Demand of Consumer Goods

Increase in the Discrepancy between Supply and Demand of Consumer Goods

Surplus currency in circulation was not a uniquely wartime phenomenon in the Soviet Union. Even in 1940, collective farm market prices, the most sensitive to this surplus, were much higher than those in state and cooperative stores for vegetables and animal products.[78]

The German invasion, the drop in production, and the allocation of material resources to the armed forces reduced considerably the total supply of consumer goods.[79] The result was a sizable drop in goods sold in the retail trade network. Their value in constant prices fell in 1942 to 34 per cent of what it had been in 1940, to 32 per cent in 1943, and rose only to 45 per cent in 1945 (see Table 70). The situation was made still worse by the increase in currency in circulation, due largely to the increase in the amount of currency held by the peasants.

Faced with the scarcity of goods, the government tried to introduce a strict wage policy. There was even a decree (issued on October 3, 1942) eliminating wage increases in remote areas and the far north.[80] But, in actual fact, the government had to yield more and more often on its wage freeze under the pressure of the labor shortage in industries working for defense as well as in other activities essential to the economy. Wage increases, then, were granted gradually in a spontaneous fashion[81] and seemed to be a source of embarrassment to the government, which refused to publish most of these provisions in

76. Data for 1940 from Kondrashev, *Tsenoobrazovanie*, p. 133; data for 1943–1945 from A. G. Zverev, *Voprosy natsionalnogo dokhoda i finansov SSSR* [Problems of USSR National Income and Finances], Moscow, 1958, p. 212.

77. Kondrashev, *Tsenoobrazovanie*, p. 133.

78. On the discrepancy between the prices on the state and cooperative market and those on the collective farm market in 1940, see my "Les fluctuations des prix de détail en Union Soviétique," *Etudes et Conjoncture*, April 1955, pp. 376–81. In the Soviet economy variations in collective farm market prices are a very good index of inflationary pressure. The demand that was not satisfied in the state stores at controlled prices turned to the collective farm market, where prices were determined by the free play of supply and demand.

79. Civilian consumption suffered the effects of both a drop in production and an increase in the share of funds that did not go into the market but went to the army or for the formation of reserves. Thus the share of retail trade in the total marketed output of flour and groats dropped from 86 per cent in 1940 to 73 per cent in 1942, that of meat and meat products from 43 to 23 per cent, that of cotton fabrics from 46 to 9 per cent, and that of leather shoes from 79 to 27 per cent (Voznesensky, *Economy*, p. 75).

80. *Ekonomicheskaia zhizn*, Book I, p. 350.

81. Although these were decisions taken by the central agencies, they seem to have been reflecting the necessities of the moment rather than the over-all policy or annual or quarterly plans drafted during the war.

Table 70   Employment, Retail Trade, and Retail Prices, 1940–1945

	Units	1940 (1)	1941 (2)	1942 (3)	1943 (4)	1944 (5)	1945 (6)
Employment (workers and employees, national economy excl. collective farms and cooperatives)							
1. Average annual number	million	31.2	27.4	18.4	19.4	23.6	27.3
2. Average annual wage	rubles	3,972					5,208
3. Wage fund, partial (official Soviet)[a]	bill. rubles	123.9					142.2
4. Wage fund, total[b]	bill. rubles	162.0					187
Retail Trade							
5. State, cooperative, and collective farm (current prices)	bill. rubles	216.2					296.5
6. State and cooperative	bill. rubles	175.1	152.8	77.8	84.0	119.3	160.1
7. Collective farm, total	bill. rubles	41.1				55.0	
8. In cities	bill. rubles	29.1					136.4
9. State and cooperative (constant prices)	1940 = 100	100	84	34	32	37	45
10. Collective farm, in cities (constant prices)	1940 = 100	100					74.9
11. Collective farm (constant prices)	1940 = 100	100		33.3	43.3	53.3	78.4
Retail Price Indexes							
12. State and cooperative trade, total	1940 = 100	100	103.9	130.6	150.0	184.1	203.1
13. Rationed[c]	1940 = 100	100			100.5		
14. Collective farm trade	1940 = 100	100					448
15. Collective farm trade, January	1940 = 100	100	103	268	1,440	1,317	754
16. Collective farm trade, April	1940 = 100	100	95	636	1,602	1,488	737
17. Collective farm trade, July	1940 = 100	100	88	693	1,467	1,160	590
18. Collective farm trade, October	1940 = 100	100	112	886	1,077	758	417
19. Collective farm trade, average	1940 = 100	100	99.5	620.8	1,396.5	1,180.8	624.5
20. State, cooperative, and collective farm trade	1940 = 100	100					325

Source

LINES 1 and 2: Tables A-3, cols. 8 and 11, and A-4, cols. 1–3 and 5.

LINE 3: Line 1 times line 2.

LINE 4–Col. 1: N. A. Voznesensky, *Five-Year Plan for the Rehabilitation and Development of the National Economy of the USSR, 1946–50* (translated from the Russian), London, 1946, p. 24. **Col. 6:** Based on partial wage fund (line 3) and share that partial was of total in 1940 (derived as 76.5 per cent from lines 3 and 4, col. 1).

LINE 5–Col. 1: Sum of lines 6 and 7. **Col. 6:** Based on state and cooperative trade (line 6) and share that it was of total retail trade (54 per cent since share of collective farm trade is given as 46 per cent in *SSSR v tsifrakh v 1957 godu* [The USSR in Figures in 1957], Moscow, 1958, p. 427).

LINE 6: *Sovetskaia torgovlia* [Soviet Trade], Moscow, 1956, p. 20.

LINE 7–Col. 1: Based on total retail trade (line 5) and share of collective farm trade in total (given as 19 per cent in B. I. Gogol *et al.*, *Ekonomika sovetskoi torgovli* [Economics of Soviet Trade], Moscow, 1955, p. 236. **Col. 5:** Estimate taken from Bergson and Heymann, *Soviet National Income, 1940–48*, p. 148.

LINE 8–Col. 1: *Sovetskaia torgovlia*, p. 179. **Col. 6:** Total retail trade (line 5) minus state and cooperative retail trade (line 6).

LINE 9: *Shagi*, p. 121. According to Malafeev (*Istoriia*, p. 407), retail trade in 1945 in 1940 prices was 73.5 billion rubles, which means that the index in 1945 would be 41.9 with 1940 = 100.

LINE 10–Col. 6: Based on collective farm trade in cities in 1940 (line 8, col. 1) and in 1945 in 1940 prices (derived as 21.8 billion rubles from trade in 1945 prices in line 8, col. 6, and price increase between 1940 and 1945 in line 19, col. 6).

LINE 11: Derived from A. V. Liubimov, *Torgovlia i snabzhenie v gody velikoi otechestvennoi voiny* [Trade and Supply during the Great Patriotic War], Moscow, 1968, pp. 161–62. For April of each year.

LINE 12: Based on trade in current prices (line 6) and in constant prices (calculated from lines 6 and 9). According to Malafeev (*Istoriia*, p. 228), the index of state and cooperative retail trade prices in the fourth quarter of 1942 was

Table 70 *continued*

156 (with June 1941 = 100); the index of food prices was 174.5 and of other products 126.4. Malafeev explains that the increase was caused largely by the increase in the price of vodka (522 per cent), for basic food prices increased only 11.6 per cent in that period. For col. 6, Malafeev's calculations (*ibid.*, pp. 234–35) yield an index of 218 (with 1940 = 100) and he gives an index of 220 (*ibid.*, p. 229). However, *Shagi* (p. 157) gives 205 for the end of the war, broken down into 225 for food products and 195 for other products.

LINE 13–Col. 4: Voznesensky, *Economy*, p. 76.

LINE 14–Col. 6: Based on Malafeev's estimates (*Istoriia*, pp. 234–35) of the average weighted index of state trade prices and collective farm trade prices for 1945 (325 with 1940 = 100), index of state and cooperative trade prices (220 with 1940 = 100), and weights (46 per cent for collective farm trade and 54 per cent for state and cooperative trade).

LINES 15-18: *Finansy i sotsialisticheskoe stroitelstvo* [Finance and Socialist Construction], Moscow, 1957, p. 39.

LINE 19: Unweighted average of lines 15-18.

LINE 20–Col. 6: Malafeev, *Istoriia*, p. 235.

a. Soviet statistics on wage funds usually cover only that part of these funds which can be calculated by multiplying total employment by average annual wage.

b. Total wage funds (given occasionally by Soviet sources, see line 4, col. 1) include, according to Bergson and Heymann (*Soviet National Income, 1940–48*, p. 125): wages paid in certain local industries and wages paid for work not included in the national economic plan, wages paid to hired workers by collective farms, earnings of artisans belonging to cooperatives, military pay, and possibly earnings of forced laborers.

c. Not all state and cooperative trade was affected by rationing, but the share that was is not known.

documents accessible to the public. Only partial information is available on how these wage increases worked.

During the first months of the war, available sources make no mention of wage increases. But the massive evacuation to the east of more than 10 million people[82] entailed additional monetary expenditures that were not compensated by production. During evacuation, workers received their average wage of the preceding three months as well as certain benefits: the monthly wage for each worker, a quarter of his wage for his wife, and one-eighth of his wage for each member of his family who was not working.[83]

The first wage increases were mentioned as of January 1, 1942, for workers in Machine and Tractor Stations.[84] These were supplemented by additional payments to be made by collective farms for plan overfulfillment to MTS workers and combine operators (decrees of May 9 and June 20, 1942).[85] In railroad transportation wages were increased as of March 1, 1942, and in the coal industry they were increased by a decree of August 21, 1942.[86] These were followed by raises for employees in the health services on December 1, 1942, for high school teachers and professors on August 1, 1943, for veterinarians and zootechnicians on January 1, 1944, and for instructors in pedagogical institutes on September 1, 1945.[87] By decrees of June 24, 1944, and June 20, 1945, addi-

82. *Shagi*, p. 120.

83. Kravchenko, *Voennaia ekonomika*, p. 100.

84. January 12, 1942, decree of the USSR Council of People's Commissars and of the Party Central Committee (*Sobranie postanovlenii*, No. 1, 1942, Art. 3).

85. *Ibid.*, No. 5, 1942, Art. 73, and No. 6, 1942, Art. 88.

86. March 16, 1942, decree of USSR Council of People's Commissars and Party Central Committee (*ibid.*, No. 2, 1942, Art. 19); and decree on workers of the People's Commissariat of the Coal Industry (*Ekonomicheskaia zhizn*, Book I, p. 349).

87. December 13, 1942, decree (*Sobranie postanovlenii*, No. 2, 1944, Art. 25); August 11, 1943, decree (*ibid.*, No. 11, 1943, Art. 197); January 9, 1944, decree (*ibid.*, No. 2, 1944, Art. 26); September 2, 1945,

tional payments were also provided to collective farmers per *trudoden* when plans were overfulfilled and crop yields exceeded.[88]

In addition to wage increases, more frequent recourse was had to bonuses. The share of bonuses in total earnings rose from 11 per cent in 1940 to 28 per cent in 1944 for engineers and technical personnel and from 4.5 to 8 per cent for workers. Wage increases were higher in industries run by Union agencies, where workers' wages rose 53 per cent between 1940 and 1944. On the whole, during the war years from 1940 to 1945, the average wages of workers and employees in the national economy increased by 29.5 per cent (see Tables A-3 and A-4). For industrial workers the increase was 42 per cent in 1944 alone.[89]

These wage increases, imposed by circumstances, had the effect of increasing considerably differentials in average wages in different branches of industry. The maximum differential, 85 per cent before the war, tripled toward the end of the war;[90] that is, it reached 255 per cent. The difference between average wages in various industries and the average wages of ferrous metal industry workers are shown for 1944 and May 1945 in Table 71.

Another effect of the wage increases was the appearance of a large quantity of surplus currency in circulation; in 1945, according to the calculations of Gosplan and the Commissariat of Finance, for each ruble in circulation one-third as much merchandise was available as in 1940.[91] The increase in nominal incomes was accompanied by a reduction in per capita real personal consumption of 35–40 per cent during the war years.[92] Soviet writers estimate that real wages of workers and employees in the national economy were reduced by 60 per cent between 1940 and 1945 (57 per cent for industrial workers).[93] In view of this and the definite improvement in the supply of goods in retail trade in 1945 (see Table 70), it can be assumed that the situation was much less favorable during 1942–1944. The government was perfectly aware of this situation and, from the very beginning of the war, settled itself into an economy of scarcity by introducing rationing, revising the methods of planning distribution, and completely reorganizing the work of the agencies in charge of supplying food to the civilian population.

Introduction of Rationing and Distinctions among Various Categories of Consumers

Rationing was introduced during the war in several successive stages. The first decree on the subject (July 18, 1941) introduced rationing in Moscow, Leningrad, and 21 cities and 17 districts in the provinces of Moscow and Leningrad.[94]

---

decree (*ibid.*, No. 9, 1945, Art. 115). Wage increases in certain areas with a harsh climate, such as the Irkutsk area and the far north, were also provided for agronomists and certain MTS workers by the February 25 and December 13, 1944, decrees (*ibid.*, No. 4, 1944, Art. 57, and No. 15, 1944, Art. 219).

88. *Ekonomicheskaia zhizn*, Book I, pp. 374 and 385.
89. Voznesensky, *Economy*, pp. 69–70.
90. *Shagi*, p. 152.
91. *Ibid.*, p. 159.
92. *Ibid.*, p. 157.
93. Malafeev, *Istoriia*, p. 235.
94. July 18, 1941, decree of USSR Council of People's Commissars (*Direktivy*, Vol. 2, pp. 705–7). See

Among the rationed food products were bread and breadstuffs, groats, maca-roni, sugar, confectionery, butter and fat, meat and meat products, and fish. Among the rationed manufactured products were cotton, linen, and rayon fabrics, ready-made clothes, hosiery, leather shoes, rubber shoes, and soap. Rationing was later extended individually to different products and different cities or provinces without becoming general for all products in the whole country.

Table 71   Index of Average Wage Differentials in Different Branches of Industry at End of World War II

	1944			May 1945,
	Workers	Engineers and Technical Personnel		Workers and Employees
Coal mining	104.6	87.1	Tank industry	125
Ferrous metal industry	100.0	100.0	Aircraft industry	117
Industry, total	82.2	70.1	Armaments	112
			Ferrous metal industry	100

Source: 1944: Calculated from Voznesensky, *Economy*, pp. 69–70; 1945: *Shagi*, p. 152.

Rationing of bread, sugar, and confectionery quickly became general. Intro-duced on August 15, 1941 (for bread only, in several other cities such as Sverd-lovsk, Cheliabinsk, Perm, and Gorky), it was extended on September 1 to 197 cities and workers' settlements and in November to all cities and workers' settlements.[95]

Rationing of meat, fish, fat, groats, and macaroni was extended in November to 38 cities[96] (Gorky, Sverdlovsk, Cheliabinsk, Novosibirsk, Kuibyshev, and others) and then gradually to all 115 big cities and industrial centers.[97] In the other cities, rationing of meat, fish, groats, and macaroni was done informally. The central agencies delivered these products to the trading agencies according to the quotas of the rationing system. The trading agencies in turn delivered them by priority to the enterprises with canteens and to certain categories of the population (teachers and doctors, for example). For bread, direct sales to the population in stores were made according to the stocks available, on presenta-tion of ration coupons (which bore no name), in amounts not exceeding the fixed ration in effect in other cities.[98] Similar principles were applied for such

---

also U. G. Cherniavskii, *Voina i prodovolstvie. Snabzhenie gorodskogo naseleniia v velikuiu otechestvennuiu voinu (1941–1945)* [War and Provisioning. Supplying the Urban Population during the Great Patriotic War, 1941–1945], Moscow, 1964, pp. 70–73.

95. Liubimov, *Torgovlia*, p. 22. See also Cherniavskii, *Voina*, p. 70.

96. Liubimov, *Torgovlia*, p. 22. According to Cherniavskii (*Voina*, p. 71), 43 cities.

97. Liubimov, *Torgovlia*, p. 22.

98. *Ibid.*, p. 23. Liubimov was the People's Commissar of Trade during 1939–1948 and seems to be presenting the official version of the regulations. The limitation of sales on presentation of coupons that bore no name does not seem to have been very efficient. On the other hand, these stores often had no supplies at all, which made prices on the collective farm markets go up (see Table 70).

other food products as vegetables and fruit, with total sales to groups of the population being determined by the local executive committees. Milk was supplied by priority to children, kindergartens, hospitals, and enterprise canteens. Salt and tea were sold only in limited quantities upon presentation of ration card coupons.[99]

The government also maintained from the outset a certain number of stores, cafés, and restaurants authorized to sell at higher prices without ration cards.[100] Products necessary for meals, for example, could be bought at a price 200 per cent above the cost of the raw materials. These stores were set up at the same time that the rationing system was introduced, but in 1942–1943, when rationing became widespread, when ration cards were introduced for travelers, and when the scarcity of resources became general, the number of these stores was reduced.[101]

Rationing of manufactured goods was introduced in 43 cities (other than those around Moscow and Leningrad) as of February 1, 1942. The number of rationed products was larger than that introduced by the decree of July 18, 1941, for Moscow and Leningrad, including linens, watches, and several household articles in addition to the others.[102] At the end of April 1942, rationing of manufactured goods was introduced in all cities and workers' settlements, and ration cards for the same products were introduced in rural settlements for certain categories of workers.[103]

The population supplied by the rationing system was divided into four categories: (1) workers and assimilated workers; (2) employees and assimilated employees; (3) their dependents and assimilated dependents; and (4) children up to 12. Workers and employees were classified into the first or second category according to the importance of the industries in which they worked. Certain categories of workers or specialists received higher rations because of their occupation. The variation in total number of calories ranged from 780 calories a day for members of families to 4,418 calories for certain miners (that is, a ratio of 1 to 5.66). The variation by branch of industry is not known. The norms of the Commissariat of Light Industry were 4 per cent higher than those of the Commissariat of the Textile Industry, those in the ferrous metal industry 39 per cent higher, those of the Commissariat of Munitions 46 per cent higher, and those of the Commissariat of the Coal Industry 60 per cent higher (during the first quarter of 1945).[104] For individual products distributed to workers, the ratio of the lowest to the highest at the end of the war was 1 to 2.4 for bread, 1 to 2.5 for meat, fish, fat, and groats, and 1 to 1.25 for sugar and confectionery.[105]

The number of people provided with bread and other food products was 76.8

99. *Ibid*.

100. These stores were set up largely for travelers and people who had not been able to get ration cards.

101. *Ibid*., pp. 23–24.

102. The rationing of these additional products was also extended to Moscow, Leningrad, and their environs.

103. *Ibid*.

104. Cherniavskii, *Voina*, p. 78.

105. *Shagi*, p. 156.

million toward the end of the war, compared with 60.6 million of urban population in 1941.[106] These people received rations that varied very little. Sugar rations, for example, were reduced in the fall of 1941 and in the spring of 1942, and the bread rations were temporarily reduced in the fall of 1943. With larger quantities available during the last two years of the war, supply was improved mainly by increasing the number of people authorized to receive larger rations. Thus, in the middle of 1942, only two-fifths of the urban population received the bread rations granted to workers and employees. This proportion increased to around 50 per cent by the end of 1944. Whereas in 1942 four-fifths of employees received the higher rations of workers, this proportion increased to eleven-twelfths toward the end of 1944.[107]

Centralized Distribution of Consumer Goods

War conditions imposed considerable changes in the organization and planning of distribution. Before the war plans for trade turnover were based on an estimate of the total effective demand of the population and its structure, but during the war these plans were based on consumption norms fixed centrally. The share of centrally allocated funds was increased considerably for the whole country as well as for the republics and provinces. Planning and centralized distribution became monthly. Distribution was effected largely by two methods.[108] The first was direct grants of supplies to agencies that were, in the official terminology, on the "centralized supply" list and called "fund holders." A list of these agencies, the most important for the economy, was transmitted for each province by the People's Commissariat of Trade, and two-thirds of the population was supplied in this way. The second method, for the rest of the population, was through the Commissariat of Trade, which transmitted supplies to its province agencies without specifying the quantities intended for various organizations.

The over-all supervision of centralized allocation was entrusted to the Commissariat of Trade, under which an Administration for Rationed Supplies was set up. Offices for the distribution of ration cards for food and industrial products were created at all administrative levels. There were altogether 3,100 of these offices[109] on January 1, 1946, employing 14,000 people. Ration cards were distributed in industrial enterprises, apartment organizations, and other agencies, which employed 400,000 people in this work, 20 per cent of whom worked full time. Strict supervision had to be established over the operation, and in 1946 supervision itself occupied about 1,900 offices of control and accounting with 12,000 employees. To this vast apparatus of distribution and control should be

106. Cherniavskii, *Voina*, p. 81. It should be noted that in December 1945 the number of people supplied with bread under the rationing system was 80.6 million, 26.8 million of whom lived in rural areas (*Shagi*, p. 156).

107. Cherniavskii, *Voina*, pp. 83–84.

108. *Ibid.*, pp. 95 and 81–85.

109. Of which 29 were republic (including autonomous republic) offices, 140 territory or province offices, 915 city offices, and 335 village offices (Liubimov, *Torgovlia*, p. 47).

added other administrative agencies, such as the permanent commissions of the local Councils of Workers' Deputies, and the trade union organizations.[110]

In enterprises and institutions the main role in the distribution of rationed resources fell to Sections for Supplying Workers (*Otdely Rabochego Snabzheniia*, abbreviated to *Orsy*). *Orsy* had existed as early as 1930–1935, but before the war they were only agencies for supplying food in certain industries (nonferrous metals, timber industry, etc.). Before the war also, special sections of the Commissariat of Trade operated under the armed forces (*Glavvoentorg*), under military detachments of the People's Commissariat of Internal Affairs (*Glavspetstorg*), and under the Navy (*Glavvoenflottorg*).[111] All these supply sections were closed, which meant that only the eligible workers, enterprises, or organizations were authorized to receive supplies. The number of *Orsy* increased considerably during the war, from 1,986 at the end of 1942 to 4,000 in January 1944 to 7,720 on August 1, 1945.[112] Several enterprises and stores of the Commissariat of Trade and other organizations serving workers and employees in many factories and construction projects were transferred to *Orsy*. As early as January 1, 1943, *Orsy* and the Offices for Supplying Food to Industry (*Prodsnaby*) had 17,500 stores, 4,300 kiosks, and 17,200 canteens; these numbers increased to 31,600 stores, 13,300 kiosks, and 29,700 canteens by January 1, 1946.[113] Their share in the total turnover of state and cooperative retail trade rose from 8 per cent in 1940 (*Prodsnaby* only) to 30 per cent in 1943 and increased still further in 1945.[114] On the whole, *Orsy* supplied 48 per cent of the population receiving rationed supplies toward the end of the war.[115]

The canteens were not managed solely by *Orsy*. But the share of *Orsy* in the total turnover of public catering increased considerably, exceeding 29 per cent during the first half of 1942 and 43 per cent during the first half of 1945.[116] This increase occurred despite a sizable expansion in the public catering system during the war (see Table 72). That the number of meals served rose faster than the total turnover of public eating places can be explained by the drop in the value of the meals served. This occurred because of changes in the assortment of foods and in the norms used and also because lower-quality products were used.[117] In some cases the rapid expansion caused defects in the organization of public catering, which were criticized in decrees.[118]

The results of rationing were not always satisfactory to the government,

110. *Ibid.*, pp. 47–48.

111. *Ibid.*, p. 87.

112. *Ibid.*, p. 62; and Cherniavskii, *Voina*, p. 100.

113. Liubimov, *Torgovlia*, p. 62. The author uses the term "public eating places" for canteens and it may include several canteens in large enterprises, but the term "canteen" corresponds better to their principal use.

114. Cherniavskii, *Voina*, p. 102. The share of *Orsy* only (excluding *Prodsnaby*) increased from 17.8 to 27.5 per cent of retail trade turnover between the first half of 1942 and the first half of 1945 (Liubimov, *Torgovlia*, p. 62).

115. Cherniavskii, *Voina*, p. 100.

116. Liubimov, *Torgovlia*, p. 63.

117. *Ibid.*, p. 113.

118. Such as the decree of November 23, 1943, on the operation of public catering in Moscow, which criticized the poor quality of products and the bad service and set a minimum assortment of products for use in preparing meals (*ibid.*, p. 122).

which wanted, on the one hand, to tie the quantities of rations delivered to the productive efforts of those receiving them and, on the other, to combat all infractions of the existing rules. In order to achieve the first objective, a decree was issued on October 18, 1942,[119] encouraging the overfulfillment of norms by providing for increased rations and priority supplies and compelling Party agencies to supervise implementation of the decree. Another decree, issued on January 22, 1943, was intended to combat infringements of the regulations on delivery of rationed products. The control agencies of the Commissariat of Trade were reorganized at this time and a new agency—the Central Administration for State Inspection of Trade—was created under the Commissariat of Trade. Party and trade union agencies were also involved in these control operations.[120]

Limitation of Sector Restricted to Centralized Planning

Strengthening controls alone would not have been sufficient to combat speculation in the situation of wartime scarcity. The government was aware of this problem and tried to cope with it by making a certain number of concessions to nonplanned sectors of production and distribution. These concessions seem to

Table 72   Public Catering, 1940–1945

	Total Number of Public Eating Places (thousands) (1)	Number of Canteens and Restaurants (thousands) (2)	Number of People Served (millions) (3)	Number of Meals Served (billions) (4)	Turnover of Public Eating Places (bill. rubles) (5)	Share of Turnover in Retail Trade (per cent) (6)
1940	87.6	44.5	10–11	8.1	22.9	13
1941	51.6	29.2			21.4	14
1942	51.4	36.0		10.8	18.2	23
1943	58.4	44.5		14.9	20.7	25
1944	70.1	53.9	25	15.8	28.5	24
1945	73.4	53.1		15.0	33.1	21

Source: Cols. 1–2: *Sovetskaia torgovlia*, p. 144; col. 3: Liubimov, *Torgovlia*, p. 116; col. 4: *Sovetskaia torgovlia*, p. 74; col. 5: *ibid.*, p. 20; col. 6: calculated from *ibid.*, p. 20.

have been most important in three series of measures. Nonrationed state trade using "market" prices was introduced, intended to compete with the collective farm market and the "bazaar."[121] The number of farms directly under industrial enterprises, transport enterprises, and other state institutions was increased. The number of private plots owned by the urban population was increased.

119. Decree of USSR Council of People's Commissars, "On Supplying Food and Industrial Products to Workers in Industrial Enterprises" (Cherniavskii, *Voina*, pp. 110–11).
120. Decree of State Committee for Defense, "On Intensifying Efforts to Combat Misappropriation and Squandering of Food and Industrial Products" (*ibid.*, pp. 111–12; and Liubimov, *Torgovlia*, p. 68).
121. A kind of flea market where individuals sell used (and a few new) manufactured goods, largely ones that cannot be found in the stores. The government simply tolerates the "bazaar."

The government did not have to authorize the free sale of agricultural surpluses since this had been done officially since 1932 on the collective farm markets,[122] but with wartime scarcity the prices on these markets reached alarming levels and in April 1943, averaged 16 times as high as in 1940 (see Table 70). If account is taken of the fact that in constant prices the volume of collective farm trade dropped less (particularly after 1943) than that of state and cooperative trade, it is easy to see why this shift in sales volume caused large sums of money to be transferred to the rural population. The high level of prices on the collective farm market was responsible for its large share in total retail trade (46 per cent in 1945—see Table 70, source note to line 5, col. 6), although in 1944 it accounted for only 14.5 per cent of the caloric content of the food consumed by the urban population (see Table 73). Moreover, the high collective farm market prices were very unstable, not only because of seasonal variations (see Table 70) but also because of the considerable discrepancies between the prices on the various markets.

In order to control collective farm market prices, the government decided, as soon as its stocks had increased a little, to "compete" with the collective farm market by reintroducing the so-called "commercial" sales that had existed in 1931–1935 and consisted of selling rationed products at higher prices, closer to those on the collective farm markets. The first 20 stores selling freely at "commercial" prices were opened in Moscow on April 15, 1944. "Commercial" stores were soon opened in such other cities as Leningrad, Kiev, and Sverdlovsk; by the beginning of 1945 they were operating in 25 cities, and in the beginning of 1946 in 130 cities. Manufactured products began to be sold in "commercial" stores during the second half of 1944.[123] The turnover of sales in these stores increased rapidly, rising from 6 billion rubles in 1944 to 16.5 billion in 1945 and to more than 66 billion in 1946.[124] Nevertheless, their main effect was to lower free or semifree prices. The government itself lowered prices for food products in the commercial stores several times. The first reduction, an average of 5 per cent, was made on July 1, 1944. After November 4, 1944, the prices of vodka and wine were reduced by 25 per cent. On February 27, 1945, there was another reduction of 6 per cent on the average in Moscow and 9 per cent in other cities. A final reduction of 15 per cent on the average was decreed on August 21, 1945.[125] It is hard to say whether these reductions preceded or followed the spontaneous drops on the collective farm market (see Table 70), but it is certain that the reintroduction of the commercial stores considerably alleviated wartime scarcity.

Even before the war, in 1940, the government had taken measures to facilitate the organization of and extend farms belonging to industrial and other enterprises.[126] Several measures were taken at the beginning of the war to promote

122. See my Planning for Economic Growth in the Soviet Union, 1918–1932, translated and edited by Marie-Christine MacAndrew and G. Warren Nutter, Chapel Hill, N.C., 1971, pp. 226–27.

123. Liubimov, Torgovlia, pp. 167–68.

124. Most of this income went into the budget under the heading of turnover tax: 4.5 billion rubles in 1944, 10.9 billion in 1945, and 38 billion in 1946 (ibid., p. 170).

125. Plotnikov, Biudzhet, p. 262.

126. September 7, 1940, decree, "On the Organization of Farms to Raise Garden Produce and Animals at Enterprises in Cities and Workers' Settlements" (Sobranie postanovlenii, No. 23, 1940, Art. 582).

Table 73   Sources of Food Supply to Urban Population, 1942–1944 (per cent of caloric content of total food supply)

Source of Supply	All Products			All Products except Bread and Flour		
	1942	1943	1944	1942	1943	1944
State funds distributed in retail trade	78.5	73.0	68.0	46.4	40.3	39.8
Farm plots belonging to enterprises or institutions	3.4	4.2	4.5	9.3	10.4	9.0
Decentralized procurement of agricultural products	1.0	0.8	0.6	2.8	2.2	1.1
Total distributed by state agencies	82.9	78.0	73.1	58.5	52.9	49.9
Private plots of urban population	8.0	9.4	12.4	22.6	24.0	25.3
Collective farm trade	9.1	12.6	14.5	18.9	23.1	24.8
Grand total	100.0	100.0	100.0	100.0	100.0	100.0

Source: Cherniavskii, *Voina*, p. 186.

these farms. The April 7, 1942, decree ordered republic and local agencies to register all uncultivated land near cities or settlements and to put it at the disposal of enterprises, organizations, and the army so that the land could be cultivated and gardens planted by workers and employees.[127] Another measure transferred farms that had previously been under the People's Commissariat of State Farms from enterprises to *Orsy*. More than 550 state and other farms were transferred to *Orsy* during 1941–1943.[128] A special decree, issued on October 18, 1942, tried to organize and plan farms belonging to 28 industrial commissariats.[129] To spur the organization of these farms, they were obliged to deliver to the state only 50 per cent of the meat, grain, and fish products that they raised and were allowed to keep the entire output of other products, mainly milk, eggs, and potatoes.[130]

In October 1942 the number of farms belonging to enterprises and organizations was about 10,000. They belonged to industrial enterprises as well as to transportation and trade enterprises, various institutions, schools, hospitals, etc., and raised mainly garden produce and some animals (mostly poultry and pigs). The largest were those belonging to the *Orsy* and the *Prodsnaby*. Their sown area increased from 2 million hectares in 1942 to more than 4 million hectares toward the end of the war. The number of cattle on the farms of the 37 industrial commissariats increased by 70 per cent between 1942 and 1945, and the number of sheep and goats doubled during the same period.[131] Between

127. April 7, 1942, decree, "On the Appropriation of Land for Farms and Gardens for Workers and Employees" (*Direktivy*, Vol. 2, p. 723).
128. Cherniavskii, *Voina*, p. 133.
129. "On Measures to Further Develop Farms of Industrial People's Commissariats" (*Direktivy*, Vol. 2, pp. 734–43).
130. Cherniavskii, *Voina*, p. 133.
131. Liubimov, *Torgovlia*, p. 148.

1942 and 1945 the production of vegetables on farms belonging to the *Orsy* of 45 commissariats increased 5.4 times, potatoes 3.7 times, and milk 2.5 times.[132] Despite these increases, the share of these farms in urban supply was around 4.5 per cent of total caloric content in 1944, this share being 9.0 per cent for all products except bread and flour (see Table 73).

The workers and employees of cities and settlements also had their own private plots before the war. The total area of these plots was small (735,000 hectares[133]), but for some crops, such as potatoes and vegetables, they accounted for about 3.5 per cent of the total sown area and supplied one-quarter of the needs of the urban population in potatoes and one-tenth in vegetables.[134]

During the war, government policy encouraging the increase in the number of private plots cultivated by urban workers and employees was the same as the policy on farms belonging to enterprises. Thus, the April 7, 1942, decree expressly provided that uncultivated land be given to that category of the population (see above). Promoting the cultivation of these private plots was entrusted, at the beginning of the war, to the Central Council of Trade Unions. A little later (on February 27, 1943), the government created under this Council the Committee to Help the Private and Collective Gardening of Workers and Employees.[135] Special agricultural sections were also organized under the city executive committees in the spring of 1943 to handle these matters.[136] At the beginning of 1942 and 1943, for the benefit of its local sections, the Central Council of Trade Unions drew up directives containing measures to facilitate gardening in cities.[137] In 1944 and 1945 these directives, which were published by the USSR Council of Ministers, set areas to be sown and drafted general plans for this work.[138] The government also granted certain favors to holders of these plots. On July 19, 1943, they were partially exempted from paying the agricultural tax, and in November 1943 the government decided that the concessions on granting private plots to urban workers and employees should hold for five to seven years and forbade the redistribution of the land by enterprise management during this time.[139]

Gardening by the urban population grew to considerable proportions during the war. From 5.9 million in 1942, the number of plots rose to 11.8 million in 1943 and to 16.5 million in 1944. The area granted for the plots, which had been reduced to 500,000 hectares in 1942 (from 735,000 in 1940—see above), was

132. Cherniavskii, *Voina*, p. 137.

133. Iu. V. Arutiunian, *Sovetskoe krestianstvo v gody velikoi otechestvennoi voiny* [The Soviet Peasantry during the Great Patriotic War], Moscow, 1963, p. 413.

134. Cherniavskii, *Voina*, pp. 137–38.

135. *SSSR*, p. 346.

136. Cherniavskii, *Voina*, p. 140.

137. Directives of January 5, 1942, and March 11, 1943 (*Ekonomicheskaia zhizn*, Book I, pp. 342 and 358).

138. Decrees of February 19, 1944 (setting an increase of at least 20 per cent over 1943 in sown area), and of February 6, 1945 (*ibid.*, Book I, pp. 371 and 382).

139. *Sobranie postanovlenii*, No. 9, 1943, Art. 153, and No. 10, 1942, Art. 154. However, these concessions were only granted conditionally. Exemption from the agricultural tax applied only to plots of less than 0.15 hectares per family with no large cattle. The permanence of the plots for five to seven years was done away with in the case of departure (other than to the army or other forced work or as a result of infirmity).

increased to 1,415,000 hectares in 1944 and to 1,705,000 hectares in 1945, with potatoes and vegetables accounting for 1,185,400 hectares of this last figure.[140] These plots supplied some 16.5 million urban families with potatoes and vegetables in 1944, for example. It should be noted that their importance, in caloric content, was almost the same as that of the collective farm market in 1944 (12.4 per cent compared with 14.5 per cent for the collective farm market—see Table 73). Furthermore, for food products other than bread and flour, they supplied around a quarter of the total caloric content of the food supply to the urban population (see Table 73).

Government Measures against Private Plots on Collective Farms

Before the war the government and the Party were very careful to keep the production and size of the private plots of collective farmers within the strict limits of the collective farm charter. A special decree of May 27, 1939,[141] condemned infractions of these regulations with the aim of preventing the collective farmers' private plots from becoming their main source of income.

The war profoundly disrupted the internal life of the collective farms. The total number of collective farmers may have dropped only slightly, but this drop was mainly in the able-bodied population because of the departure of men mobilized into the army and defense-related work. In 1944 there were only two able-bodied men per ten collective farm households, whereas there had been nine in 1940 (see Table 74).

Income from collective farming, which was not very high before the war, was sharply reduced. The total amount of grain distributed was reduced by more than two-thirds in 1943 and payments per *trudoden* were considerably decreased, except for the payment in money, the real value of which had been sharply reduced by inflation. To live on the income supplied by the collective farm would have meant starvation for a peasant family. In 1943 it received, per person, less than 200 grams of grain and about 100 grams of potatoes per day, that is, one pot of grain and one potato; they also received a few vegetables, but meat, butter, and milk were hardly distributed at all.[142] The national averages, moreover, do not reflect the actual situation on some collective farms, which paid practically nothing per *trudoden*. In 1945, for example, 5.4 per cent of the collective farms distributed absolutely no grain; 37.2 per cent paid only 300 grams of grain per *trudoden*; and 75 per cent distributed no potatoes. In fact, what collective farmers received per *trudoden* was half or a third as much as what urban workers and employees received in the way of food rations.[143]

All this explains the attention that collective farmers devoted to their private plots. They clung above all to their homes, to which these plots were attached,

140. Arutiunian, *Sovetskoe krestianstvo*, p. 413; and Cherniavskii, *Voina*, p. 141.
141. Decree of the USSR Council of People's Commissars and Party Central Committee, "On Measures to Protect the Collective Lands of Collective Farms from Being Squandered" (*Direktivy*, Vol. 2, pp. 589–94).
142. Arutiunian, *Sovetskoe krestianstvo*, p. 335.
143. *Ibid.*, pp. 346 and 335.

Table 74   Income from Collective Farming and Development of Farming and Livestock Breeding on Private Plots of Collective Farmers, 1940–1945

	Units	1940 (1)	1941 (2)	1942 (3)	1943 (4)	1944 (5)	1945 (6)
1. Collective farm population, total:	millions	75.8	40.5	41.1	47.3	64.4	64.5
2. Able-bodied population:	millions	35.4	16.5	15.1	16.6	22.0	23.9
3. Male	millions	16.9			3.6	4.5	6.5
4. Female	millions	18.6			12.9	17.6	17.4
5. Collective farm households	millions	18.7		10.8	12.8	18.0	17.9
6. Number of people per 10 households:	number	42				35	36
7. Able-bodied males	number	9				2	5
8. Able-bodied females	number	10				10	10
Income from collective farming received by collective farmers							
9. Total grain distributed for trudodni[a]	mill. m. t.	10.15	4.35	2.24	2.95	4.21	3.79
Value of trudoden:[a b]							
10. Grain	kg	1.60	1.40	0.80	0.65		0.70
11. Potatoes	kg	0.98	0.33	0.22	0.40		0.26
12. Money	rubles	0.98	1.07	1.03	1.24	1.12	0.85
Average received (in trudodni[a]) per capita per day:							
13. Grain	kg	0.50			0.18		0.19
14. Potatoes	kg	0.33			0.11		0.07
Private plots of collective farmers							
15. Sown area, total:	th. ha	4,481				4,845	4,937
16. Grain	th. ha	861				1,534	1,543
17. Industrial crops	th. ha	147				132	122
18. Vegetables and potatoes	th. ha	3,113				3,008	3,082
19. Fodder	th. ha	360				171	190
20. Sown area as per cent of total sown area	per cent	3				4.4	4.3
21. Sown area per collective farm household	ha	0.24				0.27	0.28
Livestock:							
22. Cattle	mill. head	19.2	11.8	9.7	13.4	16.5	17.9
23. Sheep and goats	mill. head	31.6	20.7	17.6	18.1	18.9	18.1
Livestock per 100 collective farm households							
24. Cattle:	head	103					100
25. Cows	head	65					60
26. Pigs	number	44					17
27. Sheep and goats	number	169					106

Source: Arutiunian, *Sovetskoe krestianstvo*, pages specified below.
Lines 1–4, cols. 1 and 4–6: p. 318; line 1, cols. 2–3: p. 390; line 2, cols. 2–3: p. 392; line 5, col. 1: p. 319; line 5, cols. 3–6: p. 388; lines 6–8, cols. 1 and 5–6: p. 320; line 9: p. 437; lines 10–12, cols. 1–6: p. 334; lines 13–14, cols. 1, 4, and 6: p. 335; line 15, cols. 1 and 5–6: sum of lines 16–19; lines 16–19, cols. 1 and 5–6: pp. 412–13; line 20, cols. 1 and 5–6: p. 345; line 21, cols. 1 and 6: p. 345; line 21, col. 5: calculated from lines 15 and 5; lines 22–23, cols. 1–6: p. 342; lines 24–27, cols. 1 and 6: p. 343.

Note: Details may not agree with totals because of rounding.

a. Hypothetical working day.
b. Including tractor drivers from Machine and Tractor Stations and combine operators paid at much higher rates.

even if the over-all collective farm population diminished considerably because of war losses. Between 1940 and 1942, the collective farm population and the number of collective farm households dropped more or less in the same proportion—46 and 42 per cent, respectively (see Table 74). In 1944, however, while the number of collective farm households almost regained its prewar level (96.2 per cent), the collective farm population dropped by 15 per cent, or 11.4 million, below the 1940 level (see Table 74). They tried to make maximum use of their plots, which to be sure, were very small—0.27 hectares on the average per collective farm household in 1944 (see Table 74). The cultivation of a private plot allowed the peasant to have all the necessary food products: potatoes, vegetables, milk, meat, and eggs. But he lacked the most basic essential—bread. Despite the increase in the share of plots sown to grain (which rose from 19 per cent in 1940 to 31–32 per cent in 1944 and 1945), the average grain harvest per household never exceeded 25 to 30 kilograms per person per year.[144] In order to obtain bread, salt, oil, and manufactured products, the collective farmer had to sell his products on the collective farm market. The rapid rise in prices on the collective farm market and the supply difficulties in cities encouraged the farmers to have recourse to barter as often as possible. Exchange with city-dwellers became more and more widespread in the villages themselves, where the city-dwellers came bringing clothes, boots, watches, and other essential manufactured products to exchange them for potatoes, butter, or grain.[145]

The government's attitude toward this increased importance of collective farmers' private plots was just the opposite of its attitude toward private plots of city-dwellers. It believed that it had to defend the very principle of collectivized agriculture. But the measures taken directly to encourage work on the collective farms[146] and the penal sanctions taken to tighten labor discipline[147] did not seem sufficient, and the government was led to take direct measures against the cultivation of private plots by collective farmers. One of the most important of these measures was the forced "purchase" of livestock owned privately by collective farmers. About 2.5 million calves were "bought" in this manner in the unoccupied areas in 1942, more than 2 million in 1943, and 1.5 million in 1944.[148] These "purchases" were made after local Party and government agencies took on obligations they could not meet to increase collective farm livestock, so this was a convenient way to fulfill their plans. Often, as was the case in Kazakhstan and many other regions, these "purchases" were not controlled by the state.[149]

144. *Ibid.*, pp. 345–47.
145. *Ibid.*, pp. 346–47.
146. Among these measures, the following should be mentioned: the increase in the number of compulsory *trudodni*, the training of tractor drivers and mechanics, the mobilization of city-dwellers for agricultural work, the increase in MTS wages, and additional payments for *trudodni* when the plan was overfulfilled (all of which have been discussed above).
147. The penalty for not fulfilling the required number of *trudodni* was "re-education" work on collective farms for up to six months. The same penalties were given, moreover, to workers and employees who left their jobs without authorization; these sanctions were specified in the 1940 decrees (Arutiunian, *Sovetskoe krestianstvo*, p. 19).
148. *Ibid.*, p. 307.
149. This practice was condemned in Kazakhstan in April 1944. But in 1942 this republic received the award of the Red Flag and first prize in the socialist competition in livestock breeding. See *ibid.*, p. 337.

The immediate consequences of this practice were the clandestine slaughtering of privately owned livestock and a considerable reduction in the total livestock privately owned by collective farmers (see Table 74). This reduction was just as great in the regions that were not occupied and had not suffered war damage as in the liberated areas. Between 1940 and 1945, in the unoccupied areas, the number of cattle privately owned by collective farmers dropped by 8.2 per cent (7.7 per cent of which was cows), of pigs by 58.3 per cent, and of sheep and goats by 43.2 per cent.[150]

The government also directly appropriated the income of peasants by taxes (see second section of this chapter). The rates of the agricultural tax depended on the level of income. In the Russian Republic these norms were increased 3.5 times for cows and five times for grain and potatoes.[151] After the 1943 reform, these taxes and the monetary taxes paid by collective farmers to the state accounted for 18 per cent of their money income in the Russian Republic. They had been only 9 per cent in 1942.[152]

While absorbing their money income by taxes, the government was "shocked" by the high income that the collective farmers received for the sale of their products on the collective farm market. The newspapers attacked speculators for profiting from the market situation, and complaints were published from women protesting the high prices set or demanded by collective farm chairmen who did not obtain the approval of the general assembly of collective farmers for those prices. Attempts were made to introduce onto collective farm markets so-called "prices fixed by common agreement," which were much lower than the market prices (one-third to one-quarter of prices for flour, one-half to one-third of prices for milk and meat). But this practice had to be abandoned because the collective farms reduced their sales on the collective farm markets by selling the same products outside the market at higher prices.[153]

Further pressure was applied to the cultivation of private plots by administrative control over the size of these plots. In unoccupied areas, such as Alma Ata, Moscow, and Kirov, as well as in formerly occupied areas, collective farmers tended to increase the size of their gardens to a hectare or even more. Agencies of the People's Commissariats of Agriculture and of State Control instituted controls and applied penal sanctions provided by the May 27, 1939, decree.[154] The elimination of "additional" land in private plots slowed down the increase in the sown area of plots (particularly in 1944 and 1945), while socialized agriculture recovered quickly.

Labor discipline on collective farms also restrained work on private plots. The collective farm, and through it the state, dictated the very form of life of the collective farmers; socialist forms of work, the link (zveno) system, and the

150. Ibid., p. 343.
151. The income norms were raised from 824 rubles in 1942 to 4,000 rubles in 1943 for grain (per hectare cultivated), from 2,638 to 14,000 rubles for potatoes, and from 1,000 to 3,500 rubles for each cow (ibid., p. 336).
152. Ibid., p. 337.
153. Ibid., p. 349.
154. Ibid., p. 344. See above.

brigade were strengthened along with discipline. Female collective farmers, who had managed to spend 35 per cent of their time working on their private plots in 1940, could spend no more than 31 per cent of it on the plots in 1945. The private plots of collective farmers, despite their enormous importance in feeding the country, continued to be treated as something of secondary importance.[155]

155. *Ibid.*, p. 351.

PART FIVE

Postwar Economic Planning and Equilibrium, 1946–1952

CHAPTER 16

Economic Plans during Reconstruction, 1946–1952

The Soviet Economy at the End of World War II

Three major factors must be taken into account in assessing the economic power of the Soviet Union at the end of World War II. First, the Soviet Union had become a major world power, largely as the result of direct territorial annexation (670,340 square kilometers, inhabited before the war by 23.6 million people[1]) carried out mainly at the expense of victims of German aggression (Czechoslovakia, Poland) or neutral countries (Lithuania, Latvia, Estonia) and even Finland, the victim of Soviet aggression in December 1939. Territorial annexation of Axis countries (Germany, Japan) or of their temporary allies (Rumania) was less important. But the major part of the Soviet Union's new power was the result of protracted military occupation and the subsequent stationing of its troops in countries that had regained the status of officially independent countries, such as Poland, Czechoslovakia, East Germany, Bulgaria, or Hungary. Thus, direct Soviet power extended beyond its official borders, which had an effect on its economy. The immediate advantages that the Soviet Union derived from the territories it occupied militarily were of three kinds: (1) reparation payments (from the countries that had belonged to the Axis—Austria, Hungary, Rumania, and Bulgaria); (2) confiscation of "ex-German" goods in these same countries;[2] and (3) payments for the upkeep of Soviet troops, their transportation, etc. In addition, factories were dismantled and requisitioned arbitrarily in all the countries, enemy or "friendly," occupied by the Soviet army. The officially calculated

---

1. Abram Bergson and Hans Heymann, Jr., *Soviet National Income and Product, 1940–48*, New York, 1954, p. 6.
2. The Soviet occupation authorities gave a very broad interpretation to the concept of "ex-German" goods. They included goods confiscated by the Nazis from nationals of the countries in question for racist (persecution of the Jews) or other reasons. Sometimes they formed on this basis joint companies, thus making permanent the advantages acquired.

total paid by the countries of Central Europe to the Soviet Union from 1945 to October 1956 has been estimated at 5 billion rubles per year (in 1938 dollars). Until 1950, East Germany alone paid 609.6 million dollars a year (in 1938 dollars).[3]

The second factor is the tremendous losses suffered by the Soviet Union during the war. Toward the end of 1945, its population was approximately 2 to 4 million less than that recorded in January 17, 1939, census for the territory before annexation. Of the total population that had lived on the actual territory at the end of 1940, losses could be set at about 30 million persons.[4] According to official Soviet estimates (which are difficult to check), direct capital losses due to war damages in prewar prices came to 679 billion rubles (that is, 128 billion prewar dollars at the official exchange rate).[5] If war expenditures and the income losses of the population and enterprises are included, total losses are estimated at 1,890 billion rubles (357 billion prewar dollars).[6]

The third factor is the power of the Communist Party, not to mention the personal power of Stalin, which had been considerably strengthened by the war. The postwar reconstruction, then, was not only the reconstruction of the economy but also the restoration of prewar political and institutional order and a return to the goals and methods of prewar administrative planning.

3. Naum Jasny, *Soviet Industrialization, 1928–1952*, Chicago, 1961, p. 246. For more detail, see Antony C. Sutton, *Western Technology and Soviet Economic Development, 1945–1965*, Stanford, 1973, Chapters 1 and 2.

4. The Soviet population at the end of 1940 can be estimated at 197.5 million from the population on January 1, 1940 (given as 194.1 million in *Narodnoe khoziaistvo v 1965 godu* [The USSR National Economy in 1965], Moscow, 1966, p. 7) and the increase during 1940 (assumed to be the same as the increase during 1939, which was calculated as 3.4 million from the population on January 1, 1940, above, and the population on January 17, 1939, which was given as 190.7 million in *Itogi vsesoiuznoi perepisi naseleniia 1959 goda. SSSR (Svodnyi tom)* [Results of All-Union Census of the Population in 1959. USSR: Summary Volume], Moscow, 1962, p. 13).

Soviet sources do not give any estimates of the 1945 population, but some sources indicate that the Soviet Union lost 20 million people during the war. (See, for example, A. Ia. Utenkov, *KPSS— organizator i rukovoditel sotsialisticheskogo sorevnovaniia v promyshlennosti v poslevoennye gody (1946–1950 gg.)* [The Communist Party of the Soviet Union—the Organizer and Leader of Socialist Competition in Industry in the Postwar Years, 1946–1950], Moscow, 1970, p. 18.) In fact, if the Soviet estimate of the population for the first postwar year (given as 178.5 million for January 1, 1950, in *Trud v SSSR* [Labor in the USSR], Moscow, 1968, p. 19) is taken as a base and annual increases of 1.5 or 1.7 per cent from 1945 to 1949 are accepted, a population of 168.2 or 166.9 million is obtained for the end of 1945. Actually, population growth was 1.7 per cent in 1950, and there was no increase of less than 1.6 per cent in any year from 1950 to 1961 (see *Narodnoe khoziaistvo SSSR v 1961 godu* [The USSR National Economy in 1961], Moscow, 1962, p. 28, and *Narodnoe khoziaistvo, 1965*, p. 42). Thus, according to the estimate accepted for 1945, a population loss of 29.3 or 30.6 million between 1940 and 1945 is obtained.

5. Nikolai A. Voznesensky, *The Economy of the USSR during World War II* (translated from the Russian), Washington, 1948, p. 97. For alternative estimates, see G. Warren Nutter, *Growth of Industrial Production in the Soviet Union*, Princeton, 1962, p. 214, n. 29.

6. In the occupied areas, complete or partial destruction and looting affected 31,850 factories, plants, and other industrial establishments (not counting small enterprises and workshops); 1,876 state farms; 2,890 Machine and Tractor Stations; 98,000 collective farms; 216,700 stores, canteens, restaurants, and other commercial establishments; 4,100 railroad stations; 36,000 post offices, telephone stations, radio stations, and other communications offices; 6,000 hospitals; 33,000 dispensaries; 976 sanatoriums; 82,000 primary and secondary schools; 334 higher educational institutions, among others (Voznesensky, *Economy*, pp. 95–97).

Fourth Five-Year Plan, 1946–1950

Drafting of Fourth Five-Year Plan

Immediately after the cessation of hostilities with Germany and notwithstanding the war still in progress with Japan, the Soviet government took measures to return to a peacetime economy. But it must be understood that this was a Stalinist peacetime, which meant an economy with high levels of military and arms expenditures. One of the first measures on reconversion was a decree of the State Committee for Defense ("On Measures to Rebuild Industry in Connection with the Reduced Production of Armaments," May 26, 1945), which dealt with the reconversion of certain enterprises to civilian production and with the problem of wages tied to the change in the production assortment.[7] The June 23, 1945, law provided for the demobilization of 13 age groups of the oldest men in the army.[8] And the State Committee for Defense was dissolved on September 4, 1945, its functions being transferred to the USSR Council of People's Commissars.

Among the measures taken immediately after cessation of hostilities with Germany was the Party Central Committee and Council of People's Commissars decree of August 19, 1945, which directed USSR Gosplan and the commissariats to draft as quickly as possible a five-year plan for the reconstruction and development of the national economy for 1946–1950 and a five-year plan for the reconstruction and development of transportation for 1946–1950.[9] The directives provided for the "complete reconstruction of the economy in the areas of the USSR occupied by the Germans, the postwar reconversion of the economy, and the further development of all areas of the USSR, which should make it possible to exceed considerably the prewar level of economic development."[10]

Unfortunately, the detailed contents of these directives are not known, but this plan seems to have been part of a project to make the Soviet economy so powerful that it would not have to fear any external danger. The economic goals that were to make this possible were summarized by Stalin in his speech of February 9, 1946: 500 million metric tons of coal, 60 million metric tons of petroleum, 50 million metric tons of pig iron, and 60 million metric tons of steel.[11] Such goals may seem naive today as indicators of economic progress,

---

7. *Direktivy KPSS i sovetskogo pravitelstva po khoziaistvennym voprosam* [Directives of the Communist Party of the Soviet Union and of the Soviet Government on Economic Matters], Moscow, 1957, Vol. 2, pp. 861–62. Industrial commissariats and enterprises directors were authorized to pay workers' wages at the rate of the preceding three months for one or two months during the period of assimilation of the new production because of the complex nature of this new production (*Ekonomicheskaia zhizn SSSR* [Economic Life of the USSR], edited by S. G. Strumilin, Moscow, 1967, Book I, p. 384).

8. *Ibid.*, Book I, p. 385. The Soviet armed forces were reduced from 11,365,000 men in May 1945 to 2,874,000 in 1948, according to Nikita Khrushchev (*Pravda*, January 15, 1960, p. 3).

9. *Ekonomicheskaia zhizn*, Book I, p. 386.

10. *Partiinoe stroitelstvo* [Party Building], No. 16, 1945, p. 33, as cited in Utenkov, *KPSS*, pp. 23–24.

11. Stalin indicated that these goals were to be realized during three five-year periods or even later. Presumably these were the usual goals of the long-term plans, often formulated for a period of approximately 10 or 15 years. See "Rech tovarishcha I.V. Stalina na predvybornom sobranii izbiratelei stalinskogo izbiratelnogo okruga g. Moskvy 9 fevralia 1946 goda" [Speech of Comrade I. V. Stalin at Pre-Election Meeting of Voters of Stalin Electoral District of Moscow on February 9, 1946], *Planovoe khoziaistvo* [Planned Economy], No. 1, 1946, p. 10.

but, as goals formulated by an all-powerful dictator, they reflect the crude idea of economic development, based on quantitative and quite rudimentary criteria, that was at the heart of the Fourth Five-Year Plan.

A draft of this plan was prepared by USSR Gosplan, and on the basis of the draft and a report on it by Gosplan Chairman Voznesenskii, the "Law on the Fourth Five-Year Plan for 1946–1950"[12] was passed by the USSR Supreme Soviet on March 18, 1946. This law provided that the USSR Council of Ministers was to examine and approve the plans drafted by the ministries and organizations. The goals of the plan were apparently given in the law in a brief form, and no breakdown by year was given. Nevertheless, even the abbreviated version makes it possible to get an idea of the government's principal choices.

Principal Goals of Fourth Five-Year Plan

Most of the goals for the fourth plan use 1940 as a base, the last prewar year for the Soviet Union. Although it may be useful, this base does not make it possible to examine the main plan choices. It seems more useful to present the principal goals with 1945 as a base, as has been done in Table 75, because that permits comparisons of the basic provisions of the Third and Fourth Five-Year Plans. The first observation is that the planned growth rates of national income and gross industrial production are *lower* in the fourth than in the third plan. According to official Soviet data (see Table 79), national income in 1945 was lower than in 1940, so it seems that the pressure on the economy had been reduced and planning was less taut. It is true that reduced production of armaments and related products caused most of the reduction in the planned growth of industrial production (160.9 in the fourth plan as opposed to 192.7 in the third plan), but total industrial production in 1945 was lower than in 1940 (127.4 billion rubles compared with 138.5 billion in 1940—see Table 79). Hence Soviet planners apparently believed that reconstruction required a reduction in growth rates, a belief not confirmed by subsequent experience in the Soviet Union itself or in a number of other countries, as, for instance, France.

Another noteworthy aspect of the plan is the breakdown of growth between producer and consumer goods.[13] According to Stalinist doctrine, producer goods should always grow more rapidly than consumer goods. But in the prewar Soviet Union the level of consumption often fell so low that even Stalinist planners felt obliged to twist the doctrine. This had been the case with the Second Five-Year Plan and the first variant of the Third Five-Year Plan, and it could not help but happen again with the first postwar five-year plan. According to the plan, producer goods were to increase by 43.1 per cent, while consumer goods were to increase by 118 per cent. For agricultural production, the 1950

12. The passage of this law did not mean that the final plan had been adopted. Rather, it was a "framework law," not binding on the government or the Party, on the basis of which the final text of the Fourth Five-Year Plan was to be drawn up.

13. Official Soviet statistics on "consumer goods" and "producer goods" are misleading if one wants to draw conclusions about Soviet consumption. Several agricultural raw materials (cotton yarn, leather, etc.) intended for eventual transformation are producer goods although they could be used to produce consumer goods.

Table 75   Comparison of Principal Goals of Third and Fourth Five-Year Plans

	Units	Third Five-Year Plan Goals for 1942		Fourth Five-Year Plan Goals for 1950	
		Physical Units (1)	Index (1937 = 100) (2)	Physical Units (3)	Index (1945 = 100) (4)
National income (1926/27 prices)	bill. rubles	173.6	180.3	177	166.2
Gross industrial production (1926/27 prices):	bill. rubles	184	192.7	205.0	160.9
Producer goods	bill. rubles	114.5	207.4	135.9	143.1
Consumer goods	bill. rubles	69.5	172.5	69.1	218.0
Gross agricultural production (1926/27 prices)	bill. rubles	30.5	151.6	29.6	211.4[a]
Railroad freight traffic	bill. m. ton–km	510.0	143.7	532	169.4
Employment, workers and employees:					
National economy	millions	32.7	121.1	33.5	122.9
Industry	thousands	11,899	117.7	11,900	125.2
Wages, workers and employees, national economy:					
Wage fund	bill. rubles	137.40	167.1	201.0	141.5
Average money wage	rubles	4,162	136.6	6,000	115.2
Average real wage	yr. preced. plan = 100		136.6[b]		305.2[a]
State and cooperative retail trade:					
In current prices	bill. rubles	206.0	163.6	275.0	171.8
In constant prices	bill. rubles	206.0[c]	163.6[c]	224.1	304.9
Labor productivity:					
Industry	yr. preced. plan = 100		165[d]		136[e]
Construction	yr. preced. plan = 100		175[f]		140[e]
Cost of production:					
Industry	yr. preced. plan = 100		89[d]		83[e]
Construction	yr. preced. plan = 100				88[e]

Source: Unless otherwise indicated, cols. 1 and 3: Table A-1, cols. 7 and 10; col. 2: based on Table A-1, cols. 7 and 2; col. 4: based on col. 3 and Table A-4, col. 15.

a. Table 79, col. 5.

b. Since the Third Five-Year Plan said nothing about a decline in retail prices, it was assumed that retail prices (and the cost of living) were to remain unchanged during the Third Five-Year Plan.

c. It was assumed that retail prices in state and cooperative trade were to remain unchanged during the Third Five-Year Plan and hence would be 1937 prices.

d. *Tretii piatiletnii plan razvitiia narodnogo khoziaistva SSSR (1938–1942)* [Third Five-Year Plan for the Development of the USSR National Economy, 1938–1942], Moscow, 1939, p. 199.

e. "Zakon o piatiletnem plane vosstanovleniia i razvitiia narodnogo khoziaistva SSSR na 1946–1950 gg." [Law on Five-Year Plan for the Reconstruction and Development of the USSR National Economy in 1946–1950], *Resheniia Partii i Pravitelstva po khoziaistvennym voprosam* [Decisions of the Party and Government on Economic Matters], Moscow, 1968, Vol. 3, p. 272.

f. E. Vasilev and Kh. Kovalzon, "Za dostoinuiu sotsialisticheskogo obshchestva proizvoditelnost truda" [For a Labor Productivity Worthy of a Socialist Society], *Planovoe khoziaistvo*, No. 3, 1939, p. 155.

goal was simply a repetition of the old 1942 goal. This reflected the Stalinist habit of planning high growth rates for agricultural production based on optimism rather than on serious study of the probable consequences of the measures adopted.

Railroad freight traffic was to grow more rapidly in the fourth plan than in the third, while industrial production was to grow more slowly. This phenomenon reflects the transformations that took place in the geographic distribution of Soviet industry. According to official Soviet estimates, in 1945 the index of gross industrial production for the whole country was 92 (in 1926/27 prices, with 1940 = 100).[14] But the same index was only 29.5 in the formerly occupied territory and 122.3 in the unoccupied territory.[15]

Employment was to increase at practically the same rate in the fourth plan as in the third plan, despite the huge number of demobilized soldiers. This is additional evidence of the immense human losses that the Soviet Union suffered during the war.

For wages and prices, the fourth plan is perhaps more "Stalinist" than the third plan. Money wages were to increase very little (only 15.2 per cent in five years), whereas real wages were to triple, thanks to an anticipated drop in the retail price index (see Table 79).

Coherence of Fourth Five-Year Plan

A first glance at the fourth plan suggests that it was a typical "Stalinist" plan but with lower industrial growth rates. Thus, the conclusion might be drawn that the plan was less taut, hence more coherent.

The drafting of the fourth plan marked the first occasion on which a summary balance of producer and consumer goods was drawn up.[16] The over-all results of these calculations are presented in Table 76. According to Soviet writers, the balance for consumer goods was originally drawn up with a sizable deficit and, despite several revisions, planned uses always exceeded resources by a billion rubles; but such a deficit was not serious, in view of the reserves of consumer goods provided in the balance.[17]

The planned balance of producer and consumer goods was part of a calculation of the balance of the national economy that included 34 tables. Among these tables, the most important was the one for social product (see Table 77). Its interest lies mainly in the publication, very rare in Soviet practice, of the volume of transfer from group B to group A for 1940 and for 1950, the last year of the 1946–1950 plan. The writers indicated on this occasion that the total production of armaments planned for 1950 had been reduced to the 1940 level.[18]

These calculations are of interest largely because they bring out the principal

14. *Narodnoe khoziaistvo, 1965*, p. 122.
15. Calculated from data given by Serge N. Prokopovicz, *Histoire économique de l'U.R.S.S.*, Paris, 1952, p. 311.
16. The first version of such a balance was presented by Voznesenskii when the annual plan for 1941 was drafted (*Po edinomu planu* [According to a Single Plan], Moscow, 1971, pp. 105–6).
17. *Ibid.*, p. 106.
18. *Ibid.*, p. 104.

Table 76   Planned Balance of Producer and Consumer Goods for 1950 (billion rubles, 1940 prices)

Producer Goods			
Total Planned Uses	498	*Total Production*	504
Consumption in production	414		
Accumulation	71.5		
Personal consumption	8		
Losses	4	Surplus of needs	
		over production	6
Increase in reserves and stocks	30.5		
Consumer Goods			
Total Planned Uses	410	*Total Resources*	409
Households and institutions (per cent)	90		
Stocks (per cent)	8.3	Deficit	1 [a]
Losses (per cent)	1.7		

Source: *Po edinomu planu*, pp. 105–6.

a. Covered by the reserves of 3 billion rubles.

Table 77   Social Product, 1940 and 1950 [a] (1940 prices [b])

	1940 Actual (billion rubles)	Five-Year Plan Goals for 1950	
		Billion Rubles	Index (1940 = 100)
Producer goods (group A)	290.0	432.0	149.0
Consumer goods (group B)	391.8	507.0	129.4
Transfer from group B to group A	+91.0	+98.0	108.0
Group A (including transfer)	355.3	504.0	141.9 [c]
Total	682.1	939.0	137.7

Source: Unless otherwise indicated, *Po edinomu planu*, p. 104. Reproduced from "Tsentralnyi Gosudarstvennyi Arkhiv Narodnogo Khoziaistva SSSR" [Central State Archives of USSR National Economy], F. 4372, op. 46, ed. khr. 249.

a. Including turnover tax.
b. The prices used here are not given directly, but all the surrounding tables in this source use 1940 prices.
c. Calculated from cols. 1 and 2.

choices of the fourth plan, as seen clearly in Table 78, which shows total national income produced and distributed and its breakdown into consumption, accumulation, and reserves. In national income produced it is interesting to note the very high "negative" production in 1944 and 1945, due probably to disinvestment.

The distribution of national income provided for increases in consumption and accumulation at the expense of reserves for military purposes as well as a change in the distribution within consumption. The increase in the share of consumption in general from 65.8 per cent in 1945 to 72.5 per cent in the 1950 plan was accompanied by a reduction in the consumption of military personnel

Table 78   Formation and Distribution of National Income, 1940, 1944, 1945, and Fourth Five-Year Plan Goals for 1950 (1940 prices)

	1940		1944		1945		Five-Year Plan Goals for 1950	
	Billion Rubles (1)	Per Cent (2)	Billion Rubles (3)	Per Cent (4)	Billion Rubles (5)	Per Cent (6)	Billion Rubles (7)	Per Cent (8)
1. National income produced:	386.2		239.3		296.7		524.5	
2. Losses	11.5		8.0		8.0		11.5	
3. Other uses or resources[a]	−2.7		−71.8		−42.4		+8.5	
4. National income distributed:	377.4	100	303.1	100	331.1	100	504.5	100
5. Consumption, total:	279.3	74.0	183.3	60.5	217.7	65.8	366.0	72.5
6. Households	264.3	70.0	150.0	49.5	188.5	56.9	351.0	69.6
7. Consumption of military personnel[b]	15.0	4.0	33.3	11.0	29.2	8.8	15.0	3.0
8. Accumulation, total:	66.1	17.5	40.6	13.4	48.8	14.7	103.5	20.5
9. In fixed capital[c]	40.5	10.7	22.7	7.5	27.9	8.4	56.6	11.2
10. In livestock	0.1	0.0	0.1	0.0	1.5	0.5	5.0	1.0
11. Increase in stocks:	25.5	6.8	17.8	5.9	19.4	5.8	38.0	7.5
12. Industrial	18.5	4.9	14.6	4.8	15.0	4.5	30.0	5.9
13. Agricultural	7.0	1.9	3.2	1.1	4.4	1.3	8.0	1.6
14. Increase in trade stocks							3.5	0.7
15. Reserves, total:[d]	32.0	8.5	79.2	26.1	64.6	19.5	35.0	6.9
16. Used for accumulation	5.0	1.3	2.3	0.8	2.3	0.7	6.0	1.2

Source: Unless otherwise indicated, cols. 1, 3, 5, and 7: *Po edinomu planu*, pp. 105–6, reproduced from "Tsentralnyi Gosudarstvennyi Arkhiv," F. 4372, op. 46, ed. khr. 249; cols. 2, 4, 6, and 8: calculated. Figure in line 11, col. 5, is given as 19.0 but is clearly a typographical error.

a. Calculated as difference between national income produced (minus losses) and national income distributed (line 4). The minus sign probably shows disinvestment (tax on reserves, reduction of capital, etc.).

b. Calculated as difference between lines 5 and 6.

c. Including the value of unfinished construction.

d. The reserves not used for accumulation seem to have gone for military purposes. *Po edinomu planu* (p. 105) mentions "the reduction planned for 1950 of the consumption of military personnel and war reserves."

from 8.8 to 3.0 per cent and an increase in the share of the civilian population from 56.9 to 69.6 per cent. The consumption of the civilian population thus returned to what it had been before the war (1940). The share of accumulation in the plan for 1950 (20.5 per cent) exceeded not only the share in 1945 (14.7 per cent) but also that in 1940 (17.5 per cent). This increase came largely from an attempt to increase industrial stocks. The share of reserves used for accumulation in 1950 returned to its 1940 level.

The data on the distribution of national income clearly show an attempt to make the plan coherent, at least from an accounting standpoint. However, it must not be forgotten that the accounting balance thus obtained is not sufficient to provide information on the coherence of the five-year plan. What matters is the sources of accumulation and the realism of the premises on which the calculation of the balances was based. The summary nature of the statistics published on the fourth plan precludes making a full evaluation of its coherence.

Nevertheless, the internal consistency of the principal indexes of the plan can be examined briefly from the data collected in Table 79.

According to the plan, the main source of growth in production during 1946–1950 was to be an increase in labor productivity. As usual in Stalinist-type plans, employment was to increase very little (22.7 per cent over 1945 and 7.4 per cent over 1940), despite sizable demobilization.[19] The increase in productivity (36 per cent over 1940 in industry and 40 per cent in construction) was based on anticipated investment. However, it should not be forgotten that calculations of investment costs could not be made with any precision in a country just out of war. Moreover, investment was estimated in so-called 1945 estimate prices—prices during rationing when wages could be frozen. Producer goods prices, particularly fuel, had changed very little during the war, which made sizable subsidies necessary.[20]

The main sources of accumulation in the Soviet budget are taxes on enterprise profits and the turnover tax. The two taxes are based on the difference between product cost and selling price (the selling price at the factory in the case of the profits tax and the retail price with a deduction for the margin of profits in the case of the turnover tax). Therefore, in order to create sources of accumulation, the movement of costs had to be watched very carefully. The plan provided for a reduction of costs of 12 to 18 per cent in the different branches of the economy (see Table 79). This reduction was apparently calculated in 1945 estimate prices, and the planned movement of the wholesale price index is not known. But the index certainly could not have been intended to rise significantly, since a reduction in state and cooperative retail trade prices of more than 40 per cent was planned (see Table 79).

Was such planning realistic? It is debatable in view of the fact that two years later, in 1948, wholesale prices were increased 50 per cent on the average (30 per cent for machine-building products).[21] The lack of precision of the investment estimates, accompanied by the underestimation of costs, inevitably jeopardized the planned investments, particularly their actual implementation. The figures in Table 79 confirm the precariousness of the plan for getting new capital investments into operation. Moreover, overfulfillment of the planned volume of investment is a reflection more of initial underestimation of costs than of improved investment performance.

The precariousness of the plan for consumption also emerges very clearly. A small increase in money wages (only 15.2 per cent in five years) was to make possible the tripling of real wages, thanks to a drop in the over-all cost of living of more than 60 per cent below 1945 (see Table 79, line 21). This drop was to occur largely through the abolition of bread, flour, groats, and macaroni rationing planned for the fall of 1946 and the rationing of all other goods during 1947.[22]

19. See footnote 8 above.
20. The subsidies paid from the state budget increased from 4.6 billion (old) rubles in 1943 to 13.9 billion rubles in 1945, 25.8 billion in 1946, and 41.2 billion in 1948 (A. G. Zverev, *Voprosy natsionalnogo dokhoda i finansov SSSR* [Problems of USSR National Income and Finances], Moscow, 1958, p. 212). See Chapter 15.
21. Jasny, *Soviet Industrialization*, p. 265.
22. Voznesensky, *Five-Year Plan*, p. 27; and "Zakon o piatiletnem plane vosstanovleniia i razvitiia

However, such a movement of retail prices, and hence real wages, was unlikely. In fact, it proved difficult to keep wages down to the planned increase in view of the rise in the prices of rationed goods that inevitably accompanied the abolition of rationing. The wage increase of 15.2 per cent (corresponding to an average wage of 6,000 rubles a year) was almost reached in 1946 (average wage of 5,700 rubles) and considerably exceeded in 1947 (average wage of 6,973 rubles).[23] Furthermore, reducing retail prices depended on success in agriculture (which did not have high priority in Stalinist planning), cost reductions in industry, and stable industrial prices—conditions that seemed highly improbable after 1946.

Difficulties in 1946 and Revisions Made in Five-Year Plan

Difficult Beginning of Fourth Five-Year Plan

Official sources point out several difficulties encountered during 1946.[24] These troubles were directly related to the transition from a wartime to a peacetime (or, rather, "cold war") economy. Several difficulties came up in reconstruction on territories formerly occupied by the Germans and in reclassifying labor. The number of workers taking courses in technical and industrial schools and in factory schools (FZO[25]) had to be increased, and workers had to be redistributed within the factories.

Additional difficulties arose because of the poor harvest in 1946. According to Soviet sources, in that year the European part of the country suffered the worst drought in 50 years. The area affected was larger than in 1921 and nearly as large as in 1891.[26] The grain harvest (barn yield) fell from 47.3 million metric tons in 1945 to 39.6 million in 1946.[27] Nevertheless, the over-all index of agricultural production (in 1958 prices) increased by 10.5 per cent between 1945 and 1946; vegetable production rose by 7.5 per cent and animal production by 20.8 per cent.[28] The immediate consequence of the poor harvest was that the abolition of rationing was put off until 1947 in a decree of September 16, 1946. This decree provided for an increase in wages and prices, hardly in line with the provisions of the Fourth Five-Year Plan.[29]

narodnogo khoziaistva SSSR na 1946–1950 gg." [Law on the Five-Year Plan for the Rehabilitation and Development of the National Economy of the USSR, 1946–1950], *Direktivy*, Vol. 3, p. 48.

23. For 1946, given in *Narodnoe khoziaistvo SSSR v 1964 godu* [The USSR National Economy in 1964], Moscow, 1965, p. 555. For 1947, calculated by Jasny (*Soviet Industrialization*, p. 408) on the basis of information in *Sotsialisticheskii trud* [Socialist Labor], No. 5, 1959, p. 51.

24. *Ekonomicheskaia zhizn*, Book I, p. 391.

25. See footnote 12 in Chapter 15.

26. *Ibid.*, Book I, p. 399.

27. *Strana sovetov za 50 let* [Land of the Soviets during Fifty Years], Moscow, 1967, p. 119.

28. *Narodnoe khoziaistvo, 1961*, p. 292.

29. *Ekonomicheskaia zhizn*, Book I, p. 396.

Table 79   Fulfillment of Principal Goals of Fourth Five-Year Plan for 1946–1950

| | | Actual Results | | Plan for 1950 | | | Actual Results in 1950 | | |
| | | | | Physical Units | Index | | Physical Units | Index | As Per Cent of Plan |
	Units	1940 (1)	1945 (2)	(3)	1940 = 100 (4)	1945 = 100 (5)	(6)	1940 = 100 (7)	(8)
National Income									
1. Official Soviet estimate (1926/27 prices)	bill. rubles	128.3	106.5	177.0	138.0	166.2	210.4	164.0	118.9
2. Bergson index (1937 ruble factor cost)	1940 = 100	100.0	100		138.0			124.0	89.9
3. Nutter index (1937 income originating weights)	1940 = 100	100.0			138.0			116	84.1
4. Moorsteen and Powell (1937 ruble factor cost)	1940 = 100	100.0	79.4		138.0			121.4	88.0
Industrial Production									
5. Official Soviet estimate, total (1926/27 prices)	bill. rubles	138.5	127.4	205.0	148.0	160.9	239.6	173.0	116.9
6. Kaplan and Moorsteen index of civilian production (1950 wholesale prices)	1940 = 100	100.0			148.0			140.4	94.9
7. Nutter index (moving weights)	1940 = 100	100.0			148.0			124	83.8
8. Official Soviet estimate, producer goods (1926/27 prices)	bill. rubles	84.8	95.0	135.9	160.3	143.1	173.3	204.4	127.5
9. Official Soviet estimate, consumer goods (1926/27 prices)	bill. rubles	53.7	31.7	69.1	128.7	218.0	66.1	123.1	95.7
Agricultural Production									
10. Official Soviet estimate (1926/27 prices)	bill. rubles	23.3	14.0	29.6	127.0	211.4	26.6	114.2	89.9
11. Official Soviet index (1958 prices)	1940 = 100	100.0	61		127.0			99.3	78.2
12. Johnson and Kahan index (1958 weights)	1940 = 100	100.0			127.0			100.8	79.4
13. Nutter index (1958 weights)	1940 = 100	100.0			127.0			97.0	76.4
Transportation									
14. Railroad freight traffic	bill. m. ton-km	415.0	314.0	532.0	128.2	169.4	602.3	145.1	113.2
Employment									
15. National economy, workers and employees	millions	31.2	27.3	33.5	107.4	122.7	38.9	124.7	116.1
16. Industry, workers and employees	thousands	10,967	9,508	11,900	108.5	125.2	14,144	129.0	118.9
Wages (national economy)									
17. Wage fund	bill. rubles	123.7	142.0	201.0	162.5	141.5	298.3	241.1	148.4
18. Average money wage, workers and employees	rubles	3,972	5,208	6,000	151.1	115.2	7,668	193.1	127.8
19. Average real wage, workers and employees (in 1940 prices)	rubles	3,972	1,602	4,890	123.1	305.2	4,357	109.7	89.1
20. Average real wage, workers and employees (index)	1940 = 100	100.0	40.3		123.1			109.7	89.1
Retail Price Index									
21. State, cooperative, and collective farm trade	1940 = 100	100.0	325		122.7	37.8		176	143.3
22. State and cooperative trade	1940 = 100	100.0	218		122.7	56.3		186	151.5

Table 79   *continued*

		Actual Results		Plan for 1950			Actual Results in 1950		
				Physical	Index		Physical	Index	As Per
	Units	1940	1945	Units	1940 = 100	1945 = 100	Units	1940 = 100	Cent of Plan
		(1)	(2)	(3)	(4)	(5)	(6)	(7)	(8)
State and Cooperative Retail Trade									
23. In current prices	bill. rubles	175.1	160.1	275.0	157.1	171.8	359.6	205.4	130.8
24. In 1940 prices	bill. rubles	175.1	73.5	224.1	128.0	304.9	192.6	110.0	85.9
Labor Productivity									
25. Industry, official Soviet index	1940 = 100	100.0			136			137	100.7
26. Industry, derived from Kaplan and Moorsteen production index	1940 = 100	100.0			136			108.8	80.0
27. Industry, derived from Nutter production index	1940 = 100	100.0			136			96.1	70.7
28. Construction, official Soviet index	1940 = 100	100.0			140			123	87.9
Cost of Production									
29. Industry (excl. price increase)	1945 = 100					83.0		79.5	95.8
30. Industry (current prices)	1945 = 100					83.0		111.4	134.2
31. Construction	1945 = 100					88.0			
32. Railroad transportation	1945 = 100					82.0			
33. MTS work	1945 = 100					84.0			

Source

COLUMN 1–Lines 1, 5, 8-10, 14-18, and 23: Table A-1, col. 5. **Line 19:** Same as line 18. **Line 24:** Same as line 23.

COLUMN 2–Lines 1, 5, 8-9, 14-18, and 23-24: Table A-4, col. 5. **Line 2:** For 1944. Abram Bergson, *The Real National Income of Soviet Russia since 1928*, Cambridge, Mass., 1961, p. 134. Converted from 1937 = 100. **Line 4:** Richard Moorsteen and Raymond Powell, *The Soviet Capital Stock, 1928–1962*, Homewood, Ill., 1966, p. 623. Converted from 1937 = 100 for gross national product. **Line 10:** Based on 1940 production (col. 1) and index for 1945 (given as 60 with 1940 = 100 in Table A-4, col. 5). **Line 11:** *Narodnoe khoziaistvo SSSR v 1958 godu* [The USSR National Economy in 1958], Moscow, 1959, p. 350. Converted from 1913 = 100. **Line 19:** Based on average money wage (line 18) and index of retail trade prices (line 21). **Line 20:** Derived from real wage (in 1940 prices) in 1945 and in 1940 (line 19, cols. 1 and 2). **Line 21:** Table 70, line 20, col. 6. **Line 22:** A. N. Malafeev, *Istoriia tsenoobrazovaniia v SSSR, 1917–1963 gg*. [History of Pricing in the USSR, 1917–1963], Moscow, 1964, p. 407. Converted from 1928 = 100.

COLUMN 3–Lines 1, 5, 8-10, 14-18, and 23-24: Table A-1, col. 10. **Line 19:** Calculated from average money wage planned for 1950 (line 18) and planned retail price index (line 21, col. 4).

COLUMN 4–Lines 1, 5, 8-10, 14-19, and 23-24: Col. 3 as per cent of col. 1. **Lines 2-4:** Assumed to be same as line 1. **Lines 6-7:** Assumed to be same as line 5. **Lines 11-13:** Assumed to be same as line 10. **Line 20:** Same as line 19. **Line 21:** It was assumed that the change in retail prices in state, cooperative, and collective farm trade as a whole in 1946–1950 was planned to be the same as in retail prices in state and cooperative trade, hence the same as in line 22. **Line 22:** Calculated from trade in current prices (line 23) and in 1940 prices (line 24). **Lines 25 and 28:** *Resheniia*, Vol. 3, p. 272. **Lines 26-27:** Assumed to be same as line 25.

COLUMN 5–Lines 1, 5, 8-10, 14-19, and 23-24: Col. 3 as per cent of col. 2. **Lines 21-22:** Derived from cols. 2 and 4. **Lines 29-31:** *Resheniia*, Vol. 3, p. 272. **Lines 32-33:** N. A. Voznesensky, *Five-Year Plan for the Rehabilitation and Development of the National Economy of the USSR, 1946–50*, London, 1946, pp. 21–22.

COLUMN 6–Lines 1, 5, 8-10, 14-18, and 23-24: Table A-1, col. 11. **Line 19:** Based on average money wage (line 18, col. 6) and index of retail prices in state, cooperative, and collective farm trade for 1950 (line 21, col. 7).

COLUMN 7–Lines 1, 5, 8-10, 14-19, and 23-24: Col. 6 as per cent of col. 1. **Line 2:** Bergson, *Real National Income since 1928*, p. 134. Converted from 1937 = 100. **Line 3:** G. Warren Nutter, "The Effects of Economic Growth on Sino-Soviet Strategy," *National Security: Political, Military, and Economic Strategies in the Decade Ahead*, D. M. Abshire and R. V. Allen, eds., New York, 1963, p. 166. Converted from 1928 = 100. **Line 4:** Moorsteen and Powell, *Soviet Capital Stock*, p. 623. Converted from 1937 = 100 for gross national product. **Line 6:** Norman Kaplan and Richard

Table 79 *continued*

Moorsteen, "Indexes of Soviet Industrial Output," RAND Research Memorandum 2495, Santa Monica, 1960, pp. 234–35. Converted from 1950 = 100. **Line 7:** G. Warren Nutter, *Growth of Industrial Production in the Soviet Union*, Princeton, 1962, p. 196. Converted from 1913 = 100. **Line 11:** *Narodnoe khoziaistvo, 1958*, p. 350. Converted from 1913 = 100. **Line 12:** D. Gale Johnson and Arcadius Kahan, "Soviet Agriculture: Structure and Growth," *Comparisons of the United States and Soviet Economies*, Joint Economic Committee, U.S. Congress, Washington, 1959, Part I, p. 204. Converted from 1928 = 100. **Line 13:** Nutter, *National Security*, p. 165. Converted from 1913 = 100. **Line 20:** Same as line 19. **Line 21:** Derived from 1950 price indexes for state and cooperative trade (line 22, col. 7) and for collective farm trade (calculated as 104 with 1940 = 100 by Basile Kerblay, *Les marchés paysans en U.R.S.S.*, Paris, 1968, p. 184) and share of collective farm trade in total trade (given as 12 per cent in *Narodnoe khoziaistvo SSSR* [The USSR National Economy], Moscow, 1956, p. 206). **Line 22:** *Narodnoe khoziaistvo SSSR v 1956 godu* [The USSR National Economy in 1956], Moscow, 1957, p. 232. **Line 25:** *Pravda*, April 16, 1951. **Line 26:** Derived from Kaplan and Moorsteen index of industrial production (line 6, col. 7) and index of industrial employment (line 16, col. 7). **Line 27:** Derived from Nutter index of industrial production (line 7, col. 7) and index of industrial employment (line 16, col. 7). **Line 28:** *Narodnoe khoziaistvo, 1956*, pp. 40 and 181. **Lines 29-30:** Malafeev, *Istoriia*, p. 406. Computed from annual changes between 1945 and 1950.

    COLUMN 8–Lines 1, 5, 8-10, 14-18, and 23-24: Table A-1, col. 12. **Lines 2-4, 6-7, 11-13, 20-22, and 25-28:** Col. 7 as per cent of col. 4. **Line 19:** Col. 6 as per cent of col. 3. **Lines 29-30:** Col. 7 (which is based on 1945 here) as per cent of col. 5.

Attempts to Maintain Five-Year Plan Goals

Nevertheless, the government tried to maintain the principal five-year plan goals for personal consumption. This effort was manifested mainly in two decrees—that of December 23, 1946, on rebuilding light industry producing consumer goods and that of February 1947 on measures to improve agriculture in the postwar years.[30] The decree on light industry declared that growth rates in the textile and light industries were not high enough to reach the five-year plan goals. Enterprises of the Ministries of the Textile Industry and Light Industry had obtained neither the necessary manpower to put back into use the equipment that had been put out of operation nor the necessary fuel, electric power, materials, spare parts, and subsidiary materials. The government criticized the attitude of local agencies that treated these industries as of little importance and made provision to increase investments, reorganize operations, and grant necessary resources to these industries.

The principal goals for these industries for 1947 through 1950 are given in Table 80. They represent increases of 2.1 to 8.6 per cent over the original five-year plan production goals (except shoes, for which the goals remained the same) and a much higher increase (from 22 to 33 per cent) over the original investment goals. In order to guarantee additional investment in the textile and light industries, the decree even stipulated that it would be necessary to reduce planned investments in other branches of the economy, enumerated in an attached list.[31] New capacities to be engaged were listed in detail by industrial combines.

    30. Decree of Council of Ministers, "On Measures to Accelerate the Rebuilding of State Light Industry Producing Consumer Goods" (*Direktivy*, Vol. 3, pp. 126–34); and decree of plenary session of Party Central Committee, "On Measures to Rebuild Agriculture in the Postwar Period" (*ibid.*, Vol. 3, pp. 147–93).
    31. This list is not reproduced in the source cited.

Table 80 Principal Goals of Adjusted Plan for Textile Industry and Light Industry for 1947–1950

| | Units | Adjusted Plan | | | | Original Plan for 1950 | Adjusted Plan as Per Cent of Original Plan for 1950 |
		1947 (1)	1948 (2)	1949 (3)	1950 (4)	(5)	(6)
Production							
Cotton fabrics	mill. meters	2,679	3,416.5	4,146.5	4,786	4,686	102.1
Woolen fabrics	mill. meters	89.2	110.5	134.4	168.4	159.4	105.6
Silk and rayon fabrics	mill. meters	61.7	84	107	151	141	107.1
Linen fabrics	mill. meters	154.8	208	294	339	420.0	80.7
Leather shoes	mill. pairs	105.3	166	206	240	240	100.0
Hosiery	mill. pairs	220.3	348	458	630	580	108.6
Investment (total for 1946–1950)							
Ministry of Textile Industry	mill. rubles			7,300		5,990[a]	121.9
Ministry of Light Industry	mill. rubles			2,900		2,180[a]	133.0
Housing Construction (total for 1946–1950)							
Ministry of Textile Industry	mill. rubles			1,800[b]			
Ministry of Light Industry	mill. rubles			600[c]			
Installation of New Capacity and Restarting of Old Capacity							
Ministry of Textile Industry							
Spinning machines, new	thous.	373	586	740	534		
Spinning machines, old	thous.	817	259	57			
Ministry of Light Industry						2,860[d]	
Spinning machines, new	thous.	41	101	95	52		
Spinning machines, old	thous.	115	121				
Leather shoes, new	mill. pairs	32	26	24	15	100[d]	
Hosiery, new	mill. pairs	75	142	106	43	345[d]	

Source: Unless otherwise indicated, cols. 1–4: *Direktivy*, Vol. 3, pp. 128–29; col. 5: Table A-1, col. 10; col. 6: col. 4 as per cent of col. 5.

a. *Direktivy*, Vol. 3, p. 128.
b. To build 3 mill. m² of floorspace.
c. To build 1 mill. m² of floorspace.
d. *Resheniia*, Vol. 3, p. 269.

The agricultural goals of the Fourth Five-Year Plan were preserved by a special decree of the plenary session of the Party Central Committee in February 1947.[32] This decree declared, first, that during the five-year plans the grain problem had been resolved in the Soviet Union (a statement repeated by G. M. Malenkov at the Nineteenth Party Congress in October 1952 and then violently attacked by Khrushchev in September 1953). It set as a goal agricultural development that would make possible "within a very short time guaranteeing an abundance of food products for the population and of raw materials for light industry and the accumulation of indispensable government food and raw material reserves."[33] A number of measures were planned to realize these goals: Party and govern-

32. *Direktivy*, Vol. 3, pp. 147–93.
33. *Ibid.*, Vol. 3, p. 149.

ment agencies, the Ministry of Agriculture, the Ministry of State Farms, and local agencies were to improve agricultural management. Agricultural plans were to be sent to provinces, territories, and republics at the same time as the general economic plans, no later than by January 1 of the planned year. Collective farm charter infringements were to be exposed and eliminated. Inadequacies in remuneration of collective farm labor were to be eliminated. The work of Machine and Tractor Stations was to be improved. Finally, new tractors, new trucks, and new agricultural machinery were to be delivered to agriculture.

These measures were strictly administrative; the main stress was on discipline and control. Goals were set to "reach" the prewar level of grain harvest during the first three years (1947, 1948, and 1949) and to exceed that level considerably by the end of the five-year plan. The goal of 127 million metric tons of grain to be harvested in 1950 was reaffirmed with gusto. Other goals gave details for sown area by region and by product, but they cannot be compared with the original goals since the latter were not sufficiently detailed.

Fulfillment of Annual Plan for 1946

Since the annual plan for 1946 was not published, it is impossible to study its fulfillment. The Central Statistical Administration announcement on plan fulfillment (see Table 81) gave only a breakdown by industrial ministries. It is amazing to find no trace of economic difficulties during 1946. Except for the Ministries of Agricultural Machine-Building, Transport Machine-Building, and the Fishing Industry of Eastern Regions, all the ministries fulfilled their plans very well. The Ministry of the Textile Industry even overfulfilled its plan by 3 per cent, and the Ministry of Light Industry fulfilled its plan to within 0.4 per cent. The Ministry of the Food Industry fulfilled 98 per cent of its plan.

These results are in obvious contradiction with what is known of developments in the Soviet economy in 1946 and with what was announced definitely in the decrees published at that time. They can be explained only as follows. First, the announcements from the Central Statistical Administration referred to the degree of fulfilling the plan in effect at the end of the year. This plan bound the enterprises administratively and was the criterion for payment of the wage fund, bonuses, and other income. Hence it included all the revisions made in the course of the year. No doubt many such revisions were made in 1946. Second, the percentages of plan fulfillment by ministries of industrial production were calculated by summing the production of different enterprises. The administrative changes made during the year could have revised considerably the volume of over-all production. Third, "constant" prices were not really constant except for production of identical quality. Because of technical progress, new products that differed from the planned assortment were introduced at prices calculated from costs and an authorized profit (cost-plus).

For all these reasons, it is tempting to compare the fulfillment of the plan in value by ministries with the fulfillment of the plan in physical terms. The available data on this subject—extremely scarce—have been gathered in Table 82. It seems that, for those industrial products for which goals were known, the

Table 81 Fulfillment of Annual Plans for Gross Industrial Production by Ministries and Economic Organizations, 1946–1952 (per cent)

	1946	1947	1948	1949	1950	1951	1952
Ministries							
Ferrous Metal Industry	99.5	101 }	111[a]	102[a]	101	104	103
Nonferrous Metal Industry	99	107 }			100.3	102	100
Coal Industry:			101	102	100.8	100.7	100.2
Coal Industry of Western Regions	105	95					
Coal Industry of Eastern Regions	97	100					
Petroleum Industry:			108	103	101	103	100.7
Petroleum Industry of Southern and Western Regions	103	106					
Petroleum Industry of Eastern Regions	105	107					
Electric Power Stations	99.7	101	103	101	102	102	100.9
Chemical Industry	105	114	116	104	105	104	102
Electrical Industry	106	108	115	105	106	103	102
Communications Equipment Industry	103	112	106	103	103	102	100.9
Heavy Machine-Building	105	105	107	106	104	100	99
Motor Vehicle and Tractor Industry	92 [b]	98	115	103	102	100.6	102
Machine Tool Industry	98	106		106	102	100	100.5
Agricultural Machine-Building	77	100	105	100	101.1	104	96
Transport Machine-Building	81	94	113	102	102	100.9	96
Machine and Instrument Building	98	107	109	103	100.6	100.9	100.7
Construction and Highway Machine-Building		115	126	103	103	106	104
Construction Materials Industry	105	101	112	104	104	102	99
Timber Industry	98	96 }	111[c]	100[c]	93[c]	94	90
Pulp and Paper Industry	110	98 }				103[d]	102[d]
Rubber Industry	96	107 }					
Textile Industry	103	103 }	106[e]	108[a]	104[e]	102[e]	100.6[e]
Light Industry	99.6	106 }					
Meat and Dairy Industry	110	107 }	100	105	102	103	100.5
Food Industry	98	109	108	104	103	107	103
Spice Industry	102	113	104				
Fishing Industry:			100	95	96	109	94
Fishing Industry of Western Regions	100.6	104					
Fishing Industry of Eastern Regions	85	96					
Local Industry and Fuel Industry of Federal Republics	102	111	105	107	106	106	103
Artisan Industrial Cooperatives			101	106	100.8	106	102
Industrial Enterprises Belonging to:							
Ministry of Cotton Growing					106	99.7	99.9
Ministry of Transportation					98	99.1	100
Ministry of Health					104	106	103
Ministry of Film Industry					110	103	107
Central Administration for Printing, Publishing, and Book Trade							104
Gross industrial production		103.5	106	103	102	103.5	101
Fulfillment of five-year plan goals [f]		100	103				

Source: 1946: *Pravda*, January 21, 1947; **1947:** *Pravda*, January 18, 1948; **1948:** *Pravda*, January 20, 1949; **1949:** *Pravda*, January 18, 1950; **1950:** *Pravda*, January 26, 1951; **1951:** *Pravda*, January 29, 1952; **1952:** *Pravda*, January 23, 1953.

a. Ministry of the Metal Industry, which included the Ministry of the Ferrous Metal Industry and the Ministry of the Nonferrous Metal Industry (in existence in 1946–1947 and 1950–1952).

b. Motor vehicle industry only.

c. Ministry of the Timber and Paper Industry.

d. Ministry of the Paper and Woodprocessing Industry.

e. Ministry of Light Industry, which from 1948 on included the textile industry.

f. Per cent fulfillment of five-year plan goals for two years in 1947 and for three years in 1948.

Table 82   1946 Annual Plan and Its Fulfillment

	Units	Planned (1)	Actual (2)	Per Cent of Fulfillment of	
				Annual Plan (3)	Third Quarter Plan (4)
Industrial Production					
1. Coal	th. m. tons		164,063		
2. Electric power	mill. kwh	48,720	48,571	99.7	
3. Steel	mill. m. tons	20.0	13.346	66.7	
4. Cement	thous. m. tons	3,505	3,373	96.2	
5. Window glass	mill. m²		39.9		
6. Bricks	millions	4,761	3,239	68.0	
7. Machine tools	units	44,000	40,300	91.6	
8. Motor vehicles	units	150,000	102,170	68.1	
9. Agricultural machinery				65.3	
10. Motor boats and barges	units			51	
11. Gold mining (Lena)				overfulfilled	
Agricultural Production					
12. Sown area, total	mill. hect.	122			
13. Sown area, collective farm	mill. hect.	89.4			
14. Area sown to flax	mill. hect.	1.13			
15. Area sown to hemp	mill. hect.	.31			
16. Flax harvest	thous. m. tons	120			
17. Flax seed harvest	thous. m. tons	65.8			
18. Hemp harvest	thous. m. tons	15.1			
19. Hemp seed harvest	thous. m. tons	11.9			
20. Raw cotton (biological yield)	thous. m. tons		1,400		
Railroad Transportation					
21. Coal	1945 = 100	114	114	100.0	not fulfilled
22. Coke	1945 = 100				103.7
23. Oil and oil products	1945 = 100		108		107
24. Ferrous metals	1945 = 100	121	121	100.0	not fulfilled
25. Ore	1945 = 100	136	136	100.0	not fulfilled
26. Firewood	1945 = 100	110	110	100.0	104.8
27. Construction materials	1945 = 100	139			112.8
28. Grain	1945 = 100	132			103.2
29. Passenger traffic	1945 = 100	109			
Inland Waterway Transportation					
30. Ministry of Inland Waterway Fleet	tons				104
31. Ministry of Inland Waterway Fleet	ton-km			103.3	115
32. Coal	ton-km			overfulfilled	118
33. Oil	ton-km			overfulfilled	132
34. Firewood	ton-km				not fulfilled
35. Cement	ton-km			overfulfilled	
36. Chemicals	ton-km			overfulfilled	
37. Grain	ton-km			overfulfilled	not fulfilled
38. Salt	ton-km			not fulfilled	not fulfilled
Deliveries to Industry					
39. Flax fiber	thous. m. tons	120.0	65.0	54.2	
40. Chemicals to textile industry	m. tons	1,200	600	50	
Deliveries to Agriculture					
41. Tractors	units			3,500 short	
42. Tractors	15-hp units			5,700 short	
Spare parts to MTS:					
43. Ministry of Transport Machine-Building				55	
44. Ministry of Heavy Machine-Building				84	

Table 82   *continued*

Source

LINE 1–Col. 2: Table A-5, col. 2. **Col. 3:** The situation was bad for all coal basins at the end of 1946 (*Cahiers de l'Economie Soviétique*, No. 7, 1947, p. 24). The coal industry experienced serious difficulties as a result of the war. It was far behind schedule and held up the development of the other branches of heavy industry, railroad transportation, and the whole national economy. Difficulties were particularly severe in the Urals and in the Kuzbass (*ibid.*, No. 8, 1947, p. 20).

LINE 2–Cols. 1–3: Table A-5, cols. 1–3.

LINE 3–Cols. 1-2: Table A-5, cols. 1 and 2. **Col. 3:** Col. 2 as per cent of col. 1.

LINE 4–Col. 1: Table A-5, col. 1. **Col. 2:** Table A-5, col. 2. **Col. 3:** Col. 2 as per cent of col. 1. Some sources (*Cahiers*, No. 7, 1947, p. 20) state that the planned goals for cement were regularly overfulfilled every quarter.

LINE 5–Col. 2: Table A-5, col. 2. **Col. 3:** Plan stated to be overfulfilled (*Cahiers*, No. 7, 1947, p. 20); 1946 output stated to be 76 per cent higher than 1945 output (Table A-4), which does not check out. See note to line 6, col. 1.

LINE 6–Col. 1: Based on 1945 output (given as 2,026 million in Table A-4, col. 5) and increase planned for 1946 (given as 135 per cent in *Cahiers*, No. 7, 1947, p. 20). It is possible that this planned increase applied not only to the Ministry of the Construction Materials Industry but also to other producers, such as local industry. **Col. 2:** Table A-5, col. 2. Another source (*Cahiers*, No. 7, 1947, p. 20) states that actual production in 1946 was 80 per cent higher than in 1945, which would yield 3,647 million. See note to col. 1 above on possible coverage. **Col. 3:** Col. 2 as per cent of col. 1.

LINE 7–Col. 1: *Cahiers* (No. 3, 1946, p. 42) states that output in 1946 was planned to reach prewar level (Table A-1, col. 5). **Col. 2:** Table A-5, col. 2. **Col. 3:** Col. 2 as per cent of col. 1.

LINE 8–Col. 1: *Cahiers* (No. 4, 1946, p. 29) states that output in 1946 was planned to double 1945 output (given as 74,700 in Table A-4, col. 5). Rounded. **Col. 2:** Table A-5, col. 2. **Col. 3:** Col. 2 as per cent of col. 1.

LINE 9–Col. 3: *Cahiers*, No. 8, 1947, p. 21. The Lipetsk plant fulfilled only 9.6 per cent of its plan (see Table 99). The Ministry of Agricultural Machine-Building fulfilled only 77 per cent of its 1946 plan (see Table 81). The percentage of fulfillment of the plan for the first half of 1946 was as follows: 95.5 for tractors, 56 for plows, 42 for combines, and 54.5 for harvesters (*Cahiers*, No. 6, 1946, p. 34).

LINE 10–Col. 3: *Cahiers*, No. 8, 1947, p. 16.

LINE 11–Col. 3: *Cahiers*, No. 7, 1947, p. 29. The annual plan for gold mining at the Lena gold mines was fulfilled in ten months. The plans for prospecting, construction of new mines, and construction of living quarters were also overfulfilled.

LINE 12–Col. 1: Sown area in 1945 (given as 113.8 mill. hectares in *Selskoe khoziaistvo SSSR* [Agriculture in the USSR], Moscow, 1971, p. 108) plus increase planned for 1946 (given as 8.2 mill. hectares in *Cahiers*, No. 4, 1946, pp. 33 and 46).

LINE 13–Col. 1: Sown area in 1945 (given as 83.9 mill. hectares in *Selskoe khoziaistvo*, 1971, p. 112) plus increase planned for 1946 (given as 5.5 mill. hectares in *Cahiers*, No. 4, 1946, pp. 33 and 46).

LINE 14–Col. 1: Based on sown area in 1945 (given as 1.0 mill. hectares in *Selskoe khoziaistvo*, 1971, p. 108) and increase planned for 1946 (given as 13.1 per cent in *Cahiers*, No. 6, 1946, p. 31).

LINE 15–Col. 1: Based on sown area in 1945 (given as .28 mill. hectares in *Selskoe khoziaistvo*, 1971, p. 108) and increase planned for 1946 (given as 10 per cent in *Cahiers*, No. 6, 1946, p. 31).

LINES 16-19–Col. 1: *Cahiers*, No. 6, 1946, p. 31.

LINE 20–Col. 1: *Ibid.* (No. 7, 1947, p. 27) states that harvest in 1946 was planned to be 40 per cent higher than in 1945, but this obviously applies to biological yield and hence has not been applied to figure for 1945 barn yield in Table A-4. **Col. 2:** *Ibid.* **Col. 3:** Even if the percentage given in note to col. 1 were applied to the barn yield in 1945 to obtain a 1946 planned harvest of 1,666 thous. m. tons, the percentage of plan fulfillment would be only 84.0. Hence it must have been much lower.

LINE 21–Col. 1: *Cahiers*, No. 4, 1946, p. 29. **Cols. 2 and 4:** *Ibid.*, No. 7, 1947, p. 20. **Col. 3:** Col. 2 as per cent of col. 1.

LINE 22–Col. 4: *Cahiers*, No. 7, 1947, p. 20.

LINE 23–Cols. 2 and 4: *Ibid.*

LINES 24-26–Col. 1: *Ibid.*, No. 4, 1946, p. 29. **Cols. 2 and 4:** *Ibid.*, No. 7, 1947, p. 20. **Col. 3:** Col. 2 as per cent of col. 1.

LINES 27-28–Col. 1: *Cahiers*, No. 4, 1946, p. 29. **Col. 4:** *Ibid.*, No. 7, 1947, p. 20.

LINE 29–Col. 1: *Ibid.*, No. 4, 1946, p. 29.

LINES 30 and 34–Col. 4: *Ibid.*, No. 7, 1947, p. 21.

LINES 31-33, 37-38–Cols. 3 and 4: *Ibid.*

LINES 35-36–Col. 3: *Ibid.*

LINE 39–Cols. 1 and 2: *Ibid.*, No. 7, 1947, p. 33. **Col. 3:** Col. 2 as per cent of col. 1.

Table 82   *continued*

LINE 40–Cols. 1 and 2: *Cahiers*, No. 7, 1947, p. 33. The number of dyes, which amounted to 120 in 1940, was reduced to 35. Certain basic dyes were not produced at all at that time.

LINES 41-42–Col. 3: *Ibid.*, No. 8, 1947, p. 22. In addition, this source mentions that the shortage of spare parts delivered resulted in 10,000 tractors not being used. Moreover, draft animals had to be used to make up for the lack of power machinery. In Kalinin Province, for instance, out of 141,000 hectares, 97,000 were worked with draft animals.

LINES 43-44–Col. 3: *Ibid.*, No. 7, 1947, p. 26.

annual plan was very poorly fulfilled; on the average, about two-thirds of the plan was fulfilled. Such a low percentage shows that the 1946 annual plan was hardly "operational" and that it was supplanted by the quarterly plans or the separate ministerial plans.

Other shortcomings can be seen in the plan, particularly in deliveries to agriculture of tractors and spare parts. The plan for transportation, on the other hand, seems to have been better fulfilled, which means that, for an industrial production of roughly two-thirds the planned size, the same quantities, probably in ton-kilometers, had to be transported.

Revision of Fourth Five-Year Plan Goals in Annual Plan for 1947

At the time the 1947 annual plan was published,[34] the Soviet government did not hide the difficulties encountered in fulfilling the 1946 plan. The text of the published plan mentions difficulties during 1946 in coal production, in consumer goods, in housing construction, in starting up new plants, and in meeting needs for machinery and construction materials. It also mentions the special attention devoted to drafting the 1947 annual plan. In particular, the consistency of the plan was studied by balances, several of which, with quarterly breakdowns, received government approval.[35]

Officially the annual plan for 1947 fitted into the framework of the Fourth Five-Year Plan, of which it was to have been the second year. In actual fact, the 1947 annual plan diverged widely from five-year plan goals implied for that year. However, it is very difficult to measure this divergence because the five-year plan published in 1946 did not contain goals for each year but showed goals only for the final year, 1950.

It is hard to estimate the Fourth Five-Year Plan goals for 1947 since the economy was in the midst of rapid expansion and certain points of departure were very low. In some instances, starting up a single factory that was out of use

34. *Komsomolskaia pravda* [Truth of the Young Communist League], March 1, 1947, pp. 1–2. This was the only one of the annual plans published between 1946 and 1953, and, moreover, it was a very brief version.

35. The following balances were approved by the government: electric power, with breakdowns by regions; solid fuels (coal, peat, oil shale); petroleum products; ferrous and nonferrous metals; equipment, tractors, agricultural machinery, and motor vehicles; timber products; construction materials (cement, roll roofing, asbestos shingles, window glass); prefabricated houses; chemical products; rubber products; pulp, paper, paperboard, and paper bags; industrial products (without further specification). At the same time measures were approved to eliminate bottlenecks and to guard against eventual disproportions for each material balance. *Ibid.*, March 1, 1947, p. 3.

during the war would be sufficient to double or triple production. In those cases, the best way to estimate the 1947 goals would be to divide the over-all physical growth during the five years into equal annual slices. A comparison of the goals of the 1947 annual plan with those of the five-year plan for 1947 thus estimated is presented in the left-hand side of Table 83. However, in cases in which production was less disrupted during the war, an equal average planned rate of growth can be used to estimate the 1947 goals. A comparison of the goals for the 1947 annual plan with the five-year plan goals for 1947 estimated in this way is presented in the right-hand side of Table 83. The comparison shows that the actual 1947 annual plan goals generally exceeded the five-year plan goals estimated by this second method, often by substantial margins.

Table 83 shows first that annual plan goals deviated considerably from the five-year plan goals, whether higher or lower, and that the deviations are slightly greater in heavy industry than in light industry. It can also be seen that the deviations from the five-year plan vary in the different branches of the economy. They are high in transportation, where the lag behind the five-year plan was increasing. The annual plan goals for wages were much higher than the five-year plan goals. This is actually a bad sign, however, since the government was trying to minimize the increase in money wages in the plan. It obviously did not succeed. The same is true of employment, but the deviation is much smaller.

The difference in the retail trade goals according to whether current or constant prices are used should also be noted. This reflects an increase in retail prices in 1946 and in the 1947 plan, which jeopardized the goals for prices and wages in the 1946–1950 plan.

Disintegration of Fourth Five-Year Plan

Economic Expansion in 1947

Soviet writers stress the fact that 1947 was the first real peacetime year for Soviet industry.[36] Soviet sources, however, do not give a direct breakdown of industrial production into civilian and military uses, which would simplify judgment of this assertion. Reconversion shows up in 1946 (see Table 84), when the reduction of 16.3 per cent in gross industrial production and of 26.8 per cent in producer goods was due to the reduction in military production. The reduction of 6 per cent in national income in 1946 also reflected the poor grain harvest and the decrease in maritime traffic. Civilian industrial production still increased 20 per cent in 1946.

Nevertheless, the extent of reconversion can be seen in Western estimates. According to G. Warren Nutter, military production dropped from 627 in 1945 (with 1937 = 100) to 92 in 1946 and only 70 in 1947, while civilian production rose from 45.9 in 1945 to 59.7 in 1946, and 77.2 in 1947 (with 1937 = 100).[37]

36. *Po edinomu planu*, p. 107.
37. Nutter, *Growth*, pp. 196–97.

Table 83   Goals for 1947: Annual Plan as Percentage of Interpolated Fourth Five-Year Plan

Assuming Equal Annual Planned Increment in Physical Growth during 1946–1950 (1)		*Assuming Equal Average Annual Planned Rate of Growth during 1946–1950* (2)	
Industry			
Producer goods		*Producer goods*	
Window glass	123.3	Looms	1,115.8
Railroad freight cars	121.2	Steam locomotives	925.3
Metallurgical equipment	109.2	Railroad freight cars	729.5
Cement	108.7	Automobiles	187.1
Industrial timber hauled	105.4	Tractors (units)	169.6
Lumber	103.7	Phosphoric fertilizer	
Asbestos shingles	102.7	(18.7% P_2O_5)	156.0
Coal	100.4	Cement	156.0
Bricks	100.1	Steam and gas turbines	148.6
Refined copper	97.7	Window glass	148.4
Crude petroleum	99.5	Asbestos shingles	139.3
Electric power	95.8	Bricks	138.5
Lead	95.5	Metallurgical equipment	136.1
Rolled steel	95.0	Industrial timber hauled	122.7
Machine tools	94.2	Lumber	114.7
Pig iron	91.0	Lead	106.9
Steel ingots and castings	90.8	Soda ash	105.8
Automobiles	89.6	Coal	103.7
Soda ash	88.0	Trucks	103.1
Caustic soda	81.6	Rolled steel	101.6
Phosphoric fertilizer		Refined copper	100.8
(18.7% P_2O_5)	79.5	Electric power	100.8
Steam locomotives	79.1	Motor vehicles, total	100.1
Ammonium sulfate	78.7	Machine tools	99.3
Tractors (units)	77.3	Pig iron	98.3
Natural gas	70.9	Buses	98.3
Buses	70.1	Steel ingots and castings	96.9
Trucks	69.2	Crude petroleum	96.7
Steam and gas turbines	65.7	Caustic soda	95.0
Motor vehicles, total	65.4	Ammonium sulfate	88.3
Looms	36.3	Natural gas	85.3
Consumer goods		*Consumer goods*	
Ginned cotton	121.7	Rubber footwear	162.8
Butter	115.4	Ginned cotton	143.3
Rubber footwear	112.1	Butter	126.3
Fish catch	103.3	Woolen fabrics	111.2
Woolen fabrics	96.1	Fish catch	109.2
Cotton fabrics	94.9	Cotton fabrics	109.1
Leather shoes	85.9	Leather shoes	106.8
Silk and rayon fabrics	79.2	Raw sugar	100.8
Raw sugar	73.0	Silk and rayon fabrics	99.1
Vegetable oil	72.3	Meat and subproducts of	
Crude alcohol	66.3	first category	97.5
Linen fabrics	66.1	Vegetable oil	83.9
Soap (40% fatty acid)	61.4	Linen fabrics	83.2
Meat and subproducts of		Crude alcohol	82.5
first category	56.7	Soap (40% fatty acid)	76.3
Agriculture			
Cattle	94.5[a]	Sheep and goats	96.7[a]
Horses	93.5[a]	Cattle	95.8[a]

Table 83   *continued*

Assuming Equal Annual Planned Increment in Physical Growth during 1946–1950	(1)	Assuming Equal Average Annual Planned Rate of Growth during 1946–1950	(2)
Sheep and goats	93.1[a]	Grain harvest, biological yield	95.7
Grain harvest, biological yield	90.8	Horses	95.3[a]
Pigs	70.2[a]	Pigs	81.5[a]
Transportation			
Average daily carloadings, RR	93.0	Motor freight traffic	97.2
Inland waterway freight traffic		Average daily carloadings, RR	95.2
(ton-km)	79.7	Inland waterway freight traffic	
Maritime freight traffic (ton-km)	78.7	(ton-km)	91.4
Motor freight traffic	71.1	Maritime freight traffic (ton-km)	86.7
Employment			
National economy, workers		National economy, workers	
and employees	106.2	and employees	106.7
Wages			
Wage fund, national economy	128.6	Wage fund, national economy	130.5
State and Cooperative Retail Trade			
Total in current prices	157.5	Total in current prices	163.3
Total in 1940 prices	93.5[b]	Total in 1940 prices	108.9[b]

Source: Calculated from 1947 annual plan goals (Table A-5, col. 4) and Fourth Five-Year Plan goals for 1947, estimated from actual results in 1945 (Table A-4, col. 5) and goals for 1950 (Table A-1, col. 10) by assuming, for col. 1, an equal annual planned increment in physical growth during 1946–1950 and, for col. 2, an equal average annual planned rate of growth during 1946–1950.

a. Data for calculations explained in source above taken from *Resheniia*, Vol. 3, p. 273; *Komsomolskaia pravda*, March 1, 1947; and *Chislennost skota v SSSR* [Head of Livestock in the USSR], Moscow, 1957, pp. 6–7.

b. 1947 annual plan goal derived as 125,000 million rubles from trade in 1940 prices in 1946 (Table A-5, col. 2) and ratio of trade planned for 1947 to 1946 trade, both in current prices (derived as 1.313 from Table A-5, cols. 2 and 4, series 233), assuming no price change was planned for 1947. Five-year plan goal for 1950 taken to be same as that for trade in constant prices (Table A-1, col. 10, series 234a) since the plan figure appears to be in 1940 prices (*Resheniia*, Vol. 3, p. 288).

Other Western writers, however, consider that the drop in military production was far smaller, although they estimate civilian production much the same.[38]

The rapidity of economic expansion in 1947 can be clearly seen in Table 84. Compared with the 1946 results, there was a real "take-off" toward an eventual rapid expansion in 1947. However, the picture suggested by the figures originally published by Gosplan[39] is a bit too favorable. The list of industrial products whose output increased considerably in 1947 over 1946 covers mostly civilian machine-building industries and the light and textile industry, which had just gotten started.[40] Agricultural production is given on the basis of the old

38. According to Richard Moorsteen and Raymond Powell (*The Soviet Capital Stock, 1928–1962*, Homewood, Ill., 1966, pp. 622–23), Soviet munitions production dropped from 420 in 1945 (with 1937 = 100) to 275 in 1946 and 245 in 1947, while civilian industrial production rose from 54.3 in 1945 (with 1937 = 100) to 67.4 in 1946 and 82.6 in 1947.

39. *Pravda*, January 18, 1948.

40. The January 18 Gosplan report (*ibid.*) gives the following indexes of growth for 1947 over 1946:

estimates, which were too high because they were based on biological yield. Sales in state and cooperative retail trade seem to be overestimated; Moorsteen and Powell derive much smaller annual increases in 1946 (9.4 per cent) and 1948 (8.2 per cent) and an actual decline in 1947 (of 8.3 per cent).[41]

Nevertheless, the rapid expansion was real, and Western estimates confirm it.[42] Official Soviet announcements mention a rapid expansion during 1947, with higher growth in each quarter than in the corresponding quarter of the preceding year: 12 per cent in the first quarter, 18 per cent in the second, 26 per cent in the third, and 30 per cent in the fourth. They claim that, during the fourth quarter of 1947, the average quarterly level of prewar industrial production was reached.[43] Such an expansion might suggest that the goals of the 1947 annual plan were well fulfilled. But, in fact, the opposite was true.

Poor Fulfillment of 1947 Annual Plan

The percentages of fulfillment of the 1947 annual plan goals that are known are presented in Table 85. The data on individual products are hardly consistent with the official figure for over-all plan fulfillment of 103.5 per cent. Besides the incompleteness of the available data, Soviet methods used to calculate gross production and the use of 1926/27 prices could explain this difference.[44] For producer goods the median fulfillment was 87.9 per cent, and for consumer goods 100.4 per cent, but it is mainly the dispersion around the median that shows what little importance was accorded the annual plan goals. In this connection, it is interesting to note that production increases in machine-building industries mentioned above[45] were quite uneven and the percentages of plan fulfillment for some machinery (grain combines, automobiles, metallurgical equipment) were the lowest of all industries for which data are available.

In agriculture, successes resulting from the good harvest of 1947 were diminished by the failure to fulfill animal husbandry plans. In transportation, employment, and wages, plan overfulfillment reflects mainly costs higher than planned.

An examination of Table 85 cannot help but give the impression that the 1947 plan was a failure. Nevertheless, economic expansion in 1947 was spectacular. This shows that a very clear distinction must be made between the success of the

---

309 for trolleybuses, 277 for main-line locomotives, 263 for spinning machines, 257 for steam turbines, 210 for sugar, 209 for tractors, 206 for agricultural machinery, 168 for rubber shoes, etc. The production of the light and textile industry increased by 33 per cent.

41. Moorsteen and Powell, *Soviet Capital Stock*, p. 635.

42. According to Nutter, the production of all Soviet industry increased 21.7 per cent in 1947 over 1946: an increase of 29.4 per cent for civilian production (of which 20.6 per cent for intermediary products, 56.8 per cent for machinery and equipment, and 32.2 per cent for consumer goods), but a drop of 23.9 per cent for military production (Nutter, *Growth*, pp. 196–97). Moorsteen and Powell (*Soviet Capital Stock*, p. 623) estimate the annual increase in national income (GNP) at 11.2 per cent in 1947 and only 13.6 per cent in 1948.

43. *Pravda*, January 18, 1948.

44. On the methods of calculating gross production and value in 1926/27 prices, see my *Planning for Economic Growth in the Soviet Union, 1918–1932*, translated and edited by Marie-Christine MacAndrew and G. Warren Nutter, Chapel Hill, N.C., 1971, p. 256.

45. See footnote 42 above.

Table 84   Official Soviet Estimates of Annual Growth Rates in 1946–1948 (per cent)

	1946 (1)	1947 (2)	1948 (3)
1. National income (constant prices)	−6.0	20	24
2. Gross industrial production:	−16.3	20.8	26.9
3. Civilian production:	20		
4. Producer goods (group A)	−26.8	23.2	28.9
5. Consumer goods (group B)	13.6	22.2	20.9
Gross agricultural production			
6. Original estimate[a]		32	
7. Revised estimate[a]	10.5	28.4	11.5
Vegetable production:			
8. Original estimate[a]		48	
9. Revised estimate[a]	7.5	40.0	12.8
Animal production:			
10. Original estimate[a]			
11. Revised estimate[a]	20.8	2.3	7.9
Grain harvests:			
12. Biological yield	−7.6	59	18.6[b]
13. Barn yield	−16.3	66.4	2.0
Transportation (ton-kilometers)			
14. Railroad	6.7	4.6	27.2
15. Inland waterway	9.7	23	27.9
16. Maritime	−14.0	18.4	0
17. State and cooperative retail trade (constant prices)	30	17	13

Source

LINE 1–Col. 1: Calculated from *Narodnoe khoziaistvo SSSR v 1970 godu* [The USSR National Economy in 1970], Moscow, 1971, p. 533. **Cols. 2 and 3:** *Ekonomicheskaia zhizn*, Book I, pp. 411 and 420.

LINES 2, 4-5, and 12-16: Calculated from Tables A-4, col. 5, and A-5, cols. 2, 5, and 8.

LINE 3–Col. 1: *Pravda*, January 21, 1947.

LINES 6, 8, 12, and 17–Col. 2: *Pravda*, January 18, 1948, p. 1.

LINES 7, 9, and 11: Calculated from *Narodnoe khoziaistvo, 1961*, p. 292.

LINE 17–Col. 1: *Pravda*, January 21, 1947, p. 1. **Col. 2:** *Pravda*, January 18, 1948. **Col. 3:** V. Sokolov and R. Nazarov, *Sovetskaia torgovlia v poslevoennyi period* [Soviet Trade in the Postwar Period], Moscow, 1954, p. 61.

a. The original estimates were probably based on biological yield. The revised estimates, based on barn yield, were first published in *Narodnoe khoziaistvo, 1958*, p. 350. The practice of using biological yield for estimates of agricultural production was attacked by Khrushchev in 1953 when he revised the data Malenkov gave for 1952.

b. A completely different figure (a drop of 2 to 5 per cent) could be obtained from official statements that grain harvest in 1948 "nearly reached the 1940 level" (*Pravda*, January 20, 1949, p. 1) and that grain harvest in 1947 "reached the prewar level."

Table 85 Fulfillment of 1947 Annual Plan (per cent)

Industry		Consumer goods	
Total value of production		Raw sugar	108.5
(1926/27 prices)	103.5	Vegetable oil	105.8
		Silk and rayon fabrics	105.5
Producer Goods		Butter	104.8
Ammonium sulfate	116.3	Woolen fabrics	103.0
Asbestos shingles	105.7	Rubber footwear	102.8
Natural gas	104.4	Ginned cotton	101.1
Machine tools	101.6	Soap (40% fatty acid)	99.7
Crude petroleum	101.3	Leather shoes	98.1
Electric power	100.3	Crude alcohol	97.9
Lumber	97.2	Fish catch	95.5
Coal	96.3	Cotton fabrics	94.1
Steam locomotives	96.3	Linen fabrics	92.2
Buses	95.7	Meat and subproducts of first category	87.8
Lead	95.7		
Rolled steel	95.3	**Agriculture**	
Pig iron	94.3	Grain harvest, biological yield	118.1
Caustic soda	93.8	Cattle	96.4
Refined copper	93.4	Horses	92.4
Steel ingots and castings	91.4	Sheep and goats	90.7
Window glass	84.3	Pigs	72.3
Industrial timber hauled	83.9		
Soda ash	83.4	**Transportation**	
Motor vehicles, total	83.1	Motor freight traffic	114.8
Sulfuric acid	83.0	Maritime freight traffic (ton-km)	108.0
Trucks	82.4	Inland waterway freight traffic	
Phosphoric fertilizer (18.7% P_2O_5)	82.4	(ton-km)	102.0
Cement	81.8	Average daily carloadings, RR	97.7
Bricks	74.9		
Steam and gas turbines	73.7	**Employment**	
Tractors (units)	72.8	National economy, workers and	
Looms	67.9	employees	101.6
Railroad freight cars	66.1	**Wages**	
Metallurgical equipment	64.4	Wage fund, national economy	103.0
Automobiles	36.7	**Retail Trade**	
Grain combines	35.9	State and cooperative, total,	
		current prices	101.9

Source: Table A-5, col. 6, except for livestock for which figures were calculated from *Komsomolskaia pravda*, March 1, 1947, and *Chislennost*, pp. 6–7.

plan and the success of the economy, a distinction too often forgotten in studies of planned economies.

The failure of the 1947 plan is all the more important since 1947 was the first year when the new regulations about annual plans were in effect. Before 1947, only quarterly plans were operational. After 1947, following a decree of the USSR Council of Ministers of August 29, 1946,[46] the government had only to approve the annual plan and budget and the annual balances and plans for the distribution of funds presented with quarterly breakdowns. Henceforward, approval was required only for the quarterly plans for the distribution of food products,

46. "On Annual and Quarterly Economic Plans" (*Direktivy*, Vol. 3, pp. 89–91).

State Bank credit, State Bank funds, and transportation (with breakdowns by month). At the same time there was a tendency to increase the number of products that had to be listed in the annual plans approved by the Council of Ministers.[47] Thus, greater attention paid by the government to the annual plans did not make these plans any more operational.

Fulfillment of Five-Year Plan in 1947

As mentioned earlier, the published text of the Fourth Five-Year Plan for 1946–1950 did not give any information on annual goals. Ordinarily, the best way to estimate the five-year plan goals for the intermediary years is to assume equal rates of growth for all five years. This method of estimation cannot be used in exceptional periods when some products reappear after a stoppage in production or begin to be mass-produced after the construction of new factories.[48] In such cases growth cannot be at equal rates for all five years; it is necessarily faster (often at double or triple the subsequent rates) soon after the construction of the first factories and thereafter is less spectacular. The authors of the fourth plan obviously had to take this problem into account in planning the output of new products (or of products that were produced in very small quantities during the war), which was to grow at high rates during the first years of the five-year period. For other products, the annual goals of the five-year plan might be based on similar growth rates for all five years. Unfortunately, it is impossible to distinguish between these two categories of products in making estimates of the five-year plan goals for 1947. For that reason, Table 86 presents estimates based on both methods: on the left-hand side, equal annual planned increments in physical growth are assumed for all five years; on the right-hand side, equal average annual planned rates of growth are assumed during the five-year period.

Chart 9 shows the estimates of the five-year plan annual goals for the production of cement, calculated by both methods. The two yield very different results. Actual production lies between these two sets of goals; that is, it is higher than the goals estimated by assuming an equal annual rate of growth for 1946–1950 and lower than the goals estimated the other way. Because its output declined sharply during the war, cement production had to increase very fast to regain its 1940 level. Hence, the first method (assuming equal annual planned increments in physical growth) seems more nearly correct. The fact that the annual plan goal for 1947 is slightly above the five-year plan goal for 1947 estimated by the first method also supports the use of this method. For many products, this procedure seems the better of the two. On the other hand, for products whose output suffered less during the war (such as steel, rolled steel, etc.), the second method (assuming equal rates of growth) seems more valid.[49]

47. See p. 66 in Chapter 4.
48. See pp. 363–64 above.
49. It could not reasonably be assumed that the production of steam locomotives, of which only eight were produced in 1945, should increase at "equal rates of growth." Production was 243 in 1946 and 674 in 1947. This last figure is lower than the annual plan goal of 700. So it is highly unlikely that this represented an 8.5-fold overfulfillment of the five-year plan goal for 1947. See Table 85.

Table 86   Fulfillment of Fourth Five-Year Plan Goals Interpolated for 1947 (per cent)

Assuming Equal Annual Planned Increment in Physical Growth during 1946–1950 (1)		*Assuming Equal Average Annual Planned Rate of Growth during 1946–1950* (2)
Industry		
Consumer goods (1926/1927 prices)	94.3	Consumer goods (1926/1927 prices)	101.6
Total value of production (1926/1927 prices)	81.3	Total value of production (1926/1927 prices)	83.6
Producer goods (1926/1927 prices)	76.9	Producer goods (1926/1927 prices)	78.1
Producer goods		*Producer goods*	
Asbestos shingles	113.5	Steam locomotives	890.9
Synthetic dyes	107.0	Looms	688.5
Window glass	104.0	Railroad freight cars	482.3
Nickel	102.0	Ground natural phosphate	171.8
Steel pipes	100.8	Asbestos shingles	153.9
Crude petroleum	100.8	Tractors (15 hp)	141.4
Lumber	99.2	Phosphoric fertilizer (18.7% P_2O_5)	128.5
Peat	98.1	Cement	127.6
Coal	96.7	Window glass	125.1
Electric power	96.1	Tractors (units)	123.5
Machine tools	95.7	Synthetic dyes	122.4
Hydroelectric power	92.3	Paper	113.9
Ammonium sulfate	91.6	Steel pipes	113.1
Iron ore	91.5	Lumber	111.5
Lead	91.5	Mineral fertilizer	110.5
Refined copper	91.2	Steam and gas turbines	109.6
Rolled steel	90.5	Nickel	107.4
Cement	88.9	Crude petroleum	105.3
Paper	88.9	Peat	103.8
Industrial timber hauled	88.4	Bricks	103.7
Coke	86.9	Hydroelectric power	103.1
Pig iron	85.8	Industrial timber hauled	103.0
Steel ingots and castings	83.0	Ammonium sulfate	102.7
Mineral fertilizer	80.9	Lead	102.4
Railroad freight cars	80.2	Iron ore	101.6
Zinc	78.8	Electric power	101.1
Caustic soda	76.5	Machine tools	100.9
Steam locomotives	76.2	Coal	99.9
Bricks	75.1	Rolled steel	96.9
Natural gas	74.0	Refined copper	94.2
Soda ash	73.4	Buses	94.0
Plywood	70.4	Coke	93.8
Metallurgical equipment	70.3	Pig iron	92.8
Buses	67.1	Plywood	90.5
Phosphoric fertilizer (18.7% P_2O_5)	65.5	Natural gas	89.0
Tractors (15 hp)	58.9	Caustic soda	88.8
Trucks	57.1	Steel ingots and castings	88.6
Tractors (units)	56.2	Soda ash	88.2
Motor vehicles, total	54.3	Metallurgical equipment	87.6
Steam and gas turbines	48.4	Zinc	87.3
Ground natural phosphate	45.5	Roofing tiles	87.0
Automobiles	32.9	Trucks	85.0
Roofing tiles	30.8	Motor vehicles, total	83.2
Looms	22.4	Automobiles	68.7
Consumer goods		*Consumer goods*	
Ginned cotton	123.1	Phonographs	1117.9
Butter	121.0	Radios	510.5
Rubber footwear	115.3	Bicycles	191.8

Table 86 *continued*

Assuming Equal Annual Planned Increment in Physical Growth during 1946–1950 (1)		Assuming Equal Average Annual Planned Rate of Growth during 1946–1950 (2)	
Cotton yarn	100.9	Rubber footwear	167.4
Radios	100.5	Motorcycles	164.4
Woolen fabrics	99.0	Ginned cotton	144.9
Fish catch	98.6	Butter	132.4
Cotton fabrics	89.3	Margarine	126.5
Leather shoes	84.3	Cameras	118.0
Confectionery	84.3	Woolen fabrics	114.6
Silk and rayon fabrics	83.6	Cotton yarn	109.6
Beer	81.1	Raw sugar	109.4
Raw sugar	79.2	Clocks and watches	106.7
Vegetable oil	76.4	Confectionery	106.6
Margarine	72.8	Leather shoes	104.8
Hosiery	68.6	Silk and rayon fabrics	104.5
Crude alcohol	64.9	Fish catch	104.3
Matches	64.0	Hosiery	103.0
Soap (40% fatty acid)	61.2	Cotton fabrics	102.7
Linen fabrics (meters)	61.0	Beer	100.0
Starch and syrup	52.2	Vegetable oil	88.8
Motorcycles	52.1	Matches	87.0
Meat and subproducts of		Starch and syrup	86.1
first category	49.8	Meat and subproducts of	
Bicycles	47.8	first category	85.7
Cameras	43.2	Crude alcohol	80.7
Clocks and watches	39.1	Linen fabrics (meters)	76.7
Phonographs	32.6	Soap (40% fatty acid)	76.0

Agriculture

Sugar beets	114.5	Sugar beets	145.4
Grain harvest, biological yield	107.3	Grain harvest, biological yield	113.1
Raw cotton, barn yield	98.6	Raw cotton, barn yield	105.7
Grain harvest, barn yield	95.2	Grain harvest, barn yield	102.4
Cattle	91.0[a]	Sunflowers, barn yield	101.2
Milk	89.2	Milk	92.4
Horses	86.8[a]	Cattle	92.3[a]
Sheep and goats	84.4[a]	Horses	88.1[a]
Sunflowers, barn yield	83.9	Sheep and goats	87.7[a]
Meat and fat,		Flax fiber, barn yield	70.4
incl. rabbit and poultry	61.0	Meat and fat,	
Flax fiber, barn yield	59.1	incl. rabbit and poultry	67.7
Pigs	50.8[a]	Pigs	59.0[a]

Transportation

Total passenger traffic,		Total passenger traffic,	
RR (pass.-km)	120.8	RR (pass.-km)	123.1
Length of network, RR	98.7	Motor freight traffic	111.6
Total freight traffic, average length		Length of network, RR	98.8
of haul, RR	94.9	Average daily carloadings, RR	95.2
Average daily carloadings, RR	90.9	Total freight traffic, RR (m. tons)	95.1
Total freight traffic, RR (m. tons)	90.0	Total freight traffic,	
Total freight traffic, RR (ton-km)	87.4	average length of haul, RR	95.1
Maritime freight traffic (ton-km)	85.0	Inland waterway freight traffic	
Motor freight traffic	81.6	(ton-km)	91.4
Inland waterway freight traffic		Total freight traffic, RR (ton-km)	90.4
(ton-km)	81.3	Maritime freight traffic (ton-km)	86.7

Table 86 *continued*

Assuming Equal Annual Planned Increment in Physical Growth during 1946–1950 (1)		*Assuming Equal Average Annual Planned Rate of Growth during 1946–1950*	(2)
Employment			
Industry	108.9	National economy, workers and employees	108.4
National economy, workers and employees	107.9	Industry	105.8
Wages			
Wage fund, national economy	132.4	Wage fund, national economy	134.4
Money wage, national economy	123.7	Money wage, national economy	124.0
State and Cooperative Retail Trade			
Total, in current prices	160.5	Total, in current prices	166.4

Source: Calculated from actual results in 1947 (Table A-5, col. 5) and Fourth Five-Year Plan goals for 1947, estimated from actual results in 1945 (Table A-4, col. 5) and goals for 1950 (Table A-1, col. 10) by assuming, for col. 1, an equal annual planned increment in physical growth during 1946–1950 and, for col. 2, an equal average annual planned rate of growth during 1946–1950.

a. Data for calculations explained in source taken from *Resheniia*, Vol. 3, p. 273, and *Chislennost*, pp. 6–7.

The equal-increments method shows substantial discrepancies from the plan goals (see Table 85). These discrepancies are larger for producer goods, especially for most machine-bulding products, even though they grew very rapidly in 1947 (see above). The situation is not quite as bad for consumer goods, but the number of products included is not as large. As for agriculture, it is interesting to see that, with the exception of sugar beets and grain, the five-year plan goals were not reached (using the equal-increments method). The failure of the animal husbandry plan is particularly striking.

That the five-year plan for transportation was not fulfilled is apparent whichever method is used. The slight overfulfillment of the plan for employment is not affected by the method used. As for the wage fund, the overfulfillment of the five-year plan goals (which varies very little in the two methods of estimation) is considerable. This reflects price and wage revisions that seem not to have been planned in the same way. In fact, it is not only the balance of wages, prices, and supply of consumer goods that differs from the five-year estimates. The whole structure of the economy differs considerably from that envisaged by the five-year plan, which seems to have disintegrated after the end of 1947.

The Postwar Collectivization Campaign and New Agricultural Plans

The Policy in the Socialist Sector of Agriculture in the Fourth Five-Year Plan

The text of the Fourth Five-Year Plan published in March 1946 did not announce new collectivization measures, but it clearly reaffirmed support for the socialist sector. The government pledged "to strengthen by all possible means the social-

Chart 9   Planned and Actual Output of Cement, 1940–1950

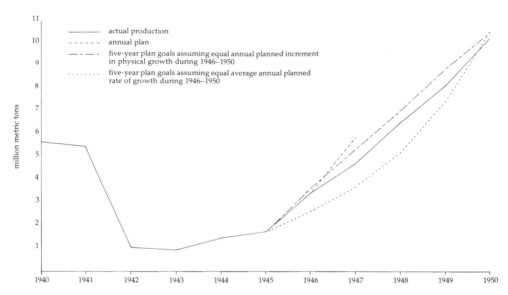

Source: For actual production: Tables A-3, A-4, and A-5; for 1947 annual plan: Table A-5; for five-year plan annual goals: estimated from actual production in 1945 and goals for 1950 (Table A-1) by assuming, in one case, an equal annual planned increment in physical growth during 1946–1950 and, in the other, an equal average annual planned rate of growth during 1946–1950.

ist sector of collective farms and the organization of Machine and Tractor Stations and state farms"; it also announced that collective farm property would be protected, the collective farm charter respected, and livestock completely restored on collective farms in areas that had been under German occupation.[50]

Repression of the Private Sector of Agriculture

The campaign against the private sector of agriculture had been announced before the war, in March 1939, at the Eighteenth Party Congress. Following the resolution of that congress, the May 27, 1939, decree stipulated that the private plots of collective farmers be limited, in accordance with the collective farm charter, to a quarter or half a hectare and, in certain districts, to one hectare.[51] In 1937 the average size of a collective farmer's private plot was just under half a hectare, and the total area of these private plots came to 9,065,000 hectares.

Nevertheless, the private sector of agriculture, represented largely by the private plots of collective and state farmers, was encouraged on several occasions. Thus, it was officially stipulated that "government assistance should be given to collective farmers in livestock breeding, in accordance with the collective farm charter"; assistance in raising pigs and bee-keeping was also stressed.[52]

50. *Direktivy*, Vol. 3, pp. 33 and 37–38.
51. Prokopovicz, *Histoire*, pp. 240–41.
52. *Direktivy*, Vol. 3, pp. 37–38.

The first measures taken against the private plots of collective farmers after the war were aimed at curtailing practices that had become prevalent during the war. A decree of September 19, 1946, criticized the practices, current during the war, of enlarging the size of plots and selling at low prices livestock, grain, seed, fodder, meat, and other products belonging to the collective farms, and it announced a check on the actual state of affairs through existing records.[53] As indicated by Serge N. Prokopovicz, the accusations of outright seizure of collective farm land by collective farmers were unfounded.[54] During the war, every ton of grain or potatoes was precious; collective farmers often cultivated the land that the collective farms allowed to lie fallow, and the administration said nothing. After the war, attempts to recover these lands from collective farmers, whose families included returned soldiers or officers, encountered active resistance.

As a result of the check-ups announced in the September 19 decree, 89 per cent of the collective farms were inspected by January 1, 1947; 4 million hectares of land taken over by various organizations and public institutions and 177,000 hectares of land held by individuals were restored to the collective farms.[55] As pointed out by Naum Jasny,[56] this campaign against private plots was based on the principle that the collective farms should fully satisfy the food needs of the collective farmers. This notion was particularly wrongheaded during the years immediately after the war when the food situation was very difficult in the Soviet Union.[57]

The campaign against private plots is mentioned in the February 1947 decree of the plenary session of the Party Central Committee,[58] one section of which is devoted to the problem of infringements of the collective farm charter. But no measures against the private plots were announced at that time.

Collectivization on the Territory Annexed during the War

The Soviet authorities were careful not to announce the complete collectivization of agriculture in the countries and territories occupied during the war. In the Baltic countries, Eastern Poland, Bessarabia, and Northern Bukovina, the government simply announced a vast agricultural reform, expropriating and physically liquidating large landowners and dividing their large and medium-sized estates among peasants who had very little or no land. The result of this policy was that, in 1946, there were more than 3 million peasant farms in the Soviet Union, most of which were in the annexed territories.[59]

The consolidation of Soviet power after World War II enabled the Communist

53. Decree of USSR Council of Ministers and Party Central Committee, "On Measures to Eliminate Infringements of the Collective Farm Charter on Collective Farms" (*ibid.*, Vol. 3, pp. 91–97).

54. Prokopovicz, *Histoire*, pp. 249–50.

55. *Izvestia* [News], March 7, 1947, and *Bolshevik*, No. 4, 1947, pp. 5–6, as cited in Prokopovicz, *Histoire*, p. 247.

56. *Soviet Industrialization*, p. 317.

57. It should not be forgotten that there was a severe drought in 1946 and that, because of the difficult food situation, the abolition of rationing had to be put off. See p. 354 above.

58. *Direktivy*, Vol. 3, pp. 147–93.

59. Harry Schwartz, *Russia's Soviet Economy*, London, 1951, p. 289.

Party to revoke concessions made during the war. A huge collectivization campaign was launched at the end of 1948 and continued into 1949 and 1950. As a result, almost all peasant farms were eliminated in the annexed territories and countries. Precise statistics on this collectivization are not available, but it is possible to reproduce partially the development of this campaign, as in Table 87. This table shows that the pace of the postwar collectivization campaign was different in the different republics. It seems to have begun first in Latvia and continued through 1949 in other annexed countries or territories. The continuation of this campaign during the last years of the Fourth Five-Year Plan would certainly have made plan fulfillment impossible had the plan not already been put aside. In addition to the agricultural contribution of the highly developed Baltic countries, the Soviet Union benefited from annexations in Belorussia and the Ukraine, where the Polish contribution accounted for nearly half (for Belorussia) or a third of the total number (after annexation) of peasant households in these republics in 1940.[60]

Amalgamation of Collective Farms and Attempts to Regroup Peasants into Agricultural Cities

The amalgamation of collective farms and organization of collective farm centers could have been carried out within the framework of the five-year plan without endangering its goals. But the scope of this campaign and its ideological implications went far beyond the framework of the plan.[61] Stalin had always preferred large-scale agricultural enterprises, for he considered them more productive and more amenable to direct control by central power.[62] His ideological preferences for diminishing urban-rural differences and for replacing the market by barter, as expressed in his last writings,[63] were directed toward enlarging and then unifying agricultural enterprises on the model of state farms. In fact, if in order to achieve communism it was necessary to abolish the market and if, as Stalin saw it, the market still existed in the Soviet Union solely because of cooperative (collective farm) ownership of the land, a vast reorganization of Soviet agriculture seemed to be called for.

The task of carrying out this reorganization seems to have fallen mainly to Nikita Khrushchev, who had just been appointed Secretary of the Party Central Committee and the Moscow Party Committee. His scheme to revamp agriculture worked basically in two directions: (1) strengthening brigades on collective farms and abolishing autonomous teams for grain crops, and (2) amalgamating small collective farms. Khrushchev's campaign was opposed to the concessions

60. After the annexation of Eastern Poland in 1940, the share of households integrated into Ukrainian collective farms in the total number of peasant households in the Ukraine fell to 71.7 per cent to climb later to 99.9 per cent in 1966 (*Ukraina za piatdesiat rokiv (1917–1967)* [The Ukraine during 50 Years, 1917–1967], Kiev, 1967, p. 35).

61. The known texts of the Fourth Five-Year Plan and of the February 1947 decree on agriculture do not mention enlarging and amalgamating collective farms.

62. On this subject, see my *Planning*, pp. 70–72.

63. I. V. Stalin, *Ekonomicheskie problemy sotsializma v SSSR* [The Economic Problems of Socialism in the USSR], Moscow, 1952.

Table 87 Results of Postwar Collectivization Campaign, 1940 and 1945–1953[a]

	Lithuania (1)	Latvia (2)	Belorussia (3)	Transcarpathian Province (Ruthenia) (4)
Number of Peasant Households Collectivized as Per Cent of Total				
1940	[b]	[b]	51.8	[c]
1945			55.7	
1947		0.1		
1948		2.4		
1949	33.9	76.7		52.9[d]
1950	72.8	90.3		82.0[d]
1951	93.1	97.7		
1952	95.9	98.4		
1953	98.9	98.7	97.2	95.9
Share of Area Sown by Collective and State Farm Peasants				
1940	[b]	[b]	60.2	
1945			55.4	
1947		0.03		
1948		2.4		
1949	30.2	80.9		27.9[d]
1950	75.7	94.7		64.9[d]
1951	95.3	99.5		
1952	98.5	99.8		
1953	99.8	99.8	99.9	97.2

Source: Col. 1: *Narodnoe khoziaistvo Litovskoi SSR* [National Economy of the Lithuanian SSR], Vilnius, 1957, p. 65. **Col. 2:** *Narodnoe khoziaistvo Latviiskoi SSR* [National Economy of the Latvian SSR], Riga, 1957, p. 67. **Col. 3:** *Dostizheniia Sovetskoi Belorussii za 40 let* [Achievements of Soviet Belorussia during Forty Years], Minsk, 1958, p. 46. **Col. 4:** *Narodnoe Gospodarstvo Zakarpatskoi Oblasti* [National Economy of the Transcarpathian Province], Uzhgorod, 1957, p. 27.

a. As of July 1.

b. Since the Soviet annexation took place in June 1940, there could hardly have been any farms collectivized by July 1, 1940.

c. Annexed only in 1945.

d. As of June 1.

granted to collective farmers after the war and to the policy of Politburo member A. Andreev, chairman of the Council for Collective Farm Affairs under the USSR Council of Ministers.[64] The campaign opened with an anonymous article published in *Pravda* on February 19, 1950, entitled "Against Deviations in the Organization of Work on Collective Farms," directed against the proponents of the team method.[65] Khrushchev soon launched a drive for the amalgamation of collective farms. In a speech to the voters of Kalinin District on March 7, 1950,[66] Khrushchev described the advantages of large agricultural enterprises and declared that many collective farmers, convinced of these advantages, wished to

64. The Council for Collective Farm Affairs was created by the October 8, 1946, decree of USSR Council of Ministers and Party Central Committee, "On the Council for Collective Farm Affairs" (*Direktivy*, Vol. 3, p. 105).

65. *Pravda*, February 19, 1950, pp. 4–5.

66. *Pravda*, March 8, 1950, p. 4.

amalgamate their farms. A whole press campaign was organized on this subject, in which the main role was played by *Moskovskaia pravda* [Moscow Truth], a newspaper directly under Khrushchev's control. Many advantages of enlarged collective farms were stressed during the campaign: better facilities for mechanization; increased specialization; introduction of mixed farming; savings on administrative personnel; hiring of specialists (agronomists, veterinarians); formation of construction brigades and brigades for draining swampland; creation of cultural funds; more careful selection of managerial personnel among Party members; creation of Party cells in almost all collective farms; and intensification of political work.[67]

The amalgamation of collective farms was to be only the first step in the reorganization. According to Khrushchev, each enlarged collective farm was to start by choosing a center to serve as the site of the farm management. Once the center was established, the collective farm, with the help of official agencies, was to draw up a plan for constructing and improving the administrative buildings of the enlarged farm and subsequently to regroup the houses of the villages and dispersed hamlets in the collective farm center. According to Khrushchev, the collective farm centers rebuilt in this way would become agricultural cities.[68] On this occasion Khrushchev proposed a whole program for housing construction on collective farms. There was to be a housing center with two-storied houses, each containing two to four apartments.[69] To economize and to limit the size of the collective farm center, private plots accompanying the houses would be reduced to one orchard and one vegetable garden of from 0.12 to 0.15 hectares, with the rest of the land being outside the agricultural city and farmed with machines—hence in a more or less communal manner.[70]

During 1950 and at the beginning of 1951 many articles were devoted to regrouping collective farms, discussing plans for various agricultural cities already under construction. But certain criticisms appeared in the winter of 1950–1951. *Pravda* published articles largely on questions of labor organization and selection of personnel and political work, while *Moskovskaia pravda* continued to publish long articles almost daily on regrouping the agglomerations and on construction. On March 4, 1951, *Pravda*, *Moskovskaia pravda*, and *Sotsialisticheskoe zemledelie* [Socialist Agriculture] published a report by Khrushchev entitled "The Construction and Organization of Collective Farms."[71] Although following the line of Khrushchev's previous declarations, this report also stressed the need for "construction that was more economical" and suggested calling the collective farm centers not "agricultural cities" as before but "collective farm villages." One day later, on March 5, the same three newspapers published a short item to the effect that a note presenting this article as "the basis for a discussion" had

67. *Notes et Etudes Documentaires*, April 11, 1952, pp. 14–17, and speeches and articles by Khrushchev in *Pravda*, March 3, April 25, and May 27, 1950, and March 4, 1951, as cited in *Notes*, April 11, 1952, pp. 36–46.

68. *Notes*, April 11, 1952, p. 21.

69. Khrushchev, *Pravda*, March 4, 1951, p. 2.

70. *Notes*, April 11, 1952, p. 22.

71. On this subject, see *ibid.*, pp. 28–29.

inadvertently been omitted. At the same time, on March 3, Minister of Agriculture Benediktov published a long article in *Sotsialisticheskoe zemledelie* [Socialist Agriculture] emphasizing the economic aspects of amalgamation and making no mention of the problem of transferring housing on the enlarged collective farms. Soon direct criticisms of the agricultural cities appeared in the press. On March 20, the secretary of the Armenian Party Central Committee, Arutiunov, declared in a speech that "certain statements confuse and trouble the group of Party activists." He asserted that the main task of the regrouped collective farms was to strengthen the collective communal economy by making maximum use of agricultural machinery, developing all branches of collective farm production, and rationally organizing the work of the collective farms. All attempts to replace this main task with others—namely those put forward by Khrushchev—only created confusion and worked against the Party policy at the present stage of collective farms. According to Arutiunov, the idea of agricultural cities was vague and the concentration of manpower in one single place was not absolutely necessary.[72] A similar position was taken a little later by Bagirov, secretary of the Azerbaidzhan Party Central Committee.[73]

After these events, the idea of agricultural cities was put off, but the amalgamation of collective farms was continued, although less intensely. Nevertheless, the number of collective farms diminished very rapidly, dropping from about 252,000[74] in 1949 to 121,353 at the end of 1950 and to 91,177 at the end of 1953.[75] Table 88 indicates the speed with which this amalgamation took place. It should be noted that the process of enlarging collective farms did not stop with Stalin's death. The number of collective farms, which was 91,177 at the end of 1953, dropped to 67,681 at the end of 1958, to 44,900 at the end of 1960, and to 33,600 at the end of 1970, recent developments being influenced most by the state farm charter.[76]

As a consequence of amalgamation, the average size of collective farms more than doubled between 1945 and 1950, and the number of collective farm households per farm also doubled. But while the average size of collective farms was 1,000 hectares in 1951, the average size of state farms was 2,600 hectares. The simultaneous enlarging of collective and state farms continued into 1958, with the average size of collective farms rising to 1,900 hectares and of state farms to 8,700 hectares.[77] A movement of such magnitude could not help but affect the agricultural plans and the prospects for implementing them.

72. Arutiunov included in his listing the regrouping of small villages, collecting them together in a single village, and building agricultural cities or collective farm villages with two-storied houses with three or four apartments (*Kommunist* [The Communist], Erevan, March 21, 1951, as cited in *Notes*, April 11, 1952, pp. 28–29).

73. *Bakinskii rabochii* [The Baku Worker], May 26, 1951, as cited in *Notes*, April 11, 1952, p. 29.

74. *Sotsialisticheskoe zemledelie*, March 3, 1951, as cited in *Notes*, April 11, 1952, p. 26. Jasny (*Soviet Industrialization*, p. 324) estimated the number of collective farms at about 260,000 in 1949.

75. *Selskoe khoziaistvo SSSR* [Agriculture in the USSR], Moscow, 1960, p. 51.

76. *Ibid.*, and *Selskoe khoziaistvo*, 1971, p. 10.

77. *Strana*, p. 117.

Table 88   Number of Collective Farms, Selected Years, 1940–1970[a]

	1940 (1)	1949 (2)	1950 (3)	1953 (4)	1958 (5)	1960 (6)	1970 (7)
USSR, total:	236,945	252,000[b]	123,747	93,256	69,129	44,944	33,561
Russian Republic:[c]	168,398		69,762	54,688	38,163	21,467	14,053
North	8,047		2,956	2,520	2,344		
Northwest	13,084		4,142	3,435	3,000	2,038	814
Center	42,757		12,340	10,534	7,523	4,628	2,801
Volga-Viatsk	24,460		8,130	6,373	4,998	2,190	1,637
Central Black Earth	20,309		7,679	6,253	4,152	1,882	1,690
Volga (Povolzhe)	12,344		8,428	6,418	3,958	3,209	2,703
Northern Caucasus	7,605		4,243	2,968	2,049	1,790	1,400
Urals	17,953		9,188	6,755	4,528	1,861	1,269
Western Siberia	14,531		6,474	4,762	2,515	1,819	866
Eastern Siberia	5,987		4,531	3,286	2,025	1,258	563
Far east	1,321		1,651	1,384	1,071	668	200
Ukraine:							
Prewar territory		26,401[d]	14,433[d]				
Postwar territory	28,637		19,527	16,245	13,345	9,745	9,244
Belorussia:							
Prewar territory		9,771[e]	3,279[f]				
Postwar territory	10,174		9,334	5,287	3,837	2,382	2,206
Uzbekistan	7,514		3,215	2,451	1,286	978	1,056
Kazakhstan	6,901		3,800	3,092	1,606	1,337	449
Georgia	4,256	3,916[g]	2,535	2,057	2,258	1,847	1,265
Azerbaidzhan	3,429		1,615	1,359	1,424	1,115	992
Lithuania			4,514	2,267	2,185	1,915	1,428
Moldavia	233		1,639	938	754	557	551
Latvia			1,794	1,474	1,249	1,122	669
Kirghizia	1,732		1,144	715	545	306	245
Tadzhikistan	3,093		1,314	589	434	353	282
Armenia	1,030		668	626	805	760	476
Turkmenistan	1,548		573	470	351	338	331
Estonia			2,313	998	887	722	314

Source: Unless otherwise indicated, cols. 1 and 3–5: *Selskoe khoziaistvo*, 1960, p. 50; cols. 6 and 7: *Selskoe khoziaistvo*, 1971, pp. 484–85.

a. End of year. Including fishing and industrial collective farms.

b. *Sotsialisticheskoe selskoe khoziaistvo* [Socialist Agriculture], March 3, 1950, as cited in *Notes*, April 11, 1952, p. 26.

c. In certain provinces of the Russian Republic the amalgamation of collective farms was especially rapid, with each new collective farm replacing, on the average, three or four old ones. The number of collective farms in five provinces changed as follows betweeen 1949 and 1950:

	1949	1950
Moscow Province	6,069	1,668
Yaroslav Province	3,890	963
Voronezh Province	3,188	1,119
Kaluga Province	3,458	1,036
Leningrad Province (approx.)	2,000	600

Taken from *Pravda*, June 25 and October 27, 1950; *Sotsialisticheskoe zemledelie*, August 19 and 29, 1950; and *Trud* [Labor], August 16, 1950, as cited in *Notes*, April 11, 1952, p. 26.

d. *Sotsialisticheskoe zemledelie*, December 28, 1950, as cited in *Notes*, April 11, 1952, p. 26.

e. *Pravda*, November 14, 1950, p. 2.

f. *Ibid*. This figure does not agree with the one given later in *Selskoe khoziaistvo*, 1960, p. 50. The difference between prewar and postwar territory is not sufficient to explain this discrepancy.

g. *Zaria Vostoka* [Dawn of the East], October 17, 1950, as cited in *Notes*, April 11, 1952, p. 26.

New Agricultural Plans

The postwar disruptions in Soviet agriculture certainly justified drafting new agricultural plans. The February 1947 decision of the plenary session of the Party Central Committee seems, indeed, to have been based on a new agricultural plan drawn up during 1946. This new plan probably was needed to preserve the original goals of the five-year plan that had been jeopardized by the drought and the poor harvest of 1946.[78] The published text was much more detailed than the provisions of the March 1946 law on the five-year plan. The February 1947 decree paid special attention to the socialist sector of agriculture, particularly to collective farms. However, the data on area to be sown covered only certain regions, and it is difficult to compare them with actual results and draw conclusions. The only agricultural goals specified with more detail in the February 1947 decree were goals for livestock breeding. The principal goals of this plan, which could be called biennial (1947–1948), are shown in Table 89. It provided for an increase in livestock in all sectors of agriculture—socialist and private. That privately held livestock were to increase proves that measures to limit the size of private plots[79] were not too extensive at this time.

The implementation of this biennial plan for livestock breeding was not very successful, especially in view of the fact that the plan for grain harvest for 1947 was overfulfilled (see Table 85). The percentages of fulfillment were generally lower in 1948 than in 1947, which suggests that the plan was not carried out very energetically. It should not be forgotten that the figures in Table 89 are averages for the whole country and that the results by provinces or by districts would certainly show much greater deviations from the plan. In 1947 the plans for breeding horses, sheep, and goats were fulfilled better on collective farms than in the country as a whole. The explanation must be weaknesses in the private sector. For beef cattle (including cows) and pigs, on the other hand, the private sector seems to have done better. The situation in the private sector deteriorated in 1948, and fulfillment of the plan in 1948 was better everywhere (except for cows) on collective farms than in the whole country. Discrimination against the private sector, hence, seems to have played an important role after 1947.

Discrimination against private-sector livestock breeding can be seen directly in the "Three-Year Plan for Livestock Breeding on Collective and State Farms in 1949–1951," published in *Pravda* on April 19, 1949 (see Table 90). First, it should be noted that this plan was officially outside the annual framework of the Fourth Five-Year Plan, which was to end in 1950, both because it set 1950 goals different from the five-year plan goals and because it was limited to the socialist sector of agriculture. The decree on deliveries of livestock products that was issued soon afterward (on May 26, 1949)[80] shows, moreover, that this was a special plan intended to guarantee delivery to the state of the most important livestock products, rather than a plan to expand agriculture in general.

---

78. See pp. 358–59 above.
79. See pp. 374–75 above.
80. Joint decree of USSR Council of Ministers and Party Central Committee (*Direktivy*, Vol. 3, pp. 341–68).

Table 89   Plan for Livestock Breeding, 1947–1948 (millions)

	1947			1948		
	Planned (1)	Actual (2)	Per Cent of Plan Fulfilled (3)	Planned (4)	Actual (5)	Per Cent of Plan Fulfilled (6)
Horses, total:	11.9	11.0	92.4	12.9	11.8	91.5
Collective farm	7.3	6.9	94.5	8.2	7.9	96.3
State farm[a]	0.34			0.37		
Beef cattle, total:	52	50.1	96.3	56.1	54.8	97.9
Collective farm	18.4	17.0	92.4	21.2	20.9	98.6
State farm[a]	1.46			1.60		
Cows, total:	24.7	23.8	96.3	27.2	24.2	89.0
Collective farm	4.4	3.8	86.4	6.0	4.6	76.7
Pigs, total:	13.4	9.7	72.4	20.3	15.2	74.9
Collective farm	4.6	3.1	67.4	6.3	5.4	85.7
State farm[a]	0.55			0.70		
Sheep and goats, total:	84.7	76.8	90.7	97.8	85.6	87.5
Collective farm	46.0	43.8	95.2	53.7	50.9	94.8
State farm[a]	3.17			3.59		
Poultry, collective farm	[b]			[c]		
Yield of milk per collective farm cow (kg per year)	[d]			[e]	1,070[f]	

Source: Unless otherwise indicated, cols. 1 and 4: *Direktivy*, Vol. 3, pp. 165–68 and 182–83; cols. 2 and 5: *Chislennost*, pp. 6–7; col. 3: col. 2 as per cent of col. 1; col. 6: col. 4 as per cent of col. 3.

a. Only those under the Ministry of State Farms.
b. Information on this plan is given in *Direktivy*, Vol. 3, pp. 165–68. Poultry on collective farms was to double between 1946 and 1947 (*ibid.*, Vol. 3, p. 170).
c. Poultry on collective farms was to triple between 1946 and 1948 (*ibid.*, Vol. 3, p. 170).
d. An increase of 15 per cent was planned between 1946 and 1947 (*ibid.*, Vol. 3, p. 166).
e. An increase of 15 per cent was planned between 1947 and 1948 (*ibid.*, Vol. 3, p. 166).
f. Given by Khrushchev (*Izvestia*, December 16, 1958, p. 3). The plan certainly could not have been fulfilled since the yield in 1945 was 945 kg (*Dostizheniia sovetskoi vlasti za 40 let v tsifrakh* [Achievements of the Soviet Regime during 40 Years in Figures], Moscow, 1957, p. 183), and a 15 per cent increase in 1947 and again in 1948 would have produced a figure considerably higher than 1,070 unless there was a catastrophic drop in 1946.

Although the three-year plan was limited to collectively owned livestock, the text of the plan also gave for the record (probably for the spring of 1949) the head of privately owned livestock (belonging to collective farmers, state farmers, and individual peasants). But nothing was said about future prospects for this livestock. In Table 90 it is assumed that the three-year livestock plan anticipated maintaining privately owned livestock at its 1949 level, but this assumption may not be correct. One reason is that the program launched in 1949 for rapid collectivization of the territory annexed during the war implied a reduction in privately owned livestock, unless it was to be compensated by an increase in privately owned livestock in other parts of the country.

The desire to strengthen the socialist sector was reflected in the increase of all the goals of the five-year plan for collective farm livestock. Since the goals for

Table 90 Three-Year Plan for Livestock Breeding on Collective and State Farms, 1949–1951, and Fulfillment of Fourth Five-Year Plan Goals in 1950

| | Three-Year Plan | | | | | | | | | Five-Year Plan Goals for 1950 | |
| | 1949 | | | 1950 | | | 1951 | | | | |
	Planned (1)	Actual (2)	Per Cent of Plan Fulfilled (3)	Planned (4)	Actual (5)	Per Cent of Plan Fulfilled (6)	Planned (7)	Actual (8)	Per Cent of Plan Fulfilled (9)	Planned (10)	Per Cent of Plan Fulfilled (11)
Livestock (millions)											
1. Beef cattle, total:	58	58.1	100.2	62.5	57.1	91.4	69.7	58.8	85.0	66.2	86.3
2. Collective farm	24	25.4	105.8	28	28.1	100.4	34	31.3	92.1	25.9	108.5
3. State farm	4.0	4.0	100.0	4.5	3.9	86.7	5.7			4.5	86.7
4. Privately owned	30[a]	28.7	95.7	30[a]	25.1	83.7	30[a]			35.8	70.1
5. Pigs, total:	20.6	22.2	107.8	24.3	24.4	100.4	30.8	27.1	88.0	31.8	76.7
6. Collective farm	10	9.6	96.0	13.0	12.3	94.6	18.0	15.5	86.1	11.1	110.8
7. State farm	3.4	3.4	100.0	4.1	3.4	82.9	5.6			4.1	82.9
8. Privately owned	7.2[a]	9.2	127.8	7.2[a]	8.7	120.8	7.2[a]			16.6	52.4
9. Sheep and goats, total:	98.2	93.6	95.3	110.2	99.0	89.8	128.0	107.6	84.1	122.5	80.8
10. Collective farm	62.4	60.4	96.8	73.0	68.3	93.6	88.0	74.0	84.1	68.1	100.3
11. State farm	9.3	9.3	100.0	10.7	8.8	82.2	13.5			10.7	82.2
12. Privately owned	26.5[a]	23.9	90.2	26.5[a]	22.9	86.4	26.5[a]			43.7	52.4
Poultry:											
13. Collective farm	65			120			200				
14. Privately owned	350[b]							under 300			
Procurements											
15. Meat and fat (live weight) (mill. m. tons)	1,930	1,800	93.3	2,300	2,300	100.0	2,700	2,600	96.3		
16. Milk (mill. m. tons)	8,000			8,900	8,479	95.3	10,000	9,515	95.1		
17. Eggs (millions)	2,102			3,000	1,912	63.7	4,200				
18. Wool (mill. m. tons)	140			158	136	86.1	188				

Source

COLUMNS 1, 4, and 7–Line 1: Sum of lines 2–4. **Lines 2-4, 6-8, and 10-13:** *Direktivy*, Vol. 3, pp. 343–47 and 357. **Line 5:** Sum of lines 6-8. **Line 9:** Sum of lines 10–12. **Lines 15-18:** *Direktivy*, Vol. 3, pp. 444, 449, 453, 454.

COLUMN 2–Lines 1-2, 5-6, and 9-10: *Chislennost*, pp. 6–7. **Lines 3, 7, and 11:** Assumed to be same as plan in col. 1. **Lines 4, 8, and 12:** Total minus collective and state farm animals. **Line 15:** *Narodnoe khoziaistvo SSSR v 1967 godu* [The USSR National Economy in 1967], Moscow, 1968, p. 336.

COLUMN 3–All lines: Col. 2 as per cent of col. 1.

COLUMN 5–Lines 1-2, 5-6, and 9-10: *Chislennost*, pp. 6–7. **Lines 3, 7, and 11:** *Narodnoe khoziaistvo, 1956*, pp. 129–30. **Lines 4, 8, and 12:** Total minus collective and state farm animals. **Line 15:** *Narodnoe khoziaistvo, 1967*, p. 336. **Lines 16-18:** *Selskoe khoziaistvo*, 1960, p. 91.

COLUMN 6–All lines: Col. 5 as per cent of col. 4.

COLUMN 8–Lines 1-2, 5-6, and 9-10: *Chislennost*, pp. 6–7. **Line 14:** Jasny, *Soviet Industrialization*, p. 318 n. **Line 15:** *Narodnoe khoziaistvo, 1967*, p. 336. **Line 16:** Estimated from Khrushchev's statement (*Izvestia*, January 28, 1958, p. 2) that the average for 1954–1957 was 62 per cent higher than the average for 1950–1953. The figures for 1950, 1953, 1955, 1956, and 1957 are given as 8,479, 10,656, 13,506, 17,337, and 20,454 thousand metric tons in *Selskoe khoziaistvo*, 1960, p. 91; the figure for 1952 is given as 10 million metric tons in Nancy Nimitz, "Statistics of Soviet Agriculture," RAND Research Memorandum 1250, Santa Monica, 1954, p. 34; and the figure for 1954 is given as 11,300 thousand metric tons in T. A. Koval, *Selskoe khoziaistvo v shestoi piatiletke* [Agriculture in the Sixth Five-Year Plan], Moscow, 1957, p. 144.

Table 90 *continued*

COLUMN 9–All lines: Col. 8 as per cent of col. 7.

COLUMN 10–Line 1: Based on 1945 figure (given as 47.6 million in *Chislennost*, p. 6) and increase planned for 1950 (given as 39 per cent in *Direktivy*, Vol. 3, p. 34). **Lines 2, 6, and 10:** Voznesensky, *Five-Year Plan*, p. 17. **Lines 3, 7, and 11:** Assumed to be same as three-year plan for 1950 (col. 4). **Lines 4, 8, and 12:** Total minus collective and state farm animals. **Line 5:** Based on 1945 figure (given as 10.6 million in *Chislennost*, p. 6) and increase planned for 1950 (given as threefold in *Direktivy*, Vol. 3, p. 34). **Line 9:** Based on 1945 figure (given as 70.0 million in *Chislennost*, p. 6) and increase planned for 1950 (given as 75 per cent in *Direktivy*, Vol. 3, p. 34).

COLUMN 11–All lines: Col. 5 as per cent of col. 10.

a. Livestock owned by collective farmers, workers and employees (largely workers on state farms), and independent peasants. The three-year plan, which gives data on "livestock belonging to the population" as of the end of 1948 or spring of 1949, does not mention any increase planned for privately owned livestock during 1949–1951, so the figures given in the plan for 1949 have been used here for 1949–1951.

The breakdown of privately owned livestock in 1949 was as follows (in thousands):

	Beef Cattle	Pigs	Sheep and Goats
Collective farmers	19,100	3,700	18,500
Workers and employees (state farm employees)	7,000	1,600	5,200
Independent peasants	3,900	1,900	2,800
Total	30,000	7,200	26,500

b. Given in the three-year plan (*Direktivy*, Vol. 3, p. 348) as the actual figure in 1949, but since it was originally published in April 1949 it could only be a plan figure. It is impossible to discover the plan's policy on privately owned poultry, which may have been different from the policy on privately owned livestock.

state farms were not given in the five-year plan, it is impossible to draw conclusions on this subject, but an increase was likely there, too.[81]

Was the three-year plan part of Khrushchev's program for the amalgamation of collective farms and the creation of agricultural cities, with barely veiled reprisals against the private sector? Nothing in the text of the plan indicates this, and it is not impossible that the five-year goals were maintained for the private sector.[82] In any case, whether envisaged by the three-year plan or not, the suppression of privately owned livestock that accompanied the amalgamation of collective farms jeopardized both the five-year plan livestock goals and the three-year plan goals for the whole country. The five-year plan for livestock was fulfilled only for collective (and probably state) farms, but it was nowhere nearly fulfilled for the whole country. It appears from Table 90 that the number of privately owned livestock in 1950 was far below the five-year plan goals (fulfillments were 52.4 per cent for pigs and sheep and goats and 70.1 per cent for beef cattle).

As for the three-year plan for livestock breeding, there is no doubt about its

81. In Table 90 the five-year plan goals for state farm livestock were estimated at the same level as in the three-year plan for 1950. These were maximum figures. Thanks to this estimate, it was possible to estimate the five-year plan goals for privately owned livestock. These figures, then, represent a minimum.

82. In Table 90 it is assumed that privately owned livestock was maintained at the level of the spring of 1949. If the five-year plan goals were maintained, the total goals for the whole country should have been considerably increased. The nonfulfillment of the three-year plan, then, would have been much worse.

failure (see Table 90). By 1950, of collectively owned livestock, only collective farm beef cattle had increased according to plan; the other categories were lagging behind. But in 1951, after the campaign for the amalgamation of collective farms, the failure of all the goals, for both collectively and privately owned sectors, was even worse. This was also the case, although not to such an extent, for procurement. The Soviet state was able to push some of the effects of the agricultural crisis onto the producers, which, in the final analysis, meant onto the peasants. Thus, collective farms and private producers had to deliver more livestock products per unit of livestock to the state than had been specified in the plans.

Fourth Five-Year Plan Put Aside and Fifth Five-Year Plan Drafted

Maintaining the Fiction of the Fourth Five-Year Plan

The disintegration of the Fourth Five-Year Plan at the end of 1947 could have led the government officially to give up its goals. In actual fact, the government tried to take advantage of the new situation and to show from the figures that it allowed to be published that any changes made in the plan were the result of unexpected successes. At the same time the goals for the annual plans for 1948–1950 were published only in very brief form and only the joint report of Gosplan and the Central Statistical Administration, published in *Pravda* on April 16, 1951, mentioned the over-all fulfillment of the fourth plan.[83]

During the whole period 1946–1950, insistence on the real and binding nature of the fourth plan remained dogma. It was taken for granted, as with the 1947 plan, that "the plan set a volume of production for the most important branches of industry that was higher than the preliminary provisions of the Fourth Five-Year Plan."[84] The official view on this subject was peremptorily reaffirmed: "USSR Gosplan demanded of all the ministries fulfillment of the principal goals of the 1946–1950 five-year plan for each year. When it became apparent in 1946–1947 that the five-year plan goals had been exceeded, Gosplan insisted that the ministries take on additional obligation in the annual plan for 1948."[85]

In 1949, it was also pointed out that "the successful development of the national economy has permitted the government to increase the plan originally set for industrial production."[86]

In reality, while claiming its fidelity to the current five-year plan, the government was turning increasingly toward long-term plans (longer than five years), partial plans on the fringe of the current five-year plan, and the plan for the following five-year period (1951–1955).

83. On the fulfillment of the five-year plan for 1946–1950, see pp. 396–402 below.
84. *Ekonomicheskaia zhizn*, Book I, p. 401.
85. *Po edinomu planu*, p. 114.
86. *Ekonomicheskaia zhizn*, Book I, p. 421.

Drafting Long-Term Plans

As early as the summer of 1947, USSR Gosplan proposed to the government that a general economic plan for 15 years be drafted.[87] Commissions and study groups, with participation of well-known researchers, planning agency personnel, and people from the economic administration agencies, were formed to handle the main problems. Several conferences were held and the commissions presented reports on prospects for technical progress, development of various branches, changes in the level of per capita consumption, and so forth, but the work was never finished,[88] apparently having been abandoned in 1949 after Voznesenskii's downfall. Long-term plans for other sectors of the national economy were also drawn up during this period (see Table 91). For example, the government decree of February 1, 1949, stipulated that the 10-year plan for rebuilding the city of Moscow (1936–1945) be carried out in 3 or 4 years and a new plan for 20 or 25 years be drawn up. Other plans concerned electrification. There was a plan for the rapid electrification of villages and rural areas for 1948–1965 and a 10-year plan (1951–1960) for the electrification of the USSR by the construction of electric power stations (see Table 91). "The long-term prospects for the development of railroad transportation for fifteen years" (probably 1951–1965) and the 10-year plans (1951–1960) for the development of various branches of the economy drafted with a limited number of indexes should also be mentioned.[89]

"The Stalin Plan for the Transformation of Nature"

After the Fourth Five-Year Plan was put into a state of abeyance in 1948, a whole series of plans for the transformation of nature was published. The best known of these plans, that of October 20, 1948, provided for planting forests and creating artificial ponds and reservoirs in huge areas of the European part of the Soviet Union in order to combat drought.[90] The reforestation and revegetation of the steppe of the European part of the country was necessary to combat drought and the *sukhovei* (hot dry wind). As Serge Prokopovicz wrote: "The sudden melting of the snow, the rapid flowing of spring waters, the formation of ravines, the erosion of the soil from the wind and wild waters, the lowering of the level of subterranean waters from the scant rainfall in summer are just as much phenomena that cause the periodic droughts and impoverishment of the Black Earth. The dry winds coming from the deserts of central Asia have a particularly harmful effect on the harvest."[91]

The law on the 1946–1950 five-year plan already provided for increased afforestation in order to protect fields from drought and intensified efforts to

87. *Po edinomu planu*, p. 115.
88. *Ibid.*, pp. 115–16.
89. *Ibid.*, p. 116.
90. Decree of USSR Council of Ministers and Party Central Committee, "On the Plan to Plant Forest Shelter Belts, to Introduce Grassland Crop Rotation, and to Create Ponds and Reservoirs to Obtain High and Stable Crop Yields in the Steppe and Forest Steppe Areas of the European Part of the USSR" (*Sobranie postanovlenii i rasporiazhenii pravitelstva SSSR* [Collection of Resolutions and Decrees of the USSR Government], November 26, 1948, No. 6, Art. 80, pp. 102–36).
91. *Histoire*, p. 183.

build ponds and reservoirs on the collective and state farms in the steppe and forest steppe areas. It also provided for an increase of 656,000 hectares of irrigated land and 615,000 hectares of drained land.[92] The February 1947 decree reiterated the government's concern without giving any specific goals. The importance attached to this matter is confirmed by the administrative measures that were announced, which included strengthening the Central Administration for Water Management under the Ministry of Agriculture (to which were attached supply organizations and study offices) and creating the post of Deputy Minister of Irrigation and Agricultural Improvements under the USSR Ministry of Agriculture.[93]

It is hard to know the exact state of these projects at the time "the Stalin plan for the transformation of nature" was launched on October 24, 1948. This decree gave specific goals for afforestation zones and the number of ponds and reservoirs or forest shelter belt stations to be built, whereas the law on the Fourth Five-Year Plan and the February 1947 decree presented these goals only in general terms. On the other hand, there were no specific goals for the area of irrigated and drained land in either the February 1947 decree or "the Stalin plan for the transformation of nature."[94]

The drought of 1946 and the difficult agricultural situation lead one to believe that the Stalin plan had several objectives. First, it was intended to make people forget the very poor fulfillment of the five-year plan provisions for afforestation and drought alleviation by proposing grandiose projects for 1949–1965. Second, it set out to rebuild Soviet agriculture, which had been jeopardized by collectivization, by means of large-scale works carried out under administrative surveillance. Finally, it was meant to replace in part the failure of the five-year plan for the development of agriculture by concrete measures going far beyond the Fourth Five-Year Plan period.

The announced goals of the October 20 decree are very impressive. First, during 1950–1965, eight huge forest shelter belts of a total approximate length of 5,300 kilometers (with a width varying from 30 to 300 meters, but mostly 60 meters) were to be planted over a vast area (along the banks of the Volga, Donets, Don, and other rivers) extending from the western borders of the Soviet Union to the Urals. Second, forest shelter belts were also to be planted in the steppe and the forest steppe areas of the European part of the Soviet Union over an area of 5,709,000 hectares (of which 3,592,000 hectares were to be planted by collective farms,[95] 580,000 hectares by state farms, and 1,536,500 hectares by the Ministry of Forestry). This work was to extend from 1949 to 1965. A small part of the program was to be carried out in 1949 (252,600 hectares) and in 1950 (282,000 hectares). Third, during 1949–1955, the Ministry of Forestry was to build wind-

92. *Direktivy*, Vol. 3, p. 35.
93. *Ibid.*, Vol. 3, pp. 174–75.
94. It is interesting to note that the results of the Fourth Five-Year Plan (*Pravda*, April 17, 1951, p. 2) make no mention of the fulfillment of the irrigation and drainage projects but do give the area of forest shelter belts planted up until 1950 (see footnote 103 below).
95. Of this, 960,500 hectares were to be planted on collective farm land with collective farm labor (*Sobranie postanovlenii*, November 26, 1948, No. 6, Art. 80, pp. 104–8).

breaks and reforest an area of 322,000 hectares. Fourth, the collective farms were to construct 41,300 artificial ponds and reservoirs and the state farms 2,928 during 1949–1955.[96]

Other measures were taken on planting trees and grass, creating 570 forest protection stations (in 1949–1951), and supplying these stations with 22,000 tractors and 5,000 machines for planting seedlings.[97] The decree also provided for the creation of a Central Administration for Forest Shelter Belts under the USSR Council of Ministers. The decree did not give any details about how all these projects were to be financed. The measures that were to be carried out by the state farms and the Ministry of Forestry naturally were the state's responsibility. But the work to be done by the collective farms was to be carried out "with the means of the collective farms with assistance from the state."[98] Ten-year loans were provided, but it is clear that this program was a heavy burden on the collective farmers.[99]

Other, still more grandiose, projects were announced during this period. Thus, engineer M. Davydov studied how the large Siberian river Ob might be diverted from its course toward the Arctic Ocean and made to flow in the bed of its tributaries, the Irtych and Tobol rivers, toward the Aral and the Caspian seas. To accomplish this, it would have been necessary to build a dam on the Ob and to dig a canal 930 kilometers long in the area of the "Gates of Turgai."[100]

Implementing "the Stalin plan for the transformation of nature" obviously would not be easy. As Prokopovicz pointed out: "The large Russian rivers have a steep right bank and a flat left one. The planting of huge forests on lands periodically flooded from the valley of the Urals, the Volga, the Don, and the Northern Donets would be no protection against the *sukhovei* [hot dry wind]. Any planting on the cliffs of the right bank of the rivers would require much care to protect it from drought and wind, and for dozens of years; for the beneficial results of these forests would be felt only in twenty-five or thirty years."[101]

According to another writer, Solomon M. Schwarz, "shelterbelts mitigate the effect of drying winds, delay the melting of snow, slow down the water course, diminish evaporation from the soil, and thus contribute to a more even and complete use of the available water resources. But they cannot increase the resources. Moreover, forests, too, consume and evaporate considerable amounts of water."[102]

Nevertheless, the Soviet press did not fail to publish "victory communiqués" during the first years after "the Stalin plan for the transformation of nature" was

96. *Ibid.*, pp. 129–30. See also Prokopovicz, *Histoire*, pp. 184–85.

97. *Sobranie postanovlenii*, November 26, 1948, No. 6, Art. 80, pp. 129–31. See also Schwartz, *Soviet Economy*, p. 299.

98. *Sobranie postanovlenii*, November 26, 1948, No. 6, Art. 80, p. 107.

99. Schwartz, *Soviet Economy*, p. 299. For the building of ponds by the collective farms, for example, the state budget assumed responsibility only for studies and projects and technical direction (*Sobranie postanovlenii*, November 26, 1948, No. 6, Art. 80, p. 130).

100. The amount of electric power produced was to reach 82 billion kwh a year and the area of land irrigated in central Asia 30 million hectares (V. Juronskii, *Literaturnaia gazeta* [Literary Gazette], January 1, 1949, p. 3, as cited in *Notes*, July 28, 1951, p. 30).

101. Prokopovicz, *Histoire*, p. 185.

102. *New Leader*, January 1, 1949, p. 15, as cited in Schwartz, *Soviet Economy*, p. 301.

launched. Thus, on September 16, 1950, *Pravda* announced that the 1950 annual plan for afforestation of the steppe and forest steppe areas of the European part of the USSR had been exceeded by the spring. More than 700,000 hectares of forest had been seeded and planted. Hundreds of new ponds and reservoirs had been built.[103] A little later, Professor Satpaev announced that the workers in the state forests in the Urals had undertaken an obligation to finish the planting in 5 years instead of 15.[104]

Soon after this, however, information on the progress of the Stalin forest shelter belt plan started becoming rarer and rarer. Only after Stalin's death, in 1954, was the silence on the subject broken; but even then no indication was given of how many of the planted trees had survived.[105] The secrecy surrounding "the Stalin plan for the transformation of nature" continued and the October 20, 1948, decree was not reproduced in the collections of government decrees on economic problems published in 1958.[106] Only extracts of the October 20 decree were published in a later edition in 1968.[107]

Construction Projects for Large-Scale Hydroelectric Power Stations

Projects for building large-scale hydroelectric power stations represented a continuation of "the Stalin plan for the transformation of nature." They consisted of plans covering six to seven years, typical of the Stalinist style of planning large-scale works and very hard to fit into the framework of traditional five-year planning. These projects, which are listed in Table 91, entailed the construction of five hydroelectric power projects: the Kuibyshev,[108] Stalingrad,[109] Kakhovka,[110] Turkmenistan,[111] and Tsimlianskaia Stanitsa[112] power stations. The scope of the planned projects was tremendous. As pointed out by Soviet writers, the largest American power stations—Grand Coulee Dam with 972,000 kw in 1947[113] and

103. A. Bovin, *Pravda*, September 16, 1950, p. 2. The report on the fulfillment of the Fourth Five-Year Plan (*Pravda*, April 17, 1951, p. 2) states that the area of forest shelter belts planted during the five-year plan was 1,350,000 hectares, 760,000 hectares of which were planted in 1950.

104. *Izvestia*, October 5, 1950.

105. Jasny, *Soviet Industrialization*, p. 328.

106. *Direktivy*, Vol. 3.

107. *Resheniia*, Vol. 3, pp. 531–48.

108. The capacity of this station was about 2 million kw; its annual production was intended to be 10 billion kwh (6.1 billion for Moscow, 2.4 billion for Kuibyshev and Saratov, and 1.5 billion for irrigation of trans-Volga land). It was to be built during 1950–1955. (*Pravda*, August 21, 1950, p. 1.)

109. The capacity of this station was 1.7 million kw; its annual production was 10 billion kwh (4 billion for Moscow, 1.2 billion for the central Black Earth regions, 2.8 billion for Stalingrad, Saratov, and Astrakhan Provinces, and 2.0 billion for irrigation and supplying water to trans-Volga and Caspian land). It was to be built during 1951–1956. (*Pravda*, August 31, 1950, p. 1.)

110. This was to have a capacity of 250,000 kw, and annual production of 1.2 billion kwh. It was to be built during 1951–1956. (*Direktivy*, Vol. 3, pp. 549–53.)

111. Comprised of one station near the Takhia-Tash Dam and two near the dams on the Grand Canal of Turkmenistan, the project was to have a total capacity of 100,000 kw. It was to be built during 1951–1957. (*Pravda*, September 12, 1950, p. 1.)

112. This was to have a capacity of 160,000 kw, and was to be built during 1950–1952 (*Direktivy*, Vol. 3, pp. 553–56).

113. *Bolshevik*, No. 17, 1950, pp. 3–4, as cited in *Notes*, July 28, 1951, p. 5. However, the same source cites *Document de la Semaine*, published by the American Information Service in February 1946, as giving a capacity of 1,424,000 kw for the Grand Coulee Dam.

Table 91 Long-Term Plans Drafted during 1946–1952

Date of Adoption or Publication	Plan	Years	Sector or Area Covered
2/9/46	Long-Range Development Goals Cited in Speech by Stalin	10–15 years	Coal, petroleum, pig iron, steel
3/18/46	Law on Five-Year Plan for Reconstruction and Development of USSR National Economy in 1946–1950	1946–1950	National economy
4/13/46	On Measures for Further Restoration of Production of Grain, Sugar Beets, and Oil Seed Crops on Collective Farms of Ukraine	1946–1948	Grain, sugar beets, oil seed crops. Ukraine. Collective farms
12/23/46	On Measures to Accelerate Recovery of State-Owned Light Industry Producing Consumer Goods	1947–1950	Light industry. USSR
12/26/46	On Increasing Sown Area and Yield of Grain Crops, Especially Spring Wheat in Eastern Regions of USSR	1947–1949	Grain. Eastern regions of USSR
2/47	On Measures to Rebuild Agriculture in Postwar Period	1947–1949	USSR agriculture
8/8/47	On Mechanization of Wood Procurements, Adaptation of New Logging Areas, and Creation of Conditions Necessary to Keep Workers, Engineers, and Technicians of USSR Ministry of Forestry	1947–1949	Logging
8/22/47	On Development of Livestock Breeding Specialized in Meat Production	1947–1948	Livestock breeding. Kazakhstan, Kirgizia, northern Caucasus, Volga, southern Urals, eastern Siberia
9/1/47	On Measures to Rebuild and Develop Inland Waterway Transportation	1947–1950	Inland waterway transport. Industry producing equipment for it
5/29/48	On Plan to Develop Rural Electrification for 1948–1950	1948–1950	Construction. Power stations. Villages
10/4/48	On Development of Fishing Industry in Far East	1949–1952	Fishing industry. Far east
10/20/48	On Plan for Afforestation, Sowing of Pasture Land, and Construction of Canals and Reservoirs to Obtain Higher and Stable Yields in Steppe and Partially Wooded Areas in European Regions of USSR	1949–1965	Afforestation plan. Cultivating steppe in European regions
2/1/49	On Drafting New General Plan for Reconstruction of City of Moscow	1950– 1969/1974	Reconstruction. City of Moscow
4/18/49	Three-Year Plan for Development of Productive Livestock Breeding on Collective and State Farms (1949–1951)	1949–1951	Livestock breeding. Collective and state farms
5/26/49	On Procurement of Animal Products	1949–1951	Procurement. Animal products. USSR
6/17/49	Ten-Year Plan for Electrification of USSR	1951–1960	Construction. Power stations
9/3/49	On Measures to Increase Productive Capacity of Sugar Refineries in 1950–1955 and on Technical Re-equipment of Sugar Industry	1950–1955	Construction and equipment of sugar refineries
1949a	General Long-Term Economic Plan for 15 Years	1951–1965	National economy
1949b	General Plan for Complete Rural Electrification in USSR	1948–1965	Electrification of USSR countryside
1949c	Development of Goals for Railroads for 15 Years	1951–1965	Railroads. USSR
1949d	Plans for Development of Different Branches of USSR Economy	1951–1960	Branches of USSR economy
5/9/50	On Reduction in Construction Costs	1950–1955	Development of production. Construction materials

Table 91   *continued*

Date of Adoption or Publication	Plan	Years	Sector or Area Covered
8/17/50	On Transition to New System of Irrigation in Order to Make More Complete Use of Irrigated Land and Increased Mechanization of Agricultural Work	1950–1953	Irrigation. Agriculture
8/21/50	On Construction of Kuibyshev Hydroelectric Station on the Volga	1950–1955	Hydroelectric station
8/31/50	On Construction of Stalingrad Hydroelectric Power Station on the Volga and on Irrigation and Supplying Water from Areas around Caspian Sea	1951–1956	Large-scale construction works. Hydroelectric station
9/12/50	On Construction of Grand Canal of Turkmenistan (Amu-Daria-Krasnovodsk) and on Irrigation and Supplying Water to Southern Areas of Plains around Caspian Sea of Western Turkmenia and to Lower Amu-Daria and Western Part of Kara-Kuma Desert	1951–	Large-scale construction works on canals. Central Asia
9/20/50	On Construction of Kakhovka Hydroelectric Power Station on the Dnieper, of South Ukrainian Canal, and of North Crimean Canal, and on Irrigation of Areas of Southern Ukraine and of Northern Crimea	1951–1957	Large-scale construction works. Hydroelectric stations, canals, irrigation, Ukraine. Crimea
12/27/50	On Construction of Volga-Don Shipping Canal and on Irrigation of Lands in Rostov and Stalingrad Provinces	1951–1956	Volga-Don canal. Irrigation
8/20/52	Directives of 19th Party Congress on Five-Year Plan for Development of USSR in 1951–1955 (draft)	1951–1955	National economy
10/10/52	Directives on Fifth Five-Year Plan for Development of USSR in 1951–1955	1951–1955	National economy

Source

2/9/46: *Planovoe khoziaistvo*, No. 1, 1946, p. 10. Goals given as 500 mill. m. tons for coal, 60 mill. m. tons for crude petroleum, 50 mill. m. tons for pig iron, and 60 mill. m. tons for steel. These do not seem to be part of a real long-term plan but rather directives.

3/18/46: *Direktivy*, Vol. 3, pp. 7–79. Law approved by the USSR Supreme Soviet.

4/13/46: *Ibid.*, Vol. 3, pp. 79–83. Decree of USSR Council of Ministers.

12/23/46: *Ibid.*, Vol. 3, pp. 126–34. Decree of USSR Council of Ministers.

12/26/46: *Ibid.*, Vol. 3, pp. 135–45. Decree of USSR Council of Ministers.

2/47: *Ibid.*, Vol. 3, pp. 147–93. Decree of Plenary Session of Party Central Committee.

8/8/47: *Resheniia*, Vol. 3, pp. 436–47. Decree of USSR Council of Ministers.

8/22/47: *Direktivy*, Vol. 3, pp. 216–21. Decree of USSR Council of Ministers.

9/1/47: *Ibid.*, Vol. 3, p. 221–33. Decree of USSR Council of Ministers.

5/29/48: *Ibid.*, Vol. 3, pp. 286–98. Decree of USSR Council of Ministers.

10/4/48: *Ibid.*, Vol. 3, pp. 314–24. Decree of USSR Council of Ministers.

10/20/48: *Sobranie postanovlenii i rasporiazhenii Soveta Ministrov SSSR* [Collection of Resolutions and Decrees of USSR Council of Ministers], No. 6, November 26, 1948, Art. 8, pp. 102–36. Joint decree of Party Central Committee and USSR Council of Ministers of October 20, 1948.

2/1/49: *Direktivy*, Vol. 3, p. 337. Joint decree of USSR Council of Ministers and Party Central Committee of February 1, 1949, stating that the previous ten-year plan for the reconstruction of the city of Moscow (1936–1945) would be fulfilled in three or four years and instructing the Moscow Central Executive Committee and the Moscow Party Committee to draw up a new plan.

4/18/49: *Ibid.*, Vol. 3, pp. 341–68. Decree of USSR Council of Ministers and Party Central Committee.

5/26/49: *Ibid.*, Vol. 3, pp. 442–67. Decree of USSR Council of Ministers and of Party Central Committee.

6/17/49: *Ibid.*, Vol. 3, p. 470. Decree of Party Central Committee confirming the draft directives for the ten-year plan for the construction of electric power stations.

Table 91 *continued*

9/3/49: *Ibid.*, Vol. 3, pp. 473–80. Decree of USSR Council of Ministers.

1949a: *Po edinomu planu*, pp. 115–16. Plan drafted by USSR Gosplan after 1947 but not finished in 1949. The exact period of the plan is not given.

1949b, 1949c, and 1949d: *Ibid.*, p. 116. Draft plans drawn up by Gosplan during 1948–1949. Dates uncertain.

5/9/50: *Direktivy*, Vol. 3, pp. 484–94. Decree of USSR Council of Ministers. The plan for the production of construction materials was part of a more general plan for the reduction of construction costs.

8/17/50: *Ibid.*, Vol. 3, pp. 540–47. Decree of USSR Council of Ministers.

8/21/50: *Pravda*, August 21, 1950, p. 1.

8/31/50: *Pravda*, August 31, 1950, p. 1. Decree of USSR Council of Ministers.

9/12/50: *Pravda*, September 12, 1950, p. 1. Decree of USSR Council of Ministers.

9/20/50: *Direktivy*, Vol. 3, pp. 549–53. Decree of USSR Council of Ministers.

12/27/50: *Ibid.*, Vol. 3, pp. 553–56. Decree of USSR Council of Ministers.

8/20/52: *Trud*, August 20, 1952, pp. 1–3. Draft of the Party Central Committee drawn up after a meeting held "a few days previously," published at the same time as the announcement of the convocation of the Nineteenth Party Congress, and signed by Stalin.

10/10/52: *Pravda*, October 10, 1952, pp. 2–4. Directives adopted after a speech by M. Z. Saburov, chairman of Gosplan. For the directives adopted by the Nineteenth Party Congress, see *Direktivy*, Vol. 3, pp. 669–91.

Boulder Dam on the Colorado River with 1,030,000 kw—had a smaller capacity than the Kuibyshev and Stalingrad (Volgograd) Hydroelectric Stations and were under construction for dozens of years.[114] For the Soviet Union, the projected power stations represented an impressive step forward. The total capacity of all Soviet hydroelectric stations was only 1,252,000 kw in 1945 and 3,218,000 kw in 1950.[115] The addition in six years of 4,210,000 kw of new capacity was to more than double existing capacity.[116]

The weak point of these projects was their cost. The government decrees do not mention it and Soviet writers stress the savings to the government from collective ownership of the land and the lack of compensation to displaced users.[117] Nevertheless, the costs must have been immense, and, after the construction of these power stations, in 1958, Khrushchev violently criticized these projects as too costly and redirected the construction of electric power stations toward thermal power stations.[118]

Integration of these projects into the five-year plans caused additional problems. It was obviously impossible to include them in the five-year plan in progress, although two construction projects (Kuibyshev and the Volga-Don) were scheduled to begin in 1950. We can hypothesize that these Stalinist projects for the "building of communism" published between August and December of 1950 were responsible for the delay in the preparation of the final text of the Fifth

114. *Bolshevik*, No. 17, 1950, pp. 3–4, as cited in *Notes*, July 28, 1951, pp. 4–5. For a comparison of Soviet and American construction projects and the length of construction, see G. Krzhizhanovskii in *Pravda*, September 3, 1950, as cited in *Articles et Documents*, September 21, 1950, pp. 1–4.

115. *Promyshlennost SSSR* [Industry of the USSR], Moscow, 1957, p. 171.

116. The total capacity of hydroelectric stations in the Soviet Union reached 5,996,000 kw in 1955, 8,498,000 kw in 1956, and 10,040,000 kw in 1957. The production of hydroelectric power increased from 12.7 billion kwh in 1950 to 29.0 billion in 1956 and 39.4 billion in 1957. See *Promyshlennost SSSR* [Industry of the USSR], Moscow, 1964, p. 232.

117. On this subject, see *Pravda*, September 3, 1950, p. 1.

118. Jasny, *Soviet Industrialization*, p. 328.

Five-Year Plan (1951–1955), along with such other obstacles as the Voznesenskii affair and the plans for agricultural cities. The emergencies resulting from the Korean War also delayed the plan.

Stalinist Plans for the Construction of Major Canals and Irrigation Systems

These plans were, to a large extent, linked to the construction of the hydroelectric stations. But while the construction of the power stations was the principal objective in the cases of the Kuibyshev and Stalingrad (Volgograd) Hydroelectric Stations, in other projects the main objective was the construction of canals and irrigation systems.

The best-known construction project was the Grand Canal of Turkmenistan.[119] Running from the Amu-Daria to Krasnovodsk on the Caspian Sea, it was to be 1,100 kilometers long. It was to be supplemented by important feeder canals for irrigation and water supply with a total length of 1,200 kilometers. It was to make possible irrigating 1,300,000 hectares of new land for agriculture, particularly for cotton crops, and supplying water to 7 million hectares of pasture land in the Kara-Kum Desert. Planting forest shelter belts and stabilizing the sand over the length of the Grand Canal were also planned to cover an area of about 500,000 hectares.[120]

Another important project was connected with the construction of the Kakhovka Hydroelectric Station on the Dnieper.[121] It envisaged two canals—the South Ukrainian Canal (going from Zaporozhe on the Dnieper to Askania Nova and then to Sivash on Lake Molochnaia) and the North Crimean Canal (going from Sivash to Kerch)—with a combined length of 550 kilometers. Another canal 60 kilometers long was to connect Askania Nova and Kakhovka, thus linking the Kakhovka reservoir with the South Ukrainian Canal. Important feeder canals 300 kilometers in length were also envisaged. The area of irrigated land was to cover 1,500,000 hectares and the area supplied with water 1,700,000 hectares. Forest shelter belts were also to be planted. The hope was to obtain stable harvest of grain and intensive cotton growing in the irrigated areas.

The third project was the construction of the Volga-Don Canal.[122] This was to include the Volga-Don Shipping Canal (between Stalingrad and Kalach), 101 kilometers in length, with 13 locks and 3 dams, along with a connection 89 kilometers long with the Tsimlianskaia reservoir and with Proletarskaia Station and 568 kilometers of feeder canals. The plan envisaged 140 pumping stations and a network for supplying water from feeder canals to irrigate an area of 750,000 hectares and supply water to an additional area of 2 million hectares.

119. *Pravda*, September 12, 1950, p. 1.
120. *Ibid.*
121. September 20, 1950, decree of USSR Council of Ministers, "On the Construction of the Kakhovka Hydroelectric Station on the Dnieper, the South Ukrainian Canal, and the North Crimean Canal and on the Irrigation of South Ukrainian and North Crimean Lands" (*Direktivy*, Vol. 3, pp. 549–53).
122. December 27, 1950, decree of USSR Council of Ministers, "On the Construction of the Volga-Don Shipping Canal and Irrigation of the Land in Rostov and Stalingrad Provinces" (*ibid.*, Vol. 3, pp. 553–56).

Among the projects mainly concerned with building canals should be included the irrigation and water supply done at the time the Kuibyshev and Stalingrad (Volgograd) power stations were built (see Table 92).

The five decrees promulgated between August 21 and December 28, 1950, make up the basic part of "the Stalin plan for the transformation of nature," of which the first part on the planting of shelter belts was published on October 20, 1948. The Soviet press of the period considered these "grandiose undertakings of the Stalinist era, essential links in the creation of the material and equipment base of a communist society."[123] The projects were to make possible more extensive utilization of water resources in order to cope simultaneously with the problems of power, irrigation, shipping, etc. The electrification of the country, so dear to Lenin,[124] was once again brought to the fore. But resounding successes in agricultural production were also anticipated: "When the new hydrotechnical projects are completed, our country will have left the capitalist countries far behind in agricultural production. Turkmenia alone, after the irrigation of its land, will grow cotton over an area half again as large as that of Argentina, Mexico, and Iran put together."[125]

The scope of the irrigation program can be seen from the following facts. The Fourth Five-Year Plan anticipated an increase of 656,000 hectares in the area of irrigated land.[126] The area of land to be irrigated in the "large-scale construction projects of communism" hence was to be almost ten times as large (6,050,000 hectares, see Table 92). This program implied that the area of irrigated land in the Soviet Union would be doubled.[127]

The results achieved here were much lower than planned. As mentioned above, the goals for irrigation were not given either in the February 1947 decree or in "the Stalin plan for the transformation of nature," and the results of the Fourth Five-Year Plan did not give the fulfillment of irrigation goals. As pointed out by Naum Jasny,[128] a significant silence was maintained on this subject after Stalin's death. The report on the fulfillment of the Fifth Five-Year Plan in 1955 mentioned only that the area of land supplied with water on collective and state farms increased by 13 per cent during the five-year period and the utilized area of this land increased by 25 per cent.[129] Later, in 1960, the statistical handbook on agriculture announced that the total area supplied with water increased from 10,083,000 hectares in 1950 to 11,128,000 hectares in 1955 and 11,223,000 hectares in 1957.[130] Hence, in seven years the increase was only 1,140,000 hectares. Comparison with the figures in Table 92 shows the extent to which aspirations

123. *Pravda*, September 3, 1950, p. 1.

124. "Lenin's famous statement that 'communism is Soviet power plus electrification of the whole country' became, for the Party and the government, the guiding light in the building of communism" (*Bolshevik*, No. 17, 1950, p. 5, as cited in *Notes*, July 28, 1951, p. 4).

125. *Vestnik Akademii Nauk* [Bulletin of the Academy of Sciences], No. 10, 1950, as cited in *Notes*, July 28, 1951, p. 5. The latter source states that the combined production of cotton in Argentina, Mexico, and Iran represented 5 per cent of the world production (*ibid.*).

126. See p. 387 above.

127. Jasny, *Soviet Industrialization*, p. 327.

128. *Ibid.*, pp. 327–28.

129. *Pravda*, April 25, 1956, p. 3.

130. *Selskoe khoziaistvo*, 1960, p. 258.

Table 92 Main Characteristics of Large-Scale Hydraulic Projects Planned in 1950

| | Construction Schedule | Electric Power | | Length of Canals (km) | Irrigated Area (th. hectares) | Area Supplied with Water (th. hectares) |
		Capacity (th. kw)	Production (mill. kwh)			
1. Kuibyshev power station	1950–1955	2,000	10,000		1,000	
2. Stalingrad (Volgograd) power station	1951–1956	1,700	10,000		1,500	11,500 ·
3. Grand Canal of Turkmenistan	1951–1957	100		1,200	1,300	7,000
4. South Ukrainian and North Crimean canals and power station	1951–1956	260	1,200[a]	910	1,500	1,700
5. Volga-Don Canal	1950–1956	160		758	750	2,000
6. Total		4,220	22,000[b]	2,868	6,050	22,200

Source

Line 1: *Pravda*, August 21, 1950, p. 1.
Line 2: *Ibid.*, August 31, 1950, p. 1.
Line 3: *Ibid.*, September 12, 1950, p. 1.
Line 4: *Direktivy*, Vol. 3, pp. 549–53.
Line 5: *Ibid.*, Vol. 3, pp. 553–56.
Line 6: Sum of lines 1–5, unless otherwise indicated.

a. Excludes production of the hydroelectric station (of 10,000 kw capacity) near the dam north of Melitopol.
b. Approximate figure (given in *Bolshevik*, No. 17, 1950, pp. 3–4, as cited in *Notes*, July 28, 1951, p. 4).

exceeded accomplishments in projects for irrigation and water supply in "the Stalin plan for the transformation of nature."

Preparation and Publication of Fifth Five-Year Plan Goals

The "large-scale construction projects of communism," with the plans to build hydroelectric power stations, canals, and irrigation systems, were fitted into the framework of the new five-year plan being prepared for 1951–1955. However, information on the actual preparatory work for this plan is not available, and all that can be done is to advance more or less tenuous hypotheses.

To judge from the normal amount of time spent preparing a five-year plan, the work should have started in 1948, that is, at about the time that the 1946–1950 five-year plan disintegrated. The multitude of long-term plans drafted during this period (see Table 91) makes one suppose that these studies were intended to inspire the authors of the fifth plan. Aside from the projects announced with so much fanfare (described above), the number of partial drafts of the new five-year plan prepared at this time was very limited. Table 91 contains only two such plans: one for building sugar refineries in 1950–1955 and another for reducing construction costs in 1950–1955. Thus, the preliminary versions of the fifth plan remain unknown. A number of factors seemed to have contributed to the delay in publishing the final text of the draft plan (which appeared on August 20, 1952—see Table 91). Gosplan was reorganized after Voznesenskii's disgrace in

1948, and there were changes in plans because of the "large-scale construction projects of communism" that were published after August 20, 1950, when the plan must already have been quite far along. There probably were revisions of the plans because of the Korean War (such revisions were made in all the plans of the people's democracies).[131] Finally, in November 1951 there were ideological discussions on the publication of a political economy textbook, which enabled Stalin to reassert with enthusiasm his theses on the building of communism in the Soviet Union.[132] This discussion concerned planning problems and the social structure in the USSR—collective farm ownership, the objective nature of economic laws and the struggle against "voluntarism," the definition of the main law of socialist production,[133] and the role of the law of the planned proportional development of the national economy. It must have had practical repercussions on the draft of the five-year plan in preparation.

Fulfillment of Fourth Five-Year Plan Goals in 1950

As mentioned earlier, important revisions were made in the fourth plan as early as 1947, when it began to disintegrate. This might bring to mind the experience of the Second Five-Year Plan[134] and the question of whether it makes sense to discuss "fulfillment of the Fourth Five-Year Plan."

In fact, when comparing the goals of the fourth plan with the actual results achieved, two types of development have to be juxtaposed—the development that the Soviet authorities considered possible and desirable and "real" development. The discrepancy between "real" development and the Fourth Five-Year Plan goals can be seen clearly in Table 93. The discrepancy lies less in the difference in the average level achieved than in the difference in the structure of production. Thus, for instance, in producer goods, the median of plan fulfillment is 95.5 per cent, but the results range from 32.1 per cent (for roofing tiles) to 139.9 per cent (for spinning machines). For consumer goods, the median is 92.5 per cent, but the dispersion range covers 36.7 to 124.6 per cent. Similar dispersions can be observed for agriculture and transportation, but for money wages and employment overfulfillment seems to have been the general rule.[135]

Nevertheless, the results diverge less from the planned production structure than in the Second Five-Year Plan, where the outcomes ranged from 3.6 to 219.5 per cent of planned targets for producer goods and from 23.5 to 182.2 per cent

131. The revisions of the Czech plans on February 24, 1951, and of the Hungarian plans on February 28, 1951, increasing industrial goals are pointed out in my *Les courants commerciaux de l'Europe Danubienne au cours de la première moitié du XX-e siècle*, Paris, 1952, p. 290. Similar increases were also made in Poland.

132. Stalin, *Ekonomicheskie problemy*.

133. This "law" was formulated rather as an objective—"to ensure maximum satisfaction of the constantly growing material and cultural needs of all society through the uninterrupted growth and improvement of socialist production based on advanced technology" (*ibid.*, p. 40). At that time Stalin asserted that the "law" of the planned proportional development of the national economy was not the basic law and that it was subordinated to the above "law."

134. See pp. 153 ff in Chapter 7.

135. The figures in Table 93 are too aggregated, but this conclusion can be drawn from the general evolution of employment and wages during 1946–1950.

Table 93 Fulfillment of Fourth Five-Year Plan in 1950 (per cent)

National income	118.9	Butter	122.2
		Confectionery	116.8
Industry		Radios	115.9
Producer goods (1926/27 prices)	127.5	Sewing machines, household	111.5
Total value of production (1926/27		Raw sugar	105.1
prices)	116.9	Matches	103.0
Consumer goods (1926/27 prices)	95.7	Clocks and watches	102.2
		Meat	98.1
Producer Goods		Woolen fabrics	97.4
Spinning machines	139.9	Cotton yarn	96.7
Steel pipes	133.4	Ginned cotton	96.2
Asbestos shingles	133.3	Meat and subproducts of first	
Lumber	126.9	category	95.1
Ground natural phosphate	120.8	Soap (40% fatty acid)	93.8
Rolled steel	117.3	Vegetable oil	93.1
Refined copper	114.3	Silk and rayon fabrics	92.0
Electric power	111.3	Motorcycles	91.2
Synthetic dyes	108.2	Beer	87.2
Metallurgical equipment	108.1	Leather shoes	84.7
Steel ingots and castings	107.6	Starch and syrup	84.6
Crude petroleum	107.0	Cotton fabrics	83.2
Coal	104.4	Hosiery	81.5
Hydroelectric power	101.8	Fish catch (incl. shellfish, whales)	79.8
Iron ore	99.1	Margarine	76.8
Automobiles	98.5	Crude alcohol	72.4
Pig iron	98.3	Linen fabrics	67.2
Mineral fertilizer	98.1	Flour (centralized resources)	65.3
Ammonium sulfate	97.9	Bicycles	61.8
Tractors (units)	97.2	Cameras	49.1
Cement	97.1	Phonographs	36.7
Bricks	96.9		
Window glass	96.1	**Agriculture**	
Phosphoric fertilizer (14% P_2O_5)	95.5	Raw cotton (barn yield)	141.7
Machine tools	95.4	Raw cotton (biological yield)	121.0
Tractors (15 hp)	94.8	Grain (biological yield)	98.0
Soda ash	93.6	Sugar beets (barn yield)	93.4
Zinc	93.2	Sugar beets (biological yield)	90.4
Coke	92.4	Total value of production	
Lead	92.3	(1926/27 prices)	89.9
Paper	89.1	Sunflowers (biological yield)	83.8
Phosphoric fertilizer (18.7% P_2O_5)	87.1	Grain (barn yield)	79.5
Industrial timber hauled	85.9	Milk	78.5
Caustic soda	83.3	Meat and fat (incl. rabbit and poultry)	76.0
Steam and gas turbines	81.9	Meat and fat (excl. rabbit and poultry	75.9
Peat	81.3	Sunflowers (barn yield)	62.2
Plywood	81.2	Flax fiber (barn yield)	51.6
Motor vehicles, total	72.6		
Railroad freight cars	69.6	**Transportation**	
Trucks	68.8	Railroad freight traffic (ton-km)	113.2
Buses	60.9	Railroad freight traffic (tons)	108.2
Natural gas	51.4	Railroad, average length of haul	104.6
Electric locomotives	46.4	Railroad, average daily carloadings	102.7
Steam locomotives	44.8	Railroad, length of network	94.9
Diesel locomotives	41.7	Inland waterway freight traffic	
Railroad passenger cars	35.1	(ton-km)	93.1
Looms	34.8	Railroad passenger traffic (pass.-km)	89.8
Roofing tiles	32.1	Motor freight traffic (ton-km)	80.5
		Maritime freight traffic (ton-km)	77.8
Consumer goods			
Rubber footwear	124.6		

Table 93 *continued*

Employment		Average money wage, national	
Industry, workers and employees	118.9	economy, workers and employees	127.8
National economy, workers and		Real wage, national economy,	
employees	116.1	workers and employees	89.1
Wages		**State and Cooperative Retail Trade**	
Wage fund, national economy,		Total in current prices	130.8
workers and employees	148.4	Total in constant prices	85.9

Source: Table A-1, col. 12.

for consumer goods (see Table 26 in Chapter 7). The same phenomenon can be seen in the case of transportation; the dispersion of plan fulfillment percentages in agriculture is similar in the second and fourth plans (from 41.7 to 126.3 per cent in the second plan and from 51.6 to 141.7 per cent in the fourth plan—see Tables 26 and 93).

It should, however, be remembered that when the planned structure of production or consumption is not followed, it is the result as much of underfulfillment as overfulfillment of the goals. It is the deviation (whether above or below) from these goals that counts. An attempt to measure these deviations has been made in Table 94. The largest deviation is for money wage (among sectors) and for machine-building (among industrial branches). The large deviations from the plan in these two cases are almost traditional in the Soviet Union. Soviet planners try to restrain money wage increases and to plan wages "at a minimum" as an element of costs. But in carrying out the plan, when faced with a choice between an unplanned increase in wages and nonfulfillment of the production plan, they always choose the first alternative.

The deviations in machine-building are easy to explain. For new products, a delay in one project to build a factory is sufficient to jeopardize the plan. But for old products, too, changes in the plans for investments, foreign trade, or domestic demand (for example, for steam locomotives) have considerable repercussions on the fulfillment of the planned goals.

Deviations from the Fourth Five-Year Plan goals were considerably smaller than in the first and second plans (see Table 94). This reduction requires explanation. First, there is the problem of measurement. With the increase in the number of series covered, indexes for lower-priority products (hence less controlled by the planners) are taken into account. Since the mean deviation is calculated as an *unweighted* mean, it is hard to draw direct conclusions from the observed differences. In any case, the number of series used in calculating the deviation was 128 for the First Five-Year Plan, rose to 208 in the second plan, and dropped to only 103 in the fourth plan. Hence it might be that, if an equal number of series had been included, the reduction in the deviation would have been much more considerable in the second plan. The reduction between the

Table 94   Mean Absolute Deviation from 100 Per Cent Fulfillment of First, Second, and Fourth Five-Year Plans (percentage points)

	Absolute Deviation Based on 1932 Results Compared with First Five-Year Plan Maximum Goals for 1932/33 (1)	Absolute Deviation Based on 1937 Results Compared with Second Five-Year Plan Goals for 1937 (2)	Absolute Deviation Based on 1950 Results Compared with Fourth Five-Year Plan Goals for 1950 (3)
1. Industry	43.8	31.1	17.4
2. Fuel and power	17.4	24.4	15.4
3. Ferrous and nonferrous metals	51.1	19.2	11.2
4. Machine-building	31.0	57.3	31.6
5. Chemicals	78.4	39.0	9.2
6. Construction materials	46.4	20.0	20.2
7. Light industry	47.3	28.4	19.8
8. Food industry	34.8	29.5	14.4
9. Agriculture	53.9	23.6[a]	22.1
10. Animal production	66.5	36.3	23.2
11. Market production	54.1	23.3	
12. Procurements		27.7	
13. Harvests (biological yield)	41.2	23.4	12.2
14. Harvests (barn yield)		7.1[b]	31.0
15. Transportation	24.5	24.3	10.3
16. Employment	50.6	21.1	17.5
17. Average money wage	30.8	66.5	27.8
18. Average real wage	60.0	39.1	10.9
19. Housing	36.7	41.4	
20. Population	11.7	11.4	
21. Retail trade (in constant prices)	35.5	50.9	14.1
22. Foreign trade (in constant prices)	40.2		
23. All groups	38.8	34.4[c]	17.2

Source: Cols. 1 and 2: Unless otherwise indicated, Table 27, cols. 1 and 2. Col. 3: The unweighted arithmetic mean of absolute deviations of the percentage fulfillments in Table A-1, col. 12, from 100 covers the series indicated below:

Line 1: unweighted arithmetic mean of lines 2–8. **Line 2:** series 5–7 and 10–12. **Line 3:** series 13–17 and 21–23. **Line 4:** series 46–47, 50–57, 59–62, and 64. **Line 5:** series 24–27, 29–31, and 34a. **Line 6:** series 35 and 37–44. **Line 7:** series 66–69, 71–72, 75–76, 78, 81–83, and 84–87. **Line 8:** series 88, 90, 92–97, 99–100, 103–5, and 107. **Line 9:** unweighted arithmetic mean of lines 10 and 13–14. **Line 10:** series 125–26. **Line 13:** series 113 and 119–21. **Line 14:** series 113a, 119a, 120a, 121a, and 122a. **Line 15:** series 149–52, 162, 166, 168, 179, and 183. **Line 16:** series 186–87. **Line 17:** series 203. **Line 18:** series 204. **Line 21:** series 234a. **Line 23:** unweighted arithmetic mean of lines 1, 9, 15–18, and 21.

Note: Some groups include aggregate series and their components. The comparison of the deviations in the two plans is made with reservations since the same series are not included in all three calculations.

a. Unweighted arithmetic mean of lines 10–14.
b. Calculated from series 113a in Table A-1, col. 3.
c. Unweighted arithmetic mean of lines 1, 9, and 15–21.

first and fourth plans, thus, could reflect a more gradual development in comparable terms.[136]

Does the reduction in the discrepancy between the plan and the results reflect a better fulfillment of the plan? In the planning process, the first four five-year plans were not really put into operation, even as a vision of growth, and they disintegrated by the third year of their proposed operation. Hence, the reduction in the discrepancy was due less to better fulfillment of the five-year plans than to a less unrealistic vision of growth. That the fourth plan was more realistic than the first and second was the result of several factors. The first plan was seriously disrupted by the leap forward of 1930; the second was made obsolete by a serious crisis in 1936 and 1937 (due to the purges and rearmament). The galloping inflation of 1930–1941 rendered all value series useless. In the second plan, the plan for money wages was exceeded by 66.5 per cent, and only 39.1 per cent of the plan for real wages was fulfilled (see Table 94).

On the other hand, several elements favored economic development immediately after the war. Reconstruction was facilitated by the technological contribution of the war years and by reparations from the conquered countries as well as appropriations from all over Eastern Europe. Joint companies also brought in considerable profits. The inflation of the war years was stopped by the currency reform of December 1947, and there was a deflationary movement after 1948 with a lowering of centrally fixed prices. Finally, despite the devastation of the war, Soviet industrialization during 1946–1950 had reached a sufficiently advanced level to have planned growth rates that were not so high and a structure of production that lent itself less to outlandish projects. "The Stalin plan for the transformation of nature," the "large-scale construction projects of communism," and even the collectivization campaign thus could not have such disturbing effects on the economy. But it must be remembered that, even with a mean deviation of 17.2 per cent, the disparity between the original goals and the actual results was still quite large, and in any case the plan was, for all practical purposes, never put into operation.

Another problem arises in evaluating the results obtained during 1946–1950, for there is a problem of measurement here, too. If the official Soviet statistics in 1926/27 prices are used,[137] they yield a tremendous increase (64 per cent) in national income between 1940 and 1950, an increase of 73 per cent for industrial production, and even an increase of 14.2 per cent for agricultural production (see Table 77 above). Western estimates reduce growth to more modest proportions (16 to 24 per cent with 1940 = 100 for national income, 24 to 40 per cent for industrial production, and −3.0 to 0.8 per cent for agricultural production, see Table 79). In any case, the progress made during the postwar years was consid-

136. These results are partially confirmed by Nutter's calculations (*Growth*, p. 206, Table 57). Calculated in value terms with standard product coverage, the deviation from planned targets does not change much for the First and Second Five-Year Plans but is quite substantial. For the Fourth Five-Year Plan, the deviation is very small for total industrial production and is considerably reduced in size for different industrial branches. According to Nutter's calculations, the conclusions do not change much for calculations with variable product coverage and for alternative weighting in 1928 and 1955 prices.

137. For criticism of 1926/27 prices, see my *Planning*, p. 256, and p. 158 in Chapter 7.

erable. Progress is also seen in the tripling of real wages between 1945 and 1950 (an increase of 9.7 per cent over 1940, see Table 79), a substantial increase even though the base was quite low.

There is another way of studying efficiency—in relation not to a base year but to the planned goals. Table 95 shows the principal indexes for such a comparison. It appears from the Western estimates that all the series representing results of economic activity (national income, industrial production, agricultural production, real wages, retail trade sales) were lower than the planned goals by 5 to 25 per cent. But the costs of obtaining these results were definitely higher than planned. Total employment (largely nonagricultural) was 16.1 per cent above plan, the wage fund 48.4 per cent, and total investments in constant prices 22 per cent.

Table 95   Comparison of Soviet and Western Estimates of Fulfillment of Fourth Five-Year Plan in 1950 (per cent)

National Income	
Official Soviet estimate:	
1. In 1926/27 prices	118.9
Western estimates:	
2. Bergson (1937 ruble factor cost)	89.9
3. Nutter (1937 income originating weights)	84.1
4. Moorsteen and Powell (1937 ruble factor cost)	88.0
Industrial Production	
Official Soviet estimates:	
5. Total (1926/27 prices)	116.9
6. Producer goods (1926/27 prices)	127.5
7. Consumer goods (1926/27 prices)	95.7
Western estimates:	
8. Kaplan and Moorsteen, civilian production	
(1950 wholesale prices)	94.9
9. Nutter, total (moving weights)	83.8
Agricultural Production	
Official Soviet estimates:	
10. In 1926/27 prices	89.9
11. In "comparable" (1958) prices	78.2
Western estimates:	
12. Johnson and Kahan (1958 weights)	79.4
13. Nutter (1958 weights)	76.4
Employment	
14. Workers and employees, national economy	116.1
Wages (national economy)	
15. Average money wage, workers and employees	127.8
16. Average real wage, workers and employees	89.1
17. Wage fund, workers and employees (current prices)	148.4
Investment	
18. Total for five years (1945 estimate prices)	122[a]
Retail Trade	
19. State and cooperative (1940 prices)	85.9

Source: Unless otherwise indicated, Table 79, col.8.

a. *Po edinomu planu*, p. 110.

But this comparison of results and planned costs does not answer the question of efficiency. The question is whether the planned goals were feasible or whether their role was simply to demand more in order to stimulate effort. In that case the plan would act only as a stimulant, one among others, and other criteria would be needed to judge its efficiency.

CHAPTER 17

Investment and Resource Balances, 1945–1953

The Burden of Investment

The principal data on investment, construction and assembly work, and the installation of fixed capital during the Fourth Five-Year Plan (1946–1950) are presented in Table 96. The plan provided for the reconstruction, new construction, and putting into operation of 5,900 state enterprises. The value of fixed capital was to reach 1,130 billion rubles (in state prices) in 1950, which would exceed the prewar level by 8 per cent.[1]

Estimation of the burden of this investment would be facilitated by knowledge of its share in national income, but unfortunately that information is not available. The total volume of investment in so-called 1945 estimate prices for the five-year period, 1946–1950, is given in Table 96. But the only figure available for total national income is for 1950, and it is given in 1926/27 prices (see Table 79 in Chapter 16). The shares of investment in national income produced for 1940, 1944, 1945, and the five-year plan goal for 1950 were given recently (in 1940 prices—see Table 78 in Chapter 16). Only 15.4 per cent in 1945, this share was to rise to 21.7 per cent by 1950. The only indication—and indirect, at that[2]—of the burden of investment in the fourth plan is to be found by comparing annual average centralized investments. The average for the 1946–1950 plan was 31.9 per cent higher than for the period January 1, 1938–June 30, 1941, and 68.9 per cent higher than during the war (see Table 96).

These few figures might give the impression that the burden of investment in the fourth plan was not very heavy. While national income in 1950 was planned to increase over 1940 by 35.8 per cent in 1940 prices (see Table 78) and by 38.0 per

1. V. Grossman, "Ob ukreplenii rezhima ekonomii v stroitelstve" [On Strengthening Economy Measures in Construction], *Planovoe khoziaistvo* [Planned Economy], No. 3, 1946, p. 36. The 1950 figure of 1,130 billion rubles in "state prices" is given without any explanation of these prices.
2. These figures were estimated from official Soviet data in July 1, 1955, prices. See Table 96, line 3.

Table 96 Investment Goals of Fourth Five-Year Plan (1946–1950) and Their Fulfillment (billion rubles, 1945 estimate prices, unless otherwise indicated)

	Actual Investment		Total Investment for 1946–1950		
	Jan. 1, 1938– June 30, 1941 (1)	July 1, 1941– Dec. 31, 1945 (2)	Planned (3)	Actual (4)	Per Cent of Plan Fulfillment (5)
1. National economy, total:			383.3	469.2	122.4
2. Centralized investment, total	132	131	250.3	306	122
3. Centralized investment, annual average	37.9	29.6	50.0	61.0	122
4. Industry, total	57.6	73.1	157.5	158.6	100.7
5. Coal			21	40.8	190
6. Nonferrous metals			12		
7. Agricultural machinery			4.5		
8. Textiles			5.99		
9. Light industry			2.18		
10. State-owned agriculture, total			19.9	23.2	117
11. Machine and Tractor Stations			8.8		
12. State farms			5.3		
13. Irrigation and land improvement			2		
14. Transportation			53.5		
15. Railroad transportation			40.1	37.8	94.3
16. Other centralized investment (communications, trade, procurements, and administration)			25.2		
17. Decentralized investment			45.0	52.2	116
18. Housing construction			42.3	49.1	116
19. Collective farm investment			38	29.1	77
20. Capital repairs			50	81.9	160
21. Construction and assembly, total:	106.9	102.5	153		
22. Ministries for Construction of Heavy Industrial Enterprises, Construction of Fuel Enterprises, Construction of Military and Naval Enterprises			55		
23. Installation of fixed capital:			234		
24. Electric power stations (mill. kw):	3.0		11.7	8.4	72
25. Hydroelectric stations (mill. kw)	0.5		2.3	2.0	87
26. Iron ore mines (mill. m. tons)			35.4		
27. Foundries (mill. m. tons)			12.8	8.9	70
28. Steel mills (mill. m. tons)			16.2	8.9	55
29. Rolling mills (mill. m. tons)			11.7	5.6	48
30. Phosphoric fertilizer (thous. m. tons)			2,720		
31. Soda ash (thous. m. tons)			813		
32. Caustic soda (thous. m. tons)			278		
33. Cement (mill. m. tons)			9.4	6.3	67
34. Window glass (mill. m²)			40		
35. Asbestos shingles (millions)			332		
36. Spinning machines (thous.)			2,860	2,200	77
37. Shoes (mill. prs)			100	76.1	76
38. Coal mines (mill. m. tons)			183	107.3	58.6
39. Coking plants (mill. m. tons)			19.1		
40. Hosiery (mill. prs)			345		

Table 96 *continued*

	Actual Investment		Total Investment for 1946–1950		
	Jan. 1, 1938– June 30, 1941 (1)	July 1, 1941– Dec. 31, 1945 (2)	Planned (3)	Actual (4)	Per Cent of Plan Fulfillment (5)
41. Salt (mill. m. tons)			1.4		
42. Grain silos and elevators (mill. m. tons)			6.4		
43. Flour mills (thous. m. tons per day)			20		
44. Construction of new railroad track (km)			7,230	2,319	32.1
45. Electrification of railroads (km)			5,325	974	18.3

Note: Data given in new rubles have been converted to old (pre-1961) rubles (1 new ruble = 10 old rubles). Data given in 1955 prices have been converted into "1945 estimate prices" by dividing by 1.082. This factor was derived from total actual investment in 1946–1950, which was given in 1955 prices (33.1 billion new rubles in *Narodnoe khoziaistvo SSSR v 1961 godu* [The USSR National Economy in 1961], Moscow, 1962, p. 536) and in 1945 estimate prices (306 billion old rubles in *Po edinomu planu* [According to a Single Plan], Moscow, 1971, p. 110).

Source

COLUMN 1–Lines 2-4 and 21: *Narodnoe khoziaistvo, 1961*, pp. 536, 542, and 550. Given in new rubles in 1955 prices and converted as explained in note above. **Lines 24-25:** Capacity at end of 1940 (given as 11.193 and 1.587 mill. kw, respectively, in *Narodnoe khoziaistvo SSSR v 1959 godu* [The USSR National Economy in 1959], Moscow, 1960, p. 193) minus capacity at end of 1937 (given as 8.235 and 1.044 mill. kw, respectively, in *ibid.*).

COLUMN 2–Lines 2-4 and 21: *Narodnoe khoziaistvo, 1961*, pp. 536, 543, and 550. Given in new rubles in 1955 prices and converted as explained in note above. **Lines 24-25:** There was a reduction in capacity between the end of 1940 and the end of 1945 (see *Narodnoe khoziaistvo, 1959*, p. 193).

COLUMN 3–Line 1: Sum of lines 2, 17, 19, and 20. **Line 2:** "Zakon o piatiletnem plane vosstanovleniia i razvitiia narodnogo khoziaistva SSSR na 1946–1950 gg." [Law on the Five-Year Plan for the Rehabilitation and Development of the USSR National Economy in 1946–1950], *Resheniia Partii i Pravitelstva po khoziaistvennym voprosam* [Decisions of the Party and Government on Economic Matters], Moscow, 1968, Vol. 3, p. 251. According to *Atlas istorii SSSR* [Atlas of USSR History], edited by K. V. Bazilevich, I. A. Golubtsov, and M. A. Zinovev, Moscow, 1950, Part III, p. 50, 135 billion rubles for new construction and 115 billion for "reconstruction." Total investment planned for Siberia and the far east is given as 35.6 billion rubles in A. Korobov, "Stroitelnaia programma novoi piatiletki" [The Construction Program of the New Five-Year Plan], *Planovoe khoziaistvo*, No. 3, 1946, p. 25. **Line 3:** Based on actual investment (col. 4) and per cent of plan fulfillment (col. 5). **Lines 4, 11, 13, 15, 18-19, and 21-45:** *Resheniia*, Vol. 3, pp. 251, 254, 257, 261, 266–67, 269, 271–72, 274, 280, and 287. **Lines 5 and 7:** P. I. Liashchenko, *Istoriia narodnogo khoziaistva SSSR* [History of the USSR National Economy], Moscow, 1956, Vol. III, pp. 571 and 575. **Lines 6, 14, 16-17, and 20:** Norman Kaplan, "Capital Investments in the Soviet Union, 1924–1951," RAND Research Memorandum 735, Santa Monica, 1951, pp. 195, 89, 80 and 89, 133 and 140–42 ("extra-limit investments"), and 133 and 142–44, respectively. **Lines 8-9:** *Direktivy KPSS i sovetskogo pravitelstva po khoziaistvennym voprosam* [Directives of the Communist Party of the Soviet Union and of the Soviet Government on Economic Matters], Moscow, 1957–1958, Vol. 3, p. 128. See also Table 80 in Chapter 16. **Line 10:** *Resheniia*, Vol. 3, p. 274. According to Kaplan ("Capital Investments," pp. 86–88), planned investment in state-owned agriculture includes 5.8 billion rubles of decentralized investment (2 million for increase in state farm livestock and 3.8 million for loans to collective farms). It is not clear whether the coverage of the planned figure here is the same as that of the actual figure in col. 4. **Line 12:** Kaplan, "Capital Investments," p. 88. Sum of 3.3 billion rubles of centralized investment and 2 billion of decentralized investment.

COLUMN 4–Line 1: Sum of lines 2, 17, 19, and 20. **Line 2:** *Po edinomu planu*, p. 110. **Lines 3-4, 10, and 19:** *Narodnoe khoziaistvo, 1961*, pp. 536, 543, and 538. Given in new rubles in 1955 prices and converted as explained in note above. **Lines 5, 15, 18, and 20:** Kaplan, "Capital Investments," pp. 207, 195, and 133. Sum of investments for the five years. **Line 17:** Based on planned investment (col. 3) and per cent of plan fulfillment (col. 5). **Lines 24, 27-29, 33, 36-38, and 44-45:** *Dostizheniia sovetskoi vlasti za 40 let v tsifrakh* [Achievements of the Soviet Regime during 40 Years in Figures], Moscow, 1957, p. 212. **Line 25:** Capacity at end of 1950 minus capacity at end of 1945 (given as 3.218 and 1.252 mill. kw, respectively, in *Narodnoe khoziaistvo, 1959*, p. 193).

COLUMN 5–Lines 1, 4-5, 10, 15, 18-20, 24-25, 27-29, 33, 36-38, and 44-45: Col. 4 as per cent of col. 3. **Line 2:** *Po edinomu planu*, p. 110. **Line 3:** Assumed to be same as line 2. **Line 17:** Assumed to be same as line 18.

cent in 1926/27 prices (see Table 79), the share of investment in 1940 prices was to increase slightly, from 18.8 per cent in 1940 to 21.7 per cent in the 1950 plan. Such an impression would, however, be incorrect for several reasons. First, national income in 1945 was definitely lower than in 1940: it was 79.4 with 1940 = 100 according to the Moorsteen and Powell estimates and 76.8 and 83.0 according to official Soviet estimates in 1940 and 1926/27 prices, respectively (see Table 79). Hence, in 1940 prices, funds allocated to household consumption in 1945 were about a third less than what they were in 1940 (see Table 78). Second, the estimates of fixed capital, national income, and investment could not have been very precise in 1945. The extent of war destruction and reconstruction difficulties could only be approximated. Third, the 1946–1950 plan was drawn up hurriedly, and it was impossible to make correct estimate costs. For many of the most important centralized construction projects,[3] financed by the Industrial Bank (*Prombank*), there were no estimate costs or financial documentation in 1945 and 1946 (see Table 97).

The situation was no better for investment projects for 1946–1950. The text of the Fourth Five-Year Plan, moreover, specified as a goal that "construction work must be carried out entirely on the basis of technical specifications and estimate costs set according to the established procedure."[4]

Although it may be difficult to make any definite estimates of the real burden of the investment program in the fourth plan, the plan was taut with only tenuous provisions made for its fulfillment.

One of its basic provisions was a 40 per cent increase in labor productivity in construction over 1940 (see Table 79). Such an increase could be obtained only through large-scale mechanization of labor, since about half of the work in construction was done manually at the beginning of 1946.[5] Voznesenskii's report called for the mechanization by 1950 of 60 per cent of excavation work, 90 per cent of rubble crushing, 95 per cent of concrete mixing, 90 per cent of mortar mixing, 60 per cent of concrete pouring, and 50 per cent of painting work.[6] Such a program required producing or importing the necessary machinery and was, in turn, dependent on other investment plans.

Another important provision concerning investment in the Fourth Five-Year Plan was the 12 per cent reduction in construction costs planned in the course of the five years (see Table 79).[7] This reduction was no doubt based in large part on the 17 per cent decrease in the cost of industrial production planned for the same period. It is unnecessary to dwell on the tenuousness of this provision. According to V. Grossman, between 1940 and 1944, construction material price

3. *Sverkhlimitnye* (above the limit) and *nizhelimitnye* (below the limit) in the Russian. According to Kaplan ("Capital Investments," p. 29), this is a synonym for centralized investment that is included in the national plan for investment and is confirmed by the USSR Council of Ministers or by the Union republic council of ministers.

4. Grossman, *Planovoe khoziaistvo*, No. 3, 1946, p. 38.

5. *Ibid.*, p. 40.

6. N. A. Voznesensky, *Five-Year Plan for the Rehabilitation and Development of the National Economy of the USSR, 1946–50* (translated from the Russian), London, 1946, p. 14.

7. Grossman (*Planovoe khoziaistvo*, No. 3, 1946, p. 37) states that the saving to be realized from this reduction should amount to 10 billion rubles.

Table 97   Distribution of Construction Projects Financed by the Industrial Bank according to Financial Specifications, 1945–1946

Financial Specifications	January 1, 1945			January 1, 1946		
	Number of Construction Projects (1)	Annual Value of Projects (mill. rubles) (2)	Share in Total Projects (per cent) (3)	Number of Construction Projects (4)	Annual Value of Projects (mill. rubles) (5)	Share in Total Projects (per cent) (6)
Construction projects financed according to estimate costs	764	3,245	30.4	1,120	5,897	45.0
Construction projects financed according to financial specifications	216	1,907	18.0	202	1,679	12.8
Construction projects without financial specifications	681	5,496	51.6	552	5,529	42.2

Source: Grossman, *Planovoe khoziaistvo*, No. 3, 1946, p. 37.

increases averaged 22.5 per cent.[8] Many of these materials were obtained from local sources through decentralized channels, and hence control over prices was even more difficult. To plan a reduction in costs on the basis of anticipated future production and construction conditions is obviously hazardous.

Difficulties in Launching the Investment Plan in 1946

Investment difficulties contributed heavily to the poor fulfillment of the 1946 annual production plan studied above.[9] However, information on this subject is scarce. According to Table 98, in constant prices, 72.7 per cent of planned centralized investment was realized in 1946. But the average level of plan fulfillment is not very significant. More detailed information by branch and sector of the economy, given in Table 99, shows that plan fulfillment was very uneven. The sectors with the poorest showing seem to have been the coal industry (see Table 82, note to line 1, in Chapter 16), ferrous metals, construction materials, agricultural machinery, and housing construction.

   Fulfillment of investment plans at a particular time does not mean that new productive capacities are actually in operation (see Chapter 11). Provisions to commission new facilities were written into the plan directly (see, for instance, Table 96, lines 23–45). So the production plan took account of both the possibilities of increasing production in existing enterprises and the plan to put new capacities into operation. The process of determining productive capacities pointed out bottlenecks and partial disproportions in production and thus new investment went to eliminate these bottlenecks. Productive capacities were determined

8. *Ibid.*, p. 41. In the People's Commissariat of Construction.
9. See pp. 359–63 and Table 82 in Chapter 16.

Table 98   Fulfillment of Annual Plans for Investment in Fixed Capital, 1946–1953

	Planned			Actual			
	Investment in Current Prices (bill. rubles) (1)	Cost Increase or Decrease (per cent) (2)	Investment in Comparable Prices (bill. rubles) (3)	Investment in Current Prices (bill. rubles) (4)	Cost Increase or Decrease (per cent) (5)	Investment in Comparable Prices (bill. rubles) (6)	Per Cent of Plan Fulfillment (7)
Centralized Investment							
1946	49.4	−3	50.9	44.2	+19.4	37.0	72.7
1947	58.8	−5	61.9	53.1	+30.8	40.6	65.6
1948	70.5	−1.7	71.7	66.2	+4.1	63.6	88.7
Centralized and Decentralized Investment							
1949	105.5	−4.5	110.5	114	+21.5	114	103.2
1950	135.6	−12.5	155.0	120	−14.4		
1951	135.7	−3	139.9	134.5	+0.1	134.4	96.1
1952	143.1			137.8	−7.7	149.3	
1953	156.1	−3.2	161.3	141.9	−1.0	143.3	88.8

Source

COLUMN 1–1946: *Zasedaniia Verkhovnogo Soveta SSSR (vtoraia sessiia). 15–18 oktiabria 1946 g.* [Meetings of USSR Supreme Soviet. Second Session, October 15–18, 1946], Moscow, 1946, p. 16. **1947:** *Sovetskie finansy* [Soviet Finance], No. 2, 1947, pp. 12–13, as cited by Kaplan, "Capital Investments," pp. 117–18. According to *Komsomolskaia pravda* [Truth of the Young Communist League], (March 1, 1947, p. 2), 1947 investment was estimated in 1945 estimate prices. **1948:** Based on actual investment (col. 4) and percentage of plan fulfillment for investment from budget, which was derived as 93.9 from planned investment from budget (60.9 bill. rubles in *Narodnoe khoziaistvo SSSR* [USSR National Economy], Vol. 2, Moscow, 1948, p. 483, as cited by Kaplan, "Capital Investments," pp. 117 and 119) and actual investment from budget (57.2 bill. rubles in A. Zverev, "Gosudarstvennyi biudzhet chetvertogo goda poslevoennoi Stalinskoi piatiletki" [State Budget of the Fourth Year of the Postwar Stalinist Five-Year Plan], *Planovoe khoziaistvo*, No. 2, 1949, p. 43). **1949:** Zverev, *Planovoe khoziaistvo*, No. 2, 1949, p. 43. **1950:** A. Zverev, "Gosudarstvennyi biudzhet zavershaiushchego goda poslevoennoi Stalinskoi piatiletki" [State Budget of the Final Year of the Stalinist Five-Year Plan], *Planovoe khoziaistvo*, No. 4, 1950, p. 16. Sum of investment from budget (106.5 bill. rubles) and investment from funds of economic organizations (29.1 bill. rubles). **1951:** *Pravda*, March 8, 1951, p. 2, as cited by Kaplan, "Capital Investments," pp. 117–18. Includes 3.7 bill. rubles for project-making outlays. See also *Zasedaniia Verkhovnogo Soveta SSSR (vtoraia sessiia). 6–12 marta 1951 g.* [Meetings of USSR Supreme Soviet. Second Session, March 6–12, 1951], Moscow, 1951, p. 25. **1952:** Zverev, *Pravda*, March 7, 1952, p. 3. **1953:** Zverev, *Pravda*, August 3, 1953, p. 3.

COLUMN 2–1946: Assumed to be same as planned decrease in cost of construction (given as 12 per cent for 1946–1950 in *Resheniia*, Vol. 3, p. 272, of which approximately one-fifth was accepted for 1946). **1947:** Assumed to be same as planned decrease in cost of construction (given as 5 per cent relative to 1945 estimate prices in *Komsomolskaia pravda*, March 1, 1947, p. 2). **1948:** Based on investment in current prices (col. 1) and in comparable prices (col. 3). **1949:** Assumed to be same as planned decrease in cost of construction (given in Zverev, *Planovoe khoziaistvo*, No. 2, 1949, p. 45). **1950:** Estimated to be half the reduction planned for cost of construction estimates as of July 1, 1950, to be achieved through economizing and a new reduction in prices (given as 25 per cent in Zverev, *Planovoe khoziaistvo*, No. 4, 1950, p. 17). **1951:** Assumed to be same as planned decrease in cost of construction below July 1, 1950, prices (given in *Zasedaniia*, 1951, p. 27). **1953:** Assumed to be same as planned decrease in cost of construction ("U.R.S.S. Le Budget de 1955," *Statistiques et Etudes Financières*, No. 78, June 1955, p. 649).

COLUMN 3–1946-1947, 1949-1951, and 1953: Based on planned investment in current prices (col. 1) and planned cost increase or decrease (col. 2). **1948:** Based on planned investment in current prices (col. 1) and saving to be realized through decrease in cost of construction in 1948 plan, which was estimated at 1.2 bill. rubles from statement (in A. Korobov, "Kapitalnoe stroitelstvo v tretem reshaiushchem godu poslevoennoi piatiletki" [Capital Construction in the Third Decisive Year of the Postwar Five-Year Plan], *Planovoe khoziaistvo*, No. 3, 1948, p. 23) that it was to amount to more than a billion rubles.

COLUMN 4–1946: *Sovetskie finansy*, No. 2, 1947, pp. 12–13, as cited by Kaplan, "Capital Investments," pp. 117–18. **1947:** Kaplan, "Capital Investments," pp. 117 and 119. Rough estimate. According to *Pravda*, February 2, 1947, p. 2, the plan was not fulfilled. **1948:** Zverev, *Planovoe khoziaistvo*, No. 2, 1949, p. 43. **1949-1953:** Table 101, line 2.

COLUMN 5–1946-1947: Table 102, line 4. For 1947, increase over 1945. **1948:** Calculated from Table 102, line 4. The prices used in the 1948 plan are not known but the estimate here (see note to col. 1, 1948) is based on Zverev's 1949 figures for actual investment which took into account the price increase of January 1, 1949. Hence the figure of

Table 98   *continued*

66.2 bill. rubles is probably in current prices, not in 1945 estimate prices. Therefore, only the cost reduction planned for 1948 and the cost increase that actually took place in that year have to be taken into account. **1949:** Calculated from Table 101, line 4. **1950:** Calculated from Table 101, line 4. For centralized and decentralized investments in current prices. **1951:** Calculated from Table 101, line 4. According to *Pravda*, January 29, 1952, p. 2, there was a reduction in construction costs. **1952:** Calculated from Table 101, line 4. According to *Pravda Ukrainy* [Truth of the Ukraine], January 24, 1953, p. 2, there was a reduction in construction costs. **1953:** Calculated from Table 101, line 4.

COLUMN 6–1946-1948 and 1951-1953: Based on investment in current prices (col. 4) and cost increase or decrease (col. 5). **1949:** Taken to be same as investment in current prices (col. 4) on the assumption that the figure is comparable to planned investment in comparable prices (col. 3).

COLUMN 7–1946-1949, 1951, and 1953: Calculated from cols. 3 and 6.

through "improved" technical norms, established from the tested experience of Stakhanovites. These were norms, then, that were revised periodically. In this way productive capacities were calculated with the help of statistics on the productivity of machines, the number of machines, and the norms of hours worked.[10]

That investment outlays are made does not mean that production plans will be met. Insofar as can be judged from the available statistics, the plans for the installation of new capacities were fulfilled less well than investment plans, with aftereffects reflected in the fulfillment of production plans. The disturbances thus created were transmitted immediately to the producer goods sector with relatively slow repercussions in the consumer goods sector, where money played a more active role.[11] These disturbances also seem to have been controlled very little, if at all, when quarterly plans were drafted. These plans appear to have played a passive role and to have been incapable of checking the movement. Much more detailed statistics would be required to establish the extent of this interaction between the "spontaneous" movement and the "equilibrium" of the economy established with the help of the quarterly plans. We can only quote commentaries on the 1947 annual plan that mention the difficulties encountered in 1946.[12]

In addition,[13] the severe consequences of the war, as well as the lagging of various branches of the national economy and the poor agricultural harvest, caused a certain number of difficulties:

1. The growth of the coal industry, which experienced the worst difficulties after the last war, delayed and held back the development of other branches of heavy industry, railroad transportation, and the whole national economy.

2. The restoration of consumer goods production lagged far behind the restoration of producer goods production.

3. The plan for housing construction was not fulfilled in 1946 and only 6 million square

10. P. Ivanov, "O planirovanii ispolzovaniia proizvodstvennykh moshchnostei" [On Planning the Utilization of Productive Capacities], *Planovoe khoziaistvo*, No. 4, 1949, pp. 11–12.

11. On this point, see the sections on equilibrium between consumer goods and demand below.

12. *Komsomolskaia pravda*, March 1, 1947, p. 1.

13. The plan mentions the success achieved in 1947 and then the bad harvest because of the drought and the measures taken to promote trade.

meters of floor space was built. The deficiencies in housing held back the formation of permanent cadres of workers and the growth of labor productivity.

4. The failure to fulfill the plan to put productive capacities into operation in several branches, particularly in the coal industry and in ferrous metals, raised the number of unfinished construction projects, increased the cost of construction, and froze sizable state funds.

5. Among the machine-building construction projects that lagged considerably behind the needs of the national economy were the electrical industry and agricultural machine-building, for the latter of which the 1946 annual plan was not fulfilled.[14]

6. The production of rails and wheels for transportation equipment, pipes for the petroleum industry, and steel sheets for the motor vehicle industry was far below the needs of the national economy.

7. Despite an increase in the production of construction materials in 1946, the requirements of the national economy were far from being satisfied; the reconstruction and development of the timber industry lagged behind the needs of the national economy.

It is interesting to note that, while this report on the plan takes account of the economic situation, including all the difficulties encountered and the propagation of the movement of disturbances, the role of the plan in combating these disturbances remains vague.

The extent of the actual investment effort remains difficult to judge. The official statistics in constant prices (see Table 100) cite an annual growth of 17 per cent for the whole national economy in 1946, with higher rates in the food and light industry (67 per cent), housing construction (55 per cent), and the coal industry (20 per cent)—all sectors, as seen above, that experienced considerable difficulties.

Uncertainty about the total volume of investment in 1946 is noted by Naum Jasny, who emphasizes that the 1945 base (90.7 per cent with 1940 = 100 in July 1, 1955, prices—see Table 101) is too high and that the total amount of construction materials available would have made it impossible to attain.[15] Jasny bases his estimates on statistics published by S. G. Strumilin for 1950 (45 per cent increase over 1940) and calculates a level of 60.9 per cent for 1945 (with 1940 = 100).[16] Later calculations by Moorsteen and Powell confirm this estimate of Jasny's showing a level of 57.0 in 1945 (with 1940 = 100) with 1950 weights and 66.1 with 1937 weights (see Table 101). The variations in investment price indexes on which these different computations are based are, in fact, very important. Whereas the official Soviet price index of July 1, 1955, implies only a 13.1 per cent increase in investment prices in 1945 over 1940, the Moorsteen and Powell indexes show increases of 55.2 and 80.0 per cent for 1937 and 1950 weights, respectively (see Table 102).

14. The 1946 plan for the electrical industry was fulfilled by 106 per cent and the plan for agricultural machine-building by only 77 per cent (see Table 81).

15. *Soviet Industrialization, 1928–1952*, Chicago, 1961, pp. 297–99. Jasny gives a chart showing the output of construction materials and the volume of investment in construction and assembly work from 1936 to 1946.

16. Strumilin's article ("Zakon stoimosti i izmerenie obshchestvennykh izderzhek proizvodstva v sotsialisticheskom khoziaistve" [The Law of Value and Measurement of Social Production Costs in a Socialist Economy]) was published in *Planovoe khoziaistvo*, No. 2, 1957, pp. 38–50.

Table 99 Information on Fulfillment of 1946 Annual Plan for Investment

Branch of Economy	Plan (1)	Fulfillment (2)	Per Cent of Plan Fulfillment (3)
1. *Rural electric power stations*	1,200 hydroelectric power stations 1,000 thermoelectric power stations		
Ferrous metal industry			
2. General reconstruction plan (USSR or only Ukraine)		In 10/46 plan fulfilled by 47 of 106 trusts under USSR Ministry for Construction of Heavy Industrial Enterprises	
3. Donbass		By 11/21/46 80% of plan for large-scale construction work fulfilled, 70% of equipment plan, and 20% of plan for rebuilding worker housing	
4. Makeev Combine	3 open-hearth furnaces 3 rolling mills	Equipment not delivered	
Construction materials			
5. RSFSR local industry:	To be put into operation	Actually put into operation by 9/1/46	
Brick enterprises	1,000	503	
Roofing tile enterprises	400	40	
Lime enterprises	400	284	

Agricultural machinery
6. Construction and reconstruction of 5 large plants:

	Industrial Area	Living Area	Industrial Area	Living Area
	(thousand m²)		(thousand m²)	
Stalingrad	35.5	36.0	18.7	18.4
Kharkov	63.2	9.0	33.0	6.0
Vladimir	12.3	15.0	1.0	5.1
Altai (Rubtsov)	12.1	25.0	0	5.3
Lipetsk	22.7	10.0	1.0	4.7

Branch of Economy	Plan (1)	Fulfillment (2)	Per Cent of Plan Fulfillment (3)
Railroad transportation			
7. Construction of new track (km)	1,375	1,200	87.3
8. Electrified track (km)	600	600	100.0
Housing			
9. Construction and reconstruction, USSR:			
Floorspace (thous. m²)	8,940	7,900	88.4
Buildings (thous.)	6,000		
Private houses (thous.)	1,900		
Credit for private construction (mill. rubles)	961		
Housing built by industrial ministries			
10. Coal, Moscow Basin, Moskvaugol Combine	Housing construction	16.5% of plan fulfilled in 8 months	
11. Ferrous metals, Magnitostroi Trust		50 buildings (31,300 m² floorspace) 286 private houses (9,500 m² floorspace) bridge over Ural River at Magnitogorsk	40

Table 99   *continued*

Branch of Economy	Plan (1)	Fulfillment (2)	Per Cent of Plan Fulfillment (3)
12. Textiles	For 1946 and 1st Q of 1947 = 525,000 m² of floorspace	113,000 m² built in 9 months 170,000 m² built in 4th Q 283,000 m² total	
13. Gold mines of Lena	Housing construction	Plan overfulfilled in 10 months	

Source

ITEM 1: *Cahiers de l'Economie Soviétique*, No. 7, 1947, p. 23

ITEMS 2, 4, and 9: *Ibid.*, p. 30.

ITEM 3: *Ibid*. These delays sometimes arose because some reconstruction trusts, being so new, had not yet had time to progress from organization to operation. They were usually due to delays in deliveries of equipment by plants (e.g., the Novokramatorsk and Elektrostal factories).

ITEM 5: *Ibid.*, p. 26.

ITEM 6: *Ibid.*, No. 8, 1947, p. 21. The poor fulfillment of the investment plans for these plants explains the shortage of tractors and parts (*ibid.*, p. 22).

ITEM 7: Plan from *ibid.*, No. 4, 1946, p. 9; and fulfillment from *ibid.*, No. 7, 1947, p. 20.

ITEM 8: Plan from *ibid.*, No. 4, 1946, p. 28; and fulfillment from *ibid.*, No. 7, 1947, p. 20.

ITEM 10: *Ibid.*, No. 7, 1947, p. 25. The Moskvaugol Combine did not fulfill its mining plan either. Neither the shafts nor the living quarters were ready for winter. A new shaft (42 Smorodinskaia) was not put into operation for five months for living quarters for the miners.

ITEM 11: *Ibid.*, p. 31.

ITEM 12: *Ibid.*, pp. 32–33. The number of people employed increased by 86,000 during the first nine months of 1946. The total number employed was 290,000 instead of the 427,000 anticipated for 1950. The lack of living quarters seems to have limited hiring, but this was only a temporary difficulty.

ITEM 13: *Ibid.*, p. 29.

Investment Planning and Economic Equilibrium in 1947

The preceding chapter discussed the considerable expansion that occurred during 1947 and the underfulfillment of the annual plan. However, since the role of the plan, as officially stated, was to guarantee economic equilibrium, it is important to examine the extent to which the investment plan was used in the attempt to eliminate bottlenecks, the results achieved, and the disturbances caused by the poor fulfillment of this plan.

In the 1947 annual plan, it is clear that investment played a major role in restoring equilibrium. The plan stressed the growth of production in branches that were lagging in 1946: fuels, mechanization of agriculture, light industry, and textiles.[17] This growth was to come primarily from an extraordinary increase in investment credits for the priority sectors (see Table 103). The plan contained a series of measures to increase production in these sectors.[18] The lag in the mechanization of labor was to be eliminated, particularly in mines, construction and timber industries, and loading work in transportation. New productive capacities in the fuel industry, electric power stations, the metal industry, the

17. *Komsomolskaia pravda*, March 1, 1947, p. 1.
18. *Ibid*.

Table 100   Average Annual Growth Rates of Investment in Various Sectors of National Economy, 1946–1953 (per cent, in comparable prices)

	1946	1947	1948	1949	1950	1951	1952	1953
National economy, total	17	10	23	20	23	12	11	4
Industry								
Coal	20	9	29					
Coal and petroleum				22	15	12	5	
Electric power stations	10	4	20	39	32	40	26	
Ferrous and nonferrous metals	16		31	18	16	20	11	
Machine-building	12[a]		15	10	9	10	12	
Construction materials				12	16	35	9	
Food and light industry	67	30	32		10		9	8
Food industry				21				
Agriculture								
Machine and Tractor Stations and state farms				54	48	6		
Transportation	14	8	11	32	22	3		
Housing construction								
Official Soviet estimates[b]	55		36	26	18	20	10	
Western estimates (1937 prices)[c]		2.1	14.3	3.6	10.3	9.4	−1.4	13.0

Source: Unless otherwise indicated, for 1946: *Pravda*, January 21, 1947, p. 1; for 1947: *Pravda*, January 18, 1948, p. 1; for 1948: *Pravda*, January 20, 1949, p. 1; for 1949: *Pravda*, January 18, 1950, p. 2; for 1950: *Pravda*, January 26, 1951, p. 2; for 1951: *Pravda*, January 29, 1952, p. 2; for 1952: *Pravda*, January 23, 1953, p. 2; and for 1953: *Pravda*, January 31, 1954, p. 3.

a. Civilian machine-building.

b. These percentages are based on value figures. The same sources, as well as *Narodnoe khoziaistvo SSSR v 1956 godu* [The USSR National Economy in 1956], Moscow, 1957, p. 176, also give the following figures on urban housing construction including reconstruction in million m³:

	State and Cooperative	Private
1946	12.6	4.8
1947	11.8	6.4
1948	14.7	6.4
1949	15.5	6.4
1950	17.8	6.4
1951	20.3	7.3
1952	20.0	7.4
1953	23.2	7.6

c. Calculated from estimates of total investment in housing construction (including reconstruction) given by Richard Moorsteen and Raymond Powell, *The Soviet Capital Stock, 1928–1962*, Homewood, Ill., 1966, p. 88.

Table 101 Investment in Fixed Capital, 1940 and 1945–1953

	1940	1945	1946	1947	1948	1949	1950	1951	1952	1953
	Part A: Billion Rubles									
1. Official Soviet estimates in July 1, 1955, prices	43.2	39.2	46.8	50.8	62.1	76.0	90.8	102.1	113.8	119.2
2. Western estimates based on official Soviet estimates in current prices	38[a]	36.3	50.7	61.1	78.2	114	120	134.5	137.8	141.9
3. Moorsteen and Powell estimates based on official Soviet estimates in current prices	39.73	40.78	50.20	58.83	74.21	122.20	123.82	134.65	140.41	148.94
4. Moorsteen and Powell estimates in 1937 prices	32.19	21.29	26.72	30.96	37.89	45.76	55.25	60.84	64.56	71.26
5. Moorsteen and Powell estimates in 1950 prices	74.19	42.28	56.30	66.39	83.89	103.25	123.74	137.34	146.40	160.07
	Part B: Indexes, 1940 = 100									
6. Official Soviet estimates in July 1, 1955, prices	100	90.7	108.3	117.6	143.8	175.9	210.2	236.3	263.4	275.9
7. Moorsteen and Powell estimates based on official Soviet estimates in current prices	100	102.6	126.4	148.1	186.8	307.6	311.7	338.9	353.4	374.9
8. Moorsteen and Powell estimates in 1937 prices	100	66.1	83.0	96.2	117.7	142.2	171.6	189.0	200.6	221.4
9. Moorsteen and Powell estimates in 1950 prices	100	57.0	75.9	89.5	113.1	139.2	166.8	185.1	197.3	215.8
	Part C: Indexes, 1945 = 100									
10. Official Soviet estimates in comparable prices		100	117	128.7	158.3	190.0	233.7	261.7	290.5	302.1
11. Official Soviet estimates in July 1, 1955, prices	110.2	100	119.4	129.6	158.4	193.9	231.6	260.5	290.3	304.1
12. Western estimates based on official Soviet estimates in current prices		100	139.7	168.3	215.4	314.0	330.6	370.5	379.6	390.9
13. Kaplan estimates based on official Soviet estimates in current prices		100	121.8	146.3	182.4	308.4	357.1			
14. Moorsteen and Powell estimates based on official Soviet estimates in current prices	97.4	100	123.1	144.3	182.0	299.7	303.6	330.2	344.3	365.2
15. Moorsteen and Powell estimates in 1937 prices	151.2	100	125.5	145.4	178.0	214.9	259.5	285.8	303.2	334.7
16. Moorsteen and Powell estimates in 1950 prices	175.5	100	133.2	157.0	198.4	244.2	292.7	324.8	346.3	378.6

Source

LINE 1: *Narodnoe khoziaistvo, 1956*, pp. 172–73.

LINE 2–1940-1950: Table 104, line 3. 1951-1953: Table 104, sum of lines 3 and 5 since project-making outlays were included in total investment in fixed capital in the state sector before 1951. When a range is given in Table 104, the average of the two figures is used here.

LINE 3: Moorsteen and Powell, *Soviet Capital Stock*, p. 391. Given for gross investment in fixed capital excluding capital repairs and based on official Soviet figures in current prices.

LINE 4: *Ibid.*, p. 387. Gross investment in fixed capital excluding capital repairs in 1937 prices.

LINE 5: *Ibid.*, p. 389. Gross investment in fixed capital excluding capital repairs in 1950 prices.

LINE 6: Calculated from line 1.

LINE 7: Calculated from line 3.

LINE 8: Calculated from line 4.

LINE 9: Calculated from line 5.

LINE 10: Recalculated from annual rates of growth (given in Table 100, line 1) to 1945 = 100. The figures are officially given in "constant prices," which, according to Kaplan ("Capital Investments," p. 121), are 1945 prices.

LINE 11: Calculated from line 1.

LINE 12: Calculated from line 2.

LINE 13: Moorsteen and Powell, *Soviet Capital Stock*, p. 391. Calculated from centralized investment for 1945–1948 and for sum of centralized and decentralized investment for 1949–1950 (see *ibid.*, p. 117).

LINE 14: Calculated from line 3.

LINE 15: Calculated from line 4.

LINE 16: Calculated from line 5.

a. In 1936/37 prices.

Table 102 Implied Price Deflators for Investment Goods, 1940 and 1945–1953

	1940	1945	1946	1947	1948	1949	1950	1951	1952	1953
					Part A: 1940 = 100					
1. Based on official Soviet estimates in July 1, 1955, prices	100	113.1	132.3	146.9	153.8	183.1	161.4	160.8	147.9	145.3
2. Based on Moorsteen and Powell estimates in 1937 prices	100	155.2	152.3	154.0	158.7	216.3	181.6	179.3	176.2	169.3
3. Based on Moorsteen and Powell estimates in 1950 prices	100	180.0	166.5	165.5	165.2	221.0	186.9	183.1	179.1	173.7
					Part B: 1945 = 100					
Based on official Soviet estimates in constant prices:										
4. Centralized and decentralized investment in current prices		100	119.4	130.8	136.1	165.3	141.5	141.6	130.7	129.4
5. Centralized investment for 1945–1948 and decentralized investment for 1949–1950 in current prices		100	104.1	113.7	115.2	162.3	152.8			
6. Based on official Soviet estimates in July 1, 1955, prices		100	117.0	129.9	136.0	161.9	142.7	142.2	130.8	128.5
7. Based on Moorsteen and Powell estimates in 1937 prices	64.4	100	98.1	99.2	102.2	139.5	117.0	115.5	113.6	109.1
8. Based on Moorsteen and Powell estimates in 1950 prices	55.5	100	92.4	91.9	91.7	122.7	103.7	101.7	99.4	96.5

Source

LINE 1–1945: Derived from Table 101, lines 7 and 6. 1946-1953: Derived from Table 101, lines 12 and 11, deflated by ratio of line 14 to line 11 for 1940.

LINE 2: Derived from Table 101, lines 7 and 8.

LINE 3: Derived from Table 101, lines 7 and 9.

LINE 4: Derived from Table 101, lines 12 and 10.

LINE 5: Derived from Table 101, lines 13 and 10.

LINE 6: Derived from Table 101, lines 12 and 11.

LINE 7: Derived from Table 101, lines 14 and 15.

LINE 8: Derived from Table 101, lines 14 and 16.

textile industry, machine-building, and railroad transportation were to be put into operation more rapidly. Finally, the capacity of the construction materials industry was to be increased considerably and the development of the timber industry was to be accelerated. This program helped guarantee high growth rates in 1947,[19] but the growth was far from matching plan provisions (see Table 85 in Chapter 16), and, while helping eliminate certain disturbances, the investment plan seems to have been responsible for creating others.

An examination of the tensions created by the 1947 investment plan is particularly difficult. The best approach would be to study the government provisions dealing with these tensions, but unfortunately only one decree of this sort was published at the time (concerning the development of inland waterway transportation), and even this decree does not give many details on the measures taken in 1947.[20] It concerns a plan of three years and four months, applying

19. See Table 84 in Chapter 16.

20. September 1, 1947, decree of the USSR Council of Ministers, "On Measures for the Reconstruction and Further Development of Inland Waterway Transportation" (*Direktivy*, Vol. 3, pp. 221–33, extracts).

Table 103   1947 Annual Plan for Investment and Its Fulfillment

	Planned		Actual		
	Billion Rubles [a] (1)	Index (1946 = 100) (2)	Billion Rubles [a] (3)	Index (1946 = 100) (4)	Per Cent of Plan Fulfillment (5)
Total Investment in National Economy					
1. In 1945 prices and norms	50.0			110	
2. In current prices	58.8		53.1	120.1	90.3
3. Occupied areas	20.5	117.1			
Investment by Sector of Economy					
4. Electric power stations	3.0			104	
5. Coal	6.3	142		109	
6. Petroleum	2.8	144			
7. Ferrous metals	4.9	130			
8. Motor vehicles					
9. Agricultural machinery and tractors		almost 150			
10. Electrical industry		more than 200			
11. Chemicals		145			
12. Rubber					73
13. Cement		almost 300			
14. Light and food industries	3.3			130	
15. Textiles and light industry:		more than 200			
16. Textiles	1.6				
17. Transportation				108	
18. Railroad transportation	6.0				
19. Dashava-Kiev pipeline	0.075				
20. Geological prospecting	2.4				
21. Housing construction					
Construction and Assembly					
22. National economy, total:	30.8				
Work done by contract:					
23. Ministry for Construction of Heavy Industrial Enterprises	5.3 ⎫				
24. Ministry for Construction of Fuel Enterprises	3.75 ⎬ 146				
25. Ministry for Construction of Military and Naval Enterprises	1.75 ⎭				
26. Ministry for Civilian Housing Construction and for Federal Republic Housing Construction	1.9				
Installation of Fixed Capital					
27. National economy, total (bill. rubles)	48.2				
28. Coal mines (mill. m. tons)	38.0				
29. Electric power stations (mill. kw)	2.0				
30. Foundries (mill. m. tons)	2.1				
31. Steel mills (mill. m. tons)	2.9				
32. Rolling mills (mill. m. tons)	3.6				
33. Coking plants (mill. m. tons)	3.8				
34. Lipetsk Tractor Plant					
35. Factory for repairing MTS equipment					
36. Construction materials					
37. Light industry					
38. Rubber industry					53.7
39. Drilling by Ministry of Petroleum Industry (thous. linear meters)	2,078				

Table 103 *continued*

	Planned		Actual		
	Billion Rubles[a] (1)	Index (1946 = 100) (2)	Billion Rubles[a] (3)	Index (1946 = 100) (4)	Per Cent of Plan Fulfillment (5)
40. Spinning machines (thous.)	414	138	373	124.3	90.1
41. Sugar (thous. m. tons of sugar beets processed per day)	15	15			
42. Alcohol (thous. liters produced per day)	200				
43. Construction of roads to transport wood (km)	4,040				
44. Opening up new and rebuilt living space in cities and workers' settlements (mill. m²)	13.8	175	13.0		
45. In destroyed areas (mill. m²)	5.8				
46. State funds (mill. m²)	12.8	213	9	150	70.3
47. Private funds (mill. m²)	1.0	53	4		400
48. Funds of ministries, institutions, and federal republics (bill. rubles)	8.8				

Source

COLUMN 1–Line 1: "O gosudarstvennom plane vosstanovleniia i razvitiia narodnogo khoziaistva SSSR na 1947 god" [On the State Plan for the Reconstruction and Development of the USSR National Economy for 1947], *Komsomolskaia pravda*, March 1, 1947, p. 2. This is only centralized investment (see Kaplan, "Capital Investments," p. 117, and see note to line 2). **Line 2:** *Komsomolskaia pravda*, March 1, 1947, p. 2. According to A. Zverev (in *Zasedaniia Verkhovnogo Soveta SSSR (tretia sessiia). 20–25 fevralia 1947 g.* [Meetings of USSR Supreme Soviet. Third Session, February 20–25, 1947], Moscow, 1947, pp. 18–19 and 24), this sum was broken down as follows: centralized investment—50.0 bill. rubles; additional expenditures of the ministries—3.6 bill. rubles; and adjustment for increase in wages and in working capital—5.2 bill. rubles. **Lines 3-7, 14, 18, 22-33, 40-42, 44, and 46-48:** *Komsomolskaia pravda*, March 1, 1947, p. 2. **Line 16:** Based on investment in light and food industries (line 14 above) and share of textiles (given as about half in *Cahiers*, No. 10, 1947, p. 17). **Line 19:** *Ibid.*, No. 8, 1947, pp. 19–20. **Line 20:** *Komsomolskaia pravda*, March 1, 1947, p. 2. Of this amount, 923 mill. rubles were in the investment plan and 1,489 mill. rubles in the budget. **Line 21:** The share of housing construction in total investment was to increase from 10 per cent in 1946 to 18 per cent in 1947 (A. Korobov, "Ob uskorenii vvoda moshchnostei i snizhenii stoimosti stroitelstva" [On Putting Capacities into Operation Faster and Reducing Construction Costs], *Planovoe khoziaistvo*, No. 3, 1947, p. 7). **Line 34:** The plan called for constructing eight workshops at the Lipetsk Tractor Plant, 23,500 m² of space for these workshops, and also 17,000 m² of living space (A. Korobov, "Kapitalnoe stroitelstvo v tretem reshaiushchem godu poslevoennoi piatiletki" [Capital Construction in the Third Decisive Year of the Postwar Five-Year Plan], *Planovoe khoziaistvo*, No. 3, 1948, p. 16). **Lines 39 and 43:** Korobov, *Planovoe khoziaistvo*, No. 3, 1947, p. 6.

COLUMN 2–Line 3: Based on 1947 plan (col. 1) and actual investment in 1947 (given as 17.5 bill. rubles in *Ekonomicheskaia zhizn SSSR* [The Economic Life of the USSR], Moscow, 1967, Book I, p. 400). According to Korobov (*Planovoe khoziaistvo*, No. 3, 1948, p. 14), investment in occupied areas amounted to 38.7 bill. rubles for 1946, 1947, and the first quarter of 1948. **Lines 5-7, 9-11, 13, and 15:** Korobov, *Planovoe khoziaistvo*, No. 3, 1947, pp. 6–7. For lines 5–7, 11, and 15, covers ministries of corresponding industries. **Lines 23-25:** *Ibid.*, p. 14. For certain trusts of the Ministry for the Construction of Heavy Industrial Enterprises, planned investment was double or triple 1946 investment. **Line 40:** Based on 1947 plan (col. 1) and actual number of spinning machines put into operation in 1946 (given as 300 thous. in *Cahiers*, No. 8, 1947, p. 27, note 2). **Line 41:** Based on 1947 plan (col. 1) and new capacity put into operation in 1946 (given as 100 thous. quintals in *ibid.*). **Lines 44 and 46-47:** Based on 1947 plan (col. 1) and amount of living space built in 1946 (given as 7.9 mill. m², of which 6.0 mill. m² was by state funds and 1.9 mill. m² by private funds, in *ibid.*, No. 9, 1947, p. 30).

COLUMN 3–Line 2: Kaplan, "Capital Investments," p. 117. Very rough approximation. **Line 22:** Instead of the planned reduction in construction costs, some construction organizations showed an increase, due largely to increased prices of materials produced at their auxiliary enterprises, exceeding wage funds, and increased overhead expenses (Korobov, *Planovoe khoziaistvo*, No. 3, 1948, p. 23). **Line 28:** An example of the poor fulfillment of the plan is the Artemugol trust of the Ministry of the Coal Industry of Western Regions, which fulfilled only 31.5 per cent of its plan for reconstruction of mines (*ibid.*, p. 16). During the first half of 1947, a total of 4 mill. m. tons of

Table 103 *continued*

capacity was put into operation (*Rapport américain sur l'évolution économique de l'Union Soviétique en 1947*, Paris, 1948, p. 8). During the first quarter of 1947, coal mines with an annual capacity of 1.3 mill. m. tons were put into operation ("Za vypolnenie i perevypolnenie gosudarstvennogo plana na 1947 god" [For the Fulfillment and Overfulfillment of the State Plan for 1947], *Planovoe khoziaistvo*, No. 2, 1947, p. 8). **Line 33:** During the first half of 1947, a total of 900,000 m. tons of capacity was put into operation (*Rapport américain*, p. 8). **Line 40:** Of the 1,190 thous. spinning machines to be put into operation in 1947, 800 thous. were machines that were not in use the previous year and 373 thous. were to be supplied by new production (*Cahiers*, No. 8, 1947, p. 27). **Lines 44 and 46-47:** Korobov, *Planovoe khoziaistvo*, No. 3, 1948, p. 16, and *Rapport américain*, p. 8.

COLUMN 4–**Lines 1, 4-5, 14, and 17:** Table 99 (for 1947). According to Korobov (*Planovoe khoziaistvo*, No. 3, 1947, p. 7), total investment in the national economy in the first four months of 1947 was 8 per cent higher than in the corresponding period of 1946. However, other sources (*Rapport américain*, p. 8) give the increase for the first nine months of 1947 as only 6 per cent over 1946. **Line 2:** Based on investment in 1947 (col. 3) and corresponding investment in 1946 (given as 44.2 bill. rubles in Kaplan, "Capital Investments," p. 117). **Line 21:** According to Korobov (*Planovoe khoziaistvo*, No. 3, 1947, p. 8), investment in housing construction during the first four months of 1947 was 21 per cent higher than during the corresponding period in 1946. **Line 40:** Based on actual figure for 1947 (col. 3) and actual number of spinning machines put into operation in 1946 (see source to col. 2, line 41). **Line 46:** Korobov, *Planovoe khoziaistvo*, No. 3, 1948, p. 16, and *Rapport américain*, p. 8.

COLUMN 5–**Lines 2, 40, and 46-47:** Based on cols. 3 and 1. **Line 8:** According to Korobov (*Planovoe khoziaistvo*, No. 3, 1947, p. 9), 77.2 per cent of the plan for the first quarter of 1947 was fulfilled by the Ministry of the Motor Vehicle Industry; but only 49.3 per cent of the plan was fulfilled by the bearing factories in the Volga region, 50.6 per cent by the Urals bearing factory, and 28.5 per cent by the Siberian bearing factory. **Line 10:** According to Korobov (*ibid.*), only 49 per cent of the plan for the first quarter of 1947 was fulfilled by the Ministry of the Electrical Industry. **Line 12:** Korobov, *Planovoe khoziaistvo*, No. 3, 1948, p. 16. Ministry of the Rubber Industry. **Line 21:** According to Korobov (*Planovoe khoziaistvo*, No. 3, 1947, p. 8), the plan was not entirely fulfilled. Fulfillment was particularly poor in the following ministries: Ferrous Metal Industry, Coal Industry of Western Regions, Coal Industry of Eastern Regions, Petroleum Industry of Southern and Western Regions, Petroleum Industry of Eastern Regions, Heavy Machine-Building, Motor Vehicle Industry, Construction Materials Industry, Rubber Industry, and Textile Industry. **Lines 23-25:** According to Korobov (*ibid.*, p. 14), the plan for these ministries was not fulfilled during the first months of 1947. The poorest performances were by the Ministry for the Construction of Heavy Industrial Enterprises (in their construction projects for ferrous and nonferrous metals and for the electrical industry) and by the Ministry for the Construction of Fuel Enterprises (in their construction projects for the coal and petroleum industries). **Line 34:** According to Korobov (*Planovoe khoziaistvo*, No. 3, 1948, p. 16), the construction organization Lipetskstroi of the Ministry for the Construction of Heavy Industrial Enterprises, in violation of the plan, split up its resources among 24 construction projects and, as a result, did not fulfill the plan. Despite the fact that the factory's investment plan was overfulfilled, only 42 per cent of the plan to open up industrial and living space was fulfilled. **Line 35:** Only 11 per cent of the plan was fulfilled by June 20, 1947 (*Cahiers*, No. 10, 1947, p. 14). **Lines 36-37:** According to Korobov (*Planovoe khoziaistvo*, No. 3, 1948, p. 16), the fulfillment of the plan to put productive capacities into operation for the corresponding ministries was much lower than that of the plan for total investment. **Line 38:** *Ibid.* Ministry of the Rubber Industry.

a. Unless otherwise indicated.

mostly to 1948–1950, which envisaged rebuilding the inland waterway fleet and outfitting it with the necessary equipment, developing inland waterway ports and equipping them with machinery, and providing supplementary financial allocations of 720 million rubles for the Ministry of the Inland Waterway Fleet for 1948–1950.[21] Subsidies were planned for the ministry to cover the difference between planned costs (calculated with a 5 per cent reduction below 1945 estimate prices, see Table 98) and actual prices.[22] This decree represented a real revision of the 1947 annual plan and of the five-year plan not only for the Ministry of the Inland Waterway Fleet but also for its numerous suppliers of equipment and for the construction agencies.

Another decree representing a substantial revision of the 1947 annual plan and the five-year plan was not published until 1968 in the new edition of the collection of decisions on economic matters.[23] It set new goals for 1947–1950 for the Ministry of the Timber Industry and the delivery of timber products. Having established that 90 per cent of timber procurements were produced by manual labor, the decree provided measures to mechanize this work, to build new roads, to mechanize the construction of these roads, and to increase timber deliveries. It contained concrete goals on the delivery of equipment (tractors, cranes, etc.) and inland waterway boats to transport wood. It also contained measures to guarantee decent working conditions for the workers and to compensate the Ministry of the Timber Industry construction organizations for the increase in the cost of construction and assembly work over the 1945 estimate costs.[24] Additional expenditures for investment in housing were also provided for 1947. It is clear that this decision implied significant revisions in the machine-building plan, in the plans of the construction organizations, and in employment to be made starting in 1947.

It can be assumed that similar revisions were also made in other sectors of the economy, such as heavy industry, particularly in the metal and coal industries, where the plan for the first quarter of 1947 was very poorly fulfilled. The difficulties experienced in these industries in the winter of 1946/47 were not overcome before April of 1947.[25]

---

21. For the Military Inland Waterway Central Administration of this ministry: 130 million rubles in 1948, 190 million in 1949, and 280 million in 1950 (fixed program) and, in addition, 120 million rubles of their own investment in 1948–1950 (*ibid.*, pp. 226–27).

22. *Ibid.*, p. 227.

23. August 8, 1947, decree of the USSR Council of Ministers, "On the Mechanization of Timber Procurements, the Opening up of New Forest Areas, and the Creation of Indispensable Conditions to Consolidate the Position of the Workers and the Engineering and Technical Staff of the USSR Ministry of the Timber Industry" (*Resheniia*, Vol. 3, pp. 436–47).

24. *Ibid.*, pp. 446–47.

25. Poor fulfillment of the Ministry of the Ferrous Metal Industry plan for the production of pig iron, steel, rolled steel, and the mining of iron ore should be emphasized. The production of pig iron increased by 10 per cent and that of rolled steel by 6 per cent over the first quarter of the preceding year, which is less than the average annual rates of growth planned for the production of ferrous metals for 1947.

These lags in ferrous metal output were due mainly to the poor preparation for winter of several plants. Moreover, the weather conditions during that winter turned out to be extremely severe. The directors of the ferrous metal plants did not prepare the ore yards at the proper time, with the result that the ore often froze. The internal transportation at the factories operated badly. Equipment was

In the absence of information on revisions of the investment plan during 1947, we can only guess at their size from data on the fulfillment of the 1947 plan, presented in Table 103. The first problem is estimating over-all plan fulfillment. Norman Kaplan's rough figures make it possible to estimate the percentage fulfillment of the investment plan in "current prices" as 90.3 (see Table 103). However, the plan figures include both centralized investment (50 billion rubles) calculated in 1945 estimate prices and certain additions. Expenditures for decentralized investment are not given. But we must also take into account the planned reduction in construction costs of 5 per cent (see Table 98) and the actual increase in investment prices that occurred between 1945 and 1947 (see Table 98). Although there are several deficiencies in the estimate,[26] the failure to fulfill the 1947 investment plan was substantial: the percentage of fulfillment might well be around 65, as shown in Table 98.

However incomplete, the data by sector of the economy seem consistent with this calculation. Sizable increases were planned for the principal sectors, as can be seen in Table 103. These sectors covered 67 per cent of total investment[27] and had planned rates of growth over 1946 ranging from 30 to 200 per cent. Hence an increase in total investment in constant prices of only 10 per cent in 1947 seems very small.

The poor fulfillment of the 1947 plan for aggregate investment seems to have been largely caused by the failure to carry out the plans for construction and assembly work. Official Soviet sources, however, give information only on the fulfillment of these plans for the first quarter of 1947 (see Table 103, source notes).

The most crucial part of the plan was the installation of fixed capital, on which the production plans were based (see Chapter 11). Data on fulfillment in this area are only fragmentary and often cover only the first quarter of 1947, but there is no doubt that these plans were very poorly fulfilled. For the first quarter of 1947, the official commentary is very clear: "Particularly inadmissible is the unsatisfactory fulfillment of the plan to put productive capacities into operation in the coal industry and in the ferrous metal industry, in combine and tractor plants, in sulfuric acid and soda enterprises, and in construction projects of the electrical industry."[28]

Moreover, Soviet writers stress the fact that the plan to put new capacities into operation was less well fulfilled than the plan for investment expenditure: "Thus, for instance, in 1947 the Ministry of the Rubber Industry fulfilled 73 per cent of the investment plan and only 53.7 per cent of the plan for putting capacities into operation. In the Ministry of Light Industry and the Ministry of

---

sent in too often for repairs that were not included in the plan; the fuel reserves that were accumulated during the summer months of 1946 turned out to be insufficient. There were difficulties in fuel deliveries in January and to some extent in February because of the poor functioning of the railroads. (*Planovoe khoziaistvo*, No. 2, 1947, p. 6.)

26. The planned reduction in costs of industrial production was 1.4 per cent (*Komsomolskaia pravda*, March 1, 1947, p. 2).

27. Heavy industry, electric power stations, and railroad transportation (*Ekonomicheskaia zhizn*, Book I, p. 401).

28. *Planovoe khoziaistvo*, No. 2, 1947, p. 9.

the Construction Materials Industry, the fulfillment of the plan for putting productive capacities into operation was much worse than fulfillment of the plan for volume of investment."[29]

In view of these results in commissioning new facilities, one might expect poor fulfillment of the production plan. Nevertheless, from Table 85 it appears that for many basic products (except construction materials) the underfulfillment of the plan did not exceed 10 per cent. There are two possible explanations for this. First, expecting poor fulfillment of the plans for putting new capacities into operation, the government was cautious in planning the contribution of these new facilities to production. Second, the government defended the key sectors during the year by revising the plans accordingly. Both explanations may be partly true. The uneven fulfillment of the production plan for different products indicates that revisions of the plans were probably made during the year. Unfortunately, the number of products cited in Table 85 is too small to draw more definite conclusions.

Even if it is not possible to establish a definite correlation between the fulfillment of investment and production plans, it is useful to examine the causes for the failure to fulfill the plans for investment (and for putting capacities into operation). One of the most important is the failure to fulfill the plans for costs. It can be estimated from Tables 98 and 102 that about a 10 per cent reduction in construction costs was anticipated in the 1947 plan.[30] Instead, there was an increase of about 9 per cent (see Table 98). (The increase was noted by official Soviet commentators.[31]) The very process of planning investment is largely responsible for the failure to meet cost targets. The deficiencies in drawing up construction estimate costs, which were mentioned earlier, were caused both by the schedules set at the time the projects were presented and by the administrative process of their approval.[32] Other disruptions, difficult to control centrally, contributed to cost overruns while the work was in progress; these involved norms for utilizing materials and equipment, their purchase prices, employment plans, and the wage plan.

Many statements of reasons for the failure to fulfill construction cost plans,

29. Korobov, *Planovoe khoziaistvo*, No. 3, 1948, p. 16.

30. Index of 104.1 in 1946 (with 1945 = 100) for investment (that is, construction and assembly plus equipment, see Table 102, line 5) and a reduction of 5 per cent (1945 = 100) planned for 1947 in the cost of construction and assembly work (see Table 98, col. 2), with the result rounded to 10 per cent. It should be noted that, according to A. Zverev ("Mobilizatsiia finansovykh resursov na vypolnenie i perevypolnenie plana 1947 goda" [Mobilization of Financial Resources for the Fulfillment and Overfulfillment of the 1947 Plan], *Planovoe khoziaistvo*, No. 2, 1947, p. 28), the reduction in the cost of industrial production anticipated in the 1947 plan was 1.4 per cent below the actual level in 1946. In fact, there was an increase of 5.8 per cent for "comparable" production (A. N. Malafeev, *Istoriia tsenoobrazovaniia v SSSR, 1917–1963 gg*. [History of Pricing in the USSR, 1917–1963], Moscow, 1964, p. 406).

31. See Korobov, *Planovoe khoziaistvo*, No. 3, 1948, p. 23.

32. Despite a certain improvement in estimate costs and in documentation during 1946 and 1947, there were still shortcomings in the work of the following ministries in this area: Transport Machine-Building, Light Industry, Meat and Dairy Industry, Construction Materials Industry, Timber Industry, and Construction of Military and Naval Enterprises. The situation was the same in 1948, and on May 1, 1948, several construction projects of these ministries did not have any technical documentation. This was one of the principal causes for the delays in construction. (*Ibid.*, p. 22.)

applicable to 1947 as well as to other years, could be cited. For the cost of construction materials, a Soviet specialist summarizes as follows: "Of crucial significance in the increased cost of construction materials are poor organization of the production of construction materials, serious deficiencies in the supply and delivery of materials to the construction sites, uneconomical and careless use of materials."[33]

The same author adds that "at many construction sites, accounting of the receiving, distribution, and expenditure of construction materials is badly organized and the technical norms established for their utilization are not observed."[34] In 1947, in particular, "the increase in construction costs at these construction agencies is the result mainly of the high cost of the materials produced in their auxiliary enterprises, exceeding the wage fund, and high administrative expenditures."[35]

In 1947 the wage fund was exceeded largely because of an unwarranted increase in the number of auxiliary workers.[36] More generally, the administrative apparatus in construction agencies was top-heavy[37] and the proportion of workers in auxiliary sectors too high.[38] The shortage of materials actually fed the inflation of these employees. In primary production the number of administrative personnel was limited by norms for administrative expenditures and the number of workers by the employment plans. There were no such norms for administrative expenditures in auxiliary production; only the total number of workers was planned. That made it possible to inflate the administrative staff. The procurement storage sector, where the size of this staff was very large because of the presence of numerous "fixers" (tolkachi),[39] provided a prominent example.

Another important disrupting factor in carrying out the investment plans was the dispersion of resources among many investment projects (see fourth section of Chapter 11). According to Minister of Finance A. G. Zverev, in 1946, "the failure to fulfill the plan to put already started construction projects into operation was seriously affected by the incorrect practice at many construction sites of

33. Grossman, *Planovoe khoziaistvo*, No. 3, 1946, p. 42.

34. *Ibid.*, p. 43.

35. Korobov, *Planovoe khoziaistvo*, No. 3, 1948, p. 23.

36. In this connection, Korobov (*ibid.*) mentions the construction agencies of the Ministry for the Construction of Heavy Industrial Enterprises and the Ministry for the Construction of Fuel Enterprises.

37. According to Grossman (*Planovoe khoziaistvo*, No. 3, 1946, pp. 43–44), the number of administrative jobs in construction was inflated and many engineers worked in trust and agency offices. He gives figures by ministry, from which it appears that the number of production workers per administrative employee ranged from 6.2 to 10.9 and averaged around 8 instead of the 10 which he considers right.

38. In the Ministry of the Aircraft Industry the number of workers in auxiliary production was 115 per cent of that in primary production; in the former People's Commissariat of the Petroleum Industry the figure is 132 per cent; and in the Ministry of the Nonferrous Metal Industry it is 123 per cent. Of the total number of auxiliary workers, 21 per cent were assigned to transportation and loading work, 38 per cent to subcontracted auxiliary enterprises, and 41 per cent to service enterprises. Out of a total administrative staff in construction of 260,000 people, 140,000, or 56 per cent, worked in auxiliary sectors. (Grossman, *Planovoe khoziaistvo*, No. 3, 1946, p. 45.)

39. *Ibid.* On *tolkachi* in general, see Joseph S. Berliner, *Factory and Manager in the USSR*, Cambridge, Mass., 1957, pp. 207–30.

dispersing material and financial resources, as well as labor, among a large number of projects instead of concentrating on the ones already started."[40] While citing examples of the dispersion of resources in 1946, Zverev exhorted the ministries and construction agencies not to do the same in 1947 and to concentrate on projects already under way.[41]

To judge from comments by a Soviet specialist on 1947 investment fulfillment, the results do not seem to have been fully satisfactory:

One of the main reasons for the failure to fulfill the plan to put productive capacities into operation is the dispersion of construction efforts among a large number of projects and sites within the projects. When the state plan is transmitted to the construction projects, some ministries and general administrations, instead of concentrating their financial, material, and labor resources primarily on the already started construction projects, distribute them among many different projects, thus compromising the state plan from the very beginning of the year. And the various construction projects are not completely supplied with indispensable construction materials and equipment.[42]

Dispersion of resources was directly responsible for the delay in commissioning new facilities, as can be seen from numerous examples.[43] It is important, nevertheless, to discover the source of this chronic trouble in investment planning. It could result from excessive decentralization of investment decision-making. However, as can be seen from Table 104, the share of decentralized investment was very low and this investment was also controlled.

To carry the analysis further, it seems useful to distinguish between "dispersion" included in the plan, dispersion at the time revisions were made in the plans by the central authorities during the year, and "spontaneous" dispersion at the enterprise level.

Examples of dispersion included in the plans were given as early as 1946 by a Soviet specialist in investment problems, who cites several incidents that probably occurred in 1945. For example, the plans of the Ordzhonikidze Plant at Kramatorsk under the Ministry of the Ferrous Metal Industry and the Stalin

40. A. G. Zverev, *O gosudarstvennom biudzhete SSSR na 1947 god* [On the State Budget of the USSR for 1947], Moscow, 1947, p. 19.

41. *Ibid.*, pp. 19–20. "Here is an example. At the construction site of the Kolomna locomotive plant under the Ministry of Transport Machine-Building (head of the capital construction section—Comrade Klavuch; director of the plant—Comrade Iakovlev), seven facilities were scheduled to be opened in 1946. Instead of concentrating the available labor and materials on these facilities, construction resources were dispersed among 44 and, as a result, not one single facility was put into operation.

"Or, again, for example, in the construction of the Sherlovaia Gora Lead Combine under the Ministry of the Nonferrous Metal Industry (head of construction—Comrade Troianov), during the first half of 1946 11 facilities were to be opened, but because the available materials and labor were dispersed among 18 facilities, not one was opened on schedule."

42. Korobov, *Planovoe khoziaistvo*, No. 3, 1948, p. 16.

43. Some construction organizations, instead of concentrating on already started construction projects, distributed their resources among a great number of projects. Thus, for example, 32 facilities were built simultaneously in the Solikam Magnesium Plant belonging to *Glavaluminium* (the Central Administration for Aluminum); on November 1, 1946, 90 per cent of the plan for construction work was fulfilled and only 33 per cent of the plan for putting capacities into operation. Out of 20 housing developments only 2 were completed, and out of 12 industrial projects not one was completed. (Zverev, *Planovoe khoziaistvo*, No. 2, 1947, p. 34.) On the dispersion of resources during the reconstruction of the Lipetsk Tractor Plant, see Table 103, notes to line 35.

Table 104   Investment in State and Cooperative Sector, 1940 and 1945–1953 (billion rubles, current prices)

	1940ᵃ	1945	1946	1947	1948	1949	1950	1951	1952	1953
1. Centralized investment	32	36.3	44.2	53.1ᵇ	66.2					
2. Decentralized investment	6	0	6.5	8	12					
3. Total centralized and decentralized investment in state sector	38	36.3	50.7	61.1	78.2	114	120	130.8	127–141	131–145
4. Capital repairs	6.6	7	9.3	11.6	14	22	26.0	28.8	31.7	35
5. Project-making outlaysᶜ								3.7	3.6–4.0	3.7–4.1
6. Collective farm investments from own resources	5.5	6.6	7	7	8	8.8	9.5	11.4	11.2	12.9
7. Total investment, excluding inventory investment	50.1	49.9	67.0	79.7	100.2	144.8	155.5	174.7	173.5–187.9	182.6–197.0
8. Inventory investment						58	30	40	40	29
9. Total investment in state and cooperative sector						203	186	215	214–228	212–226
10. Total investment as estimated by Hoeffding and Nimitzᵈ						231	206	242	248	243

Source: For 1940 and 1945–1948: Kaplan, "Capital Investments," p. 37; for 1949–1953: O. Hoeffding and N. Nimitz, "Soviet National Income and Product, 1949–1955," RAND Research Memorandum 2101, Santa Monica, 1959, p. 180 (except for line 7, which was obtained by summing lines 3–6).

a. 1936/37 prices.

b. *Etude provisoire sur la situation économique de l'Europe en 1951* (Geneva, 1952) gives 53.8 billion rubles.

c. Until 1951, included in total centralized and decentralized investment in state sector.

d. Obtained by subtracting outlays other than investment from gross national product. The fact that these estimates exceed the totals in line 9 does not necessarily imply overstatement since the latter totals exclude such minor investment categories as state reserve commodity stockpiles, gold production, net foreign balance, inventories held by organizations other than nonagricultural *khozraschet* enterprises, geological services, etc. (Hoeffding and Nimitz, "Soviet National Income," p. 181).

Plant under the Ministry of Heavy Machine-Building provided very small sums for completion of basic facilities, while allocating extensive resources to other less important facilities.[44] It is surprising that such an allocation of resources could have been written into the centralized plans. The explanation for these "deficiencies" must lie in the process of drawing up investment plans. By making use of their power within the ministry, these plants (and, presumably, others) succeeded in getting their own way. It is possible, of course, that it was rational to start several investment projects simultaneously in these plants, but the available information is insufficient for deciding the issue. These factories were trying to write a certain number of projects into the plan so that later they would have a basis for claims. If the plants had resigned themselves to making investments only to complete certain projects, would other bottlenecks have appeared later on? Such quandaries appear to reflect general defects in the plans for centralized investment which the factories tried to remedy at the microeco-

44. Grossman, *Planovoe khoziaistvo*, No. 3, 1946, pp. 45–46. The plant at Kramatorsk provided 140,000 rubles for the completion of an iron foundry, instead of the necessary 4.5 million rubles, and allocated other resources to other projects. The Stalin plant provided 3.4 million and 1 million rubles for two workshops instead of the 9 and 3 million rubles needed.

nomic level, thus causing delays in completion that were added to the delays created by the centralized plan itself.

There is another possible explanation for this enterprise behavior. In administrative planning of the Stalinist type, investment credits are a free good for enterprises. Even if the initial investment funds allocated are small and insufficient, increasing the number of construction and investment projects makes it possible to obtain sizable funds later on, precisely in order to complete construction projects "in progress." And thus arises pressure from enterprises which, poorly controlled by the central authorities, gives rise to disturbances in the same way as the increase of monetary purchasing power in a market economy for which there are no corresponding resources in existence.

Plan revisions made directly by the government during the year or at the time the quarterly plans are drawn up are clearly responsible for the dispersion of resources. Unfortunately, data on such revisions made during 1947 are very scarce (see above).

There was considerable dispersion of resources at the level of the enterprise during plan execution. Special research would be necessary to analyze fully this behavior and to estimate the extent to which investment planning itself was responsible. Breakdowns in the system of contracts with suppliers were definitely a contributing factor.[45] In any case, at the present stage of documentation, for 1945–1952 the investment sector must be regarded as the primary source of disturbances, although neither the mechanism nor the means of transmitting these disturbances to other sectors can be explained.

Investment Planning in 1948–1952

Information about the annual investment plans between 1948 and 1952 is so fragmentary that it is impossible to judge how well they were fulfilled or how effective they were. It is possible only to note the general policy that was followed and the extent to which the principal features of investment planning observed in 1946 and 1947 were maintained.

Investment Policy

Data on the distribution of investment among the various sectors of the national economy are gathered in Tables 105 and 106. The basic shares of fixed capital allocated to the different sectors are shown in Table 105. The large share allocated to heavy industry is clearly visible; that share would be even higher if working capital were included.[46] Within industry the largest share of investment

---

45. *Ibid.*, pp. 38–39.

46. Investment in working capital of state enterprises of collective farms and of private housing construction is not included in Table 105 (see Jasny, *Soviet Industrialization*, p. 304, note to Table 24), but it is included in the investment figures published when the budget was presented (see Table 106). However, the figures in Table 105 show separately total investment in housing, whereas in Table 106 these expenditures are largely included in investment by the various ministries building housing for their own workers (see *ibid.*).

Table 105   Distribution of Centralized Investment in Fixed Capital, 1938–1955 (per cent)

	Jan. 1, 1938– June 30, 1941	July 1, 1941– Jan. 1, 1946	1948	1949	1946– 1950	1951– 1955
Part A: By Branch of Industry [a]						
1. Industry, total			100.0	100.0		
2. Electric power stations			8.9	10.6		
3. Coal			20.0	20.9		
4. Petroleum			8.9	9.3		
5. Ferrous and nonferrous metals			21.0	21.1		
6. Machine-building			11.4	10.8		
7. Light (excl. textiles) and food industry			10.9	10.6		
8. Other branches			18.9	16.7		
Part B: By Sector of Economy [b][c]						
9. National economy, total	100.0	100.0			100.0	100.0
10. Industry, total	40.9	54.0			48.9	51.1
11. Heavy industry	34.4	50.3			42.9	46.2
12. Light industry	6.5	3.7			6.0	4.9
13. Agriculture	5.3	2.1			7.3	9.6
14. Transportation and communications	20.4	18.1			14.2	10.1
15. Housing construction	12.7	7.8			12.7	15.5
16. Other sectors	20.7	18.0			16.9	13.7

Source: For Part A: Kaplan, "Capital Investments," pp. 66 and 207, rough estimates (line 8 derived as residual); for Part B: *Dostizheniia*, p. 210.

a. In 1945 estimate prices.

b. In July 1, 1955, prices.

c. These state investments do not include investments of industrial ministries, which are usually included in the appropriate sector, and hence are not comparable with those in Part A.

went for coal, metals, and machine-building, which together accounted for more than half of industrial investment in 1948 and 1949 (see Part A of Table 105). In the Fourth Five-Year Plan agriculture was to receive only 7.3 per cent of total investment, about the same share as the food and light industry, which seems to be a regular feature of Stalinist economic policy. The reduction in the share of transportation in total investments below the prewar level was no doubt the result of insufficient investment, planned or not planned. Troubles in transportation ensued, as mentioned in his memoirs by then Minister of Finance A. G. Zverev: "As for the Fourth Five-Year Plan, in these years railroad transportation was a source of great concern to the government. It was being rebuilt at an unjustifiably slow pace. A disproportion had developed between traffic capacity and the volume of freight to be transported. Urgent measures were taken."[47]

Housing is another sector where investment seems to have been neglected. Its share remained the same after the war as before, even though war destruction was particularly severe in housing.

This distribution of investment could either have resulted from a government policy written into the annual plans or have been the more or less spontaneous

47. A. G. Zverev, *Zapiski Ministra* [Memoirs of a Minister], Moscow, 1973, p. 237.

Table 106   Distribution of Centralized Investment in Fixed Capital in 1948 and in 1949 Plan

	Actual Investment, 1948		Planned Investment, 1949	
	Million Rubles [a] (1)	Per Cent (2)	Million Rubles [a] (3)	Per Cent (4)
National economy, total	66,152	100.0	105,533	100.0
Industry	46,389	70.1	72,231	68.4
Agriculture	4,318	6.5	9,209	8.7
Transportation and communications	8,995	13.6	13,542	12.8
Trade and procurement	841	1.3	986	0.9
Other	5,609	8.5	9,565	9.1

Source: Cols. 1 and 3: Zverev, *Planovoe khoziaistvo*, No. 2, 1949, p. 43; cols. 2 and 4: calculated from cols. 1 and 3, respectively.

a. In current prices.

result of the process of fulfilling the investment plans (or a combination of both). The percentages of fulfillment of the annual plans presented in Table 98 above show improvement between 1948 and 1953 over the immediate postwar years of 1946 and 1947 (89–103 per cent compared with 66–73 per cent earlier). Unfortunately, such calculations cannot be made for 1950 and 1952 owing to lack of data on the planned reduction in construction costs. As rough as these calculations are, they seem consistent with the transition to a less troubled period in investment, with a gradual reconstruction of the economy. The year 1953, with the changes in plans that followed Stalin's death, saw a partial return to the practices current immediately after the war.

Does the improved fulfillment of the annual investment plans in 1948–1953 imply that these plans were less taut? This hardly seems likely since the government's attitude toward the plans and the methods of drafting them remained the same. In this connection, Zverev reports the way the balance was established for the 1950 plan:

Let us assume that plans were made [at the highest level] to increase the level of consumption by 10 per cent, investment by 12 per cent, expenditures on the army and administration by 12 per cent. . . .

Thus, for example, we come to the dividing line between the Fourth and the Fifth Five-Year Plans. Gosplan presents the draft of the next annual plan for the development of the national economy. The drafted goals are quite good. But . . . the financial deficit is 50 billion rubles.[48] It is impossible to find such a sum in the budget. When the presidium of the USSR Council of Ministers reviews the draft, they decide to form a commission to make a detailed study of the problem. I am instructed to balance the budget and present suggestions. How do I go about it? Some of the investments and other expenditures for

48. The total income of the USSR state budget in the 1950 plan was 432.0 billion rubles and expenditures were 427.9 billion, with a surplus of 4.1 billion. This budget was presented on June 13, which could have been because of the initial deficit mentioned by Zverev. (A. G. Zverev, *O gosudarstvennom biudzhete SSSR na 1950 god i ob ispolnenii gosudarstvennogo biudzheta SSSR za 1948 i 1949 gody* [On the State Budget of the USSR for 1950 and on the Fulfillment of the State Budget for 1948 and 1949], Moscow, 1950, p. 10.)

increased reproduction will have to be reduced. And, even so, the problem is still not resolved altogether. Won't we have to cut certain credits in the military establishment estimates? I present a combination of these suggestions for examination. We again review the draft with the Gosplan people and submit it to the government. This variant is accepted.[49]

In order to reach a conclusion on plan tautness, it is necessary to know how the various balances of the plan and the budget were obtained. The traditional process is well known: reduce the norms for consumption of materials, increase the norms for labor productivity, adopt the most favorable assumptions for putting investments into operation, for harvests, and for foreign trade, etc. Unfortunately, the details of these calculations are not known. But every time that they turned out to be too optimistic, not only were the plans not fulfilled but there were also unplanned cost increases that the government could not deflect onto other producer goods sectors. On the contrary, the prices of producer goods had to be maintained at the planned level. But, to do that, subsidies had to be increased, and this became common practice during 1943–1950; the total amount of subsidies paid out during these years is shown in Table 107.

Nevertheless, by 1948 it became clear that producer goods prices could not be maintained at their low prewar level, and there was an increase averaging 50 per cent (see Table 108). According to Zverev, the government agreed to this increase very reluctantly and there were subsequent decreases on January 1, 1950, July 1, 1950, and January 1, 1952.[50]

In actual fact, what matters for the equilibrium of a planned economy is not so much the absolute level of prices as the relation between planned and real costs.[51] In the case of unplanned price increases, the government can either grant subsidies or raise prices. But, either way, it reduces the total amount actually allocated to investment and thus transmits disturbances to different sectors of the economy. An examination of the main features of investment planning during 1948–1952 shows the extent to which this tendency to increase planned costs was actually reflected in this sector.

Main Features of Investment Planning in 1948–1952

One of the important causes of bottlenecks arising from the failure to fulfill the plans for putting new (or old) capacities into operation was the dispersion of resources among several construction sites or projects. The difficulties encoun-

49. Zverev, *Zapiski*, pp. 248–49.

50. *Ibid.*, p. 237; Malafeev, *Istoriia*, pp. 250, 432, and 433; and *Finansy i sotsialisticheskoe stroitelstvo* [Finance and Socialist Construction], Moscow, 1957, p. 50.

51. Wholesale prices in the Soviet Union are set at the center on the basis of the average costs of a given branch. The government makes an effort to contain rises by equalizing costs within the branch and by recourse to subsidies, as was the case during and after the war. Price changes, therefore, reflect a change in costs after a certain time lag. The price decreases that occurred after the January 1, 1949, reform were mostly in machine-building, the chemical industry, and electric power. The official index is distorted here because in these branches "comparable" products are used mostly and price rises are authorized for "new products," although they are often new only in name. Thus there is a reduction in the index of wholesale prices and a simultaneous rise in the costs of construction and equipment caused by deliveries at prices higher than those specified in the cost estimates (which contain "old" products at lower prices).

Table 107 Subsidies Paid from the State Budget, 1943–1950 (billion rubles)

	National Economy	Industry
1943	4.60	3.40
1944	8.10	6.50
1945	13.90	11.70
1946	25.80	22.40
1947	34.10	29.10
1948	45.20[a]	35.30
1949	6.00[b]	2.90[b]
1950	6.60[b]	3.10[b]

Source: Unless otherwise specified, A. G. Zverev, *Natsionalnyi dokhod i finansy SSSR* [USSR National Income and Finances], Moscow, 1961, pp. 294–95.

a. Zverev, *Zapiski*, p. 236. In his earlier book (*Natsionalnyi dokhod*, pp. 294–95), Zverev gives 41.20 bill. rubles. For all other years, the two sets of figures agree.

b. According to Zverev (*Zapiski*, p. 236), planned expenditures for the coal industry and the timber industry continued to be higher than the wholesale prices after the January 1, 1949, reform of wholesale prices. Hence the major part of the subsidies paid out in 1949 and 1950 were earmarked for these industries.

tered in this area before and after the war were discussed above.[52] Again in 1948, despite strict regulations that new construction was not to be authorized unless the work could be completed and the facility put into operation by the end of the year,[53] the results were far from satisfactory.[54] Several examples of poor utilization of funds were pointed out by Soviet commentators in this connection.[55]

The same appeals were made in 1949 and at the time the budget was presented for every year from 1950 to 1953,[56] but with disappointing results. In 1949,

52. See Chapter 11 and pp. 422–23 above.

53. *Zasedaniia Verkhovnogo Soveta SSSR (chetvertaia sessiia). 30 ianvaria–4 fevralia 1948* [Meetings of USSR Supreme Soviet. Fourth Session, January 30–February 4, 1948], Moscow, 1948.

54. According to Zverev (*Planovoe khoziaistvo*, No. 2, 1949, p. 44), "the concentration of material and financial resources on the most important already started projects is still inadequate, as a result of which in many ministries fixed capital is not put into service on schedule."

55. "Unfortunately, too often resources are dispersed on secondary projects instead of being concentrated on already started projects. Thus, at the Alma-Ata factory of the Ministry of Heavy Machine-Building, construction projects that were 75 to 95 per cent finished did not receive the necessary allocations for completion in 1948, whereas the allocations for 1948 were scattered among 22 projects that were not very advanced. In the construction of a locomotive plant at Kherson for the same ministry, the 11.2 million rubles allocated for 1948 were dispersed among 21 projects, most of which were not very advanced" ("O gosudarstvennom biudzhete SSSR na 1949 god i ob ispolnenii gosudarstvennogo biudzheta SSSR za 1947 god. Doklad ministra finansov SSSR deputata A. G. Zvereva" [On the State Budget of the USSR for 1949 and on the Fulfillment of the State Budget of the USSR for 1947. Report of USSR Minister of Finance Deputy A. G. Zverev], *Pravda*, March 11, 1949, p. 3).

56. Zverev, *O biudzhete na 1950*, p. 13; *O gosudarstvennom biudzhete SSSR na 1951 god. Doklad i zakliuchitelnoe slovo ministra finansov A. G. Zvereva* [On the State Budget of the USSR for 1951. Report and Final Speech of Minister of Finance A. G. Zverev], Moscow, 1951, p. 19; "O gosudarstvennom biudzhete SSSR na 1952 god i ob ispolnenii gosudarstvennogo biudzheta SSSR za 1950 god. Doklad ministra finansov SSSR A. G. Zvereva" [On the State Budget of the USSR for 1952 and on the Fulfillment of the State Budget of the USSR for 1950. Report of USSR Minister of Finance A. G. Zverev], *Pravda*, March 7, 1952, p. 3; *O gosudarstvennom biudzhete SSSR na 1953 god i ob ispolnenii gosudarstvennogo biudzheta SSSR za 1951 i 1952 gody. Doklad i zakliuchitelnoe slovo Ministra finansov SSSR*

Table 108   Index of Wholesale Prices in Industry,[a] 1940–1955 (1940 = 100)

	1948	1949	1950	1955
Industry, total:	181	212	170	128
Heavy industry:	111	175	140	107[b]
Electric power	114	174	160	129
Petroleum refining	100	121	103	79
Coal industry	100	310	310	260
Ferrous metal industry	100	275	195	166
Chemical and petrochemical industry	109	187	157	125
Machine-building and metal processing	115	150	114	78
Timber and wood processing industry	104	419	357	356
Pulp and paper industry	100	287	233	186
Construction materials industry	115	256	202	146
Light and food industries:	272	260	210	156
Light industry	258	271	238	192
Food industry	278	255	197	140

Source: *Narodnoe khoziaistvo SSSR v 1970 godu* [The USSR National Economy in 1970], Moscow, 1971, p. 176.

a. Including turnover tax.

b. In 1952 the wholesale prices in heavy industry were 7 per cent higher than in 1948 (*Narodnoe khoziaistvo, 1970,* p. 177, note)—that is, 118.8 per cent of 1940.

according to Zverev, "in a number of ministries material and financial resources were dispersed among many construction projects instead of being concentrated primarily on the most important facilities already under way."[57] During 1950–1953, these shortcomings showed up mainly in criticisms of the slowness with which new capacities were put into operation.[58]

The dispersion of resources among numerous construction sites and projects is, in a highly centralized planning system of the Stalinist type, largely the result of errors by the central authorities, poor synchronization of plans made at different levels of the administrative apparatus, and inadequate (or, in actual fact, unrealizable) control over the administration of enterprises. Nevertheless, the constant repetition of complaints about dispersion directed at enterprises is striking, since *ex-ante* methods of control and strict supervision during execution are very powerful means of enforcement. If the central agencies finally agree to authorize new or additional investment, that means it is *indispensable.* Instead of holding managers responsible, the central planners deserve the blame for launching badly prepared work for which there are insufficient resources. Thus the trouble lies with the concept of a "taut plan" and exaggerated confi-

---

A. G. *Zvereva na piatoi sessii Verkhovnogo Soveta SSSR* [On the State Budget of the USSR for 1953 and on the Fulfillment of the State Budget of the USSR for 1951 and 1952. Report and Final Speech of USSR Minister of Finance A. G. Zverev at the Fifth Session of the USSR Supreme Soviet], Moscow, 1953.

57. Zverev, *Planovoe khoziaistvo,* No. 4, 1950, p. 16.

58. See sources cited in footnote 56 above. According to Zverev, in 1951 "the ministries and the construction organizations and agencies must concentrate their material and financial resources on projects that are in the process of completion and must not allow them to be dispersed among many secondary projects. They must unconditionally guarantee the completion of tasks assigned by the national economic plan for the installation of fixed capital" (*O biudzhete na 1951,* p. 19).

dence in the system of priorities (rationing), where the principle of selection is supposed to be the solution to everything. In fact, it looks as though the principle of selection can work only within narrow limits. Above a certain "threshold," a disturbance to which the system of priorities does not react is propagated in the priority sectors, takes the central planner by surprise, and cancels the positive effects anticipated from the rationing system. The central planner is thus caught in his own trap and penalized for not having taken his production plan seriously. With a disintegrating production plan and an ineffective system of priorities (rationing), administrative planning gives way to a regulated market economy (*économie dirigée*), where continuous administrative orders and regulations replace the national plan.

Cost overruns were another permanent feature of investment planning in 1948–1953. The shortcomings in this area in 1947 were hardly exceptional.[59] Although it is extremely difficult to estimate these increases in planned costs, an attempt was made in Table 98. For the years for which some data exist (1948, 1951, 1953), it seems clear that costs were exceeded in general. These comparisons, however, concerned plans and results for construction costs (that is, construction and assembly work), whereas investment also includes purchase of equipment. Planned prices in this field are not known, and the official index of actual prices is based on an incomplete sample.[60]

Insofar as the national economic plan is assumed to constitute a program equilibrated with balances, cost overruns should bring about (after reserves have been used up) a situation of scarcity. Considered in real terms, this would imply that the demands of some producers could not be satisfied. Considered in monetary terms, there should be an unplanned increase in costs that the budget has to make up with additional subsidies. The government can then choose either to inflate by granting credits that are not backed by sufficient material funds or to sacrifice certain projects. Thus, the disturbance created by the unplanned increase in costs is inevitably transmitted to the other sectors.

Since this is a major source of disturbance in a planned economy, the causes for unplanned increases in costs are important. Official commentaries give a number of reasons. Estimate costs may be poorly prepared or completely lacking.[61] The pace of work may be irregular, with immobilization of equipment and labor

59. See pp. 421–23 above.

60. See footnote 51 above.

61. The poor quality of estimate costs was mentioned above in connection with the investment plan for 1946 (see p. 406 above and Table 97). According to Zverev (*Planovoe khoziaistvo*, No. 2, 1949, p. 45), "instead of trying to economize, many ministries and construction organizations allow considerable excess expenditures in drawing up estimate costs."

In 1950, too, "Often construction work is carried out without projects or estimate costs, which leads to a large amount of unnecessary work and a rise in construction costs. Thus, in the Ministry of the Coal Industry at the end of the first quarter of 1950, 112 construction projects did not have any approved technical documentation; in the USSR Ministry of the Food Industry, 15 construction projects did not have any fixed tasks; in the USSR Ministry of the Fishing Industry, 12 construction projects did not have any technical documentation" (Zverev, *Planovoe khoziaistvo*, No. 4, 1950, p. 16).

62. "The Ministry of Communications maintains three construction offices in the one town of Voronezh. None of these offices works at full capacity, which in 1948 led to an accumulation of more than 5 million rubles of deficits in the course of six months.

stoppages.[62] There is a tendency to accumulate stocks of raw materials and equipment,[63] and a tendency to exceed norms for consumption of materials.[64]

"The main reasons for the increase in construction costs lie in poor organization of work and insufficient mechanization of labor" (*Pravda*, March 11, 1949, p. 3).

"One of the reasons for the high cost of construction lies in the inadequate organization of construction and assembly work, as a result of which, in many instances, machinery and equipment are not sufficiently used and there are labor stoppages and uneconomic expenditures of materials" (Zverev, *O biudzhete na 1950*, p. 14).

"Construction machinery is often used quite inadequately and prolonged labor stoppages are allowed on the construction sites as a result of the poor organization of construction work" (*O biudzhete na 1951*, p. 18). Prolonged labor stoppages and the inadequate utilization of equipment are also pointed out by Zverev for 1951 (see footnote 63 below).

"Many construction enterprises did not carry out their assigned tasks in reducing construction costs in 1952. Thus, many organizations of the Ministry of Construction are responsible for a sizable increase in the cost of construction and assembly work as a result of serious shortcomings in the utilization of labor, machinery, and equipment, as well as other causes. The losses suffered from expenditures in excess of estimate costs and other unproductive expenditures climbed to 725 million rubles for this ministry in 1952, whereas the plan envisaged gains of 1,025 million rubles. The construction organizations of the Ministry of the Coal Industry and the Ministry of Transportation are also responsible for sizable losses" (*O biudzhete na 1953*, p. 18).

63. "The ministries and offices that handle construction should take energetic measures to avoid the excessive accumulation of equipment and materials on the construction sites.

"At certain construction sites it often happens that not only is the construction equipment in excess of what is needed but it is also useless. In various offices of the Ministry of the Chemical Industry, stocks of equipment are five times the normal requirements. At the Ministry of Transport Machine-Building, the stocks of equipment were found to be much too large. Among these reserves in excess of the plan is equipment that has been brought to the construction sites without any precise destination" (*Pravda*, March 11, 1949, p. 3).

"One of the reasons for the increase in construction costs is, in many cases, the excessively large expenditures for materials and equipment. The stocks of materials and equipment often exceed the established norms. It happens that some builders order equipment quite independently of real needs or prefer to stock up new equipment instead of using the equipment already available at the construction sites" (Zverev, *Planovoe khoziaistvo*, No. 2, 1949, p. 44).

"The high cost of construction" is also the result of "an unjustified increase in the quantity and power of the technological and auxiliary equipment of the enterprises" (Zverev, *O biudzhete na 1950*, p. 14).

"At many construction sites there are sizable stocks of useless equipment which often remains unused. At the construction sites of the Moscow-Kursk Railroad there is a large amount of equipment without precise destination and without a set schedule for its use. A sizable amount of unused equipment also exists at the construction sites of the Ministry of Electric Power Stations" (*O biudzhete na 1951*, pp. 18–19).

" The accumulation of stocks in excess of the value plan is often the result of irregular production and of serious defects in the organization of materials and equipment supply of several ministries. Thus, at the Mytishchin Machine-Building Plant of the Ministry of the Motor Vehicle and Tractor Industry, on the average for 1951, production was as follows: 18.0 per cent during the first ten days of the month, 27.1 per cent during the second ten days, and 54.9 per cent during the last ten days. Irregular work was responsible for numerous labor stoppages, a low coefficient of utilization of equipment, and the accumulation of sizable stocks in excess of the norms, the volume of which amounted to more than 11 million rubles on January 1, 1952" (*Pravda*, March 7, 1952, p. 3).

64. "The ministries, construction organizations, and long-term investment banks should intensify their efforts to reduce sharply expenditures on materials and administrative expenses in construction" (Zverev, *Planovoe khoziaistvo*, No. 2, 1949, p. 45).

"The main reasons for the increase in costs of construction work lie . . . in expenditures in excess of estimate costs planned for buying materials and in excessive expenses" (*Pravda*, March 11, 1949, p. 3).

"The increase in construction costs is influenced by the sizable expenditures for delivery of construction materials, resulting from the excessive distances they are transported, and also by superfluous overhead, administrative, and management expenses" (Zverev, *O biudzhete na 1950*, p. 14).

"A reduction in construction costs can be obtained largely through the more economical utilization of materials. The government is taking measures to set up highly mechanized enterprises which are

Plans for wages and administrative expenses are exceeded.[65] Finally, there is inadequate bank control over committed expenditures.[66]

Examination of the causes for cost overruns in construction leads to some observations about the Stalinist system. First, these are permanent causes, inherent in the system of Stalinist planning. The constant repetition of the same causes (the examples cited above could be multiplied and presented as a separate booklet) clearly shows that these are not accidents of the economic system. Second, in all cases, the government holds the executors responsible and imposes more and more strict controls. Third, if, despite these strict controls, the same thing happens year after year, the government must grant exceptions along the way, exceptions that become so common that they make the rule. In fact, the central authorities are obliged to make an exception when their orders cannot be carried out. This means that the very principle of administrative and authoritarian centralized planning is compromised. Superficial rigidity with

---

to supply construction agencies with materials and prefabricated components" (*O biudzhete na 1951*, p. 18).

"Some agencies use more construction materials than allowed by the norms. . . . In the second sector of Trust No. 5 of the Ministry for the Construction of Machine-Building Enterprises, the norms set in the estimate costs for the utilization of materials during nine months of 1951 were exceeded as follows: by 23 per cent for lumber, by 32 per cent for steel sheets, by 53 per cent for lime . . ." (other examples follow) (*Pravda*, March 7, 1952, p. 3).

65. "Instead of lowering construction costs, the management of Voronezh construction and assembly work under the Ministry of the Chemical Industry allowed them to increase, which resulted in a deficit of 82 kopeks per ruble of work done. This deficit was the result of excessive expenditures from the wage fund, materials and other unproductive expenses" (*Pravda*, March 11, 1949, p. 3).

A 3 per cent reduction in construction costs and an 11 per cent increase in labor productivity were to be obtained "by improving the organization of construction and assembly work, utilizing machinery better, and reducing expenditures for materials and administrative and management expenses" (*O biudzhete na 1951*, p. 19).

"The construction organizations did not do the necessary to reduce administrative expenditures. These expenditures were excessive in the construction organizations of the Ministries of Transportation, the Inland Waterway Fleet, Shipbuilding, Transport Machine-Building, and Machine and Instrument-Building. One of the main reasons for these high administrative expenditures lay in the inflation of the administrative and management staff" (Zverev, *Planovoe khoziaistvo*, No. 4, 1950, p. 17). See also footnote 64 above.

66. "The financial agencies, particularly the long-term investment banks which finance construction, should tighten their control over execution of the investment plan and the plan for cost reduction" (Zverev, *O biudzhete na 1950*, p. 15).

"The long-term investment banks still do an inadequate job of enforcing the financial discipline of projects and estimate costs on construction sites, utilizing materials and financial resources economically, and mobilizing internal resources on the sites. The work of the long-term investment banks must be improved and their control over the fulfillment of the goal to reduce construction costs must be tightened" (*O biudzhete na 1951*, p. 19).

"The long-term investment banks, which are required to supervise regularly the fulfillment of the goals to reduce construction costs, do not always perform this duty. For example, the Azerbaidzhan, Uzbekistan, Riazan, and Vinnitsa offices of the Industrial Bank (*Prombank*) did not supervise, as necessary, the utilization of materials and the wage fund; their checking of the documentation of projects and estimate costs of construction sites was inadequate, and they did not make sufficient efforts to tighten the financial and accounting discipline on the construction sites. The long-term investment banks should improve their work and establish strict control over every ruble spent in the process of construction" (*Pravda*, March 7, 1952, p. 3).

"It has to be pointed out that there are serious defects in the operation of the *Prombank*. Many of the agencies of this bank still exercise inadequate supervision over the fulfillment of the goals for reduction of construction costs, do not make the necessary efforts to mobilize internal resources, and do not demand strict observance of construction project and estimate costs" (*O biudzhete na 1953*, p. 18).

frequent exceptions introduces an element of spontaneity into the system and gives the real power to the agencies entitled by law or by fact to revise the plan. Fourth, by law and even more in fact, some degree of enterprise autonomy exists. Higher authorities often accuse enterprises of noneconomic behavior, but their criticisms seem based on a confusion between macroeconomic and microeconomic views. Stockpiling may seem irrational from a macroeconomic viewpoint. But, for the enterprise, it is a guarantee against shortcomings in the supply system, a measure of self-defense, and a guarantee of fulfilling its plan. The "taut" plan thus introduces a conflict between fulfillment of the plan at the microeconomic and at the macroeconomic level. Finally, the tendency to exceed norms and plans for wages also seems "noneconomic" from the macroeconomic viewpoint. But it is again the plan (primarily for gross production) that, with its arbitrary success criteria, gives rise to excessive consumption of materials. To the extent that the production plan is more important to the enterprise than the plan for costs, exceeding the wage plan is the lesser evil. That this is tolerated is clear since wage payments are strictly controlled by the State Bank.

In conclusion, the two disrupting factors discussed here—the dispersion of resources and unplanned increases in costs—appear to be inherent in the administrative and authoritarian planning system of the Stalinist type. It could even be said that this system simultaneously experiences disturbance by *demand* (dispersion of resources among too many construction projects, authorized by the initial or revised plan) and disturbance by *costs*. There is a clear similarity to inflation-causing factors in market systems if the disturbances are seen in real terms, but the role of money and prices as agents transmitting disturbances is eliminated or considerably reduced in the Stalinist command system.

To the extent that disturbances originate in the investment sector, they are propagated through the rest of the economy in two ways: by appropriation of resources needed for production, and by delays in putting new production facilities into service. The direct appropriation of resources needed for production is practically impossible to estimate for 1946–1952 from the available data. Information on failure to fulfill plans for fixed capital installation is, on the other hand, plentiful.

Fixed Capital Installation

A first approach to the problem may be attempted by comparing investment expenditures with the value of capital put into service. Table 109 contains all the data on the various five-year plan periods given in official Soviet sources. It is clear from Table 109 that the time lag between installation of fixed capital and investment made is a permanent feature of Stalinist planning. (The favorable results for the First Five-Year Plan could come from the completion of investment begun before the five-year plan period.)

Curiously enough, performance in fixed capital installation was better in the collective farm and private sector than in the state sector. The lack of separate data for collective farms is unfortunate since such data would have made it easier to draw conclusions for the private, collective farm, and state sectors

Table 109 Investment in and Installation of Fixed Capital during the First Five Five-Year Plans, 1928–1955 (billion rubles; estimate prices of January 1, 1969)

	Total			State and Cooperative			Collective Farm and Private		
	Investment (1)	Installation (2)	Per Cent (3)	Investment (4)	Installation (5)	Per Cent (6)	Investment (7)	Installation (8)	Per Cent (9)
First Five-Year Plan (Oct. 1, 1928– Dec. 31, 1932)	8.8	9.4	106.8	8.0	8.6	107.5	0.8	0.8	100
Second Five-Year Plan (1933–1937)	19.9	17.4	87.4	18.1	15.7	86.7	1.8	1.7	94.4
Third Five-Year Plan (Jan. 1, 1938– June 30, 1941)	20.6	18.6	90.3	17.8	16.0	89.9	2.8	2.6	92.9
July 1, 1941– Dec. 31, 1945	20.8	19.1	91.8	17.3	15.8	91.3	3.5	3.3	94.3
Fourth Five-Year Plan (1946–1950)	48.1	42.8	89.0	40.5	35.3	87.2	7.6	7.5	98.7
Fifth Five-Year Plan (1951–1955)	91.1	81.1	89.0	77.8	68.3	87.8	13.3	12.8	96.2

Source: Cols. 1, 4, and 7: *Narodnoe khoziaistvo, 1970*, p. 478 (for col. 7, sum of investments by collective farms and by the population for private construction); cols. 2 and 5: *ibid.*, p. 471; col. 3: col. 2 as per cent of col. 1; col. 6: col. 5 as per cent of col. 4; col. 8: col. 2 minus col. 5; and col. 9: col. 8 as per cent of col. 7.

separately. In any case, despite its marginal nature and low priority, the collective farm and private sector carried out its plans better than the state sector.

The continuing delays in fixed capital installation raise the question of the accumulation of construction in progress. This seems to have increased considerably during the Fourth Five-Year Plan and in 1951–1953, as can be seen from Table 110.

According to Jasny,[67] the share of equipment in investment is a good indicator of the completion of investments, because buildings are constructed first and then machinery is installed. This share increased from 26 to 30 per cent between 1946 and 1947, reached 34 per cent in 1950, and decreased in 1951–1953 (30 per cent in 1951, 28 per cent in 1952, and 29 per cent in 1953).[68] These figures are confirmed by data on the increase in unfinished construction during this period.

Nevertheless, an increase or decrease in the amount of unfinished construction is not in itself an indication of plan tautness. Two problems arise in this connection. First, fixed capital installation is planned in the same way as investment, so tensions can result only from the poor fulfillment of plans in this area (on condition that the plans themselves are balanced). Second, the planner can take into account the eventual failure to fulfill the plan for putting investments into operation. In that case, disturbances would occur only beyond a certain threshold or a certain degree of nonfulfillment of the plan.

The information that was available on plans for fixed capital installation

67. Jasny, *Soviet Industrialization*, pp. 305–6.
68. *Narodnoe khoziaistvo, 1956*, p. 174.

Table 110   Unfinished Construction in State and Cooperative Enterprises, 1950–1953 (end of year, actual construction costs)

	Billion Rubles	As Percentage of Total Annual Capital Investment
1950	8.7	85
1951	10.2	91
1952	11.7	95
1953	12.9	100.8

Source: *Narodnoe khoziaistvo SSSR v 1963 godu* [The USSR National Economy in 1963], Moscow, 1965, p. 460.

during 1948–1953 applied only to the first of these two problems. Failure to fulfill the plans for installation was mentioned for nearly every year, but actual figures were not given.

The 1948 plan, for instance, anticipated the concentration of resources on the most important equipment and workshops, facilities that were to be put into operation in 1948 and to yield additional production that very year. This goal was to be realized "at any cost."[69] But the results in 1948 were not satisfactory, and "the construction of a large number of projects that were to have been put into operation in 1948 was not entirely finished on schedule."[70]

For 1949, too, Minister Zverev prescribed "the intensification of the struggle for a greater concentration of material and financial resources on projects already under way."[71] Once again the results were unsatisfactory, even though the investment plan was better fulfilled in 1949.[72]

Also in 1950, the planners predicted "a considerable increase in fixed capital put into service thanks to the concentration of labor, material, and financial resources primarily on the most important facilities already started, that can be put into operation during the current year."[73] In 1951 certain accomplishments were reported in this area for 1950, but the absolute necessity of putting planned fixed capital into service was still stressed.[74] It is interesting to note that "a reduction in the investment cycle" was pointed out at the time the 1952 budget

69. Korobov, *Planovoe khoziaistvo*, No. 3, 1948, p. 17. See also pp. 427–28 above.

70. Zverev, *Planovoe khoziaistvo*, No. 2, 1949, p. 44. See also footnote 54 above.

71. *Ibid.*, p. 45.

72. "In several ministries, the installation of fixed capital was found to lag behind investment. Thus, although the Ministry for the Construction of Machine-Building Enterprises and the contract construction agencies of the Ministry of the Coal Industry fulfilled last year's investment plan, they did not completely fulfill the installation plan. This can be explained largely by the dispersion of material and financial resources among numerous construction projects instead of concentrating these resources primarily on already started projects. Such a dispersion of material and financial resources extended the construction cycle, increased the amount of unfinished construction, and increased the cost of construction work, as a result of which some organizations did not fulfill the goals for the reduction of construction costs" (Zverev, *O biudzhete na 1950*, p. 13).

73. Zverev, *Planovoe khoziaistvo*, No. 4, 1950, p. 17.

74. These accomplishments were formulated very vaguely. Mostly, the reports stressed the success of the measures taken on July 1, 1950, to reduce construction costs by an average of 25 per cent. See Zverev, *O biudzhete na 1950*, p. 14, and *O biudzhete na 1951*, pp. 17–19.

was presented by Minister Zverev,[75] whereas Table 110 shows an increase in the share of unfinished construction in total investment. In any case, Zverev announced a new appeal for strict adherence to the government's schedule for putting current investments into service.[76] But in 1952 these provisions again were not followed: "In order to guarantee the fulfillment of construction plans for 1953, we must eliminate serious shortcomings in the organization of construction which lead to considerable cost increases and delays in completion of construction work."[77]

Fulfillment of Fourth Five-Year Plan Investment Goals

The official announcement (Table 96) that the 1946–1950 five-year plan for centralized investment had been exceeded requires additional details. The estimates are in constant prices and it may therefore be assumed (if constant prices were correctly calculated) that the total volume of expenditures on centralized investment was higher than planned. At the same time it must not be forgotten that, besides centralized investments, there were decentralized investments, with plan fulfillment of 116.1 per cent, and collective farm investments, with plan fulfillment of 76.6 per cent (see Table 96), a particularly low percentage. On the other hand, much more was spent on capital repairs, which had a plan fulfillment of 163.8 per cent.

It should be noted that the degree of plan fulfillment was uneven within the centralized sector itself. In industry, for which the over-all plan seems to have been 100 per cent fulfilled, above-plan investments may be observed, mainly for certain priority sectors. For example, in the coal industry, twice as much as the planned goal was spent. Expenditures in other sectors, such as ferrous metals and electric power stations, must also have exceeded the investment plan. Hence it can be concluded that other sectors, such as light and food industries, must have had their allocations reduced.

If actual real investments exceed planned investments, it should be possible to obtain a corresponding excess of fixed capital installation over planned levels. The real goal is not the expenditure but the resulting increase in production capacities. But it can be seen from Table 96 that fulfillment of these plans was particularly poor. The results for putting rolling mills into operation (47.9 per cent of plan), for steel mills (54.9 per cent), for construction of new railroad track (32.1 per cent), and for the electrification of railroads (18.3 per cent) were particularly unsatisfactory. The highest known fulfillment—that for putting hydroelectric stations into operation—was only 87.0 per cent, and it must have been influenced by the vast plan for electric power station construction launched by Stalin toward the end of the 1940's.

The comparison of the percentages of fulfillment of the investment plan for expenditures and results (installation) shows a low efficiency of investment according to the criteria accepted by the Soviet planners themselves. The impres-

---

75. *Pravda*, March 7, 1952, p. 3.
76. *Ibid.*
77. *O biudzhete na 1953*, pp. 17–18.

sion is gained that the five-year plan represented a program of large-scale works set up in physical terms, with monetary estimates being purely secondary. The Stalinist planners seem to have measured efficiency not in terms of comparing costs and results but as real growth in production capacities relative to previous years and to results obtained in Western countries.

But do these results, measuring the relation between planned costs in the five-year plan and the installation of fixed capital, really provide information on the expenditures anticipated during the five-year period? In actual fact, the annual investment plans appear to have been very poorly fulfilled, especially during 1946–1948 (see Table 98). Exceeding the expenditures anticipated in the five-year plan, then, could have been obtained only through a considerable increase in the goals for the annual slices of the five-year plan.

Hence it looks as if the Soviet planners very quickly realized how unrealistic the financial provisions of the five-year plan for investment were and provided much larger sums in the annual plans. But these larger sums could not be released, particularly during 1946–1948. Did they at the same time cut back the original plans for fixed capital installation in order to make the annual plans more realistic? It is impossible to answer this question from the information available. Such reductions seem likely, but the constant failure to fulfill the annual plans for installation of fixed capital makes it appear that these reductions were not large enough.

On the whole, inflationary pressures during this period seem to have resulted more from the five-year plan for investment than from the annual plans. By basing the investment cycle on data in physical terms, poorly related to estimate cost and financial calculations, the five-year plan set off a chain reaction propagated through the dispersion of resources (due to unfinished projects) and through increases in planned costs, which entailed a complete revision of Stalin's designs.

CHAPTER 18

Equilibrium on the Consumer Goods Market after the War

Equilibrium on Consumer Goods Market at End of War

Accumulation of Liquid Assets by the Population

The reasons for the increase in the liquid assets held by the population during the war have been well explained by N. A. Voznesenskii:

> Money outlays of the urban (non-agricultural) population exceeded incomes by 3.6 billion rubles in 1940, and by 2.2 billion rubles in 1942, which represented a decline in the cash holdings of the urban population. However, while the decline in cash in the cities in 1940 represented also a general decline in currency in circulation, in the war year 1942 money was leaving urban areas for rural areas, increasing the overall amount of currency in circulation in the country. In 1941, as a result of large lump-sum wage and salary payments to workers and employees who were being mobilized for the Soviet Army, and also in 1943, as a result of the rapid growth of the payroll, the increase in urban trade lagged behind the money incomes of the urban population. Because of this, the amount of currency in circulation increased also in cities during the above-mentioned years.
>
> Money incomes of the agricultural population increased greatly in 1942, as against 1940, owing to the rise in retail prices in *kolkhoz* markets, where peasants sell their surpluses of agricultural commodities. Money outlays of the agricultural population also increased in 1942, in comparison with 1940, but to a lesser amount than money incomes. Money incomes of the agricultural population exceeded current outlays, which meant that a part of the money was retained in circulation channels. In rural areas this was taking place during the war year 1943 as well.[1]

In addition, the army had appropriated consumer goods, contributing to the increase in currency in circulation.

During the war a sizable amount of goods went not to the civilian population but to the army, retail trade turnover could not satisfy the existing demand, and money either

1. Nikolai A. Voznesensky, *The Economy of the USSR during World War II* (translated from the Russian), Washington, 1948, p. 81.

remained in hand or passed into the pockets of rural producers or, worse yet, to speculators who profited from the difficult times. In this way or another, money by-passed the state coffers. The normal circulation of currency was disrupted. In order to pay workers' wages on time, to finance military expenditures, etc., the government had to have recourse each time to issuing [money]. A surplus of money appeared.[2]

These factors led to an approximate 2.4-fold increase in currency in circulation during the first three years of the war (see Table 111). It is interesting to note that the increase in currency in circulation during the last year of the war was equal to that of the first three years put together (31 billion rubles). During the whole war period, currency in circulation increased 3.8 times. While this was happening, state and cooperative retail trade (in constant prices) was 32 per cent in 1943 of what it had been in 1940 and 45 per cent in 1945 (see Table 70 in Chapter 15). At the same time, between 1940 and 1945, cash payments by the State Bank for wages increased by 24 per cent.[3] Hence currency in circulation increased much more rapidly than goods available to the population. According to the calculations of USSR Gosplan and the Commissariat of Finance, for every ruble in circulation in 1945, the supply of available goods was less than one-third of what it was in 1940.[4]

Some stabilization of currency in circulation might have been expected after the end of the war. The increase in the supply of goods in retail trade, the moderate increases in wages, and the budget surpluses (3.4 billion rubles in 1945, 17.9 billion in 1946, and 24.7 billion in 1947)[5] should have encouraged a moderate growth of the currency in circulation. In any case, an examination of the money income and expenditures of households in 1940 and 1945 (see Table 112) shows that the increase in wages, salaries, other payments, military pay, pensions, and allowances (39.2 billion rubles) and the decrease in state and cooperative retail trade sales (9.9 billion—that is, a total of 49.1 billion rubles) were more than offset by the increase in direct taxes (39.0 billion rubles) and in savings (15.9 billion). Inflationary pressure was released largely through turn-over (in money terms) on the collective farm market, where purchases and sales increased by nearly 88 billion rubles between 1940 and 1945.

Money incomes and expenditures of households normally were more or less balanced during 1945–1947 (see Tables 113 and 114). However, the estimates in Tables 113 and 114 are tentative, and generous allowance should be made for error, especially for the surplus of income over expenditures (see Table 112, note a). Nevertheless, there seems to be a definite tendency for the liquid assets of the population to be absorbed by making planned household expenditures higher than income (see Table 114). Konnik confirms that this was the practice after 1946.[6] But the plans were not completely fulfilled because of unplanned increases in money wages and employment.

2. A. G. Zverev, *Zapiski Ministra* [Memoirs of a Minister], Moscow, 1973, p. 232.
3. Konnik, *Zakonomernosti*, p. 53.
4. *Shagi*, p. 159.
5. For 1945, see Table 69 in Chapter 15. For 1946 and 1947, see K. N. Plotnikov, *Ocherki istorii biudzheta sovetskogo gosudarstva* [Essays on the History of the Soviet State Budget], Moscow, 1954, p. 377, and *Bolshevik* [The Bolshevik], June 1950.
6. During the first quarter of 1945 cash payments for wages still exceeded income from trade by 172 million rubles, but during the first quarter of 1946 income from trade exceeded cash payments for

Table 111   Estimated Currency in Circulation,[a] 1937–1958 (billion rubles)

1937 (Jan. 1)	10.8
1940 (Jan. 1)	23.0
1941 (Jan. 1)	22
1944 (July 1)	53
1945 (July 1)	84
1947 (Dec. 14)	380
1947 (Dec. 22)	28
1949 (July 1)	30
1958 (annual average)	63

Source

1937: Given as .802 bill. new rubles in bank notes and .280 bill. new rubles in Treasury notes (*Money and Banking 1937/38*, League of Nations, Geneva, 1938, Vol. 2, p. 183, as cited by Raymond Powell, "Monetary Statistics" in *Soviet Economic Statistics*, edited by Vladimir G. Treml and John P. Hardt, Durham, N.C., 1972, pp. 404–6). Converted into old rubles at 1 new ruble = 10 old rubles.

1940: Estimate by Powell (*ibid.*, based on I. I. Konnik, *Dengi v period stroitelstva kommunisticheskogo obshchestva* [Money during the Period of Building a Communist Society], Moscow, 1966, p. 156, and Konnik, *Zakonomernosti vzaimosviazi tovarnogo i denezhnogo obrashcheniia pri sotsializme* [Economic Laws of the Interrelation between the Circulation of Goods and of Money under Socialism], Moscow, 1968, pp. 17, 170n., 187, and 196). In addition to the figure here, there was 1 bill. rubles in coins (see sources above). Converted into old rubles as above.

1941: Based on 1940 figure above and statement by Voznesensky (*Economy*, p. 7) that currency in circulation declined considerably on the eve of the war (assumed arbitrarily to be a decline of 1 bill. rubles). It is useful to have an estimate for the beginning of 1941 to use as a base for further calculations of the increase in currency in circulation during the war.

1945: Based on 1941 figure above and statement (in *Shagi piatiletok: Razvitie ekonomiki SSSR* [Steps of the Five-Year Plans: Development of the USSR Economy], Moscow, 1968, p. 159) that total currency in circulation increased 3.8 times during the war.

1947 (December 14): Based on December 22, 1947, figure below and statement by Konnik (*Dengi*, p. 174, as cited by Powell in *Soviet Economic Statistics*, p. 415n.) that the new currency put into circulation was 13.5 times less than that submitted for conversion.

1947 (December 22): Based on 1941 figure above and statement by Konnik (*Dengi*, p. 174, as cited by Powell in *Soviet Economic Statistics*, p. 415n.) that currency in circulation on December 22, 1947, was 1.27 times the 1940 level.

1949: Based on 1941 figure above and statement by Konnik (*Dengi*, p. 176, as cited by Powell in *Soviet Economic Statistics*, p. 406) that currency in circulation in the middle of 1949 was 1.3 to 1.4 times prewar currency (taken as 1.35).

1958: Based on 1941 figure above and "approximate calculation" by Konnik (*Zakonomernosti*, p. 69, as cited by Powell in *Soviet Economic Statistics*, p. 406) that currency in circulation in 1958 was 286 per cent of that in 1940.

a. Notes of the State Bank and the Treasury.

Table 111 shows, based on information provided by Konnik, a sizable increase (4.5 times) in currency in circulation in the two and a half years from July 1945 to December 1947. Raymond Powell considers such an increase impossible; he believes that the percentages cited by Konnik are inconsistent and that his assertion that the new currency put into circulation was 1/13.5 of that submitted for conversion is not convincing[7] (the official conversion rate was 10 to 1, but special rates were used—see below).

---

wages by 655 million rubles, during the first quarter of 1947 by 1.56 billion rubles, during the first quarter of 1948 by 755 million rubles, and during the first quarter of 1949 by 1.33 billion rubles. During the first quarter of 1950, the plan for collection of income from trade by the treasury of the State Bank was exceeded by 1.3 per cent. (Konnik, *Zakonomernosti*, p. 53.) Konnik gives the figures in new rubles (1 new ruble = 10 old rubles).

7. Powell in *Soviet Economic Statistics*, p. 415 and n. 23 on that page.

Table 112   Comparison of Money Incomes and Expenditures of Households in 1940 and 1945 (billion rubles)

	1940	1945	Increase or Decrease
Income			
Wages and salaries	123.7	142.2	+ 18.5
Other payments and military pay	38.3	42.6 [a]	+ 4.3
Income of cooperative artisans and other money income	20.6	19.1	− 1.5
Money payments to collective farmers for *trudodni*	11.3	6.8	− 4.5
Income from sale of farm products to state procurement agencies	5.0	1.6	− 3.4
Income from sale of farm products to collective farm market	25.6	120.0	+ 94.4
Pensions and allowances	7.3	23.7	+ 16.4
Stipends and scholarships	2.4	3.1	+ 0.7
Interest on loans and savings	2.8	4.1	+ 1.3
Insurance payments and credits for construction of private houses	.5 [b]	1.5	+ 1.0
Total	237.5	364.7	+ 127.2
Expenditures			
State and cooperative retail trade sales to households	162.0	152.1	− 9.9
Collective farm market sales to households	28.3	115.9	+ 87.6
Housing, services, and tuition payments	21.0	15.5	− 5.5
Trade union, party, and other dues	1.6	2.8	+ 1.2
Direct taxes	12.6	51.6	+ 39.0
Net increase in savings and loans	11.5	27.4	+ 15.9
Total	237.0	365.3	+ 128.3

Source: Unless otherwise indicated, Tables 48, 49, 113, and 114.

a. According to Konnik (*Zakonomernosti*, p. 53), cash payments for wages increased 24 per cent between 1940 and 1945. If this percentage is applied to the total of wages, salaries, other payments, and military pay, it would yield a 1945 total of 200.9 billion rubles instead of 184.8. This would result in a surplus of income over expenditures of 15.6 billion instead of a surplus of expenditures of 0.6 billion.

b. Sum of personal and property insurance payments and credits for construction of private houses (given as 7.3, 195.3, and 346 mill. rubles in *Finansy i sotsialisticheskoe stroitelstvo* [Finance and Socialist Construction], Moscow, 1957, pp. 355–57).

It is difficult to make a definitive judgment about Konnik's estimates. However, it seems impossible to deny *a priori* that there was a sizable increase in currency in circulation between the end of the war and the currency conversion of December 1947. This argument can be supported on several grounds, including some increases that do not appear in the balance of money incomes and expenditures of households estimated in Tables 113 and 114.

First, a large part of the population's money incomes had been frozen during the war, including paid vacations, military pay, certain pensions, and allowances. This money had to be released, an action that entailed lump-sum payments to individuals, rather than new income flows.

Second, substantial government expenditures were required by the two demobilization decrees of June 23 and September 26 (followed later by others). These decrees ordered the demobilization of 13 age groups of military personnel during the second half of 1945 and 2 more groups after January 1, 1946, and the return to civilian life of soldiers and noncommissioned officers who had higher, technical, or agricultural secondary education. These people were to be given clothing, food, traveling expenses, sizable cash compensation, employment within a month, and, in the case of rural people, assistance to set up their farms. Also envisaged were benefits and material assistance for the families of workers and soldiers, the war wounded, and the demobilized. The families of dead soldiers, the war wounded, and the needy families of mobilized men were entitled to loans to build or rebuild their houses. These loans amounted to 5,000 to 10,000 rubles and could be paid off in five to ten years.[8]

Third, in order to justify the currency exchange of December 1947, the Soviet authorities also claimed that the German occupation powers "had issued a large amount of counterfeit Soviet currency."[9]

Finally, between 1944 (the official Soviet estimate of currency in circulation is for "the end of the war," which means May 1945) and 1947 retail trade in current prices increased from 119.3 billion rubles to 330.8 billion[10]—that is, about 2.8 times, which must signify some increase in money wages[11] and in currency in circulation.

The Soviet Union was not the only country in Eastern Europe that saw a sizable increase in currency in circulation after the war. In Poland, currency in circulation increased from 790 million zlotys on December 31, 1945, to 1,802 million in 1946, to 2,744 million at the end of 1947, 3,921 million at the end of 1948, 5,157 million at the end of 1949, and 5,998 million at the end of 1950. After the monetary reform of October 1950 and the currency exchange at the rate of 100 to 1 (deposits in savings banks at the rate of 100 to 3), Polish currency in circulation fell to 5,773 million zlotys at the end of 1951.[12] The reasons for the growth of currency in Poland were similar to those in the Soviet Union. There was an increase in production and in trade, payment of arrears in wages frozen during the war and reparations, and the return of demobilized soldiers. Furthermore, there was speculative trade in war spoils. The increase in prices influenced the amount of money needed for economic transactions. Inflationary pressure was reinforced by the increase of currency in circulation because of the accumulation of cash by speculators.

It is interesting to note that in the Soviet Union, despite the currency exchange, generally at the rate of 10 to 1, it was possible to reduce currency in circulation 13.5-fold (according to Konnik). This might mean that a large amount of the currency could not be exchanged, either because of losses or because the holders of large sums did not dare exchange them for fear of the sanctions that

8. *Cahiers de l'Economie Soviétique*, No. 2, 1945, p. 27.

9. A. V. Liubimov, *Torgovlia i snabzhenie v gody velikoi otechestvennoi voiny* [Trade and Supply during the Great Patriotic War], Moscow, 1968, p. 159.

10. *Sovetskaia torgovlia* [Soviet Trade], Moscow, 1956, p. 20.

11. According to Konnik (*Zakonomernosti*, pp. 52–53), cash payments for wages from the treasury of the State Bank in 1945 were 24 per cent higher than in 1940 and in 1947, 73 per cent higher. Thus the increase between 1945 and 1947 was 39.5 per cent. Obviously, it is necessary to know the change in the velocity of circulation, but Konnik's estimates on this point are not very clear. On this subject, see Powell in *Soviet Economic Statistics*, p. 415.

12. The total issuance of currency in Poland was 10,381 million zlotys on June 30, 1945, 26,319 million on December 31, 1945, and 60,066 million on December 31, 1946.

I would like to thank Wilhelm Jampel, the former director general of the Polish Ministry of Domestic Trade (from 1948 to 1968), for having been kind enough to provide me with these figures and to explain the reasons for the considerable increase in currency circulation in Poland after the war.

Table 113   Money Incomes of Households, 1945–1953 (billion pre-1961 rubles)

	1945		1946		1947		1948	
	Planned (1)	Actual (2)	Planned (3)	Actual (4)	Planned (5)	Actual (6)	Planned (7)	Actual (8)
1. Wages and salaries	138.4	142.2	160.3	174.4	212.9	219.3	241.5	247.9
2. Other payments	28.5	29.2	32.7	35.8	39.8	44.2	42.8	44.0
3. Income of cooperative artisans	4.8	4.9	5.5	5.8	6.8	6.9	7.9	7.9
4. Money payments to collective farmers for *trudodni*	(6.8)	6.8	(6.6)	6.6	(7.0)	7.0	(7.5)	7.5
5. Income from sale of farm products to state procurement agencies	(1.6)	1.6	(1.2)	1.2	(2.0)	2.0	(2.4)	2.4
6. Income from sale of farm products on collective farm market	(120.0)	120.0	(145.0)	145.0	(150.7)	150.7	(49.6)	49.6
7. Military pay	(13.4)	13.4	(14.5)	14.5	(10.5)	10.5	(10.2)	10.2
8. Pensions and allowances	23.0	23.7	26.1	26.4	32.5	32.9	32.8	26.8
9. Stipends and scholarships	(3.1)	3.1	(3.7)	3.7	(3.9)	3.9	(4.1)	4.1
10. Interest on loans and savings	4.2	4.1	6.7	6.8	7.3	7.4	(1.8)	1.8
11. Other money income	13.8	14.2	16.0	17.4	21.3	21.9	24.2	24.8
12. Insurance payments	(0.5)	0.5	(0.5)	0.5	(0.5)	0.5	(0.5)	0.5
13. Credits for construction of private houses	(1.0)	1.0	(1.3)	1.3	(1.1)	1.1	(1.0)	1.0
14. Total money income	359.1	364.7	420.1	439.4	496.3	508.3	426.3	428.5

might be imposed. Hence a reduction of 13.5 times in currency in circulation is not impossible *a priori*.

Price Policy for Consumer Goods

Distribution Channels Inherited from the War / It was mentioned above that there was no diversification of distribution channels during the war to take account of the scarcity of goods and rationing. During 1945–1947 the distribution structure remained unchanged. There were several channels of distribution for rationed products: state sales at high prices in the so-called "commercial" stores and sales on the open market, the collective farm market, commission trade, and "bazaars." Sales in these channels of distribution can be evaluated in constant prices (for example, in 1940 prices) or in current prices. Table 115 shows the change in the shares of rationed sales, "commercial" sales, and collective farm market sales in total state and cooperative retail trade in current prices.[13] In this table, the very large share of trade at high, open-market prices in the total turn-

On the Polish inflation after World War II, see also Henri Wronski, *Le rôle économique et social de la monnaie dans les Démocraties Populaires. La réforme monétaire polonaise*, Paris, 1954.

13. It would also be possible to calculate, with the help of the indexes of retail prices given in Table 118 below, the share of various channels of distribution in constant prices.

1949		1950		1951		1952		1953		Line
Planned (9)	Actual (10)	Planned (11)	Actual (12)	Planned (13)	Actual (14)	Planned (15)	Actual (16)	Planned (17)	Actual (18)	No.
261.2	268.7	290.9	298.3	319.7	321.9	334.4	340.4	349.2	356.1	1
43.3	44.4	46.3	47.4	48.8	49.1	49.0	49.8	48.5	49.4	2
8.1	8.2	8.3	8.4	9.2	9.3	9.4	9.5	9.5	9.6	3
(9.3)	9.3	(11.8)	11.8	(12.9)	12.9	(13.4)	13.4	(18.4)	18.4	4
(2.6)	2.6	(2.6)	2.6	(2.6)	2.6	(2.5)	2.5	(6.6)	6.6	5
(40.1)	40.1	(43.3)	43.3	(43.2)	43.2	(45.6)	45.6	(41.5)	41.5	6
(10.5)	10.5	(15.0)	15.0	(19.0)	19.0	(23.2)	23.2	(23.6)	23.6	7
32.1	33.2	35.0	34.5	35.9	35.9	37.7	37.6	38.4	38.9	8
(4.4)	4.4	(4.5)	4.5	(4.9)	4.9	(5.2)	5.2	(5.7)	5.7	9
3.0	3.0	4.1	4.3	5.7	5.6	7.8	7.6	10.8	10.7	10
26.1	26.9	29.1	29.8	31.5	32.2	33.4	34.0	34.9	35.6	11
(0.4)	0.4	(0.4)	0.4	(0.4)	0.4	(0.4)	0.4	0.4	0.4	12
(0.8)	0.8	(0.6)	0.6	0.6	0.6	(0.6)	0.6	(0.8)	0.8	13
441.9	452.5	491.9	500.9	534.4	537.6	562.6	569.8	588.3	597.3	14

Note: Figures in parentheses are estimates based on the assumption, for lack of any other data, that planned income was the same as actual income in a given year.

Source

LINE 1: Table C-1, line 3.
LINE 2: Table C-1, line 13.
LINE 3: Table C-4, col. 3.
LINE 4: Table C-3, line 6.
LINE 5: Table C-3, line 8.
LINE 6: Table C-3, line 14.
LINE 7: Table C-1, line 7.
LINE 8: Table C-6, col. 6.
LINE 9: Table C-7, col. 5.
LINE 10: Table C-8, col. 6.
LINE 11: Based on total wages and salaries (line 1) and share of other money income in that total (assumed to be 10 per cent). See Abram Bergson and Hans Heymann, Jr., *Soviet National Income and Product, 1940–48*, New York, 1954, p. 131. O. Hoeffding and N. Nimitz ("Soviet National Income and Product, 1949–1955," RAND Research Memorandum 2101, Santa Monica, 1959, p. 66) use a rough figure of 25 bill. rubles for 1949–1955.
LINE 12–Cols. 2, 6, and 8: Assumed to be same as in 1946 (col. 4). **Col. 4:** Sum of personal and property insurance (given as 45.8 and 410.1 mill. rubles in *Finansy*, pp. 355–56). **Cols. 10, 14, 16, and 18:** Assumed to be same as in 1950 (col. 12). **Col. 12:** Sum of personal and property insurance (given as 62.5 and 354.8 mill. rubles in *Finansy*, pp. 355–56).
LINE 13–Col. 2: Interpolated between 1940 (given as 346 mill. rubles in *ibid.*, p. 357) and 1946 (col. 4). **Cols. 4 and 12:** *Ibid.* There is no way of ascertaining whether these sums were paid entirely in cash. **Cols. 6, 8, and 10:** Interpolated between 1946 (col. 4) and 1950 (col. 12). **Cols. 14, 16, and 18:** Interpolated between 1950 (col. 12) and 1955 (given as 1,016 mill. rubles in *Finansy*, p. 357).
LINE 14: Sum of lines 1–13.

Table 114 Money Expenditures of Households, 1945–1953 (billion pre-1961 rubles)

	1945		1946		1947		1948	
	Planned (1)	Actual (2)	Planned (3)	Actual (4)	Planned (5)	Actual (6)	Planned (7)	Actual (8)
1. State and cooperative retail trade sales to households	146.0	152.1	240.5	228.7	300.3	306.0	319.1	286.9
2. Collective farm market sales to households	(115.9)	115.9	(140.1)	140.1	(145.6)	145.6	(40.5)	40.5
3. Housing	(2.9)	2.9	(3.1)	3.1	(3.2)	3.2	(3.3)	3.3
4. Services	11.7	12.2	19.2	18.3	24.0	24.5	25.5	23.0
5. Tuition payments	(0.4)	0.4	(0.5)	0.5	(0.6)	0.6	(0.6)	0.6
6. Trade union dues	0.9	0.9	1.0	1.1	1.5	1.6	1.6	1.7
7. Party dues	(1.4)	1.4	(1.5)	1.5	(1.8)	1.8	(1.9)	1.9
8. Other dues	(0.5)	0.5	(0.5)	0.5	(0.5)	0.5	(1.0)	1.0
9. Direct taxes	57.1	51.6	34.5	33.8	37.2	38.3	39.8	41.8
10. Net increase in savings and loans	29.6	27.4	24.1	23.3	21.0	24.5	22.1	22.9
11. Total money expenditures	366.4	365.3	465.0	450.9	537.7	546.6	455.4	423.6
12. Surplus of income over expenditures	−7.3	−0.6	−44.9	−11.5	−39.4	−38.3	−29.1	+4.9
13. Total money income	359.1	364.7	420.1	439.4	496.3	508.3	426.3	428.5

over of retail trade is striking. This share was 51.6 per cent in 1945, 60.4 per cent in 1946, and 51.2 per cent in 1947 (Table 115, lines 2 plus 4). This shows the importance of currency held by individuals and testifies to the extent of the disequilibrium. High collective farm market prices led to large incomes for sellers, who then engaged in arbitrage between the official and collective farm markets as well as hoarding cash. The importance of the collective farm market in retail trade, which grew rapidly during the war,[14] continued afterward until the monetary reform of December 1947 (see Table 115).

Sales in "commercial" stores continued after the war. These stores were closed down only in 1947, at the time rationing was abolished.[15] Nevertheless, the number of *Orsy* fell but little between 1945 and 1954, dropping from 7,720 on August 1, 1945, to 7,582 in 1954.[16] Their turnover seems not to have decreased significantly. In 1945, 30 per cent of state and cooperative retail trade was conducted through 7,720 *Orsy* and *Prodsnaby*;[17] as late as 1956 this percentage

14. See p. 334 in Chapter 15.
15. E. Ia. Linetskii, A. F. Lelekov, and F. M. Sokolov, *Ekonomika i planirovanie sovetskoi torgovli* [Economics and Planning of Soviet Trade], Moscow, 1962, p. 42.
16. Liubimov, *Torgovlia*, p. 62; and D. V. Pavlov, *Sovetskaia torgovlia v sovremennykh usloviiakh* [Soviet Trade in Present-Day Conditions], Moscow, 1965, p. 42.
17. See p. 332 in Chapter 15, and B. I. Gogol, *Ekonomika sovetskoi torgovli* [Economics of Soviet Trade], Moscow, 1960, p. 42.

1949 Planned (9)	Actual (10)	1950 Planned (11)	Actual (12)	1951 Planned (13)	Actual (14)	1952 Planned (15)	Actual (16)	1953 Planned (17)	Actual (18)	Line No.
331.2	310.0	337.0	332.6	346.8	351.3	384.5	364.1	393.3	398.4	1
(42.2)	42.2	(46.7)	46.7	(48.3)	48.3	(51.0)	51.0	(46.4)	46.4	2
(3.5)	3.5	(3.7)	3.7	(3.9)	3.9	(4.0)	4.0	(4.2)	4.2	3
44.7	41.9	45.5	44.9	43.4	43.9	48.1	45.5	49.2	49.8	4
(0.7)	0.7	(0.7)	0.7	(0.8)	0.8	(0.8)	0.8	(0.9)	0.9	5
2.1	2.1	2.4	2.5	2.8	2.8	3.3	3.1	3.1	3.2	6
(1.9)	1.9	(1.9)	1.9	(1.9)	1.9	(1.9)	1.9	(1.9)	1.9	7
(1.0)	1.0	(1.0)	1.0	(1.0)	1.0	(1.5)	1.5	(1.5)	1.5	8
46.2	43.4	46.5	46.9	54.0	53.5	58.5	58.5	57.4	57.4	9
22.2	26.7	31.1	30.3	32.8	36.4	42.1	40.3	28.0	30.0	10
495.7	473.4	516.5	510.2	535.7	543.8	595.7	570.7	585.9	593.7	11
−53.8	−20.9	−24.6	−9.3	−1.3	−6.2	−33.1	−0.9	+2.4	+3.6	12
441.9	452.5	491.9	500.9	534.4	537.6	562.6	569.8	588.3	597.3	13

Note: Figures in parentheses are estimates based on assumption, for lack of any other data, that planned expenditures were the same as actual expenditures in a given year.

Source

LINE 1: Table C-9, col. 3.
LINE 2: Table C-10, col. 3.
LINE 3: Table C-11, col. 6.
LINE 4: Table C-12, col. 3.
LINE 5–Cols. 2, 4, and 6: Extrapolated from 1948 (col. 8). Col. 8: Bergson and Heymann, *Soviet National Income*, p. 158. Cols. 10, 12, 14, 16, and 18: Hoeffding and Nimitz, "Soviet National Income," p. 103.
LINE 6: Table C-13, col. 3.
LINE 7–Cols. 2, 4, 6, and 8: Extrapolated from 1949 on the basis of average annual wage (see Tables A-4 and A-5). Cols. 10, 12, 14, 16, and 18: Hoeffding and Nimitz, "Soviet National Income," pp. 103–4.
LINE 8–Cols. 2, 4, 6, 8, 10, 12, 14, 16, and 18: Arbitrarily estimated from 1956 dues (given as 1.5 bill. rubles in Nancy Nimitz, "Soviet National Income and Product, 1956–1958," RAND Research Memorandum 3112–PR, Santa Monica, 1962, pp. 57–58). These are said to cover dues to the Young Communist League, DOSAAF (for paramilitary training), and various sports and recreational clubs.
LINE 9: Table C-14, col. 8.
LINE 10: Table C-15, col. 3.
LINE 11: Sum of lines 1–10.
LINE 12: Line 13 minus line 11.
LINE 13: Table 113, line 14.

was still 29, even though the number of *Orsy* and *Prodsnaby* had fallen to 2,011 on January 1, 1957.[18]

Sales in canteens and restaurants (public eating places) increased in value between 1945 and 1947 and decreased in 1948 (see Table 116). The increase in the total number of public eating places after the war, however, was caused by the increase in the number of refreshment stands and bars. The number of canteens and restaurants decreased steadily until 1949 and then increased slightly in 1952–1954. At the same time the number of meals served declined considerably until 1950.

In actual fact, the prices of meals and food served in public eating places increased. An instruction was issued in 1943 providing for surcharges according to category of enterprise (there were three categories, with increases ranging up to 100 per cent from the first to the third category) and the kind of meal. In addition, surcharges were provided for sales without ration coupons. For meals or food served at refreshment stands, there was a mark-up of 200 per cent of the cost of the raw materials. Bread was sold according to the "commercial" sales system.[19]

The number of restaurants and refreshment stands selling at "commercial" prices, which was very small at the end of the war (107 restaurants and 270 refreshment stands on July 1, 1945),[20] rose considerably in 1946. The plan was to

18. *Ekonomika sovetskoi torgovli* [Economics of Soviet Trade], Moscow, 1958, p. 47. (On the *Orsy* and *Prodsnaby* see p. 332 in Chapter 15.) The *Orsy* were trading agencies granted accounting autonomy (*khozraschet*) that operated with the rights of autonomous sections of enterprises (factories, construction sites, railroads, etc.). They were managed by administrations (*Upravleniia Rabochego Snabzheniia*, abbreviated as *Ursy* or *Glavursy*). *Prodsnaby* were trading agencies serving certain branches of industry (such as nonferrous metals) that were located in remote areas. These were centralized organizations whose branches, unlike *Orsy*, were not part of the enterprises which they served and came under the sole jurisdiction of their own superior agencies. (*Ibid.*, pp. 46–47). Besides the *Orsy* and *Prodsnaby*, sales were made to special customers in "firm" stores (stores belonging to firms) of an industry (the food industry, the meat and dairy industry, the fish industry, the electrical industry, etc.) and to organizations, such as the "Dynamo" sports association. *Orsy*, *Prodsnaby*, and other "firm" stores were put under the general control of the Ministry of Trade in 1947, but the actual management remained the same as before. The statistical data on their turnover, compared with the prewar and wartime setups, are not precise because it is not clear whether they include the "firm" stores. Gogol (*Ekonomika*, p. 45) provides a little more precise information, putting the share of the *Orsy* and *Prodsnaby* in the total turnover of state and cooperative retail trade at 7.7 per cent in 1940, 19.4 per cent in 1950, and 19.2 per cent in 1959 and the share of "other trading agencies" at 11.9 per cent in 1940, 7.4 per cent in 1950, and 3.4 per cent in 1959. In 1955, according to *Sovetskaia torgovlia*, 1956 (p. 36), the share of different trade channels in total retail trade was as follows (in per cent):

State trade	68.2
Ministry of Trade	46.6
Glavursy of ministries	17.8
Specialized retail network of ministries	2.1
Procurement organizations	0.2
Other organizations	11.5
Cooperative trade	31.8
Tsentrosoiuz	29.8
Producer cooperatives	2.0

19. V. M. Roizman, *Tseny v obshchestvennom pitanii* [Prices in Public Catering], Moscow, 1965, pp. 14–16.

20. G. I. Basovskaia *et al.*, *Ekonomika torgovli* [Economics of Trade], Moscow, 1966, p. 63.

Table 115   Distribution of Retail Trade, 1945–1947 (current prices)

	1945		1946		1947	
	Billion Rubles (1)	Per Cent (2)	Billion Rubles (3)	Per Cent (4)	Billion Rubles (5)	Per Cent (6)
1. State and cooperative trade in fixed prices	143.6	48.4	181.2	39.6	244.8	48.8
2. State and cooperative trade in open-market prices ("commercial" sales)	16.5	5.6	66.0	14.4	86.0	17.1
3. Total state and cooperative trade	160.1	54.0	247.2	54.0	330.8	65.9
4. Collective farm trade	136.4	46.0	210.6	46.0	171.3	34.1
5. Total retail trade turnover	296.5	100.0	457.8	100.0	502.1	100.0

Source

LINE 1–Cols. 1, 3, and 5: Line 3 minus line 2. **Cols. 2, 4, and 6:** Calculated from cols. 1, 3, and 5 and total trade (line 5).

LINE 2–Cols. 1 and 3: Liubimov, *Torgovlia*, p. 170. **Cols. 2, 4, and 6:** Calculated from cols. 1, 3, and 5 and total trade (line 5). **Col. 5:** Based on total state and cooperative trade (line 3) and percentage that trade in flexible prices was of total (given as 26 per cent by D. V. Pavlov, "Razvitie torgovli za gody sovetskoi vlasti" [Development of Trade during the Years of the Soviet Regime], in *40 let sovetskoi torgovli* [Forty Years of Soviet Trade], Moscow, 1957, p. 9).

LINE 3–Cols. 1, 3, and 5: *Sovetskaia torgovlia*, 1956, p. 20. **Cols. 2 and 4:** Line 5 minus line 4. **Col. 6:** Calculated from col. 5 and total trade (line 5, col. 5).

LINE 4–Col. 1: Calculated from line 3, cols. 1 and 2, and line 4, col. 4. **Col. 2:** G. A. Dikhtiar, *Sovetskaia torgovlia v period sotsializma i razvernutogo stroitelstva kommunizma* [Soviet Trade during the Period of Socialism and of the All-Out Building of Communism], Moscow, 1965, p. 213. **Col. 3:** Calculated from line 3, cols. 3 and 4, and line 4, col. 4. **Col. 4:** Assumed to be same as in 1945 (col. 2). **Col. 5:** M. Lifits, "Perekhod k razvernutoi sovetskoi torgovle" [Transition to Expanded Soviet Trade], *Voprosy ekonomiki* [Problems of Economics], No. 2, 1948, p. 60, as cited in Basile Kerblay, *Les marchés paysans en U.R.S.S.*, Paris, 1968, p. 184. **Col. 6:** Calculated from col. 5 and total trade (line 5, col. 5).

LINE 5–Cols. 1, 3, and 5: Sum of lines 3 and 4.

open some 4,000 enterprises financed with both centralized and decentralized funds and also under the jurisdiction of consumer cooperatives.[21]

It appears, then, that the public catering system used two channels of distribution—one at fixed prices (with increases in 1943) and the other at prices set according to demand.

Table 115 shows a sizable increase in "commercial" sales during 1945–1947, the result of considerable effort by the government. At the time the "commercial" stores were set up, the Central Administration for "Commercial" Trade (*Glavosobtorg*), headed by the Deputy Commissar of Trade, was created in the

21. The number of these enterprises that came under the sole jurisdiction of the USSR Ministry of Trade increased as follows:

	Jan. 1, 1946	Jan. 1, 1947
Restaurants in cities	138	189
Restaurants and refreshment stands in stations	1,411	1,937
Rural cafés		4,189

(Liubimov, *Torgovlia*, pp. 177–78).

Table 116   Public Catering, 1945–1953

	Total Number of Public Eating Places (thousands[a]) (1)	Number of Canteens and Restaurants (thousands[a]) (2)	Number of Meals Served (billions) (3)	Turnover of Public Eating Places (bill. rubles) (4)	Share of Turnover in State and Cooperative Retail Trade (per cent) (5)
1945	73.4	53.1	14,952	33.1	21
1946	70.5	40.4	12,289	48.8	20
1947	82.1	38.9	10,915	68.1	21
1948	91.8	34.0	7,917	45.5	15
1949	93.5	31.3	6,234	45.5	14
1950	95.4	31.0	6,428	47.4	13
1951	101.0	31.7	6,502	50.2	13
1952	106.5	32.7	7,235	53.4	14
1953	112.9	34.2	7,926	57.1	13

Source: Cols. 1–2: *Sovetskaia torgovlia*, 1956, p. 144; col. 3: *ibid.*, p. 74; cols. 4–5: *ibid.*, p. 20.

a. At the end of the year.

system of the USSR People's Commissariat of Trade. *Glavosobtorg* had the right to place orders for a wide assortment of goods with the best enterprises, some of which were to work exclusively for *Glavosobtorg*. Very severe penalties were to be imposed for not filling these orders. Enterprises working for *Glavosobtorg* had the right to be supplied directly from industrial bases without going through the *Sbyty* of the industrial ministries. *Glavosobtorg* organizations had top priority for supply of stocks, equipment, work clothing, transportation, and other inputs.[22]

The expansion of the network of "commercial" sales outlets, other than in public catering, was considerable, as can be seen in Table 117.

Level of Prices of Consumer Goods and Services at the End of the War / Official Soviet publications make little mention of retail consumer goods prices during the war. For 1941–1945 there is only one aggregate index of prices in state and cooperative retail trade, implicitly given when retail trade turnover was published in both current and constant prices (see Table 119), and one aggregate index of collective farm market prices (average for the whole country, given by quarters—see Table 118, sources to line 8). The aggregate index, which makes no distinction between state ration prices and open-market prices or among the different groups of products, unfortunately cannot provide much information on the price policy of the Soviet authorities. To obtain even an approximate idea of this policy, it is necessary to reconstruct an index of retail prices and of the cost of living.

The estimates are presented in Table 118. The main defects of the cost-of-living index should be noted immediately; they are such that the index should

22. *Ibid.*, pp. 173–75.

Table 117   Number of "Commercial" Enterprises under the Ministry of Trade,[a] 1946–1947

	Jan. 1, 1946	Jan. 1, 1947
"Gastronom" food stores	149	568
Stores selling industrial goods	51	502
Bread stores		210
Grocery stores		200
Fodder stores		207

Source: Liubimov, *Torgovlia*, p. 178.

a. Other than enterprises in the public catering system.

be considered as showing a trend rather than representing precise measurements. First, the prices used to construct this index were found in various publications; their number was certainly not adequate, and quality comparisons among various products are difficult to check. Second, the prices for the collective farm market are not for Moscow but the average for the whole country. From the estimates of Basile Kerblay, these prices seem a little lower than the prices in effect in Moscow (see Table 119). But an index without collective farm prices would have been inadequate. Third, the base for the index here (July 1940) was taken from an earlier study by the author (see Table 118). For 1940, this study was based on well-documented American data published in the *Monthly Labor Review*, which show a sizable increase between 1938 and 1940. The Soviet authorities do not seem to accept this increase. They use 1940 weights, making theirs a Paasche index, which tends to underestimate price increases during inflation. Our index comes closer to the Laspeyres formula using the initial year of the series as a base. In any case, the high level accepted for 1940 is responsible for the apparent low retail price level during 1940–1953.

Fourth, the prices used for "commercial" sales are the "posted" prices and do not take into account reductions that were widely granted.[23] Hence the index of prices in "commercial" stores is overestimated. The most common reductions were 10 to 25 per cent. Assuming an actual average price reduction of 15 per cent, the index for food products would be 5,844 in 1944, 3,870 in 1945, and 1,510 in 1946 (with 1940 = 100). For manufactured goods, it would be 1,685 in 1944, 1,637 in 1945, and 980 in 1946. For all "commercial" prices, it would be 3,890 in 1944, 2,663 in 1945, and 1,191 in 1946. Such reductions were no longer granted after September 15, 1946. Fifth, as indicated in Table 118, note a, the index of rationed goods prices includes prices of unrationed goods sold regularly in state and cooperative trade. According to Voznesenskii, the index of rationed goods prices rose only 0.5 per cent between 1940 and 1943 (see Table 70 in Chapter 15). The available data do not enable us to make this distinction.

For all these reasons, it is desirable to compare my index with others (see Table

23. See pp. 455–61 below.

Table 118   Index of Cost of Living in Moscow, 1941–1953 (July 1940 = 100)

	Jan. 1941	1942	1943	1944	1945	1946 Up to Sept. 15	1946 After Sept. 15
1. Food products, excl. alcoholic beverages, state and cooperative retail trade, weighted average prices	102.1	111.8	109.4	448.9	567.1	555.9	506.3
2. Ration prices[a]	102.1	111.8	109.4	110.6	109.4	111.1	269.3
3. Commercial prices				6875.7	4553.2	1776.9	1157.0
4. Alcoholic beverages, state and cooperative retail trade, weighted average prices	100	622	622	715.9	650.6	613.3	600
5. Ration prices[a]	100	622	622	622	622	600	600
6. Commercial prices				2500	900	650	600
7. Food products, incl. alcoholic beverages, state and cooperative retail trade, weighted average prices	101.7	219.3	217.4	505.1	584.7	568.0	526.0
8. Collective farm market, total	99.5	620.8	1396.5	1180.8	624.5	682	682
9. State, cooperative, and collective farm retail trade	100.6	424.1	818.7	849.7	605.0	626.1	605.6
10. Tobacco and products, weighted average prices	100.0	100.0	100.0	255.7	309.7	364.7	438.0
11. Ration prices[a]	100.0	100.0	100.0	176.3	176.3	176.3	308.3
12. Commercial prices				1765	1471	882	794
13. Manufactured goods, weighted average prices	100.0	126.4	126.4	219.2	311.7	400.6	363.8
14. Ration prices[a]	100.0	126.4	126.4	126.4	126.4	126.4	152.7
15. Commercial prices				1982.9	1925.5	1153.3	943.5
16. State and cooperative retail trade, weighted average prices	101.1	186.7	185.4	406.8	490.2	509.4	471.2
17. Ration prices[a]	101.1	186.7	185.4	187.4	186.8	184.6	277.3
18. Commercial prices				4576.1	3132.6	1401.0	1003.7
19. Total state, cooperative, and collective farm retail trade	100.4	320.6	578.7	632.2	503.5	547.4	523.3
20. Heating and lighting	100.0	100.0	100.0	100.0	100.0	100.0	151.0
21. Rent and services	100.0	100.0	100.0	100.0	100.0	100.0	121.8
22. Over-all cost-of-living index	100.4	297.0	527.5	575.3	460.3	499.5	482.0

1947 Up to Dec. 15	1947 After Dec. 15	1948	1949	1950	1951	1952	1953	Line No.
411.4	232.5	231.2	206.9	164.1	147.6	130.3	111.7	1
269.2								2
816.3								3
600	600	480	321.6	256.7	236.6	235.1	203.0	4
600								5
600								6
451.1	309.9	283.6	212.2	168.4	151.7	135.1	115.9	7
719	288	205	143	130	105	104	97	8
563.4	305.1	266.3	199.7	161.1	142.9	129.1	112.7	9
434.6	312.6	303.8	292.9	234.5	200.9	200.9	178.8	10
308.8								11
794								12
304.4	152.7	152.4	142.9	116.0	111.4	110.9	98.9	13
152.7								14
736.1								15
402.7	258.4	240.9	190.9	152.4	139.4	128.3	111.4	16
277.2								17
759.8								18
476.1	255.2	229.6	182.7	147.6	133.6	124.4	109.4	19
151.0	151.0	151.0	276.7	265.1	241.9	241.9	218.6	20
121.8	121.8	122.6	157.3	157.3	157.3	149.0	160.5	21
439.9	242.6	219.8	186.8	154.8	141.0	132.3	118.2	22

Source

LINE 1–1941-1943: Line 2 since no commercial prices existed in these years. **1944-1947 (up to December 15):** Weighted average of ration price indexes (line 2) and commercial price indexes (line 3), weighted by share of "commercial" trade in total state and cooperative retail trade (derived as 5.0, 10.3, 26.7, and 26.0 per cent for 1944, 1945, 1946, and 1947, respectively, from total retail trade in *Sovetskaia torgovlia*, 1956, p. 20, and trade of people's commissariat in Liubimov, *Torgovlia*, p. 170, for 1944 and 1946, and from Pavlov in *40 let sovetskoi torgovli*, p. 9, for 1945 and 1947). **1947 (after December 15)-1948:** Weighted average of price indexes in Table D-1, lines 1–5, 7–10, 12–15, 17–21, 23, 25–26, and 28–29 (total weight for subgroup in line 31). **1949-1953:** Eugène Zaleski, "Les fluctuations des prix de détail en Union Soviétique," *Annexe Méthodologique et Statistique No. 3, Conjoncture et Etudes Economiques*, 1955, Table XXV, p. 26. Recomputed to 1940 base.

LINE 2–1941-1947: Weighted average of price indexes in Table D-1, lines 1–5, 7–10, 12–15, 17–21, 23, 25–26, and 28–29 (total weight for subgroup in line 31).

LINE 3–1944-1947: Weighted average of price indexes in Table D-2, lines 1–4, 6, 8–10, 12–16, 18, and 20–21 (total weight for subgroup in line 23).

LINE 4–1941-1943: Line 5 since no commercial prices existed in these years. **1944-1947 (up to December 15):** Weighted average of ration price indexes (line 5) and commercial price indexes (line 6), weighted by share of "commercial" trade in total state and cooperative retail trade (derived as 5.0, 10.3, 26.7, and 26.0 per cent for each

Table 118   *continued*

year, as in source to line 1, 1944–1947). **1947 (after December 15)-1948:** Price indexes in Table D-1, line 32. **1949-1953:** Zaleski, *Annexe No. 3*, Table XXVII, p. 28. Recomputed to 1940 base.

   LINE 5–1941-1947 (up to December 15): Price indexes in Table D-1, line 32.

   LINE 6–1944-1947: Price indexes in Table D-2, line 24.

   LINE 7–1941-1948: Weighted average of lines 1 and 4, weighted by subgroup weights in Table D-1, lines 31 and 33. **1949-1953:** Weighted average of lines 1 and 4, weighted by percentage shares in total cost-of-living index (derived as 55.7 and 2.7, respectively, from Zaleski, *Annexe No. 3*).

   LINE 8–1941-1945: Unweighted average of indexes given for city collective farm market prices in whole country for January, April, July, and October of each year in A. N. Malafeev, *Istoriia tsenoobrazovaniia v SSSR, 1917–1963 gg.* [History of Pricing in the USSR, 1917–1963], Moscow, 1964, p. 235. **1946-1947 (up to December 15), 1948-1950:** Kerblay, *Marchés paysans*, p. 184. Index of collective farm market prices in Moscow. **1947 (after December 15):** Based on price index for 1947 before price reform of December 16 and estimate that prices were reduced by 60 per cent after the reform, derived from statement in S. P. Figurnov, *Realnaia zarabotnaia plata i podem materialnogo blagosostoianiia trudiashchikhsia v SSSR* [Real Wages and the Increase in the Material Welfare of Workers in the USSR], Moscow, 1960, p. 158, that bazaar (*bazarnye*) prices were reduced by a factor of two or three for the main products immediately after the reform (2.5 was actually used in the calculation). **1951-1953:** *Sovetskaia torgovlia*, 1956, p. 179. Official index for collective farm market prices.

   LINE 9–1941-1946: Weighted average of lines 7 and 8, weighted by 1945 share of collective farm sales in total sales of food products (given as 51 per cent in Dikhtiar, *Sovetskaia torgovlia*, p. 213). **1947 (up to December 15):** Weighted average of lines 7 and 8, weighted by 1947 share of state and cooperative trade in total food products trade (derived as 58.1 per cent from total state and cooperative trade and share in that of food products given in *Sovetskaia torgovlia*, 1956, pp. 20 and 39, and collective farm trade in Kerblay, *Marchés paysans*, p. 184). **1947 (after December 15)-1948:** Weighted average of lines 7 and 8, weighted by 1948 share of state and cooperative trade in total food products trade (derived as 78 per cent from total state and cooperative trade and share in that of food products given in *Sovetskaia torgovlia*, 1956, pp. 20 and 39, and collective farm trade in Kerblay, *Marchés paysans*, p. 184). **1949-1953:** Weighted average of lines 7 and 8, weighted by share of state and cooperative trade in total food products trade (derived as 81.9, 81.0, 81.2, 80.8, and 82.9 per cent from total state and cooperative trade and share in that of food products given in *Sovetskaia torgovlia*, 1956, pp. 20 and 39, for 1949 and 1951–1953 and given in *ibid.*, p. 40, for 1950, and collective farm market trade in cities in *Bolshaia sovetskaia entsiklopediia* [The Large Soviet Encyclopedia], Moscow, 2nd ed., 1949–1957, Vol. 22, p. 75, as cited in Kerblay, *Marchés paysans*, p. 184, for 1949, and *Sovetskaia torgovlia*, 1956, p. 179, for 1950–1953). The data on collective farm market trade in cities cover sales by collective farmers, collective farms, individual peasants, workers, and employees with private plots, and also sales by nonagricultural households and organizations on collective farm markets and not on them at market prices (see *ibid.*). A small part of these sales are not for food products, but no attempt was made to eliminate this part in order to keep the methods consistent with those used for 1941–1948.

   LINE 10–1941-1943: Line 11 since no commercial prices existed in these years. **1944-1947 (up to December 15):** Weighted average of ration price indexes (line 11) and commercial price indexes (line 12), weighted by share of ''commercial'' trade in total state and cooperative retail trade (derived as 5.0, 10.3, 26.7, and 26.0 per cent for each year, as in source to line 1, 1944–1947). **1947 (after December 15)-1948:** Weighted average of price indexes in Table D-1, lines 34 and 35 (total weight for subgroup in line 36). **1949-1953:** Zaleski, *Annexe No. 3*, Table XXVII, p. 28. Recomputed to 1940 base.

   LINE 11–1941-1947: Weighted average of price indexes in Table D-1, lines 34 and 35 (total weight for subgroup in line 36).

   LINE 12–1944-1947: Price indexes in Table D-2, line 26.

   LINE 13–1941-1943: Line 14 since no commercial prices existed in these years. **1944-1947 (up to December 15):** Weighted average of ration price indexes (line 14) and commercial price indexes (line 15), weighted by share of ''commercial'' trade in total state and cooperative retail trade (derived as 5.0, 10.3, 26.7, and 26.0 per cent for each year, as in source to line 1, 1944–1947). **1947 (after December 15)-1948:** Weighted average of price indexes in Table D-1, lines 37–40, 42, 44, 46–47, 49, and 51–53 (total weight for subgroup in line 55). **1949-1953:** Zaleski, *Annexe No. 3*, Table XXVII, p. 28. Recomputed to 1940 base.

   LINE 14–1941-1946 (up to September 15): Index for fourth quarter of 1942 with June 1941 = 100 (given by Malafeev, *Istoriia*, p. 229, for nonfood products) accepted for all these years since information on individual products is largely unavailable. **1946 (after September 15)-1947:** Weighted average of price indexes in Table D-1, lines 37–40, 42, 44, 46–47, 49, and 51–53 (total weight for subgroup in line 55).

   LINE 15–1944-1947: Weighted average of price indexes in Table D-2, lines 28–31, 33, 35, 37, and 39 (total weight for subgroup in line 41).

   LINE 16–1941-1943: Line 17 since no commercial prices existed in these years. **1944-1948:** Weighted average of lines 1, 4, 10, and 13, weighted by subgroup weights in Table D-1, lines 31, 33, 36, and 55. **1949-1953:** Weighted

Table 118   *continued*

average of lines 7, 10, and 13, weighted by percentage shares in total cost-of-living index (derived as 58.4, 1.6, and 29.3, respectively, from Zaleski, *Annexe No. 3*).

   LINE 17–1941-1947: Weighted average of lines 2, 5, 11, and 14, weighted by subgroup weights in Table D-1, lines 31, 33, 36, and 55.

   LINE 18–1944-1947: Weighted average of lines 3, 6, 12, and 15, weighted by subgroup weights in Table D-2, lines 23, 25, 27, and 41.

   LINE 19–1941-1953: Weighted average of lines 9, 10, and 13, weighted by percentage shares in total cost-of-living index (derived as 58.4, 1.6, and 29.3, respectively, from Zaleski, *Annexe No. 3*).

   LINE 20–1941-1948: Weighted average of price indexes in Table D-1, lines 56–58 (total weight for subgroup in line 59). **1949-1953:** Zaleski, *Annexe No. 3*, Table XXVII, p. 28. Recomputed to 1940 base.

   LINE 21–1941-1948: Weighted average of price indexes in Table D-1, lines 60–64 (total weight for subgroup in line 65). **1949-1953:** Zaleski, *Annexe No. 3*, Table XXVII, p. 28. Recomputed to 1940 base.

   LINE 22–1941-1953: Weighted average of lines 19, 20, and 21, weighted by percentage shares in total cost-of-living index (derived as 89.3, 5.7, and 5.0, respectively, from Zaleski, *Annexe No. 3*).

   a. Including prices of unrationed goods sold regularly in state and cooperative trade.

119). My cost-of-living index probably overstates the increase between 1941 and 1947, most likely because of the use of "commercial" prices, which are too high, and the fact that prices in Moscow were higher than average prices for the whole country. It probably underestimates the increase for 1947–1953 because of the use of the 1940 base. It is interesting to note that my index shows a greater decline in the cost of living than does the index calculated independently by Janet Chapman. As long as no details are available about the methods used to calculate the Soviet index for 1940, the independent estimates presented here, despite their shortcomings, are useful because they make it possible to check the basic data and the methods used.

   The large disparities among indexes seen in Table 118 suggest that it would be misleading to refer to a single price level in the Soviet Union at the end of the war. Prices moved differently according to the channels of distribution. Indeed, the main thrust of retail price policy consisted of *not* allowing a uniform movement of prices for the same products. The general level represented by the cost of living was, in any case, theoretical: the cost of living varied by level of income and as a function of supply facilities open to different individuals. Moreover, there were large differences among the various components of the cost-of-living index. The prices of heating, lighting, rent, and services may have remained practically unchanged during the war, but the prices of food products and alcoholic beverages increased considerably.

   The sizable differences among the various channels of distribution are shown in Chart 10. The cost-of-living index rose substantially between 1941 and 1944 *despite* relative stability in rationed goods prices (after the 1941 jump in alcoholic beverage prices) and the reduction in prices on the collective farm market. This was due primarily to the decreasing importance of the rationed sector relative to "commercial" sales.

   The government had at least two objectives in its 1944 authorization of open-market sales at higher prices in "commercial" stores. The first was to restrain price increases on the collective farm market. Thus, prices for commercial sales[24]

Table 119   Comparison of Different Indexes[a] of Retail Prices and Cost of Living, 1941–1953 (1940 = 100)

	1941	1942	1943	1944	1945
State and Cooperative Retail Trade, Total					
Soviet indexes:					
1. Central Statistical Administration	103.9	130.6	150.0	184.1	203.1
2. *Shagi piatiletok*					205
3. Mikoyan					
4. Figurnov					
5. Malafeev		156			218
Western indexes:					
6. Jasny					
7. Chapman (1937 weights)				122	
8. Chapman (given-year weights)					
9. Zaleski, Moscow	101.1	187.7	185.4	406.8	490.2
State and Cooperative Retail Trade, Food Products (including alcoholic beverages)					
Soviet indexes:					
10. Central Statistical Administration					
11. Central Statistical Administration and Figurnov					
12. Malafeev		174.5			
13. *Shagi piatiletok*					225
Western indexes:					
14. Chapman (1937 weights)					
15. Chapman (given-year weights)					
16. Zaleski	101.7	219.3	217.4	505.1	584.7
State and Cooperative Retail Trade, Manufactured Goods (including tobacco)					
Soviet indexes:					
17. Central Statistical Administration					
18. Central Statistical Administration and Figurnov					
19. Malafeev		126.4			
20. *Shagi piatiletok*					195
Western indexes:					
21. Chapman, Moscow (1937 weights)					
22. Chapman, Moscow (given-year weights)					
23. Zaleski	100.0	126.4	126.4	219.2	311.7
Collective Farm Market					
Soviet indexes:					
24. Central Statistical Administration					
25. Malafeev	99.5	621	1,397	1,181	625
26. Figurnov					
27. Dikhtiar			1,288		560
Western indexes:					
28. Chapman (city)				1,000.0	
29. Kerblay, USSR (city)			1,260–1,320		448
30. Kerblay, Moscow	288	1,732	1,723	1,069	626

| 1946 | | 1947 | | | | | | | | |
Up to Sept. 15	After Sept. 15	Up to Dec. 15	After Dec. 15	1948	1949	1950	1951	1952	1953	Line No.
249		326	296	271	231	186	170	161	146	1
										2
		277				160		143	127	3
		321	266	228	228	183	170	161	144	4
		321				186	170	161	146	5
266		305		253	225	187	171	162	146	6
				252				164		7
				238				157		8
509.4	471.2	402.7	258.4	240.9	190.9	152.4	139.4	128.3	111.4	9
		383		314	260	203	181	166	146	10
		371		304	252	197	178	160	141	11
										12
										13
				264				150		14
				250				146		15
568.0	526.0	451.1	309.9	283.6	212.2	168.4	151.7	135.1	115.9	16
		254		218	198	165	157	156	145	17
		253		218	197	164	159	157	144	18
										19
										20
				230				180		21
				217				168		22
400.6	363.8	304.4	152.7	152.4	142.9	116.0	111.4	110.9	98.9	23
						104	105	104	97	24
										25
			372	134	103	104	105	104	97	26
										27
				175				104		28
		416								29
682		719		205	143	130				30

Table 119   *continued*

	1941	1942	1943	1944	1945
State and Cooperative Retail Trade and					
Collective Farm Market					
Soviet index:					
31. Malafeev					325
Western indexes:					
32. Chapman (1937 weights)				143	
33. Chapman (given-year weights)					
34. Zaleski, Moscow	100.4	320.6	578.7	632.2	503.5
Cost-of-Living Indexes					
35. *Politicheskaia ekonomiia*					
36. Figurnov					
37. Chapman (1937 weights)				140	
38. Chapman (given-year weights)					
39. Zaleski, Moscow	100.4	297.0	527.5	575.3	460.3

Source

LINE 1–1941-1945: Table 70, line 12. **1946-1947:** Based on 1945 and data on trade in current and constant prices in *Sovetskaia torgovlia* [Soviet Trade], Moscow, 1964, pp. 40 and 45, as cited in Dikhtiar, *Sovetskaia torgovlia*, p. 269. Figures are for whole year. **1947 (up to December 15):** Based on index for 1950 and percentage that that index was of index for fourth quarter of 1947 (given as 57 in *Narodnoe khoziaistvo v 1956 godu* [The USSR National Economy in 1956], Moscow, 1957, p. 233). **1948-1949:** Based on index for 1947 and indexes for 1948 and 1949 with the fourth quarter of 1947 = 100 (given as 83 and 71 in *ibid.*). **1950-1953:** *Ibid.*, p. 232.

LINE 2–1945: *Shagi*, p. 157.

LINE 3–1947, 1950, and 1952-1953: Calculated from data given by Mikoyan (*Etudes et Conjoncture*, No. 4, April 1955, p. 346).

LINE 4–1947 (up to December 15): Figurnov, *Realnaia plata*, p. 157. **1947 (after December 15)-1953:** Based on index for 1947 and indexes for December 1947, April 1948, March 1949, March 1950, March 1951, April 1952, and April 1953 with fourth quarter of 1947 = 100 (given as 83, 71, 71, 57, 53, 50, and 45 in *ibid.*, p. 156).

LINE 5–1942: Malafeev, *Istoriia*, pp. 228–29. Index for fourth quarter of 1942 with June 1941 = 100. **1945, 1947, 1950-1953:** *Ibid.*, pp. 407–8. Recomputed from 1928 = 100 to 1940 = 100.

LINE 6–1946-1953: Derived from ruble data in current prices and index in constant prices (given in Naum Jasny, *Soviet Industrialization, 1928–1952*, Chicago, 1961, p. 389). Figures for 1946 and 1947 are for the whole year.

LINES 7 AND 8–1944, 1948, and 1952: Janet Chapman, *Real Wages in Soviet Russia since 1928*, Cambridge, Mass., 1963, p. 355. Recomputed to 1940 = 100. The 1944 index is stated to be "less reliable than those for other years."

LINE 9–1941-1953: Table 118, line 16. 1941 figure is for January.

LINE 10–1947: Based on index for 1950 and percentage that that index was of index for fourth quarter of 1947 (given as 53 in *Narodnoe khoziaistvo, 1956*, p. 233). **1948-1949:** Based on index for 1947 and indexes for 1948 and 1949 with the fourth quarter of 1947 = 100 (given as 82 and 68 in *ibid.*). **1950-1953:** *Ibid.*, p. 232.

LINE 11–1947: Figurnov, *Realnaia plata*, p. 157. **1948-1953:** Based on index for 1947 (line 11) and indexes for 1948–1953 with the fourth quarter of 1947 = 100 (given as 82, 68, 53, 48, 43, and 38 in *Narodnoe khoziaistvo, 1956*, p. 233).

LINE 12–1942: Malafeev, *Istoriia*, pp. 228–29. Index for fourth quarter of 1942 with June 1940 = 100.

LINE 13–1945: *Shagi*, p. 157.

LINES 14 and 15–1948 and 1952: Chapman, *Real Wages*, p. 81. Recomputed to 1940 = 100.

LINE 16–1941-1953: Table 118, line 7.

LINE 17–1947: Based on index for 1950 and percentage that that index was of index for fourth quarter of 1947 (given as 65 in *Narodnoe khoziaistvo, 1956*, p. 233). **1948-1949:** Based on index for 1947 and indexes for 1948 and 1949 with the fourth quarter of 1947 = 100 (given as 86 and 78 in *ibid.*). **1950-1953:** *Ibid.*, p. 232.

LINE 18–1947: Figurnov, *Realnaia plata*, p. 157. **1948-1953:** Based on index for 1947 (line 18) and indexes for 1948–1953 with the fourth quarter of 1947 = 100 (given as 86, 78, 65, 63, 62, and 57 in *Narodnoe khoziaistvo, 1956*, p. 233).

LINE 19–1942: Malafeev, *Istoriia*, pp. 228–29. Index for fourth quarter of 1942 with June 1940 = 100.

1946 Up to Sept. 15	1946 After Sept. 15	1947 Up to Dec. 15	1947 After Dec. 15	1948	1949	1950	1951	1952	1953	Line No.
										31
				241				154		32
				228				147		33
547.4	523.3	476.1	255.2	229.6	182.7	147.6	133.6	124.4	109.4	34
									122	35
		325								36
				230				155		37
				216				149		38
499.5	482.0	439.9	242.6	219.8	186.8	154.8	141.0	132.3	118.2	39

LINE 20–1945: *Shagi*, p. 157.

LINES 21 and 22–1948 and 1952: Chapman, *Real Wages*, p. 81.

LINE 23–1941-1953: Table 118, line 13.

LINE 24–1950-1953: *Sovetskaia torgovlia*, 1956, p. 179.

LINE 25–1941-1945: Average of indexes given for January, April, June, and October of each year in Malafeev, *Istoriia*, p. 235.

LINE 26–1947-1953: Figurnov, *Realnaia plata*, p. 158.

LINE 27–1943: Based on index for 1945 and decrease between 1943 and 1945 (given as 2.3 times in Dikhtiar, *Sovetskaia torgovlia*, p. 202). **1945:** *Ibid*.

LINE 28–1944, 1948, and 1952: Chapman, *Real Wages*, p. 97. Recomputed to 1940 = 100.

LINE 29–1943, 1945, and 1947: Kerblay, *Marchés paysans*, pp. 162 and 184. For 1943, 1,260 for vegetable products and 1,320 for animal products. Figure for 1947 is for the whole year.

LINE 30–1941-1950: *Ibid*., Figures for 1946 and 1947 are for the whole year.

LINE 31–1945: Malafeev, *Istoriia*, p. 235. Annual average for 1940 = 100.

LINES 32 and 33–1944, 1948, and 1952: Chapman, *Real Wages*, p. 87. Recomputed to 1940 = 100.

LINE 34–1941-1953: Table 118, line 19. 1941 figure is for January.

LINE 35–1953: *Politicheskaia ekonomiia: Uchebnik* [Political Economy: A Textbook], Moscow, 1954, p. 462.

LINE 36–1947: Figurnov, *Realnaia plata*, p. 151.

LINES 37 and 38–1944, 1948, and 1952: Chapman, *Real Wages*, p. 87. Recomputed to 1940 = 100.

LINE 39–1941-1953: Table 118, line 22. 1941 figure is for January.

a. My indexes (lines 9, 16, 34, and 39) include trade in "commercial" stores. It is not known to what extent the other indexes include this trade.

Chart 10   Indexes of Prices and Cost of Living in Moscow, 1940–1953 (1940 = 100)

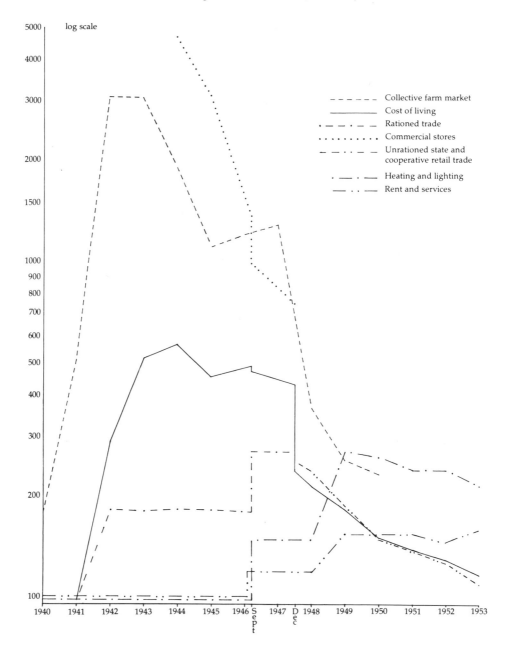

Source: Table 118, except for collective farm market prices which are explained in footnote 27.

were set a little higher than those on the collective farm market or in the commission stores (for manufactured products).[25] The second was to exert downward pressure on open-market prices so that eventually there would be uniform prices in state and cooperative retail trade.

The average level of "commercial" prices was not fixed with any precision. The quality of products sold was often higher than that of products sold on the collective farm market and in commission stores. The government also introduced discount books providing 10 to 25 per cent reductions for specified volumes of purchases per month.[26]

The government's efforts to depress collective farm market prices and to equalize prices of open-market rationed trade can be seen more clearly in Chart 11, which shows the movement of prices of food products. In 1940, the level of collective farm market prices was approximately 1.82 times that of state and cooperative retail trade prices.[27] To show the movement of the two series together in Chart 11, then, the level of the collective farm market price index is set at 182 in 1940. The equalization of the prices of "commercial" sales and those of the collective farm market can be seen clearly. The movement of "commercial" prices actually paid followed the collective farm prices closely. It can also be seen that the level of collective farm prices became higher than that of "commercial" sales after September 15, 1946—after the increase in ration prices. Kravis and Mintzes explain this movement in the following way.[28]

The cut in rations received by many people decreased the quantity of goods resold out of ration allowances on the open market. The result was a sharp increase in open-market prices for certain items. The greater convenience of shopping in open markets, owing to the overcrowding of commercial stores, has been another factor tending to increase the demand for goods on the open market. When open-market prices of certain items rose to several times the commercial-store prices following the September [1946] decree, purchase of goods in the commercial stores for resale in the open markets was stimulated. The Government, however, instituted a campaign against this type of speculation by reducing the maximum size of purchases in commercial stores, thus making it more difficult to purchase in large quantities.

Another measure against speculation was the commercial-store sale of items in combinations which discouraged resale. For instance, bread was sold together with certain types of meat in the form of a sandwich; thus, while individuals could make purchases

24. Liubimov, *Torgovlia*, p. 179.

25. Irving B. Kravis and Joseph Mintzes, "Soviet Union: Trends in Prices, Rations, and Wages," *Monthly Labor Review*, July 1947, p. 29.

26. *Ibid*.

27. According to Kerblay (*Marchés paysans*, p. 184), collective farm market prices were the same as official trade prices in 1949. (See also Figurnov, *Realnaia plata*, pp. 158–59.) The official Soviet index of prices of food products in state and cooperative retail trade was 260 in 1949 with 1940 = 100 (see Table 119). In other words, official trade prices would have to be increased 2.6-fold in order to reach the level of collective farm market prices. Kerblay calculated the index of collective farm market prices (in Moscow) as 143 in 1949 with 1940 = 100 (see Table 119). Thus, in 1940 collective farm market prices were 1.818 times higher than the official trade prices. Hence, taking official trade prices in 1940 as a base, the following index is obtained for collective farm market prices: 181.8 in 1940; 523.6 in 1941; 3,148.8 in 1942; 3,132.4 in 1943; 1,943.4 in 1944; 1,138.1 in 1945; 1,239.9 in 1946; 1,307.1 in 1947; 372.7 in 1948; 260 in 1949; and 236.3 in 1950. It should be noted that according to Jasny (*Soviet Industrialization*, p. 274), in 1940 the level of collective farm market prices was 85 per cent higher than that of official trade prices.

28. Kravis and Mintzes, *Monthly Labor Review*, July 1947, p. 30.

Chart 11   Indexes of Prices of Food Products in Moscow (excluding alcoholic beverages), 1940–1953 (1940 = 100[a])

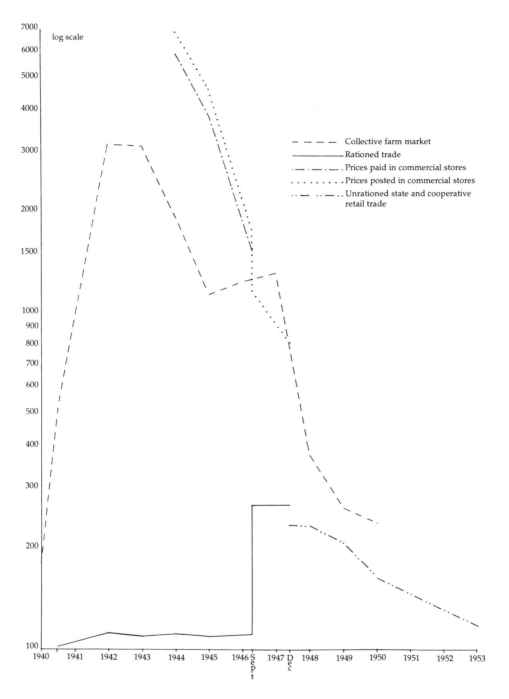

Source: Table 118, except for collective farm market prices, which are explained in footnote 27, and prices paid in commercial stores, which are given on p. 451.

a. Food prices in state and cooperative trade in 1940 = 100 for all distribution channels, i.e., state and cooperative trade prices, rationed prices, commercial store prices, and collective farm market prices.

for immediate use, speculators would be burdened with unprofitable meat and at the same time with bread which was not suitable for later sale. In addition, temporary shortages from time to time in the commercial stores also resulted in higher prices in the open markets.

It should be remembered that the food situation in 1946 was not always good. In 1946 the state trade stores had begun to sell bakery products, grocery items, and fodder at "commercial" prices without coupons. These sales had to be stopped in the fall of 1946 after the bad harvest caused by the drought.[29]

A similar comparison of "commercial" and open-market prices for manufactured goods could not be made. Indexes of the prices in commission stores at the bazaars cannot be calculated with the information available. However, it can be assumed that the movements of these prices were not very different from those of food products. The movements of the prices of "commercial" sales and of rationed trade, shown in Chart 12, were in any case very similar to those of food products.

The most significant event in the policy of equalizing fixed and open-market prices in 1945–1947 was, no doubt, the increase in prices of rationed products on September 16, 1946. According to the estimates in Table 118, the over-all increase in the prices of rationed products was 50.2 per cent. Included in this were increases of 142.4 per cent for food products excluding alcoholic beverages (there was no increase in alcoholic beverage prices, which were already high) and 20.8 per cent for manufactured goods. According to Kravis and Mintzes, the increase was 166 per cent for 14 food products (unweighted average of price changes) or 180 per cent if the size of rations is taken into account.[30]

The increases in ration prices decreed September 16, 1946, forced the government to grant wage increases; these amounted to 50 per cent for monthly wages of 200–300 rubles, 33 per cent for wages of 300–400 rubles, and 25 per cent for wages of 400–500 rubles. But the increase was only 9 per cent for wages of 900–980 rubles, and no increases were granted for wages over 1,000 rubles a month.[31] According to Kravis and Mintzes, these increases were not large enough to prevent a decline in purchasing power. The decline resulted not only from the increase in prices of rationed products but also from the cut in rations.[32] The cost-of-living index in Table 118, however, shows a slight reduction in the cost of living (3.5 per cent). But those estimates are based on the movement of "commercial" prices; differences between them and the Kravis and Mintzes estimates are within the margin of error possible in calculations based on "commercial" prices.

29. Liubimov, *Torgovlia*, p. 176.

30. Kravis and Mintzes, *Monthly Labor Review*, July 1947, pp. 30 and 32.

31. *Ibid.*, p. 35. In rubles, these monthly increases amounted to 100 rubles for wages up to 500 rubles, 90 rubles for wages up to 700 rubles, and 80 rubles for wages up to 900 rubles; nonworking pensioners received a supplement of 60 rubles and students receiving stipends 60–80 rubles a month (*ibid.*, p. 28).

32. *Ibid.*

Chart 12   Indexes of Prices of Manufactured Goods, 1940–1953 (1940 = 100)

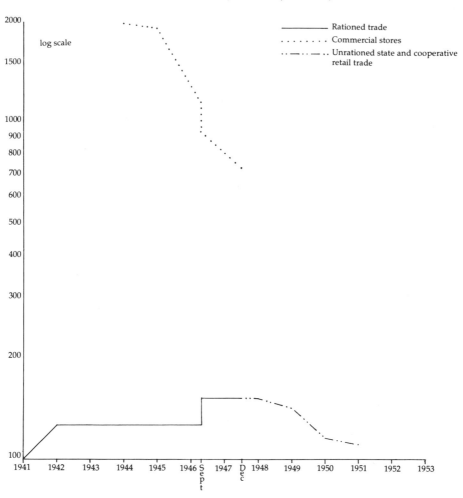

Source: Table 118.

Preparations for Eliminating Rationing

Rationing during the First Postwar Years

In view of the considerable discrepancy—a legacy of the war—between currency in circulation and goods available, the government could not abolish rationing at once. Moreover, it was forced to control money wages very strictly.[33] However, the end of the war made it possible slightly to increase food rations. The exact dates and amounts of these increases are not known, but an idea of their scope can be gained by comparing the rations of December 1943 with those of September 1945 given in Table 120. Bread and meat rations, in particular, seem to have been increased. The category of "heroes" appears in 1945, but it is not clear when it was introduced.

In addition to these rations, certain Soviet citizens could receive supplementary rations. In September 1945, "heroes" and persons assimilated to that category could receive supplementary cards (or books) giving them the right to buy, at taxed prices, any rationed product up to a certain sum (from 100 to 500 rubles).[34] This provision also applied to workers engaged in certain strenuous activities. Supplements for some kinds of work, usually provided as prepared food to workers on the job, were also common.[35] Supplements were also given to child-bearing women from the sixth month of pregnancy until the second month after the birth of the child.[36] Special ration cards, called "B cards" or "limited cards," given to certain people (the social elite, who might also receive "special worker" cards) were also mentioned at the beginning of 1946. "B cards" entitled the bearer to special monthly rations, and bearers of "B cards" received "points" (125 every six months) valuable for purchase of certain manufactured goods (the number of "points" required to buy a pair of shoes was 40).[37]

So-called "limited cards" of the "second category"[38] entitled the bearer to buy food products in stores and to purchase consumer goods at reduced prices. The people who received these cards were those who had been awarded a national order (heroes of the Soviet Union, heroes of labor, the order of Lenin, and others).[39] For industrial consumer goods (such as textiles), these "limited

33. The average annual money wages of workers and employees in the national economy increased only from 5,208 rubles in 1945 to 5,700 rubles in 1946 and 6,832 rubles in 1947 (see Tables A–4 and A–5).

34. *Cahiers*, No. 2, 1946, p. 29. These cards are referred to as "limited cards of the first category" in *Cahiers*, No. 3, 1946, p. 33.

35. *Cahiers*, No. 2, 1946, p. 29. These supplements amounted to 1–3 kilograms of meat or fish, 1.5–3 kilograms of flour and macaroni, 330–1,500 grams of fats, and 300–500 grams of sugar.

36. *Ibid.*, p. 30.

37. "B cards" entitled the bearer to the following monthly rations: white bread, 6,000 grams; flour and farinaceous products, 3,500 grams; butter, 1,800 grams; sugar, 1,600 grams; meat, 7,200 grams; alcohol or spirits, 1,600 grams; crackers, 1,000 grams; eggs, 10; toilet soap, 1 bar; household soap, 400 grams; cigarettes, 250; and unspecified quantities of dried and fresh fruit, vegetables, potatoes, and condensed milk (*Cahiers*, No. 3, 1946, pp. 32–33).

38. For the "first category," see footnote 34 above.

39. In Estonia there were no commercial stores selling at open-market prices at the beginning of 1946. Holders of ration cards were distributed among different food stores, the Gastronomes, all of which sold at the same prices. Members of the Communist Party had their own Gastronome. (*Cahiers*, No. 3, 1946, p. 33.)

Table 120   Food Rations during and after the War, 1942–1947 (grams)

	Heroes[a]		Workers				Children		
	First Class (1)	Second Class (2)	First Category[b] (3)	Second Category[c] (4)	Ordinary[d] (5)	Employees (6)	Under 12 (7)	Over 12 (8)	Non-workers[e] (9)
Bread (per day)									
1. December 1942			800	600		500	400		400
2. December 1943			650	550		450	300		300
3. September 1945	1,000	1,000	1,000	900	500	400	300[f]	400[f]	300
4. January 1947			635	544		454	318		272–0
Flour or Macaroni (per month)									
5. December 1942[g]			2,000	2,000		1,500	1,200		1,000
6. December 1943[g]			2,000	2,000		1,500	1,200		1,000
7. September 1945	3,000	2,500	2,000	1,500	1,200	800	1,500		1,200
8. January 1947[h]			2,000	2,000		1,500		1,179	1,000–0[i]
Meat and Fish (per month)									
9. December 1942			2,200	2,200		1,200	600		600
10. December 1943			2,200	2,200		1,200	600		600
11. September 1945	4,500	4,000	3,200	2,200	1,800	1,200	800	1,500	800
12. January 1947			2,200	2,200		1,200	600		600–0
Fats (per month)									
13. December 1942			800	800		400	400		200
14. December 1943			800	800		400	400		200
15. September 1945	1,000	900	900	750	400	300	300	500	300
16. January 1947			800	800		400	200		200–0
Sugar (per month)									
17. December 1942			500	500		300	300		200
18. December 1943			500	500		300	300		200
19. September 1945	500	500	500	500–400		300	400	500	400
20. January 1947			900	900		500	500		400
Salt (per month)									
21. September 1945	400	400	400	400	400	400	400	400	400
22. January 1947			400	400		400	400		400
Tea (per month)									
23. September 1945	25	25	25	25	25	25	25	25	25
24. January 1947			45	45		45	45		45–0

Source

LINES 1-2, 5-6, 9-10, 13-14, and 17-18: Lazar Volin, *Survey of Russian Agriculture*, Washington, 1951, p. 175, as cited by Solomon Schwarz, *Labor in the Soviet Union*, New York, 1951, p. 216n.

LINES 3, 7, 11, 15, 19, 21, and 23: *Cahiers*, No. 2, 1945, p. 29.

LINES 4, 8, 12, 16, 20, 22, and 24: Kravis and Mintzes, *Monthly Labor Review*, July 1947, p. 29. Given in pounds, converted into grams (1 lb = 453.59 grams), and rounded.

a. This category includes Soviet citizens holding certain decorations, researchers, and certain officials, engineers, and technicians.

b. Heavy workers, according to Schwarz (*Labor*, p. 216n.).

c. The intermediate category between ordinary workers and those engaged in strenuous work includes specialized workers, those doing harder work than the average, and those not included in the first category (*Cahiers*, No. 2, 1946, p. 29). Only for September 1945 is a distinction made between workers of the second category and ordinary workers. For the other years, they are lumped together. Schwarz (*Labor*, p. 216n.) divides workers into heavy and ordinary workers.

d. All workers not included in cols. 3 and 4.

e. According to Schwarz (*Labor*, p. 216n.), dependents. According to Kravis and Mintzes (*Monthly Labor Review*, July 1947, p. 29), dependents I–4 and IT–4, which terms are not defined.

Table 120 *continued*

f. Children were divided into categories 1, 2, and 3. It was assumed that categories 1 and 2 were under 12 and category 3 over 12.

g. Groats, according to Schwarz (*Labor*, p. 216n.).

h. Grits, according to Kravis and Mintzes (*Monthly Labor Review*, July 1947, p. 29).

i. Grits rations were eliminated entirely for dependents IT–4 in January 1947 (*ibid*).

cards" did not carry any "points." The "limited cards" were distributed by the trade unions.[40]

The criterion for receiving these privileged cards was the "responsibility" of one's job. Thus it was possible to end up with several privileged cards, for these were issued not only to individuals but also for jobs.[41] The result was that, on top of the careful measure of rations allotted to workers and social categories, a preferential system[42] was superimposed, which removed all moral justification for the sacrifices demanded of workers.

The difficulties experienced in 1946 made it impossible to maintain this system fully. The revision of prices made on September 16, 1946, was accompanied by a cut in rations for several products (see Table 120) and a reclassification of persons in less advantageous ration categories. The number of privileged cards issued was considerably reduced.[43] The first items cut back were bread and bakery products. The number of people supplied by this system, which had reached 77.1 million in January 1945 and 87.8 million by the end of the third quarter of 1946, was reduced to 60 million in October 1946.[44] The number of rural inhabitants supplied with bread was reduced and the right to rations of some people living at home and not working was abolished. Bread rations were reduced, as well as the amounts sold in "commercial" stores. The use of bread and groats as raw materials in supplementary feeding was forbidden; the use of grain for industrial production and the use of bread for consumers outside the market (such as institutions) were reduced. In October, when the unfavorable harvest forecasts were confirmed,[45] additional measures were taken to reduce grain consumption. Supplies of grain and groats in "commercial" stores were cut back; production of high-quality flour was reduced; and reductions were made in the rates of payment of grain in compensation for deliveries of cotton and agricultural raw materials. As of November 1946, the segments of the popula-

40. The trade unions fixed, in agreement with the central distribution agency, the quantity of products to be distributed to each consumer. The distribution was carried out by the trade union. (The same was true for firewood.) These allotments were reduced and consisted mainly of one warm padded garment and one pair of felt boots per year. (*Ibid.*)

41. *Ibid.*, p. 32.

42. Among those given preferential treatment were diplomats who benefited from higher rations at reduced prices (*Cahiers*, No. 4, 1946, p. 27).

43. Kravis and Mintzes, *Monthly Labor Review*, July 1947, p. 29.

44. Liubimov, *Torgovlia*, p. 202.

45. The total grain harvest for 1946 was not published. According to Nancy Nimitz ("Soviet Government Grain Procurements, Dispositions, and Stocks, 1940, 1945–1963," RAND Research Memorandum 4127–PR, Santa Monica, 1964, p. 55), the 1946 harvest can be estimated at 35–40 million metric tons compared with 47.3 million metric tons in 1945. Nimitz estimates total procurements at 15 million metric tons in 1946 compared with 20.0 million metric tons in 1945.

tion supplied with grain were set every month by the USSR Council of Ministers with a breakdown by republics, territories, and provinces, and by supply norms, on the advice of the USSR Ministry of Trade, the USSR Ministry of Agricultural Procurement, and USSR Gosplan.[46]

All this resulted in a sizable reduction of supplies for trade. Use of flour in bakeries was reduced from 2,910,000 metric tons during the third quarter of 1946 to 1,780,000 metric tons in the fourth quarter. The corresponding reductions for groats were from 183,000 to 85,000 metric tons and for sugar from 109,000 to 94,000 metric tons; sugar supplies fell further to 85,000 metric tons during the first quarter of 1947. But the number of people supplied with bread increased from 60 million in October 1946 to 63 million in 1947.[47]

Preparation for Eliminating Rationing

The shortages that followed the drought of 1946 did not make it easier to prepare to eliminate rationing. The government ordered the formation of reserve stocks for commercial storage facilities and large stores. Such a reserve was begun for industrial products during the third quarter of 1947 and for food products in the fourth quarter of 1947.

Detailed studies turned out to be necessary for the transition to sales without coupons. First, "request-calculations" were required of republics, territories, provinces, cities, *Tsentrosoiuz*, and *Glavki* for worker supply in the ministries. The resulting data were used to calculate a plan for sales of goods after the abolition of rationing.[48] This plan was based on a number of factors. First was the deliveries expected from centralized industrial stocks by quarter and by month, according to the revised rates of growth in the 1947 annual plan and to the five-year plan for 1948. Scheduled deliveries of raw materials and manufacture of agricultural products from the 1947 harvest comprised the second factor. Supplies expected from other sources (farms belonging to enterprises, decentralized purchases and procurements, state reserves, imports, etc.) were another factor. The amount of new currency anticipated as a result of the currency exchange and payments of wages, pensions, and allowances in the new currency were key financial factors. Finally, demand was anticipated for goods compared with that for 1939 and 1940, taking into account wartime changes.

The draft materials were corrected while the 1947 annual plan was being carried out. After the size of the 1947 harvest was known, it was possible to estimate the accumulation of stocks with the help of calculations by Gosplan, the Ministry of Trade, and the Ministry of Finance. Detailed studies were made to calculate the sales plan by republic and to specify the assortment of products. Abundant documentation on the new price lists and instructions on how to change prices were sent to trade agencies three days before rationing was abolished. In order to prevent excessive buying and speculation, maximum sales

46. Liubimov, *Torgovlia*, pp. 202–3.
47. *Ibid.*, p. 204.
48. *Ibid.*, pp. 212–13.

per buyer were set for some industrial and agricultural products and maximum total daily sales per store were established for certain products.[49]

Currency Exchange and Eliminating Rationing in December 1947

The main objective of the decree issued on December 14, 1947,[50] was the reform of the Soviet consumer goods market. The conditions existing at the time were as follows. First, state and cooperative retail trade turnover had increased considerably between 1945 and 1947 (from 160 billion rubles in 1945 to 331 billion in 1947—see Table 115). Second, retail trade inventories had increased considerably during 1947. From January 1 to December 1, 1947, food industry meat inventories had risen by two-thirds, animal fat stocks by 60 per cent, and sugar inventories by more than 100 per cent. In light and textile industries, stocks of cotton fabrics had risen 150 per cent, of wool by 70 per cent, of silk and rayon fabrics by 85 per cent, of clothing by more than 100 per cent, of hosiery by nearly 65 per cent, and of leather shoes by 200 per cent. On December 1, 1947, potato procurements were 5,202,000 metric tons and vegetable procurements 1,871,000 metric tons more than the previous year.[51] Third, open-market prices had been reduced several times and the prices of rationed products had been increased in 1947, so some equalization of prices in the two sectors was possible.

As pointed out by G. Kosiachenko,[52] there were two possible ways to absorb the large stocks of liquid assets held by the population. Supply could be increased (through increasing trade turnover) or there could be a currency exchange with confiscation of excess cash from the population.[53] It is clear that Stalin never seriously entertained the first possibility. Former Minister of Finance Zverev reports in his memoirs that Stalin approached him at the end of 1943 to discuss the subject of a postwar monetary reform. As early as then, Stalin and Zverev were considering confiscating surplus currency; the only problem was how and when. Zverev says that he presented a supersecret report on this subject at a Politburo meeting a year later. This report was not preserved, even in the archives of the secretary general of the Party. Another year later, at the end of 1945, Stalin again requested a report on this subject. Zverev presented a first report of about 12 pages and then, two weeks later, a second report of some 100 pages. In addition to a currency exchange, this report proposed a revision of

49. *Ibid.*, pp. 214–18.

50. Decree of USSR Council of Ministers, "On the Introduction of the Monetary Reform and the Abolition of Ration Cards for Food and Industrial Products" (*Resheniia Partii i Pravitelstva po khoziaistvennym voprosam* [Decisions of the Party and Government on Economic Matters], Moscow, 1968, Vol. 3, pp. 460–67).

51. Liubimov, *Torgovlia*, p. 216.

52. G. Kosiachenko, "Sovetskaia denezhnaia reforma" [The Soviet Monetary Reform], *Planovoe khoziaistvo* [Planned Economy], No. 1, 1948, p. 26. See also V. Moskvin, "Ot kartochnoi sistemy snabzheniia k razvernutoi sovetskoi torgovle" [From the Ration Card System of Supply to an Expanded Soviet Trade], *ibid.*, pp. 41–53.

53. A general increase in prices was not practicable because of the unequal distribution of liquid assets. Zverev envisaged a considerable deflation in the form of a reduction of incomes (wages) and of prices, but Stalin did not agree. Zverev speaks directly of the intention of creating a scarcity of money, which he calls "deflation." (Zverev, *Zapiski*, pp. 232 and 235.)

prices in heavy industry, a reduction of personal income, and a fivefold reduction of consumer goods prices. Stalin did not accept this report. A final draft drawn up with his approval provided for a currency exchange, setting uniform prices for products sold in state and cooperative trade, and the abolition of rationing. This text was prepared by a commission presided over by Zverev, which included 14 people from the Ministry of Finance and a representative of the USSR State Bank. It was ready one year before the reform, that is, toward the end of 1946.[54]

The decree published on December 14, 1947, contained four monetary provisions: currency exchange, revaluation of deposits in the State Bank, revaluation of saving banks deposits, and the conversion of loans. The currency exchange was at the rate of 10 old rubles for one new ruble and took place from December 16 to 22 (and, in some exceptional cases, until December 29). Coins were not subject to the exchange and retained their face value.

Deposits of collective farms and cooperatives in the State Bank were recalculated on the basis of five old to four new rubles. Savings bank deposits of individuals were revalued as follows: for deposits up to 3,000 rubles, one old for one new ruble; for deposits between 3,000 and 10,000 rubles, three old for two new rubles; and for deposits over 10,000 rubles, two old for one new ruble.

The conversions of the Second, Third, and Fourth Five-Year Plan loans (except for the 1947 loan, which was recalculated at par value) were done at the rate of three old rubles for one new ruble. The obligations of the 1938 lottery loan were exchanged for the December 13, 1947, lottery loan at the rate of five old rubles for one new ruble or could be bought back by the savings banks at the same rate[55]

While the Soviet government reduced the purchasing power of money, it did not change the obligations of citizens to the state or to each other. Taxes, debts, and financial obligations remained unchanged.[56]

The currency exchange obviously brought about a large reduction in currency in circulation. According to Konnik, it was reduced by a factor of 13.5, which would amount to the confiscation of some 350 billion old rubles. This represents a sum greater than the turnover of state and cooperative trade in 1947.[57] A precise estimate of the size of the actual appropriation may be impossible, but there is no doubt that a shortage of currency immediately occurred. Zverev mentions it directly.[58] Another author, G. A. Dikhtiar, blames this shortage for the unusual drop in the turnover of state and cooperative retail trade during the first quarter of 1948. According to Dikhtiar, there was usually a seasonal drop of about 10 per cent between the fourth quarter of one year and the first quarter of the following year. However, the reduction in the first quarter of 1948 was abnormal. Turnover in the fourth quarter of 1947 was 92.9 billion rubles, but only 68.8 billion in the first quarter of 1948.[59] Dikhtiar concludes that this drop

54. *Ibid.*, pp. 234–35.
55. On the monetary provisions of the December 14, 1947, decree, see *Resheniia*, Vol. 3, pp. 464–66.
56. See Zverev, *Zapiski*, p. 235.
57. On Konnik's estimates, see pp. 441–43 above.
58. Zverev, *Zapiski*, p. 235.
59. These figures are in pre-1961 rubles (1 1961 ruble = 10 pre-1961 rubles). Dikhtiar's figures are in 1961 rubles.

was caused by a currency shortage and that this phenomenon was responsible for the failure to fulfill the 1948 annual plan for the turnover of state and cooperative retail trade. Actual turnover was 310 billion rubles compared with the 345 billion planned, a fulfillment of 89.9 per cent.[60] This failure to fulfill the sales plan caused an unexpected increase in inventories, which grew from 38.7 billion (or 46 days' worth) on January 1, 1948, to 59.5 billion rubles (or 76 days' worth of sales) on January 1, 1949.[61]

Under the shelter of such a drain of liquid assets from the population, the government could easily undertake the elimination of ration cards and even a reduction in retail prices. This reduction is officially estimated at 16.5 per cent between the fourth quarter of 1947 (before December 15) and the last two weeks of December of 1947 (see Table 119). Our calculations, which may overestimate slightly the increase in "commercial" prices during the war, put it at 35.6 per cent for Moscow (see Table 119). The desire for deflation was undeniable.

Deflationary Policy of 1948–1953 and Maintenance of Inflationary Pressure

Official Reductions in Retail Prices in State Stores

The magnitude and rapidity of the currency exchange caused a disequilibrium between the liquid assets held by the population and the goods offered for sale at the newly fixed prices. This is not surprising in view of the relation between retail trade turnover and currency in circulation in 1940 and in 1948–1949. State and cooperative retail trade increased by 77.1 per cent between 1940 and 1948 and by 91.4 per cent between 1940 and 1949.[62] Currency in circulation, on the other hand, increased only 27 per cent between January 1, 1941, and December 22, 1947, and 30–40 per cent between 1940 and 1949 (see Table 111). Hence a substantial increase in the velocity of circulation of currency would have been necessary to have made up for the lack of currency. According to Konnik, the proportion of retail trade receipts in monetary holdings of the State Bank did not change much between 1940 and 1950; it was 85.7 per cent in 1940, 87.8 per cent in 1945, and 84.7 per cent in 1950.[63] Konnik's data on the velocity of circulation are, unfortunately, difficult to interpret. In any case, the shortage of currency in the hands of individuals created conditions favorable for official price decreases.

The size of the price decreases decided upon after the currency exchange of December 1947 is shown in Table 121. My index shows even greater decreases than the official Soviet index. The differences may result from several factors. First, official Soviet sources do not give the movement of the cost-of-living index from 1947 to 1953. During this time there were increases in prices of services and heating, which means that the cost-of-living index went down less than the retail price index. A second point of difference is the level of collective farm market prices accepted for 1947 after December 15. In my index, Basile Kerblay's estimate of collective farm market prices in Moscow before the reform (an index

60. Dikhtiar, *Sovetskaia torgovlia*, p. 270.
61. *Ibid*.
62. The turnover of state and cooperative retail trade was 175.1 billion rubles in 1940, 310.2 billion in 1948, and 335.1 billion in 1949 (*Sovetskaia torgovlia*, 1956, p. 20).
63. Konnik, *Zakonomernosti*, p. 50.

Table 121   Changes in Retail Prices and Cost of Living between 1947 and 1953

	1947 (after Dec. 15) (1940 = 100) (1)	1953 (2)	Col. 2 as Per Cent of Col. 1 (3)
Zaleski index (for Moscow)			
Food products	232.5	111.7	48.0
Alcoholic beverages	600.0	203.0	33.8
Tobacco and products	312.6	178.8	57.2
Manufactured goods	152.7	98.9	64.8
State and cooperative retail trade	258.4	111.4	43.1
Heating and lighting	151.0	218.6	144.8
Rent and services	121.8	160.5	131.8
Collective farm market	288.0	97	33.7
Cost of living	242.6	118.2	48.7
Official Soviet index			
State and cooperative retail trade	266	144	54.1

Source: Table 118, lines 1, 4, 10, 13, 16, 20, 21, 8, and 22, and Table 119, line 4.

of 719, with 1940 = 100) was divided by 2.5, on the strength of S. P. Figurnov's statement that bazaar prices for basic products dropped by a factor of two or three immediately after the reform.[64] This yielded an estimate of the price index as 288. On the other hand, Figurnov accepts an index of collective farm market prices of 372 (with 1940 = 100) for 1947, before the reform, and he seems to suggest that the index he gives for 1948 (134 with 1940 = 100) also applies to the last two weeks of 1947. Thus, according to Figurnov, the drop in collective farm market prices would be from an index number of 134 to 97 in 1953. This result, contrary to the implication of my index, would mean that the movement of collective farm market prices actually slowed down the general downward movement in retail prices of consumer goods.

The government stressed the benefits enjoyed by the population as a result of the price reductions, and Table 122 summarizes the effects of this policy. The presentation of the benefits is slightly misleading; the "annual" savings were theoretical because the price reductions took place either March 1 or April 1 and the population had already bought products at the "old" prices. In any case, the reduction was real and larger for food products than for manufactured goods (see Table 121), which had a considerable effect on family budgets. Prices of such products as bread, meat, and butter were reduced more than the average; prices in 1954 compared with the fourth quarter of 1947 (before December 16) were 33 per cent for bread, 36 per cent for meat and poultry, and 33 per cent for butter.[65]

Table 122 shows that price reductions were rapid but uneven. Despite an

64. Figurnov, *Realnaia plata*, p. 158.
65. *Ibid.*, p. 157.

Table 122   Effect of Reductions in Consumer Goods Prices in State and Cooperative Trade, 1947–1954

	Price Index		Annual Saving by Households in Prices of Preceding Year (billion rubles)
	Fourth Quarter[a] of 1947 = 100	As Per Cent of Preceding Year	
December 1947	83	−16.6	57
April 1948 ⎱ March 1949 ⎰	71	−14.8	48
March 1950	57	−19.8	80
March 1951	53	−6.8	28
April 1952	50	−5.7	24
April 1953	45	−10.8	50
April 1954	43	−4.0	20

Source: Figurnov, *Realnaia plata*, p. 156.

a. Before December 16, 1947.

increase in retail trade turnover between 1947 and 1954, the "annual savings" diminished and the percentages of the reductions decreased. Even the April 1, 1953, reduction, obviously politically motivated following Stalin's death, did not change the general trend. But to understand fully the effect of these price reductions, it is necessary to consider its counterpart—the effect of the policy on the money income of the population.

Slowing Down the Rise in Monetary Incomes and Financial Pressure

Household money incomes were presented in Table 113. Two categories of income are the most important: nonfarm wages and salaries, and peasant incomes. The movement of the former reflects urban incomes reasonably well, but the latter vary more widely and hence are more difficult to represent by a single index. Three sources of peasant incomes must be distinguished: money payments, sales to the state, and sales on the collective farm market.

The slowing down of the increase in money wages is very clear during the period of retail price reductions. Between 1947 and 1952 the increase was only 18.1 per cent (see Table A-5); during the war (1941–1945), despite a considerable deceleration, it had been 31.1 per cent (see Table 70 in Chapter 15). In the two postwar years, money wages increased by 31.2 per cent (see Tables A-4 and A-5); in the eight years from 1947 to 1955, they rose by only 25.6 per cent.[66] The reversal of the trend of the first five-year plans is striking. Money wages of workers and employees rose by 78.4 per cent during the First Five-Year Plan (1928–1932) and by 143.0 per cent during the Second Five-Year Plan (1933–1937).

Estimating the deceleration of growth in peasant incomes is more difficult since part of this income was obtained through sales of surplus private plot

66. Calculated from 1955 wages (in *Narodnoe khoziaistvo SSSR v 1964 godu* [The USSR National Economy in 1964], Moscow, 1965, p. 555) and 1947 wages (in Table A–5).

production on the collective farm market. The money income of peasants from their private plots is divided into two parts: sales to the state (procurement agencies at fixed prices) and sales on the collective farm market (at open-market prices). During and after the war (1941–1947), there was a considerable disproportion between these two sources of income. Income from sales to the state remained stable, while income from open-market sales increased at a dizzying pace as prices increased on the collective farm market. Indeed, in 1947, of a total of 159.7 billion rubles of money income of collective farmers, 150.7 billion—94.4 per cent—came from sales on the collective farm market (see Table 123).

Hence the reduction of collective farm market prices was the most important factor in reducing the income of collective farmers, causing them to lose more than 100 billion rubles every year. These losses were much greater than the gains derived from decreases in state and cooperative retail trade prices shown in Table 122. Clearly, these gains accrued mainly to city-dwellers.[67]

Government policy regarding peasant incomes, moreover, had been extremely restrictive since the beginning of the five-year plans. The prices that the government paid to the collective farms or collective farmers for procurements, except for technical crops, increased much more slowly than the prices of state and cooperative trade. In 1952, the index of state and cooperative retail trade prices was 1,026 (based on 1928 = 100), but the indexes of prices paid for grain, potatoes, and livestock products ranged from 119 to 400 (see Table 124).

Thus, to cut back peasant money incomes, the government did not have to take any special measures after 1947. To maintain peasant money incomes from the state at extremely low levels, it sufficed to continue paying them low prices. Table 113 shows that income from the sale of agricultural products to state procurement agencies, which was only 2 billion rubles (or 1.3 per cent of collective farm incomes) in 1947, rose only to 2.5 billion rubles in 1952 (when it constituted 4.1 per cent). The increase in 1953 to 6.6 billion rubles resulted from a change in policy after Stalin's death. Altogether, government procurement prices increased 54 per cent between 1952 and 1953.[68] But for the principal agricultural products, 1953 prices were still much lower than those received by the government in state and cooperative trade (see Table 124).

Much more serious for peasant incomes were the effects of this policy on the income of the collective farms. Collective farmers did not receive a wage for their work but participated in the net profit of the collective farm, which was distributed according to the number of *trudodni* ("labor days") earned by each of them.[69] By refusing to pay higher prices for compulsory deliveries of the production of the collective farms while allowing the prices at which they purchased goods to rise (the collective farms bought many products in the retail trade network) and by making the income of collective farms independent, in case of

67. In fact, the percentage share of state and cooperative trade in rural areas in the total trade turnover moved as follows between 1945 and 1952: 1945, 26; 1946, 23; 1947, 18; 1948, 20; 1949, 23; 1950, 24; 1951, 25; and 1952, 25 (Dikhtiar, *Sovetskaia torgovlia*, p. 275).

68. Malafeev, *Istoriia*, p. 412.

69. An actual day of work corresponded to 1.4 *trudodni* in 1954 (Henri Wronski, *Rémunération et niveau de vie dans les kolkhoz: Le troudoden*, Paris, 1957, p. 135).

Table 123   Comparison of Money Incomes and Expenditures of Households in 1947 and 1953 (billion rubles)

	1947	1953	Increase or Decrease
Income			
Wages and salaries	219.3	356.1	+136.8
Other payments and military pay	54.7	73.0	+18.3
Income of cooperative artisans and other money income	28.8	45.2	+16.4
Money payments to collective farmers for *trudodni*	7.0	18.4	+11.4
Income from sale of farm products to state procurement agencies	2.0	6.6	+4.6
Income from sale of farm products to collective farm market	150.7	41.5	−109.2
Pensions and allowances	32.9	38.9	+6.0
Stipends and scholarships	3.9	5.7	+1.8
Interests on loans and savings	7.4	10.7	+3.3
Insurance payments and credits for construction of private houses	1.6	1.2	−0.4
Total	508.3	597.3	+89.0
Expenditures			
State and cooperative retail trade sales to households	306.0	398.4	+92.4
Collective farm market sales to households	145.6	46.4	−99.2
Housing, services, and tuition payments	28.3	54.9	+26.6
Trade union, party, and other dues	3.9	6.6	+2.7
Direct taxes	38.3	57.4	+19.1
Net increase in savings and loans	24.5	30.0	+5.5
Total	546.6	593.7	+47.1

Source: Tables 113 and 114.

poor harvest, of the quantity of products sold, the government made the collective farms support the failures of the agricultural sector. The collective farms were put in a deficit financial position and the profits to be distributed per *trudoden* became ridiculously small.

The money value of the *trudoden* had been absurdly low even before the war (29 kopeks in 1933, 27 in 1934, 65 in 1935, 76 in 1936, 85 in 1937, and 109 in 1938).[70] The government has long maintained silence on this subject, but Jasny was able to calculate the data for Moscow Province, the only area for which data are available for several years (see Table 125). In 1950, an able-bodied collective farmer earned an average of 300 *trudodni* a year,[71] which gave him a money income of *165 rubles a year* from his work on the collective farm. By contrast, the average money wage of workers and employees was 7,668 rubles for the same year (see Table A-1). According to Soviet authors, in 1954 the money share of the *trudoden* averaged 43.1 per cent of the total value of the *trudoden* in the Russian Republic.[72] Thus the value of the *trudoden* in Moscow Province, including pay-

70. *Ibid.*, p. 130.

71. The number of *trudodni* earned in 1950 was 8,286 (*Narodnoe khoziaistvo SSSR* [The USSR National Economy], Moscow, 1956, p. 129) and employment in the collectivized sector of collective farms in 1950 was 27.6 million (*Selskoe khoziaistvo SSSR* [Agriculture in the USSR], Moscow, 1971, p. 13).

72. M. Solenova, "Ob oplate truda v kolkhozakh" [On the Remuneration of Labor on Collective Farms], *Kommunist* [The Communist], No. 1, 1956, p. 37.

Table 124   Comparison of State and Cooperative Retail Trade Prices and Prices Paid by the State for Agricultural Procurements, 1940–1953 (1929 = 100[a])

	1940	1947	1952	1953
State and cooperative retail trade prices	637	2,045	1,026	930
Prices paid for procurements:				
Wheat	142		119	292
Potatoes	128		146	461
Beef cattle	234		209	706
Pigs	200		171	775
Milk	243		400	808
Cotton	509		1,127	1,183
Sugar beets	369		1,012	1,457
Flax	300		1,413	1,964

Source: Malafeev, *Istoriia*, pp. 267, 408, and 412–13.

a. Except for state and cooperative retail trade prices, where 1928 = 100.

ments in kind, part of which is shown in Table 125, amounted to 383 rubles a year, less than a twentieth of the average money wage for that year.

The average value of the *trudoden* in Moscow Province seems to have been lower than that for the country as a whole, except possibly for 1948 and adjacent years. For the whole country, average money payments per *trudoden* were 1.25 rubles in 1940 and 1.40 rubles in 1952,[73] which, for 300 *trudodni* worked a year, amounts to 375 and 420 rubles, respectively, while the average annual wage increased from 3,972 to 8,066 rubles during these years.[74] During the years 1947 to 1952 total money payments increased from 7.0 to 13.4 billion rubles (see Table 113). In 1953, as a result of Khrushchev's efforts, these payments increased to 18.4 billion rubles (see Table 123), but they still amounted to less than half the money income of peasants obtained from sales on the collective farm market.

Additional pressure was put on peasant incomes through the agricultural tax. The 1939 provisions introduced income norms based on sown area and progressive rates and intended to discourage the cultivation of private plots.[75] Between 1946 and 1952, the agricultural tax increased by 78 per cent (from 5.9 to 10.5 billion rubles),[76] while, according to Table 114, all other direct taxes increased by 73 per cent (from 33.8 to 58.5 billion rubles).

Much of this discrimination against peasants came from Stalin's false idea of the material situation of collective farmers. Quite typical is an exchange of views between Stalin and Minister of Finance Zverev on this subject.[77]

73. Jasny, *Soviet Industrialization*, p. 421.
74. See Table A–1 for 1940 and A. Becker, "Soviet National Income and Product, 1958–1962," RAND Research Memorandum 4394–PR, Santa Monica, 1965, p. 100, for 1952.
75. Franklyn D. Holzman, *Soviet Taxation: The Fiscal and Monetary Problems of a Planned Economy*, Cambridge, Mass., 1955, p. 197.
76. For 1946, Zverev, *Zapiski*, p. 247; for 1952, calculated from 1953 (*ibid.*) and planned reduction in 1953 (given in Holzman, *Soviet Taxation*, p. 198).
77. "Stalin: All a collective farmer has to do to satisfy the Ministry of Finance is to sell a chicken.

Table 125   Distribution per *Trudoden* in Moscow Province, 1948–1956

	Money (rubles)	Grain (kg)	Potatoes (kg)	Vegetables (kg)
1948	0.61	0.74	3.97	1.53
1949	0.62	0.74	3.18	1.35
1950	0.55	0.64	1.99	0.96
1951	0.51	0.67	1.03	0.34
1952	0.57	0.74	1.55	0.46
1953	0.92	0.33	1.07	0.98
1954	1.81	0.63	0.60	0.80
1955	2.73	1.26	0.28	0.87
1956	3.48	1.16	1.19	0.80

Source: Jasny, *Soviet Industrialization*, p. 422.

The financial pressure exerted on agricultural income was also important for other income during the period of retail price reductions. As just mentioned, direct taxes rose by 73 per cent between 1947 and 1952, while the wage funds of workers and employees increased only 55 per cent during the same period. An additional tax was also levied through essentially obligatory loans, withheld directly from wages. Payments for loans increased from 24.5 billion rubles in 1947 to 41.2 billion rubles in 1952, that is, by 68 per cent. But the state debt also increased (from 126.1 billion rubles in 1947 to 149.8 billion in 1952 and 183.5 billion in 1953), which almost doubled the interest payments made by the government.[78] The reduction of the total amount of state loans from 36.3 billion rubles in 1952 to 17.3 billion in 1953,[79] fixed by the government, was obviously motivated by the fear of having to increase government interest payments once again. A moratorium on interest payments and the abolition of loans were declared in 1957.

*Disequilibrium on the Consumer Goods Market
and Institutionalization of Inflationary Pressures*

The deflationary policy and authoritarian reductions in retail prices were not met with unanimous approval. Criticisms on this score surfaced after Stalin's death. Dikhtiar expressed a general criticism in blaming the whole system of Soviet trade for the poor conditions after the abolition of rationing.[80] Wartime habits had led industrial enterprises to think that there was demand for their products, whatever the quality. The sales organizations of industry did not sort the products at their plants, but sent goods to trading agencies in large lots,

"Zverev: Unfortunately, Comrade Stalin, that's not exactly the way things are. For some collective farmers, even a cow wouldn't be enough to pay the tax" (Zverev, *Zapiski*, p. 244).

78. Which amounted to 5.3 billion rubles in 1947, 6.8 billion in 1952, and 9.7 billion in 1953 (Figurnov, *Realnaia plata*, p. 180). Figurnov's figures differ a little from those in Table 113.

79. *Ibid.*, p. 177. State loans signed up for in one year are partly paid in the following year, which explains the discrepancies between these figures and the ones in Table 114.

80. Dikhtiar, *Sovetskaia torgovlia*, p. 271.

without taking delivery schedules or assortment into account and without adequate packing. Provisions to eliminate these shortcomings were taken after the
war. A decree issued on November 20, 1948,[81] called for a better organization of
trade and required the Ministry of Light Industry to set assortment plans for its
production in agreement with the Ministry of Trade and *Tsentrosoiuz*, taking into
account the orders of the trading agencies. In 1951 the prewar system of orders
for goods was reinstituted; in 1949 documentation of regional trade plans was to
be improved and the Central Statistical Administration was to be required to
prepare quarterly statistics on this subject.[82] All these government provisions
did not lead to any substantial improvement in the consumer goods market
during the period of price reductions.

One of the most important criticisms of the policy of authoritarian price reductions concerned the repercussions it had on the level of wages. The deceleration
in money wage increases caused some unwanted changes in wage differentials,
altered the desired relation between wages and output, and weakened the
material incentives of workers. It also slowed down the rate of increase in wages
of the lowest paid workers.[83] With stable wages and uniform reductions in
prices, workers with the highest money incomes enjoyed the largest increases in
real income.

But the most frequent criticism centered on the uniform and automatic nature
of these reductions. Figurnov and Malafeev compare the reductions in retail
prices with the reductions in industrial costs.[84] They insist that there was no
correspondence between the movements of these two, on the whole or for the
principal products. This compromised the operation of "the law of value" and
made subsidies necessary, which took the form of reductions in the turnover
tax.[85] But these reductions were uniform over entire groups of products and did
not correspond to changes in production costs of individual products. As a
result, the discrepancy between the price and cost of certain products rose,
which caused an artificial increase in profitability. For other products, reductions
in profits or even losses occurred that were no less artificial.[86]

Many price reductions included in the reform were meaningless because the
quantities produced were not sufficient to meet demand, thus forcing the population to buy more expensive products and so, for consumers, the price reductions were illusory. In addition, the emphasis laid on basic products stimulated
an increased demand and often led to dysfunctional behavior. For example,

81. *Ibid.*, pp. 271–72.

82. *Ibid.*, pp. 272–73.

83. Figurnov, *Realnaia plata*, pp. 162–63.

84. *Ibid.*, pp. 161–62, and Malafeev, *Istoriia*, pp. 263–64.

85. Figurnov admits that these comparisons are not completely valid since they cover, on the one
hand, reductions in the retail prices of consumer goods and, on the other, the movement of costs of
all industrial products, but he considers that the general movement of prices and costs corresponds
to the figures he cites. On the reduction in retail prices, see Table 122. The reduction in industrial
production costs (in constant prices) below the preceding year is: −8.6 per cent in 1948, −6.8 per
cent in 1949, −5.4 per cent in 1950 and in 1951, −4.4 per cent in 1952, −3.7 per cent in 1953, and
−3.2 per cent in 1954 (Figurnov, *Realnaia plata*, p. 161).

86. Malafeev, *Istoriia*, p. 265.

bread was used to feed cattle in suburban areas, and alcohol was produced at home.[87]

The major disproportions tended to be self-perpetuating. In 1952, at the prevailing level of prices, total effective demand (particularly of the rural population) began to fall behind the supply of several nonfood products.[88] At the same time, low agricultural production rates caused output of food products to be insufficient to meet urban demand.[89]

One of the consequences of this situation was an unwanted increase in retail trade inventories. According to Dikhtiar, the inventories reflected disequilibrium in the consumer goods markets; inventory levels were closely linked to rates of sales. The increase in inventories that occurred between January 1, 1951, and January 1, 1953, is shown in Table 126 and reflects, in cooperative trade, the disequilibrium between supply and the liquid assets of the rural population.

Table 126   Changes in Inventories in Retail Trade between 1950 and 1952 (days of sales)

	On Jan. 1, 1951		On Jan. 1, 1953	
	Total	Consumer Cooperatives	Total	Consumer Cooperatives
Total goods	70	109	94	149
Cotton fabrics	55	57	149	157
Silk and rayon fabrics	63	128	157	213
Linen fabrics	84	72	117	137
Clothing, hats, and furs	86	158	101	176
Knitted goods	54	87	87	160
Hosiery	93	160	220	325
Leather shoes	148	237	224	324
China and glassware	216	263	253	345
Wood and construction materials	99	153	180	179

Source: *Sovetskaia torgovlia*, 1964, pp. 122–23, as cited in Dikhtiar, *Sovetskaia torgovlia*, p. 274.

As noted above, the lack of correspondence between price reductions, on the one hand, and cost reductions and production increases, on the other, caused losses to be recorded for several products, particularly food products. Therefore, it is not surprising that in 1950 and 1951 prices on the collective farm market did not fall along with the reductions in prices of food products in state trade; on the contrary, collective farm prices rose moderately (see Table 127).[90]

Malafeev asserts that speculators established certain monopoly prices on the

87. Figurnov, *Realnaia plata*, p. 163.

88. Dikhtiar, *Sovetskaia torgovlia*, p. 273. On the share of sales in rural localities, see footnote 67 above. This share was 29 per cent in 1940 (*ibid.*, p. 275).

89. Dikhtiar (*ibid.*, p. 273) also stresses the fact that the disproportion between supply and demand of food products for the urban population was caused by price reductions made without taking into account either the costs of agricultural products or the real possibilities of increasing their production.

90. Malafeev, *Istoriia*, p. 265.

Table 127   Collective Farm Market Prices as Percentage of State and Cooperative Trade Prices, 1940–1958

	Malafeev (1)	Jasny (2)
1940		185
1945		618
1947		352
1948		211
1949		85
1950	110	104
1951	117	119
1952	120	131
1953	123	142
1954	134	160
1955		160
1956	a	144
1957		137
1958		144

Source: Col. 1: Malafeev, *Istoriia*, p. 265; col. 2: Jasny, *Soviet Industrialization*, p. 274.

a. According to Malafeev (*Istoriia*, p. 265), the spread between collective farm market prices and state and cooperative trade prices increased every year from 1950 to 1956.

collective farm market and also in under-the-counter trade in industrial products for their personal gain.[91] Malafeev's observation is partly true; retailers always try to derive some gain from the services they offer. They keep a part of the difference between prices in different sectors of trade. But this gain was more the result than the cause of the disequilibrium. The real cause lay in the government policy toward retail prices, which reduced the prices and turnover of collective farm trade and deprived peasants of 100 billion rubles of their money income (see Table 123 above). Thus the Soviet government effected a huge transfer of purchasing power to the urban population. But the reduction of agricultural income caused reductions in agricultural production. Hence collective farm market prices rose willy-nilly, which spontaneously mitigated the adverse effects of the government price policy.

In reality, the policy of authoritarian reductions in retail prices accentuated the inflationary pressures on the consumer goods market. But the experience of 1947–1953 shows that the Stalinist system of administrative planning was well equipped to handle a certain degree of inflationary pressure.[92] The policy of deliberately planning a surplus of expenditures over income of the population (see Table 114 above), even though not entirely carried out, certainly made it possible to limit the damage. But there were other barriers against the propagation of inflationary pressures. The effects of the agricultural difficulties had repercussions on the peasants through remuneration based on collective farm

91. *Ibid*.
92. It is tempting to compare this situation to the capacity of market economies to support a certain degree of budgetary deficit.

profits; private agriculture was maintained as a safety valve, euphemistically called individual plots; wages and currency in circulation were strictly controlled; and retail trade was rationed at the store level.

All this made a certain degree of inflationary pressure supportable. On the other hand, recourse to such methods may be habit-forming and leads to choosing the easy way out at the expense of efficiency.

CHAPTER 19

Conclusions

Stalinist Model of Authoritarian Administrative Planning

The first conclusion to be drawn from the study of Stalinist planning is this: our understanding of the mechanisms involved is overly influenced by observation of plans drawn up in market economies. An example of the effect of that influence can be seen in my own earlier definition of planning in a collective economy: "In a collective economy, the coordination of the plans of individuals and of enterprises is, in principle, performed a priori by a central authority" and this coordination is achieved "by building a hierarchy of economic units and their plans."[1] This definition assumes that economic units draft their plans first, and the central authority subsequently coordinates them. The Stalinist experience shows that this explanation is incorrect. The main job of the Stalinist planner is not the coordination of plans. He has a more ambitious goal—to impose his vision of the future on the country. How does he impose his will? The first step takes place on paper, where the main goals chosen by the planner are set out. This step is a choice of growth strategy rather than an attempt to eliminate incompatible projects or to prevent disequilibrium. At the outset, there is, therefore, a single over-all "plan," which provides the basis for the subsequent allocation of specific tasks. The tasks include goals to be met and provision of the means to achieve them. They may be thought of as mini-plans, not yet operational, by means of which the central authority transmits its growth strategy through the channels of the hierarchy. These mini-plans become operational as they descend the economic hierarchy (each echelon adding details that become orders for the lower echelons), and specific tasks are transmitted to the basic units. During ensuing phases of the process, dossiers specifying the details of the plans are transmitted back up through the hierarchy. These dossiers are then made into the final plan; in the meanwhile, the basic units begin carrying

---

1. Eugène Zaleski, *Planning for Economic Growth in the Soviet Union, 1918–1932*, translated and edited by Marie-Christine MacAndrew and G. Warren Nutter, Chapel Hill, N.C., 1971, p. 4.

out the tasks that have been assigned to them. Thus, the final coordination of plans is done *ex post* after they have been put into operation.

Therefore, I propose another definition of Stalinist planning: it is the process of allocating tasks and resources through the channels of the hierarchy to the basic economic units. From this definition derive the following four principal features of the model.

1. Heterogeneous Nature of the Central National Plan

In the earlier volume of my work on planning, a plan was defined as "a decision taken by a subject with regard to goals to be pursued and to the means of achieving them."[2] This definition implies some choice of goals and a will to act to achieve them. The Stalinist plan does not fulfill these conditions. It includes direct or implied goals that are in the administrative dossiers which ultimately comprise the national plan, estimates of the behavior of economic units that the government influences through (nonconstraining) "economic tools" (prices, credit, subsidies, financial provisions), and estimates of the evolution of phenomena on which the government has little if any influence (climate and harvest, the situation on foreign markets, demography, the development of technical progress in the outside world).

Hence the Stalinist plan is an amalgam of results anticipated from actions taken by the government and projections made on more or less solid bases. The Stalinist experience shows that both parts of this plan are fragile, the part based on orders transmitted through hierarchical channels very often being more fragile than even bold projections.

How, then, can the Stalinist plan be defined? Since the realism of the means provided for its implementation is questionable, only the first part of the definition previously accepted can be maintained: the Stalinist national plan remains "a vision of growth,"[3] itself at the service of a development strategy.

2. Priority of Political Objectives
and of the Political Apparatus in Drafting and Implementing the Plan

Western economists tend to apply their own criteria to the Soviet plan, which usually results in their evaluating it in terms of growth in national income or some similar aggregate. But such criteria focus on only one aspect of economic policy, one which, indeed, may itself be of little importance to the planners.

In fact, Soviet authorities judge any plan primarily by how well it conforms to the ideological and political objectives of the country. The Communist Party uses its vast apparatus to advance those objectives at all levels of the hierarchy. The Soviet regime does not recognize any division of powers. The Party not only controls the legislative, executive, and judiciary branches but it also exercises religious (ideological, in the official vocabulary) and economic power.

Therefore, in studying plans, three factors must be taken into account. First,

2. *Ibid.*, p. 3.
3. *Ibid.*, p. 297.

the Party's ideological objectives have priority over such economic criteria as social welfare or growth in national income;[4] the ideological objectives represent a constraint that must always be kept in mind. Second, the Party apparatus is ubiquitous at all levels of economic life. Third, besides being an organization built on a strict hierarchy, the Stalinist Communist Party also is in the process of development.[5] The struggle for power within the Party and the repression of enemies, real or imagined, of Stalin's personal dictatorship had a decisive influence on the criteria used to judge the national plans as well as the plans at all other levels of economic management.

3. Priority of Management over Planning

In describing the Soviet economy—a centrally planned economy—the tendency is to give planning priority over management. This would be correct if the central plan, broken down among economic units in an authoritarian fashion, were actually carried out. However, this study shows that the existence of such a central national plan, coherent and perfect, to be subdivided and implemented at all levels, is only a *myth*. What actually exists, as in any centrally administered economy, is an endless number of plans, constantly evolving, that are coordinated *ex post* after they have been put into operation. The unification of these innumerable plans into a single national plan, supposedly coherent, takes place rarely (once or twice during a five-year period and once for an annual or quarterly plan); furthermore, the attempt at unification is only a projection of observed tendencies resulting from extrapolating trends based on natural forces.

In view of the changing and often ephemeral nature of the plans, management emerges as the only constant in the system. The economic administration is built on a strict hierarchy descending from the ministry (or people's commissariat) to the enterprise, subject to strict discipline, obeying orders transmitted continuously. Under each management agency, from the Council of Ministers down to the enterprises, there is a planning commission with a consulting role (see Chart 2 in Chapter 3). Of course, higher-level "consultants" (Gosplan) tend to take over certain management functions (material and equipment supply) or to intervene more or less directly in management, but then they become administrators just like the others and their "planning" becomes management.

The priority of management over planning has been the dominant feature of the Soviet economy since Stalin's time. Since management is highly centralized, this feature is characteristic of the entire model. Therefore, it seems more nearly correct to call the economy "centrally managed" rather than centrally planned.

I have devoted considerable space in this book to describing the economic administration in the Soviet Union. The purpose was to determine the extent to which the stability of central management replaced the instability of planning and in whose hands lay the real decision-making power.[6] It was found that only the restricted committee of the Council of Ministers (called the Council for Labor

4. See the formulation of the goals of the Second Five-Year Plan at the beginning of Chapter 6.
5. On this point, see pp. 9–10 in Chapter 2.
6. The distribution of the decision-making power is discussed in the following section.

and Defense for a long time, later divided into the Economic Council and the Defense Committee, and finally merged into the Council of War) had any stability as an institution. The other management agencies, ministries, central administrations (*Glavki*), and enterprises were reorganized more or less constantly, like divisions, regiments, or battalions in an army. Moreover, the institutional approach was the rule; each new problem was handled by creating a new institution or reorganizing an old one. By adding to the multiple encroachments on the specialized agencies (state committees or special commissions for labor, wages, norms, new techniques, finances, not to mention planning committees), these *ad hoc* committees further contributed to the complexity of the system. But they reinforced the priority of current management over planning and the priority of the central authority and Stalin's personal dictatorship over the economic administration.

4. *Splitting Up Economic Decision-Making in the Face of Absolute Central Power*

The title of this section suggests a surprising conclusion in an economy that has just been defined as centrally managed. However, the centralization of power does not imply an equal concentration of decision-making authority, and the formal appropriation of all power does not carry with it the ability to exercise that power. To clarify, the breakdown of actual decision-making power should be examined in three areas: management, planning, and resource allocation.

Four main levels of management can be distinguished: central authority (restricted committee of the Council of Ministers), ministry, *Glavk*, and enterprise. At each level, orders from above are made more precise by the management involved. Decision-making, then, consists of making orders from above more precise and, furthermore, in independent arbitration in cases when the higher authorities are not consulted. It is easy to show that each level has real power. The higher authorities and the ministry officially hold all the power, but as a practical matter they cannot deal with everything. Even if the decrees setting norms for raw material consumption in the production of shoes or fabrics are published in the official documents under the signature of the prime minister (Molotov, during this period), it is hard to believe that he has any personal ideas on the subject. That directors should ratify with their signatures decisions taken by other people is normal procedure, but power that is impossible to exercise is not real power. Many of the powers officially held by higher authorities were in actual fact exercised by much lower echelons who passed the responsibility off onto the higher authorities. In such a system, persons who actually make decisions thus become anonymous.

It is generally accepted that the most important management functions were held during this period by the ministry *Glavki*.[7] Their control of enterprise management tended to increase, particularly in production and finance. Never-

7. On this subject, see pp. 33–34 in Chapter 2.

theless, their freedom of action was severely limited, both from above—by the ministry and various specialized agencies—and from below—by enterprises that controlled the production funds and administered manpower.

The enterprise theoretically has the least power. Nevertheless, it is the basic management unit, has accounting autonomy and an autonomous balance sheet, and represents "the lowest unit of industry to be dealt with in plans and in checks on the execution of these plans."[8] Actually, the real decision-making power of the enterprise is greater than its official power. The enterprise is a group of workers with their own interests—notably, maximization of their income—that are not always served by the plans imposed from above. So the enterprise uses what powers remain to it (the most important being the declaration of the enterprise's real production capacities) to influence the plan in such a way as to promote its own interests. The enterprise also derives decision-making power from the fact that the many orders it receives are not always compatible and that the numerous managerial success criteria leave the enterprise a certain choice.

But the real power of the enterprise is even greater. For it is at the enterprise level that the encounter occurs between directives (planned or not) from higher agencies and technical and economic constraints. Whoever is officially entitled to change an order, it is at the execution level (i.e., the enterprise) that the feasibility of the order is established. It is at this enterprise level that planning goals meet economic reality.

The allocation of powers among the various management levels can be seen even more clearly in the process of drafting the plans.[9] The precision of the plan indexes, highly aggregated at the central level, is sharpened at each level; this sharpening consists of making decisions. There is an inverse relation between the number of indexes imposed on an enterprise and its autonomy. The number of plan indexes imposed by the central authorities increased continuously during the Stalinist planning period; however, the number imposed by intermediate echelons is not known. Nevertheless, it is sufficient to compare the number of centrally established indexes (9,490 in 1953) with the list of industrial products (more than 20 million) to realize the extent of the jurisdiction of intermediary agencies and enterprises. Moreover, plan indexes covered more than production in general and industrial production in particular.

Control over material and equipment supply is highly concentrated, largely in the ministries and the *Glavki*.[10] But Soviet enterprises notoriously engage in production for self-supply, so part of the supply system is effectively decentralized. In principle, suppliers should follow the quarterly plans for material and equipment supply. In actual fact, in times of scarcity, they hold real power over supply allocation and often willingly deal with factory "fixers" (*tolkachi*).[11] The decision-making power in material and equipment supply is, moreover, tied to that in production: refusal to deliver causes production stoppage and hence

8. David Granick, *Management of the Industrial Firm in the USSR*, New York, 1955, p. 21.
9. See pp. 62–66 in Chapter 4.
10. See pp. 88–91 in Chapter 5.
11. Joseph S. Berliner, *Factory and Manager in the USSR*, Cambridge, Mass., 1957, pp. 207–30.

brings about intervention by those authorities who have an interest in the matter. Taking these factors together, it is seen that decision-making in supply is decentralized in a very simple way. Enterprises tend to stock up, more or less legally, on scarce materials and equipment or to barter their own production. The experience of Stalinist planning shows that it was quite difficult to enforce strict priorities in supply and to contain the pressures from the "base."

Coherence of Authoritarian Administrative Plans

Stalinist planning gave rise to the practice of putting into operation plans, whether approved or not, that were not balanced or coherent. I shall try to show that the lack of coherence was the result of the planning system itself rather than of mistakes by the planners or inconsistencies of economic policy.

Formal and Real Equilibrium

The equilibrium of a Stalinist plan was obtained largely by means of balances. These balances, in physical and in value terms, were meant to ensure a correspondence between needs and resources and hence to replace the market, whose role the system tried to reduce to the minimum. Soviet authorities have been very secretive about the contents of these balances and very few of them have been published, even in aggregated form. They almost always show perfect equilibrium between resources and needs, but the equilibrium is more apparent than real.

Physical balances, which the Stalinist planners preferred, are necessarily of limited scope. They are well suited to homogeneous products like electric power, coal, or pig iron but less well suited to diversified products like fabrics or machines. These balances are necessarily aggregated, which limits their practical significance.

Value balances are the only ones possible for many products (equipment, for instance), and only from them can equilibrium between economic aggregates such as saving and investment be calculated. These balances, however, suffer from the basic defect of the administrative planning system: the prices in which they are calculated are arbitrarily fixed by the authorities and do not reflect scarcity. The total purchasing power being distributed according to the values of resources implied by the plan, there is an excess demand for some products and excess supply of others, at the prices set. What use, then, is an equilibrium of balances if the monetary purchasing power based on it cannot be used to acquire the products necessary for maintaining those balances? There is a disequilibrium from the very outset, which the central authorities deal with through a rationing system (material and equipment supply).

Another cause of the real disequilibrium of the balances arises from the very process of administrative planning. The central authorities try to "mobilize" resources by imposing a taut plan. They set "progressive" norms for labor productivity and consumption of materials (costs). These norms are allocated administratively among executors and give rise to underestimated needs and overestimated resources. The resulting general deficit in the production process is then controlled by rationing.

Constant Reorganization of Management and Planning Agencies

Reorganization of planning and management agencies should not necessarily produce a lack of coherence in the plans. As a matter of fact, the reorganization of these agencies under Stalin was not always for the purpose of meeting economic and administrative goals, but was the result of political purges within the Party and government apparatus. These reorganizations were more extensive than their number at the central level would indicate; the Soviet Union is a federal state, and every change in jurisdiction between federal and republic agencies gives rise to multiple changes.

The formal hierarchy of planning agencies did not change significantly during the Stalinist period except for attempts to create a direct administration of Gosplan in the independent republics. But the powers of USSR Gosplan and the local planning commissions changed often and their statutes were changed regularly both before and after the war. The changes in the statutes usually reflected changes in jurisdiction (especially in material and equipment supply) and showed the tenuous dividing line between planning and management in this area.

Not only did these power changes occur, but the establishment of planning commissions was far from complete before the war, especially in districts. Thus there was a separation between the plan made at the central level or by agencies under central, republic, and province authorities, on the one hand, and plans made by enterprises and local agencies, on the other.

Influence of the Planning Process

The organization of planning agencies and the procedures they use to draft a plan have a direct effect on its quality. The difficulties arising from the setup of the local planning agencies have already been mentioned. The federal structure of the management agencies to which the planning committees were attached made their work particularly difficult.

Most notably, Gosplan of the Russian Republic (RSFSR) has a huge territory under its jurisdiction, covering about three-quarters of the country. Therefore, the definition of its authority as distinct from that of USSR Gosplan raises important questions. If RSFSR Gosplan were to deal with all the economic activities on its territory, its work would to a large extent duplicate that of USSR Gosplan. Yet planning by RSFSR Gosplan for its territory was necessary for plan coherence. Since USSR Gosplan tended to interpret its functions very broadly, it appropriated the right to plan industry (and other economic activities) under Union ministries on the territory of the Russian Republic. RSFSR Gosplan, then, worked in a vacuum; USSR Gosplan did not even take account of its results. At the same time, neither Gosplan took responsibility for certain important problems. The eventual outcome was that RSFSR Gosplan handled only economic activities under the Russian Republic Council of Ministers and "took account" of the rest of the economy, which left the door open to inconsistencies.[12]

The same situation existed in Gosplans of the other federal republics and in the province and district planning committees, with the additional problem that it was only with reluctance that the management agencies on their territories transmitted the necessary information. The work of the local planning committees was also hindered for other reasons. The enterprises and agencies drafting plans tended to bypass the appropriate planning committees and address themselves directly to the higher-level planning committee. The fact that they had their own administrative hierarchies made these moves easier.

The administrative nature of the plan also complicated the drafting of a coherent plan. Of course, a common "language" had to be introduced for giving orders.[13] But it was also necessary to go beyond the initial practice of planning only the principal activity of each people's commissariat, because that omitted many auxiliary activities.[14] Even though considerable progress was made in coordinating auxiliary activities, it was clear that coordination could affect only the list of products included in the plan, a list much more aggregated than the list of products used in retrospective statistics.

Obviously, a coherent plan can be drawn up only by qualified people working under reasonable conditions. As has been pointed out,[15] however, despite the sizable increase in the Gosplan staff during the Stalinist period, working conditions were not always very good, to put it mildly. Low wages, purges, and the low regard in which their work was held all gave rise to a high turnover of personnel. Furthermore, the staff were not highly qualified, particularly after the purges of 1936–1937. How could one expect a Gosplan employee in an insecure position to draft a plan for five or more years when he had had litttle experience in his job and had very little chance of keeping the job long?

But what undoubtedly compromises most seriously the coherence of an administrative plan is the atmosphere in which it is drawn up.[16] Drafting a plan is not the same as calculating an optimum or an equilibrium. It is largely a matter of carefully filling out numerous forms in order to make up a dossier. The case for this dossier will be argued by the enterprise management before its superior agency under very sensitive conditions. The goals and the means to achieve them are imposed from the outset, and substantive questions can be raised only under the cloak of technical discussions. The administrative and authoritarian plan is considered a constraint, and the demands of the higher authorities, if taken literally, are not only mutually inconsistent but also inexecutable. The higher authorities who transmit these orders are aware of this fact and ordinarily are willing to compromise. Some planned indexes come to be regarded as more important than others and the government is more sensitive about these (depending on its policy at the moment). At the same time, all the indexes remain

12. See p. 74 in Chapter 4.
13. See beginning of Chapter 4.
14. See pp. 62–63 in Chapter 4.
15. See last section of Chapter 3.
16. See last section of Chapter 4.

mandatory and can be used as whips by the higher authorities to show dissatis-faction.[17]

In such a situation, the enterprise management tries to survive by using what-ever means it possesses; personal and political influence play important roles, and the management uses the danger of not meeting its obligations as a bar-gaining lever. A curious phenomenon appears at such times. By specifying production and fixing the means to achieve it (as though, when ordering shoes, someone fixed not only all the required attributes and the smallest details of production but also the price), the administrative plan suppresses the market. But it gives rise to much more extensive bargaining by bringing into play not only economic factors (taken into account in a competitive market economy) but also political and social pressures, where anything goes. The interests of the individual or group, supposedly eliminated by the suppression of private prop-erty, reappear during the process of determining planned targets.

What can possibly remain of plan coherence after such a planning process? The director of an enterprise who requests investment funds and manpower corresponding exactly to his needs will be in trouble since the higher authorities do not believe him and will cut back his requests considerably.[18] A higher authority who does not apply pressure to his subordinates risks compromising cost savings and productivity plans. The administrative planning process, then, forces the higher authorities to demand more than they expect to get and the executors to demand more resources than they actually require. Hence the point of equilibrium that the approved plan represents lies at the intersection of the influences of the various pressure groups that take part in the bargaining, and it is highly improbable that this point corresponds to the conditions required for coherence. Authoritarian administrative planning being essentially the study of millions of pending dossiers, approval of the plan obtained by these procedures makes coherence impossible.

*Lack of Coherence of Administrative Plans
and Limitation of Their Real Importance*

Lack of coherence in the administrative plans implies that the government cannot consider the national plan as an unalterable whole. Among the plan goals the government is forced to distinguish those that are of paramount importance from those that could eventually be neglected. Government pri-orities can be seen mainly in the management of material and equipment supply, in the course of which those who are to receive supplies are ranked according to priority lists. Material and equipment supply (rationing) is handled within the framework of the current plan, with the less important on the priority lists being neglected in the case of short supply. Other priorities are expressed in plan revisions intended to support the more important sectors or to aid sectors in trouble.

17. This vivid definition of the authoritarian administrative plan was suggested to me by a former planner of high rank who held his job for many years.
18. See the examples on pp. 76–78 and Tables 5 and 6 in Chapter 4.

In actual fact, the use of priorities means the rejection of plan goals that are beyond the limits of the supplies provided by the priority system. The enterprises and activities affected by lack of deliveries can no longer fulfill their plans, and the administrative order to produce loses much of its weight (without being actually canceled). These enterprises have to use the services of *tolkachi* and are eventually advised to try to supply themselves from "local resources"—that is, outside the system of the central plan. In other words, the lack of coherence of administrative plans and the resulting system of priorities restrict the scope of the central plan and enlarge what could be called the sphere of the regulated market economy (*économie dirigée*), that collection of activities in which the plans of enterprises and economic units are not covered by an over-all plan. But this extension of the sphere of the regulated market economy contributes to the lack of coherence in the system because the new activities that are brought into being are disrupted by the lack of supply provisions in the plan. The ensuing economic disequilibrium incites the central planner to increase still further the number of indexes in the central administrative plan and to extend still further the sphere of authoritarian administrative planning in the next plan in order better to control the disrupted sphere.

This lack of coherence of the national administrative plans is especially serious in wartime, when priority activities must have firm plans. The Soviet government understood this very well during World War II, throughout which it did not draft a single national administrative plan.[19] It replaced them with "wartime economic plans" of more restricted scope and with specific plans for sectors that enjoyed superpriority in supply. Other plans for different branches and activities were tied together only by the budget and by rationing and "floated" in the sphere of the regulated market economy.

It must not be forgotten that, besides the regulated market economy (which is not covered by the national administrative plan but nevertheless is influenced by it), there exists in the Soviet Union a sphere controlled basically by the market. It covers largely the labor market, production and sales from the private plots of collective and state farmers, production and sales of artisans not in cooperatives, and various more or less private services. The national economic plan takes the activity of this sphere into account in its estimates. Although market and administratively planned spheres are clearly distinct, they are not isolated from each other.

The failure of the sphere of the authoritarian administrative plan resulting from its lack of coherence has direct repercussions on the activity of the regulated and relatively free market sphere, activity that alleviates the defects of the plan but creates a distribution of income that is not the one desired by the authorities. Increased activity in these two markets occurred during 1932–1935, during the years of war and reconstruction (1941–1947), and every time that the central plan was badly disrupted (1939, 1950).

On the basis of these considerations, it can be concluded that administrative plans that are not coherent are viable only because other spheres exist in the

19. See Chapter 14.

Soviet economy—the spheres of the regulated market economy and of the free market—that absorb the shocks caused by the incoherent administrative plans and are sufficiently tractable and flexible to fill the gaps left in the dominant administrative sector.

Administrative Plans as Tools in a Strategy of Growth

The Economic Policy Promised by the National Plans

The term "economic policy" does not appear in the terminology currently in use in the Soviet Union. The national economic plans drafted for various periods are supposed to convey the policy and to do a better job of it than the leaders of market economy countries can. The planning theoreticians consider that economic policy as conveyed by the national plans is, by definition, superior to that which could be applied by the leaders of market economies. Does it not replace the private and individual rationale by the social and economic rationale, as Oskar Lange declared?[20] In any case, it is much more comprehensive because national authoritarian plans cover all the activities of the country and appropriate all the necessary means to impose the chosen policy. There is no doubt that the national economic plans translate into concrete and precise goals the aims of the government's economic policy. Such was also the case of the national plans in the Stalinist period. Furthermore, there is a real stability in the main objectives of Stalinist economic policy included in the five-year plans. Some of the goals of the five Stalinist five-year plans are presented in Table 128. A forceful policy of industrialization and growth emerges for the over-all period. This growth policy is manifested in very high planned indexes for national income, industrial production (with priority given to producer goods), railroad transportation, and investment. Other goals usually included in the national plans that do not appear in Table 128 were equally ambitious: catching up with and surpassing the most advanced capitalist countries, achieving complete economic independence, construction of modern factories, regional development, training of personnel, and scientific and technical progress.

The growth policy, as it appears in the five-year plans, is a policy of *balanced* growth. Although priority is given to heavy industry, the production of consumer goods is to increase at very high rates, and the planned indexes of growth of agricultural production are particularly high. Therefore, the industrialization envisaged in the authoritarian plans is supposed not only to occur without demanding any sacrifices of the people but even to bring them some immediate substantial benefits. Thus, retail trade in constant prices, real wages, and peasant incomes (which do not appear in Table 128) show impressive increases in all the plans. Other social goals of the plans—private housing construction, hospitals, schools, communal equipment, and services for the population—also show rapid increases.

Many observers who limit their investigations of Soviet industrialization to the plans then proceed to contrast this industrialization *cum* prosperity with the

20. See my *Planning*, p. 5.

"chaotic" industrialization of nineteenth-century capitalism described by, among others, Karl Marx. By what means do the Soviet planners expect to perform such a miracle? Their answer is the superiority of their system where the state has taken over all the means of production and all the levers of control. This state ownership of the means of production, they say, makes it possible to draft a rational plan and to achieve growth with abundance.

This rationalization can be seen clearly in the national economic plan, in which the economy is treated as though it were one single enterprise. The process used in the plan to achieve growth with abundance is the following. First, the plan is drafted in such a way as to show a maximum cost reduction. This is achieved by pressure from the central authorities to reduce the coefficients for utilization of materials and labor and to increase the coefficients of utilization of capital. Second, the minimization of costs, justified mainly by an order from above, makes it possible simultaneously to lower certain growth indexes and raise others. Plans for employment, freight traffic (see Table 128), and production of industrial raw materials and equipment are minimized relative to the economic results anticipated from their utilization. Thus, planning a reduction in the length of haul makes it possible to minimize the increase in freight traffic in ton-kilometers (with all the consequences implied for planning rolling stock, etc.); increasing norms makes it possible to minimize the share of new manpower; and increasing the coefficient of utilization of coal in blast furnaces makes it possible to minimize the production of coal needed for the production of pig iron. Other indexes are raised for the same reasons. The minimization of the increase in employment means increased labor productivity for the same volume of production, and the minimization of inputs makes it possible to increase the output of finished products with the same production of raw materials and semifabricated products. Third, the reduction of costs and the increase of finished production makes it possible to plan reductions in retail prices, construction costs, and even some wholesale prices. The sizable increase in production that is planned at the same time makes it possible to show considerable profits for enterprises and hence a large accumulation in the hands of the state. Fourth, and hardly surprising, then, a considerable increase in investment (see Table 128) can also be planned, which justifies a very high growth of all branches of production and national income as a result. The increase in investment, moreover, is all the greater since costs are minimized for various reasons.[21] Last, the sizable increase in national income achieved in this way makes it possible to plan a considerable rise in the standard of living, in social services, etc.

In addition to these methods of drafting the national plan, optimistic forecasts are often made in matters where the government's influence is limited, such as harvests, trends of prices on foreign markets, and climatic conditions.

Drawn up in this way, the national plan certainly expresses a policy of growth with abundance, and it is through this policy that people are to be mobilized. The problem arises when this plan is compared with reality.

21. On this subject, see Chapter 17.

Table 128   Principal Goals of Five-Year Plans, 1932–1955

	First Five-Year Plan (1932/33 goal as per cent of 1927/28)	Second Five-Year Plan	
		Prelim. (1937 goal as per cent of 1932)	Final
	(1)	(2)	(3)
1. National income (constant prices) [a]	204	238	220
2. Gross industrial production (constant prices) [a]:	236	237	214
3. Producer goods (constant prices) [a]	302	209	197
4. Consumer goods (constant prices) [a]	204	269	234
5. Gross agricultural production (constant prices) [a]	156		200
6. Railroad freight traffic (ton-km)	185		177
Employment, workers and employees:			
7. National economy	140		126
8. Industry	131		128
Wages, workers and employees, national economy:			
9. Average money wage	144		123
10. Average real wage	168		189
11. Index of cost of living, national economy	86		
Index of retail prices:			
12. State and cooperative trade	78		65
13. Total trade, incl. collective farm			
State and cooperative retail trade:			
14. In current prices	204		163
15. In constant prices	261		251
Labor productivity:			
16. Industry	210		163
17. Construction			175
Cost of production:			
18. Industry	65		74
19. Construction	59		60
20. Railroad transportation			90
21. Investment, total for five-year period (billion rubles)	102.3		133.4
22. Investment, index (preceding five-year-plan period = 100)			264

	Third Five-Year Plan		Fourth Five-Year Plan	Fifth Five-Year Plan	
	Prelim. (1942 goal as per cent of 1937) (4)	Final (5)	(1950 goal as per cent of 1945) (6)	(1955 goal as per cent of 1950) (7)	Line No.
		180	166	160	1
	200	192	161	170	2
	185	207	143	180	3
	250	172	218	165	4
		152	211	150	5
	181	144	169	140	6
		121	123	115	7
		118	125	116	8
		137	115	103	9
		137	305	135	10
		100			11
		100	56	76	12
			38		13
		164	172	130	14
		164	305	170	15
		165	136[b]	150	16
		175	140[b]	155	17
		89	83	75	18
			88	80	19
		97	82	85	20
		214	250.3		21
		167	190	190	22

Source

COLUMN 1–Lines 1-10 and 14-15: Calculated from Zaleski, *Planning*, Table A-1, cols. 1 and 5. **Lines 11-12, 16, and 19:** *Piatiletnii plan narodno-khoziaistvennogo stroitelstva SSSR* [Five-Year Plan for the Development of the USSR National Economy], Moscow, 1929, Vol. II, Part 2, pp. 40, 192, and 267. **Line 18:** *Pravda*, December 27, 1931, p. 2. **Line 21:** Zaleski, *Planning*, p. 246, Table 47, col. 7.

COLUMN 2–Lines 1-4: Table 14, col. 2, in Chapter 6. Rounded.

COLUMN 3–Lines 1-4: Table 14, col. 4. Rounded. **Lines 5-9, 15-20, and 22:** *Vtoroi piatiletnii plan razvitiia narodnogo khoziaistva SSSR (1933–1937)* [Second Five-Year Plan for the Development of the USSR National Economy, 1933–1937], Moscow, 1934, pp. 465, 713, 505, 504, 521, 509, 518, and 443. **Line 10:** Table A-1, col. 1. **Line 12:** *Vtoroi plan*, p. 531. As per cent of 1933. Prices are assumed to have remained stable between 1932 and 1933, although there was probably a slight rise. **Line 14:** Excludes alcoholic beverages and tobacco. Based on planned increase (in 1932 prices) of 250.7 (*ibid.*, p. 521) and decline in prices between 1933 and 1937 (given as .65 in *ibid.*, p. 531). See note to line 12 above. **Line 21:** Table 12, col. 2, in Chapter 6.

COLUMN 4–Lines 2-4 and 6: Table 29, col. 5, in Chapter 8.

COLUMN 5–Lines 1, 5, 7-10, and 14-18: Table 75, col. 2, in Chapter 16. Rounded. **Lines 2-4 and 6:** Table 33, col. 4, in Chapter 8. **Lines 11-12:** Estimated. See Table 75, note c, and Table A-1. **Lines 20-22:** *Tretii piatiletnii plan razvitiia narodnogo khoziaistva SSSR (1938–1942)* [Third Five-Year Plan for the Development of the USSR National Economy, 1938–1942], Moscow, 1939, pp. 199 and 26.

COLUMN 6–Lines 1-10 and 14-19: Table 75, col. 4, in Chapter 16. Rounded. **Lines 12-13 and 20:** Table 79, col. 5, in Chapter 16. Rounded. **Line 21:** Table 96, col. 3, in Chapter 17. **Line 22:** Calculated from Table 96, cols. 1 and 3, in Chapter 17.

Table 128 *continued*

COLUMN 7–Lines 1-2, 6-7, 10, 15-20, and 22: *Direktivy KPSS i sovetskogo pravitelstva po khoziaistvennym voprosam* [Directives of the Communist Party of the Soviet Union and of the Soviet Government on Economic Matters], Moscow, 1957–1958, Vol. 3, pp. 686, 669, 684, 687, 683, and 689–90. **Lines 3-4:** G. Malenkov, *Otchetnyi doklad XIX sezdu Parti o rabote tsentralnogo komiteta VKPb* [Report of the XIX Party Congress on the Work of the Party Central Committee], Moscow, 1952, p. 42. **Line 5:** Rough estimate based on planned increases for components of agricultural production (given in *Direktivy*, Vol. 3, pp. 678–79). **Line 8:** Based on planned increase in labor productivity in industry (line 16) and planned increase in industrial production (derived as 174 by weighting increases planned for producer and consumer goods in lines 3 and 4 by 60 and 40 per cent, respectively, instead of accepting the apparently too low figure of 170 given in line 2). **Line 9:** Based on planned increase in average real wage (line 10) and planned index of retail prices (unrounded figure in note to line 12 below). **Line 12:** *Pravda*, April 25, 1956, p. 3. Rounded from 76.5. **Line 14:** Based on planned increase in trade in constant prices (line 15) and planned index of retail prices (unrounded figure in note to line 12 above).

a. 1926/27 prices until 1950.
b. 1950 goal as per cent of 1940.

Launching the National Plans and Their Life-Spans

It may be surprising to see the problem of implementing plans presented in this way. In the usual terminology, plans are "drafted" and "fulfilled." However, it is sufficient to observe the process of administrative planning to understand that no plan fulfillment exists separately from the planning process as a whole. Thus, the plans are fulfilled, but by means of drafting shorter-term plans in the case of the national plans (five-year, annual, and quarterly) and "autonomous" plans (relative to the central plan) for periods of less than three months.

Theoretically, any distinction among plans for different periods simply reflects different approaches. A quarterly plan, for instance, is meant to be an integral part of the annual plan, which in turn is intended to be an integral part of the five-year plan. In actual fact, five-year, annual, and quarterly plans are drafted separately, and this raises problems about their interrelations. In fact, it means that the plan for the first quarter of the current year must be made into the quarterly slice of the annual plan for that year and the annual plan must become the first annual slice of the five-year plan to be implemented. The problem of launching the three categories of national plans—five-year, annual, and quarterly —should be examined briefly.

Five-Year Plans / Drafting five-year plans is a very long process. For the First Five-Year Plan, it took nearly four years, the first variants covering 1925/26–1929/30 and the last ones 1928/29–1932/33.[22] The other five-year plans took equally long to draft, except for the fourth, which was drawn up in haste in about six months.[23]

It is obvious that, as the drafting of a five-year plan is prolonged, the basic data used for this purpose are modified. To keep a five-year plan cohesive, a new five-year plan would have to be drafted at least every year. This procedure

22. See my *Planning*, Table 3, p. 54.
23. See pp. 347–48 in Chapter 16. The drafting of the Second Five-Year Plan lasted from 1931 to 1934, the third from 1936 to 1939, and the fifth from 1948 (see pp. 395–96 in Chapter 16) to 1952.

is known as a "sliding" plan in which every year the terminal year of the plan is pushed back one year, but the total span of the plan stays the same. In theory, it is conceivable to launch a plan every year, each annual plan being based on the new five-year projection.

In the Soviet Union, the First Five-Year Plan came the closest to being a "sliding" plan. The terminal year of the plan was pushed back every year, and the last annual plans (for 1927/28 and 1928/29) were based on preliminary variants of the five-year plan, although not too closely since the five-year and annual plans were drawn up completely separately. The final approval of the five-year plan in May of 1929, as a law mandatory for five years, put an end to this annual drafting.

Moreover, the other five-year plans (except for the fourth) were still drafted in many ways like "sliding" plans. The main difference was that, instead of the terminal year of the five-year plan being pushed back, each year the scope of the plan was contracted. Thus, at the time of the first directives in 1931, the Second Five-Year Plan was a seven-year plan (annual plan for 1931 plus provisions of the annual plan for 1932 plus five-year projections for 1933–1937). In 1932, it became a six-year plan (annual plan for 1932 plus the five-year plan for 1933–1937); in 1933, it was a five-year plan (annual plan for 1933 plus four-year plan for 1934–1937); and finally, in 1934, it became a four-year plan (annual plan for 1934 plus three-year plan for 1935–1937). The same was true of the Third and Fifth Five-Year Plans, although this fact is much harder to prove statistically.

Another important difference between sliding plans and the Stalinist five-year plans lies in the relation between the vision of growth proposed by the five-year plan and the operational annual plan based on that vision. The administrative annual plan is not of the same nature as the five-year plan of which it forms a part. It must answer the needs of the moment, and the scope of the constraints on the annual planner is much broader than those on the five-year planner. The annual plan is intended to be (without really being) operational, hence concrete and practical. Imre Vajda, a well-known Hungarian economist, described the annual plan as the summation of factory plans.[24] Without going that far, it must be admitted that there is a qualitative difference between five-year plan forecasts and annual plan provisions. Criticism of the annual plan goals was out of the question, as the Soviet planners were well aware, so the planners transposed its trends to the five-year (or long-term) plan without changes. In this way, the five-year plan tended to extrapolate the growth rates shown in the annual plan for the subsequent years. Thus, the five-year plan forecasts became dependent on the tenuous success of the annual plan.

The nonauthoritarian "sliding" plan, as it is usually conceived in the West, needs to take into account every year only the unforeseen changes in the economic situation that occur between one year and the next. A "sliding" administrative and authoritarian plan is much more complicated to draft. In addition to correcting mistaken annual forecasts of the central authorities, it must take account of draft plans made in answer to the "planned orders" it has sent out to

24. A remark made during a conference organized in Vienna at the end of September 1965 by Osterreichisches Ost- und Sudosteuropa Institut (Austrian East and Southeast European Institute).

lower units. The sum of these draft plans makes up a completely different plan from that originally drafted. The length of time involved in drafting an administrative plan makes it very difficult to correct poor economic forecasts. The process of drafting an administrative plan takes place simultaneously at all levels, and any important change risks forcing the planners to start their work all over again.

This explains why anything resembling a "sliding" plan ends with the formal adoption of the five-year plan (which usually happened in Stalinist planning toward the end of the second year of the official period). But once the law on the five-year plan has been passed, is the plan really launched? An attempt will be made to answer that question largely from the experience of the Second Five-Year Plan, which was put into operation during a "normal" period. The Third Five-Year Plan, launched in March of 1939, was upset by the outbreak of war in September 1939, and the Fourth Five-Year Plan was announced in 1946 without really being put into operation. The Fifth Five-Year Plan (1951–1955), launched by Stalin in August 1952, was put aside by the changes in policy that followed Stalin's death in March 1953.

The launching of the Second Five-Year Plan failed, and the failure was obviously due to the failure of its "first stage," represented by the annual plan for 1934.[25] This is especially significant because 1934 was a very good year (one of the three best in the 1930's, according to Naum Jasny[26]). The annual rates of growth, according to official Soviet estimates, were impressive: 14.5 per cent for national income, 17.4 per cent for gross industrial production, and 6.2 per cent for gross agricultural production.[27] Wages and the standard of living also rose considerably after the hard years of 1932 and 1933. The year 1934 was also one of the better years for percentage of fulfillment of the Stalinist annual plans.[28]

However, it must not be forgotten that successful growth and fulfillment of planned goals are not necessarily the same thing. What is important for the launching of a five-year plan is the structure of production, costs, and prices on which rest the plan estimates for the following years.[29] In this regard, the results of 1934 do not bear much resemblance to the provisions of the 1934 annual plan. Thus, the fulfillment of the plans for individual products of heavy industry ranged from 39.4 to 114.1 per cent, those of the light and food industries from

25. Taking account of the economic conditions in 1939, 1946, and 1952, the corresponding annual plans, which represented the "first stages" of the respective five-year plans, were certainly less well fulfilled than the annual plan for 1934.

26. Naum Jasny, *Soviet Industrialization, 1928–1952*, Chicago, 1961, pp. 119–76.

27. *Narodno-khoziaistvennyi plan na 1935 god* [The National Economic Plan for 1935], 1st ed., Moscow, 1935, pp. 78–79 and 83. The annual growth of industrial production was confirmed by Western calculations (19.5 per cent according to G. Warren Nutter and 19.3 per cent according to Hodgman for large-scale industry), but the growth of agricultural production was not (0.5 per cent according to Johnson and Kahan), nor was the growth of national income (see my *Planning*, Table 52, p. 259, and Table A–14, p. 387).

28. See Table 61 in Chapter 13 for 1933–1938 and the appendix for all the other years.

29. The annual plan for 1934 ("Osnovnye pokazateli narodnokhoziaistvennogo plana na 1934 g."), which was published in *Planovoe khoziaistvo* [Planned Economy], No. 5–6, 1934, pp. 195–232, was reproduced verbatim in the final text of the Second Five-Year Plan (see pp. 131–33 in Chapter 6). Possibly this was also the case for the Third, Fourth, and Fifth Five-Year Plans, but the published texts of these plans are not subdivided by year.

32.0 to 248.9 per cent, harvest and animal production from 80.3 to 133.1 per cent, etc. (see Table 20 in Chapter 7). Sources of accumulation were considerably reduced. Although in 1926/27 prices the increase in national income was 4.6 billion rubles less than planned, investment was 4 billion rubles (in current prices) below plan (much more in constant prices, since the cost of construction did not change, whereas the 1934 plan assumed a 15 per cent reduction). Unplanned increases in retail prices and sizable unplanned changes in costs[30] upset all the provisions of the five-year plan in this area.

What could the government do under these circumstances? One possible solution would have been to revise the five-year plan by adding new two-year goals (1936–1937) to the 1935 annual plan. But this was unattractive because of its limited scope.

Another solution would have been to try to maintain the goals of the current five-year plan by making the 1935 annual plan goals correspond to the interim goals implied by the five-year plan. Even if such a solution had been desirable, it is not certain that it would have been possible. The dispersion of the percentages of fulfillment of the 1934 annual plan for individual series shows that the production relations actually established differed from those that had been planned. If the plan is looked upon as a table of interindustry relations, the realized technical coefficients, stocks, and capital coefficients were completely different from those in the plan. Nevertheless, the five-year plan used these out-of-date coefficients to establish modified coefficients, on the basis of which were drafted interbranch relations and production figures for 1935.[31] The discrepancy between the true state of affairs and the basic estimates used to compute the five-year plan provisions for 1935 was thus considerably widened. To try to catch up with the five-year plan goals for 1935, the authorities would have had to use in their calculations completely unrealistic coefficients which stood no chance of being realized.

As far as the annual plan was concerned, the only solution that remained to the government was to suffer the consequences of not fulfilling the 1934 annual plan and to base the 1935 plan on the actual results without paying any attention to the five-year plan goals for 1935. This policy can be seen clearly by studying the effect of the outcome of 1934 on the revisions of the five-year plan goals for 1935 made in the annual plan for that year (see Table 23 in Chapter 7). There is a strong correlation between the degree of fulfillment of the 1934 annual plan and the discrepancy between the new and old goals for 1935. Even in cases when the correlation is weak, there is a change in preference for one product over another (grain combines over automobiles, railroad freight cars over railroad passenger cars, coal over faltering petroleum, etc.). What the government did was to maintain the rates of growth, that is, the pressure, set in the five-year plan, but to

30. See pp. 143–44 and Table 21 in Chapter 7.
31. The failure to realize the coefficients of production and costs specified in the annual plan for 1934 was even more serious, since these coefficients and costs reflected relatively modest progress. The five-year plan for 1933–1937 was drafted in such a way that new investment and the most sensitive advances were programmed for the last years of the plan. In other words, the provisions of the five-year plan were more precarious after 1935.

apply them to the actual results for 1934.[32] To maintain at any price the five-year plan targets would have meant impossible increases in growth rates for 1935.

The available data do not make it possible to judge with any precision the fate of the different parts of the five-year plan. It can be seen from Table 22 in Chapter 7 that the differences between the five-year plan for 1935 and the annual plan for 1935 do not lie simply in the rates of growth. The interindustry and interbranch relations are completely different. If the profound changes in the structure of costs (see Table 21 in Chapter 7) and of consumer goods prices are also taken into consideration, it is obvious that the "launching" of the Second Five-Year Plan was a complete failure. This failure is confirmed by Tables 23 and 24 (Chapter 7) and by the complete lack of correlation between the percentages of fulfillment of the annual plans and of the five-year plan for 1933–1937 (see Table 59 in Chapter 13). The data that are available lead one to think that this correlation was even weaker during the other Stalinist five-year plans.

What became of the five-year plans then? The projects that they inspired while they were being drafted (the "sliding" plans) and launched were continued, but in an independent fashion, and their coordination had to await another five-year plan. Other projects had to be coordinated *ad hoc* in annual plans, and most of them had to be abandoned or put off until a later date.

In studying the launching of the Stalinist five-year plans, it is tempting to draw an analogy with the launching of rockets. The launching pad corresponds to the plan for the year preceding the plan period, but in this case even the exact site and the orientation of the launching pad are not known precisely. The first stage corresponds to the annual plan (for instance, the 1934 annual plan) attached onto the five-year plan, which comprises the whole structure of plans at all levels. Badly launched because of the uncertain position of the launching pad, the five-year plan, consisting of many independent parts (many more than in a rocket), explodes into pieces because of defects in its first stage. These component parts lead an independent life; some of them are even protected because of special arrangements provided for them; but it is impossible to put them together again. We have to wait for the launching of another rocket, another plan, and that takes time.

Annual and Quarterly Plans / Just as in the case of the five-year plans, the uncertain point of departure and the long administrative process of drafting are the main obstacles to a proper launching of annual and quarterly plans. However, the problems involved in launching annual plans are quite different from those for five-year plans.

Seemingly, quarterly plans bear the same relation to annual plans as annual plans do to five-year plans; they are the shortest national plans, which are used to introduce the plans for a longer term. But, in actual fact, quarterly plans differ considerably from annual plans. It is true that they represent an attempt at coordination, on a national scale, for the shortest period, that is, they represent

32. See pp. 144–45 in Chapter 7.

the last broad-scale intervention of the government before plan implementation is entrusted to the lower echelons. The balances and the allocation plans make the quarterly plans directly operational. But there are several important differences between annual and quarterly plans.

The quarterly plans have a limited number of indexes,[33] and the process of drafting them is considerably simplified (there is no going back and forth as in the annual plan draft). They do not seem to give rise to similar government directives. From the outset, they are drafted as special slices of the annual plan and, in principle, the plan for the first quarter goes through the process of approval at the same time as the annual plan. Moreover, since 1947, the approval of quarterly plans takes place through the appproval of the quarterly slices of the annual plan and only certain parts of these plans need separate approval from the government each quarter.[34] All this means that the coordination, on a national scale, of quarterly plans is very brief and the indexes in these plans, often estimated automatically at 24–26 per cent of the annual plan goal, are simply placed side by side with the others in one document.

The first consequence of these differences between annual and quarterly plans is that decisions included in the annual plan are transmitted by two different channels: some are transmitted once every three months through the approval of the quarterly plans and others are transmitted together with the annual plan. Thus, the quarterly plan is not the only instrument (as in the case of the annual plan relative to the five-year plan) for putting the annual plan into operation, but merely one of several channels used for this purpose.

A second important consequence comes from delays in drafting annual plans. Delays in drafting a five-year plan reduce its life-span to four or three years, but the five-year plan as a whole is launched through the annual plan for its first year, which is incorporated in it like the first stage of a rocket. In contrast, delays in drafting annual plans cannot reduce their life-spans nor be mitigated by the use of "sliding" plans (since doing so would imply giving up the annual period in economic accounting). Instead, the delays give rise to a fragmentation of plans, since their component parts are launched separately at different times. This almost always happens for the first-quarter plan. Because of delays in drafting annual plans, first-quarter plans are approved separately[35] on the basis of unfinished drafts of the annual plans. The parts of the annual plan not included in the quarterly plans are sent on, in their final form, to those concerned after the annual plan has been approved by the government. During 1933–1941, this approval was received toward the middle of January, although state budgets were approved later. However, since the annual plan is the source of decisions about allocations, there remains still a further delay. As can be seen from Table E-4, it took a rather long time for the final parts of the plan to reach the districts

33. A proposal was made, for example, to "free" republic and province planning committees of the obligation to include in their quarterly plans indexes for production directly under the jurisdiction of Union commissariats. In actual fact, the published plan indexes covered mainly industry under Union jurisdiction (see p. 263 in Chapter 12).

34. Plan for the distribution of food products, the State Bank's plans for credit and cash, and the transportation plan (see footnote 3 in Chapter 12).

35. See pp. 262–63 in Chapter 12.

(often not before July), and approved plans reached different units at different times. The time needed for transmittal through the intermediary of the people's commissariats (ministries) is not known; it may be shorter, but certainly enterprises received their approved plans at different times. The situation does not seem to have changed much during 1946–1952; state budgets were approved at even later dates,[36] and it can be assumed that the various parts of the annual plan reached those concerned still later and at different times.

It should be added that the parts of the annual plan that were included in the quarterly plans also did not arrive at the same time. Because of the very short time limits granted during drafting, these plans were very often transmitted in "little bundles."[37]

In conclusion, it seems necessary to give up the idea of a single operational annual plan transmitted, even if with delays, to executors. In actual fact, from the very outset the annual plan is launched in pieces and at different times. Hence it falls apart when it is put into operation, and the incomplete and poorly coordinated quarterly plans are inadequate tools to repair the damage. Doomed to failure in that general sense, the main role of the quarterly plans is to try to meet targets for the priority sectors. This effort can be seen during 1936.[38] Despite the government's attempts to make up for the quarterly plans' initial shortcomings during the following half years and despite the setting of goals at a very high level, the attempt to maintain the goals of the 1936 annual plan by the quarterly plans was not very successful. To understand the reasons for this would entail studying the partial revisions made in the annual plan in 1936. But, in any case, this confirms the conclusion that it is neither possible nor, no doubt, desirable to make an effort to re-establish the unity of a plan that falls apart before or while it is put into operation.

Real Economic Policy of the Stalinist Period

The upshot of the preceding discussion is that economic policy, as expressed in the plans, is not implemented. The five-year plans are not actually put into operation, and the annual and quarterly plan—poorly coordinated, late, and put into operation piece-meal—represent only one of the elements of a whole network of decisions taken by the government during the year.

To the extent that the planned goals as a whole become impossible to carry out, the government is forced to make choices that it thought it could avoid thanks to the plans.[39] One way of showing the actual choices made during the Stalinist period is to compare the goals of the five-year plans summarized in Table 128 above with the percentages of their fulfillment presented in Table 129 below.

36. The only annual plan of which extracts were published during this period is the 1947 plan (*Pravda*, March 1, 1947). For the dates that the budget was approved during this period, see footnote 75 in Chapter 4.

37. See p. 262 in Chapter 12.

38. See pp. 264–67 in Chapter 12 and Appendix F.

39. The necessity to make choices is illustrated by the failure to fulfill goals in costs and productivity (see Table 129). The planned sources of accumulation are not sufficient and the cuts that are thereby imposed on investment plans have repercussions in the production sector.

Table 129 Fulfillment of Principal Goals of Stalinist Five-Year Plans, 1932–1950 (per cent)

	First Five-Year Plan (1928–1932) (1)	Second Five-Year Plan (1933–1937) (2)	Fourth Five-Year Plan (1946–1950) (3)
National Income			
1. Official Soviet estimate (1926/27 prices)	91.5	96.1	118.9
2. Jasny estimate (1926/27 "real" prices)	70.2	66.5	
3. Bergson estimate			89.9
4. Nutter estimate			84.1
Industrial Production			
5. Official Soviet estimate (1926/27 prices)	100.7	103.0	116.9
6. Jasny estimate	69.9	81.2	
7. Nutter estimate	59.7	93.1	83.8
8. Kaplan and Moorsteen estimate	65.3	75.7	94.9
9. Official Soviet estimate, producer goods (1926/27 prices)	127.6	121.3	127.5
10. Official Soviet estimate, consumer goods (1926/27 prices)	80.5	85.4	95.7
Agricultural Production			
11. Official Soviet estimates (1926/27 prices)	57.8	62.6–76.9	89.9
12. Jasny estimate	49.6	76.7	
13. Nutter estimate	50.7	69.0	76.4
14. Johnson and Kahan estimates	52.4	66.1–69.0	79.4
Transportation			
15. Railroad freight traffic (ton-km)	104.0		113.2
Employment			
16. National economy, workers and employees	144.9	93.4	116.1
17. Industry, workers and employees	173.9		118.9
Wages (workers and employees, nat. economy)			
18. Average money wage	143.9	173.6	127.8
19. Average real wage, official Soviet estimate	31.9	102.6	89.1
20. Average real wage, Zaleski estimate	26.0	65.8	
Labor Productivity, Industry			
21. Official Soviet estimate	65.1		100.7
22. Jasny estimate	41.8		
23. Nutter estimate	36.3		
24. Kaplan and Moorsteen estimate			80.0
Cost of Production			
25. Industry (current prices)	146.1	121.2	134.2
Investment			
26. In constant prices	54		122

Source

COLUMN 1–Lines 1, 5, 9-11, and 15-19: Zaleski, *Planning*, Table A-1, col. 8. **Line 2:** Based on Jasny estimate for 1932 (34.9 billion rubles in *ibid.*, p. 245, Table 46) and goal for 1932 (49.7 billion rubles in *ibid.*, Table A-1, col. 5). **Line 6:** Based on planned increase (236 in Table 128, col. 1, line 2) and Jasny's index using 1926/27 prices (165 in *ibid.*, p. 259, Table 52, col. 4). **Line 7:** Based on planned increase (236 in Table 128, col. 1, line 2) and Nutter's index using moving weights (141 in *ibid.*, p. 259, Table 52, col. 2). **Line 8:** Based on planned increase (236 in Table 128, col. 1, line 2) and Kaplan and Moorsteen's index using 1950 prices (154 in *ibid.*, p. 259, Table 52, col. 6). **Line 12:** Based on planned increase (156 in Table 128, col. 1, line 5) and Jasny's index using 1926/27 prices (77.4 in *ibid.*, p. 387, Table A-14). **Line 13:** Based on planned increase (156 in Table 128, col. 1, line 5) and Nutter's index (derived as 79.1 from index based on 1913 in his "The Effects of Economic Growth on Sino-Soviet Strategy," *National Security: Political, Military, and Economic Strategies in the Decade Ahead*, edited by D. M. Abshire and R. V. Allen, New York, 1963, p. 165). **Line 14:** Based on planned increase (156 in Table 128, col. 1, line 5) and Johnson and Kahan's index using

Table 129 *continued*

1926/27 prices (81.7 in Zaleski, *Planning*, p. 387, Table A-14). **Line 20:** Based on planned increase (168 in Table 128, col. 1, line 10) and my index (43.6 in *ibid.*, p. 392, Table A-17, col. 7). **Lines 21-23:** *Ibid.*, p. 249, Table 48, last column. **Line 25:** Based on actual increase in 1932 (given as 2.3 per cent in *Dostizheniia sovetskoi vlasti za 40 let v tsifrakh* [Achievements of the Soviet Regime during 40 Years in Figures], Moscow, 1957, p. 55) and decrease planned for 1932 (given as 30 per cent in *Piatiletnii plan*, Vol. II, Part 1, p. 267). **Line 26:** Zaleski, *Planning*, p. 246, Table 47, last column.

   COLUMN 2–Lines 1-2, 5-8, 11-12, 14, 16, and 18-20: Table 28, col. 2, in Chapter 7. **Lines 9-10:** Table 36 in Chapter 7. **Line 13:** Based on planned increase (200 in Table 128, col. 3, line 5) and Nutter's index (derived as 137.9 from "Effects," *National Security*, p. 165). **Line 25:** Based on actual decrease in 1932 (given as 10.3 per cent in *Dostizheniia*, p. 55) and decrease planned for 1932 (given as 26 per cent in *Vtoroi plan*, p. 518).

   COLUMN 3–Lines 1-25: Table 79, col. 8, in Chapter 16. **Line 26:** Table 96, col. 5, in Chapter 17.

The choices made by the government follow a pattern. Producer goods and freight traffic are regularly favored at the expense of agricultural production and consumer goods. The result is very poor fulfillment of the plan for real wages, despite an inflationary increase in money income. Several other government goals, which could not be presented in Table 129, were also carried out according to the same pattern. Construction of modern factories, economic independence, strengthening of military power, and, to a certain extent, catching up with Western countries are all objectives that are quite well fulfilled. This is not the case for housing construction, communal services, and everything that reflects the standard of living.

   Results here show a real Stalinist "model of growth." Why were they not included in the plan, which would thus have become more coherent and more realistic? A comparison of the goals in Tables 128 and 129 suggests the answer. The economic policy expressed in the plans is very attractive and popular; it flatters national ambitions and promises a better life for every individual in the immediate future. Therefore, it helps mobilize the people (especially Party militants) to implement such promising plans. The plans are put on a pedestal and surrounded with mystery, while information on their revisions is very hard to come by. A distorted presentation of the costs of growth in the final result and a misleading and rather naive presentation of achievements in standard of living are then intended to hide the real economic policy—that of austerity—and the immense cost of this authoritarian and economically inefficient planning.

Stalinist Administrative Planning and Economic Equilibrium

However defective, the authoritarian administrative plan performs an important function because of its official character. It gives the green light to the individual plans of all economic units. They are put into operation even at the beginning of the year, whatever the state of the national plan. But since they are not coordinated with the national plan at the time, that has to be done after they have been put into operation. Thus, the real problem is to discover the means used in this coordination since the administrative Stalinist system suppresses the constraining mechanisms of the market—variations in prices and costs, changes in supply and demand, bankruptcies, unemployment, and other sanctions.[40] This problem will be studied separately for the sector dominated by the authoritarian allocation of resources—largely production and investment—and the consumption sector, where money and the market play a less passive role.

Equilibrium of the Centrally Managed Sector

Official authorization, at the beginning of the year, for putting the plans of economic units into operation has major consequences for the economy as a whole. These plans no longer exist solely on paper in the offices of planning and management agencies but exist in fact. Authorization of programs for production, investment, or management gives economic units the right to request the resources necessary for their activities. Thus, the authorization has at the outset the same effects as the issuance of money in a market economy. The volume of resources that economic units can actually obtain is, however, uncertain in both systems. In a market economy, variations in prices and costs will eliminate some potential buyers and will equalize the supply and demand of a given product. In a centrally managed economy, this elimination is performed by much more complicated means.

The "purchasing power" granted by the plan is subject to various restrictions that act as brakes on undesirable effects. Money and credit are strictly controlled by the banking system, and centrally fixed prices make it possible to avoid any immediate effects on money costs. Strict rationing, carried out every three months through the offices of material and equipment supply, makes it possible to watch over priority sectors. The whole system of centralized management is there ready to act as an arbiter.

Authorization to put microeconomic plans into operation when the national plan is not coherent, or has not yet been approved, is bound to mean that the distribution of "purchasing power" granted by the plan will be at the root of the disequilibrium between the supply and demand (needs and resources) of certain products, even if these items are balanced for the whole economy. In actual fact, the Stalinist plans typically created inflationary pressure through the excess demand represented by the total "purchasing power" authorized at the microeconomic level. How, then, were these excess demands arbitrated?

The rationing offices (material and equipment supply) are obviously there to eliminate low-priority demands. But the very idea of priorities is not so simple. Allocations are made through "fund holders" (e.g., supply sections of ministries) whose directors have their own preferences. Facilities to obtain supplies or substitutes play an important part, as do the government policy of the moment and the personal connections of the enterprise director. The government is not indifferent to disturbances in microeconomic plans caused by excess demand. It intervenes by revising the plans of branches, sectors, or groups of activities and thus replaces the national plan that has been adopted by the implicit national plan that is the sum of the authorized microeconomic plans and the established

40. See my *Planning*, pp. 3–4.

priorities. In defending some goals and sacrificing others, the government limits the effects of disturbances by favoring the most important sectors and trying to limit the transmission of disturbances to sectors where they will subside most rapidly (consumer goods and personal consumption, for example).

At this stage, the limits of centralized management show up clearly. The more the central authorities appropriate power, the more cumbersome becomes the administrative process of drafting plans. Any partial revision of plans upsets the unity of the national plan. The inflexibility of the national plan causes the actual plan revisions to be made by units lower in the management hierarchy. And the lower the decision-making power descends and the shorter the time limits granted for this revision, the greater is the importance of technical-economic constraints—represented by the volume and nature of available resources—and of social constraint—manifested through enterprise incentives.

Hence, the excess demand created by the plan is eliminated by two different principles: the power actually exercised by the management hierarchy and the technical, economic, and social constraints represented by the relatively autonomous decisions taken at the microeconomic level. The dividing line between these two is not fixed, and a paradoxical phenomenon appears. The stronger government pressure is and the more the priorities established initially are upset, the more significant become the technical, economic, and social constraints. This is the case during "leaps forward" or crises. Thus, there are natural limits on the claim of the authorities to manage the economy centrally.

Hence the data on fulfillment of annual and quarterly plans calculated in this book reflect the real economic equilibrium that was established as opposed to the equilibrium provided in the national plans. This real equilibrium is the result of both the action of the management apparatus and technical, economic, and social constraints. But there remains the question of the root of the disturbances.

Fulfillment of production plans depends on many factors, but the problem is different for production obtained from available productive capacities and for the increase in production resulting from the introduction of new capacities. The latter depends largely on planned investment. Thus, the planned equilibrium fundamentally depends on investment plans, which are very difficult to establish and even more difficult to integrate into the national plan. Fulfillment of these plans in financial terms (in constant prices) does not mean their fulfillment in technical terms. Technical fulfillment does not mean actual implementation and starting of production. Investment cycles vary and are difficult to account for in annual or quarterly plans.

Inclusion of investment plans is particularly difficult because of their poor quality. We have seen that the five-year plans for investment were considerably underestimated and completely invalidated by the annual plans.[41] The annual investment plans themselves are drawn up on very tenuous grounds. Actually they consist of lists of "projects," usually but not always established by esti-

41. See, for example, Tables 96 and 98 in Chapter 17, which show how the Fourth Five-Year Plan provisions for investment were exceeded and how almost none of the annual plans during the corresponding period were fulfilled.

mate costs made by the study offices. The quality of these estimate costs is uneven, and some construction projects are begun on the basis of simple calculations or even without any financial documentation.[42]

There are two main reasons for the poor quality of the investment plans: dispersion of resources among a large number of construction projects and unexpected increases in costs. Criticisms on this subject were repeated every year during Stalinist planning (and up to the present time) and, to be sure, they have deep roots in the system. The reason for the dispersion of resources is debatable. Since dispersion of resources is held responsible for delays in putting capital into service, it could be interpreted as a preference for investments with a long cycle over those with immediate yields. This interpretation is hardly convincing. If enterprises had a choice between a long and a short cycle, they would certainly choose the latter. Actually, investment is a vital necessity for an enterprise (or for a ministry). The important thing is to obtain it, since in any case experience shows that investment may take a long time to be realized. What matters, then, is to get it written into the plan. Since the financial constraints are strong and the investment requests numerous, enterprises have no interest in revealing at the outset the real cost of the operation or its real size. Once investment has been included in the plan, the chain reaction can start; once agreement has been given to build a factory, then that factory must have machines A, B, or C, which were omitted from the cost estimates. If there is a factory, there must be quarters for the workers and there must be a canteen where they can eat, etc. Hence the dispersion of resources is more like a correction made in the original plans by the basic units[43] than faulty and incomprehensible behavior on the part of the directors. Once accepted in the plans, it produces the same effects as inflationary demand pressure because of the delay in putting fixed assets into service.

The study of investment during 1933–1952 also revealed sizable unanticipated cost increases. Only part of these increases can be attributed to unforeseen increases in wages and prices of materials and equipment. Other reasons for these increases are numerous: exceeding norms for utilization of materials and equipment, delays in delivery of materials, inflation of costs of auxiliary work, poor quality of cost estimates, accumulation of stocks, etc.[44] Unanticipated increases in costs use up resources otherwise available for current production and for investment projects already under way, cause scarcities, delay installation, and are a permanent source of inflationary pressure.

Hence it must be acknowledged that planned equilibrium in the centrally managed sector is difficult to realize not only because of the poor coordination of plans before they are put into operation but also because of the poor quality of some plans, especially in sectors as sensitive as investment.

42. See pp. 406–7 and 421 in Chapter 17.
43. See pp. 422–24 in Chapter 17.
44. See pp. 431–34 and footnotes 61–66 in Chapter 17.

Planned Equilibrium of the Market during the Stalinist Period

The Stalinist administrative plan tends to replace the equilibrium between supply and demand achieved through prices on the market by a calculation. The
balance of money income and expenditures of households is intended to play
this role. In actual fact, this calculation was hardly any better than the others
made within the framework of the national plan. It was even less precise since it
played a residual role; the results of production and investment plans and all
government policies on retail prices and finances were reflected in the calculation. Moreover, the planned equilibrium covered mainly over-all volumes at the
Union level, was less precise at province and local levels, and did not take into
account the elasticities of demand of different products relative to changes in
effective demand. The most precarious estimates on the money income side
were the incomes of peasants (who suffered the aftereffects of the harvest plans
and procurement policy[45]) and the incomes of wage-earners, which always
exceeded planned provisions. Total supply depended on fulfillment of plans
for agricultural production and consumer goods, that is, the most tenuous parts
of the plans.[46] Over-all, the planned balances of the money incomes and expenditures of households showed an excess of expenditures, implying a shrinkage
of the liquid assets of the population. Retail prices were planned to remain
stable, except for during 1948–1953 when there were planned price reductions.

The very idea of a market equilibrium achieved through balances predicting
fixed prices, but where the two sides (incomes and expenditures) are residual
magnitudes and practically unforecastable, may seem absurd. In actual fact, the
equilibrium that the Stalinist planners strove to attain on this market was not an
equilibrium between supply and demand but a certain stabilization of this
market when faced by permanent inflationary pressures. Hence the real role of
this market was to absorb disturbances coming from all sectors of the economy
and to prevent their transmission to other sectors, especially industrial production, agricultural production, and investment. Numerous barriers enabled the
government to isolate these inflationary pressures. Failure to fulfill agricultural
plans automatically reduced peasant incomes from work in the socialist sector.[47]
Excess income from wages was soaked up by increases in norms, regulation of
bonuses, direct taxes, and compulsory loans. Insufficient supply was compensated by more or less hidden price rises. But the real barrier against the propagation of inflationary forces was the organization of retail trade and the rigid
planning process. Disequilibrium between supply and demand was not allowed
to have any effect on either prices or production of the deficit good. Rationing at
the wholesale trade level meant that the store that had sold its allotment could
not receive any more supplies. Queues outside certain shops and empty shelves
became the standard picture of Soviet trade. For the deficits to be translated into
increased production, the requests of stores had to be accepted by the planning

45. See p. 221 in Chapter 10.
46. On the fulfillment of the annual plans, see Tables A-2, A-3, and A-5.
47. See pp. 474–76 in Chapter 18.

and management agencies, the next plan had to try to make up the deficits, and the plan had to be actually fulfilled. But requests for increased production and supplies of consumer goods were in competition with all the other requests of state agencies for available resources.

Without additional channels of distribution, it was impossible to maintain this "institutional" equilibrium of the market, whose main role was to act as a safety valve for the whole planning system and to absorb the disturbances by making consumers bear them. A free but controlled market, the collective farm market (and bazaar for nonfood products), made it possible to meet the shortages and enabled peasants to supplement their absurdly low income from the collective sector. Moreover, prices on this market acted as a barometer. The role of this market was particularly important in times of scarcity (1930–1934, 1939–1947); in certain periods sales on this market accounted for almost half the total value of retail trade.

The Stalinist experience showed that the "institutional" equilibrium of the market, which has been called organized, did not work during times of great scarcity. So the government reluctantly introduced rationing for different groups of products and for different cities.[48] Thus the "institutional" equilibrium of the market was replaced by direct allocation of consumer goods by state and cooperative stores and factory canteens. Of the 24 years that the Stalinist five-year plans were in operation (1928–1952), in 13½ there was direct distribution of consumer goods in the form of rations. This situation had several disadvantages from the standpoint of the government. Distribution by allotment was irregular and gave rise to privileges and abuses. It underlined the discrepancy between ration prices of "organized" trade and free prices on the collective farm market. Trading by individuals, denounced by the government as "speculation," led to the undesired result of some people getting rich. The excess liquid assets of the peasants affected the sales of manufactured products, which damaged labor discipline. Workers fled from poorly supplied places; the whole system of bonuses became ridiculous in view of the profits that could be made from the discrepancy between free prices and ration prices; and the usefulness of wages as incentives was diminished.

As soon as it thought it was in a position to do so (in 1930 and in 1944), the government tried to reduce the size of the collective farm market. It did so first by providing competition in the form of state stores selling freely at high prices. Then it influenced collective farm market prices by modifying supply and demand. Some merchandise was transferred from rationed trade to state trade at higher prices (so-called "commercial" trade) and stricter control of wages was intended to limit demand. This policy was not always successful, as, for instance, in 1946 when it was counteracted by the effects of a poor harvest,[49] but on the whole high state prices led to reductions in collective farm prices (see Charts 10, 11, and 12 in Chapter 18). A great many measures were necessary to bring free prices closer to ration prices, and in 1947 recourse was had to an

48. See my *Planning*, p. 89, and pp. 328–37 in Chapter 15.
49. See p. 463 in Chapter 18.

exchange of currency and confiscation of most of the liquid assets held by the population.[50]

The conclusion is that the organized market with its "institutional" equilibrium is a solution solely for average inflationary pressures. This equilibrium becomes unstable in times of scarcity when the organized state market takes the form of centralized distribution and when the "free" market of the state as well as of individuals (peasants) is considerably extended. Then the government is forced to have recourse to classical methods to re-establish equilibrium on this "free" market. It affects both demand and supply, controls the circulation of money, and influences the level of prices.

To judge from the years 1946–1952, the Soviet government did not show great skill in this area. The currency exchange and confiscation of liquid assets decreed at the end of 1947 deprived the peasants of a major part of the money income from their private plots and brought about a crisis in agricultural production, slowing down sales of industrial consumer goods in the country and creating a scarcity of food products in the cities.[51] The authoritarian reductions in state retail prices decreed after 1947 were made without taking into account costs and the possibilities of increasing production, which worsened the disequilibrium of the recently unified organized market. The "spontaneous" rise in prices on the collective farm market, nevertheless, partly attenuated the bad effects of the government price policy on agricultural incomes. Thus the automatism of the market, however limited, made it possible to correct the defects of authoritarian planning.

Authoritarian Planning and Spontaneity

One might be curious about the rationale of the Soviet authorities' desire to impose their will, down to the smallest detail, on economic agents through the plans. No strictly economic rationale could justify such an attitude, which seems to be a transposition to the economic sphere of the manipulation of men by a totalitarian political party. Total obedience of the citizen to the Party, of the Party to the Politburo, and of the Politburo to Stalin is the rule. Only Stalin knows the "real needs" of everybody and he claims that his orders are infallible and based on profound scientific knowledge. The citizen owes the Party and its leader absolute obedience not only as producer and consumer but also in his way of thinking.

But absolute power over men as producers is impossible; there necessarily are limits on this power, since men have to master nature and techniques and, as a result, are aware of their own powers. Wanting to impose on a man in an authoritarian fashion a certain behavior as a producer, without knowing the technical and physical interrelations of the "objects" on which he must act, amounts to wanting to impose a man's arbitrary power on nature. It also amounts to wanting to turn society into an immense computer (the dream of

50. See first section of Chapter 18.
51. See pp. 477–81 in Chapter 18.

some pseudoscientists) without taking into account man as an individual who does not always allow his desires to be dictated (even if that is the only way to be considered socialist) or his own scale of preferences to be replaced by that of the people who have power over him, however great that power.

It suffices to compare the authoritarian Stalinist plans (five-year, annual, and quarterly) with their results to see that this claim to command production the way one commands men is only an illusion. The consequences of a conscious action and continuous authoritarian prompting by the central management apparatus are largely unanticipated. In one sense, the operation of this system is not different from that of a market economy: there, too, the conscious action of entrepreneurs and the continuous prompting of the authorities produce results different from the original forecasts of either.

In my previous book,[52] the "spontaneity" of results relative to the plan was seen as the result of the constant adjustment of goals and the means to achieve them provided in the plans; the fact that the central planner found it impossible to act on forces over which he had insufficient control gave more power to the enterprise, whose behavior was only imperfectly predictable. This statement still holds but requires certain qualifications. At the outset in the Stalinist planning system there are spheres with decision-making methods based on different principles (see above). The lack of coherence in the authoritarian administrative plan makes the real decision-making power descend lower in the hierarchy. To the spontaneity of the indispensable adjustment in the plans of the centrally controlled sphere is added another spontaneity, that of decisions taken at the microeconomic level on the basis of technical, economic, and social constraints. The lack of coherence of the authoritarian administrative plan remains the principal source of spontaneity. It has to be changed by force either by the management authorities (who do not have the time to study the coherence of the plan on the national level) or by the executors. Here special attention should be drawn to the decisions taken at the intermediary level (*Glavki*), situated between the central authorities and the enterprises, which often constitute an element of spontaneity relative to the central national plan.

Another category of spontaneity mentioned in the first volume on the subject of investment decision-making[53] also appears in Stalinist planning. This is the actual limitation of the powers of the central planner in decisions taken within the framework of the plan. The technical and economic constraints are transmitted, through the counterproposals of the executors, to the higher authorities; and the shorter the time-span of the plan, the more imperative they become. That is why coordination within quarterly plans is so brief and is no longer done at the national level for shorter time-spans.

Moreover, spontaneity continually invades the process of drafting plans. Negotiations that occur in Western economies after plans have been drafted and put into operation occur in a planned economy, in an authoritarian fashion, at

52. See my *Planning*, pp. 301–2.
53. See *ibid.*, pp. 301–3.

the actual stage of drafting the plans. It is the continually repeated bargaining about setting goals[54] that limits the power of the central authorities by emphasizing the technical and economic constraints and the preferences of the enterprise.

There is a common tendency to impute the causes of disturbances and their transmission to spontaneity, hence to a phenomenon that is outside the plan. The experience of Stalinist planning shows that the main cause of disturbances lay in the plans themselves, badly coordinated and poor-quality plans (particularly in the investment sector). The spontaneous action of a lower level in the economic hierarchy usually was for the purpose of correcting the disequilibrium created by the plan. That is why the most serious disturbances occurred in the producer goods and investment sectors where money plays a passive role.

Disturbances are often transmitted spontaneously in the Stalinist economy. This is true of disturbances created both in the producer goods sector (by a kind of chain reaction caused by technical problems) and in the consumption sector (due to a disequilibrium of the free market and an insufficiently controlled organized market). But this spontaneity is certainly short-lived. The planner intervenes either through his system of priorities (material and equipment supply) or through adjustment of the plans. In both cases, he transmits the disturbance to nonpriority sectors where it can be absorbed more easily. Another type of behavior on the planner's part is also frequent. Instead of trying to correct the disturbance in order to defend the goals of the plan, he simply transmits it by reducing the rates of growth by the same proportions in the following plan (such as was done in the annual plan for 1935). Whether he plays an active role (defending goals) or a passive one, the planner thus becomes an agent transmitting disturbances.

The question can be raised of how the results of Stalinist growth should be evaluated. If the targets of national plans are used as criteria, the conclusion is that they were not really followed up. What is left of these plans is an impulse and a constant pressure with unpredictable results. From this point of view, the result was uncontrolled and largely disequilibrated growth. But if the plans are given a more modest role—that of an instrument of Stalinist economic policy that was particularly unpopular—the conclusion is that this policy of power and austerity was largely carried out. But the success was that of a dictator and of the privileged group of top Party managers, and it is no accident that the rules of the game, the effects, and the final outcome of this growth were questioned in the Soviet Union after Stalin's death.

54. See pp. 490–91 above.

Statistical Appendixes

The sources in these appendixes are cited by italicized numbers, which refer to the bibliography following Appendix F. Numbers 1–325 refer to Soviet sources and 400–500 to non-Soviet sources.

Abbreviations

bill.	billion	m^3	cubic meter
conven.	conventional	mill.	million
gm	gram	m. t.	metric ton
hl	hectoliter	pass.	passenger
hp	horsepower	prec.	preceding
kg	kilogram	prs	pairs
km	kilometer	rub.	rubles
kw	kilowatt	th.	thousand
kwh	kilowatt hour	thous.	thousand
m	meter	yr.	year
m^2	square meter		

Production

List of Output Series

List of Output Series

1	National income	*natsionalnyi dokhod*
	Industry	*Promyshlennost*
2	Gross production, total	*valovaia produktsiia vsei promyshlennosti*
3	Producer goods	*proizvodstvo sredstv proizvodstva*
4	Consumer goods	*proizvodstvo predmetov narodnogo potrebleniia*
5	Coal	*ugol*
6	Peat	*torf*
7	Coke	*koks*
8	Oil shale	*goriuchie slantsy*
9	Crude petroleum	*neft*
10	Natural gas (m³)	*gaz prirodnyi* (m³)
10a	Natural gas (tons)	*gaz prirodnyi* (t)
11	Electric power	*elektro-energiia*
12	Hydroelectric power	*gidroelektricheskaia energiia*
13	Iron ore	*zheleznaia ruda*
14	Pig iron	*chugun*
15	Steel ingots and castings	*stal*
16	Rolled steel	*prokat*
17	Steel pipes	*truby stalnye*
18	Aluminum	*aliuminii*

19	Manganese ore	*margantsevaia ruda*
20	Nickel	*nikel*
21	Zinc	*tsink*
22	Refined copper	*med*
23	Lead	*svinets*
24	Mineral fertilizer	*mineralnye udobreniia*
25	Phosphoric fertilizer (14% P_2O_5)	*fosfornye udobreniia, superfosfat* (14% P_2O_5)
26	Phosphoric fertilizer (18.7% P_2O_5)	*fosfornye udobreniia, superfosfat* (18.7% P_2O_5)
27	Ground natural phosphate	*fosforitnaia muka*
28	Potash fertilizer	*kaliinye udobreniia*
29	Ammonium sulfate	*sulfat ammoniia, sernokislyi ammonii*
30	Soda ash	*kaltsinirovannaia soda*
31	Caustic soda	*kausticheskaia soda*
32	Sulfuric acid	*sernaia kislota*
32a	Synthetic rubber	*sinteticheskii kauchuk*
33	Tires	*pokryshki*
34	Plastics	*plasticheskie massy*
34a	Synthetic dyes	*sinteticheskie krasiteli*
35	Cement	*tsement*
36	Lime	*izvest*
37	Window glass	*steklo okonnoe*
38a	Roofing tiles	*cherepitsa*
39	Asbestos shingles	*shifer*
40	Bricks	*kirpich*
41	Industrial timber hauled	*vyvozka delovoi drevesiny*
42	Lumber	*pilomaterialy*
43	Plywood	*fanera*
44	Paper	*bumaga*
45	Paperboard	*karton*
46	Machine tools	*stanki metallorezhushchie*
46a	Metallurgical equipment	*metallurgicheskoe oborudovanie*
46b	Oil equipment	*nefteapparatura*
47	Steam and gas turbines	*parovye i gazovye turbiny*
48	Steam boilers	*parovye kotly*
49	Turbogenerators	*turbogeneratory*
50	Spinning machines	*priadilnye mashiny, vatera*
51	Looms	*tkatskie stanki*
52	Tractors	*traktory*
53	Tractors (15 hp)	*traktory* (15 *ls*)
54	Motor vehicles, total	*avtomobili*
55	Trucks	*gruzovye avtomobili*
56	Automobiles	*legkovye avtomobili*
57	Buses	*avtobusy*
58	Grain combines	*kombainy zernovye*
59	Steam locomotives	*parovozy magistralnye*
60	Diesel locomotives	*teplovozy*
61	Electric locomotives	*elektrovozy*
62	Railroad freight cars	*vagony tovarnye*
63	Railroad freight cars (2-axle)	*vagony tovarnye* (2-*osnye*)
64	Railroad passenger cars	*vagony passazhirskie*

65	Excavators	*ekskavatory*
66	Ginned cotton	*khlopok-volokno*
67	Cotton yarn	*khlopchatobumazhnaia priazha*
68	Cotton fabrics	*khlopchatobumazhnye tkani*
69	Woolen fabrics	*sherstianye tkani*
70	Linen fabrics (m²)	*lnianye tkani (m²)*
71	Linen fabrics (m)	*lnianye tkani (m)*
72	Silk and rayon fabrics	*tkani shelkovye i iz iskusstvennogo shelka*
73	Knitted underwear	*trikotazhnoe bele*
74	Knitted outer garments	*verkhnie trikotazhnye izdeliia*
75	Hosiery	*chulochno-nosochnye izdeliia*
76	Leather shoes	*obuv kozhanaia*
77	Felt footwear	*valianaia obuv, fetrovaia obuv*
78	Rubber footwear	*rezinovaia obuv*
79	Rubber galoshes	*galoshi*
80	Metal beds	*krovati metallicheskie*
80a	Enameled kitchenware	*posuda zheleznaia emalirovannaia*
81	Motorcycles	*mototsikly*
82	Bicycles	*velosipedy*
83	Radios	*radiopriemniki i radioli*
83a	Refrigerators, household	*kholodilniki bytovye*
84	Sewing machines, household	*shveinye mashiny bytovye*
85	Clocks and watches	*chasy vsekh vidov*
86	Cameras	*fotograficheskie apparaty*
87	Phonographs	*patefony, grammofony*
88	Soap (40% fatty acid)	*mylo*
89	Bread and breadstuffs (large-scale industry)	*khleb i khlebnye produkty*
89a	Bread and breadstuffs (ministries and local Soviets)	*khleb i khlebnye produkty (ministerstva i mestnye sovety)*
90	Flour (total)	*muka*
90a	Flour (centralized resources)	*muka (iz tsentralizovannykh resursov)*
90b	Flour (procurements)	*muka (Komzag)*
91	Macaroni	*makarony, makaronnye izdeliia*
92	Raw sugar	*sakhar-pesok*
93	Starch and syrup	*krakhmal i patoka*
94	Fish catch	*ulov ryby*
95	Crude alcohol	*spirt syrets*
96	Vegetable oil	*maslo rastitelnoe*
97	Butter	*maslo zhivotnoe*
98	Cheese	*syr*
99	Meat	*miaso*
100	Meat and subproducts of first category	*miaso (vkliuchevaia subprodukty I kategorii)*
101	Sausages	*kolbasnye izdeliia*
102	Canned food	*konservy*
103	Confectionery	*konditerskie izdeliia*
104	Margarine	*margarin i kompound zhir*
105	Beer	*pivo*
106	Cigarettes	*papirosy*

107	Matches	*spichki*
108	Low-grade tobacco	*makhorka*
109	Salt	*sol*

Agriculture — *Selskoe khoziaistvo*

110	Total value of production (1926/27 prices)	*valovaia produktsiia (v tsenakh 1926/27 gg)*
110a	Total value of production (comparable prices)	*valovaia produktsiia (v sopostavimykh tsenakh)*
111	Vegetable production (1926/27 prices)	*produktsiia zemledeliia (v tsenakh 1926/27 gg)*
111a	Vegetable production (comparable prices)	*produktsiia zemledeliia (v sopostavimykh tsenakh)*
112	Animal production (1926/27 prices)	*produktsiia zhivotnovodstva (v tsenakh 1926/27 gg)*
112a	Animal production (comparable prices)	*produktsiia zhivotnovodstva (v sopostavimykh tsenakh)*

Harvests — *Valovoi sbor*

113	Grain, total (biological yield)	*zernovye kultury*
113a	Grain, total (barn yield)	*zernovye kultury (ambarnyi urozhai)*
114	Wheat (biological yield)	*pshenitsa*
114a	Wheat (barn yield)	*pshenitsa (ambarnyi urozhai)*
115	Rye (biological yield)	*rozh*
115a	Rye (barn yield)	*rozh (ambarnyi urozhai)*
116	Barley (biological yield)	*iachmen*
116a	Barley (barn yield)	*iachmen (ambarnyi urozhai)*
117	Oats (biological yield)	*oves*
117a	Oats (barn yield)	*oves (ambarnyi urozhai)*
118	Corn (biological yield)	*kukuruza*
118a	Corn (barn yield)	*kukuruza (ambarnyi urozhai)*

Harvests of Technical Crops — *Valovoi sbor tekhnicheskikh kultur*

119	Raw cotton (biological yield)	*khlopok-syrets*
119a	Raw cotton (barn yield)	*khlopok-syrets (ambarnyi urozhai)*
120	Sugar beets (biological yield)	*sakharnaia svekla*
120a	Sugar beets (barn yield)	*sakharnaia svekla (ambarnyi urozhai)*
121	Sunflowers (biological yield)	*podsolnechnik*
121a	Sunflowers (barn yield)	*podsolnechnik (ambarnyi urozhai)*
122	Flax fiber (biological yield)	*lnovolokno, len-dolgunets*
122a	Flax fiber (barn yield)	*lnovolokno, len-dolgunets (ambarnyi urozhai)*
123	Hemp (biological yield)	*penka, konoplia*
123a	Hemp (barn yield)	*penka, konoplia (ambarnyi urozhai)*
124	Potatoes (biological yield)	*kartofel*
124a	Potatoes (barn yield)	*kartofel (ambarnyi urozhai)*

Animal Production — *Produktsiia zhivotnovodstva*

125	Meat and fat (excl. rabbit and poultry)	*miaso i salo (bez miasa krolikov i ptitsy)*
125a	Meat and fat (incl. rabbit and poultry)	*miaso i salo (vkliuchaia miaso krolikov i ptitsy)*
126	Milk	*moloko*

| 127 | Eggs | *iaitsa* |
| 128 | Wool | *sherst* |

	Market Production	*Tovarnaia produktsiia*
129	Grain	*zernovye kultury*
130	Raw cotton	*khlopok-syrets*
131	Sugar beets	*sakharnaia svekla*
132	Flax fiber	*lnovolokno*
133	Potatoes	*kartofel*
134	Meat and fat (dead weight)	*miaso i salo (v uboinom vese)*
135	Milk and dairy products	*moloko i molochnye produkty*
136	Wool	*sherst*

	Procurements	*Gosudarstvennye zagotovki i zakupki*
137	Grain	*zernovye kultury*
138	Raw cotton	*khlopok-syrets*
139	Sugar beets	*sakharnaia svekla*
140	Sunflowers	*podsolnechnik*
141	Flax fiber	*lnovolokno*
142	Hemp	*penka*
143	Potatoes	*kartofel*
143a	Vegetables	*ovoshchi*
144	Meat and fat (live weight)	*miaso i salo (v vese zhivogo skota)*
145	Meat and fat (dead weight)	*miaso i salo (v uboinom vese)*
146	Milk and dairy products	*moloko i molochnye produkty*
147	Eggs	*iaitsa*
148	Wool	*sherst*

	Railroad Transportation	*Zheleznodorozhnyi transport*
149	Length of network	*vsia ekspluatatsionnaia dlina*
150	Average daily carloadings	*srednesutochnaia pogruzka*
151	Total freight traffic (ton-km)	*gruzooborot*
152	Total freight traffic (tons)	*perevozki, perevezeno gruzov*
153	Coal and coke	*kamennyi ugol i koks*
154	Oil and oil products	*neftianye gruzy*
155	Ferrous metals	*chernye metally*
156	Ore	*ruda vsiakaia*
157	Firewood	*drova*
158	Timber	*lesnye gruzy*
159	Mineral construction materials	*mineralnye stroitelnye materialy*
159a	Principal construction materials (stone, lime, cement, bricks)	*osnovnye mineralnye stroitelnye materialy (kamen, izvest, tsement, kirpich)*
160	Grain and flour	*khlebnye gruzy*
161	Salt	*sol*
162	Total freight traffic, average length of haul	*sredniaia dalnost perevozok, vse gruzy*
163	Coal and coke, average length of haul	*sredniaia dalnost perevozok, kamennyi ugol i koks*
163a	Oil and oil products, average length of haul	*sredniaia dalnost perevozok, neftianye gruzy*
164	Ferrous metals, average length of haul	*sredniaia dalnost perevozok, chernye metally*

164a	Firewood, average length of haul	*sredniaia dalnost perevozok, drova*
164b	Timber, average length of haul	*sredniaia dalnost perevozok, lesnye gruzy*
165	Grain and flour, average length of haul	*sredniaia dalnost perevozok, khlebnye gruzy*
165a	Ore, average length of haul	*sredniaia dalnost perevozok, ruda vsiakaia*
166	Total passenger traffic	*passazhirooborot*

	Inland Waterway Transportation	*Rechnoi transport*
166a	Length of network	*vsia ekspluatatsionnaia dlina*
168	Freight traffic under ministries and economic organizations (ton-km)	*gruzooborot (ministerstva, upravleniia)*
170	Freight traffic under ministries and economic organizations (tons)	*perevozki, perevezeno gruzov (ministerstva, upravleniia)*
171	Coal and coke	*kamennyi ugol i koks*
172	Oil and oil products	*neft i nefteprodukty*
173	Timber and firewood	*les i drova*
174	Mineral construction materials	*mineralnye stroitelnye materialy*
175	Grain and flour	*khlebnye gruzy*
176	Salt	*sol*
177	Average length of haul under ministries and economic organizations	*sredniaia dalnost perevozok (ministerstva, upravleniia)*
178	Passenger traffic (pass.-km)	*passazhirooborot*
178a	Passenger traffic (pass.)	*perevezeno passazhirov*

	Maritime Transportation (Soviet ships)	*Morskoi transport (sovetskie suda)*
179	Freight traffic (ton-km)	*gruzooborot*
180	Freight traffic (tons)	*perevozki, perevezeno gruzov*
181	Average length of haul	*sredniaia dalnost perevozok*
182	Passenger traffic (pass.-km)	*passazhirooborot*
182a	Passenger traffic	*perevezeno passazhirov*

| | *Motor Transportation* | *Avtomobilnyi transport* |
| 183 | Freight traffic (ton-km) | *gruzooborot* |

	Air Transportation	*Vozdushnyi transport*
184	Freight traffic, incl. mail	*gruzooborot (vkliuchaia pochtu)*
185	Passenger traffic	*perevezeno passazhirov*

	Employment (annual averages)	*Chislennost rabochikh (srednegodovaia)*
186	Workers and employees, national economy, excl. collective farms	*vsego rabochikh i sluzhashchikh v narodnom khoziaistve (bez kolkhozov)*
187	Industry	*promyshlennost*
188	Construction	*stroitelstvo*
188a	Construction and assembly work	*stroitelno-montazhnye raboty*
189	State-owned agriculture and logging	*selskoe khoziaistvo i lesnoe khoziaistvo*

190	State-owned agriculture (state farms, MTS, and other state establishments)	*selskoe khoziaistvo (sovkhozy, MTS, i podsobnye selskokhoziaistvennye predpriiatiia)*
191	Railroad transport	*zheleznodorozhnyi transport*
192	Maritime and inland waterway transport	*vodnyi transport*
193	Other transport (motor, etc.)	*avtomobilnye, gorodskie, i prochnye transporty*
194	Communications	*sviaz*
195	Trade, procurements, and supply	*torgovlia, zagotovki, i materialno-tekhnicheskoe snabzhenie*
196	Public eating places	*obshchestvennoe pitanie*
197	Credit institutions	*kreditnye i strakhovye uchrezhdeniia*
198	Administration	*apparat organov gosud. i khoz. upravleniia, gosud. i obshchestvennye uchrezhdeniia*
199	Education	*prosveshchenie*
200	Public health	*zdravookhranenie*

	Wage Fund, Workers and Employees	*Fond zarabotnoi platy rabochikh i sluzhashchikh*
201	National economy	*narodnoe khoziaistvo*
202	Industry	*promyshlennost*

	Average Annual Wage, Workers and Employees	*Sredniaia zarabotnaia plata rabochikh i sluzhashchikh (za god)*
203	Money wage, national economy, excl. collective farms and cooperatives	*denezhnaia zarabotnaia plata v narodnom khoziaistve*
204	Real wage, national economy, excl. collective farms and cooperatives, calculated from official Soviet index	*realnye dokhody v narodnom khoziaistve*
204a	Real wage, national economy, excl. collective farms and cooperatives, calculated from Zaleski index	
205	Money wage, industry	*denezhnaia zarabotnaia plata v promyshlennosti*

	Average Annual Money Wage, Workers	*Sredniaia denezhnaia zarabotnaia plata rabochikh (za god)*
206	Industry	*promyshlennost*
207	Iron ore	*zheleznaia ruda*
208	Coal	*ugolnaia promyshlennost*
209	Ferrous metals	*chernye metally*
209a	Machine-building	*mashinostroenie*
210	Paper	*bumazhnaia promyshlennost*
211	Chemicals	*khimicheskaia promyshlennost*
212	Textiles	*tekstilnaia promyshlennost*
212a	Cotton	*khlopchatobumazhnaia promyshlennost*
212b	Wool	*sherstianaia promyshlennost*
213	Leather	*kozhanaia promyshlennost*
214	Food	*pishchevaia promyshlennost*

	Average Annual Money Wage, Workers and Employees	*Sredniaia denezhnaia zarabotnaia plata rabochikh i sluzhashchikh (za god)*
215	Construction	*stroitelstvo*
216	Railroad transport	*zheleznodorozhnyi transport*
217	Maritime and inland waterway transport	*vodnyi transport*
218	Communications	*sviaz*
219	Trade	*torgovlia*
220	Public eating places	*obshchestvennoe pitanie*
221	Credit institutions	*kreditnye i strakhovye uchrezhdeniia*
222	Administration	*apparat organov gosud. i khoz. upravleniia*
223	Education	*prosveshchenie*
224	Public health	*zdravookhranenie*
225	State-owned agriculture	*selskoe khoziaistvo*
226	Logging and timber procurements	*lesnoe khoziaistvo i lesnye zagotovki*

	Housing	*Zhilishchnoe stroitelstvo*
227	Housing fund, urban, total	*ves gorodskoi zhilishchnyi fond*
228	Housing construction, urban, total (including reconstruction)	*zhilishchnoe stroitelstvo v gorodakh (vkliuchaia vosstanovlenie)*
228a	Housing construction, urban	*zhilishchnoe stroitelstvo v gorodakh*
229	Floorspace per inhabitant, urban	*obshchaia ploshchad v srednem na odnogo gorodskogo zhitelia*

	Population	*Naselenie*
230	Total	*chislennost naseleniia*
231	Urban	*gorodskoe naselenie*
232	Rural	*selskoe naselenie*

	Retail Trade	*Roznichnyi tovarooborot*
233	State and cooperative in current prices	*gosudarstvennaia i kooperativnaia torgovlia v tsenakh sootvetstvuiushchikh let*
234	State and cooperative in 1940 prices	*gosudarstvennaia i kooperativnaia torgovlia v tsenakh 1940 g.*
234a	State and cooperative in constant prices calculated from official Soviet price index	*gosudarstvennaia i kooperativnaia torgovlia v sopostavimykh tsenakh*
234b	State and cooperative in constant prices calculated from Zaleski price index	
234c	Food products in current prices	*prodovolstvennye tovary v tsenakh sootvetstvuiushchikh let*
234d	Food products in 1940 prices	*prodovolstvennye tovary v tsenakh 1940 g.*
235	Collective farm in current prices	*kolkhoznaia torgovlia v tsenakh sootvetstvuiushchikh let*

Tables

Table A-1 Fulfillment of Definitive Variants of Second, Third, and Fourth Five-Year Plans in 1937, 1940, 1942, and 1950

Series	Units	Second Five-Year Plan (1933–1937)		
		Goals for 1937 (1)	Results in 1937 (2)	(2) as Per Cent of (1) (3)
1. National income (1926/27 prices)	bill. rub.	100.2	96.3	96.1
Industry				
2. Gross production, total (1926/27 prices)	bill. rub.	92.7	95.5	103.0
3. Producer goods (1926/27 prices)	bill. rub.	45.5	55.2	121.3
4. Consumer goods (1926/27 prices)	bill. rub.	47.2	40.3	85.4
5. Coal	th. m. t.	152,500	127,968	83.9
6. Peat	th. m. t.	25,000	24,040	96.2
7. Coke	th. m. t.	21,300	20,028	94.0
8. Oil shale	th. m. t.	2,600	515.0	19.8
9. Crude petroleum	th. m. t.	44,300	28,501	64.3
10. Natural gas	mill. m^3	2,750	2,178.9	79.2
11. Electric power	mill. kwh	38,000	36,173	95.2
12. Hydroelectric power	mill. kwh	5,800	4,184	72.1
13. Iron ore	th. m. t.	34,000	27,770	81.7
14. Pig iron	th. m. t.	16,000	14,487	90.5
15. Steel ingots and castings	th. m. t.	17,000	17,730	104.3
16. Rolled steel	th. m. t.	13,000	12,967	99.7
17. Steel pipes	th. m. t.	1,100	923	83.9
18. Aluminum	th. m. t.	80.0	37.7	47.1
19. Manganese ore	th. m. t.	2,700	2,752	101.9
20. Nickel	th. m. t.		2.28	
21. Zinc	th. m. t.	90.0	76.5	85.0
22. Refined copper	th. m. t.	135.0	97.5	72.2
23. Lead	th. m. t.	115	62.3	54.2
24. Mineral fertilizer	th. m. t.	6,416	3,240	50.5
25. Phosphoric fertilizer (14% P$_2$O$_5$)	th. m. t.	3,000	1,963	65.4
26. Phosphoric fertilizer (18.7% P$_2$O$_5$)	th. m. t.	2,246	1,472.7	65.6
27. Ground natural phosphate	th. m. t.	2,200.0	649.9	29.5
28. Potash fertilizer	th. m. t.		355.8	
29. Ammonium sulfate	th. m. t.		761.6	
30. Soda ash	th. m. t.	700	528.2	75.5
31. Caustic soda	th. m. t.	354.0	163.7	46.2
32. Sulfuric acid	th. m. t.	2,080	1,369	65.8
32a. Synthetic rubber	th. m. t.		70.2	
33. Tires	thous.	3,000	2,698	89.9
34a. Synthetic dyes	th. m. t.		30.96	
35. Cement	th. m. t.	7,500	5,454	72.7
36. Lime	th. m. t.	4,850	4,822	99.4
37. Window glass	mill. m^2	81.4	79.3	97.4
38a. Roofing tiles	mill.	200	108.0	54.0
39. Asbestos shingles	mill.	220.0	187.0	85.0
40. Bricks	mill.	8,000	8,666	108.3
41. Industrial timber hauled	mill. m^3	170.0	114.2	67.2
42. Lumber	mill. m^3	48.0	33.8	70.4
43. Plywood	th. m^3	735.0	678.9	92.4
44. Paper	th. m. t.	1,000.0	831.6	83.2
45. Paperboard	th. m. t.	125.0	82.8	66.2
46. Machine tools	units	40,000	36,120	90.3
46a. Metallurgical equipment	th. m. t.		18.4	
47. Steam and gas turbines	th. kw	1,300	1,068	82.2

	Third Five-Year Plan (1938–1942)					Fourth Five-Year Plan (1946–1950)			
Interpolated Goals for 1940 (4)	Results in 1940 (5)	(5) as Per Cent of (4) (6)	Goals for 1942 (7)	Results in 1942 (8)	(8) as Per Cent of (7) (9)	Goals for 1950 (10)	Results in 1950 (11)	(11) as Per Cent of (10) (12)	Series No.
137	128.3	93.6	173.6	84.7	48.8	177	210.4	118.9	1
141	138.5	98.2	184	106.6	57.9	205.0	239.6	116.9	2
85.5	84.8	99.2	114.5	84.7	74.0	135.9	173.3	127.5	3
55.9	53.7	96.1	69.5	21.9	31.5	69.1	66.1	95.7	4
188,000	165,923	88.3	243,000	75,536	31.1	250,000	261,089	104.4	5
36,847	33,229	90.2	49,000	14,738	30.1	44,300	35,999	81.3	6
25,000	21,102	84.4	29,000	6,893	23.8	30,000	27,728	92.4	7
1,800	1,682.9	93.5	4,000				4,716.2		8
39,692	31,121	78.4	49,500	21,988	44.4	35,400	37,878	107.0	9
3,400	3,219.1	94.7				11,200	5,760.9	51.4	10
56,014	48,309	86.2	75,000	29,068	38.8	82,000	91,226	111.3	11
6,536	5,113	78.2	8,800			12,464	12,691	101.8	12
36,350	29,866	82.2	43,500	9,763	22.4	40,000	39,651	99.1	13
18,612	14,902	80.1	22,000	4,779	21.7	19,500	19,175	98.3	14
23,318	18,317	78.6	28,000	8,070	28.8	25,400	27,329	107.6	15
17,314	13,113	75.7	21,000	5,415	25.8	17,800	20,888	117.3	16
	966					1,500	2,001	133.4	17
80.0	59.9	74.9	132	51.9	39.3	173			18
3,696	2,557	69.2	4,500	767	17.0		3,377		19
9.78	8.66	88.5	25.8	7.4	28.7	28.9			20
125	95.0	76.0	172			125.0	116.5	93.2	21
181	160.9	88.9	273			225.0	255.0	114.3	22
98.6	89.4	90.7	134			156	144	92.3	23
	3,238					5,600	5,492	98.1	24
3,300	1,810	54.8	4,600			3,600	3,440	95.5	25
2,500	1,351.9	54.1	3,500			2,700	2,350.5	87.1	26
	381.7					400	483.2	120.8	27
591.5	532.3	90.0	830.0				750.4		28
1,215	971.7	80.0	1,660			1,950	1,908.3	97.9	29
831.4	536.1	64.5	1,125.0	65	57.7	800	748.6	93.6	30
	190.4					390	324.8	83.3	31
	1,587						2,125		32
	100					200			32a
5,558	3,007	54.1	9,000				7,401		33
	33.87					43	46.53	108.2	34a
8,308	5,675	68.3	11,000	1,100	10.0	10,500	10,194	97.1	35
6,285	4,470	71.1	7,500				6,451		36
	44.7					80	76.9	96.1	37
199.4	131.7	66.0	300.0			693.2	222.5	32.1	38a
248.3	205.6	82.8	300.0			410	546.4	133.3	39
11,050	7,455	67.5	13,000			10,500	10,179	96.9	40
159.8	117.9	73.8	200.0			187.5	161.0	85.9	41
44.0	34.8	79.1	52.4			39	49.5	126.9	42
856.5	731.9	85.5	1,000.0			810	657.5	81.2	43
1,184	812.4	68.6	1,500			1,340.0	1,193.3	89.1	44
132	120.0	90.9	180.0				291.8		45
54,000	44,000	81.5	70,000	17,087	24.4	74,000	70,597	95.4	46
	23.7			19.4		102.9	111.2	108.1	46a
	972					2,906	2,381	81.9	47

Table A-1   *continued*

		Second Five-Year Plan (1933–1937)		
Series	*Units*	*Goals for 1937* (1)	*Results in 1937* (2)	*(2) as Per Cent of (1)* (3)
48. Steam boilers	th. m²	385	170.4	44.3
49. Turbogenerators	th. kw	1,150	514.0	44.7
50. Spinning machines	units	6,500	884	13.6
51. Looms	units	32,000	4,095	12.8
52. Tractors	units	88,500	50,976	57.6
53. Tractors (15 hp)	th. conven. units	166.7	66.5	39.9
54. Motor vehicles, total	thous.	200.0	199.9	99.9
55. Trucks	thous.	140.0	180.3	128.8
56. Automobiles	thous.	60.0	18.2	30.3
57. Buses	thous.		1.4	
58. Grain combines	units	20,000	43,910	219.5
59. Steam locomotives	units	2,270	1,172	51.6
60. Diesel locomotives	units	110	4	3.6
61. Electric locomotives	units	150	32	21.3
62. Railroad freight cars	units	60,000	29,799	49.7
63. Railroad freight cars	2-axle units	118,400	59,000	49.8
64. Railroad passenger cars	units	3,500	912	26.1
65. Excavators	units		522	
66. Ginned cotton	th. m. t.	700	716.7	102.4
67. Cotton yarn	th. m. t.	611	532.9	87.2
68. Cotton fabrics	mill. m	5,100	3,448	67.6
69. Woolen fabrics	mill. m	220.0	108.3	49.2
70. Linen fabrics	mill. m²	600.0	254	42.3
71. Linen fabrics	mill. m		285.2	
72. Silk and rayon fabrics	mill. m	64.0	58.9	92.0
73. Knitted underwear	mill.	100.0	111.5	111.5
74. Knitted outer garments	mill.		45.1	
75. Hosiery	mill. prs	1,000	408.6	40.9
76. Leather shoes	mill. prs	191	182.9	95.8
77. Felt footwear	mill. prs	16.0	13.4	83.7
78. Rubber footwear	mill. prs	100.0	84.6	84.6
79. Rubber galoshes	mill. prs		55.5	
80. Metal beds	thous.		4,160	
80a. Enameled kitchenware	th. m. t.		19.0	
81. Motorcycles	thous.		13.1	
82. Bicycles	thous.	575.0	540.7	94.0
83. Radios	thous.	500.0	199.9	40.0
83a. Refrigerators, household	thous.		0	
84. Sewing machines, household	thous.	450.0	510.1	113.4
85. Clocks and watches	thous.	17,100	4,028	23.5
86. Cameras	thous.	350.0	353.2	100.9
87. Phonographs	thous.	1,500.0	675.8	45.1
88. Soap (40% fatty acid)	th. m. t.	1,000.0	495	49.5
89. Bread and breadstuffs (large-scale industry)	th. m. t.	10,500	19,131	182.2
89a. Bread and breadstuffs (ministries and local Soviets)	th. m. t.		10,510	
90. Flour (total)	th. m. t.		28,000	
90a. Flour (centralized resources)	th. m. t.		15,118	
90b. Flour (procurements)	th. m. t.	14,000	13,918	99.4
91. Macaroni	th. m. t.	510.0	263.8	51.7
92. Raw sugar	th. m. t.	2,500	2,421	96.8

	Third Five-Year Plan (1938–1942)					Fourth Five-Year Plan (1946–1950)			
Interpolated Goals for 1940 (4)	Results in 1940 (5)	(5) as Per Cent of (4) (6)	Goals for 1942 (7)	Results in 1942 (8)	(8) as Per Cent of (7) (9)	Goals for 1950 (10)	Results in 1950 (11)	(11) as Per Cent of (10) (12)	Series No.
424	175.5	41.4	780				358.7		48
	313.5						676.5		49
2,190	1,109	50.6	4,000			1,400	1,958	139.9	50
9,954	1,823	18.3	18,000			25,000	8,700	34.8	51
57,900	31,649	54.7	63,000	3,520	5.6	112,000	108,830	97.2	52
104	66.2	63.7	140.0			254.0	240.9	94.8	53
303.0	145.4	48.0	400.0			500	362.9	72.6	54
244.7	136.0	55.5	300.0	30.4	10.1	428	294.4	68.8	55
50.6	5.5	10.9	100.0			65.6	64.6	98.5	56
	3.9					6.4	3.9	60.9	57
	12,756						46,338		58
1,391	914	65.7	1,558			2,200	985	44.8	59
	5					300	125	41.7	60
	9					220	102	46.4	61
38,100	30,880	81.0	45,000			73,000	50,795	69.6	62
76,000			90,000			146,000			63
2,010	1,051	52.3	3,400			2,600	912	35.1	64
771.8	274	35.5	1,000				3,540		65
894.0	848.6	94.9	1,035.0			990	952.7	96.2	66
675	649.9	96.3	791			685.0	662.5	96.7	67
4,260	3,954	92.8	4,900	1,644	33.6	4,686	3,899	83.2	68
145.4	119.7	82.3	177.0	38.3	21.6	159.4	155.2	97.4	69
	219								70
341.5	285.5	83.6	385.0			420.0	282.2	67.2	71
68.6	76.6	111.7	76.0			141.0	129.7	92.0	72
142.6	124.4	87.2	168.0				150.4		73
58.7	58.6	99.8	70.0				47.1		74
572.1	485.4	84.8	716.0			580	472.7	81.5	75
224.8	189.5	84.3	258.0	52.5	20.3	240	203.4	84.7	76
	17.9						22.4		77
119	69.7	58.6	150			88.6	110.4	124.6	78
83.6	45.0	53.8	110						79
6,386	6,157	96.4	8,500				4,358		80
32.3	11.4	35.3	46.0				20.3		80a
20	6.8	34.0	27			135	123.1	91.2	81
852.6	255.0	29.9	1,155			1,050	649.3	61.8	82
577.0	160.5	27.8	1,170			925	1,072.4	115.9	83
	3.5		25.0				1.2		83a
562	175.2	31.2	600			450	501.7	111.5	84
	2,796					7,400	7,566	102.2	85
	355.2					530	260.3	49.1	86
934.5	313.7	33.6	1,160.0			1,000	366.8	36.7	87
721	700	97.1	925.0			870	816	93.8	88
20,400			21,300						89
	13,737						12,412		89a
	28,792						22,037		90
17,065	16,397	96.1	18,500			19,000	12,396	65.3	90a
15,132			16,000						90b
	324.2						440.2		91
3,020	2,165	71.7	3,500	114	3.3	2,400	2,523	105.1	92

Table A-1 *continued*

Series	Units	Second Five-Year Plan (1933–1937)		
		Goals for 1937 (1)	Results in 1937 (2)	(2) as Per Cent of (1) (3)
93. Starch and syrup	th. m. t.		247	
94. Fish catch	th. m. t.	1,800	1,609	89.4
95. Crude alcohol	th. hl	7,500	7,670	102.3
96. Vegetable oil	th. m. t.	750	495	66.0
97. Butter	th. m. t.	180	185	102.8
98. Cheese	th. m. t.	37.0	31.0	83.8
99. Meat	th. m. t.	1,200.0	812.1	67.7
100. Meat and subproducts of first category	th. m. t.	1,644	1,002	60.9
101. Sausages	th. m. t.		326.0	
102. Canned food	mill. 400-gm cans	2,000	982	49.1
103. Confectionery	th. m. t.	1,350	921	68.2
104. Margarine	th. m. t.	120.0	74.0	61.7
105. Beer	th. hl	7,500	8,960	119.5
106. Cigarettes	bill.	125.0	89.2	71.4
107. Matches	th. crates	12,000	7,163	59.7
108. Low-grade tobacco (*makhorka*)	th. 20-kg crates	6,000	5,343	89.1
109. Salt	th. m. t.	6,000	3,200	53.3
Agriculture				
110. Total value of production (1926/27 prices)	mill. rub.	26,160	20,123	76.9
110a. Total value of production (comparable prices)	yr. prec. plan = 100	200.1	125.2	62.6
111. Vegetable production (1926/27 prices)	mill. rub.	18,133	15,070	83.1
111a. Vegetable production (comparable prices)	yr. prec. plan = 100	185.4	120.0	64.7
112. Animal production (1926/27 prices)	mill. rub.	8,027	5,053	63.0
112a. Animal production (comparable prices)	yr. prec. plan = 100	243.8	145.3	59.6
Harvests				
113. Grain, total (biological yield)	mill. m. t.	104.80	120.29	114.8
113a. Grain, total (barn yield)	mill. m. t.	104.8	97.4	92.9
114. Wheat (biological yield)	mill. m. t.	37.84	46.8	123.7
114a. Wheat (barn yield)	mill. m. t.			
115. Rye (biological yield)	mill. m. t.	25.41	29.44	115.9
115a. Rye (barn yield)	mill. m. t.			
116. Barley (biological yield)	mill. m. t.	8.39	10.60	126.3
116a. Barley (barn yield)	mill. m. t.			
117. Oats (biological yield)	mill. m. t.	18.05	21.86	121.1
117a. Oats (barn yield)	mill. m. t.			
118. Corn (biological yield)	mill. m. t.	6.0	3.89	64.8
118a. Corn (barn yield)	mill. m. t.			
Harvests of Technical Crops				
119. Raw cotton (biological yield)	mill. m. t.	2.125	2.58	121.5
119a. Raw cotton (barn yield)	mill. m. t.			
120. Sugar beets (biological yield)	mill. m. t.	27.60	21.86	79.2
120a. Sugar beets (barn yield)	mill. m. t.			
121. Sunflowers (biological yield)	mill. m. t.	3.40	2.08	61.2
121a. Sunflowers (barn yield)	mill. m. t.			

	Third Five-Year Plan (1938–1942)					Fourth Five-Year Plan (1946–1950)			
Interpolated Goals for 1940 (4)	Results in 1940 (5)	(5) as Per Cent of (4) (6)	Goals for 1942 (7)	Results in 1942 (8)	(8) as Per Cent of (7) (9)	Goals for 1950 (10)	Results in 1950 (11)	(11) as Per Cent of (10) (12)	Series No.
	247					286	242	84.6	93
1,969	1,404	71.3	2,252	900	40.0	2,200	1,755	79.8	94
11,700	8,990	76.8	15,500			10,080	7,300	72.4	95
685	798	116.5	850	253	29.8	880	819	93.1	96
245	226	92.2	295			275	336	122.2	97
	37.3						49.1		98
1,221	1,192	97.6	1,600			1,300	1,275	98.1	99
1,523	1,501	98.5	2,014			1,636	1,556	95.1	100
493	346.3	70.2	650				491.7		101
1,420	989	69.6	1,800				1,535		102
1,234	790	64.0	1,500			850	993	116.8	103
	121					250	192	76.8	104
11,700	12,130	103.7	14,000			15,000	13,080	87.2	105
108	100.4	93.0	123				125.1		106
10,710	10,000	93.4	14,000	1,612	11.5	9,900	10,200	103.0	107
	4,600						3,800		108
	4,404						4,474		109
25,823	23,300	90.2	30,500	8,900	29.2	29,600	26,600	89.9	110
128	105.2	82.2	151.6	40	26.4	127	99.3	78.2	110a
18,176	16,300	89.7	20,600						111
121	103.3	85.4	136.7						111a
7,565	7,000	92.5	9,900						112
150	104.6	69.7	196						112a
126	118.8	94.3	130			127	124.5	98.0	113
104	95.496	91.8	108.1	29.1	26.9	102.1	81.20	79.5	113a
49	40.625	82.9	51				46.779		114
	31.746						31.076		114a
	26.1								115
	20.967						17.961		115a
	15.3								116
	12.046						6.354		116a
	21.2								117
	16.795						13.005		117a
									118
	5.120						6.644		118a
2.99	2.700	90.3	3.29			3.1	3.75	121.0	119
	2.023			1.323		2.53	3.584	141.7	119a
25.47	20.95	82.3	28.20			26	23.5	90.4	120
	18.015			2.1		22.3	20.819	93.4	120a
2.50	3.3	132.0	2.83			3.7	3.1	83.8	121
	2.578			.28		2.89	1.798	62.2	121a

Table A-1 *continued*

Series	Units	Second Five-Year Plan (1933–1937)		
		Goals for 1937 (1)	Results in 1937 (2)	(2) as Per Cent of (1) (3)
122. Flax fiber (biological yield)	th. m. t.	807	570	70.6
122a. Flax fiber (barn yield)	th. m. t.			
123. Hemp (biological yield)	th. m. t.	476		
123a. Hemp (barn yield)	th. m. t.			
124. Potatoes (biological yield)	mill. m. t.	72.97	65.63	89.9
124a. Potatoes (barn yield)	mill. m. t.			
Animal Production				
125. Meat and fat (excl. rabbit and poultry)	th. m. t.	5,090	2,370	46.6
125a. Meat and fat (incl. rabbit and poultry)	th. m. t.			
126. Milk	mill. m. t.	32.43	26.06	80.4
127. Eggs	bill.	12.25	7.5	61.2
128. Wool	th. m. t.	160	106.3	66.4
Market Production				
129. Grain	mill. m. t.	34.50	37.97	110.1
130. Raw cotton	mill. m. t.	2.104	2.54	120.7
131. Sugar beets	mill. m. t.	27.60	21.45	77.7
132. Flax fiber	th. m. t.		324	
133. Potatoes	mill. m. t.	16.400	11.68	71.2
134. Meat and fat (dead weight)	th. m. t.	2,484	1,464	58.9
135. Milk and dairy products	mill. m. t.	9.637	8.015	83.2
136. Wool	th. m. t.		80.3	
Procurements				
137. Grain	th. m. t.	30,000	31,850	106.2
138. Raw cotton	th. m. t.	2,104	2,542	120.8
139. Sugar beets	th. m. t.	27,600	21,430	77.6
140. Sunflowers	th. m. t.		1,076	
141. Flax fiber	th. m. t.	645	275	42.6
142. Hemp	th. m. t.	200	49	24.5
143. Potatoes	th. m. t.	7,620	7,021	92.1
143a. Vegetables	th. m. t.	1,500	1,477	98.5
144. Meat and fat (live weight)	th. m. t.		1,259	
145. Meat and fat (dead weight)	th. m. t.	1,334	795	59.6
146. Milk and dairy products	th. m. t.	5,841	4,990	85.4
147. Eggs	mill.		1,400	
148. Wool	th. m. t.	114	78.9	69.2
Railroad Transportation				
149. Length of network	th. km	94.0	84.9	90.3
150. Average daily carloadings	thous.	79.0	89.8	113.7
151. Total freight traffic	bill. m. ton-km	300.0	354.8	118.3
152. Total freight traffic	mill. m. t.	475.0	517.3	108.9
153. Coal and coke	mill. m. t.	125.0	116.6	93.3
154. Oil and oil products	mill. m. t.	32.0	24.7	77.2
155. Ferrous metals	mill. m. t.	23.0	26.2	113.9
156. Ore	mill. m. t.	27.0	30.5	113.0
157. Firewood	mill. m. t.	19.0	19.3	101.6
158. Timber	mill. m. t.	45.0	46.9	104.2
159. Mineral construction materials	mill. m. t.		102.4	
159a. Principal construction materials (stone, lime, cement, bricks)	mill. m. t.	40.0	41.5	103.8

	Third Five-Year Plan (1938–1942)					Fourth Five-Year Plan (1946–1950)			
Interpolated Goals for 1940 (4)	Results in 1940 (5)	(5) as Per Cent of (4) (6)	Goals for 1942 (7)	Results in 1942 (8)	(8) as Per Cent of (7) (9)	Goals for 1950 (10)	Results in 1950 (11)	(11) as Per Cent of (10) (12)	Series No.
724	565	78.0	850			800			122
	349			210		494	255	51.6	122a
									123
	133						73		123a
84.49	84.24	99.7	100.0				101.9		124
	75.874			23.5			88.612		124a
4,300	4,399	102.3	6,300	1,716	27.2	6,000	4,553	75.9	125
	4,695			1,831		6,400	4,867	76.0	125a
36.2	33.64	72.9	45.0	15.8	35.1	45	35.31	78.5	126
	12.2			4.5			11.7		127
194.1	161	82.9	290.0	125.6	43.3		175		128
	38.3						38.2		129
	2.24						3.54		130
	17.4						19.7		131
									132
	12.9						14.0		133
	2,600						2,500		134
	10.8						11.4		135
	120						138		136
37,100	36,446	98.2	41,000	12,516	30.5		32,311		137
2,968	2,237	75.4	3,290	1,329	40.4		3,539		138
26,218	17,357	66.2	30,000	1,537	5.1		19,822		139
1,390	1,500	107.9	1,650	128	7.8		1,084		140
394	245	62.2	500	108	21.6		174		141
84	44	52.4	120				33		142
10,160	8,457	83.2	13,000				6,906		143
2,025	2,970	146.7	2,500				2,043		143a
2,034	2,040	100.3	2,800	1,244	44.4		2,122		144
	1,300						1,300		145
7,107	6,453	90.8	9,000	2,877	32.0		8,479		146
2,200	2,679	121.8	2,900	672	23.2		1,912		147
146	120	82.2	220	80	36.4		136		148
91.4	106.1	116.1	96.0	62.9	65.5	123.2	116.9	94.9	149
101	97.9	96.9	110.0	42.8	38.9	115	118.1	102.7	150
441.1	415.0	94.1	510.0	218	42.7	532	602.3	113.2	151
643.9	592.6	92.0	745.0	277.2	37.2	771.0	834.3	108.2	152
161.1	152.5	94.7	200.0				266.1		153
33.0	29.5	89.4	40.0				43.2		154
33.8	27.1	80.2	40.0				43.3		155
36.9	35.2	95.4	42.0				48.4		156
24.1	23.1	95.9	28.0				18.9		157
60.7	42.8	70.5	72.0				72.4		158
109.8	111.7	101.7	115.0				157.5		159
	32.0								159a

Table A-1   *continued*

| Series | Units | Second Five-Year Plan (1933–1937) | | |
		Goals for 1937 (1)	Results in 1937 (2)	(2) as Per Cent of (1) (3)
160. Grain and flour	mill. m. t.	32.0	38.9	121.6
161. Salt	mill. m. t.		4.1	
162. Total freight traffic, average length of haul	km	632	686	108.5
163. Coal and coke, average length of haul	km	730	709	97.1
163a. Oil and oil products, average length of haul	km	785	1,228	156.4
164. Ferrous metals, average length of haul	km	780	1,004	128.7
164a. Firewood, average length of haul	km	260	261	100.4
164b. Timber, average length of haul	km	720	932	129.4
165. Grain and flour, average length of haul	km	650	689	106.0
165a. Ore, average length of haul	km	450	674	149.8
166. Total passenger traffic	bill. pass.-km	110.0	90.9	82.6
Inland Waterway Transportation				
166a. Length of network	th. km	101.0	101.1	100.1
168. Freight traffic under ministries and economic organizations	bill. m. ton-km	63.0	33.1	52.5
170. Freight traffic under ministries and economic organizations	mill. m. t.	90.0	66.9	74.3
171. Coal and coke	th. m. t.	3,505	2,100	59.9
172. Oil and oil products	th. m. t.	17,595	7,900	44.9
173. Timber and firewood	th. m. t.		35,500	
174. Mineral construction materials	th. m. t.	9,515	9,900	104.0
175. Grain and flour	th. m. t.	6,380	4,300	67.4
176. Salt	th. m. t.	1,300	1,300	100.0
177. Average length of haul under ministries and economic organizations	km	700	500	71.4
178. Passenger traffic	bill. pass.-km	7.4	3.2	43.2
178a. Passenger traffic	mill. pass.	74.0	65.2	88.1
Maritime Transportation (Soviet ships)				
179. Freight traffic	bill. m. ton-km	51.0	36.8	72.2
180. Freight traffic	mill. m. t.	40.0	29.4	73.5
181. Average length of haul	km	1,275	1,252	98.6
182. Passenger traffic	mill. pass.-km	1,400	850	60.7
182a. Passenger traffic	mill. pass.	5.6	3.0	53.6
Motor Transportation				
183. Freight traffic	bill. m. ton-km	16.0	8.7	54.4
Air Transportation				
184. Freight traffic, incl. mail	mill. m. ton-km	120.0	24.9	20.7
185. Passenger traffic	th. pass.	665.0	235	35.3
Employment (annual averages)				
186. Workers and employees, national economy, excl. collective farms	mill.	28.9	27.0	93.4
187. Industry	thous.	10,204	10,112	99.1
188. Construction	thous.	3,425	2,023	59.1
188a. Construction and assembly work	thous.		1,576	
189. State-owned agriculture and logging	thous.	4,935		
190. State-owned agriculture (state farms, MTS, and other state establishments)	thous.	3,575	2,483	69.5

	Third Five-Year Plan (1938–1942)					Fourth Five-Year Plan (1946–1950)			
Interpolated Goals for 1940 (4)	Results in 1940 (5)	(5) as Per Cent of (4) (6)	Goals for 1942 (7)	Results in 1942 (8)	(8) as Per Cent of (7) (9)	Goals for 1950 (10)	Results in 1950 (11)	(11) as Per Cent of (10) (12)	Series No.
43.0	44.6	103.7	46.0				38.8		160
									161
685	700	102.2	685	786	114.7	690	722	104.6	162
	701			886			670		163
	1,234						1,205		163a
	966						1,095		164
	252						241		164a
	1,019			632			998		164b
	736						795		165
	612						574		165a
107	98.0	91.6	120.0	37.9	31.6	98.0	88.0	89.8	166
	107.3						130.2		166a
46.3	35.9	77.5	58.0	21.5	37.1	49.3	45.9	93.1	168
89.0	72.9	81.9	108.0	41.5	38.4		91.5		170
	2,200						4,300		171
11,000	9,700	88.2	13,700				11,900		172
	40,200						50,500		173
	7,600						11,700		174
	5,200						4,500		175
	1,400						1,668		176
522	493	94.4	537	518	96.5		502		177
3.8	3.8	100.0	4.2				2.7		178
75.9	73.0	96.2	84.0	34	40.5		53.6		178a
44.8	23.8	53.1	51.0	15.7	30.8	51.0	39.7	77.8	179
37.7	31.2	82.8	44.5				33.7		180
1,189	745	62.7	1,146				1,178		181
1,000	876	89.6	1,200				1,233		182
3.8	3.1	81.6	4.5				3.2		182a
22	8.896	40.4	40.0	2.76	6.9	25	20.121	80.5	183
	33.1			20.2			195		184
	400						1,500		185
30.3	31.2	103.0	32.7	18.4	52.3	33.5	38.9	116.1	186
11,148	10,967	98.4	11,899	7,171	60.3	11,900	14,144	118.9	187
1,904	2,164	113.7	1,829				4,087		188
	1,563			861			2,569		188a
2,875	2,852	99.2	2,975				3,881		189
2,580	2,573	99.7	2,650				3,437		190

Table A-1   *continued*

Series	Units	Second Five-Year Plan (1933–1937)		
		Goals for 1937 (1)	*Results in 1937* (2)	*(2) as Per Cent of (1)* (3)
191. Railroad transport	thous.	1,666	1,512	90.8
192. Maritime and inland waterway transport	thous.	230	180	78.3
193. Other transport (motor, etc.)	thous.	880	1,092	124.1
194. Communications	thous.	336	375	111.6
195. Trade, procurements, and supply	thous.	2,285	1,991	87.3
196. Public eating places	thous.	860	395.5	46.0
197. Credit institutions	thous.	135	193	143.0
198. Administration	thous.	1,470	1,743.3	118.6
199. Education	thous.	2,065	2,303	111.5
200. Public health	thous.	1,020	1,118	109.6
Wage Fund, Workers and Employees				
201. National economy	mill. rub.	50,742	82,247	162.1
202. Industry	mill. rub.	18,148	30,385	167.4
Average Annual Wage, Workers and Employees				
203. Money wage, national economy, excl. collective farms and cooperatives	rubles	1,755	3,047	173.6
204. Real wage, national economy, excl. collective farms and cooperatives, calculated from official Soviet index	yr. prec. plan = 100	189	101.5	53.7
204a. Real wage, national economy, excl. collective farms and cooperatives, calculated from Zaleski index	yr. prec. plan = 100	189	128.7	68.1
205. Money wage, industry	rubles	1,779	3,005	168.9
Average Annual Money Wage, Workers				
206. Industry	rubles		2,820	
207. Iron ore	rubles		3,143	
208. Coal	rubles	1,875	3,626	193.4
209. Ferrous metals	rubles	1,984	3,266	164.6
209a. Machine-building	rubles	2,022	3,387	167.5
210. Paper	rubles			
211. Chemicals	rubles		3,165	
212. Textiles	rubles	1,390	2,338	168.2
212a. Cotton	rubles	1,400	2,396	171.1
212b. Wool	rubles	1,420	2,338	164.6
213. Leather	rubles	1,565		
214. Food	rubles		2,259	
Average Annual Money Wage, Workers and Employees				
215. Construction	rubles	1,794	3,087	172.1
216. Railroad transport	rubles	1,859	3,271	176.0
217. Maritime and inland waterway transport	rubles	1,977	3,397	171.8
218. Communications	rubles	1,655	2,356	142.4
219. Trade	rubles	1,533	2,528	164.9
220. Public eating places	rubles	1,200	2,045	170.4
221. Credit institutions	rubles	2,293	3,425	149.4
222. Administration	rubles	2,368	3,937	166.3
223. Education	rubles	1,960	3,442	175.6

	Third Five-Year Plan (1938–1942)					Fourth Five-Year Plan (1946–1950)			
Interpolated Goals for 1940 (4)	Results in 1940 (5)	(5) as Per Cent of (4) (6)	Goals for 1942 (7)	Results in 1942 (8)	(8) as Per Cent of (7) (9)	Goals for 1950 (10)	Results in 1950 (11)	(11) as Per Cent of (10) (12)	Series No.
1,620	1,752	108.1	1,700	1,067	62.8		2,068		191
210	203	96.7	230				222		192
1,440	1,581	109.8	1,735				1,827		193
445	478	107.4	500	273	54.6		542		194
2,280	2,465	108.1	2,500				2,705		195
490	662	135.1	560				659		196
215	262	121.9	230	129	56.1		264		197
1,890	2,139	113.2	2,000	920	46.0		1,831		198
2,645	2,930	110.8	2,900	1,600	55.2		3,752		199
1,386	1,507	108.7	1,600	975	60.9		2,051		200
111,900	123,700	110.5	137,400			201,000	298,300	148.4	201
40,747	44,750	109.8	49,567						202
3,674	3,972	108.1	4,162			6,000	7,668	127.8	203
121	109.8	90.7	137			305.2	272.0	89.1	204
121	82.8	68.4	137						204a
3,656	4,080	111.6	4,166				8,436		205
3,504	3,876	110.6	4,050				8,244		206
									207
	5,229						14,472		208
	4,719						11,472		209
	4,791						8,928		209a
	3,343						8,868		210
	4,509						8,760		211
	3,434						6,852		212
							7,296		212a
									212b
							7,250		213
	3,396						6,144		214
3,758	4,068	108.2	4,285				7,212		215
3,792	4,092	107.9	4,187				8,700		216
3,786	4,908	129.6	4,070				9,432		217
2,957	3,372	114.0	3,440				6,324		218
2,860			3,109						219
2,449			2,761						220
3,770	4,008	106.3	4,020				7,968		221
4,322	4,656	107.7	4,600				8,196		222
4,324	3,876	89.6	5,034				8,004		223

Table A-1   *continued*

Series	Units	Goals for 1937 (1)	Results in 1937 (2)	(2) as Per Cent of (1) (3)
		Second Five-Year Plan (1933–1937)		
224. Public health	rubles	1,560	2,455	157.4
225. State-owned agriculture	rubles	1,299	2,121	163.3
226. Logging	rubles	1,291	1,920	148.7
Housing				
227. Housing fund, urban, total	mill. m²	246.5	207.3	84.1
228. Housing construction, urban, total	mill. m²	19.7	3.9	19.8
229. Floorspace per inhabitant, urban	m²	5.35	3.77	71.8
Population				
230. Total	mill.	180.7	167.2	92.5
231. Urban	mill.	49.1	55.0	112.0
232. Rural	mill.	131.6	112.2	85.3
Retail Trade				
233. State and cooperative in current prices	mill. rub.	90,000	125,943	139.9
234a. State and cooperative in constant prices calculated from official Soviet price index	mill. rub.	138,500	60,060	43.4
234b. State and cooperative in constant prices calculated from Zaleski price index	mill. rub.	138,500	76,050	54.9

Source

The sources are given below by individual series for all columns except col. 4, which was estimated from actual results in 1937 (col. 2) and goals for 1942 (col. 7) by assuming an equal average annual planned rate of growth during 1938–1942.

1. National income (1926/27 prices)–**Col. 1:** *293*, p. 427. **Cols. 2 and 7:** *254*, p. 197. **Cols. 5 and 11:** *161*, p. 112. For col. 5, *290*, p. 6, gives the rounded figure of 128. **Col. 8:** Based on national income in 1940 (col. 5) and index for 1942 (given as 66 with 1940 = 100 in *285*, No. 5, 1965, p. 70). **Col. 10:** *194*, Vol. 3, p. 284.

INDUSTRY

2. Gross production, total (1926/27 prices)–**Col. 1:** *293*, p. 687. **Col. 2:** *254*, p. 197. **Col. 5:** *289*, p. 12. Also, *194*, Vol. 3, p. 252. **Col. 7:** *256*, p. 9. The two other versions of the plan (*254*, p. 197, and *255*, p. 21) give 180. **Col. 8:** Based on gross production in 1940 (col. 5) and index for 1942 (given as 77 with 1940 = 100 in *285*, No. 5, 1965, p. 70). **Col. 10:** *194*, Vol. 3, p. 252. **Col. 11:** Based on gross production in 1940 (col. 5) and index for 1950 (given as 173 with 1940 = 100 in *180*, 4/14/51).

3. Producer goods (1926/27 prices)–**Col. 1:** *293*, p. 429. **Col. 2:** *254*, p. 197. **Col. 5:** *290*, p. 6. **Col. 7:** *256*, p. 9. The two other versions of the plan (*254*, p. 197, and *255*, p. 22) give 112.0. **Col. 8:** Based on total production (series 2) and share of producer goods in total (given as 79.5% in *99*, p. 114). **Col. 10:** *475*, p. 313. **Col. 11:** Based on 1937 output (col. 2) and index for 1950 (given as 314 with 1937 = 100 in *187*, p. 33).

4. Consumer goods (1926/27 prices)–**Col. 1:** *293*, p. 429. **Col. 2:** *254*, p. 197. **Col. 5:** *290*, p. 6. **Col. 7:** *256*, p. 9. The two other versions of the plan (*254*, p. 197, and *255*, p. 23) give 68.0. **Col. 8:** Based on total production (series 2) and share of consumer goods in total (given as 20.5% in *99*, p. 114). **Col. 10:** *475*, p. 313. **Col. 11:** Based on 1937 output (col. 2) and index for 1950 (given as 164 with 1937 = 100 in *187*, p. 33).

5. Coal–**Col. 1:** *293*, p. 691. **Cols. 2, 5, and 11:** *187*, p. 140. **Col. 7:** *256*, p. 9. The two other versions of the plan (*254*, p. 202, and *255*, p. 22) give 230,000. **Col. 8:** 1943 output (given as 93,141 in *99*, p. 248) minus increase in output between 1942 and 1943 (given as 17,605 in *99*, p. 248). **Col. 10:** *194*, Vol. 3, p. 253.

6. Peat–**Col. 1:** *293*, p. 691. **Cols. 2, 5, 8, and 11:** *218*, p. 35. Includes collective farm output. **Col. 7:** *254*, p. 202. **Col. 10:** *194*, Vol. 3, p. 259.

7. Coke (6% humidity)–**Col. 1:** *293*, p. 691. **Cols. 2, 5, and 11:** *187*, p. 115. **Col. 7:** *254*, p. 203. Output of Commissariat of the Ferrous Metal Industry. **Col. 8:** Based on 1945 output (given as 13,649 in Table A-4, col. 5) and index for 1945 (given as 198 with 1942 = 100 in *99*, p. 236). **Col. 10:** *194*, Vol. 3, p. 254.

	Third Five-Year Plan (1938–1942)					Fourth Five-Year Plan (1946–1950)			
Interpolated Goals for 1940 (4)	Results in 1940 (5)	(5) as Per Cent of (4) (6)	Goals for 1942 (7)	Results in 1942 (8)	(8) as Per Cent of (7) (9)	Goals for 1950 (10)	Results in 1950 (11)	(11) as Per Cent of (10) (12)	Series No.
3,003	3,060	101.9	3,435				5,820		224
2,539	2,628	103.5	2,863				4,584		225
2,111			2,250						226
	270						290		227
		84.9		5.8			24.2		228
	5.1						4.67		229
	196.7						181.6		230
	63.9						73.0		231
	132.8						108.5		232
169,160	175,080	103.5	206,000	77,800	37.8	275,000	359,582	130.8	233
169,160	147,100	87.0	206,000	50,000	24.3	224,100	192,600	85.9	234a
169,160	110,900	65.6	206,000	37,700	18.3				234b

8. Oil shale–**Col. 1:** *293*, p. 691. **Cols. 2, 5, and 11:** *187*, p. 166. **Col. 7:** *485*, series 311.4.

9. Crude petroleum–**Col. 1:** *293*, p. 121. **Cols. 2, 5, and 11:** *187*, p. 153. **Col. 7:** *254*, p. 202. **Col. 8:** *99*, p. 133. **Col. 10:** *194*, Vol. 3, p. 253.

10. Natural gas–**Col. 1:** Based on planned output in tons (given as 2.5 mill. m. t. in *293*, p. 121) and ratio of m³ to tons for 1937 (derived as 1,100 in Table A-2, series 10). **Cols. 2, 5, and 11:** *187*, p. 156. Includes secondary extraction of gas. **Col. 10:** *291*, p. 12. Extraction of gas. *194*, Vol. 3, p. 253, gives 1,900 for gas extracted from coal and oil shale and 8,400 for natural gas.

11. Electric power–**Col. 1:** *293*, p. 691. **Cols. 2, 5, and 11:** *187*, p. 171. **Col. 7:** *254*, p. 213. **Col. 8:** *99*, p. 261. **Col. 10:** *194*, Vol. 3, p. 253.

12. Hydroelectric power–**Col. 1:** *293*, p. 106. **Cols. 2, 5, and 11:** *187*, p. 171. **Col. 7:** *254*, p. 213. **Col. 10:** Based on total electric power (series 11) and share of hydroelectric in total (given as 15.2% in *291*, p. 12).

13. Iron ore–**Col. 1:** *293*, p. 691. **Cols. 2, 5, and 11:** *187*, p. 115. **Col. 7:** *254*, p. 203. **Col. 8:** *99*, p. 230. **Col. 10:** *194*, Vol. 3, p. 254.

14. Pig iron–**Col. 1:** *293*, p. 691. **Cols. 2, 5, and 11:** *187*, p. 106. **Col. 7:** *254*, p. 203. **Col. 8:** *121*, p. 188. **Col. 10:** *194*, Vol. 3, p. 253.

15. Steel ingots and castings–**Col. 1:** *293*, p. 691. **Cols. 2, 5, and 11:** *187*, p. 106. **Col. 7:** *256*, p. 9, and *255*, p. 22. *254*, p. 203, gives 27,500. **Col. 8:** *121*, p. 188. **Col. 10:** *194*, Vol. 3, p. 253.

16. Rolled steel–**Col. 1:** *293*, p. 691. **Cols. 2, 5, and 11:** *187*, p. 106. **Col. 7:** *254*, p. 203. **Col. 8:** *121*, p. 188. **Col. 10:** *194*, Vol. 3, p. 253.

17. Steel pipes–**Col. 1:** *293*, p. 693. **Cols. 2, 5, and 11:** *187*, p. 106. **Col. 10:** *194*, Vol. 3, p. 254.

18. Aluminum–**Col. 1:** *293*, p. 430. **Col. 2:** *254*, p. 204. Excluding production from scrap. Total production given as 46.8 in *254*, p. 204. **Col. 5:** Based on 1937 output (col. 2) and index for 1940 (given as 159 with 1937 = 100 in *75*, 2/21/41, as cited in *472*, p. 460). **Col. 7:** *254*, p. 204. Excluding planned production from scrap. Planned total given as 162 in *254*, p. 204. **Col. 8:** Based on 1943 output (given as 62.3 th. m. t. in Table A-4, col. 2) and increase in 1943 over 1942 (given as 20% in *290*, p. 84). **Col. 10:** Based on 1945 output and planned increase for 1950 (given as twofold in *194*, Vol. 3, p. 256). 1945 output estimated at 86.3 from 1940 output (col. 5) and increase in 1945 (given as 44% in *75*, 4/2/46, as cited in *472*, p. 460).

19. Manganese ore–**Col. 1:** *293*, p. 691. **Cols. 2, 5, and 11:** *187*, p. 115. **Col. 7:** *254*, p. 203. Output of Commissariat of the Ferrous Metal Industry. **Col. 8:** *99*, p. 233.

Table A-1 *continued*

20. Nickel–**Cols. 2 and 5:** *485*, series 213.4. **Col. 7:** Based on 1937 output (col. 2) and index for 1942 (given as 1,130 with 1937 = 100 in *231*, No. 4–5, 1939, p. 8, as cited in *485*, series 213.4). **Col. 8:** Based on 1943 output (given as 11.2 in Table A-4, col. 2) and increase between 1942 and 1943 (given as 52% in *290*, p. 84). **Col. 10:** Based on 1945 output (Table A-4, col. 4) and planned increase for 1950 (given as 1.9–fold in *194*, Vol. 3, p. 256).

21. Zinc–**Col. 1:** *293*, p. 430. **Col. 2:** *472*, p. 421. **Col. 5:** *470*, 1/26/48, Pt. 2, p. 19. Also *472*, p. 421. **Col. 7:** Based on 1932 output (given as 13.656 in *498*, p. 307) and planned increase for 1942 (given as 12.623–fold for pig [*chushkovoi*] zinc in *65*, 3/4/39, p. 3, as cited in *485*, series 210.1). **Col. 10:** Based on 1945 output (Table A-4, col. 4) and planned increase for 1950 (given as 2.5–fold in *194*, Vol. 3, p. 256). **Col. 11:** Based on 1945 output (Table A-4, col. 4) and index for 1950 (given as 233 with 1945 = 100 in *167*, pp. 40–41).

22. Refined copper–**Col. 1:** *293*, pp. 138 and 430. **Cols. 2 and 5:** *472*, p. 420. **Col. 7:** Based on 1937 output (col. 2) and planned increase for 1942 (given as 2.8–fold in *256*, p. 13). **Cols. 10 and 11:** *433*, p. 146. For col. 11, *472*, p. 420, gives 247.0.

23. Lead–**Col. 1:** *293*, p.138. **Cols. 2, 5, and 11:** *472*, p. 421. **Col. 7:** Based on 1932 output (given as 18.717 in *498*, p. 307) and planned increase for 1942 (given as 7.152-fold in *65*, 3/4/39, p. 3, as cited in *485*, series 209.1). **Col. 10:** Based on 1945 output (Table A-4, col. 4) and planned increase for 1950 (given as 2.6–fold in *194*, Vol. 3, p. 256).

24. Mineral fertilizer–**Col. 1:** Sum of phosphoric fertilizer, 18.7% P_2O_5 (series 26), ground natural phosphate (series 27), ammonium sulfate (planned deliveries to agriculture given as 1,410 in *293*, pp. 472 and 696–97), and potash fertilizer, 41.6% K_2O. The latter is derived as 560 from planned deliveries to agriculture for 1937 of sylvanite with 15% K Cl (given as 1,680 in *293*, pp. 472 and 696–97) and ratio of potash fertilizer to sylvanite (derived as 1 to 3 from 1932 output of potash fertilizer in *485*, series 412.4, and 1932 output of sylvanite in *293*, pp. 472 and 696–97). **Cols. 2, 5, and 11:** *187*, p. 192. **Col. 10:** Sum of phosphoric fertilizer, potash fertilizer, and ammonium sulfate (given as 5,100 in *194*, Vol. 3, pp. 253 and 274), ground natural phosphate (series 27), and other mineral fertilizers such as Thomas slag and phosphoric precipitate apparently included after 1949 (roughly estimated at 100). On the enlarged coverage of mineral fertilizer after 1949, see *485*, series 407.1, notes.

25. Phosphoric fertilizer (14% P_2O_5)–**Col. 1:** *293*, p. 697. **Cols. 2, 5, and 11:** *485*, series 409.3. **Col. 7:** Planned output in 100% P_2O_5, (given as 650 in *254*, p. 204) converted into 14% P_2O_5, as in *485*, series 409.3. **Col. 10:** Planned output in 18.7% P_2O_5 (series 26) converted into 14% P_2O_5.

26. Phosphoric fertilizer (18.7% P_2O_5)–**Col. 1:** Planned output in 14% P_2O_5 (series 25) converted into 18.7% P_2O_5. **Cols. 2, 5, and 11:** *187*, p. 192. **Col. 7:** Planned output in 100% P_2O_5 (given as 650 in *254*, p. 204) converted into 18.7% P_2O_5. Kurskii (in *173*, No. 3, 1939, p. 45) gives 3,300 for output in 18.5% P_2O_5. **Col. 10:** Based on prewar output (col. 5) and increase planned for 1950 (twofold according to Pervukhin in *302*, p. 130).

27. Ground natural phosphate–**Col. 1:** *293*, p. 697. **Cols. 2, 5, and 11:** *187*, p. 192. **Col. 10:** *194*, Vol. 3, p. 275. Deliveries to agriculture.

28. Potash fertilizer–**Cols. 2, 5, and 11:** *187*, p. 192. **Col. 7:** *173*, No. 3, 1939, p. 45.

29. Ammonium sulfate–**Cols. 2, 5, and 11:** *187*, p. 192. **Col. 7:** *173*, No. 3, 1939. p. 45. **Col. 10:** Based on prewar output (col. 5) and increase planned for 1950 (twofold according to Pervukhin in *302*, p. 129).

30. Soda ash–**Col. 1:** *293*, p. 431. **Cols. 2, 5, and 11:** *187*, p. 194. **Col. 7:** *254*, p. 204. **Col. 8:** *485*, series 406.1. Estimate. **Col. 10:** *194*, Vol. 3, p. 253.

31. Caustic soda–**Col. 1:** *293*, p. 431. **Cols. 2, 5, and 11:** *187*, p. 194. **Col. 10:** *194*, Vol. 3, p. 253.

32. Sulfuric acid–**Col. 1:** *293*, p. 431. **Cols. 2, 5, and 11:** *187*, p. 196.

32a. Synthetic rubber–**Cols. 2 and 5:** *223*, p. 247. **Col. 10:** Based on 1940 output (col. 5) and planned increase for 1950 (given as twofold in *173*, No. 3, 1946, p. 30).

33. Tires–**Col. 1:** *293*, p. 458. **Cols. 2, 5, and 11:** *187*, p. 199. **Col. 7:** *254*, p. 205. Output of Commissariat of the Chemical Industry.

34a. Synthetic dyes–**Col. 2:** *472*, p. 425. **Cols 5 and 11:** *187*, p. 197. Output of Ministry of the Chemical Industry. **Col. 10:** *194*, Vol. 3, . 253.

35. Cement–**Col. 1:** *293*, p. 699. **Cols. 2, 5, and 11:** *187*, p. 277. **Col. 7:** *256*, p. 9. The two other versions of the plan (*254*, p. 205, and *255*, p. 22) give 10,000. **Col. 8:** *285*, No. 5, 1965, p. 70. **Col. 10:** *194*, Vol. 3, p. 254.

36. Lime–**Col. 1:** *293*, p. 699. **Cols. 2, 5, and 11:** *187*, p. 282. Sum of construction lime and technological lime. **Col. 7:** *254*, p. 205.

37. Window glass–**Col. 1:** *293*, p. 703. Excluding the output of industrial cooperatives. **Cols. 2, 5, and 11:** *187*, p. 312. **Col. 10:** *194*, Vol. 3, p. 254.

38a. Roofing tiles–**Col. 1:** *293*, p. 699. **Cols. 2 and 7:** *254*, p. 205. Excluding collective farm output. **Col. 5:** Total output (given as 173.3 in *187*, p. 299) minus collective farm output (estimated as 24% of total from total output for 1937 in col. 2 and noncollective farm output of 108.0 in *254*, p. 205). This was done to keep output comparable with planned output. **Col. 10:** Based on total prewar output (given as 173.3 in *187*, p. 299) and increase planned for 1950 (fourfold according to *194*, Vol. 3, p. 267). **Col. 11:** *187*, p. 299.

39. Asbestos shingles–**Col. 1:** *293*, p. 156. **Cols. 2, 5, and 11:** *187*, p. 299. **Col. 7:** *254*, p. 205. **Col. 10:** *194*, Vol. 3, p. 254.

Table A-1 *continued*

40. Bricks–**Col. 1:** *293*, p. 699. **Cols. 2, 5, and 11:** *187*, p. 291. **Col. 7:** *254*, p. 205. Excluding output of collective farms. **Col. 10:** Given as 10,000 to 11,000 in *189*, 10/23/47, p. 3, according to *426*, pp. 86 and 92, as cited in *485*, series 705.1.

41. Industrial timber hauled–**Col. 1:** *293*, p. 699. **Cols. 2, 5, and 11:** *187*, p. 249. **Col. 7:** *254*, p. 208. **Col. 10:** Based on 1940 output (col. 5) and planned increase for 1950 (given as 59% in *194*, Vol. 3, p. 267).

42. Lumber–**Col. 1:** Planned output in *293*, p. 701 (given as 43.0 for apparently limited coverage) increased by 5.0 (difference between 1937 ouput figures given in *254*, p. 208, and in more recent source, *187*, p. 261) to make series comparable with wider coverage of more recent sources. **Cols. 2, 5, and 11:** *187*, p. 261. **Col. 7:** *460*, p. 118. *254*, p. 208, gives 45, but this figure has a more limited coverage. **Col. 10:** *194*, Vol. 3, p. 254.

43. Plywood–**Col. 1:** *293*, p. 344. **Cols. 2, 5, and 11:** *187*, p. 261. Total production used rather than output of Commissariat of the Timber Industry (as in Third Five-Year Plan) since the difference was negligible, the latter amounting to 97.4% of the former in 1937 (*254*, p. 208). **Col. 7:** *254*, p. 208. Output of Commissariat of the Timber Industry. **Col. 10:** *276*, p. 70., as cited in *485*, series 702.1.

44. Paper–**Col. 1:** *293*, p. 701. **Cols. 2, 5, and 11:** *187*, p. 268. **Col. 7:** *256*, p. 9. The earlier version of the plan (*254*, p. 208) gives 1,300. **Col. 10:** *291*, p. 13. *19*, No. 3–4, 1946, pp. 7 and 9 (as cited in *485*, series 449.1, source notes) gives 1,360.

45. Paperboard–**Col. 1:** *293*, p. 703. Paperboard and fiber. The definition of paperboard was considerably enlarged in later years. **Col. 2:** *254*, p. 209. *187*, p. 268, gives a much larger figure (144.2) with a wider coverage, but the older figures are used here to maintain comparability. **Col. 5:** *485*, series 450.3. **Col. 7:** *254*, p. 209. **Col. 10:** *19*, No. 3–4, 1946, p. 9 (as cited in *485*, series 450.3) gives 175, but this figure does not seem to have comparable coverage to the 1950 output figure used here (col. 11) and hence has not been used. **Col. 11:** *187*, p. 268.

46. Machine tools–**Col. 1:** *293*, p. 695. **Cols. 2 and 7:** *254*, p. 207. **Col. 5:** Based on 1950 output (col. 11) and increase in 1950 over 1940 (given as 1.6 times in *75*, 4/20/51, p. 2). Other possible estimates are 43,500, derived from output of larger coverage (given as 58,400 in *140*, 1956, p. 55) reduced to smaller coverage as in col. 8 below; and 45,300, derived by subtracting presses and forges (given as 4,700 in *140*, 1956, p. 55) from total figure (given as 50,000 in *76*, p. 106, as cited in *485*, series 1009.1). **Col. 8:** Output of larger coverage (given as 22,935 in *99*, p. 135) reduced by ratio of smaller to larger coverage for 1937 (derived as 74.5% from col. 2 and *187*, p. 208). **Col. 10:** *194*, Vol. 3, p. 253. **Col. 11:** *187*, pp. 208–9.

46a. Metallurgical equipment–**Cols. 2, 5, and 11:** *187*, pp. 212–13. **Col. 8:** *207*, p. 140. **Col. 10:** *194*, Vol. 3, p. 253.

47. Steam and gas turbines–**Col. 1:** Planned output of steam and hydraulic turbines (given as 1,500 in *293*, p. 695) minus planned output of hydraulic turbines (estimated at 200 from 1932 output of total turbines of 314 in *293*, p. 695, and 1932 output of steam and gas turbines of 239 in *187*, p. 214). **Cols. 2, 5, and 11:** *187*, pp. 214–15. **Col. 10:** *180*, 3/21/46, p. 3, as cited in *485*, series 1012.1.

48. Steam boilers–**Col. 1:** *293*, p. 693. Output of specialized factories. **Cols. 2 and 7:** *254*, p. 206. **Col. 5:** Output of larger coverage (given as 276.3 in *187*, pp. 214–15) reduced by ratio of smaller to larger coverage for 1937 (derived as 63.5% from col. 2 and *187*, p. 214). **Col. 11:** *187*, pp. 214–15. After the war, the definition was changed. The corresponding coverage for 1937 was 268.2.

49. Turbogenerators–**Col. 1:** Planned output of steam and hydraulic turbogenerators (given as 1,400 in *186*, p. 448) minus planned output of hydraulic turbogenerators (estimated at 250 from 1932 output—derived from total output of 966 in *186*, p. 448, and output of steam and gas turbogenerators of 826 in *187*, p. 214—and planned increase for 1937). **Cols. 2, 5, and 11:** *187*, pp. 214–15.

50. Spinning machines–**Col. 1:** *293*, p. 695. **Cols. 2, 5, and 11:** *187*, pp. 234–35. **Col. 7:** *254*, p. 207. **Col. 10:** *194*, Vol. 3, p. 253.

51. Looms–**Col. 1:** *293*, p. 695. **Cols. 2 and 7:** *254*, p. 207. **Col. 5:** *28*, p. 74. **Col. 10:** *194*, Vol. 3, p. 253. **Col. 11:** *187*, p. 235.

52. Tractors (excluding garden tractors)–**Col. 1:** *293*, p. 695. **Cols. 2, 5, and 11:** *187*, pp. 228–29. **Col. 7:** *254*, p. 207. **Col. 8:** *99*, p. 136. **Col. 10:** *194*, Vol. 3, p. 253.

53. Tractors (conventional 15 hp units)–**Col. 1:** *293*, p. 695. **Cols. 2, 5, and 11:** *187*, p. 226. **Col. 7:** *254*, p. 207. **Col. 10:** *168*, p. 73.

54. Motor vehicles, total–**Col. 1:** *293*, p. 695. **Cols. 2, 5, and 11:** *187*, p. 223. **Col. 7:** *254*, p. 206. **Col. 10:** *194*, Vol. 3, p. 253.

55. Trucks–**Col. 1:** *293*, p. 695. **Cols. 2, 5, and 11:** *187*, p. 223. **Col. 7:** *254*, p. 206. **Col. 8:** *209*, p. 113. **Col. 10:** *194*, Vol. 3, p. 253.

56. Automobiles–**Col. 1:** *293*, p. 695. **Cols. 2, 5, and 11:** *187*, p. 223. **Col. 7:** *254*, p. 206. **Col. 10:** *194*, Vol. 3, p. 253.

57. Buses–**Cols. 2, 5, and 11:** *187*, p. 223. Total motor vehicles minus trucks and automobiles. **Col. 10:** *194*, Vol. 3, p. 257.

58. Grain combines–**Col. 1:** *293*, p. 695. **Cols. 2, 5, and 11:** *187*, p. 233.

59. Steam locomotives–**Col. 1:** *186*, p. 448. Sum of locomotives for freight cars (1,560) and for passenger cars (710). *293*, pp. 692–93, gives 2,800, but that figure is in conventional units. **Cols. 2, 5, and 11:** *187*, p. 220. **Col. 3:**

Table A-1 *continued*

Fulfillment in conventional units was 56.5 (*293*, pp. 692–93). **Col. 7:** *254*, p. 207. Locomotives for the Commissariat of Transportation. **Col. 8:** Production was reduced "to the minimum" (*99*, p. 136). **Col. 10:** *194*, Vol. 3, p. 253.

60. Diesel locomotives–**Col. 1:** *293*, p. 693. **Cols. 2, 5, and 11:** *187*, p. 220. **Col. 10:** *194*, Vol. 3, p. 253.

61. Electric locomotives–**Col. 1:** *293*, p. 693. **Cols. 2, 5, and 11:** *187*, p. 220. **Col. 10:** *194*, Vol. 3, p. 253.

62. Railroad freight cars (units)–**Col. 1:** Based on planned output in 2-axle units (series 63) and ratio between 1937 output in physical units (col. 2) and in 2-axle units (series 63, col. 2). **Cols. 2, 5, and 11:** *187*, p. 222. **Col. 7:** *254*, p. 207. Freight cars for the Commissariat of Transportation. **Col. 10:** Based on planned output in 2-axle units (series 63) and ratio between 1942 planned output in physical units (col. 7) and in 2-axle units (series 63, col. 7).

63. Railroad freight cars (2-axle units)–**Col. 1:** *293*, p. 693. **Col. 2:** *254*, p. 207. **Col. 7:** *254*, p. 207. **Col. 10:** *194*, Vol. 3, p. 253.

64. Railroad passenger cars–**Col. 1:** *293*, p. 693. **Cols. 2, 5, and 11:** *187*, p. 220. **Col. 7:** *254*, p. 207. **Col. 10:** *194*, Vol. 3, p. 253.

65. Excavators–**Cols. 2, 5, and 11:** *187*, p. 236. **Col. 7:** *254*, p. 207.

66. Ginned cotton–**Col. 1:** *293*, p. 528. **Cols. 2, 5, and 11:** *187*, p. 324. **Col. 7:** *254*, p. 209. **Col. 10:** *251*, No. 7–8, 1946, p. 2, as cited by *404*, p. 20.

67. Cotton yarn–**Cols. 1 and 7:** *404*, p. 31. **Col. 2:** *72*, p. 85. **Cols. 5 and 11:** *187*, p. 327. **Col. 10:** *251*, No. 7–8, 1946, p. 3, as cited in *485*, series 1208.6.

68. Cotton fabrics–**Col. 1:** *293*, p. 703. **Cols. 2, 5, and 11:** *187*, p. 328. **Col. 7:** *254*, p. 209. **Col. 8:** *285*, No. 5, 1965, p. 71. **Col. 10:** *194*, Vol. 3, p. 254.

69. Woolen fabrics–**Col. 1:** *293*, p. 703. **Cols. 2, 5, and 11:** *187*, p. 328. **Col. 7:** *256*, p. 9. *254*, p. 209, gives 175.0. **Col. 8:** Based on 1940 output (col. 5) and index for 1942 (given as 32 with 1940 = 100 in *99*, p. 115). **Col. 10:** *194*, Vol. 3, p. 254.

70. Linen fabrics (square meters)–**Col. 1:** *293*, p. 703. **Cols. 2 and 5:** *485*, series 1210.7.

71. Linen fabrics (meters)–**Cols. 2, 5, and 11:** *187*, p. 328. **Col. 7:** *254*, p. 209. **Col. 10:** *251*, No. 10, 1947, p. 4, as cited in *485*, series 1209.7.

72. Silk and rayon fabrics–**Col. 1:** *293*, p. 522. Output of state and cooperative industry. **Cols. 2, 5, and 11:** *187*, p. 328. For col. 2, *254*, p. 209, gives 57.9. **Col. 7:** *254*, p. 209. **Col. 10:** *291*, p. 13.

73. Knitted underwear–**Col. 1:** *293*, p. 703. Production of Commissariat of Light Industry only, hence not fully comparable with col. 2. **Cols. 2, 5, and 11:** *187*, p. 343. For col. 2, *254*, p. 209, gives 102.6, but that figure has a more limited coverage. **Col. 7:** *254*, p. 209.

74. Knitted outer garments–**Cols. 2, 5, and 11:** *187*, p. 343. For col. 2, *254*, p. 209, gives 39.71, but this figure has a more limited coverage. **Col. 7:** *254*, p. 209.

75. Hosiery–**Col. 1:** Based on total output in 1932 (given as 208.0 in *498*, p. 309) and planned increase for 1937 (derived as 4.7-fold from 1932 output and 1937 planned output for Commissariat of Light Industry in *293*, p. 703). **Cols. 2, 5, and 11:** *187*, p. 343. For col. 2, *254*, p. 209, gives 401.0, slightly different from later figures. **Col. 7:** *254*, p. 209. **Col. 10:** *194*, Vol. 3, p. 254.

76. Leather shoes–**Col. 1:** Based on total output in 1932 (given as 86.9 in *498*, p. 309) and percentage that 1937 plan was of 1932 output for state and cooperative industry (given as 219.5 in *293*, p. 703). See also *451*, p. 81. **Col. 2:** *187*, p. 351. *254*, p. 209, gives 164.2, which apparently does not cover total output. **Col. 5:** Total output (given as 211.0 in *187*, p. 351) reduced by 10.2% (derived from total 1937 output in col. 2 and 1937 output given in *254*, p. 209) in order to maintain comparability with plan figures. **Col. 7:** *256*, p. 9. *254*, p. 209, gives 235.0. **Col. 8:** *285*, No. 5, 1965, p. 71. **Col. 10:** *194*, Vol. 3, p. 254. **Col. 11:** *187*, p. 351.

77. Felt footwear–**Col. 1:** *186*, p. 523. Output of state and cooperative industry. **Cols. 2, 5, and 11:** *187*, p. 323.

78. Rubber footwear–**Col. 1:** *293*, p. 697. **Cols. 2, 5, and 11:** *187*, p. 199. **Col. 7:** *254*, p. 205. Output of Commissariat of the Chemical Industry. **Col. 10:** *194*, Vol. 3, p. 254.

79. Rubber galoshes–**Cols. 2 and 7:** *254*, p. 205. Output of Commissariat of the Chemical Industry. **Col. 5:** *180*, 7/5/46, as cited in *485*, series 1203.6.

80. Metal beds–**Cols. 2 and 7:** *254*, p. 208. **Cols. 5 and 11:** *188*, p. 412.

80a. Enameled kitchenware–**Cols. 2 and 7:** *254*, p. 208. **Cols. 5 and 11:** *187*, p. 364.

81. Motorcycles–**Cols. 2, 5, and 11:** *187*, p. 362. **Col. 7:** *173*, No. 3, 1939, p. 78. **Col. 10:** *194*, Vol. 3, p. 288. Output and sales.

82. Bicycles–**Col. 1:** *293*, p. 697. **Cols. 2, 5, and 11:** *187*, p. 362. **Col. 7:** Based on output of Commissariat of Machine-Building (given as 750.0 in *254*, p. 208) and ratio of output of Commissariat of Machine-Building to total output in 1937 (derived as 1.54 from *254*, p. 208, and col. 2). **Col. 10:** *194*, Vol. 3, p. 288. Output and sales.

83. Radios–**Col. 1:** *293*, p. 697. **Cols. 2, 5, and 11:** *188*, p. 407. For col. 2, *254*, p. 208, gives 194.0. **Col. 7:** *254*, p. 208. **Col. 10:** *194*, Vol. 3, p. 288. Output and sales.

83a. Refrigerators, household–**Col. 2:** *254*, p. 208. **Cols. 5 and 11:** *188*, p. 408. **Col. 7:** *254*, p. 208.

84. Sewing machines, household–**Col. 1:** *293*, p. 522. Output of state industry. **Cols. 2, 5, and 11:** *187*, p. 362.

Table A-1 *continued*

Col. 7: *254*, p. 208. Output of Commissariat of Machine-Building. **Col. 10:** *194*, Vol. 3, p. 288. Output and sales.

85. Clocks and watches–**Col. 1:** Based on 1932 output (given as 3,557 in *498*, p. 310) and index of planned increase in value of output for 1937 (derived as 480.8 with 1932 = 100 from *293*, pp. 696–97). **Cols. 2, 5, and 11:** *187*, p. 362. **Col. 10:** *194*, Vol. 3, p. 288. Output and sales.

86. Cameras–**Col. 1:** Based on planned output for state industry (given as 140.0 in *293*, p. 523) and ratio of total output to output of state industry in 1932 (derived as 2.5 from *498*, p. 310, and *293*, p. 523). **Cols. 2, 5, and 11:** *187*, p. 362. **Col. 10:** *194*, Vol. 3, p. 288. Output and sales.

87. Phonographs–**Col. 1:** *293*, p. 697. **Col. 2:** *254*, p. 208. **Cols. 5 and 11:** *187*, p. 363. **Col. 7:** *254*, p. 208. **Col. 10:** *194*, Vol. 3, p. 288. Output and sales.

88. Soap (40% fatty acid)–**Col. 1:** *293*, p. 703. **Cols. 2, 5, and 11:** *187*, p. 372. **Col. 7:** *254*, p. 210. **Col. 10:** *194*, Vol. 3, p. 254.

89. Bread and breadstuffs (large-scale industry)–**Col. 1:** *293*, p. 462. Planned output of *Tsentrosoiuz* (Union of Cooperatives) only. In 1932 this output was very close to total output, but the reorganization of the baking industry during the Second Five-Year Plan makes such comparisons in 1937 difficult. **Col. 2:** *173*, No. 5, 1939, p. 161. *254*, p. 210, gives 19.1 mill. m. t. Jasny (*450*, pp. 127 and 143) points out that much of the increased production in 1937 was due to the discouragement of home baking and its transfer to commercial enterprises. **Col. 3:** This considerable overfulfillment is exaggerated because the plan for total production is not known and the results are for total production. It arises from the commercialization of baking rather than from an increase in total bread production. **Col. 7:** *254*, p. 210.

89a. Bread and breadstuffs (ministries and local Soviets)–**Cols. 2, 5, and 11:** *316*, p. 171.

90. Flour (total)–**Col. 2:** *187*, p. 372. **Cols. 5 and 11:** *188*, p. 450.

90a. Flour (centralized resources)–**Col. 2:** *254*, p. 210. Sum of output of Commissariat of Agricultural Procurement and of Commissariat of the Food Industry. Also, see notes to series 89, col. 2. **Cols. 5 and 11:** *15*, p. 49. **Col. 7:** *254*, p. 210. **Col. 10:** *194*, Vol. 3, p. 254. Although not specified, this appears to be centralized resources.

90b. Flour (procurements)–**Col. 1:** *293*, pp. 704–5. This source also gives figures for total output of flour and groats (38.757 in 1932 and 55.35 planned for 1937), but they are not comparable with other figures (see, e.g., *187*, p. 372, and *472*, p. 449). Groats accounted for a very small part of the total. **Cols. 2 and 7:** *254*, p. 210. Output of Commissariat of Agricultural Procurement.

91. Macaroni–**Col. 1:** *293*, p. 522. Output of state and cooperative industry. **Cols. 2, 5, and 11:** *187*, p. 404.

92. Raw sugar–**Col. 1:** *293*, p. 705. **Cols. 2, 5, and 11:** *187*, p. 373. **Col. 7:** *254*, p. 210. Planned output of Commissariat of the Food Industry. **Col. 8:** *285*, No. 5, 1965, p. 71. **Col. 10:** *194*, Vol. 3, p. 254.

93. Starch and syrup–**Cols. 2, 5, and 11:** *187*, p. 372. Sum of starch and syrup. **Col. 10:** *317*, p. 41, as cited in *485*, series 1118.5.

94. Fish catch–**Col. 1:** *293*, p. 705. **Cols. 2, 5, and 11:** *187*, p. 381. **Col. 7:** *254*, p. 209. **Col. 8:** *22*, p. 62. **Col. 10:** *194*, Vol. 3, p. 254.

95. Crude alcohol–**Col. 1:** *293*, p. 705. **Cols. 2, 5, and 11:** *187*, p. 405. **Col. 7:** *254*, p. 210. **Col. 10:** *194*, Vol. 3, p. 254.

96. Vegetable oil–**Col. 1:** *173*, No. 4, 1934, p. 28. **Col. 2:** *254*, p. 210. **Cols. 5 and 11:** *187*, p. 392. **Col. 7:** *254*, p. 210. **Col. 8:** *285*, No. 5, 1965, p. 71. **Col. 10:** *194*, Vol. 3, p. 254.

97. Butter (industrial production)–**Col. 1:** *293*, p. 705. **Cols. 2, 5, and 11:** *187*, p. 386. **Col. 7:** *254*, p. 210. **Col. 10:** *194*, Vol. 3, p. 254.

98. Cheese (industrial production)–**Col. 1:** *293*, p. 705. **Col. 2:** *313*, p. 12, as cited in *472*, p. 450. Apparently excludes collective farm production. **Cols. 5 and 11:** *316*, p. 161. Excludes collective farm production.

99. Meat–**Col. 1:** *293*, p. 705. Output of Commissariat of Food Supply. **Col. 2:** *168*, p. 79. *254*, p. 210, gives 797.2 for output of Commissariat of the Meat and Dairy Industry, but the difference is minor. **Col. 5:** Based on 1950 output (col. 11) and index for 1950 (given as 107 with 1940 = 100 in *160*, p. 162). **Col. 7:** *254*, p. 210. Output of Commissariat of the Meat and Dairy Industry. **Col. 10:** *194*, Vol. 3, p. 254. **Col. 11:** *160*, p. 162.

100. Meat and subproducts of first category (industrial production)–**Col. 1:** Based on 1932 output (given as 596 in *498*, p. 311) and index for planned output of meat in 1937 (given as 275.9 with 1932 = 100 in *293*, p. 705). **Cols. 2, 5, and 11:** *187*, p. 378. Excludes collective farm production. **Col. 7:** Based on 1937 output (col. 2) and index for planned output of meat in 1942 (given as 201 with 1937 = 100 in *254*, p. 210). **Col. 10:** Based on 1940 output (col. 5) and index for planned output of meat in 1950 (derived as 109 with 1940 = 100 from series 99, cols. 5 and 10).

101. Sausages–**Col. 2:** *254*, p. 210. This figure covers 88.5% of total output (given as 368.6 in *187*, p. 380). **Col. 5:** Total output (given as 391.3 in *187*, p. 380) reduced by 11.5% (derived from total 1937 output in note to col. 2 and 1937 output corresponding to plan coverage in col. 2) in order to maintain comparability with plan figure. **Col. 7:** *254*, p. 210. **Col. 11:** *187*, p. 380.

102. Canned food–**Col. 1:** *293*, p. 705. Output of Commissariat of Food Supply. **Cols. 2 and 11:** *187*, p. 398. **Col. 5:** Total output (given as 1,113 in *187*, p. 398) reduced by 11.1% (derived from total 1937 output in col. 2 and 1937

Table A-1 *continued*

output corresponding to plan coverage in col. 7, given as 873 in *254*, p. 210) in order to maintain comparability with plan figure. **Col. 7:** *254*, p. 210. Output of three commissariats: food industry, meat and dairy industry, and fish industry.

103. Confectionery–**Col. 1:** *293*, p. 705. **Col. 2:** *254*, p. 210. **Cols. 5 and 11:** *187*, p. 401. **Col. 7:** *254*, p. 210. **Col. 10:** *317*, p. 40, as cited in *485*, series 1127.5.

104. Margarine–**Col. 1:** *293*, p. 705. **Cols. 2, 5, and 11:** *187*, p. 372. **Col. 10:** *317*, p. 38, as cited in *485*, series 1106.5.

105. Beer–**Col. 1:** *293*, p. 705. **Col. 2:** *187*, p. 372. This figure is accepted rather than the one for the output of the Commissariat of the Food Industry given in *254*, p. 210 (8,800). **Cols. 5 and 11:** *187*, p. 372. **Col. 7:** *254*, p. 210. Output of Commissariat of Food Industry. **Col. 10:** *317*, p. 39, as cited in *485*, series 1122.1.

106. Cigarettes–**Col. 1:** *293*, p. 705. **Cols. 2, 5, and 11:** *187*, p. 372. **Col. 7:** Based on 1937 output (col. 2) and planned increase for 1942 for cigarettes and tobacco under the Commissariat of the Food Industry (given as 38% in *254*, p. 210).

107. Matches–**Col. 1:** *293*, p. 703. **Col. 2:** *72*, p. 84. *187*, p. 267, gives 7,200, probably a rounded figure. **Cols. 5 and 11:** *187*, p. 267. **Col. 7:** *254*, p. 209. Output of Commissariat of the Timber Industry. **Cols. 8 and 10:** *113*, No. 6–7, 1946, pp. 13–15 and 8, as cited in *485*, series 1125.1.

108. Low-grade tobacco (*makhorka*)–**Col. 1:** *293*, p. 705. **Col. 2:** *173*, No. 5, 1939, p. 161. **Cols. 5 and 11:** *187*, p. 372.

109. Salt–**Col. 1:** *293*, p. 522. State and cooperative industry. **Col. 2:** *187*, p. 372. **Col. 5:** *287*, p. 230. *187*, p. 372, gives a rounded figure of 4,400. **Col. 11:** *287*, p. 230.

AGRICULTURE

110. Total value of production (1926/27 prices)–**Col. 1:** *293*, p. 465. **Col. 2:** *72*, p. 92. **Col. 5:** *160*, p. 286. *290*, p. 6, gives a rounded figure of 23,000 (in constant prices). **Col. 7:** *254*, p. 198. **Col. 8:** Based on 1940 output (col. 5) and index for 1942 (given as 38 with 1940 = 100 in *207*, p. 121). **Col. 10:** Based on 1940 output (col. 5) and planned increase for 1950 (given as 27% in *194*, Vol. 3, p. 273). **Col. 11:** Based on 1940 output (col. 5) and index for 1950 (given as 114 with 1940 = 100 in *285*, No. 8, 1953, p. 55).

110a. Total value of production, revised (comparable prices)–**Note:** In 1958 the Central Statistical Administration published a corrected index of agricultural production. This new index has been used here for the actual results and compared with the old planned indexes. **Col. 1:** *293*, p. 465. 1937 plan as percentage of 1932. **Col. 2:** Index for 1937 as percentage of index for 1932 (both given in *142*, p. 350). **Col. 4:** Interpolated goal for 1940 (series 110, col. 4) as percentage of 1937 (series 110, col. 2). **Col. 5:** Index for 1940 as percentage of index for 1937 (both given in *142*, p. 350). **Col. 7:** *254*, p. 198. 1942 plan as percentage of 1937. **Col. 8:** Based on 1940 index (col. 5) and index for 1942 (given as 38 with 1940 = 100 in *285*, No. 5, 1965, p. 72). **Col. 10:** *194*, Vol. 3, p. 273. 1950 plan as percentage of 1940. **Col. 11:** Index for 1950 as percentage of index for 1940 (both given in *142*, p. 350).

111. Vegetable production (1926/27 prices)–**Col. 1:** *293*, p. 465. **Col. 2:** *72*, p. 92. **Col. 5:** Based on total production (series 110) and share of vegetable production in total (calculated as 70% from *449*, p. 775). **Col. 7:** *254*, p. 198.

111a. Vegetable production, revised (comparable prices)–**Note:** See note to series 110a. **Col. 1:** *293*, p. 465. 1937 plan as percentage of 1932. **Col. 2:** Index for 1937 as percentage of index for 1932 (both given in *142*, p. 350). **Col. 4:** Interpolated goal for 1940 (series 111, col. 4) as percentage of 1937 (series 111, col. 2). **Col. 5:** Index for 1940 as percentage of index for 1937 (both given in *142*, p. 350). **Col. 7:** *254*, p. 218. 1942 plan as percentage of 1937.

112. Animal production (1926/27 prices)–**Col. 1:** *293*, p. 465. **Col. 2:** *72*, p. 92. **Col. 5:** Based on total production (series 110) and share of animal production in total (calculated as 30% from *449*, p. 775). **Col. 7:** *254*, p. 198.

112a. Animal production, revised (comparable prices)–**Note:** See note to series 110a. **Col. 1:** *293*, p. 465. 1937 plan as percentage of 1932. **Col. 2:** Index for 1937 as percentage of index for 1932 (both given in *142*, p. 350). **Col. 4:** Interpolated goal for 1940 (series 112, col. 4) as percentage of 1937 (series 112, col. 2). **Col. 5:** Index for 1940 as percentage of index for 1937 (both given in *142*, p. 350). **Col. 7:** *254*, p. 198. 1942 plan as percentage of 1937.

HARVESTS

113. Grain, total (biological yield)–**Col. 1:** *293*, p. 466. Estimates of barn yield were only introduced during the drawing up of the Second Five-Year Plan. An early version of the plan (*163*, p. 66) gives a planned harvest of 130. Later versions reduced that goal considerably (to 110.56 in *186*, p. 462, and finally to the one given here). Since biological yield may be 20–30% higher than barn yield, it is quite possible that this final goal is for barn yield. **Col. 2:** *72*, p. 94. **Cols. 5 and 11:** *469*, p. 4. **Col. 7:** *254*, p. 218. Converted from poods (1 pood = .01638 m. t.). **Col. 10:** *194*, Vol. 3, p. 273.

113a. Grain, total (barn yield)–**Col. 1:** *293*, p. 466. See note to series 113, col. 1. **Col. 2:** *242*, p. 119. **Cols. 5 and 11:** *202*, p. 202. **Col. 7:** Based on 1937 harvest (col. 2) and planned increase for 1942 (given as 11% in *254*, p. 218). **Col. 8:** *99*, p. 150. **Col. 10:** Based on 1940 harvest (col. 5) and planned increase for 1950 (derived as 6.9% from series 113, cols. 5 and 10).

Table A-1 *continued*

114. Wheat (biological yield)–**Col. 1:** *293*, p. 462. **Col. 2:** *72*, p. 94. **Cols. 5 and 11:** *432*, p. 79. **Col. 7:** *254*, p. 218. Converted from poods (1 pood = .01638 m. t.).

114a. Wheat (barn yield)– **Cols. 5 and 11:** *202*, p. 202. Sum of winter wheat and spring wheat.

115. Rye (biological yield)–**Col. 1:** *293*, p. 466. Winter rye. **Col. 2:** *469*, p. 4. **Col. 5:** Estimated from area sown to winter rye (given as 23.1 mill. hectares in *140*, p. 106) and yield (given as 11.3 centners per hectare in *190*, p. 20).

115a. Rye (barn yield)–**Cols. 5 and 11:** *202*, p. 202. Winter rye.

116. Barley (biological yield)–**Col. 1:** *293*, p. 466. **Col. 2:** *72*, p. 94. **Col. 5:** Estimated from area sown to barley (given as 10.5 mill. hectares for spring barley and .8 mill. hectares for winter barley in *179*, Vol. I, p. 7) and yield (given as 13.5 centners per hectare in *190*, p. 20).

116a. Barley (barn yield)–**Cols. 5 and 11:** *202*, p. 202. Sum of winter barley and spring barley.

117. Oats (biological yield)–**Col. 1:** *293*, p. 466. **Col. 2:** *469*, p. 5. **Col. 5:** Estimated from area sown to oats (given as 20.2 mill. hectares in *140*, p. 106) and yield (given as 10.5 centners per hectare in *190*, p. 20).

117a. Oats (barn yield)–**Cols. 5 and 11:** *202*, p. 202.

118. Corn (biological yield)–**Col. 1:** Estimated from total for corn and sorghum (given as 6.065 in *293*, p. 466). Sorghum is assumed to account for a very small fraction, since the 1932 figure for corn and sorghum is 3.49 (*293*, p. 466) and for corn alone 3.426 (*229*, p. 342). **Col. 2:** *469*, p. 5.

118a. Corn (barn yield)–**Cols. 5 and 11:** *202*, p. 202.

HARVESTS OF TECHNICAL CROPS

119. Raw cotton, (biological yield)–**Col. 1:** *293*, p. 466. **Col. 2:** *72*, p. 94. Also, *254*, p. 218. **Col. 5:** *194*, Vol. 3, p. 248. **Col. 7:** *254*, p. 218. **Col. 10:** *194*, Vol. 3, p. 273. **Col. 11:** *180*, 1/26/51, p. 2.

119a. Raw cotton (barn yield)–**Cols. 5 and 8:** *7*, p. 175. **Col. 10:** Based on 1940 harvest (col. 5) and planned increase for 1950 (given as 25% in *291*, p. 16). **Col. 11:** *201*, p. 232.

120. Sugar beets (biological yield)–**Col. 1:** *293*, p. 466. **Col. 2:** *254*, p. 218. **Col. 5:** *5*, p. 12. **Col. 7:** *256*, p. 15. *254*, p. 218, gives 30.0. **Col. 10:** *194*, Vol. 3, p. 273. **Col. 11:** *180*, 11/7/51. See also *469*, p. 6.

120a. Sugar beets (barn yield)–**Cols. 5 and 11:** *202*, p. 202. **Col. 8:** *99*, p. 150. **Col. 10:** Based on 1940 harvest (col. 5) and planned increase for 1950 (derived as 24% from series 120, cols. 5 and 10).

121. Sunflowers (biological yield)–**Col. 1:** *293*, p. 466. **Cols. 2, 5, and 11:** *469*, p. 6. **Col. 7:** *254*, p. 218. **Col. 10:** *194*, Vol. 3, p. 273.

121a. Sunflowers (barn yield)–**Cols. 5 and 11:** *201*, p. 248. **Col. 8:** *99*, p. 150. **Col. 10:** Based on 1940 harvest (col. 5) and planned increase for 1950 (derived as 12.1% from series 121, cols. 5 and 10).

122. Flax fiber (biological yield)–**Col. 1:** *293*, p. 528. **Col. 2:** *72*, p. 94. **Col. 5:** *5*, p. 12. **Col. 7:** *254*, p. 218. **Col. 10:** *194*, Vol. 3, p. 273. **Col. 11:** For a possible estimate, see Table A-5, col. 14.

122a. Flax fiber (barn yield)–**Cols. 5 and 11:** *202*, p. 202. **Col. 8:** *99*, p. 150. **Col. 10:** Based on 1940 harvest (col. 5) and planned increase for 1950 (derived as 41.6% from series 122, cols. 5 and 10).

123. Hemp (biological yield)–**Col. 1:** *293*, p. 225.

123a. Hemp (barn yield)–**Cols. 5 and 11:** *202*, p. 202. Hemp fiber.

124. Potatoes (biological yield)–**Col. 1:** Estimated from area sown to potatoes (given as 6.634 th. hectares in *293*, p. 468) and yield (given as 110 centners per hectare in *293*, p. 467). **Cols. 2 and 7:** *254*, p. 218. **Col. 5:** Estimated from area sown to potatoes (given as 7.7 mill. hectares in *285*, No. 6, 1954, p. 33) and yield (given as 109.4 centners per hectare in *285*, No. 6, 1954, p. 33). **Col. 11:** Based on 1940 harvest (col. 5) and increase in 1950 (given as 21% in *180*, 4/17/51, p. 2).

124a. Potatoes (barn yield)–**Cols. 5 and 11:** *202*, p. 202. **Col. 8:** *99*, p. 150.

ANIMAL PRODUCTION

125. Meat and fat, excl. rabbit and poultry (dead weight)–**Col. 1:** *293*, p. 466. **Cols. 2 and 7:** *254*, p. 218. **Cols. 5 and 11:** *202*, p. 333. Total meat and fat minus rabbit and poultry. **Col. 8:** Based on 1940 production (col. 5) and index for 1942 (given as 39 with 1940 = 100 in *207*, p. 144). **Col. 10:** Based on 1945 production (given as 2,419 th. m. t. in Table A-4, col. 5) and increase planned for 1950 over 1945 for meat and fat including rabbit and poultry (derived as 150% in series 125a, col. 10).

125a. Meat and fat, incl. rabbit and poultry (dead weight)–**Cols. 5 and 11:** *202*, p. 333. **Col. 8:** Based on 1940 production (col. 5) and index for 1942 (given as 39 with 1940 = 100 in *207*, p. 144). **Col. 10:** Based on 1945 production (given as 2,559 th. m. t. in Table A-4, col. 5) and increase planned for 1950 over 1945, derived as 150% from increase in number of domestic animals planned for 1950 and increase in production of meat per head planned for 1955. The former increase was derived as 84.5% over 1945 by weighting the increases planned for 1950 for cattle, sheep and goats, and pigs (given as 39%, 75%, and 200%, respectively, in *194*, Vol. 3, p. 273) by the 1945 output of beef and veal, lamb and goat meat, and pork (given as 1,328, 553, and 569 th. m. t., respectively, in *203*, p. 290). The latter increase was derived as 37% over 1950 from the increase in meat production planned for 1955 (taken as 85% from range given in *194*, Vol. 3, p. 726) and increase in number of domestic animals planned for 1955, derived as 34.7%

Table A-1 *continued*

by weighting the increases planned for 1955 for cattle, sheep and goats, and pigs (taken as 19%, 61%, and 47.5%, respectively, from ranges given in *194*, Vol. 3, p. 726) by the 1950 output of beef and veal, lamb and goat meat, and pork (given as 2,355, 690, and 1,478 th. m. t., respectively, in *203*, p. 290).

126. Milk–**Col. 1:** *293*, p. 466. **Cols. 2 and 7:** *256*, p. 218. **Cols. 5 and 11:** *202*, p. 333. **Col. 8:** Based on 1940 production (col. 5) and index for 1942 (given as 47 with 1940 = 100 in *285*, No. 5, 1965, p. 72). **Col. 10:** Based on 1945 production (given as 26.4 mill. m. t. in Table A-4, col. 5) and increase planned for 1950 over 1945, derived as 70% from increase in head of cattle planned for 1950 (given as 39% in *194*, Vol. 3, p. 273) and increase in milk production per head planned for 1955. This was derived as 24% over 1950 from the increase in milk production planned for 1955 (taken as 47.5% from range given in *194*, Vol. 3, p. 726) and increase in head of cattle planned for 1955 (given as 19% in *194*, Vol. 3, p. 726).

127. Eggs–**Col. 1:** *293*, p. 466. **Col. 2:** *449*, p. 777. Estimate. **Cols. 5 and 11:** *202*, p. 333. **Col. 8:** Based on 1940 production (col. 5) and index for 1942 (given as 37 with 1940 = 100 in *285*, No. 5, 1965, p. 72).

128. Wool–**Col. 1:** *293*, p. 466. **Cols. 2 and 7:** *254*, p. 218. Method of calculation unknown. **Cols. 5 and 11:** *202*, p. 333. Calculated in physical weight. Also given converted into unwashed wool (for col. 5, same figure; for col. 11, 180). **Col. 8:** Based on 1940 output (col. 5) and index for 1942 (given as 78 with 1940 = 100 in *285*, No. 5, 1965, p. 72). Method of calculation unknown.

MARKET PRODUCTION

129. Grain–**Col. 1:** *293*, p. 526. **Col. 2:** *469*, p. 4. **Cols. 5 and 11:** *242*, pp. 122–23.

130. Raw cotton–**Col. 1:** *293*, p. 528. Given for procurements, which cover nearly all of market production of raw cotton. **Col. 2:** *132*, p. 184. **Cols. 5 and 11:** *242*, pp. 122–23.

131. Sugar beets–**Col. 1:** *293*, p. 528. Given for procurements, which cover nearly all of marketed production of sugar beets. See *449*, p. 78. **Col. 2:** *132*, p. 184. **Cols. 5 and 11:** *242*, pp. 122–23.

132. Flax fiber–**Col. 2:** *173*, No. 7, 1939, p. 162.

133. Potatoes–**Col. 1:** *293*, p. 529. **Col. 2:** *173*, No. 7, 1939, p. 162. Given as 713.2 mill. poods for 1937/38 (1 pood = .01638 m. t.). **Cols. 5 and 11:** *242*, pp. 122–23.

134. Meat and fat–**Col. 1:** *293*, p. 529. **Col. 2:** *173*, No. 7, 1939, p. 162. Given as 89.4 mill. poods for 1937/38 for meat (1 pood = .01638 m. t.). *469*, p. 34, gives 1,400 th. m. tons. **Cols. 5 and 11:** *242*, pp. 122–23. Given simply for meat.

135. Milk and dairy products–**Col. 1:** *293*, p. 529. **Col. 2:** *173*, No. 7, 1939, p. 162. Given as 489.3 mill. poods for 1937/38 (1 pood = .01638 m. t.). *469*, p. 34, gives 8.08 mill. m. tons. **Cols. 5 and 11:** *242*, pp. 122–23.

136. Wool–**Col. 2:** *173*, No. 7, 1939, p. 162. Given as 4.9 mill. poods for 1937/38 (1 pood = .01638 m. t.). *469*, p. 41, states that marketed output amounted to 75% of total output. **Cols. 5 and 11:** *242*, pp. 122–23.

PROCUREMENTS

137. Grain–**Col. 1:** *293*, p. 527. **Col. 2:** *72*, p. 98. **Cols. 5 and 11:** *202*, p. 90. **Col. 7:** *254*, p. 232. Centralized state procurements. **Col. 8:** *99*, p. 150.

138. Raw cotton–**Col. 1:** *293*, p. 528. **Cols. 2 and 7:** *254*, p. 232. Centralized state procurements. **Cols. 5 and 11:** *202*, p. 90. **Col. 8:** *99*, p. 150.

139. Sugar beets–**Col. 1:** *293*, p. 528. **Cols. 2 and 7:** *254*, p. 232. Centralized state procurements. **Cols. 5 and 11:** *202*, p. 90. **Col. 8:** *99*, p. 150.

140. Sunflowers–**Cols. 2 and 7:** *254*, p. 232. Centralized state procurements. **Cols. 5 and 11:** *202*, p. 90. **Col. 8:** *99*, p. 150.

141. Flax fiber–**Cols. 2 and 7:** *254*, p. 232. Centralized state procurements. **Cols. 5 and 11:** *202*, p. 90. **Col. 8:** *99*, p. 150.

142. Hemp–**Col. 1:** *293*, pp. 174 and 225. **Cols. 2 and 7:** *254*, p. 232. Centralized state procurements. **Cols. 5 and 11:** *202*, p. 90.

143. Potatoes–**Col. 1:** *293*, p. 529. **Cols. 2 and 7:** *254*, p. 232. Centralized state procurements. **Cols. 5 and 11:** *202*, p. 90. State procurements and purchases. Coverage may not be entirely comparable with 1937 figures.

143a. Vegetables–**Col. 1:** *293*, p. 529. **Cols. 2 and 7:** *254*, p. 232. Centralized state procurements. **Cols. 5 and 11:** *202*, p. 90. **Col. 6:** This considerable overfulfillment of the plan is hard to explain. The explanation is hardly likely to lie in difference in coverage, but might lie in annexation of territory and increased pressure on the peasantry.

144. Meat and fat (live weight)–**Cols. 2 and 7:** *254*, p. 232. Centralized state procurements. **Cols. 5 and 11:** *202*, p. 91. **Col. 8:** *99*, p. 150.

145. Meat and fat (dead weight)–**Col. 1:** *293*, p. 529. **Col. 2:** *469*, p. 34. Centralized procurements and purchases. **Cols. 5 and 11:** *149*, p. 337.

146. Milk and dairy products–**Col. 1:** *293*, p. 129. **Cols. 2 and 7:** *254*, p. 232. Centralized state procurements. **Cols. 5 and 11:** *202*, p. 91. **Col. 8:** *99*, p. 150.

147. Eggs–**Cols. 2 and 7:** *449*, p. 79. Centralized state procurements. **Cols. 5 and 11:** *202*, p. 91. **Col. 8:** *99*, p. 150.

Table A-1 *continued*

148. Wool–**Col. 1:** *186*, p. 528. **Cols. 2 and 7:** *254*, p. 232. Centralized state procurements. **Cols. 5 and 11:** *202*, p. 91. **Col. 8:** *99*, p. 150.

RAILROAD TRANSPORTATION

149. Length of network–**Col. 1:** *293*, p. 432. **Cols. 2, 5, and 11:** *252*, p. 28. **Col. 6:** Overfulfillment of the plan is the result of annexation of new territory. **Col. 7:** Based on 1937 length (col. 2) and planned increase for 1942 (estimated as 11.0 in *255*, p. 30). **Col. 8:** *445*, p. 365. **Col. 10:** Sum of 1945 length (given as 112.9 in *252*, p. 27) and planned increase for 1950 (given as 10.3 in *445*, p. 365). *194*, Vol. 3, p. 280, gives 7.23 for construction of new lines during the Fourth Five-Year Plan, which may not include reconstruction of old lines.

150. Average daily carloadings–**Col. 1:** *293*, p. 433. **Cols. 2 and 7:** *254*, p. 222. **Cols. 5, 8, and 11:** *490*, p. 171. **Col. 10:** *194*, Vol. 3, p. 279.

151. Total freight traffic (ton-km)–**Col. 1:** *293*, p. 476. **Col. 2:** *254*, p. 222. Also, *252*, p. 32. **Cols. 5 and 11:** *252*, p. 32. **Col. 7:** *254*, p. 198. **Col. 8:** *99*, p. 281. **Col. 10:** *194*, Vol. 3, p. 279.

152. Total freight traffic (tons)–**Col. 1:** *293*, p. 476. **Cols. 2 and 7:** *254*, p. 222. For col. 2, also *252*, p. 32. **Cols. 5 and 11:** *252*, p. 32. **Col. 8:** *99*, p. 152. **Col. 10:** Total freight traffic (series 151) divided by average length of haul (series 162).

153. Coal and coke–**Col. 1:** *293*, p. 478. **Cols. 2 and 7:** *254*, p. 222. For col. 2, also *142*, p. 548. **Cols. 5 and 11:** *140*, p. 178.

154. Oil and oil products–**Col. 1:** *293*, p. 478. **Cols. 2 and 7:** *254*, p. 222. For col. 2, also *142*, p. 548. **Cols. 5 and 11:** *140*, p. 178. Also, *142*, p. 549.

155. Ferrous metals–**Col. 1:** *293*, p. 478. **Cols. 2 and 7:** *254*, p. 222. For col. 2, also *142*, p. 548, which includes scrap metal. **Cols. 5 and 11:** *140*, p. 178. Also, *142*, p. 549. Includes scrap metal.

156. Ore–**Col. 1:** *293*, p. 478. **Cols. 2 and 7:** *254*, p. 222. For col. 2, *142*, p. 548, and *252*, p. 36, give 32 for all ores including iron pyrites. **Cols. 5 and 11:** *142*, p. 549. Covers all ores including iron pyrites.

157. Firewood–**Col. 1:** *293*, p. 478. **Cols. 2 and 7:** *254*, p. 222. For col. 2, also *142*, p. 548. **Cols. 5 and 11:** *142*, p. 549.

158. Timber–**Col. 1:** *293*, p. 478. **Cols. 2 and 7:** *254*, p. 222. For col. 2, also *142*, p. 548. **Cols. 5 and 11:** *142*, p. 549.

159. Mineral construction materials–**Cols. 2 and 7:** *254*, p. 222. For col. 2, also *142*, p. 548. **Cols. 5 and 11:** *142*, p. 549.

159a. Principal construction materials (stone, lime, cement, bricks)–**Col. 1:** *293*, p. 478. **Cols. 2 and 5:** *445*, p. 303.

160. Grain and flour–**Col. 1:** *293*, p. 478. **Cols. 2 and 7:** *254*, p. 222. For col. 2, also *142*, p. 549. **Cols. 5 and 11:** *142*, p. 549.

161. Salt–**Col. 2:** *445*, p. 179.

162. Total freight traffic, average length of haul–**Cols. 1 and 7:** Total ton-kilometers (series 151) divided by total tons (series 152). **Cols. 2, 5, and 11:** *252*, p. 34. **Col. 8:** 1940 average length of haul (col. 5) plus increase in 1942 over 1940 (given as 86 km in *99*, p. 152). **Col. 10:** *194*, Vol. 3, p. 280.

163. Coal and coke, average length of haul–**Col. 1:** Estimated to be slightly less than average length of haul for coal (given as 740 in *186*, p. 474), since in 1934 and 1935 average length of haul for coke was lower than for coal (*229*, p. 420). **Cols. 2, 5, and 11:** *252*, p. 35. **Col. 8:** *18*, p. 96.

163a. Oil and oil products, average length of haul–**Col. 1:** *186*, p. 474. **Cols. 2, 5, and 11:** *252*, p. 35.

164. Ferrous metals, average length of haul–**Col. 1:** *186*, p. 474. **Cols. 2, 5, and 11:** *252*, p. 36.

164a. Firewood, average length of haul–**Col. 1:** *186*, p. 474. **Cols. 2, 5, and 11:** *252*, p. 38.

164b. Timber, average length of haul–**Col. 1:** *186*, p. 474. **Cols. 2, 5, and 11:** *252*, p. 38. **Col. 8:** *445*, p. 173.

165. Grain and flour, average length of haul–**Col. 1:** *186*, p. 474. **Cols. 2, 5, and 11:** *252*, p. 37.

165a. Ore, average length of haul–**Col. 1:** *186*, p. 474. **Cols. 2, 5, and 11:** *252*, p. 36.

166. Total passenger traffic–**Col. 1:** *293*, p. 476. **Cols. 2 and 7:** *254*, pp. 198 and 222. **Cols. 2, 5, and 11:** *252*, p. 32. **Col. 8:** Based on traffic in 1945 (given as 65.9 bill. pass.-km in Table A-4, col. 5) and index for 1945 (given as 174 with 1942 = 100 in *99*, p. 282). **Col. 10:** *443*, p. 215, and *444*, p. 16, as cited in *477*, p. 343.

INLAND WATERWAY TRANSPORTATION

166a. Length of network–**Col. 1:** *293*, p. 481. **Cols. 2, 5, and 11:** *252*, p. 115.

168. Freight traffic under ministries and economic organizations (ton-km)–**Col. 1:** *293*, p. 476. **Col. 2:** *254*, p. 223. **Cols. 5 and 11:** *252*, p. 116. **Col. 7:** *254*, p. 198. **Col. 8:** Based on 1940 traffic (col. 5) and index for 1942 (given as 60 with 1940 = 100 in *285*, No. 5, 1965, p. 73). **Col. 10:** *168*, p. 42. *194*, Vol. 3, p. 281, only gives the percentage increase over 1940 (38%).

170. Freight traffic under ministries and economic organizations (tons)–**Col. 1:** *293*, p. 480. **Cols. 2 and 7:** *254*, p. 223. **Cols. 5 and 11:** *252*, p. 116. **Col. 8:** *99*, p. 283.

171. Coal and coke–**Col. 1:** *293*, p. 480. **Cols. 2, 5, and 11:** *252*, p. 120. Coal only.

Table A-1   *continued*

172. Oil and oil products–**Col. 1:** *293*, p. 480. **Cols. 2, 5, and 11:** *252*, p. 120. **Col. 7:** *254*, p. 223.

173. Timber and firewood–**Cols. 2, 5, and 11:** *252*, p. 120.

174. Mineral construction materials–**Col. 1:** *293*, p. 480. **Cols. 2, 5, and 11:** *252*, p. 120.

175. Grain and flour–**Col. 1:** *293*, p. 480. **Cols. 2, 5, and 11:** *252*, p. 120.

176. Salt–**Col. 1:** *293*, p. 480. **Cols. 2 and 5:** *252*, p. 120. **Col. 11:** *287*, p. 238. *252*, p. 120, gives a rounded figure of 1.7 mill. m. tons.

177. Average length of haul under ministries and economic organizations–**Cols. 1 and 7-8:** Ton-kilometers (series 168) divided by tons (series 170). **Cols. 2, 5, and 11:** *252*, p. 116.

178. Passenger traffic (pass.-km)–**Col. 1:** *293*, p. 476. **Cols. 2, 5, and 11:** *252*, p. 116. For col. 2, *254*, p. 198, gives 3.1. **Col. 7:** *254*, p. 198.

178a. Passenger traffic (pass.)–**Col. 1:** *293*, p. 460. **Cols. 2, 5, and 11:** *252*, p. 116. **Col. 7:** *254*, p. 223. **Col. 8:** *99*, p. 283.

MARITIME TRANSPORTATION (Soviet ships)

179. Freight traffic (ton-km)–**Col. 1:** *293*, p. 476. **Cols. 2, 5, and 11:** *252*, p. 7. **Col. 7:** *254*, p. 198. **Col. 8:** Based on 1940 traffic (col. 5) and index for 1942 (given as 66 with 1940 = 100 in *285*, No. 5, 1965, p. 73). **Col. 10:** *168*, p. 42. *194*, Vol. 3, p. 281, only gives the increase since 1940 (2.2-fold).

180. Freight traffic (tons)–**Col. 1:** *293*, p. 713. **Cols. 2 and 7:** *254*, p. 223. **Cols. 5 and 11:** *252*, p. 95.

181. Average length of haul–**Cols. 1, 2, and 7:** Ton-kilometers (series 189) divided by tons (series 180). **Col. 5:** *490*, p. 182, series C–46. **Col. 11:** *285*, No. 7, 1956, p. 21.

182. Passenger traffic (pass.-km)–**Col. 1:** *293*, p. 713. **Cols. 2, 5, and 11:** *252*, p. 95. Converted from pass.-miles at 1 pass.-km = 0.54 pass.-miles. **Col. 7:** *254*, p. 198.

182a. Passenger traffic (passengers)–**Col. 1:** *293*, p. 713. **Cols. 2, 5, and 11:** *252*, p. 95. Excludes traffic in steamships in Central Asia. **Col. 7:** *254*, p. 223.

MOTOR TRANSPORTATION

183. Freight traffic–**Col. 1:** *293*, p. 476. **Cols. 2 and 7:** *254*, p. 198. **Cols. 5 and 11:** *252*, p. 159. **Col. 8:** Based on 1940 traffic (col. 5) and index for 1942 (given as 31 with 1940 = 100 in *285*, No. 5, 1965, p. 73). **Col. 10:** Based on 1940 traffic (col. 5) and planned increase for 1950 (given as 2.8-fold in *168*, pp. 41–42).

AIR TRANSPORTATION

184. Freight traffic, incl. mail–**Col. 1:** *293*, p. 273. **Col. 2:** *72*, p. 102. **Col. 5:** Based on 1943 traffic (given as 25.8 mill. m. ton-km in *99*, p. 284) and index for 1943 (given as 78 with 1940 = 100 in *285*, No. 5, 1965, p. 73). **Col. 8:** Based on 1940 traffic (col. 5) and index for 1942 (given as 61 with 1940 = 100 in *285*, No. 5, 1965, p. 73). **Col. 11:** Based on 1940 traffic (col. 5) and index for 1950 (given as 589 in *140*, p. 184).

185. Passenger traffic–**Col. 1:** *293*, p. 273. **Col. 2:** *72*, p. 102. **Cols. 5 and 11:** *253*, p. 34.

EMPLOYMENT (annual averages)

186. Workers and employees, national economy, excl. collective farms–**Col. 1:** *293*, p. 505. **Col. 2:** *72*, p. 104. **Cols. 5 and 11:** *140*, p. 189. For col. 5, also *99*, p. 220. **Col. 7:** Based on 1937 employment (col. 2) and planned increase for 1942 (given as 21% in *256*, p. 27). *254*, p. 228, gives 32.0 and an increase of 18.6%. **Col. 8:** *99*, p. 220. **Col. 10:** *194*, Vol. 3, p. 284.

187. Industry–**Col. 1:** *293*, p. 504. **Col. 2:** *72*, p. 104. **Cols. 5 and 11:** *140*, p. 190. **Col. 7:** *254*, p. 228. **Col. 8:** *99*, p. 115. **Col. 10:** Based on employment in 1940 (col. 5) and planned increase for 1950 (derived as 8.8% from planned increases in industrial production of 48% and in labor productivity of 36% given in *194*, Vol. 3, pp. 252 and 272).

188. Construction–**Col. 1:** *293*, p. 505. **Col. 2:** *72*, p. 104. **Col. 5:** Employment with larger coverage (given as 2,510 in *28*, p. 219) reduced to same coverage as plan figures (by 13.8% derived from 1937 employment in col. 2 and that of 2,348 given in *28*, p. 219). **Col. 7:** *254*, p. 228. **Col. 11:** *260*, p. 121. The figures given by this source for the earlier years are slightly higher than the ones used here.

188a. Construction and assembly work–**Cols. 2, 5, and 11:** *140*, p. 190. **Col. 8:** Based on employment in 1945 (given as 1,515 in Table A-4, col. 5) and index for 1945 (given as 176 with 1942 = 100 in *99*, p. 218).

189. State-owned agriculture and logging–**Col. 1:** *293*, p. 505. Sum of agriculture and logging. **Col. 2:** In the Second Five-Year Plan (*293*, p. 505) logging is part of industry, whereas in the Third Five-Year Plan (*254*, p. 229) it is a separate sector of the economy. The goals of the Second Five-Year Plan are not comparable with the results in 1937 given in *254*, p. 229, which are therefore not entered here. **Col. 4:** Calculated from 1937 figures given in *254*, p. 229. See source note to col. 5. **Col. 5:** Employment with larger coverage (given as 2,703 for agriculture and 280 for logging in *260*, p. 24) reduced to same coverage as plan figures (by 4.4% derived from 1937 employment given as 2,482.6 for agriculture and 247.9 for logging in *254*, p. 229, and given as 2,609 and 248, respectively, in *260*, p. 24). **Col. 7:** *254*, p. 229. Sum of agriculture and logging. **Col. 11:** *260*, pp. 24–25. Sum of agriculture and logging.

190. State-owned agriculture (state farms, MTS, and other state establishments)–**Col. 1:** *293*, p. 505. **Col. 2:** *72*,

Table A-1 *continued*

p. 104. **Col. 5:** Employment with larger coverage (given as 2,703 in *260*, p. 24) reduced to same coverage as plan figures (by 4.8% derived from 1937 employment in col. 2 and that of 2,609 given in *260*, p. 24). **Col. 7:** *254*, p. 229. **Col. 11:** *260*, pp. 24–25.

191. Railroad transport–**Col. 1:** *293*, p. 505. **Col. 2:** *72*, p. 104. **Cols. 5 and 11:** *140*, p. 190. **Col. 7:** *254*, p. 229. **Col. 8:** Based on total employment (series 186) and share of railroad transport workers in total (given as 5.8% in *99*, p. 115).

192. Maritime and inland waterway transport–**Col. 1:** *293*, p. 505. **Col. 2:** *77*, p. 104. **Cols. 5 and 11:** *140*, p. 190. **Col. 7:** *254*, p. 229.

193. Other transport (motor, etc.)–**Col. 1:** *293*, p. 505. **Col. 2:** *72*, p. 104. **Col. 5:** Employment with smaller coverage (given as 1,552 in *260*, p. 24) increased to same coverage as plan figures (by 1.87%, derived from 1937 employment in col. 2 and that of 1,072 given in *260*, p. 24). **Col. 7:** *254*, p. 229. **Col. 11:** *260*, p. 25.

194. Communications–**Col. 1:** *293*, p. 505. **Col. 2:** *72*, p. 104. **Cols. 5 and 11:** *140*, p. 190. **Col. 7:** *254*, p. 229. **Col. 8:** Based on employment in 1945 (given as 426 in Table A-4, col. 5) and index for 1945 (given as 156 with 1940 = 100 in *99*, p. 218).

195. Trade, procurements, and supply–**Col. 1:** *293*, p. 505. **Col. 2:** *72*, p. 104. **Col. 5:** Employment with larger coverage (given as 2,539 in *140*, p. 190) reduced to same coverage as plan figures (by 2.9%, derived from 1937 employment in col. 2 and that of 2,054 given in *140*, p. 190). **Col. 7:** *254*, p. 229. **Col. 11:** *140*, p. 190.

196. Public eating places–**Col. 1:** *293*, p. 505. **Col. 2:** *72*, p. 104. Later sources (*140*, p. 190, and *141*, pp. 204–5) give 471, but the earlier figure seems to be closer in coverage to the Second Five-Year Plan. **Col. 5:** Employment with larger coverage (given as 788 in *260*, p. 130) reduced to same coverage as plan figures (by 16.0%, derived from 1937 employment in col. 2 and that of 471 given in *260*, p. 130). **Col. 7:** *254*, p. 229. **Col. 11:** *140*, p. 190.

197. Credit institutions–**Col. 1:** *293*, p. 505. **Col. 2:** *72*, p. 104. **Cols. 5 and 11:** *140*, p. 190. **Col. 7:** *254*, p. 229. **Col. 8:** Based on total employment (series 186) and share of credit institution workers in total (given as 0.7% in *99*, p. 115).

198. Administration–**Col. 1:** *293*, p. 505. **Col. 2:** *72*, p. 104. **Col. 5:** Employment with smaller coverage (given as 1,825 in *140*, p. 190) increased to same coverage as plan figures (by 17.2%, derived from 1937 employment in col. 2 and that of 1,488 given in *140*, p. 190). **Col. 7:** *254*, p. 229. **Col. 8:** Based on total employment (series 186) and share of administration workers in total (given as 5.0% in *99*, p. 115). **Col. 11:** *140*, p. 190.

199. Education–**Col. 1:** *293*, p. 505. **Col. 2:** *72*, p. 104. **Cols. 5 and 11:** *140*, p. 190. **Col. 7:** *254*, p. 229. **Col. 8:** Based on total employment (series 186) and share of education workers in total (given as 8.7% in *99*, p. 115).

200. Public health–**Col. 1:** *293*, p. 505. **Col. 2:** *72*, p. 104. **Cols. 5 and 11:** *140*, p. 190. **Col. 7:** *254*, p. 229. **Col. 8:** Based on total employment (series 186) and share of public health workers in total (given as 5.3% in *99*, p. 115).

WAGE FUND, WORKERS AND EMPLOYEES

201. National economy–**Col. 1:** *293*, p. 505. **Col. 2:** *72*, p. 106. **Col. 5:** *288*, p. 10. **Col. 7:** Based on 1937 wage fund (col. 2) and planned increase for 1942 (given as 67% in *256*, p. 27). *254*, p. 228, gives 133.24 and an increase of 62%. **Col. 10:** Based on total planned employment (series 186) and planned average annual money wage (series 203). *194*, Vol. 3, p. 284, gives 252.3, which is the *total* wage fund. The figure for the *partial* wage fund used here is comparable with the actual figure in col. 11. See *410*, p. 125. **Col. 11:** Based on total employment (series 186) and average annual money wage (series 203).

202. Industry–**Col. 1:** *293*, p. 505. **Col. 2:** *72*, p. 106. **Col. 5:** Based on employment in industry (series 187) and average annual money wage in industry (series 205). **Col. 7:** *254*, p. 228.

AVERAGE ANNUAL WAGE, WORKERS AND EMPLOYEES

203. Money wage, national economy, excl. collective farms and cooperatives–**Col. 1:** *293*, p. 505. **Col. 2:** *72*, p. 105. **Cols. 5 and 11:** *141*, p. 555. Converted into old rubles. **Col. 7:** Based on 1937 wage (col. 5) and planned increase for 1942 (given as 37% in *256*, p. 27). *254*, p. 228, gives 4,100 and an increase of 35%. **Col. 10:** *194*, Vol. 3, p. 284.

204. Real wage, national economy, excl. collective farms and cooperatives, calculated from official Soviet index–**Col. 1:** Based on increase in money wage planned for 1937 over 1932 (given as 23% in *293*, p. 505) and decrease in retail prices in state and cooperative trade planned for 1937 over 1933 (given as 35% in *293*, p. 531) on the assumption that retail prices did not change between 1932 and 1933. **Col. 2:** *498*, p. 392, Table A-17, col. 6. Converted from 1927/28 base to 1932 base. **Col. 5:** Based on increase in money wage (derived as 130.7 for 1940, with 1937 = 100, from series 203, cols. 5 and 2) and increase in retail prices (derived as 119.0 for 1940, with 1937 = 100, from *498*, p. 391, Table A-17, col. 2). **Col. 7:** Increase in money wage between 1942 and 1937 (derived as 37% from series 203, cols. 7 and 2) assumed to apply also to real wage since *254*, p. 27, states that the consumption of workers was to increase by more than half during the Third Five-Year Plan. **Col. 10:** Table 79, line 19, col. 5. **Col. 11:** Table 79, line 19, col. 6 divided by col. 2.

204a. Real wage, national economy, excl. collective farm and cooperatives, calculated from Zaleski index–**Col. 1:** See note to series 204, col. 1. **Col. 2:** *498*, p. 392, Table A-17, col. 7. Converted from 1927/28 base to 1932 base. **Col.**

Table A-1   *continued*

3: This fulfillment is higher than the one in series 204 because my index shows a greater price increase than the official Soviet index, which is based on 1940 prices and uses the Paasche formula. **Col. 5:** Based on increase in money wage (derived as 130.7 for 1940, with 1937 = 100, from series 203, cols. 5 and 2) and increase in retail prices (derived as 157.9 for 1940, with 1937 = 100, from *498*, p. 391, Table A-17, col. 3). **Col. 7:** See note to series 204, col. 7.

205. Money wage, industry–**Col. 1:** *293*, p. 504. **Col. 2:** *72*, p. 105. **Cols. 5 and 11:** *260*, p. 138. Converted into old rubles. **Col. 7:** *254*, p. 228.

AVERAGE ANNUAL MONEY WAGE, WORKERS

206. Industry–**Cols. 2 and 7:** *254*, p. 228. **Cols. 5 and 11:** *260*, p. 138. Converted into old rubles.

207. Iron ore–**Col. 2:** *173*, No. 3, 1939, p. 163.

208. Coal–**Col. 1:** *293*, p. 509. **Col. 2:** *173*, No. 3, 1939, p. 163. **Col. 5:** Based on wage planned for 1941 for workers in the Commissariat of the Coal Industry (given as 5,475 in *60*, p. 514) and planned increase between 1940 and 1941 (given as 4.7% in *60*, p. 513). **Col. 11:** *260*, p. 140. Converted into old rubles.

209. Ferrous metals–**Col. 1:** *293*, p. 509. **Col. 2:** *173*, No. 3, 1939, p. 163. **Col. 5:** Based on wage planned for 1941 for workers in Commissariat of the Ferrous Metal Industry (given as 5,120 in *60*, p. 516) and planned increase between 1940 and 1941 (given as 8.5% in *60*, p. 513). **Col. 11:** *260*, p. 140. Converted into old rubles.

209a. Machine-building–**Col. 1:** *293*, p. 509. **Col. 2:** *173*, No. 3, 1939, p. 163. **Col. 5:** Based on wage planned for 1941 for workers in Commissariats of Heavy Machine-Building, Medium Machine-Building, and General Machine-Building (average derived as 5,055 by weighting wage given for each commissariat in *60*, pp. 519–20, by percentage share of workers of that commissariat in total number of workers of all three commissariats, derived from *60*, pp. 519–20) and planned increase between 1940 and 1941 (average derived as 5.5% by weighting each increase given in *60*, p. 513, by same share as above). **Col. 11:** *260*, p. 141. Machine-building and metalworking. Converted into old rubles.

210. Paper–**Col. 5:** Based on wage planned for 1941 for workers in the Commissariat of the Pulp and Paper Industry (given as 3,577 in *60*, p. 522) and planned increase between 1940 and 1941 for workers in Commissariat of the Paper Industry (given as 7.0% in *60*, p. 513). **Col. 11:** *260*, p. 142. Converted into old rubles.

211. Chemicals–**Col. 2:** *173*, No. 3, 1939, p. 163. **Col. 5:** Based on wage planned for 1941 for workers in Commissariat of the Chemical Industry (given as 4,761 in *60*, p. 517) and planned increase between 1940 and 1941 (given as 5.6% in *60*, p. 513). **Col. 11:** *260*, p. 141. Converted into old rubles.

212. Textiles–**Col. 1:** Estimated at slightly lower level than wage in cotton industry (given as 1,400 in *254*, p. 509). See estimation in col. 2. **Col. 2:** Derived by weighting wages of workers in cotton, wool, and linen industries (given as 2,396, 2,338, and 2,066, respectively, in *173*, No. 3, 1939, p. 163) by percentage shares of workers in these industries in total number of workers in all three industries (derived from *229*, p. 520). **Col. 5:** Based on wage planned for 1941 for workers in Commissariat of the Textile Industry (given as 3,571 in *60*, p. 522) and planned increase between 1940 and 1941 (given as 4.0% in *60*, p. 513). **Col. 11:** *260*, p. 143. Converted into old rubles.

212a. Cotton–**Col. 1:** *293*, p. 509. **Col. 2:** *173*, No. 3, 1939, p. 163. **Col. 11:** *260*, p. 143. Converted into old rubles.

212b. Wool–**Col. 1:** *293*, p. 509. **Col. 2:** *173*, No. 3, 1939, p. 163.

213. Leather–**Col. 1:** *293*, p. 509. Leather and shoe industry. **Col. 11:** *400*, p. 67. Fur, leather, and footwear. Converted into old rubles.

214. Food–**Col. 2:** *173*, No. 3, 1939, p. 163. **Col. 5:** Based on wage planned for 1941 for workers in Commissariats of the Food Industry, the Meat and Dairy Industry, and Food Supply (average derived as 3,484 by weighting wage given for each commissariat in *60*, pp. 524–27, by percentage share of workers of that commissariat in total number of workers in all three commissariats, derived from *60*, pp. 524–27) and planned increase between 1940 and 1941 (average derived as 2.6% by weighting each increase given in *60*, p. 513, by same share as above). **Col. 11:** *260*, p. 144. Converted into old rubles.

AVERAGE ANNUAL MONEY WAGE, WORKERS AND EMPLOYEES

215. Construction–**Col. 1:** *293*, p. 505. **Col. 2:** *72*, p. 105. **Cols. 5 and 11:** *260*, p. 138. Converted into old rubles. **Col. 7:** *254*, p. 229.

216. Railroad transport–**Col. 1:** *293*, p. 505. **Col. 2:** *72*, p. 105. **Cols. 5 and 11:** *260*, p. 138. Converted into old rubles. **Col. 7:** *254*, p. 229.

217. Maritime and inland waterway transport–**Col. 1:** *293*, p. 505. **Col. 2:** *72*, p. 105. **Cols. 5 and 11:** *260*, p. 138. Converted into old rubles. **Col. 7:** *254*, p. 229.

218. Communications–**Col. 1:** *293*, p. 505. **Col. 2:** *72*, p. 105. **Cols. 5 and 11:** *260*, p. 138. Converted into old rubles. **Col. 7:** *254*, p. 229.

219. Trade–**Col. 1:** *293*, p. 505. **Col. 2:** *72*, p. 105. **Col. 7:** *254*, p. 229.

220. Public eating places–**Col. 1:** *293*, p. 505. **Col. 2:** *72*, p. 105. **Col. 7:** *254*, p. 229.

221. Credit institutions–**Col. 1:** *293*, p. 505. **Col. 2:** *72*, p. 105. **Cols. 5 and 11:** *260*, p. 138. Converted into old rubles. **Col. 7:** *254*, p. 229.

Table A-1 *continued*

222. Administration–**Col. 1:** *293*, p. 505. **Col. 2:** *72*, p. 105. **Cols. 5 and 11:** *260*, p. 138. Includes cooperative organizations, which may or may not be included in *254*, p. 229. Converted into old rubles. **Col..7:** *254*, p. 229.

223. Education–**Col. 1:** *293*, p. 505. **Col. 2:** *72*, p. 105. **Cols. 5 and 11:** *260*, p. 138. Converted into old rubles. For col. 5, also *242*, p. 227. **Col. 7:** *254*, p. 229.

224. Public health–**Col. 1:** *293*, p. 505. **Col. 2:** *72*, p. 105. **Cols. 5 and 11:** *260*, p. 138. Converted into old rubles. **Col. 7:** *254*, p. 229.

225. State-owned agriculture–**Col. 1:** *293*, p. 505. **Col. 2:** *72*, p. 105. **Col. 5:** *260*, p. 138. Covers state farms and farms belonging to auxiliary enterprises. Converted into old rubles. **Col. 7:** *254*, p. 229. **Col. 11:** *260*, p. 138. Converted into old rubles. Covers state farms and auxiliary agricultural enterprises.

226. Logging–**Col. 1:** *293*, p. 505. **Col. 2:** *72*, p. 105. **Col. 7:** *254*, p. 229. Definition not comparable with that in *293*, but difference may be minor. See note to series 189, col. 2.

HOUSING

227. Housing fund, urban, total–**Col. 1:** *293*, p. 533. **Col. 2:** Housing fund at end of 1936 (given as 204.38 in *173*, No. 3, 1937, p. 244) plus housing construction during 1937 (series 228, col. 2) minus wear during 1937 (estimated at 1). **Cols. 5 and 11:** *410*, p. 10.

228. Housing construction, urban, total–**Col. 1:** *293*, p. 533. **Col. 2:** *173*, No. 6, 1938, p. 166. Stated to be half of the plan for 1938 of 7.8. **Col. 6:** Housing construction made available for occupancy between 1/1/38 and 6/30/41 (derived as 26.75 from total construction of 42 given in *141*, p. 176, and ratio of 1.57 of construction available for occupancy to total construction estimated from *254* and *293*) divided by housing construction planned for the same period (derived as 31.5 from construction planned for whole five-year period of 35 given in *255*, p. 42). **Col. 7:** See note to col. 6. **Col. 8:** *99*, p. 214. Including rebuilt housing. **Col. 11:** *141*, p. 176.

229. Floorspace per inhabitant, urban–**Col. 1:** *293*, p. 533. **Col. 2:** Total urban housing fund (series 227) divided by urban population (series 231). **Col. 5:** *285*, No. 1, 1957, p. 14. *427*, p. 331, gives 4.09. **Col. 11:** *427*, p. 331. Calculated according to prewar practice of including only actual living space (excluding corridors). Later Soviet sources (such as *285*, No. 1, 1957, and *173*, No. 4, 1958, p. 25) give total living space (including corridors). According to that method of estimation, *242*, p. 248, gives 7.

POPULATION

230. Total (end of year)–**Col. 1:** *293*, p. 503. **Col. 2:** Based on population on 1/17/39 (given as 170.6 in *140*, p. 17), and rate of increase in 1938 (derived as 20.5 per thousand inhabitants from birthrate of 38.3 per thousand and mortality rate of 17.8 per thousand given by Eason in *481*, pp. 104 and 105). **Col. 5:** Population on 1/1/40 (given as 194.1 in *260*, p. 19) plus increase in 1940 (derived as 2.6 from net increase of 13.4 per thousand given in *140*, p. 243). Also, population on 7/1/40 (given as 193 in *427*, p. 615) plus half the above increase in 1940 would yield 194.3. **Col. 11:** *260*, p. 19. 1/1/51.

231. Urban (end of year)–**Col. 1:** *293*, p. 503. **Col. 2:** Based on population on 1/17/39 (given as 56.1 in *140*, p. 17) and rate of increase in 1938 (derived as 20.5 per thousand inhabitants as in series 230, col. 2). **Col. 5:** Population on 1/1/40 (given as 63.1 in *260*, p. 19) plus increase in 1940 (derived as .8 as in series 230, col. 5). **Col. 11:** *260*, p. 19. 1/1/51.

232. Rural (end of year)–**Col. 1:** *293*, p. 503. **Col. 2:** Based on population on 1/17/39 (given as 114.5 in *140*, p. 17) and rate of increase in 1938 (derived as 20.5 per thousand inhabitants as in series 230, col. 2). **Col. 5:** Population on 1/1/40 (given as 131.0 in *260*, p. 19) plus increase in 1940 (derived as 1.8 as in series 230, col. 5). **Col. 11:** *260*, p. 19.

RETAIL TRADE

233. State and cooperative in current prices–**Col. 1:** Planned trade excluding tobacco and alcohol (given as 80,000 in *293*, p. 521) plus tobacco and alcohol (estimated at 10,000 from 1932 figure of 8.5 derived from total trade in 1932 in *498*, p. 320, series 233, and trade excluding tobacco and alcohol in 1932 in *293*, p. 521). **Col. 2:** *72*, p. 107. **Cols. 5, 8, and 11:** *232*, pp. 31 and 20. **Col. 7:** *254*, p. 199. In 1937 retail prices. **Col. 10:** *194*, Vol. 3, p. 288. This figure takes into account the planned decrease in prices during the Fourth Five-Year Plan. In constant prices, this figure is 28% higher than the 1940 figure.

234a. State and cooperative in constant prices calculated from official Soviet price index–**Col. 1:** 1937 plan in current (1937) prices (series 233) deflated by planned decrease in retail prices between 1933 and 1937 (given as 35.0% in *293*, p. 531). It was assumed that retail prices did not change between 1932 and 1933. **Col. 2:** Based on 1937 total in current prices (series 233) and the official Soviet price index for 1937 (209.7 with 1932 = 100, converted from 1927/28 base given in *498*, p. 391, Table A-17, col. 2). **Col. 5:** Based on total in 1937 prices (series 233) and the official Soviet price index for 1940 (119.0 with 1937 = 100, converted from 1927/28 base given in *498*, p. 391, Table A-17, col. 2). **Col. 7:** *254*, p. 199. In 1937 retail prices. **Col. 8:** Based on 1940 total (col. 5) and index for 1942 in constant prices (given as 34 with 1940 = 100 in Table 69 of this book). **Col. 10:** Based on 1940 total in current prices (series 233, col. 5) and planned increase in 1950 in constant prices (given as 28% in *194*, Vol. 3, p. 288). **Col. 11:** Based on 1940 total in current prices (series 233, col. 5) and increase in 1950 in constant prices (given as 10% in *140*, p. 203).

Table A-1 *continued*

234b. State and cooperative in constant prices calculated from Zaleski price index–**Col. 1:** Same as series 234a, col. 1. **Col. 2:** Based on total in current prices (series 233) and the Zaleski price index for 1937 (165.6 with 1932 = 100, converted from 1927/28 base given in *498*, p. 391, Table A-17, col. 3). **Col. 5:** Based on total in 1937 prices (series 233) and the Zaleski price index for 1940 (157.9 with 1937 = 100, converted from 1927/28 base given in *498*, p. 391, Table A-17, col. 3). **Col. 7:** *254*, p. 199. In 1937 retail prices. **Col. 8:** Based on 1940 total (col. 5) and index for 1942 in constant prices (given as 34 with 1940 = 100 in Table 70 of this book).

Table A-2   Fulfillment of Annual Plans during Second Five-Year Plan, 1933–1937

Series	Units	1933			1934		
		Planned (1)	Actual (2)	(2) as Per Cent of (1) (3)	Planned (4)	Actual (5)	(5) as Per Cent of (4) (6)
1. National income (1926/27 prices)	bill. rub.	51.0	48.5	95.1	60.2	55.8	92.7
Industry							
2. Gross production, total (1926/27 prices)	bill. rub.	50.4	46.0	91.3	55.8	54.6	97.8
3. Producer goods (1926/27 prices)	bill. rub.	28.0	25.3	90.4	30.9	30.3	98.1
4. Consumer goods (1926/27 prices)	bill. rub.	22.3	20.7	92.8	24.9	24.3	97.6
5. Coal	th. m. t.	84,200	76,333	90.7	96,750	94,160	97.3
6. Peat	th. m. t.	17,700	13,846	78.2	18,000	18,254	101.4
7. Coke	th. m. t.	12,616	10,225	81.0	13,600	14,222	104.6
8. Oil shale	th. m. t.	560.0	174.3	31.1	450	206.4	45.9
9. Crude petroleum	th. m. t.	24,400	21,489	88.1	29,260	24,218	82.8
10. Natural gas	mill. m³		1,066		1,540	1,533	99.5
10a. Natural gas	th. m. t.		968.9		1,400	1,394	99.6
11. Electric power	mill. kwh	16,300	16,357	100.3	19,000	21,011	110.6
12. Hydroelectric power	mill. kwh		1,250		2,268	2,376	104.8
13. Iron ore	th. m. t.	19,140	14,455	75.5	21,800	21,509	98.7
14. Pig iron	th. m. t.	9,000	7,110	79.0	10,000	10,428	104.3
15. Steel ingots and castings	th. m. t.	8,950	6,889	77.0	9,800	9,693	98.9
16. Rolled steel	th. m. t.	6,255	5,065	81.0	6,600	7,034	106.6
17. Steel pipes	th. m. t.	451	348	77.2	526	470	89.4
18. Aluminum	th. m. t.		4.4		13	14.39	110.7
19. Manganese ore	th. m. t.	1,400	1,021	72.9	1,700	1,821	107.1
20. Nickel	th. m. t.				.78	.84	106.6
21. Zinc	th. m. t.	23.4	16.62	71.0	30	27.15	90.5
22. Refined copper	th. m. t.	66.0	44.3	67.1	64.0	53.3	83.3
23. Lead	th. m. t.	28.5	13.66	48.0	33.0	27.20	82.4
24. Mineral fertilizer	th. m. t.		1,034			1,398	
25. Phosphoric fertilizer (14% P_2O_5)	th. m. t.	750	688.8	91.8	900	890	98.9
26. Phosphoric fertilizer (18.7% P_2O_5)	th. m. t.	561	545.0	97.1	67.4	691.9	102.7
27. Ground natural phosphate	th. m. t.		332.0		535	284.3	53.1

1935			1936			1937			
Planned (7)	Actual (8)	(8) as Per Cent of (7) (9)	Planned (10)	Actual (11)	(11) as Per Cent of (10) (12)	Planned (13)	Actual (14)	(14) as Per Cent of (13) (15)	Series No.
64.5	66.9	103.7	83.1	86.0	103.5	105.5	96.3	91.3	1
62.5	66.8	106.9	81.1	85.8	105.8	103.0	95.5	92.7	2
35.4	38.8	109.6	45.6	50.2	110.1	60.0	55.2	92.0	3
27.1	28.0	103.3	35.5	35.6	100.3	43.0	40.3	93.7	4
112,200	109,634	97.7	135,000	126,826	93.9	150,150	127,968	85.2	5
19,520	18,486	94.7	22,000	22,451	102.1	25,000	24,040	96.2	6
16,750	16,749	100.0	19,635	19,874	101.2	22,000	20,028	91.0	7
535	416.9	77.9	850	468	55.1	800	515	64.4	8
25,975	25,218	97.1	27,945	27,427	98.1	32,160	28,501	88.6	9
2,041	1,791	87.8	2,261	2,053	90.8	2,574	2,179	84.7	10
1,855	1,628	87.8	2,055	1,866	90.8	2,340	1,984	84.8	10a
24,900	26,288	105.6	32,000	32,837	102.6	40,500	36,173	89.3	11
3,419	3,676	107.5	4,852	4,013	82.7	4,503	4,184	92.9	12
27,500	26,843	97.6	28,200	27,834	98.7	31,000	27,770	89.6	13
12,500	12,489	99.9	14,500	14,400	99.3	16,012	14,487	90.5	14
11,800	12,588	106.7	16,000	16,400	102.5	20,150	17,730	88.0	15
8,650	9,446	109.2	12,200	12,454	102.1	15,623	12,967	83.0	16
635	639	100.6	1,070	859	80.3	1,175	923	78.6	17
25	25.0	100.0	37.0	32.6	88.1	50	37.7	75.4	18
2,400	2,385	99.4	2,800	3,000	107.1	3,200	2,752	86.0	19
1.67	1.02	61.1	2.72				2.28		20
44.80	46.20	103.1	66.0	63.25	95.8	91.0	76.5	84.1	21
71.0	76.0	107.0	109.5	110.8	92	145.0	97.5	67.2	22
46.0	36.44	79.2	72.0	48.69	67.6	80.0	62.3	77.9	23
	2,323			2,839			3,240		24
1,200	1,460.4	121.7	1,680	1,671	99.5	2,500	1,963	78.5	25
898	1,125.8	125.4	1,258	1,256.6	99.9	1,872	1,472.7	78.7	26
495.0	530.9	107.3	720.0	623.0	86.5	884.2	649.9	73.5	27

Table A-2 *continued*

Series	Units	1933			1934		
		Planned (1)	*Actual* (2)	*(2) as Per Cent of (1)* (3)	*Planned* (4)	*Actual* (5)	*(5) as Per Cent of (4)* (6)
28. Potash fertilizer	th. m. t.		45.8			196.0	
29. Ammonium sulfate	th. m. t.		110.9		300.0	226.0	75.3
30. Soda ash	th. m. t.	329.9	329.7	99.9	375.0	398.0	106.1
31. Caustic soda	th. m. t.	146.6	101.4	69.2		104.3	
32. Sulfuric acid	th. m. t.	700	627	89.6	805	782	97.1
32a. Synthetic rubber	th. m. t.		2.2		12	11.1	92.5
33. Tires	thous.		679		1,500	1,547	103.1
34. Plastics	th. m. t.		4.19			5.56	
34a. Synthetic dyes	th. m. t.	15.87	16.00	100.8	21.06	24.02	114.1
35. Cement	th. m. t.	4,495	2,709	60.3	4,350	3,536	81.3
36. Lime	th. m. t.		1,966		2,800	2,636	94.1
37. Window glass	mill. m²	50.5	29.8	59.0	51.9	50.1	96.5
38a. Roofing tiles (excl. collective farm output)	mill.		43.7		95.0	55.9	58.8
39. Asbestos shingles	mill.		61.4		120.0	100.2	83.5
40. Bricks	mill.		3,822		6,000	4,972	82.9
41. Industrial timber hauled	mill. m³	119.9	98.0	81.7	118.5	99.7	84.1
42. Lumber	mill. m³	31.8	27.3	85.9	31.6	30.6	96.9
43. Plywood	th. m³		425.0		497.0	500.0	100.6
44. Paper	th. m. t.	550.0	506.1	92.0	600.0	565.8	94.3
45. Paperboard	th. m. t.		49.2		60.0	52.2	87.0
46. Machine tools	units		21,000		19,000	21,131	111.2
46a. Metallurgical equipment	th. m. t.		6.5		21.6	8.5	39.4
47. Steam and gas turbines	th. kw	608	634.5	104.4	700	363.8	52.0
48. Steam boilers	th. m²	158	154.0	97.5	200	140.0	70.0
49. Turbogenerators	th. kw	439	385.0	87.7	551	335.0	60.8
50. Spinning machines	units		330		745	488	65.5
51. Looms	units		1,928		3,783	2,319	61.3
52. Tractors	units	60,500	73,700	121.8	95,000	94,000	98.9
53. Tractors (15 hp)	th. conven. units	66.7	79.9	119.8	115.3	118.1	102.4
54. Motor vehicles, total	thous.	40.0	49.7	124.3	72.0	72.4	100.6
55. Trucks and buses	thous.	30.0	39.5	131.7	55.0	55.4	100.7
56. Automobiles	thous.	10.0	10.3	103.0	17.0	17.1	100.6
57. Buses	thous.		0.3			0.7	
58. Grain combines	units	12,000	8,578	71.5	12,000	8,239	68.7
59. Steam locomotives	units	1,175	930	79.1	1,253	1,210	96.6
60. Diesel locomotives	units		1		20	8	40.0
61. Electric locomotives	units		17		40	19	47.5
62. Railroad freight cars	units		12,989		26,500	20,732	78.2
63. Railroad freight cars	2-axle units	34,400	18,126	52.7	42,000	28,957	68.9
64. Railroad passenger cars	units	1,800	1,274	70.8	2,000	1,495	74.7
65. Excavators	units		116		358	290	81.0
66. Ginned cotton	th. m. t.	417.0	378.5	90.8		419.7	
67. Cotton yarn	th. m. t.		367.3		352.9	387.7	109.9
68. Cotton fabrics	mill. m	2,750	2,732	99.3	3,059.2	2,733	89.3
69. Woolen fabrics	mill. m	92	85.2	92.6	71.9	77.9	108.3
70. Linen fabrics	mill. m²	147.0	142.7	97.1	192.0	152.7	79.5
71. Linen fabrics	mill. m		140.5			162.1	

	1935			1936			1937		
Planned (7)	Actual (8)	(8) as Per Cent of (7) (9)	Planned (10)	Actual (11)	(11) as Per Cent of (10) (12)	Planned (13)	Actual (14)	(14) as Per Cent of (13) (15)	Series No.
	291.6		514.4	406.6	79.0		355.8		28
	374.5			522.8			761.6		29
416	422.1	101.5	500.0	503.4	101.7	553.3	528.2	95.5	30
	125.9		112.0	128.2	114.5	126.0	163.7	129.9	31
965	994	103.0	1,300	1,197	92.1	1,666	1,369	82.2	32
20	25.7	128.5	42.4	46.7	110.1		70.2		32a
2,000	2,084	104.2	2,500	2,209	88.4	3,200	2,698	84.3	33
	7.64		10.32	10.66	103.3	15.56	13.8	88.7	34
22.84	25.34	110.9	27.81	30.3	109.0	37.70	30.96	82.1	34a
4,400	4,488	102.0	6,500	5,872	90.3	7,437	5,454	73.3	35
2,800	2,906	103.8	3,455	3,721	107.7	4,510	4,822	106.9	36
63.3	69.8	110.3	92.1	87.9	95.4	97.8	79.3	81.1	37
100	86.7	86.7	153	116.0	75.8	240	108.0	45.0	38a
180.0	169.2	94.0	215	209.7	97.5	252	187.0	74.2	39
6,000	5,959	99.3	8,560	8,345	97.5	10,965	8,666	79.0	40
116.1	117.0	100.8	138.5	128.1	92.5	167.9	114.2	68.0	41
33.6	35.7	106.3	42.8	40.9	95.5	48.26	33.8	70.0	42
511.3	554.3	108.4	622.0	673.9	108.3	783.6	678.9	86.6	43
620.0	640.8	103.4	787.4	763.5	97.0	955.4	831.6	87.0	44
60.8	64.1	105.4	71.2	78.0	109.6	96.4	82.8	85.9	45
26,000	23,400	90.0	32,000	32,408	101.3	41,016	36,120	88.1	46
42.2	22.7	53.8	54.8	31.8	58.0		18.4		46a
721	473.9	65.7	1,371	622.9	45.4	2,169	1,068	49.2	47
245	135	55.1	275.3	182.2	66.2	289.3	170.4	58.9	48
610.0	425.5	69.8	633	503.5	79.5	960	514.0	53.5	49
830	646	77.8	896	659	73.5	1,950	884	45.3	50
3,920	3,687	94.1	5,110	4,446	87.0	4,200	4,095	97.5	51
97,000	112,600	116.1	96,200	112,900	117.4	79,000	50,976	64.5	52
126.7	155.5	122.7	154.3	173.2	112.2	172.7	66.5	38.5	53
92.0	96.7	105.1	161.5	136.5	84.5	220.0	199.9	90.9	54
75.0	77.8	103.7	144.5	132.9	92.0	195.0	181.8	93.2	55
17.0	19.0	111.8	17.0	3.7	21.8	25.0	18.2	72.8	56
	0.9		1.45	1.33	92	2.6	1.4	53.8	57
20,000	20,169	100.8	61,000	42,600	69.8	55,000	43,910	79.8	58
1,485	1,518	102.2	1,400	1,153	82.4	1,425	1,172	82.2	59
30	4	13.3	35	13	37.1		4		60
50	34	68.0	62	46	74.2	50	32	64.0	61
63,750	69,638	109.2	45,875	27,512	60.0	43,500	29,799	68.5	62
85,000	85,675	100.8	90,000	75,900	84.3	94,600	59,000	62.4	63
650	887	136.5	905	725	80.1	1,500	912	60.8	64
735	458	62.3	650	573	88.2	630	522	82.9	65
	437.2		542.0	596.2	110.0	730.0	716.7	98.2	66
340	382.5	112.5	467.6	478.8	102.4	583.6	532.9	91.3	67
2800.7	2,640	94.3	3,215.0	3,270	101.7	4,084.1	3,448	84.4	68
72.8	84.0	115.4	90.5	101.5	112.2	108.1	108.3	100.2	69
230.0	189.7	82.5	327.7	278.1	84.9		254		70
	215.6		326.0	295.2	90.6	310.0	285.2	92.0	71

Table A-2   *continued*

Series	Units	1933			1934		
		Planned (1)	*Actual* (2)	*(2) as Per Cent of (1)* (3)	*Planned* (4)	*Actual* (5)	*(5) as Per Cent of (4)* (6)
72. Silk and rayon fabrics	mill. m	27.9	26.0	93.2	30.8	31.4	101.9
73. Knitted underwear	mill.		36.1			53.7	
74. Knitted outer garments	mill.		17.2		9.0	22.4	248.9
75. Hosiery	mill. prs	272.9	250.9	91.9	355.6	322.9	90.8
76. Leather shoes	mill. prs	96.8	90.3	93.3	67.5	69.2	102.5
77. Felt footwear	mill. prs		7.0		8.4	7.5	89.3
78. Rubber footwear	mill. prs	60.0	62.2	103.7	65.0	65.0	100.0
79. Rubber galoshes	mill. prs		49.1		51.3	50.2	97.9
80. Metal beds	thous.		1,017		1,798	1,604	89.2
80a. Enameled kitchenware	th. m. t.		8.5		14.0	16.0	114.3
81. Motorcycles	thous.		0.119			0.365	
82. Bicycles	thous.		132.4		320.0	274.5	85.8
83. Radios	thous.		22.2		150	48.0	32.0
83a. Refrigerators, household	thous.						
84. Sewing machines, household	thous.		265.8		400.0	260.9	65.2
85. Clocks and watches	thous.		4,122			4,387	
86. Cameras	thous.		115.4		140	168.6	120.4
87. Phonographs	thous.		99.3		450	204.8	45.5
88. Soap (40% fatty acid)	th. m. t.		262.3		460.0	426.4	92.7
89. Bread and breadstuffs (large-scale industry)	th. m. t.		8,065			10,329	
89a. Bread and breadstuffs (ministries and local Soviets)	th. m. t.		5,451			6,687	
90. Flour (total)	th. m. t.		27,000			31,000	
90b. Flour (procurements)	th. m. t.	9,382	8,685	92.6	10,500	9,250	88.1
91. Macaroni	th. m. t.	200.0	146.0	73.0	272.0	176.0	64.7
92. Raw sugar	th. m. t.	1,350	995	73.7	1,400.0	1,404	100.3
93. Starch and syrup	th. m. t.	143.0	144.3	100.9	193.0	193.6	100.3
94. Fish catch	th. m. t.		1,303		1,500	1,547	103.1
95. Crude alcohol	th. hl	3,880	3,385	87.2	5,500	4,720	85.8
96. Vegetable oil	th. m. t.	364.0	281.4	77.3	380.0	372	97.9
97. Butter	th. m. t.		124.4		125.3	138.0	110.1
98. Cheese	th. m. t.	15.0	12.5	83.3	15.0	16.7	111.3
99. Meat	th. m. t.	480.0	380.7	79.3	490.5	438.4	89.4
100. Meat and subproducts of first category	th. m. t.		527			649	
101. Sausages	th. m. t.	65.5	49.1	75.0		58.4	
102. Canned food	mill. 400-gm cans	850	750	88.2	850	739	86.9
103. Confectionery	th. m. t.	479	429	89.6	615	522	84.9
104. Margarine	th. m. t.	60.0	51.8	86.3	75.0	69.2	92.3
105. Beer	th. hl		4,315		4,645	4,568	98.3
106. Cigarettes	bill.	70.0	62.7	89.6	73.0	67.8	92.9
107. Matches	th. crates	9,400	6,876	73.1	10,000	9,114	91.1
108. Low-grade tobacco (*makhorka*)	th. 20-kg crates	3,100	2,579	83.2	3,200	2,967	92.7
109. Salt	th. m. t.	3,600	2,734	75.9	3,600	3,545	98.5

	1935			1936			1937			
Planned (7)	Actual (8)	(8) as Per Cent of (7) (9)	Planned (10)	Actual (11)	(11) as Per Cent of (10) (12)	Planned (13)	Actual (14)	(14) as Per Cent of (13) (15)	Series No.
35.2	38.2	108.5	49.0	51.7	105.5	58.3	58.9	101.0	72
55.5	63.4	114.2	96.2	85.9	89.3	128.6	111.5	86.7	73
19.2	26.0	135.4	34.4	35.9	104.4	44.2	39.7	89.8	74
383.5	340.7	88.8	420.4	358.7	85.3	486.7	408.6	84.0	75
77.0	84.8	110.1	121.9	139.9	114.8	190.0	182.9	96.3	76
8.7	8.9	102.3	11.3	11.2	99.1	16.5	13.4	81.2	77
75	76.4	101.9	85.0	82.0	96.5	100.0	84.6	84.6	78
56.5	55.2	97.7	58	56.3	97.1	69.0	55.6	80.6	79
2,143	1,909	89.1	2,551	2,863	112.2	3,913	4,160	106.3	80
19.0	23.4	123.2	22.5	23.0	102.2	27.6	18.95	68.7	80a
	1.202		10.0	6.7	67.0	15.0	13.1	87.3	81
350.0	324.2	92.6	800.0	557.5	69.7	900.0	540.7	60.1	82
172	128.1	74.5	517.6	334.1	64.5	652.5	199.9	30.6	83
			3.5				0		83a
400.0	402.8	100.7	450.0	490.0	108.9	510.0	510.1	100.0	84
	4,515			4,942			4,028		85
207.0	150.7	72.8	236	268.0	113.6	298.5	353.2	118.3	86
447	284.7	63.7	955.0	575.5	60.3	1,000.0	675.8	67.6	87
500	478.7	95.7	581.4	557.4	95.9	485.0	495	102.1	88
13,894	14,355	103.3	14,756	16,145	109.4	17,000	19,131	112.5	89
	7,491			7,824			10,510		89a
							15,118		90
12,000	11,994	100.0	11,700	12,655	108.2	12,600	13,918	110.5	90b
279.4	185	66.2	248.6	262	105.4	327.5	263.8	80.5	91
1,450	2,032	140.1	2,500	1,998	79.9	2,600	2,421	93.1	92
214.1	249.2	116.4	274.2	277.0	101.0	285.5	247	86.5	93
1,550	1,520	98.1	1,714	1,631	95.2	1,800	1,609	89.4	94
5,800	6,070	104.7	7,000	6,950	99.3	8,015	7,670	95.7	95
400	425.7	106.4	509.9	450.9	88.4	488.0	495.3	101.5	96
135.0	154.8	114.7	193.0	189	97.9	222.0	185.2	83.4	97
18.0	19.4	107.8	24.5	25.3	103.3	34.0	31.0	91.2	98
470.8	473.6	100.6	650.0	773.1	118.9	800.0	797.2	101.5	99
	787			995			1,002		100
50.0	108	216.0	170.0	244.4	143.8	300	326.0	108.7	101
1,084	1,119	103.2	1,274	1,172	92.0	1,425	982	68.9	102
635.2	606.4	95.5	823.4	810.1	98.4	1,073.6	921.4	85.8	103
84.0	81.8	97.4	80.0	75.0	93.8	65.0	74	113.8	104
4,755	5,186	109.1	5,978	7,436	124.4	8,600	8,960	104.2	105
75.0	78.6	104.8	88.6	84.0	94.8	102.0	89.2	87.5	106
10,200	10,730	105.2	10,700	8,194	76.6	8,000	7,163	89.5	107
3,200	3,750	117.2	5,000	5,021	100.4	5,500	5,343	97.1	108
3,940	4,350	110.4	4,643	4,166	89.7	3,340	3,200	95.8	109

Table A-2 *continued*

Series	Units	1933 Planned (1)	1933 Actual (2)	(2) as Per Cent of (1) (3)	1934 Planned (4)	1934 Actual (5)	(5) as Per Cent of (4) (6)
Agriculture							
110. Total value of production (1926/27 prices)	mill. rub.		14,017		15,600	14,591	93.5
110a. Total value of production (comparable prices)	prec. yr. = 100		94.4		107.0	105.0	98.1
111. Vegetable production (1926/27 prices)	mill. rub.		11,054		12,500	11,308	90.5
111a. Vegetable production (comparable prices)	prec. yr. = 100		96.8		111.1	103.3	93.0
112. Animal production (1926/27 prices)	mill. rub.		2,962		3,100	3,283	105.9
112a. Animal production (comparable prices)	prec. yr. = 100		86.7			110.8	
Harvests							
113. Grain, total (biological yield)	mill. m. t.	80.20	89.80	112.0	91.22	89.40	98.0
113a. Grain, total (barn yield)	mill. m. t.	80.2	68.4	85.3	91.22	67.65	74.2
114. Wheat (biological yield)	mill. m. t.		27.73		30.35	30.41	100.2
115. Rye (biological yield)	mill. m. t.		24.19		23.82	20.13	84.5
116. Barley (biological yield)	mill. m. t.		7.85		7.67	6.84	89.2
117. Oats (biological yield)	mill. m. t.		15.41		16.13	18.90	117.2
118. Corn (biological yield)	mill. m. t.		4.80		4.56	3.84	84.2
Harvests of Technical Crops							
119. Raw cotton (biological yield)	mill. m. t.	1.43	1.31	91.6	1.42	1.18	83.1
120. Sugar beets (biological yield)	mill. m. t.	12.0	8.99	74.9	14.16	11.36	80.3
121. Sunflowers (biological yield)	mill. m. t.	2.20	2.35	107.0	2.17	2.08	95.7
122. Flax fiber (biological yield)	th. m. t.	550	548	99.6	575	533	92.7
123. Hemp (biological yield)	th. m. t.		234			134	
124. Potatoes (biological yield)	mill. m. t.		49.25		57.33	51.01	89.0
Animal Production							
125. Meat and fat (excl. rabbit and poultry)	th. m. t.		1,722		1,390	1,509	108.6
126. Milk	mill. m. t.		18.83		20.0	19.71	98.6
127. Eggs	bill.						
128. Wool	th. m. t.		63.9		64.6	64.5	99.8
Market Production							
129. Grain	mill. m. t.		25.6		27.6	28.0	101.4
130. Raw cotton	mill. m. t.		1.28		1.40	1.16	82.9
131. Sugar beets	mill. m. t.		8.24		11.10		

1935			1936			1937			
Planned (7)	Actual (8)	(8) as Per Cent of (7) (9)	Planned (10)	Actual (11)	(11) as Per Cent of (10) (12)	Planned (13)	Actual (14)	(14) as Per Cent of (13) (15)	Series No.
17,251	16,181	93.8	19,673				20,123		110
116.3	112.3	96.6	124.2	91.6	73.8		122.9		110a
13,384	12,278	91.7	14,751				15,070		111
116.1	110.4	95.1	123.6	85.5	69.2		127.1		111a
3,867	3,903	100.9	4,922				5,053		112
117.2	119.4	101.9	126.1	111.6	88.5		113.5		112a
94.93	90.10	94.9	104.76	82.73	79.0	108.32	120.29	111.1	113
94.93	75.02	79.0	104.76	61.0	58.2	108.32	97.4	89.9	113a
32.51	31.33	96.4	37.95			40.89	46.8	114.5	114
23.77	21.63	91.0	24.17				29.44		115
8.03	8.45	105.2	8.94			9.17	10.60	115.6	116
17.54	18.69	106.6	19.78	13.0	65.7	19.41	21.86	112.6	117
4.17	2.98	71.15	4.40	3.87	87.9	4.73	3.89	82.2	118
1.59	1.71	107.5	1.93	2.39	123.8	2.32	2.58	111.5	119
15.25	16.21	106.3	25.42	16.83	66.2	24.5	21.86	89.2	120
2.16	1.85	85.6	2.70	1.49	55.2	2.71	2.08	76.8	121
620	551	88.9	780	530	67.9	830	570	68.7	122
									123
67.93	69.74	102.7	85.38	51.52	60.3	88.89	65.63	73.8	124
1,550	1,769	114.1	2,259	2,500	110.7	3,545	2,370	66.9	125
21.53	20.85	96.9	26.14	24.20	92.6	29.46	26.06	88.5	126
							7.5		127
72.8	79.0	108.5	91.4	96.0	105.0	120.0	106.3	88.6	128
31.0	31.01	100.0	36.30				37.97		129
							2.57		130
							21.45		131

Table A-2 *continued*

Series	Units	1933 Planned (1)	1933 Actual (2)	(2) as Per Cent of (1) (3)	1934 Planned (4)	1934 Actual (5)	(5) as Per Cent of (4) (6)
132. Flax fiber	th. m. t.						
133. Potatoes	mill. m. t.		9.31		13.0	10.55	81.2
134. Meat and fat (dead weight)	th. m. t.		962		990	1,028	103.8
135. Milk and dairy products	mill. m. t.		5.36		5.94	6.32	106.3
136. Wool	th. m. t.		41				
Procurements							
137. Grain	th. m. t.	23,600	23,285	98.6	24,938	26,072	104.5
138. Raw cotton	th. m. t.	1,346	1,235	91.8			
139. Sugar beets	th. m. t.	13,000	8,127	62.5			
140. Sunflowers	th. m. t.		797			756	
141. Flax fiber	th. m. t.			75.4			
142. Hemp	th. m. t.	60	14	23.3			
143. Potatoes	th. m. t.	5,780	5,652	97.8			
143a. Vegetables	th. m. t.	1,859	1,728	93.0			
144. Meat and fat (live weight)	th. m. t.	1,230	1,095	89.0		1,096	
145. Meat and fat (dead weight)	th. m. t.		375		554	517	93.3
146. Milk and dairy products	th. m. t.	3,964	3,580	90.3	4,120	3,832	93.0
147. Eggs	mill.			43.5			
148. Wool	th. m. t.	47.8	38	79.5		42	
Railroad Transportation							
149. Length of network	th. km		82.6		83.6	83.5	99.9
150. Average daily carloadings	thous.	58.0	51.2	88.3	68.0	55.7	81.9
151. Total freight traffic	bill. m. ton-km	183.0	169.5	92.6	215.0	205.7	95.7
152. Total freight traffic	mill. m. t.	300.0	268.1	89.4	352.0	317.1	90.1
153. Coal and coke	mill. m. t.	65.0	66.6	102.5	80.0	81.9	102.4
154. Oil and oil products	mill. m. t.	18.0	16.5	91.7	25.0	20.3	81.2
155. Ferrous metals	mill. m. t.	12.0	11.0	91.7	16.0	14.0	87.5
156. Ore	mill. m. t.	15.0	15.6	104.0	20.0	20.0	100.0
157. Firewood	mill. m. t.	15.0	14.0	93.3	16.0	15.4	96.3
158. Timber	mill. m. t.	33.0	28.6	86.7	36.0	32.4	90.0
159. Mineral construction materials	mill. m. t.		32.8			38.7	
159a. Principal construction materials (stone, lime, cement, bricks)	mill. m. t.	31.0	18.6	60.0	29.0	20.7	71.4
160. Grain and flour	mill. m. t.	26.0	26.7	102.7	30.0	25.7	85.7
161. Salt	mill. m. t.		2.95			3.51	
162. Total freight traffic, average length of haul	km	610	632	103.6	611	649	106.2
163. Coal and coke, average length of haul	km		669			658	

	1935			1936			1937		
Planned (7)	Actual (8)	(8) as Per Cent of (7) (9)	Planned (10)	Actual (11)	(11) as Per Cent of (10) (12)	Planned (13)	Actual (14)	(14) as Per Cent of (13) (15)	Series No.
							324		132
13.11	13.62	103.9	16.47				11.68		133
1,203	1,221	101.5	1,460				1,464		134
6.85	7.43	108.4	9.14				8.08		135
	58						80.3		136
27,908	28,400	101.8		25,700			31,850		137
1,515	1,702	112.3	1,878	2,315	123.3		2,542		138
15,220	15,732	103.4	17,700	15,656	88.5		21,430		139
992	882	88.9	937	636	67.9		1,076		140
312.5	315.8	101.1	342.3	269.9	78.8		275		141
62.0	52.2	84.2	58.7	30.8	52.5		49		142
6,384	6,462	101.2	5,909	5,080	86.0		7,021		143
1,783	1,623	91.0					1,477		143a
1,144	1,056	92.3	1,271	1,321	103.9		1,259		144
	519						795		145
	3,983		4,610	5,020	108.9		4,990		146
			800	785	98.1		1,400		147
	52		73.3	71	96.9	95	78.9	82.1	148
83.8	83.8	100.0	84.9	85.1	100.2	86.5	84.9	98.2	149
63.0	68.0	107.9	78.5	86.2	109.8	95.0	89.8	94.5	150
229.1	258.1	112.7	299.3	323.4	108.1	387.8	354.8	91.5	151
358.0	388.5	103.5	457.0	483.2	105.7	565.0	517.3	91.6	152
98.0	94.7	96.6	121.0	114.0	94.2	141.0	116.6	82.8	153
24.5	22.3	91.0	25.0	26.0	104.0	28.5	24.7	86.7	154
17.5	19.2	109.7	23.5	25.5	108.5	29.0	26.2	90.3	155
24.0	26.0	108.3	29.0	29.2	100.7	33.5	30.5	91.0	156
16.0	18.3	114.4	18.5	17.9	96.8	21.5	19.3	89.8	157
36.0	42.2	117.2	47.5	47.8	100.6	63.0	46.9	74.4	158
	55.7		57.5	92.0	160.0	93.5	102.4	109.5	159
23.0	29.4	127.8	34.0	35.4	104.1		41.5		159a
29.5	30.0	101.7	31.0	33.6	108.4	34.0	38.9	114.4	160
	4.50						4.10		161
640	664	103.8	655	668	102.0	685	686	100.1	162
	644			673			709		163

Table A-2 *continued*

Series	Units	1933 Planned (1)	Actual (2)	(2) as Per Cent of (1) (3)	1934 Planned (4)	Actual (5)	(5) as Per Cent of (4) (6)
163a. Oil and oil products, average length of haul	km		959			955	
164. Ferrous metals, average length of haul	km		880			963	
164a. Firewood, average length of haul	km		236			245	
164b. Timber, average length of haul	km		689			743	
165. Grain and flour, average length of haul	km		665			680	
165a. Ore, average length of haul	km		543			539	
166. Total passenger traffic	bill. pass.-km	89.0	75.2	84.5	82.0	71.4	87.1
Inland Water Transportation							
166a. Length of network	th. km		84.5		90.0	88.8	98.7
168. Freight traffic under ministries and economic organizations	bill. m. ton-km	31.6	26.0	82.3	35.5	29.0	81.7
170. Freight traffic under ministries and economic organizations	mill. m. t.	53.2	44.7	84.1	59.0	52.7	89.3
171. Coal and coke	th. m. t.		731		1,200	905	75.4
172. Oil and oil products	th. m. t.		6,823		7,800	6,852	87.8
173. Timber and firewood	th. m. t.		25,922			30,611	
174. Mineral construction materials	th. m. t.		3,230		6,300	5,111	81.1
175. Grain and flour	th. m. t.		3,229		4,200	3,481	82.9
176. Salt	th. m. t.		878		1,300	1,083	83.3
177. Average length of haul under ministries and economic organizations	km		581		602	551	91.5
178. Passenger traffic	bill. pass.-km		3.7		4.7	3.0	63.8
178a. Passenger traffic	mill. pass.		41.6			41.2	
Maritime Transportation (Soviet ships)							
179. Freight traffic	bill. m. ton-km	29.5	24.4	82.7	30.6	27.6	90.2
180. Freight traffic	mill. m. t.	18.2	16.2	89	24.6	22.6	91.9
181. Average length of haul	km	1,621	1,506	92.9	1,244	1,221	98.2
182. Passenger traffic	mill. pass.-km		870		900	903	100.3
182a. Passenger traffic	mill. pass.						
Motor Transportation							
183. Freight traffic	bill. m. ton-km		1.3			2.4	
Air Transportation							
184. Freight traffic, incl. mail	mill. m. ton-km	3.5	3.1	88.6	7.0	6.0	85.7
185. Passenger traffic	th. pass.		41.6		50	68.5	137.0

| 1935 | | | 1936 | | | 1937 | | | |
Planned (7)	Actual (8)	(8) as Per Cent of (7) (9)	Planned (10)	Actual (11)	(11) as Per Cent of (10) (12)	Planned (13)	Actual (14)	(14) as Per Cent of (13) (15)	Series No.
	1,020			1,086			1,228		163a
	980			989			1,004		164
	255						261		164a
	802						932		164b
	687						689		165
	61.6			613			674		165a
73.0	67.9	93.0		77.2		87.0	90.9	104.5	166
92.9	87.8	84.5	98.0	92.7	94.6	101.5	101.1	99.6	166a
35.0	34.0	97.1	42.9	31.2	72.7	44.8	33.1	73.9	168
59.0	64.7	109.7	75.6	70.0	92.6	87.1	66.9	76.8	170
1,360	1,446	94.1	1,925	1,695	88.1	2,750	2,100	76.4	171
7,800	7,058	90.4	8,215	6,798	82.8	8,600	7,900	91.9	172
	38,054						35,000		173
6,000	6,759	112.7	8,139	9,924	121.9	12,595	9,900	78.6	174
4,200	4,620	110.0	5,500	4,337	78.9	4,850	4,300	88.7	175
1,200	1,583	131.9	1,625	1,109	68.2	1,540	1,300	84.4	176
593	525	88.5	567	446	78.7	514	500	97.3	177
3.7	2.9	78.4	3.43	2.71	79	3.3	3.2	97.0	178
	41.5			48.2			65.2		178a
37.0	34.1	92.2	45.2	41.1	90.9	46.7	36.8	78.8	179
26.8	26.1		31.6	30.7	97	35.5	29.4	82.8	180
1,381	1,307	94.6	1,430	1,343	93.9	1,315	1,252	94.1	181
804	869	108.1	821	772	94	870	850	97.7	182
							3.0		182a
	3.5			5.5			5.9		183
10.0	9.3	93.0	20.0	21.0	105	25.0	24.9	99.6	184
111.0	96.3	86.8	167.0	158.4	94.9	180.0	235	130.6	185

Table A-2 *continued*

Series	Units	1933			1934		
		Planned (1)	*Actual* (2)	*(2) as Per Cent of (1)* (3)	*Planned* (4)	*Actual* (5)	*(5) as Per Cent of (4)* (6)
Employment (annual averages)							
186. Workers and employees, national economy, excl. collective farms	mill.	21.3	22.3	104.7	23.5	23.7	100.9
187. Industry	thous.	8,200	7,867	95.9	7,800	8,402	107.7
188. Construction	thous.	2,000	2,361	118.1	3,017	2,681	88.9
188a. Construction and assembly work	thous.						
189. State-owned agriculture and logging	thous.	3,594	4,012	111.6	4,365	4,303	98.6
190. State-owned agriculture (state farms, MTS, and other state establishments)	thous.		2,819		3,213	3,094	96.3
191. Railroad transport	thous.	1,494	1,474	98.7	1,558	1,603	102.9
192. Maritime and inland waterway transport	thous.	246	189	76.8	203	222	109.4
193. Other transport (motor, etc.)	thous.		642		572	630	110.1
194. Communications	thous.	300	258	86.0	279	295	105.7
195. Trade, procurements, and supply	thous.	1,200	1,375	114.6	1,610	1,465	91.0
196. Public eating places	thous.	543	532	98.0	590	546	92.5
197. Credit institutions	thous.		132		115	134	116.5
198. Administration	thous.		1,678		1,500	1,601	106.7
199. Education	thous.		1,463		1,550	1,569	101.2
200. Public health	thous.		681		753	739	98.1
Wage Fund, Workers and Employees							
201. National economy	mill. rub.	30,825	34,953	113.4	38,125	44,000	115.4
202. Industry	mill. rub.	12,500	12,368	98.9	13,026	15,362	117.9
Average Annual Wage, Workers and Employees							
203. Money wage, national economy, excl. collective farms and cooperatives	rubles	1,523	1,566	102.8	1,625	1,858	114.3
204. Real wage, national economy, excl. collective farms and cooperatives, calculated from official Soviet index	1932 = 100						
205. Money wage, industry	rubles	1,541	1,572	102.0	1,672	1,828	109.3
Average Annual Money Wage, Workers							
206. Industry	rubles		1,513			1,768	
207. Iron ore	rubles		1,601			1,952	

1935			1936			1937			
Planned (7)	Actual (8)	(8) as Per Cent of (7) (9)	Planned (10)	Actual (11)	(11) as Per Cent of (10) (12)	Planned (13)	Actual (14)	(14) as Per Cent of (13) (15)	Series No.
24.4	24.7	101.2	25.7	25.8	100.4	26.3	27.0	102.7	186
8,717	9,001	103.3	9,417	9,677	102.8	9,907	10,112	102.1	187
2,321	2,268	97.7	2,492	2,112	84.8	1,749	2,023	115.7	188
							1,576		188a
4,516	4,274	94.6					2,731		189
3,217	2,967	92.2	2,753	2,720	98.8	2,588	2,483	95.9	190
1,770	1,789	101.1	1,580	1,495	94.6	1,550	1,512	97.5	191
211	246	116.6	202	180	89.1	197	180	91.4	192
800	881	110.1	1,021	970	95	1,120	1,092	97.5	193
311	326	104.8	343	340	99.1	375	375	100.0	194
1,513	1,650	109.1	1,835	1,798	98.0	1,947	1,994	102.4	195
556	478	86.0	466	405	86.9	413	396	95.9	196
135	152	112.6	170	168	99	181	193	106.6	197
1,570	1,640	104.5	1,645	1,710	103.9	1,710	1,743	101.9	198
1,650	1,758	106.5	1,870	2,000	107.0	2,190	2,303	105.2	199
788	827	104.9	819	1,007	123.0	1,156	1,118	96.7	200
49,825	56,200	112.8	63,400	71,400	112.6	78,330	82,247	105.0	201
18,556	20,572	110.9	23,320	26,270	112.7	28,810	30,385	105.5	202
2,046	2,274	111.1	2,465	2,770	112.4	2,976	3,047	102.4	203
							656		204
2,129	2,285	107.3	2,476	2,715	109.7	2,908	3,005	103.3	205
2,121	2,241	105.7	2,500	2,700	108	2,881	2,820	97.9	206
	2,440						3,143		207

Table A-2 *continued*

Series	Units	1933 Planned (1)	1933 Actual (2)	1933 (2) as Per Cent of (1) (3)	1934 Planned (4)	1934 Actual (5)	1934 (5) as Per Cent of (4) (6)
208. Coal	rubles		1,591			1,903	
209. Ferrous metals	rubles		1,712			2,032	
209a. Machine-building	rubles		1,822			2,099	
210. Paper	rubles		1,330			1,459	
211. Chemicals	rubles		1,637			1,876	
212. Textiles	rubles		1,222			1,438	
212a. Cotton	rubles		1,246			1,501	
212b. Wool	rubles		1,223			1,466	
213. Leather	rubles		1,389			1,561	
214. Food	rubles		1,229			1,360	
Average Annual Money Wage, Workers and Employees							
215. Construction	rubles		1,641		1,624	2,042	125.7
216. Railroad transport	rubles	1,600	1,637	102.3	1,794	1,930	107.6
217. Maritime and inland waterway transport	rubles	1,622	1,709	105.4	1,932	2,103	108.9
218. Communications	rubles	1,474	1,450	98.4	1,489	1,571	105.5
219. Trade	rubles		1,343		1,389	1,483	106.8
220. Public eating places	rubles		1,122		1,102	1,242	112.7
221. Credit institutions	rubles		2,128		2,249	2,336	103.9
222. Administration	rubles		2,354		2,258	2,694	119.3
223. Education	rubles		1,765		1,773	1,941	109.5
224. Public health	rubles		1,413		1,441	1,545	107.2
225. State-owned agriculture	rubles		1,041		1,117	1,228	109.9
226. Logging	rubles		1,137		1,180	1,375	116.5
Housing							
227. Housing fund, urban, total	mill. m²		191.5		202.2	196.6	97.2
228. Housing construction, urban, total	mill. m²	12.0	7.2	60.0	11.2		
229. Floorspace per inhabitant, urban	m²						
Population							
230. Total (end of year)	mill.		159.2			160.0	
231. Urban (end of year)	mill.						
232. Rural (end of year)	mill.						
Retail Trade							
233. State and cooperative in current prices	mill. rub.	49,000	49,789	101.6	60,000	61,815	103.0
234. State and cooperative in 1940 prices	mill. rub.						
234c. Food products in current prices	mill. rub.		29,265			38,495	
234d. Food products in 1940 prices	mill. rub.						
235. Collective farm in current prices	mill. rub.		11,500			14,000	

	1935			1936			1937		
Planned (7)	Actual (8)	(8) as Per Cent of (7) (9)	Planned (10)	Actual (11)	(11) as Per Cent of (10) (12)	Planned (13)	Actual (14)	(14) as Per Cent of (13) (15)	Series No.
	2,556						3,626		208
	2,509						3,266		209
	2,575						3,387		209a
	1,859								210
	2,410						3,165		211
	1,830						2,338		212
	1,917						2,396		212a
	1,797						2,338		212b
	1,950								213
	1,721						2,259		214
1,987	2,538	127.7	2,715	2,884	106.2	2,887	3,087	106.9	215
2,201	2,311	105.0	2,500	2,864	114.6	3,080	3,271	106.2	216
2,382	2,533	106.3	2,861	3,000	104.9	3,335	3,397	101.9	217
1,925	1,953	101.5	1,956	2,050	104.8	2,132	2,356	110.5	218
1,760	1,876	106.6	1,887	2,256	120.0	2,333	2,528	108.4	219
1,507	1,561	103.0	1,550	1,877	121.1	1,933	2,045	105.8	220
2,566	2,678	104.4	3,216	3,280	102	3,295	3,425	103.9	221
2,740	3,124	114.0	3,250	3,645	112.2	3,870	3,937	101.7	222
2,193	2,357	107.5	2,400	3,432	143.0	4,022	3,442	85.6	223
2,160	2,160	100.0	2,356	2,348	99.7	2,355	2,455	104.2	224
1,408	1,577	112.0	1,700	1,853	109.0	1,966	2,121	107.9	225
1,547	1,525	98.6					1,920		226
202.9	200.4	98.8	209.4	204.4	97.6	210.3	207.3	98.6	227
			2.4	.81	33.8		3.9		228
							3.79		229
	161.3			163.4			166.9		230
							54.7		231
							112.2		232
80,000	81,712	102.1	100,000	106,761	106.8	131,000	125,943	96.1	233
							149,900		234
	53,400			67,800		79,100	79,482	100.5	234c
							94,600		234d
	14,500		16,500	15,607	94.6		17,800		235

Table A-2 *continued*

Source

1. National income (1926/27 prices)–**Col. 1:** *153*, p. 124. **Cols. 2 and 5:** *215*, p. 4. **Col. 4:** *173*, No. 5–6, 1934, p. 196. **Col. 7:** *155*, p. 441. **Cols. 8 and 13:** *157*, pp. 42–43. **Col. 10:** *156*, p. 390. **Col. 11:** *161*, p. 112, as cited in *417*, p. 181. **Col. 14:** *254*, p. 197.

INDUSTRY

2. Gross production, total (1926/27 prices)–**Col. 1:** Based on 1932 output (given as 43.3 bill. rubles in *293*, pp. 686–87) and increase planned for 1933 (given as 16.5% over 1932 in *153*, p. 118). **Cols. 2, 4, and 7:** *155*, p. 442. **Cols. 5 and 10:** *156*, p. 392. **Cols. 8, 11, and 13:** *157*, pp. 42–43. **Col. 14:** *254*, p. 197.

3. Producer goods (1926/27 prices)–**Col. 1:** Based on 1932 output (given as 23.1 bill. rubles in *293*, pp. 429–30) and increase planned for 1933 (given as 21.2% over 1932 in *153*, p. 118). **Cols. 2, 4, and 7:** *155*, p. 442. **Cols. 5 and 10:** *156*, p. 392. **Cols. 8, 11, and 13:** *157*, pp. 42–43. **Col. 14:** *254*, p. 197.

4. Consumer goods (1926/27 prices)–**Col. 1:** Based on 1932 output (given as 20.2 bill. rubles in *293*, pp. 429–30) and increase planned for 1933 (given as 10.5% in *153*, p. 118). **Cols. 2, 4, and 7:** *155*, p. 443. **Cols. 5 and 10:** *156*, p. 392. **Cols. 8, 11, and 13:** *157*, pp. 42–43. **Col. 14:** *254*, p. 197.

5. Coal–**Col. 1:** *153*, p. 118. **Cols. 2, 5, 8, 11, and 14:** *187*, p. 140. **Col. 4:** *173*, No. 5–6, 1934, p. 205. **Col. 7:** *155*, p. 444. **Col. 10:** *156*, p. 410. **Col. 13:** *157*, p. 65.

6. Peat–**Col. 1:** *153*, p. 45. **Cols. 2 and 5:** *215*, p. 150. **Col. 4:** *173*, No. 5–6, 1934, p. 205. **Col. 7:** *155*, p. 444. **Cols. 8, 11, and 14:** *218*, p. 35. Includes collective farm output. **Col. 10:** *156*, p. 411. **Col. 13:** *157*, pp. 66–67.

7. Coke (6% humidity)–**Col. 1:** *162a*, 1933, p. 34. **Cols. 2, 5, 8, 11, and 14:** *187*, p. 115. **Col. 4:** *173*, No. 5–6, 1934, p. 205. **Col. 7:** *155*, p. 508. Excludes Suchansk Factory of Commissariat of Transportation. Includes factory of the Leningrad municipal economy (with a plan of 25 thous. m. t.). **Col. 10:** *156*, p. 411. **Col. 13:** *157*, pp. 66–67. Commissariat of Heavy Industry.

8. Oil shale–**Col. 1:** *153*, p. 45. **Cols. 2 and 5:** *131*, Vol. 24, pp. 51 ff., as cited in *485*, series 311.4. **Col. 4:** *173*, No. 5–6, 1934, p. 66. **Cols. 7 and 10:** *156*, p. 411. **Cols. 8 and 13:** *157*, pp. 66–67. **Col. 11:** *184*, p. 100. **Col. 14:** *187*, p. 166.

9. Crude petroleum–**Col. 1:** *153*, p. 118. **Cols. 2, 5, 8, 11, and 14:** *187*, p. 153. **Col. 4:** *173*, No. 3, 1934, p. 69. Planned output of petroleum and natural gas minus planned output of natural gas. **Cols. 7 and 10:** *156*, p. 411. Planned output of petroleum and natural gas minus planned output of natural gas. **Col. 13:** *157*, p. 67.

10. Natural gas (m³)–**Cols. 2, 4, 5, 7, 8, 10, 11, and 13:** Based on output in tons (series 10a) and ratio of m³ to tons for 1937 (derived as 1,100 from col. 14 here and in series 10a). **Col. 14:** *187*, p. 156. Includes secondary extraction of gas.

10a. Natural gas (tons)–**Cols. 2 and 5:** *215*, p. 138. **Col. 4:** *155*, p. 508. **Cols. 7 and 10:** *156*, p. 411. **Cols. 8, 11, and 13:** *157*, pp. 66–67. Crude petroleum including gas minus crude petroleum excluding gas. **Col. 14:** *254*, p. 202. Crude petroleum including gas minus crude petroleum excluding gas.

11. Electric power–**Col. 1:** *153*, p. 118. **Cols. 2, 5, 8, 11, and 14:** *187*, p. 171. **Col. 4:** *173*, No. 5–6, 1934, p. 205. **Col. 7:** *155*, p. 444. **Col. 10:** *156*, p. 410. **Col. 13:** *157*, p. 65.

12. Hydroelectric power–**Cols. 2, 5, 8, 11, and 14:** *187*, p. 171. **Col. 4:** Based on 1933 output and planned increase for 1934 for regional hydroelectric power stations (given as 81.4% in *173*, No. 5–6, 1934, p. 212). **Col. 7:** Based on 1934 output and planned increase for 1935 for regional hydroelectric power stations (given as 43.9% in *155*, p. 84). **Col. 10:** Based on 1935 output and planned increase for 1936 for large (apparently the same as regional) hydroelectric power stations (given as 32% in *156*, p. 84). **Col. 13:** Based on 1937 output (col. 14) and percentage of plan fulfilled (col. 15). Estimate. **Col. 15:** Based on 1937 capacity of hydroelectric power stations (given as 1,044 th. kw in *187*, p. 171) and planned capacity for 1937 (derived as 1,124 th. kw from 1936 capacity of 956 th. kw in *187*, p. 171, and planned increase roughly estimated as 10% more than planned increase for hydroelectric stations under Commissariat of Heavy Industry given as 153 th. kw in *157*, p. 17).

13. Iron ore–**Col. 1:** *162a*, 1933, p. 34. **Cols. 2, 5, 8, 11, and 14:** *187*, p. 115. **Col. 4:** *173*, No. 5–6, 1934, p. 205. **Col. 7:** *155*, p. 508. Excludes mines belonging to factories of Omutinsk and Petrovsk-Zabaikal. **Col. 10:** *156*, p. 412. **Col. 13:** *157*, p. 69.

14. Pig iron–**Col. 1:** *153*, p. 118. **Cols. 2, 5, 8, 11, and 14:** *187*, p. 106. **Col. 4:** *173*, No. 5–6, 1934, p. 205. **Col. 7:** *155*, p. 509. **Col. 10:** *156*, p. 413. **Col. 13:** *157*, p. 69.

15. Steel ingots and castings–**Col. 1:** *153*, p. 118. **Cols. 2, 5, 8, 11, and 14:** *187*, p. 106. **Col. 4:** *173*, No. 5–6, 1934, p. 205. **Col. 7:** *155*, p. 509. **Col. 10:** *156*, p. 413. **Col. 13:** *157*, p. 69.

16. Rolled steel–**Col. 1:** *153*, p. 118. **Cols. 2, 5, 8, 11, and 14:** *187*, p. 106. **Col. 4:** *173*, No. 5–6, 1934, p. 205. **Col. 7:** *155*, p. 509. **Col. 10:** *156*, p. 413. **Col. 13:** *157*, p. 69.

17. Steel pipes–**Col. 1:** *173*, No. 5–6, 1934, p. 68. Iron pipes. **Cols. 2, 5, 8, 11, and 14:** *187*, p. 106. **Col. 4:** *173*, No. 5–6, 1934, p. 205. Iron pipes. **Col. 7:** *155*, p. 510. Iron pipes. **Col. 10:** *156*, p. 414. Iron pipes. **Col. 13:** *157*, p. 69. Iron pipes.

18. Aluminum–**Cols. 2 and 5:** *228*, p. 190. **Col. 4:** *173*, No. 5–6, 1934, p. 82. **Col. 7:** *33*, 2/4/35, p. 2, as cited in *485*, series 201.4. **Col. 8:** Based on 1934 output (col. 5) and increase in 1935 (given as 74% in *156*, p. 117). **Cols. 10-11:** *162a*, Dec. 1936, pp. 16–17. **Col. 13:** Estimate in *485*, series 201.4. **Col. 14:** *254*, p. 204.

Table A-2 *continued*

19. Manganese ore–**Col. 1:** *162a*, 1933, p. 34. **Cols. 2, 5, 8, 11, and 14:** *187*, p. 115. **Col. 4:** *154*, p. 128. **Cols. 7 and 10:** *156*, p. 412. **Col. 13:** *157*, p. 69.

20. Nickel–**Cols. 4, 7, 8, 10, and 14:** Estimates in *485*, series 213.4. For col. 4, *173*, No. 5–6, 1934, p. 82, gives 800 m. t. **Col. 5:** *62*, p. 146, as cited in *485*, series 213.4.

21. Zinc–**Col. 1:** Based on 1933 output (col. 2) and percentage of plan fulfilled (col. 3). **Col. 2:** *228*, p. 190. **Col. 3:** *173*, No. 5–6, 1934, p. 79. Given as underfulfillment of 29%. **Col. 4:** *173*, No. 5–6, 1934, p. 81. **Cols. 5 and 8:** *264*, No. 3, 1936, p. 11, as cited in *485*, series 210.1. **Cols. 7, 10, 11, 13, and 14:** Estimates in *485*, series 210.1.

22. Refined copper–**Col. 1:** *162a*, 1933, p. 34. **Cols. 2 and 5:** *228*, p. 190. **Cols. 3 and 4:** *173*, No. 5–6, 1934, pp. 79–80. **Col. 7:** *171*, No. 20, 1935, p. 6. **Cols. 8, 11, 12, and 13:** *157*, pp. 70–71. **Col. 10:** Based on 1936 output (col. 11) and percentage of plan fulfilled (col. 12). **Col. 14:** Estimate in *472*, p. 420.

23. Lead–**Col. 1:** Based on 1933 output (col. 2) and percentage of plan fulfilled (col. 3). **Cols. 2, 5, and 8:** *264*, No. 3, 1936, p. 7, as cited in *485*, series 209.1. *228*, p. 190, gives 13.67 and 27.17 th. m. t. for cols. 2 and 5. **Cols. 3 and 4:** *173*, No. 5–6, 1934, pp. 79–81. **Cols. 7, 10, 11, and 13:** Estimates in *485*, series 209.1. **Col. 14:** *472*, p. 421.

24. Mineral fertilizer–**Cols. 2, 5, 8, 11, and 14:** *187*, p. 192.

25. Phosphoric fertilizer (14% P_2O_5)–**Col. 1:** *162a*, 1933, p. 35. **Col. 2:** *154*, p. 136. **Col. 4:** *173*, No. 5–6, 1934, p. 207. **Cols. 5, 7, and 10:** *156*, p. 422. **Cols. 8, 11, and 13:** *157*, pp. 90–91. **Col. 14:** Estimate in *485*, series 409.3.

26. Phosphoric fertilizer (18.7% P_2O_5)–**Cols. 1, 4, 7, 10, and 13:** Planned output in 14% P_2O_5 (series 25) converted into 18.7% P_2O_5. **Cols. 2, 5, 8, 11, and 14:** *187*, p. 192.

27. Ground natural phosphate–**Cols. 2, 5, 8, 11, and 14:** *187*, p. 192. **Col. 4:** *173*, No. 5–6, 1934, p. 207. **Cols. 7 and 10:** *156*, p. 412. **Col. 13:** *157*, pp. 90–91.

28. Potash fertilizer–**Cols. 2, 5, 8, 11, and 14:** *187*, p. 192. **Col. 10:** *315*, No. 4, 1936, p. 197, as cited in *485*, series 412.4.

29. Ammonium sulfate–**Cols. 2, 5, 8, 11, and 14:** *187*, p. 192. **Col. 4:** *173*, No. 5–6, 1934, p. 87.

30. Soda ash–**Col. 1:** *315*, No. 7, 1934, p. 12, as cited in *485*, series 406.1. **Cols. 2, 5, 8, 11, and 14:** *187*, p. 194. **Col. 4:** *173*, No. 5–6, 1934, p. 87. **Cols. 7 and 10:** *156*, p. 422. **Col. 13:** *157*, p. 91.

31. Caustic soda–**Col. 1:** Total planned output of soda (given as 476.5 th. m. t. in *162a*, 1933, p. 35) minus soda ash (series 30, col. 1). **Cols. 2, 5, 8, 11, and 14:** *187*, p. 194. **Col. 10:** *315*, No. 4, 1936, p. 197, as cited in *485*, series 420.1. **Col. 13:** *315*, No. 7, 1934, p. 12, as cited in *485*, series 420.1. Covers only three main plants.

32. Sulfuric acid–**Col. 1:** *315*, No. 2, 1933, p. 3, as cited in *485*, series 401.3. **Cols. 2, 5, 8, 11, and 14:** *187*, p. 196. **Col. 4:** *173*, No. 5–6, 1934, p. 87. **Cols. 7 and 10:** *156*, p. 422. **Col. 13:** *157*, p. 91.

32a. Synthetic rubber–**Cols. 2 and 5:** *229*, p. 179. **Col. 4:** *173*, No. 5–6, 1934, p. 88. **Col. 7:** *171*, No. 20, 1935, p. 57. **Cols. 8, 11, and 14:** *223*, p. 247. **Col. 10:** Based on output during first quarter of 1936 (given as 10.592 th. m. t. in *175*, No. 5, 1936, p. 199) and statement that this output amounted to 25% of 1936 annual plan (in *173*, No. 5, 1936, p. 199).

33. Tires–**Cols. 2, 5, 8, 11, and 14:** *187*, p. 199. **Cols. 4 and 7:** *155*, p. 520. **Col. 10:** *156*, p. 423. Sum of ordinary and "giant" tires. **Col. 13:** *157*, p. 93.

34. Plastics–**Cols. 2, 5, and 8:** *215*, p. 172. **Col. 10:** *173*, No. 3, 1937, p. 233. **Cols. 11 and 13:** *157*, p. 93. **Col. 14:** *173*, No. 3, 1939, p. 89.

34a. Synthetic dyes–**Cols. 1, 7, 10, and 13:** *315*, No. 7, 1934, p. 23, as cited in *485*, series 415.1. **Cols. 2, 5, and 8:** *215*, p. 171. **Col. 4:** *315*, No. 3, 1934, p. 2, as cited in *485*, series 415.1. **Col. 11:** *173*, No. 8, 1937, p. 190. **Col. 14:** Estimate from *472*, p. 425, series 412.

35. Cement–**Col. 1:** *162a*, 1933, p. 34. Given for cement milling. **Cols. 2, 5, 8, 11, and 14:** *187*, p. 277. **Col. 4:** *173*, No. 5–6, 1934, p. 207. **Col. 7:** *155*, p. 521. **Col. 10:** *156*, p. 423. **Col. 13:** *157*, p. 93.

36. Lime–**Cols. 2 and 5:** *215*, p. 227. **Col. 4:** *173*, No. 5–6, 1934, p. 207. **Col. 7:** *155*, p. 523. Excludes collective farm production. **Cols. 8, 11, and 13:** *157*, pp. 92–93. **Col. 10:** *156*, p. 424. **Col. 14:** *187*, p. 282. Sum of construction lime and technological lime.

37. Window glass–**Col. 1:** Based on 1933 output (col. 2) and percentage of plan fulfilled (col. 3). **Cols. 2, 5, 8, 11, and 14:** *187*, p. 312. **Col. 3:** *162a*, 1933, p. 34. Applies to output in tons. **Col. 4:** *173*, No. 5–6, 1934, p. 210. **Col. 7:** *155*, pp. 538–39. **Col. 10:** *156*, p. 429. **Col. 13:** *157*, p. 101.

38a. Roofing tiles (excluding collective farm output)–**Cols. 2 and 7:** *155*, p. 523. **Col. 4:** *173*, No. 5–6, 1934, p. 207. **Cols. 5 and 10:** *156*, p. 424. **Cols. 8, 11, and 13:** *157*, pp. 94–95. This source also mentions a 64% fulfillment of 1936 annual plan, which perhaps refers to a revised plan. **Col. 14:** *254*, p. 205.

39. Asbestos shingles–**Cols. 2, 5, 8, 11, and 14:** *187*, p. 299. **Cols. 4 and 7:** *155*, p. 523. **Col. 10:** *156*, p. 424. **Col. 13:** *157*, p. 95.

40. Bricks–**Cols. 2, 5, 8, 11, and 14:** *187*, p. 291. **Cols. 4 and 7:** *155*, p. 522. Excludes collective farm production. **Col. 10:** *426*, p. 86. **Col. 13:** *157*, p. 95. Excludes collective farm production.

41. Industrial timber hauled–**Col. 1:** *162a*, 1933, p. 35. **Cols. 2, 5, 8, 11, and 14:** *187*, p. 249. **Cols. 4 and 7:** *155*, p. 528. **Col. 10:** *156*, p. 424. **Col. 13:** *157*, p. 95.

Table A-2 *continued*

42. Lumber–**Col. 1:** Based on 1933 output (col. 2) and percentage of plan fulfilled (col. 3). **Cols. 2, 5, 8, 11, and 14:** *187*, p. 261. **Col. 3:** *162a*, 1933, p. 34. Given for limited coverage. **Col. 4:** Based on 1934 output (col. 5) and percentage of plan fulfilled (col. 6). **Col. 6:** Derived from 1934 planned and actual output for smaller, incomplete coverage (given as 25.72 and 24.91 mill. m³, respectively, in *155*, p. 530). **Col. 7:** Based on 1934 output (col. 5) and increase planned for 1935 (given as 9.7% for incomplete coverage in *155*, p. 530). **Col. 10:** Based on 1935 output (col. 8) and increase planned for 1936 (given as 20% from *156*, p. 425). **Col. 13:** Based on 1936 output (col. 11) and increase planned for 1937 (given as 18% from *157*, pp. 94–95).

43. Plywood–**Cols. 2, 5, 8, 11, and 14:** *187*, p. 261. **Cols. 4 and 7:** Planned output of Commissariat of Timber Industry (given as 489.0 and 503.3 th. m³, respectively, in *155*, p. 530) increased by 8 th. m³ to cover total output (since that was the difference between output of commissariat and total output in 1933 and 1935). **Col. 10:** Planned output of Commissariat of the Timber Industry (given as 614.0 th. m³ in *156*, p. 426) increased by 8 th. m³ to cover total output. **Col. 13:** Planned output of Commissariat of the Timber Industry (given as 775.6 th. m³ in *157*, p. 95) increased by 8 th. m³ to cover total output.

44. Paper–**Col. 1:** *153*, p. 52. **Cols. 2, 5, 8, 11, and 14:** *187*, p. 268. **Col. 4:** *173*, No. 5–6, 1934, p. 208. **Col. 7:** *155*, p. 530. **Col. 10:** *156*, p. 426. **Col. 13:** *157*, p. 97.

45. Paperboard–**Cols. 2, 4, and 7:** *155*, p. 531. **Cols. 5 and 10:** *156*, p. 426. **Cols. 8, 11, and 13:** *157*, pp. 96–97. **Col. 14:** *254*, p. 209.

46. Machine tools–**Col. 2:** *187*, p. 207. **Col. 4:** *173*, No. 5–6, 1934, p. 206. Excludes tool-grinding machines. See *155*, p. 517, note 4. **Col. 5:** *215*, p. 71. Excludes tool-grinding machines (3,056) and polishing tools (832). **Col. 7:** *155*, p. 516, note 4. Covers plants under *Glavstankoinstrument* and other plants under the Commissariats of Heavy Industry and Local Industry planned by that *Glavk*. Includes tool-grinding machines. **Col. 8:** *156*, p. 417. Same coverage as col. 7. These figures have been used, although they do not cover total production, because the plan and actual figures are comparable. Total production was 33,900 (*187*, p. 207). **Col. 10:** *156*, p. 417. Excludes machine tools produced by the Commissariat of Agriculture. **Cols. 11 and 13:** *157*, p. 73. Covers production of Commissariats of Heavy Industry, Local Industry, Education, and Internal Affairs of the Russian Republic. Although not covering total production, these figures are closer in coverage to those used for 1936. Total production in 1936 was 44,400 (*187*, p. 207). **Col. 14:** *254*, p. 207. This seems closest in coverage to col. 13. On the coverage problem, see *485*, series 1009.1, notes.

46a. Metallurgical equipment–**Cols. 2, 4, and 7:** *155*, p. 516. Equipment for rolling mills produced by factories of Kramatorsk, Uralsk, Izhorsk, Krasnoe Sormovo, and Zlatoust. **Cols. 5, 8, and 10:** *156*, p. 419. Equipment for rolling mills. For col. 10, sum of different types of equipment. **Col. 11:** Estimate from *485*, series 1010.2.

47. Steam and gas turbines–**Col. 1:** Based on 1932 output (given as 239.0 th. kw in *498*, p. 308) and increase planned for 1933 (given as 154.5% in *173*, No. 1–2, 1933, p. 32). **Cols. 2 and 5:** *215*, p. 225. **Cols. 4 and 7:** *155*, p. 514. Steam turbines only. **Cols. 8 and 13:** *157*, p. 70–71. Steam turbines only. **Col. 10:** *156*, p. 418. Steam turbines only. **Col. 11:** *30*, p. 26, as cited in *472*, p. 440. **Col. 14:** *187*, p. 214.

48. Steam boilers–**Col. 1:** Based on 1932 output (given as 40 th. m² from *186*, p. 448) and increase planned for 1933 (given as 294.3% in *173*, No. 1–2, 1933, p. 32). **Cols. 2, 4, 5, and 7:** *155*, p. 514. Covers *Glavenergoprom*, which does not account for total production. **Cols. 8 and 10:** *156*, p. 418. For col. 10, includes 15.3 th. m² for Commissariat of Transportation. **Cols. 11 and 13:** *157*, p. 71. Comparable coverage. Total production in 1936 was 265.4 th. m² (*30*, p. 26, as cited in *472*, p. 439). **Col. 14:** *254*, p. 206. This seems the closest coverage to col. 13. Total production was 268.2 th. m² (*187*, p. 214).

49. Turbogenerators–**Col. 1:** *162a*, 1933, p. 34. **Cols. 2, 5, and 8:** *215*, p. 225. **Cols. 4 and 7:** *155*, p. 515. **Col. 10:** *156*, p. 418. Also, *162a*, Dec. 1933, p. 18. **Col. 11:** *162a*, Dec. 1936, pp. 18–19. **Col. 13:** Based on 1937 plan for all generators (given as 1,335 th. kw in *157*, p. 71) and ratio of total generators to turbogenerators (derived as 1.39 from 1936 plan for all generators of 880.0 th. kw and 1936 plan for turbogenerators in col. 10). **Col. 14:** *187*, p. 214.

50. Spinning machines–**Cols. 2 and 5:** *215*, p. 73. Given as water frames. **Cols. 4 and 7:** *155*, p. 517. **Cols. 8 and 13:** *157*, pp. 74–75. **Col. 10:** Based on 1936 output and percentage of 1936 plan fulfilled for different coverage (given as 690 units and 77%, respectively, in *157*, p. 75). **Col. 11:** *438*, p. 13. Given as other frames. **Col. 14:** *254*, p. 207.

51. Looms–**Cols. 2 and 8:** *215*, p. 73. **Cols. 4, 5, and 7:** *155*, p. 517. Covers automatic looms produced by Commissariat of Heavy Industry. **Col. 10:** Based on 1936 output (col. 11) and percentage of plan fulfilled (col. 12). **Cols. 11, 12, and 13:** *157*, p. 75. Commissariat of Heavy Industry. **Col. 14:** *254*, p. 207.

52. Tractors–**Col. 1:** *153*, p. 118. **Cols. 2, 5, 8, and 11:** *187*, p. 226. **Cols. 4 and 7:** *155*, p. 511. Excludes traction engines. **Col. 10:** *156*, p. 416. Sum of wheel, caterpillar, and cultivator tractors. Excludes traction engines. **Col. 13:** *157*, p. 83.

53. Tractors (15 hp units)–**Col. 1:** Derived from total horsepower (given as about 1 mill. in *153*, p. 53). **Cols. 2, 5, 8, 11, and 14:** *187*, p. 226. **Col. 4:** *173*, No. 5–6, 1934, p. 206. **Col. 7:** *155*, p. 511. Sum of wheel and caterpillar tractors. Excludes traction engines. **Col. 10:** *156*, p. 416. **Col. 13:** Derived from total horsepower (given as 2,590,000 in *157*, p. 83).

54. Motor vehicles, total–**Col. 1:** *153*, p. 118. **Cols. 2, 5, 8, 11, and 14:** *187*, p. 223. **Col. 4:** *173*, No. 5–6, 1934, p.

Table A-2 *continued*

206. **Col. 7:** *155*, p. 511. **Col. 10:** *156*, p. 416. **Col. 13:** *157*, p. 83.

55. Trucks and buses–**Col. 1:** *162a*, 1933, p. 34. Given as 34 thous. but, since this is a later source than *153*, the figure is assumed to have been adjusted and is therefore reduced in order to conform to total motor vehicles. **Cols. 2, 5, and 7:** *155*, p. 511. **Col. 4:** *173*, No. 5–6, 1934, p. 206. **Cols. 8, 11, and 13:** *157*, p. 83. **Col. 10:** *156*, p. 416. **Col. 14:** *254*, p. 206.

56. Automobiles–**Col. 1:** *162a*, 1933, p. 34. **Cols. 2, 5, 8, 11, and 14:** *187*, p. 223. **Col. 4:** *173*, No. 5–6, 1934, p. 206. **Col. 7:** *155*, p. 511. **Col. 10:** *156*, p. 416. **Col. 13:** *157*, p. 83.

57. Buses–**Cols. 2, 5, and 14:** *187*, p. 223. Total motor vehicles minus trucks and automobiles. **Cols. 8, 11, 12, and 13:** *157*, pp. 82–83. **Col. 10:** Based on 1936 output (col. 11) and percentage of plan fulfilled (col. 12).

58. Grain combines–**Col. 1:** *153*, p. 53. **Cols. 2, 5, and 8:** *215*, p. 77. **Col. 4:** *173*, No. 5–6, 1934, p. 206. **Col. 7:** *155*, p. 514. **Col. 10:** *156*, p. 416. **Cols. 11 and 14:** *187*, pp. 232–33. **Col. 13:** *157*, p. 79.

59. Steam locomotives–**Col. 1:** *153*, p. 118. **Cols. 2 and 8:** *215*, p. 74. **Cols. 4 and 7:** *155*, p. 513. Sum of different types. **Col. 5:** *229*, p. 163. Includes 45 locomotives that were not delivered to the Commissariat of Transportation. **Col. 10:** *156*, p. 414. Sum of different types. **Cols. 11 and 13:** *157*, p. 81. **Col. 14:** *187*, p. 220.

60. Diesel locomotives–**Cols. 2, 5, and 8:** *215*, p. 74. **Col. 4:** *173*, No. 5–6, 1934, p. 206. **Col. 7:** *155*, p. 512. **Col. 10:** *156*, p. 415. **Cols. 11 and 14:** *187*, p. 220.

61. Electric locomotives–**Cols. 2 and 5:** *215*, p. 74. **Col. 4:** *173*, No. 5–6, 1934, p. 206. **Col. 7:** *155*, p. 512. **Cols. 8, 11, and 14:** *187*, p. 220. **Col. 10:** *156*, p. 415. **Col. 13:** *157*, p. 81.

62. Railroad freight cars (units)–**Cols. 2, 5, and 8:** *215*, p. 74. Sum of different types. **Cols. 4 and 7:** *155*, p. 513. Sum of different types. **Col. 10:** *156*, p. 415. Sum of different types. **Cols. 11 and 13:** *157*, pp. 80–81. Sum of different types. **Col. 14:** *187*, p. 22.

63. Railroad freight cars (2-axle units)–**Col. 1:** *153*, p. 119. **Cols. 2, 5, and 8:** *215*, p. 74. **Col. 4:** *173*, No. 5–6, 1934, p. 206. Given as units in source but obviously should be thousands. **Col. 7:** *155*, p. 512. **Col. 10:** *156*, p. 415. **Cols. 11 and 13:** *157*, p. 81. **Col. 14:** *254*, p. 207. Output of Commissariat of Transportation.

64. Railroad passenger cars–**Col. 1:** *153*, p. 52. **Cols. 2, 5, and 8:** *215*, p. 75. Sum of different types. **Col. 4:** *173*, No. 5–6, 1934, p. 206. **Col. 7:** *155*, p. 513. **Col. 10:** *156*, p. 415. **Cols. 11 and 13:** *157*, p. 81. **Col. 14:** *254*, p. 207.

65. Excavators–**Col. 2:** *215*, p. 79. **Cols. 4 and 7:** *155*, p. 517. **Cols. 5 and 11:** *187*, p. 236. **Cols. 8 and 13:** *157*, pp. 76–77. **Col. 10:** *156*, p. 419. **Col. 14:** *254*, p. 207.

66. Ginned cotton–**Col. 1:** Based on 1932 output (given as 395.3 in *498*, p. 309) and increase planned for 1933 (given as 5.5% in *173*, No. 1–2, 1933, p. 47). **Cols. 2 and 5:** *215*, p. 202. **Cols. 8, 11, 12, and 13:** *157*, pp. 98–99. Primary cotton output. **Col. 10:** Based on 1936 output (col. 11) and percentage of plan fulfilled (col. 12). **Col. 14:** *187*, p. 324.

67. Cotton yarn–**Cols. 2 and 5:** *215*, p. 206. **Cols. 4 and 7:** *155*, pp. 534–35. Output of *Glavk* for Cotton Industry. **Cols. 8, 11, and 13:** *157*, p. 98. **Col. 10:** *156*, p. 427. **Col. 14:** *72*, p. 85.

68. Cotton fabrics–**Col. 1:** *153*, p. 119. **Cols. 2, 5, 8, 11, and 14:** *187*, p. 328. **Col. 4:** *173*, No. 5–6, 1934, p. 208. **Cols. 7 and 10:** *156*, p. 427. **Col. 13:** *157*, p. 99.

69. Woolen fabrics–**Col. 1:** Based on 1933 output (col. 2) and statement (in *173*, No. 5–6, 1934, p. 101) that 1933 plan was underfulfilled by around 7 mill. m. **Cols. 2 and 4:** *173*, No. 5–6, 1934, p. 208. **Cols. 5, 8, 11, and 14:** *187*, p. 328. **Col. 7:** *155*, pp. 534–35. **Col. 10:** *156*, p. 427. **Col. 13:** *157*, p. 99.

70. Linen fabrics (square meters)–**Col. 1:** *295*, No. 8, 1933, p. 47, as cited in *485*, series 1210.7. **Col. 2:** *215*, p. 210. **Col. 4:** *173*, No. 5–6, 1934, p. 208. **Col. 5:** *156*, p. 427. **Col. 7:** *155*, p. 535. Output of Commissariat of Light Industry. **Cols. 8, 11, and 14:** Estimates in *485*, series 1210.7. **Cols. 10–11:** *162a*, Dec. 1936, pp. 22–23. Given for linen and semilinen fabrics.

71. Linen fabrics (meters)–**Cols. 2, 5, 8, 11, and 14:** *187*, p. 328. **Col. 10:** *156*, p. 427, as cited in *485*, series 1209.7. **Col. 13:** *157*, p. 99.

72. Silk and rayon fabrics–**Col. 1:** *12*, Vol. 62, p. 253, as cited in *485*, series 1213.1. **Cols. 2, 5, 8, 11, and 14:** *187*, p. 328. **Col. 4:** *173*, No. 5–6, 1934, p. 209. **Col. 7:** *155*, p. 666. Market production. **Col. 10:** *156*, p. 427. **Col. 13:** *157*, p. 99.

73. Knitted underwear–**Cols. 2, 5, 11, and 14:** *187*, p. 343. **Col. 7:** *155*, pp. 534–35. **Cols. 8 and 13:** *157*, pp. 98–99. **Col. 10:** *156*, p. 428.

74. Knitted outer garments–**Cols. 2, 5, 8, and 11:** *187*, p. 343. **Col. 7:** *155*, pp. 534–35. **Col. 10:** *156*, p. 428. **Col. 13:** *157*, p. 99. **Col. 14:** *254*, p. 209. Output of limited coverage. Total output was 45.1 mill. (*187*, p. 343).

75. Hosiery–**Col. 1:** Based on 1933 output (col. 2) and statement (in *173*, No. 5–6, 1934, p. 101) that 1933 plan was underfulfilled by 22 mill. pairs. **Cols. 2, 5, 8, 11, and 14:** *187*, p. 343. **Col. 4:** *173*, No. 5–6, 1934, p. 209. **Col. 7:** *155*, p. 666. Market production. **Col. 10:** *156*, p. 428. **Col. 13:** *157*, p. 99.

76. Leather shoes–**Col. 1:** Based on 1933 output (col. 2) and statement (in *173*, No. 5–6, 1934, p. 101) that 1933 plan was underfulfilled by state industry by 6.5 mill. pairs. *153*, p. 119, gives 81.5, but this does not cover total planned output. **Cols. 2 and 14:** *187*, p. 351. **Cols. 4 and 5:** *155*, p. 536. Coverage incomplete but comparable for both planned and actual output. Total output was 85.4 mill. pairs (*187*, p. 351). **Cols. 7 and 8:** *156*, p. 429. Coverage

Table A-2   *continued*

incomplete but comparable for both planned and actual output. Total output was 103.6 mill. pairs (*187*, p. 351). **Col. 10:** *173*, No. 3, 1937, p. 235. **Col. 11:** *157*, p. 101. Coverage incomplete but comparable with planned output. Total output was 143.2 mill. pairs (*187*, p. 351). **Col. 13:** *157*, p. 101.

77. Felt footwear–**Cols. 2, 4, and 5:** *155*, p. 536. **Cols. 7, 8, and 10:** *156*, p. 429. **Cols. 11 and 13:** *157*, p. 101. For col. 13, sum of felt footwear (*valenki*), felt galoshes and slippers produced by Commissariat of Local Industry, and felt footwear (*fetrovaia obuv*) produced by Commissariat of Local Industry and industrial cooperatives. **Col. 14;** *187*, p. 323. Includes *fetrovaia obuv*.

78. Rubber footwear–**Col. 1:** *162a*, 1933, p. 35. **Cols. 2, 5, 8, 11, and 14:** *187*, p. 199. **Col. 4:** *173*, No. 5–6, 1934, p. 209. Commissariat of Heavy Industry. **Col. 7:** *155*, p. 519. **Col. 10:** *156*, p. 423. **Col. 13:** *157*, p. 92. Includes galoshes.

79. Rubber galoshes–**Cols. 2, 5, and 8:** *215*, p. 176. **Cols. 4 and 7:** *155*, p. 668. Market production of Commissariat of Heavy Industry. **Col. 10:** *156*, p. 423n. **Cols. 11 and 13:** *157*, p. 93. **Col. 14:** *254*, p. 205. Commissariat of Chemical Industry.

80. Metal beds–**Cols. 2, 4, 5, and 7:** *155*, p. 670. Market production. **Cols. 8, 11, and 13:** *157*, p. 89. Includes output of Commissariats of Heavy Industry, Local Industry, and Defense Industry and industrial cooperatives. **Col. 10:** *173*, No. 3, 1937, p. 233. Includes same output as col. 8 above. **Col. 14:** *254*, p. 208.

80a. Enameled kitchenware–**Cols. 2, 4, 5, and 7:** *155*, p. 669. Market production of Commissariats of Heavy Industry and Local Industry. **Cols. 8, 11, and 13:** *157*, p. 89. **Col. 10:** *156*, p. 421. **Col. 14:** *254*, p. 208.

81. Motorcycles–**Cols. 2, 5, and 8:** *215*, p. 83. **Col. 10:** *156*, p. 416. **Col. 13:** *157*, p. 89. **Col. 14:** *187*, p. 362.

82. Bicycles–**Cols. 2, 4, 5, and 7:** *155*, p. 671. Market production. **Cols. 8, 11, and 13:** *157*, pp. 88–89. **Col. 10:** *156*, p. 421. **Col. 14:** *187*, p. 362.

83. Radios–**Cols. 2 and 5:** *66*, p. 176, as cited in *472*, p. 458. **Col. 4:** *173*, No. 5–6, 1934, p. 207. **Col. 7:** *156*, p. 421. Includes production of industrial cooperatives and Commisariat of Communications. **Cols. 8 and 10:** *173*, No. 3, 1937, p. 233. Receivers. **Cols. 11 and 13:** *157*, p. 89. **Col. 14:** *188*, p. 407.

83a. Refrigerators, household–**Col. 10:** *156*, p. 421. **Col. 14:** *254*, p. 208.

84. Sewing machines, household–**Cols. 2, 4, 5, and 7:** *155*, p. 670. Market production of Commissariat of Heavy Industry. **Cols. 8, 11, and 13:** *157*, p. 89. **Col. 10:** *156*, p. 421. **Col. 14:** *187*, p. 362.

85. Clocks and watches–**Cols. 2, 5, and 8:** *215*, p. 226. **Col. 11:** *188*, p. 406. **Col. 14:** *187*, p. 362.

86. Cameras–**Cols. 2, 5, and 8:** *215*, p. 83. **Col. 4:** *173*, No. 5–6, 1934, p. 207. **Col. 7:** *155*, p. 670. Market production. **Col. 10:** *156*, p. 421. **Cols. 11 and 13:** *157*, p. 89. **Col. 14:** *187*, p. 362.

87. Phonographs–**Cols. 2 and 5:** *215*, p. 83. **Col. 4:** *173*, No. 5–6, 1934, p. 207. **Col. 7:** *155*, p. 518. Sum of output of Commissariat of Heavy Industry and industrial cooperatives. **Cols. 8, 11, and 13:** *157*, pp. 88–89. For col. 8, also *215*, p. 83. **Col. 10:** *156*, p. 421. Includes output of industrial cooperatives. **Col. 14:** *254*, p. 208.

88. Soap (40% fatty acid)–**Cols. 2 and 7:** *155*, p. 543. **Col. 4:** *173*, No. 5–6, 1934, p. 211. **Cols. 5 and 10:** *156*, p. 430. **Cols. 8, 11, and 13:** *157*, p. 103. **Col. 14:** *187*, p. 372.

89. Bread and breadstuffs (large-scale industry)–**Cols. 2 and 5:** *229*, p. 214. **Col. 7:** *155*, p. 663. Market production of baked bread. **Cols. 8, 11, and 13:** *157*, pp. 102–3. Bread and bakery products. **Col. 10:** *156*, p. 432. **Col. 14:** *173*, No. 5, 1939, p. 161. *254*, p. 210, gives 19.1 mill. m. t.

89a. Bread and breadstuffs (ministries and local Soviets)–**Cols. 2, 5, 8, 11, and 14:** *316*, p. 171.

90. Flour (total)–**Cols. 2 and 5:** Estimates in *485*, series 1126.5. **Col. 14:** *254*, p. 210. Sum of output of Commissariats of Agricultural Procurement and the Food Industry.

90b. Flour (procurements)–**Cols. 1 and 2:** *162a*, 1933, p. 35. **Cols. 2, 4, 5, and 7:** *155*, p. 663. **Cols. 8 and 10:** *156*, p. 432. **Cols. 10-11:** *162a*, Dec. 1936, pp. 24–25. Commissariat of the Food Industry. **Col. 13:** *162a*, April 1937, p. 18. **Col. 14:** *254*, p. 210.

91. Macaroni–**Col. 1:** *172*, p. 29. **Cols. 2 and 4:** *173*, No. 5–6, 1934, p. 211. For col. 2, Commissariat of Food Supply. **Cols. 5 and 10:** *156*, p. 431. **Col. 7:** *155*, p. 665. Market production. **Cols. 8, 11 and 14:** *187*, p. 403–4. **Col. 13:** *157*, p. 105.

92. Raw sugar–**Col. 1:** *172*, p. 20. **Cols. 2, 5, and 8:** *215*, p. 220. **Col. 4:** *173*, No. 5–6, 1934, p. 210. **Col. 7:** *155*, p. 665. Market production. **Col. 10:** *156*, p. 430. **Cols. 11 and 14:** *187*, p. 373. **Col. 13:** *157*, p. 103.

93. Starch and syrup–**Col. 1:** *172*, p. 25. **Cols. 2 and 4:** *173*, No. 5–6, 1934, p. 211. Commissariat of Food Supply. **Col. 5:** *229*, p. 227. **Col. 7:** *155*, p. 546. **Cols. 8 and 13:** *157*, pp. 104–5. **Col. 10:** *156*, p. 431. **Cols. 11 and 14:** *316*, p. 179. For col. 14, also *187*, p. 372.

94. Fish catch–**Cols. 2 and 7:** *155*, p. 543. **Col. 4:** *173*, No. 5–6, 1934, p. 210. **Cols. 5, 8, 11, and 14:** *187*, p. 381. **Col. 10:** *156*, p. 430. **Col. 13:** *157*, p. 103.

95. Crude alcohol–**Col. 1:** *172*, p. 23. Also, *162a*, 1933, p. 35. **Col. 2:** *162a*, 1933, p. 35. **Col. 4:** *173*, No. 5–6, 1934, p. 116. **Cols. 5 and 8:** *229*, p. 23. **Cols. 7 and 10:** *156*, p. 431. **Cols. 11 and 14:** *187*, p. 405. **Col. 13:** *157*, p. 102.

96. Vegetable oil–**Col. 1:** *172*, p. 21. **Cols. 2 and 7:** *155*, p. 664. Market production of Commissariats of Food Industry and Local Industry. **Col. 4:** *173*, No. 5–6, 1934, p. 210. **Col. 5:** *229*, p. 23. Large-scale industry, which seems to correspond to planned output. **Cols. 8, 11, and 13:** *157*, p. 102. Incomplete coverage, which seems to correspond to large-scale industry. **Col. 10:** *156*, p. 430. Incomplete coverage. **Col. 14:** *254*, p. 210. Incomplete coverage. *187*, p. 392, gives a more complete figure of 539 th. m. t.

Table A-2   *continued*

97. Butter–**Cols. 2 and 5:** *215*, p. 220. **Cols. 4 and 7:** *155*, p. 664. Market production. **Cols. 8 and 13:** *157*, p. 105. **Col. 10:** *156*, p. 431. **Col. 11:** *187*, p. 386. **Col. 14:** *72*, p. 86.

98. Cheese–**Col. 1:** *172*, p. 28. **Cols. 2 and 4:** *173*, No. 5–6, 1934, p. 211. For col. 2, Commissariat of Food Supply. **Cols. 5 and 7:** *155*, p. 664. Market production of Commissariat of the Food Industry and *Tsentrosoiuz*. **Cols. 8 and 10:** *156*, p. 431. **Cols. 11 and 13:** *157*, p. 105. **Col. 14:** *313*, p. 12, as cited in *472*, p. 450.

99. Meat–**Col. 1:** *172*, p. 20. **Cols. 2, 4, 5, and 7:** *155*, pp. 543 and 663. For cols. 4, 5, and 7, market production. Includes Commissariats of the Food Industry and Local Industry and artisan industry. **Col. 8:** Total meat output (given as 585.6 th. m. t. in *229*, p. 215) minus output of sausages (given as 112 th. m. t. in *157*, p. 102). **Col. 10:** *156*, p. 430. Commissariat of the Food Industry. **Cols. 11 and 13:** *157*, p. 104. Commissariat of the Food Industry. **Col. 14:** *254*, p. 210. Commissariat of the Meat and Dairy Industry.

100. Meat and subproducts of first category–**Cols. 2, 5, 8, 11, and 14:** *187*, p. 378.

101. Sausages–**Col. 1:** *172*, p. 28. **Cols. 2 and 5:** *229*, p. 215. Coverage may be smaller than that of col. 1. **Cols. 7, 8, and 10:** *156*, p. 430. Commissariat of the Food Industry. **Cols. 11 and 13:** *157*, p. 104. Commissariat of the Food Industry. **Col. 14:** *254*, p. 210.

102. Canned food–**Col. 1:** *172*, p. 27. **Cols. 2 and 4:** *173*, No. 5–6, 1934, p. 210. Commissariat of Food Supply. **Col. 5:** *155*, p. 544. Sum of output of Commissariats of the Food Industry, Local Industry, and Domestic Trade. **Col. 7:** *155*, p. 544. Includes output of three above-mentioned commissariats and *Tsentrosoiuz* and *Vsekopromsovet*. **Cols. 8 and 10:** *156*, p. 431. **Cols. 11 and 13:** *157*, p. 104. **Col. 14:** *187*, p. 398.

103. Confectionery–**Col. 1:** *172*, p. 24. Sum of output of Commissariat of Food Supply and industrial cooperatives. **Cols. 2 and 5:** *215*, p. 228. **Col. 4:** *173*, No. 5–6, 1934, p. 211. **Col. 7:** *155*, p. 664. Market production. **Cols. 8 and 13:** *157*, pp. 104–5. **Col. 10:** *156*, p. 431. **Col. 11:** Estimate in *485*, series 1127.5. **Col. 14:** *254*, p. 210.

104. Margarine–**Col. 1:** *172*, p. 21. **Cols. 2 and 5:** *215*, p. 220. **Col. 4:** *173*, No. 5–6, 1934, p. 210. **Col. 7:** *155*, p. 664. Market production of Commissariat of the Food Industry. **Cols. 8, 11, and 13:** *157*, pp. 104–5. Commissariat of the Food Industry. **Col. 10:** *156*, p. 431. **Col. 14:** *187*, p. 372.

105. Beer–**Cols. 2 and 5:** *229*, p. 228. State industry. **Cols. 4 and 7:** *155*, p. 672. Market production. **Cols. 8, 11, and 13:** *157*, pp. 104–5. **Col. 10:** *156*, p. 432. **Col. 14:** *187*, p. 372.

106. Cigarettes–**Col. 1:** *172*, p. 24. **Cols. 2 and 5:** *215*, p. 221. **Col. 4:** *173*, No. 5–6, 1934, p. 211. **Col. 10:** *156*, p. 431. **Col. 7:** *155*, p. 672. Market production. **Cols. 8 and 13:** *157*, pp. 104–5. **Col. 11:** *316*, p. 177. **Col. 14:** *187*, p. 372.

107. Matches–**Col. 1:** Based on 1933 output (given as 7.0 mill. crates in *173*, No. 5–6, 1934, p. 210) and statement (in *173*, No. 5–6, 1934, p. 101) that 1933 plan was underfulfilled by 2.4 mill. **Cols. 2 and 5:** *215*, p. 227. **Col. 4:** *173*, No. 5–6, 1934, p. 210. **Col. 7:** *155*, p. 672. Market production. **Cols. 8 and 11:** *113*, No. 6–7, 1946, pp. 13 and 15, as cited in *472*, p. 454. **Col. 10:** *156*, p. 426. **Col. 13:** *157*, p. 99. **Col. 14:** *72*, p. 84.

108. Low-grade tobacco (*makhorka*)–**Col. 1:** *172*, p. 24. Sum of smoking and snuff *makhorka*. **Cols. 2 and 5:** *215*, p. 221. Sum of smoking and snuff *makhorka*. **Col. 4:** *173*, No. 5–6, 1934, p. 211. **Col. 7:** *155*, p. 545. Commissariat of the Food Industry. **Cols. 8 and 10:** *156*, p. 431. **Cols. 11 and 13:** *157*, p. 105. **Col. 14:** *72*, p. 86.

109. Salt–**Col. 1:** *172*, p. 26. **Cols. 2, 5, and 8:** *229*, p. 174. **Col. 4:** *173*, No. 5–6, 1934, p. 211. **Col. 7:** *155*, p. 548. **Col. 10:** *156*, p. 431. **Col. 11:** Estimate in *472*, p. 451. **Col. 13:** Planned output of Commissariats of the Food Industry and Local Industry (given as 3,212 th. m. t. in *157*, p. 105) increased by 4% to cover total production (derived from *229*, p. 174, and *157*, p. 104). **Col. 14:** *187*, p. 372.

AGRICULTURE

110. Total value of production (1926/27 prices)–**Cols. 2 and 5:** *215*, p. 238. **Col. 4:** *173*, No. 5–6, 1934, p. 198. **Col. 7:** *155*, p. 585. **Col. 8:** *469*, p. 2. **Col. 10:** *156*, p. 433. **Col. 14:** *72*, p. 92.

110a. Total value of production (comparable prices)–**Cols. 2, 5, 8, 11, and 14:** Calculated from index (1913 = 100) in *142*, p. 350. **Col. 4:** *173*, No. 5–6, 1934, p. 198. In 1926/27 prices. **Col. 7:** *155*, p. 585. In 1926/27 prices. **Col. 10:** *156*, p. 433. In 1926/27 prices.

111. Vegetable production (1926/27 prices)–**Cols. 2 and 5:** *215*, p. 238. **Col. 4:** *173*, No. 5–6, 1934, p. 121. **Col. 7:** *155*, p. 585. **Col. 8:** *469*, p. 2. **Col. 10:** *155*, p. 433. **Col. 14:** *72*, p. 92.

111a. Vegetable production (comparable prices)–**Cols. 2, 5, 8, 11, and 14:** Calculated from index (1913 = 100) in *142*, p. 350. **Col. 4:** *173*, No. 5–6, 1934, p. 121. **Col. 7:** *155*, p. 585. **Col. 10:** *156*, p. 433.

112. Animal production (1926/27 prices)–**Cols. 2, 5, and 8:** *215*, p. 238. **Col. 4:** Total value of production (series 110) minus vegetable production (series 111). **Col. 7:** *155*, p. 585. **Col. 10:** *156*, p. 433. **Col. 14:** *72*, p. 92.

112a. Animal production (comparable prices)–**Cols. 2, 5, 8, 11, and 14:** Calculated from index (1913 = 100) in *142*, p. 350. **Col. 7:** *155*, p. 585. **Col. 10:** *156*, p. 433.

HARVESTS

113. Grain, total (biological yield)–**Col. 1:** *153*, p. 121. Probably barn yield. **Cols. 2, 5, and 8:** *215*, p. 286. **Col. 4:** *173*, No. 5–6, 1934, p. 213. **Col. 7:** *155*, p. 586. **Col. 10:** *156*, p. 435. **Col. 11:** *469*, p. 4. **Col. 13:** *157*, p. 25. Converted from poods (1 pood = .01638 m. t.). **Col. 14:** *72*, p. 94.

113a. Grain, total (barn yield)–**Col. 1:** *153*, p. 121. Assumed to be barn yield. **Cols. 2, 5, and 8:** *68*, No. 5, 1964, p.

Table A-2 *continued*

14. **Cols. 4, 7, 10, and 13:** Assumed to be the same as biological yield (series 113) since it is not known whether separate plans were made for barn yield. **Col. 11:** Total yield for 1933–1937 (derived as 364.5 mill. m. t. from average annual yield for 1933–1937 of 72.9 mill. m. t. in *142*, p. 352) minus yield for 1933 (col. 2), 1934 (col. 5), 1935 (col. 8), and 1937 (col. 14). **Col. 14:** *242*, p. 119.

114. Wheat (biological yield)–**Cols. 2 and 5:** *215*, p. 286. **Col. 4:** *173*, No. 5–6, 1934, p. 213. **Col. 7:** *155*, p. 586. **Col. 8:** *469*, p. 4. **Col. 10:** *156*, p. 436. **Col. 13:** *173*, No. 4, 1937, p. 71. **Col. 14:** *172*, p. 94.

115. Rye (biological yield)–**Cols. 2 and 5:** *215*, p. 286. **Col. 4:** *173*, No. 5–6, 1934, p. 213. Total food grain (meaning wheat and rye) minus wheat. **Col. 7:** *155*, p. 586. Total food grain minus wheat. **Col. 10:** *156*, p. 437. Total food grain minus wheat. **Cols. 8 and 14:** *469*, p. 4.

116. Barley (biological yield)–**Cols. 2 and 5:** *215*, p. 286. **Col. 4:** Estimated from planned area to be sown to barley (given as 7,677 th. hectares for spring barley in *173*, No. 5–6, 1934, p. 213, and 395 th. hectares for area actually sown to winter barley in 1934 in *215*, p. 272) and planned yield (given as 9.5 centners per hectare in *155*, p. 587). **Col. 7:** Estimated from planned area to be sown to barley (given as 7,730 th. hectares for spring barley in *155*, p. 588, and 466 th. hectares for area actually sown to winter barley in *215*, p. 272) and planned yield (given as 9.8 centners per hectare in *155*, p. 587). **Col. 8:** *469*, p. 5. **Col. 10:** Estimated from planned area to be sown to barley (given as 8,182 th. hectares for spring barley in *156*, p. 433, and estimated as 500 th. hectares for winter barley from 1935 area in col. 7 above and 1937 area of 600 in *179*, Vol. I, p. 6) and planned yield (given as 10.3 centners per hectare in *156*, p. 435). **Col. 13:** Estimated from planned area to be sown to barley (given as 8,134 th. hectares for spring barley in *157*, p. 106, and 600 th. hectares for winter barley in *179*, Vol. I, p. 6) and planned yield (given as 10.5 centners per hectare in *157*, p. 109). **Col. 14:** *72*, p. 94.

117. Oats (biological yield)–**Cols. 2 and 5:** *215*, p. 286. **Col. 4:** Estimated from planned sown area (given as 16,975 th. hectares in *173*, No. 5–6, 1934, p. 213) and planned yield (given as 9.5 centners per hectare in *155*, p. 587). **Col. 7:** Estimated from planned sown area (given as 17,365 th. hectares in *155*, p. 588) and planned yield (given as 10.1 centners per hectare in *155*, p. 588). **Cols. 8, 11, and 14:** *469*, p. 5. **Col. 10:** Estimated from planned sown area (given as 17,659 th. hectares in *156*, p. 433) and planned yield (given as 11.2 centners per hectare in *156*, p. 433). **Col. 13:** Estimated from planned sown area (given as 17,486 th. hectares in *157*, p. 106) and planned yield (given as 11.1 centners per hectare in *157*, p. 108).

118. Corn (biological yield)–**Cols. 2 and 5:** *215*, p. 286. **Cols. 4 and 7:** Estimated from planned sown area (derived as 3,649 and 3,259 th. hectares from area planned to be sown to spring corn and sorghum given as 3,752 and 3,425 th. hectares in *155*, p. 588, minus actual area sown to sorghum in 1934 and 1935, derived as 103.4 and 166.8 th. hectares from *155*, p. 588, *156*, p. 433, and *215*, p. 272) and planned yield (given as 12.5 and 12.8 centners per hectare in *155*, p. 587). **Cols. 8, 11, and 14:** *469*, p. 5. **Col. 10:** Estimated from planned sown area (given as 2,751 th. hectares in *156*, p. 482) and planned yield (given as 16.0 centners per hectare in *156*, p. 435). **Col. 13:** Estimated from planned sown area (given as 2,781 th. hectares in *157*, p. 106) and planned yield (given as 17.0 centners per hectare in *157*, p. 109).

HARVESTS OF TECHNICAL CROPS

119. Raw cotton (biological yield)–**Col. 1:** *153*, p. 121. **Col. 2:** *204*, p. 192, as cited in *472*, p. 430. **Col. 4:** *173*, No. 5–6, 1934, p. 213. **Cols. 5 and 8:** *215*, p. 287. **Col. 7:** *155*, p. 586. **Col. 10:** *156*, p. 436. **Col. 11:** *173*, No. 8, 1937, p. 196. **Col. 13:** *469*, p. 6. **Col. 14:** *72*, p. 94.

120. Sugar beets (biological yield)–**Col. 1:** *153*, p. 121. **Cols. 2, 5, and 8:** *215*, p. 287. **Col. 4:** *173*, No. 5–6, 1934, p. 213. **Col. 7:** *155*, p. 586. **Col. 10:** *156*, p. 436. **Col. 11:** *469*, p. 6. **Col. 13:** *157*, p. 25. **Col. 14:** *72*, p. 94.

121. Sunflowers (biological yield)–**Col. 1:** *153*, p. 121. **Cols. 2, 5, 8, and 14:** *469*, p. 6. **Col. 4:** *173*, No. 5–6, 1934, p. 213. **Col. 7:** *135*, p. 586. **Col. 10:** *136*, p. 436. **Col. 11:** *449*, p. 792. **Col. 13:** *157*, p. 25.

122. Flax fiber (biological yield)–**Col. 1:** *153*, p. 121. **Cols. 2 and 11:** *469*, p. 6. **Col. 4:** *173*, No. 5–6, 1934, p. 213. **Cols. 5 and 8:** *229*, p. 347. **Col. 7:** *155*, p. 586. **Col. 10:** *156*, p. 436. **Col. 13:** *157*, p. 25. **Col. 14:** *72*, p. 94.

123. Hemp (biological yield)–**Cols. 2 and 5:** *449*, p. 792.

124. Potatoes (biological yield)–**Cols. 2 and 8:** *229*, p. 345. **Col. 4:** *173*, No. 5–6, 1934, p. 213. **Cols. 5 and 11:** *469*, p. 6. **Col. 7:** *155*, p. 586. **Col. 10:** *156*, p. 436. **Col. 13:** *157*, p. 25. **Col. 14:** *254*, p. 218.

ANIMAL PRODUCTION

125. Meat and fat, excl. rabbit and poultry (dead weight)–**Cols. 2, 4, and 7:** *155*, pp. 612–13. **Cols. 5 and 10:** *156*, p. 444. **Cols. 8, 11, 13, and 14:** *469*, p. 34.

126. Milk–**Cols. 2, 4, and 7:** *155*, pp. 612–13. **Cols. 5, 8, 11, and 13:** *469*, p. 34. **Col. 10:** *156*, p. 444. **Col. 14:** *254*, p. 218.

127. Eggs–**Col. 14:** *449*, p. 777. Estimate.

128. Wool–**Cols. 2, 4, and 7:** *155*, pp. 612–13. **Cols. 5 and 10:** *156*, p. 444. **Cols. 8, 11, and 13:** *469*, p. 35. **Col. 14:** *254*, p. 218.

Table A-2 *continued*

MARKET PRODUCTION

129. Grain–**Cols. 2, 5, and 7:** *155*, p. 662. **Col. 4:** *173*, No. 5–6, 1934, p. 166. **Cols. 8 and 14:** *469*, p. 4. **Col. 10:** *156*, p. 464.

130. Raw cotton–**Col. 2:** Based on 1932/33 market production (given as 73.4 mill. poods in *173*, No. 7, 1939, p. 162, and converted at 1 pood = .01638 m. t.) and increase in 1933 (given as 6.8% in *173*, No. 5–6, 1934, p. 166). **Col. 4:** Based on 1933 market production (col. 2) and increase planned for 1934 (given as 9% in *173*, No. 5–6, 1934, p. 166). **Col. 5:** Estimated to be 20,000 m. t. smaller than total harvest (series 119 above), the same difference as in the 1934 plan (col. 4). **Col. 14:** *173*, No. 7, 1939, p. 162. For 1937/38. Converted at 1 pood = .01638 m. t.

131. Sugar beets–**Col. 2:** Based on 1932/33 market production (given as 373.4 mill. poods in *173*, No. 7, 1939, p. 162, and converted at 1 pood = .01638 m. t.) and increase in 1933 (given as 34.7% in *173*, No. 5–6, 1934, p. 166). **Col. 4:** Based on 1933 market production (col. 2) and increase planned for 1934 (given as 34.7% in *173*, No. 5–6, 1934, p. 166). **Col. 14:** *173*, No. 7, 1939, p. 162. For 1937/38. Converted at 1 pood = .01638 m. t. *449*, p. 78, gives 21.5 mill. m. t. for 1937/38.

132. Flax fiber–**Col. 14:** *173*, No. 7, 1939, p. 162. Converted at 1 pood = .01638 m. t.

133. Potatoes–**Cols. 2 and 7:** *155*, p. 662. **Col. 4:** *173*, No. 5–6, 1934, p. 166. **Cols. 5, 8, and 10:** *156*, p. 464. **Col. 14:** *173*, No. 7, 1939, p. 162. For 1937/38. Converted at 1 pood = .01638 m. t.

134. Meat and fat–**Cols. 2 and 7:** *155*, p. 662. **Col. 4:** *173*, No. 5–6, 1934, p. 166. **Cols. 5, 8, and 10:** *156*, p. 464. **Col. 14:** *173*, No. 7, 1939, p. 162. Converted at 1 pood = .01638 m. t. *469*, p. 34, gives 1,400 th. m. t.

135. Milk and dairy products–**Cols. 2 and 7:** *155*, p. 662. **Col. 4:** *173*, No. 5–6, 1934, p. 166. **Cols. 5, 8, and 10:** *156*, p. 464. **Col. 14:** *469*, p. 34.

136. Wool–**Cols. 2 and 8:** *469*, p. 35. **Col. 14:** *173*, No. 7, 1939, p. 162. Converted at 1 pood = .01638 m. t.

PROCUREMENTS

137. Grain–**Col. 1:** Based on 1933 planned procurements (col. 2) and percentage of plan fulfilled (col. 3). **Cols. 2 and 5:** *469*, p. 4. **Col. 3:** *162a*, 1933, p. 190. Fulfillment of 1933/34 plan for centralized procurements only on 1/1/34. **Col. 4:** Based on 1933 procurements (col. 2) and increase planned for 1934 (given as 7.1% in *173*, No. 5–6, 1934, p. 167, for state grain procurements including deliveries of state farms and payments in kind to MTS). **Col. 7:** *162a*, March 1936, pp. 242–43. Sum of centralized procurements and government purchases. **Cols. 8 and 11:** *449*, p. 794. For 1935/36 and 1936/37. **Col. 14:** *72*, p. 98. Includes purchases.

138. Raw cotton–**Cols. 1 and 2:** *162a*, 1933, p. 190. Centralized procurements only, for 1933/34 plan. **Cols. 7 and 8:** *162a*, March 1936, p. 242. Centralized procurements only, for 1935/36 plan. **Cols. 10 and 11:** *162a*, Dec. 1936, p. 239. Centralized procurements only, for 1936/37 plan. **Col. 14:** *254*, p. 232.

139. Sugar beets–**Cols. 1 and 2:** *162a*, 1933, p. 190. Centralized procurements only, for 1933/34 plan. **Cols. 7 and 8:** *162a*, March 1936; p. 242. Centralized procurements only, for 1935/36 plan. **Col. 14:** *254*, p. 232.

140. Sunflowers–**Cols. 2, 5, and 8:** *79*, p. 245. For col. 8, *162a*, March 1936, pp. 242–43 (sum of centralized procurements and government purchases) gives 869 th. m. t. **Col. 7:** *162a*, March 1936, pp. 242–43. Sum of centralized procurements and government purchases. **Cols. 10 and 11:** *162a*, Dec. 1936, p. 239 (including substitutes). For col. 11, *79*, p. 245, gives 731 th. m. t. **Col. 14:** *254*, p. 232.

141. Flax fiber–**Col. 3:** *162a*, 1933, p. 190. Fulfillment of 1933/34 plan for centralized procurements only on 1/1/34. **Cols. 7 and 8:** *162a*, March 1936, p. 242. Centralized procurements only, for 1935/36 plan. **Cols. 10 and 11:** *162a*, Dec. 1936, p. 239. Centralized procurements only, for 1936/37 plan. **Col. 14:** *254*, p. 232.

142. Hemp–**Cols. 1 and 2:** *162a*, 1933, p. 190. Centralized procurements only, for 1933/34 plan. **Cols. 7 and 8:** *162a*, March 1936, p. 242. Centralized procurements only, for 1935/36 plan. **Cols. 10 and 11:** *162a*, Dec. 1936, p. 239. Centralized procurements only, for 1936/37 plan. **Col. 14:** *254*, p. 232.

143. Potatoes–**Cols. 1 and 2:** *162a*, 1933, p. 190. Centralized procurements only, for 1933/34 plan. **Cols. 7 and 8:** *162a*, March 1936, p. 242. Centralized procurements only, for 1935/36 plan. **Cols. 10 and 11:** *162a*, Dec. 1936, p. 239. Centralized procurements only, for 1936/37 plan. **Col. 14:** *254*, p. 232.

143a. Vegetables–**Cols. 1 and 2:** *162a*, 1933, p. 190. Centralized procurements only, for 1933/34 plan. **Cols. 7 and 8:** *162a*, March 1936, p. 242. Centralized procurements only, for 1935/36 plan. **Col. 14:** *254*, p. 232.

144. Meat and fat (live weight)–**Cols. 1 and 2:** *162a*, 1933, p. 191. Obligatory deliveries and centralized procurements for 15 months. **Cols. 5 and 8:** *469*, p. 34. **Col. 7:** *162a*, March 1936, pp. 241 and 243. Sum of centralized procurements and government purchases. **Cols. 10 and 11:** *162a*, Dec. 1936, p. 240. Sum of centralized procurements and government purchases. **Col. 14:** *254*, p. 232.

145. Meat and fat (dead weight)–**Cols. 2, 5, 8 and 14:** *469*, p. 34. **Col. 4:** Based on 1933 procurements (col. 2) and increase planned for 1934 (given as 47.6% in *173*, No. 5–6, 1934, p. 167).

146. Milk and dairy products–**Col. 1:** *162a*, 1933, p. 191. Obligatory deliveries and centralized procurements. **Cols. 2, 5 and 8:** *469*, p. 34. For col. 2, *162a*, 1933, p. 191, gives 3,569 th. m. t. **Col. 4:** Based on 1933 procurements (col. 2) and increase planned for 1934 (given as 15% in *173*, No. 5–6, 1934, p. 167). **Cols. 10 and 11:** *162a*, Dec. 1936, p. 240. Sum of centralized procurements and government purchases. **Col. 14:** *254*, p. 232.

Table A-2 *continued*

147. Eggs–**Col. 3:** *162a*, 1933, p. 191. **Cols. 10 and 11:** *162a*, Dec. 1936, p. 240. State purchases. **Col. 14:** *449*, p. 79.
148. Wool–**Col. 1:** *162a*, 1933, p. 191. Centralized procurements and obligatory deliveries. **Cols. 2 and 5:** *469*, p. 35. **Cols. 8, 11, and 13:** *173*, No. 1, 1937, p. 41. **Col. 10:** *162a*, Dec. 1936, p. 240. Sum of centralized procurements and government purchases. **Col. 14:** *254*, p. 232.

RAILROAD TRANSPORTATION

149. Length of network–**Cols. 2, 5, 11, and 14:** *252*, p. 28. **Col. 4:** *173*, No. 5–6, 1934, p. 217. **Col. 7:** *155*, p. 624. **Cols. 8 and 10:** *156*, p. 448. **Col. 13:** *157*, p. 121.
150. Average daily carloadings–**Col. 1:** *153*, p. 122. **Cols. 2, 4, 5, and 7:** *155*, p. 623. **Cols. 8 and 10:** *156*, p. 449. **Cols. 11 and 13:** *157*, p. 123. **Col. 14:** *254*, p. 222.
151. Total freight traffic (ton-km)–**Col. 1:** Based on total freight traffic in tons (series 152) and average length of haul (series 162). **Cols. 2, 5, 8, 11, and 14:** *252*, p. 32. **Col. 4:** *173*, No. 5–6, 1934, p. 216. **Col. 7:** *155*, p. 622. Commercial traffic. **Col. 10:** *156*, p. 449. Commercial traffic. **Col. 13:** *157*, p. 123. Commercial traffic.
152. Total freight traffic (tons)–**Col. 1:** *153*, p. 122. **Cols. 2, 5, 8, 11, and 14:** *252*, p. 32. **Col. 4:** *173*, No. 5–6, 1934, p. 216. **Col. 7:** *155*, p. 622. Commercial traffic. **Col. 10:** *156*, p. 449. Commercial traffic. **Col. 13:** *157*, p. 123. Commercial traffic.
153. Coal and coke–**Col. 1:** *173*, No. 3, 1934, p. 102. **Cols. 2, 4, 5, and 7:** *155*, p. 622. **Cols. 8, 11, and 13:** *157*, pp. 122–23. **Col. 10:** *156*, p. 449. **Col. 14:** *254*, p. 222.
154. Oil and oil products–**Col. 1:** *173*, No. 3, 1934, p. 102. Oil only. **Cols. 2, 4, and 7:** *155*, p. 622. **Cols. 5, 8, and 10:** *156*, p. 449. **Cols. 11 and 13:** *157*, p. 123. **Col. 14:** *254*, p. 222.
155. Ferrous metals–**Col. 1:** *173*, No. 3, 1934, p. 102. **Cols. 2, 4, and 7:** *155*, p. 622. **Cols. 5, 8, and 10:** *156*, p. 449. **Cols. 11 and 13:** *157*, p. 123. **Col. 14:** *254*, p. 222.
156. Ore–**Col. 1:** *173*, No. 3, 1934, p. 102. **Cols. 2 and 5:** *229*, p. 418. **Cols. 4 and 7:** *155*, p. 622. **Cols. 8, 11, and 13:** *157*, pp. 122–23. **Col. 10:** *156*, p. 449. **Col. 14:** *254*, p. 222.
157. Firewood–**Col. 1:** *173*, No. 3, 1934, p. 102. **Cols. 2 and 5:** *229*, p. 422. **Cols. 4 and 7:** *155*, p. 622. **Cols. 8, 11, and 13:** *157*, pp. 122–23. **Col. 10:** *156*, p. 449. **Col. 14:** *254*, p. 222.
158. Timber–**Col. 1:** *173*, No. 3, 1934, p. 102. Timber materials. **Cols. 2 and 5:** *229*, p. 422. Building timber. **Cols. 4 and 7:** *155*, p. 622. Timber materials. **Cols. 8, 11, and 13:** *157*, pp. 122–23. Timber materials. **Col. 10:** *156*, p. 449. Timber materials. **Col. 14:** *254*, p. 222.
159. Mineral construction materials–**Col. 2:** *445*, p. 303. **Col. 5:** *229*, p. 421. **Cols. 8, 11, and 13:** *157*, pp. 122–23. **Col. 10:** *156*, p. 449. **Col. 14:** *254*, p. 222.
159a. Principal construction materials (stone, lime, cement, bricks)–**Col. 1:** *173*, No. 3, 1934, p. 102. **Cols. 2, 5, and 8:** *229*, p. 421. **Cols. 4 and 7:** *155*, p. 622. **Col. 10:** *156*, p. 449. **Cols. 11 and 14:** *445*, p. 303.
160. Grain and flour–**Col. 1:** *173*, No. 3, 1934, p. 102. **Cols. 2 and 5:** *229*, p. 422. **Cols. 4 and 7:** *155*, p. 622. **Cols. 8, 11, and 13:** *157*, pp. 122–23. **Col. 10:** *156*, p. 449. **Col. 14:** *254*, p. 222.
161. Salt–**Col. 2:** *228*, p. 397. **Cols. 5 and 8:** *215*, p. 306. **Col. 14:** *445*, p. 179.
162. Total freight traffic, average length of haul–**Col. 1:** *173*, No. 1–2, 1933, p. 44. **Cols. 2 and 7:** *155*, p. 622. **Col. 4:** *173*, No. 5–6, 1934, p. 216. **Cols. 5 and 10:** *156*, p. 449. Commercial traffic. **Cols. 8, 11, and 13:** *157*, pp. 122–23. **Col. 14:** *252*, p. 34.
163. Coal and coke, average length of haul–**Cols. 2, 5, and 8:** *229*, p. 420. **Col. 11:** *420*, p. 221. **Col. 14:** *252*, p. 35.
163a. Oil and oil products, average length of haul–**Cols. 2, 5, and 8:** *229*, p. 420. **Col. 11:** *173*, No. 6, 1939, p. 112. **Col. 14:** *252*, p. 35.
164. Ferrous metals, average length of haul–**Cols. 2, 5, and 8:** *229*, p. 420. Includes rails. **Col. 11:** *420*, p. 221. **Col. 14:** *252*, p. 36.
164a. Firewood, average length of haul–**Cols. 2, 5, and 8:** *229*, p. 422. **Col. 14:** *252*, p. 38.
164b. Timber, average length of haul–**Cols. 2, 5, and 8:** *229*, p. 421. Building timber. **Col. 14:** *252*, p. 38.
165. Grain and flour, average length of haul–**Cols. 2, 5, and 8:** *229*, p. 422. **Col. 14:** *252*, p. 37.
165a. Ore, average length of haul–**Cols. 2, 5, and 8:** *229*, p. 420. **Col. 11:** *420*, p. 221. **Col. 14:** *252*, p. 36.
166. Total passenger traffic–**Col. 1:** *173*, No. 1–2, 1933, p. 44. **Cols. 2, 5, 8, and 11:** *252*, p. 32. **Col. 4:** *173*, No. 5–6, 1934, p. 216. Given in million pass.-km but obviously should be billion pass.-km. **Col. 7:** *155*, p. 623. **Col. 13:** *157*, p. 123. **Col. 14:** *254*, p. 222.

INLAND WATERWAY TRANSPORTATION

166a. Length of network–**Cols. 2 and 4:** *173*, No. 5–6, 1934, p. 217. **Col. 5:** Derived from length of network for Commissariat of Water Transport (given as 81,240 km in *156*, p. 452) and its share in total length (derived as 91.5% from figures for both for 1935 in *156*, p. 452). **Col. 7:** Derived from length of network for Commissariat of Water Transport (given as 85,000 km in *156*, p. 452) and its share in total length (derived as 91.5% in col. 5 above). **Cols. 8 and 10:** *156*, p. 452. **Cols. 11 and 13:** *157*, p. 128. **Col. 14:** *252*, p. 115.
168. Freight traffic under ministries and economic organizations (ton-km)–**Col. 1:** Based on 1933 traffic (col. 2)

Table A-2 *continued*

and percentage of plan fulfilled (col. 3). **Cols. 2 and 7:** *155*, p. 629. **Col. 3:** *173*, No. 5–6, 1934, p. 141. **Col. 4:** *173*, No. 5–6, 1934, p. 216. **Col. 5:** *215*, p. 314. **Cols. 8 and 11:** *252*, p. 116. **Col. 10:** *156*, p. 452. **Col. 13:** *157*, p. 131. **Col. 14:** *254*, p. 223.

170. Freight traffic under ministries and economic organizations (tons)–**Col. 1:** Based on 1933 traffic (col. 2) and percentage of plan fulfilled (col. 3). **Cols. 2 and 11:** *252*, p. 116. **Col. 3:** *173*, No. 5–6, 1934, p. 141. **Col. 4:** *173*, No. 5–6, 1934, p. 216. **Cols. 5 and 8:** *215*, p. 314. **Col. 7:** *155*, p. 629. **Col. 10:** *156*, p. 452. **Col. 13:** *157*, p. 129. **Col. 14:** *254*, p. 223.

171. Coal and coke–**Cols. 2, 4, and 7:** *155*, p. 629. **Cols. 5 and 8:** *215*, p. 315. Coal only. **Col. 10:** *156*, p. 452. **Cols. 11 and 13:** *157*, p. 129. **Col. 14:** *252*, p. 120. Coal only.

172. Oil and oil products–**Cols. 2, 4, and 7:** *155*, p. 629. **Cols. 5 and 8:** *215*, p. 315. **Col. 10:** *156*, p. 452. **Cols. 11 and 13:** *157*, p. 129. **Col. 14:** *215*, p. 120.

173. Timber and firewood–**Col. 2:** *228*, p. 415. **Cols. 5 and 8:** *215*, p. 315. Timber only. **Col. 14:** *252*, p. 120.

174. Mineral construction materials–**Cols. 2, 4, and 7:** *155*, p. 629. **Cols. 5 and 8:** *215*, p. 315. **Col. 10:** Sum of plan for cement (derived as 542 th. m. t. from actual haulage of cement and percentage of plan fulfilled given in *157*, p. 129) and plan for other mineral construction materials (derived as 7,597 th. m. t. from actual haulage and percentage of plan fulfilled given in *157*, p. 129). **Cols. 11 and 13:** *157*, p. 129. Sum of cement and other mineral construction materials. **Col. 14:** *252*, p. 120.

175. Grain and flour–**Cols. 2, 4, and 7:** *155*, p. 629. **Cols. 5 and 8:** *215*, p. 315. **Col. 10:** *156*, p. 452. **Cols. 11 and 13:** *157*, p. 129. **Col. 14:** *252*, p. 120.

176. Salt–**Cols. 2, 4, and 7:** *155*, p. 629. **Col. 5:** *215*, p. 315. **Cols. 8, 11, and 13:** *157*, p. 129. **Col. 10:** *156*, p. 452. **Col. 14:** *252*, p. 120.

177. Average length of haul under ministries and economic organizations–**Cols. 2 and 7:** *155*, p. 629. **Col. 4:** *173*, No. 5–6, 1934, p. 216. **Cols. 8, 11, and 14:** *252*, p. 116. **Col. 10:** *156*, p. 452. **Col. 13:** Based on ton-km (series 168) and tons (series 170).

178. Passenger traffic (pass.-km)–**Cols. 2 and 5:** *229*, p. 451. **Col. 4:** *173*, No. 5–6, 1934, p. 216. Given in million pass.-km but obviously should be billion pass.-km. **Col. 7:** *155*, p. 629. **Col. 10:** Based on actual traffic (col. 11) and percentage of plan fulfilled (col. 12). **Cols. 8, 11, 12, and 13:** *157*, p. 131. **Col. 14:** *252*, p. 116.

178a. Passenger traffic (pass.)–**Cols. 2, 5, 8, 11, and 14:** *252*, p. 116.

MARITIME TRANSPORTATION (Soviet ships)

179. Freight traffic (ton-km)–**Col. 1:** Based on actual traffic (col. 2) and percentage of plan fulfilled (col. 3). **Cols. 2, 5, and 11:** *490*, p. 182. **Col. 3:** *173*, No. 5–6, 1934, p. 141. **Col. 4:** *173*, No. 5–6, 1934, p. 216. **Col. 7:** *155*, p. 629. Converted from ton-miles at 1 m. ton-km = 0.54 ton-miles (derived from col. 4 and *155*, p. 629). **Col. 10:** *156*, p. 453. Converted from ton-miles as above. **Col. 13:** *157*, p. 131. Converted from ton-miles as above. **Col. 14:** *252*, p. 7.

180. Freight traffic (tons)–**Col. 1:** Based on actual traffic (col. 2) and percentage of plan fulfilled (col. 3). **Cols. 2 and 4:** *173*, No. 5–6, 1934, p. 216. **Col. 3:** *173*, No. 5–6, 1934, p. 141. **Col. 5:** *490*, p. 182. **Col. 7:** *155*, p. 629. **Cols. 8, 11, 12, and 13:** *157*, p. 131. **Col. 10:** Based on actual traffic (col. 11) and percentage of plan fulfilled (col. 12). **Col. 14:** *254*, p. 223.

181. Average length of haul–**Cols. 1, 4, 7, 10, 13, and 14:** Based on freight traffic in ton-km (series 179) and in tons (series 180). **Cols. 2, 5, 8, and 11:** *490*, p. 182.

182. Passenger traffic (pass.-km)–**Cols. 2 and 4:** *173*, No. 5–6, 1934, p. 216. Given in million pass.-km but obviously should be billion pass.-km. **Cols. 5 and 8:** *229*, p. 481. Converted from pass.-miles at 1 pass.-km = 0.54 pass.-miles (derived from col. 2 and *229*, p. 481). **Col. 7:** *155*, p. 629. Converted from pass.-miles as above. **Col. 10:** Based on actual traffic (col. 11) and percentage of plan fulfilled (col. 12). **Cols. 11, 12, and 13:** *157*, p. 131. Converted from pass.-miles as above. **Col. 14:** *252*, p. 95. Converted from pass.-miles as above.

182a. Passenger traffic (pass.)–**Col. 14:** *252*, p. 95. Commissariat of the Maritime Fleet. Excludes traffic in steamships in Central Asia.

MOTOR TRANSPORTATION

183. Freight traffic–**Cols. 2, 5, 8, 11, and 14:** *252*, p. 155.

AIR TRANSPORTATION

184. Freight traffic, incl. mail–**Cols. 1 and 2:** *173*, No. 1, 1934, p. 180. All categories of traffic, probably including passenger traffic, since *173*, No. 5–6, 1934, p. 216, cites the same figure for col. 2 specified to include passenger traffic. **Col. 4:** *173*, No. 5–6, 1934, p. 216. Includes passenger traffic. **Col. 5:** *215*, p. 336. All categories of traffic. Excludes Deruluft, local airways, and *Glavk* for Northern Sea Route. **Col. 7:** *155*, p. 633. All categories of traffic. **Cols. 8, 11, 12, and 13:** *157*, p. 135. All categories of traffic. **Col. 10:** Based on actual traffic (col. 11) and percentage of plan fulfilled (col. 12). **Col. 14:** *72*, p. 102.

185. Passenger traffic–**Cols. 2 and 7:** *155*, pp. 632–33. **Col. 4:** *173*, No. 5–6, 1934, p. 216. **Cols. 5 and 10:** *156*, p. 455. **Cols. 8, 11, and 13:** *157*, p. 135. **Col. 14:** *72*, p. 102.

Table A-2 *continued*

EMPLOYMENT (annual averages)

186. Workers and employees, national economy, excl. collective farms–**Col. 1:** *153*, p. 123. **Cols. 2 and 5:** *215*, p. 355. **Col. 4:** *173*, No. 5–6, 1934, p. 222. **Col. 7:** *155*, p. 640. **Cols. 8, 11, and 13:** *157*, pp. 144–45. **Col. 10:** *156*, p. 457. **Col. 14:** *72*, p. 104. Although *140*, p. 189, gives 27.0 mill. for end of year and 26.7 for annual average, it was considered preferable to maintain contemporary sources which do not specify.

187. Industry–**Col. 1:** Based on 1932 employment (given as 8.0 mill. in *498*, p. 317) and increase planned for 1933 (taken as 2%, the planned increase for large-scale and cooperative industry derived from *153*, p. 123). **Cols. 2 and 7:** *155*, p. 640. **Col. 4:** *173*, No. 5–6, 1934, p. 222. **Cols. 5 and 10:** *156*, p. 457. **Cols. 8, 11, and 13:** *157*, pp. 144–45. **Col. 14:** *72*, p. 104.

188. Construction–**Col. 1:** *153*, p. 123. **Col. 2:** *215*, p. 355. **Col. 4:** *173*, No. 5–6, 1934, p. 222. **Cols. 5 and 10:** *156*, p. 145. **Col. 7:** *155*, p. 640. **Cols. 8, 11, and 13:** *157*, pp. 144–45. **Col. 14:** *72*, p. 104.

188a. Construction and assembly work–**Col. 14:** *140*, p. 190.

189. State-owned agriculture and logging–**Col. 1:** *173*, No. 1–2, 1933, p. 46. Total employment minus nonagricultural sector. **Cols. 2, 5, and 8:** *215*, p. 355. Sum of agriculture and forestry. **Col. 4:** *173*, No. 5–6, 1934, p. 222. Sum of agriculture and forestry. **Col. 7:** *155*, p. 640. Sum of agriculture and forestry. **Col. 14:** *72*, p. 104. Sum of agriculture and forestry.

190. State-owned agriculture (state farms, MTS, and other state establishments)–**Cols. 2 and 5:** *215*, p. 355. **Col. 4:** *173*, No. 5–6, 1934, p. 222. **Col. 7:** *155*, p. 640. **Cols. 8, 11, and 13:** *157*, pp. 144–45. **Col. 10:** *156*, p. 458. **Col. 14:** *72*, p. 104.

191. Railroad transport–**Col. 1:** *153*, p. 122. **Cols. 2, 5, and 8:** *215*, p. 355. **Col. 4:** *173*, No. 5–6, 1934, p. 222. **Col. 7:** *155*, p. 640. **Col. 10:** *156*, p. 457. **Cols. 11 and 13:** *157*, p. 145. **Col. 14:** *72*, p. 104. After 1936, data on employment in railroad transport seem to have a more limited coverage.

192. Maritime and inland waterway transport–**Col. 1:** *153*, p. 122. **Cols. 2, 5, and 8:** *215*, p. 355. **Col. 4:** *173*, No. 5–6, 1934, p. 222. **Col. 7:** *155*, p. 640. **Col. 10:** *156*, p. 457. **Cols. 11 and 13:** *157*, p. 145. **Col. 14:** *72*, p. 104. After 1936, data on employment in maritime and inland waterway transport seem to have a more limited coverage.

193. Other transport (motor, etc.)–**Cols. 2 and 5:** *215*, p. 355. For col. 5, given figure of 730 th. reduced by 100 th. to make coverage comparable. **Col. 4:** *173*, No. 5–6, 1934, p. 222. **Col. 7:** *155*, p. 640. **Cols. 8, 11, 12, and 13:** *157*, pp. 144–45. **Col. 10:** Based on actual employment (col. 11) and percentage of plan fulfilled (col. 12). **Col. 14:** *72*, p. 104. Lower figures published later, but figures for 1935–1937 here seem to be of comparable coverage.

194. Communications–**Col. 1:** *153*, p. 123. **Cols. 2 and 5:** *215*, p. 355. **Col. 4:** *173*, No. 5–6, 1934, p. 222. **Col. 7:** *155*, p. 640. **Cols. 8, 11, and 13:** *157*, pp. 144–45. **Col. 10:** *156*, p. 457. **Col. 14:** *72*, p. 104.

195. Trade, procurements, and supply–**Col. 1:** *153*, p. 123. **Cols. 2, 5, and 8:** *215*, p. 355. **Col. 4:** *173*, No. 5–6, 1934, p. 222. **Col. 7:** *155*, p. 640. **Col. 10:** *156*, p. 457. **Cols. 11 and 13:** *157*, p. 145. **Col. 14:** *72*, p. 104.

196. Public eating places–**Col. 1:** *153*, p. 123. **Cols. 2 and 5:** *215*, p. 355. **Col. 4:** *173*, No. 5–6, 1934, p. 222. **Col. 7:** *155*, p. 640. **Cols. 8, 11, and 13:** *157*, pp. 144–45. **Col. 10:** *156*, p. 457. **Col. 14:** *72*, p. 104.

197. Credit institutions–**Cols. 2 and 5:** *215*, p. 355. **Col. 4:** *173*, No. 5–6, 1934, p. 222. **Col. 7:** *155*, p. 640. Increased by 7,200 by the March 13, 1935, decree of the Central Personnel Commission. **Cols. 8, 11, 12, and 13:** *157*, pp. 144–45. **Col. 10:** Based on actual employment (col. 11) and percentage of plan fulfilled (col. 12). **Col. 14:** *72*, p. 104.

198. Administration–**Cols. 2 and 7:** *155*, p. 640. **Col. 4:** *173*, No. 5–6, 1934, p. 222. **Cols. 5 and 10:** *156*, p. 458. **Cols. 8, 11, and 13:** *157*, pp. 144–45. **Col. 14:** *72*, p. 104.

199. Education–**Cols. 2 and 5:** *215*, p.355. **Col. 4:** *173*, No. 5–6, 1934, p. 222. **Col. 7:** *155*, p. 640. **Cols. 8, 11, and 13:** *157*, pp. 144–45. **Col. 10:** *156*, p. 457. **Col. 14:** *72*, p. 104.

200. Public health–**Cols. 2 and 5:** *215*, p. 508. **Col. 4:** *173*, No. 5–6, 1934, p. 222. **Col. 7:** *155*, p. 640. **Cols. 8, 11, and 13:** *157*, p. 145. **Col. 10:** *156*, p. 457. **Col. 14:** *72*, p. 104.

WAGE FUND, WORKERS AND EMPLOYEES

201. National economy–**Col. 1:** *173*, No. 1–2, 1933, p. 46. **Cols. 2 and 5:** *215*, p. 367. **Col. 4:** *173*, No. 5–6, 1934, p. 223. **Col. 7:** *155*, p. 642. **Cols. 8, 11, and 13:** *157*, pp. 146–47. **Col. 10:** *156*, p. 458. **Col. 14:** *72*, p. 106.

202. Industry–**Col. 1:** Based on 1932 wage fund for industry (given as 11,236 mill. rubles in *498*, p. 318) and increase planned for 1933 for large-scale state and cooperative industry (derived as 11.4% from statement in *153*, p. 120, that the latter wage fund was planned to increase by 1,060 mill. rubles to reach 10,300 mill. rubles). **Cols. 2 and 7:** *155*, p. 642. **Col. 4:** *173*, No. 5–6, 1934, p. 223. **Cols. 5 and 10:** *156*, p. 458. **Cols. 8, 11, and 13:** *157*, p. 147. **Col. 14:** *72*, p. 106.

AVERAGE ANNUAL WAGE, WORKERS AND EMPLOYEES

203. Money wage, national economy, excl. collective farms and cooperatives–**Col. 1:** Based on 1932 money wage (given as 1,427 rubles in *498*, p. 318) and increase planned for 1933 (given as 6.7% in *153*, p. 123). **Cols. 2 and 5:** *215*, p. 369. **Col. 4:** *173*, No. 5–6, 1934, p. 223. **Col. 7:** *155*, p. 641. **Cols. 8, 11, and 13:** *157*, pp. 144–45. **Col. 14:** *72*, p. 105.

Table A-2 *continued*

204. Real wage, national economy, excl. collective farms and cooperatives, calculated from official Soviet index–**Col. 14:** Based on real wage in 1937 (derived as 3,627 rubles from money wage in 1937, series 201, and price index for 1937 with 1940 = 100, 84 from *498*, p. 391, Table A-17, col. 2) and real wage in 1932 (given as 553 rubles in *498*, Table A-1, p. 318).

205. Money wage, industry–**Col. 1:** Based on money wage in 1932 (given as 1,410 in *498*, p. 318) and increase planned for 1933 for large-scale state and cooperative industry (given as 9.3% in *153*, p. 120). **Cols. 2 and 7:** *155*, p. 641. **Col. 4:** *173*, No. 5–6, 1934, p. 223. **Cols. 5 and 10:** *156*, p. 458. **Cols. 8, 11, and 13:** *157*, pp. 144–45. **Col. 14:** *72*, p. 105.

AVERAGE ANNUAL MONEY WAGE, WORKERS

206. Industry–**Cols. 2 and 5:** *215*, p. 383. **Col. 7:** *155*, p. 641. **Cols. 8, 11, 12, and 13:** *157*, pp. 144–45. **Col. 10:** Based on actual wage (col. 11) and percentage of plan fulfilled (col. 12). **Col. 14:** *254*, p. 228.

207. Iron ore–**Cols. 2, 5, and 8:** *215*, p. 383. **Col. 14:** *173*, No. 3, 1939, p. 163.

208. Coal–**Cols. 2, 5, and 8:** *215*, p. 383. **Col. 14:** *173*, No. 3, 1939, p. 163.

209. Ferrous metals–**Cols. 2, 5, and 8:** *215*, p. 383. **Col. 14:** *173*, No. 3, 1939, p. 163.

209a. Machine-building–**Cols. 2, 5, and 8:** *215*, p. 383. **Col. 14:** *173*, No. 3, 1939, p. 163.

210. Paper–**Cols. 2, 5, and 8:** *215*, p. 383.

211. Chemicals–**Cols. 2, 5, and 8:** *215*, p. 383. **Col. 14:** *173*, No. 3, 1939, p. 163.

212. Textiles–**Cols. 2, 5, and 8:** *215*, p. 383. **Col. 14:** Derived as in Table A-1, col. 2.

212a. Cotton–**Cols. 2, 5, and 8:** *215*, p. 383. **Col. 14:** *173*, No. 3, 1939, p. 163.

212b. Wool–**Cols. 2, 5, and 8:** *215*, p. 383. **Col. 14:** *173*, No. 3, 1939, p. 163.

213. Leather–**Cols. 2, 5, and 8:** *215*, p. 383.

214. Food–**Cols. 2, 5, and 8:** *215*, p. 383. **Col. 14:** *173*, No. 3, 1939, p. 163.

AVERAGE ANNUAL MONEY WAGE, WORKERS AND EMPLOYEES

215. Construction–**Cols. 2 and 5:** *215*, p. 369. **Col. 4:** *173*, No. 5–6, 1934, pp. 222–23. **Col. 7:** *155*, p. 641. **Cols. 8, 11, and 13:** *157*, pp. 144–45. **Col. 10:** *156*, p. 458. **Col. 14:** *72*, p. 105.

216. Railroad transport–**Col. 1:** Based on 1932 wage (given as 1,496 rubles in *498*, p. 319) and increase planned for 1933 (given as 7% in *153*, p. 122). **Cols. 2, 5, and 8:** *215*, p. 369. **Col. 4:** *173*, No. 5–6, 1934, pp. 222–23. **Col. 7:** *155*, p. 641. **Col. 10:** *156*, p. 458. **Cols. 11 and 13:** *157*, p. 147. **Col. 14:** *72*, p. 105.

217. Maritime and inland waterway transport–**Col. 1:** Based on 1932 wage (given as 1,509 rubles in *498*, p. 319) and increase planned for 1933 (given as 7.5% in *153*, p. 122, for water transport). **Cols. 2, 5, and 8:** *215*, p. 389. **Col. 4:** *173*, No. 5–6, 1934, pp. 222–23. **Col. 7:** *155*, p. 641. **Col. 10:** *156*, p. 458. **Cols. 11 and 13:** *157*, p. 147. **Col. 14:** *72*, p. 105.

218. Communications–**Col. 1:** Based on 1932 wage (given as 1,333 rubles in *498*, p. 319) and increase planned for 1933 (given as 10.6% in *153*, p. 122). **Cols. 2 and 5:** *215*, p. 389. **Col. 4:** *173*, No. 5–6, 1934, pp. 222–23. **Col. 7:** *155*, p. 541. **Cols. 8, 11, and 13:** *157*, pp. 146–47. **Col. 10:** *156*, p. 458. **Col. 14:** *72*, p. 105.

219. Trade–**Cols. 2 and 5:** *215*, p. 369. **Col. 4:** *173*, No. 5–6, 1934, pp. 222–23. **Col. 7:** *155*, p. 641. **Cols. 8, 11, and 13:** *157*, pp. 146–47. **Col. 10:** *156*, p. 458. **Col. 14:** *72*, p. 105.

220. Public eating places–**Cols. 2 and 5:** *215*, p. 369. **Col. 4:** *173*, No. 5–6, 1934, pp. 222–23. **Col. 7:** *155*, p. 641. **Cols. 8, 11, and 13:** *157*, pp. 146–47. **Col. 10:** *156*, p. 458. **Col. 14:** *72*, p. 105.

221. Credit institutions–**Cols. 2 and 5:** *215*, p. 369. **Col. 4:** *173*, No. 5–6, 1934, pp. 222–23. **Col. 7:** *155*, p. 641. **Cols. 8, 11, 12, and 13:** *157*, pp. 146–47. **Col. 10:** Based on 1936 wage (col. 11) and percentage of plan fulfilled (col. 12). **Col. 14:** *72*, p. 105.

222. Administration–**Cols. 2 and 5:** *215*, p. 369. **Col. 4:** *173*, No. 5–6, 1934, pp. 222–23. **Col. 7:** *155*, p. 641. **Cols. 8, 11, and 13:** *157*, pp. 146–47. **Col. 10:** *156*, p. 458. **Col. 14:** *72*, p. 105.

223. Education–**Cols. 2 and 5:** *215*, p. 369. **Col. 4:** *173*, No. 5–6, 1934, pp. 222–23. **Col. 7:** *155*, p. 641. **Cols. 8, 11, and 13:** *157*, pp. 146–47. **Col. 10:** *156*, p. 458. **Col. 14:** *72*, p. 105.

224. Public health–**Cols. 2 and 5:** *215*, p. 369. **Col. 4:** *173*, No. 5–6, 1934, pp. 222–23. **Col. 7:** *155*, p. 641. **Cols. 8, 11, and 13:** *157*, pp. 146–47. **Col. 10:** *156*, p. 458. **Col. 14:** *72*, p. 105.

225. State-owned agriculture–**Cols. 2 and 5:** *215*, p. 369. **Col. 4:** *173*, No. 5–6, 1934, pp. 222–23. **Col. 7:** *155*, p. 641. **Cols. 8, 11, and 13:** *157*, pp. 146–47. **Col. 10:** *156*, p. 458. **Col. 14:** *72*, p. 105.

226. Logging–**Cols. 2, 5, and 8:** *215*, p. 369. **Col. 4:** *173*, No. 5–6, 1934, pp. 222–23. **Col. 7:** *155*, p. 641. Listed under industry. **Col. 14:** *72*, p. 105.

HOUSING

227. Housing fund, urban, total–**Cols. 2 and 4:** *173*, No. 5–6, 1934, p. 225. **Cols. 5, 7, and 10:** *156*, p. 467. 1935 plan (col. 7) revised by 7/11/35 decree of Council of People's Commissars. **Cols. 8, 11, and 13:** *157*, p. 163. **Col. 14:** Housing fund at end of 1936 (given as 204.38 mill. m² in *173*, No. 3, 1937, p. 244) plus housing construction during

Table A-2   *continued*

1937 (series 228, col. 14) minus wear during 1937. This was estimated at 1 mill. m² from difference between housing fund in 1933 (col. 2) and in 1932 (given as 185.1 mill. m² in *498*, p. 319) subtracted from housing construction in 1933 (series 228, col. 2).

228. Housing construction, urban, total–**Col. 1:** *153*, p. 69. **Col. 2:** *227*, p. 436. **Col. 4:** *173*, No. 5–6, 1934, p. 160. **Col. 10:** *162a*, Dec. 1936, p. 298. Given for 44 large towns with the following breakdown: housing for Central Executive Committees, .35 mill. m²; industrial housing, 1.07 mill. m²; and housing for transport, .19 mill. m². **Col. 11:** *162a*, Dec. 1936, p. 298. Given for 44 large towns with the following breakdown: housing for Central Executive Committees, .1 mill. m²; industrial housing, .41 mill. m²; and housing for transport, .08 mill. m². **Col. 14:** Based on 1938 plan (given as 7.8 mill. m² in *173*, No. 6, 1938, p. 166) and statement (in *173*, No. 6, 1938, p. 166) that 1938 plan was double 1937 construction.

229. Floorspace per inhabitant, urban–**Col. 14:** Total urban housing fund (series 227) divided by urban population (series 231).

POPULATION

230. Total (end of year)–**Cols. 2, 5, 8, and 11:** *491*, pp. 1–14. For col. 2, Stalin (in *241*, p. 458) gave 168 mill., which has not been used since it is clearly too high. **Col. 14:** Based on population on Jan. 17, 1939 (given as 170,467,186 in *226*, p. 8), rate of increase in 1938 (derived as 20.5 per thousand inhabitants from birthrate of 38.3 per thousand and mortality rate of 17.8 per thousand given by Eason in *481*, pp. 104–5), and amount of increase between Jan. 1 and 17 of 1939 (estimated at 140 thous.).

Table A-3   Fulfillment of Annual Plans during Third Five-Year Plan, 1938–1941

Series	Units	1938			1939		
		Planned (1)	Actual (2)	(2) as Per Cent of (1) (3)	Planned (4)	Actual (5)	(5) as Per Cent of (4) (6)
1. National income (1926/27 prices)	bill. rub.		105.0			115.0	
Industry							
2. Gross production, total (1926/27 prices)	bill. rub.	111	106.1	95.6		123.9	
3. Producer goods (1926/27 prices)	bill. rub.		62.1			73.7	
4. Consumer goods (1926/27 prices)	bill. rub.		44.0			50.1	
5. Coal	th. m. t.	153,900	133,263	86.6	148,130	146,208	98.7
6. Peat	th. m. t.		26,534			29,882	
7. Coke	th. m. t.		19,625			20,159	
8. Oil shale	th. m. t.		562				
9. Crude petroleum	th. m. t.	31,500	30,186	95.8		30,259	
10. Natural gas	mill. m³		2,200			2,200	
11. Electric power	mill. kwh	41,200	39,366	95.5		43,203	
12. Hydroelectric power	mill. kwh		5,084			4,705	
13. Iron ore	th. m. t.	32,000	26,585	83.1	32,300	29,921	92.6
14. Pig iron	th. m. t.	16,300	14,652	89.9		14,520	91.5
15. Steel ingots and castings	th. m. t.	20,300	18,057	89.0		17,564	
16. Rolled steel	th. m. t.	15,100	13,258	87.8	14,500	12,729	87.8
17. Steel pipes	th. m. t.		909			917	
18. Aluminum	th. m. t.		43.8			47.0	
19. Manganese ore	th. m. t.	3,200	2,273	71.0		2,252	

Table A-2 *continued*

231. Urban (end of year)–**Col. 14:** Based on total population (series 230) and share that urban was in total in 1939 census (derived as 32.8% from *226*, p. 9).

232. Rural (end of year)–**Col. 14:** Based on total population (series 230) and share that rural was in total in 1939 census (derived as 67.2% from *226*, p. 9).

RETAIL TRADE

233. State and cooperative in current prices–**Col. 1:** *153*, p. 67. **Cols. 2, 5, 8, and 11:** *241*, p. 584. **Col. 4:** *173*, No. 5–6, 1934, p. 199. **Col. 7:** *155*, p. 675. **Col. 10:** *156*, p. 465. **Col. 13:** *157*, p. 161. **Col. 14:** *72*, p. 107.

234. State and cooperative in 1940 prices–**Col. 14:** *124*, p. 407.

234c. Food products in current prices–**Cols. 2, 5, and 8:** *229*, p. 612. **Col. 11:** Based on total retail trade in current prices (series 233) and share of food products in total trade (given as 63.5% in *173*, No. 2, 1937, p. 95). **Col. 13:** Based on planned total retail trade in current prices (series 233) and share of food products in total trade planned for 1937 (given as 60.4% in *173*, No. 2, 1937, p. 95). **Col. 14:** *232*, p. 40.

234d. Food products in 1940 prices–**Col. 14:** Based on total retail trade in 1940 prices (series 234) and share of food products in total trade in current prices (given as 63.1% in *232*, p. 44).

235. Collective farm in current prices–**Cols. 2, 5, 8, 11, and 14:** *241*, p. 584. **Col. 10:** *171*, No. 12, 1936, p. 27.

1940			1941			
Planned (7)	Actual (8)	(8) as Per Cent of (7) (9)	Planned (10)	Actual (11)	(11) as Per Cent of (10) (12)	Series No.
	128.3			118		1
	138.5		162.0	135.7	83.8	2
	84.8		103.6	94.3	91.0	3
	53.7		58.4	41.4	70.9	4
	165,923		190,800	151,400	79.4	5
	33,229		39,615	27,431	69.2	6
	21,102		23,800			7
	1,682.9		3,900			8
	31,121		34,602	33,038	95.5	9
	3,219.1		3,779			10
	48,309		53,957	46,700	86.5	11
	5,113					12
	29,866		34,030	24,700	72.6	13
	14,902		18,000	13,816	76.8	14
	18,317		22,400	17,898	79.9	15
	13,113		15,800	12,588	79.7	16
	966		1,100			17
	59.9					18
	2,557		3,100			19

Table A-3 *continued*

Series	Units	1938 Planned (1)	1938 Actual (2)	(2) as Per Cent of (1) (3)	1939 Planned (4)	1939 Actual (5)	(5) as Per Cent of (4) (6)
20. Nickel	th. m. t.		2.51			3.49	
21. Zinc	th. m. t.		83.1			91	
22. Refined copper	th. m. t.	139.4	103.2	74.0		142	
23. Lead	th. m. t.	87	77.8	89.4		85.1	
24. Mineral fertilizer	th. m. t.		3,413			3,562	
25. Phosphoric fertilizer (14% P_2O_5)	th. m. t.		2,070			2,380	
26. Phosphoric fertilizer (18.7% P_2O_5)	th. m. t.	1,767	1,595.7	90.3		1,637.9	
27. Ground natural phosphate	th. m. t.		631.5			582.2	
28. Potash fertilizer	th. m. t.		357.9			383.2	
29. Ammonium sulfate	th. m. t.	937	828.1	88.4		958.8	
30. Soda ash	th. m. t.	613	542.7	88.5		564.7	
31. Caustic soda	th. m. t.		176.6			177.5	
32. Sulfuric acid	th. m. t.	1,588	1,544	97.2		1,625	
32a. Synthetic rubber	th. m. t.		90.0			103.0	
33. Tires	thous.		3,595			4,221	
34. Plastics	th. m. t.		17.44				
34a. Synthetic dyes	th. m. t.		35.3				
35. Cement	th. m. t.	7,050	5,688	80.7		5,197	
36. Lime	th. m. t.		4,447			4,566	
37. Window glass	mill. m²		59.6			51.3	
38a. Roofing tiles	mill.		159.1			162.6	
39. Asbestos shingles	mill.		170.3			200.8	
40. Bricks	mill.		7,586			7,594	
41. Industrial timber hauled	mill. m³	153	114.7	75.0		126.1	
42. Lumber	mill. m³		34.5			34.5	
43. Plywood	th. m³	750	666.0	88.8		671.9	
44. Paper	th. m. t.	920.0	832.8	90.5	885.0	799.8	90.4
45. Paperboard	th. m. t.		96.6		117.8	97.6	
46. Machine tools	units	40,800	39,000	95.7	46,894	40,446	86.2
46a. Metallurgical equipment	th. m. t.		17.0				
47. Steam and gas turbines	th. kw		1,135			1,377	
48. Steam boilers	th. m²		240.4				
49. Turbogenerators	th. kw		374.0				
50. Spinning machines	units						
51. Looms	units						
52. Tractors	units		49,200			48,100	
53. Tractors (15 hp)	th. conven. units		93.4			88.8	
54. Motor vehicles, total	thous.		211.1			201.7	
55. Trucks and buses	thous.		184.1			182.1	
56. Automobiles	thous.		27.0			19.6	
57. Buses	thous.		1.7			3.3	
58. Grain combines	units		22,900			14,800	
59. Steam locomotives	units		1,216			1,011	
60. Diesel locomotives	units		4			6	
61. Electric locomotives	units		32			17	
62. Railroad freight cars	units						

	1940			1941			
Planned (7)	Actual (8)	(8) as Per Cent of (7) (9)	Planned (10)	Actual (11)	(11) as Per Cent of (10) (12)	Series No.	
	8.66		17.2			20	
	95					21	
	160.9		211			22	
	89.4					23	
	3,238					24	
	1,810		2,500			25	
	1,351.9		1,870			26	
	381.7		610.0			27	
	532.3		623.0			28	
	971.7		870.0			29	
649	536.1	82.6	673.0			30	
	190.4					31	
	1,587					32	
	100.0					32a	
	3,007		4,000			33	
	14.9		13.5			34	
	33.87		39.5			34a	
	5,675		7,998	5,500	68.8	35	
	4,470		4,500			36	
	44.7		59.4			37	
	173.3		241.0			38a	
	205.6		240.0			39	
	7,455		9,138			40	
	117.9		151.6			41	
	34.8		28.9			42	
	731.9		552.5			43	
	812.4		969.8			44	
115.8	120.0	103.6	197.0			45	
51,300	44,000	85.8	58,000	44,500	76.7	46	
	23.7		45.0	20.9	46.4	46a	
	972		545			47	
	276.3		270.6			48	
	313.5		644.5			49	
	1,109		2,000			50	
	1,823		3,150			51	
	31,649		28,000			52	
	66.2					53	
	145.4		140.0			54	
	139.9		131.0			55	
	5.5		9.0			56	
	3.9		4.5			57	
	12,756		13,000			58	
	914		1,300			59	
	5		6			60	
	9		10			61	
	30,880		61,900			62	

Table A-3 *continued*

Series	Units	1938			1939		
		Planned (1)	Actual (2)	(2) as Per Cent of (1) (3)	Planned (4)	Actual (5)	(5) as Per Cent of (4) (6)
64. Railroad passenger cars	units		1,167				
65. Excavators	units		492			310	
66. Ginned cotton	th. m. t.		830.9			909.0	
67. Cotton yarn	th. m. t.		566			606	
68. Cotton fabrics	mill. m	4,035.5	3,460	85.7	3,662	3,763	102.8
69. Woolen fabrics	mill. m		113.2		110.4	122.4	110.9
70. Linen fabrics	mill. m²		249			215	
71. Linen fabrics	mill. m		269.8		290.2	257.7	88.8
72. Silk and rayon fabrics	mill. m		58.8			70.4	
73. Knitted underwear	mill.		114.9			117.0	
74. Knitted outer garments	mill.	51.2	54.0	105.5		53.7	
75. Hosiery	mill. prs	515	451.1	87.6	425.0	457.4	107.6
76. Leather shoes	mill. prs	180	173.2	96.2		184.7	
77. Felt footwear	mill. prs						
78. Rubber footwear	mill. prs		85.5			80.3	
79. Rubber galoshes	mill. prs						
80. Metal beds	thous.						
80a. Enameled kitchenware	th. m. t.						
81. Motorcycles	thous.						
82. Bicycles	thous.						
83. Radios	thous.						
83a. Refrigerators, household	thous.						
84. Sewing machines, household	thous.						
85. Clocks and watches	thous.		3,542			2,983	
86. Cameras	thous.						
87. Phonographs	thous.						
88. Soap (40% fatty acid)	th. m. t.	560.0	606	108.2		676	
89. Bread and breadstuffs (large-scale industry)	th. m. t.		16,600				
89a. Bread and breadstuffs (ministries and local Soviets)	th. m. t.	9,000	9,379	104.2		11,225	
90. Flour (total)	th. m. t.						
90a. Flour (centralized resources)	th. m. t.		15,000				
90b. Flour (procurements)	th. m. t.						
91. Macaroni	th. m. t.	290	306	105.5		388	
92. Raw sugar	th. m. t.	2,700	2,520	93.3		1,826	
93. Starch and syrup	th. m. t.	277.0	306	110.5		233	
94. Fish catch	th. m. t.	1,630	1,542	94.6		1,566	
95. Crude alcohol	th. hl		9,320			9,450	
96. Vegetable oil	th. m. t.	540	643	119.1		693	
97. Butter	th. m. t.	180	199	110.6		191	
98. Cheese	th. m. t.	33.0	30.5	92.4		33.2	
99. Meat	th. m. t.	900	1,140	126.7	1,100		

1940			1941			
Planned (7)	Actual (8)	(8) as Per Cent of (7) (9)	Planned (10)	Actual (11)	(11) as Per Cent of (10) (12)	Series No.
	1,051		900			64
	274		490			65
	848.6		860.0			66
	649.9		699.3			67
	3,954		4,337.7	3,824	88.2	68
	119.7		121.7			69
	219					70
	285.5		283.8			71
	76.6		73.0			72
	124.4		132.4			73
	58.6		55.1			74
	485.4		538.0			75
206	189.5	92.0	221.6			76
19.0	17.9	94	18.4			77
	69.7		82.0			78
	45.0		54.8			79
	6,157		5,723			80
	11.4		12.7			80a
	6.8					81
	255.0		374			82
	160.5		265.0			83
	3.5					83a
	175.2		408			84
	2,796		3,405			85
	355.2		40.0			86
	313.7		270.0			87
	700		725.0			88
			22,100			89
	13,737					89a
	28,792					90
	16,397		18,797			90a
			16,447			90b
	324.2		389.5			91
2,683	2,165	80.7	2,650	523	19.7	92
	247					93
1,750	1,404	80	1,661	1,270	76.5	94
	8,990		9,880			95
	798		737.0	685	92.9	96
	226		203.0	175.2	86.3	97
	37.3		43.5			98
1,500	1,192	79	1,240.0			99

Table A-3 *continued*

Series	Units	1938			1939		
		Planned (1)	Actual (2)	(2) as Per Cent of (1) (3)	Planned (4)	Actual (5)	(5) as Per Cent of (4) (6)
100. Meat and subproducts of first category	th. m. t.		1,447			1,639	
101. Sausages	th. m. t.	330	395	119.7			
102. Canned food	mill. 400-gm cans	1,500	1,104	73.6		1,148	
103. Confectionery	th. m. t.	891	994	111.6		999	
104. Margarine	th. m. t.	85	93	109.4		107	
105. Beer	th. hl	9,800	10,310	105.2		10,740	
106. Cigarettes	bill.		95.6			97.6	
107. Matches	th. crates		9,516			10,243	
108. Low-grade tobacco (*makhorka*)	th. 20-kg crates	5,600	5,600	100.0		4,300	
109. Salt	th. m. t.		3,500			3,800	
Agriculture							
110. Total value of production (1926/27 prices)	mill. rub.		18,529				
111. Vegetable production (1926/27 prices)	mill. rub.		12,694				
112. Animal production (1926/27 prices)	mill. rub.		5,835				
Harvests							
113. Grain, total (biological yield)	mill. m. t.		94.99			106.5	
113a. Grain, total (barn yield)	mill. m. t.						
114. Wheat (biological yield)	mill. m. t.						
114a. Wheat (barn yield)	mill. m. t.						
115. Rye (biological yield)	mill. m. t.						
115a. Rye (barn yield)	mill. m. t.						
116. Barley (biological yield)	mill. m. t.						
116a. Barley (barn yield)	mill. m. t.						
117. Oats (biological yield)	mill. m. t.						
117a. Oats (barn yield)	mill. m. t.						
118a. Corn (barn yield)	mill. m. t.						
Harvests of Technical Crops							
119. Raw cotton (biological yield)	mill. m. t.		2.69			2.79	
119a. Raw cotton (barn yield)	mill. m. t.						
120. Sugar beets (biological yield)	mill. m. t.		16.68		23.46	21.0	89.5
120a. Sugar beets (barn yield)	mill. m. t.						
121. Sunflowers (biological yield)	mill. m. t.		1.67		2.33	2.92	125.3
121a. Sunflowers (barn yield)	mill. m. t.						

1940			1941			
Planned (7)	Actual (8)	(8) as Per Cent of (7) (9)	Planned (10)	Actual (11)	(11) as Per Cent of (10) (12)	Series No.
	1,501					100
	391.3		382.0			101
	1,113		1,262.0			102
	790		1,092.0			103
	121		125.0			104
	12,130		12,860			105
112	100.4	89.6	110.0			106
	10,000		11,750	7,458	63.5	107
	4,600		5,600			108
	4,404		4,780			109
	23,300			14,500		110
	16,300					111
	7,000					112
	118.8		123.76			113
	95.496			56.300		113a
	40.625					114
	31.746					114a
	26.1					115
	20.967					115a
	15.3					116
	12.046					116a
	21.2					117
	16.795					117a
	5.120					118a
	2.70		3.01			119
	2.023		2.26	2.349	103.9	119a
	20.95		24.18			120
	18.015		20.8	2.0	9.6	120a
	3.3		2.94			121
	2.578		2.3	.88	38.3	121a

Table A-3   *continued*

Series	Units	1938			1939		
		Planned (1)	Actual (2)	(2) as Per Cent of (1) (3)	Planned (4)	Actual (5)	(5) as Per Cent of (4) (6)
122. Flax fiber (biological yield)	th. m. t.		546			633	
122a. Flax fiber (barn yield)	th. m. t.						
123a. Hemp (barn yield)	th. m. t.						
124. Potatoes (biological yield)	mill. m. t.		41.96			62.12	
124a. Potatoes (barn yield)	mill. m. t.						
Animal Production							
125. Meat and fat (excl. rabbit and poultry)	th. m. t.						
125a. Meat and fat (incl. rabbit and poultry)	th. m. t.		4,500			5,100	
126. Milk	mill. m. t.		28.86			27.2	
127. Eggs	bill.		10.5			11.5	
128. Wool	th. m. t.		137			150	
Market Production							
129. Grain	mill. m. t.		36.52				
130. Raw cotton	mill. m. t.		2.69				
131. Sugar beets	mill. m. t.		16.35				
132. Flax fiber	th. m. t.		310				
133. Potatoes	mill. m. t.		8.06				
134. Meat and fat (dead weight)	th. m. t.		2,054				
135. Milk and dairy products	mill. m. t.		8.19				
136. Wool	th. m. t.		88.5				
Procurements							
137. Grain	th. m. t.		31,500			35,000	
138. Raw cotton	th. m. t.						
139. Sugar beets	th. m. t.						
140. Sunflowers	th. m. t.		977			1,247	
141. Flax fiber	th. m. t.	222			217		
142. Hemp	th. m. t.	39			40		
143. Potatoes	th. m. t.		5,131			4,706	
143a. Vegetables	th. m. t.		1,000			1,700	
144. Meat and fat (live weight)	th. m. t.						
145. Meat and fat (dead weight)	th. m. t.						
146. Milk and dairy products	th. m. t.						
147. Eggs	mill.						
148. Wool	th. m. t.						
Railroad Transportation							
149. Length of network	th. km		85.0			86.4	
150. Average daily carloadings	thous.	95	88.0	92.6		93.4	
151. Total freight traffic	bill. m. ton-km	394.8	370.5	93.8		391.7	
152. Total freight traffic	mill. m. t.	568.0	516.3	90.9		553.6	
153. Coal and coke	mill. m. t.						

	1940			1941		
Planned (7)	Actual (8)	(8) as Per Cent of (7) (9)	Planned (10)	Actual (11)	(11) as Per Cent of (10) (12)	Series No.
	565		750			122
	349		460	130	28.3	122a
	133					123a
	84.24		97.44			124
	75.874		87.8	26.6	30.3	124a
	4,399		3,340	3,800	113.8	125
	4,695		3,968	4,100	103.3	125a
	33.64		35.9	25.6	71.3	126
	12.2			9.3		127
	161		189.4	161	85.0	128
	38.3					129
	2.24					130
	17.4					131
						132
	12.9					133
	2,600					134
	10.8					135
	120					136
	36,446			24,298		137
	2,237			2,478		138
	17,357			1,670		139
	1,500			478		140
	245			67		141
	44					142
	8,457					143
	2,970					143a
	2,040			1,500		144
	1,300					145
	6,453			5,200		146
	2,679			1,900		147
	120			119		148
	106.1			74.0		149
	97.9		103.0	86.0	83.5	150
	415.0		430.9	386	89.6	151
	592.6		624.9	549	88.0	152
	152.5		170.0			153

Table A-3 *continued*

Series	Units	1938 Planned (1)	1938 Actual (2)	1938 (2) as Per Cent of (1) (3)	1939 Planned (4)	1939 Actual (5)	1939 (5) as Per Cent of (4) (6)
154. Oil and oil products	mill. m. t.						
155. Ferrous metals	mill. m. t.						
156. Ore	mill. m. t.						
157. Firewood	mill. m. t.						
158. Timber	mill. m. t.						
159. Mineral construction materials	mill. m. t.		93.5			106.1	
159a. Principal construction materials (stone, lime, cement, bricks)	mill. m. t.		38.0			35.0	
160. Grain and flour	mill. m. t.						
162. Total freight traffic, average length of haul	km	695	718	103.3		708	
163. Coal and coke, average length of haul	km		698			700	
163a. Oil and oil products, average length of haul	km						
164. Ferrous metals, average length of haul	km		1,019			1,016	
164a. Firewood, average length of haul	km						
164b. Timber, average length of haul	km						
165. Grain and flour, average length of haul	km						
165a. Ore, average length of haul	km		602				
166. Total passenger traffic	bill. pass.-km	95.0	84.9	89.4		93.7	
Inland Waterway Transportation							
166a. Length of network	km						
168. Freight traffic under ministries and economic organizations	bill. m. ton-km		32.1			34.5	
170. Freight traffic under ministries and economic organizations	mill. m. t.		66.5			71.3	
171. Coal and coke	th. m. t.						
172. Oil and oil products	th. m. t.						
173. Timber and firewood	th. m. t.						
174. Mineral construction materials	th. m. t.						
175. Grain and flour	th. m. t.						
176. Salt	th. m. t.						
177. Average length of haul under ministries and economic organizations	km		483			484	

	1940			1941		
Planned (7)	Actual (8)	(8) as Per Cent of (7) (9)	Planned (10)	Actual (11)	(11) as Per Cent of (10) (12)	Series No.
	29.5		32.5			154
	27.1		30.5			155
	35.2		36.0			156
	23.1		20.1			157
	42.8		54.0			158
	111.7		100.0			159
	32.0					159a
	44.6		45.5			160
	700		690	732	106.1	162
	701					163
	1,234					163a
	966					164
	252					164a
	1,019					164b
	736					165
	612					165a
	98.0		91.0			166
	107.3					166a
	35.9		46.3	34	73.4	168
	72.9		87.0			170
	2,200		2,120			171
	9,700		10,940			172
	40,200		49,370			173
	7,600		9,240			174
	5,200		5,860			175
	1,400		1,720			176
	493		533			177

Table A-3 *continued*

		1938			1939		
Series	Units	Planned (1)	Actual (2)	(2) as Per Cent of (1) (3)	Planned (4)	Actual (5)	(5) as Per Cent of (4) (6)
178. Passenger traffic	bill. pass.-km		3.2			3.3	
178a. Passenger traffic	mill. pass.		68.1			69.7	
Maritime Transportation (Soviet ships)							
179. Freight traffic	bill. m. ton-km		33.7			29.8	
180. Freight traffic	mill. m. t.		30.4			30.2	
181. Average length of haul	km		1,119			987	
182. Passenger traffic	mill. pass.-km		800				
182a. Passenger traffic	mill. pass.		3.1				
Motor Transportation							
183. Freight traffic	bill. m. ton-km		6.8			7.9	
Air Transportation							
184. Freight traffic, incl. mail	mill. m. ton-km		31.7				
185. Passenger traffic	th. pass.						
Employment (annual averages)							
186. Workers and employees, national economy, excl. collective farms	mill.		27.8			30.1	
187. Industry	thous.	10,600	10,100	95.3		10,100	
188. Construction	thous.						
188a. Construction and assembly work	thous.						
189. State-owned agriculture and logging	thous.						
190. State-owned agriculture (state farms, MTS, and other state establishments)	thous.		2,142				
191. Railroad transport	thous.						
192. Maritime and inland waterway transport	thous.						
193. Other transport (motor, etc.)	thous.						
194. Communications	thous.						
195. Trade, procurements, and supply	thous.						
196. Public eating places	thous.						
197. Credit institutions	thous.						
198. Administration	thous.						
199. Education	thous.						
200. Public health	thous.						
Wage Fund, Workers and Employees							
201. National economy	mill. rub.	94,000	96,425	102.6		116,500	
202. Industry	mill. rub.	35,171	34,815	99.0		42,265	

| 1940 | | | 1941 | | | |
Planned (7)	Actual (8)	(8) as Per Cent of (7) (9)	Planned (10)	Actual (11)	(11) as Per Cent of (10) (12)	Series No.
	3.8		3.67			178
	73.0		74.0			178a
	23.8		25.2	20	79.4	179
	31.2		34.6			180
	745		728			181
	876		833			182
	3.1		3.26			182a
	8.896		9.37	6.2	66.2	183
	33.1		48	24.5	51.0	184
	400		387.0			185
	31.2		31.6	27.4	86.7	186
	10,967		11,092	9,800	88.4	187
	2,510		3,085			188
	1,563		1,958			188a
	2,983					189
	2,073		2,075			190
	1,752		1,714			191
	203		207			192
	1,552					193
	478		463			194
	2,465		2,355			195
	662		670			196
	262		275.3			197
	1,825					198
	2,930		2,875			199
	1,507		1,646			200
129,300	123,700	95.7	133,668			201
	44,750		52,230			202

Table A-3   *continued*

Series	Units	1938 Planned (1)	1938 Actual (2)	1938 (2) as Per Cent of (1) (3)	1939 Planned (4)	1939 Actual (5)	1939 (5) as Per Cent of (4) (6)
Average Annual Wage, Workers and Employees							
203. Money wage, national economy (excl. collective farms and cooperatives)	rubles		3,467			3,867	
205. Money wage, industry	rubles	3,318	3,447	103.9			
Average Annual Money Wage, Workers							
206. Industry	rubles						
208. Coal	rubles						
209. Ferrous metals	rubles						
209a. Machine-building	rubles						
210. Paper	rubles						
211. Chemicals	rubles						
212. Textiles	rubles						
214. Food	rubles						
Average Annual Money Wage, Workers and Employees							
215. Construction	rubles						
216. Railroad transport	rubles	3,454	3,732	108.0		4,116	
217. Maritime and inland waterway transport	rubles						
218. Communications	rubles						
219. Trade	rubles						
220. Public eating places	rubles						
221. Credit institutions	rubles						
222. Administration	rubles						
223. Education	rubles						
224. Public health	rubles						
225. State-owned agriculture	rubles						
Housing							
227. Housing fund, urban, total	mill. m^2	214.1					
228. Housing construction, urban, total	mill. m^2	7.8					
229. Floorspace per inhabitant, urban	m^2						
Population							
230. Total (end of year)	mill.		170.6				
231. Urban (end of year)	mill.		56.1				
232. Rural (end of year)	mill.		114.5				
Retail Trade							
233. State and cooperative in current prices	mill. rub.	140,500	140,000	99.6	184,400	165,800	89.9
234c. Food products in current prices	mill. rub.		88,100			104,600	
235. Collective farm in current prices	mill. rub.		24,399			29,900	

1940			1941			
Planned (7)	Actual (8)	(8) as Per Cent of (7) (9)	Planned (10)	Actual (11)	(11) as Per Cent of (10) (12)	Series No.
	3,972		4,230			203
	4,080		4,345			205
	3,876		4,128			206
	5,229		5,475			208
	4,719		5,120			209
	4,791		5,055			209a
	3,343		3,577			210
	4,509		4,761			211
	3,434		3,571			212
	3,307		3,373			214
	4,068		4,312			215
	4,092		4,231			216
	4,908		5,012			217
	3,372		3,492			218
	3,000		3,248			219
			2,875			220
	4,008		3,734			221
	4,656					222
	3,876		4,331			223
	3,060		3,122			224
	2,628		3,440			225
	270		273.8			227
			5.2			228
	5.1					229
	196.7					230
	63.9					231
	132.8					232
189,000	175,080	92.6	197,000	152,800	77.6	233
	110,535			96,300		234c
	41,100					235

Table A-3 *continued*

Source

1. National income (1926/27 prices)–**Col. 2:** *226*, p. 18. **Cols. 5 and 8:** *161*, p. 112. **Col. 11:** Based on national income in 1940 (col. 8) and index for 1942 (given as 92 with 1940 = 100 in *207*, p. 121).

INDUSTRY

2. Gross production, total (1926/27 prices)–**Col. 1:** *173*, No. 5, 1938, p. 20. **Col. 2:** *226*, p. 34. **Col. 5:** *412*, p. 137. **Col. 8:** *194*, Vol. 3, p. 252. **Col. 10:** *60*, p. 3. See also *288*, p. 13. **Col. 11:** Based on gross production in 1940 (col. 8) and index for 1942 (given as 98 with 1940 = 100 in *207*, p. 121).

3. Producer goods (1926/27 prices)–**Col. 2:** *226*, p. 34. **Col. 5:** *433*, p. 149. **Col. 8:** *290*, p. 6. **Col. 10:** *288*, p. 14. **Col. 11:** Based on gross production (series 2) and share of producer goods in total (given as 69.5% in *99*, p. 114).

4. Consumer goods (1926/27 prices)–**Col. 2:** *226*, p. 34. **Col. 5:** *433*, p. 149. **Col. 8:** *290*, p. 6. **Col. 10:** *288*, p. 14. **Col. 11:** Based on gross production (series 2) and share of consumer goods in total (given as 30.5% in *99*, p. 114).

5. Coal–**Col. 1:** Estimated from increase planned for 1938 (given as 17.7 mill. m. t. and 13% in *173*, No. 5, 1938, p. 21). **Cols. 2, 5, and 8:** *187*, p. 140. **Col. 4:** *173*, No. 2, 1939, p. 55. **Col. 10:** *60*, p. 3. *288*, p. 13, gives 191 mill. m. t. **Col. 11:** *99*, p. 160. Sum of output for first and second halves of year.

6. Peat–**Cols. 2, 5, 8, and 11:** *218*, p. 35. Includes collective farm output. **Col. 10:** *60*, p. 658.

7. Coke (6% humidity)–**Cols. 2, 5, and 8:** *187*, p. 115. **Col. 11:** *60*, p. 17.

8. Oil shale–**Col. 2:** *65*, 6/9/39, as cited in *472*, p. 423. **Col. 8:** *187*, p. 166. **Col. 11:** *60*, p. 660. Includes output of Estonian Republic, which amounted to 2,700 th. m. t.

9. Crude petroleum–**Col. 1:** Planned output of crude petroleum and gas (given as 33.5 mill. m. t. in *173*, No. 5, 1938, p. 21) minus actual output of gas (estimated as 2,000 th. m. t. in *485*, series 310.1). **Cols. 2, 5, and 8:** *187*, p. 153. **Col. 10:** *60*, p. 15. **Col. 11:** *99*, p. 133.

10. Natural gas–**Cols. 2 and 5:** *472*, p. 422. **Col. 8:** *187*, p. 156. Includes secondary extraction of gas. **Col. 10:** Based on planned output in tons (given as 3,435 th. m. t. in *60*, p. 16) and ratio of m³ to tons for 1937 (derived as 1,100 in Table A-2, series 10).

11. Electric power–**Col. 1:** *173*, No. 5, 1938, p. 21. **Cols. 2, 5, and 8:** *187*, p. 171. **Col. 10:** *60*, p. 12. **Col. 11:** *285*, No. 5, 1965, p. 70.

12. Hydroelectric power–**Cols. 2, 5, and 8:** *187*, p. 171.

13. Iron ore–**Col. 1:** *54*, No. 3, 1938, p. 5, as cited in *485*, series 101.3. **Cols. 2, 5, and 8:** *187*, p. 115. **Col. 4:** *173*, No. 8, 1939, p. 71. **Col. 10:** *60*, p. 16. **Col. 11:** *99*, p. 160. Sum of output for first and second halves of year.

14. Pig iron–**Col. 1:** *173*, No. 5, 1938, p. 21. **Cols. 2, 5, and 8:** *187*, p. 106. **Col. 6:** *173*, No. 8, 1939, p. 71. Covers first half year. **Col. 10:** *60*, p. 17. **Col. 11:** *121*, p. 188.

15. Steel ingots and castings–**Col. 1:** *173*, No. 5, 1938, p. 21. **Cols. 2, 5, and 8:** *187*, p. 106. **Col. 10:** *60*, p. 18. **Col. 11:** *121*, p. 188.

16. Rolled steel–**Col. 1:** *173*, No. 5, 1938, p. 21. **Cols. 2, 5, and 8:** *187*, p. 106. **Col. 4:** Estimated by doubling plan for first half of year (derived as 7,247 th. m. t. from statement in *173*, No. 8, 1939, p. 67, that 92.5% of plan for first half year was fulfilled and that the shortfall amounted to 543.5 th. m. t.). **Col. 10:** *60*, p. 18. **Col. 11:** *121*, p. 188.

17. Steel pipes–**Cols. 2, 5, and 8:** *187*, p. 106. **Col. 10:** *60*, p. 24.

18. Aluminum–**Col. 2:** *226*, p. 62. Total minus secondary aluminum. **Cols. 5 and 8:** *472*, p. 420.

19. Manganese ore–**Col. 1:** *54*, No. 3, 1938, p. 5, as cited in *485*, series 212.3. **Cols. 2, 5, and 8:** *187*, p. 115. **Col. 10:** *60*, p. 17.

20. Nickel–**Cols. 2, 5, 8, and 10:** *485*, series 213.4. Estimates.

21. Zinc–**Col. 2, 5, and 8:** *472*, p. 421. Estimates.

22. Refined copper–**Col. 1:** Based on 1937 output (given as 97.5 th. m. t. in Table A-1, col. 2) and increase planned for 1938 for blister copper (given as 43% in *173*, No. 5, 1938, p. 21). **Col. 2:** *226*, p. 62. **Cols. 5 and 8:** *472*, p. 420. Estimates. **Col. 10:** Based on 1940 output (col. 8) and increase planned for 1941 (given as 31% in *288*, p. 14).

23. Lead–**Col. 1:** *485*, series 209.1. **Cols. 2, 5, and 8:** *472*, p. 421. Estimates.

24. Mineral fertilizer–**Cols. 2, 5, and 8:** *187*, p. 192.

25. Phosphoric fertilizer (14% P_2O_5)–**Cols. 2, 5, and 8:** *485*, series 409.3. **Col. 10:** *60*, p. 56. Converted from 100% P_2O_5.

26. Phosphoric fertilizer (18.7% P_2O_5)–**Col. 1:** Based on 1937 output (given as 1,472.7 th. m. t. in Table A-1, col. 2) and increase planned for 1938 (given as 20% in *173*, No. 5, 1938, p. 21). **Cols. 2, 5, and 8:** *187*, p. 192. **Col. 10:** *60*, p. 56. Converted from 100% P_2O_5.

27. Ground natural phosphate–**Cols. 2, 5, and 8:** *187*, p. 192. **Col. 10:** *60*, p. 56.

28. Potash fertilizer–**Cols. 2, 5, and 8:** *187*, p. 192. **Col. 10:** *60*, p. 302. Deliveries to agriculture.

29. Ammonium sulfate–**Col. 1:** Based on 1937 output (given as 761.6 th. m. t. in Table A-1, col. 2) and increase planned for all nitric fertilizers for 1938 (given as 23% in *315*, No. 3, 1938, p. 3, as cited in *485*, series 414.3). **Cols. 2, 5, and 8:** *187*, p. 192. **Col. 10:** *60*, p. 302. Deliveries to agriculture.

30. Soda ash–**Col. 1:** Based on 1937 output (given as 528.2 th. m. t. in Table A-1, col. 2) and increase planned for 1938 (given as 16% in *173*, No. 5, 1938, p. 21). **Cols. 2, 5, and 8:** *187*, p. 194. **Col. 7:** Based on 1939 output (col. 5) and increase planned for 1940 (given as 15% in *315*, No. 10, 1939, p. 4, as cited in *485*, series 406.1). **Col. 10:** *60*, p. 56.

Table A-3 *continued*

31. Caustic soda–**Cols. 2, 5, and 8:** *187*, p. 194.

32. Sulfuric acid–**Col. 1:** Based on 1937 output (given as 1,369 th. m. t. in Table A-1, col. 2) and increase planned for 1938 (given as 16% in *173*, No. 5, 1938, p. 21). **Cols. 2, 5, and 8:** *187*, p. 196.

32a. Synthetic rubber–**Cols. 2, 5, and 8:** *223*, p. 247.

33. Tires–**Cols. 2, 5, and 8:** *187*, p. 199. **Col. 10:** *60*, p. 58.

34. Plastics–**Col. 2:** *485*, series 455.4. Estimate. **Col. 8:** *188*, p. 146. Synthetic tars and plastics. **Col. 10:** *60*, p. 57. Commissariat of the Chemical Industry.

34a. Synthetic dyes–**Col. 2:** *13*, p. 819. **Col. 8:** *187*, p. 197. Commissariat of the Chemical Industry. **Col. 10:** *60*, p. 57. Commissariat of the Chemical Industry.

35. Cement–**Col. 1:** *263*, No. 4, 1938, p. 9, as cited in *485*, series 709.1. **Cols. 2, 5, and 8:** *187*, p. 277. **Col. 10:** *60*, p. 664. **Col. 11:** *285*, No. 5, 1965, p. 70.

36. Lime–**Cols. 2, 5, and 8:** *187*, p. 282. Sum of construction lime and technological lime. **Col. 10:** *60*, p. 61.

37. Window glass–**Cols. 2, 5, and 8:** *187*, p. 312. **Col. 10:** *60*, p. 67.

38a. Roofing tiles–**Cols. 2, 5, and 8:** *187*, p. 299. Includes collective farm output. **Col. 10:** *60*, p. 65. Excludes collective farm output.

39. Asbestos shingles–**Cols. 2, 5, and 8:** *187*, p. 299. **Col. 10:** *60*, p. 65. Commissariat of Construction Materials.

40. Bricks–**Cols. 2, 5, and 8:** *187*, p. 291. **Col. 10:** *60*, p. 63. Excludes collective farm output.

41. Industrial timber hauled–**Col. 1:** Based on 1937 output (given as 114.2 mill. m³ in Table A-1, col. 2) and increase planned for 1938 (given as 34% in *173*, No. 5, 1938, p. 22). **Cols. 2, 5, and 8:** *187*, p. 249. **Col. 10:** *60*, p. 68.

42. Lumber–**Cols. 2, 5, and 8:** *187*, p. 261. **Col. 10:** *60*, p. 68.

43. Plywood–**Col. 1:** *173*, No. 2, 1939, p. 99. **Cols. 2, 5, and 8:** *187*, p. 261. **Col. 10:** *60*, p. 69.

44. Paper–**Col. 1:** *19*, No. 2, 1938, p. 11, as cited in *485*, series 449.1. **Cols. 2, 5, and 8:** *187*, p. 268. **Col. 4:** *19*, No. 4, 1939, p. 74, as cited in *485*, series 449.1. *173*, No. 10, 1939, p. 64, gives 1,005 th. m. t. On the discrepancies in data from different sources, see *485*, series 449.1, general note. **Col. 10:** *60*, p. 69.

45. Paperboard–**Cols. 2, 5, and 7:** *19*, No. 10, 1940, p. 62, as cited in *485*, series 450.3. The definition of paperboard was considerably enlarged in later years, but the older figures of narrower coverage are used here to maintain comparability. **Col. 4:** *173*, No. 10, 1939, p. 64. **Col. 8:** *485*, series 450.3. Estimate. *187*, p. 268, gives 150.8 th. m. t., but this is the newer, larger coverage discussed above. **Col. 10:** *60*, p. 70.

46. Machine tools–**Col. 1:** Based on actual output (col. 2) and percentage of plan fulfilled (col. 3). **Col. 2:** *433*, p. 18. **Col. 3:** *26*, Vol. 2, p. 601. Given for *Glavstankoprom*. **Col. 4:** *26*, Vol. 2, p. 602. **Col. 5:** Output of larger coverage (derived as 54,290 from output in 1937 given as 48,473 and indexes for 1937 and 1939 given as 25 and 28 with 1928 = 100 in *187*, pp. 207–8) reduced by ratio of smaller to larger coverage (derived as 74.5% in Table A-1, series 46, col. 5). **Col. 7:** *26*, Vol. 2, p. 602. Revised five-year plan figure for 1940 assumed to be same as annual plan for 1940, since 1941 annual plan figure given in same source is very close to that given in *60*. **Col. 8:** Table A-1, col. 5. **Col. 10:** *60*, p. 32. **Col. 11:** *285*, No. 5, 1965, p. 70.

46a. Metallurgical equipment–**Col. 2:** *433*, p. 146. **Col. 8:** *187*, p. 212. **Col. 10:** *60*, p. 34. Basic metallurgical equipment for the ferrous and nonferrous metal industry. **Col. 11:** Based on 1942 output (given as 19.4 th. m. t. in Table A-1, col. 8) and decrease in 1942 below 1941 (given as 7% in *99*, p. 135).

47. Steam and gas turbines–**Cols. 2, 5, and 8:** *187*, p. 216. **Col. 10:** *60*, p. 28. Definition may not be the same as for 1938–1940.

48. Steam boilers–**Col. 2:** *226*, p. 64. **Col. 8:** *187*, p. 218. **Col. 10:** *60*, p. 27. Coverage may not be same as for 1938–1940.

49. Turbogenerators–**Col. 2:** *128*, 1/21/39, p. 3, as cited in *472*, p. 441. **Col. 8:** *187*, pp. 214–15. **Col. 10:** *60*, p. 30.

50. Spinning machines–**Col. 8:** *187*, pp. 234–35. **Col. 10:** *60*, p. 36.

51. Looms–**Col. 8:** *28*, p. 74. **Col. 10:** *60*, p. 37.

52. Tractors–**Cols. 2, 5, and 8:** *187*, pp. 226 and 228. **Col. 10:** *60*, p. 42.

53. Tractors (15 hp)–**Cols. 2, 5, and 8:** *187*, p. 226.

54. Motor vehicles, total–**Cols. 2, 5, and 8:** *187*, p. 223. **Col. 10:** *60*, p. 45.

55. Trucks and buses–**Cols. 2, 5, and 8:** *187*, p. 223. Total motor vehicles minus automobiles. **Col. 10:** *60*, p. 45.

56. Automobiles–**Cols. 2, 5, and 8:** *187*, p. 223. **Col. 10:** *60*, p. 45.

57. Buses–**Cols. 2, 5, and 8:** *187*, p. 223. Total motor vehicles minus trucks and automobiles. **Col. 10:** *60*, p. 45.

58. Grain combines–**Cols. 2, 5, and 8:** *187*, pp. 232–33. **Col. 10:** *60*, p. 41. Given for combines without further specification.

59. Steam locomotives–**Cols. 2, 5, and 8:** *187*, p. 220. **Col. 10:** *60*, p. 42. Commissariat of Transportation type of locomotive.

60. Diesel locomotives–**Cols. 2, 5, and 8:** *187*, p. 220. **Col. 10:** *60*, p. 42. Commissariat of Heavy Machine-Building.

61. Electric locomotives–**Cols. 2, 5, and 8:** *187*, p. 220. **Col. 10:** *60*, p. 42. Commissariat of Electrical Industry.

Table A-3   *continued*

62. Railroad freight cars (units)–**Col. 8:** *187*, p. 222. **Col. 10:** *60*, p. 43.

64. Railroad passenger cars–**Col. 2:** *128*, 7/15/39, p. 2, as cited in *472*, p. 433. **Col. 8:** *187*, p. 220. **Col. 10:** *60*, p. 44, Commissariat of Medium Machine-Building.

65. Excavators–**Cols. 2, 5, and 8:** *187*, p. 236. **Col. 10:** *60*, p. 40.

66. Ginned cotton–**Col. 2:** *226*, p. 73. **Col. 5:** *107*, No. 8–9, 1939, p. 5. **Col. 8:** *187*, p. 324. **Col. 10:** *60*, p. 71.

67. Cotton yarn–**Cols. 2 and 5:** *404*, p. 31. **Col. 8:** *187*, p. 327. **Col. 10:** *60*, p. 71.

68. Cotton fabrics–**Col. 1:** *173*, No. 5, 1938, p. 23. **Cols. 2, 5, and 8:** *187*, p. 328. **Col. 4:** *485*, series 1205.1. **Col. 10:** *60*, p. 4. **Col. 11:** *285*, No. 5, 1965, p. 71.

69. Woolen fabrics–**Cols. 2, 5, and 8:** *187*, p. 328. **Col. 4:** *208*, No. 1, 1939, p. 6, as cited in *485*, series 1216.1. **Col. 10:** *60*, p. 43.

70. Linen fabrics (square meters)–**Cols. 2, 5, and 8:** *485*, series 1210.7.

71. Linen fabrics (meters)–**Cols. 2, 5, and 8:** *187*, p. 328. **Col. 4:** *107*, No. 1, 1939, p. 5, as cited in *485*, series 1209.7. **Col. 10:** *60*, p. 4.

72. Silk and rayon fabrics–**Cols. 2, 5, and 8:** *187*, p. 328. **Col. 10:** *60*, p. 4.

73. Knitted underwear–**Cols. 2, 5, and 8:** *87*, p. 343. **Col. 10:** *60*, 71.

74. Knitted outer garments–**Col. 1:** Based on 1937 output (given as 45.1 mill. in Table A-1, col. 2) and increase planned for 1938 (given as 13.5% in *173*, No. 5, 1938, p. 23). **Cols. 2, 5, and 8:** *187*, p. 343. **Col. 10:** *60*, p. 71.

75. Hosiery–**Col. 1:** *173*, No. 5, 1938, p. 23. **Cols. 2, 5, and 8:** *187*, p. 343. **Col. 10:** *60*, p. 71.

76. Leather shoes–**Col. 1:** *173*, No. 5, 1938, p. 23. **Cols. 2, 5, and 8:** Total output (given as 192.9, 205.7, and 211.0 mill. prs, respectively, in *173*, p. 351) reduced by 10.2% (derived in Table A-1, series 76, col. 5) to maintain comparable coverage. **Col. 7:** Planned output of state industry excluding cooperatives (given as 163 mill. prs in *173*, No. 3, 1940, p. 85) increased by 20.7% (the share of cooperatives in total output derived from *60*, p. 72). **Col. 10:** *60*, p. 72.

77. Felt footwear–**Col. 7:** Based on 1940 output (col. 8) and percentage of plan fulfilled (col. 9). **Col. 8:** *187*, p. 323. **Col. 9:** *173*, No. 4, 1941, p. 45. **Col. 10:** *60*, p. 72. Sum of *valenki* and *fetrovaia obuv*.

78. Rubber footwear–**Cols. 2, 5, and 8:** *187*, p. 199. **Col. 10:** *60*, p. 60. Sum of output of Commissariat of the Chemical Industry and Belorussian Commissariat of Light Industry plus output of Northern Bukovina (Ukrainian Republic).

79. Rubber galoshes–**Col. 8:** *180*, 7/5/46, p. 2, as cited in *485*, series 1203.6. **Col. 10:** *60*, p. 60. Sum of output of Commissariat of the Chemical Industry and Belorussian Commissariat of Light Industry plus output of Northern Bukovina (estimated at 75% of total output of rubber footwear).

80. Metal beds–**Col. 8:** *188*, p. 412. **Col. 10:** *60*, p. 169. Given for beds without further specification.

80a. Enameled kitchenware–**Col. 8:** *187*, p. 364. **Col. 10:** *60*, p. 169.

81. Motorcycles–**Col. 8:** *187*, p. 362.

82. Bicycles–**Col. 8:** *187*, p. 362. **Col. 10:** *60*, p. 171. Sum of output of Commissariat of General Machine-Building, Ukrainian Commissariat of the Metal Industry, Belorussian Commissariat of the Metal Industry, and parts for bicycles for the Grodno and Lvov factories.

83. Radios–**Col. 8:** *188*, p. 407. **Col. 10:** *60*, p. 172. Sum of output of Belorussian Commissariat of the Metal Industry and of alternating and direct current receivers produced by Commissariat of the Electrical Industry.

83a. Refrigerators, household–**Col. 8:** *188*, p. 408.

84. Sewing machines, household–**Col. 8:** *187*, p. 362. **Col. 10:** *60*, p. 171. Sum of output of Commissariat of Armaments and Ukrainian Commissariat of the Metal Industry.

85. Clocks and watches–**Cols. 2 and 5:** *188*, p. 406. **Col. 8:** *187*, p. 362. **Col. 10:** *60*, p. 171. Sum of pocket watches, wrist watches, alarm clocks, wrist watches made from pocket watch mechanisms, wall clocks, and table clocks.

86. Cameras–**Col. 8:** *187*, p. 362. **Col. 10:** *60*, p. 172. Commissariat of Internal Affairs.

87. Phonographs–**Col. 8:** *187*, p. 363. **Col. 10:** *60*, p. 172.

88. Soap (40% fatty acid)–**Col. 1:** *170*, 2/26/38, p. 1, as cited in *485*, series 1113.1. **Cols. 2 and 5:** *316*, p. 178. **Col. 8:** *187*, p. 372. **Col. 10:** *60*, p. 167.

89. Bread and breadstuffs (large-scale industry)–**Col. 2:** *226*, p. 77. **Col. 10:** *60*, p. 75.

89a. Bread and breadstuffs (ministries and local Soviets)–**Col. 1:** *173*, No. 5, 1938, p. 23. **Cols. 2, 5, and 8:** *316*, p. 171.

90. Flour (total)–**Col. 8:** *188*, p. 450.

90a. Flour (centralized resources)–**Col. 2:** *135*, No. 1, 1939, p. 3, as cited in *485*, series 1126.5, col. 3, notes. **Col. 8:** *15*, p. 49. **Col. 10:** *60*, p. 75.

90b. Flour (procurements)–**Col. 10:** *60*, p. 75.

91. Macaroni–**Col. 1:** *173*, No. 5, 1938, p. 23. **Cols. 2 and 5:** *187*, p. 403. **Col. 8:** *187*, p. 404. **Col. 10:** *60*, p. 74.

92. Raw sugar–**Col. 1:** *173*, No. 5, 1938, p. 23. Given as 27 thous. centners, but obviously should be 27 mill. centners. **Cols. 2, 5, and 8:** *187*, p. 373. **Col. 7:** Based on 1940 output (col. 8) and percentage of plan fulfilled (col. 9). **Col. 9:** *173*, No. 4, 1941, p. 45. **Col. 10:** *60*, p. 73. **Col. 11:** *285*, No. 5, 1965, p. 71.

Table A-3 *continued*

93. Starch and syrup–**Col. 1:** *170,* 2/26/38, p. 1, as cited in *485,* series 118.5. **Cols. 2 and 5:** *316,* p. 272. Sum of starch and syrup. **Col. 8:** *187,* p. 372.

94. Fish catch–**Col. 1:** *173,* No. 5, 1938, p. 23. Given for fish without further specification. **Cols. 2, 5, and 8:** *187,* p. 381. **Col. 7:** Based on 1940 catch (col. 8) and percentage of plan fulfilled (col. 9). **Col. 9:** *173,* No. 4, 1941, p. 45. Given for fish and herring. **Col. 10:** *60,* p. 73. **Col. 11:** Based on 1940 catch (col. 8) and index for 1941 (derived as 90.3 with 1940 = 100 from fish catch of Commissariat of the Fishing Industry for 1940 and 1941 in *22,* p. 62).

95. Crude alcohol–**Cols. 2, 5, and 8:** *187,* p. 405. **Col. 10:** *60,* p. 74.

96. Vegetable oil–**Col. 1:** *173,* No. 5, 1938, p. 23. **Cols. 2, 5, and 8:** *187,* p. 392. **Col. 10:** *60,* p. 73. Commissariat of the Food Industry. **Col. 11:** *285,* No. 5, 1965, p. 71.

97. Butter–**Col. 1:** *173,* No. 5, 1938, p. 23. **Cols. 2, 5, and 8:** *187,* p. 386. **Col. 10:** *60,* p. 73. Includes 197.0 th. m. t. for Commissariat of the Meat and Dairy Industry. **Col. 11:** Based on planned output (col. 10) and percentage of plan fulfilled (col. 12). **Col. 12:** Assumed to be same as for Commissariat of the Meat and Dairy Industry (derived from planned output in note to col. 10 above and actual output given as 170.0 th. m. t. in *22,* p. 59).

98. Cheese–**Col. 1:** *170,* 2/26/38, p. 1, as cited in *485,* series 1108.2. **Cols. 2 and 5:** *133,* No. 2–3, 1940, p. 6, as cited in *472,* p. 450. **Col. 8:** *316,* p. 161. **Col. 10:** *60,* p. 73.

99. Meat–**Col. 1:** *173,* No. 5, 1938, p. 23. **Col. 2:** *226,* p. 77. **Col. 4:** *170,* 12/27/38, p. 1, as cited in *485,* series 1109.2. **Col. 7:** Based on 1940 output (col. 8) and percentage of plan fulfilled (col. 9). **Col. 8:** Table A-1, col. 5. **Col. 9:** *173,* No. 4, 1941, p. 45. **Col. 10:** *60,* p. 73.

100. Meat and subproducts of first category–**Cols. 2, 5, and 8:** *187,* p. 378.

101. Sausages–**Col. 1:** *173,* No. 5, 1938, p. 23. Given as 330 tons, but obviously should be 330 thous. m. tons. **Col. 2:** *226,* p. 77. **Col. 8:** *187,* p. 380. **Col. 10:** *60,* p. 73.

102. Canned food–**Col. 1:** *173,* No. 5, 1938, p. 23. **Cols. 2, 5, and 8:** *187,* p. 398. **Col. 10:** *60,* p. 74.

103. Confectionery–**Col. 1:** *173,* No. 5, 1938, p. 23. **Cols. 2, 5, and 8:** *187,* p. 401. **Col. 10:** *60,* p. 74.

104. Margarine–**Col. 1:** *170,* 2/26/38, p. 1, as cited in *485,* series 1106.5. Margarine and compound fats. **Cols. 2 and 5:** *316,* p. 170. **Col. 8:** *187,* p. 372. Margarine and compound fats. **Col. 10:** *60,* p. 73.

105. Beer–**Col. 1:** *173,* No. 5, 1938, p. 23. Given as 980 mill. decaliters, but obviously should be 980 mill. liters. **Cols. 2 and 5:** *316,* p. 174. **Col. 8:** *187,* p. 372. **Col. 10:** *60,* p. 74.

106. Cigarettes–**Cols. 2 and 5:** *316,* p. 177. **Col. 7:** Based on 1940 output (col. 8) and percentage of plan fulfilled (col. 9). **Col. 8:** *187,* p. 372. **Col. 9:** *173,* No. 4, 1941, p. 101. **Col. 10:** *60,* p. 74.

107. Matches–**Cols. 2, 5, and 11:** *113,* No. 6–7, 1946, pp. 13 and 15, as cited in *485,* series 1125.1. **Col. 8:** *187,* p. 267. **Col. 10:** *60,* p. 69.

108. Low-grade tobacco (*makhorka*)–**Col. 1:** *170,* 2/26/38, as cited in *485,* series 1124.3. **Cols. 2 and 5:** *316,* p. 177. **Col. 8:** *187,* p. 372. **Col. 10:** *60,* p. 74.

109. Salt–**Cols. 2 and 5:** *316,* p. 176. **Col. 8:** *287,* p. 230. **Col. 10:** *485,* series 115.5.

AGRICULTURE

110. Total value of production (1926/27 prices)–**Col. 2:** *469,* p. 2. **Col. 8:** *160,* p. 286. **Col. 11:** Based on 1940 value (col. 8) and index for 1941 (given as 62 with 1940 = 100 in *207,* p. 121).

111. Vegetable production (1926/27 prices)–**Col. 2:** *469,* p. 2. **Col. 8:** Based on total production (series 10) and share of vegetable production in total (calculated as 70% from *449,* p. 775).

112. Animal production (1926/27 prices)–**Col. 2:** *469,* p. 2. **Col. 8:** Based on total production (series 110) and share of animal production in total (calculated as 30% from *449,* p. 775).

HARVESTS

113. Grain (biological yield)–**Cols. 2 and 8:** *469,* p. 4. **Col. 5:** *449,* p. 793. **Col. 10:** *469,* p. 4. *60,* p. 203, gives 7.51 bill. poods, which (converted at 1 pood = .01638 m. t.) is 123.01 mill. m. t. *288,* p. 21, gives 7.9 bill. poods, which is 129.4 mill. m. t.

113a. Grain (barn yield)–**Col. 8:** *202,* p. 202. **Col. 11:** Based on 1940 harvest (col. 8) and index for 1941 (given as 59 with 1940 = 100 in *285,* No. 5, 1965, p. 72).

114. Wheat (biological yield)–**Col. 8:** *433,* p. 88.

114a. Wheat (barn yield)–**Col. 8:** *202,* p. 202. Sum of winter wheat and spring wheat.

115. Rye (biological yield)–**Col. 8:** Table A-1, col. 5. Estimate.

115a. Rye (barn yield)–**Col. 8:** *202,* p. 202. Winter rye.

116. Barley (biological yield)–**Col. 8:** Table A-1, col. 5. Estimate.

116a. Barley (barn yield)–**Col. 8:** *202,* p. 202. Sum of winter barley and spring barley.

117. Oats (biological yield)–**Col. 8:** Table A-1, col. 5. Estimate.

117a. Oats (barn yield)–**Col. 8:** *202,* p. 202.

118a. Corn (barn yield)–**Col. 8:** *202,* p. 202.

Table A-3 *continued*

HARVESTS OF TECHNICAL CROPS

119. Raw cotton (biological yield)–**Col. 2:** *225*, p. 68, as cited in *472*, p. 430. **Col. 5:** *91*, p. 402, as cited in *472*, p. 430. **Col. 8:** *194*, Vol. 3, p. 248. **Col. 10:** *60*, p. 203.

119a. Raw cotton (barn yield)–**Cols. 8 and 11:** *7*, p. 175. **Col. 10:** Based on 1940 harvest (col. 8) and increase planned for 1941 for biological yield (calculated as 11.5% from series 119, cols. 8 and 10).

120. Sugar beets (biological yield)–**Col. 2:** *469*, p. 6. **Col. 4:** Based on area sown to sugar beets on collective and state farms (derived as 1,173.1 th. hectares from *212*, No. 14, 1939, art. 88 and p. 165) and yield on collective farms (given as 200 quintals per hectare in *212*, p. 200). **Col. 5:** *449*, p. 792. **Col. 8:** *5*, p. 12. **Col. 10:** *60*, p. 203.

120a. Sugar beets (barn yield)–**Col. 8:** *202*, p. 202. **Col. 10:** Based on 1940 harvest (col. 8) and increase planned for 1941 for biological yield (calculated as 15.4% from series 120, cols. 8 and 10). **Col. 11:** Based on 1940 harvest (col. 8) and index for 1941 (given as 11 with 1940 = 100 in *285*, No. 5, 1965, p. 72).

121. Sunflowers (biological yield)–**Col. 2:** *449*, p. 776. **Col. 4:** Based on area sown to sunflowers on collective and state farms and by individual peasants (derived as 3,109.9 th. hectares from *212*, No. 14, 1939, art. 88, p. 164) and yield on collective farms (given as 7.5 quintals per hectare in *212*, p. 160). **Col. 5:** Based on 1940 harvest (col. 8) and increase of 1940 harvest over 1939 (given as 13.2% in *288*, p. 21). **Col. 8:** *469*, p. 6. **Col. 10:** *60*, p. 203.

121a. Sunflowers (barn yield)–**Col. 8:** *201*, p. 248. **Col. 10:** Based on 1940 harvest (col. 8) and decrease planned for 1941 for biological yield (calculated as 10.9% from series 121, cols. 8 and 10). **Col. 11:** Based on 1940 harvest (col. 8) and index for 1941 (given as 34 with 1940 = 100 in *285*, No. 5, 1965, p. 72).

122. Flax fiber (biological yield)–**Cols. 2 and 8:** *5*, pp. 46 and 12. **Col. 5:** *412*, p. 82. **Col. 10:** *60*, p. 203.

122a. Flax fiber (barn yield)–**Col. 8:** *202*, p. 202. **Col. 10:** Based on 1940 harvest (col. 8) and increase planned for 1941 for biological yield (calculated as 32.7% from series 122, cols. 8 and 10). **Col. 11:** Based on 1940 harvest (col. 8) and index for 1941 (given as 38 with 1940 = 100 in *285*, No. 5, 1965, p. 72).

123a. Hemp (barn yield)–**Col. 8:** *202*, p. 202.

124. Potatoes (biological yield)–**Col. 2:** *469*, p. 6. **Col. 5:** Based on 1940 harvest (col. 8) and increase in 1940 over 1939 (given as 35.6% in *288*, p. 21). **Col. 8:** Based on area sown to potatoes (given as 7.7 mill. hectares in *285*, No. 6, 1954, p. 33) and yield (given as 109.4 centners per hectare in *285*, No. 6, 1954, p. 33). **Col. 10:** *60*, p. 203.

124a. Potatoes (barn yield)–**Col. 8:** *202*, p. 202. **Col. 10:** Based on 1940 harvest (col. 8) and increase planned for 1941 for biological yield (calculated as 15.7% from series 124, cols. 8 and 10). **Col. 11:** Based on 1940 harvest (col. 8) and index for 1941 (given as 35 with 1940 = 100 in *285*, No. 5, 1965, p. 72).

ANIMAL PRODUCTION

125. Meat and fat (excl. rabbit and poultry)–**Col. 2:** *477*, p. 327, gives 3.3 mill. m. t., but this is the old definition and therefore is not used here. **Col. 8:** *202*, p. 333. Total meat and fat minus rabbit and poultry. **Col. 10:** *60*, p. 203. Total meat and fat minus rabbit and poultry. **Col. 11:** Based on 1940 production (col. 8) and index for 1941 (given as 87 with 1940 = 100 in *285*, No. 5, 1965, p. 72).

125a. Meat and fat (incl. rabbit and poultry)–**Cols. 2, 5, and 8:** *202*, pp. 328 and 333. For col. 2, *469*, p. 34, gives 3,607 th. m. t., but that is the old definition. **Col. 10:** *60*, p. 203. **Col. 11:** Based on 1940 production (col. 8) and index for 1941 (given as 87 with 1940 = 100 in *285*, No. 5, 1965, p. 72).

126. Milk–**Col. 2:** *469*, p. 34. **Cols. 5 and 8:** *202*, pp. 328 and 333. **Col. 10:** *60*, p. 203. **Col. 11:** Based on 1940 production (col. 8) and index for 1941 (given as 76 with 1940 = 100 in *285*, No. 5, 1965, p. 72).

127. Eggs–**Cols. 2, 5, and 8:** *202*, pp. 328 and 333. **Col. 11:** Based on 1940 production (col. 8) and index for 1941 (given as 76 with 1940 = 100 in *285*, No. 5, 1965, p. 72).

128. Wool–**Cols. 2, 5, and 8:** *202*, pp. 328 and 333. **Col. 10:** *60*, p. 203. **Col. 11:** Based on 1940 production (col. 8) and index for 1941 (given as 100 with 1940 = 100 in *285*, No. 5, 1965, p. 72).

MARKET PRODUCTION

129. Grain–**Col. 2:** *469*, p. 4. **Col. 8:** *242*, p. 122.

130. Raw cotton–**Col. 2:** *132*, p. 207. Converted from poods at 1 pood = .01638 m. t. For 1938/39. **Col. 8:** *242*, p. 122.

131. Sugar beets–**Col. 2:** *132*, p. 207. Converted from poods at 1 pood = .01638 m. t. For 1938/39. **Col. 8:** *242*, p. 122.

132. Flax fiber–**Col. 2:** *173*, No. 7, 1939, p. 162. Converted from poods at 1 pood = .01638 m. t. For 1938/39.

133. Potatoes–**Col. 2:** *173*, No. 7, 1939, p. 162. Converted from poods at 1 pood = .01638 m. t. For 1938/39. **Col. 8:** *242*, p. 122.

134. Meat and fat–**Col. 2:** *173*, No. 7, 1939, p. 162. Converted from poods at 1 pood = .01638 m. t. For 1938/39. *469*, p. 34, gives 1.46 mill. m. t. for 1938 and 2.05 mill. m. t. for 1939. **Col. 8:** *242*, p. 122.

135. Milk and dairy products–**Col. 2:** *173*, No. 7, 1939, p. 162. Converted from poods at 1 pood = .01638 m. t. For 1938/39. *469*, p. 34, gives 8.01 mill. m. t. for 1938 and 8.19 mill. m. t. for 1939. **Col. 8:** *242*, p. 122.

136. Wool–**Col. 2:** *173*, No. 7, 1939, p. 162. Converted from poods at 1 pood = .01638 m. t. For 1938/39. *469*, p. 35, gives 80 th. m. t. for 1938 and 88 th. m. t. for 1939. **Col. 8:** *242*, p. 122.

Table A-3 *continued*

PROCUREMENTS

137. Grain–**Cols. 2 and 5:** *449*, p. 794. For 1938/39 and 1939/40. **Col. 8:** *202*, p. 90. **Col. 11:** *99*, p. 150.

138. Raw cotton–**Col. 8:** *202*, p. 90. **Col. 11:** *99*, p. 150.

139. Sugar beets–**Col. 8:** *202*, p. 90. **Col. 11:** *99*, p. 150.

140. Sunflowers–**Cols. 2 and 5:** *79*, pp. 245–46. **Col. 8:** *202*, p. 90. **Col. 11:** *99*, p. 150.

141. Flax fiber–**Col. 1:** *224*, No. 4, 1938, pp. 9–10. **Col. 4:** *212*, No. 23, 1939, art. 142. **Col. 8:** *202*, p. 90. **Col. 11:** *99*, p. 150.

142. Hemp–**Col. 1:** *224*, No. 4, 1938, p. 12. **Col. 4:** *212*, No. 23, 1939, art. 142. **Col. 8:** *202*, p. 90.

143. Potatoes–**Cols. 2 and 5:** *466*, p. 149. Sum of procurements and purchases by state. For 1938/39 and 1939/40. *132*, p. 118, gives slightly different figures. **Col. 8:** *202*, p. 90. Sum of procurements and purchases by state.

143a. Vegetables–**Cols. 2 and 5:** *132*, pp. 149 and 152. Sum of procurements and purchases by state. **Col. 8:** *202*, p. 90.

144. Meat and fat (live weight)–**Col. 8:** *202*, p. 91. **Col. 11:** Based on 1940 procurements (col. 8) and index for 1941 (given as 73 with 1940 = 100 in *207*, p. 147).

145. Meat and fat (dead weight)–**Col. 8:** *149*, p. 337.

146. Milk and dairy products–**Col. 8:** *202*, p. 91. **Col. 11:** Based on 1940 procurements (col. 8) and index for 1941 (given as 81 with 1940 = 100 in *207*, p. 147).

147. Eggs–**Col. 8:** *202*, p. 91. **Col. 11:** Based on 1940 procurements (col. 8) and index for 1941 (given as 71 with 1940 = 100 in *207*, p. 147).

148. Wool–**Col. 8:** *202*, p. 91. **Col. 11:** Based on 1940 procurements (col. 8) and index for 1941 (given as 99.2 with 1940 = 100 in *207*, p. 147).

RAILROAD TRANSPORTATION

149. Length of network–**Cols. 2, 5, and 8:** *252*, p. 28. **Col.. 11:** *445*, p. 365.

150. Average daily carloadings–**Col. 1:** *173*, No. 6, 1938, p. 58. **Cols. 2, 5, 8, and 11:** *490*, p. 171. **Col. 10:** *60*, p. 5.

151. Total freight traffic (ton-km)–**Col. 1:** *173*, No. 6, 1938, p. 56. **Cols. 2, 5, and 8:** *252*, p. 32. **Col. 10:** *60*, p. 5. **Col. 11:** Based on 1940 traffic (col. 8) and index for 1941 (given as 93 with 1940 = 100 in *207*, p. 148).

152. Total freight traffic (tons)–**Col. 1:** *173*, No. 6, 1938, p. 58. **Cols. 2, 5, and 8:** *252*, p. 32. **Col. 10:** *60*, p. 450. **Col. 11:** *490*, p. 170.

153. Coal and coke–**Col. 8:** *140*, p. 178. **Col. 10:** *60*, p. 450. Sum of coal and coke.

154. Oil and oil products–**Col. 8:** *140*, p.178. **Col. 10:** *60*, p. 450.

155. Ferrous metals–**Col. 8:** *140*, p. 178. **Col. 10:** *60*, p. 450.

156. Ore–**Col. 8:** *142*, p. 549. Includes pyrites. **Col. 10:** *60*, p. 540.

157. Firewood–**Col. 8:** *142*, p. 549. **Col. 10:** *60*, p. 450.

158. Timber–**Col. 8:** *142*, p. 549. **Col. 10:** *60*, p. 540.

159. Mineral construction materials–**Cols. 2 and 5:** *445*, p. 303. **Col. 8:** *142*, p. 549. **Col. 10:** *60*, p. 450.

159a. Principal construction materials (stone, lime, cement, bricks)–**Cols. 2, 5, and 8:** *445*, p. 303.

160. Grain and flour–**Col. 8:** *142*, p. 549. **Col. 10:** *60*, p. 450.

162. Total freight traffic, average length of haul–**Col. 1:** *173*, No. 6, 1938, p. 58. **Cols. 2 and 5:** *285*, No. 7, 1956, p. 15. **Col. 8:** *252*, p. 34. **Col. 10:** *60*, p. 450. **Col. 11:** *490*, p. 170.

163. Coal and coke, average length of haul–**Cols. 2 and 5:** *420*, p. 221. **Col. 8:** *252*, p. 35.

163a. Oil and oil products, average length of haul–**Col. 8:** *252*, p. 35.

164. Ferrous metals, average length of haul–**Cols. 2 and 5:** *420*, p. 221. **Col. 8:** *252*, p. 36.

164a. Firewood, average length of haul–**Col. 8:** *252*, p. 38.

164b. Timber, average length of haul–**Col. 8:** *252*, p. 38.

165. Grain and flour, average length of haul–**Col. 8:** *252*, p. 37.

165a. Ore, average length of haul–**Col. 2:** *420*, p. 221. **Col. 8:** *252*, p. 36.

166. Total passenger traffic–**Col. 1:** *173*, No. 6, 1938, p. 58. **Cols. 2, 5, and 8:** *252*, p. 32. **Col. 10:** *60*, p. 450.

INLAND WATERWAY TRANSPORTATION

166a. Length of network–**Col. 8:** *252*, p. 115.

168. Freight traffic under ministries and economic organizations (ton-km)–**Cols. 2, 5, and 8:** *252*, p. 116. **Col. 10:** *60*, p. 454. **Col. 11:** Based on 1940 traffic (col. 8) and index for 1941 (given as 95 with 1940 = 100 in *207*, p. 148).

170. Freight traffic under ministries and economic organizations (tons)–**Cols. 2, 5, and 8:** *252*, p. 116. **Col. 10:** *60*, p. 454.

171. Coal and coke–**Col. 8:** *252*, p. 120. **Col. 10:** *60*, p. 454.

172. Oil and oil products–**Col. 8:** *252*, p. 120. **Col. 10:** *60*, p. 454.

173. Timber and firewood–**Col. 8:** *252*, p. 120. **Col. 10:** *60*, p. 454. Sum of timber hauled and timber rafted.

174. Mineral construction materials–**Col. 8:** *252*, p. 120. **Col. 10:** *60*, p. 454. Sum of cement and other mineral construction materials.

Table A-3 *continued*

175. Grain and flour–**Col. 8:** *252*, p. 120. **Col. 10:** *60*, p. 454.

176. Salt–**Col. 8:** *252*, p. 120. **Col. 10:** *60*, p. 454. Includes salt transported in ships belonging to the Commissariat of the Fishing Industry.

177. Average length of haul under ministries and economic organizations–**Cols. 2, 5, and 8:** *252*, p. 116. **Col. 10:** *60*, p. 454.

178. Passenger traffic (pass.-km)–**Cols. 2, 5, and 8:** *252*, p. 116. **Col. 10:** *60*, p. 454.

178a. Passenger traffic (pass.)–**Cols. 2, 5, and 8:** *252*, p. 116. **Col. 10:** *60*, p. 454.

MARITIME TRANSPORTATION (Soviet ships)

179. Freight traffic (ton-km)–**Col. 2:** *226*, p. 107. **Col. 5:** *490*, p. 182. Estimate. **Col. 8:** *252*, p. 7. **Col. 10:** *60*, p. 5. Converted from ton-miles at 1 ton-km = 0.54 ton-miles (see Table A-2, notes to series 179, col. 7). **Col. 11:** Based on 1940 traffic (col. 8) and index for 1941 (given as 85 with 1940 = 100 in *207*, p. 148).

180. Freight traffic (tons)–**Col. 2:** *226*, p. 107. **Col. 5:** *490*, p. 182. Estimate. **Col. 8:** *252*, p. 95. **Col. 10:** *60*, p. 463. In addition, 240.4 mill. m. t. for the *Glavk* for the Northern Sea Route (*60*, p. 465).

181. Average length of haul–**Cols. 2, 5, and 8:** *490*, p. 182. **Col. 10:** Based on freight traffic in ton-km (series 179) and in tons (series 180).

182. Passenger traffic (pass.-km)–**Col. 2:** *226*, p. 107. **Col. 8:** *252*, p. 95. Converted from pass.-miles at 1 pass.-km = 0.54 pass.-miles. **Col. 10:** *60*, p. 463. Converted from pass.-miles at 1 pass.-km = 0.54 pass.-miles. In addition, 7.2 mill. pass.-miles for *Glavk* for Northern Sea Route (*60*, p. 465).

182a. Passenger traffic (pass.)–**Col. 2:** *226*, p. 107. **Col. 8:** *252*, p. 95. **Col. 10:** *60*, p. 463. In addition 4,200 pass. for the *Glavk* for Northern Sea Route (*60*, p. 465).

MOTOR TRANSPORTATION

183. Freight traffic–**Cols. 2 and 5:** *252*, p. 155. **Col. 8:** *252*, p. 159. **Col. 10:** *60*, p. 473. **Col. 11:** Based on 1940 traffic (col. 8) and index for 1941 (given as 70 with 1940 = 100 in *207*, p. 148).

AIR TRANSPORTATION

184. Freight traffic, incl. mail–**Col. 2:** *226*, p. 108. Sum of traffic under *Glavk* for Civil Aviation and *Glavk* for Northern Sea Route. **Col. 8:** Table A-1, col. 5. **Col. 10:** *60*, p. 478. Sum of Union airlines and local airlines. **Col. 11:** Based on 1940 traffic (col. 8) and index for 1941 (given as 74 with 1940 = 100 in *207*, p. 148).

185. Passenger traffic–**Col. 8:** *253*, p. 34. Since this is a rounded figure, it cannot be compared with the 1941 plan figure in col. 10. **Col. 10:** *60*, p. 478. Union airlines.

EMPLOYMENT (annual averages)

186. Workers and employees, national economy, excl. collective farms–**Cols. 2 and 5:** Based on wage fund (series 201) and average annual money wage (series 203). **Col. 8:** *140*, p. 189. **Col. 10:** *60*, p. 512. **Col. 11:** Based on 1940 employment (given as 31,192 th. in *99*, p. 220) and index for 1941 (given as 88 with 1940 = 100 in *207*, p. 121).

187. Industry–**Col. 1:** Based on 1937 employment (Table A-1, col. 2) and increase planned for 1938 (given as 5% in *173*, No. 5, 1938, p. 21). **Col. 2:** Based on 1937 employment (Table A-1, col. 2) and increase in 1938 (derived as 0.1% from increase in industrial production—11.1% from series 2, col. 2, and Table A-1, col. 2—and increase in labor productivity—given as 11.0% in *481*, p. 195). **Col. 5:** Based on 1938 employment (col. 2) and increase in 1939 (derived as 0.1% from increase in industrial production—16.8% from series 2, cols. 2 and 5—and increase in labor productivity—given as 16.7% in *481*, p. 195). **Col. 8:** *140*, p. 190. **Col. 10:** *60*, p. 512. **Col. 11:** Based on 1940 employment (col. 8) and index for 1941 (derived as 89 with 1940 = 100 from index of industrial production of 98 and index of labor productivity of 110 with 1940 = 100 in *207*, pp. 121 and 153).

188. Construction–**Col. 8:** *28*, p. 219. Larger coverage than figure used in Table A-1, col. 5. **Col. 10:** *60*, p. 512.

188a. Construction and assembly work–**Col. 8:** *140*, p. 190. **Col. 10:** *60*, p. 512.

189. State-owned agriculture and logging–**Col. 8:** *260*, p. 24. Sum of agriculture and logging. Larger coverage than figure used in Table A-1, col. 5.

190. State-owned agriculture (state farms, MTS, and other state establishments)–**Col. 2:** *431*, p. 42. **Col. 8:** *260*, p. 24. Larger coverage than figure used in Table A-1, col. 5. **Col. 10:** *60*, p. 512. For state farms and MTS. Coverage not the same as in col. 8.

191. Railroad transport–**Col. 8:** *140*, p. 190. **Col. 10:** *60*, p. 512.

192. Maritime and inland waterway transport–**Col. 8:** *140*, p. 190. **Col. 10:** *60*, p. 512.

193. Other transport (motor, etc.)–**Col. 8:** *260*, p. 24. Smaller coverage than figure used in Table A-1, col. 5.

194. Communications–**Col. 8:** *140*, p. 190. **Col. 10:** *60*, p. 512.

195. Trade, procurements, and supply–**Col. 8:** Table A-1, col. 5. **Col. 10:** *60*, p. 512.

196. Public eating places–**Col. 8:** Table A-1, col. 5. **Col. 10:** *60*, p. 512.

197. Credit institutions–**Col. 8:** *140*, p. 190. **Col. 10:** *60*, p. 512.

198. Administration–**Col. 8:** *140*, p. 190. Smaller coverage than figure used in Table A-1.

Table A-3 *continued*

199. Education–Col. 8: *140*, p. 190. Col. 10: *60*, p. 512.
200. Public health–Col. 8: *140*, p. 190. Col. 10: *60*, p. 512.

WAGE FUND, WORKERS AND EMPLOYEES

201. National economy–Col. 1: *322*, p. 9. Col. 2: *226*, p. 139. Col. 5: *442*, p. 40. Col. 7: Based on 1939 wage fund (col. 5) and increase planned for 1940 (given as 11% in *24*, No. 1, 1940, p. 8). Col. 8: *288*, p. 10. Col. 10: Based on planned number of workers and employees in the national economy (series 186) and planned average annual money wage (series 203).

202. Industry–Cols. 1, 2, and 8: Based on number of workers and employees in industry (series 187) and average annual money wage in industry (series 205). Col. 5: Based on 1938 wage fund (col. 2) and increase in 1939 (derived as 21.4% from increase in gross industrial production—in series 2, cols. 2 and 5—and percentage that increase in wage fund was of increase in gross industrial production—given as 103.9% in *124*, p. 188). Col. 10: *60*, p. 512.

AVERAGE ANNUAL WAGE, WORKERS AND EMPLOYEES

203. Money wage, national economy, excl. collective farms and cooperatives–Col. 2: *226*, p. 139. Col. 5: *442*, p. 39. Estimate. Col. 8: *147*, p. 555. Converted into old rubles. Col. 10: Based on 1940 money wage (col. 8) and increase planned for 1941 (given as 6.5% in *288*, p. 33). The figure obtained from employment and wage fund in *60*, p. 512, would be 5,547 rubles, but it is not comparable with the rest of the series here because of changes in the definition of wage fund (see Table 48, notes to line 2, in Chapter 10).

205. Money wage, industry–Col. 1: Based on 1937 money wage (Table A-1, col. 2) and increase planned for 1938 (given as 10.4% in *173*, No. 5, 1938, p. 21). Col. 2: *241*, p. 586. Col. 8: *260*, p. 138. Converted into old rubles. Col. 10: Based on 1940 money wage (col. 8) and increase planned for 1941 (given as 6.5% in *288*, p. 33).

AVERAGE ANNUAL MONEY WAGE, WORKERS

206. Industry–Col. 8: *260*, p. 138. Converted into old rubles. Col. 10: Based on 1940 money wage (col. 8) and increase planned for 1941 (given as 6.5% in *288*, p. 33).

208. Coal–Col. 8: Table A-1, col. 5. Col. 10: *60*, p. 514. Commissariat of the Coal Industry. Note: These figures are probably not comparable with those in series 203, 205, and 206 because of changes in definition in *60*.

209. Ferrous metals–Col. 8: Table A-1, col. 5. Col. 10: *60*, p. 516. Commissariat of the Ferrous Metal Industry. Note: See note to series 208.

209a. Machine-building–Col. 8: Table A-1, col. 5. Col. 10: *60*, pp. 519–20. Average of planned wages for Commissariats of Heavy Machine-Building, Medium Machine-Building, and General Machine-Building, weighted as in Table A-1, col. 5. Note: See note to series 208.

210. Paper–Col. 8: Table A-1, col. 5. Col. 10: *60*, p. 522. Commissariat of the Pulp and Paper Industry. Note: See note to series 208.

211. Chemicals–Col. 8: Table A-1, col. 5. Col. 10: *60*, p. 517. Commissariat of the Chemical Industry. Note: See note to series 208.

212. Textiles–Col. 8: Table A-1, col. 5. Col. 10: *60*, p. 522. Commissariat of the Textile Industry. Note: See note to series 208.

214. Food–Col. 8: Based on planned wage for 1941 (col. 10) and increase planned for 1941 over 1940 (given as 2.0% in *60*, p. 513). The coverage here is not the same as in Table A-1, col. 5. Col. 10: *60*, p. 524. Commissariat of the Food Industry. This does not include the Commissariats of the Meat and Dairy Industry, Fishing Industry, and Procurements.

AVERAGE ANNUAL MONEY WAGE, WORKERS AND EMPLOYEES

215. Construction–Col. 8: *260*, p. 138. Converted into old rubles. Col. 10: Based on 1940 wage (col. 8) and increase planned for 1941 for construction and assembly work (given as 6.0% in *60*, p. 513).

216. Railroad transport–Col. 1: Based on 1937 wage (Table A-1, col. 2) and increase planned for 1938 (given as 5.6% in *173*, No. 11–12, 1937, p. 20). Cols. 2 and 5: *445*, p. 328. Col. 8: *260*, p. 138. Converted into old rubles. Col. 10: Based on planned wage fund and planned number of workers and employees in railroad transport (given as 7,251.0 mill. rubles and 1,713.7 thous. in *60*, p. 512). Coverage not the same as in earlier years.

217. Maritime and inland waterway transport–Col. 8: *260*, p. 138. Converted into old rubles. Col. 10: Based on planned wage fund and planned number of workers and employees in water transport (given as 1,037.4 mill. rubles and 207.0 thous. in *60*, p. 512). Coverage not the same as in earlier years.

218. Communications–Col. 8: *260*, p.138. Converted into old rubles. Col. 10: Based on planned wage fund and planned number of workers and employees in communications (given as 1,617.0 mill. rubles and 463.0 thous. in *60*, p. 512).

219. Trade–Col. 8: *260*, p. 138. Covers trade, public eating places, procurements, and material and equipment supply. Converted into old rubles. Col. 10: Based on planned wage fund and planned number of workers and employees in trade, procurements, and supply (given as 7,648.0 mill. rubles and 2,355.0 thous. in *60*, p. 512).

Table A-3 *continued*

220. Public eating places–**Col. 10:** Based on planned wage fund and planned number of workers and employees in public eating places (given as 1,926.0 mill. rubles and 670.0 thous. in *60*, p. 512).

221. Credit institutions–**Col. 8:** *260*, p. 138. Converted into old rubles. **Col. 10:** Based on planned wage fund and planned number of workers and employees in credit and insurance institutions (given as 1,028.0 mill. rubles and 275.3 thous. in *60*, p. 512).

222. Administration–**Col. 8:** *260*, p. 138. Converted into old rubles.

223. Education–**Col. 8:** *260*, p. 138. Converted into old rubles. **Col. 10:** Based on planned wage fund and planned number of workers and employees in education (given as 12,453.0 mill. rubles and 2,875.0 thous. in *60*, p. 512).

224. Public health–**Col. 8:** *260*, p. 138. Converted into old rubles. **Col. 10:** Based on planned wage fund and planned number of workers and employees in public health (given as 5,139.0 mill. rubles and 1,646.0 thous. in *60*, p. 512).

225. State-owned agriculture–**Col. 8:** *260*, p. 138. Covers state farms and farms belonging to various agencies. Converted into old rubles. **Col. 10:** Based on planned wage fund and planned number of workers and employees on state farms and MTS (given as 7,139.0 mill. rubles and 2,075.0 thous. in *60*, p. 512). MTS may not be included in col. 8.

HOUSING

227. Housing fund, urban, total–**Col. 1:** Housing fund at end of 1937 (Table A-1, col. 2) plus housing construction planned for 1938 (series 228, col. 1) minus wear during 1938 (estimated at 1 mill. m² as in Table A-2, col. 14). **Col. 8:** *410*, p. 10. **Col. 10:** Housing fund in 1940 (col. 8) plus housing construction planned for 1941 (given as 5,236.95 th. m² in *60*, p. 493) minus wear during 1941 (estimated at 1.4 mill. m² or 0.5% of total). Excludes Commissariats of Transportation, Defense, and Navy.

228. Housing construction, urban, total–**Col. 1:** *173*, No. 6, 1938. p. 166. **Col. 10:** *60*, p. 493. Excludes Commissariats of Transportation, Defense, and Navy.

229. Floorspace per inhabitant, urban–**Col. 8:** *285*, No. 1, 1957, p. 14. See note to Table A-1, series 229, col. 5.

POPULATION

230. Total (end of year)–**Col. 2:** *140*, p. 17. **Col. 8:** Table A-1, col. 5.

231. Urban (end of year)–**Col. 2:** *140*, p. 17. **Col. 8:** Table A-1, col. 5.

232. Rural (end of year)–**Col. 2:** *140*, p. 17. **Col. 8:** Table A-1, col. 5.

RETAIL TRADE

233. State and cooperative in current prices–**Col. 1:** *182*, No. 2, 1938, p. 161. **Cols. 2, 5, 8, and 11:** *232*, pp. 20 and 31. **Col. 4:** Based on 1937 trade turnover (Table A-1, col. 2), increase during 1938, and increase planned for 1939 (the latter two increases given as averaging 21% each in *173*, No. 3, 1939, p. 146). **Col. 7:** Based on 1939 trade turnover (given as 163.4 bill. rubles in *403*, p. 254) and increase planned for 1940 (given as 15.7% in *322*, p. 69). **Col. 10:** *288*, p. 13.

234c. Food products in current prices–**Cols. 2, 5, and 11:** Based on total state and cooperative trade turnover (series 233) and share of food products in total (given as 62.9%, 63.1%, and 63.0% for 1938, 1939, and 1941, respectively, in *232*, p. 39). **Col. 8:** *232*, p. 40.

235. Collective farm in current prices–**Col. 2:** *241*, p. 584. **Cols. 5 and 8:** Based on state and cooperative trade turnover (series 233) and share of collective farm trade in total trade (given as 15.3% for 1939 and 19.0% for 1940 in *36*, p. 236).

Table A-4 Production during the War Years, 1942–1945

Series	Units	Actual 1942 (1)	Actual 1943 (2)	Actual 1944 (3)	1945 Planned (4)	1945 Actual (5)	(4) as Per Cent of (5) (6)
1. National income (1926/27 prices)	bill. rub.	84.7	94.9	112.9		106.5	
Industry							
2. Gross production, total (1926/27 prices)	bill. rub.	106.6	124.7	144.0	152	127.4	83.8
3. Producer goods (1926/27 prices)	bill. rub.	84.7	100.8	117.9	122.2	95.0	77.7
4. Consumer goods (1926/27 prices)	bill. rub.	21.9	23.9	26.1	29.8	31.7	106.4
5. Coal	th. m. t.	75,536	93,141	121,470	153,000	149,333	97.6
6. Peat	th. m. t.	14,738	21,274	22,993		22,445	
7. Coke	th. m. t.	6,893	8,220	11,495		13,649	
8. Oil shale	th. m. t.					1,387	
9. Crude petroleum	th. m. t.	21,988	17,984	18,261		19,436	
10. Natural gas	mill. m ^{3}					3,278	
11. Electric power	mill. kwh	29,068	32,288	39,214	45,880	43,257	94.3
12. Hydroelectric power	mill. kwh.					4,841	
13. Iron ore	th. m. t.	9,763	9,320	11,663		15,864	
14. Pig iron	th. m. t.	4,779	5,591	7,296		8,803	
15. Steel ingots and castings	th. m. t.	8,070	8,475	10,887	13,000	12,252	94.2
16. Rolled steel	th. m. t.	5,415	5,675	7,878		8,485	
17. Steel pipes	th. m. t.					571	
18. Aluminum	th. m. t.	51.9	62.3			86.3	
19. Manganese ore	th. m. t.	767	901	1,005		1,470	
20. Nickel	th. m. t.	7.4	11.2			15.2	
21. Zinc	th. m. t.		38.4			50	
22. Refined copper	th. m. t.		105			135	
23. Lead	th. m. t.		49.9			60	
24. Mineral fertilizer	th. m. t.					1,119	
26. Phosphoric fertilizer (18.7% P_2O_5)	th. m. t.					233.6	
27. Ground natural phosphate	th. m. t.					10.1	
28. Potash fertilizer	th. m. t.					130.7	
29. Ammonium sulfate	th. m. t.					744.7	
30. Soda ash	th. m. t.	65		156.9		235.3	
31. Caustic soda	th. m. t.					128.2	
32. Sulfuric acid	th. m. t.					781	
33. Tires	thous.					1,370	
34. Plastics	th. m. t.					27.0	
34a. Synthetic dyes	th. m. t.					15.1	
35. Cement	th. m. t.	1,100	1,000	1,500		1,845	
36. Lime	th. m. t.					1,929	
37. Window glass	mill. m ^{2}		8.2	15.5		23.3	
38a. Roofing tiles	mill.					29.6	
39. Asbestos shingles	mill.					83.6	
40. Bricks	mill.					2,026	
41. Industrial timber hauled	mill. m ^{3}			51.5		61.6	
42. Lumber	mill. m ^{3}					14.7	
43. Plywood	th. m ^{3}					192.2	
44. Paper	th. m. t.					321.1	
45. Paperboard	th. m. t					55.9	
46. Machine tools	units	22,935	23,281	34,049		38,419	

Table A-4   *continued*

Series	Units	Actual 1942 (1)	Actual 1943 (2)	Actual 1944 (3)	1945 Planned (4)	1945 Actual (5)	(4) as Per Cent of (5) (6)
46a. Metallurgical equipment	th. m. t.	19.4	24.8	26.4		26.9	
47. Steam and gas turbines	th. kw					189	
48. Steam boilers	th. m.²					90.3	
49. Turbogenerators	th. kw					185.5	
50. Spinning machines	units					11	
51. Looms	units					18	
52. Tractors	units	3,520		3,154		7,728	
53. Tractors (15 hp)	th. conven. units					14.7	
54. Motor vehicles, total	thous.			61.3		74.7	
55. Trucks	thous.	30.4	45.6	52.6		68.5	
56. Automobiles	thous.					5.0	
57. Buses	thous.					1.2	
58. Grain combines	units					323	
59. Steam locomotives	units					8	
60. Diesel locomotives	units					0	
61. Electric locomotives	units					0	
62. Railroad freight cars	units					819	
64. Railroad passenger cars	units					5	
65. Excavators	units			7		10	
66. Ginned cotton	th. m. t.					312.2	
67. Cotton yarn	th. m. t.					303	
68. Cotton fabrics	mill. m	1,644	1,635	1,779		1,617	
69. Woolen fabrics	mill. m	38.3				53.6	
71. Linen fabrics	mill. m					106.5	
72. Silk and rayon fabrics	mill. m					36.4	
73. Knitted underwear	mill.					26.6	
74. Knitted outer garments	mill.					23.4	
75. Hosiery	mill. prs					91.0	
76. Leather shoes	mill. prs	52.5	55.8	67.4		63.1	
77. Felt footwear	mill. prs					13.3	
78. Rubber footwear	mill. prs					15.1	
80. Metal beds	thous.					873	
80a. Enameled kitchenware	th. m. t.					2.5	
81. Motorcycles	thous.					4.7	
82. Bicycles	thous.					23.8	
83. Radios	thous.					13.9	
83a. Refrigerators, household	thous.					0.3	
84. Sewing machines, household	thous.					0	
85. Clocks and watches	thous.					336	
86. Cameras	thous.					0.01	
87. Phonographs	thous.					0.6	
88. Soap (40% fatty acid)	th. m. t.					229	
89a. Bread and breadstuffs (ministries and local Soviets)	th. m. t.					7,269	
90. Flour (total)	th. m. t.					14,577	
90a. Flour (centralized resources)	th. m. t.					6,724	
91. Macaroni	th. m. t.					243	
92. Raw sugar	th. m. t.	114	117	245		465	
93. Starch and syrup	th. m. t.					36	
94. Fish catch	th. m. t.	900	1,095	1,108		1,125	
95. Crude alcohol	th. hl					2,650	
96. Vegetable oil	th. m. t.	253	215	238		292	

Table A-4   *continued*

Series	Units	Actual 1942 (1)	Actual 1943 (2)	Actual 1944 (3)	1945 Planned (4)	1945 Actual (5)	(4) as Per Cent of (5) (6)
97. Butter	th. m. t.					117	
98. Cheese	th. m. t.					25.6	
100. Meat and subproducts of first category	th. m. t.					663	
101. Sausages	th. m. t.					139.6	
102. Canned food	mill. 400-gm cans					558	
103. Confectionery	th. m. t.					212	
104. Margarine	th. m. t.					28	
105. Beer	th. hl					4,050	
106. Cigarettes	bill.					25.0	
107. Matches	th. crates	1,612	1,828	1,588		2,000	
108. Low-grade tobacco (*makhorka*)	th. 20-kg crates					700	
109. Salt	th. m. t.					2,900	
Agriculture							
110a. Total value of production (comparable prices)	1940 = 100	38	37	54		60	
Harvests							
113. Grain, total (biological yield)	mill. m. t.					66	
113a. Grain, total (barn yield)	mill. m. t.	29.1	26.5	49.1		47.3	
Harvests of Technical Crops							
119a. Raw cotton (barn yield)	mill. m. t.	1.323	.708	1.13		1.19	
120a. Sugar beets (barn yield)	mill. m. t.	2.1	1.4	4.1		5.5	
121a. Sunflowers (barn yield)	mill. m. t.	.28	.78	1.02		.84	
122a. Flax fiber (barn yield)	th. m. t.	210	157	168		150	
124a. Potatoes (barn yield)	mill. m. t.	23.5	34.7	54.9		58.31	
Animal Production							
125. Meat and fat (excl. rabbit and poultry)	th. m. t.	1,716	1,672	1,848		2,419	
125a. Meat and fat (incl. rabbit and poultry)	th. m. t.	1,831	1,784	1,972		2,559	
126. Milk	mill. m. t.	15.8	16.5	22.2		26.4	
127. Eggs	bill.	4.5	3.4	3.5		4.9	
128. Wool	th. m. t.	126	100	103		111	
Market Production							
129. Grain	mill. m. t.					23.2	
130. Raw cotton	mill. m. t.					1.16	
131. Sugar beets	mill. m. t.					4.7	
133. Potatoes	mill. m. t.					11.8	
134. Meat and fat (dead weight)	th. m. t.					1,300	
135. Milk and dairy products	mill. m. t.					5.4	
136. Wool	th. m. t.					73	
Procurements							
137. Grain	th. m. t.	12,516	12,252	21,556		20,016	
138. Raw cotton	th. m. t.	1,329	726	1,131		1,161	
139. Sugar beets	th. m. t.	1,537	1,027	3,393		4,699	
140. Sunflowers	th. m. t.	128	412	560		590	
141. Flax fiber	th. m. t.	108	90	95		65	
142. Hemp	th. m. t.					4	
143. Potatoes	th. m. t.					4,500	

Table A-4   *continued*

Series	Units	Actual 1942 (1)	Actual 1943 (2)	Actual 1944 (3)	1945 Planned (4)	1945 Actual (5)	(4) as Per Cent of (5) (6)
143a. Vegetables	th. m. t.					1,800	
144. Meat and fat (live weight)	th. m. t.	1,244	1,229	1,106		1,248	
145. Meat and fat (dead weight)	th. m. t.					700	
146. Milk and dairy products	th. m. t.	2,877	2,412	2,615		2,924	
147. Eggs	mill.	672	496	851		1,145	
148. Wool	th. m. t.	80	65	64		66	
Railroad Transportation							
149. Length of network	th. km	62.9	81.6	106.0		112.9	
150. Average daily carloadings	thous.	42.8	45.7	55.7		62.2	
151. Total freight traffic	bill. m. ton-km	218	239	281		314.0	
152. Total freight traffic	mill. m. t.	277.2	313.0	371.0		395.2	
153. Coal and coke	mill. m. t.					142	
154. Oil and oil products	mill. m. t.					21.3	
155. Ferrous metals	mill. m. t.					21.3	
156. Ore	mill. m. t.					17.8	
157. Firewood	mill. m. t.					17.4	
158. Timber	mill. m. t.					26.5	
159. Mineral construction materials	mill. m. t.					41.9	
160. Grain and flour	mill. m. t.					20.2	
162. Total freight traffic, average length of haul	km	786	818	801		794	
163. Coal and coke, average length of haul	km	886				693	
163a. Oil and oil products, average length of haul	km					1,115	
164. Ferrous metals, average length of haul	km					1,123	
164a. Firewood, average length of haul	km					157	
164b. Timber, average length of haul	km	632				780	
165. Grain and flour, average length of haul	km					1,153	
165a. Ore, average length of haul	km					702	
166. Total passenger traffic	bill. pass.-km	37.9	39.4	57.6		65.9	
Inland Waterway Transportation							
166a. Length of network	th. km					117.2	
168. Freight traffic under ministries and economic organizations	bill. m. ton-km	21.5	22.3	22.3		18.6	
170. Freight traffic under ministries and economic organizations	mill. m. t.	41.5				36.6	
171. Coal and coke	th. m. t.					1,300	
172. Oil and oil products	th. m. t.					5,500	
173. Timber and firewood	th. m. t.					20,900	
174. Mineral construction materials	th. m. t.					1,800	
175. Grain and flour	th. m. t.					2,400	
176. Salt	th. m. t.					1,100	
177. Average length of haul under ministries and economic organizations	km	518				509	
178. Passenger traffic	bill. pass.-km					2.3	
178a. Passenger traffic	mill. pass.	34				38.5	

Table A-4 *continued*

Series	Units	Actual 1942 (1)	Actual 1943 (2)	Actual 1944 (3)	1945 Planned (4)	1945 Actual (5)	(4) as Per Cent of (5) (6)
Maritime Transportation (Soviet ships)							
179. Freight traffic	bill. m. ton-km	15.7	32.6	34.3		34.2	
180. Freight traffic	mill. m. t.					20.2	
181. Average length of haul	km					1,695	
182. Passenger traffic	mill. pass.-km					628	
182a. Passenger traffic	mill. pass.					1.0	
Motor Transportation							
183. Freight traffic	bill. m. ton-km	2.76	2.76	3.47		4.98	
Air Transportation							
184. Freight traffic, including mail	mill. m. ton-km	20.2	25.8	49.0		102.3	
185. Passenger traffic	th. pass.					600	
Employment (annual averages)							
186. Workers and employees, national economy, excl. collective farms	mill.	18.4	19.40	23.62		27.26	
187. Industry	thous.	7,171	7,500	8,430		9,508	
188. Construction	thous.					2,343	
188a. Construction and assembly work	thous.	861	921	1,343		1,515	
190. State-owned agriculture (state farms, MTS, and other state establishments)	thous.					2,731	
191. Railroad transport	thous.	1,067				1,841	
192. Maritime and inland waterway transport	thous.					190	
193. Other transport (motor, etc.)	thous.					1,080	
194. Communications	thous.	273	287	363		426	
195. Trade, procurements, and supply	thous.					1,747	
196. Public eating places	thous.					715	
197. Credit institutions	thous.	129				197	
198. Administration	thous.	920				1,645	
199. Education	thous.	1,600				2,551	
200. Public health	thous.	975				1,419	
Wage Fund, Workers and Employees							
201. National economy	mill. rub.					142,000	
202. Industry	mill. rub.					53,600	
Average Annual Wage, Workers and Employees							
203. Money wage, national economy, excl. collective farms and cooperatives	rubles					5,208	
204. Real wage	1940 = 100					40.3	
205. Money wage, industry	rubles					5,640	
Average Annual Money Wage, Workers							
206. Industry	rubles			5,504		5,400	
208. Coal	rubles					8,916	
Average Annual Money Wage, Workers and Employees							
215. Construction	rubles					4,956	

Table A-4 *continued*

Series	Units	Actual 1942 (1)	Actual 1943 (2)	Actual 1944 (3)	1945 Planned (4)	1945 Actual (5)	1945 (4) as Per Cent of (5) (6)
216. Railroad transport	rubles					6,300	
217. Maritime and inland waterway transport	rubles					5,916	
218. Communications	rubles					4,248	
221. Credit institutions	rubles					6,144	
222. Administration	rubles					6,048	
223. Education	rubles					5,664	
224. Public health	rubles					4,728	
225. State-owned agriculture	rubles					2,556	
Housing							
227. Housing fund, urban, total	mill. m²					200	
228. Housing construction, urban, total	mill. m²	5.8	10.5	15.7		15.0	
Population							
230. Total (end of year)	mill.					166.7	
Retail Trade							
233. State and cooperative in current prices	mill. rub.	77,800	84,000	119,300		160,100	
234. State and cooperative in 1940 prices	mill. rub.	59,500	56,000	64,800		73,500	
234c. Food products in current prices	mill. rub.	56,000	61,200	89,500		121,000	
234d. Food products in 1940 prices	mill. rub.					53,800	
235. Collective farm in current prices	mill. rub.					136,400	

Source

1. National income (1926/27 prices)–**Cols. 1-3 and 5:** Based on national income in 1940 (given as 128.3 bill. rubles in Table A-1, col. 5) and index for 1942–1945 (given as 66, 74, 88, and 83, respectively, with 1940 = 100, in *285*, No. 5, 1965, p. 70).

INDUSTRY

2. Gross production, total (1926/27 prices)–**Cols. 1-3 and 5:** Based on gross production in 1940 (given as 138.5 bill. rubles in Table A-1, col. 5) and index for 1942–1945 (given as 77, 90, 104, and 92, respectively, with 1940 = 100, in *285*, No. 5, 1965, p. 70). **Col. 4:** *69*, Vol. 5, p. 366.

3. Producer goods (1926/27 prices)–**Col. 1:** Based on total production (series 2) and share of producer goods in total (given as 79.5% in *99*, p. 114). **Col. 2:** Based on 1942 output (col. 1) and increase in 1943 (given as 19% in *99*, p. 215). **Col. 3:** Based on 1943 output (col. 2) and increase in 1944 (given as 17% in *99*, p. 215). **Col. 4:** Planned gross production (series 2) minus planned consumer goods (series 4). **Col. 5:** Based on 1940 output (given as 84.8 bill. rubles in Table A-1, col. 5) and percentage that 1945 output was of 1940 output (given as 112 in *140*, p. 47). Sum of producer and consumer goods does not add to total (series 2) due to rounding.

4. Consumer goods (1926/27 prices)–**Col. 1:** Based on total production (series 2) and share of consumer goods in total (given as 20.5% in *99*, p. 114). **Col. 2:** Gross production (series 2) minus producer goods (series 3). A similar figure is obtained from 1942 output (col. 1) and increase in 1943 (given as 9.7% in *99*, p. 215). **Col. 3:** Gross production (series 2) minus producer goods (series 3). A slightly higher figure (28.7) is obtained from 1943 output (col. 2) and increase in 1944 (given as 20% in *99*, p. 215). **Col. 4:** Based on 1944 output (col. 3) and increase planned for light industry for 1945 (given as 14% in *69*, Vol. 5, p. 366). **Col. 5:** Based on 1940 output (given as 53.7 bill. rubles in Table A-1, col. 5) and percentage that 1945 output was of 1940 (given as 59 in *140*, p. 47). Sum of producer and consumer goods does not add to total (series 2) due to rounding.

5. Coal–**Col. 1:** 1943 output (col. 2) minus increase in output between 1942 and 1943 (given as 17,605 th. m. t. in *99*, p. 248). **Cols. 2 and 3:** *99*, p. 248. **Col. 4:** Based on 1944 output (col. 3) and increase planned for 1945 (given as 26% in *69*, Vol. 5, p. 366). **Col. 5:** *187*, p. 140.

Table A-4 *continued*

6. Peat–**Cols. 1-3 and 5:** *218*, p. 35. Includes collective farm output.

7. Coke–**Col. 1:** Based on 1945 output (col. 5) and index for 1945 (given as 198 with 1942 = 100 in *99*, p. 236). **Cols. 2, 3, and 5:** *99*, p. 235.

8. Oil shale–**Col. 5:** *187*, p. 166.

9. Crude petroleum–**Cols. 1-3 and 5:** *99*, pp. 133 and 252.

10. Natural gas–**Col. 5:** *187*, p. 156. Includes secondary extraction of gas.

11. Electric power–**Cols. 1-3:** *99*, pp. 261–62. **Col. 4:** Based on 1944 output (col. 3) and increase planned for 1945 (given as 17% in *69*, Vol. 5, p. 366). **Col. 5:** *187*, p. 171.

12. Hydroelectric power–**Col. 5:** *187*, p. 171.

13. Iron ore–**Cols. 1-3 and 5:** *99*, p. 230.

14. Pig iron–**Cols. 1-3:** *121*, p. 188. **Col. 5:** *187*, p. 106.

15. Steel ingots and castings–**Cols. 1-3:** *121*, p. 188. **Col. 4:** Based on 1944 output (col. 3) and increase planned for 1945 (given as 20% in *69*, Vol. 5, p. 366). **Col. 5:** *187*, p. 106.

16. Rolled steel–**Cols. 1-3:** *121*, p. 188. **Col. 5:** *187*, p. 106.

17. Steel pipes–**Col. 5:** *187*, p. 106.

18. Aluminum–**Col. 1:** Based on 1943 output (col. 2) and increase in 1943 over 1942 (given as 20% in *290*, p. 84). **Col. 2:** Based on 1940 output (given as 59.9 th. m. t. in Table A-1, col. 5) and increase in 1943 over 1940 (given as 4% in *294*, p. 42, as cited in *485*, series 201.4). **Col. 5:** Based on 1940 output (given as 59.9 th. m. t. in Table A-1, col. 5) and increase in 1945 over 1940 (given as 44% in *75*, 4/2/46, p. 2).

19. Manganese ore–**Cols. 1-3:** *99*, p. 233. **Col. 5:** *187*, p. 115.

20. Nickel–**Col. 1:** Based on 1943 output (col. 2) and increase in 1943 over 1942 (given as 52% in *290*, p. 84). **Col. 2:** Based on 1940 output (given as 8.66 th. m. t. in Table A-1, col. 5) and increase in 1943 over 1940 (given as 29% in *14*, No. 22, 1944, p. 24, as cited in *485*, series 213.4). **Col. 5:** Based on 1940 output (given as 8.66 th. m. t. in Table A-1, col. 5) and increase in 1945 over 1940 (given as 76% in *75*, 4/2/46, p. 2).

21. Zinc–**Col. 2:** *485*, series 210.1. Estimate. **Col. 5:** *472*, pp. 421 and 461. Estimate.

22. Refined copper–**Col. 2:** *485*, series 204.1. Estimate. **Col. 5:** *472*, pp. 420 and 460–61.

23. Lead–**Col. 2:** *485*, series 209.1. Estimate. **Col. 5:** *472*, pp. 421 and 461. Estimate.

24. Mineral fertilizer–**Col. 5:** *187*, p. 192.

26. Phosphoric fertilizer (18.7% P_2O_5)–**Col. 5:** *187*, p. 192.

27. Ground natural phosphate–**Col. 5:** *187*, p. 192.

28. Potash fertilizer–**Col. 5:** *187*, p. 192.

29. Ammonium sulfate–**Col. 5:** *187*, p. 192.

30. Soda ash–**Col. 1:** *485*, series 406.1. Estimate. **Col. 3:** Based on 1945 output (col. 5) and increase in 1945 output over 1944 (given as 50% in *180*, 3/18/46, p. 2). **Col. 5:** *187*, p. 194.

31. Caustic soda–**Col. 5:** *187*, p. 194.

32. Sulfuric acid–**Col. 5:** *187*, p. 196.

33. Tires–**Col. 5:** *187*, p. 199.

34. Plastics–**Col. 5:** *188*, p. 146. Includes synthetic tars (*sinteticheskie smoly*).

34a. Synthetic dyes–**Col. 5:** *187*, p. 197. Ministry of the Chemical Industry.

35. Cement–**Cols. 1-3:** *285*, No. 5, 1965, p. 70. **Col. 5:** *187*, p. 277.

36. Lime–**Col. 5:** *187*, p. 282. Sum of construction lime and technological lime.

37. Window glass–**Cols. 2-3:** *485*, series 711.7. Estimates. **Col. 5:** *187*, p. 312.

38a. Roofing tiles–**Col. 5:** *187*, p. 299.

39. Asbestos shingles–**Col. 5:** *187*, p. 304.

40. Bricks–**Col. 5:** *187*, p. 291.

41. Industrial timber hauled–**Col. 3:** *112*, No. 1, 1946, p. 59, as cited in *485*, series 701.1. **Col. 5:** *187*, p. 249.

42. Lumber–**Col. 5:** *187*, p. 261.

43. Plywood–**Col. 5:** *187*, p. 261.

44. Paper–**Col. 5:** *187*, p. 268.

45. Paperboard–**Col. 5:** *187*, p. 268.

46. Machine tools–**Cols. 1-3:** *99*, p. 255. **Col. 5:** *187*, p. 209. Also, *99*, p. 255.

46a. Metallurgical equipment–**Col. 1:** *207*, p. 140. **Cols. 2-3:** Based on 1942 output (col. 1) and index for 1943 and 1944 (given as 128 and 136 with 1942 = 100 in *99*, p. 256). **Col. 5:** *187*, p. 213.

47. Steam and gas turbines–**Col. 5:** *187*, p. 216.

48. Steam boilers–**Col. 5:** *187*, p. 218.

49. Turbogenerators–**Col. 5:** *187*, p. 215.

50. Spinning machines–**Col. 5:** *187*, p. 235.

51. Looms–**Col. 5:** *28*, p. 74.

52. Tractors–**Col. 1:** *99*, p. 136. Excludes garden tractors. **Col. 3:** *99*, p. 257. **Col. 5:** *187*, p. 229.

Table A-4 *continued*

53. Tractors (15 hp)–**Col. 5:** *187*, p. 226.
54. Motor vehicles, total–**Col. 3:** *99*, p. 349. Estimated from statement that the Minsk factory produced 2,760 motor vehicles, which represented 4.5% of total production. **Col. 5:** *187*, p. 223.
55. Trucks–**Cols. 1-3:** *209*, p. 113. **Col. 5:** *187*, p. 223.
56. Automobiles–**Col. 5:** *187*, p. 223.
57. Buses–**Col. 5:** *187*, p. 223. Total motor vehicles minus trucks and automobiles.
58. Grain combines–**Col. 5:** *187*, p. 233.
59. Steam locomotives–**Col. 1:** Production was reduced "to the minimum" (*99*, p. 136). **Col. 5:** *187*, p. 220.
60. Diesel locomotives–**Col. 5:** *187*, p. 220.
61. Electric locomotives–**Col. 5:** *187*, p. 220.
62. Railroad freight cars–**Col. 5:** *187*, p. 222.
64. Railroad passenger cars–**Col. 5:** *187*, p. 220.
65. Excavators–**Col. 3:** Based on 1945 output (col. 5) and increase in 1945 over 1944 (given as almost 1.5–fold in *99*, p. 256). **Col. 5:** *187*, p. 236.
66. Ginned cotton–**Col. 5:** *187*, p. 324.
67. Cotton yarn–**Col. 5:** *187*, p. 323.
68. Cotton fabrics–**Cols. 1-3:** *285*, No. 5, 1965, p. 71. **Col. 5:** *187*, p. 328.
69. Woolen fabrics–**Col. 1:** Based on 1940 output (given as 119.7 mill. m in Table A-1, col. 5) and index for 1942 (given as 32 with 1940 = 100 in *99*, p. 115). **Col. 5:** *187*, p. 328.
71. Linen fabrics (meters)–**Col. 5:** *187*, p. 328.
72. Silk and rayon fabrics–**Col. 5:** *187*, p. 328.
73. Knitted underwear–**Col. 5:** *187*, p. 343.
74. Knitted outer garments–**Col. 5:** *187*, p. 343.
75. Hosiery–**Col. 5:** *187*, p. 343.
76. Leather shoes–**Cols. 1-3:** *285*, No. 5, 1965, p. 71. **Col. 5:** *187*, p. 351. Also, *285*, No. 5, 1965, p. 71.
77. Felt footwear–**Col. 5:** *187*, p. 323.
78. Rubber footwear–**Col. 5:** *187*, p. 199.
80. Metal beds–**Col. 5:** *188*, p. 412.
80a. Enameled kitchenware–**Col. 5:** *187*, p. 364.
81. Motorcycles–**Col. 5:** *187*, p. 362.
82. Bicycles–**Col. 5:** *187*, p. 362.
83. Radios–**Col. 5:** *188*, p. 407.
83a. Refrigerators, household–**Col. 5:** *187*, p. 363.
84. Sewing machines, household–**Col. 5:** *187*, p. 362.
85. Clocks and watches–**Col. 5:** *187*, p. 362.
86. Cameras–**Col. 5:** *187*, p. 362.
87. Phonographs–**Col. 5:** *187*, p. 363.
88. Soap (40% fatty acid)–**Col. 5:** *187*, p. 372.
89a. Bread and breadstuffs (ministries and local Soviets)–**Col. 5:** *316*, p. 171.
90. Flour (total)–**Col. 5:** *188*, p. 450.
90a. Flour (centralized resources)–**Col. 5:** *15*, p. 49.
91. Macaroni–**Col. 5:** *187*, p. 403.
92. Raw sugar–**Cols. 1-3:** *285*, No. 5, 1965, p. 71. **Col. 5:** *187*, p. 373. See also *285*, No. 5, 1965, p. 71.
93. Starch and syrup–**Col. 5:** *187*, p. 372. Sum of starch and syrup.
94. Fish catch–**Cols. 1-3:** *22*, p. 62. Commissariat of Fishing Industry. Given for fish without further specification. **Col. 5:** *140*, p. 89. Includes whales. Fish catch excluding whales is given as 1,109 th. m. tons in *140*, p. 89, and 998 th. m. tons for the Commissariat of the Fishing Industry in *22*, p. 62.
95. Crude alcohol–**Col. 5:** *187*, p. 405.
96. Vegetable oil–**Cols. 1-3:** *285*, No. 5, 1965, p. 71. **Col. 5:** *187*, p. 392.
97. Butter–**Col. 5:** *187*, p. 386.
98. Cheese–**Col. 5:** *187*, 1964, p. 442. Coverage is larger than that in Tables A-1, A-2, and A-3. Probably includes collective farm output. Tables A-1 and A-3 give 37.3 th. m. t. for 1940 and Tables A-1 and A-5 give 49.1 th. m. t. for 1950, whereas *188* gives 42.4 th. m. t. for 1940 and 56.4 for 1950.
100. Meat and subproducts of first category–**Cols. 1-3:** *22*, p. 59. Production varied between 41 and 54% of the prewar level. **Col. 5:** *187*, p. 378.
101. Sausages–**Col. 5:** *188*, p. 436.
102. Canned food–**Col. 5:** *187*, p. 398.
103. Confectionery–**Col. 5:** *187*, p. 401.

Table A-4 *continued*

104. Margarine–**Col. 5:** *187*, p. 372. Margarine and compound fats.
105. Beer–**Col. 5:** *187*, p. 372.
106. Cigarettes–**Cols. 1-3:** *187*, p. 372.
107. Matches–**Cols. 1-3:** *113*, No. 6–7, 1946, pp. 13 and 15, as cited in *485*, series 1125.1. **Col. 5:** *187*, p. 267. *113*, No. 6–7, 1946, pp. 13 and 15, as cited in *485*, series 1125.1, gives the slightly lower figure of 1,864 th. crates.
108. Low-grade tobacco (*makhorka*)–**Col. 5:** *187*, p. 372.
109. Salt–**Col. 5:** *187*, p. 372.

AGRICULTURE
110a. Total value of production (comparable prices)–**Cols. 1-3 and 5:** *285*, No. 5, 1965, p. 72.

HARVESTS
113. Grain, total (biological yield)–**Col. 5:** *410*, p. 9. Estimate.
113a. Grain, total (barn yield)–**Cols. 1-3 and 5:** *99*, pp. 150 and 270.

HARVESTS OF TECHNICAL CROPS
119a. Raw cotton (barn yield)–**Cols. 1 and 2:** *7*, p. 175. **Cols. 3 and 5:** *99*, p. 270.
120a. Sugar beets (barn yield)–**Cols. 1-3 and 5:** *99*, pp. 150 and 270.
121a. Sunflowers (barn yield)–**Cols. 1-3 and 5:** *99*, pp. 150 and 270.
122a. Flax fiber (barn yield)–**Col. 1:** *99*, p. 150. **Cols. 2 and 3:** Based on 1940 output (given as 349 th. m. t. in Table A-1, col. 5) and index for 1943 and 1944 (given as 45 and 48, respectively, with 1940 = 100 in *207*, p. 144). **Col. 5:** *203*, p. 201.
124a. Potatoes (barn yield)–**Cols. 1-3:** *99*, pp. 150 and 270. **Col. 5:** *203*, p. 206.

ANIMAL PRODUCTION
125. Meat and fat (excl. rabbit and poultry)–**Cols. 1-3 and 5:** Based on 1940 output (given as 4,399 th. m. t. in Table A-1, col. 5) and index for 1942–1945 (given as 39, 38, 42, and 55, respectively, with 1940 = 100 in *285*, No. 5, 1965, p. 72).
125a. Meat and fat (incl. rabbit and poultry)–**Cols. 1-3:** Based on 1940 output (given as 4,695 th. m. t. in Table A-1, col. 5) and index for 1942–1944 (given as 39, 38, and 42, respectively, with 1940 = 100 in *285*, No. 5, 1965, p. 72). **Col. 5:** *203*, p. 290.
126. Milk–**Cols. 1-3:** Based on 1940 output (given as 33.64 mill. m. t. in Table A-1, col. 5) and index for 1942–1944 (given as 47, 49, and 66, respectively, with 1940 = 100 in *285*, No. 5, 1965, p. 72). **Col. 5:** *203*, p. 287.
127. Eggs–**Cols. 1-3:** Based on 1940 output (given as 12.2 bill. in Table A-1, col. 5) and index for 1942–1944 (given as 37, 28, and 29, respectively, with 1940 = 100 in *285*, No. 5, 1965, p. 72). **Col. 5:** *202*, p. 329.
128. Wool–**Cols. 1-3:** Based on 1940 output (given as 161 th. m. t. in Table A-1, col. 5) and index for 1942–1944 (given as 78, 62, and 64, respectively, with 1940 = 100 in *285*, No. 5, 1965, p. 72). **Col. 5:** *202*, p. 329.

MARKET PRODUCTION
129. Grain–**Col. 5:** *242*, p. 123.
130. Raw cotton–**Col. 5:** *242*, p. 123.
131. Sugar beets–**Col. 5:** *242*, p. 123.
133. Potatoes–**Col. 5:** *202*, p. 86.
134. Meat and fat–**Col. 5:** *202*, p. 87.
135. Milk and dairy products–**Col. 5:** *202*, p. 87.
136. Wool–**Col. 5:** *202*, p. 87.

PROCUREMENTS
137. Grain–**Cols. 1-3 and 5:** *99*, pp. 150 and 274. For cols. 2, 3, and 5, converted from poods at 1 pood = .01638 m. t.
138. Raw cotton–**Cols. 1-3 and 5:** *99*, pp. 150 and 274.
139. Sugar beets–**Cols. 1-3 and 5:** *99*, pp. 150 and 274.
140. Sunflowers–**Cols. 1-3 and 5:** *99*, pp. 150 and 274.
141. Flax fiber–**Cols. 1-3 and 5:** *99*, pp. 150 and 274.
142. Hemp–**Col. 5:** *203*, p. 52.
143. Potatoes–**Col. 5:** *203*, p. 52.
143a. Vegetables–**Col. 5:** *203*, p. 52.
144. Meat and fat (live weight)–**Cols. 1-3 and 5:** *99*, pp. 150 and 274.
145. Meat and fat (dead weight)–**Col. 5:** *203*, p. 53.
146. Milk and dairy products–**Cols. 1-3 and 5:** *99*, pp. 150 and 274–75.
147. Eggs–**Cols. 1-3 and 5:** *99*, pp. 150 and 275.
148. Wool–**Cols. 1-3 and 5:** *99*, pp. 150 and 275.

Table A-4   *continued*

RAILROAD TRANSPORTATION

149. Length of network–**Cols. 1-3 and 5:** *445*, p. 365.

150. Average daily carloadings–**Cols. 1-3 and 5:** *490*, p. 171.

151. Total freight traffic (ton-km)–**Cols. 1-3:** *99*, p. 281. **Col. 5:** *252*, p. 32. See also *99*, p. 281.

152. Total freight traffic (tons)–**Col. 1:** *99*, p. 152. **Cols. 2 and 3:** *490*, p. 170. **Col. 5:** *252*, p. 32.

153. Coal and coke–**Col. 5:** *252*, p. 35.

154. Oil and oil products–**Col. 5:** *445*, p. 347. *252*, p. 35, gives rounded figure of 21 mill. m. t.

155. Ferrous metals–**Col. 5:** *445*, p. 347. *252*, p. 36, gives rounded figure of 21 mill. m. t.

156. Ore–**Col. 5:** *445*, p. 347. *252*, p. 36, gives rounded figure of 18 mill. m. t.

157. Firewood–**Col. 5:** *445*, p. 347. *252*, p. 38, gives rounded figure of 17 mill. m. t.

158. Timber–**Col. 5:** *445*, p. 347. *252*, p. 38, gives rounded figure of 27 mill. m. t.

159. Mineral construction materials–**Col. 5:** *445*, p. 347. *252*, p. 37, gives rounded figure of 42 mill. m. t.

160. Grain and flour–**Col. 5:** *445*, p. 347. *252*, p. 37, gives rounded figure of 20 mill. m. t.

162. Total freight traffic, average length of haul–**Col. 1:** 1940 average length of haul (given as 700 km in Table A-1, col. 5) plus increase in 1942 over 1940 (given as 86 km in *99*, p. 152). **Cols. 2-3:** *490*, p. 170. **Col. 5:** *252*, p. 34.

163. Coal and coke, average length of haul–**Col. 1:** *18*, p. 96. Coal only. **Col. 5:** *252*, p. 35.

163a. Oil and oil products, average length of haul–**Col. 5:** *252*, p. 35.

164. Ferrous metals, average length of haul–**Col. 5:** *252*, p. 36.

164a. Firewood, average length of haul–**Col. 5:** *252*, p. 38.

164b. Timber, average length of haul–**Col. 1:** *445*, p. 173. **Col. 5:** *252*, p. 38.

165. Grain and flour, average length of haul–**Col. 5:** *252*, p. 37.

165a. Ore, average length of haul–**Col. 5:** *252*, p. 36. Includes pyrites.

166. Total passenger traffic–**Col. 1:** Based on 1945 traffic (col. 5) and index for 1945 (given as 174 with 1942 = 100 in *99*, p. 282). **Cols. 2-3:** Based on 1942 traffic (col. 1) and index for 1943 and 1944 (given as 104 and 152, respectively, with 1942 = 100 in *99*, p. 282). **Col. 5:** *252*, p. 32.

INLAND WATERWAY TRANSPORTATION

166a. Length of network–**Col. 5:** *252*, p. 115.

168. Freight traffic under ministries and economic organizations (ton-km)–**Cols. 1-3:** Based on 1940 traffic (given as 35.9 bill. ton-km in Table A-1, col. 5) and index for 1942–1944 (given as 60, 62, and 62, respectively, with 1940 = 100 in *207*, p. 148). **Col. 5:** *252*, p. 116.

170. Freight traffic under ministries and economic organizations (tons)–**Col. 1:** *99*, p. 283. **Col. 5:** *252*, p. 116.

171. Coal and coke–**Col. 5:** *252*, p. 120. Coal only.

172. Oil and oil products–**Col. 5:** *252*, p. 120.

173. Timber and firewood–**Col. 5:** *252*, p. 120.

174. Mineral construction materials–**Col. 5:** *252*, p. 120.

175. Grain and flour–**Col. 5:** *252*, p. 120.

176. Salt–**Col. 5:** *252*, p. 120.

177. Average length of haul under ministries and economic organizations–**Col. 1:** Based on freight traffic in ton-km (series 168) and in tons (series 170). **Col. 5:** *252*, p. 116.

178. Passenger traffic (pass.-km)–**Col. 5:** *252*, p. 116.

178a. Passenger traffic (pass.)–**Col. 1:** *99*, p. 283. **Col. 5:** *252*, p. 116.

MARITIME TRANSPORTATION (Soviet ships)

179. Freight traffic (ton-km)–**Cols. 1-3:** Based on 1940 traffic (given as 23.8 bill. pass.-km in Table A-1, col. 5) and index for 1942–1944 (given as 66, 137, and 144, respectively, with 1940 = 100 in *285*, No. 5, 1965, p. 73). **Col. 5:** *252*, p. 7.

180. Freight traffic (tons)–**Col. 5:** *252*, p. 95. Excludes traffic in steamships in Central Asia.

181. Average length of haul–**Col. 5:** *252*, p. 95. Converted from nautical miles at 1 nautical mile = 1.853 km (the ratio given in *236*, p. 177).

182. Passenger traffic (pass.-km)–**Col. 5:** *252*, p. 95. Converted from pass.-miles at 1 pass.-mile = 1.853 pass.-km.

182a. Passenger traffic (pass.)–**Col. 5:** *252*, p. 95.

MOTOR TRANSPORTATION

183. Freight traffic–**Cols. 1-3 and 5:** Based on 1940 freight traffic (given as 8.896 bill. m. ton-km in Table A-1, col. 5) and index for 1942–1945 (given as 31, 31, 39, and 56, respectively, with 1940 = 100 in *285*, No. 5, 1965, p. 73). For col. 5, *252*, p. 155, gives a rounded figure of 5.0 bill. m. ton-km.

AIR TRANSPORTATION

184. Freight traffic, incl. mail–**Cols. 1 and 3:** Based on 1940 freight traffic (given as 33.1 mill. m. ton-km in Table

Table A-4 *continued*

A-1, col. 5) and index for 1942 and 1944 (given as 61 and 148, respectively, with 1940 = 100 in *285*, No. 5, 1965, p. 73). **Cols. 2 and 5:** *99*, p. 284.

185. Passenger traffic–**Col. 5:** *253*, p. 34.

EMPLOYMENT (annual averages)

186. Workers and employees, national economy, excl. collective farms–**Cols. 1-3 and 5:** *99*, p. 220.

187. Industry–**Col. 1:** *99*, p. 115. **Cols. 2 and 3:** Based on 1942 employment (col. 1) and index for 1943 and 1944 (given as 105 and 118 with 1942 = 100 in *99*, p. 218). **Col. 5:** *140*, p. 190.

188. Construction–**Col. 5:** *260*, p. 121.

188a. Construction and assembly work–**Col. 1:** Based on 1945 employment (col. 5) and index for 1945 (given as 176 with 1942 = 100 in *99*, p. 218). **Cols. 2-3:** Based on 1942 employment (col. 1) and index for 1943–1944 (given as 107 and 156 with 1942 = 100 in *99*, p. 218). **Col. 5:** *140*, p. 190.

190. State-owned agriculture (state farms, MTS, and other state establishments)–**Col. 5:** *260*, pp. 24–25.

191. Railroad transport–**Col. 1:** Based on total employment (series 186) and share of railroad transport workers in total (given as 5.8% in *99*, p. 115). **Col. 5:** *140*, p. 190.

192. Maritime and inland waterway transport–**Col. 5:** *140*, p. 190.

193. Other transport (motor, etc.)–**Col. 5:** *140*, p. 190.

194. Communications–**Col. 1:** Based on 1945 employment (col. 5) and index for 1945 (given as 156 with 1942 = 100 in *99*, p. 218). **Cols. 2-3:** Based on 1942 employment (col. 1) and index for 1943–1944 (given as 105 and 133 with 1942 = 100 in *99*, p. 218). **Col. 5:** *140*, p. 190.

195. Trade, procurements, and supply–**Col. 5:** *140*, p. 190.

196. Public eating places–**Col. 5:** *140*, p. 190.

197. Credit institutions–**Col. 1:** Based on total employment (series 186) and share of credit institution workers in total (given as 0.7% in *99*, p. 115). **Col. 5:** *140*, p. 190.

198. Administration–**Col. 1:** Based on total employment (series 186) and share of administration workers in total (given as 5% in *99*, p. 115). **Col. 5:** *140*, p. 190.

199. Education–**Col. 1:** Based on total employment (series 186) and share of education workers in total (given as 8.7% in *99*, p. 115). **Col. 5:** *140*, p. 190.

200. Public health–**Col. 1:** Based on total employment (series 186) and share of public health workers in total (given as 5.3% in *99*, p. 115). **Col. 5:** *140*, p. 190.

WAGE FUND, WORKERS AND EMPLOYEES

201. National economy–**Col. 5:** Based on total employment (series 186) and average annual money wage (series 203). On the definition of the wage fund, see Table C-1.

202. Industry–**Col. 5:** Based on employment in industry (series 187) and average annual money wage in industry (series 205).

AVERAGE ANNUAL WAGE, WORKERS AND EMPLOYEES

203. Money wage, national economy, excl. collective farms and cooperatives–**Col. 5:** *260*, p. 138. Converted into old rubles.

204. Real wage, national economy, excl. collective farms and cooperatives–**Col. 5:** Based on 1945 money wage in 1940 prices (derived as 1,602 rubles from 1945 money wage in series 203 and price index for 1945, given as 325 with 1940 = 100 in *124*, p. 235) and 1940 money wage (given as 3,972 rubles in series 203, Table A-1, col. 5).

205. Money wage, industry–**Col. 5:** *260*, p. 138. Converted into old rubles.

AVERAGE ANNUAL MONEY WAGE, WORKERS

206. Industry–**Col. 3:** Based on 1940 money wage (given as 3,876 rubles in Table A-1, col. 5) and increase in 1944 over 1940 (given as 42% in *290*, p. 70). **Col. 5:** *260*, p. 138. Converted into old rubles.

208. Coal–**Col. 5:** *104*, p. 323. Ministry of Coal Industry.

AVERAGE ANNUAL MONEY WAGE, WORKERS AND EMPLOYEES

215. Construction–**Col. 5:** *260*, p. 138. Covers construction and assembly work. Converted into old rubles.

216. Railroad transport–**Col. 5:** *260*, p. 138. Converted into old rubles.

217. Maritime and inland waterway transport–**Col. 5:** *260*, p. 138. Converted into old rubles.

218. Communications–**Col. 5:** *260*, p. 138. Converted into old rubles.

221. Credit institutions–**Col. 5:** *260*, p. 138. Converted into old rubles.

222. Administration–**Col. 5:** *260*, p. 138. Converted into old rubles.

223. Education–**Col. 5:** *260*, p. 138. Converted into old rubles.

224. Public health–**Col. 5:** *260*, p. 138. Converted into old rubles.

225. State-owned agriculture–**Col. 5:** *260*, p. 138. Covers state farms and farms belonging to auxiliary enterprises. Converted into old rubles.

Table A-4 *continued*

HOUSING

227. Housing fund, urban, total–**Col. 5:** Housing fund in 1940 (given as 270 mill. m² in Table A-1, col. 5) minus housing destroyed during war (given as about 70 mill. m² in *159*, p. 5).

228. Housing construction, urban, total–**Cols. 1-3 and 5:** *99*, p. 214. Includes reconstruction.

POPULATION

230. Total (end of year)–**Col. 5:** Population at end of 1951 (given as 184.8 mill. in Table A-5, col. 17) minus total increase during 1949–1951 (given as 9.5 mill. in *94*, p. 342) minus annual increase during 1946–1948 (estimated at 17.0 per thous. from data for 1950–1955 in *142*, p. 31).

RETAIL TRADE

233. State and cooperative in current prices–**Cols. 1-3 and 5:** *232*, p. 20.

234. State and cooperative in 1940 prices–**Cols. 1-3:** Based on 1940 state and cooperative trade in current prices

Table A-5 Fulfillment of Annual Plans, 1946–1952

Series	Units	1946			1947			1948		
		Planned (1)	Actual (2)	(2) as Per Cent of (1) (3)	Planned (4)	Actual (5)	(5) as Per Cent of (4) (6)	Planned (7)	Actual (8)	(8) as Per Cent of (7) (9)
1. National income (1926/27 prices)	bill. rub.		100.1			119.3			148.8	
Industry										
2. Gross production, total (1926/27 prices)	bill. rub.	103	106.6	103.5		128.8		153.3	163.4	106.6
3. Producer goods (1926/27 prices)	bill. rub.		69.5			85.6			110.2	
4. Consumer goods (1926/27 prices)	bill. rub.		36.0			44.0			53.2	
5. Coal	th. m. t.		164,063		190,300	183,249	96.3		208,242	
6. Peat	th. m. t.		27,271			30,587			34,380	
7. Coke	th. m. t.		15,396			17,535			20,894	
8. Oil shale	th. m. t.									
9. Crude petroleum	th. m. t.		21,746		25,700	26,022	101.3		29,249	
10. Natural gas	mill. m³		3,875		4,570	4,770	104.4		5,165	
11. Electric power	mill. kwh	48,720	48,571	99.7	56,300	56,491	100.3		66,341	
12. Hydroelectric power	mill. kwh		6,046			7,283			9,369	
13. Iron ore	th. m. t.		19,327			23,340			27,985	
14. Pig iron	th. m. t.		9,862		11,900	11,223	94.3		13,742	
15. Steel ingots and castings	th. m. t.	20,000	13,346	66.7	15,900	14,534	91.4		18,639	
16. Rolled steel	th. m. t.		9,578		11,600	11,057	95.3		14,219	
17. Steel pipes	th. m. t.		796			950			1,324	
19. Manganese ore	th. m. t.		1,730			2,039			2,261	
20. Nickel	th. m. t.		16.2			21.1				
21. Zinc	th. m. t.		50.9			59.0			80.3	

Table A-4 *continued*

(given as 175,080 mill. rubles in Table A-1, series 233, col. 5) and index for 1942–1944 (given as 34, 32, and 37, respectively, with 1940 = 100 in *207*, p. 121). **Col. 5:** *124*, p. 407.

234c. Food products in current prices–**Cols. 1-3 and 5:** Based on state and cooperative trade in current prices (series 233) and share of food products in that trade (given as 72.0%, 72.8%, 75.0%, and 75.6% for 1942–1945, respectively, in *232*, p. 39).

234d. Food products in 1940 prices–**Col. 5:** Based on food products in current prices (series 234c) and price index for 1945 (given as 225 with 1940 = 100 in *207*, p. 157).

235. Collective farm in current prices–**Col. 5:** Based on state and cooperative trade in current prices (series 233) and share of collective farm trade in total trade (given as 46% in *237*, p. 427).

1949			1950			1951			1952			
Planned (10)	Actual (11)	(11) as Per Cent of (10) (12)	Planned (13)	Actual (14)	(14) as Per Cent of (13) (15)	Planned (16)	Actual (17)	(17) as Per Cent of (16) (18)	Planned (19)	Actual (20)	(20) as Per Cent of (19) (21)	Series No.
	174.5			210.4			236.1			261.7		1
194.4	195.3	100.5	236.3	239.6	101.4	275.5	279.8	101.6	307.8	311.6	101.2	2
	138.2			173.8			202.7		226.4	227.3	100.4	3
	57.5			66.1			76.8		83.8	84.8	101.2	4
	235,507			261,089			281,928			300,875		5
	36,045			35,999			39,799			37,234		6
	24,339			27,728			30,692			33,733		7
				4,716.2								8
	33,444			37,878			42,253			47,311		9
	5,362			5,760.9			6,256			6,356		10
	78,257			91,226			104,022			119,116		11
	11,512			12,691			13,722			14,908		12
	32,570			39,651			44,926			52,583		13
	16,389			19,175			21,909			25,071		14
	23,291			27,329			31,350			34,492		15
	18,002			20,888			24,029			26,808		16
	1,728			2,001			2,286			2,616		17
	2,896			3,377			4,118			4,403		19
												20
	99.6			116.5			134.0			166.2		21

Table A-5   *continued*

Series	Units	1946 Planned (1)	1946 Actual (2)	1946 (2) as Per Cent of (1) (3)	1947 Planned (4)	1947 Actual (5)	1947 (5) as Per Cent of (4) (6)	1948 Planned (7)	1948 Actual (8)	1948 (8) as Per Cent of (7) (9)
22. Refined copper	th. m. t.		143		167	156	93.4		187	
23. Lead	th. m. t.		71		94	90	95.7		92	
24. Mineral fertilizer	th. m. t.		1,709.1			2,355.3		3,130	3,467.8	110.8
26. Phosphoric fertilizer (18.7% P_2O_5)	th. m. t.		560.9		970	798.8	82.4		1,411.1	
27. Ground natural phosphate	th. m. t.		50.6			75.6			238.0	
28. Potash fertilizer	th. m. t.		203.5			357.1			465.7	
29. Ammonium sulfate	th. m. t.		894.1		966	1,123.8	116.3	1,160	1,353.0	116.6
30. Soda ash	th. m. t.		257.0		406	338.6	83.4		489.4	
31. Caustic soda	th. m. t.		139.7		190	178.2	93.8		223.5	
32. Sulfuric acid	th. m. t.		725		1,200	996	83.0		1,479	
33. Tires	thous.		1,988			2,954			4,072	
34. Plastics	th. m. t.									
34a. Synthetic dyes	th. m. t.		19.5			28.1			37.97	
35. Cement	th. m. t.	3,505	3,373	96.2	5,770	4,718	81.8		6,455	
36. Lime	th. m. t.		2,692			3,301			4,355	
37. Window glass	mill. m²		39.9		56.7	47.8	84.3		59.0	
38a. Roofing tiles	mill.		63.1			90.9			135.6	
39. Asbestos shingles	mill.		169.5		220	243.0	105.7		329.0	
40. Bricks	mill.	4,760	3,239	68.0	5,420	4,059	74.9		6,105	
41. Industrial timber hauled	mill. m³		80.3		118	99.0	83.9		132.4	
42. Lumber	mill. m³		19.6		24.9	24.2	97.2		32.7	
43. Plywood	th. m³		251.6			309.4			434.7	
44. Paper	th. m. t.		516.7			647.5			778.6	
45. Paperboard	th. m. t.		97.5			140.8			180.5	
46. Machine tools	units	50,000	40,300	80.6	49,600	50,400	101.6		64,500	
46a. Metallurgical equipment	th. m. t.		37.7		62.6	40.3	64.4		78.2	
46b. Oil equipment	th. m. t.									
47. Steam and gas turbines	th. kw		245		838	618	73.7		724	
48. Steam boilers	th. m²		95.0			135.1			179.4	
49. Turbo-generators	th. kw									
50. Spinning machines	units									
51. Looms	units		580		3,300	2,240	67.9		3,990	
52. Tractors	units		13,300		38,200	27,800	72.8	75,500	56,900	75.4
53. Tractors (15 hp)	th. conven. units		28.4			65.0			132.6	
54. Motor vehicles, total	thous.	150	102.17	68.1	160	132.97	83.1	200	197.06	98.5
55. Trucks	thous.		94.6		147	121.2	82.4		173.9	
56. Automobiles	thous.		6.29		26.2	9.62	36.7		20.17	
57. Buses	thous.		1.3		2.3	2.2	95.7		3.0	
58. Grain combines	units		1,500		7,800	2,800	35.9	25,000	14,500	58.0

	1949			1950			1951			1952		
Planned (10)	Actual (11)	(11) as Per Cent of (10) (12)	Planned (13)	Actual (14)	(14) as Per Cent of (13) (15)	Planned (16)	Actual (17)	(17) as Per Cent of (16) (18)	Planned (19)	Actual (20)	(20) as Per Cent of (19) (21)	Series No.
	224			247			282			324		22
	116			144			179			210		23
4,585.3			5,492.4			5,924.7			6,394.3			24
1,930.2			2,350.5			2,472.1			2,654.8			26
	375.3			483.2			553.6			598.8		27
	594.1			750.4			820.4			904.7		28
	1,685.7			1,908.3			2,078.6			2,236.0		29
	643.2			748.6			823.7			999.1		30
	283.3			324.8			351.9			390.4		31
	1,845			2,125			2,372			2,662		32
	5,680			7,401			7,519			7,599		33
				74.5			73.3			84.4		34
	42.5			46.53			53.46			58.60		34a
	8,147			10,194		12,500	12,070	96.6		13,910		35
	5,406			6,451			7,051			7,643		36
	71.5			76.9			67.7			62.0		37
	168.6			222.5			268.1			319.1		38a
	450.5			546.4		677	695.4	102.7		878.4		39
	8,137			10,179		13,100	12,801	97.7		14,854		40
	151.3			161.0		203.4	184.5	90.7	216	184.6	85.2	41
	42.8			49.5			56.0			60.5		42
	573.4			657.5			766.6			883.1		43
	995.4			1,193.3			1,341.7			1,461.2		44
	232.1			291.8			333.9			383.7		45
	64,900			70,597			71,182			74,558		46
	99.3			111.2			109.7			123.5		46a
				2,305			2,083			2,007		46b
	1,242			2,381			2,663			2,873		47
	247.5			358.7			423.5			572.6		48
				676.5			1,425.0			1,824.0		49
				1,958			1,614			1,771		50
	6,900			8,700			7,200			10,000		51
	88,200			108,830			91,825			98,655		52
	193.8			240.9			204.3			216.2		53
	275.99			362.89			288.68			307.94		54
	226.9			294.4			229.8			243.5		55
	45.66			64.55			53.65			59.66		56
	3.4			3.9			5.3			4.7		57
	29,200			46,338			53,300			42,200		58

Table A-5 *continued*

Series	Units	1946 Planned (1)	1946 Actual (2)	(2) as Per Cent of (1) (3)	1947 Planned (4)	1947 Actual (5)	(5) as Per Cent of (4) (6)	1948 Planned (7)	1948 Actual (8)	(8) as Per Cent of (7) (9)
59. Steam locomotives	units		243		700	674	96.3		1,032	
60. Diesel locomotives	units		0			25			69	
61. Electric locomotives	units		1			16			38	
62. Railroad freight cars	units		17,298		36,000	23,800	66.1		30,474	
64. Railroad passenger cars	units									
65. Excavators	units		76			630			1,832	
66. Ginned cotton	th. m. t.		549		710.0	718	101.1	850	729	85.8
67. Cotton yarn	th. m. t.		354			460			568	
68. Cotton fabrics	mill. m.		1,901		2,700	2,541	94.1	3,070	3,150	102.6
69. Woolen fabrics	mill. m.		70.9		92.2	95.0	103.0	117	123.7	105.7
71. Linen fabrics	mill. m.		112.6		153.4	141.4	92.2		184.1	
72. Silk and rayon fabrics	mill. m.		48.7		62.0	65.4	105.5	78.5	81.7	104.1
73. Knitted underwear	mill.		46.0			61.3		104	84.3	81.1
74. Knitted outer garments	mill.		30.4			38.9			42.9	
75. Hosiery	mill. prs		133.9			196.7		317	282.0	89.0
76. Leather shoes	mill. prs		81.2		115	112.8	98.1	147	134.0	91.2
77. Felt footwear	mill. prs		15.1			15.5			17.3	
78. Rubber footwear	mill. prs		30.8		49.9	51.3	102.8		71.1	
80. Metal beds	thous.		2,106			3,149			3,912	
80a. Enameled kitchenware	th. m. t.		6.0			8.0			11.0	
81. Motorcycles	thous.		6.1			29.6			17.5	
82. Bicycles	thous.		71.5			207.6			338.2	
83. Radios	thous.		228.6			380.4			536.6	
83a. Refrigerators, household	thous.								0.3	
84. Sewing machines, household	thous.		16.0			125.0			309.2	
85. Clocks and watches	thous.		567			1,235			3,042	
86. Cameras	thous.		5.7			91.5			156.4	
87. Phonographs	thous.		55.4			130.4			207.0	
88. Soap (40% fatty acid)	th. m. t.		233		298	297	99.7	400	425	106.3
89a. Bread and breadstuffs (ministries and local Soviets)	th. m. t.		9,190			8,148			11,360	
90. Flour (total)	th. m. t.		16,399			14,079			19,680	
90a. Flour (centralized resources)	th. m. t.									

	1949			1950			1951			1952		
Planned (10)	Actual (11)	(11) as Per Cent of (10) (12)	Planned (13)	Actual (14)	(14) as Per Cent of (13) (15)	Planned (16)	Actual (17)	(17) as Per Cent of (16) (18)	Planned (19)	Actual (20)	(20) as Per Cent of (19) (21)	Series No.
	1,187			985			665			254		59
	128			125			76			75		60
	82			102			113			110		61
	43,557			50,795			28,371			24,433		62
				912			1,327			1,229		64
	2,754			3,540			3,755			3,701		65
	821			952.7			1,267			1,352		66
	613			662.5			799			838		67
	3,601			3,899			4,768			5,044		68
	148.6		168.0	155.2	92.4		175.6			190.5		69
	225.5			282.2			313.5			256.5		71
	105.0			129.7			174.3		218	224.6	103.0	72
	118.6			150.4			198.3			234.9		73
	45.1			47.1			58.9			63.5		74
	375.1			472.7			597.8			584.9		75
	163.6			203.4			239.2			237.0		76
	20.3			22.4			24.7			21.5		77
	91.8			110.4			123.1			124.0		78
	3,782			4,358			4,877			6,298		80
	16.1			20.3			23.9			29.6		80a
	92.1			123.1			125.1			104.4		81
	492.2			649.3			1,157.2		1,540	1,650.4	107.2	82
	888.0			1,072.4			1,234.0			1,296.2		83
	1.8			1.2			15.0			31.1		83a
	413.9			501.7			668.0			804.5		84
	5,934			7,566			9,645			10,486		85
	166.2			260.3			357.2			459.1		86
	339.6			366.8			454.6			558.4		87
	726			816			767			785		88
	11,205			12,412			12,604			13,474		89a
	20,486			22,037			24,447			25,791		90
				12,400								90a

Table A-5 *continued*

Series	Units	1946 Planned (1)	1946 Actual (2)	(2) as Per Cent of (1) (3)	1947 Planned (4)	1947 Actual (5)	(5) as Per Cent of (4) (6)	1948 Planned (7)	1948 Actual (8)	(8) as Per Cent of (7) (9)
91. Macaroni	th. m. t.		270			238		305	311	
92. Raw sugar	th. m. t.		466		904	981	108.5	1,805	1,666	92.3
93. Starch and syrup	th. m. t.		57			71			128	
94. Fish catch	th. m. t.		1,208		1,607	1,534	95.5		1,575	
95. Crude alcohol	th. hl		3,360		3,730	3,650	97.9		5,490	
96. Vegetable oil	th. m. t.		326		381	403	105.8		549	
97. Butter	th. m. t.		186		208	218	104.8		292	
98. Cheese	th. m. t.		27.9			35.4			46.4	
99. Meat	th. m. t.					713			891	
100. Meat and subproducts of first category	th. m. t.		793		928	815	87.8		1,016	
101. Sausages	th. m. t.								245.6	
102. Canned food	mill. 400-gm cans		583			669		836	868	103.8
103. Confectionery	th. m. t.		321			394		512	615	120.1
104. Margarine	th. m. t.		39			85			126	
105. Beer	th. hl		5,690			6,840			6,940	
106. Cigarettes	bill.		50.8			74.3		90	92.4	102.7
107. Matches	th. crates		2,400			3,300			5,300	
108. Low-grade tobacco (*makhorka*)	th. 20-kg. crates		1,200			1,300			2,000	
109. Salt	th. m. t.		3,100			3,900		5,850	4,700	
Agriculture										
110. Total value of production (1926/27 prices)	mill. rub.									
110a. Total value of production (comparable prices)	1940 = 100		67.4			86.5			96.5	
111a. Vegetable production (comparable prices)	1940 = 100		64.5			90.3			101.9	
112a. Animal production (comparable prices)	1940 = 100		76.3			78.1			84.2	
Harvests										
113. Grain, total (biological yield)	mill. m. t.		61.0		82.1	97.0	118.1		115.0	
113a. Grain, total (barn yield)	mill. m. t.		39.6			65.9			67.2	
114. Wheat (biological yield)	mill. m. t.								27.0	
114a. Wheat (barn yield)	mill. m. t.		12.5			17.4			24.3	

| | 1949 | | | 1950 | | | 1951 | | | 1952 | | |
Planned (10)	Actual (11)	(11) as Per Cent of (10) (12)	Planned (13)	Actual (14)	(14) as Per Cent of (13) (15)	Planned (16)	Actual (17)	(17) as Per Cent of (16) (18)	Planned (19)	Actual (20)	(20) as Per Cent of (19) (21)	Series No.
	364			440.2			496			617		91
	2,042			2,523			2,979			3,067		92
	214			242			236			223		93
	1,953			1,755			2,142			2,107		94
	6,870			7,300			8,100			8,910		95
	722			819			919			999		96
	317			336			355			371		97
	48.3			56.4			69.0			75.7		98
	944			1,275			835			1,091		99
	1,149			1,556			1,715			1,965		100
	351.2			491.7			575.3			553.9		101
	1,162			1,535			1,848			2,064		102
	784			993			1,158			1,286		103
	144			192			219			272		104
	9,620			13,080			15,050			16,150		105
	107.9			125.1			141.2			158.1		106
	8,000			10,200			10,800			9,100		107
	2,600			3,800			3,200			2,900		108
	4,600			4,474			4,100			4,400		109
	24,700			26,600						25,600		110
	99.3			99.3			92.2			100.7		110a
	100.6			97.4			85.8			95.5		111a
	95.6			103.5			110.5			113.2		112a
	124.0			124.5			121.2			131.0		113
	70.2			81.2			78.7			92.2		113a
				46.779			48.9			60.1		114
	23.6			31.1			32.4			43.8		114a

Table A-5 *continued*

		1946			1947			1948		
Series	*Units*	*Planned* (1)	*Actual* (2)	*(2) as Per Cent of (1)* (3)	*Planned* (4)	*Actual* (5)	*(5) as Per Cent of (4)* (6)	*Planned* (7)	*Actual* (8)	*(8) as Per Cent of (7)* (9)
115a. Rye (barn yield)	mill. m. t.		9.0			18.2			17.9	
116a. Barley (barn yield)	mill. m. t.									
117a. Oats (barn yield)	mill. m. t.									
118. Corn (biological yield)	mill. m. t.								3.2	
118a. Corn (barn yield)	mill. m. t.									
Harvests of Technical Crops										
119. Raw cotton (biological yield)	mill. m. t.		1.73			2.09			2.5	
119a. Raw cotton (barn yield)	mill. m. t.		1.643			1.701			2.200	
120. Sugar beets (biological yield)	mill. m. t.		7.24			21.0				
120a. Sugar beets (barn yield)	mill. m. t.		4.293			13.998			12.856	
121. Sunflowers (biological yield)	mill. m. t.		1.83			3.28				
121a. Sunflowers (barn yield)	mill. m. t.		.792			1.393			1.934	
122. Flax fiber (biological yield)	th. m. t.									
122a. Flax fiber (barn yield)	th. m. t.		133			170			257	
123a. Hemp (barn yield)	th. m. t.									
124. Potatoes (biological yield)	mill. m. t.									
124a. Potatoes (barn yield)	mill. m. t.		55.636			74.539			95.028	
Animal Production										
125a. Meat and fat (incl. rabbit and poultry)	th. m. t.		3,100			2,500			3,100	
126. Milk	mill. m. t.		27.7			30.2		34	33.4	98.2
127. Eggs	bill.		5.2			4.9			6.6	
128. Wool	th. m. t.		119			125		161	146	90.7
Market Production										
129. Grain	mill. m. t.									
130. Raw cotton	mill. m. t.									
131. Sugar beets	mill. m. t.									
133. Potatoes	mill. m. t.									
134. Meat and fat (dead weight)	th. m. t.									
135. Milk and dairy products	mill. m. t.									
136. Wool	th. m. t.									

	1949			1950			1951			1952			
Planned (10)	Actual (11)	(11) as Per Cent of (10) (12)	Planned (13)	Actual (14)	(14) as Per Cent of (13) (15)	Planned (16)	Actual (17)	(17) as Per Cent of (16) (18)	Planned (19)	Actual (20)	(20) as Per Cent of (19) (21)	Series No.
	18.3			18.0			19.4			15.5		115a
				6.354								116a
				13.005								117a
												118
				6.644								118a
	2.7			3.75		3.937	3.94	101.5		4.544		119
	2.535			3.584			3.727			3.780		119a
	22.3			23.5			27.5					120
	15.736			20.819			23.633			22.207		120a
	3.76			3.1								121
	1.852			1.798			1.739			2.205		121a
	600			530								122
	310			255			193			213		122a
				73								123a
				101.9			80			83		124
	89.611			88.612			58.754			69.189		124a
4,800	3,800	79.2		4,867			4,700			5,200		125a
	34.9			35.31			36.2			35.7		126
	9.1			11.7			13.3			14.4		127
	163			180			192			219		128
				38.2						40.4		129
				3.54						3.77		130
				19.7						21.98		131
				14.0						12.50		133
				2,500								134
				11.4						13.2		135
				138								136

Table A-5 *continued*

Series	Units	1946 Planned (1)	1946 Actual (2)	1946 (2) as Per Cent of (1) (3)	1947 Planned (4)	1947 Actual (5)	1947 (5) as Per Cent of (4) (6)	1948 Planned (7)	1948 Actual (8)	1948 (8) as Per Cent of (7) (9)
Procurements										
137. Grain	th. m. t.		17,500			27,500			30,200	
138. Raw cotton	th. m. t.		1,643			1,701			2,200	
139. Sugar beets	th. m. t.		3,774			12,160			11,811	
140. Sunflowers	th. m. t.		522			779			1,135	
141. Flax fiber	th. m. t.		75			93			162	
142. Hemp	th. m. t.									
143. Potatoes	th. m. t.		4,551			5,215			7,230	
143a. Vegetables	th. m. t.		1,480			2,055			1,960	
144. Meat and fat (live weight)	th. m. t.		1,400			1,400			1,700	
145. Meat and fat (dead weight)	th. m. t.									
146. Milk and dairy products	th. m. t.		4,900			5,300			6,700	
147. Eggs	mill.		1,200			700			1,100	
148. Wool	th. m. t.									
Railroad Transportation										
149. Length of network	th. km		114.1			115.5			115.8	
150. Average daily carloadings	thous.		69.8		77.5	75.7	97.7	86.8	90.3	104
151. Total freight traffic	bill. m. ton-km		335.0			350.5			446.0	
152. Total freight traffic	mill. m. t.		452.6			491.1			619.8	
153. Coal and coke	mill. m. t.	162	165	101.9		183			198	
154. Oil and oil products	mill. m. t.		22.2			26.2			30.4	
155. Ferrous metals	mill. m. t.	23.4	24.5	104.7		27.7			34.1	
156. Ore	mill. m. t.	24.2	24.2	100.0		27.8			33.1	
157. Firewood	mill. m. t.	19.1							17.7	
158. Timber	mill. m. t.		33.2			37.5			51.0	
159. Mineral construction materials	mill. m. t.	58.2							107.4	
160. Grain and flour	mill. m. t.	26.7								
162. Total freight traffic, average length of haul	km		740			714			720	
163. Coal and coke, average length of haul	km									
163a. Oil and oil products, average length of haul	km									
164. Ferrous metals, average length of haul	km									

	1949			1950			1951			1952		
Planned (10)	Actual (11)	(11) as Per Cent of (10) (12)	Planned (13)	Actual (14)	(14) as Per Cent of (13) (15)	Planned (16)	Actual (17)	(17) as Per Cent of (16) (18)	Planned (19)	Actual (20)	(20) as Per Cent of (19) (21)	Series No.
	32,100			32,311			33,600			34,700		137
	2,535			3,539			3,727			3,780		138
	15,309			19,822			23,377			21,991		139
	1,166			1,084			1,157			1,349		140
	209			174			159			189		141
				33								142
	6,960			6,906			5,195			5,554		143
	1,923			2,043			1,819			1,803		143a
1,930	1,800	93.3		2,122			2,600			3,200		144
				1,300								145
8,000	7,500	93.7		8,479			9,400			10,100		146
2,102	1,400	66.6		1,912			2,300			2,400		147
140				136						182		148
	116.0			116.9			117.8			118.6		149
101.7	104.7	103	114.7	118.1	103	123.8	127.5	103	132.9	138.2	104	150
	523.8			602.3			677.3			741.3		151
	735.3			834.3			909.2			997.0		152
	241.9			266.1			283			304		153
	36.8			43.2			48			55		154
	40.9			43.3			50			57		155
	40.4			48.4			56			66		156
	21.3			18.9			17			17		157
	63.2			72.4			77			82		158
	135.3			157.5			169			194		159
	34.6			38.8			43			44		160
	712		695	722	103.9	695	750	107.9	720	749	104.0	162
	667			670			665			661		163
	1,172			1,205			1,253			1,231		163a
	1,107			1,095			1,138			1,147		164

Table A-5 *continued*

Series	Units	1946 Planned (1)	Actual (2)	(2) as Per Cent of (1) (3)	1947 Planned (4)	Actual (5)	(5) as Per Cent of (4) (6)	1948 Planned (7)	Actual (8)	(8) as Per Cent of (7) (9)
164a. Firewood, average length of haul	km									
164b. Timber, average length of haul	km					831				
165. Grain and flour, average length of haul	km									
165a. Ore, average length of haul	km									
166. Total passenger traffic	bill. pass.-km		97.9			95.1		89.7	82.5	92
Inland Waterway Transportation										
166a. Length of network	th. km		116.7			118.8			123.3	
168. Freight traffic under ministries and economic organizations	bill. m. ton-km		20.4		24.6	25.1	102	30.3	32.1	106
170. Freight traffic under ministries and economic organizations	mill. m. t.		39.9			48.2			63.5	
171. Coal and coke	th. m. t.		1,700			2,100			2,900	
172. Oil and oil products	th. m. t.		6,100			8,000			8,700	
173. Timber and firewood	th. m. t.		22,000			26,600			36,600	
174. Mineral construction materials	th. m. t.		2,600			3,400			4,900	
175. Grain and flour	th. m. t.		2,400			2,700			3,600	
176. Salt	th. m. t.		1,300			1,400			1,700	
177. Average length of haul under ministries and economic organizations	km		511			520			506	
178. Passenger traffic	bill. pass.-km		3.2			3.1			2.6	
178a. Passenger traffic	mill. pass.		49.7			51.1			48.4	
Maritime Transportation (Soviet ships)										
179. Freight traffic	bill. m. ton-km		29.4		32.2	34.8	108	34.8	34.8	100
180. Freight traffic	mill. m. t.		20.3			24.3			26.9	
181. Average length of haul	km		1,448			1,432			1,294	

1949			1950			1951			1952			
Planned (10)	Actual (11)	(11) as Per Cent of (10) (12)	Planned (13)	Actual (14)	(14) as Per Cent of (13) (15)	Planned (16)	Actual (17)	(17) as Per Cent of (16) (18)	Planned (19)	Actual (20)	(20) as Per Cent of (19) (21)	Series No.
	229			241			263			273		164a
	941			998			1,084			1,148		164b
	863			795			873			829		165
	614			574			587			588		165a
	81.3			88.0			98.5			107.4		166
	126.1			130.2			127.9			131.1		166a
38.0	38.8	102		45.9		51.2	51.5	100.6		57.8		168
	78.0			91.5			102.8			109.8		170
	4,000			4,300			5,100			6,200		171
	10,500			11,900			12,000			12,700		172
	44,600			50,500			55,800			58,900		173
	7,500			11,700			16,100			17,900		174
	4,000			4,500			4,900			5,300		175
	1,700			1,668			1,500			1,500		176
	497			502			501			527		177
	2.5			2.7			2.9			3.0		178
	48.4			53.6			60.4			62.6		178a
	37.2		38.9	39.7	102	39.5	40.3	102	44.3	44.3	100	179
	30.9			33.7			36.5			41.2		180
	1,204			1,178			1,104			1,075		181

Table A-5 *continued*

Series	Units	1946			1947			1948		
		Planned (1)	*Actual* (2)	*(2) as Per Cent of (1)* (3)	*Planned* (4)	*Actual* (5)	*(5) as Per Cent of (4)* (6)	*Planned* (7)	*Actual* (8)	*(8) as Per Cent of (7)* (9)
182. Passenger traffic	mill. pass.-km		1,401			1,285			1,057	
182a. Passenger traffic	mill. pass.		2.0			2.7			2.4	
Motor Transportation										
183. Freight traffic	bill. m. ton-km		7.5		9.23	10.6	114.8		13.3	
Air Transportation										
184. Freight traffic, including mail	mill. m. ton-km		80		103					
185. Passenger traffic	th. pass.		1,500							
Employment (annual averages)										
186. Workers and employees, national economy, excl. collective farms	mill.		30.6		31.6	32.1	101.6		34.3	
187. Industry	thous.		10,200			11,000			12,100	
188. Construction	thous.		2,973							
188a. Construction and assembly work	thous.									
189. State-owned agriculture and logging	thous.									
190. State-owned agriculture	thous.									
191. Railroad transport	thous.									
192. Maritime and inland waterway transport	thous.									
193. Other transport (motor, etc.)	thous.									
194. Communications	thous.									
195. Trade, procurements, and supply	thous.									
196. Public eating places	thous.									
197. Credit institutions	thous.									
198. Administration	thous.									
199. Education	thous.									
200. Public health	thous.									
Wage Fund, Workers and Employees										
201. National economy	mill. rub.	160,300	174,400	108.8	212,900	219,300	103.0	241,500	247,900	102.7

	1949			1950			1951			1952		
Planned (10)	Actual (11)	(11) as Per Cent of (10) (12)	Planned (13)	Actual (14)	(14) as Per Cent of (13) (15)	Planned (16)	Actual (17)	(17) as Per Cent of (16) (18)	Planned (19)	Actual (20)	(20) as Per Cent of (19) (21)	Series No.
	1,091			1,233			1,246			1,230		182
	2.7			3.2			3.2			3.6		182a
	17.0			20.121			24.1			27.6		183
				140			180			200		184
				1,500			1,600			1,600		185
	36.1			38.9			40.7			42.2		186
	12,900			14,144			14,900			15,500		187
				4,087			4,249			4,478		188
				2,569			2,692			2,809		188a
				3,881								189
				3,437								190
				2,068								191
				222								192
				1,827								193
				542								194
				2,705								195
				659			688			720		196
				264								197
				1,831								198
				3,752								199
				2,051								200
261,200	268,700	102.9	290,900	298,300	102.5	319,700	321,900	100.7	334,400	340,400	101.8	201

Table A-5 *continued*

Series	Units	1946			1947			1948		
		Planned (1)	*Actual* (2)	*(2) as Per Cent of (1)* (3)	*Planned* (4)	*Actual* (5)	*(5) as Per Cent of (4)* (6)	*Planned* (7)	*Actual* (8)	*(8) as Per Cent of (7)* (9)
Average Annual Wage, Workers and Employees										
203. Money wage, national economy, excl. collective farms and coopera-tives	rubles		5,700			6,832		7,188	7,228	100.6
205. Money wage, industry	rubles					7,573				
Average Annual Money Wage, Workers										
206. Industry	rubles									
208. Coal	rubles		9,201			11,832			12,708	
209. Ferrous metals	rubles									
209a. Machine-building	rubles									
210. Paper	rubles									
211. Chemicals	rubles									
212. Textiles	rubles									
212a. Cotton	rubles									
213. Leather	rubles									
214. Food	rubles									
Average Annual Money Wage, Workers and Employees										
215. Construction	rubles									
216. Railroad transport	rubles		6,876			8,232			8,076	
217. Maritime and inland water-way transport	rubles									
218. Communica-tions	rubles									
221. Credit institutions	rubles									
222. Administration	rubles									
223. Education	rubles									
224. Public health	rubles									
225. State-owned agriculture	rubles									
Housing										
227. Housing fund, urban, total	mill. m^2								260	
228. Housing construction, urban, total (incl. recon-struction)	mill. m^2		17.4			18.2			21.1	
228a. Housing construction, urban	mill. m^2	8.9	6.0	67.4	13.8	13.0	94.2			

1949			1950			1951			1952			
Planned (10)	Actual (11)	(11) as Per Cent of (10) (12)	Planned (13)	Actual (14)	(14) as Per Cent of (13) (15)	Planned (16)	Actual (17)	(17) as Per Cent of (16) (18)	Planned (19)	Actual (20)	(20) as Per Cent of (19) (21)	Series No.
	7,445			7,668			7,908		·	8,066		203
				8,436								205
				8,244			8,400			8,600		206
	13,458			14,472			14,573			14,646		208
				11,472								209
				8,928								209a
				9,670								210
				8,760								211
				6,852								212
				7,296								212a
				7,250								213
				6,144								214
				7,212								215
	8,520			8,700			9,216			9,228		216
				9,432								217
				6,324								218
				7,968								221
				8,196								222
				8,004								223
				5,820								224
				4,584								225
				513								227
	21.9			24.2			27.6			27.4		228
												228a

Table A-5 *continued*

Series	Units	1946 Planned (1)	1946 Actual (2)	(2) as Per Cent of (1) (3)	1947 Planned (4)	1947 Actual (5)	(5) as Per Cent of (4) (6)	1948 Planned (7)	1948 Actual (8)	(8) as Per Cent of (7) (9)
229. Floorspace per inhabitant, urban	m²									
Population										
230. Total	mill.									
231. Urban	mill.									
232. Rural	mill.									
Retail Trade										
233. State and cooperative in current prices	mill. rub.		247,200		324,600	330,800	101.9	345,000	310,200	89.9
234. State and cooperative in 1940 prices	mill. rub.		95,500			103,000			116,400	
234c. Food products in current prices	mill. rub.		184,200			237,800			199,800	
234d. Food products in 1940 prices	mill. rub.		61,900			62,100			63,600	
235. Collective farm in current prices (urban)	mill. rub.		164,800			171,200			47,700	

Source

1. National income (1926/27 prices)–**Cols. 2, 5, 8, 11, 14, 17, and 20:** Based on national income in 1940 (given as 128.3 bill. rubles in Table A-1, col. 5) and indexes for 1946–1952 with 1940 = 100 (given as 78 for 1946 in *150*, p. 533; 93 and 116 for 1947–1948 in *34*, Bk. I, p. 411; 136 and 164 for 1949–1950 in *281*, p. 140; and 184 and 204 for 1951–1952 in *140*, p. 36). For col. 14, see also *161*, p. 112.

INDUSTRY

2. Gross production, total (1926/27 prices)–**Col. 1:** Based on gross production (col. 2) and percentage of plan fulfilled (col. 3). **Cols. 2, 5, 8, 11, 14, 17, and 20:** Based on gross production in 1940 (given as 138.5 bill. rubles in Table A-1, col. 5) and indexes for 1946–1952 (given as 77, 93, 118, 141, 173, 202, and 225, respectively, with 1940 = 100, in *140*, p. 47). **Col. 3:** *34*, Bk. I, p. 410. **Col. 7:** Based on gross production in 1947 (col. 5) and increase planned for 1948 (given as 19% in *176*, p. 108). **Cols. 10, 13, 16, and 19:** Based on gross production in 1948–1951 (cols. 8, 11, 14, and 17) and planned indexes for 1949–1952 (given as 119, 121, 115, and 110, respectively, as a percentage of preceding year in *221*, p. 58).

3. Producer goods (1926/27 prices)–**Cols. 2, 5, 8, 11, 14, 17, and 20:** Based on 1940 output (given as 84.8 bill. rubles in Table A-1, col. 5) and indexes for 1946–1952 (given as 82, 101, 130, 163, 205, 239, and 268, respectively, with 1940 = 100 in *140*, p. 47). **Col. 19:** Based on 1940 output (given as 84.8 bill. rubles in Table A-1, col. 5) and index planned for 1952 (given as 267 with 1940 = 100 in *125*, p. 38).

4. Consumer goods (1926/27 prices)–**Cols. 2, 5, 8, 11, 14, 17, and 20:** Based on 1940 output (given as 53.7 bill. rubles in Table A-1, col. 5) and indexes for 1946–1952 (given as 67, 82, 99, 107, 123, 143, and 158, respectively, with 1940 = 100 in *140*, p. 47). **Col. 19:** Based on 1940 output (given as 53.7 bill. rubles in Table A-1, col. 5) and index planned for 1952 (given as 156 with 1940 = 100 in *125*, p. 38).

5. Coal–**Cols. 2, 5, 8, 11, 14, 17, and 20:** *187*, p. 140. **Col. 4:** Based on 1946 output (col. 2) and increase planned for 1947 (given as 16% in *89*, 3/1/47, p. 1).

6. Peat–**Cols. 2, 5, 8, 11, 14, 17, and 20:** *218*, p. 35. Includes collective farm output.

7. Coke–**Cols. 2, 5, 8, 11, 14, 17, and 20:** *187*, p. 115.

8. Oil shale–**Col. 14:** *187*, p. 166.

| | 1949 | | | 1950 | | | 1951 | | | 1952 | | |
Planned (10)	Actual (11)	(11) as Per Cent of (10) (12)	Planned (13)	Actual (14)	(14) as Per Cent of (13) (15)	Planned (16)	Actual (17)	(17) as Per Cent of (16) (18)	Planned (19)	Actual (20)	(20) as Per Cent of (19) (21)	Series No.
				4.67								229
	178.5			181.6			184.8			188.0		230
	69.4			73.0			76.8			80.2		231
	109.1			108.6			108.0			107.8		232
	335,100			359,582			379,800			393,600		233
	139,600			192,600			222,400			243,400		234
	205,800			205,979			219,500			225,500		234c
	79,200			103,400			121,300			135,800		234d
	45,600			49,200			50,800			53,700		235

9. Crude petroleum–Cols. 2, 5, 8, 11, 14, 17, and 20: 187, p. 153. Col. 4: Based on 1946 output (col. 2) and increase planned for 1947 (given as 18% in 89, 3/1/47, p. 1).

10. Natural gas–Cols. 2,5, 8, and 11: Based on 1945 output (given as 3,278 mill. m³ in Table A-4, col. 5) and annual increases in 1946–1949 (given as 18.2%, 23.1%, 8.3%, and 3.8%, respectively in 285, No. 5, 1958, p. 58). Col. 4: Based on 1946 output (col. 2) and increase planned for 1947 (given as 18% in 89, 3/1/47, p. 1). Col. 14: 187, p. 156. Cols. 17 and 20: Based on 1950 output (col. 14) and annual increases in 1951–1952 (given as 8.6 % and 1.6%, respectively, in 285, No. 5, 1958, p. 58).

11. Electric power–Col. 1: Based on 1946 output (col. 2) and percentage of plan fulfilled (col. 3). Cols. 2, 5, 8, 11, 14, 17, and 20: 187, p. 171. Col. 3: 415, No. 8, 1947, p. 18. Ministry of Electric Power Stations. Col. 4: Based on 1946 output (col. 2) and increase planned for 1947 (given as 16% in 89, 3/1/47, p. 1).

12. Hydroelectric power–Cols. 2, 5, 8, 11, 14, 17, and 20: 187, p. 171.

13. Iron ore–Cols. 2, 5, 8, 11, 14, 17, and 20: 187, p. 115.

14. Pig iron–Cols. 2, 5, 8, 11, 14, 17, and 20: 187, p. 106. Col. 4: Based on 1946 output (col. 2) and increase planned for 1947 (given as 21% in 89, 3/1/47, p. 1).

15. Steel ingots and castings–Col. 1: 415, No. 3, 1946, p. 43. This figure should be accepted with great caution; it may be an estimate made while the plan was being drafted. Cols. 2, 5, 8, 11, 14, 17, and 20: 187, p. 106. Col. 4: Based on 1946 output (col. 2) and increase planned for 1947 (given as 19% in 89, 3/1/47, p. 1).

16. Rolled steel–Cols. 2, 5, 8, 11, 14, 17, and 20: 187, p. 106. Col. 4: Based on 1946 output (col. 2) and increase planned for 1947 (given as 21% in 89, 3/1/47, p. 1).

17. Steel pipes–Cols. 2, 5, 8, 11, 14, 17, and 20: 187, p. 106.

19. Manganese ore–Cols. 2, 5, 8, 11, 14, 17, and 20: 187, p. 115.

20. Nickel–Col. 2: Based on 1945 output (given as 15.2 th. m. t. in Table A-4, col. 5) and increase in 1946 (given as 6.5% in 485, series 213.4). Col. 5: Based on 1946 output (col. 2) and increase in 1947 (given as 30% for nine months of year in 485, series 213.4).

21. Zinc–Cols. 2, 5, 8, 11, 17, and 20: Based on 1950 output and annual increases in 1947–1952 (given as 16%, 36%, 24%, 17%, 15%, and 24%, respectively, in 180, 1/18/48, 1/20/49, 1/18/50, 1/26/51, 1/29/52, and 1/23/53).

Table A-5 *continued*

Col. 14: Table A-1, col. 11.

22. Refined copper–**Cols. 2, 5, 8, 11, 14, 17, and 20:** *272*, p. 420. Estimates. **Col. 4:** Based on 1946 output (col. 2) and increase planned for 1947 (given as 17% in *89*, 3/1/47, p. 1).

23. Lead–**Cols. 2, 5, 8, 11, 14, 17, and 20:** *272*, p. 421. **Col. 4:** Based on 1946 output (col. 2) and increase planned for 1947 (given as 32% in *89*, 3/1/47, p. 1).

24. Mineral fertilizer–**Cols. 2, 5, 8, 11, 14, 17, and 20:** *187*, p. 192. **Col. 7:** *98*, Pt. II, p. 1087.

26. Phosphoric fertilizer (18.7% P_2O_5)–**Cols. 2, 5, 8, 11, 14, 17, and 20:** *187*, p. 192. **Col. 4:** Based on 1946 output (col. 2) and increase planned for 1947 (given as 73% in *89*, 3/1/47, p. 1).

27. Ground natural phosphate–**Cols. 2, 5, 8, 11, 14, 17, and 20:** *187*, p. 192.

28. Potash fertilizer–**Cols. 2, 5, 8, 11, 14, 17, and 20:** *187*, p. 192.

29. Ammonium sulfate–**Cols. 2, 5, 8, 11, 14, 17, and 20:** *187*, p.192. **Cols. 4 and 7:** Based on 1946 output (col. 2) and increases planned for 1947 and 1948 (given as 8% and 30%, respectively, in *78*, No. 4, 1947, p. 1).

30. Soda ash–**Cols. 2, 5, 8, 11, 14, 17, and 20:** *187*, p. 194. **Col. 4:** Based on 1946 output (col. 2) and increase planned for 1947 (given as 58% in *89*, 3/1/47, p. 1).

31. Caustic soda–**Cols. 2, 5, 8, 11, 14, 17, and 20:** *187*, p. 194. **Col. 4:** Based on 1946 output (col. 2) and increase planned for 1947 (given as 36% in *89*, 3/1/47, p. 1).

32. Sulfuric acid–**Cols. 2, 5, 8, 11, 14, 17, and 20:** *187*, p. 196. **Col. 4:** Based on 1946 output (col. 2) and increase planned for 1947 (given as 65% in *89*, 3/1/47, p. 1).

33. Tires–**Cols. 2, 5, 8, 11, 14, 17, and 20:** *187*, p. 199.

34. Plastics–**Cols. 14, 17, and 20:** *188*, p. 146. *152*, p. 172, gives lower figures.

34a. Synthetic dyes–**Cols. 2 and 5:** Based on 1945 output (given as 15.1 th. m. t. in Table A-4, col. 5) and annual increases in 1946 and 1947 (given as 29% and 44%, respectively, in *180*, 1/21/47, and 1/18/48). **Col. 8:** Communicated by Nicholas DeWitt. **Col. 11:** Based on 1948 output (col. 8) and increase in 1949 (given as 12% in *180*, 1/18/50). **Col. 14, 17, and 20:** *187*, p. 197. Ministry of the Chemical Industry.

35. Cement–**Col. 1:** Based on 1945 output (given as 1,845 thous. m. tons in Table A-4, col. 5) and increase planned for 1946 (given as 90% in *415*, No. 7, 1947, p. 31). It is possible that this planned increase applied to only part of the total output of cement, such as the Ministry of the Construction Materials Industry, for instance. **Cols. 2, 5, 8, 11, 14, 17, and 20:** *187*, p. 277. **Col. 4:** Based on 1946 output (col. 2) and increase planned for 1947 (given as 71% in *89*, 3/1/47, p. 1). **Col. 16:** Based on 1950 output (col. 14) and increase planned for 1951 (given as 23% in *307*, p. 298).

36. Lime–**Cols. 2, 5, 8, 11, 14, 17, and 20:** *187*, p. 282. Sum of construction lime and technological lime.

37. Window glass–**Cols. 2, 5, 8, 11, 14, 17, and 20:** *187*, p. 312. **Col. 4:** Based on 1946 output (col. 2) and increase planned for 1947 (given as 42% in *89*, 3/1/47, p. 1).

38a. Roofing tiles–**Cols. 2, 5, 8, 11, 14, 17, and 20:** *187*, p. 299.

39. Asbestos shingles–**Cols. 2, 5, 8, 11, 14, 17, and 20:** *187*, p. 299. **Col. 4:** Based on 1946 output (col. 2) and increase planned for 1947 (given as 30% in *89*, 3/1/47, p. 1). **Col. 16:** Based on 1950 output (col. 14) and increase planned for 1951 (given as 24% in *307*, p. 298).

40. Bricks–**Col. 1:** Based on 1945 output (given as 2,026 mill. in Table A-4, col. 5) and increase planned for 1946 (given as 135% in *415*, No. 7, 1947, p. 31). **Cols. 2, 5, 8, 11, 14, 17, and 20:** *187*, p. 291. **Col. 4:** Based on 1946 output (col. 2) and increase planned for 1947 (given as 67% in *89*, 3/1/47, p. 1). **Col. 16:** Based on 1950 output (col. 14) and increase planned for 1951 (given as 28% in *307*, p. 298).

41. Industrial timber hauled–**Cols. 2, 5, 8, 11, 14, 17, and 20:** *187*, p. 249. **Col. 4:** Based on 1946 output (col. 2) and increase planned for 1947 (given as 47% in *89*, 3/1/47, p. 1). **Col. 16:** Based on 1951 output (col. 17) and percentage of plan fulfilled (col. 18). **Cols. 18 and 21:** *47*, No. 12, 1955, p. 30. **Col. 19:** Based on 1952 output (col. 20) and percentage of plan fulfilled (col. 21).

42. Lumber–**Cols. 2, 5, 8, 11, 14, 17, and 20:** *187*, p. 261. **Col. 4:** Based on 1946 output (col. 2) and increase planned for 1947 (given as 27% in *89*, 3/1/47, p. 1).

43. Plywood–**Cols. 2, 5, 8, 11, 14, 17, and 20:** *187*, p. 261.

44. Paper–**Cols. 2, 5, 8, 11, 14, 17, and 20:** *187*, p. 268.

45. Paperboard–**Cols. 2, 5, 8, 11, 14, 17, and 20:** *143*, p. 228.

46. Machine tools–**Col. 1:** Estimate derived from statement (*415*, No. 3, 1946, p. 42) that prewar level was to be reached in 1946. The 1940 figure used was the one accepted as "prewar" when the 1946 plan was drafted (given in *76*, p. 106, as cited in *485*, series 1009.1). **Col. 4:** Based on 1946 output (col. 2) and increase planned for 1947 (given as 23% in *89*, 3/1/47, p. 1). **Cols. 2, 5, 8, and 11:** *187*, p. 207. **Cols. 14, 17, and 20:** *187*, pp. 208–9.

46a. Metallurgical equipment–**Col. 2:** Based on 1945 output (given as 26.9 th. m. t. in Table A-4, col. 5) and increase in 1946 (given as 40% in *175*, p. 412). **Col. 4:** Based on 1946 output (col. 2) and increase planned for 1947 for foundries, steel mills, and rolling mills (given as 66% in *89*, 3/1/47, p. 1). **Cols. 5, 8, and 11:** Based on 1950 output (col. 14) and annual increases for 1948–1950 (given as 94%, 27%, and 12%, respectively, in *175*, p. 412). **Cols. 14, 17, and 20:** *187*, pp. 212–13.

Table A-5 *continued*

46b. Oil equipment–**Cols. 14, 17, and 20:** *187*, p. 213.

47. Steam and gas turbines–**Cols. 2, 5, 8, 11, 14, 17, and 20:** *187*, p. 216. **Col. 4:** Based on 1946 output (col. 2) and increase planned for 1947 (given as 242% in *89*, 3/1/47, p. 1).

48. Steam boilers–**Cols. 2, 5, 8, 11, 14, 17, and 20:** *187*, pp. 218–19.

49. Turbogenerators–**Cols. 14, 17, and 20:** *187*, pp. 214–15.

50. Spinning machines–**Col. 4:** *89*, 3/1/47, p. 1, gives 178% increase over 1946. **Cols. 14, 17, and 20:** *187*, pp. 234–35.

51. Looms–**Col. 2:** Based on 1945 output (given as 18 in Table A-4, col. 5) and increase in 1946 (given as 32–fold in *180*, 1/21/47). **Col. 4:** Based on 1946 output (col. 2) and increase planned for 1947 (given as 467% in *89*, 3/1/47, p. 1). **Cols. 5, 8, and 11:** Based on 1950 output (col. 14) and annual increases for 1948–1950 (given as 78%, 73%, and 26%, respectively, in *180*, 1/20/49, 1/18/50, and 1/26/51). **Cols. 14, 17, and 20:** *187*, p. 235.

52. Tractors–**Cols. 2, 5, 8, and 11:** *140*, p. 75. **Col. 4:** Based on 1946 output (col. 2) and increase planned for 1947 (given as 187% in *89*, 3/1/47, p. 1). **Col. 7:** *98*, Pt. II, p. 1083. **Cols. 14, 17, and 20:** *187*, pp. 228–29.

53. Tractors (15 hp)–**Cols. 2, 5, 8, 11, 14, 17, and 20:** *187*, p. 226.

54. Motor vehicles, total–**Col. 1:** Based on 1945 output (given as 74.7 th. in Table A-4, col. 5) and increase planned for 1946 (given as doubling in *415*, No. 4, 1946, p. 29). **Cols. 2, 5, 8, 11, 14, 17, and 20:** *143*, p. 216. **Col. 4:** Based on 1946 output (col. 2) and increase planned for 1947 (given as 57% in *89*, 3/1/47, p. 1). **Col. 7:** Based on 1947 output (col. 5) and increase planned for 1948 (given as 50% in *415*, No. 6, 1949).

55. Trucks–**Cols. 2, 5, 8, 11, 14, 17, and 20:** *187*, p. 223. **Col. 4:** Based on 1946 output (col. 2) and increase planned for 1947 (given as 55% in *89*, 3/1/47, p. 1).

56. Automobiles–**Cols. 2, 5, 8, 11, 14, 17, and 20:** *143*, p. 216. **Col. 4:** Based on 1946 output (col. 2) and increase planned for 1947 (given as 316% in *89*, 3/1/47, p. 1).

57. Buses–**Cols. 2, 5, 8, 11, 14, 17, and 20:** *187*, p. 223. Total motor vehicles minus trucks and automobiles. **Col. 4:** Based on 1946 output (col. 2) and increase planned for 1947 (given as 74% in *89*, 3/1/47, p. 1).

58. Grain combines–**Cols. 2, 5, 8, 11, 17, and 20:** *187*, p. 232. **Col. 4:** Based on 1946 output (col. 2) and increase planned for 1947 (given as 420% in *89*, 3/1/47, p. 1). **Col. 7:** *98*, Pt. II, p. 1084. **Col. 14:** *187*, p. 233.

59. Steam locomotives–**Cols. 2, 5, 8, 11, 14, 17, and 20:** *187*, p. 220. **Col. 4:** Based on 1946 output (col. 2) and increase planned for 1947 (given as 188% in *89*, 3/1/47, p. 1).

60. Diesel locomotives–**Cols. 2, 5, 8, 11, 14, 17, and 20:** *187*, p. 220.

61. Electric locomotives–**Cols. 2, 5, 8, 11, 14, 17, and 20:** *187*, p. 220.

62. Railroad freight cars (units)–**Cols. 2, 5, 8, 11, 14, 17, and 20:** *187*, p. 222. **Col. 4:** Based on 1946 output (col. 2) and increase planned for 1947 for 2-axle units (given as 108% in *89*, 3/1/47, p. 1).

64. Railroad passenger cars–**Cols. 14, 17, and 20:** *187*, p. 220.

65. Excavators–**Cols. 2, 5, 8, 11, 14, 17, and 20:** *187*, p. 236.

66. Ginned cotton–**Cols. 2, 5, 8, 11, 17, and 20:** *188*, p. 357. **Col. 4:** *251*, No. 4, 1947, p. 3, as cited in *485*, series 502.6. **Col. 7:** Stated (in *251*, No. 11, 1947, p. 25, as cited in *404*, p. 25) to be approximately at prewar level (Table A-1, col. 5). **Col. 14:** *188*, p. 359.

67. Cotton yarn–**Cols. 2, 5, 8, 11, 17, and 20:** *188*, p. 361. **Col. 14:** *187*, p. 327.

68. Cotton fabrics–**Cols. 2, 5, 8, 11, 14, 17, and 20:** *187*, p. 328. **Col. 4:** Based on 1946 output (col. 2) and increase planned for 1947 (given as 42% in *89*, 3/1/47, p. 1). **Col. 7:** Based on 1947 output (col. 5) and increase planned for 1948 (given as 21% in *415*, No. 12, 1948, p. 21).

69. Woolen fabrics–**Cols. 2, 5, 8, 11, 14, 17, and 20:** *187*, p. 328. **Col. 4:** Based on 1946 output (col. 2) and increase planned for 1947 (given as 30% in *89*, 3/1/47, p. 1). **Col. 7:** Based on 1947 output (col. 5) and increase planned for 1948 (given as 23% in *415*, No. 12, 1948, p. 21).

71. Linen fabrics–**Cols. 2, 5, 8, 11, 14, 17, and 20:** *187*, p. 328. **Col. 4:** Based on 1946 output (col. 2) and increase planned for 1947 (given as 36.2% in *415*, No. 8, 1947, p. 27).

72. Silk and rayon fabrics–**Cols. 2, 5, 8, 11, 14, 17, and 20:** *187*, p. 328. **Col. 4:** Based on 1946 output (col. 2) and increase planned for 1947 (given as 27.3% in *415*, No. 8, 1947, p. 27). **Col. 7:** Based on 1947 output (col. 5) and increase planned for 1948 (given as 20% in *415*, No. 12, 1948, p. 21).

73. Knitted underwear–**Cols. 2, 5, 8, 11, 14, 17, and 20:** *187*, p. 343. **Col. 7:** Based on 1947 output (col. 5) and increase planned for 1948 (given as 70% in *415*, No. 12, 1948, p. 21).

74. Knitted outer garments–**Cols. 2, 5, 8, 11, 14, 17, and 20:** *187*, p. 343.

75. Hosiery–**Cols. 2, 5, 8, 11, 14, 17, and 20:** *187*, p. 343. **Col. 7:** Based on 1947 output (col. 5) and increase planned for 1948 (given as 61% in *415*, No. 12, 1948, p. 21).

76. Leather shoes–**Cols. 2, 5, 8, 11, 14, 17, and 20:** *143*, pp. 262 and 264. **Col. 4:** Based on 1946 output (col. 2) and increase planned for 1947 (given as 42% in *89*, 3/1/47, p. 1). **Col. 7:** Based on 1947 output (col. 5) and increase planned for 1948 (given as 30% in *415*, No. 12, 1948, p. 21).

77. Felt footwear–**Cols. 2, 5, 8, 11, 14, 17, and 20:** *188*, p. 398.

Table A-5   *continued*

78. Rubber footwear–**Cols. 2, 5, 8, 11, and 14:** *187*, p. 199. **Col. 4:** Based on 1946 output (col. 2) and increase planned for 1947 (given as 62% in *89*, 3/1/47, p. 1). **Cols. 17 and 20:** *143*, p. 264.

80. Metal beds–**Cols. 2, 5, 8, 11, 14, 17, and 20:** *188*, p. 412.

80a. Enameled kitchenware–**Cols. 2, 5, 8, 11, 14, 17, and 20:** *188*, p. 413.

81. Motorcycles–**Cols. 2, 5, 8, 11, 14, 17, and 20:** *188*, p. 410.

82. Bicycles–**Cols. 2, 5, 8, and 11:** *188*, p. 410. **Cols. 14, 17, and 20:** *187*, p. 362. **Col. 19:** Based on 1951 output (col. 17) and increase planned for 1952 (given as one-third in *487*, 2/25/52).

83. Radios–**Cols. 2, 5, 8, 11, 14, 17, and 20:** *188*, p. 407.

83a. Refrigerators–**Cols. 8, 11, 14, 17, and 20:** *188*, p. 408.

84. Sewing machines, household–**Cols. 2, 5, 8, 11, 14, 17, and 20:** *188*, p. 408.

85. Clocks and watches–**Cols. 2, 5, 8, 11, 14, 17, and 20:** *188*, p. 406.

86. Cameras–**Cols. 2, 5, 8, and 11:** *188*, p. 409. **Cols. 14, 17, and 20:** *187*, p. 362.

87. Phonographs–**Cols. 2, 5, 8, and 11:** *188*, p. 411. **Cols. 14, 17, and 20:** *187*, p. 363.

88. Soap (40% fatty acid)–**Cols. 2, 5, 8, 11, 14, 17, and 20:** *188*, p. 457. Soap and detergents. **Col. 4:** Based on 1946 output (col. 2) and increase planned for 1947 (given as 28% in *89*, 3/1/47, p. 1). **Col. 7:** Based on 1947 output (col. 5) and increase planned for 1948 (given as 35% in *415*, No. 12, 1948, p. 22).

89a. Bread and breadstuffs (ministries and local Soviets)–**Cols. 2, 5, 8, 11, 14, 17, and 20:** *316*, p. 171.

90. Flour (total)–**Cols. 2, 5, 8, 11, 14, 17, and 20:** *188*, p. 450.

90a. Flour (centralized resources)–**Col. 14:** Table A-1, col. 11.

91. Macaroni–**Cols. 2, 5, 8, 11, 17, and 20:** *187*, p. 403. **Col. 7:** Based on 1947 output (col. 5) and increase planned for 1948 (given as 28% in *415*, No. 12, 1948, p. 22). **Col. 14:** *187*, p. 404.

92. Raw sugar–**Cols. 2, 5, 8, 11, 14, 17, and 20:** *187*, p. 373. **Col. 4:** Based on 1946 output (col. 2) and increase planned for 1947 (given as 94% in *89*, 3/1/47, p. 1). **Col. 7:** Based on 1947 output (col. 5) and increase planned for 1948 (given as 84% in *415*, No. 12, 1948, p. 22).

93. Starch and syrup–**Cols. 2, 5, 8, 11, 14, 17, and 20:** *316*, p. 179. Sum of starch and syrup.

94. Fish catch–**Cols. 2, 5, 8, 11, 14, 17, and 20:** *187*, p. 381. **Col. 4:** Based on 1946 output (col. 2) and increase planned for 1947 (given as 33% in *89*, 3/1/47, p. 1).

95. Crude alcohol–**Cols. 2, 5, 8, 11, 14, 17, and 20:** *187*, p. 405. **Col. 4:** Based on 1946 output (col. 2) and increase planned for 1947 (given as 11% in *89*, 3/1/47, p. 1).

96. Vegetable oil–**Cols. 2, 5, 8, 11, 14, 17, and 20:** *187*, p. 392. **Col. 4:** Based on 1946 output (col. 2) and increase planned for 1947 (given as 17% in *89*, 3/1/47, p. 1).

97. Butter–**Cols. 2, 5, 8, 11, 14, 17, and 20:** *187*, p. 386. **Col. 4:** Based on 1946 output (col. 2) and increase planned for 1947 (given as 12% in *89*, 3/1/47, p. 1).

98. Cheese–**Cols. 2, 5, 8, 11, 14, 17, and 20:** *188*, p. 442. The coverage here is larger than in earlier sources (such as *316*, p. 161) and may include collective farm production. *188* specifies only that the data cover industrial production and exclude production by households.

99. Meat–**Col. 2:** According to *180*, 1/21/47, 1946 output represented an increase of 18% over 1945 output. **Col. 4:** According to *89*, 3/1/47, p. 1, the increase planned for 1947 over 1946 output was 17%. **Cols. 5, 8, and 11:** Based on 1950 output (col. 14) and annual increases in 1948–1950 (given as 25%, 6%, and 35%, respectively, in *180*, 1/20/49, 1/18/50, and 1/26/51). **Col. 14:** *160*, p. 162. **Cols. 17 and 20:** *485*, series 1109.2. Estimates.

100. Meat and subproducts of first category–**Cols. 2, 5, 8, 11, 14, 17, and 20:** *187*, p. 378. **Col. 4:** Based on 1946 output (col. 2) and increase planned for 1947 (given as 17% in *89*, 3/1/47, p. 1).

101. Sausages–**Cols. 8, 11, and 17:** Based on 1950 output (col. 14) and annual increases in 1949–1951 (given as 43%, 40%, and 17%, respectively, in *180*, 1/18/50, 1/26/51, and 1/29/52). **Col. 14:** *187*, p. 380. **Col. 20:** Based on 1955 output (given as 770.2 th. m. tons in *187*, p. 380) and annual increases in 1953–1955 (given as 16%, 11%, and 8%, in *180*, 1/31/54, 1/21/55, and 1/30/56).

102. Canned food–**Cols. 2, 5, 8, 11, 14, 17, and 20:** *187*, p. 398. **Col. 7:** Based on 1947 output (col. 5) and increase planned for 1948 (given as 25% in *415*, No. 12, 1948, p. 22).

103. Confectionery–**Cols. 2, 5, 8, 11, 14, 17, and 20:** *187*, p. 401. **Col. 7:** Based on 1947 output (col. 5) and increase planned for 1948 (given as 30% in *415*, No. 12, 1948, p. 22).

104. Margarine–**Cols. 2, 5, 8, 11, 14, 17, and 20:** *316*, p. 170.

105. Beer–**Cols. 2, 5, 8, 11, 17, and 20:** *316*, p. 174. **Col. 14:** *187*, p. 372.

106. Cigarettes–**Cols. 2, 5, 8, 11, 14, 17, and 20:** *188*, p. 457. **Col. 7:** *415*, No. 12, 1948, p. 22. Estimate.

107. Matches–**Cols. 2, 5, 8, 11, 14, 17, and 20:** *187*, p. 267.

108. Low-grade tobacco (*makhorka*)–**Cols. 2, 5, 8, 11, 14, 17, and 20:** *316*, p. 177.

109. Salt–**Cols. 2, 5, 8, 11, 17, and 20:** *316*, p. 176. **Col. 7:** Based on 1947 output (col. 5) and increase planned for 1948 (given as 50% in *415*, No. 12, 1948, p. 22). **Col. 14:** *287*, p. 230.

Table A-5 *continued*

AGRICULTURE

110. Total value of production (1926/27 prices)–**Cols. 11, 14, and 20:** Based on 1940 output (given as 23,300 mill. rubles in Table A-1, col. 5) and indexes for 1949–1950 and 1952 (given as 106 and 114 for 1949 and 1950, with 1940 = 100, in *285*, No. 8, 1953, p. 55, and as 110 for 1952 by Khrushchev in *243*, Vol. I, p. 10).

110a. Total value of production (comparable prices)–**Cols. 2, 5, 8, 11, 14, 17, and 20:** *142*, p. 350. Recalculated from index with 1913 = 100.

111a. Vegetable production (comparable prices)–**Cols. 2, 5, 8, 11, 14, 17, and 20:** *42*, p. 350. Recalculated from index with 1913 = 100.

112a. Animal production (comparable prices)–**Cols. 2, 5, 8, 11, 14, 17, and 20:** *142*, p. 350. Recalculated from index with 1913 = 100.

HARVESTS

113. Grain, total (biological yield)–**Cols. 2, 5, 8, and 11:** *477*, p. 310. **Col. 4:** Based on sown area (derived as 92.2 mill. hectares from sown area in 1946 of 85.9 mill. hectares in *202*, p. 127, and increase planned for 1947, given as 6.3 mill. hectares in *415*, No. 7–9, 1947, p. 34) and yield, derived as 8.9 quintals per hectare from yield in 1946 (derived as 7.1 quintals per hectare from harvest in 1946 in col. 2 and sown area in 1946 of 85.9 mill. hectares in *202*, p. 127) and increase in yield in 1947 (given as 26% in *89*, 3/1/47, p. 2). **Cols. 14, 17, and 20:** *469*, p. 4.

113a. Grain, total (barn yield)–**Cols. 2, 5, 8, 11, 14, 17, and 20:** *242*, p. 119.

114. Wheat (biological yield)–**Col. 8:** *434*, No. 1, 1949, p. 6. Rough estimate. **Col. 14:** *432*, p. 79. **Col. 17:** Based on 1952 harvest (col. 20) and increase in 1952 over 1951 (given as 23% in *180*, 1/23/53). **Col. 20:** Based on 1940 harvest (given as 40.625 mill. m. t. in Table A-1, col. 5) and increase in 1952 (given as 48% in *125*, p. 48).

114a. Wheat (barn yield)–**Cols. 2, 5, 8, 11, 14, 17, and 20:** *203*, p. 161.

115a. Rye (barn yield)–**Cols. 2, 5, 8, 11, 14, 17, and 20:** *203*, p. 172.

116a. Barley (barn yield)–**Col. 14:** *202*, p. 202. Sum of winter barley and spring barley.

117a. Oats (barn yield)–**Col. 14:** *202*, p. 202.

118. Corn (biological yield)–**Col. 8:** *435*, No. 1, 1949, p. 6. Rough estimate.

118a. Corn (barn yield)–**Col. 14:** *202*, p. 202.

HARVESTS OF TECHNICAL CROPS

119. Raw cotton (biological yield)–**Col. 2:** Based on 1945 harvest (given as 1,293 th. m. t. in *404*, p. 20) and increase in 1946 (given as 34% in *180*, 1/21/47). **Col. 5:** Based on 1946 harvest (col. 2) and increase in 1947 (given as 21% in *180*, 1/18/48). **Col. 8:** *469*, p. 6. **Col. 11:** *477*, p. 315. Given as "over 2.7." **Col. 14:** *180*, 1/26/51, p. 2. **Col. 16:** *485*, series 501.5. **Col. 17:** Based on 1950 output (col. 14) and index for 1951 (given as 105 with 1950 = 100 in *140*, p. 101). **Col. 20:** *404*, p. 21.

119a. Raw cotton (barn yield)–**Cols. 2, 5, 8, 11, 17, and 20:** *203*, p. 194. **Col. 14:** *201*, p. 232.

120. Sugar beets (biological yield)–**Col. 2:** Based on 1947 harvest (col. 5) and increase in 1947 over 1946 (given as 190% in *180*, 1/18/48). **Col. 5:** *475*, p. 180. **Cols. 11, 14, and 17:** *469*, p. 6.

120a. Sugar beets (barn yield)–**Cols. 2, 5, 8, 11, 14, 17, and 20:** *203*, p. 197.

121. Sunflowers (biological yield)–**Cols. 2, 11 and 14:** *469*, p. 6. For col. 2, given as "less than 1.85." **Col. 5:** Based on 1946 harvest (col. 2) and increase planned for 1947 (given as 79% in *180*, 1/18/48).

121a. Sunflowers (barn yield)–**Cols. 2, 5, 8, 11, 14, 17, and 20:** *203*, p. 203.

122. Flax fiber (biological yield)–**Col. 11:** *469*, p. 6. Given as "more than .60 mill. m. t." **Col. 14:** Based on area sown to flax fiber (given as 1.9 mill. hectares in *140*, p. 106) and yield (derived as 2.8 quintals per hectare from five-year plan goal for yield for 1950 of 4.0 quintals per hectare, given in *449*, p. 791, and estimate that only 70% of that plan was fulfilled).

122a. Flax fiber (barn yield)–**Cols. 2, 5, 8, 11, 14, 17, and 20:** *203*, p. 201.

123a. Hemp (barn yield)–**Col. 14:** *202*, p. 202. Hemp fiber (*konoplia srednerusskaia, volokno*).

124. Potatoes (biological yield)–**Col. 14:** Based on 1940 harvest (given as 84.24 mill. m. t. in Table A-1, col. 5) and increase in 1950 (given as 21% in *180*, 4/17/51, p. 2). **Col. 17:** Rough estimate based on 1952 harvest (col. 20) and statement (in *180*, 1/21/53) that there was an increase in 1952 over 1951. **Col. 20:** *469*, p. 6. Given as "more than 83."

124a. Potatoes (barn yield)–**Cols. 2, 5, 8, 11, 14, 17, and 20:** *203*, p. 206.

ANIMAL PRODUCTION

125a. Meat and fat, incl. rabbit and poultry (dead weight)–**Cols. 2, 5, 8, 11, 17, and 20:** *202*, p. 329. **Col. 10:** Estimate based on statement that the prewar level (given as 4,695 th. m. t. in Table A-1, col. 5) was to be surpassed in 1949 (*98*, Pt. II, pp. 1062–63). **Col. 14:** *202*, p. 333.

126. Milk–**Cols. 2, 5, 8, 11, 17, and 20:** *203*, p. 287. **Col. 7:** Estimate based on statement that the prewar level (given as 33.64 mill. m. t. in Table A-1, col. 5) was to be surpassed in 1948 (*98*, Pt. II, pp. 1062–63). **Col. 14:** *203*, p. 298.

127. Eggs–**Cols. 2, 5, 8, 11, 14, 17, and 20:** *202*, p. 329.

Table A-5 *continued*

128. Wool–**Cols. 2, 5, 8, 11, 14, 17, and 20:** *202*, p. 329. Given in terms of unwashed wool. See notes to Table A-1, cols. 5 and 11. **Col. 7:** Estimate based on statement that prewar level (given as 161 th. m. t. in Table A-1, col. 5) was to be surpassed in 1948 (*98*, Pt. II, pp. 1062–63).

MARKET PRODUCTION
129. Grain–**Col. 14:** *242*, pp. 122–23. **Col. 20:** *469*, p. 4.
130. Raw cotton–**Col. 14:** *242*, pp. 122–23. **Col. 20.** *132*, p. 207. Converted from poods.
131. Sugar beets–**Col. 14:** *242*, pp. 122–23. **Col. 20:** *132*, p. 207. Converted from poods.
133. Potatoes–**Col. 14:** *242*, pp. 122–23. **Col. 20:** *132*, p. 95. For 1952/53.
134. Meat and fat (dead weight)–**Col. 14:** *242*, pp. 122–23. Given simply for meat.
135. Milk and dairy products–**Col. 14:** *242*, pp. 122–23. **Col. 20:** *469*, p. 34.
136. Wool–**Col. 14:** *242*, pp. 122–23.

PROCUREMENTS
137. Grain–**Cols. 2, 5, 8, 11, 17, and 20:** *203*, p̂. 152. **Col. 14:** *202*, p. 90.
138. Raw cotton–**Cols. 2, 5, 8, 11, 14, 17, and 20:** *203*, p. 194.
139. Sugar beets–**Cols. 2, 5, 8, 11, 17, and 20:** *203*, p. 197. **Col. 14:** *202*, p. 90
140. Sunflowers–**Cols. 2, 5, 8, 11, 14, 17, and 20:** *79*, p. 246.
141. Flax fiber–**Cols. 2, 5, 8, 11, 14, 17, and 20:** *203*, p. 201.
142. Hemp–**Col. 14:** *202*, p. 90.
143. Potatoes–**Cols. 2, 5, 8, 11, 14, 17, and 20:** *203*, p. 206.
143a. Vegetables–**Cols. 2, 5, 8, 11, 14, 17, and 20:** *203*, p. 211.
144. Meat and fat (live weight)–**Cols. 2, 5, 8, 11, 17, and 20:** *149*, p. 336. **Col. 10:** *469*, p. 34. See Table 90 in Chapter 16. **Col. 14:** *202*, p. 91.
145. Meat and fat (dead weight)–**Col. 14:** *149*, p. 337.
146. Milk and dairy products–**Cols. 2, 5, 8, 11, 17, and 20:** *149*, p. 336. **Col. 10:** *469*, p. 34. See Table 90 in Chapter 16. **Col. 14:** *202*, p. 91.
147. Eggs–**Cols. 2, 5, 8, 11, 17, and 20:** *149*, p. 336. **Col. 10:** *469*, p. 34. See Table 90 in Chapter 16. **Col. 14:** *202*, p. 91.
148. Wool–**Cols. 10 and 20:** *469*, p. 35. See Table 90 in Chapter 16. **Col. 14:** *202*, p. 91.

RAILROAD TRANSPORTATION
149. Length of network–**Cols. 2, 5, 8, 11, 14, 17, and 20:** *252*, p. 28.
150. Average daily carloadings–**Cols. 2, 5, 8, 11, 14, 17, and 20:** *490*, p. 171. **Col. 4:** Based on 1946 carloadings (col. 2) and increase planned for 1947 (given as 11% in *89*, 3/1/47, p. 2). **Cols. 7, 10, 13, 16, and 19:** Based on actual carloadings in 1948–1952 (cols. 8, 11, 14, 17, and 20) and percentage of plan fulfilled (cols. 9, 12, 15, 18, and 21). **Cols. 9, 12, 15, 18, and 21:** *180*, 1/20/49, 1/18/50, 1/26/51, 1/29/52, and 1/23/53.
151. Total freight traffic (ton-km)–**Cols. 2, 5, 8, 11, 14, 17, and 20:** *252*, p. 32.
152. Total freight traffic (tons)–**Cols. 2, 5, 8, 11, 14, 17, and 20:** *252*, p. 32.
153. Coal and coke–**Col. 1:** Based on 1945 transport of coal and coke (given as 142 mill. m. t. in Table A-4, col. 5) and increase planned for 1946 for coal (given as 14% in *415*, No. 4, 1946, p. 29). **Cols. 2 and 5:** Based on 1945 transport of coal and coke (as given above) and annual increases for 1946–1947 (given as 16% and 11%, respectively, in *180*, 11/21/47 and 1/18/48). **Col. 8:** Based on 1947 transport (col. 5) and increase in 1948 (taken to be 8% from increase of 7% for coal and 17% for coke given in *180*, 1/20/49). **Col. 11:** Based on total freight traffic in tons (series 152) and share of coal and coke in total (given as 32.9% in *83*, p. 29). **Col. 14:** *142*, p. 549. **Cols. 17 and 20:** *252*, p. 35.
154. Oil and oil products–**Cols. 2, 5, and 8:** Based on 1949 transport of oil and oil products (col. 11) and annual increases for 1947–1949 (given as 18%, 16%, and 21%, respectively, in *180*, 1/18/48, 1/20/49, and 1/18/50). **Col. 11:** Based on total freight traffic in tons (series 152) and share of oil and oil products in total (given as 5.0% in *83*, p. 29). **Col. 14:** *140*, p. 178. **Cols. 17 and 20:** *252*, p. 35.
155. Ferrous metals–**Col. 1:** Based on 1945 transport of ferrous metals (given as 21.3 mill. m. t. in Table A-4, col. 5) and increase planned for 1946 (given as 10% in *415*, No. 4, 1946, p. 29). **Cols. 2, 5, 8, and 11:** Based on 1945 transport of ferrous metals (as given above) and annual increases for 1946–1949 (given as 15%, 13%, 23%, and 20%, respectively, in *180*, 1/21/47, 1/18/48, 1/20/49, and 1/18/50). **Col. 14:** *142*, p. 549. **Cols. 17 and 20:** *252*, p. 36.
156. Ore–**Col. 1:** Based on 1945 transport of ore (given as 17.8 mill. m. t. in Table A-4, col. 5) and increase planned for 1946 (given as 36% in *415*, No. 4, 1946, p. 29). **Col. 2:** Based on 1945 transport (given above) and increase in 1946 (given as 36% in *415*, No. 7, 1947, p. 20). **Cols. 5 and 8:** Based on 1949 transport of ore (col. 11) and annual increases for 1948–1949 (given as 19% and 22%, respectively, in *180*, 1/20/49 and 1/18/50). **Col. 11:** Based on total freight traffic in tons (series 152) and share of ore in total (given as 5.5% in *83*, p. 29). **Col. 14:** *142*, p. 549. Covers all ores including iron pyrites. **Cols. 17 and 20:** *252*, p. 36.
157. Firewood–**Col. 1:** Based on 1945 transport of firewood (given as 17.4 mill. m. t. in Table A–4, col. 5) and in-

Table A-5 *continued*

crease planned for 1946 (given as 10% in *415*, No. 4, 1946, p. 29). **Col. 8:** Based on 1949 transport of firewood (col. 11) and increase in 1949 over 1948 (given as 20% in *180*, 1/18/50). **Col. 11:** Based on total freight traffic in tons (series 152) and share of firewood in total (given as 2.9% in *83*, p. 29). **Col. 14:** *142*, p. 549. **Cols. 17 and 20:** *252*, p. 38.

158. Timber–**Cols. 2, 5, and 8:** Based on 1949 transport of timber (col. 11) and annual increases in 1947–1949 (given as 13%, 36%, and 24% in *180*, 1/18/48, 1/20/49, and 1/18/50). **Col. 11:** Based on total freight traffic in tons (series 152) and share of timber in total (given as 8.6% in *83*, p. 29). **Col. 14:** *142*, p. 549. **Cols. 17 and 20:** *252*, p. 38.

159. Mineral construction materials–**Col. 1:** Based on 1945 transport of mineral construction materials (given as 41.9 mill. m. t. in Table A-4, col. 5) and increase planned for 1946 (given as 39% in *415*, No. 4, 1946, p. 29). **Col. 8:** Based on 1949 transport of mineral construction materials (col. 11) and increase in 1949 over 1948 (given as 26% in *180*, 1/18/50). **Col. 11:** Based on total freight traffic in tons (series 152) and share of mineral construction materials in total (given as 18.4% in *83*, p. 29). **Col. 14:** *142*, p. 549. **Cols. 17 and 20;** *252*, p. 37.

160. Grain and flour–**Col. 1:** Based on 1945 transport of grain and flour (given as 20.2 mill. m. t. in Table A-4, col. 5) and increase planned for 1946 (given as 32% in *415*, No. 4, 1946, p. 29). **Col. 11:** Based on total freight traffic in tons (series 152) and share of grain and flour in total (given as 4.7% in *83*, p. 29). **Col. 14:** *142*, p. 549. **Cols. 17 and 20:** *252*, p. 37.

162. Total freight traffic, average length of haul–**Cols. 2, 5, 8, and 11:** *490*, p. 170. **Cols. 13, 16, 17, 19, and 20:** *173*, No. 1, 1957, pp. 80–81. **Col. 14:** *252*, p. 34.

163. Coal and coke, average length of haul–**Col. 11:** *83*, p. 31. **Cols. 14, 17, and 20:** *252*, p. 35.

163a. Oil and oil products, average length of haul–**Col. 11:** *83*, p. 31. **Cols. 14, 17, and 20:** *252*, p. 35.

164. Ferrous metals, average length of haul–**Col. 11:** *83*, p. 31. **Cols. 14, 17, and 20:** *252*, p. 36.

164a. Firewood, average length of haul–**Col. 11:** *83*, p. 31. **Cols. 14, 17, and 20:** *252*, p. 38.

164b. Timber, average length of haul–**Col. 5:** *445*, p. 173. **Col. 11:** *83*, p. 31. **Cols. 14, 17, and 20:** *252*, p. 38.

165. Grain and flour, average length of haul–**Col. 11:** *83*, p. 31. **Cols. 14, 17, and 20:** *252*, p. 37.

165a. Ore, average length of haul–**Col. 11:** *83*, p. 31. **Cols. 14, 17, and 20:** *252*, p. 36.

166. Total passenger traffic–**Cols. 2, 5, 8, 11, 14, 17, and 20:** *252*, p. 32. **Col. 7:** Based on 1948 traffic (col. 8) and percentage of plan fulfilled (col. 9). **Col. 9:** *445*, p. 190. It is not specified if this percentage applies to pass.-km or number of passengers.

INLAND WATERWAY TRANSPORTATION

166a. Length of network–**Cols. 2, 5, 8, 11, 14, 17, and 20:** *252*, p. 115.

168. Freight traffic under ministries and economic organizations (ton-km)–**Cols. 2, 5, 8, 11, 14, 17, and 20:** *252*, p. 116. **Cols. 4, 7, 10, and 16:** Based on traffic in 1947–1949 and 1951 (cols. 5, 8, 11, and 17) and percentage of plan fulfilled (cols. 6, 9, 12, and 18). **Cols. 6, 9, 12, and 18:** *180*, 1/18/48, 1/20/49, 1/18/50, and 1/29/52. **Cols. 15 and 21:** Plan not fulfilled (*180*, 1/26/51 and 1/24/53).

170. Freight traffic under ministries and economic organizations (tons)–**Cols. 2, 5, 8, 11, 14, 17, and 20:** *252*, p. 116.

171. Coal and coke–**Cols. 2, 5, 8, 11, 14, 17, and 20:** *252*, p. 120. Coal only. **Col. 12:** Plan overfulfilled (*180*, 1/18/50).

172. Oil and oil products–**Cols. 2, 5, 8, 11, 14, 17, and 20:** *252*, p. 120. **Col. 12:** Plan overfulfilled (*180*, 1/18/50).

173. Timber and firewood–**Cols. 2, 5, 8, 11, 14, 17, and 20:** *252*, p. 120.

174. Mineral construction materials–**Cols. 2, 5, 8, 11, 14, 17, and 20:** *252*, p. 120. **Col. 12:** Plan overfulfilled (*180*, 1/18/50).

175. Grain and flour–**Cols. 2, 5, 8, 11, 14, 17, and 20:** *252*, p. 120.

176. Salt–**Cols. 2, 5, 8, 11, 17, and 20:** *252*, p. 120. **Col. 12:** Plan overfulfilled (*180*, 1/18/50). **Col. 14:** *287*, p. 238. *252*, p. 120, gives a rounded figure of 1.7 mill. m. t.

177. Average length of haul under ministries and economic organizations–**Cols. 2, 5, 8, 11, 14, 17, and 20:** *252*, p. 116.

178. Passenger traffic (pass.-km)–**Cols. 2, 5, 8, 11, 14, 17, and 20:** *252*, p. 116.

178a. Passenger traffic (pass.)–**Cols. 2, 5, 8, 11, 14, 17, and 20:** *252*, p. 116.

MARITIME TRANSPORTATION (Soviet ships)

179. Freight traffic (ton-km)–**Cols. 2, 14, 17, and 20:** *252*, p. 7. **Cols. 5, 8, and 11:** *252*, p. 95. Converted from nautical ton-miles at 1 ton-km = 0.54 ton-miles (*236*, p. 177). **Cols. 4, 7, 13, 16, and 19:** Based on traffic in 1947–1948 and 1950–1951 (cols. 5, 8, 14, 17, and 20) and percentage of plan fulfilled (cols. 6, 9, 15, 18, and 21). **Cols. 6, 9, 15, and 18:** *180*, 1/18/48, 1/20/49, 1/26/51, and 1/29/52. **Col. 12:** Plan not fulfilled (*180*, 1/18/50). **Col. 21:** Plan fulfilled (*180*, 1/24/53).

180. Freight traffic (tons)–**Cols. 2, 5, 8, 11, 14, 17, and 20:** *252*, p. 97.

181. Average length of haul–**Cols. 2, 5, 8, 11, 17, and 20:** Based on traffic in ton-kilometers (series 179) and traffic in tons (series 180). **Col. 14:** *285*, No. 7, 1956, p. 21.

Table A-5 *continued*

182. Passenger traffic (pass.-km)–**Cols. 2, 5, 8, 11, 14, 17, and 20:** *252*, p. 95. Converted from nautical pass.-miles at 1 pass.-km = 0.54 pass.-miles (*236*, p. 177). Excludes traffic in steamships in Central Asia.

182a. Passenger traffic (passengers)–**Cols. 2, 5, 8, 11, 14, 17, and 20:** *252*, p. 95. Excludes traffic in steamships in Central Asia.

MOTOR TRANSPORTATION

183. Freight traffic–**Cols. 2, 5, 8, 11, 17, and 20:** *252*, p. 155. **Col. 4:** Based on 1946 traffic (col. 2) and increase planned for 1947 (given as 23% in *89*, 3/1/47, p. 2). **Col. 14:** *252*, p. 159.

AIR TRANSPORTATION

184. Freight traffic, incl. mail–**Cols. 2, 14, 17, and 20:** *253*, p. 25. These figures differ from the series used in other tables here (e.g., Table A-1); they are specified to cover only traffic "of general use." **Col. 4:** Based on 1946 traffic (col. 2) and increase planned for 1947 (given as 29% in *89*, 3/1/47, p. 2).

185. Passenger–**Cols. 2, 14, 17, and 20:** *253*, p. 34.

EMPLOYMENT (annual averages)

186. Workers and employees, national economy, excl. collective farms–**Cols. 2, 5, 8, and 11:** *260*, p. 22. Total minus members of industrial cooperatives. **Col. 4:** *89*, 3/1/47, p. 2. **Cols. 14, 17, and 20:** *140*, p. 189. Excludes members of industrial cooperatives.

187. Industry–**Cols. 2, 5, 8, 11, 17, and 20:** Based on 1950 industrial employment (col. 14) and annual increases in 1947–1952 (derived as 8.0%, 10.4%, 6.2%, 9.8%, 5.5%, and 3.7% by dividing annual increases for gross industrial production by annual increases for labor productivity in industry for 1947–1952, both given in *180*, 1/18/48, 1/20/49, 1/18/50, 1/26/51, 1/29/52, and 1/24/53). *260*, p. 81, gives higher figures, but the older series has been used here to maintain comparability with the plan figures. **Col. 14:** *140*, p. 190.

188. Construction–**Col. 2:** *28*, p. 219. **Cols. 14, 17, and 20:** *260*, p. 121. Includes employees in construction repair offices, machine repair centers, servicing construction, and intercollective farm construction organizations. These figures are slightly higher than those in *28*, p. 219.

188a. Construction and assembly work–**Col. 14:** *140*, p. 190. *260*, p. 121, gives a slightly higher figure. See note to series 188. **Cols. 17 and 20:** *260*, p. 121.

189. State-owned agriculture and logging–**Col. 14:** *260*, pp. 24–25. Sum of agriculture and logging.

190. State-owned agriculture–**Col. 14:** *260*, pp. 24–25.

191. Railroad transport–**Col. 14:** *140*, p. 190.

192. Maritime and inland waterway transport–**Col. 14:** *140*, p. 190.

193. Other transport (motor, etc.)–**Col. 14:** *260*, p. 25.

194. Communications–**Col. 14:** *140*, p. 190.

195. Trade, procurements, and supply–**Col. 14:** *140*, p. 190.

196. Public eating places–**Cols. 14, 17, and 20:** *260*, p. 130. For col. 14, also *140*, p. 190.

197. Credit institutions–**Col. 14:** *140*, p. 190.

198. Administration–**Col. 14:** *140*, p. 190.

199. Education–**Col. 14:** *140*, p. 190.

200. Public health–**Col. 14:** *140*, p. 190.

WAGE FUND, WORKERS AND EMPLOYEES

201. National economy–**Cols. 1-2, 4-5, 7-8, 10-11, 13-14, 16-17, and 19-20:** Table C-1, line 3.

AVERAGE ANNUAL WAGE, WORKERS AND EMPLOYEES

203. Money wage, national economy, excl. collective farms and cooperatives–**Cols. 2, 5, 7, 8, 11, 14, 17, and 20:** Table C-1, line 2.

205. Money wage, industry–**Col. 5:** Based on 1954 wage (derived as 9,239 rubles from 1955 wage of 9,396 rubles from *260*, p. 138, and increase between 1954 and 1955, given as 1.7% in *405*, p. 100) and increase in 1954 over 1947 (given as 22% in *222*, No. 5, 1959, p. 52). **Col. 14:** *260*, p. 138. Converted into old rubles

AVERAGE ANNUAL MONEY WAGE, WORKERS

206. Industry–**Col. 14:** *260*, p. 138. Converted into old rubles. **Cols. 17 and 20:** Based on 1950 wage (col. 14) and increases in 1951 and 1952 (given as 2% for each year in *162*, p. 46).

208. Coal–**Cols. 2, 5, 8, and 11:** Based on 1945 wage (given as 8,916 rubles in Table A-4, col. 5) and annual increases (given as 3.2%, 28.6%, 7.4%, and 5.9% in *41*, p. 22). **Col. 14:** *260*, p. 140. Converted into old rubles. **Cols. 17 and 20:** Based on 1950 wage (col. 14) and annual increases (given as 0.7% and 0.5% in *41*, p. 22).

209. Ferrous metals–**Col. 14:** *260*, p. 140. Converted into old rubles.

209a. Machine-building–**Col. 14:** *260*, p. 141. Converted into old rubles

210. Paper–**Col. 14:** *260*, p. 141. Converted into old rubles.

Table A-5   *continued*

211. Chemicals–**Col. 14:** *260,* p. 141. Converted into old rubles.

212. Textiles–**Col. 14:** *260,* p. 143. Converted into old rubles.

212a. Cotton–**Col. 14:** *260,* p. 143. Converted into old rubles.

213. Leather–**Col. 14:** *400,* p. 67. Fur, leather, and footwear. Converted into old rubles. This figure may be too high. For the shoe industry, 5,544 is obtained from *260,* p. 143 (converted into old rubles).

214. Food–**Col. 14:** *260,* p. 144. Converted into old rubles.

AVERAGE ANNUAL MONEY WAGE, WORKERS AND EMPLOYEES

215. Construction–**Col. 14:** *260,* p. 138. Converted into old rubles.

216. Railroad transport–**Cols. 2, 5, 8, 11, 17, and 20:** *445,* p. 328. **Col. 14:** *260,* p. 138. Converted into old rubles.

217. Maritime and inland waterway transport–**Col. 14:** *260,* p. 138. Converted into old rubles.

218. Communications–**Col. 14:** *260,* p. 138. Converted into old rubles.

221. Credit institutions–**Col. 14:** *260,* p. 138. Converted into old rubles.

222. Administration–**Col. 14:** *260,* p. 138. Converted into old rubles.

223. Education–**Col. 14:** *260,* p. 138. Converted into old rubles. It is not clear if this figure is comparable to ones for earlier years since in *260* a separate figure is given for wages in science.

224. Public health–**Col. 14:** *260,* p. 138. Converted into old rubles.

225. State-owned agriculture–**Col. 14:** *260,* p. 138. Converted into old rubles. Covers state farms and auxiliary agricultural enterprises

HOUSING

227. Housing fund, urban, total–**Col. 14:** *140,* p. 163. Not comparable with earlier tables because of change in statistical definition.

228. Housing construction, urban, total, including reconstruction–**Cols. 2, 5, 8, 11, 14, 17, and 20:** *141,* p. 176.

228a. Housing construction, urban, total–**Col. 1:** *415,* July–Sept. 1947, p. 30. **Cols. 2 and 4:** *89,* 3/1/47, pp. 1–2. Sum of state and private housing construction. **Col. 5:** *180,* 1/18/48. Sum of state and private housing construction.

229. Floorspace per inhabitant, urban–**Col. 14:** *427,* p. 331.

POPULATION

230. Total (end of year)–**Cols. 11, 14, 17, and 20:** *260,* p. 19.

231. Urban (end of year)–**Cols. 11, 14, 17, and 20:** *260,* p. 19.

232. Rural (end of year)–**Cols. 11, 14, 17, and 20:** *260,* p. 19.

RETAIL TRADE

233. State and cooperative in current prices–**Cols. 2, 5, 8, 11, 14, 17, and 20:** *232,* pp. 20 and 40. **Col. 4:** *89,* 3/1/47, p. 3. Sum of 251.6 mill. rubles for state trade, 17.5 mill. for urban cooperative trade, and 55.5 mill. for rural cooperative trade. **Col. 7:** *25,* p. 270. Converted into old rubles.

234. State and cooperative in 1940 prices–**Col. 2:** Based on 1945 trade (given as 73,500 mill. rubles in Table A-4, col. 5) and increase in 1946 (given as 30% in *180,* 1/21/47). **Cols. 5, 14, 17, and 20:** *124,* p. 407. **Cols. 8 and 11:** Based on 1947 trade (col. 5) and annual increases in 1948–1949 (given as 13% for 1948 in *216,* p. 67, and as 20% for 1949 in *180,* 1/18/50).

234c. Food products in current prices–**Cols. 2, 5, 8, 11, 17, and 20:** Based on total state and cooperative trade (series 233) and share of food products in total for 1946–1949 and 1951–1952 (given as 74.5%, 71.9%, 64.4%, 61.4%, 57.8%, and 57.3% in *232,* p. 39). **Col. 14:** *232,* p. 40.

234d. Food products in 1940 prices–**Col. 2:** Based on 1945 trade in food products in 1940 prices (given as 53,800 mill. rubles in Table A-4, col. 5) and increase in 1946 (given as 15% in *180,* 1/21/47). **Cols. 5, 8, 11, 14, 17, and 20:** Food products in current prices (series 234c) deflated by price index with 1940 = 100 (derived as 383 for 1947, 314 for 1948, and 260 for 1949 from indexes of 203 for 1950 with 1940 = 100 and 82 for 1948, 68 for 3/1/49, and 53 for 3/1/50, with 4th Q 1947 = 100; and given as 203 for 1950, 181 for 1951, and 166 for 1952, all in *141,* pp. 232 and 233).

235. Collective farm in current prices (urban)–**Col. 2:** Based on state and cooperative trade in current prices (series 233) and share of urban collective farm sales in total trade (estimated as 40% from 1945 share of 46% in Table A-4, col. 5, and 1947 share of 34.1% in col. 5 below). **Col. 5:** Based on state and cooperative trade in current prices (series 233) and share of urban collective farm sales in total trade (given as 34.1% in *457,* p. 184). **Col. 8:** Based on total collective farm sales (derived as 67,200 mill. rubles from 1940 collective farm sales, given as 41,100 mill. rubles in Table A-3, col. 8; increase in 1948 over 1940, given as 22% in *285,* No. 7, 1951, p. 79; and price index of collective farm market, given as 134 in 1948 with 1940 = 100 in *42,* p. 158) and share of urban sales in total collective farm market sales (given as 71 % in *439,* p. 48, note e). **Col. 11:** *457,* p. 184. **Cols. 14, 17, and 20:** *232,* p. 19.

Investment

Table B-1   Second Five-Year Plan Investment Goals for 1933–1937, by Sector (million rubles, 1933 plan prices)

	1933 (1)	1934 (2)	1935 (3)	1936 (4)	1937 (5)
1. National economy, total socialist sector	17,989	25,111	27,991	30,309	32,000
2. Industry, total	10,030	12,976	15,358	16,034	15,147
3. Producer goods (Group A)	8,400	10,632	11,299	11,616	11,495
4. Consumer goods (Group B)	1,630	2,344	4,059	4,418	3,652
5. Agriculture, total	2,100	2,724	3,102	3,518	3,795
6. State farms	1,025	1,268	1,041	1,060	1,081
7. Machine and Tractor Stations	713	955	1,187	1,590	1,915
8. Transportation, total	3,015	4,970	5,324	5,979	7,054
9. Railroad	2,065	3,365	3,630	3,915	4,389
10. Inland waterway and maritime	520	970	910	880	1,036
11. Motor	330	486	591	881	1,167
12. Civil aviation	100	149	193	303	462
13. Communications	202	342	346	372	417
14. Trade[a]	238	410	345	360	387
15. Housing, education, and other public facilities	2,404	3,689	3,516	4,046	5,200
16. Housing, education, and other public facilities, total[b]	3,513	5,575	6,635	7,715	9,061
Not included in national economy					
17. Collective farm investment from own resources	500	700	950	1,250	1,600
18. Public participation in road building	285	310	335	365	405

Source: *293*, pp. 715–16.

a. Given as circulation and distribution in some sources (*293*, p. 447, and *171*, No. 4, 1935, p. 11) and as trade turnover in others (*156*, p. 278), but figures for same years from different sources show that the category is the same.

b. This section includes investments for housing and educational facilities that are normally included in the plans of various commissariats and other institutions and hence are included in different sectors above (such as industry or agriculture), not just in line 15.

Table B-2   Second Five-Year Plan Investment Goals for 1933–1937, by Commissariat (million rubles, 1933 plan prices)

	1933 (1)	1934 (2)	1935 (3)	1936 (4)	1937 (5)
1. National economy, total socialist sector	17,989	25,111	27,991	30,309	32,000
2. Commissariat of Heavy Industry	7,700	9,290	9,880	10,060	9,830
3. Electric power	700	990	1,025	1,275	1,360
4. Coal	650	667	700	725	758
5. Petroleum	545	770	1,000	1,175	1,210
6. Ore mining	46	57	69	83	95
7. Ferrous metals	1,665	1,825	2,025	2,000	1,825
8. Nonferrous metals	690	705	800	800	796
9. Machine-building	1,280	1,495	1,800	1,750	1,735
10. Chemical and coke-chemical	800	1,049	1,050	940	931
11. Commissariat of Light Industry	580	1,031	2,605	2,900	2,084
12. Commissariat of Timber Industry	414	571	700	865	900
13. Commissariat of Food Supply	780	997	1,150	1,200	1,213
14. Commissariat of Foreign Trade	90	116	102	90	77
15. Commissariat of Agriculture	1,340	1,878	2,165	2,555	2,822
16. Commissariat of State Farms	650	747	835	865	893
17. Commissariat of Transportation	2,165	3,707	4,016	4,190	4,622
18. Commissariat of Water Transport	506	962	886	860	1,031
19. *Glavk* for Highways	375	542	676	1,020	1,387
20. *Glavk* for Civil Aviation	115	193	251	390	551
21. Commissariat of Communications	206	349	350	375	420
22. *Tsentrosoiuz*	265	293	297	303	352
23. Industrial Cooperatives	128	139	155	190	238
24. Housing Cooperatives	86	111	150	200	259
25. Housing fund of Executive Committees	140	182	220	290	362
26. Communal construction in cities (incl. subway)	725	1,323	1,450	1,600	1,802
27. Education	240	458	600	781	1,071
28. Public health	238	349	550	760	1,178
29. Committee for Procurements of Council of People's Commissars	175	315	180	150	120
30. *Glavk* for Photography and Films	35	74	138	200	228
31. *Glavk* for Northern Sea Route	26	29	50	65	80
32. Other central agencies	1,010	1,455	585	400	480

Source: *293*, pp. 718–19.

Table B-3 Implied Price Deflators for Investment Goods in Second Five-Year Plan
(1933 annual plan prices = 100[a])

	1933[b]	1934	1935	1936	1937
1. National economy, total socialist sector	100	100	91.8	84.6	80.1
2. Industry, total	100	100	92.2	83.6	78.7
3. Producer goods (Group A)	100	100	92.1	83.6	79.0
4. Consumer goods (Group B)	100	100	92.5	83.6	78.1
5. Agriculture, total	100	100	91.5	88.7	86.4
6. State farms	100	100	88.4	88.2	87.4
7. Machine and Tractor Stations	100	100	89.3	88.7	86.2
8. Transportation, total	100	100	92.7	86.0	82.0
9. Railroad	100	100	92.9	85.8	82.1
10. Inland waterway and maritime	100	100	92.0	85.8	82.2
11. Motor	100	100	92.0	85.7	81.7
12. Civil aviation	100	100	93.3	89.1	81.8
13. Communications	100	100	93.1	90.1	87.5
14. Trade[c]	100	100	90.4	83.3	76.5
15. Housing, education, and other public facilities	100	100	89.4	82.7	76.4
16. Housing, education, and other public facilities, incl. investments by agencies[d]	100	99.9	89.8	81.2	74.3
People's Commissariat or Agency					
17. Commissariat of Heavy Industry	100	100	91.6	83.4	78.6
18. Commissariat of Light Industry	100	100	92.1	83.8	78.5
19. Commissariat of Timber	100	100	93.6	82.1	80.0
20. Commissariat of Food Supply	100	100	92.2	84.2	78.7
21. Commissariat of Foreign Trade	100	100	95.1	88.9	87.0
22. Commissariat of Agriculture	100	100	94.2	88.8	86.8
23. Commissariat of State Farms	100	100	94.3	88.7	86.8
24. Commissariat of Transportation	100	100	92.4	86.2	81.6
25. Commissariat of Water Transport	100	100	92.1	86.4	81.5
26. *Glavk* for Highways	100	100	91.7	86.8	82.2
27. *Glavk* for Civil Aviation	100	100	93.6	88.5	87.1
28. Commissariat of Communications	100	100	93.7	89.9	87.6
29. *Tsentrosoiuz*	100	100	89.9	82.8	77.6
30. Industrial Cooperatives	100	100	91.0	83.7	81.9
31. Housing Cooperatives	100	100	89.3	80.5	73.0
32. Housing fund of Executive Committees	100	100	82.7	80.3	72.9
33. Communal construction of cities (incl. subway construction)	100	100	88.9	82.9	76.5
34. Education	100	100	89.5	81.0	74.7
35. Public health	100	100	89.5	81.3	74.3
36. Committee for Procurements of Council of People's Commissars	100	100	90.0	82.7	76.7
37. *Glavk* for Photography and Films	100	100	94.2	90.0	85.5
38. *Glavk* for Northern Sea Route	100	100	94.0	83.1	86.3
39. Other agencies	100	100	89.7	82.8	78.1

Source: Based on data in current prices and in 1933 plan prices given in *293*, pp. 715–20.

a. The reduction in construction costs envisaged in the Second Five-Year Plan (*293*, p. 321) was as follows: total construction, 40%; industry, 43%; housing, 40%; agriculture, 35%; transportation, 36%; and communal economy, 38%.

b. The 1933 figures are actually preliminary results rather than plan figures since *293* was published at the end of 1934. The fact that investment prices are the same in 1933 current and in 1933 plan prices is difficult to understand since the planned decrease in construction costs of 15% was not realized. See Table B-15.

c. See Table B-1, note a.

d. Included in various sectors above (see Table B-1, note b).

Table B-4   Actual Investment during Second Five-Year Plan, 1933–1937 (million rubles, current prices)

	1933 (1)	1934 (2)	1935 (3)	1936 (4)	1937 (5)
1. National economy, total socialist sector	17,989	22,626	24,722	31,750[a]	30,200[b]
2. Industry, total	10,030	11,695	12,542	14,259[c]	15,012
3. Producer goods (Group A)	8,400	9,631	10,516	11,510	
4. Consumer goods (Group B)	1,630	2,064	2,026	2,749	
5. Agriculture, total	2,100	2,474	2,297	2,577	4,146
6. State farms	950	1,115[d]			
7. Machine and Tractor Stations	749	890[d]			
8. Transportation, total	3,015	4,250	5,455	6,922	5,774
9. Railroad	2,065	2,757	3,752	4,428	
10. Inland waterway and maritime	520	785	1,122	1,546	
11. Motor	330	560	458[e]		
12. Civil aviation	100	148[f]			
13. Communications	202	278	300	345	246
14. Trade[g]	238	486	562	904	913
15. Housing, education, and other public facilities	2,404	3,443	3,566[h]	6,743[h]	7,109
Housing, education, and other public facilities, total[i]					
16. Urban and industrial housing	1,343	1,720	1,930	2,400	
17. Communal economy	750	1,283	1,400	1,800	
18. Education	330	430	550	1,300	
19. Public health	275	360	430	800	

Source (unless otherwise indicated): **Col. 1:** *173*, No. 5–6, 1934, p. 202. Since *156*, p. 504, gives the same figures, they are presumably final ones. *229*, p. 384, also gives data on actual investment in current prices for 1933–1935, but they differ somewhat from the figures given in the annual plans and their exact coverage is not known so they have not been used here. **Col. 2:** *156*, p. 504. These figures have been used rather than the ones in *155*, p. 460, which seem to be preliminary. Also, see note to col. 1. **Cols. 3-4:** *157*, pp. 142–43. For col. 4, preliminary figures. See note a. **Col. 5:** *455*, p. 111.

a. *455*, p. 111, cites 35,500 mill. rubles (given by *61*, p. 533), which seems too high and not in line with the figures in Table 50, note to col. 5.

b. *254*, p. 26. Includes capital repairs but excludes extra-limit investment.

c. *455*, p. 111, cites 15,969 mill. rubles (given in *6*, p. 71, *61*, p. 375, and *81*, p. 16), which may reflect a difference in coverage, as in the case of *229* mentioned in note to col. 1 above.

d. *155*, p. 460. Preliminary figures.

e. *156*, p. 391. Preliminary figure.

f. Line 8 minus sum of lines 9–11.

g. See Table B-1, note a.

h. Line 1 minus sum of lines 2, 5, 8, 13, and 14.

i. Included in various sectors above (see Table B-1, note b).

Table B-5 Fulfillment of Annual Investment Plan for 1933, by Sector

| | Annual Plan Goals in Current Prices[a] (mill. rubles) (1) | Actual Investment | | As Per Cent of Annual Plan Goals for 1933 (4) |
		In Current Prices (2)	In 1933 Plan Prices (3)	
		(million rubles)		
1. National economy, total	18,000	17,989	15,480	86.0
2. Industry, total	10,108.8	10,030	8,630	85.4
3. Producer goods (Group A)	8,527.3[b]	8,400	7,230	84.8
4. Consumer goods (Group B)	1,581.5	1,630	1,400	88.5
5. Agriculture	2,147.7[c]	2,100	1,800	83.8
6. State farms		950	818	
7. Machine and Tractor Stations		749	645	
8. Transportation		3,015	2,595	
9. Railroad	2,941.1	2,065	1,777	60.4
10. Inland waterway and maritime		520	448	
11. Motor		330	284	
12. Civil aviation		100	86	
13. Communications	215	202	174	80.9
14. Trade[d]		238	205	
15. Housing, education, and other public facilities		2,404	2,069	
16. Housing, education, and other public facilities, total[e]	1,472	1,343	1,156	78.5
17. Communal economy	695	750	645	92.8
18. Education		330	284	
19. Public health	270[f]	275	237	87.8

Source: Unless otherwise indicated, col. 1: *153*, pp. 59, 78, 104, and 120–23; col. 2: *173*, No. 5–6, 1934, p. 202; col. 3: col. 2 deflated by price index (given as 1.162 in Table B-16, col. 12, line 3); and col. 4: col. 3 as a percentage of col. 1.

Note: Annual plan goals have not been calculated here, as elsewhere, as a percentage of Second Five-Year Plan goals for 1933 because the latter were actually not goals but preliminary results for 1933 since the final text of the Second Five-Year Plan was published in 1934.

a. Current prices here are assumed to be 1933 plan prices with allowance for the reduction in investment costs planned for that year (see Table B-3, note b).

b. Line 2 minus line 4.

c. Socialist sector.

d. See Table B-1, note a.

e. See Table B-1, note b.

f. Includes physical culture.

Table B-6   Fulfillment of Annual Investment Plan for 1933, by Commissariat

	Annual Plan Goals in Current Prices[a] (mill. rubles) (1)	Actual Investment		
		In Current Prices (2)	In 1933 Plan Prices (3)	As Per Cent of Annual Plan Goals for 1933 (4)
		(million rubles)		
National economy, total	18,000	17,989	15,480	86.0
Commissariat of Heavy Industry		7,530	6,480	
Electric power		700[b]	602	
Coal	707			
Petroleum	[c]			
Ferrous metals	2,197			[d]
Machine-building		1,300[e]	1,120	
Commissariat of Light Industry	730	374	322	44.1
Commissariat of Timber Industry	445	410	353	79.3
Commissariat of Food Supply	735	756	651	88.6
Commissariat of Foreign Trade		90	77	
Commissariat of Agriculture		1,340	1,153	
Commissariat of State Farms		650	559	
Commissariat of Transportation	2,941	2,165	1,863	63.3
Glavk for Highways		375	323	
Glavk for Civil Aviation		115	99	
Commissariat of Communications	215	206	177	82.3
Tsentrosoiuz		265	228	
Industrial Cooperatives		128	110	
Housing Cooperatives		86	74	
Housing fund of Executive Committees		140	120	
Communal construction		600	516	
Subway construction		125	108	
Education		240	207	
Public health		218	188	
Committee for Procurements of Council of People's Commissars		175	151	
Glavk for Photography and Films		35	30	
Glavk for Northern Sea Route		26	22	
Other central agencies		1,030	886	

Source: Unless otherwise indicated, col. 1: *153*, pp. 40, 41, 44, 52, 59, 78, and 120; col. 2: *155*, p. 461; col. 3: col. 2 deflated by price index (given as 1.162 in Table B-16, col. 12, line 3); and col. 4: col. 3 as a percentage of col. 1.

Note: Annual plan goals have not been calculated here, as elsewhere, as a percentage of Second Five-Year Plan goals for 1933 because the latter were actually not goals but preliminary results for 1933 since the final text of the Second Five-Year Plan was published in 1934.

a. See Table B-5, note a.

b. *173*, No. 5–6, 1934, p. 26. For *Glavenergo*.

c. *153*, p. 120, gives 1,310 mill. rubles for the fuel industry (coal, petroleum, peat, and oil shale).

d. According to *173*, No. 1, 1935, p. 60, "the plan for production and investment was not fulfilled in 1933, although the percentage of fulfillment (81.3) was considerably higher than in the two preceding years." According to the *Glavk* for the Metal Industry, 78.8% of the plan was fulfilled in plan prices.

e. *173*, No. 5–6, 1934, p. 43.

Table B-7   Fulfillment of Annual Investment Plan for 1934, by Sector

| | Annual Plan Goals | | | | Actual Investment | | |
| | Original | | | | | | |
	In Current Prices (million rubles) (1)	In 1933 Plan Prices (million rubles) (2)	As Per Cent of 2nd FYP Goals for 1934 (3)	Revised (mill. rubles) (4)	In Current Prices (million rubles) (5)	In 1933 Plan Prices (million rubles) (6)	As Per Cent Annual Plan Goals for 1934 (7)
1. National economy, total	25,111	24,010	95.6	23,525	22,626	18,680	77.8
2. Industry, total	12,926	12,360	95.3	11,834	11,695	9,657	78.1
3. Producer goods (Group A)	10,582	10,120	95.2	9,617	9,631	7,953	78.6
4. Consumer goods (Group B)	2,344	2,241	95.6	2,217	2,064	1,704	76.0
5. Agriculture	2,775	2,653	97.4	2,523	2,474	2,043	77.0
6. State farms	1,285	1,228	96.8	1,205			
7. Machine and Tractor Stations	990	946	99.1	889			
8. Transportation	4,970	4,751	95.6	4,826	4,250	3,509	73.9
9. Railroad	3,365	3,217	95.6	3,249	2,757	2,277	70.8
10. Inland waterway and maritime	970	927	95.6	852	785	648	69.9
11. Motor	486	465	95.7		560	462	99.4
12. Civil aviation	149	142	95.3				
13. Communications	342	327	95.6	310	278	230	70.3
14. Trade[a]	410	392	95.6	428	486	401	102.3
15. Housing, education, and other public facilities	3,688	3,526	95.6		3,443	2,843	80.6
16. Housing, education, and other public facilities, total[b]	2,089	1,997			1,720	1,420	71.1
17. Communal economy	1,516	1,449			1,283	1,059	73.1
18. Education	464	444			430	355	80.0
19. Public health	422	403			360	297	73.7

Source: Col. 1: *173*, No. 5–6, 1934, p. 202; col. 2: col. 1 deflated by price index (given as 1.046 in Table B-16, col. 12, line 4); col. 3: col. 2 as a percentage of Table B-1, col. 2; col. 4: *173*, No. 1, 1935, p. 252; col. 5: *156*, p. 504; col. 6: col. 5 deflated by price index (given as 1.211 in Table B-16, col. 12, line 5); and col. 7: col. 6 as a percentage of col. 2.

a. See Table B-1, note a.
b. Included in various sectors above (see Table B-1, note b).

Table B-8   Fulfillment of Annual Investment Plan for 1934, by Commissariat

	Annual Plan Goals				Actual Investment			
	Original						As Per Cent of Annual Plan Goals for 1934	
	In Current Prices	In 1933 Plan Prices	As Per Cent of 2nd FYP Goals for 1934	Revised (million rubles)	In Current Prices	In 1933 Prices	Calculated	Official
	(million rubles)				(million rubles)			
	(1)	(2)	(3)	(4)	(5)	(6)	(7)	(8)
National economy, total	25,111	24,010	95.6	23,525	21,500	17,750	73.9	
Com. of Heavy Industry	9,211	8,806	94.8	8,356	7,950	8,565	74.6	95.9
Electric power				799				90.0
Coal				629				94.6
Petroleum				729				94.2
Ferrous metals	2,115[a]	2,022	110.7	1,627				101.9
Nonferrous metals				680				
Machine-building	1,500[b]	1,400	93.6	2,179				93.5
Chemical and coke-chemical				1,080				99.7
Com. of Light Industry	1,031	986	95.6	744	630	520	52.7	83.0
Com. of Timber Industry	569	544	95.3	526	413	341	62.7	78.3
Com. of Food Supply[c]	997	953	95.6				66.7[d]	
Com. of Food Industry				786	718	593		89.7
Com. of Domestic Trade				52	52	43		
Com. of Foreign Trade	116	111	95.7	108	90	74	66.7	91.9
Com. of Agriculture	1,818	1,738	92.5	1,690	1,700	1,404	80.8	
Com. of State Farms	747	714	95.6	771	712	588	82.4	
Com. of Transportation	3,707	3,544	95.6	3,569	3,000	2,477	69.9	94.2
Com. of Water Transport	548	524 ⎫	94.1[e]	521	470	388	74.0	85.5
Construction of Moscow Canal	399	381 ⎭		348	300	248	65.1	
Glavk for Highways	542	518	95.6	591	550	454	87.6	101.4[f]
Glavk for Civil Aviation	193	185	95.9	179	175	145	78.4	
Com. of Communications	349	334	95.7	317	230	190	56.9	87.5
Tsentrosoiuz	293	280	95.6	256	200	165	58.9	
Industrial Cooperatives	139	133	95.7	121	110	91	68.4	
Housing Cooperatives	111	106	95.5	103	95	78	73.6	
Housing fund of Executive Committees	180	172	94.5	198	170	140	81.4	
Communal construction	974	931 ⎫	95.6[g]	868	740	611	65.6	
Subway construction	349	334 ⎭		348	440	363	108.7	
Education	458	438	95.6	472	400	330	75.3	
Public health	324	310	88.8	313	265	219	70.6	
Committee for Procurements of Council of People's Commissars	315	301	95.6	271	250	206	68.4	
Glavk for Photography and Films	74	71	95.9	67	55	45	63.4	
Glavk for Northern Sea Route				33	33	27		
Local industry	100	96						
Com. of Local Industry				531	447	369		
Other central agencies				1,386	1,035	855		

Table B-8 *continued*

Source: Unless otherwise indicated, col. 1: *173*, No. 5–6, 1934, p. 203; col. 2: col. 1 deflated by price index (given as 1.046 in Table B-16, col. 12, line 4); col. 3: col. 2 as a percentage of Table B-2, col. 2; cols. 4 and 5: *155*, pp. 461 and 468; col. 6: col. 5 deflated by price index (given as 1.211 in Table B-16, col. 12, line 5); col. 7: col. 6 as a percentage of col. 2; and col. 8: *173*, No. 4, 1936, p. 43.

a. *173*, No. 5–6, 1934, p. 76.

b. *173*, No. 5–6, 1934, p. 43.

c. The Commissariat of Food Supply was split into the Commissariat of the Food Industry and the Commissariat of Domestic Trade in 1934.

d. Sum of Commissariat of the Food Industry and Commissariat of Domestic Trade in col. 6 as a percentage of Commissariat of Food Supply in col. 2.

e. Sum of Commissariat of Water Transport and Construction of Moscow Canal in col. 2 as a percentage of Commissariat of Water Transport (which presumably includes the Moscow Canal) in Table B-2, col. 2.

f. For 10 months of 1934.

g. Sum of communal construction and subway construction in col. 2 as a percentage of communal construction in cities in Table B-2, col. 2.

Table B-9   Fulfillment of Annual Investment Plan for 1935, by Sector

	Annual Plan Goals				Actual Investment		
	Original						
	In Current Prices (million rubles) (1)	In 1933 Plan Prices (million rubles) (2)	As Per Cent of 2nd FYP Goals for 1935 (3)	Revised (mill. rubles) (4)	In Current Prices (million rubles) (5)	In 1933 Plan Prices (million rubles) (6)	As Per Cent of Annual Plan Goals for 1935 (7)
1. National economy, total	21,190	18,740	67.0	24,842	24,722	21,060	112.4
2. Industry, total	10,543	9,322	60.7	12,205	12,542	10,680	114.6
3. Producer goods (Group A)	8,481	7,499	66.4	9,986	10,516	8,957	119.4
4. Consumer goods (Group B)	2,062	1,823	44.9	2,219	2,026	1,726	94.7
5. Agriculture	1,897	1,677	54.1	2,289	2,297	1,957	116.7
6. State farms	750	663	63.7				
7. Machine and Tractor Stations	925	818	68.9				
8. Transportation	5,030	4,447	83.5	5,455	5,455	4,647	104.5
9. Railroad	3,557	3,145	86.6	3,843	3,752	3,196	101.6
10. Inland waterway and maritime	897	793	87.1	1,029	1,122	956	120.6
11. Motor	440	389	65.8	458			
12. Civil aviation							
13. Communications	286	253	73.1	305	300	256	101.2
14. Trade[a]	456	403	116.8	552	562	479	118.9
15. Housing, education, and other public facilities	2,978	2,633	74.9	4,036	3,566[b]	3,037	115.3
16. Housing, education, and other public facilities, total[c]	1,827	1,615		2,023	1,930	1,644	101.8
17. Communal economy	1,143	1,011		1,447	1,400	1,193	118.0
18. Education	437	386		530	550	468	121.2
19. Public health	443	392		470	430	366	93.4

Source: Unless otherwise indicated, col. 1: *155*, p. 460; col. 2: col. 1 deflated by price index (given as 1.131 in Table B-16, col. 12, line 6); col. 3: col. 2 as a percentage of Table B-1, col. 3; col. 4: *156*, p. 391; col. 5: *157*, p. 142; col. 6: col. 5 deflated by price index (given as 1.174 in Table B-16, col. 12, line 7); and col. 7: col. 6 as a percentage of col. 2.

a. See Table B-1, note a.
b. Line 1 minus sum of lines 2, 5, 8, 13, and 14.
c. Included in various sectors above (see Table B-1, note b).

Table B-10 Fulfillment of Annual Investment Plan for 1935, by Commissariat

| | Annual Plan Goals | | | | Actual Investment | | | |
| | Original | | | Revised (million rubles) (4) | In Current Prices (million rubles) (5) | In 1933 Plan Prices (million rubles) (6) | As Per Cent of Annual Plan Goals for 1935 | |
	In Current Prices (million rubles) (1)	In 1933 Plan Prices (million rubles) (2)	As Per Cent of 2nd FYP Goals for 1935 (3)				Calculated (7)	Official (8)
National economy, total	21,190	18,740	67.0	24,842	24,015	20,460	109.2	
Com. of Heavy Industry	7,374	6,520	66.0	8,739	8,535	7,270	111.5	81.0
Electric power	894	790	77.1	841				81.9
Coal	598	529	75.6	625				81.2
Petroleum	800	707	70.7	860	860[a]	733	103.7	81.8
Ore mining	33	29	42.0					
Ferrous metals	1,461	1,292	63.8	1,549				85.1
Nonferrous metals	642	568	71.0	857	857[a]	730	128.5	
Machine-building	1,677	1,483	82.4	2,345				78.7
Chemical and coke-chemical	867	767	73.0	1,038				82.1
Com. of Light Industry	658	582	22.3	740	700	596	102.4	73.3
Com. of Timber Industry	512	453	64.7	568	525	447	98.7	72.5
Com. of Food Industry	635	561 }	59.9[b]	797	789	672	119.8	79.5
Com. of Domestic Trade	145	128 }		200	199	170	132.8	
Com. of Foreign Trade	70	62	60.8	70	59	50	80.6	
Com. of Agriculture	1,370	1,211	55.9	1,731	1,680	1,431	118.2	
Com. of State Farms	490	433	51.9	506	475	405	93.5	
Com. of Transportation	3,937	3,481	86.7	4,244	4,150	3,535	101.6	86.2
Com. of Water Transport	537	475 }		600	576	491	103.4	73.2
Construction of Moscow Canal	275	243 }	81.0[c]	340	340	290	119.3	
Glavk for Highways	473	418	61.8	491[d]	490[d]	417	99.8	81.0
Glavk for Civil Aviation	178	157	62.5					
Com. of Communications	291	257	73.4	310	287	244	94.9	
Tsentrosoiuz	189	167	56.2	60	60	51	30.5	
Industrial Cooperatives	60	53	34.2					
Housing Cooperatives	72	64	42.7	76	75	64	100.0	
Housing fund of Executive Committees	144	127	57.7	166	160	136	107.1	
Communal construction	875	774 }	65.6[e]	689	680	579	74.8	
Subway construction	200	177 }		350	350	298	168.4	
Education	316	279	46.5	400	425	362	129.7	
Public health	321	284	51.6	330	290	247	87.0	
Committee for Procurements of Council of People's Commissars	245	217	120.6	333	325	277	127.6	
Glavk for Photography and Films	109	96	69.6	114	100	85	88.5	
Glavk for Northern Sea Route	102	90	180.0	106	90	77	85.6	
Com. of Local Industry	503	445		511	475	405	91.0	
Other central agencies[f]	1,109	981		1,991	1,861	1,585	161.6	

Table B-10   *continued*

Source: Unless otherwise indicated, col. 1: *155*, pp. 461 and 468; col. 2: col. 1 deflated by price index (given as 1.131 in Table B-16, col. 12, line 6); col. 3: col. 2 as a percentage of Table B-2, col. 3; col. 4: *156*, pp. 506–7 and 512; col. 5: *156*, pp. 506–7, preliminary results; col. 6: col. 5 deflated by price index (given as 1.174 in Table B-16, col. 12, line 7); col. 7: col. 6 as a percentage of col. 2; and col. 8: *173*, No. 4, 1936, p. 43, for 11 months of 1935 in "plan prices."

a. *171*, No. 2, 1936, pp. 8–9.

b. Sum of Commissariat of the Food Industry and Commissariat of Domestic Trade in col. 2 as a percentage of Commissariat of Food Supply in Table B-2, col. 3.

c. Sum of Commissariat of Water Transport and construction of Moscow Canal in col. 2 as a percentage of Commissariat of Water Transport (which presumably includes the Moscow Canal) in Table B-2, col. 3.

d. Under the NKVD (Commissariat of Internal Affairs).

e. Sum of communal construction and subway construction in col. 2 as a percentage of communal construction in cities in Table B-2, col. 3.

f. Given as such in source. Some smaller agencies omitted.

Table B-11   Fulfillment of Annual Investment Plan for 1936, by Sector

| | Annual Plan Goals | | | | Actual Investment | | |
| | Original | | | | | | |
	In Current Prices (million rubles) (1)	In 1933 Plan Prices (2)	As Per Cent of 2nd FYP Goals for 1936 (3)	Revised (mill. rubles) (4)	In Current Prices (million rubles) (5)	In 1933 Plan Prices (6)	As Per Cent of Annual Plan Goals for 1936 (7)
1. National economy, total	32,365	30,940	102.1	36,327	31,750	26,750	86.5
2. Industry, total	13,956	13,340	83.2	16,296	14,259	12,010	90.0
3. Producer goods (Group A)	10,647	10,180	87.6	12,976	11,510	9,697	95.3
4. Consumer goods (Group B)	3,309	3,163	71.6	3,320	2,749	2,316	73.2
5. Agriculture	2,633	2,517	71.5	2,857	2,577	2,171	86.3
6. State farms							
7. Machine and Tractor Stations							
8. Transportation	7,173	6,858	114.7	7,929	6,922	5,832	85.0
9. Railroad	4,762	4,553	116.3	5,143	4,428	3,730	81.9
10. Inland waterway and maritime	1,533	1,466	166.6	1,737	1,546	1,302	88.8
11. Motor	615	588	66.7				
12. Civil aviation							
13. Communications	393	376	101.1	440	345	291	77.4
14. Trade[a]	683	653	181.4	1,046	904	762	116.7
15. Housing, education, and other public facilities	7,527	7,196	177.9		6,743[b]	5,681	78.9
16. Housing, education, and other public facilities, total[c]	3,065	2,930			2,400	2,022	69.0
17. Communal economy	1,885	1,802			1,800	1,516	84.1
18. Education	1,278	1,222			1,300	1,095	89.6
19. Public health	700	669			800	674	100.7

Source: Unless otherwise indicated, col. 1: *156*, p. 505; col. 2: col. 1 deflated by price index (given as 1.046 in Table B-16, col. 12, line 8); col. 3: col. 2 as a percentage of Table B-1, col. 4: based on col. 5 and percentage of plan fulfillment (given in *157*, p. 143); col. 5: *157*, p. 143; col. 6: col. 5 deflated by price index (given as 1.187 in Table B-16, col. 12, line 9); and col. 7: col. 6 as a percentage of col. 2.

a. See Table B-1, note a.
b. Line 1 minus sum of lines 2, 5, 8, 13, and 14.
c. Included in various sectors above (see Table B-1, note b).

Table B-12   Fulfillment of Annual Investment Plan for 1936, by Commissariat

	Annual Plan Goals				Actual Investment		
	Original						
	In Current Prices (million rubles) (1)	In 1933 Plan Prices (million rubles) (2)	As Per Cent of 2nd FYP Goals for 1936 (3)	Revised (million rubles) (4)	In Current Prices (million rubles) (5)	In 1933 Prices (million rubles) (6)	As Per Cent Annual Plan Goals for 193 (7)
National economy, total	32,365	30,942	102.1	36,327[b]	31,750[c]	26,750	86.5
Commissariat of Heavy Industry	8,500	8,126	80.8	10,054			
Electric power	1,325	1,267	99.4				
Coal	500	478	65.9		500[d]	421	88.1
Petroleum	1,000	956	81.4				
Ore mining	50	48	57.8				
Ferrous metals	1,050	1,004	50.2				
Nonferrous metals	1,100	1,052	131.5				
Machine-building	1,960	1,874	107.1				
Chemical and coke-chemical	1,535	1,467	156.1				
Commissariat of Light Industry	1,380	1,319	45.5	1,357	1,058	891	67.6
Commissariat of Timber Industry	900	860	99.4				
Commissariat of Food Industry	1,130	1,080 }	119.1[e]	1,067	1,536	1,294	119.8
Commissariat of Domestic Trade	365	349 }					
Commissariat of Foreign Trade	68	65	72.2				
Commissariat of Agriculture	2,202	2,105	82.4				
Commissariat of State Farms	360	344	39.8				
Commissariat of Transportation	5,059	4,837	115.4				
Commissariat of Water Transport	750	717	83.4				
Construction of Moscow Canal	665	636					
Glavk for Highways	650	621	60.9				
Commissariat of Communications	400	382	101.9				
Tsentrosoiuz	62	59	19.5				
Housing Cooperatives	75	72	36.0				
Housing fund of Executive Committees	249	238	82.1				
Communal construction	951	909 }	77.7[f]				
Subway construction	350	335 }					
Education	1,100	1,052	134.7				
Public health	600	574	75.5				
Committee for Procurements of Council of People's Commissars	350	335	223.3				
Glavk for Photography and Films	260	249	124.5				
Glavk for Northern Sea Route	170	163	250.8				
Local industry	930	889					
Other central agencies[g]	4,088	4,626					

Table B-12 *continued*

Source: Unless otherwise indicated, col. 1: *156*, pp. 508 and 512; col. 2: col. 1 deflated by price index (given as 1.046 in Table B-16, col. 12, line 8); col. 3: col. 2 as a percentage of Table B-2, col. 4; cols. 4 and 5: *63*, pp. 130, 132, and 196 (for heavy industry, revised as of 9/1/36); col. 6: col. 5 deflated by price index (given as 1.187 in Table B-16, col. 12, line 9); and col. 7: col. 6 as a percentage of col. 2.

a. The official estimates of the percentage of fulfillment of the annual plan goals for 1936 for the first eight months of the year are as follows: heavy industry–50.4, electric power stations–43.1, coal–52.8, petroleum–49.4, ferrous metals–64.4, nonferrous metals–47.1, machine-building–52.1, and chemicals–49.6 (*63*, p. 196). The goals for heavy industry were apparently increased when they were revised, since the fulfillment amounted to 60.3% of the original plan approved in January 1936 and to 50.4% of the revised plan (*63*, p. 196).

b. Based on actual investment in current prices (line 1, col. 5) and percentage of plan fulfilled (given in *157*, p. 143).

c. *157*, p. 143.

d. *171*, No. 4, 1937, p. 14.

e. Sum of Commissariat of the Food Industry and Commissariat of Domestic Trade in col. 2 as a percentage of Commissariat of Food Supply in Table B-2, col. 4.

f. Sum of communal construction and subway construction in col. 2 as a percentage of communal construction in cities in Table B-2, col. 4.

g. See Table B-10, note f.

Table B-13   Fulfillment of Annual Investment Plan for 1937, by Sector

	Annual Plan Goals			Actual Investment		
	In Current Prices	In 1933 Plan Prices	As Per Cent of 2nd FYP Goals for 1937	In Current Prices	In 1933 Plan Prices	As Per Cent of Annual Plan Goals for 1937
	(million rubles)			(million rubles)		
	(1)	(2)	(3)	(4)	(5)	(6)
1. National economy, total	32,593	30,690	95.9	30,200	23,892	77.8
2. Industry, total	13,928	13,110	86.6			
3. Producer goods (Group A)	10,919	10,280	89.4			
4. Consumer goods (Group B)	3,009	2,833	77.6			
5. Agriculture	2,659	2,504	66.0			
6. State farms						
7. Machine and Tractor Stations						
8. Transportation	7,370	6,940	98.4			
9. Railroad	5,323	5,012	114.2			
10. Inland waterway and maritime	1,210	1,139	109.9			
11. Motor						
12. Civil aviation						
13. Communications	370	348	83.5			
14. Trade[a]	795	749	193.5			
15. Housing, education, and other public facilities						
16. Housing, education, and other public facilities, total[b]	2,425	2,283				
17. Communal economy	1,813	1,707				
18. Education	1,454	1,369				
19. Public health	1,025	965				

Source: Col. 1: *157*, p. 143; col. 2: col. 1 deflated by price index (given as 1.062 in Table B-16, col. 12, line 10); col. 3: col. 2 as a percentage of Table B-1, col. 5; col. 4: *254*, p. 26, including capital repairs and excluding extra-limit investments; col. 5: col. 4 deflated by price index (given as 1.264 in Table B-16, col. 12, line 11); and col. 6: col. 5 as a percentage of col. 2.

a. See Table B-1, note a.
b. Included in various sectors above (see Table B-1, note b).

Table B-14 Fulfillment of Annual Investment Plan for 1937, by Commissariat

	Annual Plan Goals			Actual Investment		
	In Current Prices *(million rubles)* (1)	In 1933 Plan Prices *(million rubles)* (2)	As Per Cent of 2nd FYP Goals for 1937 (3)	In Current Prices *(million rubles)* (4)	In 1933 Plan Prices *(million rubles)* (5)	As Per Cent of Annual Plan Goals for 1937 (6)
National economy, total	32,593[a]	30,690	95.9	30,200[b]	23,892	77.8
Commissariat of Heavy Industry	8,667[c]	8,161	83.0			80.1[d]
Coal	518[e]	488	64.4	590[f]	467	95.7
Petroleum	1,130[e]	1,064	87.9			
Ferrous metals				500[g]	396	
Commissariat of Light Industry	1,406[h]	1,324	63.5			
Commissariat of Timber Industry	1,010[d]	951	105.7			
Commissariat of Food Industry	970[d]	913 ⎱	75.3[i]			
Commissariat of Domestic Trade		⎰				
Commissariat of Agriculture	2,314[d]	2,179	77.2			
Commissariat of State Farms	300[d]	282	31.6			
Commissariat of Transportation	5,553[d]	5,229	113.1			
Commissariat of Water Transport	723[d]	681	66.1			

Source: Unless otherwise indicated, col. 2: col. 1 deflated by price index (given as 1.062 in Table B-16, col. 12, line 10); col. 3: col. 2 as a percentage of Table B-2, col. 5; col. 5: col. 4 deflated by price index (given as 1.264 in Table B-16, col. 12, line 11); and col. 6: col. 5 as a percentage of col. 2.

a. *157*, p. 143.

b. *254*, p. 26. Includes capital repairs and excludes extra-limit investments.

c. *171*, No. 3, 1937, p. 16. Includes Commissariat of the Defense Industry.

d. *182*, No. 2, 1938, p. 40.

e. *171*, No. 4, 1937, pp. 14 and 17.

f. Based on actual investment anticipated for 1938 (given as 780 mill. rubles in *173*, No. 2, 1939, p. 62) and its increase over 1937 (taken as 32.5%, given as 30–35% in *173*, No. 2, 1939, p. 62).

g. *182*, No. 2, 1938, p. 40. Given as half a million rubles for the *Glavk* of the Metal Industry.

h. *182*, No. 2, 1937, p. 117.

i. Commissariat of Food Industry in col. 2 as a percentage of Commissariat of Food Supply in Table B-2, col. 5.

Table B-15   Changes in Investment Costs, Socialist Sector, 1933–1940

| | Construction | Assembly | Equipment | Other | Total with or without Allowance for Price Changes | | Jasny Estimates (with allowance for price changes) | |
| | | | (annual percentage increase or decrease) | | Without | With | 1932 = 100 | Preceding Year = 100 |
	(1)	(2)	(3)	(4)	(5)	(6)	(7)	(8)
1933								
1. Planned	−15.0							
2. Actual	+4.6[a]	a			+1.1		105	105
1934								
3. Planned	−15.0							
4. Actual	+4.2				b	c	105	100
1935								
5. Planned	−12.0		−4.0		−8.7	−6.6		
6. Actual	−3.0				d	e	109	103.8
1936								
7. Planned	−14.5				−11			
8. Actual	+1.1	−0.5	+1.5	−1.0	−6.0	+1.0	122	111.9
1937								
9. Planned	−13.5	−13.5	−5.0	−12.5	−10.5			
10. Actual	+0.8		−3.0		−0.5		130	106.6
1938								
11. Planned					−7.0			
1939								
12. Actual					+5.5			
1940								
13. Actual					+10–15			

Source

LINE 1–Col. 1: *153*, p. 62. Also, *173*, No. 9, 1939, p. 173.

LINE 2–Col. 1: *162a*, July 1934, p. 179. **Col. 5:** *63*, p. 182. Calculated by TsUNKhU. The source gives the breakdown of this change in the cost index in 1933 (with 1932 = 100) as follows: basic wages = 87.3, additions to basic wages = 130.4, materials delivered = 105.4, administrative expenses = 93.3, and other expenses = 108.3. The same source mentions elsewhere (*63*, p. 160) that the cost of construction in 1933 remained at about the 1932 level with a slight tendency to drop, so it can be assumed that the figures cited represent the actual volume of capital investments. **Col. 7:** *450*, p. 134. **Col. 8:** Same as col. 7.

LINE 3–Col. 1: *173*, No. 5–6, 1934, p. 224. Net construction.

LINE 4–Col. 1: *162a*, Aug. 1935, p. 214. Another source (*63*, pp. 189–90) gives .98 for the first nine months of 1934 relative to the entire 1933. The breakdown is given as follows (with 1933 = 100): materials = 1.008, labor = 1.05, and administrative expenses = .84–.88. Another source (*173*, No. 7, 1934, p. 15) gives a decrease of 2 to 2.5% for the first half of 1934. Still another source (*182*, No. 3, 1935, p. 8) gives, as preliminary results for 1934, a decrease of 2.8%. But another source (*171*, No. 7, 1935, p. 5) claims the cost of construction in 1934 remained at the 1933 level and the planned reduction of 15% was not realized. **Col. 7:** *450*, p. 134. **Col. 8:** Based on lines 2 and 4, col. 7.

LINE 5–Col. 1: *155*, p. 658. With allowance for increases in prices and wages provided by 12/7/34 and 12/16/34 decrees of Council of People's Commissars. Without allowance for these increases, the reduction is 15%. **Col. 3:** *155*, p. 302. **Col. 5:** Based on 1935 plan in current prices (given as 21,190 mill. rubles in *155*, p. 302) and in 1934 prices (derived as 23,220 mill. rubles from 1934 actual investments in current prices, given as 21,500 mill. rubles in *155*, p. 302, and increase in 1935 plan in constant prices over 1934, given as 8% in *155*, p. 302). **Col. 6:** Based on 1935 plan in current prices with allowance for price changes (derived as 21,684 mill. rubles from total given as 21,190 mill. rubles in col. 5 above and amount of investments represented by increase in prices and wages, given as 494 mill. rubles in *155*, p. 460) and in 1934 prices (derived as 23,220 mill. rubles in col. 5 above).

Table B-15 *continued*

LINE 6–Col. 1: *156*, p. 269. With allowance for increases in prices and wages. Without such allowance, a decrease of 3.4% (*156*, p. 313). Turetskii (*173*, No. 1, 1937, p. 92) gives a decrease of 4% for net construction. The same author elsewhere (*171*, No. 2, 1936, p. 41) cites a reduction of 1 to 2% in cost of net construction as opposed to the 15% provided by the annual plan. According to *162a*, March 1937, p. 161, −4.4%. **Col. 7:** *450*, p. 134. **Col. 8:** Based on lines 6 and 4, col. 7.

LINE 7–Cols. 1 and 5: *156*, pp. 278 and 313. The anticipated saving was to be 2,600 mill. rubles. In order to achieve this, construction workers were to increase labor productivity by 30%, reduce administrative and economic expenditures by 25% and the cost of building materials used on construction sites by 10%.

LINE 8–Col. 1: Sum of percentage changes for construction materials, basic wages, and administrative expenditures (given as +3.6, −1.7, and −1.9, respectively, in *171*, No. 5, 1937, p. 9) weighted by their percentage shares in total investments (given as 29.7, 12.3, and 13.5, respectively, in *171*, No. 5, 1937, p. 9). **Cols. 2–4:** *171*, No. 5, 1937, p. 9. **Col. 5:** *171*, No. 3, 1937, p. 56. Preliminary data for capital formation. In another article (*173*, No. 1, 1937, pp. 92 and 94), the same author states that, according to preliminary data, the cost of construction was reduced by 5–6% as opposed to the 11% provided by the plan, and he mentions a resulting saving of approximately 1,500 mill. rubles. **Col. 6:** Sum of cols. 1–4 weighted by their percentage shares in total investments (given as 55.5, 3.5, 34.5, and 6.5, respectively, in *171*, No. 5, 1937, p. 9). **Col. 7:** *450*, p. 134. **Col. 8:** Based on lines 8 and 6, col. 7.

LINE 9–Cols. 1–4: *171*, No. 5, 1937, p. 8. **Col. 5:** *157*, p. 36. See also *171*, No. 5, 1937, p. 8.

LINE 10–Cols. 1–2: *182*, No. 2, 1938, p. 40. For construction and assembly. Another source (*173*, No. 4, 1938, p. 164) gives a reduction of 0.4% for construction for the first nine months of 1937. **Col. 3:** *173*, No. 4, 1938, p. 164. For the first nine months of 1937. **Col. 5:** Sum of cols. 1–2 and 3 weighted by their percentage shares in total investments (derived as 65.5 from sum of shares for construction, assembly, and other and given as 34.5 for equipment in *171*, No. 5, 1937, p. 9). **Col. 7:** *450*, p. 134. **Col. 8:** Based on lines 10 and 8, col. 7.

LINE 11–Col. 5: *173*, No. 6, 1938, p. 41. Given as a reduction of "more than 7%," yielding a saving of more than 2.5 bill. rubles.

LINE 12–Col. 5: *173*, No. 8, 1940, p. 28. Given for sites financed by the *Prombank*, which represent more than 90% of total investments in 1939.

LINE 13–Col. 5: *173*, No. 8, 1940, p. 29. Given for several commissariats for the first half of 1940.

a. According to *63*, p. 172, comparable data exist only for enterprises belonging to the Union of Standardized Housing Construction, for which actual production costs were 4% higher than planned and 3% higher than the preceding year.

b. Unspecified increase in construction costs mentioned in *173*, No. 1, 1937, p. 92.

c. Tumanov (*173*, No. 4, 1936, p. 44) gives the following percentage increases over planned costs for work done by enterprises themselves: Commissariat of Heavy Industry, 12.2; Commissariat of Light Industry, 8.9; Commissariat of Timber, 9.8; and Commissariat of the Food Industry, 19.1. These figures may apply only to construction and assembly.

d. Chubar (*173*, No. 6, 1936, p. 15) states that the general index of construction cost in 1935 was 96.1 with 1934 = 100, but this probably applies to construction and assembly.

e. Tumanov (*173*, No. 4, 1936, p. 44) gives the following percentage increases over planned costs for work done by enterprises themselves for the first nine months of 1935: Commissariat of Heavy Industry, 7.2; Commissariat of Light Industry, 6.1; Commissariat of Timber, 6.6; and Commissariat of the Food Industry, 26.1.

Table B-16   Indexes of Investment Prices, 1932–1941

	Moorsteen and Powell						Jasny Indexes			Zaleski Indexes		
	Investment excl. Capital Repairs (billion rubles)		Indexes									
	In 1937 Prices (1)	In Current Prices (2)	1937 = 100 (3)	1932 = 100 (4)	Preceding Year = 100 (5)	1933 Plan Prices = 100 (6)	1932 = 100 (7)	Preceding Year = 100 (8)	1933 Plan Prices = 100 (9)	1932 = 100 (10)	Preceding Year = 100 (11)	1933 Plan Prices = 100 (12)
1932												
1. Actual	20.77	17.79	85.7	100		111.1	100		111.1	100.0		111.1
1933												
2. Planned			77.1[a]	90[b]	90[b]	100.0	90[b]	90.0	100.0	90.0	90[c]	100.0
3. Actual	18.46	15.59	84.5	98.6	98.6	109.6	105	105.0	116.7	104.6	104.6[d]	116.2
1934												
4. Planned										94.1	90.0[c]	104.6
5. Actual	21.04	20.27	96.3	112.4	114.0	124.9	105	100.0	116.7	109.0	104.2[d]	121.1
1935												
6. Planned										101.8	93.4	113.1
7. Actual	26.26	25.06	95.4	111.3	99.1	123.7	109	103.8	121.1	105.7	97.0[d]	117.4
1936												
8. Planned										94.1	89.0	104.6
9. Actual	36.08	34.23	94.9	110.7	99.5	123.0	122	111.9	135.6	106.8	101.0	118.7
1937												
10. Planned										95.6	89.5	106.2
11. Actual	32.51	32.51	100	116.7	105.4	129.7	130	106.6	144.4	113.8	106.6[e]	126.4
1938												
12. Planned										105.8	93.0	117.6
13. Actual	32.97	34.34	104.2	121.6	104.2	135.1				118.6	104.2[f]	131.8
1939												
14. Actual	32.95	36.64	111.2	129.8	106.7	144.2				125.1	105.5	139.0
1940												
15. Actual	32.19	39.73	123.4	144.0	111.0	160.0				138.9	111.0	154.3
1941												
16. Actual, 1st half	16.13	22.19	137.6	160.6	111.5[g]	178.4				154.9	111.5[f]	172.1
17. Actual, 2nd half	5.44	8.31	152.8	178.3	123.8[g]	198.1				172.0	123.8[f]	191.1

Table B-16 *continued*

Source: Unless otherwise indicated, cols. 1 and 2: *465*, pp. 387 and 391; col. 3: calculated from cols. 1 and 2; cols. 4 and 5: calculated from col. 3; col. 6: calculated from col. 4; col. 7: *450*, p. 134, note b; cols. 8 and 9: calculated from col. 7; col. 10: calculated from col. 11; col. 11: derived from Table B-15, col. 6 or, if unavailable, col. 5; col. 12; calculated from col. 10.

    a. Calculated from col. 4, lines 2 and 11.

    b. Taken to be same as col. 11.

    c. Rough estimate based on reduction in cost of construction (given as 15% in Table B-15, lines 1 and 3, col. 1) and ratio of cost of total investment to cost of construction for 1935–1937 (derived as approximately 75% from Table B-15, lines 5, 7, and 9, cols. 1 and 5). Result rounded. For lack of information, it has been assumed that no price changes were envisaged in the 1933 or 1934 plans.

    d. Derived from Table B-15, col. 1.

    e. Taken to be same as col. 8. In view of the sizable changes in wholesale prices in 1937, the reduction of 0.5% in investment costs (given in Table B-15, line 10, col. 5) is not representative of the change in investment prices.

    f. Taken to be same as col. 5.

    g. Relative to whole year of 1940.

Table B-17   Fixed Capital at Replacement Cost, 1932–1938 (million rubles in domestic production prices of 1933[a])

	1932 Annual Average (1)	Jan. 1, 1933, Actual (2)	Jan. 1, 1934, Actual (3)	Jan. 1, 1935, Actual (4)
1. National economy, total	85,222	91,720	104,848	119,296
2. Industry, total	25,542	28,559	35,135	40,921
3. Producer goods (Group A)	18,412	20,965	26,685	31,302
4. Consumer goods (Group B)	7,130	7,594	8,450	9,619
5. Agriculture	11,367	12,610	14,311	16,230
6. State farms	2,700			
7. Machine and Tractor Stations	825			
8. Transportation and communications	20,560[e]	21,665	23,709	26,641
9. Transportation	19,829	20,869[f]		
10. Railroad	14,233			
11. Inland waterway and maritime	2,414			
12. Motor	3,077			
13. Civil aviation	115			
14. Communications	721	796[g]		
15. Trade[h]	1,281	1,392	1,696	2,300
16. Education	3,817 ⎫			
17. Public health	2,038 ⎪			
18. Communal services	4,744 ⎬ 25,881[i]		27,488[i]	29,894[i]
19. Housing fund[j]	14,513 ⎭			
20. Urban	12,436			
21. Rural	2,077			
22. Other	1,360			

Source: Unless otherwise indicated, cols. 1 and 14: *293*, pp. 446–47; cols. 2, 3, 4, 6, and 8: *156*, p. 278; col. 7: col. 6 as a percentage of col. 5; cols. 9 and 11: *171*, No. 4, 1937, p. 11; col. 10: col. 9 as a percentage of col. 8; col. 12: *72*, p. 40; col. 13: col. 12 as a percentage of col. 11; col. 15: col. 12 as a percentage of col. 14.

a. Imported equipment included in fixed capital was evaluated in domestic production prices (*293*, p. 447).

b. *154*, p. 48. *155*, p. 308, gives 140,000 mill. rubles.

c. Sum of lines 3 and 4.

d. Based on fixed capital on Jan. 1, 1935 (col. 4) and increase planned for 1935 (given as 20, 15, and 18% for producer and consumer goods and transportation, respectively, in *155*, p. 308). The percentage for transportation was

Jan. 1, 1936			Jan. 1, 1937			Jan. 1, 1938			Annual Average, 1938		
1935 Plan (5)	1935 Actual (6)	Per Cent of Plan Fulfilled (7)	1936 Plan (8)	1936 Actual (9)	Per Cent of Plan Fulfilled (10)	1937 Plan (11)	1937 Actual (12)	Per Cent of Plan Fulfilled (13)	FYP for 1937 (14)	Per Cent of FYP Fulfilled (15)	Series No.
139,500[b]	140,600	100.8	169,600	163,280	96.3	189,260	182,200	96.3	195,193	93.3	1
48,594[c]	48,224	99.2	58,184	58,800	101.1	68,200			75,180		2
37,532[d]	37,304	99.4	45,044	45,700	101.5	52,600			58,217		3
11,062[d]	10,920	98.7	13,140	13,100	99.7	15,600			16,963		4
	18,986		21,883	20,500	93.7	23,200			22,560		5
									6,300		6
									4,970		7
31,436[d]	30,530	97.1	36,103						40,495[e]		8
				32,700		38,700			38,469		9
				22,400		25,600			26,163		10
									4,937		11
									6,573		12
									796		13
									2,026		14
	2,990		3,730	3,450		4,030			2,390		15
									8,966		16
									4,610		17
	35,610[i]		43,190[i]	41,700[i]	96.6	48,700[i]			10,318		18
									26,811		19
									23,301		20
									3,510		21
									3,863		22

used for the total of transportation and communications. For transportation, this percentage is given as 14 in *154*, p. 48.

e. Sum of lines 9 and 14.

f. *171*, No. 4, 1937, p. 11.

g. Line 8 minus line 9.

h. See Table B-1, note a.

i. Given for housing fund, public facilities, and communal services.

j. Housing funds of industry and other branches of the economy are included in the corresponding sector above (*293*, p. 447).

Income and Expenditures

Table C-1   Estimation of Wages and Salaries, Military Pay, and Other Payments, 1945–1953

	1945		1946		1947		1948	
	Planned (1)	Actual (2)	Planned (3)	Actual (4)	Planned (5)	Actual (6)	Planned (7)	Actual (8)
1. Employment: average annual number of workers and employees in national economy (mill.)		27.3		30.6	31.6	32.1	33.6	34.3
2. Average annual wages (rubles)	5,138	5,208		5,700		6,832	7,188	7,228
3. Partial wages and salaries [a] (bill. rubles)	138.4	142.2	160.3	174.4	212.9	219.3	241.5	247.9
4. State social insurance (bill. rubles)	10.1	10.4	11.7	11.6	14.9	14.6	15.7	16.2
5. State social insurance as percentage of partial wages and salaries	7.3	7.3	7.3	6.7	7.0	6.7	6.5	6.5
6. Military personnel (thous.)	11,365	11,365	5,000	5,000	3,000	3,000	2,874	2,874
7. Military pay (bill. rubles)	13.4	13.4	14.5	14.5	10.5	10.5	10.2	10.2
8. Income of cooperative artisans (bill. rubles)	4.8	4.9	5.5	5.8	6.8	6.9	7.9	7.9
9. Wages in kind (bill. rubles)	5.0	5.0	5.0	6.0	10.0	10.0	10.0	10.0
10. Total of lines 3, 7, 8, and 9 (bill. rubles)	161.6	165.5	185.3	200.7	240.2	246.7	269.6	276.0
11. Total of lines 3, 7, 8, and 9 as percentage of total wages and salaries	85	85	85	84.9	85.8	84.8	86.3	86.3
12. Total wages and salaries (bill. rubles)	190.1	194.7	218.0	236.5	280	290.9	312.4	320.0
13. Other payments (bill. rubles)	28.5	29.2	32.7	35.8	39.8	44.2	42.8	44.0

Source

LINE 1–Cols. 2, 4, 6, 8, 10, and 12: *260*, p. 22. Total minus cooperative artisans. Col. 5: *89*, 3/1/47, p. 2. Col. 7: Estimate based on 1947 employment (col. 6) and increase planned for 1948 (assumed to be the same as the actual increase between 1946 and 1947, derived as 1.5 mill. from cols. 4 and 6). Cols. 14, 16, and 18: *140*, p. 189.

LINE 2–Col. 1: Based on actual wage (col. 2) and percentage of plan fulfilled (derived as 101.37%, half of the plan fulfillment for partial wages and salaries calculated from cols. 1 and 2 in line 3). Cols. 2, 4, and 12: *260*, pp. 137 and 138. Given as monthly wage in new rubles and converted into annual wage in old rubles (1 new ruble = 10 old rubles). Col. 6: Based on average annual wage in the national economy in 1940 (given as 3,972 rubles in Table A-1, col. 5, series 203) and increase in 1947 (given as 72% in *42*, p. 136). Col. 7: Derived from partial wages and salaries (line 3) and employment (line 1). Cols. 8 and 10: Based on 1950 wage (col. 12) and increases in 1950 over 1949 and in 1949 over 1948 (roughly estimated as 3% for both years in *402*, p. 21). Cols. 14 and 16: *405*, p. 100. Converted into old rubles. Col. 18: Based on average annual wage in 1940 (taken as 4,054 rubles, the figure officially accepted at that time, see *291*, p. 24, and *194*, Vol. 3, p. 284) and increase in 1953 (given as 101% in *177*, p. 462). *405*, p. 100, gives 8,316 rubles.

LINE 3–Cols. 1, 3, 5, 7, 9, 11, 13, 15, and 17: Based on state social insurance (line 4) and its share in partial wages and salaries (line 5). This calculation is possible since all enterprises and organizations are required to pay sums ranging from 3.7 to 10.3% into the budget for social insurance and these sums cover nearly all that budget (around 97% according to *80*). Cols. 2, 4, 6, 8, 10, 12, 14, 16, and 18: Derived from employment (line 1) and average wages (line 2).

LINE 4–Cols. 1, 3, 5, 7, 9, 13, and 15: *301, 302, 304, 305, 306, 307*, and *309*. Col. 2: *174*, p. 259. Cols. 4, 6, 8, 10, 12, and 14: *44*, No. 1, 1953, p. 27, as cited in *245*, p. 139. Col. 11: Rough estimate. Cols. 16 and 18: *285*, No. 6, 1954, p. 5. Col. 17: *258*, 7/17/53, p. 2.

LINE 5–Cols. 1, 7, 9, 11, 13, 15, and 17: Assumed to be the same as actual in cols. 2, 8, 10, 12, 14, 16, and 18, for lack of any other data. Cols. 2, 4, 6, 8, 10, 12, 14, 16, and 18: Derived from insurance (line 4) and partial wages (line 3). Col. 3: Assumed to be same as in previous year on the assumption that the wage increase in 1946 was not planned. Col. 5: Assumed to be slightly higher than in col. 6 because the same percentage would imply underfulfillment of the wage fund in this year.

1949 Planned (9)	1949 Actual (10)	1950 Planned (11)	1950 Actual (12)	1951 Planned (13)	1951 Actual (14)	1952 Planned (15)	1952 Actual (16)	1953 Planned (17)	1953 Actual (18)	Series No.
	36.1		38.9		40.7		42.2		43.7	1
	7,445		7,668		7,908		8,066		8,149	2
261.2	268.7	290.9	298.3	319.7	321.9	334.4	340.4	349.2	356.1	3
17.5	18.1	19.2	19.6	21.1	21.4	21.4	21.9	22.7	23.2	4
6.7	6.7	6.6	6.6	6.6	6.6	6.4	6.4	6.5	6.5	5
2,900	2,900	4,000	4,000	4,900	4,900	5,800	5,800	5,800	5,800	6
10.5	10.5	15.0	15.0	19.0	19.0	23.2	23.2	23.6	23.6	7
8.1	8.2	8.3	8.4	9.2	9.3	9.4	9.5	9.5	9.6	8
10.0	10.0	10.0	10.0	10.0	10.0	10.0	10.0	10.0	10.0	9
289.8	297.4	324.2	331.7	357.9	360.2	377.0	383.1	392.3	399.3	10
87	87	87.5	87.5	88	88	88.5	88.5	89	89	11
333.1	341.8	370.5	379.1	406.7	409.3	426.0	432.9	440.8	448.7	12
43.3	44.4	46.3	47.4	48.8	49.1	49.0	49.8	48.5	49.4	13

LINE 6–Cols. 1, 3, 5, 7, 9, 11, 13, 15, and 17: Assumed to be the same as actual in cols. 2, 4, 6, 8, 10, 12, 14, 16, and 18, for lack of any other data. **Cols. 2 and 8:** *180*, 1/15/60, p. 3. **Cols. 4 and 6:** *465*, p. 629. **Cols. 10, 12, 14, 16, and 18:** *407*, p. 364.

LINE 7–Cols. 1, 3, 5, 7, 9, 11, 13, 15, and 17: Assumed to be the same as actual in cols. 2, 4, 6, 8, 10, 12, 14, 16, and 18, for lack of any other data. **Col. 2:** Based on military pay in 1944 (given as 14.2 bill. rubles in *407*, p. 364) and ratio of military personnel in 1945 to that in 1944 (derived as 94.7% from line 6, col. 2, and military personnel in 1944 of 12 mill. given in *407*, p. 364). **Cols. 4 and 6:** Based on military personnel in 1946 and 1947 (line 6) and average military pay (derived as 2,900 and 3,500 rubles, respectively, by using approximate average pay in 1948, derived from *407*, p. 364, for 1947 and reducing 1947 pay by 17% to obtain 1946 pay, taking into account the 20% increase in money wages between 1946 and 1947). **Cols. 8, 10, 12, 14, 16, and 18:** *407*, p. 364.

LINE 8–Cols. 1-18: Table C-4, col. 3.

LINE 9–Cols. 1, 3, 5, 7, 9, 11, 13, 15, and 17: Assumed to be same as cols. 2, 4, 6, 8, 10, 12, 14, 16, and 18. **Cols. 2 and 4:** Assumed to be lower than in following years, taking into account changes in money wages in those years. **Cols. 6 and 8:** Assumed to be same as col. 10. **Cols. 10, 12, 14, 16, and 18:** *439*, p. 69. Rough estimate. Mainly forced labor.

LINE 10–Cols. 1-18: Sum of lines 3, 7, 8, and 9.

LINE 11–Cols. 1-3: Assumed to be the same as col. 4. Rounded. **Cols. 4-6 and 8:** Derived from lines 10 and 12. **Col. 7:** Assumed to be the same as col. 8. **Cols. 9-10:** Assumed to be slightly higher than col. 8. **Cols. 11-18:** Based on col. 10 and annual increase (assumed to be 0.5%).

LINE 12–Cols. 1-3, 7, and 9-18: Derived from lines 10 and 11. **Col. 4:** Based on 1947 total (col. 6) and increase between 1946 and 1947 (given as 23% in *180*, 1/18/48, p. 1). **Col. 5:** *89*, 3/1/47, p. 2. **Col. 6:** Based on 1948 total (col. 8) and increase between 1947 and 1948 (given as 10% in *95*, p. 167). See also *134*, p. 65. **Col. 8:** *280*, p. 24. Given as "more than 320 bill. rubles."

LINE 13–Cols. 1-18: Line 12 minus line 10.

Table C-1   *continued*

a. Two different estimates of the wage fund were published before the war. The one put out by TsUNKhU was of a more limited coverage (see *408*, pp. 107–8, and *410*, pp. 125–27) and amounted simply to the multiplication of the average annual wage in the national economy by the average annual number of workers and employees in the national economy. Such statistics were published, for example, in *254*, p. 228, for 1937 (82.2 bill. rubles) and for the 1942 plan (133.2 bill. rubles).

However, more complete statistics on the wage fund were also published before and after the war—in *60*, p. 5, for instance; in *291*, p. 24, for 1940 (162 bill. rubles) and for the 1950 plan (252 bill. rubles); and in *89*, 3/1/47, p. 2, for the 1947 plan (280 bill. rubles).

Table C-2   Estimation of Money Income of Collective Farmers, 1932–1941

	1932 Actual (1)	1933 Planned (2)	1933 Actual (3)	1934 Planned (4)	1934 Actual (5)	1935 Planned (6)	1935 Actual (7)	1936 Planned (8)	1936 Actual (9)
1. Total sales on collective farm market (bill. rubles)	7.5		11.5		14.0		14.5	16.5	15.6
2. Share of urban in total (per cent)	70	70	70	70	70	70	70	70	70
3. Urban (bill. rubles)	5.3		8.1		9.8		10.1	11.5	10.9
4. Rural (bill. rubles)	2.2		3.4		4.2		4.4	5.0	4.7
5. Share of collective farms in urban collective farm market sales (per cent)	23.1	23.1	23.1	23.1	23.1	23.1	23.1	23.1	23.1
6. Sales of collective farms on urban collective farm market (bill. rubles)	1.2		1.9		2.3		2.3	2.7	2.5
7. Sales of collective farmers on urban collective farm market (bill. rubles)	4.1		6.2		7.5		7.8	8.8	8.4
8. Index of grain sales to state procurement agencies (1937 = 100)	58.9		73.1	78.3	81.9		89.2		80.7
9. Income from sale of farm products to state procurement agencies (bill. rubles)	1.7		2.11	2.26	2.36		2.57		2.32

Source

LINE 1–Col. 1: *13*, p. 1022, as cited in *442*, p. 322. **Cols. 3, 5, 7-9, 11, 13, 15, and 17:** Tables A-2 and A-3.

LINE 2–Cols. 1-15: Assumed to be slightly lower than in 1940 (col. 17). **Cols. 16 and 18-19:** Assumed to be same as in 1940 (col. 17). **Col. 17:** Derived from lines 1 and 3.

LINE 3–Cols. 1, 3, 5, 7, 8-9, 11, 13, and 15: Derived from lines 1 and 2. **Col. 17:** *232*, p. 179. On coverage, see *439*, p. 48, note d.

LINE 4–All cols.: Line 1 minus line 3.

LINE 5–Cols. 1-10: Assumed to be same as in 1937 (col. 11). **Col. 11:** Based on sales by collective farms on urban collective farm market (given as 4.12 bill. rubles in *408*, p. 104) and total sales on collective farm market (line 1).

Table C-1 *continued*

The difference between these two estimates lies, according to Bergson (*408*, pp. 107–8), who relies on Margolin (*127* and *126*) in the inclusion in the estimates of larger coverage of the wages paid to workers in certain local industries and other activities not covered by the national economic plan, wages paid by collective farms for outside labor, military pay, and probably wages paid to forced laborers. The more complete series also seems to include wages of home workers and certain bonuses. On the other hand, the income of cooperative artisans was not included before the war but was after the war, according to *410* (p. 125). However, Hoeffding and Nimitz (*439*, p. 63) do not include the income of cooperative artisans even after the war, and the definitions they use suggest that perhaps it was not included in the official statistics on the wage fund for the 1947 plan, 1948, and the 1950 plan. Hence it is possible that the income of cooperative artisans has been included twice in Table C-1, once as listed and the second time under "other payments."

| 1937 | | 1938 | | 1939 | | 1940 | | 1941 | | Series No. |
Planned (10)	Actual (11)	Planned (12)	Actual (13)	Planned (14)	Actual (15)	Planned (16)	Actual (17)	Planned (18)	Actual (19)	
	17.8		24.4		29.9		41.1			1
70	70	70	70	70	70	70.8	70.8	70.8	70.8	2
	12.5		17.1		20.9		29.1			3
	5.3		7.3		9.0		12.0			4
23.1	23.1	9.5	9.5	9.5	9.5	12	12	12	12	5
	2.9		1.6		2.0		3.5			6
	9.6		15.5		18.9		25.6			7
	100.0		98.9		109.9		114.4		76.3	8
	2.88		2.85		3.17		5.02		2.20	9

Cols. 12–14: Assumed to be same as in 1939 (col. 15). **Cols. 15 and 17:** *439*, p. 49, note q. **Cols. 16 and 18–19:** Assumed to be same as in 1940 (col. 17).
LINE 6–All cols.: Derived from lines 3 and 5.
LINE 7–All cols.: Line 3 minus line 6.
LINE 8–All cols.: Calculated from series 137 in Tables A-2, A-3, and, for 1932, *498*, p. 313.
LINE 9–Cols. 1, 3–5, 7, 9, 13, 15, and 19: Based on 1940 income (col. 11) and index in line 8. The low figure in col. 19 is due to the German occupation of Soviet territory in 1941. **Col. 11:** *408*, p. 104. **Col. 17:** *439*, p. 116. It seemed preferable to use this estimate, which takes into account the increase in farm households because of territorial annexations at this time (see *439*, p. 117).

Table C-3 Estimation of Money Income of Collective Farmers, 1945–1953

	1945 Actual (1)	1946 Actual (2)	1947 Actual (3)	1948 Actual (4)	1949 Planned (5)	1949 Actual (6)	1950 Actual (7)	1951 Planned (8)	1951 Actual (9)	1952 Actual (10)	1953 Actual (11)
1. Money income of collective farms (bill. rubles)	20.6	20	21.3	22.7	28	28	34.2	38.6	38.6	42.8	49.6
2. Tax on income of collective farms and cooperatives (bill. rubles)		3.177			4.50			5.55	7.6		
3. Tax on income of collective farms and cooperatives as per cent of money income of collective farms		16			16.1	16.1	16.2	19.7			
4. Tax on collective farms (bill. rubles)							2.54				
5. Tax on collective farms as per cent of money income of collective farms							7.4				
6. Money payments to collective farmers for *trudodni* (bill. rubles)	6.8	6.6	7.0	7.5	9.3	9.3	11.8		12.9	13.4	18.4
7. Money payments to collective farmers for *trudodni* as per cent of money income of collective farms	33	33	33	33	33	33.2	34.5		33.4	31.3	37.1
8. Income from sale of farm products to state procurement agencies (bill. rubles)	1.6	1.2	2.0	2.4		2.6	2.6		2.6	2.5	6.6
9. Total sales on collective farm market (bill. rubles)	192.1	232.1	241.3	67.2		64.2	70.1		66.8	66.2	61.0
10. Urban (bill. rubles)	136.4	164.8	171.3	47.7		45.6	49.2		50.8	53.7	48.8
11. Rural (bill. rubles)	55.7	67.3	70.0	19.5		18.6	20.9		16.0	12.5	12.2
12. Sales of collective farms on urban market (bill. rubles)	16.4	19.8	20.6	6.8		5.5	5.9		7.6	8.1	7.3
13. Sales of collective farms on urban market as per cent of urban collective farm market sales	12	12	12	12		12	12		15	15	15
14. Income from sale of farm products on collective farm market (bill. rubles)	120.0	145.0	150.7	49.6		40.1	43.3		43.2	45.6	41.5

Source

LINE 1–Col. 1: *28*, p. 165. Col. 2: Derived from lines 2 and 3. Col. 3: Estimated as the average of 1946 and 1948 incomes (cols. 2 and 4), taking into account the movement of gross agricultural production in 1946–1948 (see *142*, p. 350). Col. 4: Based on collective farm payments to the indivisible funds (given as 3.4 bill. rubles in *75*, 12/20/49, p. 2, as cited in *410*, p. 114) and share that this was of collective farm money income (taken to be 15% from decreed range of 12–20% cited in *410*, p. 114). Bergson and Heyman use 17% but that yields a money income figure that seems too low compared with the known 1945 and 1949 figures. Cols. 5 and 8: Assumed to be same as actual (cols. 6 and 9). Col. 6: *439*, p. 35. Cols. 7, 10, and 11: *140*, p. 128. Col. 9: *73*, p. 6.

LINE 2–Col. 2: *45*, p. 345. Col. 5: *198*, p. 72. Col. 7: *58*, p. 8. Col. 8: *199*, p. 70.

LINE 3–Col. 2: Assumed to be approximately the same as in 1949 and 1950 (cols. 6 and 7). Cols. 5, 7, and 8: Derived from lines 1 and 2. Col. 6: Assumed to be same as planned (col. 5).

LINE 4–Col. 7: *58*, p. 8.

LINE 5–Col. 7: Derived from lines 1 and 4.

LINE 6–Cols. 1-4: Derived from lines 1 and 7. Col. 5: Assumed to be same as actual (col. 6). Cols. 6 and 9: *439*, p. 4. Col. 7: *482*, p. 393. Col. 10: Sum of payments for *trudodni* (given as 12.4 bill. rubles in *180*, 1/25/58, p. 2) and fixed cash payments (given as 1.0 bill. rubles in *421*, Part I, p. 274). Col. 11: *405*, p. 152.

LINE 7–Cols. 1-5: Assumed to be approximately the same as col. 6. Cols. 6-7 and 9-11: Derived from lines 1 and 6.

Table C-3 *continued*

LINE 8–Cols. 1-4: Based on 1949 income (col. 6) and index for grain procurements for 1945–1948 (derived as 62.3 for 1945, 46.7 for 1946, 77.9 for 1947, 94.1 for 1948, with 1949 = 100, from *467*, p. 55). **Cols. 6 and 9:** Rounded figure of 3.0 bill. rubles (given by *439*, p. 45) assumed to be same as in 1950 (col. 7). **Col. 7:** Based on 1952 income (col. 10) and index for 1952 with 1950 = 100 (given as 95 in *45*, p. 172). **Col. 10:** Total sales of farm products to the state (given as 27.0 bill. rubles in *28*, p. 155) minus sales to state agencies (given as 24.5 bill. rubles in *439*, p. 44). **Col. 11:** *439*, p. 45.

LINE 9–Cols. 1-3 and 6: Based on urban sales (line 10) and share of urban in total (taken to be 71%, the share given for 1949 in *439*, p. 48). **Col. 4:** Based on collective farm trade in 1940 (given as 41.1 bill. rubles in Table A-3, col. 8), increase in that trade between 1940 and 1948 (given as 22% in *285*, No. 7, 1951, p. 79), and price increase between 1940 and 1948 (given as 34% in Table 119 in Chapter 18). **Col. 7:** Based on income of collective farms from sales on collective farm market (given as 9.4 bill. rubles in *439*, p. 44) and share of that income in total sales on collective farm market (given as 13.4% in *439*, p. 48). **Col. 9:** Based on urban sales (line 10) and share of urban in total (estimated as 76% in *439*, p. 48). **Col. 10:** Based on retail sales in state and cooperative trade (given as 393.6 bill. rubles in *140*, p. 201) and share of collective farm market sales in total retail sales (given as 14.4% in *439*, p. 48). **Col. 11:** *439*, pp. 47–48. Estimate.

LINE 10–Col. 1: Total retail sales (derived as 296.5 bill. rubles from sales in state and cooperative trade, given as 160.1 bill. rubles in *232*, p. 20, and share of those sales in total, derived as 54% in *25*, p. 213) minus sales in state and cooperative trade (160.1 bill. rubles as above). This checks with rounded figure of 13.6 bill. new rubles given by *25*, p. 213. **Col. 2:** Based on retail sales in state and cooperative trade (given as 247.2 bill. rubles in *232*, p. 20) and share of urban collective farm market sales in total retail sales (estimated at 40%, midpoint between 1945 share, given in line 1 above, and 1947 share, derived as 34% from state and cooperative trade sales of 330.8 bill. rubles in *232*, p. 20, and collective farm market urban sales in col. 3). **Col. 4:** Based on total sales on collective farm market (line 9) and share of urban in total (given as 71% for 1949 in *439*, p. 48). **Cols. 3 and 6:** *457*, pp. 60, 79, and 75. **Cols. 7, 9, 10, and 11:** *232*, p. 19.

LINE 11–Cols. 1-11: Line 9 minus line 10.

LINE 12–Cols. 1-11: Derived from lines 10 and 13.

LINE 13–Cols. 1-4: Assumed to be same as in 1949 and 1950 (cols. 6 and 7). **Cols. 6-7 and 9-11:** *439*, p. 48.

LINE 14–Cols. 1-11: Line 10 minus line 12.

Table C-4   Estimation of Income of Cooperative Artisans, 1945–1953

	Number Employed (millions) (1)	Average Annual Income (rubles) (2)	Total Income (mill. rubles) (3)
1945			
1. Planned	1.3	3,710	4,823
2. Actual	1.3	3,760	4,888
1946			
3. Planned	1.4	3,942	5,519
4. Actual	1.4	4,115	5,761
1947			
5. Planned	1.4	4,860	6,804
6. Actual	1.4	4,933	6,906
1948			
7. Planned	1.5	5,269	7,903
8. Actual	1.5	5,297	7,946
1949			
9. Planned	1.5	5,379	8,069
10. Actual	1.5	5,456	8,184
1950			
11. Planned	1.5	5,551	8,327
12. Actual	1.5	5,621	8,432
1951			
13. Planned	1.6	5,777	9,243
14. Actual	1.6	5,797	9,275
1952			
15. Planned	1.6	5,859	9,374
16. Actual	1.6	5,912	9,459
1953			
17. Planned	1.6	5,914	9,462
18. Actual	1.6	5,973	9,557

Source

COLUMN 1–Lines 1, 3, 5, 7, 9, 11, 13, 15, and 17: Assumed to be same as lines 2, 4, 6, 8, 10, 12, 14, 16, and 18 for lack of any other data. **Lines 2, 4, 6, 8, 10, 12, 14, 16, and 18:** *260*, p. 22.

COLUMN 2–Lines 1, 3, 5, 9, 11, 13, 15, and 17: Based on actual income in lines 2, 4, 6, 10, 12, 14, 16, and 18 and share of plan fulfillment of partial wage fund attributable to cooperative artisans (assumed to be half of plan fulfillment percentage calculated from Table C-1, line 3). **Lines 2 and 12:** Based on average annual wage of workers and employees in industry (derived as 5,640 and 8,436 old rubles for 1945 and 1950 from *260*, p. 138) and ratio of wage of cooperative artisans to wage in industry (given as two-thirds for 1950–1955 in *482*, p. 394). **Lines 4 and 6:** Based on average annual wage of workers and employees in national economy (given in Table C-1, line 2) and ratio of wage of cooperative artisans to national economy wage (derived as 72.2% from 1945 ratio of industrial wage to national economy wage—108.3% from *260*, p. 138—and two-thirds ratio given above). **Lines 7, 8, 10, 14, 16, and 18:** Based on national economy wage (given in Table C-1, line 2) and ratio of wage of cooperative artisans to national economy wage (derived as 73.3% from 1950 ratio of industrial wage to national economy wage—110% from *260*, p. 138—and two-thirds ratio given above).

COLUMN 3–All lines: Derived from cols. 1 and 2.

Table C-5 Estimation of Pensions and Allowances, 1932–1941 (billion rubles)

		Social Insurance					
		Total (1)	Per Cent Paid in Money (2)	Amount Paid in Money (3)	Social Security (4)	Family Allowances (5)	Total Pensions and Allowances (6)
1932	Actual	2.9	73	2.1	0.2		2.3
1933	Actual	3.2	73	2.3	0.2		2.5
1934	Actual	3.4	73	2.5	0.2		2.7
1935	Actual	3.7	73	2.7	0.2		2.9
1936	Actual	5.0	73	3.7	0.2	0.1	4.0
1937	Actual	5.2	73	3.8[a]	1.3	1.0	6.1[b]
1938	Actual	6.0	60	3.6	2.0	0.9	6.5
1939	Actual	6.0[c]	60	3.6	2.3	1.1	7.0
1940	Planned	5.8[d]	60	3.5	2.9[d]	1.2[d]	7.6
1940	Actual	5.0[e]	60	3.0	3.1[f]	1.2[e]	7.3
1941	Planned	5.6[g]	60	3.4	3.5[g]	1.2[e]	8.1
1941	Actual	3.4[e]	60	2.0	4.5[e]	1.2[e]	7.7

Source: Unless otherwise indicated, cols. 1, 4, and 5: *442*, p. 330; col. 2: for 1932–1936 assumed to be the same as in 1937, which was derived from cols. 1 and 3, and for 1938–1939 and 1941 assumed to be the same as in 1940, which was given by *410*, p. 140; col. 3: derived from cols. 1 and 2; col. 6: sum of cols. 3, 4, and 5.

Note: Expenditures on pensions and allowances are listed in the budget under "social and cultural expenditures" under three programs: social insurance, social security, and family allowances (for mothers of many children and unmarried mothers). Family allowances are paid entirely in money. Social security covers mainly pensions to war invalids and "invalids of labor" paid in money. Although a small part of this assistance goes for the maintenance of rest homes of various kinds (derived as about 10% by *410*, p. 140), that part has been included here. Since a sizable amount of social insurance, which covers old-age pensions and sick benefits, goes for the maintenance of hospitals and rest homes, that amount has been deducted as not being part of the money income of households.

a. Col. 6 minus cols. 4 and 5.
b. *408*, p. 18.
c. Assumed to be same as 1939 actual above.
d. *299*, p. 246.
e. *174*, p. 329.
f. Total social and cultural expenditures minus expenditures on education, public health and physical culture, family allowances, and social insurance (all given in *174*, p. 329).
g. *300*, p. 275.

Table C-6   Estimation of Pensions and Allowances, 1945–1953 (billion rubles)

	Total (1)	Social Insurance		Social Security (4)	Family Allowances (5)	Total Pensions and Allowances (6)
		Per Cent Paid in Money (2)	Amount Paid in Money (3)			
1945						
1. Planned	5.2	75	3.9	17.7	1.4	23.0
2. Actual	5.0	75	3.8	17.8	2.1	23.7
1946						
3. Planned	7.2	70	5.0	17.0	4.1	26.1
4. Actual	7.4	70	5.2	17.6	3.6	26.4
1947						
5. Planned	9.3	65	6.0	20.6	5.9	32.5
6. Actual	9.9	65	6.4	22.0	4.5	32.9
1948						
7. Planned	9.8	60	5.9	22.6	4.3	32.8
8. Actual	9.8	60	5.9	18.4	2.5	26.8
1949						
9. Planned	11.3	65	7.3	21.4	3.4	32.1
10. Actual	11.8	65	7.7	22.3	3.2	33.2
1950						
11. Planned	12.8	67.2	8.6	22.4	4.0	35.0
12. Actual	12.7	67.2	8.5	22.3	3.7	34.5
1951						
13. Planned	13.5	70	9.5	22.3	4.1	35.9
14. Actual	13.6	70	9.5	22.3	4.1	35.9
1952						
15. Planned	14.5	70	10.2	23.0	4.5	37.7
16. Actual	14.8	70	10.4	23.0	4.2	37.6
1953						
17. Planned	14.9	70	10.4	23.5	4.5	38.4
18. Actual	15.5	70	10.9	23.5	4.5	38.9

Source

COLUMN 1–Line 1: *322*, p. 155. Line 2: *174*, p. 219. Line 3: *303*, p. 20. Lines 4, 6, 8, 10, and 12: *44*, No. 10, 1953, p. 21. Line 5: *319*, p. 25. Line 7: Assumed to be same as actual (line 8). Line 9: *173*, No. 2, 1949, p. 48. Line 11: *321*, p. 21. Total expenditures on social and cultural programs (120.7 bill. rubles) minus expenditures on education, health and physical training, family allowances, and social security. Line 13: *199*, p. 36. Line 14: Assumed to be almost the same as planned (line 13). Lines 15-18: Interpolated from total expenditures for social insurance and social security (given as 37.5, 37.8, 42.9, and 43.5 bill. rubles, respectively, in *56*, p. 7, and *180*, 3/7/52, p. 3), 1951 planned figure (line 13), and 1954 actual figure (obtained as a residual of 18.5 bill. rubles in *178*, p. 482).

COLUMN 2–Lines 1, 3, 5, 7, 9, 11, 13, 15, and 17: Assumed to be same as actual (lines 2, 4, 6, 8, 10, 12, 14, 16, and 18). Lines 2, 4, and 6: Assumed to have decreased 5% per year between 1944 (for which share can be derived as roughly 80% from *410*, p. 140) and 1948 (line 8). Line 8: *410*, p. 141. Line 10: Assumed to be slightly lower than in 1950 (line 12). Line 12: *235*, No. 6, 1951, p. 62. Given as approximately 33%. Lines 14, 16, and 18: Assumed to be slightly higher than in 1950 (line 12) and constant since expenditures on maintenance of rest homes and vacation camps decreased between 1950 and 1953 (*434*, April 1954, p. 394).

COLUMN 3–All lines: Derived from cols. 1 and 2.

COLUMN 4–Line 1: *322*, p. 155. Line 2: *174*, p. 329. Line 3: *303*, p. 20. Lines 4 and 5: *319*, p. 25. Lines 6, 10, and 12: Total expenditures on social and cultural programs minus all other items (given in *44*, No. 10, 1953, p. 21). Line 7: Assumed to be slightly higher than 1947 actual (line 6). Lines 8 and 9: *173*, No. 2, 1949, p. 48. Line 11: *321*, p. 21. Line 13: *199*, p. 36. Line 14: Assumed to be same as planned (line 13). Lines 15-18: Interpolated, as in col. 1 above, from 1951 planned figure (line 13) and 1954 actual figure (given as 24.2 bill. rubles in *178*, p. 482).

Table C-6   *continued*

COLUMN 5–Line 1: *322*, p. 155. **Lines 2 and 3:** *303*, p. 20. **Lines 4, 6, 8, 10, and 12:** *44*, No. 10, 1953, p. 21. **Line 5:** *319*, p. 25. **Line 7:** Assumed to be slightly lower than 1947 actual (line 6). **Line 9:** *173*, No. 2, 1949, p. 48. **Line 11:** *321*, p. 21. **Line 13:** *199*, p. 36. **Line 14:** *173*, No. 2, 1952, p. 27. **Line 15:** *180*, 3/7/52, p. 3. **Lines 16 and 18:** *175*, p. 527. **Line 17:** Total social insurance, social security, and family allowances (given as 42.9 bill. rubles in *56*, p. 7) minus cols. 1 and 4.

COLUMN 6–All lines: Sum of cols. 3, 4, and 5.

Note: For a general description of coverage, see note to Table C-5.

Table C-7   Estimation of Stipends and Scholarships, 1945–1953

Year[a]	Number of Students in		Total		Stipends and Scholarships (mill. rubles)	
	Higher Educat. Institutions (millions) (1)	Technical and Specialized Schools (2)	Number (millions) (3)	Index (1953 = 100) (4)	Calculated (5)	Official (6)
1945	730.2	1,007.7	1,737.9	54.2	3,104	
1946	871.7	1,174.5	2,046.2	63.8	3,654	
1947	963.6	1,231.6	2,195.2	68.4	3,917	
1948	1,032.1	1,264.0	2,296.1	71.6	4,101	
1949	1,132.1	1,309.2	2,441.3	76.1	4,358	
1950	1,247.4	1,297.6	2,545.0	79.3	4,542	4,642.0
1951	1,356.1	1,368.9	2,725.0	85.0	4,868	4,828.9
1952	1,441.5	1,477.4	2,918.9	91.0	5,212	5,253.4
1953	1,562.0	1,645.5	3,207.5	100.0	5,727	5,727.0[b]

Source: Cols. 1 and 2: *101*, p. 202; col. 3: sum of cols. 1 and 2; col. 4: calculated from col. 3; col. 5: calculated from col. 6 figure for 1953 and index in col. 4; and col. 6: *190a*, p. 46.

a. Academic years, i.e., 1945 = 1945/46.
b. 1953 plan given as 5,800 in *309*, p. 126.

Table C-8 Estimation of Interest on Loans and Savings, 1945–1953 (billion rubles)

	Savings Deposits		Average Interest Rate (per cent) (3)	Interest on Savings Deposits (4)	Interest Paid to Households on Loans (5)	Total Interest on Loans and Savings (6)
	Total on Dec. 31 (1)	Annual Average (2)				
1945						
1. Planned	6.6 + 3.0[a]	5.9 + 3.0[a]	3.25	0.29	3.86 + 2.0[a]	4.15
2. Actual	8.7	6.9	3.25	0.22	3.86 + 2.0[a]	4.08
1946						
3. Planned	12.3	10.5	3.25	0.34	3.86 + 2.5[a]	6.70
4. Actual	12	10.3	3.25	0.33	3.94 + 2.5[a]	6.77
1947						
5. Planned	13.5	12.7	3.25	0.41	4.88 + 2.0[a]	7.29
6. Actual	12.8	12.4	3.25	0.40	5.0 + 2.0[a]	7.40
1948						
7. Planned	14.3	13.5	3.25	0.44	1.40	1.84
8. Actual	14.4	13.6	3.25	0.44	1.40	1.84
1949						
9. Planned	17	15.7	3.25	0.51	2.5	3.01
10. Actual	17	15.7	3.25	0.51	2.5	3.01
1950						
11. Planned	21	19.0	3.25	0.62	3.5	4.12
12. Actual	18.5	17.7	3.25	0.58	3.7	4.28
1951						
13. Planned	22.0	20.3	3.25	0.66	5.00	5.66
14. Actual	22.5	20.5	3.25	0.67	4.95	5.62
1952						
15. Planned	27.0	24.7	3.25	0.80	7.0	7.80
16. Actual	26.0	24.3	3.25	0.79	6.8	7.59
1953						
17. Planned	36.0	31.0	3.25	1.01	9.8	10.81
18. Actual	38.7	32.3	3.25	1.05	9.7	10.75

Table C-8 *continued*

Source

COLUMN 1–**Line 1:** Based on 1944 deposits (given as 5.2 bill. rubles in *174*, p. 298) and increase planned for 1945 (given as 1.4 bill. rubles in *322*, p. 152. **Line 2:** Based on 1944 deposits (5.2 bill. rubles as above) and increase in 1945 (given as 3.47 bill. rubles in *303*, p. 14). **Line 3:** Based on 1945 deposits (line 2) and increase planned for 1946 (given as 3.6 bill. rubles in *303*, p. 14). **Lines 4 and 5:** *319*, p. 15. **Lines 6 and 7:** *320*, p. 17. **Line 8:** Based on 1949 deposits (col. 10) and increase in 1949 over 1948 (given as 2.6 bill. rubles in *321*, p. 28). **Line 9:** Assumed to be same as actual (line 10). **Line 10:** *321*, p. 28. **Line 11:** Based on 1949 deposits (line 10) and increase planned for 1950 (given as 4 bill. rubles in *321*, p. 28). **Line 12:** *55*, p. 15. **Line 13:** Based on 1950 deposits (line 12) and increase planned for 1951 (given as 3.5 bill. rubles in *55*, p. 15). **Line 14:** Based on 1950 deposits (line 12) and increase in 1951 over 1950 (given as 4 bill. rubles in *180*, 3/7/52, p. 2). **Line 15:** Based on 1951 deposits (line 14) and increase planned for 1952 (given as 4.5 bill. rubles in *180*, 3/7/52, p. 2). **Lines 16 and 17:** *56*, p. 10. **Line 18:** *285*, No. 6, 1954, p. 8.

COLUMN 2–**Line 1:** Average of 12/31/44 deposits (given as 5.2 bill. rubles in *174*, p. 298) and 12/31/45 planned deposits (col. 1, line 1). **Line 2:** Average of 12/31/44 deposits (5.2 bill. rubles as above) and 12/31/45 actual deposits (col. 1, line 2). **Lines 3, 5, 7, 9, 11, 13, 15, and 17:** Average of planned deposits in each year and actual deposits for preceding year (both in col. 1). **Lines 4, 6, 8, 10, 12, 14, 16, and 18:** Average of actual deposits in each year and actual deposits in preceding year (both in col. 1).

COLUMN 3–**All lines:** Derived as 3.25% for all years from total deposits in 1939 (given as 6.5 bill. rubles in *14*, No. 3–4, 1941, p. 7, as cited in *410*, p. 143) and interest paid on savings deposits (given as .20 bill. rubles in *322*, p. 73). According to *410*, p. 143, this rate did not change between 1939 and 1953. The interest rate for regular savings accounts was 3% in 1939 and 5% for long-term accounts (*48*, p. 308, as cited in *410*, p. 143).

COLUMN 4–**All lines:** Derived from cols. 2 and 3.

COLUMN 5–**Line 1:** Assumed to be same as actual (line 2). **Line 2:** *174*, p. 292. *303*, p. 13, gives 2.978 bill. rubles. The difference may be due to forced savings during the war (see note a). **Line 3:** *303*, p. 13. **Lines 4 and 5:** *319*, p. 15. **Line 6:** Assumed to be same as planned (line 5). Rounded. **Line 7:** Assumed to be same as actual (line 8). **Line 8:** *180*, 5/4/49, p. 1. **Line 9:** Assumed to be same as actual (line 10). **Lines 10 and 11:** *321*, p. 28. **Line 12:** *180*, 2/19/52. **Line 13:** *55*, p. 15. **Lines 14 and 15:** *180*, 2/19/52. **Lines 16 and 17:** *56*, p. 11. **Line 18:** *180*, 6/10/54, p. 2.

COLUMN 6–**All lines:** Sum of cols. 4 and 5.

a. Special savings accounts were opened for employees in compensation for accumulated leave during the war. From 1946 on, the savings banks were supposed to reimburse these deposits over four years. These reimbursements were stopped after the December 1947 currency reform. See *410*, p. 144, and *319*, p. 15.

Table C-9 Estimation of State and Cooperative Retail Trade Sales
to Households, 1945–1953

	Total Sales of State and Cooperative Retail Trade (bill. rubles) (1)	Share of Sales to Households in Total Sales (per cent) (2)	State and Cooperative Retail Trade Sales to Households (bill. rubles) (3)
1945			
1. Planned		95	146.0
2. Actual	160.1	95	152.1
1946			
3. Planned		92.5	240.5
4. Actual	247.2	92.5	228.7
1947			
5. Planned	324.6	92.5	300.3
6. Actual	330.8	92.5	306.0
1948			
7. Planned	345.0	92.5	319.1
8. Actual	310.2	92.5	286.9
1949			
9. Planned		92.5	331.2
10. Actual	335.1	92.5	310.0
1950			
11. Planned		92.5	337.0
12. Actual	359.6	92.5	332.6
1951			
13. Planned		92.5	346.8
14. Actual	379.8	92.5	351.3
1952			
15. Planned		92.5	384.5
16. Actual	393.6	92.5	364.1
1953			
17. Planned		92.5	393.3
18. Actual	430.7	92.5	398.4

Source

COLUMN 1–Line 2: Table A-4, series 233, col. 5. **Lines 4-8, 10, 12, 14, and 16:** Table A-5, series 233. **Line 18:** *232*, p. 24.

COLUMN 2–**Lines 1, 3, 5, 7, 9, 11, 13, 15, and 17:** Assumed to be same as actual (lines 2, 4, 6, 8, 10, 12, 14, 16, and 18). **Line 2:** Derived from total sales and share of sales to institutions in 1944 (given as 119.11 and 5.95 bill. rubles in *410*, p. 145). **Lines 4, 6, 8, 12, 14, 16, and 18:** Assumed to be same as in 1949 (col. 10). **Line 10:** *439*, p. 97.

COLUMN 3–**Line 1:** Based on actual sales (line 2) and percentage of plan fulfilled (assumed to be same as for turnover tax, derived as 104.2% from plan of 118.1 bill. rubles in *301*, p. 252, and fulfillment of 123.1 bill. rubles given in *175*, p. 293). **Lines 2, 4-8, 10, 12, 14, 16, and 18:** Derived from cols. 1 and 2. **Line 3:** Based on actual sales (line 4) and percentage of plan fulfilled (assumed to be same as for turnover tax, derived as 95.1% from plan of 200.8 bill. rubles in *303*, p. 9, and fulfillment of 190.9 bill. rubles in *175*, p. 377). **Line 9:** Based on actual sales (line 10) and percentage of plan fulfilled (assumed to be same as for turnover tax, derived as 93.6% from plan of 262.2 bill. rubles in *173*, No. 2, 1949, p. 40, and fulfillment of 245.5 bill. rubles in *44*, No. 1, 1953, p. 27). **Line 11:** Based on actual sales (line 12) and percentage of plan fulfilled (assumed to be same as for turnover tax, derived as 98.7% from plan of 239.1 bill. rubles in *321*, pp. 23 and 36, and fulfillment of 236.1 bill. rubles in *55*, p. 10). **Line 13:** Based on actual sales (line 14) and percentage of plan fulfilled (assumed to be same as turnover tax, derived as 101.3% from plan of 244.7 bill. rubles in *55*, pp. 10 and 29, and fulfillment of 247.8 bill. rubles in *180*, 3/7/52, p. 2). **Line 15:** Based on actual sales (line 16) and percentage of plan fulfilled (assumed to be same as turnover tax, derived as 94.7% from plan of 260.7 bill. rubles in *180*, 3/7/52, p. 2, and 3/9/52, p. 3, and fulfillment of 246.9 bill. rubles in *285*, No. 6, 1954, p. 5). **Line 17:** Based on actual sales (line 18) and percentage of plan fulfilled (assumed to be same as turnover tax, derived as 101.3% from plan of 240.4 bill. rubles in *56*, p. 9, and fulfillment of 243.6 bill. rubles in *285*, No. 6, 1954, pp. 3–17).

Table C-10   Estimation of Collective Farm Market Sales to
Households, 1945–1953

	Sales on Urban Collective Farm Market (bill. rubles) (1)	Share of Sales to Households in Total Sales (per cent) (2)	Collective Farm Market Sales to Households (bill. rubles) (3)
1945	136.4	85	115.9
1946	164.8	85	140.1
1947	171.3	85	145.6
1948	47.7	85	40.5
1949	45.6	92.5	42.2
1950	49.2	95	46.7
1951	50.8	95	48.3
1952	53.7	95	51.0
1953	48.8	95	46.4

Source: Col. 1: Table C-3, line 10; col. 2, 1945–1948: taken as a little higher than the 1948 share derived from *410*, p. 148; col. 2, 1949–1953: *439*, p. 97; col. 3: derived from cols. 1 and 2.

Table C-11   Estimation of Housing Rentals, 1945–1953

	Housing Fund, Urban, Total (mill. m²) (1)	Housing Construction		Increase in Housing Stock (mill. m²) (4)	Annual Average Living Space (mill. m²) (5)	Rent (bill. rubles) (6)
		Excluding "Decentralized" (mill. m²) (2)	Including "Decentralized" (mill. m²) (3)			
1945					186	2.9
1946			17.4[a]	11.8	194	3.1
1947			18.2[a]	12.0	202	3.2
1948			21.1[a]	14.0	214	3.3
1949	317.2	15.5	17.5	14.0	222	3.5
1950	332.1	17.8	19.8	15.8	232	3.7
1951	348.0	18.7	20.7	16.6	244	3.9
1952	364.4	18.4	20.4	16.3	255	4.0
1953	381.9	21.4	23.4	18.7	267	4.2

Source: Cols. 1 and 2: *439*, p. 100; col. 3, 1946–1948: Table A-5, series 228; col. 3, 1949–1953: *439*, p. 100; col. 4, 1946–1948: based on col. 3 and share in it of increase in housing stock (estimated at two-thirds from *439*, p. 100); col. 4, 1949–1953: *439*, p. 100; col. 5, 1945–1948: based on 1949 living space and increase each year from 1945 to 1949 (assumed to be 70% of increase in housing stock in col. 4 from *439*, p. 101); col. 5, 1949–1953: *439*, p. 100; col. 6, 1945–1948: based on col. 5 and rental rate per m² (assumed to be 15.7 rubles per year, a little lower than the one accepted for 1949–1953); col. 6, 1949–1953: based on col. 5 and rental rate per m² (given as 15.84 rubles per year in *439*, p. 99).

Note: For more detail on rental rates, see *17*. The Soviet laws on this subject, which remained the same during 1949–1953, provide for a basic rate of 30–44 kopeks per m² (according to area) for people with wages up to 145 rubles. For every 10 rubles of wage above that level the rental rate rises by 3.3 kopeks per m² until a ceiling of 13.20 rubles per m².

a. Including reconstruction.

Table C-12   Estimation of Payments for Services, 1945–1953

	State and Cooperative Retail Trade Sales to Households (bill. rubles) (1)	Ratio of Payments for Services to Sales to Households (per cent) (2)	Payments for Services (bill. rubles) (3)
1945			
1. Planned	146.0	8	11.7
2. Actual	152.1	8	12.2
1946			
3. Planned	240.5	8	19.2
4. Actual	228.7	8	18.3
1947			
5. Planned	300.3	8	24.0
6. Actual	306.0	8	24.5
1948			
7. Planned	319.1	8	25.5
8. Actual	286.9	8	23.0
1949			
9. Planned	331.2	13.5	44.7
10. Actual	310.0	13.5	41.9
1950			
11. Planned	337.0	13.5	45.5
12. Actual	332.6	13.5	44.9
1951			
13. Planned	346.8	12.5	43.4
14. Actual	351.3	12.5	43.9
1952			
15. Planned	384.5	12.5	48.1
16. Actual	364.1	12.5	45.5
1953			
17. Planned	393.3	12.5	49.2
18. Actual	398.4	12.5	49.8

Source

COLUMN 1–All lines: Table C-9, col. 3.

COLUMN 2–Lines 1-7: Assumed to be same as in 1948 (line 8). Line 8: *410*, p. 157. Estimate. Lines 9-12: Ratio in 1951–1953 (lines 13–18) raised slightly since after 1951 some services were included in trade statistics. Lines 13-18: *439*, p. 105.

COLUMN 3–All lines: Derived from cols. 1 and 2.

Table C-13   Estimation of Trade Union Dues, 1945–1953

	Index of Payments for Trade Union Dues (1946 = 100) (1)	Fulfillment of Plan for Partial Wages and Salaries (per cent) (2)	Payments for Trade Union Dues (mill. rubles) (3)
1945			
1. Planned			856
2. Actual		102.7	879
1946			
3. Planned			1,028
4. Actual	100.0	108.8	1,119
1947			
5. Planned			1,516
6. Actual	139.5	103.0	1,561
1948			
7. Planned			1,636
8. Actual	150.1	102.7	1,680
1949			
9. Planned			2,062
10. Actual	189.6	102.9	2,122
1950			
11. Planned			2,431
12. Actual	222.7	102.5	2,492
1951			
13. Planned			2,792
14. Actual	251.3	100.7	2,812
1952			
15. Planned	292.5		3,273
16. Actual	273.5	101.8	3,060
1953			
17. Planned			3,126
18. Actual	285.0	102.0	3,189

Source

COLUMN 1–All lines: *46*, p. 13.

COLUMN 2–All lines: Calculated from Table C-1, line 3.

COLUMN 3–Lines 1, 3, 5, 7, 9, 11, 13, and 17: Based on actual dues in each year (lines 2, 4, 6, 8, 10, 12, 14, and 18) and percentage of fulfillment of plan for partial wages (col. 2). **Line 2:** Based on 1946 plan (line 3) and increase planned for 1946 (given as 17% in *260*, 3/2/46). **Line 4:** Based on 1949 dues (line 10) and index in col. 1. **Lines 6, 8, 12, 14, 15, 16, and 18:** Based on 1946 dues (line 4) and index in col. 1. **Line 10:** Based on trade union membership (given as 28.5 mill. in *439*, p. 103), average annual wage in national economy (given as 7,445 rubles in Table A-5, series 203), and dues per member (given as 1% of wages in *46*, p. 12).

Note: In 1946 total trade union receipts were 2.02 bill. rubles, but dues are paid not only by wage earners but also by scholarship holders, artists, and others. Payments in kind were made by MTS workers. Since these were very small sums, they have been ignored here.

Table C-14 Estimation of Direct Taxes, 1945–1953 (billion rubles)

	Taxes and Levies on Households (1)	Local Taxes and Levies		Miscellaneous Taxes		Net War Lottery Subscriptions (6)	Cash Donations to Patriotic Funds (7)	Total Direct Taxes (8)
		Total (2)	Amount Paid by Households (3)	Total (4)	Amount Paid by Households (5)			
1945								
1. Planned	45.3		3.2	8.6	4.3	3.8	0.5	57.1
2. Actual	39.8	6.3	3.2		4.3	3.8	0.5	51.6
1946								
3. Planned	23.4		3.1	15.9	8.0			34.5
4. Actual	22.7		3.1		8.0			33.8
1947								
5. Planned	27.7		3.0	14.3	7.1			37.2
6. Actual	28.0		3.0		7.1			38.3
1948								
7. Planned	31.1		2.9	11.6	5.8			39.8
8. Actual	33.1	5.7	2.9		5.8			41.8
1949								
9. Planned	36.5	6.7	3.4	12.5	6.3			46.2
10. Actual	33.7		3.4		6.3			43.4
1950								
11. Planned	36.4		3.4		6.7			46.5
12. Actual	35.8	6.7	3.4		6.7			45.9
1951								
13. Planned	43.4	7.2	3.6		7.0			54.0
14. Actual	42.9		3.6		7.0			53.5
1952								
15. Planned	47.4		4.0		7.1			58.5
16. Actual	47.4		4.0		7.1			58.5
1953								
17. Planned	46.1		4.1		7.2			57.4
18. Actual	46.1		4.1		7.2			57.4

Source

COLUMN 1–Line 1: *322*, p. 152. **Line 2:** *175*, p. 293. **Line 3:** *303*, p. 320. **Lines 4 and 5:** *319*, p. 14. **Lines 6 and 8:** *175*, p. 379. **Line 7:** *305*, p. 320. **Line 9:** *173*, No. 2, 1949, p. 40. **Lines 10, 12, and 14:** *44*, No. 1, 1953, p. 27. **Line 11:** *321*, p. 24. **Line 13:** *55*, pp. 10 and 35. **Line 15:** *180*, 3/7/52, p. 2. **Lines 16 and 18:** *285*, No. 6, 1954, pp. 3–17. **Line 17:** *56*, p. 10.

COLUMN 2: This category (*mestnye nalogy i sbory*) covers taxes on buildings and houses, ground rent, taxes on owners of means of transportation, taxes on theatrical performances, and taxes on seaside resorts, among others. These taxes are levied on individuals and economic organizations. **Line 2:** *175*, p. 293. **Lines 8 and 9:** *173*, No. 2, 1949, p. 40. **Line 12:** *82*, p. 22. **Line 13:** *199*, p. 70.

COLUMN 3–Lines 1, 3, 5, 7, 11, 15, and 17: Assumed to be same as actual taxes (lines 2, 4, 6, 8, 12, 16, and 18). **Lines 2, 8, 9, 12, and 13:** Assumed to be half of total local taxes and levies (col. 2), as in *410*, p. 172. **Lines 4 and 6:** Interpolated between cols. 2 and 8. **Lines 10 and 14:** Assumed to be same as planned taxes (lines 9 and 13). **Lines 16 and 18:** Extrapolated from lines 12 and 13.

COLUMN 4: This category—nontax revenues and miscellaneous fees (*nenalogovye dokhody i raznye sbory*)—covers notarial fees, receipts from the weights and measures administration, revenues from printing money, receipts from road inspection, television licenses, and consular fees, among others. **Line 1:** *301*, p. 253. **Line 3:** *303*, p. 321. **Line 5:** *304*, p. 260. **Line 7:** *305*, p. 321. . **Line 9:** *306*.

COLUMN 5–Lines 1, 3, 5, 7, and 9: Assumed to be half of total miscellaneous taxes. **Lines 2, 4, 6, 8, and 10:** Assumed to be same as planned taxes (lines 1, 3, 5, 7, and 9). **Lines 11, 13, 15, and 17:** Assumed to be same as actual taxes (lines 12, 14, 16, and 18). **Lines 12, 14, 16, and 18:** Extrapolated from lines 7 and 9.

COLUMN 6–Line 1: *301*, p. 253. **Line 2:** Assumed to be same as actual (line 1).

COLUMN 7–Line 1: Assumed to be same as planned (line 2). **Line 2:** *174*, p. 259.

COLUMN 8–All lines: Sum of cols. 1, 3, 5, 6, and 7.

Table C-15   Estimation of Increase in Savings and Loans, 1945–1953
(billion rubles)

	Total State Loans[a] (including increase in savings) (1)	Loans to Cooperatives, Collective Farms, and Communal Banks (2)	Loans to Households and Increase in Savings[b] (3)
1945			
1. Planned	31.5	1.89	29.61
2. Actual	29.0	1.6	27.4
1946			
3. Planned	25.5	1.4	24.1
4. Actual	24.7	1.4	23.3
1947			
5. Planned	22.2	1.2	21.0
6. Actual	25.7	1.2	24.5
1948			
7. Planned	23.1	1.05	22.05
8. Actual	23.9	1.05	22.85
1949			
9. Planned	23.1	.9	22.2
10. Actual	27.6	.9	26.7
1950			
11. Planned	31.8	.75	31.05
12. Actual	31.0	.75	30.25
1951			
13. Planned	33.4	.6	32.8
14. Actual	37.0	.6	36.4
1952			
15. Planned	42.6	.5	42.1
16. Actual	40.8	.5	40.3
1953			
17. Planned	28.4	.4	28.0
18. Actual	30.4	.4	30.0

Source

COLUMN 1–Line 1: *301*, p. 253. **Line 2:** *175*, p. 293. **Line 3:** *302*, p. 320. **Lines 4, 6, and 8:** *175*, p. 379. **Line 5:** *304*, p. 260. **Line 7:** *305*, p. 320. **Line 9:** *173*, No. 2, 1949, p. 40. **Lines 10, 12, and 14:** *44*, No. 1, 1955, p. 27. **Line 11:** *321*, p. 24. **Line 13:** *55*, p. 10. **Line 15:** *180*, 3/7/52, p. 2, and 3/9/52, p. 3. **Line 16:** Sum of state loans (given as 36.3 bill. rubles in *175*, p. 466) and increase in savings (derived as 4.5 bill. rubles from *175*, p. 491). **Line 17:** Estimated from actual (line 18) and plan fulfillment for savings (see *486*, June 1955, p. 648). **Line 18:** *175*, p. 488.

COLUMN 2–Lines 1 and 2: Based on col. 1 and the share of collective farms and cooperatives in total war loans (derived as 6% from payments by collective farms and industrial cooperatives of 5.4 bill. rubles, given in *174*, p. 292, and total war loans, given as 89.7 bill. rubles in *175*, p. 315). **Lines 3, 5, 7, 9, 11, 13, 15, and 17:** Assumed to be same as actual (lines 4, 6, 8, 10, 12, 14, 16, and 18). **Lines 4 and 6:** Assumed to be .2 bill. rubles lower than in preceding year (see note a below). **Lines 8, 10, 12, and 14:** Assumed to be .15 bill. rubles lower than in preceding year (see note a below). **Lines 16 and 18:** Assumed to be .1 bill. rubles lower than in preceding year.

COLUMN 3–All lines: Col. 1 minus col. 2.

a. The category "state loans" in the Soviet budget covers loans not only to households but also to cooperatives, collective farmers, and communal banks. Loans to the latter institutions decreased during the postwar years, and the difference between total loans and the loans to households comes largely from the increase in savings deposits (see *434*, April 1954, p. 404, and *486*, June 1955, p. 648).

b. Including voluntary insurance.

APPENDIX D

Retail Prices

Table D-1 Ration[a] Prices, State and Cooperative Retail Trade, 1940–1948

	Unit (1)	Weight (per cent) (2)	July 1940 Rubles (3)	Index (1940 = 100) (4)	January 1941 Rubles (5)	Index (1940 = 100) (6)	1942 Rubles (7)	Index (1940 = 100) (8)	1943 Rubles (9)	Index (1940 = 100) (10)	1944 Rubles (11)	Index (1940 = 100) (12)
1. Wheat bread, best-quality white	kg	3.6	1.70	100	1.70	100	(3.80)	223.5	(3.80)	223.5	3.80	223.5
2. Rye bread	kg	3.8	0.85	100	1.00	117.6	(1.00)	117.6	1.00	117.6	1.10	129.4
3. Wheat flour (30%)	kg	2.2	4.60[b]	100	4.60[b]	100	(4.60)	100	(4.60)	100	(4.60)	100
4. Macaroni	kg	2.1	6.10	100	6.10	100	(5.00)	82.0	(5.00)	82.0	(5.00)	82.0
5. Rice	kg	2.1	8.00	100	6.50	81.3	(6.50)	81.3	(6.50)	81.3	(6.50)	81.3
6. Bread, flour, and starches		13.8										
7. Potatoes	kg	2.5	0.90[e]	100	0.90[e]	100	(0.90)	100	0.90	100	0.90	100
8. Carrots	kg	0.4	2.00	100	1.50	75	(2.00)	100	2.00[f]	100	(2.00)	100
9. Onions	kg	0.4	1.30	100	3.00	230.8	(3.00)	230.8	3.00[f]	230.8	(3.00)	230.8
10. Apples	kg	0.6	6.40	100	10.00	156.3	(10.00)	156.3	(10.00)	156.3	(10.00)	156.3
11. Potatoes, vegetables, and fruit		3.9										
12. Beef	kg	3.4	20.80	100	20.80	100	(20.80)	100	14.00	67.3	14.00	67.3
13. Pork	kg	1.4	21.40	100	20.80	97.2	(14.00)	65.4	(14.00)	65.4	(14.00)	65.4
14. Lamb	kg	1.0	14.00[i]	100	14.00	100	(14.00)	100	14.00	100	(14.00)	100
15. Chicken	kg	0.7	14.00	100	14.00	100	(14.00)	100	18.00	128.6	(18.00)	128.6
16. Meat		6.5										
17. Fish, fresh[j]	kg	3.2	(12.00)	100	(12.00)	100	(12.00)	100	(12.00)	100	(12.00)	100
18. Eggs	10	2.0	8.50	100	7.50	88.2	(8.50)	100	8.50	100	(8.50)	100
19. Milk	liter	2.0	2.10	100	2.30	109.5	(2.30)	109.5	2.20	104.8	(2.20)	104.8
20. Butter	kg	1.9	28.00	100	28.00	100	(28.00)	100	26.00	92.9	28.00	100
21. Cheese	kg	1.9	25.30	100	25.30	100	(32.50)	128.5	(32.50)	128.5	(32.50)	128.5
22. Eggs and dairy products		7.8										
23. Bacon	kg	3.7	27.00[k]	100	27.00[k]	100	(27.00)	100	(27.00)	100	(27.00)	100
24. Oil and fats		3.7										
25. Sugar, lump	kg	2.6	5.50	100	5.50	100	(5.50)	100	(5.50)	100	5.50	100
26. Sugar, granulated	kg	2.5	5.00	100	5.00	100	(5.00)	100	(5.00)	100	(5.00)	100
27. Sugar		5.1										
28. Tea	kg	1.7	100.00	100	100.00	100	(100.00)	100	(100.00)	100	(100.00)	100
29. Coffee	kg	0.4	48.20	100	49.00	101.7	(49.00)	101.7	(49.00)	101.7	(49.00)	101.7
30. Tea and coffee		2.1										
31. Food products excluding alcoholic beverages		46.1										

| 1945 | | 1946 | | | | 1947 | | | | 1948 | | |
| | | Up to Sept. 15 | | After Sept. 15 | | Up to Dec. 15 | | After Dec. 15 | | | | |
Rubles (13)	Index (1940 = 100) (14)	Rubles (15)	Index (1940 = 100) (16)	Rubles (17)	Index (1940 = 100) (18)	Rubles (19)	Index (1940 = 100) (20)	Rubles (21)	Index (1940 = 100) (22)	Rubles (23)	Index (1940 = 100) (24)	Line No.
3.80	223.5	3.80	223.5	11.25	661.8	11.25	661.8	7.00	411.8	7.00	411.8	1
1.10	129.4	1.10	129.4	3.40	400.0	3.40	400.0	3.00	352.9	3.00	352.9	2
(4.60)	100	4.60[b]	100	13.00	282.6	(13.00)	282.6	8.00	173.9	8.00	173.9	3
(5.00)	82.0	5.00[c]	82.0	15.50[d]	254.1	15.50[d]	254.1	10.00	163.9	10.00	163.9	4
(6.50)	81.3	6.50[b]	81.3	19.00[b]	237.5	(19.00)	237.5	15.40	192.5	15.40	192.5	5
												6
0.90	100	0.90	100	0.90	100	0.90	100	1.20	133.3	1.00	111.1	7
(2.00)	100	(2.00)	100	(2.00)	100	(2.00)	100	1.50	75.0	1.50	75.0	8
(3.00)	230.8	(3.00)	230.8	4.00[g]	307.7	(4.00)	307.7	3.00	230.8	3.00	230.8	9
(10.00)	156.3	(10.00)	156.3	20.00[h]	312.5	(20.00)	312.5	18.00	281.3	18.00	281.3	10
												11
14.00	67.3	14.00	67.3	30.00	144.2	30.00	144.2	35.55	170.9	35.55	170.9	12
(14.00)	65.4	14.00	65.4	34.00	158.9	(34.00)	158.9	48.00	224.3	48.00	224.3	13
14.00	100	14.00	100	34.00	242.9	(34.00)	242.9	34.00	242.9	34.00	242.9	14
16.00	114.3	14.00	100	37.00	264.3	(37.00)	264.3	36.00	257.1	36.00	257.1	15
												16
(12.00)	100	12.00	100	33.00	275	(33.00)	275	(33.00)	275	(33.00)	275	17
6.50	76.5	6.50	76.5	6.50	76.5	8.50	100	14.00	164.7	14.00	164.7	18
2.20	104.8	3.50	166.7	8.00	381.0	8.00	381.0	3.50	166.7	3.50	166.7	19
28.00	100	28.00	100	66.00	235.7	64.00	228.6	70.00	250	70.00	250	20
(32.50)	128.5	32.50	128.5	70.00	276.7	(62.50)	247.0	62.50	247.0	62.50	247.0	21
												22
(27.00)	100	27.00	100	55.00	203.7	(55.00)	203.7	44.80	165.9	44.80	165.9	23
												24
5.50	100	5.50	100	15.00	272.7	(15.00)	272.7	15.00	272.7	15.00	272.7	25
(5.00)	100	5.00	100	13.40	268.0	(13.40)	268.0	13.50	270.0	13.50	270.0	26
												27
(100.00)	100	80.00	80	90.00	90	100.00	100	160.00	160	160.00	160	28
(49.00)	101.7	(49.00)	101.7	(75.00)	155.6	(75.00)	155.6	75.00	155.6	75.00	155.6	29
												30

31

Table D-1 *continued*

	Unit (1)	Weight (per cent) (2)	July 1940 Rubles (3)	Index (1940 = 100) (4)	January 1941 Rubles (5)	Index (1940 = 100) (6)	1942 Rubles (7)	Index (1940 = 100) (8)	1943 Rubles (9)	Index (1940 = 100) (10)	1944 Rubles (11)	Index (1940 = 100) (12)
32. Vodka	liter	12.3	20.00	100	20.00	100	124.40	622	(124.40)	622	(124.40)	622
33. Alcoholic beverages		12.3										
34. Cigarettes	25	0.8	3.40	100	3.40	100	(3.40)	100	(3.40)	100	(6.00)	176.5
35. Low-grade tobacco (*makhorka*)	50 g	0.8	0.50	100	0.50	100	(0.50)	100	(0.50)	100	(0.88)	176.0
36. Tobacco and products		1.6										
37. Suit, men's wool	1	3.7	1,130	100	1,130	100	(1,130)	100	(1,130)	100	(1,130)	100
38. Dress, women's cotton	1	3.7	62.50	100	62.50	100	(62.50)	100	(62.50)	100	(62.50)	100
39. Overcoat, men's winter	1	3.7	(725)ᵐ	100	725	100	(725)	100	(725)	10	(725)	100
40. Socks, men's cotton	pr	3.7	5.00	100	5.00	100	(5.00)	100	(5.00)	100	(5.00)	100
41. Clothing		14.8										
42. Shoes, men's leather	pr	6.2	280	100	280	100	(280)	100	(280)	100	(280)	100
43. Shoes		6.2										
44. Soap, household	kg	2.6	3.10	100	3.10	100	(3.10)	100	(3.10)	100	(3.10)	100
45. Upkeep and toilet articles		2.6										
46. Crockery	plate	1.7	3.50	100	3.50	100	(3.50)	100	(3.50)	100	(3.50)	100
47. Tin pail	1	1.8	10.80	100	10.80	100	(10.80)	100	(10.80)	100	(10.80)	100
48. Household articles and furnishings		3.5										
49. Newspaper, daily	1	0.5	0.10	100	0.10	100	0.15	150	0.20	200	0.20	200
50. Books and newspapers		0.5										
51. Camera	1	0.9	1,100	100	1,100	100	(1,100)	100	(1,100)	100	(1,100)	100
52. Watch, pocket	1	0.4	300	100	300	100	(300)	100	(300)	100	(300)	100
53. Electric bulb	1	0.4	1.60	100	1.60	100	(1.60)	100	(1.60)	100	(1.60)	100
54. Appliances		1.7										
55. Manufactured goods, excluding tobacco		29.3										

1945		1946 Up to Sept. 15		1946 After Sept. 15		1947 Up to Dec. 15		1947 After Dec. 15		1948		Line No.
Rubles (13)	Index (1940 = 100) (14)	Rubles (15)	Index (1940 = 100) (16)	Rubles (17)	Index (1940 = 100) (18)	Rubles (19)	Index (1940 = 100) (20)	Rubles (21)	Index (1940 = 100) (22)	Rubles (23)	Index (1940 = 100) (24)	
(124.40)	622	120.00	600	(120.00)	600	(120.00)	600	120.00	600	96.00	480	32
												33
(6.00)	176.5	6.00	176.5	(6.00)	176.5	(6.00)	176.5	6.30	185.3	5.70	167.6	34
(0.88)	176.0	0.88[1]	176.0	(2.20)	440.0	(2.20)	440.0	2.20	440.0	2.20	440.0	35
												36
(1,130)	100	(1,130)	100	800	70.8	(800)	70.8	1,400	123.9	1,400	123.9	37
(62.50)	100	(62.50)	100	(77.00)	123.2	(77.00)	123.2	77.00	123.2	77.00	123.2	38
(725)	100	(725)	100	1,000	137.9	(1,000)	137.9	986	136.0	986	136.0	39
(5.00)	100	(5.00)	100	8.25	165.0	(8.25)	165.0	6.00	120.0	6.00	120.0	40
												41
(280)	100	(280)	100	270[n]	96.4	(270)	96.4	260	92.9	260	92.9	42
												43
(3.10)	100	(3.10)	100	(13.00)	419.4	(13.00)	419.4	13.00	419.4	13.00	419.4	44
												45
(3.50)	100	(3.50)	100	(7.80)	222.9	(7.80)	222.9	7.80	222.9	7.80	222.9	46
(10.80)	100	(10.80)	100	(14.50)	134.3	(14.50)	134.3	14.50	134.3	14.50	134.3	47
												48
0.20	200	0.20	200	0.20	200	0.20	200	0.20	200	0.20	200	49
												50
(1,100)	100	(1,100)	100	(1,100)	100	(1,100)	100	1,100	100	1,100	100	51
(300)	100	(300)	100	(568)	189.3	(568)	189.3	568	189.3	500	166.7	52
(1.60)	100	(1.60)	100	(2.40)	150	(2.40)	150	2.40	150	2.40	150	53
												54

55

Table D-1 *continued*

	Unit (1)	Weight (per cent) (2)	July 1940		January 1941		1942		1943		1944	
			Rubles (3)	Index (1940 = 100) (4)	Rubles (5)	Index (1940 = 100) (6)	Rubles (7)	Index (1940 = 100) (8)	Rubles (9)	Index (1940 = 100) (10)	Rubles (11)	Index (1940 = 100) (12)
56. Coal	m. ton	2.9	60.00	100	60.00	100	(60.00)	100	(60.00)	100	(60.00)	100
57. Oil	liter	1.4	0.65	100	0.65	100	(0.65)	100	(0.65)	100	(0.65)	100
58. Electricity, domestic use	kwh	1.4	0.25	100	0.25	100	(0.25)	100	(0.25)	100	(0.25)	100
59. Heating and lighting		5.7										
60. Rent, housing space	m²	2.4	1.11	100	1.11	100	(1.11)	100	(1.11)	100	(1.11)	100
61. Movies	ticket	0.5	3.00	100	3.00	100	(3.00)	100	(3.00)	100	(3.00)	100
62. Railroad trip	200 km	0.7	16.70	100	16.70	100	(16.70)	100	(16.70)	100	(16.70)	100
63. Postage, domestic	letter	0.7	0.30	100	0.30	100	(0.30)	100	(0.30)	100	(0.30)	100
64. Streetcar	trip	0.7	0.15	100	0.15	100	(0.15)	100	(0.15)	100	(0.15)	100
65. Services		5.0										
66. Total		100.0										

Note: Figures in parentheses are estimates made on the assumption (for lack of any precise data) that prices did not change between one year and the next.

Source

Col. 2: Based on weights calculated in my article (*496* and *495*, pp. 16–18) with the following changes. Meals in factory restaurants (canteens) were omitted for lack of data on wartime prices and their weight (28.2% of total foods excluding alcoholic beverages) was reapportioned among food products; the weight of alcoholic beverages was increased from 2.7 to 12.3% at the expense of food products. Electric bulbs were changed from the category of heating and lighting to the category of appliances. The total number of goods included here is smaller than that included in my article (46 as opposed to 83), but the weights of the subgroups were kept unchanged and the weights of the missing products were reapportioned among the remaining products in each subgroup.

Cols. 3, 5, 21, and 23: Unless otherwise indicated, *496*, p. 376.

Cols. 6, 8 ,10, 12, 14, 16, 18, 20, 22, and 24: Cols. 5, 7, 9, 11, 13, 15, 17, 19, 21, and 23, respectively, as per cent of col. 3.

Cols. 7, 9, 11, 13, 15, 17, and 19: Unless otherwise indicated, Table D-3.

a. Including prices of unrationed goods sold regularly in state and cooperative trade.

b. *459*, p. 32. For line 3, the highest price found for flour has been used here rather than the price (2.90 rubles) used in my article (*495*, pp. 68–69) since there was no way to check on the quality of the flour.

	1945		1946 Up to Sept. 15		1946 After Sept. 15		1947 Up to Dec. 15		1947 After Dec. 15		1948		Line No.
Rubles (13)	Index (1940 = 100) (14)	Rubles (15)	Index (1940 = 100) (16)	Rubles (17)	Index (1940 = 100) (18)	Rubles (19)	Index (1940 = 100) (20)	Rubles (21)	Index (1940 = 100) (22)	Rubles (23)	Index (1940 = 100) (24)	
(60.00)	100	(60.00)	100	(60.00)	100	(60.00)	100	60.00	100	60.00	100	56
(0.65)	100	(0.65)	100	(2.00)	307.7	(2.00)	307.7	2.00	307.7	2.00	307.7	57
(0.25)	100	(0.25)	100	(0.25)	100	(0.25)	100	0.25	100	0.25	100	58
												59
(1.11)	100	(1.11)	100	(1.26)	113.5	(1.26)	113.5	1.26	113.5	1.28	115.3	60
(3.00)	100	(3.00)	100	(5.00)	166.7	(5.00)	166.7	5.00	166.7	5.00	166.7	61
(16.70)	100	(16.70)	100	(27.00)	161.7	(27.00)	161.7	27.00	161.7	27.00	161.7	62
(0.30)	100	(0.30)	100	(0.30)	100	(0.30)	100	0.30	100	0.30	100	63
(0.15)	100	(0.15)	100	(0.15)	100	(0.15)	100	0.15	100	0.15	100	64
												65
												66

c. *415*, No. 7, 1947, p. 17.

d. *415*, No. 8, 1947, p. 11.

e. Price during the war (Table D-3). The prices used in my article (*496*, p. 376) of 1.20 rubles for July 1940 and 1.00 rubles for January 1941 were not used here in order not to show a drop in prices during the war, which seems very unlikely.

f. *415*, No. 4, 1946, pp. 24–25. Given as prices paid by diplomats in special stores but they are the same as ration prices.

g. Estimated according to general increase in prices in rationed state and cooperative trade.

h. Increase estimated in line with price after 12/15/47.

i. Given for January 1941 (*496*, p. 376), but, in view of wartime prices, it seems more appropriate than the price of 18.00 rubles given for April 1940 (*496*, p. 376).

j. Since no information on prices of frozen and salted fish used in my article (*496*, p. 376) was available for the war years, we have used the series on fresh fish here (given in Table D-3), which seems to be homogeneous.

k. Given for January 1941 (*459*, p. 32). These prices have been used here rather than the ones in my article (*496*, p. 376) because they correspond better with the wartime and postwar prices.

l. Based on price after 9/15/46 (col. 17) and estimated increase of 150% (derived from *459*, p. 32, which gives an unweighted average price increase of 166% for 14 food products between September 1 and October 1946).

m. Price of 999.20 rubles used in my article (*496*, p. 376) was not used in order not to show a substantial drop in price during the war, which seems very unlikely.

n. *459*, p. 35.

Table D-2 Commercial Prices, State and Cooperative Retail Trade, Moscow, 1944–1947

| | | | | | | | 1946 | | | | | |
| | | | 1944 | | 1945 | | Up to Sept. 15 | | After Sept. 15 | | Dec. 14, 1947 | |
	Unit (1)	Weight (per cent) (2)	Rubles (3)	Index (1940 = 100) (4)	Rubles (5)	Index (1940 = 100) (6)	Rubles (7)	Index (1940 = 100) (8)	Rubles (9)	Index (1940 = 100) (10)	Rubles (11)	Index (1940 = 100) (12)
1. Wheat bread, best-quality white	kg	4.6	275	16,176	175	10,294	50	2,941	46	2,706	20.00[a]	1,176
2. Rye bread	kg	4.8	55[b]	6,471	35[b]	4,118	10.00	1,176	7.50	882	(7.50)	882
3. Wheat flour	kg	2.2	140	4,828[c]	90[d]	3,103[c]	35.00	1,207[c]	24.00	828[c]	(24.00)	828[c]
4. Rice	kg	2.2	385[b]	4,813	245[b]	3,063	70.00[e]	875	45.00[e]	563	(45.00)	563
5. Bread, flour, and starches		13.8										
6. Potatoes	kg	3.9	144[f]	16,000	90[g]	10,000	27[g]	3,000	24[g]	2,667	(4.00)	444
7. Potatoes, vegetables, and fruit		3.9										
8. Beef	kg	3.7	320	1,538	220	1,058	140	673	90	433	(90)	433
9. Pork	kg	1.8	500	2,336	425	1,986	300	1,402	130	607	(130)	607
10. Chicken	kg	1.0	350	2,500	290	2,071	190	1,357	95	679	(95)	679
11. Meat		6.5										
12. Fish, fresh	kg	3.2	270[h]	2,250	180[i]	1,500	80	667	40	333	(40)	333
13. Eggs	10	2.0	200	2,353	100	1,176	100	1,176	50	588	(50)	588
14. Milk	liter	2.0	55	2,619	40	1,905	40	1,905	20	952	(20)	952
15. Butter	kg	1.9	800	2,857	540	1,929	400	1,429	240	857	(240)	857
16. Cheese	kg	1.9	485	1,917	370	1,462	215	850	170	672	(170)	672
17. Eggs and dairy products		7.8										
18. Bacon	kg	3.7	1,333[j]	4,937	1,133[j]	4,196	800	2,963	400	1,481	(400)	1,481
19. Oil and fats		3.7										
20. Sugar, lump	kg	5.1	750	13,636	500	9,091	170	3,091	70	1,273	(70)	1,273
21. Tea	kg	2.1	700	700	650	650	350	350	380	380	(380)	380
22. Tea and coffee		2.1										
23. Food products excluding alcoholic beverages		46.1										
24. Vodka	liter	12.3	500	2,500	180	900	130	650	120	600	(120)	600
25. Alcoholic beverages		12.3										
26. Cigarettes	25	1.6	60	1,765	50	1,471	30[k]	882	27[l]	794	(27)	794
27. Tobacco and products		1.6										
28. Suit, men's wool	1	3.7	4,000	354	3,760[m]	333	3,500	310	3,000	265	2,000	177

Table D-2 *continued*

	Unit (1)	Weight (per cent) (2)	1944 Rubles (3)	1944 Index 1940 = 100) (4)	1945 Rubles (5)	1945 Index 1940 = 100) (6)	1946 Up to Sept. 15 Rubles (7)	1946 Up to Sept. 15 Index 1940 = 100) (8)	1946 After Sept. 15 Rubles (9)	1946 After Sept. 15 Index 1940 = 100) (10)	Dec. 14, 1947 Rubles (11)	Dec. 14, 1947 Index 1940 = 100) (12)
29. Overcoat, men's winter	1	3.7	(7,000)	966	(7,000)	966	7,000[n]	966	5,050	697	4,000	552
30. Stockings, women's cotton[o]	pr	3.7	280	3,415	263[p]	3,207	150[q]	1,829	100	1,220	(100)	1,220
31. Socks, men's cotton	pr	3.7	120	2,400	113[p]	2,260	62[q]	1,240	45	900	(45)	900
32. Clothing		14.8										
33. Shoes, women's good-quality[r]	pr	6.2	(4,700)	1,066	4,700[s]	1,066	(2,000)	454	(2,000)	454	2,000[t]	454
34. Shoes		6.2										
35. Soap, household	kg	6.1	100	3,226	100	3,226	60[u]	1,935	54[v]	1,742	27.50	887
36. Upkeep and toilet articles[w]		6.1										
37. Newspaper, daily[x]	1	0.5	0.20	200	0.20	200	0.20	200	0.20	200	0.20	200
38. Books and newspapers		0.5										
39. Electric bulb[y]	1	1.7	50	3,125	47[p]	2,938	28.20[u]	1,763	25.40[v]	1,588	(25.40)	1,588
40. Appliances[y]		1.7										
41. Manufactured goods, excluding tobacco		29.3										
42. Sales in "commercial" shops excluding heating and lighting		89.3										

Note: Figures in parentheses are estimates made on the assumption (for lack of any precise data) that prices did not change between one year and the next.

Source

Col. 2: The weights in Table D-1 have been used here for the subgroups. In cases when certain products included in Table D-1 were excluded here for lack of data, the weights of these products were reapportioned among the remaining products of the subgroup.

Cols. 3, 5, 7, 9, and 11: Unless otherwise indicated, Table D-4.

Cols. 4, 6, 8, 10, and 12: Unless otherwise indicated, cols. 3, 5, 7, 9, and 11, respectively, as per cent of Table D-1, col. 3.

a. Estimated from the statement (in *191*, p. 435) that the new price announced on 12/15/47 when rationing was abolished (7.00 rubles in Table D-1, line 1, col. 21) "was more than two and a half times lower than" (taken as 35% of) the commercial price in effect at that time.

Table D-2 *continued*

b. Extrapolated from price in 1946 (col. 7) and evolution of prices for wheat bread between 1944 and 9/14/46.

c. 1940 price of 2.90 rubles (given in *495*, pp. 68–69, for a lower-quality flour than that used in Table D-1) used to calculate indexes here since only lower-quality flour was available in commercial stores during these years.

d. Extrapolated from price in 1944 (col. 3) and evolution of prices for wheat bread between 1944 and 1945.

e. *459*, p. 32.

f. Estimated roughly as slightly lower than 1943 price on collective farm market (given as ranging from 14 to 300 rubles in *124*, p. 232).

g. Extrapolated roughly from 1944 price (col. 3) and evolution for prices of wheat bread betweeen 1944 and 1946.

h. Estimated at two-thirds the price of herring (given as 350–450 rubles for April 1944 in *415*, No. 4, 1946, pp. 24–25).

i. Estimated at two-thirds the price of herring (given as 270–300 in *415*, No. 4, 1946, pp. 24–25).

j. Extrapolated from price in 1946 (col. 7) and evolution of prices of pork between 1944 and 1946.

k. Estimated from 1945 price (col. 5) and decrease between 1945 and 1946 (assumed to be same as reduction of 40% for manufactured goods on 7/1/46, given in *459*, p. 34).

l. Estimated from price before 9/15/46 (col. 7) and decrease after that (assumed to be same as average reduction of 10% for manufactured goods in September 1946 given in *459*, p. 34).

m. Estimated from 1944 price (col. 3) and decrease in 1945 (assumed to be same as general reduction of 6% in Moscow on 2/27/45 in "commercial" stores, given in *174*, p. 262).

n. Estimated arbitrarily as a little lower than the price that would be derived by applying the average 40% reduction of 7/1/46 for manufactured goods (given in *459*, p. 34).

o. Replaces women's cotton dress, which was used in Table D-1. The 1940 price of 8.20 rubles (*496*, p. 378) was used to calculate the indexes in cols. 4, 6, 8, 10, and 12.

p. Estimated from 1944 price (col. 3) and decrease in 1945 (taken as 6% as in note m above).

q. Estimated from 1945 price (col. 5) and decrease on 7/1/46 (given as 43% for clothing in *415*, No. 6, 1946, p. 20).

r. Replaces men's leather shoes, which was used in Table D-1. The 1940 price of 441 rubles (*496*, p. 378) was used to calculate the indexes in cols. 4, 6, 8, 10, and 12.

s. Estimated from 1946 price (col. 9) and decrease between 1945 and 9/16/46 (derived as 57.5%, sum of 42% reduction for shoes on 7/1/46, given in *415*, No. 6, 1946, p. 20, and 15.5% reduction for women's good-quality shoes in September 1946, arbitrarily increased from 10% reduction given for shoes in *459*, p. 34).

t. Estimated at lower end of range of prices for unspecified shoes in Table D-4, line 51, col. 5.

u. Estimated from 1945 price (col. 5) and decrease in 1946 (assumed to be same as average reduction of 40% for manufactured goods on 7/1/46 given in *459*, p. 34).

v. Estimated from price up to 9/15/46 (col. 7) and decrease in September 1946 (given as an average of 10% for manufactured goods in *459*, p. 34).

w. Since no data were available on prices of any items included in the subgroup "household articles and furnishings" in Table D-1, the weight of that subgroup was added to that of "upkeep and toilet articles" here.

x. The prices given here for the daily newspaper (*Pravda*) are the same as those given in Table D-1. Books and newspapers were included in manufactured goods in Table D-1 and it seemed preferable to keep them there in Table D-2 also.

y. For lack of any data on other appliances, the weight for the subgroup "appliances" is applied to electric bulbs alone.

Table D-3 Basic Ration Prices, State and Cooperative Retail Trade, Moscow, 1942–1947 (rubles)

	Unit	1942 (1)	1943 (2)	1944 (3)	1945 (4)	1946 Up to Sept. 15 (5)	1946 After Sept. 15 (6)	1947 (up to Dec. 15) (7)
Wheat bread, white								
1.	kg		3.80	3.80 (1st qual.)	3.80	3.80	11.25	11.25 (1st qual.)
2.	kg			2.80 (2nd qual.)	2.80	2.80 (1st qual.)	8.00	8.00 (2nd qual.)
3.	kg					1.70 (2nd qual.)	11	
4.	kg						5.00	
Rye bread								
5.	kg		1	1.10	1.10	1.00	3.40	3.40
6.	kg					1.10		
Wheat flour								
7.	kg					2.90	13.50	
8.	kg					4.60	13.00	
Potatoes								
9.	kg		.90	.90	.90	.90	.90	.90
Beef								
10.	kg		14.00	14.00	14.00	12	30.00	30.00
11.	kg		14–15		14–15	14.00	28	
12.	kg					14–28	46	
13.	kg						30–46	
Pork								
14.	kg					14	34.00	
15.	kg					12.00	45–48	
16.	kg						48	
Lamb								
17.	kg		14		14–18	14.00	34.00	
Chicken								
18.	kg		18		14–18	14.00	37.00	
Fish, fresh								
19.	kg					2.75–4.95	33	
20.	kg					12	40	
Eggs								
21.	10		6.50–8.50		6.50	6.50	6.50	8.50
22.	10						8.50	
Milk								
23.	liter		2.20		2.20	3.50	2.20	8.00
24.	liter					2.50	8.00	
Butter								
25.	kg		26	28.00	26.00–28.00	28.00	66.00	64.00
26.	kg		20–25		28	26.00	64.00	
27.	kg				26		64–66.00	
28.	kg						66–75.00	
Cheese								
29.	kg					29	70	
30.	kg					32.50	76	
Bacon								
31.	kg					27.00	55.00	
Sugar, lump								
32.	kg			5.50	5.50	5	13.40	
33.	kg					5.50	15.00	
Tea								
34.	kg					80.00	90.00	100.00
Vodka								
35.	liter	124.40				120.00		
Cigarettes								
36.	25					3–6		

Table D-3   *continued*

	Unit	1942 (1)	1943 (2)	1944 (3)	1945 (4)	Up to Sept. 15 (5)	After Sept. 15 (6)	1947 (up to Dec. 15) (7)
						1946		
Suit, men's wool 37.	1						800	
Overcoat, men's winter 38.	1						1000	
Stockings, women's cotton 39.	pr						33ᵃ	
Socks, men's cotton 40.	pr						8.25	
Shoes, women's good-quality 41.	pr						275	
Newspaper, dailyᵇ 42.	1	0.15	0.20	0.20	0.20	0.20	0.20	0.20

Source (unless otherwise indicated)

COLUMN 1–Line 35: Based on Jan. 1941 price (given as 20.00 rubles per liter in *496*, p. 377) and increase between June 1941 and fourth quarter of 1942 (given as 522% in *124*, p. 229).

COLUMN 2–Lines 1, 9-10, 17-18, 21, 23, and 25: *415*, No. 4, 1946, pp. 24–25. Given as prices paid by diplomats in special stores but they are the same as basic ration prices. Lines 5, 11, and 26: *415*, No. 6, 1946, p. 21. For line 11, given for meat without further specification.

COLUMN 3–Lines 1-2, 5, 9-10, and 32: *475*, p. 440. For lines 2, 10, and 32, also *459*, p. 34, and *478*, p. 222. **Lines 9 and 32:** *478*, p. 222. For line 32, also *459*, p. 34, and *475*, p. 440. **Line 25:** *459*, p. 34. Also, *475*, p. 440; *478*, p. 222; and *457*, p.178.

COLUMN 4–Lines 1, 9-10, 17-18, 21, 23, and 25: *415*, No. 4, 1946, pp. 24–25. See note to col. 2, line 1, above. For line 10, also *475*, p. 440; *459*, p. 34; and *478*, p. 222. For line 25, also *478*, p. 222. **Lines 2, 26, and 32:** *459*, p. 34. For lines 2 and 32, also *478*, p. 222. **Lines 5, 11, and 27:** *415*, No. 6, 1946, p. 21. For line 11, given simply for meat.

COLUMN 5–Lines 1, 9, 17, 21, 23, and 25: *415*, No. 4, 1946, pp. 24–25. See note to col. 2, line 1, above. For line 1, also *478*, p. 220; *415*, No. 8, 1947, p. 11; and *459*, p. 32. For line 9, also *415*, No. 8, 1947, p. 11. For line 17, also *415*, No. 7, 1947, p. 17; *457*, p. 178; *459*, p. 32; and *478*, p. 220. For line 21, also *415*, No. 3, 1946, p. 28. For line 25, also *459*, pp. 32 and 34; *478*, p. 220; *457*, p. 178; and *415*, No. 8, 1947, p. 11. **Lines 2-3:** *415*, No. 3, 1946, p. 28. For line 2, also *459*, p. 34. For line 3, also *415*, No. 6, 1946, p. 21. **Line 5:** *457*, p. 178. Also, *415*, No. 3, 1946, p. 28; *478*, p. 220; *415*, No. 8, 1947, p. 11; and *459*, p. 32. **Lines 6-7, 26, and 30:** *415*, No. 6, 1946, p. 21. For line 7, given for flour without further specification. For line 7, also *415*, No. 8, 1947, p. 11 (for unspecified flour). For line 30, given for cheese without further specification. **Lines 8, 15, 18, 31, and 33:** *478*, p. 220. Also, *459*, pp. 32 and 34. For line 33, also *415*, No. 8, 1947, p. 11. **Lines 10, 14, and 32:** *415*, No. 7, 1947, p. 17. For line 10, also *478*, p. 220. For line 32, given for sugar without further specification. **Lines 11 and 24:** *459*, pp. 32 and 34. Also, *478*, pp. 220 and 222. **Line 12:** *457*, p. 178. Also, *415*, No. 8, 1947, p. 11. **Lines 19 and 35-36:** *415*, No. 3, 1946, p. 28. **Lines 20, 29, and 34:** *415*, No. 8, 1947, p. 11. For line 29, given for cheese without further specification.

COLUMN 6–Lines 1-2, 5, 26, and 33: *475*, p. 440. For line 1, also *415*, No. 8, 1947, p. 11; *478*, p. 220; and *459*, p. 32. For line 2, also *459*, p. 34, and *478*, p. 222. For line 5, also *478*, p. 220, and *415*, No. 3, 1946, p. 28, and No. 6, 1946, p. 21. For line 33, given for sugar without further specification; also *478*, p. 220, and *459*, pp. 32 and 34. **Lines 4, 7, and 29:** *415*, No. 6, 1946, p. 21. For line 7, given for flour without further specification; also *415*, No. 8, 1947, p. 11. For line 29, given for cheese without further specification. **Lines 8, 14, 18, 25, and 31:** *478*, p. 220. Also, *459*, pp. 32 and 34 (for 30% flour). **Line 9:** *415*, No. 4, 1946, pp. 24–25. See note to col. 2, line 1, above. Also, *415*, No. 8, 1947, p. 11. **Lines 10, 20, 24, and 37-41:** *459*, pp. 32, 34, and 35. For line 10, also *475*, p. 440. For lines 10 and 24, also *478*, p. 220. **Lines 11, 16-17, and 32:** *415*, No. 7, 1947, p. 17. For line 16, also *415*, No. 8, 1947, p. 11. For line 17, also *457*, p. 178; *478*, p. 220; and *459*, p. 32. For line 32, given for sugar without further specification. **Lines 13, 15, 19, 21, 23, and 34:** *415*, No. 8, 1947, p. 11. For line 30, given for cheese without further specification. **Lines 3, 12, 28, 30, and 27:** *457*, p. 178. For line 19, also *415*, No. 8, 1947, p. 11. **Line 22:** *415*, No. 3, 1946, p. 28.

COLUMN 7–Lines 1-2, 5, 9, 21, 23, 25, and 34: *475*, p. 437. For first quarter of 1947. Line 10: *415*, No. 3, 1946, p. 28.

a. Silk stockings.
b. Price of *Pravda*.

Table D-4   Basic Commercial Prices, State and Cooperative Retail Trade, Moscow, 1944–1947 [a] (rubles)

	Unit	1944 (1)	1945 (2)	1946 Up to Sept. 15 (3)	1946 After Sept. 15 (4)	1947 (up to Dec. 15) (5)
Wheat bread, white						
1.	kg	200–275	150–200	50	60	
2.	kg	140		18.20	12.50	
3.	kg	275		30	46	
Rye bread						
4.	kg			10.15	7.50	
5.	kg			10.00		
Wheat flour						
6.	kg			35.00	24.00	
7.	kg			37.00		
Potatoes						
8.	kg				4	
Beef						
9.	kg	320	220	170	90	
10.	kg			140	80–90	
11.	kg			120		
12.	kg			50–120		
Pork						
13.	kg	500–600	500	300–320	130	
14.	kg	500	350	255–270		
15.	kg			300		
Chicken						
16.	kg	700	320	180–200	95	
17.	kg	350	260	180	195	
18.	kg			200		
Herring						
19.	kg	350–450	270–300			
20.	kg	280–420				
Fish, fresh						
21.	kg			80	40	
Eggs						
22.	10	200	100	90–110	45	
23.	10	150–200			50	
Milk						
24.	liter	60	40	40	20	
25.	liter	50	30			
Butter						
26.	kg	950–1000	650	400	240	100
27.	kg	800	540	246	140	
28.	kg	750–800	500–540	210	230	
Cheese						
29.	kg	400–750	350–500	170–350	130	
30.	kg	410–560	320–420	140–290	170	
31.	kg			192		
32.	kg			270		
Bacon						
33.	kg			800	400	
Sugar, lump						
34.	kg	800	650	250	70	
35.	kg	750	450	220	75	
36.	kg	700–740	500	170		
37.	kg			150		

Table D-4   *continued*

	Unit	1944 (1)	1945 (2)	1946		1947 (up to Dec. 15) (5)
				Up to Sept. 15 (3)	After Sept. 15 (4)	
Tea						
38.	kg	400–800	600–700	520–720	380	
39.	kg	700–800	700	350	550	
40.	kg			380		
Vodka						
41.	liter	400–640	210	150	120	
42.	liter	340–460	160	110		
Cigarettes						
43.	25	35–90	25–75			
44.	25	35–40				
Suit, men's wool						
45.	1	3000–5000		3500–5000	3000	2000–5000
46.	1					2000
Overcoat, men's winter						
47.	1				5050	4000
Stockings, women's cotton						
48.	pair	260–280			100[b]	
49.	pair	280				
Socks, men's cotton						
50.	pair	120		120–270	45	100
Shoes, women's good-quality						
51.	pair				1700	1500–3000
Soap, household						
52.	kg	50–150		50–150		25–30
Daily newspaper[c]						
53.	1	0.20	0.20	0.20	0.20	0.20
Electric bulb						
54.	1	50				

Table D-4 *continued*

Source (unless otherwise indicated)

COLUMN 1–**Lines 1, 3, 13-14, 16-17, 19-20, 22-26, 28-30, 34, 36, 38-39, 41-45, 48-50, 52, and 54:** *415*, No. 4, 1946, pp. 24–25. For line 16, roast chicken; and for line 17, uncooked chicken. For lines 48–50, certain categories of privileged people received 20% discounts and officers 35%. For line 52, given for soap without further specification. **Lines 2, 9, 27, and 35:** *478*, p. 222. For line 2, open-market price. For lines 9, 27, and 35, also *459*, p. 34.

COLUMN 2–**Lines 1, 13-14, 16-17, 19, 22, 24-26, 28-30, 34-35, 38-39, and 41-43:** *415*, No. 4, 1946, p. 24. **Lines 9, 27, and 36:** *478*, p. 222. Also, *459*, p. 34.

COLUMN 3–**Lines 1, 21, 26, 32, 34, 36-37, and 40:** *459*, pp. 32 and 34. For line 1, open-market price. For lines 1, 26, and 37, also *415*, No. 4, 1946, p. 24. For lines 26, 34, and 36-37, also *478*, pp. 221 and 222. For lines 1 and 26, also *415*, No. 8, 1947, p. 11. For line 26, also *457*, p. 178. **Lines 2, 4, 6, 27, and 31:** *415*, No. 6, 1946, p. 21 (derived from decreases announced in decree of 9/16/47). For line 6, also *478*, p. 221, and *459*, p. 32. **Lines 3, 9-10, and 18:** *478*, pp. 221–222. For line 3, open-market price. For lines 10 and 18, also *459*, p. 32. **Lines 5, 11, and 15:** *457*, p. 178. **Lines 7, 12, 17, and 33:** *415*, No. 8, 1947, p. 11. For line 7, given for flour without further specification. **Lines 13-14, 16, 22, 24, 29-30, 35, 38-39, and 41-42:** *415*, No. 4, 1946, p. 24. For line 22, also *415*, No. 8, 1947, p. 11. **Line 28:** *415*, No. 7, 1947, p. 11. **Lines 45, 50, and 52:** *415*, No. 9, 1947, p. 28. Central department store of Moscow. For line 52, given for soap without further specification. **Lines 46-47:** A reduction of 43% was announced on 7/2/46 (*415*, No. 6, 1946, p. 20). **Line 48:** A reduction of 45% was announced on 7/2/46 (*415*, No. 6, 1946, p. 20). **Line 51:** A reduction of 42% was announced on 7/2/46 (*415*, No. 6, 1946, p. 20).

COLUMN 4–**Lines 1, 21, 26, 30, 34, 38, 45, 47-48, and 50-51:** *459*, pp. 32, 34, and 35. **Lines 2, 4, 6, 27, and 29:** *415*, No. 6, 1946, p. 21 (derived from decreases announced in decree of 9/16/47). For line 4, also *457*, p. 178, and *415*, No. 8, 1947, p. 11. For line 6, also *415*, No. 8, 1947, p. 11, for flour without further specification; *478*, p. 221; and *459*, p. 32. For line 27, also *415*, No. 7, 1947, p. 17. **Lines 3, 16, 22, 28, 33, 35, 39, and 41:** *415*, No. 8, 1947, p. 11. For line 35, given for sugar without further specification. For line 41, price for a bottle. **Lines 8, 10, 13, and 23-24:** *457*, p. 178. **Lines 9 and 17:** *478*, p. 221. Also, *459*, p. 32. For line 9, also *415*, No. 8, 1947, p. 11.

COLUMN 5–**Line 26:** *415*, No. 7, 1947, p. 17. **Lines 45, 47, and 50-52:** *415*, No. 9, 1947, p. 28. Central department store of Moscow. For line 52, given for soap without further specification. **Line 46:** *415*, No. 12, 1948, p. 5. Central department store of Moscow.

a. 1942 and 1943 have been omitted here for lack of information.

b. Silk stockings.

c. Price of *Pravda*.

Management and Planning Process

Table E-1 Central Agencies Directly Subordinated to USSR Council of People's Commissars, 1933, 1937, and 1941

1933 (1)	1937 (2)	1941 (3)
	People's Commissariats [a]	
Heavy Industry	Heavy Industry	Coal Industry (U)
		Petroleum Industry (U)
		Electric Power Stations (U)
		Electrical Industry (U)
		Ferrous Metal Industry (U)
		Nonferrous Metal Industry (U)
		Chemical Industry (U)
		Rubber Industry (U)
		Construction Materials Industry (UR)
	Machine-Building	Heavy Machine-Building (U)
		Machine Tool Industry (U)
		Medium Machine-Building (U)
		General Machine-Building (U)
	Defense Industry	Aircraft Industry (U)
		Shipbuilding (U)
		Munitions (U)
		Armaments (U)
Light Industry	Light Industry	Light Industry (UR)
		Textile Industry (UR)
Timber Industry	Timber Industry	Timber Industry (UR)
		Pulp and Paper Industry (U)
Food Supply [b]	Food Industry	Fishing Industry (UR)
		Meat and Dairy Industry (UR)
		Food Industry (UR)
	Domestic Trade	Trade (UR)
Foreign Trade	Foreign Trade	Foreign Trade
		Construction (U)
Agriculture	Agriculture	Agriculture (UR)
		Agricultural Procurement
State Farms	State Farms	Grain and Animal Husbandry State Farms (UR)
Transportation	Transportation	Transportation (U)
Water Transport	Water Transport	Maritime Fleet (U)
		Inland Waterway Fleet (U)
Communications	Communications	Communications (U)
Education		
Health	Health	Health (UR)
Foreign Affairs	Foreign Affairs	Foreign Affairs (U)

Table E-1 *continued*

1933 (1)	1937 (2)	1941 (3)
Defense	Defense	{ Defense (U) / Navy (U)
Finance	Finance	Finance (UR)
Internal Affairs	Internal Affairs	{ Internal Affairs (UR) / State Security (U)
Justice	Justice	Justice (UR)
		State Control (U)

State Committees and Various Agencies

1933	1937	1941
Central Administration for Truck Transport	Administration for Truck Transport	
Central Administration for Civil Aviation	Administration for Civil Aviation	Administration for Civil Aviation
Tsentrosoiuz	*Tsentrosoiuz*	*Tsentrosoiuz*
Industrial Cooperatives	Industrial Cooperatives	Industrial Cooperatives
Subway Construction	Subway Construction	Subway Construction
Committee for Agricultural Procurement	Committee for Agricultural Procurement	
Central Administration for Photography and Films	Central Administration for Photography and Films	Committee for Film Industry
		Committee for Radio
		Committee for Arts
	Committee for Higher Education	Committee for Higher Education
Central Administration for Northern Sea Route	Central Administration for Northern Sea Route	Central Administration for Northern Sea Route
	Construction of Volga Canal / Construction of Moscow Canal }	Central Administration for Moscow-Volga Canal
	Committee for State Reserves	Committee for State Reserves
	Central Administration for Forests	Central Administration for Forests
	Central Administration for Hydrometeorological Service	Central Administration for Hydrometeorological Service
		Committee for the Press
State Planning Committee	State Planning Committee	State Planning Committee
State Bank	State Bank	State Bank

Table E-1 *continued*

1933 (1)	1937 (2)	1941 (3)
		Central Administration for Sulfate, Alcohol, and Hydrolysis
		Central Administration for Military Industrial Construction
		Committee for Sports
		Committee for Geology
		Committee for Cartography and Geodesy
		Committee For Weights and Measures
Central Union of Trade Unions	Central Union of Trade Unions	Central Union of Trade Unions
		Academy of Sciences
		Palace of Soviets
		Attorney General's Office
		Ossaviakhim (Society for Assisting Aviation and Chemistry)
Councils of People's Commissars of Federal Republics[c]		
Russian Republic	Russian Republic	Russian Republic
Ukraine	Ukraine	Ukraine
Belorussia	Belorussia	Belorussia
Transcaucasus	{ Azerbaidzhan Georgia Armenia	Azerbaidzhan Georgia Armenia
Turkmenistan	Turkmenistan	Turkmenistan
Uzbekistan	Uzbekistan	Uzbekistan
Tadzhikistan	Tadzhikistan	Tadzhikistan
	Kazakhstan	Kazakhstan
	Kirghizia	Kirghizia
		Karelo-Finnish Republic
		Moldavia
		Lithuania
		Latvia
		Estonia

Source: *300* and *67*, pp. 843–44.

Table E-1   *continued*

a. There is a distinction between Union (*obshchesoiuznye*) commissariats and Union-republic (*soiuznorespublikanskie*) commissariats. The former (indicated by U in parentheses) have jurisdiction in their field over the whole country either directly or through agencies they appoint, while the latter (indicated by UR) usually exercise their power through the corresponding federal republic commissariats and manage only a few enterprises (those on a list confirmed by the presidium of the USSR Supreme Soviet).

b. In 1934 this commissariat was split into the Commissariat of the Food Industry and the Commissariat of Domestic Trade.

c. All administrative and economic activity of these councils that does not come directly under the jurisdiction of the Union commissariats or committees or administrations attached directly to the USSR Council of People's Commissars is subject, through them, to the control of the USSR Council of People's Commissars (see Chart 1).

Table E-2   Central Agencies Directly Subordinated to USSR Council of Ministers, 1946, 1953, and 1954

1946 (July) (1)	1953 (February) (2)	1953 (March 15) (3)	1954 (April 26) (4)
		Ministries [a]	
Foreign Trade (U)	Foreign Trade (U) ⎫	Foreign and Domestic Trade	⎧ Foreign Trade (U)
Trade (UR)	Trade (UR) ⎭		⎩ Domestic Trade (UR)
Transportation	Transportation (U) ⎫	Transportation (U)	⎧ Transportation (U)
Motor Transport	Motor Transport ⎭		⎨ Motor Transport and Highways (UR)
Communications (U)	Communications (U)	Communications (U)	Communications (U)
Maritime Fleet (U)	Maritime Fleet (U) ⎫	Maritime and Inland Waterway Fleet [b]	Maritime and Inland Waterway Fleet (U)
Inland Waterway Fleet (U)	Inland Waterway Fleet (U) ⎭		
Coal Industry of Western Regions (U)			
Coal Industry of Eastern Regions (U)	Coal Industry (U) [c]	Coal Industry (U)	Coal Industry (UR)
Construction of Fuel Enterprises (U)			
Petroleum Industry of Southern and Western Regions (U)	Petroleum Industry (U) [d]	Petroleum Industry (U)	Petroleum Industry (U)
Petroleum Industry of Eastern Regions (U)			
Electric Power Stations (U)	Electric Power Stations (U) ⎫	Electric Power Stations and Electrical Industry (U)	⎧ Electric Power Stations (U
Electrical Industry (U) [e]	Electrical Industry (U) ⎬		⎨ Electrical Equipment Ind
Communications Equipment Industry (U) [e]	Communications Equipment Industry (U) ⎭		⎩ Radiotechnical Industry (U) [f]

Table E-2 *continued*

1946 (July) (1)	1953 (February) (2)	1953 (March 15) (3)	1954 (April 26) (4)
Ferrous Metal Industry (U)	Ferrous Metal Industry (U)[g]	Metal Industry (U)	Ferrous Metal Industry (UR)
Nonferrous Metal Industry (U)	Nonferrous Metal Industry (U)[g]		Nonferrous Metal Industry (UR)
Chemical Industry (U)[h]	Chemical Industry (U)[h]	Chemical Industry (U)	Chemical Industry
Rubber Industry (U)[h]			
Aircraft Industry (U)	Aircraft Industry (U)	Defense Industry (U)	Aircraft Industry (U)
Armaments (U)	Armaments (U)		Defense Industry (U)
Transport Machine-Building (U)	Transport Machine-Building (U)	Transport and Heavy Machine-Building (U)	Transport Machine-Building (U)
Heavy Machine-Building (U)	Heavy Machine-Building (U)		Heavy Machine-Building (U)
Construction and Highway Machine-Building (U)	Construction and Highway Machine-Building (U)		Construction and Highway Machine-Building (U)
Shipbuilding (U)	Shipbuilding (U)		Shipbuilding (U)
Motor Vehicle Industry (U)[i]	Motor Vehicle and Tractor Industry (U)[i]	Machine-Building (U)	Motor Vehicle, Tractor, and Agricultural Machine-Building (U)
Agricultural Machine-Building (U)[j]	Agricultural Machine-Building (U)		
Machine- and Instrument-Building (U)	Machine- and Instrument-Building (U)		Machine- and Instrument-Building (U)
Machine Tool Industry (U)	Machine Tool Industry (U)		Machine Tool Industry (U)
		Medium Machine-Building[k]	Medium Machine-Building (U)[k]
Construction of Heavy Industrial Enterprises (U)	Construction of Heavy Industrial Enterprises (U)	Construction (U)	Construction (UR)
Construction of Military and Naval Enterprises (U)[l]	Construction of Machine-Building Enterprises (U)[l]		Construction of Metal and Chemical Industry Enterprises (U)
Construction Materials Industry (UR)	Construction Materials Industry (UR)	Construction Materials Industry (UR)	Construction Materials Industry (UR)
Pulp and Paper Industry (U)[m]	Paper and Woodprocessing Industry (UR)[m]	Timber and Paper Industry (UR)	Paper and Woodprocessing Industry (U)
Timber Industry (UR)[m]	Timber Industry (UR)[n]		Timber Industry (UR)
Geology (U)	Geology (U)	[n]	Geology and Mineral Conservation (U)
Pharmaceutical Industry[o]			

Table E-2 *continued*

1946 (July) (1)	1953 (February) (2)	1953 (March 15) (3)	1954 (April 26) (4)
Light Industry (UR)[p]	Light Industry (UR)[p]		Industrial Consumer Goods (U
Textile Industry (UR)[p]			
Fishing Industry of Eastern Regions (UR)	Fishing Industry		Fishing Industry (UR)
Fishing Industry of Western Regions (UR)		Light and Food Industry (UR)	
Food Industry (UR)	Food Industry (UR)[q]		Food Industry (UR)
Spice Industry[q]			
Meat and Dairy Industry (UR)	Meat and Dairy Industry (UR)		Meat and Dairy Industry (UR)
Agriculture (UR)[r]			Agriculture (UR)
Animal Husbandry[r]	Agriculture (UR)[r]		
Industrial Crops (UR)[r]	Cotton Growing		
Agricultural Procurement (U)	Agricultural Procurement (U)	Agriculture and Procurement (UR)	Agricultural Procurement (U)
Grain and Animal Husbandry State Farms (UR)[s]	State Farms (UR)[s]		State Farms (UR)
	Forestry (UR)[t]		
Higher Education (UR)[u]	Higher Education (UR)		Higher Education (U)
Film Industry (UR)[v]	Film Industry (UR)	Culture (UR)	Culture (UR)
Labor Reserves (UR)[w]	Labor Reserves (U)		
Internal Affairs (UR)	Internal Affairs (UR)	Internal Affairs	Internal Affairs (UR)
State Security (UR)	State Security (UR)		
State Control (UR)	State Control (UR)	State Control (UR)	State Control (UR)
Health (UR)	Health (UR)	Health (UR)	Health (UR)
Foreign Affairs (UR)	Foreign Affairs (UR)	Foreign Affairs (UR)	Foreign Affairs (UR)
Armed Forces (UR)		Defense (UR)	Defense (UR)
Finance (UR)	Finance (UR)	Finance (UR)	Finance (UR)
Justice (UR)	Justice (UR)	Justice (UR)	Justice (UR)
Food Reserves[x]	x		
Material Reserves[x]	x		

Table E-2 *continued*

1946 (July) (1)	1953 (February) (2)	1953 (March 15) (3)	1954 (April 26) (4)
Urban Construction [y]	[y]		

State Committees and Various Agencies [z]

1946 (July) (1)	1953 (February) (2)	1953 (March 15) (3)	1954 (April 26) (4)
State Planning Commission [aa]	State Planning Committee (Gosplan) [aa] / State Committee for Supply (*Gossnab*) / State Committee for Supply of Food and Industrial Goods (*Gosprodsnab*) [bb]	State Planning Committee [aa]	State Planning Committee
	Central Statistical Administration [cc]	Central Statistical Administration [cc]	Central Statistical Administration
	State Committee for Construction (*Gosstroi*) [dd]	State Committee for Construction	State Committee for Construction
			Committee for State Security [ee]
State Bank	State Bank	State Bank	State Bank
	State Committee for Technology (*Gostekhnika*) [ff]		
Central Administration for Construction of Machine-Building Enterprises [l]	[l]		
Central Administration for Gas and Fuel Industry [d]	[d]		
Central Administration for Gas and Petroleum Industry Construction [d]	[d]		
Committee for Arts	Committee for Arts		
Committee for Radio Information	Committee for Radio Information		
Central Administration for Printing, Publishing, and Book Trade	Central Administration for Printing, Publishing, and Book Trade		
Central Administration for Northern Sea Route [b]	Central Administration for Northern Sea Route [b]	[b]	
Attorney General's Office	Attorney General's Office	Attorney General's Office	Attorney General's Office
USSR Academy of Sciences	USSR Academy of Sciences	USSR Academy of Sciences	USSR Academy of Sciences
Central Union of Trade Unions	Central Union of Trade Unions	Central Union of Trade Unions	Central Union of Trade Unions

Table E-2   *continued*

1946 (July) (1)	1953 (February) (2)	1953 (March 15) (3)	1954 (April 26) (4)
Tsentrosoiuz	*Tsentrosoiuz*	*Tsentrosoiuz*	*Tsentrosoiuz*
Ossaviakhim (Society for Assisting Aviation and Chemistry)	*Ossaviakhim*	*Ossaviakhim*	*Ossaviakhim*
Industrial Cooperatives	Industrial Cooperatives	Industrial Cooperatives	Industrial Cooperatives
Committee for Sports	Committee for Sports	Committee for Sports	Committee for Sports
Russian Orthodox Church Affairs [gg]	Russian Orthodox Church Affairs [gg]	Russian Orthodox Church Affairs [gg]	Russian Orthodox Church Affairs [gg]
Religious Cults [gg]	Religious Cults [gg]	Religious Cults [gg]	Religious Cults [gg]
Councils of Ministers of Federal Republics			
Russian Republic	Russian Republic	Russian Republic	Russian Republic
Ukraine	Ukraine	Ukraine	Ukraine
Belorussia	Belorussia	Belorussia	Belorussia
Uzbekistan	Uzbekistan	Uzbekistan	Uzbekistan
Kazakhstan	Kazakhstan	Kazakhstan	Kazakhstan
Georgia	Georgia	Georgia	Georgia
Azerbaidzhan	Azerbaidzhan	Azerbaidzhan	Azerbaidzhan
Lithuania	Lithuania	Lithuania	Lithuania
Moldavia	Moldavia	Moldavia	Moldavia
Latvia	Latvia	Latvia	Latvia
Kirghizia	Kirghizia	Kirghizia	Kirghizia
Tadzhikistan	Tadzhikistan	Tadzhikistan	Tadzhikistan
Armenia	Armenia	Armenia	Armenia
Turkmenistan	Turkmenistan	Turkmenistan	Turkmenistan
Estonia	Estonia	Estonia	Estonia
Karelo-Finnish Republic	Karelo-Finnish Republic	Karelo-Finnish Republic	Karelo-Finnish Republic

Source: Unless otherwise indicated, col. 1: *302*, pp. 351–52; cols. 2–3: 3/16/53 decree in *34*, Bk. II, p. 459; *67*, pp. 843–44; col. 4: *310*, pp. 547–50.

a. U in parentheses after a ministry indicates a Union ministry. UR indicates a Union-republic ministry, which exists on both the Union level and the republic level. When there is no such indication, that means the source did not specify the kind of ministry.

b. The Ministry of the Maritime and Inland Waterway Fleet also took over the functions of the Central Administration for the Northern Sea Route (3/15/53).

c. The amalgamation of the three former ministries into one took place on 12/28/48 (*34*, Bk. I, p. 418).

d. The amalgamation of the Ministries of the Petroleum Industry of the Southern and Western Regions and of the Eastern Regions took place on 12/28/48 (*34*, Bk. I, p. 418). At that time the following agencies were integrated into the new ministry: the Central Administration for the Gas and Fuel Industry (*Glavgaztopprom*) under the USSR Council of Ministers, the Central Administration for Gas and Petroleum Industry Construction (*Glavneftegazstroi*)

Table E-2 *continued*

under the USSR Council of Ministers, and the Central Administration for Petroleum Supply (*Glavneftesnab*) under the Committee for Supply (*Gossnab*). It should be noted that the People's Commissariat of the Petroleum Industry was divided into two commissariats—one for the southern and western regions and the other for the eastern regions—on 4/4/46 (*34*, Bk. I, p. 392).

e. The Ministry of the Electrical Industry, which was functioning in March of 1946 (*302*, pp. 351–52, and *34*, Bk. I, p. 395), was split up on 6/28/46, into two ministries—electrical industry and communications equipment industry.

f. This ministry was created on 1/21/54 (*310*, p. 547). It seems to have replaced the Ministry of the Communications Equipment Industry (*sredstva sviazi*). See note e.

g. These two ministries were amalgamated on 7/29/48 and split up again on 12/28/50 (*34*, Bk. I, pp. 415 and 436).

h. The Ministry of the Chemical Industry and the Ministry of the Rubber Industry were amalgamated on 8/2/48 (*34*, Bk. I, p. 416).

i. The Ministry of the Motor Vehicle Industry was transformed into the Ministry of the Motor Vehicle and Tractor Industry on 8/23/47 (*34*, Bk. I, p. 406). It should be noted that the People's Commissariat of Medium Machine-Building was transformed into the People's Commissariat of the Motor Vehicle Industry on 2/17/46 (*34*, Bk. I, p. 392), but first the tractor plants under the jurisdiction of this commissariat were removed and transferred to the People's Commissariat of Agricultural Machine-Building (*34*, Bk. I, p. 391). See also note j.

j. This commissariat was created on 1/7/46 from the enterprises of the People's Commissariat of Munitions (*boepripasy*), which was eliminated at that time, the tractor plants of the People's Commissariats of Medium Machine-Building and of Transport Machine-Building, and the agricultural machine-building plants under the jurisdiction of the People's Commissariat of Mortars (*minometnoe vooruzhenie*) (*34*, Bk. I, p. 391).

k. This ministry is mentioned in *310*, pp. 547–50. See also note i. It was not mentioned in the fulfillment of plans for industries (see Table 81). It should be noted that this ministry handled the atomic industry. It was re-established 6/26/53, with V. A. Malyshev as minister (*458*, pp. 20–21).

l. The Ministry for the Construction of Military and Naval Enterprises was amalgamated, on 3/9/49, with the Central Administration for Construction of Machine-Building Enterprises (*Glavmashstroi*) under the USSR Council of Ministers and became the Ministry for the Construction of Machine-Building Enterprises (*34*, Bk. I, p. 423).

m. The Ministry of the Timber Industry and the Ministry of the Pulp and Paper Industry were amalgamated on 7/29/48 (*34*, Bk. I, p. 415) into the Ministry of the Timber and Paper Industry. On 2/16/51 this ministry was split up again—timber, on the one hand, and paper and woodprocessing, on the other (*34*, Bk. II, p. 443).

n. The Ministry of Geology was abolished on 3/16/53, and its functions were distributed among the following ministries: Metal Industry, Coal Industry, Petroleum Industry, Chemical Industry, Construction Materials Industry, and other ministries running the mining industry (*34*, Bk. II, p. 459).

o. This ministry was created on 6/14/46 and abolished on 3/1/48 (*34*, Bk. I, pp. 394 and 413).

p. The Ministry of Light Industry and the Ministry of the Textile Industry were amalgamated on 12/28/48 (*34*, Bk. I, p. 418).

q. The Ministry of the Spice Industry (*vkusovaia promyshlennost*) was created on 7/15/46 (*34*, Bk. I, p. 395). It was amalgamated with the Ministry of the Food Industry on 1/20/49 (*34*, Bk. I, p. 422).

r. On 3/26/46 the Ministry of Agriculture (*zemledelie*) was split up into the Ministries of Agriculture and of Animal Husbandry (*34*, Bk. I, p. 393). These two ministries and the Ministry of Industrial Crops were amalgamated on 2/4/47 into the Ministry of Agriculture (*selskoe khoziaistvo*) (*34*, Bk. I, p. 402).

s. The Ministry of Grain and Animal Husbandry State Farms existed in March 1946, but it was probably abolished when the Ministry of State Farms was created on 2/4/47 (*34*, Bk. I, p. 402).

t. This ministry was created on 4/4/47 (*34*, Bk. I, p. 404).

u. This ministry was created on 4/10/46 to replace the Committee for Higher Education (*Komitet po Delam Vysshei Shkoly*) under the USSR Council of Ministers (*34*, Bk. I, p. 393).

v. This ministry was created on 3/20/46 to replace the Committee for Films (*34*, Bk. I, p. 393).

w. This ministry was created on 5/15/46 by amalgamating the Central Administration for Labor Reserves and the Committee for the Estimation and Distribution of Manpower (*34*, Bk. I, p. 394).

x. The Ministries of Food Reserves and of Material Reserves were created on 5/4/46 (*34*, Bk. I, p. 394) and were amalgamated on 7/23/48 into the Ministry of Food and Material Reserves (*34*, Bk. I, p. 415), which on 4/26/51 was transformed into the State Committee for the Supply of Food and Industrial Goods (*34*, Bk. II, p. 444). This committee seems to have been absorbed into Gosplan in 1953.

y. This ministry was created on 6/1/49 (*34*, Bk. I, p. 426) and abolished on 3/14/51 (*34*, Bk. II, p. 444), after the creation of the State Committee for Construction (*Gosstroi SSSR*).

z. This list is not complete. The committees or agencies for which no sources are given were taken from Table E-1.

aa. The State Planning Commission was transformed into the State Planning Committee (Gosplan) by the 12/15/47 decision of the Party Central Committee (*26*, Vol. 2, pp. 261–62).

bb. This committee was created on 4/26/51 (*34*, Bk. II, p. 444), replacing the Ministry of Food and Material Reserves. See also note aa.

Table E-2   *continued*

cc. The USSR Central Statistical Administration under USSR Gosplan was subordinated directly to the USSR Council of Ministers by the 8/10/48 decree (*34*, Bk. I, p. 416).

dd. This committee was created on 5/9/50 by a decision of the presidium of the USSR Supreme Soviet (*34*, Bk. I, p. 433).

ee. The Ministry of State Security was amalgamated with the Ministry of Internal Affairs after Stalin's death in March 1953. It was reformed as the Committee for State Security under the USSR Council of Ministers on 3/13/54 (*310*, p. 548).

ff. The State Committee for the Introduction of Advanced Technology in the National Economy (*Gostekhnika*) was created on 12/15/47 from the Technology Department of USSR Gosplan, the Committee on Inventions and Discoveries, the Committee on Standards, and the Technical Council on Mechanization of Labor-Intensive and Heavy Work, all of which organizations previously operated under the USSR Council of Ministers (*26*, Vol. 2, p. 262). *Gostekhnika* was absorbed into Gosplan on 2/17/51. See *500*, p. 54.

gg. *458*, p. 68. (See also Table 2 in Chapter 2.) These were councils under the USSR Council of Ministers which were established on 10/8/43 and in 1944, respectively, and were formed into the Council for Religious Affairs under the USSR Council of Ministers on 12/19/65.

Table E-3   Internal Organization of Gosplan under USSR Council of People's Commissars, 1941

Chairman
Deputy chairmen
Members of Gosplan
Departments:
  General Economic Plan:[a]
    Sections:
      Production and Capital Repairs
      Production and Circulation Expenses
      Checking on Plan Fulfillment
      Balance of the National Economy
      General Transportation Plan
      General Plan
  Capital Construction:
    Sections:
      Building Industry
      General Construction Plan
      Water Management
      Special Construction
  Finance:
    Sections:
      Financial Plan
      Budget
      Credit and Cash Plan
  Labor:[b]
    Sections:
      Labor and Wages
      Training and Allocation of Personnel
      Group: Migration
  Far Eastern and East Siberian Regions[c]
  Ural and West Siberian Regions[c]
  Central Asian and Kazakhstan Regions[c]
  Transcaucasian Regions[c]
  Southern Regions[c]
  Central Regions[c]

  Southeastern Regions[c]
  Northern and Northeastern Regions[c]
  Western Regions[c]
  General Planning of Regions and Regional
    Distribution of Enterprises[c]
  Fuel:[d]
    Sections:
      Fuel Balance
      Coal and Shale Industry
      Petroleum and Gas Industry
      Peat Industry
  Material Balances:[e]
    Sections:
      Ferrous Metal Balance
      Nonferrous Metal Balance (incl. cables)
      Timber Products Balance
      Construction Supply
      Quality Steel
  Equipment Balance:[f]
    Sections:
      Power Equipment Balance
      Balance of Machine Tools and Instruments
      Technological Equipment Balance
      Balance of Construction and Transportation
        Equipment
  Electrification:[d]
    Sections:
      Production and Allocation of Electric Power
      Construction of Electric Power Stations
  Machine-Building Industry:[f]
    Sections:
      Heavy Machine-Building
      Medium Machine-Building
      General Machine-Building

Table E-3 *continued*

Power Machine-Building
General Plan
Food Industry:
Sections:
Fishing Industry
Food Industry
Meat and Dairy Products Industry
Light Industry:
Sections:
Textile Industry
Light Industry
Balance of Raw Materials and Semifabricated
Products
Agriculture:
Sections:
Vegetable Production
Animal Husbandry
Industrial Crops
Machine and Tractor Stations
State Farms[g]
Irrigation
Domestic Trade
Sections:
Distribution of Goods
Balance of Funds
Trade
Public Eating Places
Network of Stores and Trade Costs
Culture:[h]
Sections:
Schools and Higher Educational Institutions
Arts
Natural Resources[i]
Ferrous Metallurgy: [j]
Sections:
Production and Allocation
Investment and Equipment
Quality Steel and Ferroalloys
Nonferrous Metallurgy: [j]
Sections:
Production and Allocation
Investment and Equipment
Chemical Industry:
Sections:
Production and Allocation
Investment and Equipment
Group: Special Chemicals
Air Transportation and Trucking:
Sections:
Motor Transportation
Groups:
Air Transportation
Trucking
Timber Industry:
Sections:
Timber Industry
Paper and Pulp Industry
Groups:
Forestry

Hydrolysis Industry
Railroad Transportation:
Sections:
Traffic and Operation
Investment
Water Transportation:
Sections:
Inland Waterway Transportation
Maritime Transportation (incl. northern
sea route)
Procurement:
Sections:
Procurement and Balance of Agricultural
Products
Industrial Cooperatives
Construction Materials Industry
Communal Economy and Housing:
Sections:
Communal Economy
Housing
Foreign Trade
Public Health:
Sections:
Hospitals
Children's Homes
Communications
Mobilization: [k]
Groups:
Aircraft
Munitions
Armaments
Investment (incl. People's Commissariats of
Defense, Navy, Internal Affairs, and U.G.R.
and M.P.V.O.)
General Plan
Material Balances
Personnel[l]
Other Agencies Attached Directly to Presidium:
Office of Prices[m]
Office of Inventions[n]
Office of Economizing and Substitute Products[o]
Secretariat of the Chairman and Control Group[p]
Administration and Secret Section: [q]
Economic Section
Accounting
Library
Stenography
Archives
Dispatch
Personnel
Journal *Planovoe khoziaistvo* [r]
Gosplan Publishing House [r]
Institute of Technical and Economic Information [s]
Central Administration for National Accounting [t]
Corps of Gosplan Plenipotentiaries [u]
Council of Scientific and Technical Experts[v]
Council under Gosplan[w]
Molotov Economics Academy of the Union [x]

Table E-3 *continued*

Source: 12/31/40 decree of Council of People's Commissars, "On the Structure of Gosplan under USSR Council of People's Commissars" (*212*, No. 2, 1/16/41, Art. 27).

Note: During 1933–1941 the internal organization of Gosplan was revised several times. The decrees on these revisions are the following:

4/5/35: "On the Reorganization of USSR Gosplan," decree of Central Executive Committee and USSR Council of People's Commissars (*214*, No. 19, 4/28/35, Art. 154). **9/17/37:** "On Changes in the Structure of USSR Gosplan," decree of Central Executive Committee and USSR Council of People's Commissars (*214*, No. 62, 9/27/37, Art. 270). **9/22/37:** "On Changes in the Structure of USSR Gosplan," decree of Central Executive Committee and USSR Council of People's Commissars (*214*, No. 74, 12/1/37, Art. 359). **2/2/38:** "Statute on Gosplan under USSR Council of People's Commissars," decree of USSR Council of People's Commissars (*212*, No. 7, 3/28/38, Art. 41). **4/13/39:** "On the Confirmation of the Structure of Gosplan under USSR Council of People's Commissars," decree of USSR Council of People's Commissars (*212*, No. 26, 4/27/39, Art. 161). **4/13/40:** "On the Structure of Gosplan under USSR Council of People's Commissars," decree of USSR Council of People's Commissars (*212*, No. 10, 5/17/40, Art. 254). **10/10/40:** "On the Organization of Regional Departments within Gosplan under USSR Council of People's Commissars," decree of USSR Council of People's Commissars (*212*, No. 28, 10/31/40, Art. 674). **12/31/40:** Decree cited above in source. **3/21/41:** "Statute of Gosplan under USSR Council of People's Commissars," decree of USSR Council of People's Commissars and Party Central Committee. The text of the statute could not be found. For commentaries on it, see *34*, Bk. I, p. 383, and *244*, pp. 32–33 and 37–38.

a. This department was constantly being reorganized after 1933. Until 1937 it had two main sections: administration of production and technology of production. The sections given in this table were created by the 9/17/37 decree, except for the Balance of the National Economy which was created only on 2/2/38. Labor, wages, and personnel, which were grouped into a special section on 9/17/37 (and into two sections on 4/13/39), do not appear after 4/13/40 and seem to have been transferred to the Department of Labor, which was created on 4/13/40, and maintained thereafter.

b. See note a. The special Department of Labor and Personnel mentioned in the 4/5/35 decree was eliminated on 9/17/37 and amalgamated with the Department of Culture. The Department of Personnel, created on 11/22/37, was also eliminated and amalgamated with the Department of Culture and Personnel, created on 2/2/38. Another department of personnel appeared on 12/31/40, but it seems to be the continuation of the Department for the Training of Planning Personnel, which existed from 1935 to 1940.

c. These were created by the 10/10/40 subdivision, with accompanying powers, of the sections of the Department of Regional Planning (since 2/2/38 the Department for Regional Distribution of Production and Regional Planning).

d. The Department of Fuel and Electric Power was split into two departments on 9/17/37.

e. The functions of this department were the same as those of the department created on 4/5/35, except that then it was called Material Balances and Supply Plans. The 2/2/38 decree eliminated this department, amalgamating the Section of Metal Balances with the Department of Metallurgy and the Section of Construction Material Balances and perhaps also of Wood Products Balances with the Department of Capital Construction. The former Department of Material Balances was, however, re-established on 4/13/39. It should be noted that since 4/13/40 this department no longer has a Section of General Material Balances.

f. Until 2/2/38 the drawing up and allocation of equipment balances were done in a section of the Department of Machine-Building. This department seems to have been split up, on 3/21/41, into several separate departments corresponding to the breakdown of the People's Commissariat of Machine-Building. Strumilin (*244*, p. 38) mentions separate departments established on 3/21/41 for heavy machine-building, medium machine-building, and machine tools.

g. A separate Department of State Farms was amalgamated into the Department of Agriculture on 9/17/37.

h. Reorganized several times. See note a.

i. Created on 2/2/38.

j. The Department of Mining and Metallurgy, created on 4/5/35, was changed to the Department of Metallurgy on 2/2/38 and split into two departments (Ferrous Metallurgy and Nonferrous Metallurgy) on 4/13/39.

k. The separate Section of Defense, which became a department on 9/17/37, is no longer mentioned in the 2/2/38 decree. However, it reappears in the 4/13/39 decree under the name of Department of Mobilization with the notation that the breakdown into groups is given in a secret appendix. Nevertheless, a breakdown into groups is given in the 4/13/40 decree and it is given in this table. The 12/31/40 decree does not give a breakdown into groups for this department.

l. This appears to refer to planning personnel (see note a). The separate Section of Planning Personnel mentioned in the 4/5/35 decree was maintained in the 2/2/38 decree with a breakdown into three groups: Gosplan Personnel, Republic Gosplan Personnel, and Personnel of Higher Educational Planning Institutions. This last section was re-

Table E-3 *continued*

grouped separately under Administration under Gosplan by the 4/13/39 decree, but the 4/13/40 decree re-established the previous setup. The definition given in the 12/31/40 decree is not very precise, but it may be assumed that the Higher Educational Planning Institutions, which are not mentioned anywhere else, came under the jurisdiction of the Personnel Department.

m. Created by the decree of 4/13/39.

n. Created by the decree of 2/2/38.

o. Created by the decree of 4/13/40.

p. Until the 4/13/39 decree, the Secretariat of the Chairman of Gosplan was a separate agency without any other qualification. The 4/13/39 decree mentions it at the same time as the Control Group and the Secret Group. Since the 4/13/40 decree, the Secretariat of the Chairman and the Control Group have appeared together, while the Secret Group (named a section on 12/31/40) has been included in Administration (*upravlenie delami*).

q. The 4/5/35 decree mentions only the Administration and Economic Agency without further qualification. The breakdown of this agency is the same in the decrees of 2/2/38, 4/13/39, and 4/13/40 as in this table, except that the Secret Section is part of this agency in the 2/2/38 decree (see note p).

r. The Office of Editing and Publishing in the 4/5/35 decree was split up into two separate agencies on 2/2/38.

s. The Institute of Economic Research of Gosplan was eliminated on 11/17/37. At that time the Technical and Economic Office was created. This office is not mentioned in the 2/2/38 decree. The Institute of Technical and Economic Information appears in the 4/13/39 decree.

t. Attached to Gosplan during this whole period. The 3/21/41 decree reorganized it into the Central Statistical Administration (*Tsentralnoe Statisticheskoe Upravlenie*), which remained attached to Gosplan until 1948.

u. Created by the 2/2/38 decree to check up on plan fulfillment in the republics and provinces.

v. Created on 4/13/39.

w. The 4/5/35 decree created a State Plan Commission under the Chairman of Gosplan made up of 70 people (the directors of the USSR and republic Gosplan agencies and various other people). The 2/2/38 decree mentions a council under Gosplan made up of 90 of the same kind of people. No change in this setup was mentioned until 12/31/40.

x. The 4/5/35 decree mentions the Planning Academy of the Union and the Planning Institutes of Moscow and of Leningrad as attached to Gosplan. The 2/2/38 decree does not mention these organizations. The Planning Academy is mentioned again as attached to Gosplan in the 4/13/40 decree and it is certainly the same organization that is mentioned in the 12/31/40 decree (in this table). The Planning Institute of Moscow (but not of Leningrad) is again mentioned as attached to Gosplan in the 4/13/40 decree, but it no longer appears in the 12/31/40 decree (in this table).

Table E-4   Process of Drafting Annual Plans, 1933–1941

Year of Plan	*Preliminary Work (up to May)* (1)	*First Stage of Work (June–July)* (2)
	Level A: USSR Gosplan, USSR Council of People's Commissars (SNK), Central Executive Committee (TsIK), then Supreme Soviet	
1933		
1934		"Limits" sent to republics and provinces in July
1935	Forms and indicators: decree, 4/16/34, work to end 7/1/34	"Limits" approved by SNK, 8/4/34
1936	Forms and indicators: Gosplan decree 2/22/35, work to end 5/1/35. Main "limits" to be ready 5/25/35	"Limits" to be ready and presented to SNK for approval 7/15/35
1937	Forms and indicators: Gosplan decree 4/36, work to end 5/1/36; to be sent to Gosplan chairman 5/10/36; published 9/36	"Limits," Gosplan decree, 6/10/36; work to end by 6/36; plan for local industry to be drafted by 8/1/36
1938	Forms and indicators: work not finished	"Limits," Gosplan decree, mid-June; work begins
1939	Forms and indicators: work in progress, June–July	
1940	Forms and indicators: work in progress, 6/39	
1941		
	Level B: Federal Republics and Union People's Commissariats (NK)	
1934		
1935		*Ukraine:* preliminary variant drafted 8/15/34; NKZem sent project for investment, forms, and indicators, Aug.–Sept. *RSFSR:* summary directives sent, Aug.–Sept.

Second Stage of Work (August–September)	Third Stage of Work (October–December)	Approval of Plan (after December)	Year of Plan
(3)	(4)	(5)	

Level A: USSR Gosplan, USSR Council of People's Commissars (SNK), Central Executive Committee (TsIK), then Supreme Soviet

Second Stage of Work (August–September)	Third Stage of Work (October–December)	Approval of Plan (after December)	Year of Plan
		By SNK and TsIK, 1/26/33; budget by TsIK, 1/30/33	1933
"Limits" sent to provinces late, in October		By SNK, 12/31/33; budget by TsIK, 1/4/34	1934
Trial draft of indexes by district for use of republics and provinces, until mid-Sept.	Gosplan to finish drafting plan by Nov. or beginning of Dec.	By SNK before 1/18/35; budget by TsIK, 2/8/35	1935
Trial draft of indexes by district, Aug.–Sept. 1935	Gosplan agencies to present to Gosplan chairman: production plan 11/10/35, employment plan 11/15/35, regional distribution plan 11/14/35	By TsIK, 1/14/36; budget by TsIK, 1/16/36	1936
	Gosplan to give recommendations and draft national plan 11/1/36; plan actually submitted to SNK 12/36	By SNK and TsIK, 3/29/37; budget by TsIK, 1/13/37	1937
		Industry and RR transport by SNK, 11/29/37; agricultural work by SNK, 1/27/38; animal husbandry by SNK, 7/17/38; state farms, food indus., agric. by SNK; budget by Supreme Soviet, 8/14/38	1938
	Gosplan to finish work by 10/15/38	By SNK, 11/22/38; agricul. work by SNK, 2/8/39; animal husbandry by SNK, 3/25/39; budget by Supreme Soviet, 5/31/39	1939
		By SNK, 12/17/39; budget by Supreme Soviet, 4/3/40	1940
		By SNK, 1/17/41; budget by Supreme Soviet, 3/1/41	1941

Level B: Federal Republics and Union People's Commissariats (NK)

Second Stage of Work (August–September)	Third Stage of Work (October–December)	Approval of Plan (after December)	Year of Plan
Union NK's to present plans to Gosplan 10/25/33			1934
The following plans to be presented to SNK: *Union NK's*: production plans and material supplies, 10/10/34; trade plans, 10/20/34; budget and credit plans, 11/10/34. *Federal republics*: production plans and budget, 11/1/34, delayed until 11/16/34. *Ukraine Gosplan*: work with regional planning committees, 9/27/34–10/20/34.	NKZem: goals to be sent to lower agencies by 11/1/34		1935

Table E-4 *continued*

Year of Plan	Preliminary Work (up to May) (1)	First Stage of Work (June–July) (2)
1936	*Kazakhstan*: preliminary material presented in April–May	*RSFSR*: prelim. variant approved by RSFSR SNK, 8/23/35 *Kazakhstan*: variant presented to USSR Gosplan, 9/35
1937		
1938		
1940		

Level C: Autonomous Republics, Territories, Provinces, and Regional Agencies under USSR Jurisdiction

1933		
1934	*Leningrad*: forms and indicators drafted for province, before Sept.	*Leningrad*: prelim. variant drafted and approved by province TsIK with acceptance of "limits," 7/33
1935		*Voronezh*: work started 7/34 *Stalingrad*: work started 7/34; 1st variant drafted 8/34 and sent to province organization *Western Province* (Smolensk): work started 8/34; directives and "limits" sent to district planning committees
1936	*Western Province* (Smolensk): prelim. work started 1st half May; forms and indicators drafted for province *Karelia*: first outline presented June–beginning July	*Leningrad*: work started 6/35; directives sent to province organiz.; 1st variant, 7/35 *Voronezh*: 1st variant to be presented to Gosplan in Aug.; province organiz. to present materials 7/20/35

Second Stage of Work (August–September)	Third Stage of Work (October–December)	Approval of Plan (after December)	Year of Plan
(3)	(4)	(5)	
SFSR: variant drafted plans of lower echelons coordinated, Sept.–Oct.	Union NK's to present production plans and equipment needs to SNK, 11/15/35		1936
he following plans to be presented to SNK: *Union NK's*: production plans and material and equipment supplies, 10/1/36; financial plans, 10/10/36. *Federal republics*: production plans and budgets, 10/1/36. *NKLP*: production plan, 10/36	USSR Gosplan revises plans for cotton fabrics, hemp, linen yarn, sugar beets, crude alcohol, meat, oil seed crops	Allocation of plan goals to lower echelons: NKLes, 1/15/37; NKZem, 12/31/36–1/17/37	1937
		Capital repairs "limits" approved by: NKMash, 4/11/38; NKLes, 4/27/38; NKPP, end Feb.; NKLP, 2/38	1938
NK's and federal republics to present to SNK production plans, 10/15/39, and material balances and allocation plans, 10/25/39		Employment balances presented by Belorussia, Ukraine, Azerbaidzhan, and some provinces of RSFSR, 3/1/40	1940
Level C: Autonomous Republics, Territories, Provinces, and Regional Agencies under USSR Jurisdiction			
		Final plan for cotton indus. not sent to enterprises; *Krasnaia Zaria* knitting factory plan approved 1/4/34	1933
Leningrad: "limits" expected 9/25/33; variant, to be drafted 10/25/33, delayed because of delay in transmission of "limits" from center	Leningrad: examination and revision of plans of lower echelons until 12/15/33	*Moscow*: most enterprises have not received "limits" by begin. Feb.; plan of *Mostrikotazh* approved 4/22/34; plan of Moscow Cotton Trust approved 5/34; cotton indus. plan sent to enterprises, 2nd quarter 1934	1934
Leningrad: breakdown by district, 10/34 Voronezh: plan finished according to forms of USSR Gosplan to present it to RSFSR and USSR Gosplans Stalingrad: work started on 2nd variant 9/34, RSFSR and USSR Gosplan goals		Leningrad: final text drafted by mid-April; plan expected 5/35; parts of agric. plan not yet approved, 6/35 *Western Province* (Smolensk): final text finished 5/1/35 *Crimea*: final "limits" rec'd 2–3/35	1935
Leningrad: directives and main "limits" to be approved by TsIK 8/19/35; province plan to be presented to USSR Gosplan 9/20/35	Leningrad: revisions made in cooperation with RSFSR and USSR Gosplans and breakdown by district drafted, 4th quarter		1936

Table E-4   *continued*

Year of Plan	Preliminary Work (up to May) (1)	First Stage of Work (June–July) (2)
		Stalingrad: work started 7/1/35; continued Aug.
		Western Province (Smolensk): work started 7/35 on prelim. variant of investment plan; letter sent to districts to present their projects 8/20/35
		Kirov: draft plan almost finished 8/35
		Gorky: draft plan almost finished 8/35
1937	*Leningrad*: forms and indicators drafted for province, June–July; work on 1st stage sent to planning agencies 5/29/36	*Leningrad*: 1st stage to be finished in organiz. 6/20/36 and in province planning committee 7/1/36; 1st variant to be drafted 7/36
	Stalingrad: forms and indicators drafted for province, 7/36	*Western Province* (Smolensk): districts to present projects 7/25/36
	Gorky: forms and indicators typed for province, 7/36	*Gorky*: work with districts 7/36 before 1st variant is drafted and before "limits" sent by center
	Northern Caucasus: rough draft of construction plan presented by province planning committee 7/36; methodological instructions drafted and sent to district planning committees	*Northern Caucasus*: decree of TsIK 5/17/36: plan materials to be presented 7/1/36; 1st variant to be drafted 8/10/36
1938	*Leningrad*: indicators and methodological instructions sent out in June	*Leningrad*: work on 1st variant in progress July–Aug.

Second Stage of Work (August–September)	Third Stage of Work (October–December)	Approval of Plan (after December)	Year of Plan
(3)	(4)	(5)	
Karelia: revisions made in original version Sept.–Oct.	*Northern Caucasus*: plan drafted by districts from Nov. to beginning of 1936		
Leningrad: 2nd variant drafted 9/36 to present to government *Western Province* (Smolensk): recommendations on agricult. plan to be presented to TsIK 9/1/36 *Northern Caucasus*: work on 2nd variant from 2nd half of Aug. after control figures approved by TsIK	*Western Province* (Smolensk): plan by districts completed 2nd half Jan. *Northern Caucasus*: plan by districts started 2nd half Dec.	*NKZem* and *republic* and *province organiz.*: MTS plans to be approved 3/1/37 and presented to NKZem 3/15/37; state farm plans to be presented to NKZem from 2/15/37 to 3/10/37	1937
			1938

Table E-4   *Continued*

Year of Plan	Preliminary Work	First Stage of Work (June–July)	Second Stage of Work (August–September)
	(1)	(2)	(3)

Level D: Districts or Cities with Jurisdiction of Districts

Year of Plan	Preliminary Work	First Stage of Work (June–July)	Second Stage of Work (August–September)
1933			
1934			*Leningrad*: districts received forms, instructions, and main "limits" for drafting of preliminary variant Sept.–Oct.
1935			*Leningrad*: districts received forms, instructions, and main "limits" for drafting of preliminary variant Sept.–Oct. *Western Province* (Smolensk): districts received forms, instructions, and main "limits" based on their investment demands in Aug. *Tatar Republic*: work on plan by districts not started by republic planning committee in Sept. *Western Siberia* (Barnaul District): prelim. work before "limits" in beginning Aug.; instructions sent to enterprises 9/1/34 *Moscow*: of 130 districts, 87 sent in investment estimates
1936		*Voronezh*: district planning committees asked to present on 7/20/35 material to be used in drafting of 1st variant which was to be presented to Gosplan in Aug. *Western Province* (Smolensk): district planning committees asked to present on 8/20/35 draft plans and investment demands to be used in drafting the province plan	*Western Province, Starodub District*: work started 9/35; preliminary plans drafted with organizations *Moscow*: of 130 districts, 123 sent in investment estimates

Third Stage of Work (October–December) (4)	Approval of Plan (after December) (5)	Year of Plan

Level D: Districts or Cities with Jurisdiction of Districts

Third Stage of Work (October–December)	Approval of Plan (after December)	Year of Plan
	Belorussia: plan drafted without contact with district planning committees and without distribution of "limits" by district *Kuibyshev*: district plans of Central Volga Region not drafted for lack of "limits" and instructions	1933
Leningrad: province plan distributed by district sent to district planning committees in Nov. (instead of Oct.). Revisions made after review and approval of control figures in Province Planning Committee on 12/15/34 *Kuibyshev* (Central Volga): forms and instructions sent to districts end Feb.	*Azov-Black Sea*: only 77% of district plans presented by May *Central Black Earth Region*: of 144 districts, only 63 presented plans (mostly incomplete) in May; 32% of them unsatisfactory *Kuibyshev* (Central Volga): plans completed June–July *North*: of 39 districts, 27 presented plans, mostly incomplete and less good than in 1933 *Western Siberia*: of 70 districts, 38 presented plans, incomplete and limited to new construction *Tatar Republic*: 30 district plans presented in Sept. but not examined by republic planning committee	1934
Leningrad: district plans to be presented to province planning committee 12/15/34 *Western Siberia* (Barnaul District): prelim. variant of Barnaul District plan examined by Western Siberia Planning Committee beginning Oct.	*Leningrad*: of 85 districts, 18 presented plans beginning April *Moscow*: of 130 districts, 55 presented plans 6/15/35 *Ivanovo*: of 77 districts, 19 presented plans beginning June *Kuibyshev*: of 77 districts, 10 presented plans mid-May *Kursk*: 30 districts (32%) presented plans 6/1/35 *Orenburg*: of 52 districts, 7 presented plans beginning June *Western Province*: all except 2 districts presented plans 6/15/35; plans reviewed, corrected, and approved by province planning committee 5/1/35 *Western Siberia*: 4 districts presented plans beginning May (Barnaul District 4/3/35) *Crimea-Simferopol*: plan completed 5/35	1935
Leningrad: draft of province plan drawn up by districts; 40 representatives of district planning committees to meet by 12/35 *Western Province, Starodub District*: drafting of district plan began 12/35; forms received 1/5/36 and incomplete "limits" received only 1/30/36 *Northern Caucasus*: drafting of district plan begun end Nov.; coordination with representatives of district planning committees from 12/15/35 to 1/15/36; on 1/15/36, of 43 districts, 35 sent in materials *Moscow*: Sept.–Dec., drafting of district plans (investment demands and agricultural plan); examination of plans in province planning committee from 10/20/35 to 11/15/35; forms and methodological instructions to be sent to districts in Oct. and Nov.	*Bashkiria*: 3/36, district planning committees having trouble presenting plans; plans incomplete (Abdelimov District filled out 8 tables instead of 52) *Crimea-Simferopol*: presentation of plan delayed from 3/1/36 until 3/9/36 The following no. of plans presented for approval:	1936

Province or Republic	No. of Districts	No. of Plans
Moscow	131	90
Yaroslav	36	25
Kursk	92	86
Kalinin	60	48
Orenburg	50	12
Omsk	65	18
Ivanovo	41	37
Chuvash Republic (for all of 1936)	25	16

Table E-4 *Continued*

Year of Plan	Preliminary Work	First Stage of Work (June–July)	Second Stage of Work (August–September)
	(1)	(2)	(3)
1937		*Northern Caucasus*: preliminary work of district planning committees and drafts of district investment plans to be presented 6/25/36; comments on investment plans not under district jurisdiction to be presented 7/15/36; plan for economic and cultural develop. of collective farms to be presented on 9/1/36	*Northern Caucasus*: preliminary variant of district plan to be drafted after "limits" approved by Province TsIK during 2nd half of Aug.

Abbreviations

NK = *Narodnyi Komissariat* (People's Commissariat).

NKLes = *Narodnyi Komissariat Lesnoi Promyshlennosti* (People's Commissariat of the Timber Industry).

NKLP = *Narodnyi Komissariat Legkoi Promyshlennosti* (People's Commissariat of Light Industry).

NKMash = *Narodnyi Komissariat Mashinostroeniia* (People's Commissariat of Machine-Building).

NKPP = *Narodnyi Komissariat Pishchevoi Promyshlennosti* (People's Commissariat of the Food Industry).

NKZem = *Narodnyi Komissariat Zemledeliia* (People's Commissariat of Agriculture).

SNK = *Sovet Narodnykh Komissarov* (Council of People's Commissars).

TsIK = *Tsentralnyi Ispolnitelnyi Komitet* (Central Executive Committee); since 1938 Supreme Soviet.

Source
Level A

1933–**Col. 5:** *214*, No. 6, 1933, art. 37, 38, and 39.

1934–**Col. 2:** *171*, No. 2, 1934, p. 37. **Col. 3:** *171*, No. 9, 1934, p. 36. **Col. 5:** *214*, No. 2, 1934, art. 12, 13, 14, and 15.

1935–**Col. 1:** *171*, No. 4, 1934, p. 65. **Col. 2:** *171*, No. 8, 1934, p. 66. **Col. 3:** *171*, No. 9, 1934, p. 64. **Col. 4:** *171*, No. 11, 1934, p. 56. **Col. 5:** *154*. Sent to printer 1/19/35. Plan approved by SNK (*154*, p. 3). *214*, No. 8, 1935, art. 71 and 72.

1936–**Col. 1:** *171*, No. 4, 1935, p. 58. Deadline later extended to 5/15/35. *171*, No. 11, 1935, p. 56. **Col. 2:** *171*, No. 11, 1935, p. 56. **Col. 3:** *173*, No. 3, 1936, p. 153. **Col. 4:** *171*, No. 20, 1935, p. 66. **Col. 5:** *214*, No. 4, 1936, art. 32, 33, and 34.

1937–**Col. 1:** *171*, No. 9, 1936, p. 50; *171*, No. 19, 1936, p. 10. **Col. 2:** *171*, No. 12, 1936, p. 52. For the plan for local industry, see the 7/10/35 decree of USSR Gosplan chairman Mezhlauk (*171*, No. 14, 1936, p. 48). *462*, p. 138. **Col. 4:** *171*, No. 17, 1936, p. 553; *171*, No. 17, 1936, p. 52; *171*, No. 24, 1936, p. 43. **Col. 5:** *214*, No. 24, 1937, art. 98, and No. 7, 1937, art. 22 and 23.

1938–**Col. 1:** *173*, No. 7, 1938, p. 79. **Col. 2:** *171*, No. 12, 1937, p. 38. **Col. 5:** *214*, No. 75, 1937, art. 364; *212*, No. 2, 1938, art. 5, and No. 28, 1938, art. 182. Decree of 2/3/38 in *212*, No. 4, 1938, art. 14. *297*.

1939–**Col. 1:** *173*, No. 7, 1938, p. 88. **Col. 4:** *173*, No. 10, 1938, p. 159. **Col. 5:** *173*, No. 4, 1939, p. 189 (abridged report of 3/26/39 meeting of Gosplan); *212*, No. 14, 1939, art. 88, and No. 22, 1939, art. 137; *297*.

1940–**Col. 1:** Discussed during 6/8/39 meeting of Gosplan. See *173*, No. 7, 1939, p. 129. **Col. 5:** Appendix to 31/

Third Stage of Work (October–December)	Approval of Plan (after December)	Year of Plan
(4)	(5)	

Forms and instructions for drafting district plans published by RSFSR Gosplan in 11/36	*Moscow*: complete variant of district plans to be drafted starting 12/15/36 and to be presented for approval 2/20/37	1937
Moscow: draft plans to be finished during 1st half of Dec.	*Northern Caucasus*: complete variant of district plan to be drafted starting 2nd half of Dec. The following no. of plans presented for approval, 7/36	

Province or Republic	No. of Districts	No. of Plans	
		Preliminary	Final
Moscow	131	122	46
Yaroslav	36	27	17
Kursk	92	87	49
Kalinin	60	58	20
Orenburg	50	50	7
Omsk	65	64	10
Ivanovo	41	40	34
Chuvash Republic (in July 1938)	25	16	13

17/39 Decree No. 2063 of USSR Council of People's Commissars and Party Central Committee, cited in *1*, p. 176, fn. See also *173*, No. 6, 1940, p. 114 (abridged report of Gosplan meeting). *299*.

1941–Col. 5: *60* and *300*.

Level B

1934–Col. 3: *171*, No. 2, 1934, p. 37.

1935–Col. 2, Ukraine: *171*, No. 10, 1934, p. 58. **Col. 2, RSFSR:** *171*, No. 20, 1935, p. 69. **Col. 3, Union NK's:** *171*, No. 8, 1934, p. 66. **Col. 3, federal republics:** *171*, No. 8, 1934, p. 66; *171*, No. 11, 1934, p. 56. **Col. 3, Ukraine Gosplan:** *171*, No. 10, 1934, p. 58. **Col. 4:** *171*, No. 9, 1934, p. 65.

1936–Cols. 1-2, Kazakhstan: *171*, No. 19, 1935, p. 55. **Cols. 2-3, RSFSR:** *171*, No. 20, 1935, p. 69. **Col. 4:** *214*, No. 61, 1935, art. 488.

1937–Cols. 3-4: *171*, No. 17, 1936, p. 40; *171*, No. 17, 1936, p. 52; *171*, No. 24, 1936, p. 45. **Col. 5:** *171*, No. 2, 1937, p. 52; *171*, No. 2, 1937, p. 53.

1938–Col. 5: *173*, No. 9, 1938, p. 58.

1940–Col. 3: *173*, No. 7, 1939, p. 129. **Col. 5:** *173*, No. 4, 1940, p. 58.

Level C

1933–Col. 5: *171*, No. 2, 1934, pp. 37–38.

1934–Cols. 1, 3-4: *171*, No. 9, 1934, p. 36. **Cols. 2 and 5, Moscow:** *171*, No. 2, 1934, pp. 37–38. **Col. 5:** *171*, No. 9, 1934, p. 9.

1935–Cols. 2-3, Voronezh: *171*, No. 10, 1934, p. 60. **Cols. 2-3, Stalingrad:** *171*, No. 12, 1934, p. 34. **Col. 2, Western Province:** *171*, No. 10, 1934, p. 61. **Col. 3, Leningrad:** *171*, No. 9, 1934, p. 38. **Cols. 5, Leningrad:** *171*, No. 9, 1935, p. 60; *171*, No. 11, 1935, p. 39. **Col. 5, Western Province:** *171*, No. 10, 1935, p. 60. **Col. 5, Crimea:** *171*, No. 11, 1935, p. 39.

1936–Cols. 1-2, Western Province; cols. 2-3, Leningrad; and col. 2, Stalingrad: *171*, No. 17, 1935, pp. 57–58. **Cols. 1 and 3, Karelia, and col. 2, Kirov and Gorky:** *171*, No. 19, 1935, p. 55. **Col. 2, Voronezh:** *171*, No. 15, 1936, p. 63. **Col. 4, Leningrad:** *171*, No. 2, 1936, p. 58. **Col. 4, Northern Caucasus:** *171*, No. 4, 1936, pp. 51–52.

1937–Cols. 1-3, Leningrad; col. 1, Stalingrad; and cols. 2-3, Western Province: *171*, No. 14, 1936, p. 55. **Cols. 1-2, Gorky:** *171*, No. 20, 1936, p. 57. **Cols. 1-3, Northern Caucasus:** *171*, No. 13, 1936, p. 62. **Col. 4, Western Province:** *171*, No. 5, 1937, p. 55. **Col. 4, Northern Caucasus:** *171*, No. 2, 1937, . 48. **Col. 5:** *171*, No. 2, 1937, p. 53.

1938–Cols. 1-2: *171*, No. 15, 1937, p. 48.

Table E-4   *continued*

Level D

1933–Col. 5, Belorussia: *171*, No. 11, 1934, p. 40. **Col. 5, Kuibyshev:** *171*, No. 2–3, 1935, p. 82.

1934–Col. 3: *171*, No. 4, 1936, pp. 28–29. **Col. 4:** *171*, No. 9, 1934, p. 36; *171*, No. 2–3, 1935, p. 82. **Col. 5, Azov-Black Sea, Central Black Earth Region, North, and Western Siberia:** *173*, No. 8–9, 1934, pp. 6–7. **Col. 5, Kuibyshev:** *171*, No. 2–3, 1935, p. 82. **Col. 5, Tatar Republic:** *171*, No. 9, 1934, p. 68.

1935–Col. 3, Leningrad: *171*, No. 4, 1936, pp. 28–29. **Col. 3, Western Province:** *171*, No. 10, 1934, p. 61. **Col. 3, Tatar Republic:** *171*, No. 9, 1934, p. 68. **Cols. 3-5, Western Siberia:** *171*, No. 17, 1935, p. 40. **Col. 3, Moscow:** *171*, No. 2, 1937, p. 47. **Col. 4, Leningrad:** *171*, No. 9, 1934, p. 36. **Col. 5, all except Crimea:** *171*, No. 13, 1935, p. 55. **Col. 5, Crimea:** *171*, No. 9, 1936, p. 58.

1936–Col. 2, Voronezh: *171*, No. 15, 1935, p. 63. **Col. 2, Western Province:** *171*, No. 17, 1935, pp. 57–58. **Cols. 3-4, Western Province:** *171*, No. 6, 1936, p. 59. **Col. 3, Moscow:** *171*, No. 2, 1937, p. 47. **Col. 4, Leningrad:** *171*, No. 4, 1936, pp. 28–29. **Col. 4, Northern Caucasus:** *171*, No. 4, 1936, p. 51–52. **Col. 4, Moscow:** *171*, No. 20, 1935, pp. 70–71. **Col. 5, Bashkiria:** *171*, No. 6, 1936, p. 58. **Col. 5, Crimea:** *171*, No. 9, 1936, p. 58. **Col. 5, rest:** *173*, No. 7, 1938, p. 92.

1937–Cols. 2-3: *171*, No. 13, 1936, p. 62. **Col. 4:** *171*, No. 2, 1937, p. 29. **Cols. 4-5, Moscow:** *171*, No. 22, 1936, p. 69. **Col. 5, Northern Caucasus:** *171*, No. 2, 1937, p. 48.

Table E-5   Economic Plans in Wartime, 1941–1945

Date (1)	Agency (2)	Title of Plan or Resolution (3)	Details (4)
1941			
6/6/41	USSR SNK	Plan for Mobilizing Production of Ammunition for II Half, 1941 and 1942	Put into effect 6/23/41.
6/41	KPSS TsK and USSR SNK	On Plan for State Reserves and Stocks for Mobilization for 1942	
*7/30/41	KPSS TsK and USSR SNK	Plan for Mobilization of National Economy during III Q 1941	Drafted by USSR Gosplan after recommendations of KPSS TsK and USSR SNK of 6/23/41. Replaced plan for III Q 1941 adopted 6/14/41. Relative to previous plan, production of armaments was increased 26% and retail trade reduced 12%. Materials and equipment allocated to defense industries. Investment reduced and directed to defense.
7/30/41a	GKO	On Measures for Developing Oil Extraction in Eastern Regions of USSR and Turkmenia	
*8/16/41	KPSS TsK and USSR SNK	Wartime Economic Plan for IV Q 1941 and 1942 for Volga, Urals, Western Siberian, Kazakh, and Central Asian Regions	Drafted from recommendations of GKO 7/4/41. Envisaged creation of major center of defense industries in east, development of fuel, materials, and metals base in these regions, and increase in military stocks. List of priority construction projects appended for industry and transportation. Certain agricultural goals included. Evacuation of defense industries to east main goal.
8/29/41	USSR SNK	Plan for Construction of Manganese Ore Base in Eastern Regions of USSR	Toward end of 1941, manganese from Urals began to supply metallurgical plants.
9/4/41	USSR SNK and KPSS TsK	On Revision of Plan for Work of MTS in 1941	Use of beef cattle and sometimes cows belonging to collective farms authorized to fulfill plan.
10/41		Schedule set to reopen plants evacuated in Siberia, on Volga, in Urals, Central Asia, and Kazakhstan	
9–10/41	GKO	First Wartime Plan of Work of USSR Academy of Sciences	Included more than 200 subjects presented for approval of USSR SNK and KPSS TsK.
11/9/41	GKO	On Restarting Production in Ferrous Metal Plants Evacuated to Urals and Siberia and on Increasing Production Capacities from Installing New Equipment in 11–12/41 and 1/42	Mainly schedule to reopen plants for tanks and planes and ammunition in order to start production.
*11/17/41	USSR SNK and KPSS TsK	On Production and Repair of Tractors, Combines, Agricultural Machinery, Spare Parts, and on Plan for Agric. Work for 1942	Goals set for area to be sown in Volga, Urals, Siberia, Central Asia and Kazakhstan. Certain crops increased.
11/19/41	Council of War of Leningrad Front and Leningrad Party Committee	Construction of a military road by Lake Lagoda linking Leningrad with rear of front	
12/8/41	USSR SNK	On Development of Coal Mining in Eastern Regions of USSR	Revision of plan approved 8/6/41. Daily output to increase from 180,000 tons in 11/41 to 220,000 tons in I Q and to 265,000 tons in IV Q

Table E-5 *continued*

Date (1)	Agency (2)	Title of Plan or Resolution (3)	Details (4)
12/41	USSR SNK	On Essential Measures in Ferrous and Nonferrous Metals, Construction Materials, Wood Chemistry, Fuel Supply, Electric Power, Water, RR Transportation, and Agriculture in Urals	Presented 12/12/41. Gave concrete production goals. Prepared by more than 100 people. Served as basis for SNK resolutions.
12/29/41	USSR SNK	On Reconstruction of Coal Mines in Moscow Basin	Provided production goals for mines being reconstructed, fuel supply, return of miners temporarily drafted. Plan for complete reconstruction of mines to be presented 1/15/42.
12/41a		Detailed plan to obtain skilled workers for I Q 1942	
1942			
1/3/42	GKO	On Reconstruction of Railroads	Established priority lines. Allocated materials and measures under military control in front areas.
1/6/42	USSR SNK	On Developing Fishing Industry in Basins and Rivers in Siberia and Far East	Set production goals for 1942 and 1943. Allocated equipment.
1/11/42	USSR SNK and KPSS TsK	On Stimulating Processing and Procurement of Flax and Hemp from 1941 Harvest	Provided material incentives for collective farmers.
2/5/42	USSR SNK	On Measures for Reconstruction of Coal Mines in Moscow Basin	Set goals for putting mines into operation and for production.
2/12/42	USSR SNK	On Developing Coal Mining in Vorkuta-Intynsk and on Measures Guaranteeing Transportation	
2/15/42	USSR SNK and KPSS TsK	On Certain Increases in Norms for Compulsory Delivery of Meat to State	Collective farms henceforth to deliver 3.5–5 kg per hectare of land.
2/21/42	GKO	On Essential Measures to Help Ferrous Metallurgy	
*3/3/42	USSR SNK and KPSS TsK	On State Plan for Development of Agriculture for 1942	Directives to People's Commissar of Agriculture. Norms set. Bonuses set for tractor drivers.
3/13/42	USSR SNK and KPSS TsK	On Measures to Protect Young Cattle and on Increasing Livestock on Collective and State Farms	Buying plan set to increase collective farm property. Killing of cattle under 1 yr. forbidden. Bonuses. Similar measures for sheep, pigs, and horses. Goals set for head of livestock on 1/1/43.
4/13/42	GKO	On Construction and Reconstruction of Ferrous Metal Enterprises	Concrete goals set for construction, reconstruction, and putting into operation in 1942. Directives to USSR SNK on organization of Central Office of Wartime Industrial Construction.
4/14/42	GKO	On Reconstruction and Development of Production of Metallurgical Equipment in Machine-Building and Tank Factories	Goals for producing metallurgical equipment in II Q and III Q 1942.
4/15/42	USSR SNK	On Construction of Central Power Stations in Urals	Priority construction projects set up and assimilated to military construction.
5/3–8/42	USSR Academy of Sciences	Plan for Scientific Work for 1942	Adopted by General Assembly at Sverdlovsk. Approved by USSR SNK.

Table E-5 *continued*

Date (1)	Agency (2)	Title of Plan or Resolution (3)	Details (4)
7/8/42	Ukrainian Academy of Sciences	Discussion of 1942 Plan of Academy, mainly of its cooperation with war industries	Academy session held at Ufa. Plans for industry in Urals and eastern regions (oil, metals).
*7/11/42	USSR SNK and KPSS TsK	On Harvest and Procurement of Agricultural Products for 1942	Concrete measures provided. Advance payment in agricultural products arranged for collective farmers.
7/42	USSR SNK	Plan for Mining Coal in Pechora Basin in III Q and IV Q 1942	
8/24/42	GKO	On Essential Measures to Increase Coal Mining in Kuznetsk Basin	Goals set for increased production.
8/24/42a	GKO	On Enlarging Existing Plants and Building New Ones to Produce Nitric Acid and Ammoniac	Necessitated by insufficient supply of raw materials (nitric acid, cellulose) for ammunition plants.
9/3/42	USSR SNK and KPSS TsK	On Increasing Area Sown to Grain in Uzbek, Turkmenian, Tadzhik, Kirghiz, and Kazakh Republics	Precise goals set for sown areas.
9/5/42	USSR SNK	On Exploitation of Natural Gas in Elshanka Basin, Saratov Province, and on Supplying Saratov Central Power Station	Deposits discovered in 8/42. First deliveries on 8/28/42.
9/22/42	USSR SNK and KPSS TsK	On Increasing Area Sown to Grain on State Farms of Eastern Regions of USSR	Precise goals for Altai, Krasnoiarsk, and other provinces.
9/22/42a	GKO	On Measures to Consolidate Oil Extraction in Combines of Kazakhstan and Perm and in Buguruslanneft, Syzranneft, and Other Trusts	Precise goals for sinking wells and producing oil in 1942 and part of 1943.
1943			
*1943		Wartime Economic Plan for 1943	
1/18/43	GKO	On Construction of a RR line between Leningrad and RR Network of Volkov	Difficult job making it possible to link Leningrad with inside of country.
2/7/43	GKO	On Measures for Essential Aid to Metal Industry	Superpriorities established to supply fuel, raw materials, and power to metallurgical plants.
*3/3/43	USSR SNK and KPSS TsK	On Preparing Tractors, Combines, and Agricultural Machinery of MTS for Field Work in 1943	Repairing equipment, etc.
3/18/43	USSR SNK and KPSS TsK	On Measures to Restart Production of Agricultural Machinery and Equipment	Production goals for 1943 and 1944. Metal supply.
*3/19/43	USSR SNK and KPSS TsK	On State Plan to Develop Agriculture in 1943	Setting sown areas. MTS work, etc.
*4/13/43	USSR SNK and KPSS TsK	On Measures to Increase Head of Livestock on Collective and State Farms and to Raise Their Productivity	Goals set for head of livestock. Help for collective and state farms. Reconstruction of recovered territory.

Table E-5 *continued*

Date (1)	Agency (2)	Title of Plan or Resolution (3)	Details (4)
4/14/43	GKO	On Putting into Operation New Electric Power Capacities in 1943	
4/19/43	GKO	On Plan to Build up and Increase Capacity of Ferrous Metal Industry in 1943	
4/19/43a		On Construction of Coal Mines	
4/19/43b	GKO	Order to Magnitostroi Trust to Build and Put into Operation in 1943 Blast Furnace No. 6 in Metallurgical Combine of Magnitogorsk	
*5/13/43	USSR SNK and KPSS Tsk	On Measures to Increase No. of Horses and to Improve Horse Breeding on Collective and State Farms	Numerical goals. Satisfaction of needs of Red Army.
6/43	GKO	Resolution on Providing Help to Kuznetsk Basin	Facilities for supplying materials and equipment. Administrative reorganization.
*7/18/43	USSR SNK and KPSS TsK	On Harvests and Procurement of Agricultural Products in 1943	Preparatory work, repairs, etc.
8/21/43	USSR SNK and KPSS TsK	On Essential Measures to Rebuild Economy in Areas Liberated from German Occupation	Resolutions on material aid for these areas. Facilities for supplying materials.
8/43		Plan to Develop Industry and Transportation in Urals for 1943–1947	
9/43	USSR Academy of Sciences	Resolution on Drafting Long-Range Plan for Development of Soviet Science for 8 or 10 Years	Work for 1944–1945. Recommendations drafted specifying atomic energy. Examined at 10/44 session of Academy.
9/43a	USSR Academy of Sciences	Examination of vital problems in plan for scientific work for 1944	
10/26/43	GKO	On Priority Measures to Rebuild Donbass Coal Industry	Production goals, IV Q 1943, I Q 1944. Priorities.
11/43	KPSS TsK and USSR SNK	Measures to Strengthen Grain Procurements	Special commission created with high-ranking members (Voznesenskii, Kosygin, Mikoyan, etc.).
12/2/43	GKO	On Improving Material and Equipment Supplies for RR Transportation	Priorities established.
1944			
*1944	GKO	Wartime Economic Plan for 1944	
		or	Not clear which of these the plan was.
*1944a		Plan for Development of National Economy for 1944	
1/3–5/44		Monthly, quarterly, and annual plans of 1944 in Kuznetsk and Moscow Basins and Donetsk and Lugansk Provinces	Physical goals and results for 1943 given. Obligations taken by miners and metalworkers to overfulfill planned targets.

Table E-5 *continued*

Date (1)	Agency (2)	Title of Plan or Resolution (3)	Details (4)
2/8/44	GKO	On Measures to Develop Coal Mining in Pechora Basin	
2/11/44	GKO	On Restarting Construction of Nevinnomyssk Canal and Svistukhinsk Central Power Station in Stavropol Territory	Goals for opening in 1944 and III Q 1945.
2/18/44	USSR SNK and KPSS TsK	On Building Tractor Plants and on Developing Capacities for Tractor Production for Agriculture	Precise goals for 1944 and 1945 for production and construction. Personnel and material priorities set.
2/26/44	USSR SNK	On Essential Measures to Rebuild Livestock Breeding on Collective Farms in Liberated Areas of Belorussia	
2/28/44	GKO	On Developing Production of Machine Tools in Enterprises of Commissariat for Machine Tool Building	Goals for output, construction, putting facilities into operation. Priorities set.
*3/14/44	USSR SNK and KPSS TsK	On State Plan for Development of Agriculture in 1944	Plans for sowing and for MTS work. Goals for yield per hectare of sown area.
3/14/44a	USSR SNK	On Material and Equipment Supply for Agriculture	Goals for production of tractors and agricultural machinery, fertilizer, and investment in 1944.
3/29/44	GKO	On Rebuilding Industry and Communal Economy of Leningrad	Goals for 1944.
4/16/44	GKO	On Installing New Capacities in Central Power Stations	Plan for 1944.
5/11/44	GKO	On Measures to Increase Oil Production in 1944	
5/18/44	GKO	On Economical Utilization of Electric Power in Industry	New norms set for power consumption.
5/23/44	GKO	On Establishing Housing Construction Industry on a Large Scale	Goals for 1944 and I half 1945. Priorities in material and equipment supply set.
5/27/44	Soviet of City of Leningrad	On Plan to Rebuild Economy of City of Leningrad in 1944	Precise goals. Compulsory supplementary hours of work fixed.
6/2/44	GKO	On Rebuilding Central Power Stations and Power Networks for Krivoi Rog Mining Basin and for Manganese Deposits in Nikopol	
7/11/44	GKO	On Building New Facilities and Rebuilding Ferrous Metal Enterprises during II Half 1944	
7/18/44	GKO	On Reconstruction of Coal Industry in Donbass	Output goals for 1944. Supplies. Equipment. Priorities.
*7/20/44	USSR SNK and KPSS TsK	On Harvest and Procurements of Agricultural Products in 1944	Priorities set. Work organized.
*7/30/44		Plan for RR Transportation	Results given for I Q & II Q 1944.
*8/44	USSR Gosplan	Draft of Plan for Reconstruction and Development of National Economy for 1943–1947	Goals for 1947 (1940 = 100): national income = 132; industrial production = 128; agricultural production = 93; RR transportation = 108.

Table E-5 *continued*

Date (1)	Agency (2)	Title of Plan or Resolution (3)	Details (4)
8/11/44	USSR SNK	On Reconstruction of Light Industry Enterprises in Liberated Areas of Ukraine	
10/1/44	GKO	On Emphasizing Reconstruction and Development of Coal, Oil, Metal Industries, and Electric Power Stations	Priorities. Gosplan to present plan for 1945–1946 by half-year.
10/10/44	GKO	On Measures to Guarantee Work without Dislocations in Ferrous Metal Enterprises	
*10–12/44	USSR Gosplan	Two-year plans (1945–1946) for coal and oil industries, central power stations, ferrous and nonferrous metal industry drafted on orders from GKO	
12/2/44	GKO	On Improving Material and Equipment Supply to RR Transportation	Supplies given same priorities as supplies for People's Commissariat of Defense
1945			
1/18/45	GKO	Plan for Production and Consumption of Electric Power for I Q 1945; Plan for Mining Coal and Oil Shale in I Q 1945	
*1/29/45	USSR SNK and KPSS TsK	On State Economic Plan for I Q 1945	
1/29/45	GKO	Plan for Production of Planes and Plane Motors in I Q 1945. Measures to Improve Material and Equipment Supply to Metal Enterprises	Output goals. Priorities.
2/8/45	USSR SNK	On Electrification of Countryside	Goals for construction and deliveries of equipment in 1945. Priorities.
*2/24/45	USSR SNK and KPSS TsK	On Results of Agricultural Production in 1944 and on Plan for Agricultural Work in 1945	Goals, increased yields, and production.
2/45	GKO	Resolution on Opening New Central Power Stations and on Producing Turbogenerators of 50,000 and 100,000 kw	
3/3/45	GKO	Examination of Plans to Produce Mining Machinery	Goals for production and deliveries for 1945 and I Q 1945.
*3/13/45	NKZem	On Measures to Improve MTS Work in 1945	
*3/25/45		Plan for Reconstruction and Development of National Economy in 1945	Annual plan more general than wartime plans for 1942–1945. Physical goals.

Table E-5 *continued*

Date (1)	Agency (2)	Title of Plan or Resolution (3)	Details (4)
*4/6/45	USSR SNK and KPSS TsK	On State Plan for Development of Livestock Breeding on Collective and State Farms in 1945	Precise goals.
4/13/45	GKO	On Reconstruction of Donbass Coal Mines	Output goals for 1945.
4/13/45a	GKO	On Plan for Extracting and Refining Oil in II Q 1945	
6/13/45	USSR SNK	On Measures to Reconstruct Housing, Production Buildings, and Buildings for Cultural Purposes on Collective Farms and Rural Belorussia	
6/20/45	GKO	Sending demobilized soldiers to work in ferrous metal and coal industries in III Q 1945	10,300 engineers and technicians; 69,790 skilled workers.
6/21/45	GKO	On Reconstruction of Port of Novorossisk	
6/28/45	GKO	On Increase in Oil Extraction in Baku	
*7/13/45	USSR SNK and KPSS TsK	On Harvest and Procurement of Agricultural Products in 1945	Procurement plan. Supplies.
7/14/45	USSR SNK	On Measures to Rebuild and Develop Cotton Growing in Uzbekistan	Goals for 1945, 1946, 1947. Irrigation, mechanization, fertilizers.
*7/17/45	KPSS TsK and USSR SNK	National Economic Plan for III Q 1945	First postwar plan. Precise goals.
8/5/45	GKO	On Putting New Capacities into Service in Central Power Stations in 1945 and 1946	
8/18/45	GKO	On Construction of Factories of Commissariat of Coal Industry	
*8/19/45	KPSS TsK and USSR SNK	USSR Gosplan ordered to draft, with people's commissariats and republics: 5-year plan for reconstruction and development of national economy for 1946–1950; and plan for reconstruction and development of RR transportation for 1946–1950	Planned goals were to surpass prewar level of national economy.
8/22/45	USSR SNK	On Increasing Production of Consumer Goods in Local Industrial Enterprises, Industrial Cooperatives, and Invalids' Cooperatives	Use of local raw materials facilitated. Technical aid. Material incentives.
8/26/45	GKO	On Reconstruction and Development of Motor Vehicle Industry	Production goals for 1945 and 1946. Investment goals for 1946–1950. Technological directives.

Table E-5 *continued*

Date (1)	Agency (2)	Title of Plan or Resolution (3)	Details (4)
*10/12/45	USSR SNK	National Economic Plan for IV Q 1945	
11/16/45	USSR SNK	On Reconstruction of 15 Big Cities (Smolensk, Kursk, Orel, Rostov/Don, etc.). Obligation of each city to draft a general plan	Investments of 764 mill. rubles allocated for end of 1945 and 1946.
12/21/45	USSR SNK	On Measures to Help Rebuild and Develop Chemical Industry (resolution based on GKO resolution including chemical industry among essential branches of heavy industry)	Measures to facilitate formation, allocation, and stimulation of manpower.

Note: An asterisk (*) before the date indicates a general (five-year, annual, quarterly), wartime, or sector plan. The other plans are for regions or activities, changes in priorities, or revisions of existing plans.

Abbreviations

GKO = *Glavnyi Komitet Oborony* (Chief Committee for Defense)
KPSS = *Kommunisticheskaia Partiia Sovetskogo Soiuza* (Communist Party of the Soviet Union)
MTS = *Mashino-Traktornaia Stantsiia* (Machine and Tractor Station)
NKZem = *Narodnyi Komissariat Zemledeliia* (People's Commissariat of Agriculture)
Q = Quarter
SNK = *Sovet Narodnykh Komissarov* (Council of People's Commissars)
TsK = *Tsentralnyi Komitet* (Central Committee)

Source

1941–6/6/41: *99*, p. 87; *21*, p. 87. 6/41: *69*, Vol. 1, p. 412. **7/30/41 and 8/16/41:** *290*, pp. 30–31; *220*, pp. 166–67; *69*, Vol. 2, p. 139; *207*, p. 119; *99*, p. 90; *219*, pp. 206–7; *21*, pp. 87–88; *34*, Bk. I, p. 332; *26*, Vol. 2, pp. 707–12. **7/30/41a:** *69*, Vol. 2, pp. 628–29. 8/29/41: *69*, Vol. 2, pp. 153–54. 9/4/41: *238*, p. 60. 10/41: *34*, Bk. I, p. 338. 9-10/41: *114*, p. 34. 11/9/41: *69*, Vol. 2, p. 162; *238*, p. 95. 11/17/41: *69*, Vol. 2, p. 168; *238*, p. 99. 11/19/41: *98*, pp. 665–66; *69*, Vol. 2, p. 218. 12/8/41: *69*, Vol. 2, p. 155. 12/41: *114*, p. 35. 12/29/41: *26*, Vol. 2, p. 713; *99*, p. 123. **12/41a:** *99*, p. 97.

1942–1/3/42: *26*, Vol. 2, pp. 714–19. 1/6/42: *26*, Vol. 2, pp. 719–22. 1/11/42: *212*, No. 1, 1942, Art. 1. 2/5/42: *99*, p. 123. 2/12/42: *69*, Vol. 2, p. 507. 2/15/42: *238*, p. 154. 2/21/42: *238*, p. 157. 3/3/42: *34*, Bk. I, p. 344. 3/13/42: *180*, 3/13/42, as cited in *34*, Bk. I, p. 344. 4/13/42: *26*, Vol. 2, pp. 724–25. 4/14/42: *69*, Vol. 2, p. 168. 4/15/42: *69*, Vol. 2, pp. 508–9; *238*, p. 178. 5/3-8/42: *114*, p. 38. 7/8/42: *180*, 7/8/42 and 7/10/42, as cited in *34*, Bk. I, p. 348. 7/11/42: *212*, No. 7, 1942, Art. 108. 7/42: *99*, p. 124. 8/24/42: *238*, p. 245; *69*, Vol. 2, pp. 506–7. **8/24/42a:** *69*, Vol. 2, p. 349. 9/3/42: *238*, p. 250. 9/5/42: *238*, p. 251; *69*, Vol. 2, p. 502. 9/22/42: *238*, p. 258. **9/22/42a:** *26*, Vol. 2, pp. 726–27.

1943–1943: *207*, p. 120; *220*, p. 168; *219*, p. 208; *21*, p. 88. 1/18/43: *69*, Vol. 3, p. 141. 2/7/43: *26*, Vol. 2, pp. 750–51. **3/3/43, 3/19/43, 4/13/43:** *180*, 3/3/43 and 3/19/43, as cited in *34*, Bk. I, p. 358; *26*, Vol. 2, pp. 755–64. 3/18/43: *26*, Vol. 2, pp. 753–55. **4/14/43–4/19/43b:** *69*, Vol. 3, p. 611; *238*, p. 368; *34*, Bk. I, p. 359. 5/13/43: *180*, 5/13/43, as cited in *34*, Bk. I, p. 360. 6/43: *69*, Vol. 3, pp. 153–54. 7/18/43: *180*, 7/18/43, as cited in *34*, Bk. I, p. 361; *22*, p. 198. 8/21/43: *26*, Vol. 2, pp. 765–802. 8/43: *207*, p. 123. **9/43 and 9/43a:** *114*, pp. 148–50. 10/26/43: *26*, Vol. 2, pp. 802–15. **11/43, 12/2/43:** *69*, Vol. 3, p. 190.

1944–1944: *220*, p. 168; *219*, p. 208. *21*, p. 88, mentions "wartime economic plans for 1943 and the following years." **1944a:** *114*, p. 140. The author notes that this plan envisages a leap forward in industry and agriculture. He might have been referring to a more general plan than the "wartime economic plan" mentioned above, but it is possible that he confused the "wartime economic plans" with the "plans for the development of the national economy." 1/3-5/44: *180*, 1/3/44 and 1/5/44, as cited in *34*, Bk. I, p. 369. 2/8/44: *34*, Bk. I, pp. 370–71; *238*, p. 510; *26*, Vol. 2, pp. 818–22. 2/11/44: *26*, Vol. 2, p. 817. 2/18/44: *34*, Bk. I, pp. 370–71; *238*, p. 510; *26*, Vol. 2, pp. 818–22. 2/26/44: *69*, Vol. 4, p. 674. 2/28/44: *26*, Vol. 2, pp. 822–26. 3/14/44: *180*, 3/15/44, as cited in *34*, Bk. I, pp. 371–72. **3/14/44a:** *26*, Vol. 2, pp. 827–28. 3/29/44: *26*, Vol. 2, pp. 829–34. 4/16/44: *69*, Vol. 4, pp. 582 and 675. 5/11/44: *69*,

Table E-5 *continued*

Vol. 4, p. 675. **5/18/44:** *26,* Vol. 2, pp. 834–37. **5/23/44:** *26,* Vol. 2, pp. 838–43. **5/27/44:** *34,* Bk. I, p. 373. **6/2/44:** *69,* Vol. 4, p. 676. **7/11/44:** *238,* p. 584. **7/18/44:** *26,* Vol. 2, pp. 845–54. **7/20/44:** *180,* 7/20/44, as cited in *34,* Bk. I, p. 374. **7/30/44:** *180,* 7/30/44, as cited in *34,* Bk. I, p. 374. **8/44:** *207,* p. 124. **8/11/44:** *69,* Vol. 4, p. 678. **10/1/44:** *26,* Vol. 2, pp. 854–55. **10/10/44:** *69,* Vol. 4, p. 681. **10-12/44:** *26,* Vol. 2, pp. 854–55; *219,* p. 210; *220,* p. 170; *21,* p. 92. **12/2/44:** *69,* Vol. 4, p. 604.

    1945–1/18/45: *238,* p. 674. **1/29/45:** *238,* p. 682. **1/29/45;** *69,* Vol. 5, pp. 372 and 608. **2/8/45:** *26,* Vol. 2, pp. 856–60. **2/24/45:** *34,* Bk. I, p. 382. **2/45 and 3/3/45:** *69,* Vol. 5, pp. 372–73. **3/13/45:** *230,* 3/17/45, as cited in *34,* Bk. I, p. 383. **3/25/45:** *69,* Vol. 5, pp. 365–69. **4/6/45:** *34,* Bk. I, p. 383. **4/13/45 and 4/13/45a:** *69,* Vol. 5, pp. 403–4 and 610. **6/13/45, 6/20/45:** *69,* Vol. 5, p. 612. **6/21/45:** *69,* Vol. 5, p. 756. **6/28/45:** *69,* Vol. 5, p. 612. **7/13/45:** *212,* No. 6, 1945, Art. 77. **7/14/45:** *26,* Vol. 2, pp. 862–66. **7/17/45:** *69,* Vol. 5, pp. 418–19. **8/5/45:** *238,* p. 773. **8/18/45:** *69,* Vol. 5, p. 613. **8/19/45:** *180,* 8/19/45, as cited in *34,* Bk. I, p. 388. **8/22/45:** *212,* No. 8, 1945, Art. 98. **8/26/45:** *26,* Vol. 2, pp. 874–75. **10/12/45:** *69,* Vol. 5, p. 614. **11/16/45:** *180,* 11/16/45, as cited in *34,* Bk. I, p. 388. **12/21/45:** *26,* Vol. 2, pp. 876–77.

Quarterly Planning

Table F-1   Fulfillment of Quarterly Plans in 1936 in Value Terms (million rubles, 1926/27 prices)

		First Quarter			Second Quarter		
	Annual Plan (1)	Planned (2)	Actual (3)	Per Cent of Plan Fulfilled (4)	Planned (5)	Actual (6)	Per Cent of Plan Fulfilled (7)
I. *Industrial Production*							
1. Union and local industry:[a]	61,350	14,710	15,016	102.1	15,229	15,181	99.7
2.　　Producer goods	37,768	9,278	9,446	101.8	9,858	9,574	97.1
3.　　Consumer goods	23,581	5,432	5,571	102.6	5,371	5,607	104.4
4.　Heavy industry:	33,239	7,813	8,094	103.6	8,879	8,600	96.9
5.　　Commissariat of Heavy Industry	31,340	7,402	7,656	103.4	8,344	8,096	97.0
6.　　Commissariats of local industry	1,899	410	438	106.7	535	505	94.4
7.　Timber industry:	3,340	1,090	991	91.0	718	654	91.1
8.　　Commissariat of Timber Industry	3,057	1,022	920	90.1	648	583	90.0
9.　　Commissariats of local industry	283	68	71	104.5	69	71	102.9
10.　Light industry:	12,809	3,206	3,272	102.1	3,099	3,189	102.9
11.　　Commissariat of Light Industry	7,541	1,931	1,939	100.4	1,776	1,809	101.9
12.　　Commissariats of local industry	5,268	1,274	1,333	104.6	1,324	1,380	104.2
13.　Food industry:	10,029	2,118	2,224	105.0	2,113	2,334	110.5
14.　　Commissariat of Food Industry	9,122	1,916	2,028	105.8	1,888	2,114	112.0
15.　　Commissariats of local industry	907	201	196	97.2	224	220	98.2
16.　Committee for Agricultural Procurement under Council of People's Commissars	1,748	442	401	90.6	374	360	96.3
17.　Central Administration for Photography and Films	184	42	34	82.0	46	45	97.8
18. Industrial cooperatives	5,366		1,233			1,313	
II. *Union and Local Industrial Production by Branch*[a]							
A. Producer goods							
19.　Regional electric power stations	1,480	361	384	106.5	360	360	100.0
20.　Coal industry	1,322	322	320	99.3	339	294	86.7
21.　Coke industry	385	93	98	105.4	102	100	98.0
22.　Petroleum extraction	643	157	154	98.5	171	157	91.8
23.　Petroleum refining	1,258	296	317	107.2	326	336	103.1
24.　Oil shale industry	14	3	2	78.0	3	3	100.0
25.　Iron ore industry	160	37	38	103.2	42	41	97.6
26.　Manganese ore industry	36	9	8	99.4	9	10	111.1
27.　Ferrous metal industry	3,284	798	826	103.5	882	630	71.4
28.　Nonferrous metal industry	1,256	282	258	91.7	335	290	86.6
29.　Machine-building and metalworking industries:	17,591	4,039	4,144	102.6	4,715	4,469	94.8
30.　　Central Administration for Power Machine-Building	1,437	341	378	111.0	386	399	103.4
31.　　Central Administration for Transport Machine-Building	1,075	251	227	90.5	274	235	85.8

Third Quarter			Fourth Quarter					
Planned (8)	Actual (9)	Per Cent of Plan Fulfilled (10)	Planned (11)	Actual (12)	Per Cent of Plan Fulfilled (13)	Annual Production (14)	Per Cent of Annual Plan Fulfilled (15)	Series No.
16,689	15,368	92.1	19,699	18,734	95.1	64,728	105.5	1
10,747	9,543	88.8	11,894	11,087	93.2	39,722	105.2	2
5,943	5,824	98.0	7,805	7,648	98.0	25,006	106.0	3
9,599	8,570	89.3	10,317	9,775	94.7	35,082	105.5	4
9,011	8,011	89.3	9,746	9,232	94.7	33,064	105.5	5
588	525	89.4	571	543	95.2	2,018	106.3	6
909	726	79.8	1,039	802	77.2	3,272	98.0	7
832	653	78.5	954	725	76.0	2,980	97.5	8
77	73	94.6	85	77	91.0	293	103.5	9
3,213	3,126	97.3	3,955	3,923	99.2	13,640	106.5	10
1,861	1,781	95.7	2,401	2,348	97.8	7,974	105.7	11
1,352	1,345	99.5	1,553	1,575	101.4	5,665	107.5	12
2,437	2,468	101.3	3,714	3,550	95.6	10,731	107.0	13
2,184	2,243	102.7	3,435	3,306	96.2	9,864	108.1	14
252	225	89.0	278	244	87.7	867	95.6	15
484	444	91.7	612	630	102.9	1,833	104.9	16
48	35	76.7	62	55	87.9	169	91.8	17
	1,315			1,506				18
363	352.7	97.3	426	430	100.8	1,531	103.4	19
340	296.5	87.2	388	324	83.6	1,236	93.5	20
105	98.3	93.7	107	101	94.6	398	103.4	21
173	153.6	88.6	173	159	91.8	624	100.2	22
359	340.0	94.6	363	347	95.5	1,344	106.8	23
3.6	2.3	63.1						24
41.8	38.4	91.9	42	41	95.9	158	98.8	25
9.3	8.9	96.0	9.7	9.1	93.6	36	100.0	26
746	667.3	89.5	962	954	99.2	3,516	107.1	27
384	318.7	82.9	407	346	84.9	1,188	94.6	28
5,093	4,435.6	87.1	5,607	5,251	93.6	18,276	103.9	29
400	387.5	96.9	444	461	103.8	1,631	113.5	30
295	248.1	84.1	330	279	84.6	941	87.5	31

Table F-1   *continued*

| | | | First Quarter | | | Second Quarter | | |
	Annual Plan (1)	Planned (2)	Actual (3)	Per Cent of Plan Fulfilled (4)	Planned (5)	Actual (6)	Per Cent of Plan Fulfilled (7)
32. Central Administration for Motor Vehicle and Tractor Industry	2,727	570	626	109.8	697	679	97.4
33. Central Administration for Agricultural Machine-Building	980	230	215	93.3	261	247	94.6
34. Central Administration for Machine Tool Construction	551	131	142	108.0	158	170	107.6
35. Cement industry [b]	177	43	39	91.8	56	52	92.9
36. Glass and china industry [c]	190	46	50	109.5	49	52	106.1
37. Basic chemical industry	500	122	128	104.3	133	132	99.2
38. Rubber industry	1,074	267	256	95.8	280	274	97.9
39. Technical fiber industry	265	68	72	105.9	68	72	105.9
40. Procurement of industrial timber and firewood [d]	1,409	700	586	83.7	251	205	81.7
41. Woodprocessing industry	1,315	294	314	106.9	292	289	99.0
42. Paper industry	504	121	116	95.5	121	91	75.2
43. Wood chemical industry	82	10	10	99.1	13	15	115.4
B. Consumer goods							
44. Cotton industry	3,890	970	980	100.9	922	705	76.5
45. Woolen industry	806	207	210	101.4	179	188	105.0
46. Linen industry	513	117	110	93.9	124	106	85.5
47. Silk and rayon industry	433	108	107	99.4	101	70	69.3
48. Knitted goods industry	1,065	265	272	102.5	274	279	101.8
49. Leather and shoe industry	1,395	335	361	107.6	369	403	109.2
50. Hemp and jute industry	225	57	56	99.4	58	58	100.0
51. Fat industry	421	113	112	99.1	99	103	104.0
52. Match industry	67	14	15	103.8	18	18	100.0
53. Flour milling industry [b]	1,536	379	335	88.3	316	307	97.2
54. Meat industry	1,466	272	268	98.3	199	257	129.1
55. Fish catch	107		10		36	33	91.7
56. Fish processing industry	459		53		156	150	96.2
57. Butter industry (*masloboinaia*) [e]	328	91	92	101.1	63	66	104.8
58. Butter industry (*maslodelnaia*) [e]	316		45		123	120	97.6
59. Margarine industry	111	27	33	123.5	23	22	95.7
60. Raw sugar	772		119			4.	
61. Lump sugar	362		141		65	96	147.7
62. Canned goods industry	262	28	39	140.9	27	29	107.4
63. Crude alcohol industry	279	75	93	123.2	54	63	116.7
64. Tobacco industry [b]	339	86	84	97.3	86	91	105.8
65. Low-grade tobacco industry (*makhorka*) [b]	69	16	16	97.7	17	17	100.0
66. Confectionery industry	1,050	247	257	104.1	248	271	109.3
67. Beer and nonalcoholic beverage industry	284	42	51	121.1	88	100	113.6
68. Salt industry [b]	39		6		11	11	100.0

| Third Quarter | | | Fourth Quarter | | | | | |
Planned (8)	Actual (9)	Per Cent of Plan Fulfilled (10)	Planned (11)	Actual (12)	Per Cent of Plan Fulfilled (13)	Annual Production (14)	Per Cent of Annual Plan Fulfilled (15)	Series No.
828	689.3	83.2	978	826	84.5	2,846	104.4	32
260	196.1	75.3	261	218	83.6	880	89.8	33
168	168.1	100.2	179	196	109.5	690	125.2	34
63	54.3	86.8	65	52	81.0	205	115.8	35
50	47.3	94.5	48	51	107.0	191	100.5	36
127	114.0	90.1	146	147	100.8	520	104.0	37
272	255.7	94.0	346	308	89.0	1,094	101.9	38
62	63.6	103.0	77	84	109.2	288	108.7	39
260	157.3	60.5	434	287	66.1	1,357	96.3	40
410	358.9	87.5	416	343	82.6	1,312	99.8	41
103	96.6	94.1	137	133	97.1	491	97.4	42
37	29.9	81.2	29	24	80.5	79	96.3	43
693	639.2	92.2	1,124	1,090	97.1	4,006	103.0	44
216	229.1	105.9	240	245	102.1	861	107.0	45
131	100.7	77.0	136	116	84.8	431	84.0	46
82	79.6	97.5	124	125	100.8	436	100.7	47
266	245.0	92.2	300	283	94.3	1,078	101.2	48
361	397.4	110.0	434	473	109.0	1,642	117.7	49
53	50.2	94.8	64	63	98.7	230	102.2	50
76	77.3	102.1	139	127	91.0	425	101.0	51
21	24.1	115.3	23	23	100.0	80	119.4	52
445	411.2	92.4	543	565	104.1	1,617	105.3	53
319	385.1	120.9	776	756	97.5	1,686	115.0	54
55	49.2	88.9	18	15	83.5	106	99.1	55
142	143.2	100.7	133	119	89.0	470	102.4	56
53	51.1	96.6	126	110	87.2	331	100.9	57
125	126.4	100.4	32	46	144.3	344	108.9	58
17	19.5	113.5	42	37	87.6	113	101.8	59
87	25.7	29.7	610	472	77.4	620	80.3	60
18	12.9	70.4	131	134	102.0	384	106.1	61
121	136.9	112.7	114	95	82.8	304	116.0	62
36	22.3	61.4	85	95	111.7	273	97.8	63
90	90.3	100.6	120	104	86.6	369	108.8	64
17	16.2	93.6	22	21	97.1	70	101.4	65
256	229.8	89.6	299	292	97.9	1,078	102.7	66
103	99.4	96.7	63	63	100.6	315	110.9	67
11	10.6	98.3	12	7	58.6	35	89.7	68

Table F-1 *continued*

Source

COLUMNS 1 and 3–Lines 1-17 and 19-54: *162a*, March 1936, pp. 3–5. **Line 18:** *162a*, Dec. 1936, p. 3. **Lines 55-68:** *162a*, Sept. 1936. Used because page missing from *162a*, March 1936.

COLUMN 2–Lines 1-17 and 19-54: *162a*, March 1936, pp. 3–5. **Lines 57, 59, and 62-67:** Based on actual production (col. 3) and per cent of plan fulfilled (col. 4).

COLUMN 4–Lines 1-17 and 19-54: *162a*, March 1936, pp. 3–5. **Lines 57-59 and 62-67:** *171*, No. 9, 1936, p. 41. For line 67, beer only.

COLUMN 5–Lines 1-17, 19-59, and 61-68: *162a*, May 1936, pp. 3–6.

COLUMNS 6 and 9–Lines 1-17 and 19-68: *162a*, Sept. 1936, pp. 3–6. **Line 18:** *162a*, Dec. 1936, p. 3.

COLUMN 7–Lines 1-17, 19-59, and 61-68: Based on planned production (col. 5) and actual production (col. 6).

COLUMN 8–Lines 1-17: *162a*, Sept. 1936, pp. 3–6. **Lines 19-68:** Based on actual production (col. 9) and per cent of plan fulfilled (col. 10).

COLUMN 10–Lines 1-17 and 19-68: *162a*, Sept. 1936, pp. 3–6.

COLUMN 11–Lines 1-4, 7, 10, and 13: *162a*, Dec. 1936, pp. xxxii–xxxiii. **Lines 5-6, 8-9, 11-12, 14-17, 19-23, and 25-68:** *162a*, Dec. 1936, pp. 4–9.

COLUMN 12–Lines 1-4, 7, 10, and 13: *162a*, Dec. 1936, pp. xxxii–xxxiii. **Lines 5-6, 8-9, 11-12, 14-23, and 25-68:** *162a*, Dec. 1936, pp. 3–9.

Table F-2 Fulfillment of Quarterly Plans in 1936 in Physical Units

			First Quarter			Second Quarter		
	Units	Annual Plan (1)	Planned (2)	Actual (3)	Per Cent of Plan Fulfilled (4)	Planned (5)	Actual (6)	Per Cent of Plan Fulfilled (7)
Producer goods								
1. Regional electric power stations	mill. kwh	22,000	5,300	5,685	107.3	5,400	5,415	100.3
2. Coal	th. m. t.	131,500	31,975	32,031	100.2	33,800	29,696	87.9
3. Coke	th. m. t.	19,500	4,700	4,908	104.4	5,150	5,002	97.1
4. Petroleum and gas	th. m. t.	30,000	7,350	7,213	98.1	8,036	7,319	91.1
5. Petroleum used for refining	th. m. t.	25,100	6,080	6,008	98.8	6,459	6,281	97.2
6. Oil shale	th. m. t.	850	180	127	70.6	182	132	72.5
7. Iron ore	th. m. t.	27,950	6,435	6,823	106.0	7,300	7,181	98.4
8. Manganese ore	th. m. t.	2,800	702	697	99.3	758	829	109.4
9. Pig iron	th. m. t.	14,490	3,500	3,525	100.7	3,730	3,614	96.9
10. Steel ingots and castings	th. m. t.	15,860	3,907	3,920	100.3	4,100	3,949	96.3
11. Rolled steel	th. m. t.	12,100	2,833	3,062	108.1	3,200	3,029	94.7
12. Aluminum	m. t.	37,000	8,000	7,979	99.7	9,000	7,881	87.6
13. Refined copper	m. t.	110,000	25,000	22,647	90.6	29,000	24,597	84.8
14. Phosphoric fertilizer	th. m. t.	1,320	334	384	115.0	385	363	94.3
15. Sulfuric acid	th. m. t.	1,285	306	322	105.2	350	316	90.3
16. Synthetic rubber	m. t.	42,300	9,600	10,592	110.3	11,080	9,231	83.3
17. Cement, total	th. m. t.	6,454		1,314			1,462	
18. Cement, Commissariat of Heavy Industry	th. m. t.	5,500	1,300	1,194	91.8	1,435	1,333	92.9
19. Window glass, Commissariat of Heavy Industry	th. m. t.	172.6	46	44	95.7	44	37	84.1
20. Industrial timber hauled	th. m³	118,924	82,683	69,043	83.5	13,997		
21. Lumber, Commissariat of Heavy Industry	th. m³	26,550	6,407	6,288	98.1	5,539		

Table F-1 *continued*

COLUMN 13–Lines 1-4, 7, 10, and 13: *162a*, Dec. 1936, pp. xxxii–xxxiii. **Lines 5-6, 8-9, 11-12, 14-17, 19-23, and 25-68:** *162a*, Dec. 1936, pp. 4–9.

COLUMN 14–Lines 1-17, 19-23, and 25-68: *162a*, Dec. 1936, pp. 4–9.

COLUMN 15–Lines 1-17, 19-23, and 25-68: Based on planned production (col. 1) and actual production (col. 14).

Note: The percentages in cols. 4, 7, 10, and 13 may not check out with figures in preceding columns because of rounding of figures given in original sources.

a. This definition, which is given in the reports on quarterly plans, does not cover all industry. It does not cover the production of cooperatives and of nonindustrial commissariats. Total industrial production planned for 1936 was 81.1 bill. rubles in 1926/27 prices (*156*, p. 392).

b. Does not include the production of republic commissariats of local industry.

c. Includes the production of *Glavenergo* insulators.

d. Includes only procurements of the Commissariat of the Timber Industry and the Commissariat of Heavy Industry (*Soiuzlespromtiazh*).

e. The distinction between *masloboinaia* and *maslodelnaia* is not clear.

	Third Quarter			Fourth Quarter					
Planned (8)	Actual (9)	Per Cent of Plan Fulfilled (10)	Planned (11)	Actual (12)	Per Cent of Plan Fulfilled (13)	Annual Production (14)	Per Cent of Annual Plan Fulfilled (15)	Series No.
5,450	5,315	97.5	6,300	6,365	101.0	22,781	103.2	1
34,067	29,700	87.2	38,634	32,252	83.5	123,679	93.6	2
5,300	4,863	91.8	5,400	5,110	94.6	19,883	102.0	3
8,125	7,193	88.5	8,135	7,468	91.8	29,192.1	97.3	4
6,665	6,250	93.8	6,900	6,230	90.3	24,770	98.7	5
210	118	56.2	210	96	45.6	471	55.5	6
7,195	6,729	93.5	7,460	7,185	96.3	27,918	99.0	7
765	743	97.1	800	733	91.7	3,002	107.2	8
3,803	3,591	94.4	3,803	3,665	96.4	14,395	99.3	9
4,264	3,950	92.6	4,266	4,425	103.7	16,244	102.0	10
3,322	2,891	87.0	3,323	3,420	102.9	12,402	102.1	11
10,000	8,286	82.9	11,940	8,416	70.5	32,562	88.0	12
30,500	23,956	78.5	33,500	29,532	88.2	100,732	91.6	13
289	156	54.0	377	353	93.8	1,275	95.2	14
296	226	76.4	372	338	90.7	1,201	92.9	15
12,600	12,005	95.3	15,600	14,905	95.5	46,733	110.5	16
1,801	1,546	85.8	1,932	1,522	78.8	5,845	90.6	17
	1,381		1,700	1,356	79.7	5,264	93.3	18
45	34	75.6	39.7	35.3	88.9	150.5	87.2	19
11,629	5,860	50.4	27,726	13,800	49.9	102,010	84.8	20
8,655	7,580	87.6	7,834	6,540	83.5	25,471	96.8	21

Table F-2 *continued*

	Units	Annual Plan (1)	First Quarter			Second Quarter		
			Planned (2)	Actual (3)	Per Cent of Plan Fulfilled (4)	Planned (5)	Actual (6)	Per Cent of Plan Fulfilled (7)
22. Plywood	th. m³	614	148	164	110.8	164	167	101.8
23. Paper, total	th. m. t.	730		167			173	
24. Paper, Commissariat of Timber Industry	th. m. t.	668	159	151	95.2	165	158	95.8
25. Machine tools, total	units	29,662		6,797			7,005	
26. Machine tools, Commissariat of Heavy Industry	units	23,905	5,602	5,182	92.5	6,110	5,831	95.4
27. Blast furnace equipment	m. t.	1,470	316	265	83.9	230	199	86.5
28. Open-hearth furnace equipment	m. t.	3,700	419	560	133.7	530	379	71.5
29. Rolling mill equipment	m. t.	44,500		5,322		7,800	5,715	73.3
30. Equipment for presses and forges	m. t.	12,103	2,200	1,994	90.6	3,316	2,024	61.0
31. Steam turbines	th. kw	907	201	85	42.3	220	191	86.8
32. Steam boilers[a]	th. m²	260	60	45	75.0	70	36	51.4
33. Generators for steam turbines	th. kw	633	150	56	37.3	125	65	52.0
34. Tractors	units	99,200	31,750	32,300	101.7	27,000	28,086	104.0
35. Tractors (15 hp)	units	157,267	45,817	45,020	98.3	42,000	43,156	102.8
36. Motor vehicles, total	units	157,500	19,725	19,882	100.8	38,225	33,362	87.3
37. Trucks and buses[b]	units	144,500	19,075	19,211	100.7	35,825	32,758	91.4
38. Automobiles	units	13,000	650	671	103.2	2,400	604	25.2
39. Grain combines	units	60,000	15,000	13,793	92.0	15,100	16,408	108.7
40. Steam locomotives	units	1,400	349	324	92.8	354	312	88.1
41. Railroad freight cars	units	46,375	12,930	13,242	102.4	13,720	11,392	83.0
42. Railroad freight cars (2-axle units)	units	80,000	18,800	17,947	95.5	22,400	18,587	83.0
43. Railroad passenger cars	units	933	155	142	91.6	239	172	72.0
Consumer goods								
44. Cotton yarn[c]	th. m. t.	368	93	93	100.0	93	91	97.8
45. Cotton fabrics[c]	mill. m	2,511	639	673	105.3	656	643	98.0
46. Woolen fabrics[c]	mill. m	66	17	17	100.0	15	15	100.0
47. Linen fabrics[c]	mill. m	304	69	68	98.6	77	62	80.5
48. Silk and rayon fabrics	mill. m	41	10	11	110.0	9.5	9.8	103.2
49. Knitted underwear, total[d]	thous.	52,563		12,585			13,922	
50. Knitted underwear, Commissariat of Light Industry	thous.	30,000	6,800	7,362	108.3	8,100	8,292	102.4
51. Knitted outer garments, total[d]	thous.	13,900		3,783			3,732	
52. Knitted outer garments, Commissariat of Light Industry	thous.	2,200	520	574	110.4	520	549	105.6
53. Hosiery, total[d]	th. pairs	271,486		63,819			66,169	
54. Hosiery, Commissariat of Light Industry	th. pairs	135,000	33,090	32,284	97.6	33,000	33,340	101.0
55. Leather shoes, total[d]	th. pairs	79,241		20,338			22,101	
56. Leather shoes, Commissariat of Light Industry	th. pairs	45,000	11,200	11,915	106.4	12,500	12,906	103.2
57. Rubber footwear	th. pairs	85,000	22,000	20,876	94.9	20,000	20,692	103.5
58. Flour, Commissariat of Food Industry[e]	th. m. t.	11,701	3,053	2,707	88.7	2,418	2,345	97.0

	Third Quarter			Fourth Quarter					
Planned (8)	Actual (9)	Per Cent of Plan Fulfilled (10)	Planned (11)	Actual (12)	Per Cent of Plan Fulfilled (13)	Annual Production (14)	Per Cent of Annual Plan Fulfilled (15)	Series No.	
168	162	96.4	185	168	90.4	660.4	107.6	22	
191	178.4	93.4	198	184	93.0	701.8	96.1	23	
173	163	94.2	180	168.4	93.5	641.1	96.3	24	
8,234	6,953	84.4	8,478	8,011	97.0	28,766	96.9	25	
6,800	5,819	85.6	6,800	6,688	98.4	23,769	99.4	26	
260	60	23.1	261	26	10.0	550	37.4	27	
294	284	96.6	578	619	107.1	1,842	49.8	28	
12,207	7,113	58.3	10,871	8,081	74.3	26,231	58.9	29	
2,346	1,086	46.3	2,213	1,403	63.4	6,507	53.8	30	
285	177	62.1	308	107	34.6	558	65.3	31	
80	25.7	32.1	90	61.6	68.5	168	63.0	32	
180	117	65.0	200	266	133.0	503.5	79.5	33	
29,300	28,728	98.0	25,487	26,481	103.9	115,595	116.5	34	
44,960	43,021	95.7	41,157	42,166	102.5	173,363	110.2	35	
46,875	35,845	76.5	61,331	47,483	77.4	136,572	86.7	36	
42,875	34,640	80.8	53,531	46,308	86.5	132,917	92.0	37	
4,000	1,205	30.1	7,800	1,175	15.1	3,655	28.1	38	
15,300	7,274	47.5	15,600	5,070	32.5	42,545	69.7	39	
333	232	69.7	450	285	63.3	1,153	82.4	40	
12,220	8,949	73.2	15,800	10,841	68.6	45,966	87.7	41	
23,330	16,311	69.9	30,540	20,492	67.1	75,864	84.3	42	
259	195	75.3	378	216	57.1	725	80.1	43	
97.8	90.8	92.8	103.6	103.3	99.7	377.8	102.6	44	
695	634	91.2	758	739.6	97.6	2,689	102.4	45	
23.0	18.5	80.4	20.3	20.6	100.8	71.8	108.7	46	
75.4	60.8	80.6	79.5	70.3	88.5	259.0	84.9	47	
11.5	10.9	94.8	13.7	12.9	94.1	45.3	101.9	48	
16,126	13,051	80.9	14,569	13,307	91.3	52,865	100.6	49	
	7,664		8,500	8,556	100.7	31,874	106.2	50	
4,343	3,237	74.5	4,062	3,882	95.6	14,634	105.2	51	
	535		700	837	119.6	2,495	113.4	52	
80,610	55,080	68.3	74,683	66,172	88.6	251,241	92.5	53	
	28,067		37,500	36,001	96.0	129,696	96.1	54	
22,990	21,219	92.3	25,374	25,510	100.5	89,169	112.5	55	
	12,110		14,400	14,569	100.8	51,500	114.4	56	
22,500	20,516	91.2	23,500	19,922	84.8	82,006	96.5	57	
3,270	3,184	97.4	4,147	4,418	106.5	12,655	108.3	58	

Table F-2   *continued*

	Units	Annual Plan (1)	First Quarter			Second Quarter		
			Planned (2)	Actual (3)	Per Cent of Plan Fulfilled (4)	Planned (5)	Actual (6)	Per Cent of Plan Fulfilled (7)
59. Macaroni, Commissariat of Food Industry	th. m. t.	125	33	39	118.2	37	41	110.8
60. Soap (40% fatty acid), total[f]	th. m. t.	557		145			135	
61. Soap, Commissariat of Food Industry[f]	th. m. t.	522	140	141	100.7	118	129	109.3
62. Raw sugar	th. m. t.	2,500	400	367	91.8		3	
63. Lump sugar	th. m. t.	1,000	360	389	108.1	180	264	146.7
64. Fish products, total[g]	th. m. t.	1,107		122			397	
65. Fish products, Commissariat of Food Industry[g]	th. m. t.	1,070	125	119	95.2	380	380	100.0
66. Crude alcohol	mill. dl	69,400	18,500	23,423	126.6	13,500	15,967	118.3
67. Vegetable oil, Commissariat of Food Industry[h]	th. m. t.	475	120	120	100.0	80	84	105.0
68. Butter, Commissariat of Food Industry[i]	th. m. t.	125	15	18	120.0	48	45	93.8
69. Meat, Commissariat of Food Industry	th. m. t.	650	117	108	92.3	62	87	140.3
70. Canned food, Commissariat of Food Industry	mill. 400-gm cans	1,000	124	163	131.5	125	120	96.0
71. Confectionery, Commissariat of Food Industry	th. m. t.	487	109	122	111.9	125	137	109.6
72. Margarine and compound fat	th. m. t.	80	18	22	122.2	16	16.6	103.8
73. Beer, total	th. hl	5,699		1,349			1,970	
74. Beer, Commissariat of Food Industry	th. hl	2,620	470	620	131.9	700	914	130.6
75. Cigarettes	billions	87	23	22	95.7	21	21.4	101.9
76. Matches	th. crates	10,700	2,200	2,328	105.8	2,200	2,223	101.0
77. Low-grade tobacco (*makhorka*), Commissariat of Food Industry	th. 20-kg crates	5,000	1,200	1,180	98.3	1,200	1,171	97.6
78. Cast-iron kitchenware, Commissariat of Heavy Industry	th. m. t.	4,130		679	56.6			
79. Bicycles, Commissariat of Heavy Industry	thous.	800		63.9	53.3	150	136	90.7
80. Sewing machines, Commissariat of Heavy Industry	thous.	450		86.5	78.6			
81. Phonographs and records, Commissariat of Heavy Industry	thous.	955					101	
82. Radios, Commissariat of Heavy Industry	thous.	500				130	73	72.3

| Third Quarter | | | Fourth Quarter | | | | | |
Planned (8)	Actual (9)	Per Cent of Plan Fulfilled (10)	Planned (11)	Actual (12)	Per Cent of Plan Fulfilled (13)	Annual Production (14)	Per Cent of Annual Plan Fulfilled (15)	Series No.
	41		37	39	106.0	159.5	127.6	59
98.2	101.8	103.7	178.9	159.7	89.3	542.5	97.4	60
	96.3		166.0	152.4	91.8	518.5	99.3	61
260	77	29.6	2,000	1,552	77.6	1,999	80.0	62
50	34.3	68.6	360	370	102.7	1,057.5	105.8	63
	303.3		310.8	291.4	93.8	1,114.1	100.6	64
277.6	296.1	106.7	301.0	285.0	94.9	1,080.2	101.0	65
9,100	5,711	62.8	21,000	24,072	114.6	69,174	99.7	66
75.7	67.9	89.7	170.0	150.8	88.7	422.2	94.5	67
49.0	45.3	92.4	13.3	14.9	112.0	123.5	99.0	68
135	175.4	129.9	370.0	402.3	108.7	773.1	118.9	69
485	464.2	95.7	262.3	228.7	84.5	976.6	97.7	70
	121.0		151.8	144.0	94.8	523.9	107.6	71
11	12.5	113.6	27.0	23.6	87.4	75.0	93.8	72
1,877	2,109	112.4	1,532	1,721	112.3	7,148	125.4	73
	1,005		725	822	113.4	3,361	128.3	74
21	20.8	99.0	25.6	24.1	94.3	88.1	101.2	75
2,000	1,993	99.7	1,700	1,770	104.1	8,314	87.5	76
1,260	1,204	95.6	1,530	1,465	95.8	5,021	100.4	77
			1,500					78
225	158	70.2	400	200	50.0	557.4	69.7	79
			115			490	108.9	80
237	115	48.5	300			575.5	60.3	81
135	101	74.8	240			334.1	66.8	82

Table F-2 *continued*

Source

COLUMN 1–Lines 1-16, 18, 20-22, 24, 26-28, 31-35, 37-48, 50, 52, 54, 56-59, 61-63, 66-67, 69-72, and 74-77: *162a*, March 1936, pp. 10–17. **Line 17:** *162a*, Dec. 1936, p. 20. *162a*, March 1936, p. 14, gives 5,500 th. m. t. without specification of commissariat. *162a*, Dec. 1936, p. 20, gives 5,640 th. m. t. for the Commissariat of Heavy Industry. The difference between the two figures may be explained by adjustments made during the course of the year. Note that *171*, p. 423 (cited in Table A-2), gives 6,500 th. m. t. **Lines 19, 23, 25, 29-30, 49, 51, 55, 60, 64-65, 68, and 73:** *162a*, Dec. 1936, pp. 16–25. **Line 36:** Sum of lines 37 and 38. **Line 78:** Estimated from statement in *162a*, March 1936, p. xxxiv, that production in January and February was 679,500 m. t. and represented 16.2% of the annual plan. **Lines 79-81:** Table A-2, col. 10. **Line 82:** *156*, p. 421. Includes industrial cooperatives and Commissariat of Communications.

COLUMN 2–Lines 1-16, 18-22, 24, 26-28, 30-35, 37-48, 50, 52, 54, 56-59, 61-63, 65-72, and 74-77: *162a*, March 1936, pp. 10–17. For lines 65 and 68, the decimal points are clearly misplaced. See *162a*, Dec. 1936, p. 24. **Line 36:** Sum of lines 37 and 38.

COLUMN 3–Lines 1-19, 22-23, 27-35, 37-40, 43-46, and 48-77: *162a*, Dec. 1936, pp. 16–25. **Lines 20-21, 24-26, 41-42, and 47:** *162a*, March 1936, pp. 10–15. **Line 36:** Sum of lines 37 and 38. **Lines 78-80:** *162a*, March 1936, pp. xxxiv–xxxv. Given for the Commissariat of Heavy Industry for January and February only. The percentages given for the fulfillment of the quarterly plan, therefore, represent about two-thirds of the totals for the quarter.

COLUMN 4–Lines 1-16, 18-19, 22, 27-28, 30-40, 43-46, 48, 50, 52, 54, 56-59, 61-63, 65-72, and 74-77: Based on planned production (col. 2) and actual production (col. 3). **Lines 20-21, 24, 26, 41-42, and 47:** *162a*, March 1936, pp. 10–15. **Lines 78-80:** *162a*, March 1936, pp. xxxiv–xxxv. See source to col. 3, lines 78–82.

COLUMN 5–Lines 1-16, 18-22, 24, 26-35, 37-48, 50, 52, 54, 56-59, 61-62, 65-72, and 74-77: *162a*, May 1936, pp. 10–17. For line 65, the decimal point is clearly misplaced. See *162a*, Dec. 1936, p. 24. **Line 36:** Sum of lines 37 and 38. **Lines 79 and 82:** *171*, No. 6, 1936, p. 3.

COLUMN 6–Lines 1-19, 22-35, and 37-77: *162a*, Dec. 1936, pp. 16–25. **Line 36:** Sum of lines 37 and 38. **Lines 79 and 81-82:** *171*, No. 13, p. 3.

COLUMN 7–Lines 1-16, 18-19, 22, 24, 26-48, 50, 52, 54, 56-59, 61-63, 65-72, 74-77, 79, and 82: Based on planned production (col. 5) and actual production (col. 6).

COLUMN 8–Lines 1-17, 19-35, 37-49, 51, 53, 55, 57-58, 60, 62-63, 65-70, 72-73, and 75-77: *162a*, Sept. 1936, pp. 14–21. **Line 36:** Sum of lines 37 and 38. **Lines 79 and 81-82:** *171*, No. 13, p. 3.

COLUMN 9–Lines 1-19, 22-35, and 37-77: *162a*, Dec. 1936, pp. 16–25. **Lines 20-21:** Based on planned production (col. 8) and per cent of plan fulfilled (col. 10). **Line 36:** Sum of lines 37 and 38. **Lines 79 and 81-82:** *171*, No. 18, 1936, p. 4.

COLUMN 10–Lines 1-17, 19, 22-49, 51, 53, 55, 57-58, 60, 62-63, 65-70, 72-73, 75-77, 79, and 81-82: Based on planned production (col. 8) and actual production (col. 9). **Lines 20-21:** *162a*, Sept. 1936, p. 19.

COLUMN 11–Lines 1-35 and 37-77: *162a*, Dec. 1936, pp. 16–25. For lines 44 and 58, given as 303.6 th. m. t. and 1,417 th. m. t., which are clearly mistakes in view of fulfillment percentages also given in source. **Line 36:** Sum of lines 37 and 38. **Line 78:** Estimated from statement in *162a*, Dec. 1936, p. xxxvii, that production in October and November was 858 th. m. t. and represented 57.2% of the fourth-quarter plan. **Line 79:** Estimated from statement in *162a*, Dec. 1936, p. xxxvii, that production in October and November was 112.6 thous. and represented 28.2% of the fourth-quarter plan. **Line 80:** Estimated from statement in *162a*, Dec. 1936, p. xxxvii, that production in October and November was 81.6 thous. and represented 71.0% of the fourth-quarter plan. **Lines 81-82:** *171*, No. 18, 1936, p. 4.

COLUMN 12–Lines 1-19, 22-35, and 37-77: *162a*, Dec. 1936, pp. 16–25. **Lines 20-21:** Based on planned production (col. 11) and per cent of plan fulfilled (col. 13). **Line 36:** Sum of lines 37 and 38. **Line 79:** Total annual production (col. 14) minus sum of production in first three quarters (cols. 3, 6, and 9).

COLUMN 13–Lines 1-26, 28-35, and 38-77: *162a*, Dec. 1936, pp. 16–25. **Lines 27, 36-37 and 79:** Based on planned production (col. 11) and actual production (col. 12).

COLUMN 14–Lines 1-35 and 37-77: *162a*, Dec. 1936, pp. 16–25. **Line 36:** Sum of lines 37 and 38. **Lines 79-82:** Table A-2, col. 11.

COLUMN 15–Lines 1-35, 37-58, and 60-77: *162a*, Dec. 1936, pp. 16–25. **Lines 36, 59, and 79-82:** Based on planned production (col. 1) and actual production (col. 14).

Note: The percentages in cols. 4, 7, 10, 13, and 15 may not check out with figures in preceding columns because of rounding of figures given in original sources.

a. Commissariat of Heavy Industry, specified only in *162a*, Dec. 1936.

b. Covers trucks (*gruzovye*) and trolley buses (*troleibusy*), which are listed separately in *162a*, Dec. 1936.

c. Commissariat of Light Industry, specified only in *162a*, Dec. 1936.

Table F-2 *continued*

d. Does not include the Commissariat of Local Industry of the Ukraine. For lines 53 and 55, the local commissariats of other producing regions also seem to have been omitted from the annual plan (see Table A-2, col. 10, series 75 and 76).

e. Commissariat of the Food Industry, specified only in *162a*, Dec. 1936.

f. Data on the Commissariat of the Food Industry is given only in *162a*, Dec. 1936, which gives both the total (which is the same as that given in Table A-2, col. 10, series 88) and the production of the commissariat.

g. Data on the Commissariat of the Food Industry is given only in *162a*, Dec. 1936, but the figures cited as "total" do not seem complete. However, a direct comparison cannot be made with Table A-2, which gives fish catch as opposed to fish products given here. The value of the two series can be compared in Table F-1.

h. Assumed to cover only the Commissariat of the Food Industry (although not specified as such in *162a*, March 1936, p. 16) on the basis of data in *162a*, Dec. 1936, p. 24.

i. Assumed to cover only the Commissariat of the Food Industry (although not specified as such in *162a*, March 1936 and Dec. 1936) on the basis of the total planned figure in Table A-2, col. 10, series 97.

Table F-3 Comparison of Quarterly Plans with Annual Plan in 1936 in Value Terms

	Quarterly Plan as Per Cent of Annual Plan				Per Cent of Quarterly Plan Fulfilled				Per Cent of Annual Plan Fulfilled by End of			
	I Q (1)	*II Q* (2)	*III Q* (3)	*IV Q* (4)	*I Q* (5)	*II Q* (6)	*III Q* (7)	*IV Q* (8)	*I Q* (9)	*II Q* (10)	*III Q* (11)	*IV Q* (12)
I. *Industrial Production*												
1. Union and local industry:[a]	24.0	24.8	27.2	32.1	102.1	99.7	92.1	95.1	24.5	49.2	74.3	104.8
2. Producer goods	24.6	26.1	28.5	31.5	101.8	97.1	88.8	93.2	25.0	50.4	75.6	105.0
3. Consumer goods	23.0	22.8	25.2	33.1	102.6	104.4	98.0	98.0	23.6	47.4	72.1	104.5
4. Heavy industry:	23.5	26.7	28.9	31.0	103.6	96.9	89.3	94.8	24.4	50.2	76.0	105.4
5. Commissariat of Heavy Industry	23.6	26.6	28.8	31.1	103.4	97.0	89.3	94.7	24.4	50.3	75.8	105.3
6. Commissariats of local industry	21.6	28.2	31.0	30.1	106.7	94.4	89.4	95.2	23.1	49.7	77.3	105.9
7. Timber industry:	32.6	21.5	27.2	31.1	91.0	91.1	79.8	77.2	29.7	49.3	71.0	95.0
8. Commissariat of Timber Industry	33.4	21.2	27.2	31.2	90.1	90.0	78.5	76.0	30.1	49.2	70.5	94.2
9. Commissariats of local industry	24.0	24.4	27.2	30.0	104.5	102.9	94.6	91.0	25.1	50.2	76.0	103.2
10. Light industry:	25.0	24.2	25.1	30.9	102.1	102.9	97.3	99.2	25.5	50.4	74.8	105.5
11. Commissariat of Light Industry	25.6	23.6	24.7	31.8	100.4	101.9	95.7	97.8	25.7	49.7	73.3	104.5
12. Commissariats of local industry	24.2	25.1	25.7	29.5	104.6	104.2	99.5	101.4	25.3	51.5	77.0	106.9
13. Food industry:	21.1	21.1	24.3	37.0	105.0	110.5	101.3	95.6	22.2	45.4	70.1	105.5
14. Commissariat of Food Industry	21.0	20.7	23.9	37.7	105.8	112.0	102.7	96.2	22.2	45.4	70.0	106.2
15. Commissariats of local industry	22.2	24.7	27.8	30.7	97.2	98.2	89.0	87.7	21.6	45.9	70.7	97.6
16. Committee for Agricultural Procurement under Council of People's Commissars	25.3	21.4	27.7	35.0	90.6	96.3	91.7	102.9	22.9	43.5	68.9	105.0
17. Central Administration for Photography and Films	22.8	25.0	26.1	33.7	82.0	97.8	76.7	87.9	18.5	42.9	62.0	91.8
18. Industrial Cooperatives									23.0	47.4	72.0	100.0

Table F-3 *continued*

	Quarterly Plan as Per Cent of Annual Plan				Per Cent of Quarterly Plan Fulfilled				Per Cent of Annual Plan Fulfilled by End of			
	I Q (1)	II Q (2)	III Q (3)	IV Q (4)	I Q (5)	II Q (6)	III Q (7)	IV Q (8)	I Q (9)	II Q (10)	III Q (11)	IV Q (12)
II. *Union and Local Industrial Production by Branch*[a]												
A. Producer goods												
19. Regional electric power stations	24.4	24.3	24.5	28.8	106.5	100.0	97.3	100.8	25.9	50.3	74.1	103.
20. Coal industry	24.4	25.6	25.7	29.3	99.3	86.7	87.2	83.6	24.2	46.4	68.9	93.
21. Coke industry	24.2	26.5	27.3	27.8	105.4	98.0	93.7	94.6	25.5	51.4	77.0	103.
22. Petroleum extraction	24.4	26.6	26.9	26.9	98.5	91.8	88.6	91.8	24.0	48.4	72.3	97.
23. Petroleum refining	23.5	25.9	28.5	28.9	107.2	103.1	94.6	95.5	25.2	51.9	78.9	106.
24. Oil shale industry	21.4	21.4	25.7		78.0	100.0	63.1		14.3	35.7	52.1	
25. Iron ore industry	23.1	26.3	26.1	26.3	103.2	97.6	91.9	95.9	23.8	49.4	73.4	99.
26. Manganese ore industry	25.0	25.0	25.8	26.9	99.4	111.1	96.0	93.6	22.2	50.0	74.7	100.
27. Ferrous metal industry	24.3	26.9	22.7	29.3	103.5	71.4	89.5	99.2	25.2	44.3	64.7	93.
28. Nonferrous metal industry	22.5	26.7	30.6	32.4	91.7	86.6	82.9	84.9	20.5	43.6	69.0	96.
29. Machine-building and metalworking industries:	23.0	26.8	29.0	31.9	102.6	94.8	87.1	93.6	23.6	49.0	74.2	104.
30. Central Administration for Power Machine-Building	23.7	26.9	27.8	30.9	111.0	103.4	96.9	103.8	26.3	54.1	81.0	113.
31. Central Administration for Transport Machine-Building	23.3	25.5	27.4	30.7	90.5	85.8	84.1	84.6	21.1	43.0	66.1	92.
32. Central Administration for Motor Vehicle and Tractor Industry	20.9	25.6	30.4	35.9	109.8	97.4	83.2	84.5	23.0	47.9	73.1	103.
33. Central Administration for Agricultural Machine-Building	23.5	26.6	26.5	26.6	93.3	94.6	75.3	83.6	21.9	47.1	67.2	89.
34. Central Administration for Machine Tool Construction	23.8	28.7	30.5	32.5	108.0	107.6	100.2	109.5	25.8	56.6	87.1	122.
35. Cement industry[b]	24.3	31.6	35.6	36.7	91.8	92.9	86.8	81.0	22.0	51.4	82.1	111.
36. Glass and china industry[c]	24.2	25.8	26.3	25.3	109.5	106.1	94.5	107.0	26.3	53.7	78.6	105.
37. Basic chemical industry	24.4	26.6	25.4	29.2	104.3	99.2	90.1	100.8	25.6	52.0	74.8	104.
38. Rubber industry	24.9	26.1	25.3	32.2	95.8	97.9	94.0	89.0	23.8	49.3	73.2	101.
39. Technical fiber industry	25.7	25.7	23.4	29.1	105.9	105.9	103.0	109.2	27.2	54.3	78.3	110.
40. Procurement of industrial timber and firewood[d]	49.7	17.8	18.5	30.8	83.7	81.7	60.5	66.1	41.6	56.1	67.3	87.
41. Woodprocessing industry	22.4	22.2	31.2	31.6	106.9	99.0	87.5	82.6	23.9	45.9	73.1	99.
42. Paper industry	24.0	24.0	20.4	27.2	95.5	75.2	94.1	97.1	23.0	41.1	60.2	86.
43. Wood chemical industry	12.2	15.9	45.1	35.4	99.1	115.4	81.2	80.5	12.2	30.5	67.0	96.
B. Consumer goods												
44. Cotton industry	24.9	23.7	17.8	28.9	100.9	76.5	92.2	97.1	25.2	43.3	59.7	87.
45. Woolen industry	25.7	22.2	26.8	29.8	101.4	115.0	105.9	102.2	26.1	49.4	77.8	108.
46. Linen industry	22.8	24.2	25.5	26.5	93.9	85.5	77.0	84.8	21.4	42.1	61.7	84.
47. Silk and rayon industry	24.9	23.3	18.9	28.6	99.4	69.3	97.5	100.8	24.7	40.9	59.3	88.
48. Knitted goods industry	24.9	25.7	25.0	28.2	102.5	101.8	92.2	94.3	25.5	51.7	74.7	101.
49. Leather and shoe industry	24.0	26.5	25.9	31.1	107.6	109.2	110.0	109.0	25.9	54.8	83.3	117.
50. Hemp and jute industry	25.3	25.8	23.6	28.4	99.4	100.0	94.8	98.7	24.9	50.7	73.0	101.
51. Fat industry	26.8	23.5	17.8	33.0	99.1	104.0	102.1	91.0	26.6	51.1	69.4	99.
52. Match industry	20.9	26.9	31.3	34.3	103.8	100.0	115.3	100.0	22.4	49.3	85.2	119.
53. Flour milling industry[b]	24.7	20.6	29.0	35.4	88.3	97.2	92.4	104.1	21.8	41.8	68.6	105.
54. Meat industry	18.6	13.6	21.8	52.9	98.3	129.1	120.9	97.5	18.3	35.8	62.1	113.
55. Fish catch		33.6	51.4	16.8		91.7	88.9	83.5	9.35	40.2	86.2	100.

Table F-3 *continued*

		Quarterly Plan as Per Cent of Annual Plan				Per Cent of Quarterly Plan Fulfilled				Per Cent of Annual Plan Fulfilled by End of			
		I Q (1)	II Q (2)	III Q (3)	IV Q (4)	I Q (5)	II Q (6)	III Q (7)	IV Q (8)	I Q (9)	II Q (10)	III Q (11)	IV Q (12)
56.	Fish processing industry		34.0	30.9	29.0		96.2	100.7	89.0	11.5	44.2	75.4	101.4
57.	Butter industry (*masloboinaia*)[e]	27.7	19.2	16.2	38.4	101.1	104.8	96.6	87.2	28.0	48.2	63.8	97.3
58.	Butter industry (*maslodelnaia*)[e]		38.9	39.6	10.1		97.6	100.4	144.3	14.2	52.2	92.2	106.8
59.	Margarine industry	24.3	20.7	15.3	37.8	123.5	95.7	113.5	87.6	29.7	49.5	67.1	100.5
60.	Raw sugar			11.3	79.0			29.7	77.4	15.4	15.9	19.3	80.4
61.	Lump sugar		18.0	5.0	36.2		147.7	70.4	102.0	39.0	65.5	69.0	106.0
62.	Canned goods industry	10.7	10.3	46.2	43.5	140.9	107.4	112.7	82.8	14.9	26.0	78.2	114.5
63.	Crude alcohol industry	26.9	19.4	12.9	30.5	123.2	116.7	61.4	111.7	33.3	55.9	63.9	98.0
64.	Tobacco industry[b]	25.4	25.4	26.5	35.4	97.3	105.8	100.6	87.6	24.8	51.6	78.3	108.9
65.	Low-grade tobacco industry (*makhorka*)[b]	23.2	24.6	24.6	31.9	97.7	100.0	93.6	97.1	23.2	47.8	71.3	101.7
66.	Confectionery industry	23.5	23.6	24.4	28.5	104.1	109.3	89.6	97.9	24.5	50.3	72.2	100.0
67.	Beer and nonalcoholic beverage industry	14.8	31.0	36.3	22.2	121.1	113.6	96.7	100.6	18.0	53.2	88.2	110.4
68.	Salt industry[b]		28.2	28.2	30.8		100.0	98.3	58.6	15.4	43.6	70.8	88.7

Source

COLUMNS 1–4–All lines: Derived from Table F-1, cols. 2, 5, 8, and 11, respectively, and col. 1.
COLUMNS 5–8–All lines: Table F-1, cols. 4, 7, 10, and 13, respectively.
COLUMN 9–All lines: Derived from Table F-1, cols. 3 and 1.
COLUMN 10–All lines: Derived from Table F-1, cols. 3, 6, and 1.
COLUMN 11–All lines: Derived from Table F-1, cols. 3, 6, 9, and 1.
COLUMN 12–All lines: Derived from Table F-1, cols. 3, 6, 9, 12, and 1.

Note: For notes a–e, see corresponding notes in Table F-1.

Table F-4   Comparison of Quarterly Plans with Annual Plan in 1936 in Physical Units

	Quarterly Plan as Per Cent of Annual Plan				Per Cent of Quarterly Plan Fulfilled				Per Cent of Annual Plan Fulfilled by End of			
	I Q (1)	II Q (2)	III Q (3)	IV Q (4)	I Q (5)	II Q (6)	III Q (7)	IV Q (8)	I Q (9)	II Q (10)	III Q (11)	IV Q (12)
Producer goods												
1. Regional electric power stations	24.1	24.5	24.8	28.6	107.3	100.3	97.5	101.0	25.8	50.5	74.6	103.5
2. Coal	24.3	25.7	25.9	29.4	100.2	87.9	87.2	83.5	24.4	46.9	69.5	94.1
3. Coke	24.1	26.4	27.2	27.7	104.4	97.1	91.8	94.6	25.2	50.8	75.8	102.0
4. Petroleum and gas	24.5	26.8	27.1	27.1	98.1	91.1	88.5	91.8	24.0	48.4	72.4	97.3
5. Petroleum used for refining	24.2	25.7	26.6	27.5	98.8	97.2	93.8	90.3	23.9	49.0	73.9	98.7
6. Oil shale	21.2	21.4	24.7	24.7	70.6	72.5	56.2	45.6	14.9	30.5	44.4	55.6
7. Iron ore	23.0	26.1	25.7	26.7	106.0	98.4	93.5	96.3	24.4	50.1	74.2	99.9
8. Manganese ore	25.1	27.1	27.3	28.6	99.3	109.4	97.1	91.7	24.9	54.5	81.0	107.2
9. Pig iron	24.2	25.7	26.2	26.2	100.7	96.9	94.4	96.4	24.3	49.3	74.1	99.3
10. Steel ingots and castings	24.6	25.9	26.9	26.9	100.3	96.3	92.6	103.7	24.7	49.6	74.5	102.4
11. Rolled steel	23.4	26.4	27.5	27.5	108.1	94.7	87.0	102.9	25.3	50.3	74.2	102.5
12. Aluminum	21.6	24.3	27.0	32.3	99.7	87.6	82.9	70.5	21.6	42.9	65.3	88.0
13. Refined copper	22.7	26.4	27.7	30.5	90.6	84.8	78.5	88.2	20.6	42.9	64.7	91.6
14. Phosphoric fertilizer	25.3	29.2	21.9	28.6	115.0	94.3	54.0	93.8	29.1	56.6	68.4	95.2
15. Sulfuric acid	23.8	27.2	23.0	28.9	105.2	90.3	76.4	90.7	25.1	49.6	67.2	93.5
16. Synthetic rubber	22.7	26.2	29.8	36.9	110.3	83.3	95.3	95.5	25.0	46.9	75.2	110.5
17. Cement, total			27.9	29.9			85.8	78.8	20.4	43.0	67.0	90.5
18. Cement, Commissariat of Heavy Industry	23.6	26.1		30.9	91.8	92.9		79.7	21.7	45.9	71.1	95.7
19. Window glass	26.7	25.5	26.1	23.0	95.7	84.1	75.6	88.9	25.5	46.4	66.6	87.1
20. Industrial timber hauled	69.5	11.8	9.78	23.3	83.5		50.4	49.9	58.1			86.0
21. Lumber, Commissariat of Heavy Industry	24.1	20.9	32.6	29.5	98.1		87.6	83.5	23.7			
22. Plywood	24.1	26.7	27.4	30.1	110.8	101.8	96.4	90.4	26.7	53.9	80.3	107.7
23. Paper, total			26.2	27.1			93.4	93.0	22.9	46.6	71.0	96.2
24. Paper, Commissariat of Timber Industry	23.8	24.7	25.9	26.9	95.2	95.8	94.2	93.5	22.6	46.3	70.7	95.9
25. Machine tools, total			27.8	28.6			84.4	97.0	22.9	46.5	70.0	97.0
26. Machine tools, Commissariat of Heavy Industry	23.4	25.6	28.4	28.4	92.5	95.4	85.6	98.4	21.7	46.1	70.4	98.4
27. Blast furnace equipment	21.5	15.6	17.7	17.8	83.9	86.5	23.1	10.0	18.0	31.6	35.6	37.4
28. Open-hearth furnace equipment	11.3	14.3	7.95	15.6	133.7	71.5	96.6	107.1	15.1	25.4	33.1	49.8
29. Rolling mill equipment		17.5	27.4	24.4		73.3	58.3	74.3	12.0	24.8	40.8	58.9
30. Equipment for presses and forges	18.2	27.4	19.4	18.3	90.6	61.0	46.3	63.4	16.5	33.2	42.2	53.8
31. Steam turbines	22.2	24.3	31.4	34.0	42.3	86.8	62.1	34.6	9.37	30.4	49.9	61.7
32. Steam boilers[a]	23.1	26.9	30.8	34.6	75.0	51.4	32.1	68.5	17.3	31.2	41.0	64.7
33. Generators for steam turbines	23.7	19.7	28.4	31.6	37.3	52.0	65.0	133.0	8.85	19.1	37.6	79.6
34. Tractors	32.0	27.2	29.5	25.7	101.7	104.0	98.0	103.9	32.6	60.9	89.8	116.5
35. Tractors (15 hp)	29.1	26.7	28.6	26.2	98.3	102.8	95.7	102.5	28.6	56.1	83.4	110.2
36. Motor vehicles, total	12.5	24.3	29.8	38.9	100.8	87.3	76.5	77.4	12.6	33.8	56.6	86.7
37. Trucks and buses [b]	13.2	24.8	29.7	37.0	100.7	91.4	80.8	86.5	13.3	36.0	59.9	92.0
38. Automobiles	5.00	18.5	30.8	60.0	103.2	25.2	30.1	15.1	5.16	9.81	19.1	28.1
39. Grain combines	25.0	25.2	25.5	26.0	92.0	108.7	47.5	32.5	23.0	50.3	62.5	70.9
40. Steam locomotives	24.9	25.3	23.8	32.1	92.8	88.1	69.7	63.3	23.1	45.4	62.0	82.4
41. Railroad freight cars	27.9	29.6	26.4	34.1	102.4	83.0	73.2	68.6	28.6	53.1	72.4	95.8
42. Railroad freight cars (2-axle units)	23.5	28.0	29.2	38.2	95.5	83.0	69.9	67.1	22.4	45.7	66.1	91.7
43. Railroad passenger cars	16.6	25.6	27.8	40.5	91.6	72.0	75.3	57.1	15.2	33.7	54.6	77.7

Table F-4 *continued*

	Quarterly Plan as Per Cent of Annual Plan				Per Cent of Quarterly Plan Fulfilled				Per Cent of Annual Plan Fulfilled by End of			
	I Q (1)	*II Q* (2)	*III Q* (3)	*IV Q* (4)	*I Q* (5)	*II Q* (6)	*III Q* (7)	*IV Q* (8)	*I Q* (9)	*II Q* (10)	*III Q* (11)	*IV Q* (12)
Consumer goods												
44. Cotton yarn[c]	25.3	25.3	26.6	28.2	100.0	97.8	92.8	99.7	25.3	50.0	74.7	102.7
45. Cotton fabrics[c]	25.4	26.1	27.7	30.2	105.3	98.0	91.2	97.6	26.8	52.4	77.7	107.1
46. Woolen fabrics[c]	25.8	22.7	34.8	30.8	100.0	100.0	80.4	100.8	25.8	48.5	76.5	107.7
47. Linen fabrics[c]	22.7	25.3	24.8	26.2	98.6	80.5	80.6	88.5	22.4	42.8	62.8	85.9
48. Silk and rayon fabrics	24.4	23.2	28.0	33.4	110.0	103.2	94.8	94.1	26.8	50.7	77.3	108.8
49. Knitted underwear, total[d]			30.7	27.7			80.9	91.3	23.9	50.4	75.3	100.6
50. Knitted underwear, Commissariat of Light Industry	22.7	27.0		28.3	108.3	102.4		100.7	24.5	52.2	77.7	106.2
51. Knitted outer garments, total[d]			31.2	29.2			74.5	95.6	27.2	54.1	77.4	105.3
52. Knitted outer garments, Commissariat of Light Industry	23.6	23.6		31.8	110.4	105.6		119.6	26.1	51.0	75.4	113.4
53. Hosiery, total[d]			29.7	27.5			68.3	88.6	23.5	47.9	68.2	92.5
54. Hosiery, Commissariat of Light Industry	24.5	24.4		27.8	97.6	101.0		96.0	23.9	48.6	69.4	96.1
55. Leather shoes, total[d]			29.0	32.0			92.3	100.5	25.7	53.6	80.3	112.5
56. Leather shoes, Commissariat of Light Industry	24.9	27.8		32.0	106.4	103.2		100.8	26.5	55.2	82.1	114.4
57. Rubber footwear	25.9	23.5	26.5	27.6	94.9	103.5	91.2	84.8	24.6	48.9	73.0	96.5
58. Flour, Commissariat of Food Industry[e]	26.1	20.7	27.9	35.4	88.7	97.0	97.4	106.5	23.1	43.2	70.4	108.1
59. Macaroni, Commissariat of Food Industry	26.4	29.6		29.6	118.2	110.8		106.0	31.2	64.0	96.8	128.0
60. Soap, (40% fatty acid), total[f]			17.6	32.1			103.7	89.3	26.0	50.3	68.5	97.2
61. Soap, Commissariat of Food Industry[f]	26.8	22.6		31.8	100.7	109.3		91.8	27.0	51.7	70.2	99.4
62. Raw sugar	16.0		10.4	80.0	91.8		29.6	77.6	14.7	14.8	17.9	80.0
63. Lump sugar	36.0	18.0	5.00	36.0	108.1	146.7	68.6	102.7	38.9	65.3	68.7	105.7
64. Fish products, total[g]				28.1				93.8	11.0	46.9	74.3	100.6
65. Fish products, Commissariat of Food Industry[g]	11.7	35.5	25.9	28.1	95.2	100.0	106.7	94.9	11.1	46.6	74.3	100.9
66. Crude alcohol	26.7	19.5	13.1	30.3	126.6	118.3	62.8	114.6	33.8	56.8	65.0	99.7
67. Vegetable oil, Commissariat of Food Industry[h]	25.3	16.8	15.9	35.8	100.0	105.0	89.7	88.7	25.3	42.9	57.2	89.0
68. Butter, Commissariat of Food Industry[i]	12.0	38.4	39.2	10.6	120.0	93.8	92.4	112.0	14.4	50.4	86.6	98.6
69. Meat, Commissariat of Food Industry	18.0	9.54	20.8	56.9	92.3	140.3	129.9	108.7	16.6	30.0	57.0	118.9
70. Canned food, Commissariat of Food Industry	12.4	12.5	48.5	26.2	131.5	96.0	95.7	84.5	16.3	28.3	74.7	97.6
71. Confectionery, Commissariat of Food Industry	22.4	25.7		31.2	111.9	109.6		94.8	25.1	53.2	78.0	107.6
72. Margarine and compound fat	22.5	20.0	13.8	33.8	122.2	103.8	113.6	87.4	27.5	48.3	63.9	93.4
73. Beer, total			32.9	26.9			112.4	112.3	23.7	58.2	95.2	125.4
74. Beer, Commissariat of Food Industry	17.9	26.7		27.7	131.9	130.6		113.4	23.7	58.5	96.9	128.3
75. Cigarettes	26.4	24.1	24.1	29.4	95.7	101.9	99.0	94.3	25.3	49.9	73.8	101.5
76. Matches	20.6	20.6	18.7	15.9	105.8	101.0	99.7	104.1	21.8	42.5	61.2	77.7
77. Low-grade tobacco (*makhorka*), Commissariat of Food Industry	24.0	24.0	25.2	30.6	98.3	97.6	95.6	95.8	23.6	47.0	71.1	100.4

Table F-4 *continued*

	Quarterly Plan as Per Cent of Annual Plan				Per Cent of Quarterly Plan Fulfilled				Per Cent of Annual Plan Fulfilled by End of			
	I Q (1)	*II Q* (2)	*III Q* (3)	*IV Q* (4)	*I Q* (5)	*II Q* (6)	*III Q* (7)	*IV Q* (8)	*I Q* (9)	*II Q* (10)	*III Q* (11)	*IV Q* (12)
78. Cast-iron kitchenware, Commissariat of Heavy Industry				36.3	56.6				16.4			
79. Bicycles, Commissariat of Heavy Industry		18.7	28.1	50.0	53.3	90.7	70.2	50.0	8.0	25.0	44.7	69.
80. Sewing machines, Commissariat of Heavy Industry				25.6	78.6				19.2			
81. Phonographs and records, Commissariat of Heavy Industry			24.8	31.4			48.5					
82. Radios, Commissariat of Heavy Industry		26.0	27.0	48.0		72.3	74.8					

Source

COLUMNS 1-4–All lines: Derived from Table F-2, cols. 2, 5, 8, and 11, respectively, and col. 1.

COLUMNS 5-8–All lines: Table F-2, cols. 4, 7, 10, and 13, respectively.

COLUMN 9–All lines: Derived from Table F-2, cols. 3 and 1.

COLUMN 10–All lines: Derived from Table F-2, cols. 3, 6, and 1.

COLUMN 11–All lines: Derived from Table F-2, cols. 3, 6, 9, and 1.

COLUMN 12–Lines 1-19, 22-77, and 79: Derived from Table F-2, cols. 3, 6, 9, 12, and 1. **Line 20:** *157,* pp. 42–63. Given for *lesorazrabotki* for Commissariat of the Timber Industry.

Note: For notes a–i, see corresponding notes in Table F-2.

Bibliography

A. Soviet Sources (1–325)

1. Alampev, P. M. *Ekonomicheskoe raionirovanie SSSR* [Economic Regionalization of the USSR]. Moscow, 1959.

2. Allakhverdian, D. *Natsionalnyi dokhod SSSR* [National Income of the USSR]. Moscow, 1952.

3. Ananov, I. N. *Ministerstva v SSSR* [Ministries in the USSR]. Moscow, 1960.

4. Anisimov, N. I. *Selskoe khoziaistvo SSSR za 30 let* [Agriculture in the USSR during 30 Years]. Moscow, 1947.

5. _____. *Selskoe khoziaistvo v novoi stalinskoi piatiletke* [Agriculture in the New Stalinist Five-Year Plan]. Moscow, 1946.

6. Arakelian, A. *Osnovnye fondy promyshlennosti SSSR* [Fixed Capital in USSR Industry]. Moscow, 1938.

7. Arutiunian, Iu. V. *Sovetskoe krestianstvo v gody velikoi otechestvennoi voiny* [The Soviet Peasantry during the Great Patriotic War]. Moscow, 1963.

8. *Atlas istorii SSSR* [Atlas of USSR History]. K. V. Bazilevich, I. A. Golubtsov, and M. A. Zinovev, eds. Moscow, 1950.

9. *Bakinskii rabochii* [The Baku Worker]. Newspaper.

10. Basovskaia, G. I., *et al. Ekonomika torgovli* [Economics of Trade]. Moscow, 1966.

11. *Bibliograficheskie materialy po vtoromu 5-letnemu planu tiazheloi promyshlennosti* [Bibliographical Material on the Second Five-Year Plan for Heavy Industry]. Moscow-Leningrad, 1934.

12. *Bolshaia sovetskaia entsiklopediia* [The Large Soviet Encyclopedia]. 2nd ed. Moscow, 1949–1957.

13. *Bolshaia sovetskaia entsiklopediia, SSSR* [The Large Soviet Encyclopedia, the USSR]. Supplementary volume. Moscow, 1947.

14. *Bolshevik* [The Bolshevik]. Journal of Central Committee of Communist Party.

15. Borodin, A. V. *Semiletnii plan razvitiia sistemy khleboproduktov, 1959–1965* [Seven-Year Plan for the Development of a System of Bread Products, 1959–1965]. Moscow, 1959.

16. Braginskii, B. I., and Koval, N. S. *Organizatsiia planirovaniia narodnogo khoziaistva SSSR* [Organization of Planning of the USSR National Economy]. Moscow, 1954.

17. Broner, D. L. *Kurs zhilishchnogo khoziaistva* [Course in Housing]. Moscow, 1946.

18. Budnitskii, I. M. *Ekonomika ugolnoi promyshlennosti SSSR* [Economics of the Coal Industry in the USSR]. Moscow, 1959.

19. *Bumazhnaia promyshlennost* [The Paper Industry]. Monthly journal of Technical-Economic Council of the Paper Industry.

20. Bychek, N. R. *Organizatsiia planirovaniia narodnogo khoziaistva SSSR* [Organization of Planning of the USSR National Economy]. Moscow, 1956.

21. Chadaev, Ia. E. *Ekonomika SSSR v period Velikoi Otechestvennoi Voiny, 1941–1945* [The Economy of the USSR during the Great Patriotic War, 1941–1945]. Moscow, 1965.

22. Cherniavskii, U. G. *Voina i prodovolstvie. Snabzhenie gorodskogo naseleniia v velikuiu otechestvennuiu voinu (1941–1945)* [War and Provisioning. Supplying the Urban Population during the Great Patriotic War, 1941–1945]. Moscow, 1964.

23. *Chislennost skota v SSSR* [Head of Livestock in the USSR]. Moscow, 1957.

24. *Dengi i kredit* [Money and Credit]. Monthly journal of USSR Ministry of Finance.

25. Dikhtiar, G. A. *Sovetskaia torgovlia v period sotsializma i razvernutogo stroitelstva kommunizma*

[Soviet Trade during the Period of Socialism and of the All-Out Building of Communism]. Moscow, 1965.

26. *Direktivy KPSS i sovetskogo pravitelstva po khoziaistvennym voprosam* [Directives of the Communist Party of the Soviet Union and of the Soviet Government on Economic Matters]. Moscow, 1957–1958.

27. *Dostizheniia Sovetskoi Belorussii za 40 let* [Achievements of Soviet Belorussia during Forty Years]. Minsk, 1958.

28. *Dostizheniia sovetskoi vlasti za 40 let v tsifrakh* [Achievements of the Soviet Regime during 40 Years in Figures]. Moscow, 1957.

29. Dubinskii, G. L. *Organizatsiia snabzheniia narodnogo khoziaistva v Respublike i ekonomicheskom raione* [Organization of Supplies to the National Economy in the Republic and in the Economic Region]. Moscow, 1964.

30. *Dvadtsat let sovetskoi vlasti* [Twenty Years of Soviet Power]. Moscow, 1937.

31. *XXIV Sezd Kommunisticheskoi Partii Sovetskogo Soiuza* [Twenty-Fourth Congress of Communist Party of Soviet Union]. Moscow, 1971.

32. *Ekonomicheskaia gazeta* [Economic Gazette]. Weekly journal of Central Committee of Communist Party.

33. *Ekonomicheskaia zhizn* [Economic Life]. Newspaper of USSR Ministry of Finance and USSR State Bank.

34. *Ekonomicheskaia zhizn SSSR. Khronika sobytii i faktov, 1917–1965. Kniga I: 1917–1950. Kniga II: 1951–1965.* [Economic Life of the USSR. Chronology of Events and Facts, 1917–1965]. 2nd ed. S. G. Strumilin, ed. Moscow, 1967.

35. *Ekonomika materialno-tekhnicheskogo snabzheniia* [The System of Material and Equipment Supply]. E. Iu. Lokshin, ed. Moscow, 1960.

36. *Ekonomika sovetskoi torgovli* [Economics of Soviet Trade]. Moscow, 1955.

37. *Ekonomika sovetskoi torgovli* [Economics of Soviet Trade]. Moscow, 1958.

38. *Elektrifikatsiia i toplivo respublik Srednei Azii vo vtoroi piatiletke* [Electrification and Fuel in the Republics of Central Asia in the Second Five-Year Plan]. Tashkent, 1932.

39. Emdin, A. Ia. *Metodologiia planirovaniia i organizatsiia materialno-tekhnicheskogo snabzheniia* [Methods of Planning and Organizing Material and Equipment Supply]. Moscow, 1966.

40. Evenko, I. A. *Voprosy planirovaniia v SSSR na sovremennom etape* [Problems of Planning in the USSR at the Present Stage]. Moscow, 1959.

41. Feitelman, N. G. *Sebestoimost uglia i puti ee snizheniia* [Cost of Production of Coal and Ways of Reducing It]. Moscow, 1956.

42. Figurnov, S. P. *Realnaia zarabotnaia plata i podem materialnogo blagosostoianiia trudiashchikhsia v SSSR* [Real Wages and the Increase in the Material Welfare of Workers in the USSR]. Moscow, 1960.

43. *Finansovoe i khoziaistvennoe zakonodatelstvo* [Financial and Economic Legislation]. Journal.

44. *Finansy i kredit SSSR* [Finance and Credit in the USSR]. Monthly journal of USSR Ministry of Finance.

45. *Finansy i sotsialisticheskoe stroitelstvo* [Finance and Socialist Construction]. Moscow, 1957.

46. *Finansy professionalnykh soiuzov* [Finances of the Trade Unions]. Moscow, 1957.

47. *Finansy SSSR* [Finance in the USSR]. Monthly journal of USSR Ministry of Finance.

48. *Finansy SSSR za XXX let* [Thirty Years of Soviet Finances]. Moscow, 1947.

49. *Generalnyi plan elektrifikatsii SSSR. Materialy k Vsesoiuznoi Konferentsii* [General Electrification Plan for the USSR. Materials for the All-Union Conference]. G. I. Lomov, ed. Moscow-Leningrad, 1932–1933.

50. *Geograficheskoe razmeshchenie pishchevoi promyshlennosti vo vtorom piatiletii* [The Geographical Distribution of the Food Industry in the Second Five-Year Plan]. I. N. Dolinskii and M. F. Sass, eds. Moscow-Leningrad, 1932.

51. Gibshman, A. E., *et al. Ekonomika transporta* [The Economics of Transportation]. Moscow, 1957.

52. Gogol, B. I. *Ekonomika sovetskoi torgovli* [Economics of Soviet Trade]. Moscow, 1960.

53. ――――, *et al. Ekonomika sovetskoi torgovli* [Economics of Soviet Trade]. Moscow, 1955.

54. *Gornyi zhurnal* [Journal of Mining]. Monthly journal of All-Union Scientific Engineering and Mining Society.

55. *O gosudarstvennom biudzhete SSSR na 1951 god. Dolad i zakliuchitelnoe slovo Ministra finansov A. G. Zvereva* [On the State Budget of the USSR for 1951. Report and Final Speech of Minister of Finance A. G. Zverev]. Moscow, 1951.

56. *O gosudarstvennom biudzhete SSSR na 1953 god i ob ispolnenii gosudarstvennogo biudzheta SSSR za 1951 i 1952 gody. Doklad i zakliuchitelnoe slovo Ministra finansov SSSR A. G. Zvereva na piatoi sessii Verkhovnogo Soveta SSSR* [On the State Budget of the USSR for 1953 and on the Fulfillment of the State Budget of the USSR for 1951 and 1952. Report and Final Speech of USSR Minister of Finance A. G. Zverev at the Fifth Session of the USSR Supreme Soviet]. Moscow, 1953.

57. *Gosudarstvennyi bank SSSR* [The USSR State Bank]. V. F. Popov, ed. Moscow, 1957.

58. *Gosudarstvennyi biudzhet SSSR i biudzhety soiuznykh respublik* [The USSR State Budget and the Budgets of the Union Republics]. Moscow, 1962.

59. *Gosudarstvennyi plan razvitiia narodnogo khoziaistva Soiuza SSR v 1938 g.* [State Plan for the Development of the National Economy of the USSR in 1938]. Moscow, 1938.

60. *Gosudarstvennyi plan razvitiia narodnogo khoziaistva SSSR na 1941 god* [State Plan for the

Development of the USSR National Economy for 1941]. Moscow, 1941 (reprinted by the American Council of Learned Societies, 1948).

61. Granovskii, E. L., and Markus, B. L. *Ekonomika sotsialisticheskoi promyshlennosti* [Economics of Socialist Industry]. Moscow, 1940.

62. *Handbook of the Soviet Union*. New York, 1936.

63. *Industrializatsiia SSSR, 1933–1937* [Industrialization of the USSR, 1933–1937]. Moscow, 1971.

64. *Industrializatsiia SSSR, 1938–1941* [Industrialization of the USSR, 1938–1941]. Moscow, 1973.

65. *Industriia* [Industry]. Newspaper of USSR Ministries of the Fuel Industry, of Electric Power Stations and the Electrical Industry, and of the Chemical Industry.

66. Ioffe, Ia. A. *SSSR i kapitalisticheskie strany, 1913–1937* [The USSR and the Capitalist Countries, 1913–1937]. Moscow, 1939.

67. *Istoriia Sovetskoi Konstitutsii (v dokumentakh) 1917–1956* [History of the Soviet Constitution in Documents, 1917–1956]. Moscow, 1957.

68. *Istoriia SSSR* [History of the USSR]. Monthly journal of the Academy of Sciences.

69. *Istoriia Velikoi Otechestvennoi Voiny* [History of the Great Patriotic War]. Moscow, 1960–1963.

70. *Itogi vsesoiuznoi perepisi naseleniia 1959 goda. SSSR (Svodnyi tom)* [Results of All-Union Census of the Population in 1959. USSR: Summary Volume]. Moscow, 1962.

71. *Itogi vypolneniia pervogo piatiletnego plana razvitiia narodnogo khoziaistva Soiuza SSR* [Fulfillment of the First Five-Year Plan for the Development of the USSR National Economy]. Moscow-Leningrad, 1933.

72. *Itogi vypolneniia vtorogo piatiletnego plana razvitiia narodnogo khoziaistva SSSR* [Results of the Fulfillment of the Second Five-Year Plan for the Development of the USSR National Economy]. Moscow, 1939.

73. Ivanov, F. Ts. *Organizatsiia finansovogo khoziaistva v kolkhozakh* [Organization of Finances on Collective Farms]. Moscow, 1954.

74. Ivanov, G. A., and Pribluda, A. S. *Planovye organy v SSSR* [Planning Agencies of the USSR]. Moscow, 1967.

75. *Izvestia* [News]. Daily newspaper of USSR Council of Deputies.

76. *Kalendar spravochnik, 1948 god* [Almanac for 1948]. Moscow, 1948.

77. Kareva, M. P. *Konstitutsiia SSSR* [The USSR Constitution]. Moscow, 1948.

78. *Khimicheskaia promyshlennost* [The Chemical Industry]. Monthly journal of Ministry of the Chemical Industry.

79. *Khlebooborot i elevatorsko-skladskoe khoziaistvo SSSR za 40 let* [Grain Trade and Grain Elevators during 40 Years in the USSR]. Moscow, 1957.

80. Khokhliachev, I. V., and Shcherbin-

Samoilov, S. A. *Uchet i otchetnost po gosudarstvennomu sotsialnomu strakhovaniiu* [Calculations and Accounting in State Social Insurance]. Moscow, 1944.

81. Khromov, P. *Amortizatsiia v promyshlennosti SSSR* [Amortization in USSR Industry]. Moscow, 1939.

82. Kisman, N., and Slavnyi, I. *Sovetskie finansy v piatoi piatiletke* [Soviet Finances in the Fifth Five-Year Plan]. Moscow, 1956.

83. Kochetov, I. V. *Zheleznodorozhnaia statistika* [Railroad Statistics]. Moscow, 1953.

84. Koldomasov, Iu. I. *Planirovanie materialno-tekhnicheskogo snabzheniia narodnogo khoziaistva v SSSR* [Planning of Material and Equipment Supply in the USSR National Economy]. Moscow, 1961.

85. *Kommunist* [The Communist]. Journal of Central Committee of Communist Party.

86. *Kommunist* [The Communist]. Newspaper (Erevan).

87. *Kommunisticheskaia partiia v borbe za uprochenie i razvitie sotsialisticheskogo obshchestva (1937 god–iiun 1941 goda)* [The Communist Party in the Struggle to Strengthen and Develop the Socialist Society, 1937–June 1941]. Moscow, 1962.

88. *Kommunisticheskaia Partiia v period Velikoi Otechestvennoi voiny, 1 iiun, 1941–1945* [The Communist Party during the Great Patriotic War, June 1, 1941–1945]. Moscow, 1961.

89. *Komsomolskaia pravda* [Truth of the Young Communist League]. Daily newspaper of Young Communist League.

90. Kondrashev, D. D. *Tsenoobrazovanie v promyshlennosti SSSR* [Price Formation in USSR Industry]. Moscow, 1956.

91. Kondrashev, S. K. *Oroshaemoe zemledelie* [Irrigation for Farming]. Moscow, 1948.

92. Konnik, I. I. *Dengi v period stroitelstva kommunisticheskogo obshchestva* [Money during the Period of Building a Communist Society]. Moscow, 1966.

93. _____. *Zakonomernosti vzaimosviazi tovarnogo i denezhnogo obrashcheniia pri sotsializme* [Economic Laws of the Interrelation between the Circulation of Goods and of Money under Socialism]. Moscow, 1968.

94. Koshelev, F. P. *Novyi etap v razvitii narodnogo khoziaistva SSSR* [A New Stage in the Development of the USSR National Economy]. Moscow, 1954.

95. _____. *Osnovnye itogi vypolneniia pervoi poslevoennoi stalinskoi piatiletki* [Main Results of Fulfillment of the First Postwar Stalinist Five-Year Plan]. Moscow, 1951.

96. Koval, T. A. *Selskoe khoziaistvo v shestoi piatiletke* [Agriculture in the Sixth Five-Year Plan]. Moscow, 1957.

97. *KPSS o vooruzhennykh silakh Sovetskogo Soiuza* [The Communist Party of the Soviet

Union on the Soviet Armed Forces]. Moscow, 1969.

98. *KPSS v rezoliutsiiakh i resheniiakh sezdov, konferentsii i plenumov Ts. K.* [The Communist Party of the Soviet Union: Resolutions and Decisions at Congresses, Conferences, and Plenary Sessions of the Central Committee]. 7th ed. Parts I and II. Moscow, 1953.

99. Kravchenko, G. S. *Voennaia ekonomika SSSR, 1941–1945* [The Wartime Economy of the USSR, 1941–1945]. Moscow, 1963.

100. Kuibyshev, V. V. *Izbrannye proizvedeniia* [Selected Works]. Moscow, 1958.

101. *Kulturnoe stroitelstvo SSSR* [Cultural Construction of the USSR]. Moscow, 1956.

102. Kurskii, A. D. *Narodno-khoziaistvennyi plan na 1938 god i ego vypolnenie* [The National Economic Plan for 1938 and Its Fulfillment]. Moscow, 1938.

103. _____. *Tretia stalinskaia piatiletka* [Third Stalinist Five-Year Plan]. Moscow, 1940.

104. *Kuznetskii ugolnyi bassein* [Kuznetsk Coal Basin]. Moscow, 1959.

105. *K voprosu o tekhnicheskikh sdvigakh vo vtoroi piatiletke. Materialy* [On the Problem of Technological Progress in the Second Five-Year Plan. Materials]. I. M. Burdianskii *et al.*, eds. Moscow, 1932.

106. Lazarev, B. M. *Upravlenie sovetskoi torgovlei* [Management of Soviet Trade]. Moscow, 1967.

107. *Legkaia promyshlennost* [Light Industry]. Journal of USSR Ministry of Light Industry.

108. Lenin, V. I. *Grozhiashchaia katastrofa i kak s nei borotsia* [The Impending Catastrophe and How to Combat It]. Moscow, 1917.

109. _____. *"'Left-Wing' Communism—An Infantile Disorder," Selected Works.* New York and Moscow, 1967.

110. _____. *Selected Works.* New York and Moscow, 1967.

111. _____. *Sochineniia* [Works]. 2nd ed. Moscow-Leningrad, 1919–1926.

112. *Les* [Timber]. Monthly journal of Chief Timber Supply under USSR Council of Ministers.

113. *Lesnaia promyshlennost* [The Timber Industry]. Monthly journal of USSR Ministry of the Timber Industry.

114. Levshin, B. V. *Akademiia Nauk SSSR v gody Velikoi Otechestvennoi Voiny, 1941–1945* [The USSR Academy of Sciences during the Great Patriotic War, 1941–1945]. Moscow, 1966.

115. Liashchenko, P. I. *Istoriia narodnogo khoziaistva SSSR* [History of the USSR National Economy]. Moscow, 1956.

116. Lifits, M. *Ekonomika sovetskoi torgovli* [The Economics of Soviet Trade]. Moscow, 1950.

117. _____. *Sovetskaia torgovlia* [Soviet Trade]. Moscow, 1948.

118. Linetskii, E. Ia.; Lelekov, A. F.; and

Sokolov, F. M. *Ekonomika i planirovanie sovetskoi torgovli* [Economics and Planning of Soviet Trade]. Moscow, 1962.

118a. Lipinski, Edward. *Karol Marks i zagadnienia wspolczesnosci* [Karl Marx and Contemporary Problems]. Warsaw, 1969.

119. *Literaturnaia gazeta* [Literary gazette]. Weekly journal of Union of Writers.

120. Liubimov, A. V. *Torgovlia i snabzhenie v gody velikoi otechestvennoi voiny* [Trade and Supply during the Great Patriotic War]. Moscow, 1968.

121. Livshits, R. S. *Razmeshchenie chernoi metallurgii SSSR* [Location of the Ferrous Metal Industry in the USSR]. Moscow, 1958.

122. Lokshin, E. Iu. *Planirovanie materialno-tekhnicheskogo snabzheniia narodnogo khoziaistva SSSR* [Planning of Material and Equipment Supply in the USSR National Economy]. Moscow, 1952.

123. Lomovatskii, E. G., and Gromova, G. M. *Upravlenie gosudarstvennoi vnutrennei torgovlei v SSSR* [Management of State Domestic Trade in the USSR]. Moscow, 1957.

124. Malafeev, A. N. *Istoriia tsenoobrazovaniia v SSSR, 1917–1963 gg.* [History of Pricing in the USSR, 1917–1963]. Moscow, 1964.

125. Malenkov, G. *Otchetnyi doklad XIX sezdu Partii o rabote tsentralnogo komiteta VKP(b)* [Report of the XIX Party Congress on the Work of the Party Central Committee]. Moscow, 1952.

126. Margolin, N. S. *Balans denezhnykh dokhodov i raskhodov naseleniia* [Balance of Money Income and Expenditures of Households]. Moscow, 1940.

127. _____. *Voprosy balansa denezhnykh dokhodov i raskhodov naseleniia* [Questions of the Balance of Money Income and Expenditure of the Population]. Moscow, 1939.

128. *Mashinostroenie* [Machine-Building]. Newspaper of Ministry of Machine-Building and Ministry of the Defense Industry.

129. *Materialnye balansy v narodnokhoziaistvennom plane* [Material Balances in the National Economic Plan]. G. I. Grebtsov and P. P. Karpov, eds. Moscow, 1960.

130. Medvedev, Roy A. *Let History Judge: The Origins and Consequences of Stalinism.* New York, 1973.

131. *Mineralno-syrevaia baza SSSR* [Mineral Raw Material Resources of the USSR]. Moscow, 1935–1936.

132. Moiseev, M. I. *Ekonomicheskie osnovy gosudarstvennykh zagotovok selskokhoziaistvennykh produktov* [The Economic Bases of State Procurements of Agricultural Products]. Moscow, 1955.

133. *Molochnaia promyshlennost SSSR* [The USSR Dairy Industry]. Monthly journal of USSR Ministry of the Meat and Dairy Industry.

134. Mstislavskii, P. *Neuklennyi podem*

blagosostoianiia sovetskogo naroda [A Steady Rise in the Well-Being of the Soviet People]. Moscow, 1952.

135. *Mukomole i elevatorsko-skladskoe khoziaistvo* [Flour Milling and Storage]. Monthly journal of USSR Minstry of Agricultural Procurement.

136. *Narodne Gospodarstvo Zakarpatskoi Oblasti* [National Economy of the Transcarpathian Province]. Uzhgorod, 1957.

137. *Narodnoe khoziaistvo Latviiskoi SSR* [National Economy of the Latvian SSR]. Riga, 1957.

138. *Narodnoe khoziaistvo Litovskoi SSR* [National Economy of the Lithuanian SSR]. Vilnius, 1957.

139. *Narodnoe khoziaistvo SSSR* [The USSR National Economy]. Moscow, 1948.

140. *Narodnoe khoziaistvo SSSR* [The USSR National Economy]. Moscow, 1956.

141. *Narodnoe khoziaistvo SSSR v 1956 godu* [The USSR National Economy in 1956]. Moscow, 1957.

142. *Narodnoe khoziaistvo SSSR v 1958 godu* [The USSR National Economy in 1958]. Moscow, 1959.

143. *Narodnoe khoziaistvo SSSR v 1959 godu* [The USSR National Economy in 1959]. Moscow, 1960.

144. *Narodnoe khoziaistvo SSSR v 1960 godu* [The USSR National Economy in 1960]. Moscow, 1961.

145. *Narodnoe khoziaistvo SSSR v 1961 godu* [The USSR National Economy in 1961]. Moscow, 1962.

146. *Narodnoe khoziaistvo SSSR v 1963 godu* [The USSR National Economy in 1963]. Moscow, 1965.

147. *Narodnoe khoziaistvo SSSR v 1964 godu* [The USSR National Economy in 1964]. Moscow, 1965.

148. *Narodnoe khoziaistvo SSSR v 1965 godu* [The USSR National Economy in 1965]. Moscow, 1966.

149. *Narodnoe khoziaistvo SSSR v 1967 godu* [The USSR National Economy in 1967]. Moscow, 1968.

150. *Narodnoe khoziaistvo SSSR v 1970 godu* The USSR National Economy in 1970]. Moscow, 1971.

151. *Narodnoe khoziaistvo SSSR v 1974 godu* [The USSR National Economy in 1974]. Moscow, 1975.

152. *Narodnoe khoziaistvo SSSR, 1922–1972* [The USSR National Economy, 1922–1972]. Moscow, 1972.

153. *O narodnokhoziaistvennom plane i finansovoi programme pervogo goda vtoroi piatiletki. Doklady i rezoliutsii, III Sezd TsIK SSSR, Ianvar 1933* [On the National Economic Plan and Financial Program of the First Year of the Second Five-Year Plan. Reports and Resolutions, Third Congress of USSR Central Executive Committee, January 1933]. Leningrad, 1933.

154. *Narodno-khoziaistvennyi plan na 1935 god* [The National Economic Plan for 1935]. 1st ed. Moscow, 1935.

155. *Narodno-khoziaistvennyi plan na 1935 god* [The National Economic Plan for 1935]. 2nd ed. Moscow, 1935.

156. *Narodno-khoziaistvennyi plan na 1936 god* [The National Economic Plan for 1936]. Vol. I. 2nd ed. Moscow, 1936.

157. *Narodno-khoziaistvennyi plan Soiuza SSR na 1937 god* [The USSR National Economic Plan for 1937]. Moscow, 1937.

158. *Nashe stroitelstvo* [Our Construction]. Monthly journal of USSR Gosplan.

159. Nikolaev, Arsenii Ivanovich. *Zhilishchnoe stroitelstvo v shestoi piatiletke* [Housing Construction during the Sixth Five-Year Plan]. Moscow, 1956.

160. Notkin, A. I. *Materialno-proizvodstvennaia baza sotsializma* [Material and Production Base of Socialism]. Moscow, 1954.

161. ———. *Ocherki teorii sotsialisticheskogo proizvodstva* [Essays on the Theory of Socialist Reproduction]. Moscow, 1948.

161a. Ordzhonikidze, G. K. *Statii i rechi* [Articles and Speeches]. Moscow, 1957.

161b. *Organizatsiia upravleniia* [Organization of Management]. Journal.

162. Orlovskii, I. A., and Sergeeva, G. P. *Sootnoshenie rosta proizvoditelnosti truda i zarabotnoi platy v promyshlennosti SSSR* [The Relation of the Growth of Labor Productivity and Wages in USSR Industry]. Moscow, 1961.

162a. *Osnovnye pokazateli vypolneniia narodno-khoziaistvennogo plana* [Main Indicators of the Fulfillment of the National Economic Plan]. Monthly report of USSR Gosplan Central Statistical Administration.

163. *Osnovnye ukazaniia k sostavleniiu vtorogo piatiletnego plana narodnogo khoziaistva SSSR (1933–1937)* [Basic Instructions for Drafting the Second Five-Year Plan for the USSR National Economy, 1933–1937]. Moscow, 1932.

164. *Partiinoe stroitelstvo* [Party Building]. Journal.

165. Pavlov, D. V. *Sovetskaia torgovlia v sovremennykh usloviiakh* [Soviet Trade in Present-Day Conditions]. Moscow, 1965.

166. *Perspektivy Donbassa vo vtoroi piatiletke* [Prospects for the Donbass in the Second Five-Year Plan]. N. S. Popov, ed. Kharkov, 1931–1932.

167. Pervushin, S. A., *et al. Ekonomika tsvetnoi metallurgii* [The Economics of the Ferrous Metal Industry]. Moscow, 1956.

168. *O piatiletnem plane vosstanovleniia i razvitiia narodnogo khoziaistva SSSR na 1946–1950 gg.* [On the Five-Year Plan for the Reconstruction and Development of the USSR National

Economy, 1946–1950]. Moscow, 1946.

169. *Piatiletnii plan narodno-khoziaistvennogo stroitelstva SSSR* [Five-Year Plan for the Development of the USSR National Economy]. Moscow, 1929.

170. *Pishchevaia industriia* [The Food Industry]. Newspaper of USSR Ministry of the Food Industry.

171. *Plan* [Plan]. Journal of USSR State Planning Committee for 1933–1937.

172. *Plan promyshlennosti Narkomsnaba na 1933 god* [Plan for Industry of People's Commissariat of Food Supply for 1933]. Moscow-Leningrad, 1933.

173. *Planovoe khoziaistvo* [Planned Economy]. Monthly journal of USSR State Planning Committee.

174. Plotnikov, K. N. *Biudzhet sotsialisticheskogo gosudarstva* [Budget of the Socialist State]. Moscow, 1948.

175. ———. *Ocherki istorii biudzheta sovetskogo gosudarstva* [Essays on the History of the Soviet State Budget]. Moscow, 1954.

176. *Po edinomu planu* [According to a Single Plan]. Moscow, 1971.

177. *Politicheskaia ekonomiia: Uchebnik* [Political Economy: A Textbook]. Moscow, 1954.

178. *Politicheskaia ekonomiia: Uchebnik* [Political Economy: A Textbook]. 2nd ed. Moscow, 1955.

179. *Posevnye ploshchadi SSSR* [Cultivated Area of the USSR]. Moscow, 1957.

180. *Pravda* [Truth]. Daily newspaper of Central Committee of Communist Party.

181. *Pravda Ukrainy* [Truth of the Ukraine]. Daily newspaper of the Communist Party of the Ukraine.

182. *Problemy ekonomiki* [Problems of Economics]. Monthly journal of the Economics Institute.

183. *Problemy genplana elektrifikatsii SSSR* [Problems of the General Electrification Plan for the USSR]. 2nd ed. Moscow, 1932.

184. Probst, A. E. *Osnovnye problemy geograficheskogo razmeshcheniia toplivnogo khoziaistva SSSR* [Basic Problems in the Geographic Distribution of the USSR Fuel Industry]. Moscow-Leningrad, 1939.

185. *Le procès du bloc des droitistes et des Trotskistes antisoviétiques* (March 2–13, 1938). Moscow, 1938.

186. *Proekt vtorogo piatiletnego plana razvitiia narodnogo khoziaistva SSSR (1933–1937 gg.)* [Draft of Second Five-Year Plan for the Development of the USSR National Economy, 1933–1937]. Vol. I. Moscow, 1934.

187. *Promyshlennost SSSR* [Industry of the USSR]. Moscow, 1957.

188. *Promyshlennost SSSR* [Industry of the USSR]. Moscow, 1964.

189. *Promyshlennost stroitelnykh materialov* [The Construction Materials Industry]. Newspaper of USSR Ministry of the Construction Materials Industry.

190. *Pshenitsa v SSSR* [Wheat in the USSR]. Moscow-Leningrad, 1957.

190a. *Raskhody na sotsialno-kulturnye meropriiatiia po gosudarstvennomu biudzhetu SSSR* [Expenditures on Social Cultural Measures in the State Budget of the USSR]. Moscow, 1958.

191. *Razvitie sotsialisticheskoi ekonomiki SSSR v poslevoennyi period* [Development of the Socialist Economy of the USSR in the Postwar Period]. Moscow, 1965.

192. *Rekonstruktsiia gorodov SSSR, 1933–1937* [Reconstruction of the Cities of the USSR, 1933–1937]. N. Ushakov, ed. Moscow, 1933.

193. *Report of Court Proceedings in the Case of the Anti-Soviet Trotskyist Center Heard before the Military Collegium of the Supreme Court of the USSR (January 23–30, 1937)*. Moscow, 1937.

194. *Resheniia Partii i Pravitelstva po khoziaistvennym voprosam* [Decisions of the Party and Government on Economic Matters]. Moscow, 1967–1968.

195. *Rezoliutsiia Vsesoiuznoi Konferentsii po sostavleniiu generalnogo plana elektrifikatsii SSSR 7–14 maia 1932 g.* [Resolution of the All-Union Conference on Drafting a General Electrification Plan for the USSR, May 7–14, 1932]. Moscow-Leningrad, 1932.

196. Roizman, V. M. *Tseny v obshchestvennom pitanii* [Prices in Public Catering]. Moscow, 1965.

197. Rovinskii, N. N. *Gosudarstvennyi biudzhet SSSR* [State Budget of the USSR]. Moscow, 1944.

198. ———. *Gosudarstvennyi biudzhet SSSR* [State Budget of the USSR]. Moscow, 1949.

199. ———. *Gosudarstvennyi biudzhet SSSR* [State Budget of the USSR]. Moscow, 1951.

200. Rubin, A. M. *Organizatsiia upravleniia promyshlennostiu v SSSR (1917–1967 gg.)* [Organization of Industrial Management in the USSR, 1917–1967]. Moscow, 1969.

201. *Selskoe khoziaistvo SSSR* [Agriculture in the USSR]. Moscow, 1958.

202. *Selskoe khoziaistvo SSSR* [Agriculture in the USSR]. Moscow, 1960.

203. *Selskoe khoziaistvo SSSR* [Agriculture in the USSR]. Moscow, 1971.

204. *Selskoe khoziaistvo SSSR, ezhegodnik 1935* [USSR Agricultural Yearbook for 1935]. Moscow, 1936.

205. *XVII Sezd Vsesoiuznoi Kommunisticheskoi Partii, 26 ianvaria–10 fevralia 1934 g.* [Seventeenth Congress of the USSR Communist Party, January 26–February 10, 1934]. Moscow, 1934.

206. *Severnyi Krai vo vtoroi piatiletke. Vtoroi piatiletnii plan Severnogo Kraia na 1933–1937 gg. Pervyi variant* [The Northern Territory in the Second Five-Year Plan. The Second Five-Year Plan of the Northern Territory for 1933–1937. First Variant]. M. Ia. Rozner, ed. Arkhangelsk, 1932.

207. *Shagi piatiletok: Razvitie ekonomiki SSSR* [Steps of the Five-Year Plans: Development of the USSR Economy]. Moscow, 1968.

208. *Sheristianoe delo* [The Wool Industry]. Monthly journal of All-Union Wool Society.

209. Shigalin, G. I. *Narodnoe khoziaistvo SSSR v period velikoi otechestvennoi voiny* [USSR National Economy during the Great Patriotic War]. Moscow, 1960.

210. *Silami millionov razrabotat plan postroeniia sotsializma. Direktivnye ukazaniia VTsSPS i Gosplana SSSR ob uchasti rabochikh i ITR v razrabotke plana vtoroi piatiletki* [The Efforts of Millions Are Drafting the Plan to Build Socialism. Directives of the Union of Trade Unions of USSR Gosplan on the Participation of Workers, Engineers, and Technicians in Drafting the Second Five-Year Plan]. Moscow, 1932.

211. *Sistema pokazatelei i formy tablits k sostavleniiu vtorogo piatiletnego plana narodnogo khoziaistva SSSR* [The System of Indexes and Forms to Draft the Second Five-Year Plan for the USSR National Economy]. Moscow-Leningrad, 1932.

212. *Sobranie postanovlenii i rasporiazhenii pravitelstva SSSR* [Collection of Resolutions and Decrees of the USSR Government]. Serial publication.

213. *Sobranie postanovlenii i rasporiazhenii Soveta Ministrov SSSR* [Collection of Resolutions and Decrees of USSR Council of Ministers]. Serial publication.

214. *Sobranie zakonov i rasporiazhenii raboche-krestianskogo pravitelstva SSSR* [Collection of Laws and Decrees of the Workers' and Peasants' Government of the USSR]. Irregular serial publication, 1933–1937.

215. *Socialist Construction in the U.S.S.R.* (translated from the Russian). Moscow, 1936.

216. Sokolov, V., and Nazarov, R. *Sovetskaia torgovlia v poslevoennyi period* [Soviet Trade in the Postwar Period]. Moscow, 1954.

217. *40 let sovetskoi torgovli* [Forty Years of Soviet Trade]. Moscow, 1957.

218. *40 let torfianoi promyshlennosti SSSR, 1917–1957* [40 Years of the USSR Peat Industry, 1917–1957]. Moscow-Leningrad, 1957.

219. Sorokin, G. M. *Planirovanie narodnogo khoziaistva SSSR* [Planning of the USSR National Economy]. Moscow, 1961.

220. ———. *Planning in the USSR: Problems of Theory and Organization* (translated from the Russian). Moscow, 1967.

221. ———. *Voprosy ekonomiki, planirovaniia, i statistiki* [Problems of Economics, Planning, and Statistics]. Moscow, 1957.

222. *Sotsialisticheskii trud* [Socialist Labor]. Monthly journal of State Committee for Labor and Wages.

223. *Sotsialisticheskoe narodnoe khoziaistvo SSSR v 1933–1940 gg.* [The USSR Socialist National Economy in 1933–1940]. Moscow, 1963.

224. *Sotsialisticheskoe selskoe khoziaistvo* [Socialist Agriculture]. Monthly journal of USSR Ministry of Agriculture.

225. *Sotsialisticheskoe selskoe khoziaistvo, 1938* [Socialist Agriculture in 1938]. Moscow, 1939.

226. *Sotsialisticheskoe stroitelstvo Soiuza SSR, 1933–1938* [Socialist Construction in the USSR for 1933–1938]. Moscow-Leningrad, 1939.

227. *Sotsialisticheskoe stroitelstvo SSSR* [Socialist Construction in the USSR]. Moscow, 1934.

228. *Sotsialisticheskoe stroitelstvo SSSR* [Socialist Construction in the USSR]. Moscow, 1935.

229. *Sotsialisticheskoe stroitelstvo SSSR* [Socialist Construction in the USSR]. Moscow, 1936.

230. *Sotsialisticheskoe zemledelie* [Socialist Agriculture]. Daily newspaper of USSR Ministry of Agriculture.

231. *Sovetskaia geologiia* [Soviet Geology]. Monthly journal of State Committee for Geology.

232. *Sovetskaia torgovlia* [Soviet Trade]. Moscow, 1956.

233. *Sovetskaia torgovlia* [Soviet Trade]. Moscow, 1964.

234. *Sovetskie finansy* [Soviet Finance]. Monthly journal of USSR Ministry of Finance.

235. *Sovetskoe gosudarstvo i pravo* [Soviet State and Law]. Monthly journal.

236. *Spravochnik mer* [Handbook of Measures]. Moscow, 1956.

237. *SSSR v tsifrakh v 1957 godu* [The USSR in Figures in 1957]. Moscow, 1958.

238. *SSSR v Velikoi Otechestvennoi Voine, 1941–1945* [The USSR during the Great Patriotic War, 1941–1945]. Moscow, 1964.

239. Stalin, I. V. *Ekonomicheskie problemy sotsializma v SSSR* [The Economic Problems of Socialism in the USSR]. Moscow, 1952.

240. ———. *Sochineniia* [Works]. Moscow, 1952.

241. ———. *Voprosy Leninizma* [Problems of Leninism]. 11th ed. Moscow, 1947.

242. *Strana sovetov za 50 let* [Land of the Soviets during Fifty Years]. Moscow, 1967.

243. *Stroitelstvo kommunizma i razvitie selskogo khoziaistva* [The Building of Communism and Development of Agriculture]. Moscow, 1962.

244. Strumilin, S. G. *Planirovanie v SSSR* [Planning in the USSR]. Moscow, 1957.

245. Suchkov, A. *Dokhody gosudarstvennogo biudzheta SSSR* [Revenue from USSR State Budget]. Moscow, 1955.

246. *Sudebnyi otchet po delu anti-sovetskogo i pravo-Trotskistskogo Bloka* [Court Proceedings of the Trial of the Anti-Soviet and Rightist Trotskyite Bloc]. Moscow, 1938.

247. *Sudebnyi otchet po delu antisovetskogo Trotskistskogo Tsentra* [Court Proceedings of the Trial of the Anti-Soviet Trotskyite Center]. Moscow, 1937.

248. *Sudebnyi otchet po delu Trotskistskogo-Zinovevskogo Tsentra* [Court Proceedings of the Trial of the Trotskyite-Zinoviev Center]. Moscow, 1936.

249. Tamarchenko, M. L. *Sovetskie finansy v period Velikoi Otechestvennoi Voiny* [Soviet Finances during the Great Patriotic War]. Moscow, 1967.

250. *Tekhnika molodezhi* [Technology for Youth]. Journal.

251. *Tekstilnaia promyshlennost* [The Textile Industry]. Monthly journal of USSR Ministry of the Textile Industry.

252. *Transport i sviaz SSSR* [Transport and Communications in the USSR]. Moscow, 1957.

253. *Transport i sviaz SSSR* [Transport and Communications in the USSR]. Moscow, 1967.

254. *Tretii piatiletnii plan razvitiia narodnogo khoziaistva SSSR (1938–1942)* [Third Five-Year Plan for the Development of the USSR National Economy, 1938–1942]. Moscow, 1939.

255. *Tretii piatiletnii plan razvitiia narodnogo khoziaistva SSSR. Doklad V. Molotova* [Third Five-Year Plan for the Development of the USSR National Economy. Report by V. Molotov]. Moscow, 1939.

256. *Tretii piatiletnii plan razvitiia narodnogo khoziaistva SSSR. Rezoliutsiia XVIII Sezda VKPb po dokladu tov. V. Molotova* [Third Five-Year Plan for the Development of the USSR National Economy. Resolution of the Eighteenth Party Congress on the Report of Comrade V. Molotov]. Moscow, 1939.

257. Trotskii, Lev. *Stalin: An Appraisal of the Man and His Influence* (translated from the Russian). New York, 1967.

258. *Trud* [Labor]. Daily newspaper of the Trade Unions.

259. *Trud v SSSR* [Labor in the USSR]. Moscow, 1936.

260. *Trud v SSSR* [Labor in the USSR]. Moscow, 1968.

261. *Trudy Pervoi Vsesoiuznoi Konferentsii po razmeshcheniiu proizvoditelnykh sil SSSR* [Papers of the First All-Union Conference on the Geographical Distribution of the Productive Forces of the USSR]. Moscow, 1932.

262. Tseitlin, I. Ia.; Sokolova, E. P.; and Kurman, M. V. *K metodologii planirovaniia naseleniia na vtoruiu piatiletku* [On Methods of Planning Population for the Second Five-Year Plan]. Leningrad, 1932.

263. *Tsement* [Cement]. Monthly journal of the Cement Union.

264. *Tsvetnye metally* [Nonferrous Metals]. Monthly journal of the Metal Industry.

265. *Ukazaniia i formy k sostavleniiu balansov i planov materialno-tekhnicheskogo snabzheniia na 1936 god* [Instructions and Forms for Drafting Balances and Plans for Material and Equipment Supply in 1936]. Moscow, 1935.

266. *Ukazaniia i formy k sostavleniiu finansovykh planov na 1936 god* [Instructions and Forms for Drafting Financial Plans for 1936]. Moscow-Leningrad, 1935.

267. *Ukazaniia i formy k sostavleniiu materialnykh balansov i planov snabzheniia oborudovaniem, materialami i syriem na 1937 god* [Instructions and Forms for Drafting Material Balances and Plans for Equipment, Material, and Raw Material Supply in 1937]. Moscow, 1936.

268. *Ukazaniia i formy k sostavleniiu narodno-khoziaistvennogo plana na 1935 god* [Instructions and Forms for Drafting the National Economic Plan for 1935]. Moscow, 1934.

269. *Ukazaniia i formy k sostavleniiu narodno-khoziaistvennogo plana na 1936 god* [Instructions and Forms for Drafting the National Economic Plan for 1936]. Moscow, 1935.

270. *Ukazaniia i formy k sostavleniiu narodno-khoziaistvennogo plana na 1937 god* [Instructions and Forms for Drafting the National Economic Plan for 1937]. Moscow, 1936.

271. *Ukraina za piatdesiat rokiv (1917–1967)* [The Ukraine during Fifty Years, 1917–1967]. Kiev, 1967.

272. *Upravlenie narodnym khoziaistvom SSSR, 1917–1940 gg.* [Management of USSR National Economy, 1917–1940]. Moscow, 1968.

273. *The USSR in Figures for 1975* (translated from the Russian). Moscow, 1976.

274. Utenkov, A. Ia. *KPSS—organizator i rukovoditel sotsialisticheskogo sorevnovaniia v promyshlennosti v poslevoennye gody (1946–1950 gg.)* [The Communist Party of the Soviet Union—the Organizer and Leader of Socialist Competition in Industry in the Postwar Years, 1946–1950]. Moscow, 1970.

275. Valler, L. B. *Sbergatelnoe delo v SSSR* [Savings in the USSR]. Moscow, 1950.

276. Vasilev, P., and Nevrozov, N. *Lesnoe khoziaistvo i lesnaia promyshlennost SSSR* [Forestry and the Timber Industry in the USSR]. Moscow, 1948.

277. Venediktov, A. V. *Gosudarstvennaia sotsialisticheskaia sobstvennost* [State Socialist Property]. Moscow-Leningrad, 1948.

278. ———. *Organizatsiia gosudarstvennoi promyshlennosti v SSSR* [Organization of State Industry in the USSR]. Vol. II. Leningrad, 1961.

279. *Vestnik Akademii Nauk* [Bulletin of the Academy of Sciences]. Monthly journal of the USSR Academy of Sciences.

280. Vikentev, A. N. *Natsionalnyi dokhod SSSR v poslevoennoi period* [USSR National Income in the Postwar Period]. Moscow, 1957.

281. ———. *Ocherki razvitiia sovetskoi ekonomiki v chetvertoi piatiletke* [Essays on the Development of the Soviet Economy in the Fourth Five-Year Plan]. Moscow, 1952.

282. *Vodnyi transport k sedmomu sezdu Sovetov SSSR* [Water Transportation at the Seventh

USSR Congress of Soviets]. Moscow, 1935.

283. *Voenno-ekonomicheskie voprosy v kurse politekonomii* [Military and Economic Problems in the Political Economy Course]. P. V. Sokolov, ed. Moscow, 1968.

284. Volkov, N. A. *Vysshie i tsentralnye organy gosudarstvennogo upravleniia SSSR i soiuznykh respublik v sovremennyi period* [Superior and Central Agencies of the State Administration of the USSR and the Union Republics in the Contemporary Period]. Kazan, 1971.

285. *Voprosy ekonomiki* [Problems of Economics]. Monthly journal of USSR Academy of Sciences.

286. *Voprosy organizatsii i ratsionalizatsii proizvodstva vo vtoroi piatiletke* [Problems of Organization and Rationalization of Production in the Second Five-Year Plan]. I. Burdianskii, ed. Moscow-Leningrad, 1933.

287. *Voprosy ratsionalizatsii perevozov vazhneishykh gruzov* [Problems of Rationalizing the Transportation of the Most Important Commodities]. V. P. Potapov and B. I. Safirkin, eds. Moscow, 1957.

288. Voznesenskii, N. A. *Economic Results of the U.S.S.R. in 1940 and the Plan of National Economic Development for 1941* (translated from the Russian). Moscow, 1941.

289. _____. *Voennaia ekonomika SSSR v period otechestvennoi voiny* [The Economy of the USSR during World War II]. Moscow, 1947.

290. Voznesensky, Nikolai A. *The Economy of the USSR during World War II* (translated from the Russian). Washington, 1948.

291. Voznesensky, N. A. *Five-Year Plan for the Rehabilitation and Development of the National Economy of the USSR, 1946–50* (translated from the Russian). London, 1946.

292. *Vtoraia ugolnaia baza SSSR—Kuzbass* [Second Coal Basin of the USSR—Kuzbass]. Moscow, 1935–1936.

293. *Vtoroi piatiletnii plan razvitiia narodnogo khoziaistva SSSR (1933–1937)* [Second Five-Year Plan for the Development of the USSR National Economy, 1933–1937]. Moscow, 1934.

294. Vyshinskii, A. *Sovetskoe gosudarstvo v otechestvennoi voine* [The Soviet State during the Patriotic War]. Moscow, 1944.

295. *Za rekonstrukstiiu tekstilnoi promyshlennosti* [For the Reconstruction of the Textile Industry]. Monthly journal of the Scientific Research Institute of the Textile Industry.

296. "Zakon o piatiletnem plane vosstanovleniia i razvitiia narodnogo khoziaistva SSSR na 1946–1950 gg." [Law on the Five-Year Plan for the Rehabilitation and Development of the USSR National Economy in 1946–1950], *Resheniia Partii i Pravitelstva po khoziaistvennym voprosam* [Decisions of the Party and Government on Economic Matters]. Vol. 3. Moscow, 1968, pp. 246–319.

297. *Zasedaniia Verkhovnogo Soveta SSSR (vtoraia sessiia). 10–21 avg. 1938 g.* [Meetings of USSR Supreme Soviet. Second Session, August 10–21, 1938]. Moscow, 1938.

298. *Zasedaniia Verkhovnogo Soveta SSSR (tretia sessiia). 25–31 maia 1939 goda* [Meetings of USSR Supreme Soviet. Third Session, May 25–31, 1939]. Moscow, 1939.

299. *Zasedaniia Verkhovnogo Soveta SSSR (shestaia sessiia). 29 marta–4 aprelia 1940 g.* [Meetings of USSR Supreme Soviet. Sixth Session, March 29–April 4, 1940]. Moscow, 1940.

300. *Zasedaniia Verkhovnogo Soveta SSSR (vosmaia sessiia). 25 fevralia–1 marta 1941 g.* [Meetings of USSR Supreme Soviet. Eighth Session, February 25–March 1, 1941]. Moscow, 1941.

301. *Zasedaniia Verkhovnogo Soveta SSSR (odinadtsataia sessiia). 24–27 aprelia 1945 g.* [Meetings of USSR Supreme Soviet. Eleventh Session, April 24–27, 1945]. Moscow, 1945.

302. *Zasedaniia Verkhovnogo Soveta SSSR (pervaia sessiia). 12–19 marta 1946 g.* [Meetings of USSR Supreme Soviet. First Session, March 12–19, 1946]. Moscow, 1946.

303. *Zasedaniia Verkhovnogo Soveta SSSR (vtoraia sessiia). 15–18 oktiabria 1946 g.* [Meetings of USSR Supreme Soviet. Second Session, October 15–18, 1946]. Moscow, 1946.

304. *Zasedaniia Verkhovnogo Soveta SSSR (tretia sessiia). 20–25 fevralia 1947 g.* [Meetings of USSR Supreme Soviet. Third Session, February 20–25, 1947]. Moscow, 1947.

305. *Zasedaniia Verkhovnogo Soveta SSSR (chetvertaia sessiia). 30 ianvaria–4 fevralia 1948 g.* [Meetings of USSR Supreme Soviet. Fourth Session, January 30–February 4, 1948]. Moscow, 1948.

306. *Zasedaniia Verkhovnogo Soveta SSSR (piataia sessiia). 10–14 marta 1949 g.* [Meetings of USSR Supreme Soviet. Fifth Session, March 10–14, 1949]. Moscow, 1949.

307. *Zasedaniia Verkhovnogo Soveta SSSR (vtoraia sessiia). 6–12 marta 1951 g.* [Meetings of USSR Supreme Soviet. Second Session, March 6–12, 1951]. Moscow, 1951.

308. *Zasedaniia Verkhovnogo Soveta SSSR (tretia sessiia). 5–8 marta 1952 g.* [Meetings of USSR Supreme Soviet. Third Session, March 5–8, 1952]. Moscow, 1952.

309. *Zasedaniia Verkhovnogo Soveta SSSR (piataia sessiia). 5–8 avgusta 1953 g.* [Meetings of USSR Supreme Soviet. Fifth Session, August 5–8, 1953]. Moscow, 1953.

310. *Zasedaniia Verkhovnogo Soveta SSSR (pervaia sessiia). 20–27 aprelia 1954 g.* [Meetings of USSR Supreme Soviet. First Session, April 20–27, 1954]. Moscow, 1954.

311. Zavoroshkova, I. P. *Proizvoditelnost truda v ugolnoi promyshlennosti SSSR* [Labor

Productivity in the USSR Coal Industry].
Moscow, 1957.

312. *Zheleznodorozhnyi transport SSSR v dokumentakh kommunisticheskoi partii i sovetskogo pravitelstva, 1917–1957* [Railroad Transportation in the USSR in Documents of the Communist Party and Soviet Government, 1917–1957]. Moscow, 1957.

313. Zhemchuzhina, P. S. *The Food Industry of the USSR* (translated from the Russian). Moscow, 1939.

314. *Zhenshchina v SSSR* [Women in the USSR]. Moscow, 1960.

315. *Zhurnal khimicheskoi promyshlennosti* [Journal of the Chemical Industry]. Monthly journal of the Council of the Chemical Industry.

316. Zotov, V. P. *Pishchevaia promyshlennost Sovetskogo Soiuza* [The Soviet Food Industry]. Moscow, 1958.

317. _____. *Razvitie pishchevoi promyshlennosti v novoi piatiletke* [Development of the Food Industry in the New Five-Year Plan]. Moscow, 1947.

318. Zverev, A. G. *O gosudarstvennom biudzhete SSSR na 1944 god i ispolnenii gosudarstvennogo biudzheta SSSR za 1940, 1941 i 1942 gody* [On the State Budget of the USSR for 1944 and on the Fulfillment of the USSR State Budget for 1940, 1941, and 1942]. Moscow, 1944.

319. _____. *O gosudarstvennom biudzhete SSSR na 1947 god* [On the State Budget of the USSR for 1947]. Moscow, 1947.

320. _____. *O gosudarstvennom biudzhete SSSR na 1948 god i ob ispolnenii gosudarstvennogo biudzheta SSSR za 1946* [On the State Budget of the USSR for 1948 and on the Fulfillment of the State Budget of the USSR for 1946]. Moscow, 1948.

321. _____. *O gosudarstvennom biudzhete SSSR na 1950 god i ob ispolnenii gosudarstvennogo biudzheta SSSR za 1948 i 1949 gody* [On the State Budget of the USSR for 1950 and on the Fulfillment of the State Budget for 1948 and 1949]. Moscow, 1950.

322. _____. *Gosudarstvennye biudzhety Soiuza SSR 1938–1945 gg.* [State Budgets of the USSR for 1938–1945]. Moscow, 1946.

323. _____. *Natsionalnyi dokhod i finansy SSSR* [USSR National Income and Finances]. Moscow, 1961.

324. _____. *Voprosy natsionalnogo dokhoda i finansov SSSR* [Problems of USSR National Income and Finances]. Moscow, 1958.

325. _____. *Zapiski Ministra* [Memoirs of a Minister]. Moscow, 1973.

B. Non-Soviet Sources (400–500)

400. *Annual Economic Indicators for the U.S.S.R.* Joint Economic Committee, U.S. Congress. Washington, 1964.

401. *Articles et Documents.* Periodical of Documentation Française.

402. Barker, G. R. "Soviet Labour," *Bulletins on Soviet Economic Development*, June 1951, pp. 1–28.

403. Baykov, Alexander. *The Development of the Soviet Economic System.* Cambridge, 1950.

404. Becker, Abraham S. "Cotton Textile Industry of the U.S.S.R." Council for Economic and Industry Research report A-12. Washington, 1955.

405. _____. "Soviet National Income and Product, 1958–1962." RAND Research Memorandum 4394-PR. Santa Monica, 1965.

406. Bergson, Abram. "A Problem in Soviet Statistics," *Review of Economics and Statistics*, November 1947, pp. 234–42.

407. _____. *The Real National Income of Soviet Russia since 1928.* Cambridge, Mass., 1961.

408. _____. *Soviet National Income and Product in 1937.* New York, 1953.

409. Bergson, Abram; Bernaut, Roman; and Turgeon, Lynn. "Prices of Basic Industrial Products in the U.S.S.R., 1928–50," *Journal of Political Economy*, August 1956, pp. 303–28.

410. Bergson, Abram, and Heymann, Hans, Jr. *Soviet National Income and Product, 1940–48.* New York, 1954.

411. Berliner, Joseph S. *Factory and Manager in the USSR.* Cambridge, Mass., 1957.

412. Bettelheim, Charles. *L'économie soviétique.* Paris, 1950.

413. *Biennial Census of Manufacturers: 1933.* Washington, 1936.

414. Brzezinski, Zbigniew K. *The Permanent Purge.* Cambridge, Mass., 1956.

415. *Cahiers de l'Economie Soviétique.* Serial. Paris.

416. *Cahiers de l'I.S.E.A.* Serial. Paris.

417. Calvez, Jean-Yves. *Revenu national en URSS.* Paris, 1956.

418. Carrère d'Encausse, Hélène. *L'Union Soviétique de Lénine à Staline, 1917–1953.* Paris, 1972.

419. Chapman, Janet. *Real Wages in Soviet Russia since 1928.* Cambridge, Mass., 1963.

420. Clark, Gardner. *The Economics of Soviet Steel.* Cambridge, Mass., 1956.

421. *Comparisons of the United States and Soviet Economies.* Joint Economic Committee, U.S. Congress. Washington, 1959.

422. Cooper, J. M. *Defense Production and the Soviet Economy, 1929–1941.* Centre for Russian and East European Studies, University of Birmingham, Series SIPS, No. 3, 1976.

423. Dallin, David J., and Nicolaevsky, Boris I. *Forced Labor in Soviet Russia.* New Haven, Conn., 1947.

424. Davies, R. W. *The Development of the Soviet Budgetary System.* Cambridge, Mass., 1958.

425. Deutscher, I. *Stalin: A Political Biography.* New York, 1949.

426. DeWitt, Nicholas. "Cement, Brick and Other Mineral Construction Materials Industries

in the USSR." Council for Economic and Industry Research report A-18. Washington, 1955.

427. *Dimensions of Soviet Economic Power.* Joint Economic Committee, U.S. Congress. Washington, 1962.

428. Dobb, Maurice. *Soviet Economic Development since 1917.* London, 1951.

429. *Document de la Semaine.* American Information Service, Paris.

430. Duchene, Gérard. *Essai sur la logique de l'économie planifiée soviétique, 1965–75.* Paris, 1976.

431. Eason, Warren. "The Agricultural Labor Force and Population of the USSR: 1926–41." RAND Research Memorandum RM-1248. Santa Monica, 1954.

432. *Economic Survey of Europe in 1954.* United Nations. Geneva, 1955.

433. *Etude provisoire sur la situation économique de l'Europe en 1951.* United Nations. Geneva, 1952.

434. *Etudes et Conjoncture.* Journal. Paris.

435. Galenson, Walter. *Labor Productivity in Soviet and American Industry.* New York, 1955.

436. Gelard, Patrice. *Les systémes politiques des états socialistes.* Vol I: *Le Modéle soviétique.* Paris, 1975.

437. Grancik, David. *Management of the Industrial Firm in the USSR.* New York, 1955.

437a. Guitton, Henri. *Maîtriser l'économie.* Paris, 1967.

438. Gwyer, Joseph. "Notes on U.S.S.R. Production of Textile Machinery, Pumps, and Compressors." Council for Economic and Industry Research report A-43. Washington, 1955.

439. Hoeffding, O., and Nimitz, N. "Soviet National Income and Product, 1949–1955." RAND Research Memorandum 2101. Santa Monica, 1959.

440. Holloway, David. "Soviet Military R and D: Managing the 'Research-Production Cycle,'" *Soviet Science and Technology. Domestic and Foreign Perspectives.* John R. Thomas and Ursula M. Kruse-Vaucienne, eds. Washington, 1977.

441. Holzman, Franklyn D. "Soviet Inflationary Pressures, 1928–1957: Causes and Cures," *Quarterly Journal of Economics,* May 1960, pp. 167–88.

442. ———. *Soviet Taxation: The Fiscal and Monetary Problems of a Planned Economy.* Cambridge, Mass., 1955.

443. Hunter, Holland. *The Economics of Soviet Railroad Policy.* Cambridge, Mass., 1949.

444. ———. "Soviet Railroads Since 1940," *Bulletins on Soviet Economic Development,* September 1950, pp. 10–20.

445. ———. *Soviet Transportation Policy.* Cambridge, Mass., 1957.

446. Jasny, Naum. *Essays on the Soviet Economy.* New York, 1962.

447. ———. "Indices of Soviet Industrial Production, 1928–1954." Council for Economic and Industry Research report A-46. Washington, 1955.

448. ———. "Labor and Output in Soviet Concentration Camps," *Journal of Political Economy,* October 1951, pp. 405–19.

449. ———. *The Socialized Agriculture of the USSR.* Stanford, 1949.

450. ———. *Soviet Industrialization, 1928–1952.* Chicago, 1961.

451. ———. *The Soviet 1956 Statistical Handbook: A Commentary.* East Lansing, 1957.

452. ———. *The Soviet Price System.* Stanford, 1951.

453. ———. *Soviet Prices of Producers' Goods.* Stanford, 1952.

454. Johnson, D. Gale, and Kahan, Arcadius. "Soviet Agriculture: Structure and Growth," *Comparisons of the United States and Soviet Economies.* Joint Economic Committee, U.S. Congress. Washington, 1959, Part I, pp. 201–37.

455. Kaplan, Norman. "Capital Investments in the Soviet Union, 1924–1951." RAND Research Memorandum 735. Santa Monica, 1951.

456. ———, and Moorsteen, Richard. "Indexes of Soviet Industrial Output." RAND Research Memorandum 2495. Santa Monica, 1960.

457. Kerblay, Basile. *Les marchés paysans en U.R.S.S.* Paris, 1968.

458. *Key Officials of the Government of the USSR.* Part I: *The Soviet Union, 1917–1966.* Munich, 1966.

459. Kravis, Irving B., and Mintzes, Joseph. "Soviet Union: Trends in Prices, Rations, and Wages," *Monthly Labor Review,* July 1947, pp. 28–35.

460. Lamer, Mirko. "Woodworking Industries of the USSR." Council for Economic and Industry Research report A-37. Washington, 1955.

460a. Lavigne, Marie. *Les économies socialistes soviétiques et européenes.* Paris, 1970.

461. Lesage, Michel. *Les régimes politiques de l'U.R.S.S. et de l'Europe de l'Est.* Paris, 1971.

462. Miller, Jack. "Soviet Planners in 1936–37," *Soviet Planning: Essays in Honour of Naum Jasny.* Oxford, 1964, pp. 116–43.

463. *Money and Banking 1937/38.* Vol. 2. League of Nations. Geneva, 1938.

464. Moorsteen, Richard. *Prices and Production of Machinery in the Soviet Union, 1928–1958.* Cambridge, Mass., 1962.

465. ———, and Powell, Raymond. *The Soviet Capital Stock, 1928–1962.* Homewood, Ill., 1966.

466. Nimitz, Nancy. "Soviet Agriculture since the September 1953 Reforms." RAND Research Memorandum 1552. Santa Monica, 1955.

467. _____. "Soviet Government Grain Procurements, Dispositions, and Stocks, 1940, 1945–1963." RAND Research Memorandum 4127-PR. Santa Monica, 1964.

468. _____. "Soviet National Income and Product, 1956–1958." RAND Research Memorandum 3112-PR. Santa Monica, 1962.

469. _____. "Statistics of Soviet Agriculture." RAND Research Memorandum 1250. Santa Monica, 1954.

470. *Notes et Etudes Documentaires.* La Documentation Française. Periodical. Paris.

471. Nutter, G. Warren. "The Effects of Economic Growth on Sino-Soviet Strategy," *National Security: Political, Military, and Economic Strategies in the Decade Ahead.* D. M. Abshire and R. V. Allen, eds. New York, 1963.

472. _____. *Growth of Industrial Production in the Soviet Union.* Princeton, 1962.

473. Powell, Raymond P. "Monetary Statistics," *Soviet Economic Statistics.* Vladimir G. Treml and John P. Hardt, eds. Durham, N.C., 1972. pp. 397–432.

474. *Problèmes Soviétiques.* Journal. Munich.

475. Prokopovicz, Serge N. *Histoire économique de l'U.R.S.S.* Paris, 1952.

476. *Rapport américain sur l'évolution économique de l'Union Soviétique en 1947.* Paris, 1948.

477. Schwartz, Harry. *Russia's Soviet Economy.* London, 1951.

478. Schwarz, Solomon. *Labor in the Soviet Union.* New York, 1951.

479. _____. *New Leader,* January 1, 1949.

480. Souvarine, Boris. *Stalin: A Critical Survey of Bolshevism* (translated from the French). New York, 1939.

481. *Soviet Economic Growth.* Abram Bergson, ed. Evanston, Ill., 1953.

482. *Soviet Economic Prospects for the Seventies.* Joint Economic Committee, U.S. Congress. Washington, 1973.

483. *Soviet Economic Statistics.* Vladimir G. Treml and John P. Hardt, eds. Durham, N.C., 1972.

484. *Soviet Planning: Essays in Honour of Naum Jasny.* Jane Degras and Alec Nove, eds. Oxford, 1964.

485. *Statistical Abstract of Industrial Output in the Soviet Union, 1913–1955.* National Bureau of Economic Research. New York, 1956.

486. *Statistiques et Etudes Financières.* Periodical. Paris.

487. "Summary of World Broadcast." Serial.

488. Sutton, Antony C. *Western Technology and Soviet Economic Development, 1945–1965.* Stanford, 1973.

489. Swianiewicz, S. *Forced Labour and Economic Development.* London, New York, Toronto, 1965.

489a. Volin, Lazar. *Survey of Russian Agriculture.* Washington, 1951.

490. Williams, Ernest W., Jr. *Freight Transportation in the Soviet Union.* Princeton, 1962.

491. Wool, Harold. "Statistics of Population, Labor Force, and Employment in the Soviet Union." Unpublished working memorandum, National Bureau of Economic Research. New York, 1959.

492. Wronski, Henri. *Rémunération et niveau de vie dans les kolkhoz: Le troudoden.* Paris, 1957.

493. _____. *Le rôle économique et social de la monnaie dans les Démocraties Populaires. La réforme monétaire polonaise.* Paris, 1954.

494. Zaleski, Eugène. *Les courants commerciaux de l'Europe Danubienne au cours de la première moitié du XX-e siècle.* Paris, 1952.

495. _____. "Les fluctuations des prix de détail en Union Soviétique," *Annexe Méthodologique et Statistique No. 3. Conjoncture et Etudes Economiques,* 1955.

496. _____. "Les fluctuations des prix de détail en Union Soviétique," *Etudes et Conjoncture,* April 1955.

497. _____. "Investissements en Sibérie occidentale et croissance du Kuzbass," *Cahiers de l'I.S.E.A.,* No. G-8, 1960, pp. 99–163.

498. _____. *Planning for Economic Growth in the Soviet Union, 1918–1932.* Translated and edited by Marie-Christine MacAndrew and G. Warren Nutter. Chapel Hill, N.C., 1971.

499. _____. *Planning Reforms in the Soviet Union, 1962–1966.* Translated by Marie-Christine MacAndrew and G. Warren Nutter. Chapel Hill, N.C., 1967.

500. _____, et al. *Science Policy in the U.S.S.R.* OECD. Paris, 1969.

Index of Persons

Index of Subjects

transportation; Maritime transportation; Motor transportation; Railroad transportation

Transportation, People's Commissariat or Ministry of, 15, 18, 62, 78, 125, 204, 245, 257, 288, 315, 360, 432n, 433n, 644, 648, 650, 653, 656, 659, 703, 706

Transport Machine-Building, People's Commissariat or Ministry of, 19n, 359–62, 421n, 423n, 432n, 433n, 707, 711

Trials, political, 11–12, 167–68, 248
  See also Purges; Sabotage

Trucks, 150–51, 154, 188, 196, 200, 270–71, 359, 365, 369, 371, 397, 526–27, 552–53, 580–81, 604, 616–17
  and buses, 140, 146–47, 189n, 195, 744–45, 752

Trudoden or *trudodni* (hypothetical working day or days)
  number of, 311, 339n, 474–76
  payments for, 328, 337–38, 339n
  —in kind, 220, 337–38, 475–77
  —in money, 221–23, 337–38, 442, 444–45, 475–77
  See also Employment; Labor

Trusts, 3, 24–25, 27, 31, 33, 44–45, 67, 85–86, 89, 92–93
  definition of, 28–29
  powers of, 28, 30, 38
  statutes on, 28–29, 35–38

Tsentrosoiuz, 82, 448n, 468, 478, 644, 648, 650, 653, 656, 704, 710

TsUNKhU. See Central Administration of Statistics and National Accounting

Tuition payments, 442, 446–47, 475

Turbines, 296
  hydraulic, 140, 188, 196, 200
  steam, 130, 265, 267, 744–45, 752
  steam and gas, 140, 146–47, 150–51, 154, 195, 272, 365, 369, 371, 397, 524–25, 552–53, 580–81, 604, 616–17

Turbogenerators, 140, 146–47, 150–51, 154, 195, 271, 526–27, 552–53, 580–81, 604, 616–17

Turkmenistan Hydroelectric Power Station, 389

U

Unemployment, 186, 504
Urban Construction, Ministry of, 20, 22, 709
Utilization Commission, 84–85, 91, 94, 97

V

Vegetable oil, 140, 152, 154, 178, 188, 196, 200, 272, 277, 365, 369, 372, 397, 528–29, 554–55, 582–83, 604, 620–21, 746–47, 753

Vegetable production, 141, 154, 188, 195–96, 199, 354, 368, 528–29, 556–57, 584–85, 620–21

Vegetables, 208n, 336–39, 465n
  price of, 688–89, 694
  procurements, 155, 188, 196, 469, 530–31, 558–59, 586–87, 606, 624–25

Vodka, price of, 334, 690–91, 694, 697, 700
"Voluntarism," 259, 308, 396
Vouchers (*raznariady*), 101
VSNKh (Supreme Council of the National Economy), 15, 18, 22, 26, 28–30, 32, 35–38, 97, 119n, 169n
  control of supply and sales, 84–88, 91, 94

W

Wage fund, 63, 90, 192, 252, 276, 349, 355–57, 359, 373, 401, 422, 433n, 477
  in industry, 141, 152, 155, 189, 196, 201, 274, 278, 281, 534–35, 562–63, 590–91, 607
  in national economy, 136, 141, 152, 155, 183, 189, 193, 196, 201, 274, 277, 281, 326–27, 366, 369, 373, 398, 534–35, 562–63, 590–91, 607, 628–29

Wages, 36, 144, 149, 153, 165, 190, 193–95, 199, 202–4, 218–19, 252, 272, 292, 293n, 325, 327–28, 347, 349–50, 353–57, 364, 367, 396, 421, 433–34, 440, 463, 489, 498, 507, 509
  differentials in, 328–29, 478
  in kind, 668–69
  money. *See* Wages, money
  real, 135–36, 138, 143–44, 153, 156–59, 182, 185, 196, 206, 228, 259, 278, 349–50, 353, 355–57, 398–401, 492, 494–95, 503–4
  and salaries, 220–23, 440, 442, 444–45, 473, 475, 668–69, 683

Wages, money, 55, 138–39, 143, 153, 157, 185–86, 201, 275, 278, 280, 440, 443, 465, 475–76, 478, 668–69
  in administration, 141, 152, 156, 196, 221n, 274, 534–35, 564–65, 592–93, 608, 630–31
  in chemical industry, 534–35, 564–65, 592–93, 630–31
  in coal industry, 155, 534–35, 564–65, 592–93, 607, 630–31
  in communications, 141, 152, 156, 196, 201, 534–35, 564–65, 592–93, 608, 630–31
  in construction, 141, 152, 155, 196, 201, 274, 534–35, 564–65, 592–93, 607, 630–31
  in cotton industry, 156, 534–35, 564–65, 630–31
  in credit institutions, 141, 152, 156, 196, 201, 534–35, 564–65, 592–93, 608, 630–31
  in education, 141, 152, 155, 196, 201, 221n, 274, 534–35, 564–65, 592–93, 608, 630–31
  in ferrous metal industry, 156, 534–35, 564–65, 592–93, 630–31
  in food industry, 534–35, 564–65, 592–93, 630–31
  in industry, 141, 152, 156, 196, 201, 274, 277, 281, 324, 328, 534–35, 562–63, 592–93, 607, 630–31
  in iron ore industry, 534–35, 562–63
  in leather industry, 534–35, 564–65, 630–31
  in logging, 141, 156, 536–37, 564–65
  in machine-building, 156, 534–35, 564–65, 592–93, 630–31